Batsford Chess Openings

GARY KASPAROV, RAYMOND KEENE

Introductions by Jonathan Tisdall

Research Editor: Eric Schiller

American Chess Promotions, Macon, Georgia

First published in the United States 1982
by American Chess Promotions
© Raymond Keene 1982

ISBN 0 7134 2112 6

Printed in Great Britain
for the publishers
American Chess Promotions
3055 General Lee Road
Macon, Georgia 31204

A BATSFORD/AMERICAN CHESS PROMOTIONS CHESS BOOK
Adviser: R.G.Wade OBE
Technical Editor: P.A.Lamford

Contents

Symbols

+	Check
± ∓	Slight advantage
± ∓	Clear advantage
± ∓	Winning advantage
∞̄	With Compensation
=	Level position
∞	Unclear position
!	Good move
!!	Outstanding move
!?	Interesting move
?!	Dubious move
?	Weak move
??	Blunder
corr.	Correspondence
Ol	Olympiad
Z	Zonal
IZ	Interzonal
L	League
Ch	Championship
½f	Semi-final

Note on Attribution

Whenever possible analysis has been credited to its originator. However, our own analysis and assessments have generally been credited only when they were prepared specially for this volume, or in order to distinguish them from another writer's work.

RDK

Acknowledgments

First and foremost I would like to thank Gary Kasparov for his contribution. He initially agreed to co-operate on this project when we met at the Malta Olympiad in December 1980, and I went over the final version with him at the Moscow Interzonal of September 1982. Gary already enjoys a fearsome reputation as a player and is widely regarded as the natural successor in the Spassky-Fischer-Karpov line of world champions. Those of us operating in London soon became accustomed to his clear-cut analysis and comments, penned from Baku or Moscow in his distinctive green ink, and I hope that this book will establish his reputation as a theoretician, fully on a level with his outstanding play.

Many thanks to IM Jonathan Tisdall, who not only contributed considerable analysis and prepared the strategic introductions to each opening but also spent much time revising sections of the work through 1982; to Eric Schiller, whose research was invaluable in constructing the informational framework of our grid system; and to Graham Hillyard, who managed to typeset the book from a very complex and difficult manuscript, and who, together with our expert proofreader Richard Sams, pointed out many errors of commission and omission. My thanks, too, to the Batsford home team: Peter Kemmis Betty and IM Bob Wade OBE, who originally conceived the project, and Paul Lamford, who controlled and collated all corrections. Important suggestions and amendments were made by Tim Taylor and IMs Mark Ginsburg and William Watson, while IM/GM John Fedorowicz and FM Andrew Whiteley contributed theoretically. John Henshaw and Carey Groves also deserve thanks for help with proofreading and typing respectively.

Ray Keene
London, September 1982

It was an interesting task for me to take part in the creation of this openings encyclopaedia. We have tried to produce an optimal combination of traditional theoretical judgments on all opening systems and important innovations from recent practice. I think that this book will be extremely useful for all tournament competitors.

Gary Kasparov
Moscow, September 1982

Bibliography

Reference Books
Comprehensive Chess Openings, Volumes 1-3   Y.Panov and Y.Estrin (Pergamon, 1980)
Encyclopaedia of Chess Openings, Volumes A-E   A.Matanović (Sahovski Informator/
   B.T.Batsford)

Other Openings Books
Alekhine's Defence   V.Hort (A & C Black, 1982)
English: 1 ... P-K4   J.L.Watson (B.T.Batsford, 1979)
English: 1 ... N-KB3 Systems   J.L.Watson (B.T.Batsford, 1979)
English: 1 ... P-QB4   J.L.Watson (B.T.Batsford, 1980)
English: Franco, Slav and Flank Defences   J.L.Watson (B.T.Batsford, 1981)
English: Four Knights   N.E.Povah (B.T.Batsford, 1982)
Flank Openings (revised edition)   R.D.Keene (British Chess Magazine 1980)
French Defence: Tarrasch Variation   R.D.Keene & S.Taulbut (B.T.Batsford, 1981)
Grünfeld Defence   M.Botvinnik and Y.Estrin (Pitman 1980)
Grünfeld Defence: Exchange Variation   M.Pein (B.T.Batsford, 1981)
King's Indian Defence: 4 e4   E.Geller, (B.T.Batsford, 1980)
King's Indian Defence: g3 Systems   E.Geller, (B.T.Batsford, 1980)
Morra (Smith) Gambit   J.Flesch, (B.T.Batsford, 1981)
Nimzo-Indian 4 e3: Nimzowitsch, Hübner and Taimanov Systems   C.W.Pritchett
   (B.T.Batsford, 1980)
Nimzowitsch Defence   T.D.Harding (B.T.Batsford, 1981)
The Pirc for the Tournament Player   J.D.M.Nunn (B.T.Batsford, 1980)
Queen's Gambit: Chigorin Defence   J.L.Watson (B.T.Batsford, 1982)
Queen's Gambit Declined: Semi-Slav   T.D.Harding (B.T.Batsford, 1981)
Queen's Indian Defence   E.Geller (B.T.Batsford, 1982)
Sicilian: 2 c3   M.Chandler (B.T.Batsford, 1981)
Sicilian Dragon: Classical and Levenfish Variations   D.Levy (B.T.Batsford, 1981)
Sicilian: Keres Attack   J.Kinlay (B.T.Batsford, 1981)
Sicilian: Lines with ... e5   T.D.Harding & P.R.Markland (B.T.Batsford, 1981)

   Other less recent opening works, too numerous to mention, were also of use in providing
source material.

Periodicals
The Chess Player, Volumes 1-16
Informator, Volumes 1-32
Modern Chess Theory
Tournament Chess, Volumes 1-3

Introduction

This book was conceived to fill a gap in the extensive list of Batsford chess publications. Batsford already publish the five volume *Encyclopaedia of Chess Openings*, but our feeling was that both the price and the complexity of these highly specialised technical volumes were soaring beyond the reach and the needs of the average player. Accordingly, we have attempted to create a single, inexpensive volume, covering all openings to a depth that will hopefully be adequate for all social, club and county players, plus competitors in weekend tournaments. The latter may indeed perceive this lightweight compendium as a particular boon when assembling their weekend luggage. The compression required to pack coverage of all openings into some 300 pages may render our book's utility more problematic for Masters and Grandmasters on the international circuit, but we hope that the new suggestions by myself and Gary Kasparov, and our selection of material, may be helpful even for this exalted class of player.

The key points of this book are as follows:

● Co-operation by an expert international team from the USSR, USA and England, headed by Gary Kasparov and myself.

● All openings are covered.

● Ease of reference. All notes connected to the rows of main moves appear on one and the same double-spread, thus avoiding all that tedious juggling with separate pages to find the right note which one associates with so many other reference books.

● Strategic introductions, ideas and historical background to each opening.

● The material is very up to date.

● All moves appear in FIDE-approved international figurine algebraic notation.

In order to squeeze the material into a size of book which we hope will be regarded as good value, we have had to make a number of ruthless decisions to scrap or reduce coverage of lines we consider less important, and we apologise in advance if the reader finds that his favourite variation has been heavily pruned. Although Gary and I have played many openings during the course of our careers we are obviously more expert in some lines (e.g. the Queen's Indian Defence or the Modern Defence) than in others. For some topics we have had to rely more heavily on received opinion than on our own experience, but we hope that the reader will not detect significant differences in the quality of the varying modes of material.

Ray Keene
London, September 1982

Unusual Openings (1 b4; 1 g4; 1 ♘c3; 1 g3)

Under this heading comes a collection of infrequently essayed first moves. In general, they have been shunned because they are more committal and have less central influence than more orthodox debuts.

1 b4 Sokolsky's Opening, or the Orangutan as it was dubbed by Polish GM Tartakower after a visit to the zoo during the New York 1924 International tournament. Too eccentric to achieve popularity, it is restricted to sporadic appearances in the hands of maverick players.

1 g4 Grob's Attack, now championed by England's free spirit Michael Basman, has considerable psychological impact but does little to improve the White position. Black does well to develop sensibly.

1 ♘c3 The Dunst Opening has been employed of late by Mestrović, Sahović and Bellon. It is obscure and unambitious.

1 g3 Benko's Opening is the most reputable of the bunch, and first received attention when Benko used it to defeat Tal and Fischer in succession at the 1962 Candidates tournament in Curaçao. Extremely flexible, it keeps the option of transposing into more common positions or using certain defensive formations with an extra tempo. Larsen and Miles have also unleashed the move at the Grandmaster level with considerable success.

1 d3 This move usually introduces a transposition to the King's Indian Attack or Modern Defence reversed. Other moves, considered in note 1, are included only for the sake of completeness.

	1	2	3	4	5	6	7	8	9	
	Unusual Openings									
1	d3[1]	♘f3	g3	♗g2	c3[3]	♘bd2	0-0	♕c2	b3	∞
	e5[2]	♘c6	d5	♘f6	a5[4]	♗e7	0-0	b6	♗b7[5]	
2	g3[6]	♗g2	e4	♘e2	0-0	d4	♘xd4	♘c3	♘db5	=
	g6	♗g7	e5[7]	♘e7	0-0	ed	d5	de	♘a6[8]	
3	...	♗g2	d3	♘d2	e4	♘gf3	0-0			=
	d5	c6	♘f6	e5	♗c5	♘bd7	0-0[9]			
4	...	♗g2	d3[10]	♘f3	0-0	♘c3	e4	♘e2	♘d2	±
	e5	d5	c6[11]	♘d7[12]	♗d6[13]	♘e7	d4	h6	♘b6[14]	
5	g4[15]	h3[16]	♗g2	d4	c4	♘c3	g5	h4	♗h3	∓
	d5	e5	c6[17]	e4	♗d6	♘e7	♗e6	♘f5	0-0[18]	
6	♘c3[19]	d4[20]	♕xd4	♕h4	♗d2	e4	0-0-0	♔b1	a3·	∓
	c5	cd	♘c6	g6	♗g7	d6	♕a5	♗e6	a6[21]	
7	...	e4	♘ce2	♘g3[23]	♘f3	♗b5+	♗a4	♗b3	♗xe6	=
	d5	d4[22]	e5	♗e6	f6	c6	♘d7	♘c5	♘xe6[24]	
8	b4[25]	b5	♗b2	e3	d4[27]	♘f3	c4	♘c3	ed	=
	a5[26]	♘f6	d6	g6	♗g7	0-0	c5	cd	♕c7[28]	
9	...	♗b2	e3	♘f3[30]	c4	c5	♘d4	♖xb1		=
	d5	♘f6[29]	♗f5	e6	♘bd7	♗e7	♗xb1	c6[31]		
10	...	♗b2	♗xe5	c4	♘f3	♗b2	cd	♗xf6	e3[34]	=
	e5	♗xb4[32]	♘f6	0-0	♘c6	d5	♕xd5[33]	gf		

[1] Usually transposes to the King's Indian Attack, Modern Defence Reversed etc. Other initial moves are considered innocuous, but may transpose to "reversed" openings with White having an extra tempo. Some possibilities:

1 a3 (Anderssen) nowadays intends a reversed Sicilian, Benoni or St George. 1 ... g6!

1 c3 (Saragossa) intends a reversed Caro Kann or Modern. 1 ... c5!? 2 g3 (2 e4 – Sicilian; 2 d4 cd 3 cd d5 – Exchange Slav) 2 ... ♘c6 3 ♗g2 d5 =.

1 f3 is only playable in conjunction with ♘h3-f2, e.g. 1 ... d5 2 g3 e5 3 ♘h3 c5 4 ♗g2 ♘c6 5 ♘f2 ♘f6 6 0-0 ♗e7 =.

1 h3? e5 or d5 =.

1 h4? d5 2 d4 c5?! (2 ... ♘f6! Myers) 3 e4! de 4 d5 ♘f6 5 ♘c3 ♘bd7 6 ♗g5 ∞ Myers-Neuer, New York 1971.

1 e3 intends a reversed French, Queen's Gambit, Queen's Indian or Sicilian. Possible is 1 ... e5 2 d4 ed 3 ed d5, giving a normal Exchange French! Also: 1 ... d5 2 f4 – Bird; 1 ... c5 2 b3 – Larsen.

1 ♘a3 (Durkin Attack) generally intends the follow-up c4. All sensible replies equalise.

1 ♘h3 (Amar Opening) 1 ... d5 2 g3 e5 3 ♗g2 h5 (3 ... f5 4 0-0 ♘f6 5 c4 dc 6 ♕a4+ ♗d7 7 ♕xc4 ± Tartakower-Moroni, 1932) 4 d4 ed 5 ♕xd4 ♘c6 6 ♕a4! ♗d7 7 ♘f4! ∞ Amar-Tartakower, Paris 1932.

[2] Other replies transpose elsewhere.

[3] A Modern Defence reversed; 5 c4!?

[4] 5 ... ♗d6!?

[5] 10 a3 ♖e8 11 ♖d1 ♗c5 ∞ Petrosian-Polugayevsky, USSR Ch 1973.

[6] Hungarian Attack (Benko-Bilek-Barczay Opening), frequently transposing to other openings.

[7] 3 ... c5 – Closed Sicilian.

3 ... d6 – Pirc or Modern Defence.

[8] Forintos-Lengyel, Kecskemet 1972.

[9] Bilek-Geller, Havana 1971.

[10] 3 c4!? dc! 4 ♕a4+ ♗d7 5 ♕xc4 ♘c6 =.

[11] 3 ... ♘c6 4 ♘f3 ♘f6 5 0-0 ♗g4!? (5 ... ♗e7 – King's Indian Attack) 6 h3 ♗f5 7 ♘c3 ♕d7 8 ♔h2 (Tal-Kupreichik, USSR 1981) 8 ... 0-0-0

9 ♗g5 d4 ∞ Tal.

[12] 4 ... ♗d6 5 0-0 ♘e7 6 c4 ♗f5 7 cd cd = Kavalek-Blatny, Czechoslovak Ch 1962.

[13] 5 ... ♘e7 Korchnoi.

[14] 10 f4 f6 11 fe fe 12 c3 ± Christiansen-Korchnoi, Lone Pine 1981.

[15] Grob's Opening.

[16] Basman.

2 ♗g2 c6 3 g5 (3 c4?! dc 4 b3 cb 5 ♕xb3 e5 6 ♘c3 ♕b6 ∓) 3 ... h6! 4 h4 hg 5 hg ♖xh1 6 ♗xh1 ♘d6 7 ♘f3 ♗g4 8 d5 e5 ∓.

[17] 3 ... ♘c6 4 c4 dc 5 ♕a4 (5 b3 ♗e6 6 bc ♗c5 7 ♘c3 ♘ge7 8 ♘f3 ♘g6 9 d3 0-0 = Basman-Whitehead, Manchester 1981) 5 ... ♘ge7 6 ♘f3 ♘g6 7 ♘c3 ♗e6 8 h4 ♗b4 9 ♘g5 ♗d7 10 ♗d5 0-0 ∞ Basman-Miles, Manchester 1981.

[18] Basman-Keene, Manchester 1981.

[19] Dunst Opening.

[20] 2 ♘f3 ♘c6 3 d4 cd 4 ♘xd4 g6 5 ♗f4 ♘f6! =.

[21] Intending ... ♕d8, ... b5.

[22] 2 ... de 3 ♘xe4 ♗f5 4 ♕f3 ♕d5 5 ♘d6+ ♕xd6 6 ♕xf5 ♘c6 7 ♗b5 ♘f6 = Marroleni-Foguelman, Argentina 1969.

[23] 4 ♘f3!? ♗d7 5 d3 c5 6 c4 (Myers-Bills, California 1955) 6 ... b5!? 7 cb ♕a5+ ∞/∓.

[24] Figueroa-Marcussi, Argentina 1963.

[25] Sokolsky Opening.

[26] **1 ... f5!?** 2 ♗b2 ♘f6 3 g3 e6 4 b5 ♗e7 5 c4 0-0 6 ♘f3 d6 ∞ Schaufelberger-Bhend, Lugano 1970.

1 ... c6!? intending 2 ♗b2 ♕b6.

[27] 5 f4 ♗g7 6 ♘f3 e5 7 fe ♘g4 8 ♗c4 0-0 9 0-0 d5 = Barendregt-Kuijpers, Amsterdam 1966.

[28] Sokolsky-Luik, Amsterdam 1966.

[29] 2 ... ♕d6!? (Andersson) 3 b5 ♕b4 4 ♗e5!? Tisdall.

[30] 4 f4 e6 5 b5 c5 6 ♘f3 ♘bd7 7 ♗e2 ♗d6 8 0-0 0-0 =.

[31] Katalimov-Litvinov, USSR 1971.

[32] 2 ... f6 3 b5 (3 e4 ♗xb4 4 ♗c4 ♘c6 5 f4 d6 6 c3 ♗a5 7 ♘e2 ♕e7 8 0-0 ♗b6 ∓ Sokolsky-Zagorovsky, USSR 1968) 3 ... d5 4 e3 ♗e6 5 d4 e4 ∞.

[33] 7 ... ♘xd5 8 g3 intending ♗g2 =.

[34] Boleslavsky.

Larsen Attack   Bird's Opening

1 b3 was tried by Nimzowitsch in the 1920s but had to wait another 40 years before Larsen made it really respectable. We therefore choose the name Larsen Attack, as there are simply too many Nimzowitsch openings! In common with other flank openings White's idea is to control the centre by indirect means and avoid committing his central pawns too early. White's reticence allows Black to equalise in a number of ways. His most ambitious counter is 1 ... e5, which leads to an unbalanced position with equal chances.

1 f4 was popularised by the English master Henry Bird in the latter half of the last century, but its history goes back a millenium earlier. The strategic ideas of Bird's Opening, in particular control of e5, are similar to those in the more popular Dutch Defence (1 d4 f5). White's extra tempo is not enough to counterbalance the fact that 1 f4 is a basically innocuous move. The From Gambit 1 f4 e5 is periodically 'refuted' but at present looks good enough for at least equality. White's best may be to transpose into the King's Gambit by 2 e4.

	1	2	3	4	5	6	7	8	9	
				Larsen Attack		**1 b3**				
1	b3	♗b2	♘f3	e3	♗e2	0-0	d3	♘bd2	♖e1	=
	b5[1]	♗b7	♘f6	a6	e6	♗e7	d5	♘bd7	b4[2]	
2	...	♗b2	f4[3]	e3	♘f3	♗d3	0-0	♘c3	a3	∞
	b6	♗b7	e6	♘f6	c5	♘c6[4]	♕c7	a6	d5[5]	
3	...	♗b2[6]	e3	♘f3	♗e2	0-0	d3	♘bd2	a3	=
	c5	♘c6	♘f6	g6	♗g7	b6	♗b7	e6	♕e7[7]	
4	...	...	c4	g3	♗g2	♗xf6!?	♘c3	h4!	♘f3	=
	...	♘f6	d6	♘c6	g6!?	ef	h5!	♗h6!	♗g4[8]	
5	...	♗b2	e4!?[9]	g3	♗g2	♘e2	0-0	♖e1	a4	=
	♘f6	g6	d6[10]	♗g7	0-0	e5[11]	♖e8![12]	c5!	♘c6[13]	
6	...	♗b2	e3	♗b5[14]	f4	♘f3	0-0	a4	♗xc6	±
	d5	c5	♘c6	♗d7	♘f6	e6	♗e7	0-0	♗xc6[15]	
7	...	...	h3	♘f3	e3	♗e2	d3	♘bd2[16]	a3	∞
	...	♗g4	♗h5	♘d7	♘gf6	e6	♗d6	♕e7	c6[17]	
8	...	...	♘f3	e3	c4	♗e2	0-0	d3[19]	♘bd2	=
	...	♘f6	♗g4[18]	c6	♘bd7	e6	♗d6	0-0	♕e7[20]	
9	...	♗b2	c4	e3[22]	cd	a3	♕c2	♘f3	♘c3	=
	e5	♘c6[21]	♘f6	d5	♘xd5	♗d6	0-0	♕e7	♘xc3	
10	...	...	e3	f4	♘f3	♗b5	0-0	fe	♘g5	∞
	...	...	g6[23]	♗g7	d6	♗d7	♘f6	de	0-0[24]	
11	...	...	...	♗b5	♘e2	0-0	♗xc6	d4	c4	=
	...	...	♘f6	d6	♗d7	a6	♗xc6	♕e7	g6[25]	

[1]   1 ... c6 2 ♗b2 (2 e4 – Caro Kann) 2 ... d5 3 e3 ♗f5!?; 3 ♘f3 ♗g4!?
  1 ... e6 2 ♗b2 (2 e4 – French) 2 ... ♘f6 3 f4 d5 4 ♘f3 ♗e7 5 g3!?
  1 ... f5 2 ♗b2 ♘f6 3 c4 g6 4 d4 ♗g7 5 g3 d6 6 ♗g2 c6 7 ♘f3 – Leningrad Dutch; 3 d3 d6 4 e4 e5 5 ef ♗xf5 6 ♘e2 ♘c6 = Planinc-Bilek, Vrsać 1971. 2 ♘f3 b6 3 ♗b2 ♗b7 4 g3 ♗xf3?! 5 ef e6 6 f4 ♘f6 7 ♗g2 c6 8 0-0 ♗e7 9 ♕e2 ± Nimzowitsch-Tartakower, Carlsbad 1923.

[2]   Timman-Böhm, Amsterdam 1975.

[3]   3 e3 f5?! (3 ... ♘f6) 4 ♗e2 ♘f6 (4 ... ♗xg2 5 ♗h5+ g6 6 ♗f3! ±±) 5 ♗xf6! ef 6 ♗f3 ±/± Larsen-Bellon, Palma de Mallorca 1971.

[4]   6 ... ♗e7!?

[5]   Larsen-Wade, Hastings 1972/73.

[6]   2 c4 b6! 3 ♗b2 ♗b7 4 ♘f3 ♘f6 5 e3 e6 = Petrosian-Saidy, San Antonio 1972.

[7]   Andersson-Keene, Montilla 1974.

[8]   Keene-Bellon, Menorca 1974.

[9]   3 g4!? h6 (3 ... ♗g7 4 g5 ♘h5 5 ♗xg7 ♘xg7 6 ♕c1 0-0 7 ♕b2 d5!? 8 ♗g2 c6 9 ♘f3 ♘d7 10 d4 ± Holmov-Oplachkin, Kirgizh 1966; 7 ... d6! intending 8 ... e5, 9 ... f5 = Soltis) 4 h4 ♗g7 5 c4 c5 6 ♘f3 d6 7 ♖g1 e5 8 g5 hg 9 hg ♘g4 ∓ Wade-Gilberto, Cienfuegos 1975.
  3 ♘f3 ♗g7 4 e3 0-0 5 ♗e2 (5 c4 – note 7) 5 ... d6 6 d4 e5 7 c4 ♘bd7 8 ♘c3 ♖e8 9 ♕c2 c6 10 0-0 ♕e7 11 ♖fd1 e4! ∞ Lein-Lapenis, Riga 1968.

[10]   3 ... ♗g7 4 e5 ♘d5 5 ♘f3 c5 6 ♘c3 (Smyslov-Adorjan, Amsterdam 1971) 6 ...

♘xc3 ∞.

[11]   6 ... c5!? 7 d4 ♘bd7 8 0-0 ♖b8 9 a4 b6 Larsen-Uitumen, Lugano Ol 1968.

[12]   7 ... c5!? 8 ♘bc3! ♘c6 9 h3 ♖b8 10 f4 b5 11 d3 ± Bagirov-Kapengut, USSR Ch 1972.

[13]   Bellon-Polugayevsky, Palma de Mallorca 1972.

[14]   4 f4 d4 5 ♗b5 ∞.

[15]   10 ♘e5 ± Zaitsev-Klovan, USSR Ch 1967.

[16]   8 g4 ♗g6 9 g5 ♘h5 10 ♖g1 h6 11 h4 gh 12 hg ♕e7 ∓.

[17]   10 c4 0-0 11 g4 (11 0-0 e5 ∓) 11 ... ♗g6 ∞ Bronstein-Tal, USSR Ch 1972.

[18]   3 ... e6 – Réti.

[19]   8 d4?! 0-0 9 h3 ♗h5 10 ♘bd2 ♕e7 = Stein-Vaganian, USSR Ch 1971.
  8 cd!? cd 9 ♘d4 ♗xe2 10 ♕xe2 0-0 11 f4 ♖c8 12 ♘c3 a6 = Petrosian-Mecking, Las Palmas 1975.

[20]   10 ♘d4 ♗xe2 11 ♕xe2 ±/= Andersson-Hort, Göteborg 1971.

[21]   2 ... d6 3 e3 ♘c6 4 ♗b5 a6 5 ♗xc6 bc 6 f4 ef 7 ♕f3 d5 8 ♕xf4 ± Schneider-Ghinda, Kiel 1979.

[22]   4 ♘f3 e4 5 ♘d4 ♗c5 ∓ Larsen-Spassky, Belgrade 1970.

[23]   3 ... d5?! 4 ♗b5 ♗d6 5 c4 dc 6 ♘f3! ♗g4 (6 ... cb 7 ♕xb3 ∞ Gligorić) 7 bc ♘f6 8 ♕c2 ♘d7 9 ♗xc6 bc 10 ♕e4 ± Pazos-Ahmed, Skien 1979. 5 f4!?

[24]   10 ♗a3 ∞ Forintos-Hoen, Skopje Ol 1972.

[25]   Bellon-S.Garcia, Palma de Mallorca 1971.

Bird's Opening   1 f4

	1	2	3	4	5	6	7	8	9	
1	f4	c4!?[1]	♘f3	b3	♗b2	g3	♘a3	♘c2	♗g2	=
	d5	e6	c5[2]	♘c6	d4	f5	♘f6	♘e4	a5[3]	
2	...	♘f3	e3	♗e2	0-0	d3	♕e1	♕h4	♘bd2	=
	...	♘f6[4]	g6[5]	♗g7	0-0	c5	♘c6	b6	♕c7[6]	
3	...	g3	♗g2	d3[7]	♘f3	fe	e4[8]	0-0	♘c3	=
	♘c6	g6	♗g7	d6	e5	de	♘ge7	0-0	♘d7[9]	
4	...	fe[10]	ed	♘f3	g3[12]	♘h4	d4	♘g2	c3	∞
	e5	d6	♗xd6	g5[11]	g4	♘e7	♘g6	♘c6	h5[13]	

[1]   Mujannah.

[2]   Double Mujannah.

[3]   10 0-0 ♗e7 Laroche-De Riviere 1867.

[4]   2 ... g6 3 g3 ♗g7 4 ♗g2 ♘f6 5 c4 c6 6 ♕b3 0-0 7 ♘c3 d4 8 ♕d1 c5 9 ♘f2 ♘c6 = Lombardy-Portisch, Monaco 1969.

[5]   3 ... e6 4 d3 c5 5 ♗e2 ♗e7 6 0-0 ♘c6 = Pelikan-Flohr, Podebrady 1936.

[6]   10 e4 de 11 de ♘b4 = Minev-Johansson, Halle 1967.

[7]   4 ♘c3 e5 5 d3 d6 6 ♘f3 ♘ge7 7 0-0 0-0 =.

[8]   7 ♗g5 ♘ge7 8 e4 ♗g4 9 ♕d2 ♕d7 = Knaak-Malich, GDR Ch 1973.

[9]   Lutikov-Gligorić, Sarajevo 1967.

[10]   2 e4 – 1 e4 e5 2 f4.

[11]   4 ... ♘f6 5 d4 ♗g4 6 ♕d3 c5 7 ♕e4+ ♗e6 8 ♗g5 ♗xh2 9 ♕xe6 ♕h4+ 10 ♔d2 fe 11 ♖xh2 ♕g5+ 12 ♔e3 ♘xh2 13 ♕xe6+ and now 13 ... ♕e7!? O'Kelly.

[12]   5 d4 g4 6 ♘e5 ♗xe5 7 de ♕xd1+ 8 ♔xd1 ♘c6 =.

[13]   10 e4 h4 11 e5 ♗e7 ∞ Larsen-Zuidema, Beverwijk 1964.

5

Réti Opening

Brainchild of the hypermodern movement, the Réti attempts to control and influence the centre from a distance. It avoids immediate theoretical debate and postpones the conflict, a slow positional development of the struggle being the customary result. Because of its shy personality the game can tend toward Black systems with an extra move, and the reversed Benoni and King's Indian Attack (rows 1-3; see also French I, rows 5-6 and Sicilian: Introduction, row 7) make up significant portions of the opening's theory. Another frequent choice is the Neo-Catalan, where White delays or omits entirely the advance d4.

Although indirect, this opening still maintains good chances of a small but tangible plus and should appeal to those who prefer a non-theoretical struggle.

	2	3	4	5	6	7	8	9	10	
Réti						**1 Nf3 d5**				
1	g3	Bg2	0-0	d3	Nbd2[3]	e4	c3[5]	ed	a4	=
	Nf6[1]	g6[2]	Bg7	0-0	Nc6	e5[4]	a5	Nxd5	h6[6]	
2	...	...	0-0	b3[7]	Bb2	d3	Nbd2[8]	Re1[10]	e4	±
	...	c6	Bf5	e6	Be7	h6	Bh7[9]	0-0	a5[11]	
3	...	...	...	d3	Nbd2	h3[14]	Qe1	e4	e5[15]	∞
	...	...	Bg4	Nbd7[12]	e6[13]	Bh5	Be7	0-0	Ne8[16]	
4	...	Bg2	d4	0-0	Nxd4	Nb3	c4	cd	Nc3	±
	c5	Nc6[17]	e6[18]	cd[19]	Bc5	Bb6[20]	Nge7	Nxd5	Nxc3[21]	
5	c4[22]	Na3[23]	Nxc4	b3	Bb2	g3	Bg2	0-0	Nh4	±
	dc	c5[24]	Nc6	f6	e5	Nge7	Nd5[25]	Be7	0-0[26]	
6	...	e3[27]	ed	Nxd4	Nc3	d3	Qe2[31]	Be3	0-0-0	=
	d4	Nc6[28]	Nxd4	Qxd4	e5[29]	Ne7[30]	Bd7	Qd6	0-0-0[32]	
7	...	g3	Bg2	0-0[34]	b4	Ng5	Nxe4	Bxe4	Re1	=
	...	Nc6[33]	e5	Nf6[35]	e4	Bxb4	Nxe4	Bh3	Qf6[36]	
8	...	g3	Bg2	b3[38]	Bb2	Qc2[40]	0-0	d3	Nbd2	±
	c6	Nf6[37]	g6	Bg7	Qb6[39]	Na6[41]	0-0	Rd8	Bg4[42]	
9	...	...	...	b3[43]	Bb2	0-0	Nc3	d3[45]	e4	=
	...	...	Bf5	e6	Nbd7	Be7[44]	0-0	e5[46]	de[47]	
10	...	...	...	...	...	...	d3	Nc3[48]	Qc2	=
	...	...	...	...	...	h6	Bc5	0-0[49]	Bh7[50]	

1 2 ... ♘c6 3 ♗g2 e5 4 d3 ♘f6 5 0-0 ♗e7 6 a3 0-0 7 b4 e4 8 ♘fd2 ♗f5 (8 ... ed 9 cd ± Day-Timman, Malta Ol 1980) 9 ♘c3 ed 10 cd ± Miles-Sosonko, Reykjavik 1980.

2 3 ... ♗f5 4 0-0 e6 5 d3 ♗e7 6 ♘bd2 0-0 7 ♘h4 ♗g6 8 ♘xg6 ± Bielicki-Letelier, Mar del Plata 1962.

   3 ... e6 4 d3 – French.

3 6 ♘c3 c6 7 e4 de 8 de ♕xd1 9 ♖xd1 ♘a6 = Lange-Stahlberg, Hamburg 1955.

4 7 ... de 8 de e5 9 c3 b6 10 ♖e1 a5 11 ♕c2 ± Najdorf-Unzicker, Palma de Mallorca 1969.

5 8 ed ♘xd5 9 ♖e1 a5 10 ♘c4 ♘de7 11 ♗d2 f6 12 a4 ♗e6 ∓ Sergiyevsky-Korchnoi, Sochi 1966.

6 11 ♘c4 = Polugayevsky-Sveshnikov, Sochi 1974.

7 5 d3 e6 6 ♘bd2 h6 7 ♕e1 ♗e7 8 e4 ♗h7 9 ♕e2 0-0 = Dely-Hort, Sarajevo 1964. 9 ♘e5!? ♘bd7 10 ♘xd7 ♘xd7 11 f4 ± Vaganian-Sveshnikov, Sochi 1980.

8 8 e3 ♗h7 9 ♕e2 a5 10 a4 ♘a6 11 ♘c3 ♘c5 = Larsen-Polugayevsky, Le Havre 1966.

9 8 ... a5 9 a3 0-0 10 ♘e5 ♘a6 11 e3 ♗h7 12 ♕e2 ♕b6 oo Lein-Polugayevsky, USSR Ch 1967.

10 9 ♕e1 0-0 10 e4 a5 11 a4 ♘a6 12 e5 ± Vladimirov-Haritonov, USSR 1977.

11 11 a4 ± Polugayevsky-Hort, Sarajevo 1975.

12 5 ... ♕c7 6 ♘bd2 e5 7 e4 de 8 de h6 9 h3 ± Keene-Castro, Lugano Ol 1968.

13 6 ... e5 7 e4 de 8 de ♕c7 9 ♕e1 ♘c5 10 ♘c4 ± Panno-Korchnoi, Palma de Mallorca 1972.

14 7 e4 ♗e7 8 ♕e1 de 9 de 0-0 = Christoph-Geller, Bath 1973.

15 10 ♘h2 e5 11 f4 ef 12 gf de 13 de ♘c5 ∓ Kirov-Geller, Skara 1980.

16 11 g4 ♗g6 12 ♘h2 ♘c7 oo Geller.

17 3 ... g6 4 0-0 ♗g7 5 d4 cd 6 ♘xd4 ± is a Grünfeld reversed.

18 4 ... ♘f6 5 0-0 ♗g4 6 dc e5 7 c4 ♗xc5 8 cd ♕xd5 9 ♘c3 ♕xd1 10 ♖xd1 ± Petrosian-Sosonko, Las Palmas 1980.

19 5 ... ♗d7!? 6 dc!? ♗xc5 7 c4 d4 8 ♘d2 e5 9 ♘b3 ♗b6 10 e3 de 11 ♗xe3 ♗xe3 12 fe ♕e7 oo Osnos.

20 7 ... ♗e7!? 8 c4 ♘f6 9 cd ed! – Tarrasch Defence.

21 11 ♕xd8+!? ♔xd8 12 bc ♗d7 13 c4 ± Speelman-Mestel, Hastings 1979/80.

22 Réti.

23 3 ♕a4+ ♗d7 (3 ... ♘c6 4 ♘c3 ♘f6 5 g3 ♘d5 6 ♕xc4 ♘b6 7 ♕b3 g6 = Janata-Lehmann, West Germany 1969) 4 g3 a6 5 ♕xc4 b5 6 ♕c2 ♗b7 7 ♗g2 c5 = Ernst-Kieninger, Germany 1940.

24 3 ... ♘f6 4 ♘xc4 g6 5 b4 ♗g7 6 ♗b2 = Jansa-Estevez, Luhacovice 1973.

25 Better is 8 ... ♘f5 (Alekhine).

26 Botvinnik-Fine, Nottingham 1936.

27 3 b4 f6 4 e3 e5 5 ♗b2 (5 ed? e4 6 ♘h4 ♕xd4 ∓ Liberzon-Ree, Amsterdam 1977) 5 ... c5 6 ed cd 7 a3 ♘h6 8 ♗d3 a5 = Kramer-Tartakower, 1937.

28 3 ... c5 4 d3 ♘c6 5 ed cd 6 g3 e5 7 ♗g2 ♗d6 8 0-0 ♘ge7 9 a3 a5 10 ♘bd2 ± Speelman-Miles, British Ch 1979.

29 6 ... ♘f6 7 d3 c6 8 ♗e3 ♕d7 9 d4 ± Alekhine-Euwe, match 1937.

30 7 ... ♘f6 8 ♗e2 c6 9 ♗e3 ♕d8 10 d4 ed 11 ♕xd4 ♕xd4 12 ♗xd4 ± Panno-Polugayevsky, Petropolis IZ 1973.

31 8 ♗e3 ♕d8 9 d4 ed 10 ♕xd4 ♕xd4 11 ♗xd4 ♘c6 = Langeweg-Hort, Amsterdam 1978.

32 Bagirov-A.Mikhalchishin, USSR Ch 1978.

33 3 ... c5 4 b4 cb 5 a3 ba 6 ♗xa3 ♘c6 7 d3 g6 8 ♗g2 ± Larsen-Portisch, Palma IZ 1970.

34 5 d3 ♗b4+ 6 ♘fd2 (better is 6 ♘bd2) 6 ... a5 7 ♘a3 ♘f6 8 ♘c2 ♗f5 9 0-0 0-0 ∓ Vadasz-Vaganian, Erevan 1980.

35 5 ... e4 6 ♘e1 ♘f6 7 d3 ed = Bilek.

36 Psakhis-Zhuravlev, USSR 1979.

37 3 ... dc 4 ♗g2 b5 5 a4 ♗b7 6 b3 cb 7 ♕xb3 a6 8 ab ab 9 ♖xa8 ♗xa8 10 ♘e5 with compensation, Schmid-Schaufelberger, Switzerland 1970.

38 5 ♕c2 ♗g7 6 0-0 0-0 7 d3 ♖e8 8 ♗f4 ♘bd7 9 cd ♘xd5 = Jakobsen-Romanishin, Amsterdam 1973.

39 6 ... 0-0 7 0-0 ♗g4 8 d3 ♗xf3 9 ♗xf3 ♖e8 10 ♘d2 a5 11 a3 ± Larsen-Panno, Buenos Aires 1980.

40 7 ♕c1 ♗e6 8 ♘d4 ♘bd7 9 ♘xe6 fe 10 0-0 0-0 11 d3 ♘g4 = Romanishin-Pomar, Göteborg 1971.

41 7 ... ♗e6!?

42 Miles-G.Garcia, Hastings 1974/75.

43 5 cd cd 6 ♕b3 ♕c8 7 ♘c3 e6 8 d3 ♘c6 9 ♗f4 ♗e7 10 0-0 0-0 11 ♖ac1 ± Korchnoi-Karpov, Moscow (match) 1974.

44 7 ... ♗d6 8 d3 0-0 9 ♘c3 ♕e7 10 ♖e1 e5 11 cd cd 12 e4 de = Katetov-Tomović, Czechoslovakia v Yugoslavia 1947.

45 9 ♘h4 ♗g4 10 h3 ♗h5 11 g4 d4! 12 ♘b1 ♗xg4 13 hg ♘xg4 with an attack, Smyslov-Bronstein, Zürich C 1953.

46 9 ... h6!?

47 11 de ♘xe4 12 ♘xe4 ♗xe4 13 ♘xe5 ♗xg2 14 ♔xg2 ♘xe5 = Filip-Geller, Göteborg IZ 1955.

48 9 ♘bd2 0-0 10 ♕c2 ♕e7 11 e4 de 12 de ♗h7 13 a3 a5 = Keres-Euwe, AVRO 1938.

49 9 ... ♗h7?! 10 e4 de 11 0-0 12 ♕e2 ♕e7 13 e5 ± Eliskases-Euwe, Buenos Aires 1947.

50 11 e4 de 12 de ♕e7 13 ♕e2 e5 = Sajtar-Milner Barry, Helsinki Ol 1952.

	2	3	4	5	6	7	8	9	10	
11	c4	g3	♗g2	b3[51]	♗b2	0-0	d3	♘bd2[53]	a3	±
	c6	♘f6	♗g4	e6	♘bd7	♗e7[52]	0-0	♖e8	a5[54]	
12	...	g3	♗g2	♕a4+[56]	♕xc4	♕c2[59]	0-0[60]	♘c3	d4	=
	e6	♘f6	dc[55]	♘bd7[57]	c5[58]	b6	♗b7	♗e7	cd[61]	
13	...	...	...	0-0	b3[62]	♗b2	e3[63]	ed	♖e1	∞
	...	...	♗e7	0-0	c5	♘c6	d4[64]	cd	♕b6[65]	
14	...	...	...	...	...	♗b2	e3[66]	♘c3	bc	=
	...	...	...	...	b6	♗b7	c5[67]	dc[68]	♘c6[69]	

[51] 5 cd ♗xf3! (5 ... cd 6 ♘e5 ♗c8 7 0-0 e6 8 ♘c3 ♗e7 9 d4 ± Smyslov-Darga, Amsterdam IZ 1964) 6 ♗xf3 cd 7 0-0 e6 8 ♘c3 ♘c6 9 d3 ♗e7 = Keene-Geller, Teesside 1975.

[52] 7 ... ♗c5 8 d3 0-0 9 ♘bd2 ♕c7 10 h3 ♗xf3 11 ♘xf3 ± Korchnoi-Sakharov, USSR Ch 1965.

[53] 9 ♘c3 a5 10 ♕c2 ♖e8 11 e4 de 12 de ♗xf3 13 ♗xf3 e5 = Pirc-Damjanović, Yugoslavia 1963.

[54] 11 ♖e1 ♗f8 12 ♘e5 (12 e4? ♘c5) 12 ... ♘xe5 13 ♗xe5 ♗d6 14 ♗xd6 ♕xd6 15 d4 ± Larsen-Petrosian, Buenos Aires (*Clarin*) 1979.

[55] 4 ... c6 5 b3 (5 d4 – Catalan) 5 ... a5 6 0-0 a4 7 ba dc 8 ♕c2 ♕a5 9 ♕xc4 ♕xa4 = Geller-Bronstein, USSR 1964.

[56] 5 ♘a3 ♗xa3 6 ba 0-0 7 ♕c2 ♕d5 8 ♕xc4 b6 = Adamski-A.Petrosian, Leipzig 1977.

[57] 5 ... ♗d7 6 ♕xc4 ♗c6 7 0-0 ♘bd7 8 ♕c2 e5 9 ♘c3 ♗c5 10 d3 0-0 11 e4 ± Smyslov-Suetin, USSR Ch 1952.

[58] 6 ... a6 7 0-0 b5 8 ♕c2 ♗b7 9 a4 c5 10 ab ab 11 ♖xa8 ♕xa8 = Smyslov-Szily, Budapest 1952.

[59] 7 0-0 b6 8 ♘c3 ♗b7 9 e4 a6 10 ♕e2 b5 = Mokalov-Sher, USSR 1976.

[60] 8 ♘e5 ♘d5 = Nei.

[61] 11 ♘xd4 ♗xg2 12 ♔xg2 ♕c8 13 e4 0-0 = Polugayevsky-Keres, USSR Ch 1973.

[62] 6 ♕c2 c5 7 cd ♘xd5 8 ♘c3 ♘c6 9 a3 a5 = Smyslov-Portisch, Palma de Mallorca 1967.

[63] **8 cd** ♘xd5 9 ♘c3 ♗f6 10 ♕c1 b6 11 ♘xd5 ed 12 d4 ♘xd4 13 ♘xd4 cd = Adamski-Filip, Stockholm 1975.

8 d3?! d4 9 e4 e5 10 h3 ♘e8 $\mp$ Gudmundsson-Taylor, USA 1981.

[64] 8 ... b6 9 ♘c3 ♗a6!? 10 d3 ♖c8 11 e4 d4 12 ♘b5 ± Miles-Spassky, Baden 1980.

[65] **10 ...** ♖e8 11 d3 ♗f8 12 a3 a5 13 ♘e5 ♘xe5 14 ♖xe5 ♘d7 15 ♖b5! ± Tal-Zhuravlev, USSR Ch 1967.

10 ... ♕b6 11 d3 ♖e8 12 ♘a3 e5 13 ♘c2 ♗f8 ∞ Schmidt-Geller, Nice Ol 1974.

[66] 8 cd ♘xd5 9 ♘c3 c5 10 ♘xd5 ♗xd5 = Larsen-Savon, Ljubljana/Portorož 1977.

[67] 8 ... a5 9 ♘c3 ♘e4 10 ♘xe4 de 11 ♘d4 ± Miles-Kurajica, Vrbas 1980.

[68] 9 ... ♘c6 10 cd ♘xd5 11 ♘xd5 ♕xd5 12 d4 ♘a5 13 ♗a3 ♖fd8 14 ♖c1 ± Toran-Filip, Skopje Ol 1972.

[69] 11 ♕e2 ♕c7 12 d3 a6 13 ♖ab1 ♖ab8 14 ♗a1 ♘a7 = Vaganian-Tal, Erevan 1980.

English

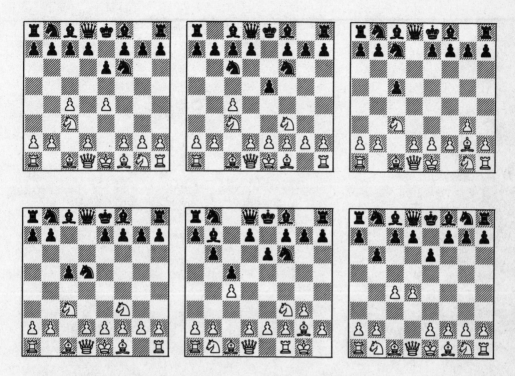

Disparaged once for being uninspired and uninspiring, the English has reached acceptance through a gradual, almost imperceptible process. As positional understanding has developed, so has appreciation of the finer points of this opening.

White's first move prepares a grip on the d5 square and much of the strategy will, not surprisingly, correspond to that of the Sicilian. The English can, however, be a real chameleon. Besides its similarity to a Sicilian with colours reversed, it can transpose at a moment's notice into the King's Indian, Grünfeld, Queen's Gambit, Nimzo-Indian or Dutch, as well as following its own unique paths.

Black is not at a loss for playable options:

1 c4 ♘f6 (The "Anglo-Indian") embraces a number of defences akin to the Nimzo-Indian, King's Indian and Grünfeld where White foregoes the move d4, giving these formations an independent turn. 2 ♘c3 e6 3 e4 (The **Mikenas Variation**) is a sharp attempt to get an edge without allowing Black the opportunity to head for quiet waters.

1 ... e5 (The "King's English") is a natural reply and leads to a variety of reversed Sicilian positions, of which the **English Four Knights** (1 c4 e5 2 ♘c3 ♘f6 3 ♘f3 ♘c6) is, at present, the most deeply researched.

1 ... c5 is sharper than its reputation and its range includes the **Symmetrical Variation**, the **English Two Knights**, the **Keres-Parma Variation**, the **Rubinstein Variation** and the 'Asymmetrical" Variation, the last two options demanding serious theoretical preparation due to their complexity and popularity.

The "Queen's English" (systems with ... b6) encompasses the fashionable **Hedgehog** (1 c4 c5 2 ♘f3 b6 3 g3 ♗b7 4 ♗g2 ♘f6 5 0-0 e6) and the obscure complications of the **English Defence** (1 c4 e6 2 d4 b6).

	2	3	4	5	6	7	8	9	10	
1	♘c3 d5	cd ♘xd5	g3 g6	♗g2 ♘xc3[2]	bc ♗g7	h4 h6[3]	♘h3 0-0	♕b3 ♘d7	♘f4 e6[4]	±
2	... ...	... ...	... ...	... ...	... ...	♘f3 0-0	0-0 c5[5]	♕a4! ♘d7[6]	♖b1 e5[7]	±
3	... ...	... ...	... ...	... ...	... ...	♖b1 ♘d7[8]	♘f3 0-0	0-0 e5[9]	d4 c6[10]	±
4	... ...	... ...	... ...	... ♘b6[11]	♘f3[12] ♗g7	0-0 0-0	d3 ♘c6	♗e3[13] e5[14]	♕c1 ♘d4[15]	±
5	... ...	... ...	... ...	... ...	d3 ♗g7	♗e3 0-0[16]	♕c1[17] ♖e8	♗h6 ♗h8	h4 ♘c6[18]	∞
6	... ...	... ...	♘f3 g6	♕a4+[19] ♗d7[20]	♕c2[21] ♘b6	d4 ♗g7	e4 0-0	♗e3 ♘c6	d5 ♘e5[22]	=
7	... ...	... ...	... ...	e4 ♘xc3[23]	bc ♗g7	♗a3! 0-0[24]	d4 ♘d7	♗d3 c5	0-0 b6[25]	±
8	... ...	... ...	... ...	... ...	dc ♕xd1+	♔xd1 ♘d7[26]	♗c4 ♗g7	♖e1 c6	♔c2 0-0[27]	±
9	... ...	... ...	... ...	g3 ♗g7	♗g2 e5[28]	♕a4+[29] c6	♘xd5 ♕xd5	0-0 ♘d7	d3 ♘c5[30]	±/=

[1] **1 ... g5** ±±. "Chess is not skittles" (Kasparov).

1 ... c6 2 ♘c3 ♘f6 3 e4 (3 d4 d5 – Slav) 3 ... d5 4 e5 d4 5 ef dc 6 bc (6 fg!?) 6 ... ef 7 d4 ♗d6 = Seirawan-Christiansen, US Ch 1978.

1 ... f5 is likely to transpose to the Dutch, or lines of the "King's English" with a later ... f5.

1 ... g6 2 e4 (here we mention the Adorjan System – transpositional possibilities in this line are numerous and obvious) 2 ... e5 3 d4 ♘f6 4 ♘f3 ♗b4+ 5 ♗d2 ♗xd2+ 6 ♕xd2 ♘xe4 7 ♕e3 d5 8 de ♘c6 9 ♘a3 ♗f5 10 ♘c2 ± Portisch-Sax, Rio de Janeiro IZ 1979.

1 ... e6 is another highly transpositional line. One independent branch is 2 ♘f3 d5 3 g3 c6 4 b3 b5 5 ♗g2 ♗a6 6 cd cd 7 0-0 ♘f6 intending ... b4 = Romanishin-Kurajica, Costa Catalana 1977.

[2] Smyslov Defence.

[3] 7 ... h5 8 ♘h3 0-0 9 ♕b3 ♘c6 10 ♘f4 e6 11 0-0 ♕d7 12 d4 ± Sliwa-Johannessen, Marianske Lazne 1961.

[4] 11 d4 c5 12 e3 ♖b8 (Langeweg-Johannessen, Zevenaa 1961) 13 a4 ±.

[5] 8 ... ♘d7 9 d4!? (9 ♖b1 – 7 ♖b1) 9 ... ♘b6! 10 ♗f4 ♘d5 11 ♗d2 c5 12 ♕b3 cd ∞ Romanishin-Gutman, USSR 1975.

[6] 9 ... ♘c6 10 ♖b1 ♘a5!? (10 ... ♕c7 11 d4 ♗d7 12 ♗f4! ♕c8 13 ♕a3 ±/± Stein-Polugayevsky, Leningrad 1971) 11 d3 b6 12 ♕h4 ♗b7 13 ♗h6 ♗xf3 14 ♗xf3 ♗xh6 15 ♕xh6 ♖c8 (Karpov-Korchnoi, 30th Game 1978) 16 h4! intending h5 ± Watson.

[7] 11 d3 a6 12 ♘g5 ♖b8 13 ♘e4 ♕c7 14 ♗e3 (14 c4!? intending ♘c3-d5 Watson) 14 ... h6 15 f4 ∞ (Tal-Bagirov, USSR Ch 1972) 15 c4 ± Watson.

[8] 7 ... ♘c6!? 8 ♘f3 0-0 9 0-0 b6! 10 ♗a3 ♖b8 11 ♕a4 ♗d7 12 ♕c2 ♗e8 = Nikolayevsky-Savon, USSR Ch 1966/67.

[9] 9 ... c5?! 10 d4 ♕a5 11 ♕b3 ♘b6 12 ♕a3 ±/± Gheorghiu-Stoica, Bucharest 1973.

9 ... ♘b6 10 ♕c2 (10 ♘d4 ♗xd4 11 cd ♕xd4 12 d3! ∞ Watson) 10 ... ♗d7 11 d3 ♗a4 12 ♕d2 ♗c6 13 c4 ♖e8 14 ♕f4! ±/±.

[10] 11 e4 ♕a5 12 ♕c2 ed 13 cd ♘b6 14 ♗d2 (Botvinnik-Smyslov, 16th Game 1958) 14 ... ♕h5! =. 14 ♗e3 intending 14 ... ♗e6 15 a4! ± Botvinnik.

[11] Czech Variation. Now White may transpose to the Neo-Grünfeld with d4.

[12] 6 h4 h6! 7 d3 ♘c6 8 ♘f3 ♗g7 9 ♗d2 e5 ∓ Marszalek-Savon, Warsaw 1969.

[13] 9 ♗d2 e5 10 ♘e4!? (10 ♕c1 – 9 ♗e3) 10 ... a5 11 ♘c5 ♘d7! ∞ Rashkovsky-Tukmakov, USSR Ch 1972.

9 a4 a5 10 ♗e3 e5 11 ♘b5 ± Dvoretsky-Gulko, USSR Ch 1973.

[14] 9 ... h6 10 ♕c1 ♔h7 11 ♖d1 e5 12 ♘c5! ♖e8 13 e3 a5 14 d4 e4 15 ♘e5 ♘xe5 16 de ± Tal-Jansa, Skopje Ol 1972.

[15] 11 ♗h6 ♗xf3+ 12 ♗xf3 c6 13 ♗xg7 ♔xg7 14 b4 ± Robatsch-Polugayevsky, Sochi 1967.

[16] 7 ... ♘c6 8 ♗xc6+! bc 9 ♗d2! ± Benko.

7 ... a5 8 ♕d2 h6 9 ♖c1 c6 10 f4 ♘8d7 11 ♘f3 ♘f6 12 h3 a4 ∞ Hurme-Koskinen, Finnish Ch 1980.

7 ... h6 8 ♕c1 ♘8d7 9 ♘f3 ♘f6 10 0-0 c6 (Simić-Bagirov, Vrnjacka Banja 1974) 11 ♖b1 ±.

[17] 8 ♕d2 ♘8d7 9 ♘f3 ♘f6 10 ♗h6 a5 11 0-0 c6 12 ♗xg7 ♔xg7 13 ♖ab1 ♘bd5 14 e4 ±/± Larsen-Hort, Amsterdam (IBM) 1980.

[18] 11 ♗xc6 bc 12 ♘f3 ♗g4 14 (Watson-Rohde, New York 1977) 13 ♘d2! ∞ Watson.

[19] Stein Attack. 5 ♕b3 ♘b6 6 g3 ♗g7 7 ♗g2 0-0 8 0-0 ♘c6 9 d3 h6 =.

[20] 5 ... ♘c6 6 ♘e5 ♘b4 7 a3 ♗g7 8 ab ♗xe5 9 e3 0-0 10 b5 ♘b8 11 ♗e2 c6 12 d4 ♗g7 13 0-0 cb 14 ♕xb5 ±/± Pachman-Hölzl, Biel 1980.

5 ... c6 6 ♕d4 ♖g8!? (6 ... ♘f6 7 ♕xd8+ ♔xd8 8 ♘e5 ±) 7 e4 ♗g7 ∞ Bagirov-Novak, Stary Smokovec 1981.

[21] 6 ♕h4 ♗c6 7 ♘e5 ♗g7 8 ♘xc6 ♘xc6 9 ♕e4 e6 10 e3 0-0 11 ♗c4 ♘ce7 12 0-0 c5 13 ♗e2 ♖c8 ±/= Kuligowski-Ftacnik, Malta Ol 1980.

[22] 11 ♘xe5 ♗xe5 12 ♖d1 ♕c8 13 f4 ♗g7 14 ♗e2 c6! = Benko-Szabo, Hastings 1973/74.

[23] 5 ... ♘b6 6 d4 ♗g7 7 h3 0-0 8 ♗e2 c6 9 0-0 ♘a6 10 ♗g5 ± Kaiszauri-Silva, London 1980.

[24] 7 ... b6 8 ♗c4 0-0 9 0-0 ♘c6 10 d4 ♘a5 11 ♗d3 ± Korchnoi-Timman, Leeuwarden (6) 1976.

[25] 11 ♕e2 ♗b7 (Averkin-Korchnoi, USSR Ch 1973) 12 e5! Yudovich.

[26] 7 ... f6!? (Najdorf-Mecking, Wijk aan Zee 1978) 8 e5 ∞.

[27] 11 ♗e3 ± Romanishin-Grigorian, USSR Ch 1976.

[28] 6 ... 0-0 7 0-0 ♘c6 (7 ... e5!) 8 d4 – Grünfeld Defence.

6 ... e5 is Korchnoi's Variation.

[29] 7 ♘xd5 ♕xd5 8 0-0 0-0 9 d3 ♘c6 10 ♗e3 ♕d6! = Mecking-Korchnoi, match (10) 1974.

7 0-0 0-0 8 d3 ♘e7 – 1 ... e5.

[30] Podgayets-Tukmakov, USSR 1974.

	5	6	7	8	9	10	11	12	13	
10	e4	♘ge2	0-0	d3³³	h3	♗e3	f4	f5		∞
	d6	e5³¹	♘bd7³²	c6	a6!	b5	♗b7	d5!³⁴		
11	♘f3	0-0	d3	♖b1	a3	♘d2	b4	ab	cd	=
	d6	e5	♘bd7	a5	c6!³⁵	♘b6!	ab	d5	cd³⁶	
12	...	...	...	♖b1³⁷	b4	b5	♖e1³⁹	♗h1	♕c2	∞/±
	...	...	♘c6	♗d7³⁸	♕c8	♘e7	♗h3	h6	♘g4⁴⁰	
13	...	...	...	...	a3	b4⁴²	ab	b5	e3	=
	...	...	...	a5	♘d4⁴¹	ab	c6	♗g4!	♘xf3+⁴³	
14	...	...	...	...	...	♘d2⁴⁴	h3	♔h2	b4	=
	...	...	...	...	♖e8	♗g4	♗e6	h6	ab⁴⁵	

	4	5	6	7	8	9	10	11	12	
15	g3⁴⁸	♗g2	a3	d4	0-0	b3!	♗b2			±
	0-0	d5	♗e7⁴⁹	c6	♘bd7	b6				
16	♕b3	a3	e3⁵⁰	♗e2	0-0	♘a4!				∞
	c5	♗a5	0-0	d5	♘c6	b6!?⁵¹				
17	♕c2	a3	♕xc3	e3	b3	♗b2	♗e2	0-0⁵²	♗xc4	=
	d5	♗xc3	0-0	a5	♘bd7	b6	♗b7	dc!	♘c5⁵³	
18	...	g3⁵⁴	♗g2	0-0	e3⁵⁵	♘e5	♗xa8	♗g2		∞
	c5	♘c6	0-0	♕e7	b6⁵⁶	♘xe5!	♗a6	♗xc4⁵⁷		
19	...	a3	g3⁵⁹	♗g2	0-0	d3	♖b1			=
	...	♗a5⁵⁸	0-0	♘c6	♕e7	a6⁶⁰	♗c7!			
20	...	a3	♕xc3	b4	♗b2	e3	d3	bc	♗e2	=
	0-0	♗xc3	b6	a5!?⁶¹	d6	e5	c5	bc	♘c6⁶²	

[31] 6 ... c6 7 0-0 a6 8 a4 a5 9 d3 ♘a6! 10 h3 ♘b4 = Hofland-van der Vliet, Dutch Ch 1977.

[32] 7 ... ♗e6 8 d3 (8 b3! ±) 8 ... ♕c8 9 f4 c6 10 b3 ± Dely-F.Portisch, Hungary 1978.

7 ... c6 8 d3 a6 9 h3 (9 a4!? a5 10 h3 ♘a6 ∞) 9 ... b5 10 b3 ∞.

[33] 8 f4 c6 9 h3 b5 10 d3! ♕b6+ 11 ♔h1 ∞ Seirawan-Sigurjonsson, Wijk aan Zee 1980.

[34] Watson.

[35] 9 ... ♘h5 10 e4 ♘c5 11 ♗e3 f5 12 ef ♗xf5 13 ♘e1 ♗c8 14 ♘c2 ±/= Andersson-Liberzon, Skara 1980.

[36] Ree-Polugayevsky, Amsterdam 1970.

[37] 8 ♗d2 h6 9 ♘e1 ♘h5 10 ♖c1 f5 11 ♘d5 f4 12 c5 ±/= Sunye-Littlewood, Hastings 1980/81.

[38] 8 ... ♗f5 9 e4!? (9 ♗g5!?) 9 ... ♗g4 10 h3 ♗xf3 11 ♗xf3 ♘d4 12 ♗g2 c6 13 b4 ± Watson.

8 ... h6 9 b4 ♗e6 10 b5 ♘e7 11 a4 ± Miles-Belyavsky, Hastings 1974/75.

8 ... ♘d4 9 b4 ∞.

8 ... ♘h5 9 b4 f5 10 ♘d5 f4 11 b5 ♘xd5 12 cd ± Watson-Agrachov, USA 1977.

8 ... ♖e8 9 ♘d2 ♗e6 10 ♘d5 (Watson-NN) 10 ... ♗xd5! 11 cd ♘e7 intending ... c6 = Watson. 9 ... ♗g4! Watson. 9 a3 a5 – 8 ... a5.

[39] 11 c5!?

[40] 14 ♘d5 ∞ Shatskes-Muchnik, Moscow 1966.

[41] 9 ... ♘h5 10 b4 ab 11 ab f5 12 b5 ♘e7 ∞/± Andersson-Smejkal, Amsterdam 1973.

9 ... h6 10 b4 ab 11 ab ♗e6 12 b5 ♘e7 13 ♗b2 ♕d7!? (13 ... ♘d2 14 ♖a1! ± Smyslov-Rashkovsky, USSR Ch 1977) 14 ♖e1 ♘h7 15 ♖a1 f5 16 ♕c2 ± Hernandez-van Tilbury, Havana 1980.

[42] 10 e3!? ♘xf3+ 11 ♗xf3 c6 =.

10 ♘d2?! c6 11 b4 ab 12 ab d5 ∓ Smejkal-Smyslov, Biel IZ 1976.

[43] 14 ♗xf3 ♗xf3 15 ♕xf3 d5 ½-½ Spiridonov-Szekely, Zamardi 1970.

[44] 10 b4 ab 11 ab e4 12 de ♘xe4 13 ♘xe4 ♖xe4 = Kivipelto-Westerinen, Finland 1970.

[45] 14 ab d5 = Petrosian-Keres, USSR Ch 1957.

[46] 3 g3 d5! – Catalan.

[47] 3 ... b6 – English ... b6 systems.

3 ... d5 4 d4 – Queen's Gambit.

3 ... ♗b4 is the Nimzo-English.

[48] 4 a3 ♗xc3 5 dc! d6 6 g3 e5 7 ♗g2 0-0 8 0-0 ♕e7 =.

[49] 6 ... ♗xc3 7 bc ♘c6! (Watson) ±/=.

[50] 6 e4!? (Watson) intending 6 ... ♗xc3 7 ♕xc3 ♘xe4? 8 ♕xg7 ♕f6 9 ♕xf6 ♘xf6 10 b4 ±. 6 ... ♘c6! ∞.

6 g3 ♘c6 7 ♗g2 d5 8 0-0 ♗xc3 9 ♕xc3 d4! ∞ Polugayevsky-Korchnoi, Sochi 1966.

[51] 9 ... ♕e7 10 ♕c2 ♘d7 11 d4 ±/ ± Karpov-Timman, Groningen 1968.

[52] 11 cd!? ♗xd5 12 d3 ♘c5 13 e4! (Watson) ±.

[53] Furman-Makarichev, USSR Ch 1973.

[54] 5 e3 ♘c6 6 b3 0-0 7 ♗b2 ♖e8 8 ♗e2 (Petrosian-Velimirović, Vršac 1981) 8 ... d5!? Petrosian.

[55] 8 d3 h6 9 e3!?

8 ♖d1 ♗xc3! 9 ♕xc3 e5 ∞/= Vaganian-Romanishin, USSR Ch 1975.

[56] 8 ... ♗xc3 9 ♕xc3 e5 10 b3 d6 11 ♗b2 h6 (Uhlmann-Balashov, Halle 1976) 12 d3! Watson.

[57] Watson.

[58] 5 ... ♗xc3 6 ♕xc3 ♘c6 7 b4 b6 8 e3 0-0 9 ♗b2 ♗b7 10 ♗e2 d6 11 0-0 e5 = Zichichi-Garcia, Malta Ol 1980.

[59] 6 e3!? ♘c6 7 d4 d6 8 ♗d3 0-0 9 0-0 ♕e7 ±/ ± Taimanov.

[60] 9 ... h6 10 e3 (10 ♖b1 a6 11 e3 ♖b8 12 d4 d6 13 dc dc_14 ♘a4 ♖d8 15 ♗d2 ♗xd2 16 ♘xd2 ♗d7 =/∓ Jelen-Velimirović, Yugoslav Ch 1981) 10 ... d6 11 b3 ♗d7 12 ♗b2 ± Lombardy-Polugayevsky, Reykjavik 1978.

[61] 7 ... ♗b7 8 ♗b2 d6 9 e3 ± Suba-Tal, Sochi 1977.

[62] Knott-Cafferty, British Ch 1980.

	3	4	5	6	7	8	9	10	11	
1	...	♘f3[2]	d4	♗d3	♗d2[3]	cd	e5	♗xc3	0-0[4]	=
	♘c6[1]	b6	♗b4	0-0	d5	ed	♗xc3	♘e4		
2	...	♘f3	d4[5]	♘xd4	f3	♗e3	♕d2	♕xc3	fe	∞
	e5!?	♘c6	ed	♗b4	0-0	♖e8	♗xc3	♘xe4	♕h4+[6]	
3	...	e5	♘f3[8]	♕c2	dc	♗f4	cd	h3[10]		±
	d5	♘e4[7]	c5[9]	♘xc3	♘c6	♗e7	ed			
4	...	...	ef	bc[11]	♘f3	♗d3	0-0	♗e4	♖b1	=
	...	d4	dc	♕xf6	e5	♗d6	0-0	♘c6	♗f5[12]	
5	...	...	...	...	d4	♗e2[14]	♗f3	♘xf3	♕a4+	±
	...	...	...	...	b6[13]	♗b7	♗xf3	♗d6	c6[15]	
6	...	...	...	...	...	♕e2[16]	de[17]	♕e3[18]	♘e2	=
	...	...	...	...	e5	♗e7	♕g6	♘c6	♕e6[19]	
7	...	cd	e5	♘f3[20]	♕b3	♕xd5	♗b5	♘xd5		=
	...	ed	♘e4	♗f5!	♘c5	♘c6	♕xd5	0-0-0[21]		
8	...	e5	d4	♕xd4	♕e4	♘f3	ed	♕d3[24]	♗d2	=
	c5	♘g8	cd	♘c6	d6[22]	♕a5[23]	♗xd6	♗e7	♘b4[25]	
9	...	...	...	...	...	♗d2	♕g4	♕xg7	♕xf6	=/∞
	...	...	...	...	♗b4	d6	♘xe5	♕f6	♘xf6[26]	
10	...	...	♘f3	d4	♘xd4	♗f4	♕b3	♕a4!	0-0-0	∞
	...	...	♘c6	cd	♕c7!?	♘xe5[27]	a6	♘e7	♘7c6[28]	

	8	9	10	11	12	13	14	15	16	
11	♗f4	♗g3	♘db5	♕a4[31]	h4[32]	0-0-0	h5	♗xf4	h6	=
	♘g6[29]	♘f6[30]	e5	♗e7	0-0	♕b6!	♘f4	ef	g6[33]	
12	♘db5	f4[35]	f5[36]	fe[37]	♕xd8+	♘d4				±
	f6[34]	♘f7	a6!?	de	♔xd8					
13	...	♘d6+	♕xd6	♗e3[38]	♗b6	♗xd8[40]	♘c7	c5	♗b6	∞
	a6	♗xd6	f6	♘e7[39]	♘f5	♘xd6	♔e7	♘e8	d5[41]	
14	♕a4	♗g5	0-0-0	c5[44]	♘e4	♘xf5	♕b3+			∞
	♘e7[42]	f6[43]	fg	♔f7	♘f5	ef				
15	...	♘b3	♗f4	♗g3	♗b5	0-0-0	♗d3	c5[45]		∞
	♗c5	♗e7	♘g6	♘f6	e5	0-0	d6			
16	...	♘db5[46]	c5	♘e4	♘xc5	♕d4	♗f4	♗g3	♗xb5[49]	∞
	♕c7	♕b8	♗xc5[47]	a6[48]	ab	♘e7!	♘7g6	0-0		

14

[1] Kevitz Defence.

[2] 4 d4 Bb4 5 e5!? Ne4 6 Qc2 Nxc3 7 bc ± Roos-Strech, Malta Ol 1980. 4 ... d5! =.

[3] 7 0-0!?

[4] Bernard-Kisubi, Malta Ol 1980.

[5] 5 a3 d6 Watson.

[6] Cramling-Hess, Reggio Emilia 1979/80.

[7] 4 ... Nfd7 5 cd ed (5 ... Nxe5 6 d4 Ng6 7 Bb5+ c6 8 dc Nxc6 9 Nf3 Be7 10 0-0 0-0 11 Re1 ±/=) 6 d4 c5 7 Nf3 Nc6 8 Bb5 a6 9 Bxc6 bc 10 0-0 Be7 11 dc Nxc5 12 Nd4 ± Smyslov-Farago, Hastings 1976/77.

[8] 5 Nxe4 de 6 Qg4 Nc6 7 Qxe4 Qd4 8 Qxd4 Nxd4 oo/= Sveshnikov-Kovan, USSR 1977. 6 ... Bd7 7 Qxe4 Bc6 8 Qe3 Na6 9 d4 Nb4 10 Kd2 a5 11 a3 Na6 12 Ke1! Be7 13 Bd2 a4 14 Bc3 0-0 15 Nf3 ± Chandler-Mednis, New York 1980.

[9] 5 ... Nc6 6 Qc2! f5 7 ef Nxf6 8 d4 ±.

[10] Watson.

[11] 6 fg cd+ 7 Bxd2 Bxg7 8 Qc2 Nc6 9 Nf3 Qe7 10 Bc3 Bxc3+ = Shatskes.

[12] Alburt-Mednis, New York 1980.

[13] 7 ... c5 8 Nf3 h6 9 Bd3 cd (9 ... Nd6!?) 10 cd Bb4+ 11 Kf1!? Nc6 12 Bb2 Bc5!? 13 Bc2 0-0 14 Qd3 Rd8 15 Rd1 Kf8 16 Qe4 ± Seirawan-Korchnoi, Wijk aan Zee 1980.

[14] 8 Nf3 Bb7 9 Bd3 h6 10 Qe2 Bd6 = Hübner-Unzicker, Bad Kissingen 1980.

[15] 12 Bg5 Qf5 13 0-0 0-0 ±/= Watson-Kane, San Francisco 1976.

[16] 8 Nf3 ed 9 Bg5 Qe6 10 Be2 f6 11 Nd4 Qf7! = Mateu-Rivas, Spanish Ch 1981.

[17] 9 Qxe5 Qxe5 10 de Nc6 11 Nf3 Bg4 12 Be2 0-0-0 13 Bf4 Rhe8 (Chekhov-Zaichik, USSR 1980) 14 Rd1 =.

[18] 10 h4 Nc6 11 h5 Qf5 12 Nf3 f6 13 h6 g6 14 ef Qxf6 15 Nd4 Nxd4 16 cd 0-0 + Guil.Garcia-Gild.Garcia, Cienfuegos 1980.

[19] 12 Nd4 Qxe5 13 Nxc6 Qxe3 14 Bxe3 bc 15 Be2 Nf6 = Sveshnikov-Makarichev, USSR Ch 1979.

[20] 6 d4 Qh4!? 7 Qc2 Bb4 oo.

[21] Gipslis-Roizman, Moscow 1965.

[22] 7 ... f5?! 8 Qe2 a6 9 Bd2 ± Bagirov-Abakorov, Baku 1959.

7 ... f6!? 8 f4 Nh6 9 Nf3 f5 10 Qe2 Bb4 11 Bd2 ± Whitehead-Lobo, USA 1980.

7 ... Qa5!? 8 Nf3 f5?! 9 ef Nxf6 10 Qc2 Ne5? 11 Be2 Nxf3+ 12 Bxf3 Qe5+ 13 Qe2! ± Christiansen-Kudrin, US Ch 1981. 10 ... d5!?

Christiansen.

[23] 8 ... de 9 Nxe5 Bd7!? 10 Nxd7 Qxd7 11 Bg5! ± Seirawan-Kudrin, US Ch 1981. 9 ... Nf6!? 10 Nxc6 Qb6 11 Qf3 bc 12 g3 Bb7 13 Bg2 Rb8! = Korchnoi-Andersson, Johannesburg 1981.

[24] 10 Bd3 Nf6 11 Qe2 (Pribyl-Adamski, Bucharest 1975) 11 ... 0-0 =.

[25] 12 Qb1 Qd8 13 a3 Nc6 = Seirawan-Peters, US Ch 1980.

[26] Rogoff-Csom, Biel 1976.

[27] 8 ... a6 9 Nxc6 Qxc6 10 Be2!? (Watson) intending Bf3.

[28] Watson.

[29] 8 ... f6 9 Bxe5 fe 10 Qh5+ g6 11 Qxe5 Qf6 12 Qe3 Bh6 = Tukmakov-Zhidkov, USSR 1980. 9 Qa4! oo Yusupov-Yudasin, USSR Ch 1981.

[30] 9 ... e5 10 Qe2!? Watson.

[31] 11 Bd3 a6 12 Qa4 Bc5 13 0-0-0 0-0 = Miles-Zaltsman, Lone Pine 1978.

[32] 12 0-0-0 =.

[33] Watson-Zaltsman, New York 1979.

[34] 8 ... Ng6 9 Ne4! Watson.

[35] 9 Bf4 a6 10 Nd6+ Bxd6 11 Qxd6 Nf7 =/∓ Timman-Karpov, Las Palmas 1977.

9 Be3 a6 10 Nd6+ Bxd6 11 Qxd6 Ne7 12 Bb6 Nf5 13 Bxd8 Nxd6 oo Shvedchikov-Yudasin, USSR Ch 1981.

[36] Keene.

[37] 11 Nd4!? Qc7!?

[38] 11 Bf4 – note 35.

[39] 11 ... Nf7 12 Qg3 Ne7! 13 Qxg7 Nf5 14 Qg4 Nxe3 oo Keene-Partos, Montreux 1977.

[40] 13 Qc5 d6 14 Qa5 Qe7 15 0-0-0 0-0 16 f4 Nc6 = Hernandez-Rodriguez, Havana 1980.

[41] 17 cd+ Nxd6 18 Bc5 Nf7 (18 ... b6 19 Bxb6 Nf5 20 0-0-0 Bb7 21 Bc5+ ± Kaiszauri-Botterill, London 1980) 19 Bc4!? (Watson) oo.

[42] 8 ... Nf6 9 Bd3 Ng6 10 h4 h5 11 Bd3 ±.

[43] 9 ... Qb6 10 0-0-0 Ng7 11 Ndb5 f5 12 Bd3 ±/± Murey-Kosenkov, USSR 1975.

[44] Watson.

[45] Watson.

[46] 9 Be2 Nc6 10 Ndb5 Qb8 11 Be3 a6 12 Nd4 ∓ Watson.

[47] 10 ... a6 11 Nd6+ Bxd6 12 ed Qxd6 13 Bf4 ± Watson.

[48] 11 ... Be7 12 Bf4 Nf3+ 13 gf Bxf4 14 Rd1 Watson.

[49] Watson-Rantanen, London 1978.

	2	3	4	5	6	7	8	9	10	
1	g3	d4¹	♕xd4	♘c3	♕e3+	♘b5	♗xe3			∞
	g6	ed	♘f6	♘c6	♕e7!	♕xe3	♔d8²			
2	...	♗g2³	e3⁴	♘e2	d4	ed	0-0	♘1c3		∞
	♘c6	g6	♗g7	d6	ed!	♘ge7	0-0			
3	...	♕a4	♗g2	♕c2	b4	♗b2⁵				∞
	c6	♘a6!?	♘c5	d5	♘e6					
4	...	♘f3	♘d4	cd	♗g2	d3	♘b3	♗d2	♕xd2	±
	...	e4	d5	cd⁶	♘f6	♗c5	♗b4+	♗xd2+	0-0⁷	
5	...	♗g2	♘c3	♘d5!	e3	♘e2	0-0	d3⁸		±
	♘f6	♘c6	♗b4	♗c5	0-0	♖e8	♗f8			
6	...	♘f3⁹	♘d4	cd	♕xd5	♘b3¹⁰	h3	♘c3	a3	=
	...	c6	e4	d5	♕xd5	♕h5	♕g6	♗b4	♗e7¹¹	
7	♘f3	♘d4	e3	ed	d5	♕e2	♘c3	d3	de	∞∞
	e4	♘c6	♘xd4	♕f6!?	♗c5	♕g6	♘f6	0-0	♘g4¹²	
8	d3	♘f3	♘c3	g3	♗g2	0-0	a3	♖b1	b4	=
	c6¹³	d6	f5	♘f6	♗e7	a5	0-0	♔h8	ab¹⁴	
9	e3	cd¹⁶	♘c3	♘f3	♗e2	d4	♘xd4	♘f3		=
	d5!?¹⁵	♕xd5	♕a5	c6	♗d6	ed	♕c7	♘f6		
10	♘c3	g3	♗g2¹⁸	d4	♘h3	0-0²¹	f3	cd	♗g5	=
	f5	♘f6¹⁷	c6¹⁹	e4²⁰	♘a6	♘c7	d5	cd	♗e7²²	
11	...	e3	d4	♘h3²³	♕b3	♕xc3	♗e2	0-0		±
	...	♘f6	e4	♗b4	♗xc3+	♘c6?!²⁴	d6	0-0²⁵		
12	...	d4	♕xd4	♕e3+!	♘h3	♕d2	a3	♕xc3²⁸		±
	...	ed?!²⁶	♘c6	♔f7²⁷	♘f6	♗b4?!	♗xc3			
13	...	e3²⁹	bc	e4	ef	d3	♘e2	♘g3	♗e2	∞
	♗b4	♗xc3	d6³⁰	f5!	♗xf5	♘e7	0-0	♗g6	♗e8³¹	
14	...	e3³²	d4	de	♕xd8+	b3	♗b2	0-0-0		=
	d6	f5	♘f6	de	♔xd8	c6	♔c7	♘bd7³³		
15	...	d4	♕xd4	♕d2	b3³⁴	e4	♘ge2	♖b1	ab	=/±
	...	ed	♘c6	♘f6	♗e6	a5	a4	ab	g6³⁵	
16	...	g3	♗g2	d3	f4³⁷	♘f3	0-0	♗xf4		=
	...	♘c6³⁶	♘f6	g6	♗g7	0-0	ef	h6³⁸		
17	...	...	♗g2	♘f3	0-0	d4	h3	♗xf3	♕xd4³⁹	±
	...	♗g4	c6	♘f6	♘bd7	♗e7	♗xf3	ed		

	2	3	4	5	6	7	8	9	10	
18	...	...	♗g2[40]	d3	f4[42]	gf[43]	♘f3	♖g1[44]		±
	...	♗e6	♘c6[41]	♕d7	ef	♗e7	♗h3			
19	...	...	...	d3	♘f3	0-0	c5!	cd	b3	±
	...	...	c6	♘f6	♗e7	0-0	h6	♗xd6	♘bd7[45]	
20	...	...	♗g2	d3[46]	♘f3	0-0	b4[47]			±
	...	f5	♘f6	♗e7	0-0	♔h8				
21	...	...	d4	de	♕xd8+	♗g2	b3	♗b2[48]		=
	...	...	♗e7!	de	♗xd8	♘f6	c6			

[1] 3 ♘c3 ♘c6 – King's English III.

[2] Larsen.

[3] 3 ♘c3 – King's English III, row 5 ff.

[4] 4 ♘c3 – King's English III, row 9 ff.

[5] Hartoch-Korchnoi, Dutch Ch 1977.

[6] 5 ... ♕xd5 – row 6.

[7] 11 ♘c3 ed ∓ Watson.

[8] Watson.

[9] 4 d4 ed 5 ♕xd4 d5 6 cd (6 ♘f3 dc! = Larsen-Hübner, Tilburg 1981) 6 ... cd 7 ♘f3 ♘c6 ∞ Andersson-Portisch, Tilburg 1981.

[10] 7 ♘c2 ♕h5 8 h3 ♕g6 9 ♘c3 ♗d6 10 ♘e3 0-0 = Shamkovich-Baumbach, USSR 1970.

[11] 11 d3 = Petrosian-Pytel, Bath 1973.

[12] 11 ♘d1 d6 12 f3 ♘e5 ∞ Murey-Udov, Moscow 1966. Black intends ... f5.

[13] 2 ... ♘c6 3 ♘c3 – 2 ♘c3. 2 ... g6 3 g3 – 2 g3.

[14] 11 ab ♗e6 = Averbakh-Kotov, USSR 1953.

[15] Transposition into any line where White plays e3 is also possible. This line is independent.

[16] 3 d4 ed 4 ed (4 ♕xd4 ♘f6 =) 4 ... c6 – Caro Kann.

[17] 3 ... d6 – row 20.

[18] 4 ♘f3 – row 20.

[19] 4 ... ♗b4 5 ♕c2 ♘c6 6 a3 ±.

[20] 5 ... d6 6 de de 7 ♕xd8+ ♔xd8 8 ♗g5 ±.

[21] 7 ♗g5, 7 f3 Larsen.

[22] 11 ♘f4 (11 ♕b3 h6 ∞) 11 ... ♘e6! = Uhlmann-Larsen, Leningrad IZ 1973.

[23] 5 a3 c6 6 f3 d5 7 ♗e2! ±.

[24] 7 ... 0-0 Watson.

[25] Réti-Romih, London 1927.

[26] 3 ... d6! (Watson) 4 de de 5 ♕xd8+ ♔xd8.

[27] 5 ... ♗e7 6 ♘d5 ±.

[28] Shatskes.

[29] 3 ♘f3 ♗xc3 4 bc d6 (4 ... ♕e7!? Tarjan) 5 c5! ± Rohde-Tarjan, USA 1980.

3 ♘d5!? ♗a5 4 b4 c6 5 ba cd 6 cd ♕xa5 (6 ... ♘f6) 7 ♕b3 ♘f6 8 ♘f3! d6 9 ♗a3 ± Smejkal-Dely, Hradec Kralove 1981.

[30] 4 ... ♘f6 5 ♘e2 (Spiridonov-Chekhov, Polanica Zdroj 1981) 5 ... d5!? 6 cd ♕xd5 7 ♘g3 h5!? Chekhov.

[31] 11 ♘e4 ♘g6 ∞ Knežević-Gurgenidze, Olomouc 1976.

[32] 3 ♘f3!? f5 4 d4 e4 5 ♘g5 (5 ♘d2 ♘f6 6 e3 c6 7 f3 d5 8 ♕a4!) 5 ... h6 6 ♘h3 g5 7 ♘g1! ♗g7 8 h4 g4 9 e3 ± Portisch-Seirawan, Mar del Plata 1982.

[33] Miles-Larsen, Las Palmas 1977.

[34] 6 g3 ♗e6 7 ♘d5 (7 e4 ♘e5 8 b3 b5! Watson) 7 ... ♘e5 8 b3 ♘e4!? ∞ Taimanov-Smyslov, USSR Ch 1967.

[35] Hübner-Balashov, Rio de Janeiro IZ 1979.

[36] 3 ... ♘f6 transposes passim.

[37] 6 ♘f3, 6 e4 – 1 ... ♘f6.

[38] Botvinnik.

[39] Dorfman-Bronstein, USSR Ch 1975.

[40] 4 b3 d5! =. 4 ♘f3 c6 5 b3 (5 d4) ± Watson. 5 ... ♕d7!? =.

[41] Tröger's Variation.

[42] 6 ♘d5 ♘d8 7 ♘f3 c6 8 ♘e3 ♗h3 9 ♗xh3 ♕xh3 10 d4 ± Portisch-Buljovčić, Vršac 1971. 6 ... g6 7 ♘f3 ♗g7 8 ♘g5 ♘d8 9 ♘xe6 fe 10 ♘c3 c6 11 ♖b1 ♗e7 12 b4 ± Korchnoi-Qi, Buenos Aires Ol 1978.

[43] 7 ♗xf4 ±.

[44] Stein-Ljubojević, Yugoslavia v USSR 1972.

[45] 11 ♗b2 ♕e7 12 ♕c2 ± Averbakh-Balashov, USSR 1973.

[46] 5 e3 c6 6 d4 ♗e7 (6 ... e4 ∞) 7 ♘ge2 0-0 (7 ... ♗e6 =) 8 b3 ♘bd7 9 ♗b2 e4! (Nunn) ∓.

[47] Benko-Larsen, Winnipeg 1968.

[48] Taimanov-Vaganian, Leningrad 1977.

	3	4	5	6	7	8	9	10	11	
1	♘f3[1]	♘g5[2]	d3![4]	de	♘xf7[7]	e5	ef	e4	f4	±/∞
	e4?!	b5![3]	bc[5]	h6[6]	♔xf7	d5	♗e6	d4	♗b4[8]	
2	...	d4	♘g5	g4	♗g2	♘gxe4	♘xe4			±
	d6	e4[9]	♗f5	♗xg4	♘c6	♘xe4	♗e7![10]			
3	g3	♗g2	♘f3	0-0	d3	♖b1	b4	b5		=
	d6	♗e7	0-0	♘c6	h6	♗e6	♕d7			
4	...	♕a4	♗g2	♘f3	d4	0-0				=
	c6[11]	d6	♘bd7	g6[12]	♗g7	0-0				
5	...	d4	♕xd4	♗g2[14]	cd	♘f3	♕a4	0-0		=
	...	ed	d5[13]	♗e6!	cd	♘c6	♗c5	0-0[15]		
6	...	♗g2	cd	♕b3	♘xd5	♘xf6+	♕d3	♗e4	♕xe4	∞
	...	d5[16]	cd	♘c6!	♘d4	gf![17]	♗f5	♗xe4	♕c7[18]	
7	...	♘f3!	♘d4	cd	♘b3	♗g2	d3[22]	0-0	bc[23]	=
	...	e4[19]	d5[20]	♕b6!	cd	♗f5[21]	♗b4	♗xc3		
8	...	♕c2	a3	♕xc3	♗g2	♕c2	d3	♘f3		∓
	♗b4[24]	0-0	♗xc3	d5!	d4	a5	♖e8	c5[25]		
9	...	♘f3[26]	♘d4	♘c2	dc	♗e3	♗g2	♘b4	cb	±
	...	e4	♘c6	♗xc3[27]	h6	♕e7	d6	♘xb4	0-0[28]	
10	...	♗g2	e4[29]	bc[30]	♘e2	cd	ed	♖b1		∓
	...	0-0	♗xc3!	c6!	d5	cd	♘xd5	♖e8[31]		
11	...	...	d3	♕b3[33]	♘f3	♘d4	ed	♕c2		∓
	...	...	c6![32]	♘a6!	e4	ed	♘c5	d5[34]		
12	...	...	♘f3	0-0	♘d4[36]	bc	d3	ed		=
	...	...	♖e8[35]	e4	♗xc3[37]	♘c6	ed	h6[38]		
13	...	cd	♗g2	♘f3	0-0	b4!	a4	♗a3	b5[41]	±
	d5	♘xd5	♘e7[39]	♘bc6	g6[40]	a6	♗g7	0-0		
14	...	...	...	♘f3![42]	d4	♘xd5	♘d2	0-0	♘b3[44]	±
	...	...	c6	♕c7[43]	ed?!	♕a5+	cd	♗e6?		
15	...	...	...	bc	d3	♘f3	0-0	h3	♕a4	=/±
	...	...	♘xc3	♘c6	♗c5!	0-0	♗g4	♗h5	♖e8[45]	

	4	5	6	7	8	9	10	11	12	
16	b3[46]	♗b2	♘f3	♗g2	0-0	e4	d3	b4	cb	=
	♗g7	d6	0-0	c6	♖e8[47]	♘bd7	a6	b5	ab[48]	
17	♗g2	♘f3	d3	0-0	♖b1[49]					=
	♗g7	♘c6	d6	0-0						

18

[1]   3 d3 transposes to other lines.

3 e4 (intending f4 and a kingside attack)
3 ... ♗c5 4 d3 d6 5 h3 ♘c6 6 ♗e3 0-0 7 ♕d2 ♘d4
8 g4 c6 9 ♗g2 a6! ∓ Sliwa-Keres, Moscow 1956.

3 ♕c2 c6 4 ♘f3 d6 5 g3 ♗e7 6 ♗g2
0-0 7 0-0 intending d4, ♖d1 (Watson).   3 ... g6
4 ♘f3 d6 5 e3 ♗g7 6 b3 0-0 7 ♗b2 =.

3 e3 c6 4 ♘f3 e4 (4 ... d6 5 d4 ♘bd7
6 ♗e2 ♗e7 ∞ Watson-Gruchacz, Lone Pine
1976) 5 ♘d4 d5 (5 ... ♗b4 6 ♕c2 ♗xc3
7 ♕xc3 0-0 ∞ Watson-Pope, Berkeley 1977)
6 cd cd 7 d3 ♗e7 8 ♗e2 0-0 9 0-0 ♘bd7 10 de de
(Watson-Mirkin, Providence 1977) 11 ♕c2 ♘c5
12 ♖d1 ♕b6 13 b3 ♗d7 14 ♗b2 ∞.   3 ... d6 and
3 ... ♘c6 are also playable.   3 ... ♗b4!?

[2]   4 ♘d4 =.   4 ♘g1 ∓/=.

[3]   Bellon Gambit.

[4]   5 ♘xb5 c6 6 ♘c3 d5 7 cd cd 8 d3 (8 e3 ♗d6
9 ♘h3 g5 oo Biyiasis-Regan, New York 1977)
8 ... h6 9 ♘h3 ♘c6 10 g3 ♗g4! 11 d4! 12 ♕b1
♕a5+ 13 ♗d2 ♕b6 14 f3 ♕xb2 15 ♕c1 ♕xc1+
16 ♗xc1 ♘b4 17 ♘a3 ♗d7 =/oo Sznapik-
Bellon, Cienfuegos 1976.

5 ♕c2 bc 6 ♘gxe4 ♗b7 7 ♘xf6+ ♕xf6 =/oo
Raičević-Suba, Novi Sad 1974.

5 ♘5xe4 ♘xe4 6 ♘xe4 bc 7 ♕a4 c6 =.

5 cb d5 6 d4 a6 7 g3 ab 8 ♘xb5 ♗g4 9 ♘c3
h6 oo Malich-Nun, Decin 1976.

[5]   4 ... ed 5 ed ♗b4!? 6 ♕b3 ♘c6 intending
... ♘d4 oo.   6 cb ♕e7+ 7 ♗e2 ±.   6 ... ♗b7
intending 7 ... ♕e7+ oo.

[6]   6 ... ♘c6 7 e3 ♗b4 8 ♗xc4 0-0 9 0-0
♗xc3 10 bc h6 11 f4!! hg 12 fg ♘h7 13 g6 ±
Keene-Wockenfuss, Bad Lauterberg 1977.

[7]   7 ♘f3 ♗b7 8 e5 ♘e4 9 ♘xe4 ♗xe4
10 ♘d2 ±/oo.

[8]   12 f5 ±.

[9]   4 ... ♘bd7 – Old Indian.

[10]   Watson.

[11]   The Keres System.

[12]   Or 6 ... ♗e7 intending ... 0-0, ... a6, ... b5 =.

[13]   Cf the Alapin-Sveshnikov Sicilian 1 e4 c5
2 c3 d5 3 ed ♕xd5.

[14]   6 ♘f3 ♗e7 7 ♗g2 c5 = Pfleger-Keres,
Bamberg 1968.

6 cd? cd 7 ♗g5 ♘c6 =.

6 ♗g5 ♗e7 7 cd (7 ♘f3 dc! 8 ♕xd8+
♔xd8 8 e4 h6! 9 0-0-0+ ♔e8 10 ♗xf6 gf =)
Shatskes.

[15]   Pirc-Keres, Yugoslavia v USSR 1956.

[16]   4 ... d6 – King's Indian or Old Indian.

[17]   8 ... ♕xf6 9 ♕d3! =.

[18]   Zamikovsky-Zurakhov, Kiev 1958, and
now 12 ♔f1 oo.

[19]   4 ... d6 5 d4 – Old Indian.

[20]   5 ... ♗c5 (Bronstein) 6 ♘b3 d6 7 ♗g2 ♗f5
8 0-0 ♘bd7 9 d3 ed 10 ed 0-0 = Smyslov-
Bronstein, Monte Carlo 1969.

[21]   5 ... ♕b6!? (Tal) 6 e3 (6 ♘b3 a5!; 6 ♘c2 d5
7 ♗g2 ♘f5 8 0-0 ♗e7 =) 6 ... d5 7 ♕c2 ♗d7
8 a3 a5 intending ... ♘a6 =.

[21]   Keres.   8 ... a5?! 9 d3 a4 10 ♗e3 ♕b4
11 ♘d4 a3 12 ♘c2! ± Botvinnik-Tal, match (9)
1961.

[22]   9 0-0 (Shatskes) d4! 10 ♘b1 ♘c6 = Watson.

[23]   Reshevsky-Keres, Los Angeles 1963.

[24]   Smyslov/Kapengut or Modern Variation.

[25]   Cuellar-Kuzmin, Leningrad IZ 1973.

[26]   4 ♕b3 ♘c6 5 ♘d5 ♗c5! 6 e3 0-0 = Karpov-
Korchnoi, match (25) 1978.

[27]   6 ... 0-0!? 7 ♗g2 ♖e8 8 0-0 ♗xc3 9 dc –
3 ♘f3 ♘c6 4 g3.

[28]   Larsen-Petrosian, Milan 1975.   12 c5! ♖d8
13 cd ♖xd6 14 ♕c1 ± Petrosian.

[29]   5 ♕b3 ♘c6! 6 ♘d5 ♗c5 7 e3 e4! 8 ♘xf6+
♕xf6 9 ♗xe4 ♖e8 10 d3 d6 = Korchnoi-Tseitlin,
Leningrad 1973.

[30]   6 dc d6 7 ♕e2 ♘bd7 8 ♘f3 ♘c5 9 ♘h4 a6!
10 b3 b5 11 ♗a3 ♘fd7 12 0-0 ♗b7 13 f3 ♗c6! ∓
Korchnoi-Mecking, match (1) 1974.

[31]   Stein-Gheorghiu, Las Palmas 1973.   11 ...
♖e8 ∓ Kapengut. 11 ... ♘b6 ∓ Pribyl-Hecht,
Luhacovice 1972.

[32]   Cf 1 e4 c5 2 ♘f3 ♘c6 3 ♗b5 d6 4 c3.

[33]   6 ♗d2 d5! = Brasket-Timman, Lone
Pine 1978.

6 ♘f3! = Watson.

[34]   Kapengut.

[35]   5 ... ♘c6 – 3 ♘f3 ♘c6 4 g3 ♗b4 5 ♗g2 0-0.

[36]   7 ♘e1 ♗xc3 8 dc d6 9 ♕c2 ♘bd7 ∓.

[37]   7 ... ♘c6 – note 35.

[38]   Kapengut.

[39]   5 ... ♗e6, 5 ... ♘b6 – 3 ♘f3 ♘c6 4 g3 d5.
5 ... ♘e7 Opocensky.

[40]   7 ... ♘f5 8 b4! a6 9 ♗b2 ♗e7 10 a3! ±
Smyslov-Jimenez, Havana 1965.

[41]   Zwaig-Romanishin, Hastings 1976/77.

[42]   6 ♘xd5 cd 7 ♕b3 ♗e6! 8 ♕xb7 ♘d7 9 ♕b3
♖b8 10 ♕d1 ♗c5 ==/∓ Taimanov.

[43]   6 ... ♕d6!?

[44]   Euwe-Meuldur, Amsterdam 1933.

[45]   11 ♕a4 ♖e8 = (±/= Taimanov).

[46]   4 ♗g2 ♗g7 5 ♘f3 ♘c6 6 d3 d6 7 0-0 0-0
9 ♖b1 is discussed in the English Four Knights.

[47]   8 ... ♕e7 9 d3 ♘bd7 10 e3 a6 11 d4 ♖e8 =
Lombardy-Evans, USA 1970.

[48]   13 a4 ba 14 ♖a4 ♗b7 = Andersson-Torre,
Manila 1974.

[49]   This move order is not playable according
to Watson as White has 6 d4! ed 7 ♘xd4 0-0
8 0-0 ♖e8 9 ♘xc6 or 9 ♘c2 ±, or even 6 0-0 0-0
7 d4, which is the Uhlmann Variation of the
King's Indian Defence. We therefore follow
(see Anglo-Indian I) a move order with ... e5
deferred: 1 c4 ♘f6 2 ♘c3 g6 3 g3 ♗g7 4 ♗g2
0-0 5 ♘f3 d6 6 0-0 e5 7 d3 ♘c6 8 ♖b1.

	3	4	5	6	7	8	9	10	11	
1	♘f3	e3	d4	d5	♗e2?!	♕c2	0-0	♖d1		=/⩲
	g6	♗g7	d6	♘ce7	f5	♘f6	0-0	h6[1]		
2	...	d4	♘xd4[2]	♘xc6	g3	♗g2	0-0	♕c2	b3	±/=
	...	ed	♗g7	bc	♘e7	0-0	♖b8	d6	c5[3]	
3	...	d4	♘g5[4]	♘h3	f3?![5]	ef	d5[6]	♔d2		∓
	f5	e4	h6	g5!	ef	♗g7	♕e7+	♘d4[7]		
4	...	d4	g3	d5	♗g2	h3	♗xf3	e4	h4![8]	±
	d6	♘f6	♗g4	♘b8	♗e7	♗xf3	0-0	♘fd7		
5	g3	♗g2	d3	e3	ef	♘ge2	♘e4![10]	♘2c3[11]		±
	f5	♘f6	♗c5[9]	f4!?	d6	0-0	♕e8			
6	...	...	e3	d4	f3	♘ge2	0-0	♘xc3	♕xf3	±
	...	...	♗e7[12]	e4[13]	0-0	♗b4	♗xc3[14]	ef	d6[15]	
7	...	♗g2	♘d5!	e3	♘e2	0-0	d3	cd	f4![16]	±
	♘f6	♗b4	♗c5	0-0	♖e8	♗f8	♘xd5	♘e7		
8	...	♗g2	♘d5	b4	♖b1	d3	e4	♘e2	♘e3[18]	∞
	d6	g6[17]	♗g7	♗e6	♕d7	♘d8	f5	c6		
9	...	♗g2	e3	♘ge2	d4!	♘xd4	ed	0-0	♖e1	±
	g6	♗g7	d6	♗e6[19]	ed![20]	♘xd4	♕d7	♘e7	0-0[21]	
10	...	...	...	...	0-0[22]	♖b1	a3	d3		=
	...	...	...	♘ge7	0-0[23]	a5	♗f5	♕d7[24]		
11	...	...	d3	e3[25]	h3![27]	♖b1	a3	b4	a4[28]	∞
	...	...	d6	h5[26]	♗e6	♕d7	♘ge7	♘d8		
12	...	...	...	♖b1	b4[29]	b5	a4	♗a3		=
	...	...	...	♗e6	♕d7	♘d8	♘e7	h6[30]		
13	...	...	♖b1	e3	b4	b5	♘ge2	bc	♕a4	=
	...	...	♘h6[31]	d6	0-0	♘e7	c6	bc	♕c7[32]	
14	...	...	...	b4	e3	♘f3	♘xe5	♖b3		∓
	...	...	♘f6!	0-0	♘e7	d5!	♗f5	♘e4[33]		
15	...	...	e4[34]	♘ge2	0-0	d3	♘xd4	♘e2	b4!	±
	...	...	♘f6	d6	0-0	♘d4	ed	c5	♘d7[35]	
16	...	...	...	♘ge2	h4	d3	f3	♘d5	♗e3[36]	±
	...	...	d6	h5	♘h6	0-0	♗e6	♔h7		
17	...	...	...	♘ge2	d3	0-0	♘d5	ef[37]		=
	...	...	♘ge7	0-0	d6	f5	h6!			
18	...	...	...	...	...	...	♘d5	♗e3[38]	♖c1	±/=
	...	...	...	...	...	♗e6	f5	♕d7	♖f7[39]	
19	...	...	...	...	...	...	h3	♔h2	♘d5	∞
	...	...	...	...	...	...	♕d7	f5	♖f7[40]	
20	...	...	♘f3	d3	0-0	♖b1	b4	b5	a4[41]	∞
	...	...	♘ge7	d6	h6	♗e6	♕d7	♘d8	♗h3[42]	

1 c4 e5 2 ♘c3 ♘c6 3 g3 g6 4 ♗g2 ♗g7 5 ♘f3 ♘ge7 6 d3 d6 7 0-0 0-0 8 ♖b1

	8	9	10	11	12	13	14	15	16	
21	...	a3	b4	ab	b5	♘d2!	e3	♕c2	♘a4[44]	±
	a5[43]	h6	ab	♗e6	♘d4	♗c8	♘e6	c6		
22	...	♗d2[45]	♕c1	♗h6	♗xg7	♘g5	f4	♘f3		=
	f5	a5![46]	♗e6	♕d7	♔xg7	♗g8	h6	a4[47]		

[1] Tolush-Smyslov, Bucharest 1953.

[2] 5 ♘d5 ♗g7 6 ♗g5 ♘ce7 7 ♘xd4 h6 8 ♗h4 g5 9 ♗g3 ♘xd5 10 cd c5 ∞ Taimanov/Watson.

[3] 12 ♗b2 ♗b7 13 ♗xb7 ♖xb7 14 ♘e4 ± Gheorghiu-Suba, Romanian Ch 1977.

[4] 5 ♘d2 ♘f6 6 e3 g6 7 a3 ♗g7 8 b4 0-0 = Korchnoi-Aronin, Spartakiad 1959.
 5 g5 ♗e7 6 ♗xe7 ♘cxe7 7 ♘d2 ♘f6 8 e3 0-0 = Tarjan-Gheorghiu, Cleveland 1975.

[5] 7 e3 ♘f6 8 ♗e2 ♗g7 9 ♗h5+ ♔f8 = Watson.

[6] 9 ♗e3 Browne.

[7] Seirawan-Browne, Lone Pine 1979.

[8] Uhlmann-Calvo, Madrid 1973.

[9] 5 ... ♗b4 6 ♘f3 0-0 7 0-0 ♗xc3 8 bc d6 9 ♖b1 ♕e8 ±.

[10] 9 0-0 ♕e8 10 ♘a4?! (10 ♘e4! Watson) 10 ... ♗d4! 11 ♘xd4?! (11 fe!) 11 ... ed 12 a3 (12 h3 h5! ∓ Saidy-Fischer, New York 1969) 12 ... a5 ∞∞ Karpov-Bellon, Madrid 1973.

[11] Watson.

[12] 5 ... g6 6 ♘ge2 ♗g7 7 d4 e4 8 0-0 d6 9 f3 ef 10 ♗xf3 ± Tal-Klaput, Poland 1966.

[13] 6 ... d6 7 b4! ±.

[14] 9 ... ♖e8 10 ♘d5! intending ♕b3 ±.

[15] 12 ♗d2 ♗d7 13 ♖ae1 ♕e8 14 ♕d1! ± Botvinnik-Simagin, USSR Ch 1952.

[16] Rogoff-Blumenfeld, Lone Pine 1976.

[17] 4 ... ♗e6 5 d3 ♕d7 6 ♘f3 ♗h3 7 ♗xh3 ♕xh3 8 ♘d5 ♕d7 9 0-0 ± Hübner-Ljubojević, Tilburg 1981. 6 ♖b1! ± Seirawan-Suttles, Vancouver 1981.

[18] Watson.

[19] The Hort Variation.
 6 ... ♘f6 7 d4 0-0 8 0-0 ♗d7 9 h3 ± Polugayevsky-Lutikov, Harkov 1967.
 6 ... f5 7 d3 ♘f6 8 ♖b1 0-0 9 b4 ± Smyslov-Liberzon, Riga 1968.
 6 ... h5!? 7 d4 ed! (Razuvayev) 8 ed h4 9 ♗e3 ± Watson.
 6 ... ♘h6 (Taimanov) 7 0-0 0-0 8 d3 ♗e6 9 h3 ± Forintos-Taimanov, Skopje 1970.
 6 ... ♗d7 7 d4! ♕c8 8 ♘d5! ± Ilivitsky-Alatortsev, USSR Ch 1948.

[20] 7 ... ♗xc4? 8 d5 ♗xe2 9 ♕xe2 ♘b8 10 ♕b5+! ♘d7 11 ♕xb7 ♖b8 12 ♕xa7! ♘c5 13 ♕a5! ♘d3+ 14 ♔e2 ♘xc1+ 15 ♖hxc1 ♖xb2+ 16 ♔f1 ±/± Rind-Morrison, Manchester 1980.

[21] 12 d5 ♗f5 13 h3! (Quinteros-Hort, Vinkovci 1972) 13 ... h5 ±.

[22] 7 d4 ed 8 ed 0-0 9 0-0 ♗g4 10 f3 ♗f5 11 g4 ♗c8 12 d5 ♘e5 ∓ Sadomsky-Murey, corr. 1965.
 7 ♖b1 ♗f5! 8 d3 ♕d7 9 ♘d5 (Popov-Nikitin, 1970) 9 ... 0-0! intending 10 0-0 ♘xd5 = Watson.

[23] 7 ... h5 8 h4 g5 9 hg h4 10 ♘e4! ±/±. 8 ... ♗g7 ∞.

[24] Bakulin-Murey, Moscow 1968.

[25] 6 f4 ♘ge7 7 ♘f3 h6! 8 0-0 ♗e6 9 ♗d2 (Flohr-Steiner, 1933) 9 ... ef! =/∓ Watson.
 6 ♗d2 ♘ge7 7 ♘f3 0-0 8 0-0 ♗d7 9 ♖b1 ♕c8 = Petrosian-Boleslavsky, Zürich C 1953.
 6 ♘h3!? ∞ Stoyko-Watson, New York 1975.
 6 ♘f3 ♘f6 7 0-0 0-0 8 ♖b1 - 1 c4 ♘f6 2 ♘c3 g6 3 g3 ♗g7 4 ♗g2 0-0 5 ♘f3 ♘c6 6 0-0 d6.

[26] 6 ... ♘ge7 and 6 ... ♘f6 are also playable.

[27] 7 h4? ♘h6 8 ♘ge2 ♗g4 9 ♕d2 0-0 ∓ Hug-Calvo, Palma de Mallorca 1972.

[28] Watson.

[29] 7 ♘h3!? h6 8 f4 ♕d7 9 ♘f2 ♘ge7 10 ♘d5 ♘d8 11 0-0 ∞.

[30] Botvinnik-Liberzon, Moscow 1968.

[31] Taimanov's idea.
 5 ... a5 6 a3 d6 7 b4 ab 8 ab ♗f5 9 d3 ± Pachman-Szabo, Solingen 1968.
 5 ... d6 6 b4 f5 7 b5 ♘ce7 8 e3 ♘f6 9 d4 e4 10 ♘ge2 0-0 11 0-0 ± Smyslov-Levy, Hastings 1969/70.

[32] 12 0-0 (Portisch-Schmid, Monaco 1969) 12 ... f5 =.

[33] Kapengut-Gulko, USSR 1970.

[34] Botvinnik System.

[35] 12 bc dc 13 f4 ± Petrosian-Bertok, Zagreb 1965.

[36] Portisch-Gulko, Biel 1976.

[37] 10 ♖b1 ♔h7 11 f4 fe! ∓ Barcza. 10 ef ♘xf5! =.

[38] 10 ♖b1 ♕d7 11 b4 ♖ae8 12 b5 ♘d8 13 ♗a3 ± (Taimanov), = (Watson).

[39] 12 ♕d2 ♖af8 13 f3! ± Csom-Gulko, Biel 1976.

[40] Hort-Spassky, match (4) 1977.

[41] 11 ♗a3 a6! =.
 11 ♖e1 0-0 12 a4 f5 13 ♕c2 ♖f7 ∞ Watson.

[42] 12 ♗a3 b6! =.

[43] 8 ... ♗d7!? Pachman-Penrose, 1954.

[44] Nikolayevsky-Peterson, USSR TU Ch 1967.

[45] 9 ♕c2!? Watson.

[46] 9 ... h6 10 b4 ♕e8 11 ♘d5 ♘xd5 12 cd ± Stolyar-Hasin, USSR Ch 1956.

[47] Analysis by Watson.

King's English: Four Knights   1 c4 e5 2 ♘c3 ♘f6 3 ♘f3 ♘c6

	4	5	6	7	8	9	10	11	12	
1	e3[1]	Qc2[3]	Qxc3	a3	d3	b3	cd	Qc2[6]		±
	Bb4[2]	Bxc3[4]	Qe7	0-0	a5[5]	d5	Nxd5			
2	...	...	...	...	b4[7]	cd	Qb3	Bc4	Bxd5	±
	...	...	...	a5	d5[8]	Nxd5	Be6[9]	e4[10]	Bxd5[11]	
3	...	...	Nd5	Qf5[12]	Nxf6+	Qh5	Bd3[14]	cd	dc	∞
	...	0-0	Re8	d6	gf[13]	d5	e4	ed	bc[15]	
4	g3	cd	Bg2	0-0	d4	bc	Nd2	e3	c4[17]	±
	d5[16]	Nxd5	Be6	Be7	Nxc3	e4	f5	0-0		
5	...	...	...	0-0	a3[18]	d3	Be3	Nxd5	Rc1	±
	...	...	Nb6	Be7	a5[19]	Be6	Nd5	Bxd5	0-0[20]	
6	...	...	...	...	d3	0-0	b4	Be3	Bxb6!	±
	...	...	...	...	Be6[21]	0-0	f6	Qe8	ab[22]	
7	...	Nxe5	Kxf2	e4[23]	d3	h3	Be2	Kg2	Be3	∓
	Bc5	Bxf2+	Nxe5	c5	d6	0-0!	Ne8	Nc7	Ne6[24]	
8	...	Bg2	0-0[25]	e3	h3	d3	g4	Nh4	b3[26]	±
	...	d6	0-0	Bg4	Bh5	Qd7	Bg6	Rae8		
9	...	Bg2[27]	Bxf3	d3	0-0	Qc2	Ne4	c5	de	=
	Nd4!?	Nxf3+	Bc5![28]	0-0	h6	c6	Be7	Nxe4	d6[29]	
10	...	Nd5	cd	Nxd4	Bg2	0-0				=
	Bb4	Nxd5[30]	Nd4	ed	Be7	c5[31]				
11	...	Bg2	Nd5	Nh4	0-0	d3	Qxd3	Qc2	Be3[32]	=
	...	0-0	e4	Bc5	Re8	ed	Ne5	c6		

1 c4 e5 2 ♘c3 ♘f6 3 ♘f3 ♘c6 4 g3 ♗b4 5 ♗g2 0-0 6 0-0

	6	7	8	9	10	11	12	13	14	
12	...	bc	d3	e4	Nh4	Be3	Rb1[35]	Rb2	f4[36]	∞
	Bxc3	d6[33]	Bd7[34]	Kh8!	Ng8	Be6	b6	Nge7		
13	...	Nd5	cd	Ne1[37]	e3	d3	Nc2	dc		=
	Re8	Nxd5	Nd4	c6	Nb5!	Nc7	Bf8	dc[38]		
14	...	Ne1	dc!	Nc2	Ne3	Qc2	f4	ef	f4	=
	e4	Bxc3	h6[39]	Re8	d6	b6[40]	ef	Bb7		
15	...	Ng5	bc!	Qc2[41]	cd	d3	Qb2!	Bf4	Nxe4	±
	...	Bxc3	Re8	d5[42]	Qxd5	Bf5	b6	h6	Nxe4[43]	

[1] 4 Qa4!? Murei.

4 e4?! (Nimzowitsch) 4 ... d6 5 d4 Bg4! =.

4 d4 ed 5 Nxd4 Bb4 =.

4 b3 d5 5 cd Nxd5 6 Bb2 Nxc3 7 Bxc3 Bd6 = Korchnoi-Gipslis, USSR 1976.

4 a3 g6 5 g3 (5 d4!?) 5 ... Bg7 6 Bg2 0-0 7 0-0 d6 8 d3 =, or 8 Rc1 h6! =.

4 d3 Bb4 5 Bd2 0-0 6 e3 Re8 7 Be2 Bf8 8 0-0 d6 9 a3 Ne7 10 b4 Ng6 11 Qc2 Bf5 = Larsen-Lombardy, Orense 1975.

[2] 4 ... Be7 5 d4 ed 6 Nxd4 0-0 7 Be2 d5 8 Nxc6 bc 9 0-0 Bd6 10 b3?! Qe7 11 Bb2 dc ∓ Timman-Karpov, Montreal 1979.

[3] 5 Nd5 e4 6 Ng1 0-0 7 a3 Bd6 8 Qc2 Re8 9 Nge2 b5!·10 Ng3 bc 11 Bxc4 Bb7 ∓ Adorjan-Romanishin, Riga IZ 1979.

[4] Romanishin Variation.

[5] 8 ... d5 9 cd Nxd5 10 Qc2 a5 11 b3 f5 12 Bb2 f4 13 e4 Nf6 14 h3 ± Ermenkov-Bisguier, Lone Pine 1980.

[6] Anikayev-Romanishin, USSR Ch 1979.

[7] Keene.

[8] 8 ... ab 9 ab Rxa1 10 Qxa1 e4 11 b5! ef 12 bc bc 13 gf 0-0 14 Bb2 Ne8 15 Bd3! ± Seirawan-Barbero, Skien 1979.

[9] 10 ... Nb6 11 b5 a4 12 Qc2 Na5 13 Bb2 ± .

[10] 11 ... a4 12 Qc2 ±.

11 ... Qd6 ±.

[11] 13 Qxd5 ef 14 gf ab 15 Bb2 ba 16 Bxg7 Rg8 17 Bc3 ±.

[12] Stean/Keene Variation.

[13] 8 ... Qxf6 9 Qxf6 gf 10 a3 Bc5 11 b3 ± Piasetski-Rajković, Stip 1977.

[14] 10 a3 Bf8 11 d4 Be6 12 Bd3 h6!? (12 ... e4 13 Bc2 Ne7 14 Nd2 f5 15 cd Qxd5 16 f3 f4! 17 Nxe4 Qxh5 18 Nf6+ Kh8 19 Nxh5 fe =/∓) 13 cd Qxd5 14 e4 Qb3! =/∞ Fedorowicz-Tarjan, Hastings 1977/78.

[15] 13 b3 (13 a3?! ∓ Watson-Shirazi, Lone Pine 1980) ∞.

[16] 4 ... g6 5 d4! ed 6 Nxd4 Bg7 7 Bg2 0-0 8 0-0 Re8 9 Nxc6 bc 10 Qa4! a5 11 Rd1 ± Uhlmann-Rajković, Hastings 1972/73.

[17] Smejkal-Ivkov, Wijk aan Zee 1972.

[18] 8 a4 a5 9 d3 Be6 10 Be3 0-0 =.

8 b3 (Simagin) 0-0 9 Bb2 Bg4 10 Rc1 f5 ∞/= Simagin-Benchuk, Moscow 1967.

[19] 8 ... 0-0 9 b4 Be6 10 d3 f6 (10 ... f5 11 Bb2! ±) 11 Bb2 Qe8 12 Nd2 Qf7 13 Rc1 a6 (Adorjan-Timman, Wijk aan Zee 1981) 14 Nce4! ±.

8 ... Be6 9 d3 f5 10 b4 Bf6 11 e4 0-0 12 ef Bxf5 13 Ne4 Bxe4!? 14 de Qxd1 15 Rxd1 Rad8 ∞.

[20] 13 Qa4 Re8 ± Botvinnik-Flohr, Wageningen 1958. 13 ... Bd6 14 Bc5 Ne7 15 e4 Bc6 16 Qc2 ± Polugayevsky-Hübner, Bugojno 1982.

[21] 8 ... Bg4 9 Be3 0-0 10 Qc1!? ±.

8 ... 0-0 9 Be3 f5 (9 ... Bg4 10 Qc1 ±) 10 Qc1 Kh8 11 Rd1 Bf6 12 d4 ± Pribyl-Kozlov, Stary Smokovec 1976.

[22] 13 d4! ed 14 Nxd4 ± Vaganian-Psakhis, Erevan Z 1982.

[23] 7 d4!? Nxc4 8 e4 d5 9 Bxc4 dc 10 Qa4+ c6 11 Qxc4 0-0 12 Re1 Bh3! Bergström-Widenkeller, Hallsberg 1977/78.

[24] 13 Qd2 Nc6 14 Raf1 Ned4 15 Bh5 Be6 16 Nd5 Rb8 17 Rf2 b5 ∓ Hickman-Camaratte, US corr. Ch 1972/75.

[25] 6 d3 a6!? 7 0-0-0-0 8 a3 h6 9 b4 Ba7 10 Rb1 Re8 11 e3 (Kots-Mikenas, USSR Ch 1962) 11 ... Bf5 ∞.

[26] Uhlmann-Thormann, GDR 1975.

[27] 5 Nxe5 Qe7 6 f4 (6 Nd3?? Nf3 mate!) 6 ... d6 7 Nd3 Bf5 8 Qf2 ∞.

[28] 6 ... Bb4?! 6 Qb3 ± Bronstein-Polugayevsky, Petropolis IZ 1973.

6 ... Be7 7 d4 d6 8 Bg5 ± Gheorghiu-Portisch, Skopje Ol 1972.

[29] 13 Rd1 Qc7 =.

[30] 5 ... Bc5 6 Bg2 0-0-0 7 0-0 d6 8 e3 (8 d3 Nxd5! 9 cd Nd4 = Larsen-Kuzmin, Bled/Portorož 1979) 8 ... Bg4!? Korchnoi-Karpov, match (15) 1981.

[31] Suba-Georgadze, Lublin 1974.

[32] Gheorghiu-Szmetan, Torremolinos 1976. 12 ... cd 13 Bxc5 Qc7 =.

[33] 7 ... Re8!? may be better.

[34] 8 ... e4 9 Ng5! ∞/± Povah.

[35] 12 Qd2 Nge7 13 f4 ef 14 Bxf4 f6 ∓ Uhlmann-Korchnoi, Leningrad 1977.

[36] Watson.

[37] 9 Nxd4 ed 10 b3 b6 (10 ... d6!?) 11 Bb2 Bc5 12 e3 Ba6 13 Re1 Qf6! (Uhlmann-Portisch, Skopje Ol 1972) 14 Qc1 intending b4 ∞.

[38] Petrosian-Kuzmin, USSR Ch 1974.

[39] 8 ... Re8 9 Qc2 Ne5 10 b3 h6 11 f4 ef 12 ef ± Ribli-Browne, Manila 1976.

[40] 11 ... a5 12 f4! ef 13 ef ± Uhlmann-Plachetka, Trencianske Teplice 1979.

[41] 9 f3 ef 10 Nxf3 d5! 11 cd Qxd5! 12 Nd4 Qh5 13 Nxc6 bc 14 e3 Bg4 15 Qa4! Re6! (15 ... Be2 16 Rxf6! Povah) 16 Ba3! ∞ Stefanov-Kertesz, Romanian Ch 1977.

[42] 9 ... Qe7 10 d3 ed 11 ed b6 12 Bd2! Bb7 13 Rae1 Qf8 14 Bf4 ± Holmov-Kapengut, USSR 1978.

[43] 15 de Bxe4 16 Rfd1 Qc4 17 f3 ± Lyavdansky-Kapengut, Kiev 1977.

	5	6	7	8	9	10	11	12	13	
1	a3[1]	♖b1[3]	e4[4]	d3	♘ge2	0-0	♘b5!	d4	♗e3	±
	e6[2]	a5	d6	♘ge7	0-0	♖b8	b6	♗a6	♖b7[5]	
2	...	♖b1[6]	e3	♘ge2	b3	♘b5	♘ec3	d3	♘d5	=
	d6	a5	e5	♘ge7	♖b8	0-0	f5	♗e6	♗f7[7]	
3	...	♖b1[8]	♛a4[9]	b4[10]	cb	♘xb5	e3	♘e2	0-0[12]	=
	a6	♖b8	♘d4!	b5![11]	♘xb5	♖xb5	♛c7	♗b7		
4	b3	♗b2	d3[14]	♗xc6!	♛d2	f4!	♘f3	fe	♛g5![15]	±
	♘f6[13]	0-0	e6	bc	d6	♛e7	e5	de		
5	...	♗b2	h4[16]	h5	cd	♖c1[17]				∞
	e6	♘ge7	d5	0-0	♘xd5					
6	...	♗b2	♘f3	♛c1	0-0	e3	♘e2	♘e1	f4	∞
	d6	e6	♘ge7	0-0	f5	e5	h6	g5	gf[18]	
7	e4[19]	♘ge2	d3	0-0	♖b1	a3	b4	ab	cb	±
	e6[20]	♘ge7	0-0	d6	a6[21]	♖b8	cb	b5	ab[22]	
8	...	♘ge2	0-0	d3[23]	♗e3[25]	♛d2	♖b1	f3	b4	±/=
	♘f6	0-0	d6	♘e8[24]	♘d4	♖b8	♗g4	♗d7	♘c7[26]	
9	e3	♘ge2	0-0[28]	b3[29]	♗b2	d3	♛d2	♖ad1[30]		±
	e5[27]	♘ge7	0-0	d6	♖b8	a6	b5	♗e6		
10	...	♘ge2	♘f4!?[31]	0-0	b3	♗b2	d3	♛e2	♖fd1	∞
	e6	♘ge7	0-0	d6	a6	b5	♗b7	♖b8	♛d7[32]	
11	♘f3	0-0	cd	♘g5[33]	d3!?[34]	♘xd5	♘h3[35]			=
	♘f6	d5	♘xd5	e6	0-0!	ed				
12	...	...	...	♘xd5	d3	♗e3	♘d4[37]	♘xc6		∞
	...	...	...	♛xd5	0-0	♗d7[36]	♛d6	♗xc6[38]		
13	...	...	...	...	...	a3	♖b1	♗e3[39]		=
	...	...	...	...	...	b6	♗b7	♘d4[40]		
14	...	...	a3	♖b1	d3	♗d2				=
	...	0-0	d6[41]	♘e8	♘c7	♖b8!				
15	...	...	d3	♖b1	a3	b4	ab	cb		=
	...	...	d6	♖b8	a6	cb	b5	ab[42]		
16	...	...	d4	♘xd4	♛xd4	♛d3[43]	♗e3	♗d4	♛d1	=
	...	...	cd	♘xd4	d6	a6![44]	♘g4!	♘e5	♖b8![45]	

[1]   5 d3 Rb8 6 e3 (6 Qd2 Qa5!) 6 ... a6 7 a4 d6 =.

[2]   5 ... e5 6 b4! d6 7 Rb1 Nge7 8 e3 ±.
   5 ... Nf6 6 Rb1 a5 7 Nf3 0-0 8 0-0 d6 9 d3 Ne8 10 Bd2 Nc7 11 Na4! ± Benko-Zuckerman, US Ch 1967.
   5 ... b6 6 Rb1 Bb7 7 d3 e6 8 h4! h5 9 Nh3 d6 10 Bf4 Qd7 11 Ng5! Rd8 12 0-0 Be5! 13 Qd2 Qe7 (Watson-Forintos, Lone Pine 1976) 14 Rae1 ±.
   5 ... a5 6 Nf3 e6 7 d4! Nxd4 8 Nxd4 Bxd4 9 Nb5 ∞∞. 8 ... cd 9 Nb5 Ne7 10 Nd6+ Kf8 11 c5.

[3]   6 b4 Nxb4! 7 ab cb 8 d4 (8 Nb5 Bxa1 ∓ Lobron-Kavalek, Bochum 1981) 8 ... bc 9 e3 Ne7 ∓ Smyslov-Hartston, Hastings 1972/73.

[4]   7 h4 Nge7 8 h5 d5 9 cd ed 10 d3 (Watson-Fuller, Harrow 1979) 10 ... 0-0.

[5]   14 a4 ± Smejkal-Andersson, Biel 1976.

[6]   6 e3 Nh6!? 7 Nge2 Nf5 8 Rb1 a5 9 b3 h5! 10 h3 e5 11 Bb2 h4 12 g4 Nfe7 13 d4 cd 14 ed 0-0 15 d5 Nb8 16 b4 f5 with counterplay, Seirawan-Short, Hastings 1979/80.

[7]   14 0-0 = Hort-van der Sterren, Lone Pine 1979.

[8]   6 Nf3 transposes elsewhere.

[9]   7 b4 cb 8 ab b5 9 c5 a5 10 Ba3! ±.

[10]   8 e3 b5 9 cb Nxb5 10 Nge2 Nf6! 11 0-0 0-0 = Rajković-Gheorghiu, Lone Pine 1979.

[11]   8 ... cb!? 9 Rxb4 Qc7! 10 Nd5 Qc6! = Rajković-Matulović, Yugoslavia 1979.

[12]   Seirawan-Reshevsky, Lone Pine 1979.

[13]   5 ... Nh6!?
   5 ... e5 6 Bb2 Nge7 7 e3 – 5 e3.

[14]   7 Nf3 d5 8 cd Nxd5 9 Qc1 Nxc3 10 Bxc3 Nd4 = Larsen-Belyavsky, Las Palmas 1974.
   7 Nh3 d5!? 8 Nxd5 Nxd5 9 Bxg7 Kxg7 10 cd Bxh3 11 Bxh3 Qxd5 = Watson.

[15]   Larsen-Bétancourt, Lanzarote 1976.

[16]   7 Na4? Bxb2 8 Nxb2 0-0 = Smyslov-Fischer, Palma de Mallorca IZ 1970.
   7 Qc1!? Gulko.

[17]   Watson.

[18]   14 ef Be6 15 d3 Qd7 16 Nf3 =/∞ Kuligowski-Murmi, Tjentiste 1975.

[19]   Botvinnik Variation.

[20]   5 ... e5 6 Nge2 Nge7 7 d3 d6 8 0-0 0-0 9 a3 ± Ivkov-Torre, Campiglio 1973.

[21]   9 ... b6 10 a3 Bb7 =/±.

[22]   14 d4! d5 15 Bf4 Rb6 16 Qb3! ± Reshevsky-Kostro, Lugano Ol 1968.

[23]   8 a3 a5 9 Rb1 Bg4 10 f3 (10 h3 Bxe2! =) 10 ... Bd7 11 d3 Ne8 12 Be3 = Taimanov-Gurgenidze, USSR Ch 1958.

[24]   8 ... a6!? 9 h3! Rb8 10 a4! Ne8 11 Be3 Nc7 12 d4 ± Taimanov-Suetin, Riga 1954.

8 ... Bd7 9 h3 Qc8!? 10 Kh2 Ne8 11 Be3 ±.

[25]   9 h3!? Nc7 10 g4 Nd4 11 f4 f5 = Taimanov.

[26]   14 f4 =/±.

[27]   5 ... Nh6 6 Nge2 Nf5 7 b3 a6 8 Bb2 0-0 9 d3 d6 10 0-0 Bd7 11 Qd2 ± Andersson-Miles, Tilburg 1977.
   5 ... Nxc3!? 6 bc b6 7 Ne2 Bb7 8 d3 d6 9 0-0 Qd7 10 e4 ∞ Speelman-Commons, Lone Pine 1978.

[28]   7 a3 d6 8 Rb1 a5 9 Nd5 0-0 10 0-0 Bg4! = Lysenko-Karpov, Rostov 1971.

[29]   8 a3 d6 9 d3 Be6 10 Nd5 Rb8 11 Nec3 a6 12 Rb1 b5 = Bertok-Adorjan, Birmingham 1973.

[30]   Lein-Polugayevsky, Tbilisi 1967.

[31]   7 0-0 0-0 8 d4 cd 9 Nxd4! d5! 10 cd Nxd4 11 ed Nxd5 12 Re1 Qb6! = Keene-Hecht, Dortmund 1973. 12 Nxd5 ed 13 Be3 Be8 =.

[32]   14 Rd2 f5 = Hort-Planinc, Banja Luka 1974.

[33]   8 Qb3 e6 9 Qb5!? (9 Qc4? b6 10 d3 0-0 ∓ G.Garcia-Dzhindzhihashvili, Wijk aan Zee 1979) 9 ... Qb6! intending 10 Qxb6 ab! or 10 Qc4 Qb4! Watson.

[34]   9 Nge4?! b6 10 Qa4 Bd7! 11 Nxd5 ed 12 Nc3 Qe7 13 Qf4 Bc6 14 b4 0-0 15 bc d4! ∓ Timman-Polugayevsky, match (3) 1979.

[35]   Watson.

[36]   10 ... Qd6 11 Rc1 Nd4 12 Nxd4! cd 13 Bd2 Bg4 14 h3 Be6 15 Qa4! ± Palatnik-Timoshenko, USSR 1973.
   10 ... Bxb2!? 11 Rb1 Bf6! 12 Qa4 Nb4 13 a3 (13 Rfc1 Bd7 14 Qd1 b6! ∞ Watson) 13 ... Na2 14 Ng5! ± Jansa-Pribyl, Luhacovice 1973.

[37]   11 d4 cd 12 Nxd4 Qc4 13 Nxc6 Bxc6 14 Bxc6 bc = Espig-Smejkal, Leipzig 1977.

[38]   13 Bxc6 Qxc6 14 Rc1 Qe6! 15 Rxc5 Qxa2 16 Rb5! b6 17 Qa1! Qe6 ∞ – Bagirov-Mikhalchishin, Tbilisi 1980.

[39]   Portisch-H.Olafsson, Lone Pine 1978.

[40]   13 b4 cb 14 ab Rfc8 = Watson.

[41]   7 ... a6 8 Rb1 Rb8 9 b4 cb 10 ab b5 11 cb ab 12 d4 d5 (Larsen-Ivkov, Palma de Mallorca 1967) 13 Ne5! ±.

[42]   Portisch-Tal, match 1965.

[43]   10 Bg5 h6! 11 Bd2 Be6 12 Qd3 Qd7 13 e4 Bh3 =.

[44]   10 ... Qa5 11 Bd2 ±.
   10 ... Nd7 11 Qc2! Nc5 12 Bg5 =.
   10 ... Bf5 11 e4 Be6 12 Bd2 Qd7 13 b3 a6 14 Qe2 Nc5 15 Rac1 b5!? 16 cb ab 17 Rc2! ±/± Smejkal-Popov, Wijk aan Zee 1975.

[45]   14 Rc1 Be6 15 Nd5 (15 b3 Qa5!?) 15 ... b5 16 cb Bxd5 (16 ... ab 17 Nb4!) 17 Bxd5 ab 18 Qd2 = Tal-Torre, Leningrad IZ 1973.

	5	6	7	8	9	10	11	12	13	
17	♘f3	h4!	d3	h5	♗xh6!	hg	♕c1!	♖xh8+	♕h6[46]	±
	♘h6	d6	♖b8	♗d7	♗xh6	hg	♗g7	♗xh8		
18	...	a3[47]	♖b1	cb	b4	ab	0-0	h3	♗xf3	=
	a6	♖b8	b5	ab	cb	d6![48]	♗g4!	♗xf3	♕d7[49]	
19	...	0-0[50]	a3[51]	♖b1	b4	e3	♕e2	♖d1		=
	d6	♘h6	0-0	♖b8	♘f5	♗d7	e6	b6[52]		
20	...	h4!?	h5	cd	d3	hg	♗d2			∞
	e6	d5![53]	♘ge7	ed	h6	fg	g5[54]			
21	...	0-0	d3[55]	♗f4![56]	♖b1	a3	♕a4[58]			∞
	...	♘ge7	0-0	d5[57]	b6	♗b7				
22	...	a3!?	b4	ab	♗a3	♕a4	0-0	♖ab1	♘a2[60]	=
	...	♘ge7	cb[59]	♘xb4	♘ec6	a5	0-0	♖b8		
23	...	0-0	♘e1	d3	♘c2	♖b1	b4	bc	♘e3[61]	=
	e5	♘eg7	0-0	♖b8	a6	d6	♗e6	dc	b6	
24	...	...	d3	a3	♖b1	♗d2[62]	♘e1	♘c2	cd	=
	...	...	0-0	d6	a5!	♖b8!	♗e6	d5	♘xd5[63]	

[46]   Botvinnik-Gligorić, Moscow 1956.
[47]   6 d3 ♖b8 7 0-0!? b5 8 cb! ab 9 ♗e3 ♘d4 10 ♖c1 ± Polugayevsky-Malich, Bad Lebenstein 1963.   7 ... d6!?
[48]   10 ... ♘f6 11 0-0 0-0 12 d4 transposes elsewhere.
[49]   14 ♗g2 e6 15 e3 ♘ge7 = Alekseev-Goikhman, Moscow 1968.
[50]   There are many transpositional possibilities.
[51]   7 b3!? 0-0 8 ♗b2 ♖b8! 9 d3 a6 10 ♕d2 b5 Watson.
[52]   Hort-Spassky, match (13) 1977. 13 ♖b3!?.
[53]   6 ... h6 7 b3 ♘ge7 8 ♗b2 ± Fedorowicz-Shamkovich, Hastings 1977/78.
[54]   Ribli-Sosonko, Amsterdam 1980.
[55]   7 e3 0-0 8 d4 d6 = Byrne.

   7 e4 d5!? Watson.
   7 d4!? ♘xd4! 8 ♘xd4 cd 9 ♘b5 d5 = Yusupov-Cordes, Graz 1978.   9 ... ♕b6!?
[56]   8 a3 d5 9 ♗d2 b6 10 ♖b1 ♗b7 11 b4? cb 12 ab dc 13 dc ♖c8 ∓ Petrosian-Fischer, Belgrade 1970.   11 cd =.
[57]   8 ... d6 9 ♕c1 ♗f5 10 ♖b1 ♕e7 11 ♖e1! ♗d7 12 ♘e4! ± Malich-Ciocaltea, Halle 1974.
[58]   Watson (∞/±).
[59]   7 ... ♘xb4? 8 ab cb 9 ♘e4 ♗xa1 10 ♕a4 ♗g7 11 ♘d6+ ♔f8 12 ♘g5 ♗f5 13 ♘gxf7! ±.
[60]   Watson.
[61]   Barcza-Karpov, Caracas 1970.
[62]   10 ♘e1 ♗e6 (intending ... d5) 11 ♘c2!? d5 ∞.
[63]   Evans-Karpov, San Antonio 1972.

	4	5	6	7	8	9	10	11	12	
1	...	♘b5	cd	♘5c3	♘d2[3]	♘b3!	♘a4	♕xd5	e4	±
	e5!?[1]	d5!?[2]	♕a5+	b5	b4	♕d8	♕xd5	♘xd5	♘f6[4]	
2	...	...	...	♘5c3	e3	♘d2[5]	a3	b4	♘c4	±
	...	...	♗c5!?	0-0	e4	♖e8	♗f5	♗f8	♘bd7[6]	
3	...	♘c3	♘b5	cd	a3!	bc	e3	♗d3	♘d4	±
	e6	♗b4	d5	ed	♗xc3+	0-0	♘e4	♗d7	♕a5[7]	
4	...	...	♘db5[8]	♗f4	cd	dc	♕xd8+	♖d1+	♘d6	∞
	...	♘c6	d5	e5	ef	bc	♔xd8	♗d7	♖b8[9]	
5	...	g3	♘d2	♘b3	e3[10]	♗g2	0-0	♗xb7	♕e2	±
	...	♕a5+	♘c6	♕c7!	b6	♗b7	♘e5	♕xb7	♗e7[11]	
6	...	...	♘c3	♗d2	♕xd2	♗g2	0-0	♖fd1[12]		±
	...	...	♘e4	♘xd2	a6	♗e7	0-0			
7	...	...	♘d2[13]	♘2b3[14]	♗g2	♗d2	♖c1	♕xd2	♘c5	∞∞
	...	♕c7	♗c5	0-0!	♗b4+[15]	♕xc4	♗xd2+	♕a6	♕b6[16]	
8	...	...	♗d2	♗xb4	♘c3	♘db5	♘c7+	♕d2	♘xe6+!	=
	...	♗b4+	♕b6[17]	♕xb4+	♕xb2	♕b4	♔d8	♘e4!	fe[18]	

[1]   **4 ... d5** 5 cd ♘xd5 6 e4 ♘b4 7 ♘b5!? ♕xd1+ 8 ♔xd1 ♘8a6 9 a3 ♘c6 10 ♘1c3 ♗g4+ 11 f3 0-0-0+ 12 ♔c2 ± Savon-Karasev, Moscow 1974.
    4 ... a6 5 ♘c3 d5 6 ♘b3! ±.

[2]   Kevitz.

[3]   8 a3?! b4! 9 ♕a4+ ♕xa4 10 ♘xa4 ♘xd5! = Adamski-Barlov, Prague 1981.

[4]   13 f3 Bétancourt-Bellon, Lanzarote 1976.

[5]   9 ♗e2?! ♗e7 (9 ... ♗f5!? 10 a3 ♘bd7 11 b4 ♗d6 12 ♗b2 a6 13 ♘d2 ♘e5 ∞ Kärner-Barczay, Tallinn 1981; 9 ... ♖e8 10 a3 ♘bd7 11 ♘d2 ♘b6 ∞ Mamužić-Barczay, Subotica 1981; 9 ... ♘a6!?) 10 ♘d2 ♖d8 11 a3 ♘xd5 12 ♘xd5 ♖xd5 13 ♕c2 ♗f5 14 b4 ♗b6 15 ♗b2 ∞ Mikhalchishin-Kasparov, USSR Ch 1981.

[6]   13 ♗b2 ♖c8 14 ♘b5! ± Ljubojević-Bukić, Yugoslavia 1981.

[7]   13 0-0 ♘a6 14 c4 ± Jimenez-Polugayevsky, Palma de Mallorca IZ 1970.

[8]   6 g3 ♗c5 7 ♘b3 ♗b4 ±.

[9]   13 ♘xf7+ ♔e8 14 ♘d6+! (14 ♘xh8 ♖xb2 ∓) 14 ... ♗xd6 15 ♖xd6 ♖xb2 16 ♖d2 ∞ Andersson-Timman, Bugojno 1982.

[10]   8 ♗g2 ♘e5 9 0-0 ♘xc4 10 ♕c2 d5 11 ♘xc4 dc 12 ♘d2 c3! =.

[11]   13 e4! ± D.Pavlović-Karlsson, Niš 1981.

[12]   Rashkovsky-Tukmakov, Baku 1977.

[13]   6 ♗g2 ♕xc4 7 0-0 ♘c6 8 ♘xc6 dc 9 ♗g5 ♗e7 10 ♘c3 0-0 11 ♘e4 ∞ Durić-Antonov, Pernik 1981.
    6 ♗c3!? ♕xc4 7 e4!?
    6 ♗g5!?

[14]   7 ♘b5? ♕c6! 8 ♘f3 ♘e4 ∓.

[15]   8 ... ♗e7?! 9 ♕d3 a6 10 0-0 d6 11 ♗d2! ± Rashkovsky-Kasparov, USSR 1981.

[16]   13 ♘a4 ♕d8 14 ♘b5 ∞∞.

[17]   6 ... ♗c5 7 ♘b3 ♗e7 8 ♗g2 ♘c6 9 0-0 b6 10 ♘c3 0-0 ∞ Rashkovsky-Savon, Lvov 1981.
    6 ... ♗xd2+ 7 ♕xd2 ±.

[18]   13 ♘xe4 ♕xd2+ 14 ♔xd2 b6! = Petursson-Forintos, Ljubljana 1981.

1 c4 c5 2 Nc3 Nf6 3 g3

	3	4	5	6	7	8	9	10	11	
1	... e6	Nf3[1] Nc6[2]	Bg2 Be7	0-0 a6	d4 cd	Nxd4 0-0	b3 Qc7	Bb2 d6	Rc1 Nxd4[3]	±
2	... ...	... ...	... ...	 d5	cd Nxd5[4]	d4 Nxc3[5]	bc 0-0	e4[6] b5[7]	d5 ed[8]	∞
3	... ...	... ...	... ...	... ...	... ...	... ...	... ...	... cd	cd b6[9]	∞
4	... ...	... ...	... ...	... ...	... ...	... 0-0	e4 Ndb4[10]	dc[11] Bxc5	e5[12]	±
5	... ...	... ...	... ...	... ...	... ...	... ...	... Nb6	d5 ed	ed Nb4[13]	∞/±
6	... ...	... ...	... ...	... ...	... ...	Nxd5 ed	d4 0-0	Be3 c4[14]	Ne5 Bf5[15]	∞
7	... ...	... ...	... ...	... ...	... ...	... ...	... ...	dc Bxc5	a3[16] a5[17]	=

1 c4 c5 2 Nc3 Nf6 3 g3 d5 4 cd Nxd5 5 Bg2 Nc7[18]

	6	7	8	9	10	11	12	13	14	
8	f4[19] e6	Nf3 Nc6	b3 Be7	Bb2 0-0	Rc1 Nf6[20]	Ba1!? Rb8	0-0 Qe7	Ne4 Bxa1	Rxa1 Rd8	=
9	... g6	b3 Bg7	Bb2 0-0	Nf3[21] Nc6	0-0 Qd7	Rc1 Rd8	Ba1 Rb8	Ne4 Nd4		=/∞
10	b3 e5	Bb2 Be7	Rc1 f6[22]	Nh3! Be6[23]	f4 Qd7	Nf2 Nc6	fe fe[24]			∞
11	Qa4+ Bd7	Qc4[25] Nc6	Qxc5 e5[26]	Qe3 Nb4!	Qxe5+ Be7	Kf1 0-0	Qe4 f5![27]	Qb1 f4		∞
12	d3 Qd7[28]	Nf3! Nc6	0-0 e5	Nd2[29] Be7	Nc4 0-0[30]	Bxc6 Qxc6	Nxe5 Qe6[31]	Nf3 b5	Bf4 Nd5	=
13	... e5	Be3 Ne6[32]	Rc1 Nd7	Nf3 Rb8	0-0 Be7[33]	Nd5 0-0	Nxe7+ Qxe7	Nh4 g6[34]		±
14	... ...	Qb3 Nc6[35]	Bxc6+ bc	Nf3 f6	Be3 Bd7!	Ne4[36] Ne6	Rc1 Qb6	N3d2 Be7[37]		=
15	... ...	f4!? ef[38]	Bxf4 Be7[39]	Qa4+ Nd7	Nf3 0-0	0-0 Nb6	Qc2 Ncd5	a3 Rxf4[40]	gf f5	∞/=

1 c4 c5 2 Nc3 Nf6 3 g3 d5 4 cd Nxd5 5 Bg2 Nc7 6 Nf3 Nc6

	7	8	9	10	11	12	13	14	15	
16	b3 e5	Bb2 f6[41]	Rc1[42] Bg4	h3[43] Bh5	Nh4 Qd7	Ne4 Ne6	0-0			∞
17	Qa4 Bd7	Qe4 g6[44]	Ne5 Bg7	Nxd7 Qxd7	0-0 0-0[45]	a3 Rac8	b4 Ne6	Rb1 b6	Nd5 Ncd4[46]	∞

[1] 4 ♗g2 d5! 5 cd ed ∓.

[2] Keres-Parma System.
 4 ... d5 5 cd ed – QGD Tarrasch.
 4 ... a6!? 5 ♗g2! ♗e7 6 0-0 0-0 7 b3 ±.

[3] 12 ♕xd4 ± Csom-Augustin, Pula 1975.

[4] 7 ... ed – QGD Tarrasch.

[5] 8 ... cd?! 9 ♘xd5! ed (9 ... ♕xd5 10 ♘xd4! ±) 10 ♘xd4 0-0 11 ♗e3 ± Portisch-Darga, Amsterdam 1969.

[6] 10 ♖b1 ♕c7 11 ♗f4 ♗d6 12 ♗xd6 ♕xd6 13 ♕a4 ±.

[7] **10 ... b6** 11 d5! ±.
 10 ... ♕c7 11 ♗f4 ♗d6 12 ♗e3 b6 13 ♕c2 ♗a6! 14 f4! ±/= Watson.

[8] 12 ed ♘a5 13 ♘e5 oo Watson/Peters.

[9] **11 ... ♗f6?** 12 ♗b2! b6 13 ♖b1 ♗b7 14 d5! ed 15 ed ♘a5 16 ♘e5! ♗xe5 17 ♗xe5 ± Christiansen-Portisch, Linares 1981.
 11 ... b6! 12 ♗e3 ♗b7 oo Quinteros-Tringov, Bar 1977.

[10] 9 ... ♘f6 10 dc ♗xc5 11 e5 ±.

[11] 10 a3 cd 11 ab dc 12 bc b6 = Filip-Pachman, Moscow 1967.

[12] 11 e5 ♗e7 12 a3 ± Korchnoi-Hübner, Johannesburg 1981.

[13] **12 ♘e5!?** ♗f6 13 f4 ♗f5! oo Tukmakov-Platonov, USSR 1977. 14 ♗e3!?
 12 ♘e1 ♗f6 (12 ... ♘c4!?) 13 ♗e3 ♗xc3 14 bc ♘4xd5 15 · ♗xc5 ♖e8 16 ♗d4 oo/± Chernin-Petursson, World Jr Ch 1979.

[14] 10 ... ♗f6 11 dc! ♗xb2 12 ♖b1 ♗f6 (Portisch-Keres, Petropolis IZ 1973) 13 ♘d4! ± Csom.

[15] **12 b3?!** ♖c8! 13 bc ♘xe5 ∓ Tal-Alburt, USSR Ch 1975.
 12 ♕a4! ♘xe5 13 de d4 14 ♗f4 g5 15 ♗d2 ♕c7 16 ♖ac1 oo Tal. 16 ... ♖fc8 17 b3 oo.

[16] **11 ♕c2** ♗b6 12 ♘g5 g6 13 ♕d1! (Miles-Tarjan, Riga IZ 1979) 13 ... ♘d4! =.
 11 ♘g5 g6 12 ♕c2 ♗xf2+ 13 ♖xf2 hg 14 ♕d2 d4 =.
 11 ♗g5 f6 12 ♖c1 ♗b6 13 ♗d2 d4! =/∓.
 11 b3 ♗g4! 12 ♗b2 d4 = Watson-Carlson, Las Cruces 1974.

[17] 12 ♘e1 ♗e6 13 ♘d3 ♗d6 14 ♗f4 ♗e7 =/± .

[18] Rubinstein System, also arising from 1 c4 ♘f6 2 ♘c3 d5 3 cd ♘xd5 4 g3 c5 5 ♗g2 ♘c7.
 5 ... ♘b4?! 6 ♘f3 ♘8c6 7 0-0 ±.

[19] 6 ♕b3?! ♘c6 7 ♗xc6+ bc 8 ♕a4 ♕d7 (8 ... ♗d7!?) 9 ♘f3 f6 10 d3 e5 11 0-0 ♘e6 12 ♗e3 ♖b8 oo Quinteros-Portisch, Mar del Plata 1981.

[20] 10 ... ♖b8 11 ♘e4 b6 12 ♕c2 ± Korchnoi-Balanel, 1959.

[21] 9 ♕c1 ♘ba6 10 ♘f3 ♘e6 =/∓ Korchnoi-Ragozin, USSR Ch 1956.

[22] 8 ... 0-0!? =.

[23] 9 ... 0-0 10 f4 ♘c6 11 0-0 ♗e6 12 fe fe 13 ♖xf8+ ♕xf8 14 ♘e4 oo/± Taimanov-Zhuravlev, Riga 1968.

[24] 12 ... ♘xe5 13 ♘ce4! ±/± Taimanov.

[25] 9 ♕b3 ♗c6! 10 ♗xc6+ ♘xc6 ∓.

[26] 8 ... ♘e6!? 9 ♕e3 ♘ed4 10 ♗e4 e5 oo Hanken-Peters, Los Angeles 1979.

[27] 12 ... g6 13 ♕b1 ± Nikolayevsky-Kudrianov, USSR 1966.

[28] 6 ... ♘c6 7 ♗xc6+! bc 8 ♕a4 ±.

[29] 9 a3 ♗e7 10 ♖b1 f6 11 ♗d2 (Smyslov-O'Kelly, Budapest 1952) 11 ... ♖b8! = Watson.

[30] 10 ... f6 11 f4 ± Taimanov.

[31] Watson.

[32] **7 ... ♘c6?** 8 ♗xc6+ ±/±.
 7 ... ♗e7 8 ♖c1 ♘ba6 9 ♘f3 f6 10 ♘d2 (Plachetka-Pribyl, Decin 1977) 10 ... ♖b8! intending 11 ... b6 = Plachetka.

[33] Watson.

[34] Analysis.

[35] 7 ... ♘d7 8 ♘f3 ♗e7 9 ♘d5 ♘xd5 (9 ... ♘e6?! 10 0-0 0-0 11 a4 ± Geller-Madera, Buenos Aires 1954) 10 ♕xd5 ♕c7! 11 ♗e3 ♖b8! 12 ♖c1 b6 = Watson.

[36] 11 0-0 ♘e6! 12 ♘a4 ♖b8 ∓ Balashov-Rashkovsky, USSR 1965.

[37] Rasch-B.Stein, 1975.

[38] **7 ... ♗d6** 8 fe ♗xe5 9 ♕a4+ ± Schwarz.
 7 ... ♘d7 8 ♕a4! ef 9 ♗xf4 ♘e6 10 ♘h3! ± Watson.

[39] 8 ... ♗d6? 9 ♕a4+! ± Filip-Ragozin, Prague 1956.

[40] Watson.
 13 ... ♗e6?! 14 e4 ± Tal-Gipslis, Riga 1954.

[41] 8 ... ♗e7 9 ♖c1 f6 10 0-0 0-0 11 ♘a4 ♘a6! 12 e3 ♗e6 13 d4 cd 14 ed ± Furman-Witkowski, Polanica Zdroj 1967.

[42] 10 0-0 ♗g4 11 h3!? Watson.

[43] 10 ♘a4 ♘e6 11 ♗a3 b6! ∓ Shatskes.

[44] 8 ... ♘e6 9 e3 g6 10 d4 cd 11 ed ♗g7 12 ♗e3! f5 13 ♕d5 ♘b4 (13 ... f4!? oo Watson) 14 ♕b3 ♘d3+ 15 ♔e2 f4! 16 ♔xd3 fe 17 ♔xe3 (Romanishin) 17 ... ♖f8!? Watson.

[45] 11 ... ♖ac8!?

[46] **15 ... ♘ed4!?** Schmidt.
 15 ... ♘cd4 16 ♗b2 f5!? (16 ... ♖fe8!?) 17 ♕e3 c4 oo Kasparov-Kapengut, Minsk 1978.

Keres-Parma; Rubinstein 1 c4 c5 2 ♘c3 ♘f6
3 g3 d5 4 cd ♘xd5 5 ♗g2 ♘c7 6 ♘f3 ♘c6 *continued*

	7	8	9	10	11	12	13	14	15	
18	♕a4	0-0[47]	♕c4[49]	b4	bc	♕e4[51]	♘g5	♖b1	♘a4	±/∞
	♕d7	g6[48]	b6	♗g7![50]	b5!	b4	♗b7	♘a6[52]	h6[53]	
19	a3	b4[54]	bc[55]	0-0[56]	a4	♗a3	♖c1			=
	g6	♗g7!	♘e6	♘xc5	0-0[57]	♕a5	♗e6[58]			
20	...	b4	bc	0-0	♗b2	♘e4[61]	♖c1	d4	♗a1	=
	e5	f6[59]	♗xc5	0-0	♗e6[60]	♗e7	♘a6	♕b6!	♖ad8[62]	
21	d3	♘d2[63]	♘c4[64]	♘e3	0-0	♗d2[66]	f4[67]	gf		∞
	e5	♗d7	b5!	♖c8[65]	♘d4	♗e6	ef	g6		
22	0-0	♘a4[68]	b3[70]	♘c3	♗b2	♖c1	♘e1!	♘e4	♘d3	∞
	g6	e5[69]	b5[71]	♖b8	♗g7	♘e6[72]	♗d7	♕e7	c4[73]	
23	...	d3[74]	♘d2	♘c4	♗xc6	♘xe5	♗e3[77]			⹀
	e5	♗e7[75]	♗d7!	0-0[76]	♗xc6	♗e8				

[47] **8 ♕e4!?** (Shatskes/Taimanov) 8 ... ♕g4!? (Watson).
  8 d3 ♘e6!? 9 0-0 g6 =.

[48] 8 ... e5 9 e3 ♗e7 10 ♖d1 (Watson) ±.

[49] 9 e3 ♗g7 10 ♖d1 ♘e6! =.
  9 ♘e1!? Watson.

[50] 10 ... cb 11 ♘g5 ♘e5 12 ♕xb4 ± Uhlmann.

[51] 12 ♕b3 b4 13 ♘g5 0-0 (Uhlmann-Liebert, East German Ch 1976) 14 ♕a4 ♘d4! 15 ♕xb4 h6! ∞ Watson.

[52] 14 ... h6? 15 ♖xb4!! ♘xb4 16 ♕xb7 hg 17 ♕xb4 ♖c8 18 c6 ± Mikhalchishin-Chekhov, USSR 1977.

[53] 16 ♘h3 ♘d8 17 ♕c2 ♗xg2 18 ♔xg2 ♖c8 ∞ Watson.

[54] 8 ♘a4 ♘e6 9 b3 ♗g7 10 ♗b2 = Watson.

[55] 9 ♖b1 ♗f5! 10 ♖b2 c4 ∓ E.Meyer-Portisch, Lone Pine 1978.

[56] 10 ♗b2 ♘xc5 11 ♘a4 ♗xb2 12 ♘xb2 ♗e6 13 0-0 0-0 14 ♖c1 ♕a5 ∓ Andersson-Portisch, Biel 1976.

[57] 11 ... ♗e6 12 ♗a3 ± Christiansen-Peters, USA 1979.

[58] Watson.

[59] 8 ... cb 9 ab b5! 10 0-0 ♗xb4 (Godes-Karasev, USSR 1979) 11 ♗b2 0-0 12 ♖c1 ∞.

[60] 11 ... ♘e6 =.

[61] 12 ♕a4!? Watson.

[62] Gofstein-Karasev, USSR 1976.

[63] 8 ♗e3 ♗d7 9 0-0 ♗e7 10 ♘d2 0-0 11 f4 ef 12 gf (Holmov-Alburt, Vilnius 1975) 12 ...

♖ac8 =.

[64] 9 0-0 transposes below.

[65] 10 ... ♘d4 11 ♗xa8 ♕xa8 ∞ Bronstein.

[66] 12 ♘ed5 = Pachman.

[67] 13 a4? a6 14 ab ab 15 ♖a7 ♗e7 ∓ Olafsson-Bronstein, Reykjavik 1974.

[68] 8 d3 ♗g7 9 ♘d2 0-0 10 a3 b6 = Watson.

[69] 8 ... ♘e6!? Watson.

[70] 9 d3 ♗d7 10 a3 ♘e6 (10 ... b5!?) 11 ♗e3 b6 12 b4 cb 13 d4! ed 14 ♘xd4 ♖c8 15 ab (Romanishin-Palatnik, Kiev 1973) ♗xb4!? ∞.

[71] **9 ... e4?** 10 ♘e1 ±.
  9 ... ♘e6 10 ♗b2 ♗g7 11 ♘e1 ± Watson.
  9 ... ♗g4!? intending ... ♘e6, ... ♗xf3, ... ♘d4.

[72] 12 ... f5!? intending ... ♕d6.

[73] 16 bc bc 17 ♖xc4 ♘ed4! intending ... ♗e6 ∞.

[74] **8 b3** ♗e7 9 ♘e1 (Abramov) 9 ... ♗g4! 10 ♗xc6+ bc 11 ♗a3 ∞.
  8 ♘e1 (Shatskes) ♗d7 9 ♘d3 f6! 10 b3 ♗g4! 11 ♗xc6+ bc 12 f3 ♗f5! 13 ♘f2 ∞/± Watson.
  8 a3 f6 9 d3 ♗e7 10 ♘d2 (Ogaard-Rosenlund, Aarhus 1976) 10 ... ♗d7! 11 ♘c4 0-0 12 f4 ef = Watson.

[75] 8 ... ♘e6 9 ♘d2 ♗d7 10 ♘c4 f6 11 f4 ef 12 ♗xf4! ± Pavlov-Nacht, Romania 1973.

[76] 10 ... f6 11 f4 b5 12 ♘e3 ef 13 gf! ♖b8 14 ♘ed5 ♘xd5 (14 ... 0-0 15 f5! ±) 15 ♘xd5 ± Seirawan-van der Wiel, Wijk aan Zee 1980.

[77] **13 ...** ♘e6/♘d5/♗f6 are all ∞.

	5	6	7	8	9	10	11	12	13	
1	e4[1]	bc	♗b5+[3]	♗c4	♗d5	a4	♕b3	♗xc6		∞
	♘xc3	g6[2]	♗d7	b5!?[4]	♘c6	b4	e6	♗xc6[5]		
2	...	dc	♔xd1	♗e3	♔c2!	♗e2	♖fd1	♖d2	♖ad1	±
	...	♕xd1+	♘c6	e6[6]	♗d7	♗e7	0-0-0	f6	♗e8[7]	
3	...	♗c4	♔e2	♔f1	b4[9]	♘d5	♗b2	♗xg7	♕c1!?[11]	∞∞
	♘b4	♘d3+[8]	♘f4+	♘e6	cb[10]	g6	♗g7	♘xg7	♘c6[12]	
4	...	...	♗xe6	♔f1	♘g5	♘xe6	♘xc5!	♕h5+	♕xc5	±
	...	♗e6	♘d3+[13]	fe	♘c6[14]	♕d7	♘xc5	g6	♕d3+[15]	
5	...	♗b5+	d4!	a3	♕xd8+	ab	♗xb2	0-0		∞
	...	♘8c6	cd	dc	♔xd8	cb[16]	e6!	f6[17]		
6	d4	bc	♗f4[19]	e3	♕d2	♗e2	♖b1	cd	♔xd2	=
	♘xc3[18]	g6	♗g7	♕a5	0-0	♘c6	cd	♕xd2+	♖d8[20]	
7	e3	bc	♗b5+[22]	0-0	a4	d4	♗d3!	♖b1	e4	±
	♘xc3[21]	g6	♘d7	♗g7	0-0	a6	b6	♗b7	♕c7[23]	

[1]   5 g3 transposes to Anglo-Indian I, Keres-Parma or Rubinstein systems.

[2]   6 ... ♘c6 7 ♗c4 ±.

[3]   **7 ♗a3 ♕c7 8 ♕b3!? ♗g7 9 ♕d5!? ♘d7 10 ♗b5 0-0 11 ♗xd7 ♗xd7 12 ♕xc5 ♗c6 13 0-0 ♕f4! ∞** O'Kelly-J.Schmidt, corr. 1952.
   7 ♕a4+!? Watson.

[4]   8 ... ♘c6!? Watson.

[5]   Korchnoi-Zaltsman, Lone Pine 1979.

[6]   8 ... b6!? intending 9 ♗b5 ♗b7 Watson.

[7]   **13 ... ♘a5? 14 e5! ±/±** Cvetković-Palatnik, USSR v Yugoslavia 1976.
   13 ... ♗e8! 14 ♖xd8+ ♘xd8 15 e5 ±/= Cvetković/Watson.

[8]   6 ... e6 7 0-0 ♘8c6 8 d3 ♘d4 9 ♘xd4 ± Nimzowitsch-Rubinstein, Dresden 1926.

[9]   9 ♘e5!? ♘c6! Peters/Keene.

[10]   9 ... g6 10 bc ♗g7 11 ♗xe6 ♗xe6 12 d4 ♘c6 13 ♗e3 ♗g4 14 ♘e2 f5 15 h3 fe 16 hg ef 17 gf ± Seirawan-Miles, London 1982.

[11]   13 ♘xb4 0-0 14 d4 ♗g4 = Hübner-Portisch, match 1980.

[12]   14 d4 ♗e6! 15 h4 ♖c8 16 h5! ∞∞ Seirawan-Peters US Ch/Z 1981.

[13]   7 ... fe? 8 0-0 ♘8c6 9 ♘g5 ♗d7 10 ♕g4 ±/±.

[14]   **9 ... ♕d7 10 ♕f3! ♘e5 11 ♕h3 ♕d3+ 12 ♕xd3 ♘xd3 13 ♔e2 ♘f4+ 14 ♔f3! e5** (Vadasz-Lukacs, Hungarian Ch 1977) 15 d4! (Moiseyev) ±.
   9 ... ♕b6!? (Polugayevsky-Tal, Riga IZ 1979) 10 ♕f3!? intending 10 ... ♘e5 11 ♕h3 or 10 ... c4!? 11 ♕f7+ ♔d7 ∞ Watson.

[15]   14 ♔g1 (Timman-Stean, Amsterdam Z 1978) 14 ... 0-0-0!? Stean.

[16]   10 ... c2!? 11 ♗xc6 bc 12 ♘e5! ♔e8 (Böhm-Langeweg, Dutch Ch 1979) 13 ♗e3! ± Stean.

[17]   Watson.

[18]   5 ... cd 6 ♕xd4 ♘xc3 7 ♕xc3 ♘c6 8 e4 e6 = Miles-Ribli, Baden Baden 1981.

[19]   7 e4 – Grünfeld.

[20]   Portisch-Timman, Tilburg 1980.

[21]   5 ... e6 – Semi-Tarrasch.

[22]   **7 d4** – Grünfeld.
   7 ♕a4+ ♘d7 =.

[23]   14 ♖e1 e6 15 e5!? ± Karpov-Korchnoi, match (12) 1981.

	1	2	3	4	5	6	7	8	9	
1	... b6	♘c3 e6	e4 ♗b7	♘f3 ♗b4[1]	♕b3![2] ♘a6[3]	♗e2[4] ♘e7	0-0 0-0	d3 f5	e5	∞
2	... ...	♘f3 ♗b7[5]	g3 ♗xf3!?[6]	ef c5	d4 cd	♕xd4 ♘c6	♕d2 g6	b3 ♗g7	♗b2[7] ♗xb2[8]	±
3	... ...	d4 ♗b7	♘c3[9] ♘f6[10]	♕c2[11] d5[12]	cd ♘xd5	e4[13] ♘xc3	bc e5	♘f3![14] ed	♗b5+ c6[15]	±
4	... ...	... e6	a3[16] ♘f6[17]	♘c3[18] ♗b7[19]	d5 b5!?[20]	e4 b4![21]	ab ♗xb4	♗d3 ed	cd ♕e7[22]	∞
5	... ...	... ...	e4 ♗b7	♗d3[23] f5	ef ♗xg2[24]	♕h5+ g6	fg ♗g7	gh+ ♔f8	♘e2! ♘f6[25]	∞
6	... ...	... ...	♘c3 ♗b7	e4 ♗b4	f3 ♕h4+[26]	g3 ♗xc3+[27]	bc ♕h5	♘h3[28] f5	♘f4 ♕f7[29]	∓
7	... ...	... ...	... ...	... ...	♗d3[30] f5	♕h5+[31] g6	♕e2 ♘f6	f3[32] ♘c6![33]		=
8	... ♘f6	♘f3 e6	g3 b6	d3 ♗b7	♗g2 ♗e7	0-0 0-0[34]	♘c3 d5[35]	♕c2[36] d4	♘a4[37] c5[38]	∞
9	... ...	... ...	... ...	♗g2 ♗b7	0-0 ♗e7	♘c3[39] 0-0	♖e1 d5![40]	cd ♘xd5[41]	♘xd5[42] ed[43]	=
10	... ...	... ...	♘c3 b6	e4 ♗b7	♗d3!?[44] c5[45]	e5[46] ♗g4[47]	h3 ♗xf3	♕xf3 ♘xe5	♕xa8 ♗xd3+[48]	∞
11	... c5	♘f3[49] b6	g3 ♗b7	♗g2 ♘f6	0-0[50] e6	♘c3 ♗e7[51]	d3[52] d5![53]	♘e5 0-0	f4 ♕c8!	=

[1] 4 ... c5 5 d4 cd 6 ♘xd4 a6 7 ♗e2 ♕c7 8 0-0 ♘f6 9 f3 ∞ Fedorowicz-Regan, US Jr Ch 1976.

[2] 5 ♕c2 f5? 6 ef ♗xf3 7 gf ♘f6 8 fe 0-0 9 d4 de 10 ♗e3 c5 11 0-0-0 ± Cekro-Arapović, Sarajevo 1981. 5 ... ♘e7.
5 ♗d3!? ♘e7 6 0-0 0-0 7 ♖e1 f5 8 a3 ♗xc3 9 dc = Friedgood-Keene, Cape Town 1976.

[3] 5 ... ♗xc3 6 ♕xc3 ♗xe4 7 ♕xg7 (7 d3!? Speelman) 7 ... ♕f6 8 ♕xf6 ♘xf6 9 ♗e2 ♖g8 10 d3 ± Smejkal-Miles, Reykjavik 1978.
5 ... a5!?

[4] 6 a3 ♘c5! ∓.

[5] 2 ... e6 generally transposes below.

[6] 3 ... ♘f6 4 ♗g2 e6 5 ♘c3 ♗b4 6 ♕c2 0-0 7 b3 d5 8 0-0 = Hjartarsson-Benjamin, Gausdal 1978.

[7] 9 ♘c3 ♘d4 (9 ... b5!) 10 ♗g2 b5 11 ♗b2 bc 12 ♘d5 ∞ Rajković-Schüssler, Smederevska Palanka 1979.

[8] 10 ♕xb2 ♘f6 11 ♘c3 ± Rajković.

[9] 3 ♗g5!? f6 4 ♗d2 e6 5 ♘c3 f5 6 ♘f3 ♘f6 7 g3 ♘c6 8 e3 ♗b4 9 ♗g2 ± Smejkal-Miles, Baden 1980. 7 ... g6 8 ♗g2 ♗g7 9 0-0 0-0 (Hölzl-Miles, Baden 1980) 10 ♕b3 intending ♖ad1 ± Byrne, Mednis.

[10] 3 ... e6 transposes below.

[11] 4 d5!? e5!? Sahović. 4 ... e6 – 2 ... e6.

[12] 4 ... e6. 4 ... c5.

[13] 6 ♘f3 ♘xc3 7 bc g6 8 e4 ♗g7 9 ♗b5+ ♘d7 Quinteros-Planinc, Ljubljana 1973.

[14] 8 de ♕h4! 9 ♗b5+ ♘d7 10 ♘f3 ♕xe4+ 11 ♕xe4 ♗xe4 12 ♘g5 ♗xg2 13 ♖g1 f6 ∓ Euwe-Alekhine, Budapest 1921.

[15] 10 ♗c4 ± Spielmann-Chekhover, Moscow 1953.

[16] 3 d5 ♕h4!? (3 ... ♘f6 4 g3 ♗b4+ 5 ♗d2 ♕e7 6 ♗g2 c6! 7 dc dc 8 ♘c3 0-0 = Tempone-Miles, Reykjavik 1978) 4 ♘c3 ♗b4 5 ♗d2 ♘f6 6 e3 ♗xc3 7 ♗xc3 ♘e4 8 ♕c2 ♘xc3 9 ♕xc3 0-0 10 g3 ♕e4 11 f3 ♕g6 12 ♘e2 ♗b7 13 0-0-0 d6 14 g4 ♘d7 15 h4 ♘f6 16 ♕xf6 ♘xf6 17 e4 ♘d7 = Karpov-Miles, Bugojno 1978.

[17] 3 ... c5!? 4 d5 ed 5 cd ♗a6 6 ♘f3 d6 7 g3 g6 (Zuodor-Keene, Lausanne 1977) 8 ♗g2! ♗g7 9 0-0 ♘e7!? ∞.

[18] 4 ♘f3 – Queen's Indian.
4 d5 ♗a6!

[19] 4 ... d5!? 5 cd ♘xd5 6 e4 ♘xc3 7 bc ♗b7 8 ♗d3 c5 ±/= Stean-Miles, Amsterdam Z 1978.

[20] 5 ... ♗d6 6 ♘f3! 0-0 7 ♗g5! ♗e7 8 ♗f4 ♘h5

32

9 ♗g3 ♘f6 10 ♘d4 ∞ Sosonko-Planinc, Ljubljana 1977.

21 6 ... bc 7 ♗xc4 ed 8 ed ± Farago-Bednarski, Polanica Zdroj 1978.

22 10 ♕e2 0-0 11 ♘f3 ♖e8 12 0-0 ∞ Möhring-Espig, Eggesin 1978.

23 **4 d5** ed 5 ed (5 cd ♘f6 intending ... ♗b4+) 5 ... ♗b4+ =.
4 f3 f5 5 ef ♕h6 6 fe ♘f5! 7 ♗e2 ♗d6 8 h4! 0-0 (8 ... ♘xh4) 9 ♘bc3 ♕f6?! (9 ... de) 10 c5 ♗e7 (Ree-Miles, Wijk aan Zee 1979) 11 ♗g5 ♕xe6 12 ♕b3 ± Miles.

24 5 ... ♗b4+!? 6 ♔f1 ♘f6 ∞∞.

25 10 ♕h4 ♗xh1 11 ♗g5 ♘c6 **12 ♘f4** (Browne-Miles, Tilburg 1978) 12 ... e5!? 13 ♘g6+ ♔f7 14 de (14 ♘xe5+ ♘xe5 15 de ♖e8 16 f4 d6) 14 ... ♖xh7! 15 ♕f4 ♕h3 16 ef ♗xf6 ∓.
12 ♘d2! b5!? (12 ... e5 13 0-0-0 e4 14 ♗xe4 ♗xe4 15 ♘xe4 ♖xh1 16 ♕xf7 ♗f7 17 ♘ec3 ±/± Magerramov-Psakhis, Riga 1980) 13 cb ♘b4 14 ♗g6 ♗b7 15 ♘f4 ♗e7 16 ♘h5 ♕f8 17 d5 ♘bxd5 18 ♘e4 ∞ Flear-Plaskett, British Ch 1982.

26 5 ... f5 6 ef ♕h6!? 7 fe ♘f5! 8 ♘ge2 de 9 ♗f4 0-0 10 ♕d2 ♕h4+ 11 ♘g3 ♗d6 ∞ Panno-Miles, Buenos Aires 1980.

27 6 ... ♕h5 7 ♘h3 ♗xc3+ 8 bc f5 9 ♘f4 ♕f7 10 ef ♕xf5 11 ♗h3 ♕a5! ∞.

28 8 c5? f5 9 ef (Young-Basman, London 1976) 9 ... ♕xf5 10 ♗d3 ♕f7 ∓.

29 10 ef ♕xf5 11 ♗d3 (11 ♗h3 – note 27) 11 ... ♕f7 12 ♗e4 ♘c6 13 d5 ed 14 ♖xd5 0-0-0 ∞ Donner-Miles, *Master Game* 1978.

30 5 d5 ♕e7 6 ♗e3 ed 7 ed ♘f6 8 ♗d3 c6 Haik-Benjamin, London 1978.

31 6 ♕e2 ♘f6 7 f3 0-0! =. 7 ♗g5 fe 8 ♗xf6 ♕xf6 9 ♗xe4 ♗xe4 10 ♕xe4 0-0 = Garces-Keene, Lausanne 1977.

32 8 ♗g5 fe 9 ♗xf6 ed!? 10 ♕e5 (10 ♗xd8 de ∓) 10 ... ♘c6 11 ♗xd8 ♘xe5 12 ♗f6 ♘xc4! ∓.

33 8 ...fe?! 9 fe ♗xc3+ 10 bc ± Botvinnik-Wallis, Leicester 1967.
8 ... 0-0!? 9 ♗g5 ♗e7 Basman.
8 ... ♘c6! =.

34 6 ... d5!?

35 7 ... d6 8 e4 ♘bd7 9 ♖e1 ♖e8 10 d4 c5 (Shamkovich-Garcia Palermo, Lone Pine 1978) 11 ♘c2! Watson.

36 8 cd ♘xd5 9 ♕xd5 ♗xd5 10 ♗d2 c5 11 ♗c3 ♘d7 12 ♖e1 ♗f6 13 a4 ♕c7 = Schmidt-Saren, Helsinki 1972.

37 9 ♘b5 c5 10 e4 ∞ Watson.

38 10 a3 ♘bd7 11 b4 e5 12 ♖b1 e4 13 ♘h4 ed

14 ed ∞ Schmidt-Unzicker, European Team Ch 1973.

39 6 d4 – Queen's Indian.

40 7 ... ♘e4 8 ♘xe4 ♗xe4 9 d3 ♗b7 (Petrosian-Portisch, 11th match game 1974) 10 e4! ± Watson.
7 ... c5? 8 e4! d6 9 d4 ±.

41 8 ... ed 9 d4 ♘bd7 10 ♕b3! c5 11 dc ♘xc5 12 ♕d1 ♘e6 13 ♘b5 ± Petrosian-Gulko, USSR Ch 1975.

42 9 e4!? ♘xc3 10 bc c5 11 d4 cd 12 cd ♘c6 13 ♗b2! ± Seirawan-Timman, Las Palmas 1981.

43 10 d4 ♘d7 11 ♗f4 c5 = Portisch-Karpov, match (3) 1975.

44 5 ♕e2 ♗b4! 6 e5 ♘g8 7 d4 ♘e7! 8 ♕d3 d5 9 ed cd 10 a3 ♗xc3+ 11 ♕xc3 ♘d7! = Uhlmann-Karpov, Skopje 1976.

45 5 ... d5!? 6 cd ed 7 e5 ♘e4!? 8 ♗c2 ♗e7 9 0-0 0-0 10 d4 f5! ∞ Watson. 8 0-0 ♘c5 9 ♗b5+ c6 10 d4 (Chekhov-A.Ivanov, USSR 1978) 10 ... cb 11 dc bc ∞

46 6 0-0 ♘c6 7 e5 ♘g4 8 ♗e4 ♕c8 9 d3! ♘gxe5 10 ♘xe5 ♘xe5 11 f4 ♘c6 12 f5 ± g6 13 ♗g5 gf 14 ♗xf5! ♗e7 15 ♕h5 ♗xg5 16 ♕xg5 ♗e7 17 ♗e4 ♗xe4 18 ♘xe4 ♕c6 19 ♖xf7! ♔xf7 20 ♕f6+ ♔g8 21 ♕xe7 ♖f8 22 ♖f1! 1-0 Tal-van der Wiel, Moscow IZ 1982.

47 6 ... ♘g8!? 7 ♗e4 ♗xe4 8 ♘xe4 ♘c6 9 0-0 f5 = Lewis-Short, British Ch 1981.

48 10 ♔e2 ♘b4 (10 ... ♘f4+ 11 ♔f1 ♘c6 12 ♕xd8+ ♔xd8 13 b3 ± Korchnoi-Polugayevsky, 1st match game 1977) 11 d3 ∞.

49 2 ♘c3 b6 3 ♘f3 ♘f6 4 e4 d6 5 d4 cd 6 ♘xd4 ♗b7 7 ♕e2 e6 8 g4!? ♘c6 9 ♘xc6 ♗xc6 ± Cvetković-Veličković, Yugoslavia 1981.

50 5 ♘c3 e6 6 d4 cd 7 ♕xd4 ♘c6 = Uhlmann-Andersson, East Germany v Sweden 1977.

51 **6 ... d5** 7 ♗e5! ∞.
6 ... ♘c6 7 e4 ♕b8!? 8 d4 cd 9 ♘xd4 ♘xd4 10 ♕xd4 ♗d6! = Smejkal-Larsen, Biel 1976.

52 **7 ♖e1** d5 8 cd ed 9 d4 0-0 10 ♗g5 ♘a6 (10 ... ♘e4!? Filip) 11 ♖c1 ♖e8 (11 ... ♘e4, 11 ... h6 Tal) 12 e3 (Romanishin-Tal, USSR Ch 1977) 12 ... ♘e4 = Tal.
7 b3 0-0 8 ♗b2 d6 9 e3 ♘c6 10 ♖e1 ♖c8 11 ♖c1 ± Petrosian-Dolmatov, USSR 1981. 9 ... ♘bd7 10 d4 a6 (Speelman-Kasparov, Graz 1981) 11 ♕e2 intending ♖fd1 ±.
7 d4 – next section.

53 7 ... 0-0 8 e4 d6 9 b3 a6 10 ♗b2 ♖e8 11 ♕e2 (11 ♖c1 ♗f8 12 ♖c2 intending ♖d2 Watson) 11 ... ♘c6 = Smejkal-Andersson, IBM 1979.

Hedgehog and Double Fianchetto				1 c4 ♘f6 2 ♘c3 e6[1] 3 ♘f3 b6					
4	**5**	**6**	**7**	**8**	**9**	**10**	**11**	**12**	
e4	♗d3	♗c2	d4	♘xd4	0-0[2]	b3	♗b2	♘xc6	±
♗b7	d6	c5	cd	♗e7	0-0	a6	♘c6	♗xc6	

1 c4 ♘f6 2 ♘c3 e6 3 ♘f3 b6 4 g3 ♗b7 5 ♗g2 c5 6 0-0 ♗e7 7 d4 cd 8 ♕xd4[3]									
8	**9**	**10**	**11**	**12**	**13**	**14**	**15**	**16**	
...	♖d1	♕f4	b3	♗b2	e4	♕e3	♘e1	♘c2	±
0-0[4]	♘c6	d6[5]	♕b8	♖d8[6]	a6	♕a7	♖ab8	♗a8[7]	
...	♗g5!?[8]	♗xf6	♕f4	♖fd1	♘e4	♕xe4	♘d4	b3	±
d6	a6	♗xf6	0-0	♗e7	♗xe4	♖a7	♕c8![9]	♖e8[10]	
...	♖d1	♘g5	♔xg2	♕f4	♘ce4!?	♘xf6+	♘xh7!	♕e4	±
...	a6	♗xg2	♘c6	♖a7	♖d7	♗xf6	♖xh7	♖h5[11]	
...	...	♘g5	♔xg2	♘ge4	♘xe4	b3	f3[12]		=
...	♘bd7!?	♗xg2	0-0	♘xe4	♕c7	♖fd8			
...	...	b3	e4	♗a3	e5	♕xe5	♘a4[15]	♕b2	±
...	...	a6	♕c7[13]	♘c5	de	♕c8[14]	♘cd7![16]	♗xa3[17]	
...	...	...	...	♗b2[18]	♕e3	♘d4	♕d2	♖e1	∞
...	...	...	♕b8	0-0	♖e8	♗f8	♕a7	♖ad8![19]	

1 c4 c5 2 ♘f3 ♘f6 3 g3 b6 4 ♗g2 ♗b7 5 0-0 g6[20]								
6	**7**	**8**	**9**	**10**	**11**	**12**	**13**	**14**
♘c3	d4[21]	♘xd4[23]	♔xg2	b3	f3	cd	♘xd5	♗e3	±
♗g7	cd[22]	♗xg2	♕c8[24]	♕b7+	d5	♘xd5	♕xd5	♘c6[25]
b3	♗b2	♘c3	♖c1	d4	♕d3	e4	de	♘d5	∞
♗g7	0-0	e6!?[26]	♕e7	d6	♘c6	e5	de	♕d6[27]

[1]   2 ... c5 3 ♘f3 b6 4 e4 (4 d4 cd 5 ♘xd4 ♗b7 6 ♗g5!? d7 7 ♗xf6 gf oo; 6 f3! intending 7 e4 ±) 4 ... d6 5 d4 cd 6 ♘xd4 ♗b7 7 ♕e2 e6 8 g3 (8 g4!? oo Cvetković) 8 ... a6 9 ♗g2 ♕c7 10 0-0 ♗e7 11 ♗e3 ♘bd7 12 ♖ac1 ± Korchnoi-Csom, Rome 1981.

[2]   9 ♗a4+!?. The row is Polugayevsky-Petrosian, USSR Cup 1982.

[3]   8 ♘xd4 ♗xg2 9 ♔xg2 ♕c8 10 ♕d3 ♘c6 11 ♘xc6 ♕xc6+ 12 e4 0-0 13 ♗d2 ♖ac8 14 b3 ♖fd8 15 ♕f3 a6 16 ♖fe1 d6 = Hort-Tal, Havana Ol 1966.

[4]   8 ... ♘c6 5 ♕f4 ♕b8 6 ♕xb8 ♖xb8 11 ♗f4 ♖c8 12 ♘b5 ± Smyslov-Tal, Moscow 1963.

[5]   10 ... ♕b8 11 e4! ± Karpov-Petrosian, Milan 1975.

[6]   12 ... a6 13 ♘g5! ± Smyslov-Andersson, Biel 1976.

[7]   Taimanov-Holmov, USSR Ch 1967.

[8]   9 b3 a6!? (9 ... ♘bd7!?; 9 ... 0-0!?) 10 ♗a3 ♘c6 11 ♕f4 d5 12 ♗xe7 ♘xe7 13 ♖fd1 ♕b8 14 ♕xb8 ♖xb8 15 cd ♘fxd5 16 ♘xd5 ♗xd5 17 ♖ac1 ± Andersson-Gheorghiu, Moscow IZ 1982.

[9]   15 ... ♕c7 16 b3 ♖c5 17 a4 ♕c7 18 ♕b1 ♖fc8 19 ♖a2 ♗f8 20 e3 ♕e7 21 ♖c2 ± Andersson-Seirawan, London 1982.

[10]   17 a4!? ♕c5 18 ♖a2 ♗f6 19 ♖ad2 ♖c7 20 ♕b1! ♗e7! 21 b4 ± Karpov-Kasparov, USSR 1981. 18 ... ♗f8!?

[11]   17 ♕xc6 ♖c5 18 ♕e4 ♕c7 19 ♗e3 ♖xc4 20 ♕a8+ ♕c8 21 ♕xc8+ ♖xc8 22 ♖ac1! ♖xc1 23 ♖xc1 ♖b7 24 b3 ± Csom-Dizdarević, Sarajevo 1981.

[12]   Krnić-de Firmian, Niš 1981. 15 ... ♘f6! = Krnić.

[13]   11 ... 0-0? 12 ♗a3! ♘c5 13 e5! de 14 ♕xd8 ♖fxd8 15 ♘xe5 ♗xg2 16 ♔xg2 ♗f8 17 ♗xc5! ♗xc5 18 ♘a4 ♔f8 19 b4! ♗d4 20 ♘c6 ♗xa1 21 ♘xd8 b5 22 ♘b6 ♖b8 23 c5 ± de Firmian-Zivanović, Smederevska Palanka 1981.

[14]   14 ... ♖c8? 15 ♕xc7 ♖xc7 16 ♗c1 ♘fe4 17 ♘xe4 ♗xe4 18 ♗f4 ♖c8 19 ♗d6 ± Gutman-

de Firmian, Lone Pine 1981.

[15]   15 ♕e3!? 0-0?! 16 ♖a4! ♘g4 17 ♕e1 ♕c7 18 ♘xc5 ♗xc5 19 ♗xc5 ♕xc5 20 h3 ± Cebalo-Ftacnik. 15 ... ♘fd7!? 16 ♖a4 ♖b8 oo Ftacnik.

[16]   15 ... ♘fd7? 16 ♕xg7 ♗f6 17 ♕h6 ♗xa1 18 ♖xa1 ± Ribli-Christiansen, Indonesia 1982.

[17]   17 ♕xa3 b5 18 ♘b2 ± Keene-Psakhis, Dortmund 1982. 18 cb!? ab 19 ♖ac1 ♕b8 20 ♘d4 intending ♘c6.

[18]   12 ♗a3 ♘c5 13 ♕d2 (13 e5 de 14 ♕xe5 ♕c8 – row 6; 14 ... ♕a7!?; 14 ... 0-0!?) 13 ... 0-0 14 ♗b2 ♖c8 oo Seirawan-Polugayevsky, Mar del Plata 1982.

[19]   17 ♖ad1 ♘c5 18 h3 ♕a8 oo Velikov-Ribli, Herkulana 1982.

[20]   The Double Fianchetto Defence.

[21]   7 d3!? 0-0 8 e4 ♘c6 9 ♗g5 d6 10 ♕d2 ♖e8 11 ♖ae1 ♘d7 12 ♕h4 ± Najdorf-Diez del Corral, Montevideo 1954.

[22]   7 ... ♘e4 8 ♘xe4 ♗xe4 9 d5 0-0 (9 ... b5 10 ♘d2 ♗xg2 11 ♔xg2 ♕b6 12 e4 0-0 13 h4 ± Schmidt-Ornstein, Erevan 1976) 10 ♗h3 ♗xf3 11 ef e5 12 f4! ef 13 ♗xf4 ♗xb2 14 ♖b1 ♗f6 15 ♕a4! ± oo Karpov-Timman, Amsterdam 1981.

[23]   8 ♕xd4!? ♘c6 9 ♕d3 ♖c8 10 e4 ♘g4 11 ♗f4 ♘ge5 12 ♘xe5 ♘xe5 13 ♗xe5 ♗xe5 14 f4 ♗xc3 15 ♕xc3 0-0 = Korchnoi-Miles, Baden Baden 1981. 11 ♕d2!? ♘ce5 12 ♘xe5 ♘xe5 13 b3 b5 14 ♘xb5 ♘xc4 15 bc ♗xa1 16 ♕h6 oo Miles.

[24]   9 ... 0-0 10 e4 ♘a6 11 b3 ♘c5 12 f3 ♘e8 (Keene-Ljubojević, Nice Ol 1974) 13 ♗e3 ±.

[25]   15 ♘xc6 ♕xc6 16 ♖c1 ± Polugayevsky-Spassky, Manila 1976.

[26]   8 ... ♘a6 9 d4 d5 10 ♘e5! e6 (10 ... cd 11 ♕xd4 ♘b4 12 ♖ad1 ♘d7 13 f4 ±) 11 dc! bc?! 12 cd ed 13 ♘d3! ± Andersson-Miles, Malta Ol 1980. 11 ... ♘xc5 12 cd ed ± Andersson.

[27]   15 ♗c3 ♖fe8 oo Gross-Smejkal, Marianske Lazne 1978. 16 a3!? Watson.

35

Dutch Defence

Although this defence has served as a useful tool for players such as Morphy, Alekhine, Botvinnik and Larsen, it has never achieved universal popularity. Black stakes an early claim to the e4 square and envisages an eventual attack with the advance of his kingside pawns. The defects of this strategy are a weakening of his position (particularly the square e6) and some difficulty in harmoniously completing his development. White's trump is the advance e4 which, when successfully executed, allows him a tangible advantage in space and activity as well as highlighting the weaknesses in Black's camp.

The **Staunton Gambit** (2 e4 fe 3 ♘c3) is a dangerous attempt to expose Black's position to an early assault. It is certainly sound, but Black's defensive resources are sufficient to hold the balance.

The **Stonewall Variation** is the most double-edged. Black, making no secret of his aggressive intentions on the kingside, commits himself to potentially fatal dark-squared weaknesses and a congested queenside if his onslaught on the other flank fails to produce results.

The **Leningrad** is a more temperate variation. White's best choice is to fianchetto his king's bishop, post his king's knight on h3 and prepare the thematic e4. He retains the better chances, but Black's position is flexible and quite playable. The Fluid Formation (6 ... d6) is the main line and Black's best chance for full equality. Here again, the first player's struggle for an edge hinges upon his ability to implement a timely e4.

	2	3	4	5	6	7	8	9	10	
				Dutch: Introduction and Staunton Gambit			**1 d4 f5**			
1	♕d3[1]	g4?![3]	h3	f4!?[5]	♕xg3	c3				∓
	d5[2]	fg	g3![4]	♘f6	♗f5	♘e4				
2	...	♗f4	♘f3	c4	♘c3	g3				=
	...	e6	♘f6	♗e7	0-0					
3	h3[6]	g4	hg	e4	♗g5!	f3	♘c3	♕d2		∞
	♘f6[7]	fg	♘xg4[8]	d6[9]	g6[10]	♘f6	c6	♗e6[11]		
4	♘c3	♗g5[12]	♗xf6	e3	♗d3	♕f3	h3[13]	♘ge2	de	∞
	♘f6	d5	ef	c6	♗d6	g6	♘d7	♘e5!!	fe[14]	
5	♘f3	♗g5	♘bd2	e3	♗d3	♕e2	♗xe7	♗xe4	♘e5	=
	♘f6	e6	d5	♗e7	0-0	♘e4	♕xe7	fe	♘d7[15]	
6	...	c3[16]	♗g5	♘bd2	e3	♘e5	♘df3	♘xe5	♗xe7	=
	...	e6	♗e7	d5	0-0	♘bd7	♘xe5	♘d7	♕xe7[17]	
7	♗g5	♘c3	e4[18]	♘xe4	♘c3	♗d3	♘ge2	0-0	de	=
	g6!	♗g7	fe	d5	♘f6[19]	♘c6	0-0	e5	♘xe5[20]	

1 d4 f5 2 e4²¹ fe

	3	4	5	6	7	8	9	10	11	
8	Nc3 / Nf6	f3²² / ef	Nxf3 / g6	Bg5²³ / Bg7	Bc4 / c6	d5! / d6	Qd2 / e6	de / d5	Bb3 / Bxe6²⁴	=
9	... / ...	... / Nc6	fe / e5	de / Nxe5	Nf3 / Nd6	Nb5! / Nxf3+	Qxf3 / Be5	Bf4 / Qe7	0-0-0 / 0-0²⁵	∞
10	... / ...	Bg5 / e6?!	Nxe4 / Be7	Bxf6 / Bxf6	Qh5!+ / g6	Qh6 / Nc6	Nf3 / Qe7²⁶	Nxf6+ / Qxf6	0-0-0 / b6²⁷	±
11	... / ...	... / b6²⁸	f3²⁹ / e3!	Bxe3³⁰ / e6	Qd2³¹ / d5	0-0-0 / c5	Bb5+ / Bd7	Bxd7+ / Qxd7	Nh3 / Nc6³²	∓
12	... / ...	... / Nc6	d5³³ / Ne5	Qd4 / Bf7	Bxf6³⁴ / ef	Nxe4 / f5!	Ng3 / g6	h4³⁵ / Bh6³⁶		=

[1] Alapin Variation.

[2] **2 ... e6?** 3 g4! fg 4 h3 ±/ ±±.
2 ... d6?! 3 e4 fe 4 Nxe4 Nf6 5 Qh4 ±. 3 g4!? fg 4 h3 Nf6! 5 Bg5 ∞∞.
2 ... g6 3 e4! fe 4 Qxe4 Nf6 5 Qh4 ±. 3 h4!? Nf6 4 h5! Nxh5 5 Rxh5! gh 6 Qxf5 d6 7 Qxh5+ Kd7 8 Nf3 ∞∞/±.

[3] 3 g3 – 2 g3.

[4] 4 ... g6? 5 hg Bg7 6 Rxh7! Rxh7 7 Qxg6+ ±±.

[5] 5 fg =. 5 Qxg3 Nc6 =.

[6] Korchnoi Variation.

[7] 2 ... e6?! 3 g4! fg 4 Qd3! – 2 Qd3 e6.

[8] 4 ... Ne4!?

[9] 5 ... d5.

[10] 6 ... c6 (intending ... Qa5+) 7 d5?! Qb6!

[11] Korchnoi-Kaenel, Biel 1979.

[12] **3 e4** – 2 e4.
3 g4 d5! =.

[13] 8 h4 h5 = Smejkal-Zwaig, Raach 1969.

[14] Keene-Bellin, Hastings 1975/76. Black intends ... e4.

[15] 11 Nxd7 Bxd7 12 f4 = Nemet-Clemens, Hamburg 1980.

[16] Barcza System.

[17] 11 Nxd7 Bxd7 = Castaldi-Canal, Venice 1953.

[18] 4 Nf3 Nf6 5 Bxf6 Bxf6 6 e4 fe 7 Nxe4 d5 ∞ Ivkov/Sokolov.
4 h4 h6 5 Bf4 Nf6 6 f3 d6 7 e4 e5 8 de Nh5 Ivkov/Sokolov.

[19] 6 ... Nc6!? 7 Bb5 Nh6 8 Bxh6 Bxh6 9 Qf3 Be6 ∞ Misimić-Knežević, Smederevska Palanka 1977. 8 Qf3!? Ivkov/Sokolov.

[20] Bogoljubow-Sämisch, Berlin 1936.

[21] The Staunton Gambit.

[22] **4 g4** (Tartakower) h6! and now:
5 h4 d5 6 Bh3 Nc6 7 Bf4 g5! 8 Be5 Be6 ∞.
5 f4 d5 6 Be2 g6! 7 g5 hg 8 fg Nh5 9 Bxh5 Rxh5 10 Nge2 Bg4! ∓ Harding.
5 f3 d5 6 Bg2 e5! = Kuzminikh.
5 g5 hg 6 Bxg5 d5 7 f3 Bf5 8 Bg2 e3! (Pachman and Schneider) ∓.

[23] 6 Bf4 Bg7 7 Qd2 0-0 8 0-0-0! d5! 9 Ne5 (9 Re1!? Pachman) 9 ... Nbd7 (9 ... c5!? intending ... Qa5) 10 Bh6 c6 11 Be2 Nxe5 12 de ∓.

[24] Harding.

[25] **11 ... Kd8** 12 Qg3 ±. **11 ... 0-0!?** ∞.

[26] 9 ... Nxd4?! 10 Nxd4 Bxd4 11 0-0-0 Bf6 12 h4! ± Knaak-Ftacnik, Trnava 1980.

[27] Knaak.

[28] Nimzowitsch's Variation.

[29] 5 Bxf6 ef 6 Bc4 g6 7 Nd5 c6 8 Bxe4 d5 ∓.

[30] 6 Bc4 e6 7 d5 Bb4 8 de d5 9 e7 ∞/∓.
6 Bd3 e6 7 Qe2 d5!? ∞.

[31] 7 Nh3!? Bb7 8 Be2 Qe7 (8 ... Bb4!? ∞) 9 0-0 Nc6 10 f4 0-0-0 11 Bf3 ± Lisitsin-Korchnoi, Leningrad 1951.

[32] 12 Rhe1 0-0-0 ∓ Johner-Nimzowitsch, Carlsbad 1929.

[33] 5 f3 e5! 6 d5 Bd4 7 Nxe4 Be7 8 Bxf6 Bxf6 9 Qd2 0-0 10 0-0-0 d6 11 c3 Nf5 = Horberg-Larsen, Stockholm 1966/67.

[34] 7 h4 c6 8 0-0-0 Qb6! 9 Bxf6 gf 10 Qxe4 Qxf2 ∞/=.
7 Bh4 g5! 8 Bg3 Bg7 9 0-0-0 c6 10 Nxe4 Qb6 ∓.

[35] 10 0-0-0 Bh6+ 11 f4 (11 Kb1 0-0 = Nimzowitsch) 11 ... 0-0 12 Nf3 Bg7 13 Qd2 b5! ∞.

[36] 11 d6 0-0 12 Bc4 Bg7 13 Qd3 Bxb2 14 Rb1 Qf6 15 Ne2 Be5 16 dc Qxc7 = Gudmundsson-Donner, Amsterdam 1950.

Dutch: Classical; Stonewall; Dutch Indian   **1 d4 f5**

	2	3	4	5	6	7	8	9	10	
1	c4[1]	♘c3	e3[3]	♗d3	♘f3	♗d2	♕c2	a3	♗xc3	=
	e6	♘f6[2]	b6	♗b7	♗b4	0-0	a5	♗xc3	♘e4[4]	
2	...	♘f3	♘c3	♗f4	e3	♗d3	0-0	c5!	b4[7]	±/±
	...	d5[5]	c6	♘f6	♗d6[6]	0-0	♕e7	♗c7		
3	...	g3	♗g2	♗d2[9]	♘f3	0-0	♕xd2[10]	♕c2		=
	...	♘f6	♗b4+[8]	♕e7!	0-0	♗xd2	♘e4	d6[11]		
4	...	...	...	♘c3	♕b3	d5	de	♗f4	♖d1	=
	...	...	♗e7[12]	0-0	♘c6	♘e5	de	♘fd7	♕e8[13]	

1 d4 f5 2 c4 e6 3 g3 ♘f6 4 ♗g2 ♗e7 5 ♘c3 0-0

	6	7	8	9	10	11	12	13	14	
5	e3[14]	♘ge2	b3	0-0	♗b2	♕d3	f3	♗xc3	♕d2	±
	d5	c6	♘e4[15]	♘d7	♘df6	♗d7[16]	♘xc3	♘e8	a5[17]	
6	...	♘ge2	0-0	d5	e4	ef	f3[19]	♗e3	♕d2	=
	d6	c6[18]	e5	♕e8	♕h5	♗xf5	♕g6	♘bd7	cd[20]	

1 d4 f5 2 c4 e6 3 g3 ♘f6 4 ♗g2 ♗e7 5 ♘f3 0-0

	6	7	8	9	10	11	12	13	14	
7	0-0	♘bd2[22]	♕c2	♘e5	♘d3	♘f3	b3	♘fe5	♘xd7	±
	d5[21]	c6[23]	♕e8[24]	♘bd7	♘e4	♘d6	b6	♗b7	♕xd7[25]	
8	...	b3[26]	♗a3	♕c1	♘bd2	♕xa3	♖ac1	♖fd1	cd	=
	...	c6	♘bd7[27]	♘e4	♗xa3	b6	♗b7	♕f6	ed[28]	
9	...	♘c3	♕c2[29]	♘e5	♘xe4	♗f4	♘xd7![31]	♖ad1[32]		±
	...	c6	♘e4	♘d7	fe[30]	♗f6	♕xd7			

1 d4 f5 2 c4 e6 3 g3 ♘f6 4 ♗g2 ♗e7 5 ♘f3 0-0 6 0-0 d6

	7	8	9	10	11	12	13	14	15	
10	♘c3[33]	b4	ba	d5	de	♘d4	h3	♕d3	♘xf5	∞
	♕e8[34]	a5	♘c6	♘xa5	c6	♕h5	♘xc4	d5	♗b4[35]	
11	...	♖e1	e4	♘xe4	♖xe4	♕e2[37]	♗d2	de	♘xe5	∞
	...	♕g6!	fe	♘xe4	♘c6[36]	♗f6	e5	♘xe5	♗xe5[38]	
12	...	♕c2	♗g5!	♖ad1	de	♗xf6	c5	♘d5	♕xc5	±
	...	♕h5	♘c6[39]	e5	♘xe5	♗xf6	dc	♕f7	♘xf3+[40]	
13	...	b3	♗a3!	e3	c5	♘d2	♖axd1	♘f3	♘e5	±
	...	♕h5	g5	♖f7	♗d7	♕xd1	d5	♖g7	♗e8[41]	
14	...	...	♗b2	e3	♕e2	e4	♘xe4			±/∞
	...	a5	♘a6!	c6	♗d7	fe	♕h5[42]			
15	...	♖e1	♕c2	bc	e4	♕xe4	♗g5	♗h3	♗xf6	±
	a5	♘e4	♘xc3	♕e8	fe	♕f7	♗f6	h6	♕xf6[43]	
16	...	♕c2	a3	d5	♘g5	♖d1	dc	♘f3	b3	±
	...	♘c6	e5	♘b8	c6	♖e8	bc	♕c7	♘a6[44]	
17	...	b3	♗b2	♖c1	♕c2	e4	♘xe4	♕xe4	♕c2	±
	...	c6[45]	♘a6	♘c7	♖b8	fe	♘xe4	♗f6	♗d7[46]	
18	...	...	...	...	e3!	♕e2	e4	♘xe4		±/∞
	...	...	...	♕e8	♘c7	♗d7	fe	♕h5[47]		

¹ 2 g3 ♘f6 3 ♗g2 e6 and now:
   4 ♘h3 (Blackburne's Variation) 4 ... ♗e7
5 0-0 0-0 6 c4 d6 7 ♘c3 ♘e8 8 e4 fe 9 ♘f4
(9 ♘xe4 ♘c6! =) 9 ... c6 10 ♘cxe4 ♘xe4
11 ♗xe4 e5 = Reshevsky-Botvinnik, The Hague
1948.
   4 ♘f3 b5 (4 ... ♗b4+ 5 c3! ♗e7 6 0-0 0-0
7 c4! – main lines) 5 ♘e5 c6 6 ♘d2 ♕b6 7 e4
♕xd4 8 ♘5f3 ♕c5 9 ef ♕xf5 10 0-0 ∞ Petrosian-
Larsen, San Antonio 1972.
² 3 ... ♗b4 4 ♗d2 ♘f6 5 e3 0-0 6 ♗d3 d6 7 ♕c2
c5 8 ♘f3 ♘c6 9 0-0-0 ♗d7 10 h3 ± Tolush-
Bronstein, USSR Ch 1957.
³ 4 a3 ♗e7 5 e3 0-0 6 ♗d3 d5 7 ♘f3 c6 8 0-0
♘e4 9 ♕c2 ♗d6 = Maroczy-Tartakower,
Teplitz Schönau 1922.
⁴ 11 0-0-0 d5 = Flohr-Bondarevsky, USSR
Ch 1951.
⁵ 3 ... ♗b4+ 4 ♗d2 ♕e7 5 ♕c2 =. 5 g3 –
row 3.
⁶ 6 ... ♗e7 7 ♗d3 0-0 8 0-0 ♘e4 9 ♗xe4! ±
Rabar-Milicević, Yugoslavia 1959.
⁷ 10 b4 ±/± Bukić-Sines, Cateske Toplice
1968.
⁸ The Dutch Indian.
⁹ 5 ♘d2 0-0 6 ♘f3 a5 7 0-0 b6 8 ♘e5 ♖a7!
9 ♘d3 ♗b7 = Botvinnik-Larsen, Leiden 1970.
¹⁰ 8 ♘bxd2 d6 9 ♕b3 e5 10 c5+ ♔h8 11 cd cd
12 de de 13 ♘c4 ♘c6 14 ♕c3 e4 =/∓ Whiteley-
Bellin, England 1976.
¹¹ Foltys-Gligorić, Prague 1946.
¹² 4 ... d5 5 ♘f3 c6 6 0-0 ♗d6 7 ♘c3 ♘bd7
(7 ... 0-0 8 ♕c2 ♕e8 9 c5 ♗c7 10 ♗f4 ♕e7 ±)
8 ♕c2 0-0 9 cd cd 10 ♘b5 ♗b8 11 ♗f4 ♗xf4
12 gf ∓ Bogoljubow-Tartakower, New York
1924.
¹³ 11 ♘b5 ♗d8 = Gereben-Tartakower, Budapest 1948.
¹⁴ Botvinnik-Bronstein Variation.
¹⁵ 8 ... ♗d7 9 ♗b2 ♗e8 10 ♘f4 ♗f7 11 ♘d3
♘bd7 12 ♕c2 ♖c8 13 c5 b6 14 b4 ± Korchnoi-
Spassky, match (8) 1977/78.
   8 ... ♗d6 9 0-0 ♕e7 10 ♕c2 ♘e4 (Bronstein-
Botvinnik, match 1951) 11 ♗b2 intending f3 ±.
¹⁶ 11 ... g5 12 cd ed 13 f3 ♘xc3 14 ♗xc3 g4
15 fg ♘xg4 16 ♗h3 ♘h6 17 ♘f4 ♗d6 18 b4! ±
Bronstein-Botvinnik, match 1951.
¹⁷ 15 ♘f4 ♗f7 16 ♘d3 ± Petrosian.
¹⁸ 7 ... e5!? 8 d5 c5 9 0-0 = Bellin.
¹⁹ 12 c5 ♗h3 13 cd ♗xd6 14 dc ♗xc6 15 ♕xd6
♖ad8 16 ♕c5 ♗g4 17 f3 ♗xg2 18 fg ♖xf1+
19 ♔xg2 ♕f7 ∞ Botvinnik.
²⁰ Botvinnik-Bronstein, match (1) 1951.
²¹ The Stonewall Variation.
²² 7 ♕c2 c6 8 ♗f4 ♕e8 9 ♘bd2 ♕h5 10 ♖ae1
♘bd7 = Sokolov-Berkovich, USSR 1973.
²³ 7 ... b6!? 8 b3 c5!?
²⁴ 8 ... b6 9 ♘e5 ♗b7 10 ♘d3 ♘dbd7 11 b4

♖e8 12 a4 ♗d6 13 ♘f3 ♘e4 14 c5 bc 15 bc ♗c7
16 ♗f4 ♗xf4 17 gf! ± Portisch-Radulov,
Budapest v Sofia 1969.
   8 ... ♘e4 9 ♘e5 ♘d7 10 ♘d3 ♘f6 11 ♘f3 g5
12 ♖b1 ♕e7 (Johansson-Olafsson, Reykjavik
1968) 13 ♘fe5 ±.
²⁵ 15 c5 ♘e4 16 f3 ± Botvinnik.
²⁶ Botvinnik's Variation.
²⁷ 8 ... ♗xa3 9 ♖xa3 ♕e7 10 ♕c1 ♘bd7
11 ♕b2 b6 12 ♖ac1 ♗b7 13 ♖fd1 a5 14 e3 ♘e4
15 ♘e5 ♘xe5 16 de ± Bilek-Marić, Bordeaux
1964.
   8 ... b6 9 ♗xe7 ♕xe7 10 ♘e5 ♗b7 11 ♘d2
♘bd7 12 ♘xd7 ♘xd7 13 e3 ♖ac8 14 ♖c1 c5
15 ♕e2 ♘f6 16 cd ♗xd5 17 ♗xd5 ed 18 ♘f3 ±
Botvinnik-Bronstein, match (7) 1951.
²⁸ 15 ♘e1 a5 16 ♘df3 f4 17 ♘d3 fg 18 hg
(18 fg!? Botvinnik) 18 ... ♖ae8 = Szabo-
Botvinnik, Budapest 1952.
²⁹ 8 ♕d3 ♘e4 9 ♘e5 ♘d7 10 ♘xd7 ♗xd7
11 f3 ♘xc3 (Grünfeld-Tartakower, Teplitz
1922) 12 bc! dc 13 ♕xc4 ♕b6 14 ♗f4 ± Grünfeld.
   8 ♕b3 ♔h8 9 ♘e5 (9 ♗f4 Capablanca:
9 ... b6!? Bellin) 9 ... ♘bd7 10 ♘xd7 ♗xd7 =
Capablanca-Botvinnik, Moscow 1936.
   8 b3 ♘e4 9 ♗b2 ♘d7 10 ♕c2 ♗f6 =.
   8 ♕c2! intending 8 ... ♕e8 9 ♗g5! ±
Chekhover.
³⁰ 10 ... ♘xe5!? 11 ♘d2 ♘f7 12 ♘f3 b6 =
Larsen.
³¹ 12 ♖ad1 ♗xe5 13 ♗xe5 ♘xe5 14 de ♕e7 =
Smejkal-Larsen, Leningrad IZ 1973.
³² Larsen.
³³ 7 b3 ♕e8 8 ♗b2 a5 9 ♘bd2 ♘c6 10 a3 ♗d8 =
Averbakh-Boleslavsky, Zürich C 1953.
³⁴ The Classical Ilyin-Zhenevsky System.
³⁵ Klüger-Farago, Hungarian Ch 1968/69.
³⁶ 11 ... e5 12 ♖e3! Krogius-Shilov, Irkutsk
1962.
³⁷ 12 ♖e1 ♗b4 13 ♖e2 e5 14 de ♗g4 15 ♕b3
♕d3 16 ♕xd3 ♘xd3 17 ♖e3 ♘xc1 18 ♖xc1 =
Neikirch-Minev, Sofia 1954.
³⁸ 16 ♗c3! ♗xc3 17 bc c6 18 ♖e7 ♗g4! ∞
Matulović-Milić, Yugoslav Ch 1959.
³⁹ 9 ... h6 10 ♗xf6 ♗xf6 11 e4 ♘c6 12 ♘b5!
(12 ♖ad1 e5 =) 12 ... ♕f7 13 ♖ad1 ♔h8 14 ♖fe1
e5 15 de ♗xe5 16 c5 ± Olafsson-Kan, Nice Ol
1974.
⁴⁰ Savitsky-Riumin, USSR 1933.
⁴¹ Kozma-Bhend, Munich Ol 1958.
⁴² ± Taimanov.   ∞ Bellin.
⁴³ 16 ♖e3 ±.
⁴⁴ 16 ♗b2 ± Smyslov-Filipowicz, Bath 1973.
⁴⁵ 8 ... ♘a6 9 ♗b2 c6 10 e3 ♖b8 11 ♕e2 ♗d7
12 e4 ± Ghitescu-Roos, Bagneux 1981.
⁴⁶ 16 ♘d2 ± Rossetto-Alvarez, Mar del Plata
1969.
⁴⁷ See note 42.

39

Dutch: Leningrad 1 d4 f5 2 g3[1]

	2	3	4	5	6	7	8	9	10	
1	...	h4[3]	h5	♖xh5	e4	♕xh5+	ef	♕h4	♗h3	∞
	g6[2]	♘f6	♘xh5	gh	♗g7	♔f8	♕e8	♕f7	♘c6[4]	
2	...	♘d2	e4	♘xe4	♘g5	♗h3	♗xf5	f4		=
	...	♗g7	fe	d5	♘h6	♘f5	♗xf5	♕d7[5]		
3	...	♗g2	♘h3[6]	c4[8]	♘c3	♗f4	d5	de	♗e3	=
	...	♗g7	♘f6[7]	0-0	d6	c6	e5	♘a6!	♕e7[9]	
4						d5[10]	0-0!	de	b3[12]	=
						c6[11]	e5	♗xe6	♘a6[13]	
5			♘f3	0-0	♘c3[14]	♖e1	d5	♘d4	f4	=
			♘f6	0-0	d6	♘c6	♘e5	♖b8!	♘f7[15]	
6					b3	♗b2	♘bd2	a4	♖e1	∓
					d6[16]	e6	a5	♘a6	♘e4[17]	
7			...	0-0	c4	♘c3	♖b1	b3	e4	∓
			c6	♘h6[18]	d6	0-0	a5	♘f7	fe[19]	
8							♕c2[20]	♖d1	b3[21]	=
							♘a6	♗d7	♘f7	

1 d4 f5 2 g3 g6 3 ♗g2 ♗g7 4 ♘f3 ♘f6 5 0-0 0-0

	6	7	8	9	10	11	12	13	14	
9	c4	b3	♗b2	♘bd2	a3	♕c2	c5	♖ac1	♘c4	=
	d6	c6[22]	♕c7	a5	♘a6	♗d7	♔h8	♖ac8	♗e6[23]	
10	...	...	...	♘bd2	a3[24]	♖e1	e4	♘xe4	♖xe4	=
	...	...	...	a5	♘a6	♕c7	♗d7	fe	♗f5[25]	
11	...	d5	♘c3	♘e1[26]	♘c2	a4	♖b1	h3	♘a3	±
	...	c5	♘a6	♖b8	♘c7	b6	♘g4	♘e5	a6[27]	
12	...	...	♘d4	♘c3[28]	♘xe4	♕xd4	♘g5			=
	...	c6	♕b6	♘e4	♕xd4	♗xd4	c5[29]			
13	...	♘c3	d5[30]	♘xe5	e4!	ef!	♗e3	♗d4	♖e1	±
	...	♘c6	♘e5	de	e6[31]	ef[32]	e4[33]	♖e8	b6[34]	
14	...	...	...	♕d3[35]	b3	♗b2	♖ae1	♗a1	bc	±
	...	...	♘a5	c5	a6[36]	♖b8	b5	bc	♖b4[37]	
15	...	...	b3[38]	♗b2	♕c2	c5	cd	♘e5	♕c1	=
	...	c6	a5[39]	♘a6	♕c7	f4!	♕xd6	♘b4	♘fd5[40]	
16	...	...	d5	e4	cd	♗g5	ef			∓
	...	...	e5[41]	cd!	♘a6	h6	♕xf6	gf[42]		
17	...	...	...	de	b3	♗b2	♗g5	♕d2	♘xe6	=
	...	...	...	♗xe6	♘a6	♘c5	♕e7	♖ad8	♕xe6[43]	
18	...	...	...	...	♕d3	♘g5[44]	♗f4	♕xd6[46]	♕xf4	∞
	...	...	...	...	♘a6	♗c8[45]	♘h5	♘xf4	h6[47]	

[1] For White second moves other than 2 c4 see Dutch: Introduction and Staunton Gambit.

2 c4 usually transposes to the text, but here are a few independent possibilities after 2 ... g6:

3 h4 h5 (3 ... ♘f6 4 h5 ♘xh5 5 ♖xh5 ∞; 3 ... ♗g7 4 h5 d6 5 ♘f3 – Forintos-Pederson, Athens 1969 – 5 ... c6 ∞) 4 ♘c3 d6?! (4 ... ♘f6 ∞/±) 5 e4 ♘f6 6 ♗d3 ♗g7 7 ef ♘c6 (7 ... gf? 8 ♕f3! Milić) 8 fg ♘xd4 9 ♘ce2! ♘xe2 10 ♘xe2 c6 ± Milić-Puc, Vrnjačka Banja 1966.

3 g3 ♗g7 4 ♗g2 ♘f6 5 ♘c3 0-0 6 e3 d6 7 ♘ge2 e5 8 0-0 c6 9 de de 10 ♕c2 e4 = Aloni-Raisa, Leipzig Ol 1960.

3 ♘c3 ♘f6 4 f3!? ♗g7 5 e4 d6 Harding.

4 ♘f3 ♗g7 5 e3 0-0 6 ♗d3 (6 ♗e2 d6 7 0-0 ♕e8 8 b3 e5 9 de de 10 ♗a3 ♖f7 = Lundin-Kotov, Stockholm 1959/60) 6 ... d6 7 0-0 ♘c6 8 d5 ♘e5 9 ♘xe5 de 10 c5 ♘d7 = Madsen-Potter, corr. Ol 1958/61.

4 ♘f3 ♗g7 5 ♗f4 d6 6 h4!? ♘h5 7 e3 0-0 (7 ... ♘d7) 8 c5! ± Larsen-Lutikov, Moscow 1959.

4 ♗g5 ♗g7 5 ♘f3 d6 6 e3 0-0 7 ♗e2 c6 8 0-0 ♕e8 9 ♗xf6 ♗xf6 = Stolyar-Lutikov, RSFSR Ch 1957.

² 2 ... ♘f6 3 ♗g2 d6 (The Hort-Antoshin Variation) 4 c4 c6 5 ♘c3 ♕c7 (5 ... e5 6 de de 7 ♕xd8+ ♔xd8 8 ♘f3 e4 9 ♘g5 ♔e8 10 f3 h6 11 ♘h3 ef 12 ♗xf3 = Bannik-Antoshin, USSR Ch 1957) 6 ♘f3 e5 7 0-0 e4 8 ♖e1 ♗e7 9 f3 ef 10 ef 0-0 11 ♗d3 ♗e6 12 b3± Udovčić-Antoshin, Yugoslavia v USSR 1969.

³ 3 c4 transposes either below or into note 1.
⁴ Bilek-Barcza, Balatonfüred 1958.
⁵ Intending ... h6, ... ♕e6, ♗e4 Schwarz.
⁶ The Carlsbad Variation.
⁷ 4 ... ♘c6 5 d5 ♘e5 6 ♘c3 ♘f6 7 ♘f4 (7 e4!) 7 ... c6! 8 ♘d3 ♘f7! 9 0-0 0-0 = Rubinstein-Bogoljubow, Carlsbad 1923.
⁸ 5 ♘f4 0-0 6 h4 ♘c6 7 h5 ♕e8 8 hg hg 9 ♘c3 ♕f7 = Alekhine-Tartakower, Carlsbad 1923.
⁹ Slov-Korchnoi, USSR 1950.
¹⁰ 7 0-0 e5! 8 de de 9 ♕xd8 ♖xd8 10 ♘d5 ♖d7 = R.Byrne-Pelikan, Mar del Plata 1961.
¹¹ 7 ... ♘a6 8 0-0 ♘c5 9 ♖b1! e5 10 de ♗xe6 11 ♘f4! (11 b3 a5!? ∓/∞ Flesch-Klüger, Hungarian Ch 1958/59) 11 ... ♗xc4 12 ♘a4 ♗f7 13 ♘xc5 dc (Toth-Dely, Kecskemet 1972) 14 ♗xb7 ♖b8 15 ♗g2 ± Botvinnik.
¹² 10 ♕d3!?
¹³ 11 ♗b2 ♕e7 12 ♘g5 ♗d7 =.

11 ♘g5 ♕e7 12 ♘xe6 ♕xe6 13 ♗b2 ♘e4 14 ♕c1 d5 15 cd cd 16 ♘xe4 de 17 ♗xg7 ♔xg7 = Taimanov-Holmov, USSR Ch 1975.

¹⁴ 7 c4 c6 transposes below.
¹⁵ Wahia-Blom, Leipzig Ol 1960.
¹⁶ 6 ... b5!? 7 c4 bc 8 bc c5 9 ♗b2 ♕b6 10 ♕c1 ♘c6 = Olafsson-Larsen, Beverwijk 1961.
¹⁷ Baumbach-Gheorghiu, Bucharest 1962.
¹⁸ The Basman Variation.
¹⁹ 11 ♘xe4 d5! ∓ Rellstab-Basman, Hastings 1973/74.
²⁰ 8 ♘g5 e5 9 de de 10 ♕xd8 ♖xd8 11 e4 ♘f7 12 ♗xf7 ♔xf7 13 ♗g5 (13 f4!?) ♖e8 14 f4 ♔g8 = Basman.
²¹ Keene-Basman, Hastings 1973/74.
²² 7 ... e5 8 de ♘g4 9 ♘c3 (9 ♗b2 ♘c6) 9 ... de 10 ♗a3 e4 11 ♗xf8 ♕xf8 12 ♘d4 e3 13 f4 ♘f2 14 ♖xf2 ef+ 15 ♔xf2 ♘a6 ∞ Wexler-Uhlmann, Buenos Aires 1960.
²³ Portisch-Uhlmann, Stockholm IZ 1962.
²⁴ 10 ♕b1!? f4! =/∞ Eliskases-Ghitescu, Tel Aviv Ol 1964.

²⁵ 15 ♖e1 ♖ae8 =.
²⁶ 9 ♖b1 ♖b8 10 b3 ♘c7 11 ♗b2 a6 12 e3 b5 13 ♘e2 ♗d7 14 ♗c3 ♘a8! 15 ♘g5! ± Keene-Ree, Paignton 1970.
²⁷ 15 f4 ♘d7 16 e4! fe 17 g4! = Botvinnik.
²⁸ 9 ♘b3 e5!? 10 dc (10 de ♗xe6 11 ♕xd6 ♗xc4 =) 10 ... ♘xc6 11 ♕xd6 ♖d8 12 ♕c5 (12 ♕a3 ♗e6 13 c5 ♕c7 ⊙⊙) 12 ... ♘d4 13 ♕xb6 ♘xe2+ 14 ♔h1 ab = Harding.
²⁹ Yudovich. 12 ... ♗d7, 13... ♘a6 = Taimanov.
³⁰ 8 b3 ♘e4 9 ♗b2 e5 10 de ♘xc3 11 ♗xc3 de 12 ♕d5+ ♔h8 13 ♕xd8 ♖xd8 14 ♘g5 ♖e8 15 ♖ad1 h6 16 ♘f7+ ♔g8 17 ♗xc6 bc 18 ♘d8 ± Pomar-Peredes, Barcelona 1977. 15 ... e4 ±.
³¹ 10 ... f4 11 b4 g5 12 ♖e1 a6 13 ♗b2 ♕e8 14 ♖c1 ♘g4 15 f3 ♘e3 (Farago-Pouttainen, Budapest 1975) 16 ♖xe3! fe 17 g4! ± Botvinnik.
³² 11 ... gf!? Botvinnik.
³³ 12 ♘g4!? 13 ♗c5 ♖e8 Botvinnik.
³⁴ Collins-Sherwin, New York 1957.
³⁵ 9 ♘d2 c5 10 a3 ♗d7 11 ♕c2 ♕c7 12 b3 a6 13 ♗b2 b5 14 ♘d1 bc 15 bc ♖ab8 16 ♗c3 ♘g4 17 ♗xg7 ♔xg7 18 ♕c3+ ♔g8 19 ♘b2 ♖b7 20 ♘d3 ± Botvinnik-Matulović, USSR v Rest of the World 1970.
³⁶ 10 ... ♘e4 11 ♗b2 a6 12 ♖ac1! (12 ♘d2 b5 13 ♘dxe4 fe 14 ♗xe4 bc 15 bc ♖b8 ⊙⊙ Udovčić-Matulović, Yugoslav Ch 1960) 12 ... b5 13 ♗a1! ±
³⁷ 15 ♘d2 ♘g4 16 a3 ♖b8 17 ♕c2 ± Nikolac-Bertok, Yugoslavia 1969.
³⁸ 8 ♕c2 ♕c7 9 e4 fe 10 ♘xe4 ♘xe4 11 ♕xe4 ♗f5 12 ♕h4 e5 13 de de 14 ♗h6 ♘a6 15 ♖ad1 ♖ae8 16 ♕g5 ♗xh6 17 ♕xh6 ♗g4 18 ♗h3 ♗xh3 = Gofstein-Bikhovsky, USSR 1977.
³⁹ 8 ... ♘a6 9 ♗b2 ♘c7 10 ♕c2 ♖b8! 11 a4 a5 12 ♖ad1 ♘a6 13 d5 ♕b6 14 ♘d4 ♗d7 15 e3 ♘c5 16 ♖b1 ♗be8 = Smyslov-Lutikov, USSR 1976.
⁴⁰ 16 ♖xd5 cd 17 a3 ♘c6 =.
⁴¹ 8 ... ♗d7 9 ♘d4 ♕b6 10 e3 ♘a6 11 ♖b1 (Palatnik-Gulko, Kiev 1973) 11 ... ♘c7 12 dc bc 13 b4 e5 ∞/=. 11 b3 ♘c5 12 ♗b2 a5 = Spiridonov-Aakesson, Polanica Zdroj 1981.

8 ... ♕a5 (Liebert) 9 ♗e3 ♕b4 10 ♕b3 (10 ♕d3!?) 10 ... ♕xb3 11 ab ∞ Goodman-Harding, England 1975.
⁴² Tsvetkov-Kotkov, Bulgaria v RSFSR 1957.
⁴³ 15 ♖ad1 ♖fe8 16 ♕c2 ± Bukić-Rakić, Ljubljana 1981.
⁴⁴ 11 ♗f4 d5 (11 ... ♕a5!? 12 ♘g5± Bergström-Graveus, Swedish Ch 1981) 12 ♘g5 ♘c5 13 ♕c2! ± Andersson-Marić, Banja Luka 1979.
⁴⁵ 11 ... ♖e8!? 12 ♘xe6 ♖xe6 13 ♗g5 h6 14 ♗d2 ♕e7 = Holm-Clemens, Hamburg 1980.
⁴⁶ 13 ♗d2 ♘c5 14 ♕c2 a5 = Ivkov-Soylu, Budva Z 1981.
⁴⁷ 15 ♘f3 g5 16 ♕c1 ♗e6 17 ♖d1 (Simagin-Hasin, Moscow Ch 1956) 17 ... ♕e7! (Simagin) 18 ♘d4 ♗xc4 or 18 b3 ♖ad8 ∞.

41

Catalan

With the early fianchetto of his king's bishop White sidesteps more traditional varieties of the Queen's Gambit in order to follow a more positional path. By eyeing the long diagonal White's bishop can exert annoying pressure on the black b-pawn, hampering the easy development of his queenside.

The Closed Catalan is solid but cramped and the task of equalising is gradual and arduous. By careful play, however, Black may balance the chances.

The Open Catalan (with ... dc) has enjoyed tremendous popularity of late due to its straightforward bid for active counterplay. Black can try the risky strategem of holding on to his extra c-pawn or negotiate its return so as to mobilise his forces quickly and execute the freeing break ... c5. White's hopes for a plus depend on preventing this liberation, and if he is successful the black QBP can become a fixed target on the half open c-file, a victim of the line-opening strategy which Black hoped would equalise. At present the well-prepared defender can find his way to comfortable equality but, like all fashionable variations, the body of theory is constantly shifting and developing.

Catalan I   1 d4 ♘f6 2 c4 e6 3 g3

	3	4	5	6	7	8	9	10	11	
1	...	♗d2	♗g2	♘f3	0-0[2]	♕c2	♖d1	♗g5	♘c3	=
	♗b4+	♗e7[1]	0-0	d5	♘bd7[3]	c6	b6[4]	♗b7	♖c8[5]	
2	...	dc[6]	♘f3	♗g2	♗d2	e3!	♘c3[7]			∞
	c5	♗xc5	♘c6	♕a5+!?	♕b6	♕xb2				
3	...	♗g2[8]	♘f3	♘xd4	♘f3	0-0	e3	ed	♗f4	±
	d5	c5	cd	e5[9]	d4[10]	♘c6	♗e7[11]	ed	0-0[12]	
4	...	...	...	0-0	♘xd4	♘b3[14]	cd	♗d2	♘c3[15]	±
	...	...	♘c6	cd	♗c5[13]	♗e7	♘xd5	0-0		
5	...	...	♕a4+	♕xc4	♘f3	♘c3	♕d3[18]	0-0		=
	...	dc	♗d7	♗c6	♘bd7[16]	♘b6[17]	♗b4	0-0[19]		
6	...	...	...	♘f3	♘c3	0-0	dc[21]	♕xc4	♕h4	= •
	...	...	♘bd7	a6[20]	c5	♖b8	♗xc5	b5	♗b7[22]	
7	...	...	...	♕xc4	♘f3[23]	♕c6[24]	♗f4	♗g5	♗xe7	=
	...	...	...	a6	b5	♖b8	♘d5	♗e7	♕xe7[25]	

1 d4 ♘f6 2 c4 e6 3 g3 d5 4 ♗g2 dc 5 ♘f3

	5	6	7	8	9	10	11	12	13	
8	...	♕a4	♗d2	♗xb4	a3	♕xb5	♔d2!	♕xc6+	♕xc4	±
	♘c6	♗b4+[26]	♘d5	♘xb4	b5	♘c2+	♘xa1	♗d7	♖b8[27]	
9	...	a4	♘e5[28]	0-0	b3	ab	♕xb3	e4	d5	±
	b5	c6	♘d5	♗b7	cb	cb	a6	♘f6	ed[29]	
10	...	♘bd2[30]	0-0	♘xc4	♕a4+	♕xc4	♗e3	♘e5	♗xd4	±
	♘bd7	♘b6[31]	c5	♘xc4	♗d7	♕b6[32]	♖c8	cd	♗c5[33]	
11	...	♘e5[34]	♗e3	dc	♗d4	♘xc4	0-0	♕xd4	♕c5[37]	±
	a6	c5[35]	♘d5	♕c7	♗xc5	0-0	♗xd4[36]	♘c6		

1   4 ... ♗xd2+ 5 ♕xd2 (5 ♘xd2 d6 6 ♘f3 ♘c6 7 ♗g2 0-0 8 0-0 e5 9 d5 ♘e7 10 e4 ♘fd7 – Alatortsev-Levenfish, USSR Ch 1937 – 11 b4 a5 12 a3!? Taimanov; 10 e3!?) 5 ... d6 (5 ... d5 leads to favourable Catalan structures, as Black lacks his good bishop; 5 ... ♘e4 6 ♕c2 f5 7 ♗g2! d5 8 ♘f3 0-0 9 0-0 ± Taimanov – a Dutch without the dark-squared bishops favours White) 6 ♘f3 ♘c6 7 ♗g2! 0-0 8 ♘c3 e5 9 d5!? Taimanov.

    4 ... ♕e7 5 ♗g2 ♘c6 (5 ... 0-0 6 ♘f3 – Bogo-Indian) 6 ♘f3! ♗xd2+ 7 ♘xd2 ± – Bogo-Indian.

2   7 ♕b3!? b6 8 cd ed 9 ♘c3 ♗b7 10 0-0! Taimanov.

3   7 ... dc 8 ♕c2 a6 9 a4 ♘bd7 10 ♘a3 ♖b8 11 ♘xc4 b6 12 ♘fe5 ± Razuvayev-Hanov, USSR 1979.

4   9 ... b5!? 10 c5 a5 11 ♗e1 ♘e4 12 ♘bd2 f5 13 ♘b3 ♕c7 14 ♘c1 e5 15 ♘d3 ♗f6 16 de ♘xe5 17 ♘fxe5 ♗xe5 18 f3 ♘f6 19 ♕d2 ± Speelman-Kovačević, Maribor 1980.

5   12 e4 h6 =/± Smejkal-Belyavsky, Moscow 1981.

6   4 ♘f3 – English.

7   Taimanov.

8   4 ♘f3 dc 5 ♕a4+ ♘bd7 6 ♕xc4 b6 7 ♗g2 ♗b7 8 0-0 c5 9 ♖d1 a6 10 dc ♘xc5 11 b4 ♗e7 12 ♗b2 b5 13 ♘d4 ♖c8 14 ♘bd2 0-0 15 a3 (Karpov-Korchnoi, match 1974) 15 ... ♕b6 =.

9   6 ... ♗c5 7 0-0 0-0 8 ♘b3 ♗b6 9 ♘c3 dc 10 ♘d2 ♘d4 11 e3 ♕d3 12 ♕a4 ♘bd7 13 ♕xc4 ±/± Bilek-Kozma, Leipzig Ol 1960.

10   7 ... e4 8 ♘d4 ♗b4+ 9 ♘c3 0-0 10 0-0 ♖e8 11 ♘xd5! ♗xd5 12 cd ♕xd5 13 ♕a4 ± Pytel-Ghitescu, Bucharest 1973.

11   9 ... ♗c5 10 ed ed 11 ♖e1+ ♗e6 12 ♘g5 0-0 13 ♘xe6 (13 ♖xe6? fe 14 ♘xe6 ♕b6 15 ♘xf8 ♖xf8 16 ♕b3 ♗g4! ∓ Alburt-Palatnik, USSR 1978) 13 ... fe 14 ♘d2 (14 ♖xe6? d3 15 ♗xc6 bc 16 ♗e3 ♗d4 17 ♘c3 ♕d7 ∓ Nenashev-Kasparov, USSR 1978) 14 ... ♕d6 15 ♘e4 ♘xe4 16 ♗xe4 e5 17 a3 a5 18 ♕d3 h6 19 ♗d2 a4 = Rashkovsky-Gorshkov, USSR 1979.

12   12 ♘e5 ± Alburt-Furman, USSR Ch 1975.

13   7 ... ♕b6 8 ♘b5 dc 9 ♘c3 ±/± Damjanović-Lutovac, Yugoslav Ch 1963.

14   8 ♘xc6 bc 9 ♕c2 ♗e7 10 ♖d1 0-0 = Zagoriansky-Taimanov, USSR 1949.

15   Reshevsky-Bronstein, Amsterdam IZ 1964.

16   7 ... ♗d5 8 ♕d3! ± Ravinsky-Abramov, USSR 1949.

17   8 ... ♗e7?! 9 0-0 0-0 10 ♕d3 ♘d5 11 e4 ♘xc3 12 bc ± Szabo-Ragozin, Budapest v Moscow 1949.

18   9 ♕b3 ♘e4 10 0-0 ♘xc3 11 ♕xc3 ♗e4 12 ♘e5 ♗xg2 13 ♔xg2 ♕d5+ 14 f3 (Antoshin-Balashov, USSR 1971) 14 ... c5 ∞ ECO.

19   Golombek-Aitken, Munich 1954.

20   6 ... ♗e7 7 ♕xc4 0-0 8 0-0 c5 9 ♖d1 ± Golombek-Szabados, Amsterdam 1950.

21   9 ♕xc4 b5 10 ♕d3 ♗b7 11 ♗e3 cd 12 ♗xd4 ♘c5 13 ♖fd1 0-0 14 ♖ac1 ♕e7 = Taimanov.

22   12 ♗g5 0-0 = ECO.

23   7 ♕c2 c5 8 ♘f3 b6 9 0-0 ♗b7 = Donner-Darga, 1966.

24   8 ♕d3 ♗b7 9 0-0 c5 = Müller-Tartakower, Venice 1949.

25   Szabo-Geller, Zürich C 1953.

26   6 ... ♘d7!? ECO.

27   14 b4 c5 15 ♘c3! cb 16 ab a5 17 ♖xa1 ± Taimanov.

28   7 0-0 ♗b7 8 ♘e5 a6 9 b3 cb 10 ♗b2 ♕b6 11 ♕xb3 ♘bd7 12 ♘xd7 ♘xd7 13 ♘d2 ♗e7 ∞ Tukmakov-Korchnoi, Leningrad IZ 1973.

29   14 ed ± Nesis-Zelinsky, corr. 1976.

30   6 0-0 ♖b8 7 a4 b6 8 ♕c2 ♗b7 9 ♕xc4 c5 10 ♘c3 cd 11 ♕xd4 ♗c5 12 ♕d3 0-0 = Smyslov-Klovan, USSR 1974.

31   6 ... c5 7 ♘xc4 ♘b6 8 ♘xb6 ♕xb6 9 0-0 ♗e7 10 dc ♗xc5 11 ♘e5 0-0 12 ♘d3 ♗e7 13 ♗e3 ± Keene-Botterill, England 1970.

    6 ... b5!? 7 ♘e5 ♗xe5 8 ♗xa8 ♕xd4 ∞.

32   10 ... b5 11 ♕c2 ♖c8 12 ♗g5 cd 13 ♕d3 ♗e7 14 ♘xd4 0-0 15 ♖ac1 ±.

33   14 ♘xd7! ♔xd7 (14 ... ♘xd7 15 b4! ♕xb4 16 ♕xb4 ♗xb4 17 ♗xb7 ±± Radashkovich-Razuvayev, USSR 1971) 15 ♖fd1 ♔e7 ± ECO.

34   6 0-0 b5 7 ♘e5 ♘d5 8 ♘c3 ♗b7 9 ♘xd5 ed 10 e4!? de (10 ... c6? 11 ed cd 12 ♕h5+ ±±) 11 ♕h5+ g6 12 ♘xg6 fg 13 ♕e5+ ♕e7 14 ♕xh8 ♘d7 ∞ Sosonko-Korchnoi, Bad Kissingen 1981.

35   6 ... ♗b4+ 7 ♘c3 ♘d5 8 ♗d2 b5 9 0-0!? ♗xc3 10 bc 0-0 11 a4 c6 12 e4 ♘b6 13 ab cb 14 f4 ♗b7 15 f5 ef 16 ♖xf5 f6 17 ♘g4 ± Szymczak-Chekhov, Polanica Zdroj 1981.

    6 ... ♖a7!? 7 0-0 b6 8 ♘c3 ♗b7 9 ♕a4+ ♘fd7 10 ♗xb7 ♖xb7 11 ♘c6! ± Neishtadt-Scheffer, corr. 1966.

36   11 ... ♖d8!? Averbakh.

37   Neishtadt.

	5	6	7	8	9	10	11	12	13	
12	...	0-0	♕a4[38]	♘xd4	♗xc6+	♖d1	♕xd1	♗g5[39]	♗e3	∞
	c5	♘c6	cd	♕xd4	♗d7	♕xd1+	♗xc6	♘e4[40]	h5[41]	
13	...	...	...	...	...	...	...	♘d2	bc	∞
	...	...	...	...	...	...	...	c3![42]	0-0[43]	
14	...	...	...	♕xc4	♕d3	dc	♘c3	♘b5	♘d6	=
	...	...	♗d7	b5!	♖c8[44]	♗xc5	b4!?[45]	0-0	♘d4[46]	
15	...	...	...	dc	♕xc4	♘c3	♖d1	♗e3	♘g5	±
	...	...	...	♗xc5[47]	♗e7	0-0	♖c8[48]	a6	♘e5[49]	
16	...	...	...	...	♕c2	♘e5[50]	♘c3	♘xd7	♕a4[52]	∞
	...	...	...	♘a5	♗xc5	♕b6[51]	♗d4	♘xd7		
17	...	...	...	...	...	...	♗d2	♗xa5	♘xd7	∞
	...	...	...	...	...	h6	♖c8	♕xa5	♘xd7[53]	
18	...	...	...	...	...	...	♘c3[54]	♘xc4	♖d1	∞
	...	...	...	...	...	♖c8	♘c6[55]	0-0	♘d4[56]	

[38] 7 ♘e5 ♗d7 8 ♘xc6 ♗xc6 9 ♗xc6+ bc 10 ♕a4 cd 11 ♕xc6+ ♘d7 12 ♕xc4 ♗c5 13 b4 ♗b6 14 a4 a6 = Panno-Browne, Manila IZ 1976.

[39] 12 ♕c2 ♗e7 13 ♕xc4 0-0 14 ♘f3 ♖fd8 15 ♗e3 ♘d5 16 ♘xd5 ♗xd5 = Polugayevsky-Andersson, Moscow 1981.

[40] 12 ... ♗e7 13 ♘d2 b5 14 a4 0-0 15 ab ♗xb5 16 ♘e4 ± Tukmakov-Alburt, Odessa 1976.

[41] 14 f3 ♘f6 15-♘d2 ♖d8 16 ♕c1 h4 17 ♘xc4 hg 18 hg ♖d5! ∞ Mochalov-Sturua, USSR 1979.

[42] 12 ... h5 13 ♘xc4! ♖d8 14 ♕c2 h4 15 ♗f4 hg 16 ♗xg3 ± Gutman.

[43] 14 ♕b3 ♗c5 15 h3 ∞ Gutman-Kraidman, Ramat Hasharon 1980.

[44] 9 ... c4 10 ♕c2 ♖c8 11 e4 ± Vukić-Pfleger, Ybbs 1968.

[45] 11 ... ♘b4 12 ♕d1 ♗c6 13 ♗g5 ♕xd1 14 ♖fxd1 h6 15 ♗xf6 gf ± Trifunović-Gereben, Beverwijk 1963.

[46] 14 ♗f4 ♘d5 15 ♗g5 g6 16 ♘ge4 ♘xf4 17 gf ♗b6 18 ♖xc8 ♗b5 19 ♕h3 ♘xe2+ 20 ♔h1 ♕xc8 ∞/+ Alburt-Andersson, Hastings 1980/81. 15 ♗e3 ♘xf3+ 16 ♕xf3?! f6 ∓ Balashov-Ljubojević, Buenos Aires 1980.

[47] 8 ... ♘e5!? 9 ♕c2 ♘xf3+ 10 ♗xf3 ♕c8 11 ♗e3 ♗xc5 12 ♗xb7 ♕xb7 13 ♗xc5 ♖c8 14 ♗a3 h5 ∞/= Rashkovsky-Belyavsky, USSR Ch 1980/81.

[48] 11 ... ♕a5 (Bolbochan-Flores, Argentina 1951) 12 ♕b3 ± ECO.

[49] 14 ♕b3 ♘c4 15 ♕xb7± Uhlmann-Unzicker, Leipzig Ol 1960.

[50] 10 ♗d2 ♖c8 11 ♗c3 (Visier-Linden, Utrecht 1943) 10 ... ♘c6! + ECO.

[51] 10 ... ♗b5 11 ♘c3 a6 12 ♘xb5 ab 13 b4! ∞ Barcza-Fuchs, Sofia 1957.

[52] Raulenberg-Unzicker, Essen 1948.

[53] Wexler-Martin, Argentina 1957.

[54] 11 ♗d2 b5 12 ♘xd7 ♘xd7 13 ♕c3 ♘c6 14 ♗xc6 ♖xc6 15 ♕xg7 ♕f6 = Barcza-Bogoljubow, Munich 1942.

[55] 11 ... b5 12 ♗g5! ± Barcza-E.Richter, Marianske Lazne 1948.

[56] 14 ♕d3 ♘d5 15 ♘e4 ♘b4 16 ♕d2 ♗b5 ∞ Averbakh.

	6	7	8	9	10	11	12	13	14	
1	...	♘e5	dc	♘xc4	b3	♕c2[3]	♗a3	♖c1	♗b2!	±
	dc	c5	♕c7[1]	♕xc5[2]	♖d8	♘c6	♘b4	♖b8	♕h5[4]	
2	...	...	♘xc6[5]	♘a3[6]	ba	♕a4	♕xc6	♕c5	♗f4	∞
	...	♘c6	bc	♗xa3	♘d5	♘b6	♖b8	♗a6	♘d5[7]	
3	...	♕c2	a4	♕xc4	♗g5[10]	♘c3	♗xe7	♘xd5	♕c2	=
	...	a6[8]	♗d7[9]	♗c6	♘bd7	♘d5	♕xe7	ed	a5[11]	
4	...	...	...	♖d1	♘c3	♗xf3	♗xc6[13]	a5	♕a4	±
	...	...	...	♗c6	♗xf3[12]	♘c6	bc	♖b8	♗b4[14]	
5	...	...	♕xc4	♕c2	♗f4	♖d1[15]	♕c1	♘c3	♗g5	=
	...	...	b5	♗b7	♘c6	♘b4	♖c8[16]	♘bd5	c5[17]	
6	...	...	...	...	♗g5	♗xf6[18]	♘bd2	♘b3	♕c3	=
	...	...	...	...	♘bd7	♘xf6	♖c8	♗e4	♘d5[19]	
7	...	...	...	...	♗d2	♘c3	♘xd4	♘xe6	♘xf8	=
	...	...	...	...	♘c6[20]	♘xd4	♗xg2	♕c8	♕h3[21]	
8	...	...	...	...	...	e3	♗xb4	a3	♘bd2	±
	...	...	...	...	...	♘b4[22]	♗xb4	♗d6	♕e7[23]	

[1] 8 ... ♗xc5 9 ♘c3 ♕e7 10 ♗g5 h6 11 ♗xf6 ♕xf6 12 ♘xc4 ♘c6 13 ♘e4 ♕e7 14 e3 ♖d8 15 ♕b3 ± Panno-Mecking, Mar del Plata 1971.

[2] 9 ... ♗xc5 10 ♘c3 ♖d8 11 ♗f4! e5?! 12 ♗xe5 ♗xf2+ 13 ♖xf2 ♖xd1+ 14 ♖xd1 ♕e7 15 ♗xf6 gf 16 ♘d5 ± ECO.

[3] 11 ♘bd2 ♘c6 12 ♗a3 ♕h5 13 ♗xe7 ♘xe7 14 e4 ♕xd1 15 ♖fxd1 ♗d7 16 ♘d6 ± Vadasz-B.Lengyel, Hungarian Ch 1975.

[4] 15 ♗f3 ± Alburt-Reshevsky, US Ch/Z 1981.

[5] 8 ♗xc6 bc 9 ♘xc6 ♘e8 10 ♘xe7+ ♕xe7 11 ♕a4 e5 12 de ♕xe5 13 ♕xc4 ♗e6 = Kirov-Geller, Sochi 1976.

[6] 9 ♗xc6 ♖b8 10 ♘c3 ♘d5 11 ♕a4 ♘b4 12 ♗g2 a6 13 a3 ♗d7 14 ♕d1 ♘c6 15 d5 ♘a5 oo Gheorghiu-Robatsch, Finland 1972.

[7] 15 ♕xa7 ♖b6 16 ♗xd5 ♕xd5 17 ♗xc7 ♗b7 18 f3 ♖b2 19 ♖ab1 oo Palatnik-Razuvayev, USSR 1973.

[8] 7 ... c5 8 dc ♕c7 9 ♕xc4 ♕xc5 10 ♕xc5 ♗xc5 11 a3 ± Korchnoi-Panov, USSR 1954.

[9] **8 ...** c5 9 dc ♗xc5 10 ♘bd2 ♘c6 11 ♘xc4 ♕e7 12 ♘fe5 ♘d4 13 ♕d1 ± Polugayevsky-Ivkov, Amsterdam 1972.
   8 ... ♘c6 9 ♕xc4 ♘d5 10 ♘bd2 ♖d8 11 e3 ♕h5 12 e4! ± Korchnoi-Tal, Moscow 1968.

[10] 10 ♗f4 ♘bd7! (10 ... ♘d5 11 ♘c3 ♘xc3 12 bc ± Mednis-Barczay, Szolnok 1975) 11 ♘c3 ♘b6 12 ♕b3 a5 13 ♖fd1 ♖a6 14 ♕c2 ♘bd5 = Petrosian-Ivanović, Vrbas 1980.

[11] 15 e3 g6 16 ♖fc1 ♖fc8 17 ♗h3 f5 = Lein-Kogan, US Ch/Z 1981.

[12] 10 ... ♗b4 11 ♗g5 ♗xc3 12 bc ♗e4 13 ♕b2 ♕d5 14 ♗xf6 gf 15 ♘e1 ♗xg2 16 ♘xg2 ♘d7 17 ♘e3 ♕c6 18 d5 ± Kogan-Byrne, US Ch/Z 1981.

[13] 12 e3 ♘d5 13 ♕e2 ♘a5 14 ♖b1 c6 15 e4 ♘b4 16 d5 ♘d3 17 ♗e3 ♘b3 18 ♕c2 ♘b4 19 ♕e2 ½-½ Romanishin-Geller, USSR Ch 1981.

[14] 15 ♘a2 ♕d6 16 ♗f4 ± Rashkovsky-Geller, USSR Ch 1981.

[15] 11 ♘bd2?! ♖c8 12 a3 ♘xd4 13 ♘xd4 ♗xg2 14 ♗xe6 ♘d5 15 ♘xf8 ♗xf1 16 ♘xf1 ♗xf8 + Speelman-Velimirović, Maribor 1980.

[16] 12 ... ♕c8 13 ♗g5 c5 14 ♗xf6 gf 15 a3 ♘d5 16 e4 ♘b6 17 d5 ed 18 ♘h4 oo Smejkal-Byrne, Baden 1980.

[17] 15 ♘xd5 ♘xd5 16 dc ♕e8 17 ♗xe7 ♕xe7 18 ♕d2 ♖xc5 19 ♖ac1 ½-½ Rubinetti-Geller, Malta Ol 1980.

[18] 11 ♘bd2 ♖c8 12 ♘b3 ♗e4 13 ♕d2 c5 14 dc ♘xc5 15 ♘xc5 ♖xd2 16 ♗xd2 ½-½ Whitehead-Sigurjonsson, Lone Pine 1981.

[19] 15 ♕c1 c5 16 ♘xc5 ♕b6 = Andersson-Karpov, Moscow 1981.

[20] 10 ... ♘bd7 11 ♗a5 ♖c8 12 ♘bd2 ♘b8 13 ♖ac1 ♘c6 14 ♘b3 ♘xa5 15 ♘xa5 ♗e4 16 ♘c6 ♗xc2 17 ♘xd8 ♗e4 18 ♘c6 ♗xc6 19 ♖xc6 ± Speelman-Taulbut, British Ch 1981.

[21] 15 ♗g5 ♗xf1 16 ♖xf1 ♖xf8 17 ♗xf6 ♗xf6 = Polugayevsky-Lengyel, Budapest 1964.

[22] 11 ... ♖a7!? 12 ♖fc1 ♗a8 13 ♘e1 ♘d8!? oo/± Speelman-Tisdall, Brighton 1980.

[23] 15 e4 e5 16 ♘h4! ± Sosonko-Morrison, Amsterdam 1978.

Catalan II *continued* 1 d4 ♘f6 2 c4 e6 3 g3 d5 4 ♗g2 ♗e7 5 ♘f3 0-0 6 0-0

	6	7	8	9	10	11	12	13	14	
9	...	cd	e4	♘c3	♘xd4	♘xc6	♕e2	♗e3	♖fd1	±
	c5	♘xd5	♘b6[24]	cd	♘c6[25]	bc	e5	♗e6	♕c7[26]	
10	...	♘c3	♘e5	cd	♗f4	♖c1	♗xe5	e4	♘e2[30]	±
	c6	b6	♗a6[27]	cd	♘fd7[28]	♘xe5	b5[29]	b4		
11	...	♘c3	e4	a4[33]	♕e2	♖d1	♘e5	♗e3	♘xc4	=
	♘bd7	dc[31]	c6[32]	a5	♘b6	♗b4	♕e7	♗d7	♘xc4[34]	
12	...	b3	♗b2[35]	♘c3	♘d2	e4	♘cxe4	♘xe4	♕e2	±
	...	c6	b6	♗a6[36]	♖c8	de[37]	♘xe4	♘f6	♘xe4[38]	
13	...	♕c2	b3	♖d1[40]	♘c3	cb	♘xb5	a4	♕a2	∞
	...	c6[39]	b6	♗b7	b5[41]	cb	♕a5	♖fc8	♗a6[42]	
14	...	...	...	♗b2	♘c3[43]	♖ad1	e4	♘xe4	♕xe4	=
	...	...	...	♗b7	♖c8	♕c7	de	♘xe4	c5[44]	
15	...	...	...	c5	♘bd2[45]	♗b2				
	...	...	b5	♘e4	f5	♗f6[46]				
16	...	...	♘bd2	b3[48]	♗b2	e4[50]	ed	dc[51]	♘xc4	=
	...	...	b6[47]	♗b7[49]	♖c8	c5	ed	dc	b5[52]	

---

[24] 8 ... ♘f6 9 ♘c3 cd 10 ♘xd4 ♘c6 11 ♘xc6 bc 12 ♕c2 ± Keres-Stahlberg, match 1938.

[25] 10 ... ♗f6 11 ♘db5 ♘c6 12 ♗e3 ♘c4 13 ♗c5 ± Fine-Kashdan, New York 1938.

[26] 15 ♖ac1 ♕b7 ± Neishtadt.

[27] 8 ... ♗b7 9 e4 dc 10 ♘xc4 ♗a6 11 b3 b5 12 ♘e3 b4 13 ♘e2 ♘bd7 13 ♗b2 ♖c8 15 ♖e1 ♘b6 16 ♘f4 ♗b7 17 ♖c1 c5 18 d5 ± Quinteros-Tatai, Bauang 1973.

[28] 10 ... ♘bd7 11 ♘c6 intending ♘xe7 ± Neishtadt.

[29] 12 ... ♘d7 13 ♗f4 ♖c8 14 ♖e1 b5 15 e4 ± Davidson-Landau, Holland 1932.

[30] Szabo-Böök, Saltsjöbaden IZ 1948.

[31] 7 ... c6 8 ♕d3 b6 9 e4 ♗a6 10 b3 ♖c8 11 ♖d1 c5 12 ed ed 13 ♗b2 ± Romanishin-Cirić, Dortmund 1976.

[32] 8 ... c5 9 d5 ed 10 ed ♘b6 11 ♘e5 ± Ragozin-Rudakovsky, USSR Ch 1945.

[33] 9 ♕e2 b5! 10 ♖d1 ♗b7 ∓.

[34] 15 ♕xc4 (Botvinnik-Lasker, Moscow 1936) 15 ... e5 16 de ♘g4 = Neishtadt.

[35] 8 ♗a3 b6 9 ♗xe7 ♕xe7 10 ♘c3 ♗a6 = Keres-Averkin, USSR Ch 1973.

[36] 9 ... ♗b7 10 e3 ♖c8 11 ♕e2 ♕c7 12 ♖ac1 ♕b8 13 ♖fd1 ♖fd8 14 ♘e5 ± Najdorf-Foltys, Amsterdam 1950.

[37] 11 ... dc 12 ♘xc4 ♗xc4 13 bc e5 14 d5 ± *ECO*.

[38] 15 ♕xe4 ± Raičević-Radulov, Vrnjačka Banja 1974.

[39] 7 ... b6 8 cd ♘xd5 9 ♘c3 ♗b7 10 ♘xd5 ♗xd5 11 e4 ♗b7 12 ♗f4! ± Keene-Robatsch, Madrid 1971.

[40] 9 ♘c3 ♗a6! 10 ♘d2 b5 11 cb cb 12 a3 ♕b6 = Quinteros-Andersson, Manila 1974.

[41] 10 ... ♖c8 11 e4 de 12 ♘xe4 c5 13 ♘xf6+ ♗xf6 14 ♘g5 ♗xg5 15 ♗xb7 ♖c7 16 ♗e4 ± Bronstein-Cirić, Sarajevo 1971.

[42] 15 ♗d2 ♕b6 16 ♗f1 ♘e4 17 e3 ♘xd2 18 ♕xd2 ♘f6 ∞ Espig-Spassky, Tallinn 1975.

[43] 10 ♘bd2 a5?! 11 a3? (11 e4! Larsen) 11 ... c5 12 cd?! ed 13 a4 ♖c8 14 ♘a1 a6 15 ♕d1 ♖e8 ∓ Najdorf-Larsen, Buenos Aires 1980.

[44] Bertok-Cirić, Yugoslav Ch 1961.

[45] 10 ♗b2!? Sosonko-Larsen, Amsterdam 1980.

[46] Schmidt-Csom, Olot 1975.

[47] 8 ... b5 9 c5 ♕c7 10 ♘b3 e5 11 ♘xe5 ♘xe5 12 ♗f4 ♘fg4 13 e4 ± Botvinnik-Rabinovich, USSR 1938.

[48] 9 e4 ♗b7 10 e5 ♘e8 11 b3 ♖c8 12 ♗b2 c5 13 cd cd 14 ♕d1 ♗xd5 15 ♗xd4 ♕c7 16 ♖c1 ♕b7 = Taimanov.

[49] 8 ... ♗a6 9 ♗b2 ♖c8 10 e4 c5 11 ed ed = Voronkov-Antoshin, USSR 1956.

[50] 11 ♖ac1 c5 12 ♕b1 dc 13 ♘xc4 b5 14 ♘cd2 ♕a5 = Panno-Najdorf, Mar del Plata 1972.

[51] 13 ♕f5?! dc 14 ♘xc4 ♗e4 15 ♕f4 b5 ∓ Furman-Zagorovsky, USSR 1951.

[52] Smyslov-Benko, Monte Carlo 1968.

46

1 d4: Miscellaneous

	1	2	3	4	5	6	7	8	9	
1	...	c4	♘f3[2]	♘c3	d5	e4	g3	h4	♗e2	±
	d6[1]	e5	♘c6	♗g4	♘ce7	♘g6	♗e7	♘f6	h6[3]	
2	...	a4!?[4]	e4	♗d3	ef	♕h5+	fg	gh+	hg♕+	±
	b5	b4	♗b7	f5!?[5]	♗xg2	g6	♗g7	♔f8	♔xg8[6]	
3	...	d5!?[8]	f4[9]	e4	f5	♔d2	fg	♔e1	♔xd1[11]	∞
	♘c6[7]	♘e5	♘g6	e5[10]	♕h4+	♕xe4	♕xd5+	♕xd1+	hg	

1   1 ... e6 2 c4 ♗b4+ (Keres) 3 ♗d2 ♕e7 4 e4 d5 5 ♗xb4 ♕xb4+ 6 ♕d2! ♕xd2+ 7 ♘xd2 ± . 6 ... ♘c6 7 ♘c3!

2   **3 de** de 4 ♕xd8+ ♔xd8 = Seirawan.

    3 ♘c3 ♘c6?! (3 ... ed! 4 ♕xd4 ♘c6) 4 d5 ♘ce7 5 g3 f5?! 6 ♘f3 ♘f6 7 ♗g2 c5 8 ♘g5 ± Csom-Suttles, Indonesia 1982.

3   Donner.

4   **2 e4** – 1 e4 a6 2 d4 b5.

    2 ♘f3 ♘f6 (Polish Defence) 3 g3 e6 4 ♗g2 ♗b7 5 0-0 ♗e7 6 ♗g5 a6 7 ♘bd2 d5?! 8 ♘e5 ♘bd7 9 c4! ±/± Timman-Miles, London 1982. 7 ... d6!? 7 ... c5!? 7 ... h6!?

5   **4 ... ♘f6** and **4 ... e6** are ±.

6   10 ♕g4 ♗xh1 (Alekhine-Prins, 1933) 11 h4 ± *ECO*. Cf Owen's Defence. Maybe 9 ♘f3!?

7   1 ... e5?! (Englund or Charlick's Gambit)

2 de ♘c6 3 ♘f3 ♕e7 4 ♕d5 f6 5 ef ♘xf6 6 ♕b3 d5 7 ♘c3 d4 8 ♘b5 ♗g4 9 ♘bxd4 ♘xd4 10 ♘xd4 0-0-0 11 c3 ± *ECO*.

8   **2 ♘f3!** d5 3 c4 – Chigorin's Defence. **2 ... d6** 3 e4 ♘f6 4 ♘c3 ♗g4 5 ♗b5!? (5 ♗e3 ±) Hulak-Miles, Indonesia 1982.

    2 e4! – Nimzowitsch Defence.

9   **3 ♗f4** ♘g6 4 ♗g3 e5.

    3 e4 e6 4 ♘f3 ♗xf3+ 5 ♕xf3 ♕f6!

    3 b3?! ♘g6 4 ♗b2 ♘f6 5 ♘f3 e6!

10   4 ... e6 5 ♘f3 ed 6 ed ♗c5 7 ♕d3 d6 8 ♗e2 ♘f6 9 ♘c3 0-0 10 ♗d2 ♘g4 11 ♘d1 ♖e8 12 h3 ♘f6 13 g4 ♘e4 14 ♖h2 ♘h4 15 ♘g5 ♘xg5 16 fg ♕e7 17 ♕g3 ♗g1! 18 ♖f2 ♗xf2+ 19 ♕xf2 ♕e4 20 ♘e3 ♕h1+ 21 ♗f1 ♘f3+ 22 ♔d1 ♘xg5 0-1 Gerusel-Miles, Porz 1981.

11   Weinitschke-Bogoljubow, Elster 1938.

	2	3	4	5	6	7	8	9	10	
1	♗f4[1]	♘c3	f3	e4	♗b5	♗xc6+	♘ge2	♕c1	♗e3[4]	±
	d6[2]	♗f5[3]	♘c6	♗g6	a6	bc	♖b8	♘h5		
2	♘c3	dc	♘f3	♗d2	e3	♗d3	0-0	e4	♘xe4[6]	±
	c5[5]	♕a5	e6	♗xc5	♕d8	d5	♘c6	de		
3	c3	f3[7]	e4	♗e3	♗d3	♘e2	0-0	♘d2	♖c1	=
	b6	♗b7	e6	c5	♗e7	0-0	d6[8]	♘bd7	♕b8[9]	
4	♗g5[10]	e4	♗xf6	♘f3	♘c3	♕d2	0-0-0	h4	g3	±
	e6[11]	h6	♕xf6	d6	g6	♕e7	a6	♗g7	b5[12]	
5	...	♗h4[13]	f3[15]	♘c3	♘xd5[16]	♗f2	e4			=
	♘e4	d5[14]	♘d6	c5	♘f5	cd	de			
6	...	♗xf6[17]	d5	♕c1[19]	e3	c3	♗c4	♘f3	♗xb5	∞
	c5	gf[18]	♕b6	f5	♗g7	e6	♕d6	b5	♕xd5[20]	
7	...	♘c3	♕xd4	♕h4	e4[22]	f4[23]	e5	♘b5	♘d6+	∞
	...	cd[21]	♘c6	e6	♗e7	b5!	b4	a6	♗xd6[24]	
8	♘f3	♗g5[26]	♗xf6[27]	e4	♘bd2[29]	c3	♘c4	♗d3	♕e2	=
	e6[25]	h6	♕xf6	d6[28]	g5!?	♘d7	♗g7	♕e7	b6[30]	
9	...	...	e3[31]	♘bd2	♗d3	c4	♔e2!?[33]	♕a4[34]		∞
	...	c5!	♕b6	♕xb2	d5[32]	♕c3	♘bd7			
10	...	♗f4	e3	♗d3[35]	♗g3	c4	♘c3	♗e4	♘xe4	∞
	b6	♗b7	e6	♘h5[36]	♗e7	d6	c5	♗xe4	0-0[37]	
11	...	♗g5	♘bd2	e3	♗d3	c3	0-0	♕e2		=
	...	♗b7	c5	e6	♗e7	0-0	♘c6	♘d5[38]		
12	...	♘c3	♗g5	e3	♘e5	♗b5+	♗d3	f4	♕f3	±
	...	♗b7	d5	e6	♗e7	c6!	♘bd7	a6	c5[39]	
13	...	♗f4[40]	♘bd2[41]	e4[42]	c3	♗b5	de	♗e3	b4	=
	g6	♗g7	0-0	d6	♘c6	e5	de	♕d6	b6[43]	
14	...	♗g5	♘bd2	e3	c3[44]	♗d3	0-0	♕e2	♖fd1	=
	...	♗g7	0-0	c5	b6	♗b7	d6	♘c6	cd[45]	
15	...	g3	♗g2	0-0	b3[46]	de	♗b2	e4	♘c3	=
	...	♗g7	0-0	d6	e5[47]	♘fd7	♘c6	de	b6[48]	
16	...	d5	♗g5	♗xf6	e4	♗e2	a4	ab	♖xa8	±
	c5	b5!?	♗b7[49]	ef	a6[50]	♗d6	♕b6	ab	♗xa8[51]	

---

[1] **2 f3 d5** = (3 e4!? – 1 d4 d5 2 e4).
  2 ♘d2 c5 3 e3 b6 4 ♗e2 ♗b7 5 ♗f3 ♘c6 6 ♘e2 g6 7 c3 ♗g7 = Nenarokov-Grigoriev, USSR 1924.

[2] 2 ... g6 3 ♘c3 ♗g7 4 e4 d6 – Pirc.

[3] 3 ... g6! 4 e4 – Pirc.

[4] Strother-Henner, 1964.

[5] 2 ... g6 3 ♗g5 (3 e4 – Pirc) 3 ... ♗g7 4 ♕d2 c5

5 dc h6 6 ♗f4 ♘a6 7 e4 ♘xc5 8 f3 ♕a5 oo Tapaszto-Dely, Hungary 1954.

2 ... d5 – 1 d4 d5 2 ♘c3 ♘f6.

[6] Müller-J.Rodriguez, Halle 1974.

[7] 3 ♘f3 – 2 ♘f3.

[8] 8 ... d5!?

[9] Intending ... ♖c8.

[10] Trompowski.

[11] 2 ... d5 3 ♗xf6!? (3 ♘c3 – Richter-Veresov) 3 ... ef! 4 e3 c6 intending ... ♗d6 =.

[12] 11 ♗h3 b4 12 ♘d5 ± Botvinnik.

[13] 3 ♗f4 d5 (3 ... c5 4 dc ♘c6 5 ♕d5 f5! 6 ♕xf5 d5 7 ♕h5+ g6 8 ♕h4 ♘d4 = Tolush-Boleslavsky, USSR Ch 1945; 4 d5 ♕b6! =; 4 f3 ♕a5+ 5 c3 ♘f6 6 d5 d6 7 e4 g6 =) 4 f3 (4 ♗d2 ♘xd2! 5 ♕xd2 ♗f5 6 ♘f3 e6 oo) 4 ... ♘f6 5 e4 de 6 ♘c3 ♘d5 7 ♘xd5 ♕xd5 = Horvath-Rovid, Hungary 1976.

[14] 3 ... g5 4 f3 gh 5 fe c5 6 e3 ♕b6 7 ♕f3 (7 ♘d2!? cd 8 ed ♕xd4 9 ♕h5 ♕xb2 10 ♖b1 oo ECO) 7 ... ♕xb2 (7 ... ♗h6 8 ♘c3 e6 9 ♔f2 ±) 8 ♘bd2 ♕c3 9 ♗d3 ♗h6 10 0-0 ♗xe3+ 11 ♔h1 ♗xd2 12 ♘xd2 ♘c6 13 ♖xf7! (Balashov-Furman, USSR Ch 1969) 13 ... h3! 14 gh cd oo ECO.

[15] 4 ♗d2 ♘d6!? (4 ... ♘xd2 5 ♕xd2) 5 e3 c6 =.

[16] 6 dc ♘f5 7 ♗f2 d4 8 ♘e4 ♘c6 9 g4 ♘e3 10 ♗xe3 de oo/+ Shereshevsky-Tukmakov, USSR 1981.

[17] 3 d5 ♕b6 4 ♘c3!? ♕xb2 5 ♗d2 ♕b6 6 e4 e5 7 f4 d6 8 fe de 9 ♘f3 ♗d6 10 ♗c4 oo Pribyl-Hazai, Varna 1978. 3 ... ♘e4! 4 ♗h4 (4 ♗f4) 4 ... ♕b6 5 ♕c1 g5 6 ♗g3 ♗g7 7 c3 ♕h6! intending ... ♘xg3.

[18] 3 ... ef 4 c3 ♕b6 5 ♕d2 ♗e7 6 e3 0-0 7 ♗e2 ♖e8 8 ♘f4 cd 9 cd ♗b4 10 ♘c3 ± Chaplinsky-Estrin, USSR 1977.

[19] 5 ♘d2 ♕xb2 6 e3 f5 7 ♖b1 ♕f6 8 ♗d3 ♗h6 9 ♘e2 d6 10 ♘g3 f4 11 ♘h5 ♕h4 12 ♘f4 ♗xf4 13 ef ♕xf4 14 0-0 oo Hort-Hartston, Hastings 1972/73.

[20] 11 0-0-0 12 c4 ♕b7 13 ♘c3 ♘c6 14 ♕d2 a6 15 ♗a4 ♕c7 oo Holmov-Polugayevsky, USSR Ch 1959.

[21] 3 ... ♕a5 4 ♗xf6 gf 5 e3 cd 6 ed e6 7 d5 ♗a3 8 ♕c1 ♕b4 9 ♖b1 ♕xc3+ 10 bc ♗xc1 11 ♖xc1 b6 + Tseitlin-Pokojowczyk, Slupsk 1978.

[22] 6 0-0-0 ♗e7 7 e4 a6 8 f4 b5 9 e5 b4 10 ef gf 11 ♘e4 fg 12 fg ♕a5 oo Vaganian-Knaak, Tallinn 1979.

[23] 7 ♘f3 ♕a5 8 ♗d3 h6 9 0-0 ♕d4! 10 ♘xd4 ♕xg5 11 ♕xg5 hg 12 e5 ♘g4 13 ♘f3 f5 +.

[24] 11 ed ♘d4 oo Nei-Taimanov, USSR 1981.

[25] 2 ... d6 usually transposes to other openings after ... g6.

2 ... b5 – 1 d4 b5.

[26] 3 g3 b5! 4 ♗g2 ♗b7 5 0-0 c5 6 c3 ♗e7 = Petrosian-Portisch, Varese (IZ play-off) 1976. 6 ♗g5!?

3 ♗f4 c5 4 c3 cd 5 cd b5 6 e3 a6 = Knežević-Velimirović, Yugoslav Ch 1978.

3 e3 c5 4 ♗d3 b6 5 ♘bd2 ♗e7 6 0-0 0-0 7 c3 ♗a6 8 ♗xa6 ♘xa6 9 ♕e2 ♕c8 = Kozomara-Barczay, Sarajevo 1968.

[27] 4 ♗h4 g5 5 ♗g3 ♘e4 6 ♘bd2 ♘xg3 7 hg ♗g7 8 c3 d6 9 e3 ♘c6 10 ♗d3 ♗d7 oo Petrosian-Botvinnik, USSR Ch 1951.

[28] 5 ... d5 6 ♘bd2 c5 7 ♗b5+ ♗d7 8 ♕e2 cd 9 ed ♗b4 10 0-0 ±.

5 ... b6 6 ♗d3 ♗b7 7 ♘c3 d6 8 0-0 ♘d7 =.

[29] 6 ♘c3 ♘d7 7 ♗d3 e5 8 0-0 c6 = Kozomara-Pachman, Sarajevo 1964. 6 ... g6 – row 4.

[30] Yusupov-Gurgenidze, USSR 1981.

[31] 4 c3 ♕b6 5 ♕c2 cd 6 cd ♘c6 7 e3 d5 8 ♘c3 ♗d7 9 ♗b5 ♘e4 = Marshall-Tartakower, Berlin 1928.

4 e4?! (Wagner Gambit) 4 ... cd 5 e5 h6 6 ♗h4 g5 + Marshall-Nimzowitsch, Berlin 1928.

[32] 6 ... ♘c3 7 0-0 d5 8 ♖e1 c4 9 ♗f1 ♘c6 10 ♗xf6 gf 11 e4 oo Alexeyev-Balashov, USSR 1972.

[33] 8 ♘e5 ♘c6 9 ♖c1 ♕a3 10 ♘xc6 bc 11 ♕c2 ♖b8 + Spassky-Miles, Tilburg 1978.

[34] ECO.

[35] 5 ♘bd2 ♘h5 6 ♗g3 ♗e7 7 ♗d3 ♘xg3 8 hg h6 = Petrosian-Reshevsky, Lugano Ol 1968.

[36] 5 ... ♗e7 6 c3 ♘e4 = Hromadka-Gilg, Prague 1937.

[37] Bronstein-Reshko, USSR 1971.

[38] Marshall-Capablanca, Kissingen 1928.

[39] 11 0-0 ± Gereben-O'Kelly, Torremolinos 1962.

[40] 3 e3 c5 =.

3 b3 ♗g7 4 ♗b2 d6 =.

[41] 4 e3 – King's Indian or Colle.

[42] 5 e3 d6 (intending ... ♗g4) 6 h3 c5 7 c3 cd 8 cd ♘c6 = Bronstein-Gurgenidze, USSR 1957.

[43] 11 0-0 ♗d7 = Keres-Boleslavsky, USSR 1965.

[44] 6 ♗c4!?

[45] 11 cd h6 = Hort-Smyslov, Wijk aan Zee 1972.

[46] 6 c4 – King's Indian.

[47] 6 ... ♘bd7 7 ♗b2 e5 8 de ♘g4 9 ♘bd2 ♘gxe5 10 ♘xe5 ♘xe5 = Filip-Fischer, Portorož IZ 1958.

[48] Polugayevsky-Stein, USSR Ch 1969.

[49] 4 ... ♕b6 5 ♘c3 b4 6 ♘a4 ♕a5 7 ♗xf6 gf (7 ... ♕xa4 8 b3 ♕a5 9 ♗b2 ±) 8 c4 ±.

4 ... ♘e4 5 ♗h4 ♕a5+ 6 ♘bd2 ♗b7 7 a4! ♗xd5 8 ab ♕b4 9 c4 ± Nogueiras-Vaganian, Mexico 1980.

[50] 6 ... ♕e7? 7 ♘bd2 ♗xd5 8 ♗xb5 ± (8 ... ♗xe4? 9 0-0! ±).

6 ... c4 7 a4! a6 8 ♗e2 ♗c5 9 0-0-0-0 10 ab ab 11 ♖xa8 ♗xa8 12 ♘c3 ♕b6 13 b3 ± Browne-Quinteros, Buenos Aires 1979.

[51] Browne-Korchnoi, Wijk aan Zee 1980.

1 d4 ♘f6 2 c4

	2	3	4	5	6	7	8	9	10	
1	...	de	♘f3[3]	♗d2	e3	♘c3	♕xd2	♘d5	♗e2	±
	e5[1]	♘e4[2]	♗b4+[4]	♗c5	♘c6	♘xd2	0-0	a5	♖e8[5]	
2	...	...	♘f3[6]	e3	a3	b3	♘c3	♗e2	♘xe5	±
	...	♘g4	♗c5	♘c6	a5	0-0	♖e8	♗cxe5	♘xe5[7]	
3	...	...	♗f4	♘d2[9]	♘f3	a3	♘xe5	e3	♕xd2	±
	...	...	♗b4+[8]	♘c6	♕e7	♘gxe5!	♘xe5	♗xd2+	d6[10]	
4	...	♘c3[12]	de	♕xd8+	♘f3	♗d2	g4	g5	h4	±
	d6[11]	e5[13]	de	♔xd8	♘fd7[14]	c6	a5	♘a6	♘ac5[15]	
5	...	...	♘f3	e4	♗e2[17]	0-0	d5	♕c2	cd	±
	...	...	♘bd7[16]	♗e7	0-0	c6	♘c5	cd	♕c7[18]	

[1] Budapest Defence.
2 ... b6!? 3 ♘c3 ♗b7 4 ♕c2! d5 5 cd ♘xd5 6 ♘f3! e6 7 e4 ♘xc3 8 bc ♗e7 9 ♗b5+ c6 10 ♗d3 ±.

[2] Fajarowicz Variation.

[3] 4 ♕c2 d5 5 ed ♗f5 6 ♘c3 ♘xd6 7 e4 ♘xe4 8 ♗d3 ♘xf2 9 ♗xf5 ♘xh1 10 ♘f3 ♗d6 11 ♘e4 ♗xh2 ∞ *ECO*.

[4] 4 ... ♘c6?! 5 a3 d6 6 ♕c2 ±/±.

[5] 11 ♕c3 ♗b4 12 ♘xb4 ab 13 ♕d2 ♕e7 14 0-0 ♕c5 15 ♕d5 ♕xd5 16 cd ♘xe5 17 ♖fc1 c6 18 ♘xe5 ♖xe5 19 ♘f3 ♖a5! ±.

[6] 4 e4 ♘xe5 5 f4 ♘ec6! 6 ♗e3 ♘a6 7 ♘c3 ♗c5 8 ♕d2 d6 9 ♘f3 0-0 ∞/= Schüssler/Wedberg.

[7] 11 0-0 d6 12 ♗b2 ±.

[8] 4 ... ♘c6 5 ♘f3 ♗b4+ 6 ♘c3 ♗xb4+ 7 bc ♕e7 8 ♕d5 f6! 9 ef ♘xf6 10 ♕d3 d6 11 e3 ♘e4 12 ♗e2 0-0 13 ♕c2! ± Rubinstein.

[9] 5 ♘c3 ♘c6 – note 8.

[10] 11 ♗e2 0-0 11 0-0 b6 ±/= Schüssler/Wedberg.

[11] Old Indian.

[12] 3 ♘f3 ♗g4 4 ♕b3 ♘c8 5 h3 ♗xf3 6 ♕xf3 g6 7 g3 ♗g7 8 ♗g2 ♘c6 9 e3 0-0 10 ♘c3 e5 (Keene-Larsen, Orense 1975) 11 d5! ∞/±.

[13] 3 ... ♗f5 4 g3! (4 f3 e5! ∞) 4 ... e5 5 ♗g2 c6 6 d5! ±.

[14] 6 ... ♘bd7 7 ♖g1! ± Karasev-Dvoretsky, USSR Ch 1976.

[15] 11 ♗e3 ± Spassky-Gheorghiu, Siegen 1970.

[16] 4 ... e4 5 ♘d2 ♗f5 6 g4! ± – King's English.

[17] 6 g3 0-0 7 ♗g2 c6 8 0-0 ♖e8 9 ♖e1 ♗f8 10 h3 a6 11 d5 cd (11 ... a5?! 12 ♗e3 ♕c7 13 ♘d2 ♘c5 14 ♗f1 ♗d7 15 ♖b1 ± Keene-Schmid, Gstaad 1973) 12 cd b5 13 b3 ♘b6 14 a4 b4 15 ♘b1 a5 ∞ Sloth-Taimanov, Copenhagen 1965.

[18] 11 ♘fd2 ♗d7 12 a4 ♖ac8 13 ♖a3 ♘e8 14 ♕d1 ♗g5 15 b4 ♘a6 16 ♕b3 f5 17 ♘c4 ±/± Kasparov-Larsen, Bugojno 1982.

1 d4 d5

	2	3	4	5	6	7	8	9	10	
1	e4?!¹	♘c3	f3³	♘xf3⁵	♘e5	g4	♗g2	h4	0-0⁷	∓
	de²	♘f6	ef⁴	♗f5⁶	e6	♗g6	c6	♗b4	♘bd7⁸	
2	♗g5	♗xf6	e3	dc	c4	♕xd8+	♗xc4	♘c3	♖c1	=
	♘f6⁹	gf¹⁰	c5	e6	dc	♔xd8	♗xc5	♔e7	♗d7¹¹	
3	♘c3	♗g5¹²	♗xf6	e3	♗d3	♕xd3	e4	♘f3	♘xe4	=
	♘f6	♗f5¹³	gf	c6	♗xd3	e6	♘d7	de	f5¹⁴	
4	...	...	f3¹⁵	e4	fe	de	♗xf6¹⁷	e6	♗c4	∞
	...	♘bd7!	c6¹⁶	de	e5	♕a5	gf	fe	♗b4¹⁸	
5	♘f3	♗g5¹⁹	e3	♘bd2	c3	♗d3	0-0	♕b1²²	♗h4	=
	♘f6	e6²⁰	c5	♗e7²¹	♘bd7	b6	0-0	h6	♗b7	
6	...	e3²³	♗d3	b3²⁵	♗b2	0-0	a3²⁶	♘e5	♘d2	∞
	...	e6²⁴	c5	♘c6	♗d6	0-0	b6	♗b7	a6²⁷	

---

¹ 2 e3 ♘f6 3 ♗d3 c5 4 c3 ♘c6 5 f4 (Stonewall) 5 ... cd (5 ... ♗g4!?) 6 ed g6 intending ... ♗f5 =.

² 2 ... e6 – French.
2 ... c6 – Caro-Kann.

³ Blackmar-Diemer Gambit.

⁴ 4 ... ♗f5!? 5 fe ♘xe4 6 ♕f3 ♘xc3 7 ♕xf5 ♘d5 8 a3 ♕d7! 9 ♕f2 g6 ∓.
4 ... c6!? 5 ♘xe4 (5 fe e5! O'Kelly) 5 ... ♗f5 ∓.

⁵ 5 ♕xf3 g6! 6 ♗f4 (6 ♗e3 intending ♗c4) 6 ... ♗g7 7 0-0-0 (7 ♘b5!?) 7 ... 0-0 8 ♗d3 ♘c6! =/∓ Micklewaite-Harding, corr. 1974/75.

⁶ 5 ... g6 (Bogoljubow) 6 ♗c4 ♗g7 7 ♘e5 (7 ♕e2!?; 7 ♗g5!?; 7 0-0 0-0 8 ♕e1 ♘bd7! 9 ♕h4 ♘b6 10 ♗b3 a5 11 a4 ♗g4!? Pachman) 7 ... 0-0 8 ♗g5 (8 ♕e2!? ∞) 8 ... ♘c6 9 ♘xc6 bc 10 ♕d2 ♘d5 11 0-0-0 =.

⁷ 10 ♗g5 ♕a5 11 ♗d2 ♘bd7 12 a3 ♗xc3 13 ♗xc3 ♕c7 ∓.

⁸ 11 ♘xd7 ♕xd7 12 h5 ♗xc3 13 bc ♗e4 14 h6 ♗xg2 15 hg ♖g8 16 ♔xg2 ♘e4! 17 ♕f3 f5! ∓ Harding.

⁹ 2 ... ♗f5 3 c4 ♗xb1 4 ♖xb1 e6 5 ♗xd8 ♗b4+ 6 ♕d2 ♗xd2+ 7 ♔xd2 ♔xd8 8 cd ed 9 e3 ± Taimanov.

¹⁰ 3 ... ef?! 4 e3 c6 5 ♗d3 ♗d6 6 ♕f3 ±.

¹¹ Lombardy-Ivkov, Amsterdam 1974.

¹² Richter-Veresov Attack.

¹³ 3 ... g6 4 ♘f3 (4 ♕d3!? ♗g7 5 e4 de 6 ♘xe4 ♘xe4 7 ♕xe4 c6 8 0-0-0 ♗f5 9 ♕e3 ♘d7 10 ♖e1 ± Alburt) 4 ... ♘bd7 5 e3 ♗g7 6 ♗d3 0-0 7 0-0 c5 8 ♖e1 b6 9 e4 ± Miles-Andersson, London 1982.
3 ... c6 4 ♗xf6 gf 5 e4 ∞.

¹⁴ 11 ♘ed2 ♗g7 12 0-0 0-0 = Alburt-Dzhindzhihashvili, USSR 1973.

¹⁵ 4 ♘f3 g6 (4 ... h6 5 ♗h4 e6 6 e4 g5! ∞ Zartobliwy-Wojtyla,* Cracow 1946) 5 e3 ♗g7 6 ♗d3 0-0 7 0-0 c6 (7 ... c5 – note 13) 8 ♖e1 ♖e8 9 e4 de 10 ♘xe4 ♘xe4 11 ♖xe4 ♘f6 = Alburt-Zaitsev, USSR 1973.

¹⁶ 4 ... c5!? 5 dc ♕a5. 5 e4 cd 6 ♕xd4 e5! ∓ Bellon-Keene, Dortmund 1980.

¹⁷ 8 ef ♕xg5 9 fg ♗xg7 10 ♕d2 ♕xd2+ 11 ♔xd2 ♘c5 12 ♗d3 ♗e6 13 ♘f3 0-0-0 14 ♔e2 b5! ∓ Alburt-Tal, USSR Ch 1972.

¹⁸ 11 ♘e2 ♘e5 12 ♗b3 ♖g8 13 a3! ∞ Rosetto-Gufeld, Camaguey 1974. 12 ... ♗d7!? ∞ Gufeld.

¹⁹ 3 ♗f4 c5 4 e3 ♘c6 5 c3 ♕b6 =. 5 ♘c3 ♗g4 6 ♗b5 e6 7 h3 ♗h5 8 g4 ♗g6 9 ♘e5 ♕b6 10 a4 ∞ Nimzowitsch-Alekhine, Vilnius 1912.

²⁰ 3 ... ♘e4 4 ♗h4 (4 ♗f4 c5! 5 e3 ♕b6 6 ♕c1 =) 4 ... c5 5 e3 ♕b6 6 ♕c1 ♘c6 =.

²¹ 5 ... ♕b6 6 ♗xf6 gf 7 c4 cd 8 ed dc 9 ♗xc4 ♘c6 10 0-0 ♗d7 11 d5 ed 12 ♕e2+ ♘e7 13 ♗xd5 0-0-0 14 ♗xf7 ± Spassky-A.Zaitsev, USSR Ch 1963.

²² 9 ♘e5 ♘xe5! 10 de ♘d7 11 ♗f4 f5 12 ef ♗xf6 ∞.

²³ Colle System.

²⁴ 3 ... g6 4 ♗d3 ♗g7 =.
3 ... ♗f5 4 ♗d3 e6! = Alekhine.

²⁵ Rubinstein's Attack.

²⁶ 8 ♘bd2 ♕e7 9 ♘e5 cd 10 ed ♗a3 11 ♗xa3 ♕xa3 = Bogoljubow-Capablanca, New York 1924.

²⁷ 10 ... a6! 11 f4 b5 12 dc ♗xc5 ∞ Dus Hotimirsky-Nimzowitsch, Carlsbad 1907.

* *later John Paul II*

Queen's Gambit

Miscellaneous

Of Black's various ways of refusing rather than declining the Queen's Gambit, the most dynamic are the **Albin Countergambit** (2 ... e5) and the **Chigorin Defence** (2 ... ♘c6). The Albin is an infrequent choice that has probably been underestimated. White is well advised to spurn the prospect of a material plus in return for the bishop pair and a small but tangible edge. The Chigorin has been attracting more followers of late but cannot be said to have gained full respectability. White seems able to wend his way through to a slight superiority in most cases but the complexion of the defence is unusual and consequently it is hard to handle.

Queen's Gambit Accepted *(2 ... dc)*

Black's temporary loss of central control does not seem to handicap him, but his subsequent hopes of keeping the balance must be based on undermining White's d4 pawn with either ... e5 or ... c5. In the latter case he should familiarise himself with the standard isolated queen's pawn positions that can also arise from the Nimzo-Indian, Semi-Tarrasch and Panov Caro-Kann.

The QGA has had a dependable reputation for over sixty years now. Marshall, Capablanca, Rubinstein, Bogoljubow, Bronstein, Smyslov, Petrosian, Portisch, Korchnoi and Tal have all played both sides of the position – a sure sign of its vitality.

Queen's Gambit Declined *(2 ... e6)*

Not the most enterprising choice of defence, the Queen's Gambit Declined sets out to neutralise White's opening advantage. The Black position requires accuracy in order to avoid permanent congestion but if it is well handled Black can achieve level prospects.

The **Exchange Variation** (3 Nc3 Nf6 4 cd ed) leads to a formation well studied and well mapped and it is a handy position to know. White strives to fracture the Black queenside with the 'minority attack' (b4-b5) in order to create and fix a pawn weakness on c6 or d5. In the meantime Black balances kingside counterplay with keeping a watchful eye on his queen's wing. A rarer treatment involves White castling long and launching a full-scale kingside attack. This policy entails considerable risk but White may have a minuscule plus.

The **Ragozin** (3 Nc3 Nf6 4 Nf3 Bb4) is a hybrid system which often transposes into the Nimzo-Indian. It has not achieved wide popularity because of White's option to simplify to a small but lasting edge.

The **Cambridge Springs** (3 Nc3 Nf6 4 Bg5 Nbd7 5 e3 c6 6 Nf3 Qa5) is yet another solid variation that is enjoying a revival, largely through the efforts of Yusupov and Smyslov.

The **Orthodox Variation** (3 Nc3 Nf6 4 Bg5 Be7 5 e3 0-0 6 Nf3 Nbd7) is the classical answer to the Queen's Gambit. Black methodically seeks equality by negotiating exchanges and achieving either ... e5 or ... c5. White can preserve some semblance of an advantage but the sterile nature of the line makes it hard to realize.

The **Lasker Defence** (3 Nc3 Nf6 4 Bg5 Be7 5 e3 0-0 6 Nf3 h6 7 Bh4 Ne4) aims at a quick balance by a rapid exchange of material. Like other variations in this section it is not clear whether Black equalizes or still labours under a microscopic disadvantage. In either case he should be able to keep matters under control.

The **Tartakower (Makagonov-Bondarevsky) System** (3 Nc3 Nf6 4 Bg5 Be7 5 e3 0-0 6 Nf3 h6 7 Bh4 b6) has been a favourite of Soviet World Champions, figuring prominently in the repertoires of Petrosian, Spassky and Karpov. It is more complex strategically than the orthodox. White can maintain a structural advantage but Black gains compensatory piece activity.

	2	3	4	5	6	7	8	9	10	
1	...	cd	Nf3	Qb3	Nc3	e4	ef	a3	Qxb7	±
	Nf6[1]	Nxd5[2]	Bf5	e6	Nc6	Nxc3	Nd5	Qd6	Rb8[3]	
2	...	cd	e4	dc	Nc3	b4!	Qc2	a3	Nxd5	±
	c5	Nf6[4]	Nxe4	Nxc5	e6	Qf6	Nca6	ed	Qe5+[5]	
3	...	Nc3[6]	cd	Qb3	Nf3!	a3	Qxc3	Bg5	e3	±
	Bf5	e6	ed	Nc6	Bb4[7]	Bxc3+	Nf6	0-0	h6[8]	
4	...	de	Nf3	g3	Nbd2	Bg2	0-0	Qa4	b4!	±
	e5	d4	Nc6	Be6	Qd7	Bh3[9]	0-0-0	h5	Bxg2[10]	
5	...	...	...	...	Bg2	0-0	Qd3[12]	Rd1	Qxf3	±
	...	...	...	Bg4	Qd7	0-0-0[11]	Nge7!	Bxf3	Bg6[13]	
6	...	Nf3[14]	cd[15]	gf[16]	e3	Nc3	Bd2	bc	cd	=
	Nc6·	Bg4	Bxf3	Qxd5	e5[17]	Bb4	Bxc3	ed	Nge7[18]	
7	...	Nc3	Nf3[19]	e4[21]	Be3	gf	d5	h4[22]		∞
	...	dc!	Nf6[20]	Bg4	Bxf3	e5	Ne7	Nd7!		

1 Marshall.

2 3 ... ♕xd5 4 ♘c3 ♕a5 5 ♗d2! ±.

3 11 ♕a6 ♗e7 12 ♗b5 ± Lipnitsky-Bondarevsky, USSR Ch 1951.

4 Rubinstein.

5 11 ♘e3 ♗e6 12 ♗b2 ♕c7 13 ♗b5+ ♘c6 14 ♘f3 ± Bondarevsky.

6 3 cd ♗xb1 4 ♕a4+ c6 5 ♖xb1 ♕xd5 6 ♘f3 ♘f6 7 e3 ⩲.

7 6 ... ♘b4?! 7 e4! de 8 ♘e5 ♕e7 9 a3 +−.

8 11 ♗xf6 ♕xf6 12 ♗e2 ⩲ Ree-Sahović, Amsterdam 1979.

9 7 ... 0-0-0 8 0-0 h5!? 9 b4 (9 h4 ♘h6 intending ... ♘g4) 9 ... ♗xb4 10 ♖b1 h4 11 ♕a4 hg 12 ♖xb4 ♘xb4 13 ♕xb4 ♗h3! =∞ Vladimirov-Wolfsen, USSR 1964.

10 11 ♔xg2 ♗xb4 12 ♖b1 ± Anishenko-Kupreichik, USSR 1964.

11 7 ... ♗h3 8 e6! ♗xe6 9 ♕a4 0-0-0 10 ♖d1 ⩲ Dzhindzhihashvili-Manievich, Israeli Ch 1978.

12 8 ♘bd2 h5 9 h4 ♘ge7 10 ♕a4 ♔b8 11 ♘b3 ♘g6 12 ♘a5 (12 ♗g5!?) 12 ... ♘xa5 13 ♕xa5 ♕f5! =∞ Browne-Mestel, Las Palmas IZ 1982.

13 11 ♕h5 ♔b8 12 ♗f4 ⩲ Korchnoi-Veinger, Beersheva 1978.

14 3 cd ♕xd5 4 ♘f3 (4 e3 e5 5 ♘c3 ♗b4 6 ♗d2 ♗xc3 7 bc ed 8 cd ♘f6 = Taylor-Watson, Calgary 1975) 4 ... e5! 5 ♘c3 (5 de!?) 5 ... ♗b4 6 e3 (6 ♗d2 ♗xc3 7 ♗xc3 e4! = Petrov-Ravinsky, USSR 1940) 6 ... ed 7 ed ♘f6!? (7 ... ♗g4 8 ♗e2 ♗xf3 9 ♗xf3 ♕c4 = Marshall-Capablanca, Lake Hopatcong 1926) 8 ♗e2 ♘e4 9 ♗d2 ♗xc3! 10 bc ♘a5 ∞ Nyholm-Alekhine, Stockholm 1912.

15 **4 ♕a4** ♗xf3 5 ef (5 gf a6!? intending 6 ♘c3 e6!) 5 ... e6 6 ♘c3 ♘e7 7 cd ed 8 ♗b5 a6 9 ♗xc6+ ♘xc6 10 0-0 ♕d7 11 ♖e1+ ♗e7 ∞.

4 ♘bd2!? dc 5 e3 e5.

4 ♘c3 e6 5 e3 ♗b4! 6 ♕b3! ♗xf3 7 gf ♘ge7 8 ♗d2 0-0 9 f4 ♖b8 10 0-0-0 dc 11 ♗xc4 b5 ∞.

4 e3 e5!? (4 ... e6 ±/=) 5 ♕b3 ♗xf3 6 gf ♘ge7! 7 ♘c3 ed 8 ♘xd5 ♖b8 9 e4 ♘g6 10 ♗d2 ♗d6 11 f4 (Steinitz-Chigorin, match 1889) 11 ... ♕h4! ∞.

16 **5 dc** ♗xc6 6 ♘c3 ♘f6 (6 ... e6 7 e4 ♗b4 8 f3 ♕h4+ 9 g3 ♕f6 10 ♗e3 0-0-0! ∞) 7 f3 e5 8 de ♘d7 9 e4 ♗b4 10 ♕b3 ♕h4+ 11 g3 ♕e7 12 ♗e2 ♘xe5 13 ♗f4 ♘g6 14 0-0-0 ♘xf4 15 gf (Henley-Miles, Indonesia 1982) 15 ... 0-0! =.

5 ef!? ♕xd5 6 ♗e3 e6! 7 ♘c3 ♕d7 =.

17 6 ... e6 7 ♘c3 ♕h5!? (7 ... ♕d7 8 f4 ⩲; 7 ... ♗b4 8 ♗d2 ♗xc3 9 bc ±) 8 f4 ♕xd1+!? 9 ♔xd1 0-0-0 10 ♔e2 ♘f6! ∞ Gligorić-Sahović, Bled-Portorož 1979. 8 ♗g2!?

18 **10 ... ♘f6!?** 11 ♗e2 0-0-0 12 ♕b3 ♖he8 13 ♕xd5 ♘xd5 ∞.

10 ... ♘ge7 11 ♖b1 0-0-0! =. 11 ♖c1 ♕xa2!. 11 ♗g2!?

19 **4 d5!?** ♘e5 5 f4 (5 ♕d4 f6!? Watson) 5 ... ♘g4! 6 e4 e5 7 f5 h5! Smyslov. 5 ... ♘g6? 6 e4 ± Gunawan-Keene, Indonesia 1982.

4 e3 e5! 5 d5 ♘a5 6 ♕a4+ c6 7 b4 (Oksam-Rey, Rotterdam 1923) 7 ... cb! 8 ab ♕b6! intending 9 ♕xa5 ♕xa5 10 ♖xa5 ♗b4.

20 **4 ... a6!?** 5 ♕a4 b5!. 5 e4!?. 5 d5 ♘b8 6 e4!?

4 ... ♗g4 5 d5 ♗xf3 6 ef ♘e5 7 ♗f4 ♘g6 (Keene-Cuartas, Dortmund 1982) 8 ♗xc4!! ♘xf4 9 ♗b5+ c6 10 dc +−.

21 5 d5 ♘a5! 6 ♕a4+ c6 7 b4! b5! 8 ♕xa5 ♕xa5 9 ba b4 10 ♘d1 cd 11 a3!? ∞/⩲.

22 9 ♗xc4 a6!? (9 ... ♘g6 10 ♕b3! ⩲ Enklaar-Cortlever, Wijk aan Zee II 1972).

	3	4	5	6	7	8	9	10	11	
1	e3	♗xc4[2]	ed	♘c3	♘f3	0-0	♗g5	bc	♕d3	=
	e5[1]	ed	♗b4+[3]	♘f6	0-0	♗g4	♗xc3[4]	♕d6	♘bd7[5]	
2	♘c3	d5[7]	e4	♗g5	♗xf6	♗xc4	♘e2	0-0	♗b3	=
	e5[6]	c6[8]	♘f6	♗b4	♕xf6	0-0	♘d7	♘b6	♗d7[9]	
3	e4	d5[11]	♗xc4	♘c3	♘xd5[14]	♗xd5	♕b3	♘f3[15]		=
	c5[10]	e6[12]	♘f6[13]	ed	♘xd5	♗e7	0-0			
4	...	e5[16]	♗xc4	♗b3[17]	♘e2[18]	♘bc3	♗f4	0-0	♕d2	∓
	♘f6	♘d5	♘b6	♘c6	♗f5	e6	♘b4	♗e7	♘4d5[19]	
5	...	♘f3[20]	♗d2[22]	♘bxd2[23]	♗xc4	0-0	e5	♕b3	♕xb7	∓
	e5	♗b4+[21]	♗xd2+	ed	♘c6[24]	♘f6[25]	♘d5[26]	♗e6[27]	♘a5	
6	...	...	♗xc4[28]	♘bd2	0-0[30]	e5	♘h4	♘df3	♗xe6	±
	...	ed	♗b4+[29]	♘c6	♕f6[31]	♕g6	♕g4	♗e6	fe[32]	
7	♘f3	e4[34]	a4	♘e5	♘c3	♘xc4	♗f4	♕d2	♗h6	∞
	♘d7[33]	♗b6	a5	♘f6	♘fd7!	g6	c6	♗g7	0-0[35]	
8	...	e4[36]	a4	b3!	♘c3	ab	♖xa8	bc		=
	a6	b5[37]	♗b7	♗xe4[38]	♗b7	ab	♗xa8	e6[39]		
9	...	e3	♗xc4	h3[41]	♕b3[43]	gf	♗e2	dc	a4	±
	...	♗g4[40]	e6	♗h5[42]	♗xf3[44]	b5	c5[45]	♗xc5	b4[46]	
10	...	♕a4+	♕xc4	g3	♗g2	0-0	♕b3	♘bd2		=
	♘f6	c6[47]	♗f5[48]	♘bd7	e6	♗e7	♕b6	0-0[49]		
11	...	♘c3	e4[51]	e5	a4[53]	bc	g3	♗g2	♘h4!	±
	...	a6?![50]	b5[52]	♘d5	♘xc3[54]	♕d5[55]	♗b7[56]	♕d7	c6[57]	

1 3 ... b5? 4 a4 c6? 5 ab cb? 6 ♕f3 ±±.

2 4 de ♕xd1+ 5 ♔xd1 ♗e6 ∓.

3 **5 ... ♘c6!?** 6 ♘f3 ♘f6 7 ♕b3 ♗b4+ 8 ♘c3 0-0 =.
   5 ... ♗d6!? ∞.

4 9 ... ♘c6 10 ♘d5 ♗e7 11 ♘xe7+ ♕xe7 12 h3! ♗xf3 13 ♕xf3 ♘xd4 14 ♕xb7 ± Stahlberg-Gligorić, match 1949.

5 Taimanov.

6 **3 ... a6** 4 e4!? b5 5 ♘f3 ∞.

7 4 e3 ed – cf row 1.

8 **4 ... a6** 5 e4 b5 6 a4 b4 7 ♘a2 f5 8 ef ♗xf5 9 ♗xc4 ♘f6 (Golombek-Alekhine, Margate 1935) 10 ♘e2 ∞.
   4 ... ♘f6 5 ♗g5 c6 transposes.

9 Benitez-Szilagyi, Moscow Ol 1956.

10 **3 ... ♘c6** 4 ♗e3 (4 ♘f3 ♗g4 5 ♗e3 e6 6 ♘c3 ♘f6 7 ♗xc4 ♗b4 ∞) 4 ... ♘f6 5 ♘c3 ♗g4 6 ♗xc4 ♘xe3 7 fe e6 ± Bagirov-Dobrovolsky, Stary Smokovec 1981.

11 4 ♘f3 cd 5 ♕xd4 ♕xd4 6 ♘xd4 ♘d7 7 ♗xc4 ♘c6 =.

12 **4 ... ♘f6** 5 ♘c3 b5 6 e5 b4 7 ef bc 8 bc ♘d7 (8 ... gf/e6 9 ♗xc4 ±) 9 ♕a4 ef! 10 ♗f4 ♕b6 11 ♗xc4 ♗d6 ± Rashkovsky-Grigorian, USSR Ch 1973.

13 **5 ... ed?** 6 ♗xd5 ♘f6?? 6 ♗xf7+.

14 7 ed a6 8 a4 ♗d6 =.

15 Taimanov. 11 ♗xb7?? c4 ∓∓.

16 **4 ♘c3 e5** 5 d5?! ♗c5 6 ♗xc4 ♗g4 ∓ Steinitz-Blackburne, London 1899. 5 ♘f3 ed 6 ♕xd4 ♕xd4 7 ♘xd4 ♗b4 8 f3 a6 9 ♗xc4 b5 10 ♗e2 c5 11 ♘c2 ♗a5 = Rashkovsky-Lerner, Lvov 1981.

17 **6 ♗d3 ♘c6** 7 ♘e2 (Bukić-Petrosian, Banja Luka 1979) 7 ... ♗b4 8 ♗e4 c6 = Petrosian.

18 **7 ♗f3!?**

19 Miles-Portisch, Buenos Aires Ol 1978.

20 **4 d5 ♗c5!?/4 ... a6!?**
    4 de ♕xd1+ 5 ♔xd1 ♘c6 6 f4 ♗g4+ (6 ... f6!? =) intending ... 0-0-0.

21 **4 ... ♘f6?!** 5 ♗xc4 ♘xe4!? 6 0-0 ♗e7 7 ♘xe5 ♘d6 8 ♗b3 ±/= Bagirov-Mukhin, USSR 1975.

22 **5 ♘bd2?** c3! ∓.
    5 ♘c3 ed 6 ♕xd4 ♕xd4 7 ♘xd4 ♗d7 (7 ... ♘f6 8 f3 ±; 7 ... c6 8 ♗xc4 ♘e7 9 ♗e3 ±) 8 ♗xc4 ♘c6 9 ♘db5 0-0-0 =. 6 ♘xd4!? ♕e7?! (6 ... ♘e7) 7 ♗xc4! ♕xe4+ (7 ... ♘f6) 8 ♗f1! (Alburt-Romanishin, Kiev 1978) 8 ... ♕g4!? ∞ Alburt.

23 **6 ♕xd2** ed 7 ♕xd4 ♕xd4 8 ♘xd4 ♗d7 9 ♗xc4 ♘c6 10 ♘xc6 ♗xc6 = Bagirov-Matulović, Titovo Užice 1978.

24 7 ... ♘h6!? 8 0-0 0-0 (8 ... c5?! 9 ♘b3 ♕e7

10 Rc1 b6 11 Bd5 Bb7 12 Nxc5!! ± Partos-Miles, Biel 1977) 9 Nb3 Qe7 = Bagirov-Shkola, USSR 1966.

[25] 8 ... Qf6 (Bagirov-Romanishin, USSR Ch 1978) 9 Nb3/ Re1 ±.

[26] 9 ... Ng4 10 h3 Nh6 11 Nb3 Nf5 ±/= Zak-Makarichev, USSR 1964.

[27] 10 ... Nce7?! 11 Bxd4 (11 Ne4) ± Bagirov-Petrushin, USSR Ch 1st L 1977.

[28] 5 Qxd4 Qxd4 6 Nxd4 Bc5 =.

[29] 5 ... Nc6?! 6 0-0 Be6 7 Bxe6 ±.

[30] 7 a3 Bxd2+ 8 Qxd2 Bg4 ∓ Neistadt.

[31] 7 ... Nf6!? 8 e5 Nd5 9 Nb3 Nb6! 10 Bb5 Bd7 11 Nbxd4 Nxd4 12 Nxd4 (Yusupov-Rufenacht, Mexico 1978) 12 ... 0-0 13 Bd3 ±.

7 ... Be6 8 Bxe6 fe 9 Nb3 Qd7 10 Nbxd4 ± Taimanov-Peterson, USSR Team Ch 1964.

[32] 12 Qb3 ± Yusupov-Mikhalchishin,USSR Ch 1981.

[33] 3 ... b5? 4 a4 c6 5 e3 Qb6 6 ab cb 7 Ne5! Bb7 8 b3 ±.

3 ... c5 4 e3 cd 5 Bxc4 ±.

3 ... e6 4 e4 c5 5 Bxc4 cd 6 Nxd4 Nf6 7 Nc3 Bc5 8 Be3 ± Capablanca-Bogoljubow, Moscow 1925. 4 ... b5!?

3 ... c6 4 e3 Bg4 5 Bxc4 e6 ±.

3 ... Bg4 4 Ne5 Bh5 5 Nc3 (5 g4 f6 ∞) 5 ... Nd7 6 Qa4 c6 7 Nxd7 Qxd7 8 Qxc4 intending e4, Be3 ± Alekhine. 6 Nxc4 Ngf6 ∞/±.

[34] 4 Nbd2?! b5 ∓ Borisenko-Dorfman, USSR 1975.

4 e3 Nb6 5 Nbd2 Be6 6 Qc2 ∞/± (6 Ng5? Bd5 7 e4 e6! ∞ Nikolac-Kovačević, Yugoslavia 1976).

[35] Gavrikov-Gulko, USSR Ch 1981.

[36] 4 Nc3 b5 5 e4 ∞.

4 a4 Nf6 5 e3 Bf5 6 Bxc4 e6 7 0-0 Nc6 8 Nc3 Bg6 (8 ... Bb4!) 9 h3 Bd6 10 Re1 0-0 11 e4 ± Tukmakov-Kuzmin, Erevan Z 1982.

[37] 4 ... Bg4 5 Bxc4 e6 6 0-0 Nd7 7 Nc3 c5 8 d5 e5 9 a4 ± Borisenko-Flohr, USSR Ch 1950.

[38] 6 ... e6 7 bc bc ∞/=.

[39] 10 ... b4 11 d5! ±.

10 ... e6 11 Nxb5 Bb4+ 12 Nd2 Bxf3 13 gf Bxd2+ 14 Qxd2 c6 15 Nc3 Ne7 = Vaiser-Bagirov, USSR 1971.

[40] 4 ... Be6?! (Winawer) 5 Nc3 d5 6 Nxd5 Qxd5 7 Qc2 e6 8 Bxc4 Bb4+ 9 Be2! ±.

4 ... b5?! 5 a4 Bb7 6 b3! ±.

[41] 6 Qb3 Bxf3 7 gf b5 8 Be2 Nd7 9 a4 b4 10 Nd2 Ngf6 11 Ne4!? c5 12 Nxc5 ± Taimanov.

6 Nc3 Nf6 7 0-0 (7 Qb3 Bxf3 8 gf b5 9 Be2 Nbd7 10 Qd1!? c5 11 d5! ±) 7 ... Nc6 (7 ... Nbd7 8 e4 b5 9 Be2 b4 10 e5 bc 11 ef ∞ Liberzon-Flohr, USSR 1963) 8 Be2 Bd6 9 b3 0-0 10 Bb2 Qe7 intending ... Ba3 =.

6 d5 ed 7 Bxd5 Qe7! 8 Qd4 (8 Qb3 c6!) 8 ... Qb4+ 9 Nc3 Nf6! =

[42] 6 ... Bxf3 7 Qxf3 Nc6 8 0-0 Nf6 9 Nc3 Bd6 10 Rd1 0-0 11 a3 e5 ± Geller-Sajtar, Helsinki Ol 1952.

[43] 7 Nc3 Nf6 8 g4!? Bg6 9 Ne5 Ndb7 10 Nxg6 hg 11 g5 Ng8!? 12 Qf3 Rb8 13 h4 c5 ∞/± Mochalov-Vorotnikov, USSR 1981.

[44] 7 ... b5?? 8 Bxb5+.

7 ... Ra7!?

7 ... Nc6!?

[45] 9 ... Nd7! – cf note 41.

[46] 12 Nd2 Nd7 13 Nc4 (Pirc-Gligorić, Yugoslav Ch 1946) 13 ... Be7 ∞/±.

[47] 4 ... Nc6 5 Nc3 d5 6 Qxc4 (6 e4 Nb6 7 Qd1 Bg4 ∞) 6 ... Ndb4 (6 ... Be7 7 e4 Nb6) 7 Qb3 Nxd4 8 Nxd4 Qxd4 9 Be3 Qe6 10 Qa4+ Bd7 = Andersson-Korchnoi, Johannesburg 1981.

4 ... Nbd7 5 Qxc4!? e6 6 Nc3 Nb6 7 Qd3 c5 8 e4 cd 9 Nxd4 Bc5 10 Nb3 Qxd3 11 Bxd3 ± Palatnik-Korsunsky, USSR 1976.

4 ... Qd7 5 Qxc4 Qc6 6 Na3! ± Alekhine-Fine, Kemeri 1937.

[48] 5 ... g6 6 Nbd2 Qd5 7 e3 Bg7 8 b3 ± Gheorghiu-Bastian, Baden Baden 1981.

5 ... Bg4 6 Nbd2 Nbd7 7 g3 e6 8 Bg2 Bd6 = Portisch-Polugayevsky, Hungary v RSFSR 1963.

[49] Taimanov-Geller, USSR Ch 1963.

[50] 4 ... Bf5 5 e3 (5 Ne5 e6 6 f3 Nfd7 7 Nxc4 Nc6 8 e4 Bg6 9 Bf4 f6 10 Be3 Bf7 ∞/= Sosonko-Hort, Tilburg 1980) 5 ... e6 6 Bxc4 Nbd7 7 0-0 c6 8 Re1 Be7 (Langeweg-Gheorghiu, Beverwijk 1968) 9 e4 Bg4 10 Be3 ±.

[51] 5 a4 Nc6 6 e4 Bg4 7 Be3 e5 (7 ... Na5!? ∞) 8 de Nd7 9 Bxc4 Ndxe5 10 Nxe5!? Nxe5 =.

5 e3 b5 6 a4 b4 7 Nb1 e6 8 Bxc4 Bb7 9 0-0 Nbd7 10 Nbd2 c5 = Miles-Kuzmin, Reykjavik 1978.

[52] 5 ... c5 6 d5 e6 7 a4! ed 8 e5 Ng8 (8 ... d4? 9 Bxc4! ±) 9 Qxd5 ± Vladimirov-Hodos, USSR 1958.

[53] 7 Bg5 Nxc3 8 bc f6! ∓.

[54] 7 ... Bb7 8 e6 fe (8 ... f6 9 Ne4 ±) 9 Ng5 Nxc3 10 bc ∞/=.

7 ... c6 8 ab Nxc3 9 bc cb 10 Ng5 f6 11 Qf3 Ra7 12 e6 Nb6!? 13 d5 fg 14 Be3! Qc7 15 Be2 ± Knaak-Thormann, East Germany 1980.

[55] 8 ... Bb7 9 e6! f6 (9 ... fe – cf note 54) 10 Be3 d5 11 Qb1! ± Shamkovich.

[56] 9 ... Bf5 10 Bg2 e6 11 0-0 Qb7 12 Nh4 Be4 13 Bxe4 Nxe4 14 Re1 Qb7 15 d5 ± Gligorić-Buljovčić, Novi Sad 1979.

9 ... Be6 10 Bg2 Qb7 11 0-0 Bd5 12 e6! Bxe6 13 Ng5 Bd5 14 Bxd5 Qxd5 15 ab ± Balashov-Miles, Bugojno 1978.

[57] 12 f4 e6 13 f5! ef 14 0-0 g6 15 Bg5 ± Kavalek-Miles, Wijk aan Zee 1978.

	4	5	6	7	8	9	10	11	12	
12	e3	♗xc4	0-0	♘c3	♕e2	♗b3	♖d1	♗c2[61]		∞
	g6[58]	♗g7	0-0[59]	♘fd7[60]	♕b6	a5	a4			
13	e3	♗xc4	h3[62]	♘c3	g4	♘e5	♘xg6	♗f1[63]	♗g2	=/±
	♗g4	e6	♗h5	a6	♗g6	♘bd7	hg	e5	ed[64]	
14	...	...	♘c3	h3[65]	0-0	e4[67]	g4	de	♘xe5	=
	...	...	♘bd7	♗h5	♗d6[66]	e5	♗g6!	♘xe5	♗xe5[68]	
15	...	...	...	...	...	...	♗e2	de	♘d4[69]	=
	...	...	...	...	...	...	0-0	♘xe5	♗c5[70]	
16	e3	♗xc4	♕e2[72]	dc	0-0	e4[74]	e5[75]	ef	♕xc4	=
	e6	c5[71]	a6	♗xc5	♘c6![73]	b5	bc	gf	♕b6[76]	
17	...	...	0-0	♕e2	♖d1	ed	♘c3	♗d3	♗g5	±
	...	...	♘c6[77]	cd	♗e7	0-0	♘a5[78]	b6	♗b7[79]	

1 d4 d5 2 c4 dc 3 ♘f3 ♘f6 4 e3 e6 5 ♗xc4 c5 6 0-0 a6

	7	8	9	10	11	12	13	14	15	
18	♕e2	♖d1[81]	dc[82]	♗d3	a4	♖xa4	♘c3			=
	♘c6[80]	b5	♕c7	♘b4[83]	ba	♖b8	♗xc5			
19	...	♘c3!?	d5[85]	♘xd5	♗xd5	b3	♗b2	h3[86]		±/=
	...	♕c7[84]	ed	♘xd5	♗d6	0-0	♗g4			
20	...	♗b3[87]	♘c3[88]	dc	e4	e5[90]	ef	♕c4	♕xc3	±
	b5	♘c6	♗e7[89]	♗xc5	b4	bc	gf[91]	♕b6	♘d4[92]	
21	...	...	♖d1	♘c3	d5[94]	♘xd5	♗xd5	♖xd5	e4	±/∞
	...	♗b7	♘bd7	♕b8[93]	ed	♘xd5	♗xd5	♕b7!	♗e7[95]	
22	a4	♕e2	dc[98]	e4	e5	♘xd4	♘a3	♖xa3	b3	±
	♘c6[96]	♗e7[97]	♗xc5	♘g4[99]	♘d4	♕xd4	♗xa3[100]	♘xe5	♕c5[101]	
23	...	...	♖d1	ed	♘c3	♗d3[104]	♗b1	a5!?[106]		±
	...	cd	♗e7[102]	0-0	♘d5[103]	♘cb4	b6[105]			

[58] 4 ... b5? 5 a4 c6 (5 ... b4 6 ♗xc4 e6 7 0-0 ♗b7 8 ♘bd2 ♘bd7 9 e4! ± Taimanov-Benediktsson, Reykjavik 1968) 6 ab cb 7 b3 ±.

4 ... ♗e6 5 ♘c3 c6 (5 ... ♗d5 6 ♘e5 intending f3, e4 ±; 5 ... g6 6 ♗g5 ♗d5 7 e4 h6 8 ♗xd5! ±) 6 a4 g6 7 e4 ♘a6 8 ♗g5! ♘c7 9 e5 intending ♘xe6, ♗xc4.

4 ... ♘bd7!? 5 ♗xc4 ♘b6 6 ♗d3 (6 ♗e2 ♗f5 Miles-Bellon, Amsterdam Z 1978) ∞.

[59] 6 ... c5!? 7 d5 (7 dc ♕c7 ∞/±) 7 ... 0-0 8 ♘c3 ♘e8 9 ♕e2 ♘d6 10 ♗d3 e5 ± Bobotsov-Mechkarov, Bulgarian Ch 1954.

[60] 7 ... c5 8 dc ±

7 ... ♗g4 ±.

[61] 11 ... ♘c6! 12 ♘e5! ∞ Bolig-Gheorghiu, Vrnjačka Banja 1963.

[62] 6 ♕b3 ♗xf3 7 gf ♘bd7 8 ♕xb7 c5 ∞, e.g. 9 dc ♗xc5 10 ♘c3 0-0 11 f4 ♘b6! 12 ♗e2 ♘fd5 Quinteros-Miles, Amsterdam 1977.

6 ♘bd2 ♘bd7 7 ♕b3 ♘b6 (7 ... ♗b8!?) 8 ♘e5 ♗h5 9 0-0 ♗d6 10 a4 ± I.Ivanov-Lerner, USSR 1979.

6 a3!? a6?! 7 b4 ♗d6 8 ♗b2 ♘c6 9 ♘bd2 ± Belyavsky-A.Petrosian, USSR Ch 1st L 1977.

[63] 11 g5 ♘d5 12 ♕g4!? =/± Tal.

[64] 13 ed ♖b8 =/± Ribli-Timman, Las Palmas

IZ 1982.
65 7 0-0 ♗d6 8 e4 e5 =.
  7 e4 ♗b4!
  7 ♗e2 ♗d6 8 e4 ♗b4 = Gligorić-Miles, Bugojno 1978.
66 8 ... ♗e7!? 9 e4 ♘b6 10 ♗e2 (10 ♗d3 0-0 11 ♗e3 ♖c8) 10 ... ♗g6! 11 ♗d3 0-0 12 ♗e3 ♖c8 13 ♕e2 c5 14 ♖fd1 cd 15 ♗xd4 ♗c5 = Smejkal-Matulović, Vršac 1981.
67 9 ♗e2 0-0 10 b3 ♕e7 11 ♗b2 e5 = Spassky-Andersson, Turin 1982.
68 13 f4 ♕d4+ 14 ♔xd4 ♗xd4+ 15 ♔h2 ♗xc3 16 bc ♗xe4 17 g5 ♗d5 18 ♖e1+ ♔f8! = Ftacnik-Matulović, Vršac 1981.
69 12 ♘xe5 ♗xe2 13 ♘xf7 (13 ♕xe2 ♗xe5 14 ♗g5 ♕e8 = Balashov-Miles, Tilburg 1977) 13 ... ♗xd1 14 ♘xd8 ♖axd8 (14 ... ♗c2!? ∞) 15 ♖xd1 ♗e5! 16 ♖xd8 ♖xd8 17 f3 ♗xc3/ 17 ... ♖d3 ∞.
70 12 ... ♗g6?! 13 ♗g5 (13 f3!?) 13 ... ♗e7 (13 ... ♖e8? 14 ♘db5 ± Portisch-Spassky, match 1977) 14 f3 ♗c5 15 ♗e3 ± Diesen-Matulović, Bajmok 1978.
  12 ... ♗xe2 13 ♕xe2 ♘g6 14 ♖d1 (14 ♘f5!? ♗e5 15 ♗g5 ♕e8 16 ♗xf6! ± Tarnai-Cordes, corr. 1979; 14 ♘db5!?) 14 ... ♕c8 15 ♗g5 ♗e5 ∞/= Browne-Miles, Reykjavik 1980.
  12 ... ♗c5 13 ♘b3 (13 ♗xh5 ♗xd4 15 ♗g5? ♗xc3 16 bc ♕xd1 17 ♗xd1 ♘xe4 18 ♗f4 ♘d3! ∓; 14 ♘d5! c5! = Hübner-Miles, Wijk aan Zee 1979) 13 ... ♕xd1 14 ♗xd1 ♗b6 = Portisch-Miles, 1978.
71 5 ... ♗e7?! 6 0-0 0-0 7 ♘c3 b6 8 ♕e2 ♗b7 9 e4 c5 10 ♖d1 cd 11 ♘xd4 ♖c8 12 e5 ± Lasker-Teichmann, Hastings 1895.
72 6 a3 a6 7 dc ♕xd1+ 8 ♔xd1 ♗xc5 9 b4 ♗d6 = Ribli-Portisch, Tilburg 1978.
73 8 ... b5?! 9 ♗d3 ♘c6 (9 ... 0-0 10 e4 e5!? 11 a4 b4 12 ♘bd2 ± Polugayevsky) 10 ♘c3!? (10 e4 ♘b4 =) 10 ... ♗b7 11 e4 (Korchnoi-Hübner, match 1980/81) 11 ... 0-0? 12 e5 ♘d7 13 ♗xh7+!. 11 ... ♕b6 ∞.
74 9 ♘c3 e5!
75 10 ♗d3 ♘b4 =.
  10 ♗b3 e5 =.
76 13 ♘c3 ♕b4 = Furman-Suetin, USSR Ch 1960.
77 6 ... cd 7 ed ♘c6 8 ♘c3 ♗e7 9 ♖e1 0-0 10 a3/ 10 ♗f4 ±. 9 a3 0-0 10 ♕d3 ±. 9 ♗e3 0-0 10 ♘e5 ±. 9 ♕e2. 9 ♗g5.
78 10 ... ♘b4 11 ♗g5 ♘bd5 12 ♖ac1 ± Alekhine-Hönlinger, Vienna 1936.
79 13 ♗xf6!?
  13 ♖ac1 ♘d5 14 ♕e4! g6 15 ♕h4 f6 16 ♗h6 ± Rashkovsky-Flesch, Lvov 1981.
  13 ♘e5 ♘d5! =.
80 7 ... cd 8 ed ♗e7 9 ♘c3 b5 10 ♗b3 ♗b7 11 ♗g5 (11 ♘e5 0-0 12 ♘xf7?! ♖xf7 13 ♕xe6

♕f8 ∓) 11 ... 0-0 12 ♖fe1 ♘c6 (12 ... ♘bd7!? 13 d5! ±) 13 ♖ad1 ±.
81 8 a4 – rows 22 and 23.
82 9 ♗d3 c4 10 ♗c2 ♗b4 11 ♘c3 ♗xc2 12 ♕xc2 ♗b7 13 d5 ♕c7 14 e4 e5 15 ♗g5 ♘d7 =/∓.
83 10 ... ♗xc5 11 a4 ba! ∞.
84 8 ... b5 9 ♗b3 – row 21.
85 9 dc ♗xc5 10 e4!?
86 Korchnoi-Radulov, Leningrad IZ 1977.
87 8 ♗d3 cd 9 ed ♗e7 10 a4 ba 11 ♖xa4 ♗b7 12 ♘c3 0-0 13 ♗g5 ♗c6 14 ♖aa1 a5 15 ♖fd1 ♘bd7 = Szabo-Portisch, Kecskemet 1962.
88 9 ♖d1 c4 10 ♗c2 ♕b4 – note 82.
89 9 ... ♗b7 10 ♖d1 ♕c7 11 d5 ed 12 e4 0-0-0 13 ♗xd5 ♘xd5 14 ♗xd5 ±/±.
90 12 ♘a4 ♗e7 13 ♗e3 ± Botvinnik.
91 13 ... ♕xf6 14 ♘c4 cb 15 ♕xc5 ♗d7 16 ♗xb2 ♕xb2 17 ♖ad1 ± Botvinnik.
92 16 ♘xd4 ♗xd4 17 ♗a4+ ♔e7 18 ♗e3 ± Euwe-Alekhine, match 1937.
93 10 ... ♗d6 11 e4 cd 12 ♖xd4! ♗c5 13 ♖d3! ♘g4 14 ♗g5 ♕b6 15 ♘d5! ♕a5 16 ♖f1 ♖c8 17 ♘f4 ± Petrosian-Bertok, USSR 1962.
94 11 e4!? cd 12 ♘xd4 ♗d6 (Reshevsky-Portisch, Amsterdam IZ 1964) 13 e5!? Panov/Estrin.
  11 ♘e5!?
95 16 ♗g5 ♘b6 17 ♖ad1 ±/∞ Panov/Estrin.
96 7 ... cd 8 ed ♗c6 9 ♘c3 ♗e7 10 ♗e3 (10 ♖e1; 10 ♗g5) 10 ... 0-0 11 ♕e2 intending ♖ad1 ±.
97 8 ... ♕c7 9 ♘c3 ♗d6 (9 ... ♗e7 10 ♖d1 0-0 11 b3 ±) 10 ♖d1 0-0 (10 ... e5 11 ♘d5 ± Gheorghiu-Radulov, Helsinki 1972) 11 h3 b6 (11 ... e5 12 de ♘xe5 13 ♘xe5 ♗xe5 14 ♘d5 ±) 12 d5 ed 13 ♗xd5! ♗b7 14 e4 ♖ae8 15 ♗g5 ± Portisch-Radulov, Nice Ol 1974.
98 9 ♖d1 ♕c7 10 ♘c3 0-0 11 b3 ±.
99 10 ... ♕c7 11 e5 ♘g4!?
100 13 ... ♘xe5 14 ♗e3! ± Neistadt.
101 16 ♖a2 ♘xc4 17 bc ♗d7 18 ♗a3 ♕f5 (Botvinnik-Petrosian, match 1963) 19 ♕b2 ±. 19 ♕d2!?
102 9 ... d3 10 ♗xd3 ♕c7 11 ♘c3 ♗e7 12 h3 0-0 13 e4 ♘d7 14 ♗e3 ♘b4 15 ♗c4 ♘c2 16 ♕xc2 ♕xc4 17 ♖ac1 ± Zagorovsky-Romanov, corr. 1966.
103 11 ... ♘b4 12 ♘e5 ♗d7 13 ♗f4 ♗c6 14 ♘xc6 bc 15 a5 ± Gligorić-Miagmasuren, Sousse IZ 1967.
104 12 ♕e4 ♘cb4 13 ♘e5 ♖a7 (13 ... b6? 14 ♘c6!! ± Vukić-Sibarević, Banja Luka 1979) 14 ♗b3 ♗f6 15 ♕h4 b6 16 ♕g3 (Petrosian-Spassky, Moscow 1971) 16 ... ♔h8! = Kotov.
  12 h4!?
  12 ♗d2 ±.
105 13 ... ♗d7 14 ♘e5 ♗c6 15 ♖a3!?/15 ♕g4 ±.
106 14 ♕e4!? ±.
  14 a5!? ± Browne-Portisch, Lone Pine 1978.

	4	5	6	7	8	9	10	11	12	
1	cd / ed	Bf4 / c6	e3[1] / Bf5	Nge2[2] / Nd7	Ng3 / Ng6	Be2 / Ngf6[3]	h4 / h5	Bf3 / Qb6	Qe2 / a5[4]	=
2	... / ...	... / ...	... / ...	g4 / Be6	h3[5] / Nd6!?	Nge2 / Ne7	Qb3 / Bc8	Bg2 / 0-0[6]		∞
3	... / ...	... / ...	... / ...	... / ...	... / Nf6	Bd3 / c5	Nf3 / Nc6	Kf1 / 0-0[7]	Kg2 / Rc8[8]	±

[1] 6 Qc2?! g6 7 0-0-0 Nf6 8 f3 Na6 9 e4 Nb4 (Korchnoi-Spassky, match 1968) 10 Qd2 =/∓.

[2] 7 Bd3 Bxd3 8 Qxd3 Nd7 9 Nf3 Ngf6 = Georgadze-Lerner, USSR Ch 1979.

[3] 9 ... Nf8? 10 h4! ±/± Portisch-Ivkov, Rio de Janeiro IZ 1979.

[4] 13 Bg5 Ba6 14 Qxa6 Rxa6 15 0-0-0 Nd6 = Bagirov-Lerner, USSR Ch ½-final 1979.

[5] 8 Bd3 Nd7 9 Nf3 h5 10 h3 Qb6 11 0-0-0 hg 12 hg Rxh1 13 Qxh1 g5 14 Bg3 Bxg4 15 Rd2 Be6 16 Qh2 0-0-0 17 Nb5!? ± Miles-Georgadze, Porz 1981/82.

   8 h4 Nd7 9 h5 Qb6! 10 Rb1 Ngf6 11 f3 h6 12 Bd3 c5 13 Nge2 Rc8 14 Kf1 0-0 15 g5 hg 16 Bxg5 ± Knaak-Geller, Moscow 1982.

[6] 11 ... Ng6?! 12 Bxd6 Qxd6 13 h4 ± Korchnoi-Spassky, match 1968.

   11 ... 0-0!? ∞.

[7] 11 ...cd 12 Nxd4 Bxd4 13 ed h5!? 14 g5 Ne4 15 Bxe4! de 16 d5 Bf5 17 Nxe4 ±.

[8] 12 ... Rc8 13 Rc1 ± Korchnoi-Karpov, match (13) 1981.

   12 ... cd 13 Nxd4 Nxd4 14 ed ± Botvinnik-Petrosian, match 1963.

   12 ... Re8!? intending ... Nd7-f8 Romanovsky.

	5	6	7	8	9	10	11	12	13	
1	Bf4 / c6[1]	Qc2[2] / Be7	Nf3 / Nbd7[3]	e3 / 0-0[4]	Bd3 / Re8	g4[5] / Nf8	h3 / Ng6	Bh2 / Bd6	Bxg6 / hg[6]	∞
2	Bg5 / c6	Qc2 / Be7	Nf3 / g6	e3 / Bf5	Bd3 / Bxd3	Qxd3 / Nbd7[7]	Bh6[8] / Ng4	Bf4 / 0-0[9]		±
3	... / ...	... / ...	e3 / Nbd7	Bd3 / Nh5[10]	Bxe7[11] / Qxe7	0-0-0[12] / Nb6	Nf3 / Ng4	Rdg1?! / Bxf3	gf / 0-0-0[13]	=
4	... / ...	... / ...	... / ...	... / Nf8	Nge2[14] / Ne6	Bh4 / g6	0-0-0 / Ng7	f3 / 0-0	g4 / Re8[15]	±
5	... / ...	... / ...	... / ...	... / 0-0	Nge2 / Re8	0-0-0 / Nf8	h3[16] / Qa5[17]	Kb1 / Be6	f4 / Rac8[18]	=
6	... / ...	... / ...	... / ...	... / ...	Nf3[19] / Re8	0-0-0 / Nf8	Rdg1[20] / Be6	g4!? / Rc8[21]	Bxf6 / Bxf6[22]	∞
7	... / ...	... / ...	... / ...	... / ...	... / ...	0-0 / Nf8	Rab1[23] / Ne4[24]	Bxe7 / Qxe7	b4 / a6[25]	=
8	... / ...	... / ...	... / ...	... / ...	... / ...	... / ...	Rae1 / Ng6[26]	Ne5 / Ng4	Bxe7 / Qxe7[27]	=
9	... / ...	... / ...	... / ...	... / ...	... / ...	... / ...	Bxf6 / Bxf6	b4 / Bg4	Nd2 / Qd6[28]	∞

[1] 5 ... Bd6 6 Ng3 c6 7 Qc2 Bxg3 8 hg g6 9 e3 Bf5 10 Bd3 Bxd3 11 Qxd3 Nbd7 12 Nge2 Qe7 = Steiner-Kotov, Venice 1950.

[2] 6 e3 Bf5 7 Nf3 Be7 8 Bd3 Bxd3 9 Qxd3 Nbd7 10 h3! 0-0 11 0-0 Re8 12 Rab1 a5 13 a3 a4! = Georgadze-Lerner, USSR 1979.

[3] 7 ... g6 8 e3 Bf5 9 Bd3 Bxd3 10 Qxd3 Nbd7 11 0-0 0-0 12 h3 Re8 13 Rab1 a5 14 Qc2 Bf8 15 a3 Nb6 16 Ne5 Nfd7 17 Nd3 Nc4 = Smyslov-Geller, match 1955.

7 ... Na6 8 a3 Nc7 9 e3 0-0 10 Bd3 Ne6 11 Be5 g6 12 0-0 Ng7 13 b4 a6 14 Bxf6 Bxf6 15 a4 Bf5 16 Bxf5 Nxf5 17 b5 ± Petrosian-Rossetto, Portorož 1958.

[4] 8 ... Bf8 9 Bd3 Ng6 (9 ... Ne6 10 Be5! g6 11 h3 0-0 12 0-0-0 Ng7 13 g4 ± Smyslov-Rossetto, Mar del Plata 1962) 10 Bg3 0-0 11 0-0 Nh5 12 Rab1 Bxg3 13 hg ± Geller-Horowitz, USSR v USA 1954.

8 ... Nh5 9 Bg3 Nf8 10 Bd3 Be6 11 0-0-0 Qa5 12 Nd2 Nxg3 13 hg 0-0-0 ± Bronstein-Keres, USSR Ch 1952.

[5] 10 0-0-0 Bf8 11 h3 a5 12 g4 a4 ∞.

10 0-0 Bf8 11 Rab1 Nh5 12 Be5 f6 13 Bg3 Be6 14 b4 Nxg3 15 hg Bf7 16 b5 c5 17 dc Bxc5 18 Na4 ± Taimanov-Holmov, Moscow 1956.

[6] 14 Ne5 c5 15 0-0-0 Be6 intending ... Qa5 ∞ Samarian.

[7] 10 ... 0-0 11 Bxf6 Bxf6 12 b4 a6 13 0-0 Be7 14 Rab1 ± Uhlmann-Donner, Havana 1964. 12 ... Qd6!?

[8] 11 h4 0-0 12 Bh6 Re8 13 h5 Ne4 14 hg hg 15 Kf1 Bf8 16 Bxf8 Rxf8 17 g3 Kg7 18 Kg2 Qe7 = Spassky-Petrosian, USSR Ch 1959.

11 0-0 0-0 12 Rab1 a5 13 a3 Re8 14 Bxf6 Nxf6 15 b4 Bd6 16 b5 c5 = Uhlmann-Portisch, Stockholm IZ 1962.

[9] Samarian.

[10] 8 ... h6 9 Nh4 0-0 10 Nge2 (10 Nf3 Re8 11 0-0 Ne4 12 Nxe4! Bxh4 13 Bh7+ Kh8 14 Bd3 Be7 15 Rab1 Bd6 16 b4 ± Cherubim-Stränger, Duisburg 1951; 15 ... a5!? Samarian) 10 ... Re8 11 f3! c5 12 0-0 a6 13 Rad1 b5 14 Bf2 c4 15 Bf5 Nb6 16 Ng3 ± Botvinnik-Larsen, Noordwijk 1965.

[11] 9 h4!? (Reshevsky) 9 ... Bxg5 10 hg Qxg5 11 Nh3 Qe7 12 0-0-0 ∞. 9 ... h6 10 Bxe7 Qxe7 11 0-0-0 ∞ Samarian.

[12] 10 Nge2 g6! intending ... f5 =. 10 ... Nf8? 11 0-0-0 g6 12 e4! de 13 Bxe4 Nf6 14 d5 ± Hasin-Chistiakov, Moscow Ch 1959.

[13] 14 Na4 Nxa4 15 Qxa4 Qb8 16 Kb1 Qh4! = Samarian.

[14] 9 Nf3 Ne6 10 Bh4 g6 11 0-0-0 0-0 12 Rab1 a5 13 a3 Ng7 14 b4 ab 15 ab Bf5 16 b5 ± Szabo-Stahlberg, Zürich C 1953.

[15] 14 Bf2 Bxg4!? 15 fg Nxg4 16 Nf4 Bg5 17 h4 ±.

[16] 11 f3 Qa5 12 h4! (12 Kb1? Ng4! ∓) Samarian.

11 Bxf6 Bxf6 12 Rdg1 Bg4 13 h3 Bxe2 14 Nxe2 Rc8 = Samarian.

[17] 11 ... Ne4 12 Bxe7 Qxe7 13 Bxe4 de 14 g4 f5 15 gf Bxf5 16 Ng3 Bg6 17 h4 h6 18 h5 Bh7 19 d5 ± Chekhover-Artsukevich, Leningrad Ch 1960.

11 ... Kh8!? 12 g4 Ng8 13 Bxe7 Nxe7 14 g5 Rc7 15 Rdg1 Bd7 16 h4 Be8 17 Ng3 Ne7 18 f4 c5 19 dc Rxc5 20 Kb1 b5 = Müller-Champetsky, corr. 1935.

[18] Antoshin-Klovan, USSR Team Ch 1964.

[19] 9 g4 (Euwe) 9 ... Re8!? 10 Bxf6 Bxf6 11 g5 Be4!?

[20] 11 h4 Be6! 12 Kb1 Rc8 13 h5 Qa5 14 Bxf6 Bxf6 15 Bf5 c5 16 Bxe6 fe 17 Nd2 Na6 18 Rhe1 Nd7 19 Qe2 Qc6 = Polugayevsky-Klovan, USSR Ch 1963.

[21] 12 ... Nxg4 13 Bxe7 Qxe7 14 Rg3 Samarian.

[22] 14 g5 Ne7 15 h4 c5 16 h5 cd 17 ed g6 18 hg fg 19 Kb1 Bb4 ∞/= Zlotnik-Panov, Kishinev 1963.

[23] 11 Ne5 Ng4! 12 Bxe7 Qxe7 13 Nxg4 Bxg4 14 Bf5 Qg5 = Flohr-Keres, Semmering 1937.

[24] 11 ... Bg4 12 Nd2! Bh5 13 Rfc1 Bg6 14 Bxg6 hg 15 Bxf6 Bxf6 16 b4 ± Pachman.

11 ... Ng6 12 b4 Bd6 13 Rfe1 (13 b5 Bd7 14 bc bc 15 Bf5 Rc8! Keres) 13 ... Bg4 14 Nh4 Bh5 15 h3 h6 16 Bxf6 Bxf6 17 Nf5 Nh4 18 Nxd6 Qxd6 19 f4 Bg6 = Gligorić-Robatsch, Beverwijk 1967.

[25] 14 a4 Ng6 (14 ... a5!?) 15 b5 ab 16 ab Nxc3 17 Qxc3 Bg4 18 Bxg6 (18 Nd2 =) 18 ... Bxf3! 19 gf hg 20 Rfc1 = Božić-Ugrinović, Yugoslavia 1970.

[26] 11 ... Ne4 12 Bxe7 Qxe7 13 Bxe4 de 14 Nd2 f5 15 f3 ef 16 Nxf3 Be6 17 e4 fe 18 Rxe4 Rad8 19 Re5 h6 20 Ne4 ± Marshall-Rubinstein, Moscow 1925. 20 ... Qc7!? Bogoljubow.

11 ... g6 12 Ne5 Ne6 13 Bh6 Ng7 14 f3 Bf5 = Keene-Csom, Palma 1971.

[27] 14 Nxg4 Bxg4 15 f3 Bd7 16 e4 Qb4 17 Ne2 ± (17 Qf2 Nf4 = Bagirov-Zilberstein, USSR Ch 1972).

[28] 13 ... Rc8 14 Bf5 Bxf5 15 Qxf5 g6 16 Qd3 Qd6 17 Rfb1 ± Reshevsky-Miagmasuren, Sousse IZ 1967.

13 ... Be7!?

13 ... Qd6 14 Rab1 Rac8 15 Bf5 Bxf5 16 Qxf5 g6 17 Qd3 a6 18 Nb3 Rc7 19 a4 Bd8! 20 b5 ab 21 ab Rxe7 22 Rfc1 Nc7 23 g3 h5 24 bc bc 25 Ne2 Qf6 26 Nd2 Qh7 27 Kg2 h4 ∞ Bagirov-Vooremaa, Riga 1968.

QGD   1 d4 d5 2 c4 e6 3 ♘c3 ♘f6 4 ♘f3

	4	5	6	7	8	9	10	11	12	
1	...	cd[1]	♗f4	♕c2[2]	e3	♗d3	0-0	h3[4]		±
	♘bd7	ed	c6	♗e7[3]	0-0	♖e8	♘f8			
2	...	a3[6]	bc	♕a4+	♕xc4	e3[8]	♗e2	0-0	♖d1	=
	♗b4[5]	♗xc3+	dc	♗d7[7]	♗c6	0-0[9]	♘bd7	♖e8	♘e4[10]	
3	...	♕a4+	♘e5[11]	♘xd7[12]	a3[14]	bc	e3	♕c2[16]	cd	=
	...	♘c6	♗d7	♕xd7[13]	♗xc3+[15]	0-0	a6	♘a5	ed[17]	
4	...	...	cd	♗g5	♗xf6[20]	e3[21]	♗e2[22]	0-0	♖ac1	=
	...	...	ed[18]	h6[19]	♕xf6	0-0	♗e6	a6	♖fc8[23]	
5	...	cd	♗g5	♗h4	♗g3	♖c1[26]	♕a4+	♘e5	♘xd7	∓
	...	ed[24]	h6	g5[25]	♘e4	h5!	♘c6	♗d7	♕xd7[27]	
6	...	...	...	♗xf6	♖c1[28]	a3	♖xc3	e3	♗e2[30]	±
	...	...	...	♕xf6	0-0	♗xc3+	c6	♗f5[29]	♘d7[31]	
7	...	♗g5	♗xf6[33]	e3	♖c1[34]	a3	♖xc3	♖xc4	♗d3	±
	...	h6[32]	♕xf6	0-0	♖d8[35]	♗xc3+[36]	dc	c6	♘d7[37]	
8	...	...	e4[38]	♗xc4	♘xd4	bc	♗xf6	0-0	f4	±
	...	dc	c5[39]	cd[40]	♗xc3+[41]	h6	♕xf6	0-0	♗d7[42]	
9	...	...	...	e5	♕a4+	0-0-0	♘e4[45]	ef	♗h4	±/∞
	...	...	...	cd[43]	♘c6	♗d7[44]	♗e7	gf	♖c8![46]	
10	...	♗f4[47]	e3	dc	♕c2[49]	♖d1	a3	♘d2	♗g5	=
	♗e7	0-0	c5[48]	♗xc5	♘c6[50]	♕a5	♗e7[51]	e5[52]	d4[53]	
11	...	...	...	...	cd	♘xd5	a3[55]	♗d3	0-0[57]	±
	...	...	...	...	♘xd5[54]	ed	♘c6	h6[56]	♗d6[58]	
12	...	...	dc	e3[59]	cd	♗e2	0-0	♗e5	♖c1	±
	...	c5	♘a6	♘xc5	ed	0-0	♗e6	♖c8	a6[60]	

[1] 5 ♗f4 dc 6 e3 ♘d5 (6 ... ♘b6 7 ♘d2± Minev) 7 ♗xc4 ♘xf4 8 ef ♘b6 (8 ... ♗e7 9 d5? ♘b6 10 ♗b5+ ♔f8! ∓ Portisch-Byrne, Biel IZ 1976; 9 ♕c2 intending 0-0-0 ± Byrne) 9 ♗d3 ♘d5 10 g3 ♗e7 =.

[2] 7 e3 ♘h5 8 ♗d3 ♘xf4 9 ef ♗d6 10 g3 0-0 11 0-0 ♖e8 ∓ Alekhine-Lasker, New York 1924. 8 ♗g5 = Kotov-Euwe, Groningen 1946.

[3] 7 ... ♘h5 8 ♗g3 ♗e7 9 e3 ± Petrosian.

[4] **11 ♖ab1** ♘h5 12 ♗e5 f6 (12 ... ♘g6? 13 h3! ♗e6 14 ♗h2 ± Benko-Taylor, New York 1976) 13 ♗g3 ♘xg3 14 hg a5 ±/=.
   11 h3!?

[5] Ragozin.

[6] 5 e3 – Nimzo-Indian, Taimanov.
   5 ♕c2 dc 6 e3 b5 7 a4 c6 8 ab cb 9 ♘d2 ♗xc3 10 ♗xc3 ♘c6 ∓ Dubinin-Savitsky, USSR Ch 1934.

[7] 7 ... ♘bd7 8 e3 0-0 9 ♕xc4 b6 10 ♗e2 ♗b7 11 0-0 c5 = Alekhine-Fox, Bradley Beach 1929.

[8] 9 ♗g5!?

[9] 9 ... ♘bd7 10 ♕b4 a5 11 ♕b1 ♘e4 12 c4 0-0 13 ♗b2 f5 14 ♗e2 ♘g5 15 ♕d1 ± Petrosian-

Uusi, USSR 1958.

[10] 13 ♗b2 ♘d6 14 ♕a2 ♗a4 = Ragozin.

[11] 6 e3 0-0 7 ♗d2 (7 ♗d3 ♕e7 8 0-0 ♗d7 9 ♕c2 dc 10 ♗xc4 e5 ∓ Model-Ragozin, USSR 1934) 7 ... ♗d7 8 ♕c2 dc 9 ♗xc4 ♗d6 10 ♘g5 e5 11 ♘d5 = Eliskases-Averbakh, Stockholm IZ 1952.

[12] 7 ♘xc6 ♗xc3+ 8 bc ♗xc6 9 ♕b3 dc 10 ♕xc4 ♘e4 11 ♗e3 0-0 12 f3 ♘d6 13 ♕d3 ♗b5 14 ♕c2 e5 ∓ Freyman-Ragozin, USSR Ch 1934/35.

[13] 7 ... ♘e4!? 8 ♗d2! ♘xd2 9 cd! ed 10 ♘e5 ± Minev.

[14] 8 e3 e5 9 de d4 10 a3 ♗xc3+ 11 bc de 12 ♗xe3 ♘g4 ∓ Spielmann-Fine, Zandvoort 1936.

[15] 8 ... ♘xd4?? 9 ab! ±± Minev.

[16] 11 ♗e2 b5 12 cb ab 13 ♕xb5 ♖fb8 14 ♕d3 ♘a5 ∞ Tolush-Sokolsky, USSR 1938.

[17] Porreca-Minev, Zagreb 1955.

[18] **6 ... ♘xd5** 7 ♗d2 ♕a5 8 ♕b3 ± Minev.
   6 ... ♘xd5 7 ♗d2 0-0 8 e3 a6 9 ♕c2 ♗d6 10 a3 ♘f6 11 ♗d3 e5 12 de ± Minev.

[19] 7 ... 0-0 8 e3 ♕d6 9 ♗xf6 ♕xf6 10 ♗e2 ♗e6

11 0-0 a6 12 ♖fd1 ♗d6 = Keres-Bronstein, Tallinn 1973.

20 8 ♘h4 0-0 9 e3 g5! 10 ♗g3 ♘e4 11 ♖c1 h5 ∞ Mikenas-Kirilov, USSR 1949.

21 9 ♘e5 0-0 10 ♘xc6 ♗xc3+ 11 bc bc 12 e3 ♕g6 13 ♕a3 ♖b8 ∓ Pavlov-Estrin, USSR 1953.

22 10 ♗b5 ♗g4 11 ♘d2 ♘xd4 12 ed ♕xd4 13 a3 ♗xc3 14 bc ♕e5+ ∞∞ Forintos-Medina, Siegen Ol 1970.

23 12 ... ♗d6 13 ♕b3 ♘e7 14 ♘a4 b6 15 ♘c3 ♖fb8 16 ♕d1 ♖d8 17 ♖e1 ± Petrosian-Antoshin, USSR Ch 1955.

12 ... ♖fc8 13 ♘e1 ♗d6 14 ♘d3 ♘e7 15 ♘c5 ♗xc5 16 dc ♖d8 = Petrosian-Averbakh, USSR Ch 1954.

24 5 ... ♕xd5 6 e3 c5 7 ♗d3 0-0 8 0-0 ♗xc3 9 bc ♘bd7 10 ♕c2 cd 11 cd b6 12 e4 ±.

25 7 ... c5 8 e3 g5 9 ♗g3 ♘e4 10 ♗b5+ ♔f8 11 dc ♘xc3 12 bc ♗xc3+ 13 ♔e2 ♗xa1 14 ♕xa1 ∞∞ Kasparov-Sosonko, Tilburg 1981.

26 9 ♘d2!? ♘xc3 10 bc ♗xc3 11 ♖c1 ∞∞ Zahariev-Cvetković, Bulgaria 1975.

27 13 f3 ♘xg3 14 hg 0-0-0 ∓ Ubilava-Bagirov, USSR 1980.

28 8 ♕b3 c5 9 e3 (9 a3!?) 9 ... 0-0 10 ♗e2 ♘c6 11 0-0 c4 = Kovalenko-Estrin, USSR 1948.

29 11 ... a5 12 ♗d3 ♗g4 13 h3 ♗h5 14 g4 ♗g6 15 ♘e5 ♗xd3 = Denker-Fischer, US Ch 1959/60.

30 12 ♕b3 ♘d7! 13 ♕xb7 ♖fb8 14 ♕xc6 ♘xc6 15 ♖xc6 ♖xb2 ∞∞.

31 13 0-0 ♕e7 14 b4 ± Suba-Nikolic, Istanbul 1980.

32 5 ... ♘bd7 6 cd ed 7 e3 c5 8 ♗d3 c4 9 ♗f5 ♕a5 10 ♕c2 ± Bogoljubow-Spielmann, Dortmund 1928.

33 6 ♘h4?! dc 7 e3 b5.

34 8 a3 ♗xc3+ = Razuvayev.
8 ♗e2 dc 9 ♗xc4 c5 10 0-0 cd 11 ed ♘c6 =.

35 8 ... c6 9 ♗d3 ♘d7 10 0-0 dc 11 ♘e4 ♕c7 12 ♖xc4 ♗a5 13 ♗b1 ± Averbakh-Andersson, Palma de Mallorca 1972.

36 9 ... ♗f8 10 cd ed 11 ♘b5 ± Razuvayev.

37 Razuvayev-Lerner, USSR Ch 1980.

38 6 e3? b5 7 a4 c6 8 ♗e2 ♘bd7 9 0-0 ♕b6 ∓ Thomas-Eliskases, Noordwijk 1938.

39 6 ... b5 7 e5 h6 8 ♗h4 g5 9 ♘xg5 hg 10 ♗xg5 ♘bd7 11 ♕f3 ± Hansen-van Scheltinga, Aalborg 1948.

40 7 ... ♕a5 8 ♗xf6 ♗xc3+ 9 bc ♕xc3+ 10 ♘d2 gf 11 dc! ♘d7 12 0-0 ± Christoffel-Burghold, Montreux 1939.

41 8 ... ♕a5 9 ♗xf6 gf 10 0-0 ♗d7 11 ♖c1 ♘c6 12 a3 ♗xc3 13 ♖xc3 ♕e5 14 ♘b5 ± Podgorny-Barcza, Karlovy Vary 1948.
8 ... ♕c7 9 ♕b3 ♗c5 10 ♗xf6 gf 11 0-0! ♕xd4 12 ♕xb4 ± Averbakh.

42 13 e5 ♕e7 14 ♖b1 ± Gipslis.

43 7 ... h6 8 ef hg 9 fg ♖g8 10 dc ± Gipslis.

44 9 ... h6 10 ef hg 11 fg ♖g8 12 ♘xd4 ♗d7 13 ♘e4 ± Vidmar-Bogoljubow, Nottingham 1936.

45 10 ef gf 11 ♘xd4 ♗xc3 12 bc fg 13 ♕xc4 ♕f6 ∓ Budo-Levenfish, USSR Ch 1937.

46 12 ... ♘a5 13 ♕c2 e5 14 ♘xd4 ed 15 ♖xd4 ♘c6 16 ♖xd7 ♕xd7 17 ♗xf6+ ♗xf6 18 ♗xf6 ♖g8 19 ♗xc4 ± Neishtadt.
12 ... ♖c8! 13 ♔b1 ♘a5 14 ♕c2 e5 15 ♘xd4 ed 16 ♖xd4 ♕b6 ∞.

47 5 ♗g5 – Orthodox Defence.

48 6 ... b6 7 cd ed 8 ♗d3 ♗b7 9 h3 c5 10 0-0 ♘bd7 11 ♖c1!? (11 ♕e2 c4 12 ♗c2 a6 ∓ Korchnoi-Petrosian, match 1980) intending 12 dc bc 13 ♕e2 ± Stean.

49 8 a3 dc 9 ♗xc4 ♕xd1+ 10 ♖xd1 a6 11 ♗d3 ♘bd7 12 ♘e5 b5 = Gipslis-Marović, Zagreb 1965.

50 8 ... dc 9 ♗xc4 ♘bd7 10 0-0 ♘h5 11 ♗g5 ± Minev.

51 10 ... ♖e8 11 ♘d2 e5 12 ♗g5 ♘d4 13 ♕b1 ♗f5 14 ♗d3 e4 15 ♗c2 ± Korchnoi-Karpov, match 1978.

52 11 ... ♗d7 12 ♗e2 ♖fc8 13 0-0 ♕d8 14 cd ed 15 ♘f3 ± Karpov-Spassky, Montreal 1979.

53 13 ♘b3 and now:
13 ... ♕b6?! 14 ♗xf6 ♗xf6 15 ♘d5 ♕d8 16 ♗d3 g6 17 ed ♘xd4 18 ♘xd4 ed 19 ♘xf6+ ♕xf6 20 0-0 ♗e6 21 ♖fe1 ± Korchnoi-Karpov, match 1978. 21 f4!? intending f5. 21 ♗e4!? intending ♖d2.
13 ... ♕d8! 14 ♗e2 a5! (14 ... h6 15 ♗xf6 ♗xf6 16 0-0 ♗e6 17 ♘c5 ± Korchnoi-Karpov, match 1978) 15 ed (15 0-0 a4 16 ♘c1 ♗e6 ∓ Farago-Geller, Novi Sad 1979) 15 ... a4 16 ♘xa4 ♘xd4 17 ♘xd4 ed ∞∞ Portisch-Belyavsky, Moscow 1981 and Korchnoi-Karpov, match (11) 1981.

54 8 ... ed 9 ♗e2 ♘c6 10 0-0 ♗e6 11 ♖c1 ♖c8 12 a3 h6 13 ♗g3 ♗b6 14 ♘e5 ± Fischer-Spassky, match 1972.
8 ... ♕a5 9 ♗d3 (9 de ± Farago) 9 ... ♘xd5 10 0-0 ♘xc3 11 bc ♗e7 12 ♕c2 ± Farago-Zaitsev, Sochi 1980.

55 10 ♗d3 ♗b4+ 11 ♔e2 ♗d6 = Smyslov-Belyavsky, Moscow 1981. 11 ... ♗g4!? Speelman.

56 11 ... ♗e6?? 12 ♗xh7+ ±±.
11 ... ♗d6!?
11 ... ♕e7!?

57 12 ♗c2!? intending ♕d3 ± Farago.

58 13 ♕a4 ♗xf4 14 ♕xf4 ± Farago-Grünfeld, Malta Ol 1980.

59 7 ♗d6 ♘xc5 8 ♗xe7 ♕xe7 9 cd ed 10 e3 ± Portisch-Bobotsov, Amsterdam 1971.

60 13 h3 b5 14 ♗d3? d4 ∓ Petrosian-Spassky, match 1969. 14 ♘d4 ±.

	4	5	6	7	8	9	10	11	12	
1	... ♘bd7	♘f3 ♗b4[1]	cd ed	e3[2] c5	♗d3 c4[3]	♗c2 ♕a5	0-0 ♗xc3	bc ♕xc3[4]	♕b1 0-0[5]	±
2	... ...	... ...	... ...	... ...	... ...	♗f5 ♕a5	0-0 ♗xc3	bc ♘e4[6]	♕c2 ♘xg5[7]	±
3	... ...	... c6	♕c2[8] dc	e4 b5	e5 h6	♗h4 g5	♘xg5 hg	♗xg5[9] ♗b7![10]		∞
4	... ...	e3 c6	♕c2[11] ♕a5	cd[12] ♘xd5	e4 ♘xc3	♗d2 ♕a4	♕xc3 a5	♘f3 ♗b4	♕c1 0-0[13]	=
5	... ...	... ...	♘f3 ♕a5[14]	♗xf6 ♘xf6	♗d3 ♗b4[15]	♕b3 dc	♗xc4 0-0	0-0 ♗xc3	bc b6[16]	∞
6	... ...	... ...	... ...	cd ♘xd5	♕d2[17] ♘7b6[18]	♗d3 ♘xc3	bc ♘d5	♖c1 ♘xc3	0-0 ♗b4[19]	∞
7	... ...	... ...	... ...	♘d2 dc[20]	♗xf6 ♘xf6	♘xc4 ♕c7	♗e2[21] ♗e7	a3 ♘d5	♖c1 0-0[22]	±
8	... ...	... ...	... ...	... ♗b4	♕c2 0-0	♗h4 c5[23]	♘b3 ♕a4	♗xf6 ♘xf6	dc ♗xc3+	=
9	... ...	... ...	... ...	... ...	... ...	♗e2 e5	de ♘e4	♘dxe4 de	0-0 ♗xc3[24]	∞
10	... ...	... ...	... ...	... ...	... ...	... ...	♗xf6 ♘xf6	de ♘e4	cd ♘xc3[25]	±
11	... ...	... ...	... ...	... ...	... ...	... ...	0-0 ♗xc3[26]	bc ♘e4	♘xe4 de[27]	±
12	... c5[28]	cd ♕b6	de cd[29]	ef+ ♔xf7	♘a4 ♕a5+[30]	♗d2 ♗b4!	♕b3+ ♘d5	♗xb4 ♕xb4+	♕xb4 ♘xb4[31]	∞
13	... ...	... ...	♗xf6! ♕xb2	♖c1![32] gf	e3 cd	ed ♗b4	♗b5+ ♗d7	♗xd7+ ♘xd7	♘ge2[33]	±
14	... ...	... cd	♕xd4[34] ♗e7	e4 ♘c6	♕d2 ♘xe4[35]	♘xe4 ed	♗xe7 ♕xe7	♕xd5 0-0[36]	f3 ♘b4[37]	±

[1] Manhattan Variation.

[2] 7 ♕a4 ♗xc3+ 8 bc 0-0 9 e3 c5 10 ♗d3 c4 11 ♗c2 ± Capablanca-Spielmann, New York 1927.

[3] 8 ... ♕a5 9 0-0 ♗xc3 10 bc ♕xc3 11 ♖c1 ♕a5 12 dc ♘xc5 13 ♗xf6 gf 14 ♘d4 ∞∞.

8 ... 0-0 9 0-0 ♗xc3 10 bc c4 11 ♗c2 ♕a5 (Alekhine-Vidmar, New York 1927) 12 ♘e5! ±.

[4] 11 ... ♘e4 12 ♗h4! ♘df6 13 ♘e5 ♗e6 14 f3! ± Euwe.

[5] 13 e4 de 14 ♗d2 ♕a3 15 ♗b4 ♕a6 16 ♗xf8 ef (Maroczy-Tenner, New York 1927) 17 ♗b4! ± Euwe.

[6] 11 ... ♕xc3? 12 ♗xf6 gf 13 ♕a4 intending 14 ♖fc1 ± Euwe.

[7] 13 ♘xg5 h6 14 ♘h3 0-0 15 f3 ± Euwe.

[8] 6 ♕b3 ♗e7 7 e3 0-0 8 ♗e2 a6 9 0-0 b5 10 cd cd 11 ♖fc1 ♗b7 = Portisch-Larsen, Linares 1981.

6 e4 de 7 ♘xe4 ♗e7 8 ♘c3 0-0 9 ♕c2 e5! 10 0-0-0 ed 11 ♘xd4 ♕a5 = Alekhine-Lunden, Orebro 1935.

[9] Kotov-Troitsky, USSR 1938.

[10] Euwe.

[11] 6 ♗d3 ♕a5 (6 ... ♗e7 – QGD Orthodox) 7 ♗h4 dc 8 ♗xc4 b5 = Capablanca-Alekhine, match 1927.

6 a3 ♗e7 7 ♘f3 ♘e4 8 ♗xe7 ♕xe7 9 ♕c2 (9 ♗xe4 de 10 ♘d2 f5 = Euwe-Bogoljubow, match 1941) 9 ... ♘xc3 10 ♕xc3 0-0 = Pirc-Rabar, Yugoslav Ch 1946.

[12] 7 ♗h4 ♗b4 8 ♗d3 dc! 9 ♗xc4 0-0 10 ♘e2 e5 = Euwe/van der Sterren.

[13] Capablanca-Alekhine, match 1927.

[14] Cambridge Springs Variation.

[15] 8 ... ♗e7 9 0-0-0-0 10 e4 de 11 ♘xe4 ±.

[16] 13 ♘e5 ♗b7 14 ♘xf7!? (14 ♗e2 c5! = Capablanca-Ed.Lasker, New York 1924) 14 ... ♔xf7 (14 ... ♖xf7 15 ♗xe6 ♖f8 16 f3 ± Euwe/van der Sterren) 15 ♗xe6+ ♔g6 16 e4 ∞∞.

[17] 8 ♕b3 ♗b4 9 ♖c1 e5 10 ♗c4 (10 e4 ♘xc3 11 bc ♗a3 12 ♖d1 ed 13 ♖xd4 ♗c5 14 ♖d2 0-0 ∓ Marshall-Rubinstein, Berlin 1928) 10 ... ♘7b6 (10 ... ed 11 ♗xd5 cd 12 ed 0-0 13 0-0 ♘b6 = Euwe/van der Sterren) 11 ♗xd5 ♘xd5 12 ♘xe5 ♗e6 = Euwe and Weenink v Alekhine and van den Bosch, Amsterdam 1931.

[18] 8 ... ♗b4 9 ♖c1 0-0 (9 ... h6 10 ♗h4 0-0

11 ♗c4 ♘7b6! Euwe/van der Sterren; 11 e4!) 10 e4 ♘xc3 11 bc ♗a3 12 ♖b1 e5 13 ♗d3 ♖e8 (13 ...ed 14 cd ♕xd2+ 15 ♘xd2 ♘b6 16 ♘c4? ♘xc4 17 ♗xc4 ♖e8 ∓ Trifunović-Bergkvist, Dubrovnik 1950; 16 0-0 ♗e6 17 ♘b3 ±) 14 0-0 b6! 15 ♕e2! ∞∞ Euwe/van der Sterren.

[19] 13 a3!? ♕xa3 14 ♖a1 ♕b3 ∞∞ Alekhine-Euwe, match 1935.

[20] Rubinstein Variation.

[21] 10 g3 c5 11 ♗g2 cd 12 ♕xd4 ♗d7 = van der Sterren-Flear, London 1980.

[22] 13 0-0 ♗d7 14 b4 ♖fc8 15 ♕b3 ♕d8 16 ♖fd1 ♗e8 ± Timman-Hort, Amsterdam 1980.

[23] 9 ... e5 10 de ♘e4 11 ♘dxe4 de 12 e6 ♘e5! 13 ef+ ♖xf7 14 0-0-0 ♗f5 (Neistadt) 15 a3 ♘d3+ 16 ♔b1 ♗xc3 17 ♕xc3 ♕xc3 18 bc ♖e8 19 ♗xd3 ed 20 ♔c1 ±.

[24] 13 bc f6 14 ♗h4 ♕xe5 15 ♗g3 ♕e7 16 ♖fd1 ♖e8 ∞∞.

[25] 12 ... ♗f5?! 13 ♘dxe4 ♗xe4 14 ♗d3 ♗xg2 15 ♖g1 ♗xd5 16 ♗xh7+ ♔h8 17 ♗d3 ± Euwe/van der Sterren.

12 ... ♘xc3! 13 bc ♗xc3 14 ♖ac1 ±/= Bukić-Nikolac, Yugoslavia 1976.

[26] 10 ... ed 11 ♘b3 ♕c7 (11 ... ♕b6!? Keene-Yusupov, England v USSR Telex match 1982) 12 ♘xd4 dc 13 ♗xc4 ± Sämisch-Kashdan, Frankfurt 1930.

10 ... ♗d6 11 ♘b3 ♕c7 12 cd ed 13 ♘xd4 ♘xd5 14 ♘xd5 ±/= Neistadt.

[27] 13 ♕xe4 (13 ♗e7!?) ± Taylor-Nikolac, Eerbeek 1978.

[28] Dutch-Peruvian Gambit.

[29] 6 ... ♕xb2 7 ♗d2! cd 8 ♖b1 ♕a3 9 ♘b5 ±.

6 ... ♗xe6? 7 d5 ♕xb2 8 ♘a4 ±±.

[30] 8 ... ♗b4+! 9 ♗d2 ♗xd2+ 10 ♕xd2 ♕b5 11 b3 ♘c6 12 ♘f3 ♖e8! ∞∞ Borisenko.

[31] 13 ♖c1! ∞∞ Grechkin-Matsukevich, corr. 1965.

[32] 7 ♕c1!? ♕xc1+ 8 ♖xc1 gf ∞∞ S.Garcia-Kavalek, Wijk aan Zee 1972.

[33] Spassky-Uitumen, Sochi 1966.

[34] 6 ♕a4+!? ♘bd7! 7 ♗xf6 ♕xf6 8 ♘b5 ♘b6! ∓ Evans-Prins, Helsinki Ol 1952.

[35] 8 ... ♘xd5!? 9 ed ♗xg5 10 f4 ♗h4+ 11 g3 ed 12 gh ♕xh4+ 13 ♔f2 ♕e7+ 14 ♕e2 ♗e6 ∞∞.

[36] 11 ... f5 12 ♗b5! ±/±.

[37] 13 ♕c4! ♗e6 14 ♕c5! ±/± Korchnoi.

| QGD: Orthodox | 1 d4 d5 2 c4 e6 3 Nc3 Nf6 4 Bg5 Be7 5 e3 0-0 6 Nf3 Nbd7 |

	7	8	9	10	11	12	13	14	15	
1	Qc2[1]	0-0-0[2]	Kb1!	Bxc4	Bxf6	Ne5[4]				±
	c5	Qa5	dc	h6![3]	Nxf6					
2	...	h4[5]	0-0-0	g4	Bxc4	Be2	Bxf6	Qe4!	Rhg1[7]	±
	h6	c5	Qa5	dc[6]	Nb6	Bd7	gf	Bd6		
3	Rc1	cd[8]	Bxe7	Be2	0-0	dc	b4	Nxe4	Qa4[9]	±
	c5	Nxd5	Nxe7	b6	Bb7	Nxc5	Ne4	Bxe4		
4	...	Bd3[10]	Bxc4	Bxe7	0-0[12]	Rxc3	de[13]	Nxe5	f4	=
	c6	dc[11]	Nd5	Qxe7	Nxc3	e5	Nxe5	Qxe5	Qe4[14]	
5	...	cd	Bd3	0-0	Qc2[15]	Ne5[16]	Bxe7	Nxg4		=
	a6	ed	c6	Re8	Nf8	Ng4	Qxe7	Bxg4[17]		
6	...	c5	Bd3[18]	de	Bf4	Bb1	ef[20]			=
	...	c6	e5![19]	Ne8	Nxc5	f5				

[1]   7 Bd3 (Botvinnik) 7 ... dc 8 Bxc4 c5 9 0-0 a6 10 a4 (Litvinov-Balashov, USSR 1972) 10 ... cd 11 ed b6 = Petrosian.
   7 Qb3 c6 8 Be2 (Alekhine-Bogoljubow, match 1934) 8 ... b6 9 0-0 Bb7 =.

[2]   8 Rd1 Qa5 9 Bd3 h6 10 Bh4 dc 11 Bxc4 Nb6 12 Be2 cd 13 ed Bd7 ±/= Samarian.

[3]   10 ... a6 11 h4! b5 12 Bd3 Bb7 13 Bxh7+ Kh8 14 Ne5 ± Pachman-Tsvetkov, Sofia 1949.

[4]   Samarian.

[5]   8 Bxf6 Bxf6 9 0-0-0!? Samarian.

[6]   10 ... hg 11 hg Ne4 12 Nxe4 de 13 Qxe4 g6 14 Ne5 ± Chudova-Kogan, USSR 1951.

[7]   Hasin-Diaconescu, corr. 1969/70.

[8]   8 dc Qa5!

[9]   Geller-Larsen, match 1965.

[10]   8 a3 a6 9 Qc2 b5 10 cd cd 11 Na2 Ne8 12 Qc6 Rb8 = Ornstein-Hurme 1978.
   8 Qc2 Ne4! 9 Bxe7 Qxe7 10 Nxe4 de 11 Qxe4 Qb4+ Alekhine-van den Bosch, Amsterdam 1936.

[11]   8 ... a6 and now:
   9 a4 dc 10 Bxc4 Nd5 11 Bxe7 Qxe7 12 0-0 Nxc3 13 bc b5 =.
   9 0-0!? dc 10 Bxc4 b5 11 Bd3 = Gligorić-Bobotsov, Praia da Rocha 1969.

[12]   11 Ne4 (Alekhine) 11 ... N5f6 12 Nxf6+ Qxf6 13 0-0 e5 14 e4 ed 15 Qxd4 Qxd4 16 Nxd4 ± Petrosian-Portisch, USA 1966.

[13]   13 Qc2 ed 14 ed Nb6! 15 Re1 Qd8! 16 Bb3 Nd5 17 Bxd5 Qxd5 18 Rc5 Qd8! 19 Ng5 g6 20 Qe4 h6 = Guil.Garcia-Ree, Wijk aan Zee 1979.
   13 Re1 e4 14 Nd2 Nf6 15 Qb1 Bf5 = Schuster.

[14]   16 Bd3 Qxe3+ 17 Kh1 Qe7 18 f5 Qf6! ∓.
   16 Bb3 Bf5 17 Qh5 g6 18 Qh6 Rad8! = Schuster.

[15]   11 Bb1!? Nf8 12 Ne5 (Uhlmann-Csom, Amsterdam 1970) 12 ... Nfd7 = Samarian.

[16]   12 Na4!? Ng6 13 Nd2 Bd6 14 g3 Bh3 15 Rfe1 h6! = Gligorić-Bisguier, Hastings 1961/62.

[17]   Pfleger-Jakobsen, BRD v Denmark 1978.

[18]   9 b4 a5 10 a3 ab 11 ab b6 12 Bf4 (12 Bd3 Ba6! 13 0-0 Bxd3 14 Qxd3 Ne8! =) 12 ... bc 13 bc Ra3! ∓ Alekhine-Henneberger, Berne 1925.

[19]   9 ... b6?! 10 cb Qxb6 11 0-0! ± Hort-Portisch, Madrid 1974.

[20]   Gligorić-Marović, Yugoslavia 1977.

1 d4 d5 2 c4 e6 3 ♘c3 ♘f6 4 ♗g5 ♗e7 5 ♘f3 0-0

	6	7	8	9	10	11	12	13	14	
1	♖c1	♗h4	cd	♘xd5	♗xe7	g3	♗g2[3]	♘e5	♖xc7	∓
	h6	b6[1]	♘xd5	ed	♕xe7	♖e8[2]	♗a6	♘d7!	♖ac8![4]	

1 d4 d5 2 c4 e6 3 ♘c3 ♘f6 4 ♗g5 ♗e7 5 e3 0-0

	6	7	8	9	10	11	12	13	14	
2	♖c1	♗h4	♗xf6	cd	♕f3[6]	♗c4!	♗b3	♘ge2	♘f4	±
	h6[5]	b6	♗xf6	ed	♗e6	c6	♕d7	♘a6	♖ae8[7]	
3	...	...	cd	♘xd5	♗xe7	♗e2[9]	♗f3[11]	♘e2	0-0	∞
	...	...	♘xd5[8]	ed	♕xe7	c5[10]	♖d8[12]	♘c6	♗a6[13]	
4	♘f3	♗xf6	♗d3	cd	h4?![14]	♗xh7+	♘g5+	♕c2	h5[15]	∓
	b6	♗xf6	♗b7	ed	c5	♔xh7	♔h6	g6	♔xg5![16]	
5	...	cd	♖c1	♘e5	♗xe7	♗d3[19]				±
	...	ed[17]	♗e6	♘fd7[18]	♕xe7					

[1]   7 ... dc 8 e3 (8 e4!? ♘c6 ∞) 8 ... c5 9 ♗xc4 cd 10 ed ♘c6 11 0-0 ♘h5 12 ♗xe7 ♘xe7 = Korchnoi-Karpov, match (9) 1981.

[2]   **11 ... ♗b7!?** 12 ♗g2 c5 13 0-0 c4! 14 ♘e5 b5 15 b3 ♘d7 = Hort-Spassky, Göteborg 1971.

11 ... ♗e6?! 12 ♗g2 c5 13 ♘e5! ±.

[3]   12 ♖c3!? ♘a6 13 ♕a4 b5! 14 ♕a5 ♕e4 15 ♔d2 ♗e6 16 b3 b4 17 ♖e3 ♕b1 ∓ Seirawan-Karpov, TV World Cup 1982.

[4]   **15 ♖xd7?** ♕b4+ 16 ♔f1 ♕xd4! ∓∓.

15 ♖xc8 ♖xc8 16 0-0 ♘xe5 17 de ♕xe5 = Uhlmann-Veresov, East Germany v Byelorussia 1970.

[5]   6 ... b6 7 cd ed 8 ♗d3 ♗e6 9 ♘ge2! c5 10 ♘f4 ♘bd7 11 0-0 h6 12 ♗xe6 fe 13 ♗f4 ± Euwe-Denker, New York 1948/49.

[6]   10 g3!? ♗e7 11 ♗g2 c6 12 ♘ge2 ♘d7 13 0-0 ♘f6 14 ♗f4 ♗d6 15 ♘ce2 ± Korchnoi-Cirić-Wijk aan Zee 1968.

[7]   15 0-0 ± Bronstein-Geller, Amsterdam C 1956.

[8]   8 ... ed 9 ♗d3 ♗b7 10 f3 c5 11 ♘ge2 ♘bd7 12 0-0 ♖e8 13 ♗f2 ♗d6 14 ♖e1 ± Botvinnik-Pilnik, Budapest 1952.

[9]   **11 g3** ♗f5 12 ♗g2 ♗e4 13 ♗xe4 de 14 ♘e2 (Korchnoi-Petrosian, USSR Ch 1958) 14 ... ♖d8! intending ...c5 = Samarian.

11 ♘e2 ♖d8 12 ♘f4 c5 13 ♗e2 ♗b7 14 0-0 ♘d7 15 ♕a4 ♘f6 16 ♕a3 ±/ ± Taimanov-Geller, Kislovodsk 1966.

[10]   **11 ... ♕b4+** 12 ♕d2 ♕xd2+ 13 ♔xd2 c6 14 ♘f3 ♗b7 15 ♘e5 ♖c8 16 b4 ± Najdorf-Pilnik, Mar del Plata 1955.

11 ... ♗e6 12 ♗f3 c5 13 ♘e2 ♘d7 14 0-0 c4

[11]   12 dc bc 13 ♕xd5!? ♗b7 14 ♕xc5 ♕xc5 15 ♖xc5 ♗xg2 16 ♗f3 ♗xh1 17 ♗xh1 ♘d7 18 ♖c7 ∞/± Neistadt.

[12]   12 ... ♗b7 13 ♘e2 c4 14 b3 b5 15 ♘c3 ♕d7 16 bc bc 17 0-0 ♖e8 18 ♖b1 ♗c6 19 ♕c1 intending ♕a3 ± Euwe-Minev, Amsterdam 1954.

[13]   15 ♖e1 ∞ Samarian.

[14]   10 ♕c2! h6 11 h4 c5 12 0-0-0 ♘c6 13 g4 cd 14 ed ♕d6 15 ♔b1 ± Taimanov-Petrosian, USSR Team Ch 1959.   15 ... ♕f4 ± Taimanov (15 ... ♘b4? 16 ♕d2 ♘xd3 17 ♕xd3 intending g5 ±).

[15]   Spielmann-Rubinstein, Vienna 1923. 14 ... ♔g7 15 hg ♗xg5 16 ♖h7+ ♔f6 16 0-0-0 c4 ∞.

[16]   Spassky.

15 hg ♗g7! intending ... ♔f6 ∓.

15 f4+ ♔h6 16 hg+ ♔g7 17 ♖h7+ ♔g8 18 0-0-0 ♗g7 19 ♖dh1 ♘f6 20 gf+ ♖xf7 21 g4 cd?! (21 ... ♘d7! ∓ Spassky) 22 g5 ♕f5 23 ♖xg7+ (23 ♕h2!? Samarian) 23 ... ♔xg7 24 ♕h2 ♖f8 25 g6 ♕xg6! 26 ♖g1 dc! 27 ♖xg6+ ♔xg6 ∓∓ Teschner-Spassky, Riga 1959.

[17]   7 ... ♘xd5 8 ♗xe7 ♕xe7 9 ♖c1 (9 ♘xd5 ed 10 ♗e2 ♗e6 11 ♕b3 c5 12 ♕a3 ± Mecking-Donner, Lugano Ol 1968) 9 ... ♗b7 10 ♗d3 c5 11 ♘xd5 ed 12 dc bc 13 ♕c2 ♘d7 14 ♗xh7+ ♔h8 15 ♗f5 d4 16 ♕e2! intending 16 ... de 17 0-0 ef+ 18 ♕xf2 ± Samarian.

[18]   9 ... c5! intending 10 ♗e2 ♘e4 or 10 ♗d3 ♘fd7.

[19]   Gligorić-Petrosian, Skopje Ol 1972.

	6	7	8	9	10	11	12	13	14	
6	Nf3	Bh4	Rc1[20]	cd[21]	Bxe7	Nxd5	Bd3!	0-0	dc	=
	h6	b6	Bb7	Nxd5	Qxe7	Bxd5	Rc8	c5	Rxc5[22]	
7	...	...	Qc2	Bxf6[24]	cd	0-0-0	dc[26]	c6[27]	Nd4	=
	...	...	Bb7[23]	Bxf6	ed	c5![25]	Nd7!	Bxc6	Bb7[28]	
8	...	...	cd	Bxe7	Nxd5[30]	Rc1	Qa4	Qa3	Bb5[33]	=
	...	...	Nxd5[29]	Qxe7	ed	Be6[31]	c5[32]	Rc8		
9	...	...	...	...	...	Bd3	Rc1	dc	0-0	±
	...	...	...	...	...	Be6[34]	c5	bc	Nd7[35]	
10	...	...	Bxe7	cd[36]	bc	Qb3	c4	Bxc4	Qc3[39]	∞
	...	Ne4	Qxe7	Nxc3	ed	Rd8[37]	dc[38]	Nc6	Bg4[40]	
11	...	...	...	Qc2	Nxe4[41]	Qxe4	Nd2	Rb1[42]	Bd3	∞̄
	...	...	...	c6!?	de	Qb4+	Qxb2	Qxa2	f5[43]	
12	...	...	...	...	Qxc3	Bd3[44]	Bxc4	0-0	e4	±/=
	...	...	...	Nxc3	c6	dc	Nd7	b6	Bb7[45]	
13	...	Bxf6	Qc2[46]	0-0-0[47]	ed	h4	Kb1![49]			∞
	...	Bxf6	c5!	cd	Nc6!	Qc7[48]				
14	...	...	Qd2	dc[51]	Bxc4	Ne4	Rd1	b4	a3	=
	...	...	c5!?[50]	dc	Nd7	Be7	Qc7	a5	ab	
15	...	...	Rc1	Bd3	cd	b4	b5	Rc2	0-0	∞
	...	...	c6	Nd7	ed![52]	Be7	Ba3	Nf6	Bd6[53]	
16	...	...	cd	b4	a3	Be2	0-0	a4	b5	±
	...	...	ed	Nc6[54]	a6	Re8	Ne7	Be6		

[20] **8 Bd3 Bb7** 9 0-0 c5 10 Rc1 Nbd7 11 Qe2 Rc8 12 Bg3 cd 13 ed dc 14 Bxc4 ± Karpov-Geller, Moscow 1981.
8 Qb3 Bb7 9 Bxf6 Bxf6 10 cd ed 11 Rd1 Re8 12 Bd3 c5 13 dc Nd7! 14 c6 Bxc6 15 0-0 Nc5 = Polugayevsky-Tal, Alma Ata 1980.
8 Be2 Bb7 9 Bxf6 Bxf6 10 cd ed 11 0-0 c5 12 dc Bxc3 13 bc bc 14 Rb1 ± Kasparov-Torre, Moscow 1981.

[21] 9 Bxf6 Bxf6 10 cd ed 11 b4 c6 12 Be2 Nd7 13 0-0 ±/= Korchnoi-Spassky, match 1977.

[22] 15 Rxc5 Qxc5 16 Qa4! Nc6! (16 ... Bc6?! 17 Qf4 Nd7 18 b4 Qf8! 19 Ba6 ± Gligorić-Kurajica, Hastings 1971/72) 17 e4 Nb4 18 ed Nxd3 19 de fe 20 b3 Rd8 21 Qg4 Qd5 = Uhlmann-Spassky, Solingen 1974.

[23] 8 ... c5 9 dc! bc 10 Rd1 Qa5 11 Be2 Nc6 12 0-0 Nb4 13 Qb1 Ba6 14 Ne5! ± Simagin-Golovko, Moscow Ch 1950.

[24] 9 0-0-0!? Nbd7 10 Rg1 c5 11 Be2 Ne4

[25] 11 ... Nc6!? 12 a3 Na5 13 h4 c5! 14 g4 cd 15 Nxd4 Nc6 ∞ Borisenko-Lein, USSR Ch 1967.

[26] 12 g4 cd 13 ed Nc6 14 h4 g6 15 h5! (15 g5 hg 16 h5 Kg7 17 hg fg 18 Bb5 g4 ∓ Uhlmann-Spassky, Moscow 1967) 15 ... Kg7 16 hg fg 17 Bg2 Rc8 18 Kb1 ± Mikenas-Liberzon, USSR Ch 1970.

[27] 13 Nxd5?! Nxc5! 14 Bc4 b5 15 Nxf6+ Qxf6 16 Bd5 Rac8 ∞ Kasparov-Zaitsev, Baku 1980.
13 cb?! Qxb6 ∞̄.

[28] 19 Be2 =.

[29] 8 ... ed 9 Bd3 Bb7 (9 ... Be6 10 0-0 Nbd7 11 Rc1 c5 12 Bb1 Rc8 13 Ne5 ± Sanguinetti-Michel, Buenos Aires 1945) 10 0-0 Nbd7 11 Rc1 c5 12 Bf5 Re8 13 Qc2 Nf8 14 Ne5 ± Olafsson-Petrosian, Candidates' 1959.

Tolush-Korchnoi, USSR Ch 1957. [under footnote 24]

30 10 Rc1 Bb7 11 Be2 Nf6 12 0-0 Nbd7 13 Qa4 c5 14 Rfd1 Rfd8 15 Qa3 Qf8 = Najdorf-Petrosian, Göteborg IZ 1955.

31 **11 ... Rd8!?** (Gligorić) 12 Qa4 Bb7 13 Be2 c5 14 Qa3 Nd7 15 0-0 a6 16 Rfd1 Rdc8 17 Ne1 Qg5! = Marcović-Pirc, Ljubljana 1947.
  11 ... Bb7 12 Qa4 c5 13 Qa3 Rc8 14 Bd3! Nd7 15 Bf5 Rc7 16 Bxd7 Qxd7 17 0-0 ± Neistadt.

32 **12 ... Rc8!?** 13 Bd3 (13 Be2 c5 14 Qa3 a5 15 0-0 Qa7! 16 dc bc 17 Rc3 Nd7 18 Rfc1 Rcb8 19 Ne1 a4 20 Nd3 c4 = Szily-Marović, Beverwijk 1967) 13 ... c5 14 dc bc 15 0-0 Nd7 (15 ... a5! Samarian) ∞.

33 **14 ... a6?!** 15 dc bc 16 0-0 Ra7 17 Be2 Nd7 18 Nd4 Qf8? 19 Nxe6 fe 20 e4! ± Fischer-Spassky, match 1972.
  14 ... Qb7!? 15 dc bc 16 Rxc5 Rxc5 17 Qxc5 Na6! 18 Qxa6 Rxa6 19 Qa3 Qc4 20 Qc3 (20 Nd2 Qg4 21 Rg1 d4! ∓ Timman-Geller, Hilversum 1973) 20 ... Qxa2 (20 ... Rb8!? Samarian) 21 0-0 = Szabo-Kavalek, Amsterdam 1973.

34 **11 ... Qg4!?** 12 0-0 Nd7 13 h3 Bxf3 14 Qxf3 Nf6 15 Rfe1 ± Kopayev-Perfiliev, USSR corr. Ch 1948.

35 15 e4! ± de 16 Bxe4 Rab8 17 b3 Rfc8 18 Re1 Qf6 19 Bb1 g6 20 Nd2 Rb4 21 Ne4 Qg7 22 Qd6 ± Florian-Gligorić, Yugoslavia v Hungary 1947.

36 9 Rc1 c6 10 Bd3 Nxc3 11 Rxc3 dc 12 Rxc4 Nd7 =.
  9 Nxe4 de 10 Nd2 f5 11 Rc1 (11 c5!? e5 12 Qb3+ Kh8 13 Nc4 ed 14 ed Nc6 15 0-0-0 ∞ Spassky-Lutikov, USSR Ch 1961; 15 ... b6!?; 15 ... Rb8!? Samarian) 11 ... Nd7 12 Qc2 c6 13 c5 e5! = Bogoljubow-Eliskases, match 1939.

37 **11 ... c6** 12 Rb1!? Nd7 13 Bd3 Nf6 14 a4 ± Neistadt.
  11 ... Qd6 12 c4 dc 13 Bxc4 Nc6 14 Be2 Be6 15 Qc3 Rb4 16 Kd2! Qd6 17 Rfc1 Bd5 18 Ne1 Rfe8 19 Kf1 Re7 20 Kg1 ± Pachman-Donner, Beverwijk 1965.

38 **12 ... Be6?!** 13 Qxb7 (13 c5 b6 14 Ne5 ± Fine) 13 ... dc 14 Qxa8 Qa3 (14 ... Qb4+ 15 Nd2 c3 16 Bd3 Bd5! 17 Qxa7 Nc6! 18 Qc5 Qxc5 19 dc Bxg2 20 Rg1! Rxd3 21 Rxg2 Rxd2 22 Rc1 Ne5 23 Rxc3 ±± Neistadt) 15 Rb1 Bd5 16 Qxd5 Rxd5 17 Rxb8+ Kh7 18 Rb1 ±.
  12 ... Nc6 13 dc Na5!? 14 Qc3 b6! 15 Bd3 Bb7 16 0-0 Bxd5 ∞ Samarian.

39 14 Be2 Rd6! 15 0-0 Be6 16 Qc3 (16 Qxb7? Rb8 intending 17 Nxd4 ∓) 16 ... Rd5 17 Rfc1 Re8 18 Ne1 f5 ∓ Korelov-Holmov, USSR Ch 1962.

40 15 0-0 Bxf3! 16 gf Qf6 17 Be2 Rd6 18 Kh1 Re8 19 Rae1 (Stahlberg-Piazini, Buenos Aires Ol 1939) 19 ... Qh4! =.

41 10 Bd3 Nxc3 11 Qxc3 dc - row 12.

42 13 Qb1 Qc3! 14 Qc1 Qxc1+ 15 Rxc1 Nd7 = Trifunović-Najdorf, match 1949.

43 15 Qh4! Qa3 16 Ke2 Qd6 17 g4 c5 18 dc Qxc5 19 Rhg1 ∞ Samarian.

44 11 cd ed 12 Bd3 intending 0-0, b4, b5 etc Samarian.

45 15 Rfe1 and now:
  15 ... c5 16 d5 ed 17 ed Qf6! 18 Qxf6 Nxf6 = Schwarz.
  15 ... Rfe8 16 Rad1 c5 17 Bb5! Red8 18 d5 ± Geller-Krogius, USSR Ch 1971.
  15 ... Rac8? 16 Rad1 Rfd8 17 b4 c5! (Radev-Hinkov, Bulgaria 1968) 18 dc bc 19 b5 ±.

46 8 Qb3 dc 9 Bxc4 c5 10 dc Nd7 11 Ne4 Nxc5 12 Nxf6+ Qxf6 13 Qc2 b6 14 0-0 Bb7 15 Nd4 Rac8 16 Qe2 e5 17 Nb3 b5! ∓ Réti-Tartakower, Hastings 1926/27.

47 9 dc Qa5 10 Be2! dc 11 0-0 Bxc3! 12 Qxc3 Qxc3 13 bc Nd7 14 c6 bc 15 Rfd1 Nb6 16 Ne5 Bb7 17 Nxc4 Ba6! = Winter-Bondarevsky, England v USSR 1947.

48 **11 ... dc** 12 Bxc4 Nxd4 13 Qe4 e5 14 Nxe5 Bf5 15 Nxf7! Rxf7 16 Bxf7+ Kxf7 17 Rxd4 ± Samarian.
  11 ... Qa5!? Müller.

49 **12 ... Qf4** 13 Ne2! Qe4 14 Qxe4 de 15 Nd2 Bxd4 16 Nxd4 Nxd4 17 Nxe4 e5 = Tal-Krogius, USSR Ch 1956.
  12 ... Rd8!? 13 c5 b6! 14 Nb5 Qb8 15 Nd6 (15 cb Qxb6 16 g4 e5! ∓ Shianovsky-Bannik, Leningrad 1956) 15 ... bc 16 dc Qb4 17 a3 Qa5 18 g4 (Ivkov-Guimard, Buenos Aires 1955) 18 ... Rxd6!? 19 cd Qb8 ∞ Samarian.

50 **8 ... b6** 9 cd ed 10 Be2 (10 Rd1 Be6 11 g3 Nd7 12 Bg2 Be7 13 0-0 c6 14 Qc2 Rc8 15 Ne5 ± Petrosian-Spassky, match 1969) 10 ... Bb7 11 0-0-0 Qe7 12 h4 Nd7 13 g4 g6 14 g5 hg 15 hg Bxg5 16 Rdg1 intending Bd3, e4 ± Jimenez-Ostojić, Havana 1965.
  8 ... Nc6 9 Rc1 a6 (9 ... dc 10 Bxc4 e5 11 d5 Ne7 12 Ne4 Nf5 13 Bb3! ±/±) 10 Be2 g6 11 0-0 Bg7 12 Rfd1 ± Polugayevsky-Belyavsky, USSR 1982.

51 9 cd cd 10 Nxd4 ed 11 Bb5! ±.

52 10 ... cd 11 0-0 b6 12 Qe2 a6 13 e4 Bb7 14 e5! Be7 15 Nd2 Re8 16 f4 Nf8 17 Qh5 Bb4 18 Rf3 f5 19 g4! ± Bobotsov-Kurajica, Wijk aan Zee 1970.

53 15 bc bc 16 e4!? de 17 Nxe4 Re8!? (17 ... Bc7!? ∞ Yusupov-Georgadze, USSR 1979) 18 Re1 Nxe4 19 Rxe4 Bd7 = Lputian-Grigorian, Erevan 1980.

54 **9 ... Re8** 10 Be2 Be7 11 Qb3 c6 12 0-0 Bd6 13 b5 Nd7 14 Rfc1 Nf6 15 bc bc 16 Na4 ± Holmov-Klovsky, USSR 1966.
  9 ... c6!? Samarian.

Tarrasch and Semi-Tarrasch

Tarrasch

This was once the focus for turbulent arguments between its inventor Siegbert Tarrasch and the rest of the chess world. Modern chess 'technology' is better placed to understand the dynamics of this defence. Voluntarily accepting an isolated d-pawn as well as granting White the ideal blockading square d4, Black receives excellent piece activity and open files as compensation. Revived and revamped by Keres, Spassky, Gligorić and Nunn, its most dedicated adherent is now Marjanović. Theory now gives White the nod, and if he is well prepared he can keep the upper hand because of Black's permanent liability, the isolated d-pawn. The mechanics of overcoming Black's energetic counterplay and nurturing this theoretical plus is a complex task and a study of Ulf Andersson's virtuoso handling of the White position is well worth while.

It should be noted here that the main-line positions of the Tarrasch and Semi-Tarrasch often arise from the English, Réti and Catalan Openings.

The **von Hennig-Schara Gambit** is a lively bit of speculation. Black offers a pawn in return for quick development and the opportunity to castle long, guaranteeing an aggressive game and open combat. White should be able to keep his pawn and, correspondingly, the advantage, though he must be careful.

In the **Swedish Variation**, characterised by an early ... c4, Black avoids the tribulations of an isolated d-pawn and hopes to generate a healthy queenside initiative. Its drawback is the unwieldy pawn structure and Black must tread very carefully to insure that a well-timed e4 break for White does not shatter his position. White is for choice but once again matters are far from simple.

The **Rubinstein Variation** is the Main Line and the crux of the Tarrasch argument. White's deployment is absolutely logical, the fianchettoed bishop bringing pressure to bear on Black's weak d-pawn. Black may fall just short of equality but his position is both active and extremely playable.

Semi-Tarrasch

In the Semi-Tarrasch Black captures on d5 with his king's knight, so avoiding the isolated queen's pawn. White gets an enduring initiative but Black has ample opportunity to pull level. His position is quite solid and he need not fear a kingside onslaught by White provided that the centre does not fall into enemy hands.

	4	5	6	7	8	9	10	11	12	
1	♘f3	♘xd4	♘db5	♘d5	e4!	♕a4	♗g5	♗xf6	b4[1]	±
	cd	e5	d4	♘a6	♘f6	♗d7	♗e7	gf		
2	...	♗g5[2]	♘xd4[3]	♘f3[4]	♘d5	♗xf6	e4	♘xe3		=
	♘f6	cd	e5!	d4	♗e7	♗xf6	de	♕xd1+		
3	e3	♘f3	cd	♗e2[7]	♘xd4	0-0				=
	♘f6	♘c6[5]	ed[6]	cd!	♗d6	0-0				

1 d4 d5 2 c4 e6 3 ♘c3 c5 4 e3 ♘f6 5 ♘f3 ♘c6

	6	7	8	9	10	11	12	13	14	
4	dc[8]	a3	♗e2	cd	bc	a4	♗a3	♗xc5		=
	♗xc5	a5[9]	♘e4	♘xc3	ed	♗f5	♕e7	♕xc5[10]		
5	a3	dc	b4	♗b2	cd	♘b5	♗e2	ba	0-0	±
	♗e7[11]	♗xc5	♗d6	0-0	ed	♗b8	a5[12]	♘xa5	♖a6[13]	
6	...	dc	b4	♗b2	♕c2	♗e2	♗xc4	♗d3	0-0	=
	a6	♗xc5[14]	♗a7	0-0	♕e7	dc	b5	♗b7	♖ac8[15]	
7	...	...	...	cd	♗b2	♗e2	0-0	♖c1	♘a4	∞
	...	...	♗d6	ed	0-0	♗e6	♖c8[16]	♕e7	♘e4[17]	
8	...	ed	♗d3[18]	♗xc4	0-0	♗e3[19]	♗d3	♕e2	♖ad1	=
	cd	♗e7	dc	0-0	a6	b5	♗b7	♖c8	♕c7[20]	
9	...	...	♗d3	bc	♗xc4	0-0[21]	♕d3	♗f4	♖fe1	=
	...	♘e4	♘xc3	dc	♗e7	0-0	b6	♗b7	♖c8[22]	

[1] Collijn.
[2] Pillsbury Variation.
[3] 6 ♕xd4 ♗e7 (6 ... ♘c6 7 ♗xf6! gf 8 ♕h4 dc 9 ♖d1 ♗d7 10 e3 ♗e7! =; 10 ... ♘e5 11 ♘xe5 fe 12 ♕xc4 ± Pillsbury-Lasker, Cambridge Springs 1904) 7 cd ed 8 e3 ♘c6 9 ♗b5 0-0 10 ♕a4 ♘e4! 11 ♘xe4 de 12 ♗xc6 bc 13 ♗xe7 ♕xe7 = Donner-Euwe, Beverwijk 1950.
[4] 7 ♘db5 a6! 8 ♕a4 (8 ♘xd5 ab! 9 ♘xf6+ ♕xf6! ∓∓ Fine-Yudovich, Moscow 1937) 8 ... ♗d7 9 cd ♗c5 ∓ Samarian. 9 ... ♕b6 ∓.
[5] 5 ... cd 6 ed – Caro-Kann, Panov.
[6] 6 ... ♘xd5 – Semi-Tarrasch.
[7] 7 ♗b5 a6 8 ♗xc6+ bc 9 0-0 ♗d6 10 ♕a4 ♕c7 11 e4 ±/± Kasparov-Agzamov, USSR Ch 1981. 7 ... ♗d6! =.
[8] 6 ♗d3 dc 7 ♗xc4 cd 8 ed ♗e7 9 0-0 0-0 10 ♖e1 b6 11 a3 ♗b7 12 ♗a2 ♕d6 13 ♗e3 ♖ac8 = Langeweg-Sosonko, Wijk aan Zee 1975.
[9] 7 ... 0-0 8 b4 ♗d6 9 ♗b2 ♕e7 10 ♗e2 ♖d8 = van Scheltinga-Langeweg, Beverwijk 1962.
[10] Langeweg-Hort, Amsterdam 1970.
[11] 6 ... dc 7 ♗xc4 a6 8 ♗d3 cd 9 ed ♗e7 10 0-0 0-0 11 ♗c2 b6 12 ♖e1 ♖a7 13 ♕d3 ♖d7 14 ♗e3 ♗b7 15 ♖ad1 ± Vaganian-Bronstein, USSR Ch 1973.
    6 ... ♘e4 7 ♗d3 (7 ♕c2!? Algeo) 7 ... ♘xc3 8 bc ♗e7 9 0-0 dc 10 ♗xc4 0-0 11 ♕e2 ♗d7 12 ♗b2 ♖c8 13 e4 ♕c7 14 ♗d3 e5 15 d5 ♘a5 16 c4 ± Vasyukov-Zhuravlev, USSR 1974.
[12] 12 ... ♗e6 13 0-0 ♕e7!? Parma.
[13] 15 ♗e5! ± Botvinnik-Tal, match 1960.
[14] 7 ... dc 8 ♕xd8+ ♖xd8 9 ♗xc4 ♗xc5 10 b4 ♗a7 11 0-0 ♗d7 12 ♗b2 ♖c8 13 ♗d3 ♘c6 14 ♖fd1 ♗b8 15 ♘a4 ± Vidmar-Mieses, Carlsbad 1907.
[15] 15 ♕e2 = Benko-Lombardy, USA 1969.
[16] 12 ... ♕e7 13 ♕d2 ♖ad8 14 ♖fd1 ♗b8 15 b5 ab 16 ♘xb5 ♘e4 ∞ Holmov-Suetin, USSR 1956.
[17] 15 ♕d3 ♖fd8 16 ♘c5 ∞ Dzhindzhihashvili-Mašić, Tbilisi 1970.
[18] 8 c5 ♘e4 9 ♕c2 f5 (9 ... ♘xc3 10 ♕xc3 a5 11 ♗b5 0-0 =) 10 ♗b5 0-0 11 0-0 g5 12 ♗xc6 bc 13 ♘e5 ♗f6 (Ivkov-Fischer, Zagreb 1970) 14 f4 =.
[19] 11 ♗g5 b5 12 ♗a2 b4 13 ab ♘xb4 14 ♗b1 ♗b7 ∓ Sveshnikov.
    11 ♗a2 ♕d6 12 h3 ♖d8 13 ♗e3 b5 = Anikayev-Sveshnikov, USSR Ch 1979.
    11 b4 b5 12 ♗b3 ♗b7∓ Abramov-Ravinsky, USSR 1958.
[20] Rashkovsky-Sveshnikov, USSR 1975.
[21] 11 ♗d3 0-0 12 ♕e2 ♘f6 13 0-0 g6 14 ♗f4 b6 = Rodriguez-Nunn, Amsterdam 1975.
[22] 15 ♖e3 ♘a5 16 ♗a2 ♗d5 ∓ Pavlenko-Liberzon, USSR 1966.
    15 ♗a2 = Parma.

	4	5	6	7	8	9	10	11	12	
				Tarrasch	1 d4 d5 2 c4 e6 3 ♘c3 c5 4 cd					
1	...	♕a4+[2]	♕xd4	♕xd5[3]	♘f3[4]	♕b3				∞
	cd!?[1]	♗d7	ed	♘c6	♘f6	♗b4[5]				
2	...	...	...	...	...	♕d1	e3	♗e2[7]	♘d4	∞
	...	...	...	...	...	♗c5[6]	♕e7	g5	0-0-0[8]	
3	...	e4	d5	♗f4	♗b5+	♘h3	♗c4	a4	♕d2	∓
	ed	de	f5[9]	♗d6	♔f7	♘f6	a6	♖e8	♕e7[10]	
4	...	dc	♗e3	♘f3	♘d2	♘b3	fe	♕xd5	♕e4	∞
	...	♘f6[11]	♘c6	♕a5	♘g4	♘xe3	♕d8	♗e6	♗e7[12]	
5	...	♘f3	♗g5[14]	♗xe7	e3	♘xd4	♘b3	♗d3		=
	...	♘c6[13]	♗e7	♘gxe7	cd	♕b6	♗e6	0-0		
6	...	...	g3[15]	♗g2[17]	0-0	♘e5	♘xc6	♘a4[18]	b3	±
	...	...	c4[16]	♗b4	♘ge7	0-0	bc	♘f5	♖e8[19]	
7	...	...	...	...	...	e4	ed	♗g5	♘xd5	±
	...	...	...	...	...	0-0[20]	♘xd5	♗e7[21]	♗xg5[22]	
8	...	...	...	♗g2	♗e3![23]	0-0	♘xd4	♕a4	♖ad1	±/=
	...	...	♘f6	♗g4	♗e7	cd	0-0	♕d7	♗h3[24]	

	9	10	11	12	13	14	15	16	17	
		1 d4 d5 2 c4 e6 3 ♘c3 c5 4 cd ed 5 ♘f3 ♘c6 6 g3 ♘f6 7 ♗g2 ♗e7 8 0-0 0-0[25]									
9	dc[26]	♘a4	♗f4	♖c1	a3	b4	♖b1!	♕xb1	♖d1![28]	±
	d4	♗f5[27]	♗e4	♕d5	♘a5	♘b3	♗xb1	d3		
10	...	♗g5[29]	♗xf6	♘d5[30]	♘d2	♖c1	♘b3	♘c5	♕a4	±
	♗xc5	d4	♕xf6	♕d8	♖e8[31]	♗d6	♗e5	♖b8	♗d6[32]	
11	...	...	...	...	h3[33]	♘f4	♘xe6	♕b3		±
	...	...	...	...	♗g4!?	♗e6	♗b6!	fe	♕e7[34]	
12	b3	♗b2	♘a4	♖c1	♘xd4	♗xd4	e3	♖e1		±
	♘e4[35]	♗f6	♖e8	cd	♘xd4![36]	♗f5	♕e7[37]	h6[38]		
13	♗e3	♖c1[40]	♘e5	de	ef	♕a4[41]				±
	♗g4[39]	♖c8	♘xe5	d4	♗f6					
14	...	♗f4	dc	e3[42]	h3	♖c1[43]	♗e5	♘xe5		∞
	♘g4!?	♗e6	♗xc5	h6	♘f6	g5!	♘xe5	♗b6[44]		
15	♗g5	♘e5	f4![46]	fe![47]	♗xe7	bc	e4	a4	♕h5	±
	c4[45]	♗e6	♘xe5	♘e4	♘xc3	♕xe7	♕d7	♖fd8	♖ac8[48]	
16	...	dc	♗xf6	♘xd5	♘c7	♕c1	♖axc1	♘xe6	e3[50]	∞
	♗e6	♗xc5	♕xf6	♕xb2	♖ad8	♕xc1	b6[49]	fe	h6[51]	

1 von Hennig-Schara Gambit.
2 5 ♕xd4 ♘c6 6 ♕d1 ed 7 ♕xd5 ♗e6?! 8 ♕xd8+ ♖xd8 9 e3 ♘b4 10 ♗b5+ ♗e7 11 ♔f1! ♘f6 12 ♘f3 ♘c2 13 ♖b1 ♗f5 14 ♗d2 ± Smyslov-Estrin, USSR 1951. 7 ... ♗d7! – 5 ♕a4+.
3 7 ♘xd5?! ♘c6 8 ♕d1 ♘f6 9 ♗xf6+ ♕xf6 ∓.

4 8 ♗g5 ♘f6 9 ♕d2 h6 10 ♗h4 g5 11 ♗g3 ♕a5 12 e3 0-0-0 13 ♘b5 ♕xd2+ 14 ♔xd2 ♗g4+ ∞ Taimanov-Zagorovsky, USSR 1949.
5 Intending ... ♗e6 ∞.
6 9 ... ♗b4 10 ♗d2 0-0 11 e3 ±.
7 11 ♗b5!? 0-0-0 12 ♕e2 g5 13 ♗d2 g4 14 ♘d4 ♗xd4 15 ed ♕d6 16 0-0-0 ± Clément-Villup,

corr. 1971. 11 ... 0-0! =.

[8] 13 0-0 g4 14 b4! ∞ (14 ♗b5 ♘xd4! ∓) 14 ... ♗xb4 (14 ... ♘xb4 15 ♗a3! ±) 15 ♗b2 (Polugayevsky-A.Zaitsev, USSR 1969) 15 ... ♖hg8! intending ... ♘e5-f3, ... ♗d6, ... ♕e5.

[9] 6 ... ♘f6 7 ♗g5 ♗e7 8 ♗b5+ ♗f8 9 ♘ge2 a6 10 ♗a4 b5 11 ♗c2 ♗b7 12 0-0 h6 13 ♗h4 b4 = Bronstein-Aronin, Moscow 1962.

[10] 13 0-0-0 ♗g8 14 ♘g5 ♘bd7 15 ♘e6 (Starck-Baumbach, Colditz 1967) 15 ... b5! 16 ab ♘b6 ∓ Euwe.

[11] 5 ... d4 6 ♘a4 b5 7 cb ab 8 b3 ♘f6 9 e3 ♗d7 10 ♕xd4 ♘c6 11 ♕b2 ♘e4 12 a3 b5 13 ♗d3 ♕a5+ 14 ♔e2 ♗f5 15 ♕b1 ± Haberditz.

[12] 13 ♘d4 0-0!? ∞ Euwe.

[13] 5 ... ♘f6 6 ♗g5 ♗e6 7 ♗xf6 ♕xf6 8 e4! de 9 ♗b5+ ♗d7 10 ♘xe4 ♕b6 11 ♕xd7+ ♔xd7 12 0-0 ± Alekhine-Kusman, New York 1924.

[14] 6 ♗f4 ♘f6 7 e3 cd 8 ♗xd4 ♗b4 9 ♘xc6 bc 10 ♕a4 ♕b6 = Hort-Espig, Tallinn 1975.

6 e3 – Symmetrical.

[15] Schlechter-Rubinstein Variation.

[16] Swedish Variation.

[17] 7 e4 de 8 ♗g5 ♕xd4! 9 ♗e3 ♕xd1+ 10 ♖xd1 h6 11 ♘d5 ♗b4+ 12 ♔xb4 ♘xb4 13 ♖xe4 ♘c2+ 14 ♔d2 ♘xe3 = A.Zaitsev-Mikenas, USSR Ch 1962.

[18] 11 e4 de 12 ♗xe4 ♗xc3 13 bc ♗d5 14 ♕c2 f5 15 ♗g2 ♗e6 16 ♖e1 ♕d6 17 ♕e2 ♖ae8 18 ♖xc4 f4 19 ♗e4 fg 20 hg h5 ∞ Golombek-Stoltz, Marianske Lazne 1947.

[19] 13 bc ♗a6 14 ♖b1 ♗f8 15 ♖e1 ♗c4 16 a3 ± Smyslov-Barcza, Bucharest 1953.

[20] 9 ... de 10 ♘xe4 0-0 11 ♕c2 ♕d5 12 ♗e3 ♘g6 13 ♘h4 ♕b5 14 ♘xg6 hg 15 a3 ♗e7 16 d5 ♘a5 17 d6 ± Reshevsky-Stahlberg, Zürich C 1953.

[21] 11 ... f6!? 12 ♘xd5! ♕xd5 13 ♗e3! ± Adorjan-Tisdall, New York 1981.

[22] 13 ♘xg5 ♕xg5 14 ♗e3! ± Euwe.

[23] 8 ♗g5 ♗xf3 9 ♗xf3 ♘xd4 10 ♗xd5 ♗e7 11 ♗xf6 ♗xf6 12 ♕a4+! b5! 13 ♘xb5 0-0! 14 ♗xa8 ♕xa8 15 0-0-0 ♘xb5 16 ♕xb5 ♖b8 17 ♕d3 ♖xb2 ∞ Gutman-Karasev, Leningrad 1978.

8 ♘e5 ♗e6! 9 ♘xc6 bc 10 0-0 cd 11 ♕xd4 ♗e7 12 e4 0-0 13 ed ♘xd5! 14 ♘xd5 cd 15 ♗f4 ♗f6 16 ♗e5 ♗xe5 17 ♕xe5 ♕b6! 18 b3 ♖ac8 = Krogius.

[24] 13 ♗xh3! ♕xh3 14 ♘f3 ±/=.

[25] 8 ... ♗e6? 9 dc ♗xc5 10 ♘a4 ♗e7 11 ♗e3 0-0 12 ♖c1 ±.

[26] 9 ♗f4!? ♗g4 (9 ... ♗f5!?; 9 ... ♗e6!?) 10 dc ♗xc5 11 ♘e5 ♗e6 12 ♘a4 ♗d6 13 ♘xc6 bc 14 ♗xd6 ♕xd6 15 ♕d4! ± Moiseev-Malevinsky, USSR 1979.

9 a3 ♗e6 10 dc ♗xc5 11 b4 ♗e7 12 ♗b2 ♖c8 = Rubinstein-Tarrasch, Teplitz-Schönau 1922.

[27] 10 ... h6!? intending ... ♗c8-g4xf3/♘h7-g5.

[28] Black's whole position hangs.

[29] 10 ♘a4 ♗e7 11 ♗e3 ♗g4 12 ♘d4 ♕d7 13 ♘xc6 bc = Tatai-Rajković, Italy 1972.

[30] 12 ♘e4 ♗e7 13 ♘xc5 ♕xc5 14 ♖c1 ♕b6 15 ♕d2 ♗g4 16 ♘g5 ♖ad8 = Ivkov.

[31] 13 ... a6 14 ♖c1 ♗a7 15 ♘c4 ♖b8 16 ♘f4 b5 17 ♘d6 ♗xd6 18 ♖xc6 ♕d8 19 ♕c2 ± Kasparov-Gavrikov, USSR Ch 1981/82.

13 ... ♗h3 14 ♗xh3 ♕xd5 15 ♗g2 ±.

[32] 18 ♖fe1 ±/= Timman-Ivkov, Geneva 1977.

[33] 14 ♘f4 ♖e8 15 ♘f3 ♕d6 16 ♖c1 ♗b6 = Leski-Cvitan, Groningen 1980/81.

[34] 18 ♗e4! ± Kuligowski.

[35] 9 ... ♗g4 10 dc! ♗xc5 11 ♗b2 ♖c8 12 h3 ♗e6 13 e3 ♕e7 14 ♗e2 ± Uhlmann-Espig, Halle 1981.

9 ... ♖e8 10 ♗b2 ♗g4 11 dc ♗xc5 12 ♘a4 (12 ♖c1!?) 12 ... ♗f8 13 h3 ♗f5 14 ♖c1 ♘e4 15 ♘d4 ♗d7 16 ♘c3 ±/= Mikenas-Malevinsky, USSR 1979.

[36] 13 ... ♗d7 14 e3!? ♖c8 15 ♖e1 ♕a5?! 16 ♘xc6 ♗xc6 17 ♗xe4! ♗xb2 18 ♖c5! ♕b4 19 ♗f5 ♖cd8 20 ♖xc6 bc 21 ♘xb2 ± Spiridonov-Marjanović, Puma 1978.

[37] 15 ... ♕d7!?

[38] Uhlmann-Marjanović, Sarajevo 1980. White intends ♘b2-d3-f4, a3, b4 ±/=.

[39] 9 ... c4?! 10 ♘e5 ♗e6 11 ♘xc4 dc 12 d5 ♘xd5 13 ♗xd5 ♘f6 14 ♗xf6+ ♕xf6 15 ♗xc6! bc 16 ♕d4 ± Miles-Petursson, Reykjavik 1980.

9 ... cd 10 ♘xd4 ±.

[40] 10 h3!? ♗xf3 11 ♗xf3 ♕d7 12 dc ♖ad8 13 ♗d4 ± Miles-Fernandez, Las Palmas 1980.

[41] Euwe.

[42] 12 ♘e1 ♗d4 13 ♘d3 (13 ♘c2?! ♗xc3 14 bc ♕a5 ∞) 13 ... ♘f6 14 ♖c1 h6 15 ♘a4 ♘e4 Flohr-Lasker, Moscow 1935.

12 ♕c2 h6 13 ♖ad1 ♖ad8 = Larsen-Sarapu, Sousse IZ 1967.

[43] 14 g4!? Taimanov.

[44] Taimanov.

[45] 9 ... ♗g4 10 dc d4 11 ♘a4 ±.

9 ... ♗f5 10 ♖c1 h6 11 ♗xf6 ♗xf6 12 dc d4 13 ♘b5 ±.

[46] 11 ♘xc6 ∞.

[47] 12 de d4 13 ef gf 14 ♗h6 dc 15 bc ♕b6+ 16 e3! ♕xe3+ 17 ♔h1 ∞/±.

[48] 18 ♖f4 ♗c7 19 ♖af1 ± Kasparov-Hjorth, Dortmund 1980.

[49] 15 ... ♗b6?! 16 ♘xe6 fe 17 ♖c4 h6 18 ♖e4 ♖fe8 19 e3 ♖d6 20 h4 ♗d8 21 ♖b1 ± Lein-Farago, Moscow v Budapest 1971.

15 ... ♗e7!? 16 ♘xe6 fe 17 ♖c4 ♗f6 18 ♖b1 ♖d6! 19 h4 h6 = Ornstein-L.Schneider, Eksjö 1981.

[50] 17 ♗h3 ♖f6! = Euwe/van der Sterren.

[51] 18 ♖c4 ♖f6 ∞ Knaak-Espig, GDR Ch 1980.

	9	10	11	12	13	14	15	16	17	
17	♗g5	♘xd4	♗e3	♕a4[53]	♖ad1	♗c1	♕b5!	♗f4![54]		±
	cd	h6[52]	♗g4	♘a5	♘c4	♕c8	♘b6			
18	...	...		♕a4	♖ad1	♕b3![55]	♕c2	♕b1![56]		±
	...	...	♖e8	♗d7	♗f8	♘a5	♖c8			
19	...	...	...	♖c1	♕c2	h3	♖fd1	♘xc6	♗xa7[59]	±
	...	...	...	♗f8	♗g4	♗h5[57]	♖c8[58]	bc		

52 10 ... ♖e8!?
53 12 h3 ♗e6 13 ♖c1 ♕d7 14 ♘xe6 fe 15 ♕b3 ♖f7 =/∓ Antoshin-Palatnik, USSR 1981.
54 Kasparov-Palatnik, Moscow 1981.
55 14 ♘xd5!? ♘xd5 15 ♗xd5 ♘b4 16 ♗xf7+

♔xf7 17 ♕b3+ ∞ Stean-Gligorić, Skara 1980.
56 16 ♕d3?! ♗g4 = Polugayevsky-Gligorić, Bugojno 1980.
57 14 ... ♗e6!?
58 Ftacnik-Ekström, Prague 1979.
59 Ftacnik.

Semi-Tarrasch   1 d4 d5 2 c4 e6 3 ♘c3 ♘f6 4 ♘f3 c5 5 cd ♘xd5[1]

	6	7	8	9	10	11	12	13	14	
1	g3	♗g2	0-0	e4	a3	ab	bc	♗f4	♕b3	=
	♘c6	♗e7	0-0	♘db4[2]	cd	dc	b6	♗b7	♕c8[3]	
2	...	...	...	♘xd5	dc	♗g5[4]	♖c1	♗d2	♕b3	=
	...	...	...	ed	♗xc5	f6	♗b6	♗g4	♔h8[5]	
3	...	...	...	...	...	♕c2	♘g5	♕d1	♕b3	=
	...	...	...	...	...	♗b6	g6	♗d4!	♗f6![6]	
4	e4	bc	cd	♗c4	♗e2	♗d2	d5	ed	0-0	±
	♘xc3	cd	♘c6	b5[7]	♗b4+	♕a5	ed	♘e7	♗xd2[8]	

1 d4 d5 2 c4 e6 3 ♘c3 ♘f6 4 ♘f3 c5 5 cd ♘xd5
6 e4 ♘xc3 7 bc cd 8 cd ♗b4+ 9 ♗d2 ♗xd2+ 10 ♕xd2 0-0[9]

	11	12	13	14	15	16	17	18	19	
5	♗c4	0-0	a4[10]	♖fe1	♗d3	a5	♖xa5	♖a4[12]		±
	♘d7	b6	♗b7	♖c8	♘b8	ba[11]	♘c6			
6	...	0-0	♖ad1[14]	♖fe1	d5	ed	♘e5!	♘c6!	dc	±
	♘c6	b6[13]	♗b7	♘e7?!	ed	♘f5	♘d6	♗xc6?	♘c4[15]	
7	...	...	...		d5	♗d3	e5[17]	♕f4	♗h7+	∞
	...	...	...	♖c8	♘a5	♕d6!?[16]	♕xd5	h6	♔xh7	

1 d4 d5 2 c4 e6 3 ♘c3 ♘f6 4 ♘f3 c5 5 cd ♘xd5 6 e3 ♘c6

	7	8	9	10	11	12	13	14	15	
8	♗c4	♗xd5	dc	0-0	b3	♗b2	♘a4	♘d4[18]		±/=
	♗e7	ed	♗e6	♗xc5	0-0	a6	♗a7			
9	...	ed	0-0	bc	♗d3	♕c2	♗h6	h4		±
	cd[19]	♗e7	♘xc3	0-0	b6	g6	♖e8	♗f6[20]		

1 d4 d5 2 c4 e6 3 ♘c3 ♘f6 4 ♘f3 c5 5 cd ♘xd5
6 e3 ♘c6 7 ♗c4 cd 8 ed ♗e7 9 0-0 0-0 10 ♖e1

	10	11	12	13	14	15	16	17	18
10	... ♗f6[21]	♘e4 b6	a3 ♗b7	♕d3 ♖c8	♘fg5 ♗xg5	♗xg5 f6	♗d2 ♕d7	♖ad1 ♘ce7[22]	=
11	... a6	♗d3 ♘cb4[23]	♗b1 b5	♘e4 ♘f6	a3 ♘bd5	♘c5 ♕b6	♕c2 a5[24]	∞	
12	... ♘xc3	bc b6	♗d3 ♗b7	h4![25] ♗xh4[26]	♘xh4 ♕xh4	♖e3[27]	±		

1 d4 d5 2 c4 e6 3 ♘c3 ♘f6 4 ♘f3 c5 5 cd ♘xd5 6 e3 ♘c6 7 ♗d3

	7	8	9	10	11	12	13	14	15
13	... ♗e7	0-0 0-0	a3[28] b6	♕c2[29] g6	b4 ♘xc3	♕xc3 ♗d7	dc ♗f6	♘d4 bc	bc ♘xd4[30]	∞∞

[1] 5 ... cd!? 6 ♕xd4 ed (6 ... ♘xd5 7 e4 ♘xc3 8 ♕xc3 ♘c6 9 ♗b5 ♗d7 10 ♗d2 ♗b4 11 ♕e3±) 7 e4! ♘c6 (7 ... de? 8 ♕xd8+ ♔xd8 9 ♘g5 ♗e6 10 ♘xe6+ ± Bisguier-Hearst, US Ch 1954) 8 ♗b5 a6 (8 ... ♘xe4 9 0-0 ±; 8 ... ♗d7 9 ♗xc6 ♗xc6 10 ed ♗xd5 11 ♘e5 ±, intending ♕a4+) 9 ♗xc6+ (9 ed ab 10 dc bc 11 ♕xd8+ ♔xd8 12 ♘e5 b4 13 ♘e2 ♔e8 14 ♘d4 ♘d5 = Vuković/van der Tak) 9 ... bc 10 ♘e5 ♗b7 11 ed ♘xd5 (11 ... ♗e7 12 ♕f4! cd 13 ♕a4+ ±) 12 0-0 ♗e7 13 ♘xc6! ♗xc6 14 ♕xg7 ♖f8 15 ♖e1 ♕d6 (Najdorf-Keres, Zürich C 1953) 16 ♘xd5! ♕xd5 17 ♗f4! ♖d8 (17 ... 0-0-0 18 ♖xe7 ♖g8 19 ♖c7+ ±±) 18 ♗h6! ♔d7 19 ♖ad1 ♖g8 20 ♖xd5+ ♗xd5 21 ♖xe7+! ±± Benkö-Klüger, Budapest 1955.

[2] 9 ... ♘xc3 10 bc cd 11 cd b6 12 ♗b2 (12 ♗e3 ♗b7 13 ♖c1 ♘a5?! 14 ♗d3 ♖c8 15 ♖xc8 ♕xc8 16 ♖c1 ♕a8 17 d5! ± Quinteros-Tringov, Bar 1977) 12 ... ♗f6 13 ♕e2 ♗b7 14 ♖fd1 ± Gulko-Grigorian, USSR Ch 1977.

[3] 15 ♖fd1 ♖d8 16 ♘d4 a6 = Polugayevsky-Radulov, Skara 1980.

[4] 11 b3 ♗f5 12 ♗b2 ♗e4 13 ♖c1 ♕e7 14 ♕d2 f6 15 ♖fd1 ♖fd8 16 e3 ♖ac8 = Vukić-Raičević, Yugoslav Ch 1978.
   11 a3 a5 (11 ... ♗f5 12 b4 ♗b6 13 ♖a2 ♗e4 14 ♖d2 ♕e7 15 ♗b2 ± Portisch-Spassky, Bugojno 1978) 12 ♘e1 ♗e6 13 ♘d3 ♗d6 14 ♗f4 ♗e7 15 ♖c1 ♕b6 = Mednis/Peters.

[5] 15 e3 d4 16 ed ♗xf3 17 ♕xf3 ♘xd4 = Portisch-Keres, San Antonio 1972.

[6] 15 ♗xd5 ♘d4 16 ♗h1 ♘xe2 17 ♗e3 (17 ♕xd8 ♖axd8 18 ♘e4 ♘xc1! 19 ♘xf6+ ♗g7 20 ♘h5+ gh! = Miles) 17 ... ♕xd5 18 ♗xd5 ♗xb2 = Miles-Tarjan, Riga IZ 1979.

[7] 9 ... ♗b4+ 10 ♗d2 ♗xd2+! - row 6.

[8] 15 ♘xd2 0-0 16 ♘b3 ± Polugayevsky-Mecking, Petropolis IZ 1973.

[9] San Sebastian Variation.

[10] 13 ♖ad1 ♗b7 14 ♖fe1 ♖c8 15 ♗d3 ♖e8 16 ♕e3 ♖c3 17 e5 ♕c7 18 ♘g5 ± Korchnoi-Najdorf, Wijk aan Zee 1971.

[11] 16 ... ♘c6 17 ab (Petrosian-Tal, USSR 1972) 17 ... ♕xb6 18 ♖eb1 ±.

[12] Parma.

[13] 12 ... ♕d6 13 ♖ad1 ♖d8 14 ♖fe1 ♗d7 15 d5! ed 16 ed ♘e7 17 ♘g5! ± Browne-H.Olafsson, Reykjavik 1980.

[14] 13 ♖fd1?! ♘a5 14 ♗d3 ♗b7 15 ♕e3 ♖c8 16 ♖ac1 ♕e7 17 ♗xc8 ♖xc8 18 ♖c1 ♖xc1+ 19 ♕xc1 ½-½ A.Zaitsev-Polugayevsky, USSR Ch 1968/69.

[15] Petrosian-Korchnoi, match (6) 1977.

[16] 16 ... ed 17 e5 ♕e7 18 ♘d4 ♘c6 (18 ... g6!?) 19 ♘f5! ± Ghitescu-M.Vuković, Smederevska Palanka 1971.

[17] 17 ♘g5!? intending 17 ... h6 18 ♘h7 ∞ Keene.   17 ... e5 Timman.

[18] Larsen-Tal, match (1) 1969.
   14 ... ♗d7 ±/=.

[19] 7 ... ♘f6 – Queen's Gambit Accepted.

[20] Langeweg-Platonov, Wijk aan Zee 1970.

[21] 10 ... ♘f6 11 a3 – Queen's Gambit Accepted.

[22] Tal-Petrosian, USSR 1966.

[23] 11 ... ♘f6 – Nimzo-Indian.

[24] Botvinnik-Makagonov, USSR 1943.

[25] 13 ♕c2 g6 14 ♗h6 ♖e8 15 ♕d2 ♖c8 16 ♖ac1 ♗f6 17 ♗f4 ♗g7! 18 ♗xg7 ♔xg7 19 ♘g5 ♕c7 ∞ Pachman-Kozma, Czechoslovakia 1959.

[26] 13 ... ♘a5 14 ♘g5! h6 15 ♕h5 ± Razuvayev-Farago, Dubna 1979.

[27] Razuvayev.

[28] 9 ♘xd5 ♕xd5 10 e4 ♕d8 11 dc ♗xc5 12 e5 ± Kasparov-Begun, USSR 1978.

[29] 10 ♕e2 ♗b7 11 ♖d1 ♕c7 12 ♗d2 (Vidmar-Kotov, Groningen 1946) 12 ... ♘xc3 ∞ Parma.

[30] 16 ed ♗c6 ∞∞ Portisch-Tal, Palma 1966.

Nf6 4 Nf3 c5 5 cd Nxd5 6 e3 Nc6 7 Bd3 cd 8 ed Be7 9 0-0 0-0

	10	11	12	13	14	15	16	17	18	
14	a3	bc	Qe2	Rd1	a4	Ba3	Bb5			=
	Nxc3	b6	Bb7	Bf6	Rc8	Re8	Qd5[31]			
15	...	Be4[32]	Qd3	Bh6	Bxg7	Rfe1	Ne5	Qd2	Rac1	=
	Bf6	Nce7	g6[33]	Bg7	Kxg7	b6	Bb7	Rc8	Nf5[34]	
16	Re1	Bg5	a3	Bc2	Rc1[36]	Qd3	Bh6	h3		∞
	Nf6	b6[35]	Bb7	Rc8	Re8	g6	Qd6	Bf8[37]		
17	...	...	Qe2	Rad1	Bb1	Ne5	Qd3	bc	Qh3	±
	...	...	Bb7	Nb4	Rc8	Nbd5	Nxc3	Qd5	Rxc3[38]	
18	...	a3	Bc2	Qd3	Bh6	Rad1	h4!?	Nxd5	Qd2	±
	...	b6	Bb7	g6[39]	Re8	Rc8	Nd5	Qxd5	Qd6[40]	
19	...	Bb1	a3	Ne5	Qd3	Qh3	Bg5	Ba2	Bh6[41]	±
	Ncb4	Nf6	Nbd5	Bd7	Bc6	Re8	g6	Nh5		
20	...	Be4	Bg5!	Nxg5	Nf3	bc				=
	Bf6	Qd6[42]	Bxg5	h6	Nxc3[43]	Bd7				
21	...	...	Qc2	Bh6	Bg5	Bd2	Qb3	Bxd5	Ne4	=
	...	Nce7	g6	Bg7	f6	Bd7	Bc6	ed	Rf7[44]	
22	...	...	Ne5	Bh6	Qd2	Rad1	Rxe4	Rh4	Bxg7	=
	...	...	g6[45]	Bg7	Nf6	Nxe4	b6	Nf5	Kxg7[46]	
23	...	...	...	...	Bxg7!	Qb3	Nxd5	ab	Bf3	±
	...	...	...	...	Kxg7	Qb6[47]	Qxb3	ed	Be6[48]	

[31] Petrosian-Rajković, Sarajevo 1972.
[32] 11 Bc2 Nxc3 12 bc e5 13 d5 Ne7 14 Be4 Bf5 15 Bxf5 Nxf5 16 Qb3 (Levenfish-Ilyin Zhenevsky, USSR Ch 1937) 16 ... e4! ∞ Parma.
[33] 12 ... h6 13 Ne5! Nxc3 14 Qxc3 Nf5 (14 ... Qd6 15 b4 Rd8 16 Bb2 ± Karpov) 15 Be3! Nd6 16 Bf3 Bd7 17 Qb4! Bb5 (17 ... Be7 18 Qb3!) 18 Rfe1 a5 19 Qb3 Ba6 20 Rad1 ± Karpov-Timman, Moscow 1981.
[34] 19 Ng4 Qh4 = Lengyel-A.Zaitsev, Debrecen 1970.
[35] 11 ... a6!? intending ... b5 Parma.
[36] 14 Qd3 g6 15 Rad1 Re8 16 Ba4 a6 17 Bxc6 Rxc6 18 Ne5 Rc7 ∞ Bilek-Holmov, Kecskemet 1962.
[37] Hort-Mukhin, Luhacovice 1973.
[38] 19 f3 h6 20 Bxf6 Bxf6 21 Be4 Qxe4 22 Rxe4 Bxe4 23 Nd7 ± Polugayevsky-Hasin, USSR Ch 1961.
[39] 13 ... Rc8 14 d5! ed 15 Bg5 g6 16 Rxe7 Qxe7 17 Nxd5 Nxd5 18 Bxe7 ± Smyslov.
[40] 19 Be4! ± Ribli-Gheorghiu, Warsaw Z 1979.
[41] Polugayevsky-Sahović, Belgrade 1969. 18 ... Bf8 ±.
[42] 11 ... Nxc3 12 bc Qa5 13 Qd3 g6 14 Bh6 Rd8 15 Qe3 ± Novak-Trmal, CSSR 1979.
[43] 14 ... Bd7?! 15 Bxd5! ed 16 Ne5 Bc6 17 Nxc6 Qxc6 18 Rc1 ± Gheorghiu-Petursson, USA 1979.
[44] 19 Nc5 Nf5 = Spassky-Petrosian, match 1966.
[45] 12 ... Bd7 13 Qd3 g6 14 Bh6 Bg7 15 Bxg7 Kxg7 16 Nxd5 ± Gligorić-Eliskases, Buenos Aires 1960.
[46] 19 Rh3 Bb7 = Liberzon-Podgayets, USSR 1968.
[47] 15 ... Nf6 16 Rad1 ± Gheorghiu-Arnason, USA 1978.
[48] 19 Nd3 b6 20 Nf4 ±.

Slav and Semi-Slav

The Slav is a sensibly motivated defence to the Queen's Gambit. It is based on the same solid philosophy as the Orthodox defences, but here Black opts to bolster the centre without hemming in his queen's bishop, a source of congestion in the more classical lines of the QGD. The pawn on c6 paves the way for later expansion on the queenside, though this plan is best illustrated in the Meran Variation of the Semi-Slav (see below).

Both the Slav and Semi-Slav have received a great deal of attention, and the Czech Variation of the Slav in particular is extremely popular. The defence combines solidity with reasonable long-term chances to play for an edge. The Semi-Slav is the more passive of the two, with a variety of ultra-sharp and well examined lines at White's disposal. The Slav and Semi-Slav have, however, proved themselves durable systems and the prepared defender can essay them with confidence.

Slav

The **Exchange Variation** (3 cd cd) is the system that takes the fun out of playing the Slav. White's extra tempo in a symmetrical position gives him a chance to establish a slim but lasting pull at no risk. Black should hold the balance but this possibility robs the defence of much of its dynamic potential.

Czech Variation (3 ♘f3 ♘f6 4 ♘c3 dc 5 a4 ♗f5).   A favourite of Smyslov, this safe and simple line provides Black with excellent prospects for full equality.

Semi-Slav

Marshall Gambit (3 ♘c3 e6 4 e4!?).   Black does best to accept the challenge, though White's compensation is always evident. A difficult and obscure variant.

Abrahams Variation (3 ♘c3 e6 4 ♘f3 dc).   A provocative and double-edged try for Black. White may be able to prove a small edge but it is a harrowing task.

Botvinnik System (3 ♘f3 ♘f6 4 ♘c3 e6 5 ♗g5).   A violent system that leads to baffling tactical complications. Serious investigation is a must for the prospective defender.

Meran Variation (3 ♘f3 ♘f6 4 ♘c3 e6 5 e3 ♘bd7 6 ♗d3 dc 7 ♗xc4 b5).   An enormous complex which embraces a large body of theory. Black's chances are sufficient for equality.

Finally we consider a hybrid of the Slav and Grünfeld Defences which can arise from either opening and from various move orders.

	3	4	5	6	7	8	9	10	11	
1	♘c3[1]	♗g5[2]	♘xe4	♕d2	e3	f3	♗h4	♗g3	0-0-0	±
	♘f6	♘e4[3]	de	♗f5	♘bd7	h6	g5	e5	♕e7[4]	
2	...	e4[5]	♘f3[7]	♕xd4	♘xd4	f3	a4	♘d1	♗f4![8]	±
	dc	e5[6]	ed	♕xd4	♘f6	b5	b4	♗a6		
3	...	cd[9]	e4	♗b5+	de	♕d5!	♘e2	♗c4	♗f4[11]	±
	e5	cd	de	♗d7	♘c6[10]	♗b4	a6	♕e7		
4	cd	♘f3[12]	♘c3	♗f4	e3	♗g3	♗d3	♘e5	de	=
	cd	♘f6	♘c6	e6[13]	♗d6	0-0!	♖e8	♗xe5	♘d7[14]	
5	...	...	...	...	...	♗d3	0-0	♗e5	♖c1	=
	...	...	...	...	♗e7	0-0	♘h5	f5[15]	♘f6[16]	
6	♘f3	e3	♘c3	♗e2	0-0	b3	♗b2	dc	bc	=
	♘f6	g6[17]	♗g7	0-0	♗e6[18]	c5!	♘c6	dc	♘d7[19]	
7	...	...	...	♗d3!	0-0	dc	♗xc4	e4	e5	±
	...	...	...	0-0	c5!?[20]	dc	♘bd7	♘xc5	♘g4[21]	
8	...	♘c3	♕b3!	cd	♗g5	e3	♗d3			±
	...	g6	♗g7	cd	♘c6[22]	e6	0-0			
9	...	...	e3	a4	♘b1[23]	♕c2	♗xc4	♕xc4	♘bd2	=
	...	dc	b5	b4	♗a6	e6	♗xc4	♕d5	♘bd7[24]	
10	...	...	e4	e5[25]	a4[26]	ab	bc	♘g5	♕h5	∞
	...	...	b5	♘d5	e6[27]	♘xc3	cb	♗b7	g6[28]	
11	...	...	a4	e4[29]	♗xc4	♗e3	0-0	♕e2[31]	♖ac1	±
	...	...	♘a6	♗g4	e6	♗e7	0-0[30]	♘b4	♗h5[32]	
12	...	...	...	♘e5[33]	g3	♗g2	♘xc4	♗d2	♕b3	=
	...	...	♗g4	♗h5	e6	♗b4[34]	♘d5	♘b6	a5[35]	
13	...	...	...	...	f3	♘xc4	♘e4[36]	♗d2	♕xd2	∞
	...	...	...	...	♘fd7	e5	♗b4+[37]	♗xd2+[38]	0-0[39]	

78

[1] **3 g3? dc!**
3♘d2 ♘f6 =.
3 e3 ♗f5 4 ♘c3 e6 =.

[2] 4 e3 ♗f5 5 cd cd 6 ♕b3 ♗c8 (6 ... ♕b6 7 ♘xd5 ♘xd5 8 ♕xd5 ♕b4+ 9 ♗d2 ♕xb2 10 ♖c1 Tal-Fuchs, Kislovodsk 1964) 7 ♘f3 ±.

[3] 4 ... dc!? 5 a4 ♘a6 6 e4 ♘b4 7 ♘f3 ♗g4 8 e5 h6 9 ♗e3 ♘fd5 10 ♗xc4 e6!? (10 ... ♗xf3 11 ♕xf3 ♘c2+ 12 ♔e2 ±) ∞.

[4] 12 fe ♗xe4 13 ♗d3 ± Nei-Chicovani, Tallinn 1967.

[5] 4 a4 e5 5 de ♕xd1+ 6 ♔xd1 ♘a6 = Tan-Euwe, Zandvoort 1936.

[6] 4 .... b5 5 a4 b4 6 ♘a2 ±.

[7] 5 ♗xc4?! ed 6 ♘f3 dc! 7 ♗xf7+ ♔e7 8 ♕b3 cb 9 ♗xb2 ♕b6 10 ♗a3 c5 11 ♗xg8 ♖xg8 12 ♕xg8 ♕a5+ 13 ♔e2 ♕a6+! ∓ Botvinnik.

[8] Nei-Roisman, Pärnu 1964.

[9] 4 de d4 5 ♘e4 ♕a5+ 6 ♘d2 ♘bd7 7 e6! fe 8 g3 e5 9 ♗g2 ♘f6 10 ♘h3 ± Simagin-Nei, USSR Ch 1960.

[10] 7 ... ♗b4 8 ♗d2 ♗xc3 9 ♗xd7+ ♕xd7 10 ♗xc3 ± Langeweg-Donner, Amsterdam 1965.

[11] Müller-Haas, corr. 1922.

[12] 4 ♘c3 ♘f6 5 ♗f4 ♕b6 6 ♕b3 ♕xd4 7 e4 e6! =.

[13] **6 ... ♗f5** 7 e3 e6 8 ♗b5 (8 ♘e5!? ♘d7 9 ♘xc6 bc 10 ♗a6 ± Keene-Sigurjonsson, Skopje Ol 1972) 8 ... ♘d7 9 ♕a4 ♕b6 (9 ... ♖c8 10 0-0 a6 11 ♗xc6 ♖xc6 12 ♖fc1 ± Ivanov-Chernikov, Kalinin 1977) 10 ♘h4 ♗e4 11 ♖c1! ± (11 f3? ♗d3 12 ♗xd3 ♕xb2) P.Littlewood-Torre, Hastings 1980/81.

6 ... ♕b6 7 a3! ± (7 ... ♕xb2?! 8 ♘a4! ♕b5 9 ♗d2! intending 10 e3/10 e4 Darius-Hennings, East German Ch 1982).

[14] 12 f4 (Portisch-Petrosian, Moscow 1967) 12 ... ♘c5! = Taimanov.

[15] 10 ... f6 11 ♗g3 ♘xg3 12 hg ±.

[16] 12 ♗xf6 gf! = Capablanca-Lasker, New York 1924.

[17] 4 ... ♗g4 5 h3! ♗xf3 6 ♕xf3 e6 7 ♗d3 ♘bd7 8 ♘c3 ± Korchnoi-Yusupov, Lone Pine 1981. 6 ... g6 7 ♘c3 ♗g7 (Taimanov-Yusupov, USSR 1981) 8 ♕d1 0-0 9 ♕b3 ± Taimanov.

[18] 7 ... ♗g4 8 cd (8 b3 ♘bd7 9 ♗b2 ± Karpov-Smyslov, Moscow 1981) 8 ... cd 9 ♕b3 b6 10 h3 ♗xf3 11 ♗xf3 e6 12 ♗d2 ± Timman-Smyslov, Las Palmas IZ 1982.

[19] Balashov-Smyslov, Moscow 1981.

[20] 7 ... ♗g4 8 h3 ♗xf3 9 ♕xf3 e6 10 ♖d1 ♘bd7 11 b3! (11 e4?! e5! Smyslov) 11 ... ♖e8 12 ♗b2

♕e7 13 ♗f1! ± Furman-Zacharian, Odessa 1960.

7 ... ♗f5 8 ♗xf5 gf 9 b3! ± Najdorf-Sanguinetti, Mar del Plata 1958.

7 ... e6 8 b3 ♘bd7 9 ♗a3! ±.

[21] **12 ♗g5 ♘xe5 13 ♘xe5! ±** Bronstein-Simagin, USSR 1964.
12 ♕e2!? intending 13 h3.

[22] 7 ... e6 8 e4 de 9 ♗b5+ ±.

[23] 7 ♘a2 e6 8 ♗xc4 ♗b7! ∞/= Reshevsky-Smyslov, USSR v USA 1945.

[24] Stahlberg-Euwe, Stockholm 1937.

[25] 6 ♕c2 e6 7 ♗e2 ♗b7 8 0-0 ♘bd7 9 ♖d1 a6 = Holmov-Bagirov, Moscow 1960.

[26] 7 ♘g5!? h6 8 ♘ge4 e6 9 a4 b4 10 ♘b1 ±.

[27] **7 ... ♗f5 (Flohr) 8 ab ♘b4 9 ♗xc4! ♘c2+ 10 ♔e2 ♘xa1 11 ♕a4 ♗c2 12 ♕xa1 ∞/±** Lilienthal.
7 ... ♗e6 7 ♘g5! ±.

[28] **11 ... ♕d7 12 ♗e2! (12 ♘xh7?! ♘c6 13 ♘xf8? – Kasparov-Kupreichik, USSR 1979 – 13 ... ♕d4!! ∓) 12 ... h6? 13 ♗f3 ±** Kasparov-Petursson, Malta Ol 1980.
11 ... g6 12 ♕g4 ♗e7 13 ♗e2 ♘bd7 14 ♗f3 (Geller-Unzicker, Stockholm 1952) 14 ... ♕c8! ∞ Taimanov.

[29] 6 e3 ♗g4 7 ♗xc4 e6 8 0-0 ♘b4 9 ♕e2 ♗e7 10 ♖d1 0-0 11 a5! ±/= Uhlmann-Teschner, Stockholm IZ 1962.

[30] 9 ... ♘b4 10 a5! 0-0 11 ♕b3! ± Pomar-Teschner, Stockholm IZ 1962.

[31] **10 h3 ♗h5 11 g4 ♗g6 =.**
10 ♗e2 ♘b4 11 ♘e5 ±.

[32] 12 ♖fd1 ♕a5 13 h3 ± Portisch-Torre, Moscow 1981.

[33] 6 e3 e6 7 ♗xc4 ♘a6 – row 11. 7 ... ♗b4 8 h3 ♗h5 9 ♕e2 ♘bd7 10 0-0 – Euwe System.

[34] 8 ... a5 9 ♗xc4 ♘a6 10 0-0 ♗e7 11 h3 ± Spassov-Popov, Bulgarian Ch 1975.

[35] 12 ♘xb6 ♕xb6 13 ♗e3 (Farago-Dieks, Amsterdam 1975) 13 ... ♕a6! Taimanov.

[36] 9 ♘xe5 ♘xe5 10 de ♘d7 (=) 11 f4 ♗b4 12 ♕c2 ♕e7 13 e4 g5! ∞ Timman-Petrosian, Las Palmas IZ 1982.
9 e4 ♕h4+! 10 g3 ♕f6 11 de ∞.
9 h4!?

[37] 9 ... ♘b6?! 10 ♘xe5 f6 11 ♘d3! ± Taimanov. 11 a5! Timman.

[38] 10 ... ♕e7 11 ♗xb4 (11 de 0-0 =) 11 ... ♕xb4+ 12 ♕d2 ♕xd2+ 13 ♔xd2 ed 14 ♘ed6+ ♔e7 (Bagirov-Podgayets, Tbilisi 1973) 15 ♘xb7! c5 16 g4 ♗g6 17 ♗g2 ± Taimanov.

[39] 12 de b5! 13 ab cb 14 ♕d5 ♘c6! ∞.

	6	7	8	9	10	11	12	13	14	
Slav: Czech System				**1 d4 d5 2 c4 c6 3 ♘f3 ♘f6 4 ♘c3 dc 5 a4 ♗f5**					
1	♘e5	f3	e4	fe	♗d2	♘xe4	♕e2	♔xd2	♔c2	±
	e6[1]	♗b4	♗xe4	♘xe4	♕xd4	♕xe4+	♗xd2+	♕d5+	♘a6[2]	
2	...	...	...	...	♕f3!?	♕xf7+	♗g5+!	♕xe6+	♕xd7+!	±
	...	...	...	...	♕xd4	♔d8	♔c8	♘d7	♕xd7[3]	
3	...	...	♘xc4	♗g5	♗h4	dc	♕xd8	e4	♗f2	±
	...		0-0[4]	h6!	c5	♗xc5[5]	♖xd8	♗h7	♗b4[6]	
4	...	...	♗g5	dc	♕xd5	e4	♘xc4	♗xf6	♘d6![8]	±
	...		c5[7]	♕d5!	ed	de	0-0	gf		
5	...	♘xc4	g3	de	♗f4	♕c1	♘xd6+	♗g2	0-0	±
	♘bd7	♕c7	e5	♘xe5	♖d8[9]	♗d6	♕xd6	0-0	a5[10]	
6	e3[11]	♗xc4	0-0[12]	♕e2	♘a2	♗d3	♘c3	bc	e4	±
	e6	♗b4	a5	♘e4	♗d6	♗g6	♘xc3	♘bd7	0-0[13]	
7	...	...	...	♕b3[14]	♘a2	♘h4!	f3	g4	♘c3	±
	...	...	♘bd7!?	a5!?[15]	♗e7	♗g4[16]	♗h5	♗g6		
8	...	...	...	♘h4	f3	g4	♘xg6[17]	♕b3	g5	±
	...	...	0-0	♗g4	♗h5	♗g6	hg	♕e7	♘d5[18]	
9	...	...	...	...	f3	♘xg6	♕c2!	♖fd1	♔h1	±
	...	...	...	♘bd7	♗g6	hg	a5	♕b6	♖ac8[19]	
10	...	...	...	♕e2	♘a2!	♗d3	♘e1!	♘xd3	♘c3[21]	±
	...	...	...	♘e4	♗e7	♗g5[20]	♗xd3	♘a6		
11	...	...	...	...	♖d1	e4	h3	g4	♘h4[23]	±
	...	...	...	♗g4	♘bd7	♗e7	♗h5[22]	♗g6		
12	...	...	...	...	e4[24]	♗d3	e5[25]	♘e4[26]	h3	∞
	...	...	...	♘bd7	♗g6	♗h5!	♘d5	♗e7	♗g6[27]	

[1] 6 ... ♘a6 7 e3 ♘b4 8 ♗xc4 e6 (8 ... ♘c2+? 9 ♕xc2 ♗xc2 10 ♗xf7 mate) 9 0-0 ♗e7 10 ♕e2 0-0 11 e4 ± Geller-Gufeld, USSR Ch 1960.

[2] 15 ♘xc4! ± Tolush-Furman, USSR 1952.

[3] 15 ♘xd7 ♘xc3 16 bc! ♗xc3+ 17 ♔d1 ♗xa1 18 ♘c5 ∞/± Borisenko-Aronin, USSR 1950.

[4] 8 ... c5 9 dc ♕xd1+ 10 ♔xd1 0-0 11 e4 ♗g6 12 ♘d6! ± Agzamov-Belyavsky, USSR Ch 1981.

[5] 11 ... ♕xd1+ 12 ♖xd1 ♗c2 13 ♖c1 ♗h7 14 e4 ♘c6 15 ♗e2 ♗xc5 16 ♗f2 ± Bagirov-Shvedshikov, Moscow 1971.

[6] 15 ♗e2 ♘c6 16 0-0 ♘d4 17 ♗xd4 ♖xd4 18 ♖fd1 ± Taimanov.

[7] 8 ... h6!? 9 ♗h4! c5 10 dc ♕d5 11 ♕xd5 ± Taimanov-Simić, Vrnjačka Banja 1974.

[8] Belavenets.

[9] 10 ... ♘fd7 11 ♗g2 ♖d8 12 ♕c1 f6 13 0-0 ♗e6 14 ♘e4 ± Euwe-Alekhine, match 1935.

[10] 15 ♕e3 ♘fg4 16 ♕b6 ♕b4 17 ♕xb4 ab 18 ♘a2 ♘g6 19 ♗c1! ± Browne-Miles, Bali 1982.

[11] Euwe Variation.

[12] 8 ♕b3 ♕e7 9 a5 0-0 10 0-0 c5 = Spielmann-Eliskases, match 1932.

[13] 15 Rb1 Rb8 16 Nd2 ± Boleslavsky-Smyslov, USSR Ch 1952.
[14] 9 Nh4 Bg4 (9 ... Bg6 10 g3 0-0 11 Qb3 Qb6 12 Nxg6 hg 13 Rd1 ± Kasparov-Belyavsky, Tilburg 1981) 10 f3 Bh5 11 g4 Bg6 12 Nxg6 hg 13 e4 0-0 14 g5! Nh5 15 f4 c5 16 Na2 Ba5 17 Be2! ± Knaak-Meduna, Trnava 1981.
[15] 9 ... Qb6!? 10 e4 Bg6 11 Bxe6! fe 12 a5 Bxa5 13 Qxe6+ Kd8 14 e5 Re8 15 Qh3! ∞ Gavrikov-Dorfman, USSR Ch 1981.
[16] 11 ... Bg6 12 g3! ± Kasparov-Belyavsky, USSR Ch 1981.
[17] 12 e4 Nbd7 13 Bg2 c5!? Portisch-Hort, Petropolis IZ 1973.
[18] 15 e4 Nb6 16 Na2 Bc5!! 17 Be3 Nxc4 18 Qxc4 Bb6 ∓. 16 Be2! c5 17 Na2! Ba5 18 dc Qxc5+ 19 Be3 ± Karpov. 17 ... Nc6!?

[19] 15 Rb1! ± Borisenko-Ignatiev, USSR Ch 1966.
[20] 11 ... Nd7 12 Qc2 ±/± Gligorić-Unzicker, Bath 1973.
[21] Flohr-Capablanca, AVRO 1938.
[22] 12 ... Bxf3 13 Qxf3 e5 14 d5 Bxc3 (14 ... Nb6 15 Bb3 cd 16 a5! ±) 15 bc ± Yusupov-Velikov, Bulgaria 1981.
[23] Flohr-Yanofsky, Saltsjöbaden 1948.
[24] 10 Rd1 Bg6! = Kuzmin-Kupreichik, USSR Ch 1981.
[25] 12 Bf4 Re8! 12 ... e5? 13 de Ng4 14 Qc2 Qe7 15 Be2! ±/±±.
[26] 13 Nxd5 cd 14 Qe3 Be7 ± Polugayevsky-Tan, Manila IZ 1976. 14 ... Bg6!? =.
[27] 15 Neg5!? ∞ Palatnik-Meduna, Hradec Kralove 1981.

| Semi-Slav: e4 gambit | | | | **1 d4 d5 2 c4 c6 3 Nc3 e6** | | | | |

	4	5	6	7	8	9	10	11	12	
1	e4	Nxe4	Bd2[3]	Bxb4	Ne2	Bf8![4]	Bxg7	Qd6!	Kd2	=
	de[1]	Bb4+[2]	Qxd4	Qxe4+	Na6	Ne7	Nb4	Nd3+	Nf5[5]	
2	...	...	...	...	Be2	Bd6	Nf3[7]	Ne5	0-0!	=
	...	...	...	...	Na6[6]	b6	Bb7	f6	fe[8]	
3	...	...	...	...	...	Ba5	Nf3	Qd6	Ne5	=
	...	...	...	...	...	Bd7	Nf6	Qf5	Qxf2+[9]	
4	...	...	...	...	...	Bxc5	Qd4	Bf3	Bb4	=
	...	...	...	...	c5	Qxg2	Nd7	Qg5	Qe5+[10]	

[1] 4 ... Nf6 5 Bg5 de 6 Nxe4 ±. 5 e5 Nfd7 6 Nf3 ±.
4 ... Bb4 5 e5 Ne7 6 Nf3 Nf5 7 cd cd 8 a3 Be7 9 Bd3 Nc6 10 Bc2 h5 11 b4 a6 12 Bb2 b5 ∞ Borisenko-Shaposhnikov, USSR Ch 1958.
[2] 5 ... e5?! 6 de Qa5+ 7 Bd2 Qxe5 8 Bd3 Na6 9 Nf3 Qc7 10 Qe2 Be6 11 Neg5 ± Karpov-Ivanović, Skopje 1976.
5 ... Nf6 6 Nxf6+ Qxf6 7 Nf3 Bd6?! 8 Bd3 h6 9 0-0 g5 10 Bd2 g4 11 Ne5 ± Janošević-Tomović, Yugoslavia 1959.
[3] 6 Nc3 Nf6 7 Be3 0-0 8 Nge2 Nbd7 9 a3 Bd6 10 Ng3 e5 = Rabar-Puc, Yugoslav Ch 1949.
[4] 9 Ba5 b6 10 Qd6 (10 Nc3? Bb7! 11 Bxg7 Nb4!) 10 ... ba 11 Rd1 f6 12 Rd4! Qb1+ 13 Rd1 = Shamkovich.
[5] 13 Qxd3 Qxd3+ 14 Kxd3 Nxg7 = Holmov-

Novotelnov, Baku 1951.
[6] 8 ... Qxg2?! 9 Bf3 Qg6 10 Ne2 Na6 11 Ba3 Ne7 12 Rg1 ± Wood-Alexander, British Ch 1948.
[7] 10 Qa4!? Bb7 11 0-0-0 0-0-0 12 Bf3 Qf5 13 Ne2 ± Shamkovich.
[8] 13 Bh5+ g6 14 Re1 Qh4 15 Bg4 Rd8 16 Rxe5 Nc5! 17 b4 Nh6 18 bc Qxg4 19 Qxg4 Nxg4 20 Rxe6+ Kd7 21 Re7+ Kc8 22 Rae1 bc 23 Rc7+ Kb8 24 Rb1 Rxd6 25 Rbxb7+ = Ragozin.
[9] 13 Kxf2 Ne4+ 13 Kf3 Nxd6 14 Rad1 Be7 16 Rxd6 Kxd6 17 Nxf7+ Ke7 18 Nxh8 Rxh8 19 Bc3 = Taimanov.
[10] 13 Ne2 Qxd4 14 Nxd4 Ne5! 15 0-0-0 Bd7 16 Bxb7 Rb8 17 Bd6 Rxb7 18 Bxe5 f6 19 Bd6 Ne7 = ECO.

Semi-Slav: Anti-Meran Systems   1 d4 d5 2 c4 c6 3 ♘f3 ♘f6 4 ♘c3 e6

	5	6	7	8	9	10	11	12	13	
1	♕b3[1]	♕xc4	g3!?	♗g2	0-0	♕d3	♘a4	♕c2		=
	dc[2]	b6[3]	♗e7	0-0	b5	b4	♗a6	♘bd7		
2	♗g5	♗xf6[5]	e3[6]	♗d3	0-0	c5!	b4	e4[8]		=
	h6[4]	♕xf6	♗d6[7]	♕e7	♘d7	♗c7	0-0			
3	...	a4[9]	e4	bc	e5	♖c1	♗e3	♕c2	ef	=
	dc	♗b4	♗xc3+[10]	♕a5	♘e4	♘d7	♘b6	f5	♘xf6[11]	
4	...	e4	a4[12]	e5	ef![14]	fg	h4!	♖xh4	♖h8[15]	±
	...	b5	♗b4?![13]	h6	hg	♖g8	gh	♘d7		
5	...	...	e5	♗h4[16]	ef[17]	♘e5[18]	a4!?[19]	♗e2	♗f3	∞
	...	...	h6	g5	gh	♕xf6	♗b4[20]	c5!?	cd[21]	
6	...	...	...	...	♘xg5	♘xf7[22]	♘xh8	♕d2[23]	0-0-0	±
	...	...	...	...	♘d5?!	♕xh4	♗b4	c5	cd[24]	
7	...	...	...	...	...	♗xg5	ef	g3[26]	d5	±
	...	...	...	...	hg	♘bd7[25]	♗b7	c5[27]	♘b6?[28]	
8	...	...	...	...	...	...	g3	♗xf6	ef	∞
	...	...	...	...	...	...	♖g8!?[29]	♘xf6	♗b7[30]	
9	...	...	...	...	...	...		♘e4	♗xd8	±±
	...	...	...	...	...	...	b4	♘xe4!?	♔xd8[31]	
10	...	...	...	...	...	...	...	ef[32]	d5	±
	...	...	...	...	...	...	...	♗b7	c5 ♗h6[33]	

1 d4 d5 2 c4 c6 3 ♘f3 ♘f6 4 ♘c3 e6 5 ♗g5 dc 6 e4 b5 7 e5 h6
8 ♗h4 g5 9 ♘xg5 hg 10 ♗xg5 ♘bd7 11 ef ♗b7 12 g3 c5 13 d5 ♕b6

	14	15	16	17	18	19	20	21	22	
11	♗g2	0-0	♘a4[35]	a3[37]	ab	♗e3!	♗xd5	♕e2	♖fc1	±
	0-0-0	b4[34]	♕b5[36]	♘b8[38]	cb	♗xd5	♖xd5	♘c6	♘a5[39]	

1 5 ♕c2?! dc! 6 e4 b5 7 ♗e2 ♗b7 8 0-0 ♘bd7 ∓.
5 ♕d3 b6 6 e4 ♗a6! ∓.

2 5 ... ♘bd7 6 g3 ♗d6 7 ♗g2 ± Sokolsky-Pachman, Moscow 1947.
5 ... ♗e7 6 ♗g5 ♘bd7 7 e3 0-0 8 ♗d3 ±.
5 ... ♕b6!?

3 6 ... b5 7 ♕b3 ♘bd7 8 ♗g5 a6 9 e3 c5 10 ♗e2 c4 = Bukić-Bagirov, Banja Luka 1976.

4 5 ... ♘bd7(!) – QGD Cambridge Springs (6 e3 ♕a5) or Carlsbad (6 cd ed 7 e3).

5 6 ♗h4 dc 7 e4 g5 8 ♗g3 b5 (8 ... ♗b4!?) 9 ♕c2! g4! 10 ♘e5 ♕xd4 11 ♖d1 ♕b6 12 ♗e2 ♘bd7 ∞/= Whiteley/Harding.

6 7 a3 dc 8 ♘e5 c5!? 9 ♘xc4 cd 10 ♘b5 ♕d8 11 ♕xd4 ♕xd4 12 ♘xd4 ♗d7 = Kasparov-Sveshnikov, USSR Ch 1981.
7 ♕b3 dc intending ... ♘d7 ± Pachman-Vitelky, Czech Ch 1952. 7 ... ♘d7! 8 e4 de 9 ♘xe4 ♕f4 ∞.

7 7 ... ♘d7 8 ♗d3 dc 9 ♗xc4 ♗d6 10 0-0 ♕e7 11 ♖c1 0-0 12 ♘e4 ± Petrosian-Dorfman, USSR Ch 1976.

8 Polugayevsky-Mecking, match 1977.

9 6 e3 b5 7 a4 ♗b4 8 ♘d2 a6 9 ab ♗xc3 10 bc cb 11 ♕f3 d5 12 ♕g3 ♘bd7 13 ♗e2 ∞ ECO.

10 7 ... b5?! 8 e5 h6 9 ♗h4 g5 10 ♘xg5 ±/±.
7 ... c5 8 ♗xc4 cd 9 ♘xd4 ±.

11 14 ♖a1! 0-0 15 ♘e5 ♘fd5 16 ♗d2 c5 = Donner-Pomar, Lugano 1959.

12 7 ♕c2 h6 8 ♗h4 g5 9 ♗g3 g4 10 ♘e5 ♕xd4

11 Rd1 Qb6 12 Be2 Nbd7 13 0-0 Be7 14 Nxg4
Nxg4 15 Bxg4 = Spassky-Pachman, Moscow
1967.
[13] **7 ...** **Qb6** 8 Bxf6 gf 9 Be2 a6 (9 ... Nd7
10 0-0 Bb4 11 d5 Bxc3 12 bc Nc5 – Stepuchov-
Bronstein, Moscow 1946 – 13 dc ±) 10 0-0 Bb7
11 d5 cd 12 ed b4 13 a5 Qc7 14 de! bc
15 Nd4! ∞/± Tal-Keller, Zürich 1959.
  7 ... b4 8 Nb1 h6 9 Bxf6 Qxf6 10 Bxc4 Qg6
11 Nbd2 Qxg2 12 Rg1 Qh3 13 Qe2 ∞.
[14] 9 Bh4 g5 10 Nxg5 hg 11 Bxg5 Qa5
12 Bxf6 ∞.
[15] Ehlvest-Andrianov, USSR 1981.
[16] 8 Bxf6 gf 9 a4 (Geller) 9 ... a6 10 ef (10 ab?!
cb 11 Nxb5 ab!) 12 Rxa8 Bb4+ 13 Ke2 Bb7
14 Ra1 Nc6 15 Qc2 Qd5 ∓) 10 ... xf6 11 Ne5
Nd7 12 Nxc6 b4 13 Ne4 Qf4 14 Ng3 Qc7
15 d5 Bb7 (Kamishev) ∓.
[17] 9 Bg3 Nd5! 10 Nd2 Nd7 11 Nde4 Qa5
(Taimanov) =/∓.
[18] Intending 11 Nxf7 Kxf7 12 Qh5+.
[19] **11 g3** Nbd7 12 Qe2 (12 f4 Bb7! 13 Bg2
Nxe5! 14 de Qd8! Pelitov-Minev, Bulgaria
1959) 12 ... Nxe5 13 de Qe7 14 Bg2 Bb7
15 0-0 Qg7 16 f4 0-0 ∞ Bronstein-Botvinnik,
USSR Ch 1951.
  11 Be2?! Nbd7 12 0-0!? (12 Nxc6 Bb7
13 Bf3 a6 14 0-0 Qg7! 15 a4 b4 16 Ne4 Qf4+ ∓
Nielsen-Böök, Stockholm 1947) 12 ... Nxe5
13 de Qxe5 14 Bf3 Bb7 15 Re1 Qd6! 16 Nxb5
Qxd1 17 Rxd1 cb 18 Bxb7 Rb8 19 Bc6+
Ke7 ∓ Ree-Hamann, Netanya 1968.
[20] **11 ... Bb7** 12 Be2 (12 ab c5! 13 b6 cd
14 Qa4+ Kd8 15 Qa5 Bd6! 16 ba Ke7 17 abQ
Rhxb8 ∓∓ ECO) 12 ... c5 13 Nxb5 Na6
14 Qh5 Rh7 15 0-0 Rg7 16 Bf3! Bxf3 17 Qxf3
Qxf3 18 Nxf3 h3 19 g3 ± Zak.
  11 ... b4 12 Ne4 Qf4 (12 ... Qf5 13 f3 ±)
13 Qe2 c3 (13 ... f5? 14 Nxf6+) 14 bc bc 15 g3
Qf5 16 Qe3 intending g4 ± Korchnoi.
[21] 14 Qxd4 Nd7 15 Bc6 (15 Bxa8 Nc5!)
15 ... 0-0 16 Bxd7 Bxd7 17 Qg4+ Kh8 18 Nxd7
Bxc3+ 19 Ke2 Qd8 ∞ Korchnoi.
[22] 10 Nf3 Qa5 11 Rc1 Bb4 12 Qd2 Nd7
13 Be2 Nb6 14 0-0 Na4 15 Bf6 Rg8 16 Qxh6
Bxc3 17 bc Naxc3 18 Rc2 Bb7 ∞ Minev.
[23] 12 Rc1 Qe4+!? 13 Be2 Nf4 14 a3! Nxg2+
15 Kf1 Ne3+ 16 fe Qxh1+ 17 Kf2 Qxh2+
18 Ke1 ± Timman-Ljubojević, Buenos Aires
1980. 12 ... c5? 13 dc Nd7 14 Be2 ± Lilienthal-
Ragozin, USSR Ch 1943.
[24] 14 Qxd4 Qg5+ 15 f4 Nxf4 16 Ne4 Ne2+
17 Kb1 Nxd4 18 Nxg5 Nbc6 19 Nf3 Nxf3 20 gf
Nxe5 21 Rhg1 ± Gligorić.
[25] 10 ... Be7 11 ef Bxf6 12 Bxf6 Qxf6
13 Be2 ±/±.
[26] 12 Be2 Qb6 (12 ... Qc7!? 13 h4 b4 14 Ne4
c5 ∞/∓) 13 a4 0-0-0 14 a5 Qa6 ∓ Nei-Böök,

Tallinn 1965. 14 ... Qc7!? ∓.
[27] 12 ... Qb6 13 Bg2 c5 14 d5 – row 11.
[28] 14 de! Qxd1+ 15 Rxd1 Bxh1 16 e7 a6
17 h4! Bh6 18 f4! ± Polugayevsky-Torre,
Moscow 1981.
[29] **11 ... Bh6!?**
  11 ... Qa5?! 12 ef b4 13 Ne4 Ba6 14 Be2
0-0-0 15 0-0 Qf5 16 Qc2 ± Shashkin-Kochiev,
USSR 1972.
[30] 14 Bg2 Qb6 15 0-0 0-0-0 16 Qh5 Rg6
17 Ne4 Rxd4 18 Qh7 Qc7 ∞ Korchnoi-Bellon,
Las Palmas 1981.
[31] **14 Bxc4** Nb6 15 Bd3 f5 16 ef! (16 Bxe4? fe
17 Qe2 a5 ∓ Shestoporov-Agrinsky, Leningrad
1967) 16 ... Nxf6 17 0-0 Nbd5 18 Qe2 a5 ∞
Radchenko.
  14 Qf3!? Taimanov.
  14 Bg2! ±±.
[32] 12 Bg2 Rg8 13 Bxf6 (13 h4!? Rxg5 14 hg
Nd5 15 g6! Qa5 16 gf+ Kd8 17 Bxd5 cd
18 0-0 ∞ Taimanov) 13 ... Nxf6 14 ef Qxf6
(14 ... Qc7!?) 15 a4 (15 Nxb5 0-0-0!) 15 ... b4
16 Ne4 Qf5 17 Rc1! ± Liberzon-Lombard,
Biel IZ 1976.
[33] **13 ... Bh6!?** 14 Bxh6 (14 Nxb5!?) 14 ...
Rxh6 15 Bg2 b4! 16 Ne4 Nf6 17 Nxc5 Bd5 ∞
Bagirov-Yusupov, USSR 1981. 15 Qd2! ±.
  13 ... 0-0-0 14 0-0 Ne5 15 de! ± Hollis-
Baumbach, corr. 1976.
[34] 15 ... Ne5 16 Qe2 Bd6 17 a4 b4 18 a5 Qa6
19 Ne4 Bxd5 20 Bf4 Bb8 21 Nxc5 Qc6 22 Ne4
a6 23 Rfd1 ± Hollis-Donner, Hastings 1965/66.
[35] **16 de** Bxg2 17 e7 Bxe7 18 fe Rdg8 ∓.
  16 Rb1!? Bh6 (16 ... Qa6?! 17 de Bxg2
18 e7! Bxf1 19 Bxf1! ± Uhlmann-Alexandria,
Halle 1981) 17 f4! (17 Qc1 Bxg5 18 Qxg5
Nf8 ∓) 17 ... a6! (Yusupov-Sveshnikov, USSR
Ch 1981) 18 de ∞ Sveshnikov.
[36] 16 ... a6? 17 a3! b3 18 Nc3 Qb6 19 Qg4
Nxd5 20 Nxd5 Bxd5 21 Bxd5 Rxd5 22 Rfd1! ±
Razuvayev-Vaiser, USSR 1981.
[37] 17 de? Bxg2 18 e7 Bxf1 19 edQ+ Kxd8
20 Kxf1 Qc6! 21 Kg1 Bd6 22 f4 Re8 23 Kf2
Kc7 ∓ Ubilava-Timoshenko, USSR 1981.
[38] 17 ... ed 18 ab ab 19 Be3! ±/± Haritonov-
Dorfman, USSR 1981.
[39] **22 ... c3** 23 Nxc3! (23 Nxb5 Rxb5 24 Nxc3)
23 ... bc 24 Qxb5 Rxb5 25 Rxc3 Kd7
26 Ra6! ± Rashkovsky-Timoshenko, USSR
1981.
  22 ... Kb7?! 23 Rxc4 Qa5 24 b3! ±.
  22 ... Na5!? 23 b3! c3 24 Nxc3! bc 25 Rxc3+
Kd7 (25 ... Kb7? 26 Qc2 Bd6 27 b4! ±) 26 Qc2
Bd6 27 Rc1 Qb7 28 b4! Qxb4 29 Rb1 Qg4
30 Bxa7!! e5 (30 ... Be5 31 Rc5! Rxc5 32 Qxc5!
Nc6 33 Qd3+! Kc8 34 Rd1! Nb8 35 Rc1! ±±
Kasparov-Dorfman, USSR Ch 1981) 31 Qa2! ±
Kasparov-Timoshenko, USSR Ch 1981.

Semi-Slav: Abrahams or Noteboom Variation   1 d4 d5 2 c4 c6 3 ♘f3 e6 4 ♘c3 dc

	5	6	7	8	9	10	11	12	13	
1	e4[1]	♗e2	0-0	a4	♗g5	e5	♗h4	♗g3	♘e4	∞
	b5	♗b7	♘f6	a6	♘bd7	h6	g5	♘h5	♕b6[2]	
2	a4	e3[3]	♗d2	ab	♗xc3	d5	de	♘d4	♘xb5	±
	♗b4	b5	♕e7[4]	♗xc3	cb	♘f6	fe[5]	0-0	♘e4[6]	
3	...	...	...	ab[7]	♗xc3[8]	b3	bc	♗b2	♗d3	±
	...	...	a5	♗xc3	cb	♗b7	b4	♘f6	♘bd7[9]	
4	...	...	...	...	...	...	d5	bc	♗xf6	∞/=
	...	...	...	...	...	...	♘f6	b4	♕xf6[10]	

[1]   5 e3 b5 6 a4 b4! 7 ♘e4 ♗a6 =.
[2]   14 ♘d6+ ♗xd6 15 ed ∞ Petrosian-Averbakh, USSR Ch 1950.
[3]   6 e4 b5 7 ♗d2 a5 8 ♕b1!? Novotelnov-Solyar, Leningrad 1956.
[4]   7 ... ♕b6 8 ♘e5 ♘f6 9 ab cb 10 b3 ± Tamaczy-Sokolov, Yugoslavia 1952.
[5]   11 ... ♗xe6 12 ♘d4 0-0 13 ♕f3 ♗d5 14 ♕g3 ± Taimanov.

[6]   14 ♗xc4! ♘xf2 15 ♕h5 ± van Scheltinga-Alexander, Hilversum 1947.
[7]   8 ♘e5!? ♘f6 9 ♕f3 ♗xc3 10 bc ♕d5 11 ♕g3 0-0 12 f3 ♘e8 13 e4 ±/± Mileika-Kirpichnikov, Latvian Ch 1966.
[8]   9 bc!? cb 10 ♕b1!? Boleslavsky.
[9]   14 0-0 ♕c7 15 ♖e1 0-0 16 c5 ± Holmov-Bikhovsky, Moscow 1967.
[10]   14 ♕a4+ ♘d7 15 ♘d4 e5! 16 ♘b3 ♔e7 ∞/=.

Semi-Slav: Meran (Introduction)   1 d4 d5 2 c4 c6 3 ♘f3 ♘f6 4 ♘c3 e6 5 e3

	5	6	7	8	9	10	11	12	13	
1	...	c5[2]	b4	♗b2	♗e2	0-0	♘a4	♗d3	♘e5[4]	±
	a6[1]	♘bd7	g6	♗g7	0-0	♕e7[3]	♘e4	f5		
2	...	♕c2	♗d2[6]	0-0-0[7]	cd	♔b1	♘b5	dc	♗b4[9]	∞
	♘bd7	♗d6[5]	0-0	c5[8]	ed	♖e8	♗f8	♘xc5	b6	
3	...	...	b3	♗e2!	cd	♘xd5[10]	de	♗b2		=
	...	...	0-0	e5	♘xd5	cd	♘xe5	♗b4+		
4	...	...	e4	♘xe4	♕xe4	de	ed[11]	♕xe8		∞
	...	...	de	♘xe4	e5	0-0	♖e8	♕xe8+		
5	...	♗d3	0-0[12]	e4	♘xe4	b3	♗b2	♕e2	♘xd4	±
	...	♗e7	0-0	de	b6	♗b7	c5	cd	♘c5[13]	
6	...	...	a3	0-0	♕c2	♗xc4	♗d2	de	♘xe5	±
	...	♗b4	♗a5[14]	0-0	dc	♗c7	e5	♘xe5	♗xe5	
7	...	...	0-0	e4	♗xc4	♗g5	♖e1	♗b3	h3	=
	...	♗d6	0-0	dc[15]	e5	♕e7	♘b6	♗g4	♗xf3[16]	

	5	6	7	8	9	10	11	12	13	
8	...	...	e4	♘xe4	♗xe4	0-0	♗c2	♖e1	♕xd4	±
	...	...	de	♘xe4	0-0	h6[17]	e5	ed	♗c5[18]	
9	...	...	♗xc4	♗e2	e4	e5	ef	fg	♗xb2	=
	...	dc	b5	a6	b4	bc	cb	♗xg7![19]	♕a5+[20]	
10	...	...	...	♗b3	♘e2	0-0	♘f4	♖e1	♘g5	=
	...	...	...	b4[21]	♗b7	♗e7	0-0	c5[22]	♗d5[23]	

---

[1] **5 ... ♗e7** 6 ♗d3 dc (6 ... ♘bd7!? – row 5) 7 ♗xc4 b5 8 ♗d3 b4 9 ♘a4 ♗a6 10 0-0 0-0 11 ♘e5 ±.
5 ... ♗d6 6 ♗d3 ♘bd7 – 5 ... ♘bd7 6 ♗d3 ♗d6.

[2] **6 ♗d3** dc 7 ♗xc4 b5 8 ♗d3 c5 = (cf. QGA).
6 cd ed 7 ♗d3 ♗d6 =.
6 ♕c2!? ♘bd7 (6 ... dc 7 ♗xc4±) – 5 ... ♘bd7 6 ♕c2 a6.

[3] **10 ... ♕c7** 11 h3! e5 12 de ♘xe5 13 ♘d4 ±.
10 ... ♘e8 11 e4 de 12 ♘xe4 ♘df6 13 ♘xf6+ ♗xf6 14 ♘e5 ±.
10 ... ♖e8 11 a4 ♕e7 12 b5 e5 13 bc bc 14 a5 ed 15 ed ♖b8 16 ♕c2 ♘e4 17 ♗d3 ♕d8 18 ♘a4! ± Matanović-Simonović, Yugoslav Ch 1949.

[4] Pachman.

[5] **6 ... a6** 7 b3 ♗d6 8 e4 ±.
6 ... ♗b4 7 ♗d2 0-0 8 0-0 c5 9 ♔b1 cd 10 ♘xd4 ♘e5 11 ♘xd5! ± Polugayevsky-Szabo, Marianske Lazne 1959.
6 ... ♗e7 7 b3 0-0 8 ♗b2 b6 9 ♗e2 ♗b7 10 0-0 ♖c8 11 ♖ad1 ♕c7 12 ♗d3 ♗d6 13 e4 ± Stoltz-Kottnauer, Groningen 1946.

[6] **7 ♗d3** 0-0 8 0-0 dc 9 ♗xc4 e5 10 h3 ed 11 ♘xd4 ♘e5 12 ♗e2 ♘g6 13 ♗d2 ♗c7 14 ♖ad1 ♖e8 15 ♗c1 ♕e7∓ Forintos-Korchnoi, Moscow 1975. 12 ... ♖e8 13 ♖d1 ♕e7 14 a3 ♘g6! = Forintos-Ivanović, Vukovar 1976.

[7] **8 ♗d3** ♕e7 9 0-0-0 e5!? 10 e4?! dc 11 ♗xc4 ed 12 ♘xd4 ♘e5 13 ♗e2 ♗c5! 14 ♖e1 ♖d8 ∓ Lutikov-Vaganian, Moscow 1972.
8 ♗e2 ♕e7 9 0-0 ±.
8 h3!?

[8] **8 ... ♕e7** 9 e4!? de 10 ♘xe4 ♘xe4 11 ♕xe4 e5 12 ♗g5! ±.
8 ... ♘g4 9 ♗e1 f5 10 h3 ♘h6 11 ♗e2 ♘f6 12 ♘e5 ♗f7 13 f4! ♘e4 14 ♘xe4 de 15 g4 ♗d7 16 c5! ± Taimanov-Karaklajić, Yugoslavia v USSR 1957.
8 ... e5 9 cd cd 10 ♘b5 ♗b8 11 de ♘xe5 12 ♗c3 ♕e7 13 ♗d4 b6 14 ♘c3 ±.

8 ... dc 9 e4! e5 10 ♗xc4 b5 11 ♗b3! ♕e7 12 ♖he1 ± Sokolov.
8 ... b5!? 9 cb c5 10 e4! ♗b7 11 ed ed 12 ♕f5 ♖e8 13 ♗d3 cd 14 ♘xd4 ♘e5 15 ♗b1 g6 16 ♕g5 ♘eg4 17 ♕h4 ♖e5 18 ♗f4 ± Vladimirov-Fuchs, Leningrad 1967.

[9] 14 ♘bd4 ♗d7 15 ♗b5 ♖c8 16 ♕e2 ♘fe4 ∞ Kärner-Vaganian, Tallinn 1968.

[10] 10 ♗b2 ♗b4 11 0-0 ♗xc3 12 ♗xc3 ♘xc3 13 ♕xc3 ed 14 ♘xd4 ♕f6 15 b4 ♖d8 16 ♖fd1 h6 ∞ Reshevsky-Euwe, New York 1951.

[11] 11 ♗f4!? ♗b4+ 12 ♔e2 ∞.

[12] **7 b3** 0-0 8 ♗b2 b6 9 ♕c2 ♗b7 10 ♘e5 c5 ±.
7 e4 de 8 ♘xe4 ♘xe4 9 ♗xe4 ♘f6 10 ♗c2 0-0 11 ♕d3 ♕a5+ 12 ♗d2 ♗b4 13 0-0-0 ♗xd2+ 14 ♖xd2 b5 15 c5 ♕xa2 16 ♘e5 g6 17 h4 ± Alatortsev-Zamikhovsky, USSR Ch 1931.

[13] 14 ♘xc5 bc 15 ♘f3 ♕c7 16 ♘e5 ♖ad8 17 ♖fe1 ♖d6 18 ♗c3 ♗a8 19 ♕e3 ♖fd8 20 ♕h3 g6 21 ♖e3 ♖h5 22 ♕g4 ± Vaganian-Petrosian, USSR 1975.

[14] 7 ... ♗xc3+ 8 bc 0-0 9 0-0 b6 10 cd ed 11 a4 ± ECO.

[15] 8 ... de 9 ♘xe4 ♘xe4 10 ♗xe4 e5? 11 de ♘xe5 12 ♘xe5 ♗xe5 13 ♗xh7+ ♔xh7 14 ♕h5 ±± Geller-Kopilov, USSR Ch 1951.

[16] 14 ♕xf3 ♘bd7 15 d5 h6 16 ♗e3 cd 17 ♖xd5 ♗c5 18 ♗xb7 ♖b8 19 ♗c6 ♖xb2 = Gligorić-Pachman, Sarajevo 1961.

[17] 10 ... c5 11 ♗c2 ♕c7 12 ♖e1 ± Vaganian-Miles, Hastings 1974/75.

[18] 14 ♕f4 ± Taimanov.

[19] 12 ... ba♕ 13 gh♕ ♕a5+ 14 ♗d2 ♕xd1+ 15 ♗xd1 ♕f5 16 0-0 ♗b7 17 d5! ± Benko-Pytel, Hastings 1973/74.

[20] Ragozin-Böök, Saltsjöbaden 1948.

[21] 8 ... ♗b7 9 0-0 ♗e7?! (9 ... b4! – 8 ... b4) 10 ♖e1 0-0 11 e4! ± Klüger-Polgar, Hungarian Ch 1965.

[22] Korchnoi-Tal, Havana 1963.

[23] 14 ♘xd5 ed 15 dc ♘xc5 16 ♗c2 ♘fe4 = Tal.

Semi-Slav: Meran		1 d4 d5 2 c4 c6 3 ♘f3 ♘f6 4 ♘c3 e6 5 e3 ♘bd7 6 ♗d3 dc 7 ♗xc4 b5							
	8	9	10	11	12	13	14	15	16
1	♗d3	♘a4	e4[2]	e5	0-0	♖e1	♘xd4	♕h5	♕e2	=
	b4	c5[1]	cd[3]	♘d5	♗e7	0-0	♕c7	g6	♗b7[4]	
2	...	♘e4	♗xe4	♕a4[6]	♘d2	a3	♘c4	♕b3		±
	...	♘xe4[5]	♗b7	♕b6	♖c8	ba	♕a6[7]	♘b6[8]		
3	...	0-0[9]	♘e4[10]	♘xf6+	e4	♕c2	♗e3[12]	♖fd1	dc	±
	♗b7	b4	♗e7[11]	♘xf6	0-0	h6	♖c8	c5	♘g4[13]	
4	...	e4	♘a4	e5	♘xc5[14]	dc	0-0[16]	♘d2	♕c2	±
	...	b4	c5	♘d5	♘xc5[15]	♗xc5	h6[17]	♘c3	♕d5[18]	
5	...	...	...	...	0-0	♖e1	♗g5[20]	♘d2	♗xa6	±
	...	...	...	...	cd	g6[19]	♕a5[21]	♗a6	♕xa6[22]	
6	...	e4[23]	e5	♗f4[26]	♘e4	♔f1	h3	♗xh6	a4[27]	±
	a6	c5[24]	♘g4[25]	cd	♗b4+	♗b7	♘h6	gh		
7	...	...	...	♘xb5[28]	♕a4[29]	♘bxd4	0-0	h3	hg	±
	...	...	cd	♘g4	♗b7[30]	♕b6	♗c5	♗xf3	♗d5[31]	
8	...	...	...	...	ef	fg	♕e2	0-0	♖d1	±
	...	...	...	ab	♕b6[32]	♗xg7	0-0	♗b7	e5[33]	
9	...	...	...	...	♘xe5	♕f3[34]	♔e2	♕g3	♘f3	=
	...	...	...	♘xe5	ab	♗b4+	♖b8	♕d6	♕xg3[35]	
10	...	...	d5	b3[37]	0-0	a4	bc	♘e2	♘g3	±
	...	...	e5[36]	♗d6	0-0	c4[38]	b4	♘c5	♕c7[39]	
11	...	...	...	...	bc	♗d2	♗c2[40]	♘e2	♗xe4	±
	...	...	...	c4	♗b4	bc	♕a5	♘xe4	c3[41]	
12	...	...	...	de	♗c2	0-0	♕e2[44]	♘g5	f4	∞
	...	...	c4	fe[42]	♗b7[43]	♕c7	♗d6[45]	♘c5	e5[46]	

---

1 9 ... ♗b7 10 e4 – row 4.

2 10 ♘xc5 ♘xc5 11 dc ♗xc5 12 e4 ♗b7 13 e5 ♘d5 – row 4.

3 10 ... ♗b7 – row 4.

4 Taimanov.

5 9 ... ♗b7 10 ♘xf6+ ♘xf6 11 ♕a4 ♗e7 12 ♗d2 a5 13 e4 ♘d7 ± Taimanov.

  9 ... ♗e7 10 ♘xf6+ ♘xf6 11 e4 c5 12 0-0-0 13 ♕c2 ♘d7 14 ♖d1 ± Ragozin-Lundin, Saltsjöbaden IZ 1948.

6 11 0-0 – note 11.

7 14 ... ♕b4+ 15 ♕xb4 ♗xb4+ 16 ♗d2 ♗xd2+ 17 ♔xd2 ♔e7 18 ♖xa3 ± Kavalek.

8 15 ... ♕b5 16 ♕xb5 cb 17 ♗b7 ♖c7 18 ♘xa3 ♖xb7 19 ♗d2 ± Portisch-Ree, Wijk aan Zee 1975.

  15 ... ♘b6 ± Kavalek.

9 9 a3 b4 10 ab ♗xb4 11 0-0 c5 = Larsen.

10 10 ♘a4 c5 – cf. row 4.

11 10 ... ♘xe4 11 ♗xe4 ♗e7 12 ♘d2 (12 ♕c2±)

12 ... 0-0 13 b3 ♖c8 14 ♘c4 ♘f6 15 ♗f3 ♘d5 16 a3 ± Portisch-Polugayevsky, Portorož 1973.

10 ... c5 11 ♘xf6+ gf (11 ... ♘xf6 12 ♗b5+ ±) 12 e4 ± Peev-Barczay, Varna 1974.

[12] 14 e5 ♘d7 15 ♗h7+ ♔h8 16 ♗e4 ♕b6 17 ♗e3 c5 18 dc (Korchnoi-Polugayevsky, 3rd match game 1977) 18 ... ♘xc5 = R.Byrne.

[13] 17 ♗d4 e5 18 h3 ed 19 hg (Korchnoi-Polugayevsky, 7th match game 1977) 19 ... ♗xc5!? ±.

[14] 12 dc ♕a5 (12 ... ♘xc5!? 13 ♘xc5 ♗xc5 – 12 ♘xc5 ♘xc5 13 dc ♗xc5) 13 0-0 ♗xc5 14 ♖e1 ♘5b6 15 ♘xb6 ♕xb6 16 ♕e2 ± Rukavina-Korchnoi, Leningrad IZ 1973.

[15] 12 ... ♗xc5 13 dc ♘xc5 (13 ... ♖c8!? Larsen) 14 ♗b5+ ♔f8 15 ♗d4 ♕b6 16 ♗c4 ±.

[16] **14 ♗b5+?** ♔e7 15 0-0 ♕b6 $\mp$ Uhlmann-Larsen, match (4) 1971.

14 ♘g5!? (Polugayevsky) 14 ... ♕c7 15 0-0 ♕xe5 16 ♕a4+ ♔e7 17 ♘xf7 ♔xf7 18 ♕d7+ ♗e7 19 ♕xb7 ∞.

[17] 14 ... 0-0 15 ♗xh7+ ♔xh7 16 ♕c2+ ±±.

[18] 17 ♘f3 ♖d8 18 ♘e1 ♗d4 19 ♗d2 ♘b5 20 ♗xb4 (Polugayevsky-Mecking, Manila 1975) 20 ... ♗xe5 21 ♖d1 ± Polugayevsky.

[19] 13 ... ♗e7 14 ♘xd4 0-0 (14 ... ♕a5 15 ♗b5+) 15 ♕h5 g6 16 ♕h6 ±.

[20] 14 ♗b5!? a6 15 ♗g5 ♕c8 16 ♗f1 ± Nikitin.

[21] 14 ... ♗e7 15 ♗h6 ♗f8 16 ♗d2!? (16 ♗g5 ♗e7 etc; 16 ♕d2!? ♗c6 17 ♗xf8 ♔xf8 18 ♗e4 ♕a5 19 b3 ♗xa4 20 ♕h6+ ♔g8 21 ba ∞ Tukmakov-Polugayevsky, USSR Ch 1977) 16 ... ♖c8 17 ♘xd4 ♗g7 18 ♘f3 ± Vasyukov-Votruba, Leningrad 1974.

[22] 17 ♘e4 ♗g7 18 ♘ac5 ♘xc5 19 ♘xc5 ♕b5 20 ♕xd4 0-0 21 ♘e4 ± Tukmakov-Sveshnikov, Lvov 1978.

[23] **9 a4 b4** 10 ♘e4 ♗b7 11 0-0 c5 =.

9 0-0 c5 10 ♕e2 ♗b7 11 ♖d1 ♕c7 12 e4 cd 13 ♘xd4 ♗c5 = Sämisch-Capablanca, Moscow 1925.

[24] 9 ... b4 10 ♘a4 c5 11 e5 ♘d5 12 0-0 ♗b7 13 ♖e1 ± Portisch-Wade, Havana 1964.

[25] 10 ... ♘d5? 11 ♘xd5 ed 12 dc ±.

[26] **11 ♗e4** ±/∞.

11 ♗g5 ±/∞.

[27] Klüger-Florian, Hungarian Ch 1951.

[28] 11 ♘e4 ♘d5 12 0-0 h6 13 a4 b4 14 a5 ♗b7 15 ♖e1 ♗e7 = Bronstein-Dorfman, USSR Ch

1975.

[29] **12 ♗e4** ab 13 ♗xa8 ♕a5+ =.

12 ♘bxd4 ♗b4+ =.

[30] **12 ... ♖b8** 13 ♘d6+ ♗xd6 14 ed ±.

12 ... ♘c5 13 ♘d6+ ±.

12 ... ♘gxe5 13 ♘xe5 ♘xe5 14 ♘c7+ ±.

[31] 17 ♘b3 0-0 18 ♕xd7 ♗xb3 19 ♗xh7+ ♔xh7 20 ♕d3+ ♔g8 21 ♕xb3 ♖xb3 22 ab ♖fb8 (Trifunović-Gligorić, Amsterdam 1950) 23 ♖a4! ♖xb3 24 ♖c4 ± Korchnoi.

[32] 12 ... ♗b7 13 0-0 ♕b6 14 fg ♗xg7 – 12 ... ♕b6.

[33] 17 ♗xb5 ♕d6 18 ♗d2 ±.

[34] **13 ♗xb5+** ♗d7! 14 ♗xd7 ♕a5+ 15 ♗d2 ♕xb5 16 ♘xf6+ gf 17 ♕e2 = Trifunović-Schmid, Oberhausen 1961.

13 0-0 ♕d5 14 ♕e2 ♗a6 15 ♗g5 ♗e7 =.

[35] 17 hg ♕d6 18 ♗f4 ♗xf4 19 gf ♗d7 20 ♘xd4 ♔e7 21 ♖ac1 ♖hc8 = Szabo-Stahlberg, Saltsjöbaden IZ 1948.

[36] **10 ... ed** 11 e5! ♘g4 12 ♗g5 ±.

10 ... ♘b6 11 de ♗xe6 12 ♕e2 ±.

[37] 11 0-0 c4 12 ♗c2 ♗c5 =.

[38] 13 ... b4 14 ♘b1 intending ♗bd2, ♘c4 ±.

[39] 17 ♗e3 a5 18 ♗xc5 ♗xc5 19 ♘d2 ± Baumbach-Jovčić, corr. 1972.

[40] 14 ♗xc4? ♕c7 15 ♕b3 ♗xc3 16 ♗xc3 ♘xe4 $\mp$.

[41] 17 ♘xc3 ♗xc3 18 0-0 ♗xd2 19 ♘xd2 0-0 20 ♘c4 ♕b4 21 d6 (21 ♕c2 ±) 21 ... ♖a7 22 ♗d5 ± Honfi-Kempe, corr. 1978/79.

[42] 11 ...cd? 12 ed+ ♕xd7 13 0-0! ♗b7 14 ♖e1 ♗b4 15 ♘e5 ♕e6 16 ♘xd3 ♗xc3 17 ♘f4 ♕d7 18 bc ± Karpov-Tal, Bugojno 1980. 14 ♗g5!? ♗e7 15 e5!? ♘e4 16 ♗xe7 ♘xc3 17 bc ♕xe7 18 ♕xd3 ± Farago-Iskov, Esbjerg 1981.

[43] 12 ... ♕c7 13 0-0 ♗c5!? ∞ Georgadze-Yusupov, USSR Ch 1980/81.

[44] 14 ♘g5 ♘c5 (14 ... ♕c6 15 ♕f3! ± Gligorić-Ljubojević, Linares 1981) 15 f4 h6! 16 e5 ♘d3! 17 ♗xd3 0-0-0! $\mp$ Gligorić-Yusupov, Vrbas 1980.

[45] 14 ... 0-0-0 15 e5 ♘d5 16 a4 b4 (Ogaard-Westerinen, Gausdal 1981) 17 ♘xd5! ♗xd5 18 ♗g5! ±/± Bukić.

[46] **17 fe** ♗xe5 18 ♘f3 ♗xc3 19 bc 0-0 ∞ Dorfman-Sveshnikov, USSR Ch 1978.

17 a4 b4! 18 ♘d5 ♘xd5 19 ed 0-0-0 20 ♕xc4 ef 21 ♗xf4 ∞ Tukmakov-Dolmatov, USSR Ch 1979.

87

Slav-Grünfeld   1 d4 ♘f6 2 c4 g6 3 g3 d5 4 ♗g2 ♗g7 5 ♘f3 c6

	6	7	8	9	10	11	12	13	14	
1	♕a4[1]	0-0	cd	♕a3	♘c3	♕b4	♗f4	♘e5	♕b3[3]	±
	0-0	♘bd7[2]	♘b6	cd	♘c4	e6	♖e8	♗f8		
2	♘bd2	0-0	♘e5	♘df3	de	cd	♗e3	♖c1		=
	0-0	a5[4]	♘bd7	♘xe5	♘e4	cd	♗e6	♕d7[5]		
3	cd	0-0	♘c3	♘xe4[6]	♘e5[7]	♕b3+	♘c4	e3[9]	♗d2	=
	cd	0-0	♘e4	de	f6[8]	e6	♘c6	f5	♕d5[10]	
4	...	...	♘e5	f4![11]	♘c3	♘xg4	♘xd5	e3	♘xb6	±
	...	...	♘g4	♕b6?![12]	♗e6	♗xg4	♗xd4+	♗xd1	ab[13]	
5	...	♘c3!	♘e5	0-0	♘xc6	♕a4	♗f4	♕d2	♖ac1	±
	...	0-0	♘c6	e6[14]	bc	♘d7	♗a6	♖e8	♗b5[15]	
6	...	...	...	♗g5	♗f4	♕d2	♗xe5	♗xg7	0-0![16]	±
	...	...	e6	h6	♘fd7	♗xe5	♘c6	♔xg7		

[1] 6 ♘e5 0-0 7 0-0 dc 8 ♘xc4 ♗e6 9 b3 ♗d5 = Furman-Gufeld, USSR Ch 1972.

[2] 7 ... ♘fd7! 8 cd ♘b6 = Panno/Andersson.

[3] Portisch-Ivkov, Petropolis IZ 1973.

[4] 7 ... ♗f5 8 b3 ♘e4 9 ♗b2 ♕a5 10 a3 ♘d7 11 b4 ± Ribli-Andersson, Wijk aan Zee 1973. 9 ... ♘d7 10 ♘h4 ♘xd2 11 ♕xd2 ♗e6 12 ♖ac1 ±.
7 ... ♗g4 8 b3 ♘bd7 9 ♗b2 ♗xf3 10 ♗xf3 ± Pfleger-Vizantiadis, Skopje Ol 1972.
7 ... ♘bd7 8 b3 b5 9 ♗b2 ♗a6 10 c5 ± Vukić-Macles, Biel 1972.
7 ... ♘e4 8 ♕b3! ±.

[5] Olafsson-Uhlmann, Havana Ol 1966.

[6] 9 ♘e5 ♘xc3 10 bc ♘d7 (10 ... ♘c6 11 ♘xc6 bc 12 ♕a4 ♕b6 13 ♗a3 ♕a6! =) 11 ♘xd7 ♕xd7 = Smejkal-Uhlmann, Raach 1969.
9 ♕b3 ♘c6 10 ♖d1 ♘a5 11 ♕b4 ♘xc3 12 ♕xc3 ♗f5 =/∓ Donner-Botvinnik, Palma 1967.

[7] 10 ♘g5 ♕xd4 11 ♘xe4 ♘c6 12 ♕b3 ♗f5 13 ♘c3 ♕b6 14 ♕xb6 ab 15 ♗e3 ♖a6 = Petrosian-Geller, USSR Ch 1958.

[8] 10 ... ♘d7 11 ♗xe4 (11 ♘c4!?) 11 ... ♘xe5 12 de ♗h3 13 ♖e1 ♕d1 14 ♖xd1 ♗xe5 =.

[9] 14 f3!?

[10] 15 ♖ac1 e5 = Pfleger-Ghitescu, Hamburg 1965.

[11] 9 ♘xg4 ♗xg4 10 ♘c3 ♘c6 11 h3 ♗d7!? (11 ... ♗e6 12 e4!? ♘xd4 13 ed ♗d7 14 ♗g5 ♘f5 15 ♖e1 h6 16 ♗f4 ♖e8 17 ♖c1 ± Christiansen-Browne, Buenos Aires 1981) 12 e3 e6 13 b3 ♕a5 = Polugayevsky-Kasparov, Moscow 1981.

[12] 9 ... ♘xe5 10 fe ± Averbakh.

[13] 15 ♖xd1 ± Averbakh-Kupreichik, USSR 1981.

[14] 9 ... ♘xe5 10 de ♘g4 11 ♖xd5 ♘xe5 12 ♕b3 e6 13 ♘c3 ♕a5 14 ♖d1 ♖b8 15 ♗d2 ♗d7 16 a4 ♕b6 17 ♕xb6 ab 18 b3 ± Schmidt-Uhlmann, Poland v East Germany 1974.
9 ... ♗f5 10 ♘xc6 bc 11 ♘a4 ♘d7 12 b3 e5 13 de ♗xe5 14 ♗h6 ♖e8 15 ♖c1 ♖c8 16 ♕d2 = Botvinnik-Smyslov, match 1957.

[15] 15 ♘c3 ♗a6 16 ♖fd1 ♖c8 17 ♗h6 ♗f6 18 h4 e5 19 de ♗xe5 20 ♗h3 ± Larsen-Krogius, Le Havre 1966.

[16] Miles-Andersson, London 1980.

Grünfeld Defence

Austrian theoretician Ernst Grünfeld's creation is based on one of the fundamental strategies of the hypermodern school: that a large pawn centre can be a target as well as a strategical asset. This defence retains its viability and has served its skilful exponents – Smyslov, Fischer, Korchnoi and more recently Timman and Adorjan – as an ambitious and reliable weapon.

The Exchange Variation (4 cd ♘xd5 5 e4) has been the main theoretical battleground for the defence. In the Classical Exchange (white knight on e2) White establishes the vaunted pawn centre as a basis for a direct attack, while Black tries to negotiate its collapse. The play is highly complex but Black's resources have weathered White's various attempts, and the Modern Exchange (white knight on f3) has replaced it in recent practice. Long thought to be innocuous, the finer points of this variation were brought to light by English GM Tony Miles. In contrast to the more aggressive ♘e2, here White tries to maintain a small plus by safeguarding his centre and often plays for a lasting pull in the ending. At present White appears able to stay on top here, but the delicate nature of the position makes it a fertile field for new ideas and the verdict on this difficult line will always be subject to change.

Less direct methods for White try a more gradual approach of occupying the centre, Black being compensated with quick development and lasting opportunities to undermine White's handiwork. The most dangerous of these is the Smyslov System (4 ♘f3 ♗g7 5 ♕b3) which periodically enjoys a prominent place in the theoretical limelight. White also has a number of quiet tries (lines with ♗f4 or ♗g5) but the consensus is that Black can achieve equality in all lines.

The Neo-Grünfeld is a closely related system. White delays the development of his queen's knight in order to chase the black knight on d5, which can no longer exchange itself on c3. This line offers White prospects of a slight edge, but the player who is content to quietly fight back against the white centre will probably also find these positions to his liking.

	Neo-Grünfeld I			1 d4 Nf6 2 c4 g6 3 g3 Bg7 4 Bg2 d5 5 cd Nxd5					
	6	7	8	9	10	11	12	13	14	
1	e4	d5[2]	a3	Nc3	Be3!	ab	Bxd4	Nge2		=
	Nb4[1]	c6	Qa5	cd	d4[3]	Qd8	Bxd4	Bxc3+[4]		
2	Nc3	bc	e3	Ne2	0-0[5]	a4[6]	Ba3	Re1	Nf4	=
	Nxc3	c5!	0-0	Nd7	Rb8	b6	Ba6	Qc7	Rfd8[7]	
3	...	...	...	...	0-0	a4[8]	Rb1	Ba3	Nf4	=
	...	...	...	Nc6	Qa5	Rd8[9]	Qc7	b6	Ba6[10]	
4	...	e3	Nge2	0-0	d5[12]	e4	ed[13]			=
	Nb6	0-0	e5	Re8[11]	c6	cd				
5	...	Nf3	e3[14]	0-0	d5	e4	Bg5	Be3	Bxb6	±
	...	Nc6	0-0	e5[15]	Na5	c6	f6!	cd	Qxb6[16]	
6	...	...	...	...	...	e4	a4[17]	a5	Qb3[18]	∞
	...	...	...	...	Ne7	Bg4	c6	Nc4	Nxa5[19]	
7	...	...	...	...	...	...	h3	Qxf3	Rd1	∞
	...	...	...	...	...	...	Bxf3	c6	cd[20]	
8	Nf3	0-0	dc	Ng5!	Nc3	Nf3	Rxd1	Be3![23]	Rac1	±
	0-0	c5	Na6	Ndb4	h6[21]	Qxd1[22]	Be6	Nc2	Nxe3[24]	
9	...	...	Nc3	d5	e4	Bg5	Bf4	ed	Qe2	∞
	...	Nb6	Nc6	Na5[25]	c6	h6	cd	Nac4	g5[26]	

[1] 6 ... ♘b6?! 7 ♘e2 ♘c6 8 d5 ♘b8 (8 ... ♘a5!? Hartston) 9 0-0 0-0 10 a4 e6 11 ♘bc3 ed 12 ed ♖e8 13 ♕b3 c6 14 ♗e3 ± Donner-Larsen, Santa Monica 1966. 7 ... e5 8 d5 c6 9 ♘bc3 cd 10 ed 0-0 11 0-0 ♘c4 (11 ... ♗f5 12 b3! Boleslavsky) 12 ♘e4 ♗f5 13 ♘2c3 ♗xe4 14 ♘xe4 ♘d6 15 ♗g5 ± Stahlberg-Smyslov, Candidates' 1950.

[2] 7 ♕a4+ ♘8c6 8 d5 ♘d3+ 9 ♔f1 (9 ♔d2 ♘xb2) 9 ... ♘xc1 10 dc b5 11 ♕c2 ♗xb2! ∓ Boleslavsky.

[3] 10 ... ♘4c6 11 ed ♗xc3+ 12 bc ♕xc3+ 13 ♗d2 ♕e5+ 14 ♘e2 ♘d4 15 ♗c3 ±/ ±±. 11 ... ♘e5!? Marić.

[4] 13 ... ♗b6 14 ♕b3 ±.
13 ... ♗xc3+ 14 ♕xc3 ♕xd1+ 15 ♖xd1 ♘a6 =.

[5] 10 a4 ♖b8 11 a5 b5 12 ab ab 13 0-0 ♗b7 14 e4 cd 15 cd ♘c5 16 ♖a7 ♗a6 = Gligorić-Taimanov, Havana 1967 (∓ Hartston).

[6] 11 e4 b5 12 ♗e3 ♗a6 13 a3 ♘b6 14 ♖a2 ♘c4 15 ♗g5 ♕d7 16 ♕c1 e5 17 d5 f6 ∓ Gligorić-Uhlmann, Moscow 1967.

[7] 15 ♕b3 ♘f6 16 ♖ad1 e5 = Trifunović-Uhlmann, Leipzig 1965.

[8] 11 ♕b3 ♗g4! ∓ Hartston.

[9] 11 ... cd 12 cd ♕h5 13 ♖b1 ♗h3? 14 ♗xh3 ♕xh3 15 ♖xb7 ♖fd8 16 ♗a3 ± Korchnoi-Gligorić, Leningrad v Belgrade 1965.

[10] 15 ♖e1 ♗c4 Taimanov-Ilivitsky, USSR Ch 1952.

[11] 9 ... ed 10 ♘xd4 ♘bd7 11 a4 a5 12 b3 ♖e8 13 ♗a3 ± Korchnoi-Gufeld, USSR Ch 1967.
9 ... cd!? Hartston.

[12] 10 a4 a5 11 b3 ♘c6 12 d5 ♘b4 13 e4 c6 14 dc bc 15 ♕xd8 ♖xd8 16 ♗e3 ♖b8 17 ♖fd1 ♖xd1+ 18 ♖xd1 ♗e6 ∓ Osnos-Savon, USSR Ch 1967.

[13] Hartston.

[14] 8 ♗f4 0-0 9 0-0 ♗e6 10 e3 h6 11 h4 ♘b4! 12 e4 ♗c4 13 ♘e2 c5 ∓/ ∓ Ravinsky-Dubinin, USSR 1949. 9 ... ♘xd4 10 ♕xd4 ♗xd4 (10 ... e5 11 ♘c6! ±) 11 ♘b5 e5 12 ♗h6 ♖e8 13 e3 ♗c5 14 ♕xd8 = Cherepkov-Savon, USSR Ch 1967.

[15] 9 ... ♖e8 10 ♘e1 e5 11 d5 ♘a5 12 e4 (12 ♘c2!?) 12 ... c6!? 13 ♘c2 cd 14 ed ♖ac4 15 b3 ♘d6 16 ♗b2 e4 ∞ Furman-Jansa, Leningrad 1970.
9 ... a5 10 d5 ♘b4 11 e4 c6 12 a3 ♘a6 13 dc bc 14 ♕c2 ± Olafsson-Sigurjonsson, Reykjavik 1966.

[16] 14 ... ab 15 ♕xd5+ ♔h8 16 ♖fd1 ♕e7 17 ♕b5 ♕c5 18 ♖d5 ± Smejkal-Lombardy, Siegen Ol 1970.

[17] 12 ♕b3 c6 13 ♘h4!? cd 14 ed (Podgayets-E.Vladimirov, USSR 1975) 14 ... ♘ec8! =. 13 ♗e3 cd 14 ed ♖c8 intending ... ♘f5 = Ree-Timman, Wijk aan Zee 1975.

[18] 14 a6 ba 15 dc ♕xd1 intending ... ♘xc6 = Botvinnik/Abramov.

[19] 14 ... cd 15 ♘xd5 ♘xd5 16 ♕xc4 ♘e7 17 ♗e3 ± Hübner-Rogoff, Biel IZ 1976.
14 ... ♘xa5 15 ♕a2 (15 ♕a4 b6 16 b4 ♘c4 17 dc a6! 18 ♗g5 b5 19 ♗xe7! ♕xe7 20 ♘d5 ♕d6 21 ♕c2 ♖a7 22 ♘d2 ♖xd2 23 ♕xd2 ♕xc6 24 ♕e3 ∞; 17 ... ♕d3! 18 ♕b3 ♗xf3 19 ♗xf3 ♕xf3 20 ♕xc4 ♘xc6! intending ... ♖ac8 =) 15 ... b6 16 b4 ♘b7 17 ♗g5 c5 18 d6 ♘xd6! 19 ♘d5 ♘xd5! 19 ♗xd8 ♘xb4 20 ♕b2 ♗fxd8 ∓ Azmaiparashvili-Gavrikov, USSR 1980. 19 bc! ♘c3! ∞ Gavrikov.

[20] 15 ♘xd5 ♘bxd5 16 ♗g5 h6 17 ♖xd5 ♕e8 18 ♗xe7 =. 15 ... ♘exd5!? 16 ed ♘d6 17 ♕b3 ♖fd8 18 ♗d2 ♖d7 ∞ Lapenis-Bagirov, USSR 1980.

[21] 10 ... ♕xd1 11 ♖xd1 ♘xc5 12 ♗e3 ♘e6 13 ♖ac1 ♘c6 14 ♘d5 ± Geller-Sandor, Göteborg 1967.
10 ... ♘xc5 11 ♗e3 ♘ca6 12 a3 ♘c6 13 ♖c1 h6 14 ♘ge4 ± Eliskases-Wexler, Buenos Aires 1954. 12 ♕b3! h6 13 a3 ±.

[22] 11 ... ♗f5 (Estrin) 12 ♘h4! ♕xd1 13 ♖xd1 ♗c2 14 ♖d2 g5 15 ♗xb7 gh 16 ♗xa6 hg 17 hg ♗f5 18 ♗b7 ♖ab8 19 c6 ♗c8 20 a3 ±± Rokhlin-Estrin, corr. 1969.

[23] 13 ♗f4 ♘xc5 14 ♗e5 f6 = Boleslavsky.
13 ♗d2 ♘xc5 14 ♘b5 ♘xa2 15 ♘c7 ♗b3 16 ♘xa8 ♗xd1 17 ♖xd1 ♗b3 18 ♘c7 ♖d8 ∞ Krogius-Navarovsky, Budapest 1965.
13 ♘e1 ♘xc5 14 ♗g3 ♖ac8 15 ♘b5 ♘a4 16 ♘xa7 ♖cd8 17 a3 ♘d5 = Gligorić-Olafsson, Los Angeles 1963.

[24] 15 fe ♘xc5 16 b4! ♘a6 17 a3 ♗b3 18 ♖d7 ♖fd8 19 ♖xd8+ ♖xd8 20 ♘d4 ± Portisch-Klüger, Hungarian Ch 1964.

[25] 9 ... ♘b4 10 e4 c6 11 a3! ♘a6 12 dc bc 13 ♕c2 ♕c7 14 b3 e5 15 ♗e3 f6 16 ♖fc1 ♗e6 17 ♗f1 ♕b7 18 ♘a4 ± Sokolsky-Simagin, corr. 1951.

[26] 15 ♗c1 ♗g4 16 h3 ♗h5 17 g4 ♗g6 18 ♘d2 ♖c8 19 ♘de4 ♕d7 20 f4 gf 21 ♗xf4 ♘xb2 22 ♕xb2 ♗xe4 23 ♗xe4 ♖xc3 ∞ Gufeld-Taimanov, USSR 1969. 18 h4 ♕d7 19 hg ♕xg4 20 gh ♗f6 ∞ Krogius-Hort, Varna 1969.

91

Neo-Grünfeld II   1 d4 ♘f6 2 c4 g6 3 g3 ♗g7 4 ♗g2 d5 5 ♘f3 0-0 6 0-0 dc

	7	8	9	10	11	12	13	14	15	
1	♕a4[1]	♖d1[2]	♕xc4	♕b3	♘c3	♕c2	♕d2	♕f4	d5[4]	∞
	♘c6	♘d7	♘b6	a5	a4	♗f5	♘c4[3]	♗c2		
2	♘a3	♘xc4	dc	♘ce5	♗e3	♖c1				=
	♘a6[5]	c5	♗e6	♘xc5	♘fe4![6]	♖c8![7]				
3	...	♘xc4	b3	♗b2	♖c1	ba	♘fe5	♔xg2	♔g1[10]	±
	♘c6	♗e6	♗d5[8]	a5	a4[9]	♖a6	♗xg2	♕a8	♖xa4[11]	
4	...	...	...	...		a3[12]	e3	♕e2	♖fd1	±
	...	...	...	...	♕c8	♖d8	♕e6	h6	♗e4[13]	
5	...	bc	♘c4	♘ce5[14]	♗b2	e3	♕e2	♘xe5	♔xg2	=/∓
	c3	c5	♘c6	♗f5!	♗e4	♕c7	♘xe5	♗xg2	♘e4[15]	
6	...	...	♘e5	♘xc6	♕d3[17]	cd	♘c2			=
	...	...	♘c6!?[16]	bc	cd	♘d5	a5[18]			

---

[1] **7 ♘c3?!** ♘c6 8 d5 ♘b4 9 ♘e5 e6 10 de ♗xe6 11 ♗xb7 ♖b8 12 ♗g2 ♘fd5 13 ♘xd5 ♗xe5 14 ♗f4 ♗xb2 15 ♗xc7 ♕d7 ∓ Boleslavsky.
7 ♘bd2?! b5 8 ♘e5 ♘d5 ∓.
7 ♘e5?! ♘e8!

[2] 8 ♕xc4 ♗e6 9 ♕a4 ♘d5 10 ♘c3 ♘b6 11 ♕d1 ♗xd4 12 ♘xd4 ♕xd4 13 ♕xd4 ♗xd4 14 ♘b5 ♗e5 15 ♗xb7 = Pirchalava-Kasparian, USSR 1949.

[3] 13 ... ♕d7!? Ivkov.

[4] Ivkov-Andersson, Wijk aan Zee 1971.

[5] **7 ... c6** 8 ♘xc4 ♗e6 9 ♕c2 ♗d5 10 ♘cd2 ♘a6 ∓ Botvinnik/Abramov.
7 ... ♗e6 8 ♘g5 ♗d5 9 e4 h6 10 ed ±.
7 ... ♘bd7 8 ♘xc4 ♘b6 9 ♘a5 c6 10 b4 ± Hartston.

[6] 11 ... ♕a5 12 ♕d2 ♕xd2 13 ♘xd2 ♘cd7 14 ♘xd7 ♘xd7 15 ♖ac1 ± Hartston.

[7] Botvinnik/Abramov.

[8] 9 ... a5!? 10 ♗b2 a4 11 ♘g5 ♗d5 12 e4 ♗xc4 13 bc h6 14 ♘h3 a3 15 ♗c3 ♘d7 16 ♖c1 (16 e5 ♘b6 17 ♖b1 ♘a4 ∞ Iljevski-Fischer, Skopje 1967) 16 ... e5 17 d5 ♗e7 (17 ... ♘d4? 18 ♗xd4 ed 19 f4 ±± Portisch-Iljevski, Skopje 1968) 18 ♗b4 ±.   13 ... a3! 14 ♗c3 ♘d7 ∓.

[9] 11 ... ♕b8!? intending ... ♖d8, ... a4, ... ♕a7 Sahović.

[10] 15 ♘xc6 bc 16 a5 c5+ 17 ♔g1 ♖d8 18 e3 cd

19 ed c5 = Vogt-Ghizdavu, Bucharest 1974.

[11] 16 a3 ♖a6 17 ♕c2 ± Pomar-Andersson, Olot 1971.

[12] 12 e3 ♖d8 13 ♕e2 ♕e6 14 ♘ce5 ± Pfleger.

[13] 16 ♗f1! ± Padevsky-Whiteley, Nice Ol 1974.

[14] **10 ♗a3** cd 11 cd ♗e6 12 ♘ce5 ♗d5 13 ♘xc6 ♗xc6 =.
10 ♘fe5 ♘d5! Gipslis.
10 ♗b2 ♗e6 11 ♘fe5 ♘xe5 12 ♘xe5 ♗d5 13 ♗xd5 (13 f3 ♘d7! Gipslis) 13 ... ♕xd5 14 c4 ♕d6 15 d5 e6! ∓ Lengyel-Gipslis, Tallinn 1975.

[15] Schüssler-Kasparov, Graz 1981.

[16] 9 ... ♘d5 10 ♘d2 (10 ♗b2 ♘c6! 11 ♘ac4 ♘xe5 12 ♘xe5 ♘b6! 12 ♗a3 ♗xe5 14 de ♕c7 ∓ Gipslis; 11 ... ♗e6!?) 10 ... ♘c6 11 ♘xc6 bc 12 ♖c1 cd (12 ... ♖b8!? Gipslis; 12 ... ♕a5 13 c4 ♕xa3 14 cd ± Gipslis) 13 cd ♗xd4 14 ♗h6 ♗g7 15 ♗xg7 ♔xg7 16 ♖xc6 ♗e6! 17 ♖c5 ♕d6 18 ♕d4+ ♘f6! 19 ♕xd6 ed 20 ♖a5 (20 ♗xa8 dc ∓) 20 ... ♖ab8 21 ♖a1 (21 ♖xa7=) 21 ... ♖b2 22 ♘b5 (Csom-Gaprindashvili, Olot 1973) 22 ... a6! 23 ♘d4 (23 ♘xd6 ♖d8 ∓) 23 ... ♗c4 ∓ Gipslis.

[17] **11 ♗xc6?** ♗h3 12 ♖e1 ♘d5! 13 ♗b2 ♖b8 ∓ Panchenko-Malanyuk, Harkov 1980.
11 ♕a4 ♘d5 12 ♕xc6 ♗e6 ∞.

[18] Analysis.

	4	5	6	7	8	9	10	11	12	
1	♕b3[1]	♕xc4	♕b5+[2]	♕b3	♘f3	e4	h3[5]	♗e3	♕c2	∓
	dc	♗e6	♗d7[3]	♘c6[4]	♗g7	0-0	♖b8	b5	b4[6]	
2	♗g5	cd[7]	bc	♘f3	e3	♗b5+[9]	c4	0-0	cb	=
	♘e4!	♘xc3[8]	♕xd5	c5	♗g7	♗d7	♕e4	♗xb5	♘d7[10]	
3	...	♗h4	e3[12]	♕b3	ed	♖d1[15]	♗xc4	♘f3	0-0	∞
	...	c5[11]	♕a5[13]	cd[14]	♗h6!	dc	♘d6	0-0	♕c7[16]	
4	♗f4	e3[17]	♖c1	dc	cd	♕c2	e4	♘f3	♘d2	±
	♗g7	0-0	c5[18]	♕a5[19]	♘e4!?[20]	♕xc5	♘ba6	b5	f5[21]	
5	...	...	cd	♘xd5	♗xc7	♘e2!	f3	♘c3	♗f4[24]	∞
	...	...	♘xd5	♕xd5	♘c6[22]	♗g4	♖ac8[23]	♕e6		
6	...	...	dc	♖c1[25]	♗xc4	♘f3	0-0	♗b3	♕e2	=
	...	c5	♕a5	dc	0-0	♘c6	♕xc5	♕a5	♘h5[26]	
7	cd	♘f3	♕b3[27]	♗g5	♗h4	♕c2	♖d1	e3	♕b1	∞
	♘xd5	♗g7	♘b6!	h6	♗e6	♘c6	0-0	♘b4	♗f5[28]	

[1] 4 f3 ♗g7 5 e4 de 6 fe c5! 7 d5 e6 8 ♘f3 0-0 9 ♗e2 ed 10 ed =.
  4 g4 dc 5 g5 ♘fd7 6 e4 ♗g7 7 ♗xc4 ♘b6 8 d5 ♘xc4 9 ♕a4+ ♕d7! 10 ♕xc4 ♕g4 11 ♕e2 ∓.

[2] 6 ♕d3 c5 7 dc ♘c6 8 ♘f3 ♗g7 9 e4 0-0 10 ♕b5 ♕c7 11 ♗e2 ♖fd8 12 0-0 a6 13 ♕a4 ♖ac8 ∓ Belavenets-Yudovich, Moscow 1936.

[3] 6 ... ♘c6 7 ♘f3 ♗d5! 8 e4 ♗b4 9 ♕a4 ♗d7 10 ♕d1 e5 11 a3 ed 12 ♕b1 ♗a6 13 b4 ♘axb4 14 ab ♗xb4+ 15 ♗d2 ♕e7 16 ♗d3 ♗xd2+ 17 ♘bxd2 ± Petrosian-Benko, USA 1963.

[4] 7 ... ♗c6 8 ♘f3 ♗g7 9 e3 0-0 = Fine-Flohr, Semmering-Baden 1937.

[5] 10 ♕xb7 ♖b8 11 ♕a6 ♘b4 12 ♕e2 c5 ∞ Botvinnik/Estrin.

[6] Forintos-Adorjan, Wijk aan Zee 1971. Black intends ... b3 and ... ♘b4 ∓.

[7] 5 ♗f4 ♘xc3 6 bc ♗g7 7 e3 c5 8 ♘f3 0-0 9 cd ♕xd5 10 ♗e2 cd 11 cd ♕a5+ = Korchnoi-Uhlmann, Buenos Aires 1960.

[8] 5 ... ♘xg5 6 h4 ♘e4! 7 ♕xe4 ♕xd5 = Canal-Gligorić, Dubrovnik Ol 1950.

[9] 9 c4 ♕d8! intending ... ♕a5+, ... ♘c6 ∓.

[10] 13 ♖c1 b6 = Alekhine-Grünfeld, Vienna 1922.

[11] 5 ... ♘xc3 6 bc dc 7 e3 ♗e6 8 ♖b1 b6 9 ♗e2 ♗h6 10 ♘f3 c6 11 ♘e5 ♗g7 12 f4 ♗d5 13 0-0 ♘d7 14 ♘xc4 ±Taimanov-Fischer, match 1971.
  5 ... ♘g7 6 e3 ♘xc3 7 bc c5 8 cd cd 9 ♗b5+ ♗d7 10 ♗xd7+ ♘xd7 11 cd ♕a5+ 12 ♕d2 ♕xd5 13 ♘f3 e5! = Averbakh-Antoshin, USSR 1970.

[12] 6 cd ♘xc3 7 bc ♕xd5 8 e3 ♗g7 9 ♕f3 ♕d8 10 ♗b5+ ♘d7 = Bagirov-Tseitlin, USSR 1970.

[13] 6 ... ♗g7 7 cd – note 12.

[14] 7 ... ♘c6 8 ♘f3 cd 9 ed ♘xc3 10 bc ♗e6 11 ♗e2 ♗g7 12 0-0 0-0 13 c5! ± Taimanov-Filip, Wijk aan Zee 1970.

[15] 9 ♘f3 g5! 10 ♗g3 g4 11 ♘e5 ♗d2+ 12 ♔d1 ♗xc3 13 bc f6 ∓ Yuferov-Razuvayev, Chelyabinsk 1972.

[16] 13 ♗d3 ♗e6 ∞ Gorchakov-Gulko, Kiev 1973.

[17] 5 ♕a4+ ♗d7 6 ♕b3 ♘c6 7 e3 ♘a5 8 ♕b4 c5! 9 ♕xc5 ♖c8 10 ♕b4 dc 11 ♘f3 b5 12 d5 ♘b7 ∓ (intending ... a5) Boleslavsky.
  5 ♘f3 – 4 ♘f3.

[18] 6 ... c6! 7 ♘f3 – 4 ♘f3.

[19] 7 ... ♗e6 (Botvinnik) 8 ♘f3 ♘c6 9 ♗e2 ♘e4 10 0-0! ♗xc3 11 bc dc 12 ♘d4 ♗xc5 13 ♗h6 ± Portisch-Schmidt, Skopje Ol 1972.

[20] 8 ... ♖d8 9 ♗c4 ♗e6 10 e4! ♘xe4 11 ♘e2 ± Pomar-Tatai, Malaga 1969.

[21] 13 e5 ♗b7 14 ♗e2 b4 15 ♘c4 ♕d8 16 ♘a4 ± Portisch-Sax, Teesside 1972. 14 ... e6!?

[22] 8 ... b6 9 ♗e2 ♘a6 10 ♗g3 e5! 11 de ♕a5+ 12 ♔f1 ♗xe5 ∞ Pachman.
  8 ... ♘a6 9 ♗xa6 ♗xg2 10 ♕f3 ♕xf3 11 ♘xf3 ba = Lengyel-Gligorić, Enschede 1963.

[23] 10 ... ♗xf3?! 11 gf ♕xf3 12 ♖g1 ♕xe3 13 ♗f4 ♕e4 14 ♗g2 ♕f5 15 ♗xc6! bc 16 ♕d2 ± Ivkov-Bouwmeester, Leipzig Ol 1960.

[24] 12 ... ♘xd4!? 13 fg ♖fd8 14 ♗d3 ♘c6 ∞ Nei-Simagin, corr. 1967/68.
  12 ... ♗xd4 13 fg g5! 14 ♗xg5 ♖fd8 ∞ Fedder-Ribli, Groningen 1971.

[25] 7 ♕a4+ ♕xa4 8 ♘xa4 ♘e4 9 f3 ♗d7 =.
  7 cd ♘xd5 8 ♕xd5 ♗xc3+ 9 bc ♕xc3+ 10 ♔e2 ♕xa1 11 ♗e5 ♕c1 (11 ... ♕b1!? ∞ Gheorghiu-Barry, USA 1974) 12 ♗xh8 ♗e6 13 ♕xb7 ♕c2+ 14 ♔f3 ♕f5+ = Vaughan-Purdy, corr. 1945.

[26] 13 ♗g5 ♗g4 = Hort.

[27] Romanishin.

[28] 13 e4 ♗g4 14 d5 g5 15 ♗g3 f5! ∞.

Grünfeld: 5 e3, 5 ♕b3   1 d4 ♘f6 2 c4 g6 3 ♘c3 d5 4 ♘f3 ♗g7

	5	6	7	8	9	10	11	12	13	
1	e3[1]	b4[3]	♗b2	♗d3[5]	♗xc3	h3	♕xf3	de	♕g3	=
	0-0[2]	♘e4[4]	c6	♘xc3	♗g4[6]	♗xf3	e5	♘d7	♕e7[7]	
2	...	♗d2	dc	cd	♗c4	0-0	♘d4	♕e2	♖fd1	=
	...	c5[8]	♘a6[9]	♘xc5[10]	♗f5[11]	♖c8	♗e4	♘xd5	♘b6[12]	
3	...	♗e2	♗xc4	d5	e4	♗d3	0-0[15]	♗c2	a3	=
	...	dc[13]	c5	♘e8[14]	♘d6	e5	c4	b5	♘d7[16]	
4	...	cd	♗c4	bc	0-0	♕e2[19]	♗a3	♖ac1	♗b2	=
	...	♘d5	♘xc3[17]	c5	♕c7[18]	♗g4	♘d7[20]	♕a5	♖ac8[21]	
5	...	♕b3	♗d2	♗d3	0-0	cd[24]	e4[25]	♘xd5	♘xf6+	=
	...	c6[22]	e6[23]	♘bd7	b6	ed	c5	cd	♗xf6[26]	
6	♕b3	♕xc4	e4	♗e2	♗e3[31]	gf	f4	0-0-0	♕c5	=
	dc[27]	0-0[28]	♘c6[29]	♗g4[30]	♗xf3	e6	♘d7	♘b6	♗f6[32]	
7	...	...	...	♗f4[33]	♖d1[34]	♖xd4	e5	♕b5	♗e3	±
			♘a6	c5	cd	♕b6	♗e6	♘h5	♕xb5[35]	
8	...	...	...	♗e3[37]	♗e2	♖d1	♕c5	h3[40]	gf	=
			♗g4[36]	♘fd7[38]	♘c6	♘b6[39]	♕d6	♗xf3	♖fd8[41]	
9	...	...	...	...	♕b3	♖d1	♗e2	♘g1[45]	♘gxe2	±
					♘b6[42]	e6[43]	♗c6[44]	♗xe2	♕e7[46]	
10	...	...	...	...	...	...	d5[47]	♗e2	gf	±
						♘c6	♘e5	♗xf3+[48]	♗h5[49]	
11	...	...	...	♗f4[50]	♕xc7	♗xc7	e5	♘xd5[51]	♗e2	=
			a6	b5	♕xc7	♗b7	♘d5	♗xd5	♖c8[52]	
12	...	...	...	♕b3	e5	h4[53]	e6	ef+	♕d1	∞
				b5	♘fd7	c5[54]	c4	♔h8	♘c6[55]	

[1] 5 ♕a4+ ♗d7 6 ♕b3 dc 7 ♕xc4 (7 ♕xb7? ♘c6 8 ♗f4 ♖b8 9 ♕xc7 ♕xc7 10 ♗xc7 ♖xb2 ∓ Kovacs-Paoli, Vienna 1949) 7 ... 0-0 8 e4 ♘a6 9 ♗e2 c5 10 d5 e6 = Gipslis.

[2] 5 ... dc 6 ♗xc4 – Queen's Gambit Accepted.

[3] Makogonov.

[4] 6 ... a5 7 b5 c5 8 bc bc 9 ♗a3 ± Makagonov-Novotelnov, USSR 1951.

6 ... b6 7 ♗b2 c5 8 bc bc 9 ♖c1 cd 10 ♘d4 ♗b7 11 ♕b3 ♘c6 = Taimanov-Schmidt, Albena 1974.

[5] 8 ♕c2!? Pytel.

[6] 9 ... dc 10 ♗xc4 ♘d7 11 0-0 ♘b6 12 ♗b3 ♕d6 = Holmov-Korchnoi, USSR Ch 1954.

[7] 14 f4 f6 15 e6 ♘b6 16 f5 ½-½ Ivkov-Pytel, Zemun 1980.

[8] 6 ... c6 7 ♗d3 ♘a6 8 cd ♘b4 9 ♗e2 ♘bxd5 10 0-0 ♗f5 11 ♕b3 ± Smyslov-Hort, Skopje 1969.

[9] 7 ... dc? 8 ♗xc4 ♕a5 9 ♘b5 ± Bagirov.

[10] 8 ... ♘xd5 9 ♗xa6 ba 10 0-0 ♖b8 11 ♘a4 ♗d7 12 ♖c1 ± Polugayevsky-Boleslavsky, USSR 1962.

[11] 9 ... a6 10 a4 (10 b4? b5! 11 bc bc 12 e4 e6 = Radoičić-Krnić, Yugoslavia 1979) 10 ... ♗f5 11 0-0 ♖c8 12 ♕e2 ♘fe4 = Borisenko-Shamkovich, USSR 1959.

[12] 14 ♘xe4 ♘xe4 15 ♗b3 ♘xd2 = Zaltsman-Chandler, New York 1980.

[13] 6 ... c5 7 0-0 cd 8 ed ♘c6 9 h3 ♗f5 10 ♗e3 dc 11 ♗xc4 ♖c8 = Bisguier-Karpov, Skopje Ol 1972.

[14] 8 ... e6 9 de ♕xd1 10 ♔xd1 ♗e6 11 ♗xe6 fe 12 ♔e2 ± Petrosian-Botvinnik, match (5) 1963.

[15] 11 de ♗xe6 12 0-0 ♘c6 13 ♗g5 ♕d7 14 ♕d2 ♘d4 ∓ Razuvayev/Nesis.

16 Anton-Nesis, corr. 1980.
17 7 ... ♘b6 8 ♗b3 c5 9 0-0 (9 dc ♕xd1 10 ♗xd1 ♘bd7 11 ♘d5 ♘c6 = Letelier-Gligorić, Havana 1967) 9 ... cd 10 ed ♘c6 11 d5 ♘a5 12 ♗g5 h6 13 ♗e3 ♗g4 = Kavalek-Hort, Las Palmas 1973.
18 9 ... ♘c6 10 ♗a3 cd 11 cd a6 12 ♖c1 b5 13 ♗xf7+ ♖xf7 14 ♖xc6 ± Rubinstein-Alekhine, Vienna Ol 1922.
19 10 ♗e2 ♘c6 11 ♗b2 b6 12 ♕c2 ♗b7 ∞ Simagin-Smejkal, Moscow v Prague 1968.
20 11 ... ♗xf3?! 12 ♕xf3 cd 13 ♗d5 ♘c6 14 cd ♕d7 15 ♖fc1 ♖ac8 16 h4 ± Keres-Pachman, Marianske Lazne 1965.
21 14 a3 cd 15 cd ♘b6 = Najdorf-Korchnoi, Hastings 1971/72.
22 6 ... e6 7 ♗e2 ♘c6!? 8 cd e9 ♗d2 ♘e7 ∞ Bisguier-D.Byrne, New York 1955.
   6 ... dc 7 ♗xc4 ♘bd7 8 ♗g5 e6 9 ♗xe6! fe 10 ♘xe6 ♕e7 11 ♘xc7+ ♔h8 12 ♘xa8 ♘g4 13 ♗d2 ♕h4 14 0-0-0 ± Pachman.
23 7 ... b6 8 cd cd 9 ♘e5 ♗b7 10 ♗b5 a6 11 ♗e2 ♘bd7 12 f4 ± Alekhine.
24 10 e4 de 11 ♘xe4 c5 = Bagirov.
25 11 ♖ad1 ♗b7 12 e4 de 13 ♘xe4 ♘xe4 14 ♗xe4 ♘f6 15 ♗c2 ♘d5 = Reshevsky-Flohr, AVRO 1938.
26 14 ♗b4 ♘c5 15 ♗xc5 bc 16 ♖ac1 ♕b6 = Sokolsky-Gotthilf, USSR 1936.
27 5 ... c6 6 cd cd 7 ♗g5 e6 8 e3 0-0 9 ♗d3 ♘c6 10 h3 ± Bagirov-Gurgenidze, USSR 1959.
28 6 ... ♗e6? 7 ♕b5+ ± Smyslov.
29 7 ... b6 8 e5 ♘fd7 (8 ... ♗e6 9 ef! ±) 9 ♕d5 c6 10 ♕e4 ♗b7 11 h4 ± Bronstein-Bogatiryev, USSR 1947.
   7 ... ♘bd7 8 ♗e2 ♘b6 9 ♕b3 c6 10 h3 ± Smyslov.
30 8 ... ♘d7 9 ♗e3 ♘b6 10 ♕c5 ♗g4 11 d5 ♘d7 12 ♕a3 ± Petrosian-Botvinnik, match 1963.
31 9 d5 ♘a5 10 ♕a4 ♗xf3 11 ♗xf3 c6 12 0-0 cd 13 ed ♖c8 ∞ Vaganian-Shamkovich, Rio de Janeiro IZ 1979.
32 Dubinin-Smyslov, USSR Ch 1947.
33 8 ♕a4 c5 9 d5 ♕b6 10 ♗xa6 ba 11 0-0 e6 12 ♖e1 ♗b7 = Nesis-G.Andersson, corr. 1980.
34 9 0-0-0? cd 10 ♘xd4 ♗d7 11 f3 ♖c8 12 ♕b3 ♘c5 = Korchnoi-Tukmakov, Moscow 1971.
35 14 ♗xb5 f6 15 ♖a4 ± Portisch-Timman, Wijk aan Zee 1972.
36 Smyslov.
37 8 ♘e5 ♗e6 9 d5 ♗c8 10 ♗e2 e6 11 ♗f4 ed

12 ed ♘e8 13 0-0 ♘d6 = Kotov-Lilienthal, Pärnu 1947.
38 8 ... ♘c6 9 d5 ♗xf3 10 gf ♘e5 11 ♕e2 c6 12 f4 ♘ed7 13 ♗g2 ± Botvinnik-Smyslov, Gröningen 1946.
39 10 ... ♗xf3 intending 11 ... e5 is also good – Fischer.
40 12 ♕d6 cd = Fischer.
41 14 d5 ♘e5 15 ♘b5 ♕f6 16 f4 ♘ed7 17 e5 ♕xf4! 18 ♗f4 ♘c5 = Botvinnik-Fischer, Varna Ol 1962.
42 9 ... ♘c6 10 ♕xb7 ♘a5 11 ♕a6 c5 12 dc ♖b8 13 ♗b5 ± Polugayevsky-Simagin, USSR 1960.
   9 ... c5 10 d5 ♗xf3 11 gf ♕b6 12 f4 ♘a6 13 ♕xb6 ♗xc3+ 14 bc ab 15 ♔d2 ± Botvinnik/Abramov.
43 10 ... e5 11 ♗e2 ed 12 ♗xd4 ♗xd4 13 ♘xd4 ♗xe2 14 ♘dxe2 ± Bondarevsky-Flohr, Saltsjöbaden IZ 1948.
44 11 ... ♗xf3? 12 ♗xf3 ♘c6 13 e5 ± Hort-Navarovsky, Luhacovice 1969.
45 12 e5 ♘e7 13 h3 ♗xf3 14 ♗xf3 ♘f5 15 0-0 c6 16 ♗e4 ♘d5 17 ♗g5 ♕b6 ∞ Grigorian.
46 14 0-0 ♖fd8 15 a3 ♘a5 16 ♕b5 ♘ac4 17 ♗g5 f6 18 ♗c1 ± Ivkov-Jansa, Skara 1980.
47 11 e5?! a5! 12 ♗e2 ♘b4 13 a3 ♗e6 14 d5 ♘6xd5 = Sosonko-Timman, Holland 1980.
48 12 ... ♕c8 13 ♘e5 ♗e2 14 ♘e2 ♗e5 15 ♗h6 ± Bondarevsky/Keres.
49 13 ... ♗h3 14 ♖g1 ♕c8 15 f4 ♗d7 16 f5 ± Sherwin-Pavey, USA 1955.
   13 ... ♗h5 14 ♖g1 ♕d7 15 ♗g3 c6 16 dc ♕xc6 17 ♘b5 ± Portisch-Gheorghiu, Manila 1974.
50 8 a4 b5!
   8 ♕a4!?
   8 ♗e2 b5 9 ♕b3 ♗b7 10 e5 ±.
   8 e5 ♘fd7 9 e6 fe 10 ♕xe6+ ♔h8 11 ♘g5 ♘c6 12 ♘f7+ ♖xf7 13 ♕xf7 ♘xd4 = Adorjan.
51 12 ♗a5 ♘f4 13 0-0-0 ♘h3! = Balashov-Barczay, Skopje 1970.
52 14 ♗a5 ♘c6 15 ♗c3 b4 = Ivkov-Ree, Wijk aan Zee 1971.
53 10 ♗e3 ♘b6 11 a4 ♗e6 12 ♕d1 b4 13 ♘e4 ♗d5 14 ♗d3 ♘c4 = Tukmakov-Tseshkovsky, USSR 1979.
54 10 ... ♘b6 11 h5 ♗e6 12 ♕d1 c5 ± Lputian-Mark Tseitlin, USSR 1980.
55 13 ... ♘f6? 14 ♘e5 ♗e6 15 ♘xg6+! hg 16 h5 ±± Lputian.
   13 ... ♘c6 ∞ Lputian-Romanishin, USSR Ch 1980/81.

	Grünfeld: 5 ♗g5, 5 ♗f4		1 d4 ♘f6 2 c4 g6 3 ♘c3 d5 4 ♘f3 ♗g7						
	5	6	7	8	9	10	11	12	13
1	♗g5	e4[2]	♗xc4[3]	♕xd4	♘xd4	♘xc6	0-0	♖ac1	♗d2	±
	dc[1]	c5	cd	♕xd4	♘c6[4]	bc	♘g4	h6	0-0[5]	
2	...	cd[6]	bc	e3[7]	♗e2[9]	0-0	cd	♗h4	♘d2	±
	♘e4	♘xc3	♕xd5	c5[8]	♘c6	cd[10]	0-0	♗f5[11]	♖ac8[12]	
3	...	...	♘xg5	♘f3[14]	e3	♗e2	b4[16]	♕b3	♖c1	=
	...	♘xg5	e6[13]	ed	0-0[15]	c6	♗e6	♘d7	a6[17]	
4	...	...	...	♕d2	♘f3[19]	e3	♗e2	0-0	b4	=
	...	...	...	h6[18]	ed	0-0	c6	♗e6	♘d7[20]	
5	...	♗h4	bc	e3[21]	♕b1[23]	♘d2	♗e2	♗f3	cd[26]	=
	...	♘c3	dc	♗e6[22]	b6	0-0[24]	c5[25]	cd	♘d7[27]	
6	...	...	cd[28]	bc	e3	♗e2	cd[30]	♘d2	♗f3	=
	...	c5	♘c3	♕xd5	♘c6	cd[29]	b6	♗b7	♕d7[31]	
7	♗f4	e3[33]	♖c1[34]	♕b3[36]	gf[38]	♗e5[39]	♗xc4	♗f1	♗g2	=
	0-0[32]	c6	♗g4[35]	♗xf3[37]	♕d7	dc	b5	♕f5	♘bd7[40]	
8	...	...	dc[41]	♖c1[43]	♗xc4	♗b3[46]	0-0	h3	♕e2	=
	...	c5	♕a5[42]	dc[44]	♕xc5[45]	♘c6	♕a5[47]	♗f5	♘e4[48]	
9	...	♖c1	e3[49]	♘g5	e4	ed	♗xg5	♗xc4	♗b3	∞
	...	dc	♗e6[50]	♗d5	h6	hg	♘xd5[51]	♘b6	♘c6[52]	
10	...	...	dc	e3[54]	♗e2[55]	0-0	bc	♘g5	♗xc4	±
	...	c5	♗e6[53]	♘c6	♘e4[56]	♘xc3	dc	♗d7[57]	♘a5[58]	

[1]   5 ... c6 6 e3 ♕a5 7 ♗xf6 ♗xf6 8 cd cd 9 ♕b3 e6 10 ♗b5 ± Holmov-Zaitsev, USSR Ch 1969.
[2]   6 e3 ♗e6 7 ♘d2 c5 8 dc ♘d5 ± Petrosian-Savon, USSR Ch 1969.
[3]   7 d5 b5 8 e5 b4 9 ef ef 10 ♕e2+ ♔f8 11 ♗e3 ± Hort.
[4]   9 ... ♘xe4 10 ♘xe4 ♗xd4 11 0-0-0 ± Dorfman.
[5]   Dorfman-Smyslov, Lvov 1978.
[6]   6 ♗f4 ♘xc3 7 bc c5 8 e3 0-0 9 cd cd 10 cd ♕xd5 = Taimanov-Hort, Harrachov 1966.
[7]   8 ♕b3 ♗e6 9 ♕xd5 ♗xd5 10 e3 ♘d7 11 ♘d2 h6 12 ♗h4 f5 13 f3 c5 = Langeweg-Hort, Beverwijk 1970.
   8 ♕a4+ ♗d7 9 ♕a3 ♘c6?! (9 ... c5 = Gipslis) 10 e3 h6 11 ♗h4 ♕a5? 12 ♗e7 ±± Taimanov-Kozma, Oberhausen 1961.
[8]   8 ... ♘c6 9 ♗e2 0-0 10 0-0 e5 11 ♗h4 ed 12 cd ♗f5 13 ♘d2 ♖fe8 14 ♗f3 ± Taimanov-Kapengut, USSR 1969.
[9]   9 ♗b5+ ♘c6 10 0-0 ♗g4 11 e4 ♕xg5 12 ♘xg5 ♗xd1 = Maciejewski-Schmidt, Polish Ch 1973.
[10]   10 ... 0-0 11 c4 ♕e4 12 d5 ♗xa1 13 ♕xa1 ♘d4 14 ed ♕xe2 15 ♗h6 ± Knaak-Pribyl, Olomouc 1972.
[11]   12 ... b6?! 13 ♘d2 ♗b7 14 ♗f3 ♕d7 15 ♖c1 ± Bagirov.
[12]   14 ♗f3 ♕d7 15 ♘b3 ♕e8 ± Bagirov-

Grigorian, Baku 1972.
[13]   7 ... e5 8 ♘f3 ed 9 ♘xd4 c5 10 ♘f3 b5 ∞ Tatai-Fletzer, Venice 1966.
   7 ... c6 8 dc ♘c6 9 e3 (9 d5 Gligorić) 9 ... e5 10 d5 ♕xg5 11 dc 0-0 ∞ Hübner-Kavalek, Montreal 1979. 8 ♘f3 cd 9 e3 0-0 10 ♗e2 ♘c6 = Petrosian-Korchnoi, USSR Ch 1973.
[14]   8 ♘h3 ed 9 ♘f4 0-0 10 g3 (10 ♘fd5 c6 ∓) 10 ... ♖e8 11 ♗g2 ♘c6 12 0-0 ♘xd4 ∓ Furman-Savon, USSR Ch 1969.
   8 ♕a4+ ♗d7 9 ♕b3 ♕xg5 10 ♕xb7 0-0 11 ♕xa8+ ♗xd4 ∞ Misutkov-Gulko, USSR 1972.
[15]   9 ... c6 10 b4 ♗f8!? 11 ♕b3 ♗d6 12 ♗e2 0-0 13 0-0 ♘d7 = Kaufman-Chandler, USA 1979.
[16]   11 0-0 ♗e6 12 ♖c1 ♘d7 13 ♘a4 ♕e7 14 ♖e1 ♖fc8 15 ♘d3 b6 = Robatsch-Hübner, Munich 1979.
[17]   14 ♘a4 ♕e7 15 ♘c5 ♘xc5 16 ♖xc5 f5 17 g3 f4! ∞ Kuuskmaa-Banas, corr. 1980.
[18]   8 ... ed 9 ♕e3+ ♔f8 10 ♕f4 ♗f6 11 h4 h6 12 ♘f3 c6 13 e4! (13 e3 ♗e6 14 ♗d3 ♘d7 15 0-0-0 ♕b8! = Bisguier-Korchnoi, Lone Pine 1979) 13 ... de 14 ♘xe4 ± Lechtynsky-Torre, Baku 1980. 12 ... ♔g7! Hort.
[19]   9 ♘h3!? ed 10 ♕e3+ ♔f8 11 ♘f4 c5! =. 10 ♘f4 0-0! 11 g3 ♘c6 ∞ Karpov-Adorjan, Budapest 1973.
[20]   14 ♖ac1 ♘b6 15 b5 ♕d6 16 bc bc 17 ♕c2 ±

Nogueiras-Honfi, Kecskemet 1979.   14 ... ♘f6 15 b5 ♘e4 = Nogueiras.

[21] 8 ♕a4+ ♗d7 (8 ... ♕d7!?9 ♕xc4 b6 intending ... ♗a6 Gipslis) 9 ♕xc4 ♗c6 10 e3 ♘d7 = Gipslis.

[22] 8 ... b5 9 a4 c6 10 ab (10 ♗e2 a6 11 ♘d2 0-0 12 ♘f3 ♖a7 13 0-0 h6 ∞ Lengyel-Gulko, Sombor 1974) 10 ... cb 11 ♘e5 ♗b7 (11 ... ♘xe5? 12 ♕f3 ±) 12 ♖b1 a6 13 ♘xc4 ± Minić. 12 ... ♕a5!? Gipslis.

[23] 9 ♖b1 b6 10 ♘d2 0-0 11 ♘xc4 ♗d5 12 ♕d2 ♕d7 13 ♘a3 c5 = Mecking-Fischer, Buenos Aires 1970.

[24] 10 ... c5 11 ♗xc4 ♗xc4 12 ♘xc4 ♕d5 13 ♕b5 ± Tukmakov.

[25] 11 ... ♗d5 12 0-0 c5 ∞ Tukmakov.

[26] 13 ♗xa8? dc ∓ Tukmakov.

[27] 13 ... ♗d5? 14 ♗xe7! ±±.
13 ... ♗d7 14 ♗xa8 ♕xa8 15 0-0 ♗d5 16 f3 ♗h6 ⎯∞⎯ Toth-Tukmakov, Valletta 1980.

[28] 7 ♘xd5 ♕a5+ 8 b4 cb 9 ♕b3 ♘c6 with counterplay.

[29] 10 ... e5 11 de ♕e6 12 0-0 0-0-0 13 ♕d6 ♘xe5 14 ♕xc5 b6 15 ♕e7 ♖e8 16 ♕xe6 ♗xe6 ⎯∞⎯ Minev-Forintos, Baja 1971.

[30] 11 ed e5 12 de ♕a5 13 0-0 0-0 14 ♕b3 ♘xe5 15 ♘d4 ♗d7 (15 ... ♗g4 16 ♖xg4 ♘xg4 17 ♕xb7 ♕xc3 18 ♘c6 ± Gligorić-D.Byrne, San Antonio 1972) 16 ♖ad1 ♖ac8 17 ♕xb7 ♖xc3 18 f4 ♖c7 = G.Garcia-Schmidt, Leipzig 1973.

[31] 14 ♖c1 ♘a5 15 ♗xb7 ♕xb7 16 ♕a4+ ♕d7 17 ♕a3 0-0 = Shamkovich-Smejkal, Polanica Zdroj 1970.

[32] 5 ... c6 6 e3 ♕a5 7 ♕b3 ±.

[33] 6 cd ♘xd5 7 ♘xd5 ♕xd5 8 ♗xc7 ♘c6 9 e3 ♗f5 10 ♗e2 ♖ac8 11 ♘g3 ♕a5+ 12 ♕d2 ♘b4 ∓ Anikayev-Georgadze, USSR 1973.

[34] 7 ♗e2 dc 8 ♗xc4 ♗g4 9 h3 ♗xf3 10 ♕xf3 ♕a5 11 0-0 ♘bd7 12 ♖ab1 ♘b6 13 b4 ♕f5 = Najdorf-Milić, Bled 1950.

7 ♕b3 ♕a5 8 ♘d2 ♘bd7 9 ♗e2 ♘h5 10 ♗xh5 dc 11 ♘xc4 (11 ♕d1 = Belyavsky) 11 ... ♕xh5 12 0-0 b5 13 ♘a5 e5 = Belyavsky-Gutman, USSR Ch 1977.

7 h3 ♕b6 (7 ... ♘bd7!?) 8 ♕b3 =.

[35] 7 ... ♗e6 8 ♘g5 ±.

7 ... ♕a5 8 ♕d2 ♗e6 9 cd ♘xd5 10 ♘xd5 ♕xd2+ 11 ♔xd2 ♗xd5 12 ♘c4 ± Pomar-Gheorghiu, Palma de Mallorca 1968.

[36] 8 h3 ♗xf3 9 ♕xf3 ♕a5 10 ♗d3 ♘bd7 11 0-0 dc 12 ♗xc4 e5 = Najdorf-Flohr, Budapest 1950.

[37] 8 ... ♕b6 9 ♕xb6 ab 10 cd ♘xd5 11 ♘xd5 cd 12 a3 ♘c6 13 ♗b5 ± Langeweg-Donner, Wijk aan Zee 1974.

[38] 9 ♕xb7? ♗g4 10 ♕xa8 ♕b6 ⫢ Uhlmann.

[39] 10 h4!? dc 11 ♗xc4 b5 ∞ Uhlmann.

[40] 14 ♗xf6 ♗xf6 15 ♘e4 ♖ac8 = Dimitrievich-Tseitlin, Kragujevac 1974.

[41] 7 ♕b3 cd 8 ♘xd4 dc 9 ♗xc4 ♘bd7 10 ♗g3 ♘h5 11 ♖d1 ♕xg3 12 hg ♕a5 = Capablanca-Botvinnik, AVRO 1938.

[42] 7 ... ♘e4 8 ♖c1 ♘c3 9 bc dc 10 ♕xd8 ♖xd8 11 ♗xc4 ♘d7 12 ♗g5 ♖e8 13 ♗b5 a6 14 ♗a4 h6 15 c6 (15 ♗h4 g5 16 c6 ♘c5! 17 cb ♗xb7 18 ♗xe8 gh ∓ Ribli-Timman, Amsterdam 1978) 15 ... ♘c5 16 cb ♗xb7 17 ♗xe8 hg 18 ♗xf7+ = F.Portisch-Vadasz, Budapest 1978.

[43] 8 cd ♘xd5 9 ♗e5 ♘xc3 10 ♕d2 ♗xe5 11 ♘xe5 ♕xc5 12 ♕xc3 ♕xc3+ ∓ Udovčić-Korchnoi, Oberhausen 1961.

8 ♕a4 ♕xc5 9 ♕b5 ♕xb5 10 ♘xb5 ♘a6 = Rosetto-Gligorić, Mar del Plata 1950.

[44] 8 ... ♘e4 9 ♗e5 ♗xe5 10 ♘xe5 ♘a6 11 cd ♘axc5 ⎯∞⎯ Uhlmann.

8 ... ♖d8 9 ♕b3 ♘e4 10 cd ♘d7 11 ♘d4 ♘dc5 ⎯∞⎯ Farago-Rajna, Hungarian Ch 1974.

[45] 9 ... ♘c6 10 0-0 ♕xc5 11 ♘b5!? ♕h5 12 ♘c7 ± Belyavsky-Tukmakov, Lvov 1978.

[46] 10 ♘b5 ♗e6! 11 ♘c7 (11 ♗e6 ♕b5 12 ♗b3 ♘c6 ∓ Ftacnik) 11 ... ♗c4 12 b3 ♕a5 13 ♕d2 ♕d2 14 ♘d2 ♗d5 15 ♘a8 ♗g2 ⎯∞⎯ Ftacnik-Uhlmann, Bucharest 1978.

[47] 11 ... ♕h5 12 h3 e5 13 ♗h2 ♖d8 14 ♘d2! ± Larsen-Tal, Bled (match) 1965.

[48] Hort-Uhlmann, Moscow 1971.

[49] 7 e4 ♗g4 8 ♗xc4 ♗xf3 9 gf (9 ♕xf3 ♘h5! ∓ Shamkovich) 9 ... ♘h5 10 ♗e3 e6 11 ♘e2 a6 12 ♘g3 ♕h4 = Shamkovich-Grigorian, USSR 1973.

[50] 7 ... c5 8 ♗xc4 cd 9 ♘xd4 ♘bd7 10 ♘f3 a6 11 0-0 b5 12 ♗d5 ± Farago-Adorjan, Hungarian Ch 1971.

[51] 11 ... b5 12 h4 c6 13 ♕f3 cd 14 h5 with an attack, Bronstein-Zilberstein, USSR 1973.

[52] 13 ... ♘xd4 14 ♘b5 ♗xb2 15 ♖xd8 ♖xd8 16 ♖xc7 ± Korchnoi.

13 ... ♘c6 14 ♘e2 ♕a5 15 ♗c2 ♕d5 16 h4 ∞ Kakageldiev-Tukmakov, USSR Ch 1978.

[53] 7 ... ♕a5? 8 cd ♖d8 9 ♗d2! ♕xc5 10 e4 ± Petrosian-Gurgenidze, USSR Ch 1960.

7 ... dc 8 ♕xd8 ♖xd8 9 e3 ♘a6 10 c6 bc 11 ♗xc4 ♘d5 12 ♗e5 ♘b6 13 ♗e2 f6 14 ♗g3 c5 = Korchnoi-Stein, USSR Ch 1963.

[54] 8 ♘d4 ♘c6 9 ♘xe6 fe 10 e3 ♕a5 11 ♕a4 ♕xc5 12 ♕b5 ♕xb5 13 cb ♘a5 14 ♗e2 ♖ac8 = Portisch-Evans, Havana 1964.

[55] 9 ♘g5 ♗g4 10 f3 e5! 11 ♗g3 d4 12 fg dc 13 ♕xd8 ♖fxd8 14 ♖xc3 h6 15 ♘f3 ♘e4 ∓ Botvinnik-Gligorić, Tel Aviv Ol 1964.

[56] 9 ... ♕a5 10 0-0 dc = Visier-Gligorić, Montilla 1978.

[57] 12 ♕xd1 13 ♖fxd1 ± Bukić.

[58] 14 ♗d5 ♖c8 15 ♕d3 e5 16 ♘xf7 ∞ Pinter-Jansa, Bajmok 1980.

14 ♗e2 ♖c8 15 e4 ♖xc5 16 ♗e3 ± Hamann-Schmidt, Skopje Ol 1972.

97

Modern Main Line	1 d4 ♘f6 2 c4 g6 3 ♘c3 d5 4 ♘f3 ♗g7 5 cd ♘xd5 6 e4 ♘xc3 7 bc								
	7	8	9	10	11	12	13	14	15
1	...	♗e2[2]	0-0[4]	♕c2![5]	d5	♗g5	♖ad1	♕xe4	♕h4	±/±
	0-0[1]	b6[3]	♗b7	c5	♘d7[6]	f5	fe	♘f6	♕d6[7]	
2	...	♖b1	♗e2	0-0	♕d3	cd	♗g5[10]			±
	c5	0-0[8]	b6[9]	♗b7	cd	e6				
3	...	♗b5+	♗xd7+	0-0	cd	♗e3	d5![13]	♘xe5	♖c1	=
	...	♗d7[11]	♕xd7[12]	cd	♘c6	0-0	♘e5![14]	♗xe5	♖fc8[15]	
4	...	...	0-0[16]	cd	♗e3[18]	♗xc6	♖c1	♕d2[20]	♘xd2	≈
	...	♘c6	cd![17]	0-0	♗g4	bc	♕a5![19]	♕xd2		
5	...	♗e2	cd	♗e3	♗d2	d5!	♖b1	♔f1	♘xe5!	±
	...	cd[21]	♘c6	♕a5+	♕a3	♘b4[22]	♘d3+	♘e5[23]		
6	...	...	♗e3[24]	e5	cd	0-0	♕d2	♖fd1		∓
	...	♘c6	♗g4[25]	cd	0-0	♕d7	♖fd8	♖ac8[26]		

1 d4 ♘f6 2 c4 g6 3 ♘c3 d5 4 ♘f3 ♗g7 5 cd ♘xd5 6 e4 ♘xc3 7 bc c5 8 ♗e2 0-0									
	9	10	11	12	13	14	15	16	17
7	♗e3	♖c1	0-0	dc!	♕a4	♗b5	♕xb5			±
	b6[27]	e6	♗b7	♗xe4[28]	♘c6	♗xb5	♕c8[29]			
8	0-0	♗e3[31]	♕b3	cd	♖ad1	h3	♗xf3	♕xb4	e5	±/=
	♗g4[30]	♕a5	cd	♘c6	♕b4	♗xf3	♖fc8	♘xb4	♖c7[32]	
9	...	♗e3[33]	♕d3![35]	cd	♖ac1	♖fd1	d5	♕xd5	♕d7	=
	b6	♗b7[34]	cd[36]	♘c6	e6	♕d6	ed	♕c7	♕xd7[37]	
10	...	♗g5	♕d3	♗e3[39]	cd	♖ad1	d5[40]	ed	♕a3	=
	...	♗b7	h6![38]	cd	e6!	♘c6	ed	♘e7	♘xd5[41]	

1 d4 ♘f6 2 c4 g6 3 ♘c3 d5 4 ♘f3 ♗g7 5 cd ♘xd5 6 e4 ♘xc3 7 bc c5 8 ♗e3								
	8	9	10	11	12	13	14	15	16
11	...	♖c1[42]	♗e2	♕d2	♗h6	♕xh6	gf	h4	h5	∞
	♗g4	0-0	♕a5[43]	e6	♗xh6	♗xf3	cd	dc	g5[44]	
12	...	♗c4[45]	♖c1	♗e2	cd	0-0	d5[46]			±
	♘c6	0-0	♘a5	cd	b6	♗b7				
13	...	♕d2	♖b1	cd	♔xd2	d5![48]	ed	♗c5![49]		±
	♕a5	♘c6[47]	cd	♕xd2+	e6	ed	♘a5			
14	...	♖c1	♕d2	d5![52]	ed	c4	♔xd2[53]			±
	0-0!	♕a5[50]	e6[51]	ed	♘d7	♕xd2+				
15	...	...	...	cd	♔xd2[54]	♗b5[55]	ef	♗c4+	♔e2[56]	=
	...	...	cd	♕xd2+	♘c6	f5!	♖xf5	♔h8		

[1] 7 ... b6 8 ♗b5+ c6 9 ♗c4 0-0 10 0-0 ♗a6 11 ♗xa6 ♘xa6 12 ♕a4 ♕c8 13 ♗g5 ♕b7 16 ♖fe1 (Kasparov-Pribyl, Skara 1980) 14 ... ♖fe8 ±.

[2] 8 ♗e3 c5 – 7 ... c5.
8 ♗a3!? ♘c6 (8 ... ♗d7!? intending ... c5, ... ♕a5) 9 ♗d3 ± Kasparov/Nikitin.

[3] 8 ... c5! – 7 ... c5.

[4] 9 ♗g5!? ♗b7 10 ♕c2 c5 11 ♖d1 cd 12 cd ♕c8 13 ♕d3 ♕g4 14 d5 ± Bronstein-Veingold, Tallinn 1979.

[5] 10 ♕d3 ♕d7! 11 ♗f4 ♕c6 12 d5 ♕a4 13 ♕e3 c6 = Alburt-Kuzmin, Kiev 1978.

[6] 11 ... c4!? ± Speelman.

[7] Speelman-Pein, London 1979.

[8] 8 ... ♘c6?! 9 d5! ♘xc3+ 10 ♗d2 ♗xd2+ 11 ♕xd2 ♘d4 (11 ... ♘a5 12 ♗b5+!; 11 ... ♘b8 12 ♕c3) 12 ♘xd4 ±.

[9] **9 ...** ♘c6 10 d5 ♗xc3+ 11 ♗d2 ♗xd2+ 12 ♕xd2 ♕d4 13 ♘xd4 ±/± Kasparov-Natsis, Malta Ol 1980. 12 ... ♘a5 13 h4! f6 (13 ... ♗g4? 14 h5 ♗xh5 15 g4! ♗xg4 16 ♕h6) 14 h5 g5 15 ♘xg5 fg 16 ♕xg5+ intending 16 ... ♔f7 17 h6 or 16 ... ♔h8 17 h6 ∞. 10 ... ♘e5!

9 ... ♕a5 10 0-0! ♕xa2 11 ♗g5 ♕e6 12 e5! ♖d8 13 ♕a4 ♘c6 14 ♕b3 ♗e6! 15 ♕xb7! ± Bagirov-Lukin, USSR 1982.

[10] Eingorn-Malanyuk, USSR 1979.

[11] 8 ... ♘d7 9 0-0-0-0 10 ♗g5 (10 a4 a6 11 ♗c4 ♕c7 12 ♕e2 – Stein-Karpov, USSR 1972 – 12 ... e5 ∞) 10 ... cd 11 cd ♘f6 12 ♖e1 ♘g4 13 ♖b1 a6 14 ♗f1 b5 15 a4 ba 16 ♕xa4 ♗d7 17 ♕a3 ± Palatnik-Faibisovich, USSR 1978.

[12] 9 ... ♘xd7 ±.

[13] 13 ♕a4 ♖fd8 14 ♖ad1 b6 15 d5 ♘a5 = Mitchell-Alekhine, Margate 1923.

[14] **13 ...** ♗xa1? 14 ♕xa1 ♘b4 15 ♗h6 ±.
13 ... ♘a5? 14 ♗d4!
13 ... ♘b4 14 ♗d4!

[15] 16 ♕b3 b6 = Tukmakov-Vaganian, Baku 1977.

[16] 9 ♖b1 0-0 10 d5 ♘a5 11 0-0 e6 12 ♗g5 f6 13 ♗e3 b6 14 ♕c2 ed = Olafsson-Stean, Las Palmas 1978.

[17] 9 ... ♕a5!? 10 ♕b3 0-0 11 ♗xc6 bc 12 ♕a3 ♕xa3 13 ♗xa3 ± Larsen-Hort, *Master Game* 1978.

[18] 11 ♗xc6 bc 12 ♗a3 ♗g4 13 ♗c5 ♖e8 = Smejkal-Portisch, Rio de Janeiro IZ 1979.

[19] 13 ... ♕d7 14 h3! ♗xf3 15 ♕xf3 ♖ab8 16 ♖c4 ± Portisch-Vadasz, Hungary 1976.

[20] 14 ♖xc6!? ♕xa2 15 ♕d3 ∞.

[21] **8 ...** ♕a5!? 9 ♗d2 ♘c6 10 d5 ±.
8 ... ♗g4 9 ♕b3!?

[22] 12 ... ♘e5 13 ♖xe5 ♗xe5 14 ♗b5+ ±/± Stean-Morrison, Amsterdam Z 1978.

[23] Palatnik-Faibisovich, USSR 1977.

[24] 9 d5!?

[25] 9 ... cd 10 cd 0-0 11 0-0 ♗g4 12 d5! ±.

[26] Smejkal-Sales, Rio de Janeiro 1978.

[27] 9 ... ♕a5 10 0-0 ♕xc3 11 ♖c1 ♕a3 12 ♖xc5 ♕xa2 13 ♘g5 ♗a6 14 ♖c2 ♕a5 15 e5 ∞ Husek-Ftacnik, CSSR Ch 1978.

[28] 12 ... ♕xd1 13 ♖fxd1 ♗xe4 14 ♘d2 ♗c6 15 ♘c4 ♘d7 16 ♖d6 ♖fc8 17 ♖xc6 ♖xc6 18 ♗f3 ♖ac8 19 ♗xc6 ♖xc6 20 ♖d1 ♘xc5 21 ♖d8+ ♗f8 22 ♗h6 ♘d7 23 ♘e5 ±± Tal.

[29] 15 ... ♕d7 16 c4 bc 17 ♖fd1 ♕c6 18 ♗xc5 ♖c8 19 ♘d4 f6 20 ♗e3 e5 21 ♕b3 ♕e6 22 ♖d6! ± Tal-Ribli, Skara 1980.

[30] **9 ...** cd 10 cd ♘c6 11 ♗e3 ♗g4 12 d5 ♘e5 13 ♘xe5 (13 ♖b1 ♘xf3+ 14 gf ♗h3 15 ♖b7 ♗xf1 16 ♗xf1 ∞ Becker-Grünfeld, match 1922) 13 ... ♗xe2 14 ♕xe2 ♗xe5 15 ♖b1 ♕d7 16 f4 ♗g7 17 ♕b5! ♕xb5 18 ♖xb5 ±/± Plachetka-Banas, Stary Smokovec 1977.

9 ... ♘d7 10 ♕d3 ♕c7 11 ♖b1 b5! 12 ♗g5!

a6 13 a4!? ba 14 ♗xe7 ± Hartston-Sax, Buenos Aires Ol 1978.

[31] 10 d5!? ♗xc3 11 ♗h6 Hartston.

[32] 18 ♖c1 ♖ac8 19 ♖xc7 ♖xc7 20 ♖b1! ±/± Karpov-Ljubojević, Montreal 1979.

[33] 10 ♗a3!? intending 10 ... ♗b7 11 e5 cd 12 cd ♘a6 13 d5! ♕d7 14 ♖c1 ♖fd8 15 e6 Portisch.

[34] 10 ... cd 11 cd ♗b7 12 d5! ♗xa1 13 ♕xa1 ♘d7 14 ♗h6 f6 15 ♗xf8 ♔xf8 16 ♘d7 ± Platonov-Bagirov, USSR Ch ½-final 1971.

[35] 11 e5 cd 12 cd ♘a6 13 ♕a4 ♘c7 ∓ Rubinstein-Alekhine, match 1924.

[36] 11 ... e6 12 ♖ad1 cd 13 cd ♕d6 14 ♖c1 ♖e8 15 ♕e3 ♗a6 ∞ Hort-Hübner, match (2) Hamburg 1979.

[37] 18 ♖xd7 ♘a5 19 e5! ♗c6 20 ♖c7 ♖fc8 21 ♖xc8+ ♖xc8 22 ♗a6 ♖d8 23 ♘d4 ♗d5 24 f4 ♗f8 25 ♖c7 ♗c5! = Korchnoi-Timman, Wijk aan Zee 1978.

[38] 11 ... ♗d7 12 ♖ad1 e6? 13 d5 ed 14 ed ± Hartston-Sax, Tallinn 1979.

[39] 12 ♗h4 cd 13 cd ♕d7 14 ♖ad1 e6! 15 d5 ♘a6! 16 ♕b1 ed 17 ♗b5 ♕d6 18 ed f5 ∞ Alburt-Jansa, Decin 1977.

[40] 15 ♕d2 ♔h7 16 d5 ed 17 ed ♘e7 18 ♗c4 ♖c8 ∓/∓ Chandler-Birnboim, Manchester 1979.

[41] 18 ♗c4 ♕e7 19 ♕xe7 ♘xe7 = Alburt-Tukmakov, Decin 1977.

[42] 9 ♕a4+!? ♘c6 (Kasparov-Razuvayev, USSR Ch 1979) 10 ♘e5 ♗xe5 11 de ♕c7 12 f4! ± Tal-Fernandez, Malaga 1981.

[43] 10 ... cd 11 cd e6 12 0-0 ♘c6 13 d5 ed 14 ed ±/± Petursson-Shamkovich, Lone Pine 1980.

[44] 17 f4 f6 ∞ Fernandez-Banas, Trnava 1980.

[45] 9 ♖c1 cd 10 cd 0-0 11 d5 ±/± Korchnoi-Miles, Vienna 1979.

[46] Knaak-Uhlmann, GDR 1975.

[47] 9 ... 0-0 – 8 ... 0-0.

[48] 13 ♗b5 ♗d7 14 d5 ed 15 ed ♘a5 16 ♖he1 0-0-0! = Pytel-Schmidt, Lublin 1979.

[49] Schmidt.

[50] 9 ... cd 10 cd e6 11 ♗c4 ♘c6 12 0-0 ♘a5 13 ♗d3 b6 14 h4! ±/± Kaplan-Liberzon, Lone Pine 1980.

[51] 10 ... ♗g4 11 ♗e2 ♘d7 12 d5 c4 13 ♗d4 ♗xf3 14 gf ♖ac8 ± Itkis-Tseshkovsky, USSR 1980.

[52] 11 ♗e2 (Browne-Sax, London 1980) 11 ... cd 12 cd ♕xd2+ 13 ♔xd2 f5!? =.

[53] Pein.

[54] 12 ♘xd2 e6 13 ♘b3! ± Karpov-Hübner, Tilburg 1980.

[55] 13 d5 ♖d8 14 ♔e1 (14 ♔c2!? Korchnoi 14 ... ♘b4! (14 ... ♘a5 15 ♗g5 f6 16 ♗d2 b6 17 ♖c7! ± Kasparov-Romanishin, Moscow 1981) 15 ♗d2 (15 a3!? ♕a2 16 ♖c4 ∞) 15 ... ♘a6 = Keene-Jansa, Esbjerg 1981.

[56] Krnić.

	7	8	9	10	11	12	13	14	15	
1	...	♘e2[2]	0-0[3]	♗e3	f4[6]	f5	♗d3	ef	♕d2	=
	0-0[1]	♘c6	b6[4]	♗b7[5]	e6	♘a5	ef	♖e8	♕d5[7]	
2	...	...	h4[8]	h5[10]	♗d3[11]	hg	♗e3	cd	d5	∞
	...	b6	♘c6[9]	♘a5	e5[12]	fg[13]	ed[14]	c5	♗xa1[15]	
3	...	...	0-0[16]	♕d3[17]	e5[18]	♘f4	♕h3	♗e2	♗e3	±
	...	♕d7	b6	♗b7	♘c6	e6	♘a5	c5	cd[19]	
4	...	♘e2	♗e3	cd	♗d5[22]	♗xc6[23]	d5	♗d4	♕d2	±
	c5	♘c6[20]	cd	b5[21]	♗d7	♗xc6	♗d7[24]	♖a5+[25]	♕xd2+[26]	

	10	11	12	13	14	15	16	17	18	
5	...	♗d3	♖c1[29]	d5	♗b1	de	♕xd8[32]	♘d4	f4	±
	♘a5[28]	b6	♗b7[30]	c4[31]	e6	fe	♖axd8	♔f7	♘c6[33]	
6	...	♖c1[34]	f4[36]	f5	♗d3	cd	♖b1	♘xd4[39]	♗xd4	=
	♕c7	♖d8[35]	♗g4[37]	♘a5[38]	cd	♕b6	♗xd4	♕xd4	♗xd1[40]	
7	...	...	♕e1	♖d1	cd	♖fxe1	♗b5[42]	♗xc6	d5	=
	...	...	♕a5[41]	cd	♕xe1	b6	♗b7	♗xc6	♗a4[43]	
8	...	...	h3	f4	♕e1[45]	♗d3	g4[46]	♗xe4	♘g3	=
	...	...	b6[44]	e6	♘a5	f5	fe[47]	♗b7	♘c4[48]	
9	...	...	♕d2	♗b3	♗f4	♗g3	♗d5	de	f4	±
	...	...	♘e5[49]	♘g4	e5	♕e7[50]	♗e6	c4	♗xd5[51]	

1 7 ... b6 8 ♕f3 0-0 9 e5 ♗a6 10 ♗b3! ♕c8 11 ♘e2 ♗b7 12 ♕g3 c5 13 h4 cd 14 h5 ± Niklasson-Simić, Stockholm 1975/76.

   7 ... ♘c6 8 ♘e2 ♕d7?! 9 ♗b5 ± Timman-Olafsson, Buenos Aires (*Clarin*) 1980.

2 8 ♗e3!? ♘c6 9 ♘f3 ♘a5 10 ♗e2 c5 11 ♖c1 ± Knaak-Uhlmann, Halle 1976. 8 ... b6 9 h4 ♗b7 10 ♕f3 ♕d7 11 ♘e2 h5 12 ♗g5 ± Knaak-Uhlmann, GDR Ch 1978. 8 ... c5 9 ♕d2 ♕a5 10 ♖d1 ± Möhring-Pavlov, Trnava 1979.

3 9 h4 ♘a5 10 ♗b3 c5 11 h5 ♘xb3 12 ab cd 13 cd ♗d7 ∓ Spassky-Stein, USSR 1964.

4 9 ... ♘a5 10 ♗d3 ♕d7 11 ♗e3 ♖d8 12 ♖b1 c5 13 f4 e6 14 f5 ef 15 ef ± Ilivitsky-Korchnoi, USSR 1964.

   9 ... e5 10 d5 ♘a5 11 ♗b3 c5 12 c4 b6 13 ♘c3 f5 ∞ Butnorius-Tseshkovsky, USSR 1980.

5 10 ... ♘a5 11 ♗d3 c5 Joksić.

6 11 f3 e6 (11 ... ♘a5 12 ♗d3 c5 ∞ Hort) 12 ♖b1 ♕d7 13 ♗b5 ♕e7 14 ♕c1 ♘a5 15 ♖d1 c6 16 ♗d3 e5 17 ♗h6 = Hort-Hübner, Hamburg (match) 1979.

7 15 ... ♗e4?! 16 ♗g5! f6 17 ♗xe4 ♖xe4 18 ♕d3 ± Spassky-Hübner, Tilburg 1979.

   15 ... ♕d5 16 ♘f4 ♕c6 17 ♖ae1 ♘c4 18 ♗xc4 ♕xc4 = Joksić.

8 9 0-0 ♗b7 10 f3 ♘c6 - note 6.

   9 ♗d5!? c6 10 ♗b3 ♗b7 11 ♗g5 ♕d7 12 0-0 c5 13 d5 ± Pinter-Groszpeter, Hungarian Ch 1978. 10 ... ♗a6 11 h4 e6 12 h5 ± A.Schneider-Groszpeter, Zamardi 1979.

9 9 ... ♗a6 10 ♗xa6 ♘xa6 11 h5 c5 12 hg hg 13 ♕d3 ♕c8 14 ♕g3 ± Fuderer-Filip, Göteborg IZ 1955.

10 10 ♗d5!? ♗b7 11 h5 e6 12 ♗b3 ♘a5 13 hg hg 14 ♕d3 ± Petran-Krnić, Belgrade 1977. 10 ... ♗d7 11 h5 e6 12 ♗b3 ♘a5 13 e5 c5 14 ♕d3 ± Tarjan-Strauss, USA 1978. 10 ... ♕d7 11 h5

(11 ♗a3?! ♖d8 12 h5 e6 13 ♗b3 ♗a6 14 hg hg 15 ♘f4 ♘xd4! ∓ Petran-Kosa, Hungary 1978) 11 ... ♗a6? (11 ... e6) 12 hg hg 13 ♘f4 e6 14 ♕g4! ± Spassky-Timman, Amsterdam (match) 1977.

[11] 11 ♗b3 e5 12 hg hg 13 ♗e3 ♕e7 14 ♕d2 ♘xb3 15 ab ed 16 ♗xd4 f6 +̄ Gligorić-Hartston, Nice Ol 1974.

[12] 11 ... c5 12 hg fg 13 ♗e3 cd 14 cd ♗e6 15 d5 ♗xa1 16 ♕xa1 ± Benjamin-Sax, London 1975.

[13] 12 ... hg? 13 ♗h6 f6 14 ♕d2 ♕e7 15 0-0-0 ± Petrosian-Stean, Moscow 1975.

[14] 13 ... ♗b7 14 ♕d2 ♕e7 15 d5 c6 16 dc ♗xc6 +̄ Gligorić-Larsen, Palma de Mallorca IZ 1970. 16 c4!? Larsen.

[15] 16 ♕a1 ♘c6 17 a3 ♕d6 18 f4 ∞̄ Timman-Adorjan, London 1975.

[16] 9 h4!? b5 (9 ... ♕g4?! 10 h5) 10 ♗d5 c6 11 ♗b3 a5 12 h5 a4 13 ♗c2 c5 14 hg fg 15 ♗h6± Polugayevsky-Gulko, USSR Ch 1978.

[17] 10 e5 ♗a6 11 ♗xa6 ♘xa6 12 f4 c5 13 f5 ♘c7 14 f6 ef 15 ef ♗h8 16 ♗f4 ♘d5 17 ♗e5 ♖fe8 +̄ Möhring-Mark Tseitlin, Trnava 1979.

[18] 11 f4 ♘c6 12 f5 ♘a5 13 ♗b3 ♘xb3 14 ab a5 15 ♗g5 c5? 16 d5 ± Rodriguez-Larsen, Orense 1975. 15 ... gf ∞ Larsen.

[19] 16 cd ♖fd8 17 ♖ad1 ± Gligorić-Vaganian, Yugoslavia v USSR 1975.

[20] 8 ... ♘d7 9 0-0 ♕c7 10 ♗f4 e5 11 de ♘xe5 12 ♗d5 0-0 13 ♗g3 ♗e6 14 ♘f4 ± Portisch-German, Stockholm IZ 1962.

[21] 10 ... ♕a5+ 11 ♗d2 ♕a3 12 ♖b1 0-0 13 0-0 ♗g4 14 d5 ± Gulko-Spiridonov, Sofia 1967.

[22] 11 ♗d3!? intending 12 ♖c1 ±.

[23] 12 ♖c1 ♖c8 13 0-0 0-0 14 ♗xc6 ♖xc6 15 ♖xc6 ♗xc6 16 d5 ♗d7 17 ♕d2 a5 18 ♖c1 b4 19 ♘d4 e6 20 ♘c5! ± Polugayevsky-Bagirov, USSR Ch 1978.

[24] 13 ... ♗xa1? 14 ♕xa1 ±±.

[25] 14 ... 0-0!?

[26] 16 ♔xd2 0-0 17 ♖xg7 ♔xg7 18 ♘d4± Amos-Martz, Mayaguez 1973.

[27] 9 ... ♘d7 10 ♗g5 h6 11 ♗e3 ♕c7 12 ♖c1 a6 13 ♕d2 ± Bronstein-Botvinnik, match 1951.

[28] 10 ... ♗g4 11 d5!? ♘a5 12 ♗d3 c4 13 ♗c2 ♗xc3 14 ♖b1 ∞̄ Polugayevsky-Timman, Breda (match) 1979.

10 ... b6 11 ♖c1 ♗b7 12 d5 ♘e5 13 ♗b3 c4 14 ♗c2 e6 15 de ♘d3! ∞ Polugayevsky-Miles, Wijk aan Zee 1979. 11 dc ♕c7 12 ♘d4!?

[29] 12 dc bc 13 ♗xc5 ♕c7 14 ♗d4 e5 15 ♗e3 ♘c4 16 ♕c1 ♖d8 17 ♖d1 ♗e6 18 ♗c2 ♖xd1+ 19 ♗xd1 ♗f8 +̄ Rocha-Keres, Hastings 1964/65.

[30] 12 ... cd 13 cd e6 Knaak.

[12] ... e6?! 13 dc ± Polugayevsky-Korchnoi, Evian C 1977.

[31] 13 ... ♕d7?! 14 c4 ♗a6 15 f4 e6 16 f5 ± Donner-Darga, Hengelo 1968.

[32] 16 f4!? ± Uhlmann.

[33] Knaak-Smejkal, Halle 1974.

[34] 11 dc?! ♘e5 12 ♗b3 ♘g4 13 ♗f4 ♕xc5 ∓ Karpov.

11 ♗f4 ♕a5 12 d5 ♘e5 13 ♗b3 c4 14 ♗c2 e6 ∞ Gipslis.

11 ♕c1 ♗d7 12 ♖b1 cd 13 cd ♖ac8 = Gulko-Tal, USSR 1970.

[35] 11 ... b6 12 ♗f4 ♕d8 13 d5 ♘a5 14 ♗d3 c4 15 ♗c2 e6 16 ♕d2 ± Shashin-Faibisovich, USSR 1974.

[36] 12 ♕a4 ♗d7 13 ♕a3 ♗f8 14 f4 e6 15 ♕b2 b5 (15 ... ♘a5 16 ♗d3 b5 17 f5 ef 18 ♘g3 ± Knaak-Ftacnik, GDR v CSSR 1978) 16 ♗d3 c4 (16 ... f5 ∞) 17 ♗b1 f5 18 g4 ± Knaak-Szymczak, Sandomierz 1976.

[37] 12 ... ♘a5 13 ♗d3 f5 14 ef ♗xf5 15 ♗xf5 gf 16 ♘g3 ± Ivkov-Jimenez, Havana 1965.

[38] 13 ... gf 14 h3 (14 ♗xf7+ ♔xf7 15 ♕b3+ e6 16 ♘f4 ♕d7 17 ef ♘a5! ∓ Spassky-Shishkin, USSR 1959) 14 ... ♗xe2 15 ♕xe2 cd 16 cd ♕d6 = Pribyl-Banas, Stary Smokovec 1972.

[39] 17 ♖xb6 ♗xe3+ 18 ♔h1 ab 19 ♕b1 ♖ac8 +̄ Rashkovsky-Korchnoi, USSR Ch 1973.

[40] 19 ♗c3 = Karpov.

[41] 12 ... e6 13 f4 ♘a5 14 ♗d3 f5 15 ♖d1 b6 16 ♕f2 cd 17 ♗xd4 ♗xd4 18 cd ♗b7 19 ♘g3 ± Spassky-Fischer, Santa Monica 1966.

[42] 16 d5 ♘e5 17 ♗b5 ♗d7 18 ♘d4 ♗xb5 19 ♘xb5 ♖d7 = Gligorić-Hartston, Praia da Rocha 1969.

[43] Pachman-Smejkal, CSSR Ch 1968.

[44] 12 ... a6 13 ♗b3 ♘a5 14 ♗f4 ♕d7 15 dc ♘xb3 16 ab a5 17 ♕c2 ♕b5 18 ♗e3 a4 = Gligorić-Hort, Siegen Ol 1970.

[45] 14 g4 ♘a5 15 ♗d3 f5 16 ♘g3 fe 17 ♘xe4 ♗b7 ∞ Leander-Ornstein, Switzerland 1972.

[46] 16 ♕f2 ♗b7 17 ♘e5 c4 18 ♗c2 ♘c6 19 g4 ♗e7 20 ♔h2 ♕c6 ∓ Gligorić-Smyslov, Yugoslavia v USSR 1959.

[47] 16 ... ♗b7 17 ♘g3 ♕d7 18 gf cd 19 fe ♕xe6 20 f5 ± Spassky-Stein, Moscow 1971.

[48] Spassky-Fischer, Siegen Ol 1970.

[49] 12 ... a6 13 ♗h6 ♗h8 14 a4 ♘a5 15 ♗a2 ♗d7 16 ♘f4 e6 17 e5 ± Rashkovsky-Kupreichik, USSR 1974.

[50] 15 ... ♗h6 16 ♗xe5! ♕xe5 17 ♕xh6 ♕xe4 18 ♗xf7+! ± Muratov-Kremenetsky, USSR 1974.

[51] 19 ed ♕c5+ 20 ♘d4 ♖xd5 21 ♕e2 ♕c8 22 ♖ce1 ± Toth-Castro, Rome 1980.

101

	10	11	12	13	14	15	16	17	18	
10	...	...	...	Rfd1	cd	Rxd2	d5	Bd3	Nd4	±
	...	...	Qa5	cd[52]	Qxd2[53]	Bd7	Na5	b6	Rac8[54]	
11	...	cd	f3	Rc1[57]	Rxc4	Qb3	Rfc1[59]	Kf2	Rxc4	=
	cd	Bg4[55]	Na5[56]	Nxc4	Bd7	Qa5[58]	Rac8	Rxc4	Rc8[60]	
12	...	...	...	Bd3	Rc1[61]	d5[62]	Qe1	Qb4	Rc5	=
	...	...	...	Be6	Bxa2	Bb3	e6[63]	ed	Bc4[64]	
13	...	...	...	...	d5	Qxa1	Rb1[66]	Bh6	e5	±
	...	...	...	...	Bxa1[65]	f6	Bd7[67]	Rf7	fe[68]	

---

[52] **13 ... Bd7** 14 Bh6 cd 15 Bxg7 Kxg7 16 Qf4 Be8 17 cd ± Gligorić-Ogaard, Manila 1975.
13 ... Bg4 14 f3 (14 Qb2 Qb6 = Geller-Georgadze, USSR Ch 1978) 14 ... Ne5 15 Bd5 Rxd5 16 ed Nc4 17 Qd3 Nb2 18 Qb1 Nxd1 19 Qxb7 ± Razuvayev-Tukmakov, USSR Ch 1979.

[53] 14 ... Bg4 15 f3 Bd7 16 d5 Qxd2 17 Rxd2 Na5 18 Bd3 e6 19 Bf4 ± Pachman-Ornstein, Stockholm 1974/75.

[54] Tarjan-Algeo, USA 1980.

[55] 11 ... Na5 12 Bd3 b6 13 Rc1 e6 14 Qd2 Bb7 15 h4! Qd7 16 h5 ∞ Baumbach-Mallee, corr. 1980. 16 Bh6! ± Baumbach.

[56] 12 ... Bd7 13 Rb1 e6 14 Qd2 Na5 15 Bd3 a6 16 Bg5 ± Spassky-Milev, Bucharest 1953.

[57] **13 Bf7+** Rf7 14 fg Rf1+ 15 Kf1 Qd7 16 h3 Qe6 ∞ Panteleev-Prahov, Bulgaria 1970.
13 Bd5 Bd7 14 Rb1 a6 15 Bxb7 (15 a4 e6 16 Ba2 b5 17 d5 Nc4 ∞ Browne-Mecking, Manila IZ 1976) 15 ... Ra7 16 Bd5 Bb5 17 a4 Bxe2 18 Qxe2 e6 19 Bc4 Bxd4 20 Rfd1 Be3+ 21 Qxe3 Rd7 22 Be2 Nc6 23 Rdc1 Nb8 24 Rb6 ± Veingold-Lechtynsky, Tallinn 1979. 22 ... Rxd1+ 23 Rxd1 Qc8 = Polugayevsky-Mecking, match 1977 and Spassky-Timman, Bugojno 1978.

[58] 15 ... b5 16 Rc5 Qb6 17 d5 Qb7 18 Rfc1 Rfc8 19 Bd4 ± Shashin-Korchnoi, USSR 1973.

[59] 16 Nc3 b6 17 Rc1 Rfc8 = Littleton-Gligorić, The Hague 1966.

[60] 19 Rxc8+ Bxc8 20 d5 Qc7 = Gligorić-Tarjan, Lone Pine 1975.

[61] 14 Qa4 a6 15 d5 b5 16 Qb4 Bxa1 17 Rxa1 Bd7 18 Qd4 f6 19 e5 = Gligorić-Portisch, San Antonio 1972.

[62] 15 Qa4 Be6 16 d5 Bd7 17 Qb4 b6 18 Ba6 ½-½ Spassky-Shamkovich, Sochi 1967.

[63] 16 ... a6? 17 Qf2 ±±. 16 ... b6 17 Bd4 ∞∞ Karpov.

[64] 19 Bxc4 Nxc4 20 Rxd5 Qxd5 (20 ... Nxe3!? 21 Rxd8 Rfxd8 22 Rb1 a5!? 23 Qxb7 a4 ∓; 23 Qb3 a4! 24 Qe3 a3 ∓) 21 ed Nxe3 =.
19 Rxa5 Bxd3 20 Rxd5 Bxe2 21 Rxd8 Rfxd8 22 Re1 a5!? 23 Qxb7 Bc4 ∞∞.

[65] 14 ... Bd7 15 Rc1 ±.

[66] 16 Bh6 Re8 17 Bh1 Rc8 18 Qd4 Bd7 19 Rb1!? (19 Qxa7 Bc4 20 h4 Ne5 21 Rb1 Bb5 22 Re1 Ra8 ∞ Furman-Suetin, USSR Ch 1954) 19 ... b6 20 e5 ∞ Deze-Pribyl, Zalaegerszeg 1977.

[67] **16 ...** Kg7 17 Qc3 Bf7 18 Qd2 Kh8 19 Bd4! ± Petran-Schmidt, Belgrade 1977.
16 ... b6 17 Bh6 Re8 18 Nf4 (18 Qd4 Bd7 19 e5 ±) 18 ... Bd7 19 e5 ± Tarjan-White, USA 1978.

[68] 19 Qxe5 Qb8 20 Qxb8+ Rxb8 21 Bd2 Bf5 22 Bxf5 Rxf5 23 Bxa5 Rxd5 ± Youngworth-Liberzon, Lone Pine 1980. 19 ... b5 20 Bd2 Rc8 (20 ... Nb7 21 Bc3 Rf6 22 Ng3) 21 Bc3 ± Tarjan-Frasco, USA 1978.

Benoni and Benko Gambit

The Benoni, a relatively recent addition to Black's defensive arsenal against 1 d4, owes much of its popularity to the successes of ex-World Champion Mikhail Tal. The Modern Benoni (1 d4 ♘f6 2 c4 c5 3 d5 e6 4 ♘c3 ed 5 cd d6) offers the inventive and enterprising player a wealth of tactical opportunities. Black's counterplay springs from his queenside pawn majority (activated by the break ... b5), pressure along the half-open e-file and the strength of his fianchettoed king's bishop. White, on the other hand, enjoys more freedom and has an opportunity for pawn storms in the centre and on the kingside, as well as having an appealing target in the shape of Black's all-important pawn on d6. If White can undermine this pawn, the cornerstone of Black's position, the defender will often find himself beset with insurmountable problems.

White's most popular choices of late have been the **Main (Classical) Line** (6 e4 g6 7 ♘f3 ♗g7 8 ♗e2 0-0 9 0-0) and the resurgent **Fianchetto Variation** (6 ♘f3 g6 7 g3). Other continuations of interest are:

Mikenas Variation (6 e4 g6 7 f4). White's most violent option, too turbulent to have ever achieved universal acceptance as a reliable system.

Systems with ♗g5. For a short time this set-up scored great successes but now Black can once again face it with confidence.

Nimzowitsch (6 ♘f3 g6 7 ♘d2). A very direct attempt to stifle the Benoni positionally. Black's lead in development should suffice to provide him with equality.

6 e4/♘f3 g6 7 ♗f4. Many surprising tricks are hidden in the paths of these systems, which are still relatively unexplored. They offer White fresh possibilities and may well appear more frequently in the future.

Brethren systems, the **Schmid Benoni** and the **Czech (Old) Benoni**, complete the family tree. The Schmid Benoni (1 d4 c5), rarely seen, is a quiet and fairly passive continuation. The Czech Benoni (3 d5 e5) is also out of fashion. Black's position is congested and a bit ponderous, but it remains solid.

Benko Gambit

It is sad that the only river ever to have given its name to a chess opening should have been forced to cede this honour to a mere mortal. But the fact that an article written in 1946 by one Argunov who happened to live in Kuibishev on the River Volga considered the moves 1 d4 ♘f6 2 c4 c5 3 d5 b5 is generally considered less significant than the fact that grandmaster Pal Benko has by his games and writings transformed this little esteemed opening into one of Black's most successful defences to 1 d4.

If White accepts the pawn by 4 cb a6 5 ba ♗xa6 Black obtains a slight lead in development and (more important) lasting pressure on the queenside, where White's b-pawn is particularly vulnerable. White's king's bishop is also a problem piece. If he plays e4 he is forced to waste time castling artificially after ... ♗xf1 ♔xf1 followed by g3 and ♔g2. If he fianchettoes the bishop it is relegated to a passive position.

It is frustrating for White that even if he manages to reach an ending a pawn up such endings are rarely theoretically won – indeed they often favour Black. White's most promising strategy may be to forget the fact that he is a pawn up, consolidate his position and play for a break in the centre by e5.

Although in theory White may be able to obtain some advantage by accepting the pawn, he has in practice achieved such little success by doing so that attention has focussed on the various ways of declining it. Several of these allow White to obtain at least an equal game without suffering the indignities often attendant upon accepting the gambit. In particular, 4 cb a6 5 ♘c3 is very effective against an unwary opponent, and the little explored 4 a4 is also not easy for Black to meet.

Benko Gambit   1 d4 ♘f6 2 c4 c5 3 d5 b5

	4	5	6	7	8	9	10	11	12	
1	a4!?[1] / bc[2]	♘c3 / d6[3]	e4 / g6[4]	f4 / ♗g7	♘f3 / 0-0	♗xc4 / ♗a6	♕e2[5] / ♗xc4	♕xc4 / ♕b6	0-0 / ♘bd7[6]	±
2	... / b4	♘d2[7] / d6[8]	e4 / g6	b3[9] / ♗g7	♗b2 / 0-0	f4 / e5!	de[10] / fe			=
3	♘f3 / ♗b7[11]	a4[12] / a6	ab / ab	♖xa8 / ♗xa8	♘c3 / ♕a5	♘d2 / b4	♘b3 / ♕b6[13]			∞
4	cb / a6[14]	e3[15] / g6	♘c3 / ♗g7[16]	a4[17] / 0-0	♗d2! / e6[18]					∞/±
5	... / ...	f3 / g6[19]	e4 / d6	a4 / ♗g7	♘c3![20] / 0-0	♗d2[21] / e6	♗c4[22]			∞/±
6	... / ...	♘c3 / ab	e4 / b4	♘b5 / d6	♗f4 / g5![23]	♗xg5[24] / ♘xe4	♗f4 / ♗a6[25]	♗d3 / ♕b6	♕e2 / ♘d7[26]	∞
7	... / ...	... / ...	... / ...	... / ...	♘f3 / g6	e5[27] / de	♘xe5[28] / ♗g7	♗c4 / 0-0	0-0 / ♗b7[29]	∞̄
8	... / ...	ba / ♗a6[30]	♘c3 / d6	♘f3[31] / g6	g3 / ♗g7	♗h3 / ♘bd7[32]	0-0 / ♘b6	♖e1 / 0-0	♗f4 / ♗c4[33]	∞̄

1 d4 ♘f6 2 c4 c5 3 d5 b5 4 cb a6 5 ba ♗xa6 6 ♘c3 d6 7 ♘f3 g6 8 g3 ♗g7 9 ♗g2 0-0[34] 10 0-0 ♘bd7

	11	12	13	14	15	16	17	18	19	
9	♖b1[35] / ♕a5[36]	a3 / ♖fb8	♗d2![37] / ♘g4	♕c2 / ♘4e5	♘xe5 / ♘xe5					∞
10	♕c2 / ♕a5	♗d2[38] / ♖fb8	h3 / ♘e8	♖fe1 / ♘c7	b3 / c4	♖ac1 / cb	ab / ♘b5	♘xb5 / ♕xb5	♕e4[39] / ♕xb5	±

1 d4 ♘f6 2 c4 c5 3 d5 b5 4 cb a6 5 ba ♗xa6 6 ♘c3 d6 7 e4 ♗xf1 8 ♔xf1 g6

	9	10	11	12	13	14	15	16	17	
11	g4[40] / ♗g7	f3[41] / 0-0	♘ge2 / e6!	♔g2 / ed	♘xd5 / ♘c6	♘ec3 / ♘xd5	ed / ♘b4!	h4 / f5[42]		∓
12	g3 / ♗g7	♔g2 / 0-0	♘f3[43] / ♘bd7	♖e1[44] / ♕a5	♖b1[45] / ♖fb8	♖e2 / ♖b7!	♗g5 / ♖ab8	♕c1 / ♕a6![46]		∓
13	... / ...	... / ...	... / ...	h3 / ♘b6	♖e1 / ♕d7	♕c2[47] / ♕b7	♗g5 / h6	♗xf6 / ♗xf6[48]		=

---

[1] 4 ♘a3 b4 5 ♘c2 e5 6 g3 d6 7 ♗g2 g6 Benko.
4 b3 bc 5 bc d6 =.
4 ♕c2 bc 5 e4 e6! 6 ♗xc4 ed 7 ed d6 8 ♘c3 ♗e7 =.
4 ♘d2 bc 5 e4 d6 6 ♗xc4 g6 7 f4 ♗g7 8 ♘gf3 0-0 9 0-0 ♘bd7 =.
4 e4 ♘xe4 5 ♕f3 ♕a5+ 6 ♘c3 ♘xc3 7 ♗d2 b4 8 bc b3 9 ♕d1 b2 10 ♖b1 ♕xa2 ∓.
4 f3 bc 5 e4 d6 6 ♗xc4 g6 7 ♘c3 ♗g7 8 ♘ge2 0-0 9 0-0 ♘bd7 10 ♗f4 = Levy.
4 g3 g6 5 ♗g2 d6 6 cb a6 7 b6 ♕xb6 8 ♘c3 ♗g7 =.
4 ♗g5 ♘e4 5 ♗f4 ♕a5+ 6 ♘d2 d6 7 b4! ♕xb4 8 ♖b1 ♕c3 9 ♖xb5 ♘xd2 10 ♗xd2 ♕xc4 ∞.

[2] 4 ... ba?! 5 ♕xa4 g6 6 ♗f4 intending d6 ±.

[3] 5 ... e6 6 e4 ed 7 ed d6 8 ♗xc4 ♗e7 9 ♘f3 ±.

[4] 6 ... e5!?
6 ... ♗a6?! 7 f4! e6 8 ♘f3 ♗e7 ±.

[5] 10 ♗xa6!? ♘xa6 11 e5 ±.

[6] 13 e5! ± Peev-Ungureanu, Poiana Brasov 1973.

[7] 5 g3!? ♗b7?! 6 ♗g2 e5 7 e4 d6 8 ♘e2 g6 9 0-0 ♘bd7 10 ♕d3 ± Balcerowski-Georgadze, Decin 1975.

[8] 5 ... e5 6 e4 d6 7 b3 ♗e7 8 ♗b2 ♘bd7 9 g3 ♘f8 10 h4 h5 11 ♗h3 ± Vaisman-Ghizdavu, Romania 1974.

[9] 7 f4!? ♗g7 8 ♘f3 0-0 9 ♗d3!? ∞.

[10] 10 fe ♘g4! ∓.

[11] 4 ... b4?! 5 ♗g5 d6 6 ♘bd2 ♘bd7 7 e4 g6

8 ♗e2 ♘g7 9 h3 0-0 10 0-0 ± Doda-Forintos, Polanica Zdroj 1968.

[12] 5 ♕b3 ♕b6 6 ♘c3 b4 =.

5 cb ♘xd5 6 ♘c3 ♗b7 7 ♕a4 d5 =.

5 ♕c2 d6 6 e4 b4 7 ♘e2 ♗g7 8 ♘g3 e6 = Hartoch-Keres, Amsterdam 1971.

5 g3 g6 6 ♗g2 ♗g7 7 0-0 0-0 8 ♖e1 d6 9 e4 bc = Klaman-Keres, USSR Ch 1957.

5 ♗g5 ♘e4 6 ♘c3 ♘xg5 7 ♘xg5 b4 =.

[13] Kan-Keres, USSR Ch 1955.

[14] 4 ... ♗b7 5 ♘c3 ♕a5 6 ♗d2 e6 7 e4 ± Stahlberg-Stoltz, Sweden 1933.

4 ... e6 5 ♘c3 ed 6 ♗g5 d4 7 ♘d5 ♗e7 8 ♗xf6 ♗xf6 9 ♕c2 d6 10 g3 ♗b7 11 ♗g2 ±.

[15] 5 b6 d6 (5 ... ♕xb6 6 ♘c3 g6 7 ♘f3 d6 8 ♘d2 ♗g7 9 e4 0-0 =) 6 ♘c3 ♘bd7 7 ♘f3 g6 8 e4 ♗g7 9 ♗e2 0-0 10 0-0 ♘xb6! = Pfleger-Benko, Skopje Ol 1972.

[16] 6 ... ab 7 ♗xb5 ♕a5 8 ♘ge2 e6 9 de fe 10 ♕b3 ±.

6 ... d6 7 ba ♗g7 8 ♗b5+ ♘bd7 (8 ... ♘fd7 9 ♘ge2 0-0 10 0-0 ♘xa6 11 e4 ±) 9 ♘ge2 0-0 10 0-0 ± Szabo-Fedorowicz, Lone Pine 1977.

[17] 7 e4 d6 (7 ... 0-0!? 8 a4 ♗b7! 9 e5 ♘e8 10 ♘f3 d6 Farago-Deze, Novi Sad 1979) 8 ba 0-0 9 f3 ♘xa6 10 ♗c4 ♘d7 11 ♘ge2 ♘e5 12 ♗b3 c4 =.

7 ba 0-0 8 ♘f3 d6 9 ♗e2 ♗xa6 10 0-0 ♘bd7 =.

7 ♘f3 0-0 8 ba d6 9 e4 ♕a5 10 ♘d2 ♗xa6 11 ♗xa6 ♕xa6 12 ♕e2 ♘fd7 13 a4 ♕xe2+ 14 ♔xe2 ♘a6 15 ♖b1 f5!? ∞ Portisch-Benko, Palma de Mallorca 1971.

[18] 8 ... d6? 9 ♗c4 ± Levy.

[19] 5 ... e6!?

[20] 8 a5 ab 9 ♗xb5+ ♘fd7! ∞ Korchnoi-Miles, Amsterdam 1976.

8 ♕b3!? e6 9 b6!? ∞ Schüssler-Borik, Dortmund 1979.

[21] 9 ♗c4 ♘bd7 10 ♘ge2 ♘e5 11 b3 ♘fd7! ∞ Chandler-Alburt, Hastings 1980/81.

[22] Levy.

[23] 8 ... ♘xe4? 9 ♗d3 ±.

8 ... ♘a6 9 ♘f3 g6 10 e5 ♘h5 11 ♕a4 ±.

8 ... ♘bd7 9 ♘f3 ♘h5 10 ♗g5 ♘hf6 11 ♘fd4!? Szabo. 11 ♗f4 ♘h5 =. 11 ♕e2 ♖a5! ∓ Zaitsev-Benko, Szolonok 1975.

[24] 9 ♗e3 ♘xe4 10 ♗d3 ♘f6 11 ♗xg5 ♗g7 ∓.

9 ... ♕a5 10 e5 ♘e4 11 ♘f3 ♗g7 12 ♗d3 ± Donner-Nun, Hradec Kralove 1978/79.

[25] 10 ... ♖a5!?

[26] 13 a4 ♗xb5 14 ♗xb5 ♘f6 15 ♗c6 0-0-0! ∞.

[27] 9 ♗f4!?

9 ♗c4 ♗g7 10 0-0-0-0 11 e5 de 12 ♘xe5 ♘e4! 13 ♖e1 ♘d6 14 ♘xd6 ed ∞ Keene.

[28] 10 d6!? ed 11 ♗g5 ♗e7 12 ♗xf6 ♗xf6 13 ♘xd6+ ♔f8 14 ♗c4 ♖a7! ∞.

[29] 13 d6 e6 14 ♘c7 ♘d5 15 ♗xd5 (Yudovich-Kremenetsky, USSR 1975; 15 ♘xa8? ♗xe5)

[15] ... ed 16 ♘d3 ♕xd6! 17 ♗f4 ♕b6! 18 ♘xa8 ♗xa8 ∞ Levy.

[30] 5 ... e6 6 ♘c3 ♘xd5 7 ♘xd5 ed 8 ♕xd5 ♘c6 9 e3 (9 ♘f3 ♗xa6! ∞) 9 ... ♗e7 10 ♗c4 0-0 11 ♘f3 ♗xa6 12 ♗d2! ± Pytel-Ungureanu, Lublin 1972!.

[31] 7 f4 g6 8 ♘f3 ♗g7 9 e4 ♗xf1 10 ♖xf1 0-0 11 ♔f2 ♘bd7 12 ♔g1 ♕b6 13 ♕e1 ♕b7 14 ♕d2 c4 ∞ Lombard-Benko, Costa Brava 1975.

[32] 9 ... 0-0 10 0-0 ♘bd7 11 ♕c2 ♕a5 12 ♗d2 ♖fb8 13 ♖ab1 ± Hort.

[33] 12 ... ♘fd7 13 ♕c1 ♗b7 14 e4 ♘c4 15 ♗h6! ± Levy.

12 ... ♘c4 13 ♕c1 ♕a5 14 ♖b1 ♖fb8 15 ♘d2 ♘e8! 16 ♖xc4 ♗xc4 ∞ Tukmakov.

[34] 9 ... ♘bd7 10 0-0 ♘b6!? 11 ♖e1 0-0 – 9 ... 0-0 10 0-0 ♘bd7 11 ♖e1 ♘b6.

[35] 11 h3 ♕a5 12 ♗d2 ♖fb8 13 ♕c2 ♘e8 14 ♖fe1 ♘c7 15 h4 ♘b5 ∞ Sosonko-Levy, Haifa Ol 1976.

11 ♗f4 ♕a5 12 ♕c2 ♖fb8 13 b3 ♘e8 intending ... ♘c7-b5 Levy.

11 ♗g5 h6! 12 ♗d2 ♕b6 13 ♕c2 ♖fb8 =.

11 ♖e1 ♘b6! 12 e4 ♘fd7 13 ♕c2 ♘c4 14 ♖d1 ♕a5 15 ♗f1 ∞.

[36] 11 ... ♘e8 12 ♗d2 ♕b6 13 b3 ♘c7 14 ♘h4 ♗b7 15 e4 ♗xc3 16 ♗xc3 ♖xa2 ∞ Mukhin-Georgadze, USSR 1972.

[37] 13 ♖e1?! ♘e8 14 ♗d2 ♗c4 15 h3 ♕a6 16 ♘h2 (Laver-Benko, USA 1968) 16 ... ♖b3! + Tukmakov.

[38] 12 h3 ♖fb8 13 ♖d1 ♘b6 =.

12 ♗g5 ♖fb8 13 ♖ab1 ♘b6 =.

12 ♖b1 ♘b6 13 ♖d1 ♘c4 14 ♘d2 ♘d7 =.

[39] Donner-Browne, Wijk aan Zee 1975.

[40] 9 ♘ge2 ♗g7 10 h3 0-0 11 ♔g1 ♕a5 12 ♖b1 ♘bd7 13 ♗e3 ♖fb8 14 ♕c2 ♘e5 15 b3 ♕a6 16 ♔h2 ♕d3 17 ♕xd3 ♘xd3 ∞ Bilyap-Palatnik, Albena 1975.

[41] 10 g5!? ♘h5 11 ♘ge2 ♘c8 12 ♔g2 ♕g4 Knaak-Pokojowczyk, Polanica Zdroj 1979.

[42] Visier-Benko, Malaga 1969. 17 g5? c4 ∓∓.

[43] 11 f4 ♘a6! 12 ♘f3 ♕b6 13 ♖e1 ♘b4 14 ♖e2 ♕a6 15 a4 ♖fb8 16 ♖a3 (intending ♘b5, ♘d2-c4) 16 ... ♕c4! 17 ♘d2 ♕d3! = Malich-Ciocaltea, Vrnjačka Banja 1972.

[44] 12 ♕e2 ♕b6! 13 ♖d1 ♕a6 14 ♕c2 ♘g4 15 h3 ♘ge5 16 ♗xe5 ♘xe5 (Gerusel-Georgadze, Dortmund 1979) 17 b3!? ∓.

12 ♘d2 ♕a5 13 ♘c4 ♕a6 14 ♕e2 ♖fb8 15 ♖e1 ♖b4 16 ♘a3 ♘e5 ∞.

[45] 13 ♗d2 ♖fb8 14 ♕c2 ♘g4 15 ♘d1 ♕b5 16 ♗c3 ♘de5 ∓ Makogonov-Korsunsky, USSR 1975.

[46] Knaak-Tseshkovsky, Leipzig 1975. .

[47] 14 e5? de 15 ♘xe5 ♕b7 16 ♕b3 e6! ∓ Taylor-Benko, Philadelphia 1975.

[48] Gligorić-Benko, Lone Pine 1975.

Schmid Benoni   1 d4 c5

	2	3	4	5	6	7	8	9	10	
1	dc[1] / ♕a5+[2]	♘c3[3] / ♘f6	♘f3 / ♘c6	♘d2 / ♕xc5	e4 / d6	♘c4 / ♘g4!	♘e3 / ♘xe3	♗xe3 / ♕a5	♗c4 / g6[4]	=
2	d5 / d6[5]	e4 / ♘f6[6]	♘c3 / g6	♗b5+ / ♗d7[7]	♗xd7+[8] / ♘bxd7	a4 / ♗g7	f4 / ♕a5	♗d2 / 0-0[9]	♘f3 / e6[10]	=
3	... / ...	... / ...	... / ...	♘f3 / ♗g7	♗b5+ / ♘bd7[11]	a4 / 0-0	0-0 / a6	♗e2 / ♖b8	♘d2 / ♘e8[12]	=
4	... / ...	... / ...	... / ...	... / ...	♗e2 / 0-0[13]	0-0 / e6[14]	de / ♗xe6	♘g5[15] / ♘c6[16]	f4 / ♘d4[17]	=
5	... / e5	e4 / d6	f4 / ef	♗xf4 / ♕e7[18]	♘c3 / a6	a4 / g5	♗g3 / ♘d7	♘f3 / ♗g7[19]		∞
6	... / ...	... / ...	♗d3 / ♗e7	♘e2 / ♘f6[20]	♘d2 / 0-0	a4 / ♘e8	0-0 / ♗g5	♘c4 / ♘d7	a5 / ♗xc1[21]	=
7	... / ...	... / ...	♘c3 / ♘f6[22]	f4 / ef	♗xf4 / ♗e7[23]	♗e2 / 0-0	♘f3 / ♖e8[24]	0-0 / ♘bd7	♘d2 / ♘f8[25]	±

---

[1] 2 e4 – Sicilian.
2 e3 ♘f6 3 ♘f3 e6 4 c4 d5 – Semi-Tarrasch.
2 ♘f3?! cd 3 ♘xd4 d5 4 g3 e5 5 ♘b3 ♘c6 6 ♗g2 ♗e6 7 0-0 f5 ∓ Tatai-Mariotti, Rome 1977.

[2] 2 ... e6 3 ♘c3 ♗xc3 4 ♘e4! ♘f6 (4 ... ♗e7 5 ♘d6+ ±) 5 ♘xc5 ♕a5+ 6 ♕d2 ♕xc5 7 ♘g5 ± Romanishin-Vaisman, Moscow 1977.

[3] 3 ♗d2!?

[4] 11 ♗d4?! ♖g8 12 0-0 ♘xd4 13 ♕xd4 ♗g7 ∓ Smith-Browne, San Antonio 1972.

[5] 2 ... e6 3 e4 ed 4 ed d6 5 ♘f3 ♘f6 6 ♘c3 ♗e7 7 ♗e2 0-0 8 0-0 ♘a6 = Vaganian-L.Bronstein, Sao Paulo 1977.

[6] 3 ... g6 4 ♗d3 ♗g7 5 c3 ♘a6 6 ♘e2 ♘c7 7 0-0 ♘h6?! 8 f3 e6 9 c4 ± Bardeleben-Pollock, Hastings 1895. 4 ♘c3!?

[7] 5 ... ♘bd7!?

[8] 6 a4! Larsen.

[9] 9 ... ♕b4 10 ♕e2 ♕xb2 11 ♖b1 ♕xc2 12 ♖c1! (12 e5? ♘xd5) 12 ... ♕b2 13 e5 ∞ Larsen.

[10] 11 0-0 c4? 12 ♔h1 ♖ae8 13 de fe 14 ♕e2 ♕c5 15 a5! ± Larsen-Rodriguez, Las Palmas 1976. 11 ... ♕c7! = Larsen.

[11] 6 ... ♗d7 7 a4 0-0 8 0-0 ♘a6 9 ♗xa6?! (9 ♖e1 =) 9 ... ba 10 ♘d2 ♖b8! ∓ Dorfman-Tal, USSR Ch 1977.
6 ... ♘fd7 7 a4 0-0 8 0-0 ♘a6 9 ♗f4 ♘c7 10 ♗e2 f5!? ∞ Larsen-Browne, Atlantic City 1972.

[12] Holmov-Stein, Kislovodsk 1966.

[13] 6 ... ♘a6 7 0-0 ♘c7 8 a4 a6 9 ♘d2 ♗d7 10 ♘c4 b5 11 e5! ± Botvinnik-Schmid, Leipzig Ol 1960.

[14] 7 ... ♗g4 8 ♘d2! (8 ♗g5 ♗xf3! 9 ♗xf3 ♘bd7 10 ♗e2 ♖c8 11 ♖e1 c4 = O'Kelly-Stein, Havana 1968) 8 ... ♗xe2 9 ♕xe2 ♘bd7 10 ♘c4 ♘b6 11 ♘e3 ± Stein-Bilek, Moscow 1967.

[15] 9 e5 de 10 ♕xd8 ♖xd8 11 ♘xe5 ♘d5 12 ♘xd5 ♗xd5 13 ♘d3 ♘c6! = Velimirović.

[16] 9 ... ♘c8? 10 ♗f4 h6 11 ♘f3 ♘e8 12 e5 ± Smyslov-Balcerowski, Polanica Zdroj 1966.

[17] 11 f5 gf 12 ♗d3 (12 ef ♗xf5 ∓) 12 ... ♗d7 13 ef ♗c6 = Kovačević-Velimirović, Zagreb 1972.

[18] 5 ... ♕h4+?! 6 g3 ♕e7 7 ♘f3! (7 ♘c3?! g5 8 ♗e3 ♘d7 9 ♘f3 h6 10 ♕d2 ♘gf6 11 0-0-0 ♘g4 ∓ Bogoljubow-Alekhine, match 1934) 7 ... ♕xe4+ 8 ♔f2 ♗g4 9 ♗b5+ ±.

[19] Kasparov.

[20] 5 ... ♗g5 6 ♘d2 ♘e7 7 0-0 ♘g6 8 a4 h6 9 c3 ±.

[21] Baumbach-Pietzsch, Bad Liebenstein 1963.

[22] 4 ... ♗e7 5 ♘f3 ♗g4 6 h3 ♗xf3 7 ♕xf3 ♗g5 8 ♗xg5 ♕xg5 9 ♘b5 ♕d8 10 ♕g4 ♔f8 11 ♘xd6 ♘f6! 12 ♕c8 ♕xc8 13 ♘xc8 ♘xe4 14 ♗d3 ± Kasparov-Dolmatov, USSR 1977.
4 ... g6!? 5 f4 ef 6 ♗xf4 ♘f6 7 ♘f3 ♘h5 8 ♗g5 ♗e7 9 ♗h6 ♘g4 ∞ Visier-Larsen, Palma de Mallorca 1969.
4 ... ♘e7 5 ♘f3 (5 g3 ♘g6 6 h4 ♗e7 7 h5 ± Alekhine-Castillo, Buenos Aires Ol 1939; 5 ... g6!?) 5 ... ♘g6 6 h4 h5 7 g3 ♗e7 8 ♘h2 ♘f8 9 ♗e2 g6 10 ♘f1 ♘bd7 ± Kostich-Spielmann, Göteborg 1920.

[23] 6 ... g6!? – note 22.

[24] 8 ... ♗g4 9 ♘d2 ♗xe2 10 ♕xe2 ♘bd7 11 0-0 a6 12 ♘c4 ± Maximovich-Ciocaltea, Niš 1977.

[25] Bellon-Fraguela, Montilla 1976.

Czech Benoni   1 d4 ♘f6 2 c4 c5 3 d5 e5

	4	5	6	7	8	9	10	11	12	
1	♘c3	e4	♗d3	♘ge2	0-0[2]	a3	b4			=
	d6	♗e7[1]	0-0	♘h5	♗g5	g6	b6[3]			
2	...	...	♘f3	♗d3[4]	h3	♗h6	g4	♕e2	0-0-0	±
	...	...	0-0	♘e8	g6[5]	♘g7	♘d7	♘f6	♔h8[6]	
3	...	...	g3	♗g2	♘ge2	f4	gf	0-0	♕d3	±
	...	...	0-0[7]	♘e8	♗g5[8]	ef	♗h6[9]	♗g4		

[1]   5 ... g6 6 ♗e2 ♘bd7 7 ♘f3 ♘h5 ∞ Keene-Mestel, Esbjerg 1981.

[2]   8 ♘g3 ♘f4 9 ♗xf4 ef 10 ♘h5 ♗g5 11 g3 f5! 12 ef ♗xf5 = Pfleger-Gheorghiu, Hastings 1963/64.

[3]   Skalkotas-Plachetka, Ybbs 1968.

[4]   7 ♗e2 ♘e8 8 0-0 ♘d7 9 a3 g6 10 ♗h6 ♗g7 11 ♕d2 ± Savon-Bannik, USSR 1969.

[5]   8 ... a6 9 g4 ♘d7 10 ♕e2 g6 11 ♗h6 ♗g7 12 0-0-0 ± Spassky-Ghitescu, Beverwijk 1967.

[6]   13 ♖dg1 ± Shashin-Korotkevich, USSR 1975.

[7]   6 ... b5 7 cb a6 8 ♘f3 0-0 9 ♘d2 ± Portisch-Damjanović, Monte Carlo 1968.

[8]   8 ... ♘d7 9 0-0 g6 10 ♗h6 ±.

[9]   10 ... ♗h4+ 11 ♘g3 f5 12 e5! de 13 fe f4 14 0-0 fg 15 ♖xf8+ ♔xf8 16 hg! ± Eperjesi-Androvitzky, Hungary 1971.

Benoni I: Early Divergences   1 d4 ♘f6 2 c4 c5 3 d5

	3	4	5	6	7	8	9	10	11	
1	...	♘c3	e4	♗d3	♘ge2[1]	0-0[2]	a4[3]	f4	♕xd3	±
	d6	g6	♗g7	0-0	a6	♘bd7	♘e5	♘xd3	♖b8[4]	
2	...	♘c3	cd	d6!?	♗g5	♕d2	0-0-0	f3	e4	±
	e6	ed	g6	♕b6[5]	♗g7[6]	0-0	♖e8	♘c6	♘d4[7]	
3	...	...	...	♘f3	♗g5!?	♗h4	♗g3	e3[9]	hg	±
	...	...	d6	g6	h6[8]	g5	♘h5	♘xg3	♗g7[10]	
4	...	...	...	...	♘d2[11]	♘c4	♗g5	♗f4	♗xd6	∞
	...	...	...	...	♗g7	0-0	h6	b6	♖e8[12]	

[1]   7 ♘f3 – King's Indian.
7 f4 a6 8 ♘ge2 (8 a4!) 8 ... b5! 9 cb ab 10 ♘xb5 ♗a6! 11 ♘ec3 c4! 12 ♗c2 (12 ♗xc4 ♗xb5 13 ♗xb5 ♖xe4! ∓) 12 ... ♗xb5 13 ♘xb5 ♕a5+ 14 ♘c3 ♘fd7! (Hernandez-Kasparov, Banja Luka 1979) 15 0-0! ∞.

[2]   8 ♗f4 ♕a5 9 ♕d2.b5 10 0-0 ♘bd7 11 ♘g3 ♘g4 ∞ Volovich-Shamkovich, Moscow 1961.

[3]   9 f4 b5 ∞ Perez-Korchnoi, Havana 1963.

[4]   12 h3 ♘e8 13 ♗e3 ♗d7 14 ♖b1 ± Pachman-Szabo, Buenos Aires 1960.

[5]   6 ... ♗g7 7 e4 0-0 8 f4 ♘c6 9 e5 ♘e8 10 ♘f3 ± van den Berg-Nievergelt, Berlin 1965.

[6]   7 ... ♘h5 8 ♗d5! f6 9 0-0-0 ±.

[7]   12 ♘ge2 ♕xd6 13 ♘xd4 cd 14 ♕xd4 ± Uhlmann.

[8]   7 ... ♗g7 8 ♘d2 0-0 9 e3 h6 10 ♗h4 a6 11 a4 ♘bd7 12 ♗e2 ♕e7 13 0-0 ♖b8 14 ♕c2 ± Furman-Bebchuk, USSR 1964.

[9]   10 ♘d2 ♗g7 11 e3 ♘xg3 12 hg 0-0 = Botvinnik-Tal, match 1960.

[10]   12 ♗d3 ♘d7 13 ♕c2 a6 14 a4 ♖b8 15 0-0 0-0 16 ♖ab1 ♕e7 17 ♖fc1 intending 18 b4 ± Furman-Tal, Tallinn 1971.

[11]   7 ♗f4!? ♗g7 8 ♕a4+ ♗d7 9 ♕b3 ♕c7 10 e4 0-0 11 ♗e2 (11 e5 ♘e8 12 ♗e2!? ♘h5 13 ♗e3 de 14 0-0 ∞ S.Garcia-Kasparov, Baku 1980) 11 ... ♘h5 12 ♗e3 a6 13 0-0 b5 14 a4 ± Sosonko-Vasyukov, Reykjavik 1980.

[12]   12 ♗g3 ♘e4 13 ♘xe4 ♖xe4 14 e3 b5 15 ♘d6!? (15 ♘d2 ♖b4 16 b3 c4! 17 a3 ♖xb3 18 ♗e2 – Chandler-Denman, Brighton 1979 – 18 ... ♕a5 ∓ Cabrilo) 15 ... ♖b4 16 ♗e2 ♗xb2 17 0-0! ∞ Petrosian.

Benoni II: Fianchetto Variation   1 d4 ♘f6 2 c4 c5 3 d5 e6
4 ♘c3 ed 5 cd d6 6 ♘f3 g6 7 g3 ♗g7 8 ♗g2 0-0 9 0-0 ♘bd7[1] 10 ♘d2

	10	11	12	13	14	15	16	17	18	
1	...	a4	h3	♘de4	♘xe4					∞
	♖e8	♘e5	g5	♘xe4	h6[2]					
2	...	a4	h3[3]	♘c4	♘a3	a5	♘c4	♕b3	♕xc4	=
	a6	♖e8	♖b8[4]	♘b6	♗d7	♘c8	♗b5	♗xc4	♘d7[5]	
3	...	...	...	...	♘a3	♔h2[6]	f4	e3	♕d3	=
	...	...	...	♘e5	♘h5	f5	♘f7	♗d7	♕c8[7]	

[1]   9 ... ♖e8 10 ♗f4! ±.
9 ... ♕e7!?
9 ... ♘a6 10 ♘d2 (10 h3!? ♘c7 11 e4 ♘d7 12 ♗f4 ♕e7?! 13 ♖e1 f6 14 ♖b1 ± Csom-Wedberg, Malta Ol 1980; 12 ... ♘e8!?) 10 ... ♘c7 11 ♘c4 and now:
11 ... b5 12 ♘xd6 ♕xd6 13 ♗f4 ♕b6 14 d6 ±/± Ogaard-Basler, Switzerland 1979.
11 ... ♘fe8 12 a4 b6 13 ♗d2 (13 ♕b3 ♗a6 14 ♘b5 ♕d7 ∞ Youngworth-Shamkovich, Lone Pine 1978) 13 ... ♖b8?! (13 ... ♗a6!?) 14 ♘b5 ♘xb5 15 ab ♘c7 16 ♖xa7 ± Tal-Mnatsakanian, USSR 1959.
11 ... ♘h5 12 a4 f5 13 e3 b6 14 ♕c2 ♗a6 15 b3 ± Marović-Honfi, Maribor 1971.

[2]   Uhlmann-Larsen, Beverwijk 1961.

[3]   12 ♘c4 ♘e5 (12 ... ♘b6 13 ♘a3 ♗d7 14 e4 ♖b8 15 ♖e1 ♘c8 16 ♗f1 b5 17 ab ab 18 ♘axb5 ♘xe4 ∞ Didishko-Kernozitsky, USSR 1965)
13 ♘a3 ♘h5 14 h3!? (14 e3?! f5?! 15 ♗d2 ♗d7 ∞ Unzicker-Hübner, Bad Kissingen 1980; 14 ... b5 15 f4 b4 16 fe ba 17 ♖xa3 ♗xe5 ∓).

[4]   12 ... ♘h5 13 ♘h2 f5 14 f4 ♘df6 15 e4 fe 16 ♘dxe4 ♘xe4 17 ♘xe4 ♘f6 18 ♗g5 h6 19 ♘e6 ♗xe6 20 de d5 21 ♖e1 ∞ Raskin-Bangiev, USSR 1973.

[5]   19 ♔h2 ♘e5 = Vukić-Gliksman, Yugoslav Ch 1968.
19 e4!? =.
19 ♕d3?! ♘e5 20 ♕c2 ♘a7! 21 ♖d1 ♘b5 ∓ Liberzon-Yusupov, Lone Pine 1981.
19 ♖a3 ♘e7 20 ♕a2 ♘f5! 21 e3 ♘e5 ∓ Rubinetti-Gheorghiu, Buenos Aires 1979.

[6]   15 e4 ♗d7!? 16 a5 ♕xa5 17 g4 ♘f6 18 g5 ♘h5 19 f4 ♘c4 20 ♘xc4 ♕xa1 21 ♘xd6 ∞ Hulak-Nunn, Toluca IZ 1982.

[7]   19 a5 b5 =.

Benoni III   1 d4 ♘f6 2 c4 c5 3 d5 e6 4 ♘c3 ed 5 cd d6 6 e4 g6

	7	8	9	10	11	12	13	14	15	
1	f3[1]	♗g5[2]	♗e3	♕d2	♘ge2	♘c1	a4	♗e2	0-0	∞
	♗g7	h6[3]	0-0[4]	♔h7	♘bd7	a6	♖b8	♗e8[5]	♘c7[6]	
2	♗d3	♘ge2	0-0[7]	♗g5	♗h4[9]	♗g3				∞
	♗g7	0-0	b6[8]	h6	g5!?[10]	♘h5				
3	...	...	...	a4	h3[11]	f4	♗e3[12]	♘g3	♗c2	±
	...	...	a6	♕c7	♘bd7	♖b8	♖e8	c4	♘c5[13]	
4	...	...	...	h3[14]	♗g5	♕d2	♗c2	a3	♘g3	∞
	...	...	♖e8	♗d7	♕c7	c4	b5	♘a6	b4[15]	
5	f4	e5	♘b5[17]	♘d6+	♘b5	d6+	♘c7	♗e2[18]	♘f3!?[20]	∞
	♗g7	♘fd7[16]	de	♔e7	♖e8	♔f8	ef+	♘c6![19]		
6	...	...	...	...	♘xc8+	♘f3[21]	fe	♗b5	♘xe5	∞/=
	...	...	...	...	♕xc8	♖e8	♘xe5	♘bd7	♔f8![22]	
7	...	...	...	...	...	...	♗c4	0-0	♗b5	∞
	...	...	...	...	...	...	♔f8	♘b6	♖d8[23]	

¹ 7 ♗b5+ ♘bd7 8 a4 a6 9 ♗e2 ♗g7 10 ♘f3 0-0 11 0-0 ♖e8 = Forintos-Vaganian, Kirovakan 1978.

7 g3 ♗g7 8 ♗g2 0-0 9 ♘ge2 a6 10 a4 ♘bd7 11 0-0 ♖b8 12 a5 b5 13 ab ♛xb6 14 h3 ♖e8 = Novotelnov-Plater, Moscow 1947.

7 ♘ge2 ♗g7 8 ♘g3 0-0 9 ♗e2 ♘a6 10 0-0 ♘c7 11 a4 ♖b8 12 ♖b1 b6 = Szabo-Borik, Dortmund 1974.

² 8 ♗e3 0-0 9 ♛d2 a6 10 a4 ♖e8 11 ♘ge2 ♛a5 12 ♖a3 ♘bd7 13 ♘b1 ♛c7 14 ♘ec3 = Alvarez-Wexler, Mar del Plata 1960.

³ 8 ... a6 9 a4 ♘bd7 10 ♘h3! h6 11 ♗e3 ♘e5 12 ♘f2 g5 13 ♗e2 ♛e7 14 ♛d2 ♗d7 15 a5 ± Gulko-Kasparov, USSR 1981. Cf. Sämisch King's Indian.

⁴ 9 ... ♘bd7 10 ♘h3! 0-0 11 ♘f2 a6 12 a4 ♖e8 13 ♗e2 ♖b8 14 0-0 ± Despotović-Kelečević, Yugoslav Ch 1968.

⁵ 14 ... ♛c7 15 0-0 ± Franco-Littlewood, Varna Ol 1962.

⁶ 16 ♔h1 b5 ∞ Gulko-Polugayevsky, USSR Ch 1974.

⁷ 9 ♗g5 h6 10 ♗f4 b6 11 ♛d2 ♔h7 12 ♘g3 ♗a6 13 h4 ♖xd3 14 ♛xd3 h5 15 ♗g5 ♛c8 16 e5 ♘g4 17 ed c4 ∞ Klaman-Blehchin, USSR 1965.

⁸ 9 ... ♘a6 10 ♗g5 h6 11 ♗f4 g5 12 ♗d2 ♖e8 13 ♘g3 ± Ghitescu-Martin, Olot 1979. 10 f3 ♗d7 11 ♗g5 ♖c8 12 ♗c4 ♘c7 13 a4 a6 14 a5 h6 ∞ Rivas-Suba, Spain 1980.

⁹ 11 ♗f4 ♗a6 12 ♘g3!? (12 a4 ♖e8 13 h3 ♛e7 14 ♘g3 c4 15 ♗c2 ♘bd7 16 ♛d2 ♛f8 17 ♗e3 ♘c5 ∞ Bergen-Tal, Skopje Ol 1972) 12 ... ♗xd3 13 ♛xd3 a6 14 ♖ae1 ♘g4 15 h3 ♘e5 16 ♗xe5 de!? (Kasparov-Ghitescu, Malta Ol 1980; 16 ... ♗xe5 17 f4 ♗d4+ 18 ♔h1 ♘d7 19 e5! de 20 f5 ∞) 17 ♖d1 ±.

¹⁰ 11 ... ♗a6 12 f4 (12 f3 ♗xd3 13 ♛xd3 a6 14 ♖ae1 ♘bd7 15 f4 ♛c7 16 ♘g3 c4 = Banfalui-Suetin, Debrecen 1963) 12 ... ♛c8 13 h3 ♗xd3

¹¹ 14 ♛xd3 ♘bd7 (Bašagić-Minić, Sarajevo 1966) 15 ♔h1!? ±.

¹¹ 11 ♘g3 ♘bd7 12 ♛e2 ♖e8 13 f4 c4 ∞ Bilek-Stein, Amsterdam IZ 1964.

¹² 13 ♘g3 c4 14 ♗c2 b5 15 ab ab 16 ♗e3 b4 17 ♖a7 ♛d8 18 ♘a4 ♖b5 19 b3 c3 = Bertok-Portisch, Stockholm IZ 1962.

¹³ 16 ♛f3 b5 17 ab ab 18 e5! de 19 fe ♖xe5 20 ♗d4 ♖g5 21 ♘ge2! (21 ♘ge4? ♘g4! ∓) 21 ... ♗f5 22 ♛e3! ± Knaak-Postler, East Germany 1976.

¹⁴ 10 ♘g3 ♘a6 11 h3 ♘c7 12 a4 b6 13 ♗f4 ♗a6 14 ♗xa6 ♖xa6 15 ♛d2 c4 ∞ Hartston-Ribli, Moscow 1977.

¹⁵ 16 ab ♘xb4 ∞ Spassky-Ljubojević, Manila IZ 1976.

¹⁶ 8 ... de?! 9 fe ♘fd7 10 e6 fe 11 de ♛e7!? (11 ... ♗xc3+ 12 bc ♛e7 13 ♘f3 ♛xe6+ 14 ♗e2 ± Steijn-Parr, Beverwijk II 1964) 12 ♘d5 ♛xe6+ 13 ♛e2 ♛xe2+ 14 ♗xe2 0-0! 15 ♘c7 ♘c6 16 ♘xa8 ♘b4 ∞ Lputian-Magerramov, USSR 1979.

¹⁷ 9 ed 0-0 10 ♘f3 ♘f6 11 ♗e2 ·a6 12 a4 ♛xd6 13 ♘e5 b6 14 0-0 ♖a7 15 ♗f3 = Podolnyi-Vasilzhuk, Moscow 1956.

¹⁸ 14 ♘xe8 ♛xe8!+ 15 ♗e2 ♘e5! ∓ Smirnov-Kapengut, Minsk 1979.

¹⁹ 14 ... ♛h4+ 15 ♔f1 ∞ Kapengut.

²⁰ 15 ♘xe8?! ♛xe8 16 ♘f3 ♘d4 17 ♘xd4 ♗xd4 18 ♗xf4 ♘e5 ∞/∓ Kapengut.
15 ♘f3!? ∞.

²¹ 12 d6+ ♔f8 13 ♘f3 e4! 14 ♘g5 h6 15 ♘xf7 ♔xf7 16 ♗c4+ ♔f8 17 f5 (Maffeo-Partos, USA 1973) 17 ... ♘c6! ∓ Larsen.

²² 15 ... ♗xe5 16 0-0 ±.
15 ... ♔f8 16 0-0 ♖xe5 17 ♗f4 c4! 18 ♛d4! ∞/= Shakarov-Shumlensson, corr. 1976/77.

²³ 16 fe ♖xd5 17 ♛e1 ♘c6 18 ♗xc6 ♛xc6 19 ♛h4 ♔g8 20 ♘g5 ∞ Mikenas-Suetin, USSR Ch 1962.

Benoni IV   1 d4 ♘f6 2 c4 c5 3 d5 e6 4 ♘c3 ed 5 cd d6 6 e4 g6 7 f4 ♗g7

	8	9	10	11	12	13	14	15	16	
1	♗b5+	♗d3	a4	♘f3	♘d2	♘c4	♘e2	♗d2	♗c3![4]	±
	♘fd7[1]	a6[2]	♕b6[3]	0-0	♗d4	♕c7	♗g7	b6		
2	...	...	♘f3	0-0	a4[7]	e5!?[9]	♖e1	♖e2	d6	∞
	...	0-0	♘a6[5]	♘c7[6]	a6[8]	♖b8	♖e8[10]	de	♘e6[11]	
3	...	a4	♘f3	0-0	♗d2[14]	♗e2	♕b3!?[16]	♔h1	ab	∞
	...	0-0	♘a6[12]	♘b4[13]	a6[15]	♖e8	♖b8[17]	b5	ab[18]	
4	♘f3	♗e2	♗b5	♘xe4	♔f2	♘xd6	♘c4	♕e2	♗e3	∞
	0-0	b5[19]	♘xe4	♕a5+	♕xb5	♕b6[20]	♕a6	♗d7	♗b5[21]	
5	...	...	e5	fe	♗xb5[22]	0-0	♗e2	♗xf3		=/±
	...	...	de	♘g4	♘xe5	♗g4	♗xf3	♘bd7[23]		
6	...	...	...	...	♗g5!	ef	♕d2	♘xb5	0-0	±
	...	...	...	...	f6[24]	♗xf6	♗f5	♘d7	♕b6[25]	
7	...	...	0-0[26]	♘d2[28]	♕xe2	♕f3	a4	♔h1	e5	∞
	...	♗g4	♘bd7[27]	♗xe2	♖e8	♕e7[29]	c4	♘c5	de[30]	

1 d4 ♘f6 2 c4 c5 3 d5 e6 4 ♘c3 ed 5 cd d6 6 e4 g6 7 f4 ♗g7 8 ♘f3 0-0 9 ♗e2 ♖e8

	10	11	12	13	14	15	16	17	18	
8	0-0	♘xe4	♗d3	f5	♘g5[32]	fg	♕a4			∞
	♘xe4	♖xe4	♖e8	♘d7[31]	♘f6	fg				
9	e5	fe	♗g5[33]	ef	♕d2[34]	0-0	h3	♕xg5	♕h6	=
	de	♘g4	f6	♗xf6	♗f5	♘d7	♗xg5	♘e3	♘xf1[35]	
10	...	...	...	0-0	d6[37]	♘d5	♘e7+	de	♔h1	=
	...	...	♕b6	♗f5[36]	♕xb2	♘e5	♖xe7[38]	♘bc6	♘f3[39]	
11	♘d2	a4	0-0	♗f3	♕c2	♘xc4	♕xc1	♗xg4	♕d1	∞
	c4	♘bd7	♘c5	♗h6	♘d3	♘xc1	♗g4[40]	♘xg4	f5[41]	
12	...	♗xg4[42]	g3	♕xg4	♘b5	h3	♘xe4	0-0[43]	♘c3	∞
	♘g4	♕h4+	♕xg4	♗xg4	♘a6	♖xe4+	♗xf3	♗xe4	♗d3[44]	
13	...	a4	♗xg4[46]	g3	♕xg4	♔f2	h3	♔g2	bc	∞
	a6	♘g4[45]	♕h4+	♕xg4	♗xg4	♘d7	♗d4	♗xc3	♗e2[47]	
14	...	0-0	a4	♗f3	♘c4[49]	ab	♘a5[50]	e5	d6[51]	∞
	♘a6	♘c7	a6[48]	♖b8	b5	ab	♗d7	de		

[1] **8 ... ♗d7?** 9 e5 ♘h5 10 ♘f3 de 11 fe ♗xb5 12 ♘xb5 0-0 13 0-0 ♕d7 14 ♘c3 ± O'Kelly-Diez del Corral, Madrid 1957.

8 ... ♘bd7? 9 e5 de 10 fe ♘h5 11 e6 fe 12 de 0-0 13 ♘f3! ♖xf3 (13 ... ♘df6 14 ♕xd8 ♖xd8 15 e7 ♖d6 16 ♘g5! ± Nei) 14 ♕xf3 ♗xc3+ 15 bc ♘e5 16 ♕e4 ♕f6 17 e7! ♕xe7 18 0-0 ♗f5 (18 ... ♘f6 19 ♕h4!) 19 ♕d5+ ♔g7 20 ♗g5 ♕xg5 21 ♕xe5+ ♔h6 22 ♖ae1 ± Kapengut.

[2] 9 ... ♕h4+!? 10 g3 ♕e7 11 ♘f3 0-0 12 0-0 ♘b6!? 13 ♔g2 ♗g4 14 h3 ♗xf3 15 ♕xf3 ♘8d7 ∞ Lukacs-Psakhis, USSR 1981.

[3] 10 ... ♕a5 11 ♗d2 ±.

[4] **16 ♕b3?!** ♖a7 17 0-0 ♖b7 18 ♘a3 ♘f6 19 h3 ♕e7 20 ♘c3 ♘h5 21 ♔h2 g5! = Alatortsev-Aronin, 18th USSR Ch.
16 ♗c3! Kapengut.

[5] 10 ... b6!? 11 0-0 (11 ♕e2 ♖e8 12 0-0 f5!? 13 ♘g5 ♘f8 14 ♕c2 fe 15 ♘gxe4 ♗f5 intending ... e4 Kapengut) 11 ... ♗a6 12 ♕e2! (12 a4 c4 13 ♗c2 ♘c5 14 ♗e3 ♘d3!?; 14 ♘b5!? ♖e8 15 e5 Kapengut) 12 ... ♗xd3 13 ♕xd3 a6 14 a4 ♖e8 15 ♔h1 ± Mititelu-Novak, Budapest 1959.

[6] **11 ... ♘b4** 12 ♗e2! ♖e8 13 a3 ♘a6 14 ♘d2 ♘c7 15 ♗f3 ♖b8 16 ♘c4 ± Farago-Grünberg, Graz (Student Ol) 1972.
11 ... ♘b6 12 ♗e3 ♗g4! =. 12 h3! ±.
11 ... ♖b8 12 ♔h1 ♘c7 13 a4 a6 14 f5 b5

15 ab ♘xb5 16 ♗g5 ♗f6 17 ♘xb5 ab 18 ♕d2 c4
19 ♗c2 b4 ∞ Zaichik-Taborov, USSR 1976.
14 a5 ♖e8 15 ♗e3?! b5! 16 ab ♖xb6 17 ♖a2 =
Hartston-Nunn, England 1977.   15 ♕e1!?

[7]   12 ♘d2 ♘f6! 13 h3 ♘h5! 14 ♕f3 b5
15 ♘xb5 ♘xb5 16 ♗xb5 ♖b8 17 a4 a6 18 ♗c6
♗d4+ 19 ♔h1 ♕h4 20 ♖a3 (Farago-Filipowicz,
Polanica Zdroj 1974) 20 ... g5 21 fg ♗e5
22 ♗g1 ♗d4+ ½-½.   16 ... ♗d4+ 17 ♔h1 ♕h4
18 ♔h2 ♖b8 19 a4 a6 20 ♗d3 (20 ♗c6 ♖b4! ∓)
20 ... ♘xf4 21 ♘c4 ♘xd3 22 ♕xd3 f5! ∓
Kapengut.

[8]   12 ... ♖e8 13 ♖e1 ♘a6 14 h3 ♘b4 15 ♗f1 a6
16 ♗e3 f5 17 ♗g5 ♘f8 18 e5! ± Lukacs-Sapi,
Hungary 1977.

[9]   13 ♕e1 ♖b8 14 e5 ♘b6 15 f5! de 16 f6 ±
Gulko-Savon, Lvov 1978.   13 ... ♘f6 14 ♗d2
b6 15 ♖d1 ♖b8 16 e5 ♘fxd5 17 ♗e4 de 18 fe
h6 ∞ Gulko-Cvetković, Sukhumi 1966.

[10]   14 ... b5 15 e6! fe 16 de ♘xe6 17 ♖xe6 ♘e5
18 fe ♗xe6 19 ♗g5 ♕b6 20 ♗e4 ± Kapengut.

[11]   17 ♘d5 ∞.

[12]   10 ... a6 11 ♗e2! ± Kasparov-Kuijpers,
Dortmund 1980.

[13]   11 ... ♘c7 12 ♖e1 (12 ♗d3 – 9 ♗d3) 12 ...
♘xb5 13 ab later.

[14]   12 ♗e3 a6 13 ♗e2 (13 ♗c4 ♖b8 14 ♗f2 ♘b6
15 ♗e2 ♗g4 Kapengut) 13 ... ♘f6 (13 ... b6
14 h3 ♘f6 15 ♗c4 ± Doroshkevich-Gorshkov,
Leningrad 1973) 14 h3 ♖e8 15 e5 de 16 ♗xc5
♘fxd5 (Kapengut) ∞.

[15]   12 ... ♘f6 13 h3 ±.

[16]   14 ♗e1 ♘b6 15 a5 ♘d7 intending ... b5 =.
15 h3 f5!.   15 ♗h4 ♗f6 16 ♗xf6 ♕xf6 17 ♕d2
♗g4 Kapengut.

[17]   14 ... ♘f6 15 e5 de 16 fe ♘fxd5 17 ♗g5
♕d7 18 ♖ad1 ±.
14 ... ♘b6 15 h3 ♗xc3 16 bc ♖xe4 17 ♖ae1
♘4xd5 18 a5 c4 19 ♕a3 ♘d7 20 ♕xd6 ±
Kapengut.

[18]   17 ♗xb5 ♗xc3 18 bc ♖xb5 19 cb ∞.

[19]   9 ... ♘a6 10 e5 de 11 fe ♘g4 12 ♗f4 ♖e8
13 e6 fe 14 d6 ♗d7 15 ♕d2 ♘b4 16 0-0 ♖f8
17 h3 ±/± Cobo-Ciocaltea, Havana 1965.

[20]   13 ... ♕a6 14 ♖xc8 ♖xc8 15 ♖e1 ♘d7
16 ♔g1 ♖e8 17 a4 c4 18 a5 ♘c5 19 ♘e5 ±
Malich-Garces, Tel Aviv Ol 1964.

[21]   17 ♖hc1 ♖e8 ½-½ A.Zaitsev-Bogdanović,
Sochi 1967.

[22]   12 ♗f4?! b4 (12 ... ♘d7 13 e6 fe 14 de ♖xf4
15 ♕d5 ♔h8 16 ♕xa8 ±/± Keres-Spassky,
match 1965) 13 ♘e4 ♘d7 14 e6 fe 15 de ♖xf4
16 ♕d5 ♔h8 17 ♕xa8 ♘b6 18 ♕c6 ♘e3 ∓.

[23]   = Geller. ± Spassky.

[24]   12 ... ♕b6 13 0-0 c4 14 ♔h1 a6 15 d6 ♗e6
16 ♘d4 ♘xe5 17 ♗e7 ± Ritov-Zhuravlev, USSR
1973.

[25]   17 ♗c4 ± Sosonko-Reshevsky, Amsterdam

1977.

[26]   10 e5?! ♗xf3 11 ♗xf3 de 12 fe ♘fd7 ∓.
10 h3 ♗xf3 11 ♗xf3 ♘bd7 ∞.

[27]   10 ... ♖e8?! 11 e5! de 12 fe ♗xf3 13 ♗xf3
♖xe5 14 ♗f4 ♖e8 15 ♕b3 ± Liptay-Vasyukov,
Budva 1963.
10 ... ♗xf3 11 ♗xf3 ♘bd7 12 ♔h1! a6
13 ♗e3 ♖e8 14 g4 ± Doroshkevich-Tal, USSR
Ch 1975.

[28]   11 a4 ♖e8 12 h3 ♗xf3 13 ♗xf3 c4 =.

[29]   13 ... a6 14 a4 ♖c8 15 a5 ± Witkowski-
Adamski, Polish Ch 1968.
13 ... ♕a5 14 a4 ♕b4 15 ♔h1 a6 16 a5 b5
17 ab ♘xb6 18 g4 ± Peev-Honfi, Cienfuegos
1976.

[30]   17 fe ♕xe5 ∞ Peev-Tseshkovsky, Albena
1977.

[31]   13 ... gf 14 g4! ±.
13 ... ♗xf5 14 ♗xf5 gf 15 ♗g5! ∞.   15 g3!?

[32]   14 g4!? ECO.

[33]   12 ♗f4!? ♘xe5 13 0-0 ♘bd7 14 d6! ♖b8
(14 ... ♘xf3+ 15 ♗xf3 ♘e5 16 ♘b5 ♗f5
17 ♘c7 ± Szabo-Zuckerman, Las Vegas 1973)
15 ♘d5?! b5! ∞ Szabo-Ciocaltea, Budapest
1973. 15 ♘b5! ∞.
12 e6!? fe 13 0-0 ed 14 ♘xd5 ♗e6 15 ♗c4
♘e5 ∞/∓ Niemala-Tal, Riga 1959.

[34]   14 ♗f4!? ♘e3 15 ♗xe3 ♖xe3 16 0-0 ECO.

[35]   19 ♘g5 ♕e7 20 d6 (Szabo-Timman, Amsterdam 1975) 20 ... ♕g7! 21 ♗c4+ ♔h8 22 ♘f7+ =.

[36]   13 ... ♘xe5 14 d6 c4+ 15 ♔h1 ♘d3 16 ♗xd3
cd 17 ♕xd3 ♗e6 18 ♖ac1 ± ECO.

[37]   14 ♘a4!? Filip.

[38]   16 ... ♔h8 17 ♘xf5 ± Filip.

[39]   19 ♗xf3 ♕xa1 20 ♕xa1 ♗xa1 21 ♖xa1 f6
22 ♗xc6 bc 23 ♖d1 ♖e8 = Filip.

[40]   16 ... ♗d7 17 b3 ♕c7 18 ♕e3 ± Padevsky-
Ciocaltea, Havana Ol 1966.

[41]   19 h3 ♖c8 20 hg ♖xc4 21 g5 ♗g7 22 ef gf
23 ♕d3 ♕c8 ∞ Boleslavsky.

[42]   11 ♘c4 h5 12 ♗xg4 ♗xg4 13 ♕d3 ∞.

[43]   17 ♘f2? ♖e8 18 ♔f1 ♗e2+ 19 ♔g2 ♗xb5 ∓.

[44]   19 ♖d1 c4 ∞.

[45]   11 ... ♘bd7 12 0-0 c4 (12 ... ♕c7?! 13 ♔h1 c4
14 e5! de 15 ♘xc4 e4 16 f5 ± Alexandria-
Chiburdanidze, match 1981) 13 ♗f3 ♕c7
14 ♔h1 ♖b8 15 a5 b5 16 ab ± Grigorian-
Lutikov, USSR 1971.

[46]   12 ♘c4 h5 ∞.

[47]   19 ♖e1 ♗d3 20 ♖e3 c4 21 ♗a3 ∞.

[48]   12 ... b6 13 ♔h1 ♗a6 14 ♖e1 ♗xe2 15 ♖xe2
♘g4 16 h3 ♕h4 17 ♕f1 f5 18 ♘f3 ♕h5 19 e5 de
20 fe ♘xe5 21 d6 ± Savon-Belyavsky, USSR
Ch 1973.   17 ... ♘h6 ± Kotov.

[49]   14 e5 de 15 fe ♘fxd5 16 ♘xd5 ♘xd5
17 ♘c4 ∞.

[50]   16 ♘d6!? ♕xd6 17 e5 ECO.

[51]   Baranov-Vilup, USSR 1960.

	7	8	9	10	11	12	13	14	15	
1	...	a4	♗e2	♗xf3	0-0	♗f4	♗e2	♗g3	♕c2	±
	a6	♗g4[1]	♗xf3	♗g7	♘bd7	♕b8	0-0	♖e8	♕c7[2]	
2	...	♕a4+	♕b3	♗f4	♗e2	e5	ed	♗d2	♘d1	=
	♗g7	♗d7[3]	♕c7	0-0	b5[4]	♘h5![5]	♕a5	♖e8	♕b6[6]	
3	...	♗g5	♗h4	♗g3	♗b5+	♗e2	hg	♘d2	a4	∞
	...	h6	g5?!	♘h5	♔f8	♘xg3	♘d7	a6	♕e7[7]	
4	...	...	...	...	...	e5!	fg	♗d3	♗xc4	±
	...	...	...	...	...	♘xg3	a6[8]	c4[9]	b5[10]	
5	...	...	...	♘d2	♕c2[11]	♗e2	0-0	♖ae1	b3	∞
	...	...	a6!	b5	0-0	♘bd7	♖b8	♕c7	♖e8[12]	
6	...	♗e2	♗g5[13]	♗h4	♗g3	♘d2	♗xf4	0-0	♗g4	±
	...	0-0	h6	g5	♘h5	♘f4	gf	a6	f5[14]	
7	...	...	...	...	...	...	hg	a4	♘c4	=
	...	...	...	...	...	♘xg3	a6	♘d7	♕e7[15]	
8	...	...	...	...	...	...	...	ef	♘c4	=
	...	...	...	...	...	...	f5	♗xf5	♕e7[16]	
9	...	...	...	...	...	...	...	♘c4	♕c2[18]	=
	...	...	...	...	...	...	♘d7	♕e7![17]	♘f6[19]	
10	...	...	0-0	♗f4	a4	♘d2	♖e1	♗xa6	♘c4	±
	...	...	♘a6[20]	♘c7[21]	b6	♖e8	♗a6	♘xa6	♗f8[22]	
11	...	...	...	h3[23]	♗xf3	♗f4[25]	♕c2[26]	g4	♗g3	±
	...	...	♗g4	♗xf3	a6[24]	♖e8	♕c7	h6	♘bd7[27]	
12	...	...	...	a4[28]	♗g5[29]	♗h4	♘d2	♗g3	h3	±
	...	...	a6	♘bd7	h6	♖e8	♕c7	♘e5	♖b8	
13	...	...	...	...	♗g5[30]	♘d2	♕xe2	f4	♕f3	∞
	...	...	...	♗g4	♘bd7[31]	♗xe2	♖e8	♕c7	c4[32]	
14	...	...	...	...	♗f4	♗xf3	♕d2	♗h6	♗xg7	±
	...	...	...	...	♗xf3	♘e8[33]	♘d7	♘ef6	♔xg7[34]	
15	...	...	...	...	...	♘d2	♕xe2	♗e3	g4[36]	±
	...	...	...	...	♖e8	♗xe2	♘h5	♘d7[35]	♘hf6[37]	

¹ 8 ... ♗g7 can transpose to rows 12-15 below.

² 16 f4 ± Wexler-Bronstein, Mar del Plata 1960.

³ 8 ... ♘bd7!? 9 ♗f4 0-0 10 ♗e2˙(10 ♘xd6?? ♘b6) 10 ... a6 11 ♕c2 =. The move order 7 ♗f4 ♗g7 8 ♕a4+ forces 8 ... ♗d7.

⁴ 11 ... ♘h5 12 ♗e3 ♗a6 13 ♘d2 f5 14 ef gf 15 ♗xh5 ∞ Portisch-Larsen, San Antonio 1972.

11 ... ♖e8 12 e5?! ♘h5 13 ♗e3 (13 ed? ♗xc3+ 14 ♕xc3 ♖xe2! ∓̄) 13 ... de 14 0-0 ∞̄ S.Garcia-Kasparov, USSR 1980.

⁵ 12 ... de 13 ♗xe5 ♕a5 14 0-0 b4 15 ♗xf6 ♗xf6 16 ♘e4 ± Toth-Valenti, Rome 1976.

⁶ 16 ♗e3 ♕a5+ 17 ♗d2 =.

⁷ 16 ♕c2 ♗d4 17 ♖f1 ♔g7 18 0-0-0 b5! 19 ab (Mecking-Keene, Hastings 1966/67) 19 ... ab ∞.

⁸ 13 ... de 14 0-0 a6 15 ♗d3 ±/ ± Miles-Hernandez, Biel 1977.

⁹ 14 ... ♕b6 15 ♘d2 ♗xe5 16 ♘c4 ♗xc3+ 17 bc ♕c7 18 0-0 ±± Miles-Wedberg, Stockholm 1976.

¹⁰ 16 ♗b3 ♕b6 17 ♕e2 ± Gulko-Savon, USSR Ch 1977.

¹¹ 11 a4 b4 12 ♘cb1 0-0 13 ♗d3 ♖e8 14 0-0 ♕c7 15 ♕c2 ♘bd7 16 ♘c4 b3! ∓ Suetin.

¹² 16 ♔h1 g5 17 ♗g3 ♘e5 18 f4 = Hartston-Nunn, London 1977.

¹³ 9 ♗f4 a6 10 a4 ♘h5 11 ♗e3 ♘d7 =.

¹⁴ 16 ♗xf5 ♗xf5 17 ef ♖xf5 18 ♕g4± Olafsson-Nievergelt, Zürich 1959.

¹⁵ 16 ♕c2 ♘e5 17 ♘b6 ♖b8 18 ♘d1 f5 = Kanko-Soos, Havana Ol 1966.

¹⁶ 16 ♘e3 ♘d7 17 ♘xf5 ♖xf5 18 0-0 ♘e5 = Wade.

¹⁷ 14 ... ♘b6 15 ♘e3 f5 16 ef ♗xf5 17 g4! ♗g6 18 ♗d3 ± Boleslavsky.

¹⁸ 15 0-0?! ♘f6 16 ♕c2 ♗d7! 17 a4 ♖fe8 18 ♖fe1 ♖ad8 ∓ Uhlmann-Gligorić, Havana Ol 1966.

¹⁹ 16 ♘e3 ♖e8 17 f3 g4 18 ♔f2 ♖b8 19 a4 a6 20 ♗d3 c4 21 ♗xc4 ♕c7! ½-½ Donner-Gligorić, Eersel (match) 1968.

²⁰ 9 ... b6 10 ♗g5 h6 11 ♗h4 ♗a6 12 ♘d2

♗xe2 13 ♕xe2 a6 14 a4 ♖e8 15 f4 ± Miles-Robatsch, Biel 1977.

9 ... ♘bd7 10 ♘d2 ♖e8 11 a4 ♖b8 12 ♘c4 ♘e5 13 ♘e3 f5 14 f4 ± Eliskases-R.Garcia, Buenos Aires 1964.

²¹ 10 ... ♘h5 11 ♗g5 ±.

²² 16 ♕d2!? Rossetto-Incutto, Mar del Plata 1970.

²³ 10 ♘d2 ♗xe2 11 ♕xe2 ♘bd7! 12 a4 a6 = transposes below.

²⁴ 11 ... ♘bd7 12 ♗f4 ± Gligorić-Matulović, Palma 1967.

²⁵ 12 a4!?

²⁶ 13 ♖e1 ♘fd7 14 a4 ± Nunn.

²⁷ 16 ♗g2 c4 17 f4 ♘c5 Janošević-Reshevsky, Netanya 1971.

²⁸ 10 e5!? de 11 ♘xe5 ♘bd7! 12 ♘xd7 ♗xd7 ∞ Dorfman-Dolmatov, USSR 1981.

²⁹ 11 ♘d2 ±.

³⁰ 11 h3 ♗xf3 12 ♗xf3 ♘bd7 13 ♗f4 ♕c7 14 a5 ♖fe8 15 ♕c2 c4 ∞ Portisch-Kasparov, Tilburg 1981.

³¹ 11 ... h6 12 ♗h4 ♘bd7 13 ♘d2 ♗xe2 14 ♕xe2 ♖e8 15 ♖ad1 (15 f4 ♕c7 ∞) 15 ... g5 (15 ... ♕c7!? ECO) 16 ♗g3 ♘e5 17 f4 gf 18 ♗xf4 ± Savon-Vogt, Halle 1974.

³² 16 ♔h1 ♖ac8 17 ♖ac1 ♕b8 18 ♗xf6 ♘xf6 19 e5 de 20 f5 ♕c7 21 ♘de4 ∞ Gligorić-Pfleger, Hastings 1971.

³³ 12 ... ♕e7 13 e5 de 14 d6 ♕e6! 15 ♖e1 ♘bd7 16 ♗xb7 ♖ab8 17 ♗xa6 ♖xb2 ∞ A.Schneider-Szalanczy, Balatonbereny 1981.

³⁴ 16 ♗e2 ♕e7 17 f3 ± Lukacs-Ničevski, Pernick 1977.

³⁵ 14 ... ♗d4?! 15 ♕d3 ♗xe3 16 ♕xe3 ♘d7 17 g4 ± Pytel-Ničevski, Albena 1973.

³⁶ 15 a5 ♕h4! 16 ♘c4 ♘f4 17 ♕f3 ♘e5 18 ♘xe5 ♗xe5 19 g3 ♕h5 = Belyavsky-Kasparov, USSR 1979.

³⁷ 16 h3 h5 17 g5 ♘h7 18 f4 ♗d4 19 ♔h1 ♗xe3 20 ♕xe3 ± Szabo-Koshansky, Sarajevo 1972.

16 f3 h6 17 ♔h1 ♘e5 18 ♖g1 b5!? ∞ Portisch-Kasparov, Moscow 1981.

16 f4!? ±.

Benoni VI: Main Line   1 d4 ♘f6 2 c4 c5 3 d5 e6
4 ♘c3 ed 5 cd d6 6 e4 g6 7 ♘f3 ♗g7 8 ♗e2 0-0 9 0-0 ♖e8

	10	11	12	13	14	15	16	17	18	
1	♕c2	♖e1	♗f4	♗g5	♗xf6[2]	h3[3]				=
	♘a6	♗g4[1]	♘h5	♗f6	♕xf6					
2	...	a3	♖e1	♗f4	b4	♘xe4	♘fd2	♗xd6	♖xa1	=
	...	♘c7	♖b8[4]	b5	♘xe4	♗f5	♘xd5	♗xa1	♕d6[5]	
3	...	♗f4	♕b1	♗g5	♗e3[7]	a3	♘g5	♗xh5	♘gxe4	=
	...	♘b4!	♘h5[6]	f6	f5	fe	♘d3	gh	c4[8]	
4	♘d2	a4[9]	♖a3[10]	♕c2	♘xc4	♗xc4	♗d3[13]			±
	♘bd7	♘e5	♗d7[11]	c4[12]	♘xc4	♘xc4	♖c8			
5	...	a4	♕c2	h3	a5	ab	♘b3	♘a5	♘c6[17]	±
	a6	♘bd7[14]	♖b8	♕c7	b5	♘xb6[15]	♕e7[16]	♗d7		
6	...	...	...	♖a3	h3	♘f3	hg	♘h2	♖e1[19]	±
	...	...	♘e5	♕e7[18]	g5	g4	♗xg4	♗d7		
7	...	♖e1[20]	a4	h3	♗b5	♗c6	♘f3	dc	♗f4	±
	♘a6	♘c7	b6	♖b8	♖e7	♗d7	♗xc6	♕e8	♕xc6[21]	

---

1 d4 ♘f6 2 c4 c5 3 d5 e6 4 ♘c3 ed 5 cd d6 6 e4 g6
7 ♘f3 ♗g7 8 ♗e2 0-0 9 0-0 ♖e8 10 ♘d2 ♘a6 11 f3 ♘c7

	12	13	14	15	16	17	18	19	20	
8	a4	♔h1[22]	♘c4	♘e3	♗d2	♖b1	ab	b4	♖a1	±
	♘d7	b6	♘e5	♖b8[23]	a6	b5	ab	c4	f5[24]	
9	...	a5[25]	ab	♘b5	♘xc7	g4	♗b5	♕b3	g5	∞
	b6	♖b8	ab	♘h5	♕xc7	♘f6	♗d7	h5	♗xb5[26]	
10	...	♘c4	♗g5[27]	♖b1[28]	♗xc4	b4	ab	♗d3	♗c2	±
	...	♗a6	♕d7	♗xc4	a6	b5	ab	c4	♖a3[29]	
11	...	...	...	♗e3	♗xc4	♕d2	♖ab1	b4	ab	±
	...	...	h6	♗xc4[30]	a6	♔h7	♖b8	b5	ab[31]	
12	...	...	...	♗h4	♗xc4	♗f2	♖e1	♗f1	♘e2[33]	±
	...	...	...	♗xc4[32]	g5	a6	♘d7	♘e5		

[1] **11 ...** ♘**b4!?** 12 ♕b3 ♗g4 13 a3 ♗xf3 14 gf ♘a6 15 ♕xb7 ♘c7 (Kozma-Polugayevsky, Kislovodsk 1972) 16 ♗g5 h6 17 ♗h4 g5 18 ♗g3 ♘h5 ∞̄.

11 ... ♖**b8** 12 ♗f4 ♘b4 13 ♕b1 ♘h5 14 ♗g5 f6 15 ♗h4 g5 16 ♘d2 ♘f4 17 ♗g3 ♘xe2+ 18 ♖xe2 f5 19 ef ♖xe2 20 ♘xe2 ♕f6 21 ♘e4! ∞ Shaposhnikov-Yudovich.   19 a3?! f4! ∓.

[2] 14 ♗d2 c4!?

[3] Keene.

[4] 12 ... b5 13 ♗xb5 ♘xb5 14 ♘xb5 ♘xd5 15 ♖d1 ♗a6 16 ♘xd6 ♕xd6 17 ♖xd5 ♕e7 ∞̄ Boleslavsky.

[5] 19 ♘xd6 ♗xc2 20 ♘xe8 ♖xe8 21 ♗xb5 ♖d8 = Veksler-Shestoperov, USSR 1973.

[6] 12 ... ♘xe4 13 ♘xe4 ♗f5 14 ♘fd2 ♘xd5 15 ♗g3 ♗h6 16 ♗b5 ♘xd2 17 ♗xe8 ♕xe8 18 ♘xd6 ± Peterson-Hodos, USSR 1964.

[7] 14 ♗d2 f5 15 a3!?

[8] 19 ♕d1 ♗f5 = Portisch-Adamski, Raach 1965.

[9] **11 h3** a6 12 a4 g5! 13 ♘c4 ♗xe4 14 ♘xe4 ♖xe4 15 ♗d3 ♖h4! ∓̄ Bukić-Wedberg, Bajmok 1980.

11 ♕c2 ♘e5 12 b3 ♘h5?! 13 ♗xh5 gh 14 ♗b2 ± Polugayevsky-Nunn, Skara 1980.

[10] 13 ♕c2 ♘h5 14 ♗xh5 gh 15 ♘d1 b6 16 ♖a3 ±.

[11] **12 ... b6!?**

12 ... a6 13 ♕c2 – 10 ... a6.

12 ... g5 13 ♕c2 a6 14 a5 ♖b8 15 ♘f3 ♘xf3+ 16 ♗xf3 ♘g4 ∞ Vaisman-Veliković, Zrenjanin 1980.

[12] 13 ... ♖c8 14 f4 ♘eg4 15 ♘c4 ♕e7 16 h3 ± Petrosian-Ljubojević, Milan (match) 1975.

[13] Analysis.

[14] 11 ... b6 12 ♕c2 ♘bd7 13 ♘c4 ♘e5 14 ♘xe5 ♖xe5 15 ♗f4 ♖e8 16 h3 ± Szymczak-Robatsch, Lublin 1976.

[15] 15 ... ♖xb6 16 ♖a3 (Petrosian-Quinteros,

Lone Pine 1976) 16 ... ♖b4!? Byrne, Mednis.

[16] 16 ... c4!?

[17] Bukić-Velimirović, Yugoslav Ch 1975.

[18] 13 ... g5 14 a5 g4 15 b3 ♘h5 16 ♘c4 ± Petrosian-Lukin, USSR 1978.

[19] Donner-Velimirović, Amsterdam 1976.

[20] **11 ♗xa6** ba 12 f3 ♗d7 13 a4 ♘h5 14 ♘c4 ♗d4+ 15 ♔h1 ♗xc3 16 bc ♕f6 17 ♕c2 g5 ∞.

11 ♖b1 ♗d7 12 ♖e1 ♖b8 13 b3 b5 14 ♗b2 ♘c7 15 ♕c2 ♕e7 16 ♘d1 ♗h6 17 f3 ♘h5 18 ♘f1 ♘xd5! 19 ed ♗f5 ∞ Gligorić-Tal, Portorož C 1959.

11 ♔h1 ♘c7 12 a4 ♖b8 13 f3 b6 14 ♘c4 ♗a6 15 ♗g5 ♕d7 16 b3 ♘h5 ∞ Portisch-Nunn, London 1982.

[21] 20 ♗xd6 ± Pelts-Sorokin, USSR 1975.

[22] 13 ♘c4 ♘e5 14 ♘e3 f5 15 ef gf 16 f4 ♘g6 17 ♔h1 ♕f6 18 ♗d3 ♗d7 19 ♕h5 ♘e7 ∞ Trois-Letelier, Mar del Plata 1973.

[23] 15 ... f5 16 f4 ♘f7 17 ef gf 18 ♗d3 ♕f6 19 ♕c2 ♘h6 20 ♗d2 ± Hesse-Espig, Leipzig 1973.

[24] 21 ef gf 22 f4 ♘f7 ± Adorjan.

[25] 13 ♔h1!? ♖b8 (13 ... ♘d7!? – 12 ... ♘d7) 14 ♘c4 ♗a6 15 ♗g5 h6 16 ♗e3 ♗xc4 17 ♗xc4 a6 18 ♕d3 ♕c8 19 ♗f4! ± Polugayevsky-Bouaziz, Riga IZ 1979.

[26] Vranesic-Matulović, Siegen Ol 1970.

[27] 14 ♗f4 ♘h5 15 ♗e3 f5 =.

[28] 15 ♕d2 ♗xc4 16 ♗xc4 a6 17 ♖fe1 b5 18 ♗f1 ba 19 ♖xa4 ± Keres-Bobotsov, Amsterdam 1971.

[29] 21 ♘e2 ± Evans-Kane, US Ch 1973.

[30] 15 ... ♘h5!? 16 ♕d2 g5 ∞ Portisch-Rajna, Hungary 1980.

[31] 21 ♗e2 c4 22 ♖a1 ♖a8 23 ♗d4 ± Reshevsky-Matulović, Palma de Mallorca IZ 1970.

[32] 15 ... ♕d7 16 ♕d2 g5 17 ♗f2 ♗xc4 18 ♗xc4 ±.

[33] Belyavsky-Rogulj, USSR v Yugoslavia 1977.

115

King's Indian Defence

A perennial favourite of aggressive, ambitious players such as Fischer, Bronstein, Gligorić and co-author Kasparov, the King's Indian is an old defence re-armed with modern ideas. Black allows White to establish a broad pawn centre with e4, hoping to use it as a target or work around it. White must take care not to release the Indian Bishop, whose latent power down the long diagonal gives the defence added bite. The locking of the centre leaves the players to their own devices in their separate sectors, which leads in general to White storming the queenside and Black pulling out all the stops on the kingside. Obviously, this hostile indifference to the plans of the opponent causes unbalanced play, and Black does not need to completely equalise in order to gain dynamic chances.

The **Classical Line** (4 e4 d6 5 ♘f3 0-0 6 ♗e2 e5 7 0-0) is the most analysed and the most often encountered. White claims an edge in space, and settles down to the task of breaking into the queenside, usually via the c-file, before Black's kingside counterattack reaches frightening proportions.

The **Sämisch** (5 f3) is now considered White's most reliable choice, combining aggression with solidity. Maintaining options of attack on either side of the board, White has a plethora of viable plans from which to choose and Black must play with great care against all of them.

The **Four Pawns Attack** (5 f4) swings in and out of fashion depending on the outcome of constant theoretical arguments about its soundness. Too violent and chaotic to gain widespread acceptance, it is nevertheless enjoying a renaissance as latest results have favoured White. How long it will be before the Attack fades from the scene once again remains to be seen. A volatile weapon, it can often backfire, and should only be chosen by those who relish living dangerously.

White's other major alternative is the **Fianchetto Variation** (g3). A quiet positional continuation, its scheme is to focus the king's bishop on the centre in order to nurture White's spatial plus. Black's position is quite solid and he can confidently adopt the system which best suits his style, with the Panno Variation (6 ... ♘c6) being the sharpest and least explored.

Systems with ♗g5 for White include the **Smyslov** (4 ♘f3, 5 ♗g5) and the **Averbakh** (4 e4, 5 ♗e2, 6 ♗g5). The Smyslov is an indirect and positionally esoteric line. Very rarely encountered, and slightly underestimated, it carries a subtle sting that can catch the unwary defender by surprise, though Black can equalise by accurate play. The Averbakh, with links to the Benoni and the Maroczy Bind, tries to provoke Black into weakening his pawn structure by tempting him to kick the annoying bishop off the d8-h4 diagonal. The play is much more complex than in the Smyslov, and White can develop a formidable initiative if not carefully watched. Its greatest adherent is undoubtedly East German grandmaster Wolfgang Uhlmann.

Miscellaneous and Smyslov System					1 d4 ♘f6 2 c4 g6 3 ♘c3				
3	4	5	6	7	8	9	10	11	
1 ...	♘f3	♗f4	♗g5	♗e3	♕d2	h3	g4	hg	∞
♗g7[1]	d6	♘h5!?[2]	h6	0-0	♔h7	f5	fg	♗xg4[3]	
2 ...	...	♗g5	♗h4	♗g3	e3	♗e2	♘d2	hg	=
...	...	h6	g5	♘h5	e6	♘d7	♘xg3	0-0[4]	
3 ...	...	...	e3	♗e2	♕d2	0-0	h3	♗xf3	=
...	...	0-0	c5	♕a5	♗g4	♘bd7	♗xf3	♖ac8[5]	
4 ...	...	...	...	♗e2	♕c2[6]	♖d1	0-0	♗h4	∞
...	...	...	♘bd7	c6	e5	♕e7	h6	g5![7]	
5 ...	...	e3	♗e2	0-0	b3	♗a3	♘xd4	♕c2	=
...	...	0-0	♘bd7	e5	♖e8	ed	♘c5	♘fe4[8]	

[1] 3 ... b6 4 e4 c5 5 d5 d6 6 f4 ♘g4 7 h3 ♘h6 8 ♘f3 ♘d7 9 ♗d3 a6 10 0-0 ± Pietzsch-G.Garcia, Havana 1965.
  3 ... c5 4 d5 e6?! 5 de fe 6 ♗g5 ♗g7 7 ♕d6 ♕e7 8 ♘b5 ± Lococo-Rosetto, Mar del Plata 1973.
[2] 5 ... 0-0 6 e3 c5 7 ♗e2 cd 8 ed ♗g4 9 h3 ♗xf3 10 ♗xf3 ♕b6 11 ♕b3 ♘c6 12 ♕xb6 ab 13 ♗e3 ♘d7 14 0-0-0 e5 15 de ♘dxe5 = Vadasz-Vasyukov, Hungary 1970.
[3] 12 ♘h4?! e5! 13 de ♘c6! 14 ed ♕xd6 ∓ Vaganian-Kupreichik, USSR Ch 1979.
[4] 12 ♕c2 f5 13 f4 c5 14 0-0-0 cd 15 ed g4 = Antunac-Quinteros, Wijk aan Zee II 1973.
[5] 12 ♗xb7 cd 13 ed ♖xc4 14 ♘d5 ♕xd2 15 ♘xe7+ ♔h8 16 ♗xd2 ♖b8 ½-½ Smyslov-Geller, USSR 1966.
[6] 8 0-0 h6 9 ♗h4 g5 10 ♗g3 ♘h5 11 ♘d2 ♘xg3 12 hg ♘f6! 13 b4 e5! = Smyslov-Gligorić, Zagreb 1970.
[7] 12 ♗g3 ♘h5 13 de de 14 ♘d2 (14 ♗xe5? ♘xe5 15 ♘xe5 ♕xe5 16 ♗xh5 g4 ∓) ½-½ Bagirov-Ciocaltea, Baja 1971: 14 ... ♘f4!? 15 ef! ef 16 ♗xf4 gf ∞ Hartston.
[8] 12 ♘xe4 ♘xe4 13 ♗b2 a5 14 ♘b5 ♗xb2 = Barcza-Bolbochan, Helsinki Ol 1952.

Fianchetto Variation		1 d4 ♘f6 2 c4 g6 3 ♘c3 ♗g7 4 ♘f3 d6 5 g3 0-0 6 ♗g2							
	6	7	8	9	10	11	12	13	14
1	...	0-0	d5	♘d2	e4	♖e1	a3	♘f3	♗e3	±
	c6	♕a5	♕b4	♗d7	a5	♘a6	♕b6	♘c5	cd[1]	
2	...	...	h3	d5[3]	♘d4	cd	♗e3[6]	♕d2	♖fb1!	±
	...	...	♗e6[2]	cd[4]	♗d7[5]	♖c8	♘a6	♘c5	♘a4[7]	
3	...	...	...	e4[8]	♘xd4	♗e3!?	a3	b4	♖e1	∞
	...	...	e5	ed	♕c5[9]	♕xc4	♕a6	♗d7	b6[10]	
4	...	0-0	d5[11]	e4	b4[13]	♗b2	ef	♘h4!	f4	±
	♘c6	e5	♘e7	♘e8[12]	h6[14]	f5	gf	♘f6	e4[15]	
5	...	...	...	c5	cd	e4[17]	a4	ef	a5[18]	=
	...	...	...	♘e8[16]	cd	h6	f5	gf	♘c7[19]	
6	...	...	♘e1[21]	e4	♘c2	f3	♗e3	♕d3	♔xg2[24]	±
	...	♗f5[20]	♕c8[22]	♗h3	♖e8[23]	a6	♖b8	♗xg2		
7	...	...	d5[25]	b3[27]	♗b2	♘d2	♕c2	♖fe1	♘d1	±
	...	♗g4	♘a5[26]	c5[28]	a6	♖b8	b5	♕c7	♖b7[29]	

[1] 15 cd a4 16 ♖b1 ♖fc8 17 h3 ♕c7 18 ♘d4 ±.

[2] 8 ... ♕h5? 9 ♘g5 ♘a6 10 ♗f3 ♕h6 11 h4 ±± Barcza-Trapl, Decin 1975.
8 ... ♗f5 9 ♘d2 e5 10 d5 c5 11 a3 ♘a6 12 e4 ♗d7 13 ♘b3 ♕d8 14 ♗g5 ± Marović-Petrosian, Amsterdam 1973.

[3] 9 ♘d2 ♘a6 10 a3 ♕b6 11 e3 c5 12 d5 ♗d7 13 ♖e1 ♕d8 14 ♖b1 ± Marović-Bertok, Zagreb 1965.

[4] 9 ... ♗d7 10 e4 ♖c8 11 a3 cd 12 cd ♕b6 13 ♕e2 ♕a6 14 ♕e3 ♗e8 15 ♖e1 ± Smejkal-Jakobsen, Raach 1969.

[5] 10 ... dc? 11 ♘xe6 fe 12 ♗xb7 ±±.
10 ... ♘e4? 11 ♘xd5 ♗xd5 12 ♘b3 ♕b6 13 ♕xd5 ♘xg3 14 ♖e1 ♘f5 15 ♕xb7 ±± Smejkal-Wright, Hastings 1968/69.

[6] 12 ♘b3 ♕d8 13 e4 ♗e8 14 ♗e3 ♘bd7 15 ♗d4 ♘b6 16 f4 ± Csom-Ostojić, Sao Paulo 1973.

[7] 15 b4 ♕d8 16 ♘xa4 ♗xa4 17 b5 ± Browne-Vukić, Banja Luka 1979.

[8] 9 d5 cd 10 cd ♘a6 11 ♘d2 ♗d7 12 ♘de4 ♘e8 13 a3 ♕d8 14 ♕b3 b6 15 a4 ♘c5 16 ♕a3 ± Vukić-Martinović, Yugoslavia 1974.

[9] 10 ... ♘a6?! 11 ♗e3 ♖e8 12 ♖e1 ♕c7 13 ♕d2 ± Mikhalchishin-Martinović, Baku 1980. 13 ♕c2!? ♘c5 14 b4 ♘e6 15 ♖ad1 ± Mikhalchisin.

[10] 15 ♔h2 ♘e8 16 ♕d2 ♕c8 17 ♗h6 a6 18 ♗xg7 ♔xg7 19 ♘c2! ∞ Vadasz-Mestel, Esbjerg 1979.
15 f4!? ♕c8 16 g4 ∞ Florian.

[11] 8 de?! de 9 ♗g5 ♗e6 10 ♘d5 (10 ♘d2 h6 11 ♗xf6 ♗xf6 12 ♘d5 ♗g7 13 ♘e4 ♘d4! 14 e3 c6! 15 ed cd 16 ♘c5 e4! ∓ Keene-Mestrović, Hastings 1971) 10 ... ♗xd5 11 ♗xf6 ♕xf6

12 cd ♘e7 13 e4 c6 = Thorbergsson-Stein, Reykjavik 1972.

[12] 9 ... ♘d7 10 b4 h6 11 ♘d2! f5 12 ef gf 13 ♗b2 ♘f6 14 c5 ♖f7 15 ♘c4 ± Tukmakov-Vukić, Ybbs 1968.

[13] 10 ♘e1?! f5 11 ef gf 12 f4 ♘g6 13 ♘d3 ♘f6! 14 ♔h1 ♖e8 = Boleslavsky.
10 ♘d2!? h6 11 ♔h1 f5 12 ef! ♘xf5 13 ♖c1 ♕e7 14 ♘e4 ± Smyslov-Doroshkevich, USSR Ch 1967.

[14] 10 ... f5?! 11 ef! (11 ♘g5 ♘f6 ∞ Uhlmann) 11 ... ♘xf5 12 ♘g5 a6 13 ♖b1 ♘d4 14 ♘e2 ♗g4 15 f3 ♘xe2+ 16 ♕xe2 ♗f5 17 ♖b3 ± Stein-Donner, Amsterdam 1969.

[15] 15 ♕d2 ♗d7 16 ♖ac1 ± Uhlmann.

[16] 9 ... dc? 10 ♘xe5 ♘fxd5 11 ♘xd5 ♗xe5 12 ♗g5 f6 13 ♘xf6+! ±±.
9 ... e4 10 ♘g5 dc 11 ♘gxe4 ♘fxd5 12 ♘xd5 ♘xd5 13 ♗g5 f6 14 ♕xd5+! ♕xd5 15 ♘xf6+ ♗xf6 16 ♗xd5+ ±.

[17] 11 ♕b3 h6 12 ♘d2 (12 e4 f5 13 ef gf 14 ♘d2 ♘g6 15 ♘c4 ♖f7 16 a4 ♗f8 17 ♗d2 ♘g7! ∞ Vaganian-Stein, USSR Ch 1970) 12 ...fg 13 ♘c4 f4 14 ♘e4 ♘f5 15 ♗d2 ♘d4 16 ♕d3 ± Barczay-Osvath, Hungarian 1965.

[18] 14 ♘d2!? Korchnoi.

[19] ·Korchnoi-Bogdanović, Sarajevo 1969.

[20] 7 ... ♗d7!? 8 d5 ♘a5 9 ♘d2 c6!? (9 ... c5 10 ♕c2 e5 11 a3 b6 12 b4 ♘b7 13 ♖b1 ♕c7 14 ♘d1?! ♘g4 15 h3 ♘h6 16 ♘e4 ♖ac8! ∓ Despotović-Velimirović, Yugoslavia 1969; 11 b3!?) 10 dc ♗xc6 11 e4 ♖c8 12 a4 ♕b6 13 ♖a3 e6 14 ♘a2 ♗d7 = Portisch-Spassky, Tilburg 1981.

[21] 8 d5 ♘a5 9 ♘d2 c6! 10 e4 ♗g4 11 f3 ♗d7 12 ♔h1 ♖c8 13 ♕e2 ♕b6 = Shamkovich-Westerinen, Leningrad 1967.

8 Rel ♘e4 9 ♘d5! Re8 10 ♘e3 ♗d7
11 d5 ♘b8 12 ♕c2 ♘c5 13 ♗d2 ± Geller-
Westerinen, Göteborg 1968.
[22] 8 ... ♕d7 9 d5 ♘a5 10 e4 ♗h3 11 ♕e2 c5
12 f4 ♗xg2 13 ♔xg2 a6 14 e5 ± Korchnoi-
Westerinen, Leningrad 1967.
[23] 10 ... e5!? 11 d5 ♘e7 ± Korchnoi.
[24] Bronstein-Tseitlin, USSR Ch 1971.
[25] 8 h3 ♗xf3 9 ♗xf3 ♘d7 10 e3 e5 11 d5 ♘e7
12 e4 f5 13 ♗d2 ♘f6! 14 b4 ♕d7 ∞ Mecking-
Korchnoi, Sousse IZ 1967.
[26] 8 ... ♗xf3?! 9 ef! ♘e5 10 ♕e2 Re8 11 b3 e6

12 f4 ♘ed7 13 de Rxe6 14 ♕c2 Rb8 15 ♗b2 a5
16 a3 ± Adorjan-Spiridonov, Polanica Zdroj
1971.
[27] 9 ♕d3!? c5 10 h3 ♗d7 11 e4 e5 12 de ♗xe6
13 b3 a6 14 ♗f4 ♘e8 15 Rad1 ± Filip-Unzicker,
Vienna 1957.
  9 ♘d2 c5 10 h3 ♗d7 11 ♕c2 e5! 12 de ♗xe6
13 b3 ± Schmidt-S.Garcia, Wijk aan Zee II 1972.
[28] 9 ... ♘xd5? 10 ♘xd5 ♗xa1 11 ♗d2 c6
12 ♘xe7+! ±.
[29] 15 ♗c3 ± Korchnoi-Ciocaltea, Skopje Ol
1972.

Fianchetto Variation   *continued*   1 d4 ♘f6 2 c4 g6 3 ♘c3 ♗g7
4 ♘f3 d6 5 g3 0-0 6 ♗g2 ♘bd7 7 0-0 e5

	8	9	10	11	12	13	14	15	16	
1	b3[1]	♕c2[3]	Rd1	♘g5	fe	e4	e3	♘f3	♘xe4	=
	Re8[2]	c6[4]	e4	e3!	♘f8[5]	♕e7	♗h6[6]	♘xe4	♕xe4[7]	
2	♕c2	♘xd4	Rd1	♘cb5	♕xc4	♘xb5	a4[9]	♕b3	♘d4	
	ed	♘b6!	♘xc4	a6	ab	♗d7[8]	d5	c6	♕c8[10]	
3	e4	♕c2	Rd1	b3[12]	♘xd4	f3	Rb1	♘ce2	♗f4	=
	c6	Re8	♕e7[11]	ed	♘c5	a5	♘fd7	♘e5	♕c7[13]	
4	...	♗e3[14]	♗g5	♗c1	h3	♗e3	♕c2	Rad1	b4	±
	Re8	♘g4	f6[15]	♘h6	♘f7	♘f8	c6	♕c7	♗d7[16]	
5	...	♘xd4	h3	Re1	♘db5[17]	♗e3	b3[19]	Re2	♘d4	∞
	ed	♘c5	Re8	a5	♘fd7[18]	♘e5	♘ed3	c6	a4!?[20]	

[1] 8 de de 9 ♕c2 c6 10 Rd1 ♕e7 11 e4 ♘e8
12 ♗g5 f6 13 ♗e3 f5 14 ♕d2 ♘b6 15 ♗g5 ♕f7
16 b3 f4 = Yabra-Polugayevsky, Siegen Ol 1970.
[2] 8 ... c6?! 9 ♗a3 ed 10 ♘xd4 ♘c5 11 b4! ♘e6
12 ♘xe6 ♗xe6 13 b5 ±.
[3] 9 ♗b2 c6 10 e4 ed 11 ♘xd4 ♘c5 12 ♕c2 a5
13 Rad1 ♕b6 14 a3!? ♘g4 15 h3 ♗xd4 16 Rxd4
♕xb3 17 ♕e2 ♘e5 18 f4 ♗e6 19 fe de ∞
Karlsson-Rantanen, Helsinki 1981.
[4] 9 ... ed!? 10 ♘xd4 ♘c5 11 ♗a3 c6 12 Rad1
♕a5 13 ♗b2 ♕b6 14 h3 a5 = van Scheltinga-
Gligorić, Amsterdam 1971.
[5] 12 ... ♘g4? 13 e4 ♗h6 14 ♗f3! ♘xh2?!
15 ♘xf7! ± Geller.
[6] 14 ... h6? 15 ♘f3 ♘xe4 16 ♘xe4 ♕xe4
17 ♕xe4 Rxe4 18 ♘e5! ±±.
[7] 17 ♕xe4 Rxe4 18 ♘g5 (18 ♘e5?? ♗xe3+
19 ♔d1 ♗xd4 ∓∓) Donner-Szabo, Buenos
Aires 1955: 18 ... Re8! 19 ♘e4 Rd8 = Geller.
[8] 13 ... ♘e8?! 14 ♘c3 ± Tal-Lehmann, Palma
de Mallorca 1966.
[9] 14 ♗xb7 Rb8 15 ♗c6 d5! =/∓ Geller.
[10] Geller.
[11] 10 ... ♕c7 11 b3 b5 12 ♗a3 ed 13 ♘xd4

bc 14 ♘a4 ♘e5 15 bc ♘fd7 16 Rac1 ±
Boleslavsky.
[12] 11 d5?! c5 12 ♘e1 ♗g4 (12 ... ♔h8!?
intending ... ♘g8 Ermenkov) 13 h3 h6 14 ♗e3
a6 15 Rab1 b6 16 b4 Ra7 17 bc bc 18 ♘a4 f5! ∞
Karpov-Ermenkov, Malta Ol 1980.
[13] Boleslavsky.
[14] 9 d5 ♘c5 10 ♘e1 a5 11 h3 (11 ♘d3 ♘xd3
12 ♕xd3 Rf8 13 b3 ♘d7 14 a3? f5! ∓ Mikenas-
Boleslavsky, USSR Ch 1950) 11 ... ♘h5! =.
[15] 10 ... ♗f6?! 11 ♗c1! ♗g7 12 h3 ♘f6 13 ♗e3
with gain of tempo (±) Geller.
[16] 17 d5 ± Geller.
[17] **12 Rb1!?**
   12 ♕c2 – Main Line (next section).
[18] 12 ... ♗e6?! 13 e5! de 14 ♕xd8 Raxd8
15 ♘xc7 ♗e7 16 ♘xe6 Rxe6 17 ♗e3 b6
18 Rad1 ± Boleslavsky.
[19] 14 ♘xc5 dc 15 ♕xd8 Rxd8 16 ♘xc7 Rb8
17 Red1 ♗e6! 18 ♘xe6 fe 19 ♗f1 ♘c6 ∞
Boleslavsky.
[20] 17 Rd2 ab 18 Rxd3 (18 ab? Rxa1 19 ♕xa1
♗xd4 20 ♗xd4 ♘xb3 ∓∓) 18 ... ♘xd3 19 ♕xd3
ba 20 Rxa2 Rxa2 21 ♘xa2 ♕a5 ∞/∓∓ Geller.

Fianchetto Variation: Main Line 1 d4 Nf6 2 c4 g6 3 Nc3 Bg7
4 Nf3 d6 5 g3 0-0 6 Bg2 Nbd7 7 0-0 e5 8 e4 c6[1] 9 h3

	9	10	11	12	13	14	15	16	17	
1	...	d5[3]	Ne1	Nd3	Be3	Qd2	a4	ef	f4	±
	Qb6[2]	c5[4]	Ne8	a6	Qc7	Rb8	f5	gf	Nb6[5]	
2	...	...	Ne1[6]	cd	Nd3	Qxd3	Rb1	Be3	Qe2	=
	...	Nc5	cd	Bd7	Nxd3	Rfc8	Nh5!	Qb4	Rc4[7]	
3	...	Re1	d5[8]	Be3	Qd2	Nh2	a4	Qe2	Bf3[11]	±
	...	Re8	c5[9]	a6[10]	Rf8	Qe7	Nh5	b6		
4	...	...	Nxd4	Na4[14]	Bf4	b3	Bd2	Bc3	Nb2	±
	...	ed[12]	Re8[13]	Qa5	Ne5	Nfd7	Qd8	Bc5	a5[15]	
5	...	Qc2	Nxd4	Nce2	cd	ed	Qxc5	Rd1	Be3	∞
	Qa5	ed[16]	Qc5	d5[17]	cd	Re8	Nxc5	Bd7	Nce4[18]	
6	...	Re1	d5	cd	Bf1	Bd2!	b4	a4	Qxa4	±
	...	Re8[19]	cd	b5	a6[20]	Qc7	Bb7	ba	Rec8[21]	
7	...	...	Nxd4	Bf1	Be3	Nxe6	Kg2![23]	f3		±
	...	ed	Ne5[22]	Re8	Be6	Rxe6	Rae8	a6[24]		
8	...	Be3	Nd2	Bxd4	Qf3[26]	Qd3	b3	Bxg7	f4	∞
	...	Nb6![25]	ed	Be6	Qe8[27]	Rd8	f5	Kxg7	fe[28]	
9	...	Re1	Qc2	Nxd4	Be3[30]	Rab1	b4	ab	f3[31]	∞
	Re8	a5	ed	Nc5[29]	a4	Bd7	ab	Qe7	Nh5[32]	
10	...	...	...	...	...	Rad1	Re2	Red2	Bf1[34]	=
	...	...	...	...	...	Nfd7	Qa5	Ne5[33]	a3[35]	
11	...	...	Rb1	b3	Nxd4	Bf4	Be3	Qd2		±
	...	...	Qe7	ed	Nc5	Nfd7	Nf8	Nfe6[36]		
12	...	...	...	Nxd4	Bf4	Qd2![38]	Be3	b4	ab[39]	±
	...	...	...	ed	Nc5	a4[37]	Nh5	Qc7	ab	

---

[1] 8 ... a6!? 9 Re1 (9 d5!? Browne) 9 ... ed 10 Nxd4 Ne5 11 b3 c5 12 Nc2 b5 (12 ... Rb8?! 13 Bb2 b5 14 f4! Bg4 15 Qd2 Nf3+ 16 Bxf3 Bxf3 17 Qd3 Bg4 18 Ne3 ± Browne-Kavalek, Novi Sad) 13 cb (Vukić-Martinović, Zemun 1980) 13 ... Qa5!? ∞ Vukić.

[2] 9 ... a5 10 Be3 a4 11 Qc2 Qa5 12 Rab1 b5 13 cb cb 14 de de 15 b4 ab 16 Qxb3 Ba6 17 Rfc1 ± Boleslavsky.
 9 ... a6 10 Rb1 b5 11 c5 b4 12 Na4 d5 13 de Nxe4 14 Nd4 ± Pachman-Tatai, Netanya

1973.

[3] 10 Rb1 Qb4 11 de Nxe5 12 Nxe5 de 13 Qd3 Nd7 = Berger-Gligorić, Amsterdam IZ 1964.
 10 c5?! dc 11 de Ne8 12 Bg5 Nxe5 13 Nxe5 (13 Be7 Qxb2 14 Rc1 b6 ∓) 13 ... Bxe5 14 Na4 Qc7 15 Nxc5 Bxb2 16 Rb1 (Kirov-Jansa, Vrsac 1975) 16 ... Be5! ∓ Jansa.

[4] 10 ... Ne8 11 Rb1 f5 12 Ng5 Ndf6 13 dc bc 14 c5 ± Geller-Wade, Stockholm IZ 1952.
 10 ... cd 11 cd Nc5 12 Qe2!? Bd7 13 Be3 Rfc8 14 Rab1 ± Antoshin-Barczay, Budapest

120

1969.

[5] 18 b3 e4 19 ♘f2± Barcza-Tringov, Ljubljana 1969.

[6] 11 ♖e1!? ♗d7 12 ♖b1 a5 13 ♗f1 ♕c7 14 b3.

[7] 18 ♖fc1 ♖ac8 19 ♔h2 f5 = Botvinnik-Tal, match 1960.

[8] 11 ♖e2?! ed 12 ♘xd4 ♕b4 13 ♖c2 ♘c5 14 ♗d2 ♕b6 15 ♗e3 a5 16 ♖b1 ♕d8 17 f3 ♘fd7 18 ♗f2 ♘e5 19 ♗f1 a4 = Lengyel-Geller, Budapest 1969.

[9] 11 ... ♘c5 12 ♖b1 a5 13 ♗e3 ♕c7 14 ♘d2 ♗d7 15 ♗f1 ♖ab8 16 a3 cd 17 cd b5 18 b4 ♘d3 19 ♗xd3 ♕xc3 20 ♖b3± Najdorf-Tal, Belgrade 1970.

[10] 12 ... ♕d8 13 ♖f1 ♖e7 14 ♖e1 ♘e8 15 ♘d3 f5 16 ♕d2 ♘ef6 17 ♗g5 ± Marović-Enklaar, Amsterdam 1973.

[11] Ribli-Biyiasis, Manila IZ 1976.

[12] 10 ... a5!? 11 ♖b1 ed 12 ♘xd4 ♘g4! 13 ♘ce2 ♘ge5 14 b3 ♗xc4 15 ♘c2! ♘c5 16 ♗g5 ♘b2 ∞ Ilic-Klauser, Switzerland 1979.

[13] 11ˑ... ♘e8!? 12 ♘f3 (12 ♘ce2 ♘c7 13 ♘b3!? ♕b4 14 ♘c3 a5 15 ♘d2 a4 16 a3 ♕a5 ∓ Bukal-Smyslov, Linz 1980; 13 ♗f4 ♘e5 14 ♕c2?! c5 15 ♘b3 a5 16 ♖ad1 a4 17 ♘d2 ♘e6 ∓ Raičević-Bukal, Linz 1980) 12 ... ♘e5 13 ♘xe5 de 14 ♗e3 ♕a5 15 a3 ♗f6 16 b4 ± Nikolić-Hausner, Banja Luka 1981.

[14] 12 ♘b3 a5 13 ♘a4 ♕b4 14 ♘d2 ♘c5 15 ♘xc5 ♕xc5 16 ♕e2 a4 = Geller-Didishko, USSR 1981.

[15] 18 a3 ♘e6 19 ♘xe6 ♗xe6 20 ♕c2± Karpov-Balashov, Moscow 1981.

[16] 10 ... b5!? 11 de ♘xe5 12 ♘xe5 de 13 ♗d2 b4 14 ♕a4 ± Boleslavsky. 11 ... de!?

[17] 12 ... ♖e8 13 ♗e3 ♕e5 14 ♘c3 ♘c5 (Hollis-Gligorić, Hastings 1962/63) 15 ♖ad1! ± Boleslavsky.

[18] 18 ♗xe4 ♖xe4 19 ♘c3 ♖e5 20 ♘f3 ♖h5 ∞∞ Mokalov-Bobolovich, USSR 1975.

[19] 10 ... b5?! 11 cb cb 12 d5 ♗b7 13 ♗d2 a6 14 a4 ba 15 ♘xa4 ♕c7 16 ♖c1 ♕b8 17 b4 ± Kavalek-Saidy, Netanya 1969.

[20] 13 ... b4 14 ♘a4 ♗a6 15 ♗xa6 ♕xa6 16 b3 ♘b6 17 ♘xb6 ♕xb6 17 ♗e3 ±Geller-Mecking, Sousse IZ 1967.

[21] 18 ♕b3 ♘b6 19 ♖ec1 Ribli-Szilagyi, Hungarian Ch 1974.

[22] 11 ... ♘b6!? 12 ♗f1 ♖e8 13 ♘b3! ♕h5 14 ♕xh5 ♘xh5 15 g4! ♘f6 ♗f4 (Marović-Bilek, Yugoslavia 1974) 16 ... ♗e6 ± Geller.

11 ... ♖e8?! 12 ♗e3 ♘b6 13 c5! ♘c4 14 ♘b3 ♕d8 15 cd ♘xd6 16 ♗d4 ♘c4 17 ♕e2

♗e6 18 ♖ad1 ♕e7 19 f4 ± Polugayevsky-Uhlmann, Amsterdam 1972.

[23] 15 a3? ♘xe4! ∓∓ Vaisman-Levin, USSR 1967.

15 ♔h1?! ♖ae8 16 a3 ♘ed7 17 ♗g2 ♘b6 18 ♕e2 ♕a6 19 c5 ♘xe2 20 ♖xe2 dc 21 ♗xc5 ♘fd7 ∓/∓ Nikitin-Polugayevsky, USSR Ch 1967/68.

[24] Boleslavsky/Geller.

[25] 10 ... ed 11 ♘xd4 ♘b6 12 ♘b3 ♕h5 (12 ... ♕b4 13 e5 ♘fd7 14 a3 ♕xc4 15 ed ± Klassup-Koblents, Riga 1963) 13 ♕xh5 ♘xh5 14 g4 ♘f6 15 ♘a5 ♗e6 16 ♖fd1 ♘xc4 17 ♘xc4 ♗xc4 18 ♖xd6 ♖fc8 19 f4± Quinteros-Polugayevsky, Siegen Ol 1970.

[26] 13 ♘b3? ♕b4 14 e5 de 15 ♗c5 ♕xc4 16 ♗xf8 ♖xf8 17 ♖e1 ♘fd5 ∓ Zaltsman-Soltis, Lone Pine 1974.

13 ♕e2? c5 14 ♗e3 ♕b4 15 e5 ♘fd7 16 ed ♕xb2 ∓ Smejkal-Minić, Ljubljana/Portorož 1973.

[27] 13 ... ♘fd7 14 ♗xg7 ♔xg7 15 b3 ♖ad8! 16 ♖ac1 ♘e5 17 ♕e3 ♕c5 = Boleslavsky.

[28] 18 ♘dxe4 d5 ∞ Ilivitsky-Yukhtman, USSR 1957.

[29] 12 ... d5 13 cd ♘xd5 14 ♘xd5 ♗xd4 15 ♗e3! ± Sokolov.

[30] 13 ♗f4 ♘fd7 14 ♘b3 a4 15 ♗xc5 ♘xc5 16 ♖ad1 ♕a5 17 ♗d2 ± Keene-Ciocaltea, Bath 1973. 14 ... ♗e5!? Boleslavsky.

[31] 17 ♖bd1 ♘fxe4! 18 ♗f4 f5 19 ♘xe4 ♘xe4 20 f3 g5 21 ♗c1 ♗xd4+ 22 ♖xd4 ♕e5 ∓ Smejkal-Planinc, Ljubljana/Portorož 1973.

[32] Minić.

[33] 16 ... ♕b4 17 ♘b1 ♘b6 18 ♘a3 ♗d7 19 ♘e2 ± Averbakh-Dittmann, Dresden 1956.

[34] 17 b3!? Boleslavsky.

[35] 18 b3 ♘f3+! = Diesen-Browne, Lone Pine 1976.

[36] Jansa-Honfi, Zalaegerszeg 1969.

[37] 13 ... ♕b6 14 ♘b3 ♘e6 15 ♗xd6! a4 16 c5 ♕a7 17 e5 ♘d7 18 ♘d2 ♘exc5 19 ♘de4 ± Portisch-Planinc, Vrsac 1971.

13 ... ♕h5 14 ♗e3 ♕c7 15 ♕d2 ♘f6 16 ♕c2 ♗d7 17 ♖bd1 ± Donner-Kavalek, Lugano 1970.

[38] 14 ♘c2?! ♘fd7 15 ♕xd6 a3! ∓ Portisch-Planinc, Madrid 1973.

14 b4 ab 15 ab ♘h5 (15 ... h6!? 16 ♕c2 – Petrosian-Quinteros, Manila 1974 – 16 ... ♘g4! 17 ♖bd1 ♘e5 18 ♗c1 ♕b6 = Geller) 16 ♗e3 ♖a3 17 g4 ♘f6 18 ♕c1 ♖a8 = Pachman-Browne, Mannheim 1975.

[39] Filip.

121

Exchange Yugoslav — 1 d4 ♘f6 2 c4 g6 3 ♘c3 ♗g7 4 ♘f3 d6 5 g3 0-0 6 ♗g2 c5 7 0-0[1] ♘c6 8 dc dc

	9	10	11	12	13	14	15	16	17	
1	♗f4	♗e3	♕d2	♖fd1[3]	♗xf3	ef	♖xd2	bc	♖d7	=
	♘h5[2]	♘d4	♗g4	♗xf3	♘xf3+	♕xd2	♗xc3	b6	♖fe8[4]	
2	♗e3	♕a4[5]	♘xa4	♗g5	♗xc5	♘e4	♗xe4	♘xc5	♘xb7	=
	♕a5	♕xa4	b6	♗b7	h6	♘xe4	bc	♖ab8	♖xb7[6]	
3	...	♗xc5[7]	♗a3	♘d4	♕xd4	♕f4	♕e3	♕xc3	bc	
	♗e6	♕a5	♗xc4	♘xd4	♖ac8	♘h5	♗xc3	♕xc3	♗xe2[8]	

[1] 7 d5 (7 dc dc 8 ♕xd8 ♖xd8 9 ♘e5!?) and now:
7 ... e6 8 de ♗xe6 9 ♘g5 ♗xc4 10 ♗xb7 ♘bd7 ∞, but note 1 d4 ♘f6 2 c4 g6 3 ♘f3 ♗g7 4 g3 d6 5 ♗g2 0-0 6 0-0 c5 7 d5 e6? 8 de ♗xe6 9 ♘g5 ♗xc4 10 ♗xb7 ♘bd7 11 ♘a3! ±.
7 ... ♘a6 8 0-0 ♘c7 9 a4 ♖b8 10 ♗a2 a6 11 a5 e6 (11 ... b6!?) 12 de ♘xe6 13 e3 ± Korchnoi-Gligorić, Belgrade 1964.

[2] 9 ... ♘d4 10 ♗e5 ♘c6 11 ♕xd8 ♖xd8 12 ♗c7 ♖d7 13 ♗f4 ♘d4 14 ♖fd1 ♘h5 15 ♗d2 ♖d8 16 ♘xd4 cd 17 ♘d5 e6 18 ♘e7+ ♔h8 19 ♖ac1 ± Gligorić-Vukčević, Yugoslav Ch 1958.
9 ... ♕xd1 10 ♖axd1 ♗e6 11 ♘e5 ♘h5 12 ♘xc6 bc 13 ♗e3 ♗xc4 14 ♖d2 ♖ac8 15 ♗xc5 ± Johansson-Letelier, Moscow Ol 1956.

[3] 12 ♖ad1 ♗xf3 13 ef!? e6 14 ♘e4 b6 15 b4 ± Larsen-Ribli, Riga IZ 1979.

[4] 18 ♖ad1 ♘g7 = Geller-Gligorić, Stockholm IZ 1962.

[5] 10 ♗d2 ♗f5 11 ♘d5 ♕d8 12 ♘h4 ♗g4 13 h3 ♗d7 14 ♗c3 e5! 15 e3 ♖e8 = Smejkal-Gligorić, Hastings 1968/69.
10 ♘d5!? e6 11 ♗d2 ♕d8 12 ♘c3 ♘d4! 13 ♗f4 ♘h5 14 ♗e3 e5 =.

[6] 18 ♗xc6 ♖xb2 19 ♗f3 ♖c8 =.

[7] 10 ♕a4 ♘d4 11 ♖ad1 ♗d7 12 ♕a3 ♘c2 13 ♕xc5 b6 14 ♗g5 h6 15 ♕f4 g5 16 ♕e5 ♖c8! ∞ Grigorian-Kasparov, USSR Team Ch 1981.

[8] 17 ... ♖c7 = Tal.
17 ... ♗xe2 18 ♖fe1 ♗a6 19 ♗xe7 ♖fe8 =.

Panno I — 1 d4 ♘f6 2 c4 g6 3 ♘c3 ♗g7 4 ♘f3 d6 5 g3 0-0 6 ♗g2 ♘c6 7 0-0 a6[1]

	8	9	10	11	12	13	14	15	16	
1	b3[2]	a4[3]	h3	♘h4	e4	g4	♘b5	hg	f3	∞
	♖b8	a5	♗f5	♗d7	♕c8	h5	hg	♗xg4	♘xe4!?[4]	
2	h3	e4	cb	♖e1	d5	de	a3	ab	♘d4	=
	♖b8[5]	b5[6]	ab	e6	♘e7	♗xe6	b4	♖xb4	♗d7[7]	
3	...	...	e5[8]	de	♖xd1	e6	cb	♘g5	♗e3	∞
	...	...	de[9]	♕xd1	♘d7	fe	ab	♘d4	c5[10]	
4	...	...	...	e6[11]	d5	cd	♘d4	b4	f4	∞
	...	...	...	♘d7!?	fe	ed[12]	♘a5	♘e5	♘ac4	c5!?[13]
5	...	...	...	cb	♘g5	♗xc6	♘xb5	♘a7	♘f3	±
	...	...	...	ab	de	ed	♖b6[14]	h6	♗a6[15]	
6	♗e3	♘d2	♖c1[17]	de	b3	♘d5	♘xf6+	♘xc4		=
	...	b5	♗d7[16]	e5[18]	♘xe5	♖e8[19]	bc	♗xf6	♘xc4	

[1] 7 ... ♖b8!? 8 d5 ♘a5 9 ♘d2 c5 10 ♕c2 e5 11 de? (11 a3 b6 12 b4 ♘b7 13 ♘b5 ♖a8 14 ♗b2 ♘h5 15 e4 a6 16 ♘c3 f5 17 ef gf 18 ♖ae1 cb 19 ab a5 = Liberzon-Gufeld, USSR Ch 1969; 11 b3! intending ♗b2, e4 ± Ribli) 11 ... ♗e6 12 b3 d5 13 cd ♘xd5 14 ♗b2 ♘b4 15 ♕c1 ♘ac6 16 a3 ♘d4! Ribli-Liberzon, Reykjavik 1975.

[2] 8 ♘d5 ♗g4! Portisch-Timman, Montreal 1979.
8 ♕d3 ♗f5 (8 ... ♘d7!?) 9 e4 ♗g4 10 d5 ± Csom-Keene, Indonesia 1982.
8 e3?! ♖b8 9 ♕e2 b5 10 ♘d2 ♘a7 11 b3 ♗g4 ∓ Euwe.

[3] 9 ♗b2 b5 10 cb ab 11 ♖c1 b4 12 ♘b1 ♘a7! 13 ♗e1! c6 14 ♘d3 ♗a6 15 ♕c2 ♘d7 16 ♖fd1 ♕b6 ± Romanishin-Keene, Dortmund 1982 (16 ... ♕c8 ± Romanishin-Tukmakov, USSR Z 1982). 15 ... ♘d5!?

[4] 16 ... ♗d7 17 f4 ♗g4 18 ♕d2 ∞ Pomar-Keene, Palma de Mallorca 1971.
16 ... ♘xe4!? Pomar.

[5] 8 ... e5 9 d5 ♘e7 10 e4 ♘e8 11 ♗d2 ± Smejkal-Haag, Polanica Zdroj 1972.

[6] 9 ... e5 10 ♗e3 ed 11 ♘xd4 ± Krogius-Rashkovsky, Sochi 1973.
9 ... ♘d7 10 ♗e3 ♘a5 11 b3 b5 12 cb ab

13 ♕d2 c6 14 ♗h6 b4 15 ♗xg7 ♔xg7 16 ♘e2 ♘f6 17 ♕e3 ± Hübner-Hartston, Ybbs 1968.
[7] 17 ♘c2 ♖b8 18 ♘e3 ♗e6 19 ♘ed5 = Czerna-Geszosz, Hungarian Ch 1975.
[8] 10 ♕e2 ♘d7 11 ♗e3 e5 12 de ♘dxe5 ∓ ECO.
[9] 10 ... ♘e8 11 cb ab 12 ♗f4 ♗d7 13 ♖e1 b4 14 ♘e4 h6 15 g4 f5 16 ef ±.
[10] 17 ♘ce4 e5 18 ♗xd4 cd 19 ♖ac1 ∞.
[11] 11 ♘g5 ♘xd4! 12 ♕xd4 ♘xe5 13 ♕h4 h6 14 ♘e4 e6 15 ♕xd8 ♖xd8 16 cb ab ∞ Boleslavsky. 13 ♕d1! ± Keene.
[12] 12 ... ♘a5 13 cb ed 14 ♘d4 ♘f6 15 ♘xd5 ab 16 ♗d2! ± Geller-Chiburdanidze, USSR 1981.
[13] 16 ... ♘f7!? 17 ♘c6 ♕e8 18 ♘xb8 ♗f5! (Hübner-Nunn, South Africa 1981) 19 ♗d2!? ∞ Hübner.

16 ... c5! 17 dc ♘xc6 18 ♘xc6 ♕b6+ 19 ♔h2 (19 ♖f2!?) 19 ... ♗xc3 20 ♘xe7+ ♔h8 21 ♘xc8 ♖bxc8 22 ♖b1 ♖ce8 = Geller-Gufeld, USSR 1981.

[14] 14 ... ♘e5!? intending 15 ♘xd4 ♖b6 ∞.
[15] 17 ♖e1 ♘b8 18 ♗e4 ♕d7 19 b3 d3 20 ♗e3 c5 21 ♗xc5 ± Nikolić-Nunn, Wijk aan Zee 1982.
[16] 10 ... ♘a5 11 cb ab 12 b4 ♘c4 13 ♘xc4 bc 14 b5 ♗b7 15 a4 ♗xg2 16 ♔xg2 ±.

10 ... ♗b7 11 ♖c1 ♘a5 12 cb ab 13 b4 ♘c4 14 ♘xc4 bc 15 d5 e6 16 a3 ♕d7 17 ♗d4 ed ∞ Poutiainen-Pinter, Budapest 1975.
[17] 11 cb ab 12 d5 ♘a5 13 b4 ♘c4 14 ♘xc4 bc 15 b5 ♘c8 16 ♕a4 ♗xh3 = Smejkal-Adorjan, Vrnjačka Banja 1972. 15 ... e6!? 16 de fe 17 a4 d5 18 ♗d4 ♕e7 ∓ Božić.
[18] 11 ... ♘a5 12 cb ab 13 b4 ♘c4 14 ♘xc4 bc 15 b5 d5! 16 ♗g5 c6 (Saidy-Gheorghiu, Las Palmas 1973) 17 a4 =.
[19] 13 ... ♗e6?! 14 f4 ♘ed7 15 ♗a7 ♖a8 16 ♗f2 ♖b8 17 e4 ± Korchnoi-Lee, Lugano Ol 1968.

13 ... b4 14 ♘d5 ♘e8 15 c5 ♗b5 16 cd ± Osnos-Partos, Zinnowitz 1971.

Panno II		1 d4 ♘f6 2 c4 g6 3 ♘c3 ♗g7 4 ♘f3 d6							
		5 g3 0-0 6 ♗g2 ♘c6 7 0-0 a6 8 d5 ♘a5 9 ♘d2 c5 10 ♕c2 ♖b8							
	11	12	13	14	15	16	17	18	19
1	b3	♗b2	♖ae1	♘d1	e3	♘e4	bc	♗a3	f4	±
	b5	e5[1]	♘h5	♗h6	♗f5	bc	♕b6	♗g7	ef[2]	
2	...	...	de	cb	♘ce4	♘xe4	♕xb2	♘c3	♘d5	±
	...	e6	♗xe6?!	ab	♘xe4	♗xb2	f5	b4[3]	h6[4]	
3	...	...	...	cb	♘ce4[5]	♖ad1	♘xf6+	♗xf6	♘e4[6]	=
	...	...	fe	ab	♗b7	♕e7	♗xf6	♕xf6	♗xe4[7]	
4	...	...	♖ab1	e4	♖fe1	bc	♘d1[9]			±
	...	...	♖e8	♗d7	bc[8]	♘g4				
5	...	...	bc	♘cb1	♗c3	h3[11]	e4	♕d3	♘a3	=
	...	bc	♗h6	♗d7	♕c7[10]	♗g7	e5	♘h5	f5	
6	...	...	f4	bc	♖ae1[12]	gf	e3	♘d1	♗e4	∞/∓
	...	♗h6	bc	e5	ef	♘h5	♗g7	♗f5	♗xb2[13]	

[1] 12 ... ♗d7?! 13 ♖ab1 e5 14 de fe 15 ♘ce4! ♘xe4 16 ♗xg7 ♘xd2?! 17 ♗xf8 ♗xb1 18 ♗xd6 ♘a3 19 ♕c1 ±± Korchnoi-Ciocaltea, Hamburg 1965.
[2] 20 gf ♖fe8 21 ♘df2 ♘f6 22 ♘xf6+ ♗xf6 23 e4 ± Langeweg-Westerinen, Wijk aan Zee 1970.
[3] 18 ... ♕f6 19 ♕d2 b4 20 ♘d5 ♗xd5 21 ♗xd5+ ± Keene-Sharpe, England 1967.
[4] 20 ♖ad1 ± Panchenko-Peev, Lublin 1975.
[5] 15 ♖ad1 d5 16 e4 ♘c6 ∓.
[6] 19 ♗xb7!? ♗xb7 20 ♕d3 b4! 21 ♘e4 ♕e7 22 f4! d5 23 ♘g5 ±. 19 ... ♖xb7!?
[7] 20 ♗xe4 d5 21 ♗g2 ♖bc8 22 e3 ♗fd8 23 ♖b1 ♖c7 24 ♖fc1 ♘b7 = Donner-Penrose, Holland v England 1966.
[8] 15 ... ♗h6? 16 de! ♗xe6 17 ♘d5 ♗g7 18 ♘xf6+ ♗xf6 19 ♗xf6 ♕xf6 20 e5! ♗f5! 21 ef ♗xc2 22 ♖ac1 ± Spassky-Ivkov, Santa Monica 1966.
[9] Spassky.
[10] 15 ... e5 16 ♘a3 ♖b4?! 17 ♗xb4 cb 18 ♘ab1 ♕c7 (18 ... ♕b6 19 ♘b3 ♘b7 20 ♘1d2 ♖c8 21 a3 ± Petrosian-Toran, Bamberg 1968) 19 e3 ♗f5 20 ♘e4 ♘xd5! 21 ♘bd2 ♘c3 22 g4 ♗xg4 23 ♘xc3 bc 24 ♕xc3 ♘b7 ∞/± Kasparov.
[11] 16 ♘b3!? ♗a4 17 e3 ± Ribli-Bouaziz, Las Palmas IZ 1982.
[12] 15 de ♗xe6 16 ♘d5 ♗xd5?! 17 cd ± Browne-Timman, Wijk aan Zee 1980. 16 ... ♖xb2! 17 ♕xb2 ♗g7 18 ♕a3 ♘xc4 19 ♗xc4 ♗xd5 ∞ Hübner-Nunn, Wijk aan Zee 1982.
[13] 20 ♘xb2 ♖xb2!! 21 ♕xb2 ♗xc4 22 ♘xc4 ♗xe4 ∞/∓ Kasparov.

4 e4 Miscellaneous 1 d4 ♘f6 2 c4 g6 3 ♘c3 ♗g7 4 e4 d6[1]

	5	6	7	8	9	10	11	12	13	
1	♘ge2	♘g3	d5	♗e2	cd	♗e3	0-0	♗g5	♖e1	=
	0-0	e5	c6	cd	a5	♘a6	h5	♗d7	♕b6[2]	
2	...	...	d5[3]	♗e2	ed	a4	♗f4	♕d2	0-0	=
	...	c5	e6	ed	a6	♖e8	♕c7	♘bd7	b6[4]	
3	♗d3	♘ge2	d5	0-0	ef	f4	♖b1	♘xf4	♗xf4	=
	0-0	e5[5]	♘h5	f5	gf	♘d7	ef	♘xf4	♘e5[6]	
4	h3	♘f3	♗e3	♗d3	e5[8]	e6	♘g5	h4[9]		±
	0-0[7]	c6	a6	b5	♘fd7	fe	♘f6			
5	...	...	d5	♗d3	ed[10]	♕e2[12]	♕xe7	♔d1	♗g5	±
	...	c5	e6	ed	♕e7+[11]	♖e8	♖xe7+	♘bd7	h6[13]	
6	...	...	d5	♘h2	♗e2	♗f3	g3![15]	♗g2	♗e3	±
	...	e5[14]	♘h5	♕e8	♗f4	f5	♘xh3	fe	♗f5[16]	
7	...	...	...	♗e3	♘h2	♗e2	♗f3	h4	g3	∞
	...	...	♘a6!	♘h5	♕e8	♘f4	f5	♕e7	♘b4!![17]	
8	♗g5	♗h4	d5	♕d2[20]	♗g3	♗e2	hg	♘f3	0-0	±
	h6[18]	c5	♕a5[19]	g5[21]	♘h5	♘xg3	a6	♘d7	♖b8[22]	

[1] 4 ... 0-0 5 e5 ♘e8 6 ♗f4 (6 ♘f3 d6 7 ed ♘xd6 8 h3 ♘f5 9 d5 c6 ∓) 6 ... d6 7 h3 c5 8 dc ♕a5 9 ed ed 10 cd ♗xc3+ 11 bc ♕xc3+ 12 ♗d2 ♕e5+ 13 ♗e2 ∞ Minev.

[2] 14 ♕d2 ♘g4 15 ♖d1 ♘c5 = Forintos-R.Byrne, Monte Carlo 1968.

[3] 7 dc dc 8 ♗e3 ♕a5 =.

[4] 14 ♗h6 ♗h8 15 h3 ½-½ Szabo-Petrosian, Sarajevo 1972.

[5] 6 ... c5 7 d5 e6 8 0-0 ed 9 ed ♘e8 10 f4 f5 11 ♗e3 ♘d7 12 ♔h1 ♘c7 13 ♘g1 ♗xc3 14 bc ♘f6 15 ♘f3 ♘e4 = Diaz-Matulović, Vrbas 1976.

[6] 14 ♘e2 ♕e8 15 ♕d2 ♗d7 16 b3 ♕g6 = R.Byrne-Weinstein, US Ch 1960/61.

[7] 5 ... e5 6 d5 (6 de!? de 7 ♕xd8+ ♔xd8 8 f4! ± ECO) 6 ... ♘bd7 7 ♗g5 h6 8 ♗e3 ♘c5 9 ♕c2 a5 10 0-0-0 0-0 11 ♘f3 ♘h5 12 ♕d2 ♘h7 13 g4 ♘f4 14 ♘xe5 ± Gheorghiu-Uhlmann, Monte Carlo 1968.

5 ... c5 6 dc (6 d5 b5 7 cb a6 8 ba 0-0 - Mititelu-Bilek, Budapest 1960 - 9 ♘f3 ±) 6 ... ♕a5 7 ♗d3 ♕xc5 8 ♘f3 0-0 9 ♗e3 ♕a5 10 0-0 ♘c6 11 a3 ± Dzhindzhihashvili-Popov, Batumi 1966.

5 ... c6 6 ♗e3 a6 7 ♘f3 b5 8 e5 ♘fd7 9 ed ed 10 ♗g5 (10 ♗d3!?) 10 ... ♘f6 11 ♕e2 (11 ♗e2!?) 11 ... ♔f8 Bronstein-Pilnik, Beverwijk 1963.

[8] 9 0-0 ♘bd7 10 ♖c1 e5 11 d5 bc 12 ♗xc4 c5 = Book-Gufeld, Tallinn 1969.

[9] Portisch-Minić, Zagreb 1965.

[10] 9 cd b5! = Engels-Euwe, The Hague 1929.

[11] 9 ... ♖e8+ 10 ♗e3 ♘a6 (10 ... ♗h6 11 0-0 ♗xe3 12 fe ♖xe3 13 ♕d2 ±) 11 0-0 ♗d7 12 ♗g5 h6 13 ♗f4 ♕e7 14 ♖e1 ♕f8 15 ♕b3! ± Quinteros-Ghitescu, Olot 1974.

[12] 10 ♗e3? ♘h6! =.

[13] 14 ♗h4 g5 15 ♗g3 ♘e8 16 ♔d2 ♘e5 17 ♘xe5 ♗xe5 18 ♗xe5 ♖xe5 19 f4 gf 20 ♖af1 ± Bagirov-Borisenko, USSR 1974.

[14] 6 ... ♘c6 7 ♗e3 e5 8 d5 ♘e7 9 g4 c6 10 ♘d2 b5 11 dc b4 12 ♘d5 ♘xc6 13 ♗g5 ♗e6 14 ♘f3 ± Larsen-Westerinen, Helsinki 1969.

[15] 11 h4 ♘a6 12 g3 ♘c5!! 13 gf ef ∞ Kavalek-Quinteros, Bauang 1973.

[16] 14 ♘g4 ♘f4 15 gf h5 16 ♘h2 ♘d7 17 fe ± Bagirov-Vukić, Banja Luka 1976.

[17] **14 ♕b3** ♘fd3+ 15 ♔e2 f4 16 ♗d2 (Kavalek-Kasparov, Bugojno 1982) 16 ... ♘xf2!! ∓.

14 gf fe!

14 0-0! g5 ∞.

[18] 5 ... 0-0 6 ♘f3 h6 7 ♗h4 g5 8 ♗g3 ♘h5 9 ♗e2 e6 10 d5 f5 11 ♘d4 ♘xg3 12 hg fe = Uhlmann-Fischer, Havana Ol 1966.

[19] 7 ... e6 8 de ♗xe6 9 ♗d3 ♘c6 10 ♘ge2 g5 11 ♗g3 ♕d7 12 0-0 0-0-0 13 f4 gf 14 ♘xf4 h5 15 ♗h4 ♖dg8 ∞ Stahlberg-Penrose, Leipzig Ol 1960.

[20] 8 ♗d3? g5 9 ♗g3 ♘xe4 10 ♗xe4 ♗xc3+ 11 bc ♕xc3+ 12 ♔f1 f5 13 ♖c1 (13 ♘e2 ♕f6 14 ♗c2 f4 15 h4 ♖f8 ∓ Stein-Geller, USSR 1966) 13 ... ♕f6! (13 ... ♕g7 14 h4 fe 15 ♕h5+ ♔d8 16 hg ±) 14 ♕h5+ ♔d8 15 h4 g4! 16 ♗d3 f4 17 ♗xf4 ♕xf4 18 ♘e2 ♕f6 ∓ Radomsky-Timoshenko, USSR 1976.

[21] 8 ... 0-0!?

[22] 14 a4 ±.

Four Pawns Attack			1 d4 ♘f6 2 c4 g6 3 ♘c3 ♗g7 4 e4 d6 5 f4 0-0[1]					
6	**7**	**8**	**9**	**10**	**11**	**12**	**13**	**14**

	6	7	8	9	10	11	12	13	14	
1	♘f3[2]	♗e2	♗e3	♗xf3	d5[5]	♕d3	b4!	♕xc4	♕d3	±
	♗g4[3]	♘fd7	♗xf3[4]	♘c6	♘a5	c6	♘xc4	cd	de[6]	
2	...	♗e2	♘xd4	♗e3	♗xc6[9]	♘xd8	♖xd1	♔e2	c5!	±
	c5[7]	cd	♘c6	♗g4[8]	♗xe2	♗xd1	♖fxd8	♖dc8	♘e8[10]	
3	...	...	...	♗e3	♗f3	♘b3	♗xc5	♗f2	♗xc5	∞
	...	...	♘a6!?	♘c5	♗h6!	e5	ef	dc	♘d7![11]	

		1 d4 ♘f6 2 c4 g6 3 ♘c3 ♗g7 4 e4 d6 5 f4 0-0 6 ♘f3 c5 7 d5 e6[12]							

	8	9	10	11	12	13	14	15	16	
4	♗e2[13]	ed[14]	0-0	♗d3	h3	a3	g4	♕xd3	cb	∞
	ed	♖e8[15]	♗f5[16]	♕d7[17]	♘a6	♘c7	♗xd3	b5!?	♖eb8[18]	
5	...	e5!?	cd	0-0	♗xf4	♕d2	h3	♗xf3	d6	∞
	...	♘fd7[19]	de	ef	♘f6	♗g4	♗xf3	♘bd7	♖b8[20]	
6	...	...	fe	♗g5	cd	0-0	♘xe5	♗c4[22]	d6[24]	±
	...	...	de	♘g4	♕a5	♘xe5	♖e8[21]	♗xe5	♘d7[23]	

1   5 ... c5 6 dc ♕a5 7 ♗d3 ♕xc5 8 ♘f3 ♘c6 9 ♕e2 0-0 10 ♗e3 ♕a5 11 0-0 ♗g4 12 ♖ac1 ♘d7 13 ♕f2 ♗xf3 14 gf a6 ∞ Bisguier-Petrosian, USA v USSR 1954.   6 d5 – rows 6-8.

2   6 ♗e2?! e5! 7 de de 8 ♕xd8 ♖xd8 9 fe ♘fd7 10 e6 fe 11 ♘f3 ♘a6 12 0-0 ♖e8 13 ♗e3 b6 = Brinck Claussen-Savon, Orebro 1966.

3   **6 ... ♘bd7?!** 7 ♗e2 e5 8 de de 9 fe ♘g4 10 ♗g5 ♕e8 11 ♘d5 ±.
  6 ... ♘c6 7 ♗e2 ♗d7 8 ♗e3 e5 9 fe de 10 d5 ♘cb8 11 c5 a5 12 0-0 ♘a6 13 ♘a4 ± Alekhine-Yates, New York 1924.

4   8 ... ♘c6?! 9 d5 ♗xf3 10 gf!? ±.

5   10 0-0 e5 11 fe de 12 d5 ♘d4! ∓.

6   15 ♗xe4 d5 16 ♗xd5! ♘b6 17 ♖d1 ♗xc3+ 18 ♕xc3 ♗xd5 19 ♕e5 e6 20 ♗d4 ±.

7   6 ... e5 7 de! de 8 ♕xd8 ♖xd8 9 ♘xe5 ♖e8 10 ♗d3 ♘a4 (10 ... ♘a6 11 0-0 ♘b4 12 ♗b1 Geller) 11 ♗xe4 f6 12 ♗d5+! (Geller) 12 ... ♔f8 13 ♗f7! ♖e7 14 ♘d5 fe 15 ♘xe7 ±±.

8   **9 ... ♘g4** 10 ♗xg4 ♗xd4 11 ♗xd4 ♗xg4 12 ♕xg4! ♘xd4 13 ♕d1 ± Pomar-Geller, Stockholm IZ 1962.
  9 ... ♘xd4 10 ♗xd4 e5 11 fe de 12 ♗c5! ♖e8 13 ♕xd8 ♖xd8 14 ♖f1! ♖e8 15 0-0-0 ±.

9   10 ♗xg4 ♘xg4 11 ♕xg4 ♘xd4 12 ♕d1 ♘c6 =.
  10 ♘f3 e5! 11 fe de 12 0-0 ♕a5 13 ♕e1 ♖ad8 =/∓ Uhlmann-Geller, Debrecen 1959.

10   15 cd ed 16 ♗d4 ♖c6 ± Uhlmann-Gligorić, Sarajevo 1963.

11   15 ♗xf8 ♕h4+ 16 ♔d2 ♗xf8 17 ♕e1 ♕e7 ∞ Stahlberg-Stein, Erevan 1965.

12   7 ... b5!? 8 cb a6 9 a4!? (9 ba ♕a5 10 ♗d2 ♗xa6 11 ♗xa6 ♘xa6 12 0-0 c4 ∞ Muchado-A.Rodriguez, Cuba 1981; 11 ... ♕xa6 ∞ Kochiev)

9 ... e6 (9 ... ♕a5 10 ♗d2 ♕b4 11 ♕c2 c4!? 12 ♘d1 ♕c5 13 ♗e3 ♕b4 14 ♗d2 = Kaplun-Kochiev, USSR 1981) 10 de ♗xe6 11 ♗e2 ab 12 ♗xb5 ♘a6 13 0-0 ♘b4 ∞ Gorelov-Gufeld, USSR 1981.

13   8 de fe (8 ... ♗xe6 9 ♗d3 ♘c6 10 f5 ♗d7 11 0-0 ♖e8 12 ♗g5 ± Ree-Polugayevsky, Sochi 1976) 9 ♗d3 ♘c6 10 0-0 ♘d4! 11 ♗g5?! e5! 12 f5 h6 13 ♘h3 gf 14 ef b5! ∞/∓ Christiansen-Kasparov, Moscow IZ 1982.

14   9 cd – Benoni IV.

15   **9 ... ♘h5!?** 10 0-0 ♗xc3 11 bc ♘g7 12 f5! ♗xf5 13 ♗f4! ∞.
  9 ... ♘e8!? intending 10 ... ♘c7.

16   10 ... ♘g4!?

17   11 ... ♘e4?! 12 ♘xe4 ♗xe4 13 ♗xe4 ♖xe4 14 ♘g5! ♖e7 15 f5 ♘d7 16 fg hg 17 ♕g4 ±.
  14 ... ♗xc4 15 ♕e2! ± ECO.

18   Geller.

19   **9 ... ♘g4!?** 10 cd de 11 h3! e4! 12 ♘xe4 ♘f6 13 ♘c3!? ∞∞
  9 ... ♘e4!? (Goodman) 10 cd ♘xc3 11 bc ♗g4 12 0-0 de 13 fe ♗xf3 14 ♖xf3! ♗xe5 15 ♗h6 ∞ Tisdall.

20   Nei-Polugayevsky, USSR Ch 1966/67.
  17 ♖ae1! ± Geller.   17 a4!? ∞∞ Petrosian.

21   **13 ... ♘xf3+** 14 ♖xf3 ♗g4 15 ♖xf7!? ♖xf7 16 ♗xg4 ∞∞ Nun-Gerszenyi, corr. 1970. 14 ♗xf3!? ∞∞.
  13 ... ♗f5 14 ♘xe5 ♗xe5 15 g4! ♗d4+ 16 ♔h1 ♘d7 17 ♘e4 ♗b5 18 b4! ± Tisdall-Taulbut, Brighton 1980.

22   15 ♗b5!? 15 d6!? Tisdall.

23   15 ... ♕b4! intending 16 ♕f3 ♗f5 17 g4 ♕xb2! Hartston.

24   Nei-Westerinen, Estonia v Finland 1966.

Averbakh 1 d4 ♘f6 2 c4 g6 3 ♘c3 ♗g7 4 e4 d6 5 ♗e2 0-0 6 ♗g5

	6	7	8	9	10	11	12	13	14	
1	...	♕d2	d5	♗f3	h4	♘ge2	dc	♘d5	♘ec3	±
	♘bd7[1]	e5	♘c5	a5	c6	b5	bc	♘e6	♖a6[2]	
2	...	♗e3	e5[3]	de	♖xd1	♗xc5	♘d5	f4	h3	±
	h6	c5	de[4]	♕xd1+	♘g4	♘xe5	♘bc6	♘g4	♘f6[5]	
3	...	...	d5	♕d2[7]	f3	♘h3	♘f2	0-0-0	g4[8]	∞
	...	e5	♘bd7[6]	h5	♘h7	♘c5	a5	b6		
4	...	dc	♗d2	♘f3	0-0	♗xf3	♗e2	♖c1	b3	=
	c5!	♕a5	♕xc5	♗g4[9]	♗xf3	♘c6	♘d7	a6	♖ac8[10]	
5	...	d5	♗d2	♘f3	ed	0-0	h3	♗xf3	a4[12]	±
	...	♕a5	e6	ed	♗g4	♘bd7[11]	♗xf3	a6		
6	...	...	a4	♗d2	♘f3	cd[13]	0-0	♕c2	h3	∞
	...	a6	♕a5	e6	ed	♖e8	♕c7	♗g4	♗xf3[14]	
7	...	...	cb	a4[15]	♗d2	♕c2[18]	♗xb5	f3	♘xb5	⊙⊙
	...	b5	a6	♕a5[16]	♕b4[17]	ab	♗a6!	♗xb5	♕xb5[19]	
8	...	...	♘f3	ed	♗h4?![21]	0-0	♗g3	♘d2	fg	∞
	...	e6	ed	h6[20]	♘a6	g5	♘h5	♘xg3	f5[22]	
9	...	...	♕d2	ed	0-0-0	f3	♘h3	♘f2	♖he1	±
	...	...	ed	♕b6	♖e8[23]	♘bd7	a6	♕a5	♘b6[24]	
10	...	...	...	...	♘f3	0-0	h3	♗xf3	a4	±
	...	...	...	♖e8	♗g4	♘bd7	♗xf3	a6	♕e7[25]	

1 d4 ♘f6 2 c4 g6 3 ♘c3 ♗g7 4 e4 d6 5 ♗e2 0-0 6 ♗g5 c5 7 d5 h6

	8	9	10	11	12	13	14	15	16	
11	♗e3	h3[26]	ed	♘f3	g4	0-0	♗xf3	♗f4	♕d3	=
	e6	ed	♖e8	♗f5	♗e4	♗xf3	♘bd7	♘b6	♘fd7[27]	
12	...	de	♕d2[28]	h3	♘f3	0-0	♖ad1	♖fe1	♗f4	=
	...	♗xe6	♔h7	♘c6	♕e7	♖ad8	♖fe8	♕f8	♘d4[29]	
13	...	♕d2	ed[30]	h3	♗d3[32]	♘f3	♘xe5	0-0	a4	±
	...	ed	♔h7	♖e8[31]	♘bd7[33]	♘e5	♖xe5	a6	♘h5[34]	
14	...	...	...	...	...	♘f3	♗b1	a3[35]	♖xb1	=
	...	...	...	...	♘a6	♘b4!	♗f5!	♗xb1	♘a6[36]	
15	♗f4	de	♗xd6	♘f3	♗xb8[37]	♕c2	g3	♘d2		±
	e6	♗xe6	♖e8	♕b6!?	♖axb8	♘h5	♗h3	♘f6[38]		
16	...	...	...	...	0-0	e5[39]	♘xd4	♕xd4[40]	♗xe5	=
	...	...	...	♘c6	♘d4	♘d7	cd	♘xe5	♕xd4[41]	

[1] 6 ... Nc6 7 Nf3 Bg4 8 d5 ±.
  6 ... c6 7 Qd2 Re8 8 f4 h6 9 Bh4 Qa5 10 Nf3 Bg4 11 0-0 Nbd7 12 Rab1 Qc7 13 e5 ± Bertok-Damjanović, Yugoslav Ch 1955.

[2] 15 c7! Nxc7 16 h5 ± Olafsson-Savon, Moscow 1971.

[3] 8 dc Qa5 9 Qd2 Qxc5 10 Nf3 Bg4 11 Rc1 Nc6 12 Be3 Qb4 13 Qd2 Bxf3 14 gf ♔h7 = Sanguinetti-Liberzon, Biel Z 1976.

[4] 8 ... Nfd7 9 ed ed 10 Nf3 ± Vaganian.

[5] 15 Bf3! ± Shereshevsky-Dementiev, USSR 1976.

[6] 8 ... c6 9 Qd2 cd 10 cd ± Uhlmann-Gligorić, Vrbas 1977.

[7] 9 g4 Nc5 10 f3 a5! 11 h4 h5 12 g5 Nh7 13 Nh3 f6 ∓ Gunnarsson-Keene, Reykjavik 1976.

[8] 14 ... h4? 15 g5 ± Uhlmann-Westerinen, Solingen 1979.
  14 ... hg 15 fg f5 16 gf gf 17 ef Qh4 ∞ Polugayevsky.

[9] 9 ... b6!? 10 0-0 Bb7 11 Be3 Qc7 12 Nd2 Nbd7 13 Rc1 e6 14 f3 Rad8 ∞ Nieves-Ree, Madrid 1982.

[10] 15 Be3 Nd4! = Fuller-Evans, Haifa Ol 1976.

[11] 11 ... Bxf3 12 Bxf3 Nbd7 13 Qc2 Rfe8 14 Be2 Re7 intending ... Rae8 ±.

[12] 14 ... Qc7 15 a5! ± Farago-Andersson, Cienfuegos 1977.

[13] 11 ed Qc7! 12 0-0 Nbd7! 13 a5 Rb8 = Litinskaya-Chiburdanidze, USSR 1979.

[14] 15 Bxf3 Nbd7 16 a5 c4! = Gligorić.

[15] 9 Qd2!? Qa5 10 f3! ± Forintos-Reshevsky, Dubna 1979.
  9 ba?! Bxa6 ∞∞.

[16] 9 ... h6!? 10 Bd2 e6 11 de Bxe6 12 Nf3 ab 13 Bxb5 Na6 14 0-0 Nc7! (14 ... Nb4?! 15 Be3 ±) 15 Re1 Nxb5 16 Nxb5 (16 ab Rxa1 17 Qxa1 d5 ∞∞) 16 ... d5 17 ed Nxd5 18 Ne5 Re8 (Tukmakov-Kasparov, USSR Ch 1981; 18 ... Qh4?! 19 Qc2! ±) 19 Nc4! ±.

[17] 10 ... Nbd7?! 11 Ra3! ± Kasparov-Spassky, Tilburg 1981.

[18] 11 Qb1!? 11 f3!?

[19] 15 ab Rxa1+ 16 Bc1 Nbd7 ∞∞.

[20] 9 ... Re8 10 0-0 Bg4 11 h3 Bxf3 12 Bxf3 Nbd7 13 Be2 Qb6 14 Qc2 ♔h8 15 f4 ± Litvinov-Doroshkevich, USSR 1967.

[21] 10 Be3! – 7 ... h6.

[22] Puc-Ostojić, Yugoslav Ch 1965.

[23] 10 ... Bf5 11 f3 intending g4 ±.

[24] 15 Nce4 Qxd2+ 16 Rxd2 Nxe4 17 Nxe4 ± Hasin-Vasyukov, USSR 1957.

[25] 15 Rae1 Qf8 16 Bd1 ± Uhlmann-Gligorić, Hastings 1970/71.

[26] 9 Nf3 ed 10 ed (10 cd b5! ∓) 10 ... Bg4 11 0-0 Nbd7 12 h3 Bxf3 13 Bxf3 Re8 = Steiner-Endzelins, corr. 1974/78.

[27] Averbakh-Geller, USSR 1974.

[28] 10 h3 Qa5 11 Bd2 Nc6 = Antoshin-Liberzon, Luhacovice 1971.

[29] Donner-Gligorić, Amsterdam 1971.

[30] 10 cd Qe7 11 f3 h5 12 h4 Nbd7 13 Nh3 Ne5 ∞ Lombard-Byrne, Skopje Ol 1972.

[31] 11 ... Na6 12 Bd3 (12 Nf3 Bf5 13 Bd3 Qd7 14 0-0 Rfe8 15 Rfe1 Nb4 16 Bxf5 Qxf5 17 a3 Nc2! = Uhlmann-Fischer, Siegen Ol 1970) 12 ... Nc7 (12 ... Re8 – 11 ... Re8) 13 a4 a6 14 Nf3 Rb8 15 a5 b5 ∞ Deze-Masić, Sombor 1972.

[32] 12 Nf3 Bf5 13 0-0 Ne4 14 Nxe4 Bxe4. 15 Ne1!? (15 Rae1 Nd7! 16 Nh2 b5 ∞ Kavalek) 15 ... Nd7 16 Rc1 b5! ∞ Karlsson-Sznapik, Helsinki 1981.

[33] 12 ... b5 13 Nxb5 Ne4 14 Qc2 Ng3 15 fg Rxe3+ 16 ♔f2 ∞∞ Euwe.

[34] 17 Rae1 ± Belyavsky-Vogt, Sukhumi 1970.

[35] 15 Bxf3 gf 16 a3 f4! Minev. 16 0-0 Ne4! ∓.

[36] 17 Qd3 Qe7 = Spassov-Ermenkov, Bulgarian Ch 1973.

[37] 12 e5!? Nfd7 (12 ... Qxb2!? 13 Nb5?! Na6 14 Rb1 Qxa2 15 Ra1 =; 13 Qc1!?) 13 Nb5 Na6 14 0-0 Rad8 (14 ... Bg4) 15 Qc1! ± Alexandria-Chiburdanidze, match 1981.
  12 Qd2 Bxc4! 13 Bxc4 Nxe4 14 Nxe4 Rxe4+ 15 Be2 Nc6! 16 0-0 Nd4 ∓.

[38] 15 ... f5?! 16 Bxh5 gh 17 0-0-0 ± Schmidt-Kupreichik, Polanica Zdroj 1981.

[39] 13 Bxc5? Nxe2+ 14 Qxe2 Nc8 ∓.
  13 Nxd4 cd 14 Qxd4 Nxe4! Adorjan.

[40] 15 Nb5 Ne5 16 c5 d3! ∞ Uhlmann-Schmidt, Brno 1975.

[41] 17 Bxd4 Bxd4 18 Rac1 Rad8 19 b3 Bxc3 20 Rxc3 Rd2 21 Bf3 Rxa2 22 Bxb7 Rb8 23 Bf3!? (23 Bc6 Ra3 = Uhlmann-Schmidt, Polanica Zdroj 1975; 23 Be4 Ra3 24 Bc2 a5 25 Re3 Ra2! =) 23 ... Ra3 24 Bd1 a5 25 Rc1 Rc8 26 Re1 a4 27 ba Rxc4 = Polugayevsky-Kasparov, Bugojno 1982.

Sämisch I 1 d4 ♘f6 2 c4 g6 3 ♘c3[1] ♗g7 4 e4 d6[2] 5 f3

	5	6	7	8	9	10	11	12	13	
1	...	♘ge2	♗g5	d5	♘c1	cd	a4	♘b3	a5	±
	e5	c6	♘bd7	♘b6	cd	0-0	a6	♗d7	♘c8	
2	...	♗e3	♗d3[4]	♘ge2[5]	0-0	♕d2[6]	♗xc4	♗b3	♘a4	±
	c6	a6[3]	b5	♘bd7	0-0	bc	♘b6	a5	♘fd7[7]	
3	...	♗e3[8]	♗d3!?[10]	dc[11]	e5[12]	f4	♘f3	e6	♗xc5	∞
	0-0	a6[9]	c5	dc	♘fd7	♘c6	f6	♘b6	♗xe6[13]	
4	...	...	♕d2[14]	♘ge2	0-0-0	♔b1	dc[17]	♘d5	♕xa5	±
	...	♘bd7	c5	a6[15]	♕a5	b5[16]	dc	♘xd5[18]	♘xe3[19]	
5	...	...	♗d3[20]	♘ge2	e5[23]	♗e4	dc	♗xc5	♗e3	±
	...	b6	a6[21]	c5[22]	♘e8[24]	♖a7	bc	♖d7	♗b7[25]	
6	...	...	♘h3	d5	0-0[27]	cd	♗g5	a4		∞
	...	...	♗b7	c5[26]	e6	ed	♖e8	♘bd7	a6[28]	
7	...	...	...	♘ge2	d5[29]	♗g5	f4	a4	0-0	±
	...	...	...	c5	e6	♘bd7	a6	♕c7	ed[30]	
8	...	...	♘ge2[31]	♘xd4	♕d2[34]	cd[35]	e5	f4	♗b5!	±
	...	e5	ed[32]	c6[33]	d5	cd	♘e8	f6	fe[36]	
9	...	...	d5	♕d2	0-0-0	ef[40]	♘h3	♗g5	♗d3	±
	...	...	♘h5[37]	f5[38]	♘d7[39]	gf	♘df6	♕e8	♗d7[41]	
10	...	...	...	♗d3	cd	♕d2[44]	ef	♘ge2	0-0	=
	...	...	c6	cd[42]	♘e8[43]	f5	gf	♘d7	♔h8[45]	
11	...	...	...	♘ge2	cd	g4	h3	♗g5	♕d2	=
	...	...	...	cd	♘bd7[46]	h5	a6	♕b6	♘h7[47]	
12	...	...	...	♕d2	cd	0-0-0![49]	♔b1	♘ge2	b4!	±
	...	...	...	cd	♘a6[48]	♗d7	♘c5	b5	♘a4[50]	
13	...	...	...	...	...	g4!	gf	0-0-0	♗f2	±/±
	...	...	...	...	♘e8	f5	gf	f4	♘d7[51]	
14	...	...	...	...	...	♘ge2	g4[52]	h3[53]	0-0-0	∞
	...	...	...	...	...	♘bd7	a6	h5!	♘h7 h4[54]	

[1] 3 f3!? d5 4 cd ♘xd5 5 e4 ♘b6 6 ♘c3 ♗g7 7 ♗e3 0-0 8 f4 ♘c6! ∞.

[2] 4 ... 0-0 5 f3 c5!? 6 d5 (6 dc b6 7 cb ♕xb6 ∞∞) 6 ... d6 leads to ♗g5 systems or the Benoni.

[3] 6 ... 0-0 7 ♗d3 e5 8 ♘ge2 (8 d5 – row 10) 8 ... ed 9 ♗xd4 d5! = Hübner-Gligorić, Leningrad IZ 1973.

[4] 7 a4 a5 intending 8 ... ♘a6 =.
7 c5!? 0-0 8 ♘ge2 ♘bd7 9 ♘f4 ±. 9 ... b5!?

[5] 8 e5!? ♘fd7 9 f4 ♘b6 10 b3 ∞ Portisch-

Kavalek, Wijk aan Zee 1975.

[6] 10 b3 ♗b7 11 ♕d2 e6 12 ♖ad1 ♖e8 = Gligorić-Kavalek, Manila 1975.

[7] 14 ♖fc1 ♗a6 ± Saidy-Bednarski, Tel Aviv Ol 1964.

[8] 6 ♗g5 c5 (6 ... ♘c6!? 7 ♘ge2 a6 8 ♕d2 ♖b8 9 0-0-0 b5 10 ♗e3!? ∞) 7 d5 e6 8 ♕d2 ed 9 cd h6 10 ♗e3 (10 ♗xh6? ♘xe4 intending ... ♕h4+) 10 ... ♔h7 11 ♘ge2 a6 12 a4 ♘bd7 13 ♘g3 ♖b8 14 ♗e2 ♘e8 15 0-0 ♘c7 (Keene-Liu Wenze, Peking 1981) 16 ♖ab1 ±.

[9] 6 ... c5 7 dc dc 8 ♕xd8 ♖xd8 9 ♗xc5 ♘c6 10 ♘d5 ♘xd5 11 cd ±/± Karpov-Barle, Ljubljana 1975.

[10] 7 ♕d2 ♘c6 – 6 ... ♘c6.

[11] 8 ♘ge2 ♘c6 9 d5 ♘e5 10 a4 ± Romanishin-A.Rodriguez, Cienfuegos 1977.

8 d5!? e6!?

[12] 9 ♗xc5 ♘c6 10 ♗e3 ♘d7 11 ♘h3 ♗xc3+ 12 bc ♘de5 ∓ Schneider-Bergin, Kaspinsk 1965.

[13] 14 ♕e2 ♗f7 (Piasetski-Eslon, Alicante 1977) 15 0-0! Piasetski.

[14] 7 ♘h3 e5 8 d5 ♗c5 9 g4 c6 ∞.

7 ♗d3 e5! 8 d5 ♘h5 9 ♘ge2 f5! = Najdorf-Fischer, Bled 1961.

[15] 8 ... cd 9 ♘xd4 ±/±.

8 ... ♖e8 9 dc ♘xc5 10 ♘d4 ♗e6 ± Szabo-Pilnik, Mar del Plata 1955.

[16] 10 ... ♖e8 11 ♘c1 (11 g4 b5 12 g5!?) 11 ... cd 12 ♗xd4 ♘c5 13 a3 ± Bobotsov-Panchev, Sofia 1957.

[17] 11 ♘d5? ♘xd5! 12 ♕xa5 ♘xe3 13 ♖d3 ♘xc4 14 ♕e1 ♖b8! ∓/∓ Beyen-Klompus, corr. 1968.

[18] 12 ... ♕d8? 13 ♗xc5!

[19] 14 ♖c1 ± Saidy-Commons, US Ch 1974.

[20] 7 ♕d2 c5 8 ♘ge2! (8 d5 ♖e8! intending ... ♘bd7-e5) 8 ... ♘c6 9 d5 ♘e5 10 ♘g3 e6 11 ♗e2 ed 12 cd a6 13 a4 ♗d7 14 0-0 b5! ∞ Ghitescu-Schaufelberger, Bath 1973.

[21] 7 ... c5? 8 e5! intending ♗e4 ±±.

[22] 8 ... ♘fd7!? 9 f4 ± Razuvayev.

[23] 9 d5 ♘bd7 10 ♘g3 b5!? 11 cb ♘e5 ∞∞ Belkadi-Petrosian, Siegen Ol 1970.

[24] 9 ... ♘fd7 10 ed ed 11 0-0 ♘c6 12 ♗c2 ±.

[25] 14 ♗xb7 ♖xb7 15 b3 ± Gligorić-Torre, Manila 1975.

[26] 8 ... e5 9 d5 ♘c8 10 ♘g1! ± Portisch-Vukić, Bugojno 1978.

[27] 10 ♕d2 ed 11 cd ± Darga-Ree, Beverwijk 1967.

[28] 14 ♘f2 ♕c7 15 b3 c4! ∞∞ Boyd.

[29] 9 0-0 ♘c6 10 ♗c2 e5 11 de de 12 ♗g5 ± Botvinnik-Stein, USSR 1964.

[30] 14 ed ± Gligorić-Parr, Lone Pine 1975.

[31] 7 de de 8 ♕xd8 ♖xd8 9 ♘d5 ♘xd5 10 cd c6 11 ♗c4 cd 12 ♗xd5 ♘c6 13 ♖d1 ♘d4 14 ♔f2 ♗e6 =.

[32] 7 ... ♘bd7 8 ♕d2 ♘b6 (8 ... a6 9 d5 ♘h5 10 0-0-0 ±/±) 9 b3 ed 10 ♘xd4 ± Hasin-Spassky Leningrad 1954.

7 ... c6 8 ♕b3 (8 ♕d2 ed!? 9 ♗xd4 ♗e6 = Neikirch-Panno, Portorož IZ 1958) 8 ... ♘bd7 9 0-0-0 ♕a5 10 ♔b1 ± Barczay-Geller, Havana 1971.

[33] 8 ... ♘c6 9 ♗e2 ♗d7 10 0-0 a6 11 ♕d2 ♖e8 12 ♖fd1 ± Slusky-Kirpichnikov, USSR 1974.

[34] 9 ♘c2 ♖e8 10 ♕d2 ♗e6 11 0-0-0 ± Ilivitsky-Gurgenidze, Moscow 1955.

[35] 10 ed cd =.

[36] 14 fe ♕h4+ 15 g3 ♕e7 ±.

[37] 7 ... c5?! 8 g4 ♗e8 9 h4 ± Tal-Boleslavsky, USSR Ch 1958.

7 ... ♘bd7 or 7 ... ♗e8 8 ♕d2 ±.

[38] 8 ... ♕h4+?! 9 g3 ♘xg3 10 ♕f2 ♘xf1 11 ♕xh4 ♘xe3 12 ♗e2! ± Karpov-Velimirović, Skopje 1976.

[39] 9 ... f4 10 ♗f2 ±.

9 ... a6 10 ef gf 11 ♘ge2 ±.

[40] 10 ♗d3 fe 11 ♘xe4 ♘f4 12 ♗c2 ± Hort-Stein, Los Angeles 1968.

[41] 14 ♖hg1 ♘h8 15 ♘f2! ± Möhring-Uhlmann, Leipzig 1975.

[42] 8 ... b5!? 9 ♕d2! bc 10 ♗xc4 c5 11 ♘ge2 ± Tarjan-Plachetka, Odessa 1976.

[43] 9 ... ♘a6 10 ♘ge2 ♗d7 11 0-0 ♘c5 12 ♗b5! ±/±.

9 ... ♘h5 10 ♘ge2 f5 11 ef gf 12 0-0 ±/± Portisch-Gligorić, Milan 1975.

9 ... ♘bd7 10 ♘ge2 ♘c5 11 ♗c2 ±.

[44] 10 ♘ge2 ♗h6! 11 ♗f2 ♘d7 12 0-0 f5 = Furman-Suetin, USSR ½-final 1956. 11 ♗xh6!? ♕h4+ 12 ♘g3 ♕xh6 13 ♕d2 ♕h4! = Szabo-Sznapik, Helsinki 1979.

[45] Polugayevsky-Geller, Petropolis IZ 1973.

[46] 9 ... ♘a6 10 g4 ♗d7 11 ♘g3 ± Boyd.

[47] Raisa-Dittman, Leipzig Ol 1960.

[48] 9 ... a6 10 ♗d3 intending ♘ge2, 0-0 ±.

[49] 10 ♗b5 ♘h5 11 ♘ge2 f5 12 ef gf 13 0-0 ♘c7 14 ♗c4 ±/± Timman-Balashov, Sochi 1973.

[50] 14 ♘xa4 ba 15 ♘c3 ♘e8 16 ♗d3! ± Gheorghiu-Timman, Moscow 1981.

[51] 14 ♔b1 ±/± Larsen-Donner, The Hague 1958.

[52] 11 ♘c1 ♘h5 12 ♘d3 b5 13 0-0-0 ♘b6 14 ♘b4 ♗d7 ∓ Szabo-Petrosian, Amsterdam C 1956.

[53] 12 ♗g5 hg 13 fg ♘c5 14 ♘g3 ♗xg4 15 b4 ∞ Botvinnik-Tal, match (10) 1960.

[54] 14 ♔b1 ∞.

129

Sämisch II 1 d4 ♞f6 2 c4 g6 3 ♞c3 ♝g7 4 e4 d6 5 f3 0-0 6 ♝e3 ♞c6

	7	8	9	10	11	12	13	14	15	
1	♛d2[1]	0-0-0	♝h6[2]	d5[3]	♞ge2	♝xe2	g4	♝e3		=
	a6	♖b8	e5	♞d4	♞xe2+	♔h8	♞g8	f5[4]		
2	♞ge2	♛d2[6]	♞c1	d5[7]	♞b3	dc	♞xd4	♝xd4	cd	∞
	♖b8[5]	♖e8	e5	♞d4	c5	bc	ed	d5!?[8]	cd[9]	
3	...	...	h4	0-0-0[11]	♝h6[12]	♛e3[14]	d5	♞g3	♝d3	∞
	...	...	h5[10]	a6	♝h8[13]	e5	♞a5	c5	b5![15]	
4	...	...	0-0-0	♛e1[16]	h4	g4[18]	fg	e5	e6	∞
	...	...	a6	♝d7[17]	h5	hg	♝xg4	♞h5	fe[19]	
5	...	...	♖b1	b4	cb	d5	♞d4	♞cxb5	de	±
	...	...	a6[20]	b5[21]	ab	♞e5	♝d7	e6	fe[22]	
6	...	♛d2[23]	0-0-0[25]	g4[27]	d5	♞g3	c5	c6	♛xc3	=
	a6	♖b8[24]	b5[26]	e5	♞a5	♝d7	b4	bc	♞xc6[28]	
7	...	...	♝h6	h4	♝xg7[31]	h5	♞d5	hg	♛h6	∞
	...	...	b5[29]	e5[30]	♔xg7	♔h8[32]	bc	fg	♞h5[33]	
8	...	...	h4	♝h6[35]	♝xg7[36]	d5[37]	cb	b4!	♛c1	±
	...	...	h5[34]	b5	♔xg7	♞a5?![38]	ab	♞c4	e6[39]	
9	...	...	...	h5![40]	d5![42]	♞g3	♞d1	♞f2	b3![44]	±
	...	...	b5	e5[41]	♞a5	b4[43]	c6	♝d7		
10	...	...	...	d5	♞g3	h5	♝h6	♛xh6	♝e2	=
	...	e5	...	♞a5	c5	♝d7	♝xh6	b5	♛e7[45]	
11	...	...	♞c1	♞b3	♞xd4	0-0-0[46]	♝h6	♛xh6	♝e2	∞
	...	...	e5	ed	♞e5	c6	♝xh6	♛e7	♝e6[47]	
12	...	...	...	...	...	♝xd4	♝e2	0-0	cb	=
	...	...	...	...	...	♞xd4	♝e6	c6[48]	ab[49]	
13	...	...	...	...	...	♝e2[50]	♞xc6	0-0[51]	♖ad1	=
	...	...	...	...	...	♝d7	♞h5	bc	♖e8 c5![52]	
14	...	...	...	d5	♞b3	ab	g4[54]	h3	gh	=
	...	...	...	♞d4	♞xb3[53]	c5	h5	♞h7	♛h4+[55]	
15	...	...	...	...	♞1e2	♝xe2	0-0-0!	c5	♝f2	±
	...	...	...	...	♞xe2[56]	♞h5	f5	f4	♝f6[57]	

[1] 7 ♝d3 e5 8 d5 (8 ♞ge2? ♞g4!) 8 ... ♞d4 9 ♞ge2 ♞d7 10 ♛d2 c5 11 dc bc 12 b4 ♝b7 13 0-0 f5 ∓ Sliwa-Ghitescu, Marianske Lazne 1961.

[2] 9 h4 e5 10 d5 ♞d4 11 ♞ge2 c5 12 dc bc 13 ♞xd4 ed 14 ♝xd4 ♝e6 ∞ Averbakh-Bogdanović, Titovo Uzice 1966.

[3] **10 ♞ge2 b5** 11 h4 bc 12 ♝xg7 ♔xg7 13 h5 ♞g8 ∞ Razuvayev-Kupreichik, USSR 1974.
10 ♝xg7 ♔xg7 11 ♞ge2 b5 12 h4 h5! =.

[4] Boleslavsky.

[5] 7 ... e5 8 d5 ♞e7 9 g4 c6 10 ♞g3 ±.

[6] 8 ♞c1 e5 9 ♞b3 ed 10 ♞xd4 ♖e8 (10 ... ♞h5!? 11 ♝e2 ♞f4 ∓ Ree-Keene, Caorle 1972) 11 ♛d2 d5! 12 cd ♞xd5 13 ♞xd5 ♞xd4 = Gligorić-Kavalek, Manila 1974.

[7] 10 ♞b3 - note 6.

[8] 14 ... c5!? 15 ♝e3 d5 16 cd ♞xd5 ∞.

[9] 16 e5 ♞h5! 17 0-0-0 ♝xe5 18 ♝xe5 ♖xe5 ∞.

[10] 9 ... a6 10 h5 b5 11 hg fg 12 ♝h6 ♝h8 13 cb ab 14 ♞f4 ± Raičević-Mestel, Hastings 1979/80.

[11] 10 ♝h6 ♝h8 11 0-0-0 a6 transposes.

[12] 11 ♛e1 ♝d7 - row 4.

[13] **11 ... e5** 12 ♝xg7 ♔xg7 13 d5 ♞e7 14 ♔b1 ♝d7 15 ♞c1 ± Ornstein-Dueball, Glucksberg 1977.
11 ... b5 12 g4! ±/±.

[14] Intending e5.

[15] **16 ♞f1** ♞d7 17 g4 ♞b6 18 gh ♞bxc4 19 ♛g1 ♝h7 20 hg+ fg ∞ Barden.
16 cb? c4! intending ... ab ∓.

[16] 10 g4 b5 11 h4 h5!? ∞.

[17] 10 ... b5 12 h4 h5 13 e5! ±/± Spassky-Keene, Dortmund 1973.

18 Intending 13 gh ♘xh5 14 ♘g3 – Ciocaltea.
19 16 ♖g1 ♗f5 17 ♘g3 ♘xg3 18 ♕xg3 e5 19 ♗h3 ♕d7 20 ♖df1 =∞ Ghitescu-Whiteley, Nice Ol 1974.
20 9 ... a5 10 g3 e5 11 d5 ♘e7 12 ♗g2 c6 Petrosian.
21 10 ... e5!? 11 d5 ♘e7 12 g3 c6 ∞ Antoshin-I.Zaitsev, Polanica Zdroj 1970. 10 ... ♗d7 11 g3! ⩲ Grosch-Veröci, Budapest 1977.
22 16 ♗e2 d5 (16 ... ♘xf3+?! 17 gf e5 18 0-0 ed 19 ♘xd4 ± Polugayevsky-Gufeld, USSR Ch 1975) 17 ed ♘xd5 18 ♗g5 ♗f6 19 ♗xf6 ♕xf6 20 0-0 ♘f4 21 ♔h1 ⩲ Boleslavsky.
23 **8 ♖b1** b5 9 cb ab 10 d5 ♘e5 11 ♘d4 e6! 12 de fe 13 ♘dxb5 ♘h5 =∞ Boleslavsky.

8 a3 ♗d7 9 b4 ♕b8! 10 ♕d2 ♖e8 11 g3 b5 =.

8 ♘c1 e5 9 d5 (9 ♘b3 ed 10 ♘xd4 ♘xd4 11 ♗xd4 c6 12 ♗e2 b5 ∞ Lein-Mestrović, Sarajevo 1968) 9 ... ♘d4 10 ♘b3 ♘xb3!? (10 ... c5!? 11 dc bc 12 ♘xd4 ed 13 ♗xd4 ♖b8 14 ♕d2 ♕a5 15 ♖c1 ♖d8! = A.Rodriguez-Kuzmin, Minsk 1982) 11 ♕xb3 c5 12 dc bc 13 0-0-0 ♕e7! 14 ♕b6 ♗b7 ∞ Timman-Kasparov, Moscow 1981.
24 8 ... ♖e8 9 ♘c1 e5 10 d5 (10 ♘b3 ed 11 ♘xd4 ♘e5 12 ♗e2 c5 13 ♘c2 ♗e6 =) 10 ... ♘d4 11 ♘1e2 c5 12 dc ♘xc6 13 ♘d5 b5! ∞ Belyavsky-Kasparov, Moscow 1981. 9 h4!? h5 10 ♘c1 (10 0-0-0 b5! 11 ♘f4 e5 12 de ♘xe5 13 cb ab 14 ♗xb5 ♗d7 15 ♗e2 ♕b8 =∞ Kraidman-Domnitz, Tel Aviv 1966) 10 ... e5 11 d5 ♘d4 12 ♘b3 ♘xb3 =.
25 **9 ♖b1** b5 10 cb ab 11 b4 e5 12 d5 ♘e7 13 g4 c6 ∞/=.

9 a3!? b5 10 cb ab 11 b4 ♖e8 12 ♖c1 ♗d7 13 d5 ♘e5 14 ♘d4 e6 15 de ♗xe6 16 ♗xb5 ♗c4? 17 ♘c6! ♘d3+ 18 ♔d1 ♗b3+ 19 ♖c2 ± Pytel-Sznapik, Polish Ch 1973. 9 ... ♗d7 10 b4 b5 11 cb ab 12 d5 ♘e5 13 ♘d4 e6 14 de fe 15 ♘dxb5 ♘h5!? 16 ♕c1 ∞ Veremeichik-Didishko, Minsk 1976/77.

9 ♖c1 ♗d7 10 g3 b5 11 cb ab 12 ♗g2 e5! =/⩱ Antoshin-Nezhmetdinov, USSR 1962.

9 ♖d1 ♗d7 10 ♘c1 e5 11 d5 ♘d4! = Portisch-Boey, Havana Ol 1966.

9 d5 ♘a5 10 ♘g3 c5 11 ♖c1 ♗d7 12 ♗d3 b5 ⩱ Lutikov-Gufeld, USSR 1980.
26 9 ... ♗d7 10 ♗h6 b5 11 h4 e5 12 ♗xg7 ♔xg7 13 g4 ♘g8 14 g5 ± Benko-Harris, USA 1968. 13 ... h5!?
27 10 h4 bc?! 11 h5 ♘xh5? 12 g4 ♘b4 13 ♘f4! ± Hillyard-J.Littlewood, British Ch 1977. 10 ... e5 11 d5 ♘a5 12 ♘g3 b4 13 ♘b1 ⩲ Knaak-Gufeld, Jurmala 1978.
28 Kraidman-Portisch, Manila 1974.
29 9 ... e5 10 ♗xg7 ♔xg7 11 h4 h5 12 0-0-0 b5 13 d5 ♘a5 14 ♘g3 (Gheorghiu-Anastopoulos, Sofia 1967) 14 ... b4! =.
30 10 ... bc 11 h5 ♘b4! 12 ♘g3 ♗xh6 13 ♕xh6 ♘c2+ = Murey-Zhelnin, USSR 1974.
31 11 0-0-0!?
32 12 ... ♔g8 13 hg fg 14 0-0-0 ⩲ Balashov-I.Zaitsev, USSR Ch 1970.
33 16 g4 ♖xb2 17 gh gh ∞ Bagirov-Gufeld, USSR 1973. 18 ♖c1!?
34 9 ... ♗d7 10 h5 b5 11 hg fg 12 ♘f4 ⩲/±.
35 **10 ♘d5** b5 11 ♘xf6+ ef! 12 g4 f5! ∞.

10 0-0-0 b5 11 ♘f4 e5 12 de ♘xe5 13 c5 ⩲/± Qi-Blackstock, China 1981, and Ree-Nunn, Wijk aan Zee 1982.
36 11 0-0-0 e5! 12 ♗xg7 ♔xg7 13 de ♘xe5 14 ♘f4 (14 ♘g3 b4! ∓ Tarjan-Quinteros, Cleveland 1975) 14 ... bc 15 ♗e2 ♖h8! 16 g3 ♘fd7 ⩱ Gligorić-Quinteros, Lone Pine 1980.
37 12 0-0-0 e5 13 cb ab 14 de ♘xe5 15 ♘f4 b4? 16 ♘cd5 ⩲/± Rivas-Mestel, Marbella Z 1982.
38 12 ... ♘e5!? 13 cb ab 14 ♘d4 b4! intending 15 ♘cb5 e6!? (16 f4 ed! 17 fe ♘xe4 ∓) ∞/⩲.
39 16 ♘d4 ± Ornstein-Martinović, Niš 1977.
40 10 cb ab 11 ♗h6 e5 12 ♗xg7 ♔xg7 13 h5 ♕e7 ∞ Scherbakov-Zhelnin, USSR 1976.
41 10 ... bc 11 hg fg 12 ♘f4 ⩲ Romanishin-Tseshkovsky, Vilnus 1975.
42 11 0-0-0 ed 12 ♘xd4 ♘xd4 13 ♗xd4 ♗e6 = Ree-Mortensen, Malta Ol 1980.
43 12 ... bc?! 13 0-0-0 ♘d7?! 14 hg fg 15 ♘b1 ± Timman-Kasparov, Bugojno 1982.
44 Petursson-Sznapik, Ljubljana 1981.
45 Gheorghiu-Andersson, Las Palmas 1972.
46 **12 ♖d1!** c5 13 ♘c2 ♗e6 14 ♕xd6 ♕xd6 15 ♖xd6 ♘xc4 =.

12 ♗e2 c5! 13 ♘c2 ♗e6 14 b3 (14 ♘d5 b5! ∓ Varnusz-Portisch, Hungarian Ch 1961) 14 ... ♕a5 = Belyavsky-Gufeld, USSR 1979.
47 16 h4 c5 17 ♘xe6 fe 18 g4 b5 ∞ Koginov-Ruban, Leningrad Ch 1966.
48 13 ... c5 14 ♗e3 b5!? 15 cb ab 16 ♘xb5 d5 17 ed ♘xd5 18 ♗xc5 ♗e5 ∞ Andrianov-Krementsky, Moscow Ch 1982.
49 16 b3 ♕e7?! 17 ♖ac1 ♖fd8 18 ♖fd1 ⩲ Grigorian-Karasev, USSR Ch 1971. 16 ... ♕a5!? Schwarz. 16 ... d5 17 e5 ♘d7 18 f4 f6 Karpov/Razuvayev.
50 12 a4 ♖e8 13 ♗e2 ♘h5 14 ♘xc6 bc 15 0-0 ♕e7 ∓ Kozlovskaya-Golovei, USSR 1966.
51 14 c5 d5 15 ♗xa6 de Schwarz.
52 16 ♖fe1 ♘f6 17 b3 ♗c6 18 ♗d3 ♕c8 =.
53 11 ... c5?! 12 dc bc (12 ... ♘xb3 13 c7! ♕xc7 14 ab ± Lyavdansky-Levin, Vladimir 1962) 13 ♘xd4 ed 14 ♗xd4 ⩲ Smiltiner-Stepak, Tel Aviv 1971.
54 **13 b4?!** cb 14 ♘a4 b5 15 cb ab 16 ♕xb4 ♘e8 17 ♘c3 ♗h6! ∓ Bobotsov-Ivkov, Beverwijk 1968.

13 ♗d3 ♘d7 14 g4 ♕h4+ = Langeweg-Bilek, 1964.
55 16 ♕f2 ♕xf2+ 17 ♔xf2 gh = Boleslavsky.
56 11 ... c5 12 dc ♘xc6 13 ♘c1 ♗e6 ∞/⩲ Agrinsky-Gruzman, corr. 1969.
57 Kaufman-Morris, USA 1979.

	6	7	8	9	10	11	12	13	14	
1	... ♗g4	♗e3 ♘fd7	♘g1 ♗xe2	♘gxe2 e5[2]	d5[3] f5	f3 ♗h6!	♕d2 ♗xe3	♕xe3 f4	♕f2 ♘c5[4]	=
2	... ...	... ...	h3 ♗xf3	♗xf3 ♘c6[5]	♘e2 e5	d5 ♘e7	h4! f5[6]	h5 f4	♗d2 ♘f6[7]	±
3	... ...	... ...	0-0 c5[8]	d5 ♘a6[9]	h3[10] ♗xf3	♗xf3 ♘c7[11]	♗e2 a6	a4 ♕b8[12]	f4 e5[13]	±
4	... ...	0-0 c5	d5[14] ♘a6[15]	♗g5[16] ♘c7[17]	♘d2[18] ♗xe2	♕xe2 ♘d7	f4 ♕e8[19]	♖ae1 a6	♕d3 b5[20]	±
5	... ♘c6	d5 ♘b8[21]	0-0[22] e6	♗g5[23] h6	♗h4 ed	cd ♖e8	♘d2 c6	♖c1 a6	♗g3 cd[24]	±
6	... c6	0-0 a6	e5[25] ♘e8	♗f4 b5	♖e1 f6	ed ed	h3 ♔h8	♖c1 g5	♗e3 h6[26]	±
7	... c5	0-0[27] ♘c6	d5 ♘a5	a3 b6	b4 ♘b7	♖b1 e6[28]	♕c2 a6	de ♗xe6	♖d1 ♕c7[29]	±
8	... e5	de de	♕xd8 ♖xd8	♗g5 ♖e8[30]	0-0-0[31] h6	♗e3[32] c6	♘e1 ♗e6[33]	f3 ♗f8	b3 ♘a6[34]	=
9	... ...	♗e3 ♘c6?![35]	d5 ♘e7	♘d2 c5[36]	g4[37] ♘e8	g5[38] ♗h3[39]	♖g1 a6	a4[40] ♖b8	♗g4 ♗xg4[41]	±
10	... ...	... ed	♘xd4 ♖e8	f3[42] c6	♗f2! d5	ed cd	c5 ♘c6	0-0 ♘h5	♕d2 ♗e5[43]	±
11	... ...	... ♕e7	d5[44] ♘g4	♗g5 f6	♗h4 h5[45]	♘d2[46] a5	a3 ♘h6	f3 ♘f7	♗d3 ♗h6[47]	±

[1] 6 ♗e3!? e5 7 de de 8 ♕xd8 ♖xd8 9 ♘d5 ♖d7 10 ♘xf6+ ♗xf6 11 c5 ± Larsen-Kavalek, Bugojno 1980. 6 ... c5 7 d5 e6. 6 ... ♘bd7 intending ... c5.

[2] 9 ... c5 10 0-0 ♘c6 11 d5 ♘a5 12 b3 a6 13 ♖b1 ♕b8 14 a4 e5 (Ivkov-Szabo, Amsterdam 1972) 15 de intending 16 ♕d2 ± Ivkov. 15 ♕d3!? intending 16 b4 ± Geller.

[3] 10 0-0 a5 11 ♕d2 ♘c6 12 f3 ed 13 ♘xd4 ± Kasparov-Vukić, Banja Luka 1979.

[4] 15 ♔d2 a5 =.

[5] 9 ... e5 10 d5 f5 11 h4 h6 12 h5 f4 13 ♗d2 g5 14 ♗g4 ± Gligorić-Ničevski, Yugoslavia 1968.

[6] 12 ... h5! ±.

[7] Keene-Fuller, Sydney 1979.

[8] 8 ... ♘c6 9 d5 (9 ♘e1!? ♗xe2 10 ♘xe2 e5 11 d5 ♘e7 12 ♘d3 ± Kagan-Szabo, Winnipeg 1967) 9 ... ♗xf3 10 ♗xf3 ♘a5 11 ♗e2 ♗xc3 (11 ... c5 12 ♖c1 a6 13 ♕d2 ♖e8 14 b3 ± Olafsson-Vasyukov, Moscow 1959; 11 ... ♘e5 12 ♕a4 c6 13 ♖ac1 cd 14 ♘xd5 e6 15 ♘xd5 e6 16 ♘c3 ± Darga-Tal, Bled 1961) 12 bc e5 13 de! fe 14 f4 ♕e7 15 ♕a4 b6 (Cuellar-Tal, Leningrad IZ 1973) 16 ♖f2! intending 17 ♖af1 ±.

[9] 9 ... ♕a5!? 10 ♕c2 (10 ♕d2 ♘b6 11 ♖ac1 ♗xf3 12 gf f5 13 ♔h1 ♘8d7 14 ♖g1 ± Sokolsky-Shamkovich, USSR Ch 1954) 10 ... ♘a6 11 a3 ♖fc8?! 12 h3 ♗xf3 13 ♗xf3 ♕d8 14 ♗g4 ♖cb8 13 f4 ± Fedorowicz-Watson, New York 1979. 11 ... ♖fb8; 10 h3!?

[10] 10 a3 ♘c7 11 ♖b1 f5 12 b4 ♗f6 13 ♕c1 f4 = Korchnoi-Hug, Zürich (match) 1977.

10 ♕d2 ♖e8 11 h3 ♗xf3 12 ♗xf3 ♘c7 13 ♗e2 a6 14 a4 ± Petrosian-Hamann, Copenhagen 1960.

[11] 11 ... ♕a5 12 ♕c2 ♖fb8 13 ♗e2 ♕d8 14 ♕d2 ♘c7 15 ♗h6 ± Torre-Blackstock, London 1977. 12 ♕d2!?

[12] 13 ... ♖e8 14 ♕d2 ♘f8 15 ♖ad1 ♕b8 16 f4 ± Schmid-Poutiainen, Nice Ol 1974.

13 ... ♖b8 14 ♕d2 ♖e8 15 ♗g5 ± Kestler-Eising, Hamburg 1965.

[13] 14 ... e6 15 e5 de 16 de ♖xe6 17 ♕xd7 ef 18 ♗f2 ♖d8 19 ♕e7 ± Diez del Corral-Szabo, Palma de Mallorca 1969.

14 ... e5!? Westerinen.

[14] 8 ♗e3 ♗xf3 (8 ... ♘a6 9 ♖e1 ♖c8 10 d5! ♘c7 11 h3 ± Smyslov-Filipowicz, Polanica Zdroj 1966; 8 ... cd!? Tisdall) 9 ♗xf3 cd 10 ♗xd4 ♘c6 11 ♗e3 ♕a5 12 a3 ♘e5 13 ♗e2 ♖fc8 14 b4 ± Kapengut-Peev, Lublin 1973.

[15] 8 ... e6 9 de fe! 10 ♘g5 ♗xe2 11 ♘xe2 (11 ♕xe2 ± ECO) 11 ... ♕d7 12 ♘f4 (12 e5 ±) 12 ... ♖e8 13 e5 de 14 ♘fxe6 h6! ∓ Bednarski-

Timman, Tbilisi 1971.

8 ... a6 9 a4 ♘bd7 10 ♗g5 ♕c7 11 ♕d2 ♖ae8 12 h3 ♗xf3 13 ♗xf3 e6 14 b3 ± Karpov-Spassky, Leningrad (match) 1974.

[16] 9 ♘g5!? ♗xe2 10 ♕xe2 h6 11 ♘f3 ♘c7?! 12 ♖d1! ± Stein-Velimirović, USSR v Yugoslavia 1972. 11 ... ♖e8! intending 12 ... e6 = Stein.

9 ♗f4 ♘c7 10 a4 a6 11 a5 ♖b8 12 ♘e1 ♗xe2 13 ♕xe2 b5 14 ab ♖xb6 15 ♘d3 ± Hecht-Filipowicz, Bath 1973.

9 ♖e1!?

[17] 9 ... h6 10 ♗e3 (10 ♗h4 ♘c7 11 ♕d2 ♗xe2 12 ♕xe2 e5 13 de ♘xe6 14 ♖ad1 ♘d4 15 ♕d3 g5 16 ♗g3 ♘h5 = Jansa-Forintos, Sochi 1974) 10 ... ♘c7 11 ♖e1!? a6 12 ♕d2 ♔h7 13 e5 ♘d7 14 ed ed 15 ♗g5! ♘f6 16 ♗h4 ± Taimanov-Cobo, Havana 1967.

[18] 10 h3 ♗xf3 11 ♗xf3 a6 12 a4 ± Stahlberg-Orbaan, Beverwijk 1956.

[19] 12 ... a6 13 e5 f6 14 ed ed 15 ♗h4 ± Saborido-Bilek, Praia da Rocha 1969.

[20] 15 b3 ± Petrosian-Taimanov, USSR 1959.

[21] 7 ... ♘e5 8 ♘xe5 de 9 0-0 c6 10 ♗g5 h6 11 ♗e3 ♕c7 12 ♕d2 ♔h7 13 f3 ♘e8 14 ♖ad1 ♗d7 15 b4 ± Kluger-Sax, Hungarian Ch 1972.

7 ... ♘b4 8 0-0 ♗g4 9 ♗e3 c5 10 h3 ♗xf3 11 ♗xf3 ♘a6 12 ♕d2 ± Dorfman-Karasev, USSR 1975.

[22] 8 ♗g5 h6 9 ♗e3 c5 10 ♕d2 ♘a6 11 0-0 ♗d7 12 f4 ♕c8 13 h3 ± Najdorf-Cordovil, Siegen Ol 1970.

8 h3 e5 9 g4 c6 10 ♗e3 cd 11 cd a6 12 ♘d2 b5 13 h4 ± Furman-Milić, USSR v Yugoslavia 1957.

[23] 9 de ♗xe6 10 ♘d4 ♗d7 11 ♗e3 ♘c6 12 f3 a6 13 ♕d2 ♖e8 14 ♖ac1 ± Bukić-Lilienthal, Szombathely 1966.

9 ♕c2 c6 10 de ♗xe6 11 ♖d1 ♕e7 12 ♗f4 ♖d8 13 ♖d2 ± Schmid-Westerinen, Havana 1967.

[24] 15 ed ± Toran-Westerinen, Malaga 1967.

[25] 8 h3!? b5 9 e5 ♘e8 10 ♗f4 ♘d7 11 ♕d2 ♗b7 12 ed ed 13 ♖ad1 ± Hort-Westerinen, Nice Ol 1974.

8 ♖e1 b5 9 e5 ♘e8 10 ♗g5 ♖a7!? 11 ♗h4 ♖b7 12 cb? (12 c5!? Mecking) 12 ... ab 13 d5 b4! 14 dc ♘xc6 15 ♘d5 ♘a5! 16 ♖c1 ♗e6 17 ♘f4 ♗d7 ∓ Cooper-Petrosian, Nice Ol 1974.

8 ♘d2!? b5 9 e5 ♘fd7 (9 ... ♘e8!?) 10 ed ed 11 ♘de4! ♘b6 12 ♗g5 f6 13 ♗f4 d5 14 ed ± Lombardy-Westerinen, Torremolinos 1974.

8 a4 a5 9 h3 ♘a6 10 ♗e3 ♘d7 11 ♕d2 ♖e8 12 ♖ad1 ♕c7 13 ♘h2! e5 14 f4 ± Ungureanu-Taimanov, Bucharest 1973. 11 ... e5!?

[26] 15 b4 a5 16 a3 ab 17 ab bc 18 d5! ±/± .

[27] 7 d5 e6 8 0-0 ♖e8 9 ♗f4! ed 10 ed ♘e4 11 ♘xe4 ♖xe4 12 ♕d2 ± Sosonko-Keene, Hastings 1975/76.

[28] 11 ... e5 12 ♘e1 ♘e8 13 ♗e3 f5 14 f3 ♘f6 15 ♘d3 ± Troianescu-Bobotsov, Balatonfüred 1958.

[29] 15 b5 a5 16 h3 ± Kozma-Popov, Budapest 1960.

[30] 9 ... ♘bd7 10 0-0-0 (10 ♘d5 c6 11 ♘e7+ ♔h8 12 ♘xc8 ♖dxc8 13 ♘d2 ♘c5 = Flohr-Geller, USSR Ch 1949) 10 ... ♖f8 11 ♘e1 c6 12 ♘c2 ♘c5 13 f3 a5 14 b3 ♖fe8 15 ♖d2 ± ECO.

9 ... ♘a6!? 10 ♘d5 ♖d6 11 ♗xf6 ♗xf6 12 ♘xf6+ ♖xf6 13 a3 ♗g4 = Knežević-Zaitsev, Dubna 1976.

[31] 10 ♘d5!? ♘xd5 11 cd c6 12 ♗c4 b5 13 ♗b3 ♗b7 14 ♖c1 ♖c8 15 ♗e3 a5 = Schmidt-Uhlmann, Decin 1979.

[32] 11 ♗h4 ♘a6 12 ♘d2 c6 13 f3 ♘h5 14 ♗f2 ♘f4 15 ♗f1 ♗f8 = Pomar-Donner, Madrid 1960.

[33] 12 ... ♘g4 13 ♗xg4 ♗xg4 14 ♖d2 ♘d7 15 b3 ± Ritov-Antoshin, USSR 1962.

12 ... ♘bd7 13 ♘c2 ♘f8 14 ♖d2 ♘g4 15 ♗xg4 ♗xg4 16 b3 ± Ritov-Kalinsky, USSR 1967.

[34] 15 ♘c2 ♔g7 16 ♖d2 ♘d7 17 ♖hd1 ♘b6 18 ♔b2 ♘c5 19 g3 a5 = Nei-Tal, Tallinn 1973.

[35] Related lines with ♗e3 - Orthodox III.

[36] 9 ... ♘e8 10 c5 f5 11 f3 f4 (11 ... ♘f6 12 ♘c4 b6 13 cd cd 14 a4 ± Portisch-Jimenez, Havana 1964) 12 ♗f2 g5 13 ♘c4 ♘g6 14 ♖c1 ♖f7 15 ♕b3 ± Kozma-Sandor, Beverwijk II 1969.

9 ... ♘d7 10 b4 f5 11 f3 a5 12 ba ♖xa5 13 ♘b3 ♖a8 14 c5 ± Magerramov-Lechtynsky, Baku 1980.

[37] 10 a3 ♘e8 11 b4 f5 12 f3 b6 13 ♘b3 ♘f6 14 g4 ♘d7 15 h4 ♗e8 oo Bilek-Ivkov, Sarajevo 1962.

[38] 11 ♕c2 a6 12 f3 ♗d7 13 a4 b6 14 ♖b1 f5 = Gufeld.

[39] 11 ... f5 12 gf ♗xf6 13 h4 a6 14 h5 ± Petkević-A.Petrosian, USSR 1974.

[40] 13 a3 ♖b8 14 b4 b6 15 ♖b2 ± Taimanov-Stefanov, Kislovodsk 1966.

[41] 15 ♕xg4 b6 16 ♖b1 ± Portisch-Andersson, Siegen Ol 1970.

[42] 9 ♕c2 ♕e7 10 f3 c6 11 ♗f2 ♘h5 12 g3 ♘d7 13 0-0 ♘e5 14 ♖fe1 ♘f6 oo Simagin-Petrosian, USSR 1966.

[43] 15 g3 ♗h3 16 ♖fe1 ♘g7 (Taimanov-Stein, USSR Ch 1965) 17 ♘db5 ± Barden.

[44] 8 de de 9 ♘d5 ♘xd5 10 cd c6 11 d6 ♕e6 12 ♘g5 ♕e8 13 ♕d2 f6! 14 ♘f3 ♗e6 15 0-0 ♕f7 16 ♕a5! ♖c8 (Bukić-Ivanović, Yugoslavia 1978) 17 b4 ♗f8 18 ♖fd1 ♘d7 oo Ivanović.

[45] 10 ... a5 11 f3! Kristiansen.

[46] 11 h3 ♘h6 12 ♘d2 c5! = Kasparov-Chiburdanidze, Baku 1980.

[47] 15 ♕e2 ♘d7 16 ♗c2 ± Smejkal-Moles, Skopje Ol 1972.

Petrosian System	7	8	9	10	11	12	13	14	15	
1 d4 ♘f6 2 c4 g6 3 ♘c3 ♗g7 4 e4 d6 5 ♘f3 0-0 6 ♗e2 e5 7 d5										
1	...	♗e3	♗g5	♗h4[2]	♘d2	♗g3	ef	♘de4	♘xe4	=
	♘bd7	♘g4[1]	f6	♘h6[3]	g5	f5	♘f6	♘xe4	♗xf5[4]	
2	...	♗g5	♗h4	♘d2	g4[6]	f3[7]	♗f2	♖b1	0-0	±
	...	h6[5]	a5	♘c5	a4	c6	♕a5	♗d7	cd[8]	
3	...	...	...	0-0	♘d2![9]	b4	f3	♖c1	♔h1	±
	...	...	a6	♕e8	♘h7	♘g5[10]	f5[11]	♕e7	♘f6[12]	
4	...	...	...	♗g3	h4[14]	fg	♘xh4	♗g4	♗xc8	±
	...	...	g5	♘h5[13]	♘xg3	gh	♕g5	♘c5[15]	♖axc8[16]	
5	...	...	...	...	...	hg	♕c2	ef	♗xf4	±
	...	...	...	...	♘f4	hg	f5[17]	♘c5	♗xf5[18]	
6	...	...	...	...	...	♘h2[19]	fg	0-0	♗d3[22]	∞
	...	...	...	...	g4	♘xg3[20]	h5	♗h6[21]	♘c5[23]	
7	...	♗g5[24]	♗d2[25]	♕c1[27]	h4	♗xf4	♕xf4	♕d2		±
	c5	h6	♘h5[26]	♔h7	♘f4	gf	f5	♕e7[28]		
8	...	...	♗h4	♗g3	♘d2	0-0[29]	♕xe2	a3	f3	=
	...	...	g5	♘h5	♘f4	♘xe2+[30]	♘d7	♖e8	♘f8[31]	
9	...	0-0[32]	♗g5	♗h4	♘e1	♘d3	f3	b3[35]		=
	a5	♘a6	h6	♕e8	♗d7[33]	♘h7[34]	b6			
10	...	♗g5	♗h4	♘d2	0-0[38]	b3[39]	f3[40]	a3	♔h1!?[41]	±
	...	h6	♘a6[36]	♕e8[37]	♗d7	♘h7	h5	♗h6	♗e3[42]	

[1] 8 ... ♘c5 9 ♘d2 a5 10 a3 ♗d7 11 b4 ab 12 ab ♖xa1 13 ♕xa1 ♘a6 14 ♕a3 ± *ECO*.
    8 ... ♕e7 9 ♘d2 a5 10 a3 (10 0-0 ♘e8 – Ornstein-Savon, Erevan 1976 – 11 a3 f5 12 ef gf 13 f4 ∞) 10 ... ♘e8 11 b4 f5 12 f3 ± Savon.

[2] 10 ♗d2 f5 11 ef?! gf 12 ♘g5 ♘c5 13 b4 e4 14 bc e3 15 fe ♕xg5 ∓ Ungureanu-Gheorghiu, Bucharest 1967. 11 ♘g5 ∞ *ECO*.

[3] 10 ... h5 11 h3 ♘h6 12 g4 hg 13 hg g5 14 ♗g3 ♘xg4 15 ♘h2 ♘xh2 16 ♖xh2 ∞ Naranja-Planinc, Nice Ol 1974.

[4] 16 ♗d3 g4 17 ♕d2 ♗xe4 18 ♗xe4 ♘f5 19 ♕d3 ♕g5 = Mecking-Gligorić, Palma de Mallorca IZ 1970.

[5] 8 ... a5 9 ♘d2 h6 10 ♗e3 ♘e8 11 g4 (11 ♕c2 f5 12 f3 ♘c5 13 ♘b3 b6 14 ♘xc5 bc 15 0-0-0 ♕e7 16 ♗d3 f4 17 ♗d2 ± Visier-Olsson, Lugano Ol 1968) 11 ... b6 12 h4 ♘c5 13 h5 g5 14 f3 ♗d7 15 ♕c2 c6 16 0-0 cd 17 cd ♖c8 18 ♖fc1 ± Zinser-van Kleef, Strasbourg 1973.

[6] 11 b3 ♗d7 12 a3 ♕e8 13 ♖c1 ♘h7 14 b4 ab 15 ab ♘a6 16 ♕b3 ± Littlewood-Franklin, Hastings 1963/64.

[7] 12 h3 ♗d7 13 ♕c2 ♕b8 14 f3 ♕a7 15 ♗f2 ± Damjanović-Bertok, Zagreb 1959.

[8] 16 cd b5 17 a3 ± Mecking-Panno, Buenos Aires 1967.

[9] 11 ♘e1?! ♘h7! (11 ... ♘c5!? 12 ♕c2 ♘fxe4 13 ♘xe4 ♘xe4 14 ♕xe4 f5 15 ♕c2 g5 16 ♗g3 f4 17 ♗d3 e4 18 ♗xe4 ♕e5 19 ♖b1 fg 20 hg ♗g4 ∞ Neikirch-Tal, Portorož IZ 1958) 12 f3 f5 13 ♘d3 f4 14 b4 g5 15 ♗f2 h5 16 c5 ♕g6 17 ♖c1 ♘df6 ∓ Sanchez-Fischer, Mar del Plata 1959.

[10] 12 ... ♗f6 13 ♗xf6 ♘hxf6 14 ♘b3 ♕e7 15 ♕d2 ♔h7 16 ♕e3! ♘g8 17 c5 ± Tal-Fischer, Bled/Zagreb 1959.

[11] 13 ... ♗f6 14 ♗f2 ♗e7 13 ♕c2 f5 14 ♗d3 fe 17 ♘cxe4 ± Malich-Hesse, GDR Ch 1973.

[12] 16 c5 ♘h5 17 c6! b6 18 ef gf 19 g3 ♗f6 (19 ... ♗f6 20 f4 ef 21 gf ♘ge4 22 ♗h5! ± Petrosian) 20 f4 ♘g7 21 ♘c4 ef 22 gf b5 23 ♘d2 ♘e4 24 ♗xf6 ♖xf6 (Petrosian-Gligorić, Bled/Zagreb 1959) 25 ♘b3! ± Petrosian. 20 a4!? e4 21 f4 ± Matanović.

[13] 10 ... a5 11 ♘d2 c6 12 0-0 cd 13 cd ♘c5 (Tal-Portisch, Riga 1959) 14 f3 intending ♗f2 ±.
    10 ... ♘xe4 11 ♘xe4 f5 12 ♘fd2 fe 13 ♘xe4± Mikhalchishin-Kovacs, Debrecen 1967.
    10 ... ♘c5 11 ♘d2 a5 12 h4 ♘h7 13 ♘b3 ± Gligorić-Aloni, Netanya 1965.

[14] 11 0-0 ♘f4 12 ♘e1 ♘xe2+ 13 ♕xe2 f5 14 ef ♘f6 15 ♘d3 ♗xf5 16 f3 ♕e8 = Boleslavsky.

[15] 14 ... ♕e3+?! 15 ♕e2 ♕xg3+ 16 ♔d1 ± Ivkov-Timman, Wijk aan Zee 1972.
    14 ... ♘f6 15 ♗xc8 ♖xg3+ 16 ♔f1 ♖fxc8 17 ♘f5 ± Addison-Saidy, New York 1965/66.

[16] 16 ♘f5 ♘h7 17 ♕f3 ♖g8 18 ♖h5 ♕f6 19 g4 ± Ivkov-Suetin, Yugoslavia v USSR 1967.

[17] 13 ... ♘xe4 14 ♕xe2 f5 15 ef ♘c5 16 ♘d2 ± Ilivitsky-Nezhmetdinov, USSR 1965.

13 ... ♘xg2+ 14 ♔d2 ♘f4 (14 ... g4 15 ♖ag1 gf 16 ♗xf3 ♘f4 17 ♗xf4 ef 18 e5 f5 19 ef ♘xf6 20 ♕g6 ±± Kanko-Littlewood, Havana Ol 1966; 14 ... ♕f6 15 ♖ag1 ♘f4 16 ♘xg5 ±± Kottnauer-Linton, 1970) 15 ♗xf4 gf 16 ♖ag1 ± Gligorić.

13 ... ♘c5 14 b4 ♘a6 15 a3 c5 16 dc bc 17 0-0-0 ±.

[18] 16 ♗xg5 ♗xc2 17 ♗xd8 ♖axd8 18 ♔d2 ♗g6 19 ♖af1 ± Brinck Claussen-Larrain, Havana Ol 1966.

[19] 12 ♘d2 f5 13 ef ♘df6 (13 ... ♘xg3 14 fg ♘c5 15 0-0 ♗xf5 16 ♖xf5 ♗xf5 17 ♗xg4 ♖f8 18 ♘de4 ∓ Wright-Huss, England 1973) 14 ♗xg4 ♘xg3 15 fg ♘xg4 16 ♕xg4 ♗xf5 17 ♕e2 e4 18 0-0 ♕d7 19 ♕e3 c5 ∞ Hort-Vogt, Leipzig 1973.

[20] 12 ... f5 13 ef ♘xg3 14 fg ♘c5 15 ♘xg4 ♗xf5 16 0-0 ♕e7 17 ♕d2 ♗xg4 18 ♗xg4 e4 19 ♖xf8+! ♖xf8 20 ♖e1 ± Bukić-Gligorić, Budva 1967.

[21] 14 ... a5 15 ♗d3 ♘c5 16 ♕e2 ♗d7 17 ♖f2 f6 18 ♘f1 ♗h6 19 ♘e3 ♗xe3 20 ♕xe3 ± Yurkov-Korzin, USSR 1965.

[22] 15 ♗xg4!? hg 16 ♘xg4 ♗g7 17 ♕f3 ♘c5 (17 ... f5 18 ef ♘f6 19 ♘xf6+ ∞) 18 ♘e3 a5 19 ♖ad1 ∞ Milić.

[23] 15 ... c6 16 ♔h1 ♘f6 17 ♗c2 ± Keres-Walther, Tel Aviv Ol 1964.

15 ... ♘f6 16 ♕e2 ♗d7 17 ♖f2 ♘e8 18 ♘f1 ♗g7 19 ♘e3 ± Ziembinski-Stilling, corr. 1974.

15 ... ♘c5 16 ♗c2 a5 17 ♕e2 f6 18 ♖f2 (Hort-Janošević, Wijk aan Zee 1970) 18 ... ♗d7 ∞ Hort.

[24] 8 0-0 ♘e8 9 ♘e1 ♘d7 10 ♘d3 f5 11 ef gf 12 f4 ♕e7 13 ♔h1 e4 14 ♘e1 ♘df6 15 ♘c2 ♕f7 16 ♘e3 ♕g6 = Gligorić-Quinteros, Leningrad IZ 1973.

[25] 9 ♗e3?! ♘g4 10 ♘d2 f5 11 ef ♗xf5 12 0-0 e4 13 ♘g5 ♘xh2 ∓ Hamann-Holmov, Kislovodsk 1966.

9 ♗xf6?! ♗xf6 10 h4 a6 11 h5 ♗g7 12 ♕d2 ♖h8 13 ♘d1 ♗g4 14 ♘e3 ♗xf3 15 ♗xf3 ♘d7 16 ♗g4 ♗g5 ∓ Naranja-Gheorghiu, Manila 1974.

[26] 9 ... ♘e8 10 ♕c1! ♔h7 11 h4 f5 12 h5 ±.

9 ... ♘bd7 10 ♕c1 ♔h7 11 h4 ♖h8 12 ♘h2 h5 13 ♘f3 ♔g8 14 a3 ± Poch-Najdorf, Mar del Plata 1971.

9 ... ♔h7 10 ♕c2 a6 11 a3 ♘h5 12 g3 ♗h3 13 ♖f2 ♘d7!? ± ECO.

[27] 10 g3!? ♘d7 11 ♕c2 ♘df6 12 h3 ♗d7 13 a4 ♕e7? 14 ♘h4! ± Larsen-Quinteros, Mar del Plata 1981. 10 ... ♗h3!?, 13 ... ♕c8!? Larsen.

[28] 14 ... fe?! Portisch-Stein, Amsterdam 1964.
14 ... ♕e7?! ± Euwe.

[29] 12 ♔f1!? ♘d7 13 ♗g4 ♘df6 14 ♗xc8 ♖xc8 15 h4 g4 16 ♔g1 ± Kapengut-Abramisov, USSR 1966.

[30] 12 ... a6 13 a3 ♘d7 14 b4 b6 15 ♖b1 f5 16 ef ♘xe2+ 17 ♕xe2 ♘f6 18 bc bc 19 h4 ± Bobotsov-Barcza, Sochi 1966.

12 ... ♘d7 13 ♗g4 ♘f6 14 ♗xc8 ♕xc8 15 ♖e1 ♘g6 16 ♘f1 ± Furman-Zhidkov, USSR 1962.

[31] 16 ♗f2 ♘g6 17 g3 ♘e7 18 b4 b6 19 ♖fb1 f5 = Ivkov-Korchnoi, Havana 1963.

[32] 8 ♗e3 ♘g4 9 ♗g5 f6 10 ♗h4 ♘a6 (10 ... ♕e8!? 11 ♘d2 f5 12 h3 ♘f6 13 g4 ♘xe4 14 ♘dxe4 fe 15 ♘xe4 ♘a6 16 f3 ∞ Durić-Tringov, Vrnjačka Banja 1975; 10 ... ♗h6 11 ♘d2 ♘f7! = Hort) 11 ♘d2 ♘h6 12 f3 ♗d7 13 0-0 ♘f7 14 ♘b3 b6 15 ♘c1 ♘c5 16 ♘d3 ♕e8 17 b3 f5 = Gligorić-Geller, Belgrade 1970.

[33] 11 ... g5!? 12 ♗g3 ♘xe4 13 ♗xe4 f5 14 ♗h5 ♕e7 15 f3 fe 16 fe ♖xf1+ 17 ♔xf1 ♘c5 =.

[34] 12 ... b6 13 b3 (13 f3 ♘h5! = ECO) 13 ... ♘c5 14 ♘xc5 bc 15 ♖b1 ♘h7 16 f3 f5 17 ♗f2 = Polugayevsky-Uhlmann, Palma de Mallorca IZ 1970.

[35] Intending a3, b4 ECO.

[36] 9 ... g5 10 ♗g3 ♘h5 11 h4! g4 12 ♘d2 ♘xg3 13 fg h5 14 0-0 ♗h6 15 ♗d3 ± Mecking-Cuellar, Sousse IZ 1967.

[37] 10 ♗d7 11 g4 ♕e8 12 ♗g3 ♘h7 13 h4 ♘c5 14 h5 ♗g5 15 hg fg 16 b3 ♕e7 17 a3 ± Planinc-Bogdanović, Yugoslav Ch 1968.

10 ... ♕d7 11 a3 ♘h7 12 f3 f5 13 b4 ab 14 ab ♖b8 15 ♖b1 ♘f6 16 ♗f2 ♕e7 17 b5! ± Petrosian-Lutikov, USSR Ch 1961.

[38] 11 g4?! ♘h7 12 ♘f1 ♘g5 13 h3 ♕e7! 14 ♗g3 f5 ∓ Ornstein-Uhlmann, Polanica Zdroj 1975.

11 a3 ♗d7 12 b3 ♘h7 13 f3 h5 14 ♗f2 ♗h6 15 ♖b1 ♕e7 (15 ... f5 16 b4 ab 17 ab ± Bukić-Suradiradja, Stip 1976) 16 b4 ab 17 ab ± Hort-Vukić, Novi Sad 1976.

[39] 12 a3?! a4 13 ♘b5 ♗xb5 14 cb ♘c5 15 ♕c2 ♘fd7 16 f3 h5 ∓ Rubinetti-Panno, Palma de Mallorca IZ 1970.

12 ♖c1 ♘h7 13 ♘b5 h5 14 f3 ♗h6 15 ♖c3 f6 = Antoshin-Bogdanović, Sarajevo 1970.

12 ♔h1 ♘h7 13 f3 h5 14 ♘b3 b6 15 ♘c1 ♗h6 16 ♘d3 ♗e3 17 ♖e1 ♘c5 = Petrosian-Hort, Lugano Ol 1968.

[40] 13 ♖b1 h5 14 h3?! ♗h6 15 a3 ♘c5 16 b4 ab 17 ab ♘a4 18 ♘xa4 ♖xa4 ∓ Bukić-Geller, Budva 1967.

[41] 15 ♖b1 ♗e3+ 16 ♗f2 ♘c5!? 17 ♗xc5 ♘xc5 18 b4 ab 19 ab ♘a4 = Antoshin-Chiburdanidze, Baku 1980.

15 ♗f2 ♕e7 16 ♕c2 h4 17 ♖fd1 f5 18 ♖ab1 ♕g5 19 b4 ab 20 ab ♘f6 = Petrosian-Stein, USSR 1967.

[42] 16 ♖b1 ♘c5 17 ♕c2 f5 18 b4 ab 19 ab ♘a4 20 ef ± Zlotnik-Yuferov, USSR 1980.

135

	7	8	9	10	11	12	13	14	15	
1	...	♘xd4	f3[1]	♔h1[3]	cd	♗g5!	fe	♘db5!	♗f4	±
	ed	♖e8	c6[2]	d5	cd	de[4]	♘bd7	♖e5!	♘xe4[5]	
2	...	...	...	♗e3	♕d2	♖ad1	h3	a4	♘c2	±
	...	...	♘c6	♘e5[6]	c6	♕c7[7]	a6	♕a5	♗e6[8]	
3	...	♖e1	♘xd4	♗f1	h3[9]	hg	g5	♗e3[11]	♕d2	±
	c6	ed	♖e8	♘g4	♕f6[10]	♕xd4	♘d7	♕e5[12]	♕e7[13]	
4	...	d5	♘e1![15]	♗g5	♗h4	a3	b4	♕b3	ab	±
	...	c5[14]	♘bd7[16]	h6	a6	♕c7	b5	cb	bc[17]	
5	...	...	cd	♗g5	♗h4	♗g3	♘d2	♘c4![20]	f3	±
	...	cd	♘bd7[18]	h6	g5[19]	♘h5	♘f4	♘f6	♕e7[21]	
6	...	♗e3	♗xd4[22]	♕c2	♖ad1	♖fe1	♗e3	♘b5	♗f4	∞
	...	ed	♖e8	♘bd7[23]	♕e7	c5[24]	♘xe4	♘df6	♗f5[25]	
7	...	♗e3[26]	d5	♗g5	♗h4	♘d2	♗xg4	f3	♕xf3	±
	♘bd7	♖e8	♘g4	f6	♘f8	h5	hg	gf	♘h7[27]	
8	...	...	♗g5	♗d2[28]	♕c2	♘xd4	♖ad1	♕c1	ef	±
	...	♘g4	f6	♘h6[29]	ed	♘e5	f5	♘hf7	gf[30]	
9	...	...	♕c2	♖ad1	d5	dc	♕d2	b3	♗xc5	±
	...	c6	♖e8	♕c7	a6[31]	bc	♖b8	♘c5	dc[32]	
10	...	...	...	♗g5	♗h4[34]	de	b4	a3	c5	±
	...	...	♘g4	f6[33]	♘h6	de	♕e7	♘f7	♖e8[35]	
11	...	...	d5	♘e1	♘d3	♕b3	a4	♖ae1	♔h1	±
	...	...	c5[36]	♘e8[37]	♘b6	a5	♘d7	♕e7	♔h8[38]	
12	...	...	♕c2[39]	♗g5	♗h4[40]	♖ad1	a3	♗g3	♖fe1	±
	...	a5	♘g4	f6	c6[41]	♕e7	♘h6	♘f7	♖e8[42]	

[1] 9 ♕c2?! ♘xe4 10 ♘xe4 ♗xd4 11 ♗g5 f6 12 ♖ad1 fg 13 ♖xd4 ♗f5 14 c5 ♘c6 15 ♗c4+ ♔g7 16 ♕c3 ♘xd4 17 ♖xd4+ ♘h6 ∓∓ Rosetto-Larsen, Amsterdam IZ 1964.

[2] 9 ... ♘bd7 10 ♗g5 c6 11 ♕d2 ♕b6 12 ♗e3 ♕c7 13 ♖ac1 ♘b6 14 ♖fd1 ± Rellstab-Najdorf, Bled 1950.

[3] 10 ♘c2 d5 11 cd cd 12 ed ♗f5 (12 ... ♕b6+ 13 ♔h1 ♘a6 14 ♗e3!! ♕xb2 15 ♗d4 ± Hort-Barczay, Dortmund 1982; 14 ... ♖xe3 15 ♘a4) 13 ♗c4 ♕b6+ 14 ♔h1 ♘a6 ∞ Botez-Gheorghiu, Romanian Ch 1966.

[4] 12 ... ♘c6 13 ♗b5! ♕b6 14 ♘xc6 bc 15 ♗xf6 ♗xf6 16 ♘xd5 cd 17 ♗xe8 ± Tal.

[5] 16 ♗xe5 ♗xe5 17 ♘xe4 ♕h4 18 h3! ♕xe4 19 ♕b3! ± Tal-Spassky, Montreal 1979.

[6] 10 ... ♘d7!?

[7] 12 ... ♕e7 13 ♖fe1 ± Cobo-Pietzsch, Salgotarjan 1967.

[8] 16 b3 ± Aloni-Domnitz, Netanya 1968.

[9] 11 ♖e2 ♕f6 12 ♘f3 ♕e5 13 ♘xe5 de 14 ♗e3 ♘d7 15 ♖d2 ♘f8 16 c5 ♘e6 17 ♕a4 ♕e7 18 b4 ♘d4 ∓ Averbakh-Suetin, Budapest 1970.
    11 ♘f3 ♕b6 12 ♕c2 a6 13 h3 ♘e5 14 ♘xe5 de 15 ♗e3 ♕d8 = Zaichik-Djurić, Tbilisi 1980.

[10] 11 ... ♕b6 12 hg ♗xd4 13 ♕d2! intending ♘a4 ± Rashkovsky.

[11] 14 ♗f4 ♕xd1 15 ♖axd1 ♘e5 16 ♗e3 ♘c5 = Smyslov-Geller, Zürich C 1953.
    14 ♕xd4 ♗xd4 15 ♗f4 ♘e5 16 ♗d2 ♘c5 17 f3 ♗e6 = Taimanov-Keene, Hastings 1975/76.

[12] 14 ... ♕xd1?! 15 ♖axd1 ♗e5 16 f4 ♗xc3

17 bc ♖xe4 18 ♖xd6 ± Rashkovsky.

[13] **15 ... ♘b6?!** 16 ♗f4 ♕d4 17 ♕xd4 ♗xd4 18 ♗xd6 ♗e6 19 ♖ad1 ♗xc3 20 bc ♗xc4 21 ♗xc4 ♘xc4 22 ♗c5! ± Rashkovsky-Szabo, Sochi 1973.

15 ... ♕e7 16 ♖ad1 ♘c5 17 f3!? ± Euwe.

[14] 8 ... a5 9 ♗g5 h6 10 ♗h4 ♘a6 11 ♕d2 ♘c5 12 b3 ♗d7 13 f3 ♖c8 14 ♖c1 ♕e8 15 a3 ± Goldenberg-Cruz, Argentina 1961.

[15] 9 ♗g5 h6 10 ♗h4 ♕b6 11 ♘d2 ♗d7 12 ♖b1 a5 13 a3 ♘a6 14 ♕c2 ♖fb8 15 b3 ♕d8 = Gligorić-Donner, Madrid 1960.

[16] **9 ... ♘e8** 10 ♘d3 f5 11 f4 ♘d7 12 ♗e3 ♕e7 13 ef gf 14 fe ♘xe5 15 ♘xe5 ♗xe5 16 ♕d2 ± van Scheltinga-Toran, Beverwijk 1957.

9 ... a6 10 ♗g5 h6 11 ♗e3! ♘bd7 12 a3 ♘e8 13 ♕d2 ♔h7 14 ♘d3 ± Trifunović-Toran, Palma de Mallorca 1966.

[17] 16 ♗xc4 ± Donner-Kurajica, Wijk aan Zee 1970.

[18] **9 ... ♘a6** 10 ♘d2 ♘e8 11 ♘c4 f5 12 f3 f4 13 a4 g5 14 ♘b5 ♖f6 15 g4! fg 16 ♗xg5 ♕d7! 17 hg ♖g6 18 ♗h4 ♗f6 19 ♔f2! ± Hübner-Kaplan, Houston 1974.

9 ... ♘e8 10 a4 h6 11 a5 f5 12 ef gf 13 g3 ♘a6 14 ♘h4 f4 15 ♖a3 ♗h3 16 ♗g4 ± Korchnoi-Suetin, USSR Ch 1967.

[19] 11 ... a5 12 ♘d2 ♘c5 13 f3 ♗d7 14 ♗f2 ♘e8 15 a4 ♖c8 16 ♖a3 ± Cafure-R.Garcia, Argentina 1965.

[20] 14 ♗g4? ♘c5 15 ♗xc8 ♖xc8 16 ♘b3 ♘cd3 17 ♗xf4 ♗xb2! ∓∓ Donner-Olafsson, Beverwijk 1961. 17 ♕b1 (± Euwe) 17 ... ♘xb2! ∓∓ Tisdall.

[21] 16 ♗f2 ♗d7 17 a4 ± Geller-Puig, Oberhausen 1961.

[22] 9 ♘xd4 ♖e8 10 f3 d5 11 cd cd 12 ♕b3 de 13 ♗c4 ♖f8 14 ♖ad1 ♕e7 15 fe ♘c6 = Nei-Stein, USSR Ch 1967.

[23] 10 ... ♕e7 11 ♖fe1 c5!? intending 12 ♗e3 ♘xe4 13 ♘xe4 ♕xe4 14 ♕d2 ∞ Tal.

[24] 12 ... ♘e5 13 h3! ♘h6 14 b4 b6 15 c5! bc 16 ♘xe5 de 17 ♗xc5 ♕b7 18 ♘a4 ± Tal-Dvoretsky, USSR Ch 1974.

[25] 16 ♘h4 ♗d7 17 ♗xd6 ♘xd6 18 ♘xd6 ♖eb8 ∞/± Vlam-Scheeren, Wijk aan Zee II 1982.

[26] 8 d5 ♘c5 9 ♕c2 a5 10 ♗g5 (10 ♘d2/ 10 ♗h6 =) 10 ... h6 11 ♗e3 b6 12 ♘d2 h5! ∞.

[27] 16 ♗f2 f5 (16 ... ♕e7!? Gligorić) 17 ♕g3 f4? (17 ... ♘f8 ±) 18 ♕xg6 ♔h8 19 ♗h4 ± Najdorf-Geller, Moscow 1967.

[28] 10 ♗h4 ♘h6 11 ♗g3 ♘f7 12 ♕c2 ♘g5 13 ♘xg5 fg 14 de ♘xe5 15 c5 ± Bukić-Marović, Yugoslavia 1968.

[29] 10 ... c6 11 h3 ♘h6 12 b4 f5 13 ♗g5 ♕e8 14 d5 ♘f7 15 ♗c1 ♘f6 16 ♘g5 ± Reshevsky-R.Byrne, Sousse IZ 1967.

[30] 16 ♕c2 ± Spassov-Sahović, Vrnjačka Banja 1976.

[31] 11 ... c5 12 ♘e1 ♘f8!? Commons.

[32] 16 ♘e1 ♕e7 17 ♕d6 ± Shamkovich-I.Zaitsev, USSR 1968.

[33] **10 ... ♕e8** 11 de de 12 b4 f5 13 c5 h6 14 ♗d2 f4 15 ♖ad1 ± Simagin-Udovčić, USSR v Yugoslavia 1961.

10 ... ♕b6 11 h3 f6 12 ♗d2 ♘h6 13 ♗e3 ♕c7 14 ♕d2 ♘f7 15 ♖fd1 ± Timman-Ree, Holland 1972.

[34] 11 ♗d2 f5 (11 ... a5 12 ♖ad1 ♕e7 13 h3 ♘h6 14 c5 dc 15 de fe 16 ♗g5 ♕e8 17 ♘a4 ± Reshevsky-Stein, Sousse IZ 1967) 12 ♗g5 (12 ef ed! 13 ♘xd4 ♗xd4 14 ♗xg4 ♘e5 15 ♗h3 ♕h4 16 ♘e2 ♗b6 ∓ Möhring-Plachetka, Trnava 1979) 12 ... ♕e8 (12 ... ♗f6!?) 13 de ♘dxe5 14 ♘xe5 ♕xe5 15 ♗xg4 fg ∓ Adamski-Möhring, Rzeszow 1980.

[35] 16 ♘d2 ♘f8 17 ♘b3 ± Ivkov-Janošević, Wijk aan Zee 1970.

[36] 9 ... cd 10 cd ♘g4 (10 ... a6 11 ♘d2 ♘e8 12 ♕c2 f5 13 f3 ♕h4 14 a4 ♗h6 15 ♗f2 ± Unzicker-Kottnauer, Aibling 1968) 11 ♗g5 f6 12 ♗h4 h5 13 ♘d2 ♘h6 14 f3 ♘f7 15 ♗f2 ♗h6 16 ♘c4 ± Hort-Herink, Havirov 1970.

[37] 10 ... ♔h8 11 ♘d3 ♘g8 12 ♕d2 f5 13 ef gf 14 f4 e4 15 ♘f2 ± Grigorov-Ermenkov, Bulgarian Ch 1975.

[38] 16 ♕c2 b6 17 ♗d2 ♘c7 18 ♗d1 ±⁻Miles-Sigurjonsson, Amsterdam 1976.

[39] 9 de!? de 10 ♕c2 ♘g4 11 ♗d2! c6 12 ♘a4 h6 13 h3 ♘gf6 14 ♗e3 ± Uhlmann-Knaak, Leipzig 1980.

[40] 11 ♗d2 ed 12 ♘xd4 ♘c5 13 ♘b3 (13 h3 f5! 14 hg ♗xd4 15 ef gf 16 ♗h6 fg! ∓ intending 17 ♗xf8 g3 ∞ Miles-Cramling, Gausdal 1980) 13 ... ♘xb3 14 ab f5 15 ♗xg4 fg 16 ♘d5 c6 17 ♘e3 ♗e6 18 ♗c3 ♗e5 = R.Byrne-Vukčević, USA 1969.

[41] **11 ... g5?!** 12 ♗g3 ♘h6 13 ♘b5 ♘f7 14 ♖ad1 ♖e8 15 c5! ± Hort-Bertok, Vinkovci 1968.

11 ... ♘h6 12 ♖ad1 g5 13 ♗g3 f5 14 ef ed 15 ♘xd4 ± Bukić-Ničevski, Yugoslavia 1980.

[42] Hort. 15 ... ♕d8?! 16 ♗f1 ♖e8 17 h3 ♕b6 (Hort-Bukić, Skopje 1968) 18 c5! ±.

137

Classical II	1 d4 ♘f6 2 c4 g6 3 ♘c3 ♗g7 4 e4 d6 5 ♘f3 0-0 6 ♗e2 e5 7 0-0 ♘bd7							
8	**9**	**10**	**11**	**12**	**13**	**14**	**15**	**16**

	8	9	10	11	12	13	14	15	16	
1	♖e1	♘xd4	f3	♘db5	♗e3	♘xb5	♕d2	♖ad1	♗f1	±
	ed[1]	♘c5	a5[2]	♗d7	♗xb5	♕e7	a4	♖fd8	♘e8[3]	
2	...	♗f1	h3	♘xd4	hg	♗e3	♖xe3	♗e2	b3[5]	±
	c6	♕b6!?	ed	♘g4	♗xd4[4]	♗xe3	♘e5	♗e6		
3	...	...	♖b1	b3?!	♘xd4	f3	cd	ed	♕xe1	=
	...	a5	♖e8	ed	♘c5[6]	d5	♘xd5	♖xe1	♗xd4+[7]	
4	...	...	...	d5	♘d2	♘b3[10]	♖xc1	♕xb3	g3	±
	...	...	...	♘c5[8]	♗h6[9]	♗xc1	♘xb3	c5	♘h5[11]	
5	...	...	...	...	b3	dċ[12]	♕c2[14]	♗a3[15]	♖bd1	±
	...	...	...	...	♗d7	♗xc6[13]	♖c8	♕b6	♖cd8[16]	
6	...	...	...	♘xd4	♗f4[17]	f3!	cd	ed	♕xe1	±
	...	...	ed	♖e8	♘c5	d5	♘xd5	♖xe1	♗xd4+[18]	

[1] **8...** ♘g4?! 9 h3 (9 ♗g5 f6 10 ♗h4 g5 11 ♗g3 ♘h6 12 ♕d2 ♘f7 13 ♖ad1 g4 14 ♘h4 ed 15 ♘b5! ± Bilek-G.Garcia, Havana 1965) 9... ed 10 ♘xd4 ♗xf2 11 ♔xf2 ♕h4+ 12 ♔f1 f5 13 ♘f3 fe 14 ♕d5+ ± *ECO*.
8... ♖e8 9 d5 a5 10 ♗g5 h6 11 ♗h4 g5 12 ♗g3 ♘h5 13 ♘d2 ♘f4 14 ♗g4 ♘c5 15 ♗xc8 ♕xc8 16 ♘f1 ± Najdorf-Andersson, Wijk aan Zee 1971.
8... h6 9 ♕c2! ♘h7 10 de de 11 ♗e3 ♖e8 12 ♖ad1 ± Andersson-Kasparov, Moscow IZ 1982.

[2] **10...** ♘h5?! 11 ♗e3 ♗e5 12 g3 ♗g7 13 ♕d2 ± Taimanov-Nezhmetdinov, USSR Ch 1957.
10... c6 11 ♗e3 ♖e8 12 ♘c2 ♕e7 13 ♕d2 ♘e6 14 ♖ad1 ♗f8 15 ♗h6 ± Kottnauer-Benko, Gastein 1948.
10... ♖e8 11 ♗e3 ♘fd7 12 ♕d2 ♘f8 13 b4 ♘ce6 14 ♘b3 ♘d7 15 ♖ad1 ± Najdorf-Bolbochan, Buenos Aires 1965.

[3] Taimanov-Kestler, Hamburg 1965.

[4] 12... ♕xd4 13 ♕xd4!? (13 g5 ♕e5 14 ♗e3 f6!? 15 ♕d2 fg 16 ♖ad1! g4 17 ♗d4! ♕xd4 18 ♕xd4 ♗xd4 19 ♖xd4 ± Ftacnik-Vogt, Tallinn 1981; 17 ♕xd6? ♕e8! ∓ Vilela-Vogt, Halle 1981) 13... ♗xd4 14 ♗h6 ♖e8 15 ♖ad1 ± Stean.

[5] Timman-Hug, Haifa Ol 1976.

[6] 12... ♘g4!? 13 f3 ♕b6 14 ♘e2 ♘ge5 15 ♗e3 ♘c5 16 ♘g3 h5 ∞ Portisch-Donner, Varna 1958.

[7] 17 ♗e3 ♕f6 18 ♗xd4 ♕xd4+ 19 ♔h1 ♗d7 20 ♖d1 ♕b4 = Dzhindzhihashvili-Kivlan, USSR 1975.

[8] 11... c5 12 a3 ♘g4 13 ♗g5 f6 14 ♗h4 g5 15 ♗g3 ♘f8 16 ♘d2 ♘g6 17 ♗d3 ♘f4 18 ♘f1 f5 19 ♗c2 ± Furman-S.Garcia, Madrid 1973.

[9] 12... ♗g4 13 f3 ♗d7 14 ♘b3 ♗xb3 15 ♕xb3 c5 16 ♗g5 h6 17 ♗h4 ± Korchnoi-Geller, USSR Ch 1967.
12... ♗d7 13 b3 ♕b8 14 a3 cd 15 cd ♖c8 16 ♕f3 ♘e8 17 ♗b5 ± Hort-Minić, Varna 1969.

[10] 13 b3 ♖f8 14 a3 ♘cd7 15 b4 ab 16 ab c5 17 ♘b5 ♘e8 = Sofrevski-Vasyukov, Skopje 1970.

[11] 17 ♘b5 f5 18 ef ♗xf5 19 ♕e3 ± Cvetković-Honfi, Belgrade 1977.

[12] 13 ♗g5 h6 14 ♗d2 ♖f8 15 a3 cd 16 cd b5 (16... a4 17 ba! ± Malich) 17 b4 ab 18 ab ♘a4 19 ♘xb5 ♘g4! ∞ Malich-Knaak, East German Ch 1975.

[13] 13... bc 14 h3 ♕c7 15 ♗a3 ♘h5 16 ♘a4! ♗f8 17 ♘xc5 dc 18 ♕d2 ♘g7 19 ♖bd1 ± Popov-Knaak, Polanica Zdroj 1976. 14... ♗f8!?

[14] 14 ♗d3!? Csom.

[15] 15 ♗g5 ± Csom.

[16] 17 ♕b1 ♗h6 18 h3 ♖f8 19 ♘d2 ♖c8 20 ♖c1 ± Knaak-Möhring, Leipzig 1975.

[17] **12 h3?!** ♘c5 13 f3 ♘h5 14 ♗e3 ♗e5 15 ♕d2 ♕f6 16 ♘ce2 ♘g3! ∓ *ECO*.
12 f3 d5 13 cd ♘xd5 (13... cd 14 ♘db5 ±) 14 ♔h1 ♗xc3 15 bc ♘c5 16 ♗e3 ♗f8! = *ECO*.

[18] 17 ♗e3 ♗xe3+ 18 ♕xe3 ± Tal-Grigorian, USSR Ch 1977.

	8	9	10	11	12	13	14	15	16	
1	d5	♘d2	b4	f3	c5	♘c4	a4[2]	♗a3	b5	±
	♘e7	♘d7	f5	♘f6	f4[1]	g5	♘g6	♖f7	♗f8[3]	
2	...	...	♖b1[5]	b4	a4[6]	a5	♕a4	♕a3	♗d1	=
	...	c5[4]	♘e8	b6	f5	♔h8	♗d7	♘g8	♘ef6[7]	
3	...	♗d2	♖c1[9]	♘g5	♘e6	de	c5[10]	cd	♘b5	±
	...	♘e8[8]	f5	h6	♗xe6	♕c8	♕xe6	cd	♕d7[11]	
4	...	b4	g3[13]	♘g5	f3	c5	hg	♘e6	de	=
	...	♘h5[12]	f5	♘f6	f4[14]	fg	h6	♗xe6	d5[15]	
5	...	♘e1	f3	g4[16]	♘d3[18]	♘f2	♗d2	a3	♖b1	=
	...	♘d7	f5	♘f6[17]	c6	♔h8	a5	♗d7!	♕b8[19]	
6	...	...	♘d3	♗d2[20]	f3	c5	cd	♘f2	♕c2	∞
	...	...	f5	♘f6[21]	f4	g5	cd	♘g6	h5[22]	
7	...	...	...	...	...	...	♕c2[23]	♖fc1	cd	±
	...	...	...	...	...	...	♘g6	♖f7	cd[24]	

[1]   12 ... a5 13 ba dc 14 ♘c4 ♗d7 15 ♖b1 ♘c8 16 ♗e3 ± Geller-I.Zaitsev, USSR Ch 1969.

[2]   **14 ♕b3** ♘g6 15 ♗a3 ± Stein-Sahović, Vrnjačka Banja 1971.
14 ♗a3!?

[3]   **17 a5!?** Bukić-Marjanović, Yugoslavia 1970.
17 b6! Fedorowicz.

[4]   **9 ... ♗d7** 10 b4 c6 11 ♗a3 a6 12 dc ♗xc6 13 ♖e1 b5 14 ♗f1 ♕b6 15 ♘b3 ± Korchnoi-I.Zaitsev, USSR Ch 1970.
9 ... a5!?

[5]   10 dc bc 11 b4 d5 12 ♗a3 a6! = Keene-Quinteros, Haifa Ol 1976.

[6]   12 bc bc 13 ♘b3 f5 14 f3 ♔h8 15 ♗d2 ♘g8 = Stein-Panno, Las Palmas 1973.

[7]   17 ♗a4 ♗h6 18 bc bc 19 ♖xd7 ♕xd7 20 ef gf = Ree-Gligorić, Wijk aan Zee 1975.

[8]   **9 ... c5** 10 dc bc 11 ♗g5! ♗e6 (11 ... c5 12 ♕d3! ±) 12 c5 ♘e8 13 cd ♘xd6 14 ♕a4 f6 15 ♗e3 ♕c7 16 ♖ac1 ± Korchnoi-Byrne, Leningrad IZ 1973. 11 ... ♕c7 ±.
9 ... ♘d7 10 b4 f5 11 ef gf 12 ♕b3 ♘f6 13 c5 ♔h8 = Kozma-Uhlmann, Leipzig 1975.

[9]   10 b4 f5 11 ♕b3 ♘f6 12 ef gf (12 ... ♘xf5!?) 13 c5 ♔h8 14 cd cd 15 ♖ac1 ♗d7 16 a4 a6 = Boleslavsky.

[10]   14 ♕b3 c6 15 f4 ± Ftacnik-Georgiev, Gröningen 1976/77.

[11]   17 ♗b4 ♘c6 18 ♗xd6 ± Geller-Minić, Skopje 1968.

[12]   **9 ... ♘e8** 10 c5 h6 11 ♘d2 f5 12 ♘c4 ♘f6 13 f3 f4 14 a4 g5 15 ♗a3 ♘g6 16 b5 ♘e8 17 a5 ♖f7 18 b6 ± Smyslov-Ciocâltea, Sochi 1963.
9 ... a5!? 10 ba c5!? 11 ♘d2 ♕xa5 12 ♘b5 ♕d8 13 ♗b2 ♘e8 14 a4 ♗h6 15 ♖a3 f5 ∞ Sosonko-Ligterink, IBM 1979. 11 ♗d2!?
9 ... ♘d7 10 c5! dc 11 bc ♘xc5 12 ♗a3 ∞∞ Liebert-Postler, East German Ch 1971.

[13]   10 c5 ♘f4 11 ♗xf4 ef 12 ♖c1 a5 13 cd cd 14 ♕d2 ab 15 ♘b5 f5 ∞ Byrne/Mednis.

[14]   12 ... c6 13 ♗e3 f4 14 ♗f2 fg 15 hg a5 16 ba ♕xa5 ∞ Hoad-Hindle, British Ch 1967.

[15]   17 ed ♘fxd5 18 ♘xd5 ♘xd5 19 ♗c4 c6 20 ♖b1! ♔h7 21 ♖b3 ♕e7! = Taimanov-Bilek, Leningrad v Budapest 1957.

[16]   11 ♘d3 f4 12 b4 g5 13 a4 ♘g6 14 c5 ∞ Damjanović-Minić, Yugoslav Ch 1962.

[17]   **11 ... h5** 12 g5 h4 13 ♘d3 f4 14 ♘h1 ♔f7 15 c5 ♖h8 16 ♕b3 b6 17 cd cd 18 ♕a3 ± Larsen-Tal, match (1) 1965.
11 ... f4 12 h4 c5 13 a3 ♔h8 14 ♗d2 ♘g8 15 ♘g2 ♘f6 16 ♘e1 ♗e7 17 b4 ♘gf6 18 ♘a4 ♘e8 19 ♗f2! ± Gligorić/Matanović.

[18]   12 ♗e3 c6! 13 ♘d3 f4 14 ♗f2 g5 15 h3 c5 16 ♖b1 h5 17 b4 b6 18 bc bc 19 ♕a4 a6 20 ♕a3!? intending ♘a4 ∞ Byrne/Mednis.

[19]   17 b3 ♖f7 18 ♕c1 ♕c7 19 b4 ab 20 ♖xb4 ♖af8 = Taimanov-Kavalek, Montilla 1977.

[20]   11 f3?! f4 12 ♖c1 g5 13 ♕c2 h5! ∓.

[21]   **11 ... f4?** 12 ♗g4! ±.
11 ... fe 12 ♘xe4 ♘f5!? (12 ... ♘f6 13 ♘xf6+! ± Polugayevsky-Tal, Alma-Ata 1980) 13 ♗g4 ♘f6 14 ♗g5 ♕d7 15 ♗xf6 ♗xf6 16 c5 ♗g7 17 ♖c1 ♕f7! 18 cd cd 19 ♗xf5 gf 20 ♘xd6 ♕xd5 ∓ Meduna-A.Rodriguez, Prague 1980. 13 f3!?
11 ... c5 (Fischer) 12 f4!? ef (12 ... a6 13 a4 ef 14 ♗xf4 ♗xc3 15 bc fe 16 ♘e1 ♘f6 17 g4 ± Belyavsky-Vogt, Havana 1976) 13 ♗xf4 ♗xc3 14 bc fe 15 ♘e1 (Ftacnik-Egmond, Amsterdam II 1977) 15 ... ♘f5!? ∞ Stean.

[22]   17 h3 ♖f7 18 ♖fc1 g4 19 fg hg 20 hg ♘h7 21 ♘b5 ∞ Sosonko-Kavalek, Tilburg 1980.

[23]   **14 cd cd** 15 ♘f2 h5 16 h3 ♘g6 ∞.
14 ♖c1 ♘g6 15 cd cd 16 ♘b5 ♖f7 ∞.

[24]   17 ♘f2 ♗f8 18 a4 h5 19 h3 ± Fedorowicz.

Nimzo-Indian Defence

Aron Nimzowitsch's greatest contribution to opening theory, this defence offers Black excellent chances to play for a win without exposing himself to unnecessary risk. His third move exerts indirect influence on the e4 square, a pressure necessary to avoid the construction of a formidable White pawn centre. Acquiring the bishop pair is easily accomplished by White but the resulting configurations make it a difficult and laborious project to attain the open lines that would allow them to cause damage. In return for ceding the two bishops, Black achieves a substantial lead in development and often saddles White with a pair of weak c-pawns which may come under attack for the duration of the game. A successful White strategy hinges on a number of thematic possibilities: the liberation of the bishop pair, the successful advance of his central pawn wedge or gradual aggressive inroads afforded by his space advantage.

An opening system of vast strategical subtlety and complexity, the Nimzo-Indian has been adopted, at one time or another, by nearly every modern GM. With its durability and dynamism, it is the QP equivalent of the Ruy Lopez, offering a stern test of skill to both players.

The **Sämisch Variation** (4 a3) is an arrogant reaction, investing a tempo to force Black to implement his strategy of doubling the white c-pawns. White tries to start an immediate attack by expanding in the centre and smoking out the opposing king. This show of aggression is not to be taken lightly and Black needs to be well acquainted with the dangers which lie in store for him in order to react properly.

The **Leningrad Variation** (4 ♗g5), analysed by Zak and bestowed upon his pupil, Boris Spassky, had an ephemeral spell of popularity. The line allows several ways for Black to equalize but a few players, notably Timman, continue to employ it for White.

The **Classical Variation** (4 ♕c2) is too tame to pose a real threat to the Nimzo-Indian. White's idea is to annex the bishop pair without incurring structural damage, but this is accomplished at the cost of neglecting his development. The positions that result are rather sterile and opportunities for dynamic play are limited.

Spielmann's Variation (4 ♕b3) is similar in plan to the Classical but the placement of White's queen is more awkward and so it, too, promises little for the ambitious player with the white pieces.

The **Rubinstein Variation** (4 e3) continues to be the main line of the Nimzo-Indian. White develops patiently but efficiently, planning a methodical opening of lines and gradual central expansion. Black, with a solid position and a superior pawn structure, has adequate resources and this dynamic balance forms the critical argument of the Nimzo-Indian.

Our final section (♘c3, ♘f3 and ♗g5 by White) forms a bridge between the Nimzo-Indian and Queen's Indian. In practice it has arisen much more frequently from 3 ♘f3 move orders.

1 d4 ♘f6 2 c4 e6 3 ♘c3 ♗b4

	4	5	6	7	8	9	10	11	12	
1	f3¹	d5	g3	♗d2	e3	♗g2⁴	♘ge2	♕c2⁵		=
	c5²	♘h5³	f5	0-0	d6	e5	♕e8			
2	♕b3	dc	♘f3⁶	♗d2	♕c2	a3⁹	♗xc3	b4¹⁰	♗b2	=
	c5	♘c6	♘e4⁷	♗xc5	f5⁸	♗xc3	0-0	♘e4	d6¹¹	
3	...	...	...	...	♘xd2	e3¹³	♗e2	0-0-0¹⁴	♘f3	=
	...	...	...	♘xd2	f5¹²	0-0	♗xc5	b6¹⁵	♗b7¹⁶	

¹ **4 ♕d3** c5 5 d5 0-0 6 ♗d2 ed 7 cd d6 8 g3 b6 9 ♗g2 ♗a6 10 ♕c2 ♘bd7 11 ♘h3 ♖e8 12 ♘f4 ♗xc3 13 ♗xc3 ∓ Gipslis.
4 ♗d2 0-0 (4 ... b6?! 5 f3! ♘c6 6 a3 ♗e7 7 d5 ♘b8 8 e4 e5 9 ♗d3 ± Duchamp-Baratz, Nice 1931) 5 ♘f3 b6 6 g3 ♗b7 7 ♗g2 d6 8 0-0 ♘bd7 9 a3 ♗xc3 10 ♗xc3 ♘e4 11 ♕c2 f5 = Bondarevsky-Kottnauer, Moscow 1947.

² **4 ... d5** 5 a3 ♗e7 (5 ... ♗xc3+ – Sämisch) 6 e4 de 7 fe e5 8 d5 ♗c5 9 ♗g5 ♗d4! 10 ♗d3 h6 11 ♗h4 c6 12 ♘ge2 g4 13 ♕c2 ♗xe2 14 ♘xe2 ♗e3 15 ♘g3 g6 16 ♘f1 ♗d4 17 0-0-0 ♘bd7 Gheorghiu-Keres, Hastings 1964/65.

³ **5 ... d6** 6 ♗d2 0-0 7 e4 ♖e8 8 ♘ge2 e9 cd a6 10 a4 ♘bd7 11 ♘g3 ♖b8 12 ♗e2 ♘e5 13 0-0 ± Spassky-Cherepkov, USSR 1957.
5 ... ♗xc3+ 6 bc ♕a5 7 ♗d2 d6 8 e4 0-0 9 ♗d3 ♘bd7 10 ♘e2 ♘e5 11 ♗g5 ♘fd7! 12 de ♘b6 13 ef+ ♔xf7 14 0-0 h6 15 ♗d8 ♗e6 16 ♗xb6 ♕xb6 17 ♕b1 ♕a6 = Taimanov.

⁴ **9 de?** ♗xe6 10 ♘d5 ♗xd5 11 ♗xb4 ♗c6 12 ♗d2 ♘d7 13 ♘h3 ♕f6 14 ♖b1 ♖ae8 ∓ Portisch-Forintos, Hungarian Ch 1969.

⁵ Taimanov.

⁶ **6 ♗d2** ♗xc5 7 e3 0-0 8 ♘f3 d5 9 cd ed 10 ♗e2 d4 11 ed ♘xd4 12 ♘xd4 ♗xd4 13 0-0 ♗e6 Luckis-Salo, Warsaw 1935.
6 ♗g5 h6 7 ♗xf6 ♕xf6 8 e3 0-0 9 ♘f3 a5! 10 a4 ♕e7 11 ♗e2 ♗xc5 12 0-0 b6 = Zimmermann-Grünfeld, corr. 1937.

⁷ **6 ... 0-0** 7 ♗g5 (7 a3 ♗xc5 8 e3 ♕e7 9 ♗e2 ♖d8 10 0-0 d5 11 cd ed 12 ♖d1 d4 13 ed ♘xd4 14 ♘xd4 ♗xd4 15 ♗f4 ♗e6 ∓ Paulsen-Enevoldsen, Denmark 1941) 7 ... h6 9 ♗h4 g5 10 ♗g3 ♘e4 11 e3 ♕a5 12 ♖c1 f5 (11 ... ♘xc5!? intending 12 ♕c2 ♕xa2 Gipslis) 12 ♗d6 ♘xd6 13 cd ♗xd6 = Winter-Capablanca, Hastings 1929/30.

⁸ **8 ... 0-0** 9 a3 ♗xc3 10 ♗xc3 a5 11 g3 ♕e7 12 ♗g2 e5 13 0-0 a4 14 ♘d2 d6 15 b4 ab 16 ♘xb3 ± Stahlberg-Nimzowitsch, (match) 1934.

⁹ **9 g3** 0-0 10 ♗g2 d5 (10 ... d6 11 ♖d1 e5 12 a3 ♗xc3 13 ♗xc3 ♕e7 14 0-0 ♗e6 =; 10 ... b6 11 0-0 ♗b7 12 ♖fd1 a6 13 a3 ♗xc3 14 ♗xc3 ♘e4 = Eliskases-Staehelin, Warsaw 1935) 11 cd ed 12 a3 d4 13 ab ♘xb4 14 ♕d1 ♗e6 15 0-0 = Mitchell-Colle, Hastings 1930/31.
9 e3 0-0 10 ♗e2 b6 11 0-0 ♗b7 12 a3 ♗xc3 =.

¹⁰ **11 g3** ♗e7 12 ♗g2 d6 13 ♖d1 =.
11 ♘d2 a5 12 e3 b6 13 ♗e2 ♗b7 14 0-0 a4 =.
11 e3 ♘e4 (11 ... a5 12 ♗e2 ♕e7 13 ♘d2 e5 14 b3 d6 15 0-0 ♗e6 16 f4 ± Eliskases-Herzog, corr. 1931) 12 ♗e2 b6 13 0-0 ♗b7 14 ♖fd1 ♕e7 = Mitchell-Lilienthal, Hastings 1933/34.

¹¹ **12 ... a5** 13 b5 ♘e7 14 e3 b6 15 ♗e3 ♗b7 = Regedzinski-Steiner, Teplice 1930.
12 ... b6 13 g3 (13 g4? ♘xf2 14 ♔xf2 fg 15 ♖g1 ♕h4+ 16 ♔e3 ♕h6+ 17 ♔d3 d5 18 ♕c1 dc+ 19 ♕xc4 ♖d8+ ∓ Botvinnik-Myasoyedov, USSR 1931; 13 e3 ♗b7 14 ♗e2 ♖c8 = Dake-Steiner, Mexico City 1935) 13 ... ♗b7 14 ♗g2 ♖c8 15 ♘d2 ♗xd2 16 ♕xd2 ♘a5 17 ♗xb7 ♘xb7 18 ♖c1 ± Euwe.
12 ... d6 13 e3 (13 g3 ♕e7 14 ♗g2 e5 = Levenfish) 13 ... e5 14 ♗e2 ♗e6 15 0-0 b6 = Foguelman-Ramirez, Mar del Plata 1962.

¹² **8 ...** ♗xc5 9 g3 0-0 10 ♗e2 b6 11 0-0-0 ♕e7 12 ♘f3 ♗b7 13 ♗d2 ♖ac8 14 ♖hd1 ♖fd8 15 ♔b1 ♘a5 16 ♕a4 ± Gipslis.

¹³ **9 g3** ♕a5 10 ♖c1 b6 11 ♗g2 ♗b7 12 0-0 ♗xc3 13 ♕xc3 ♕xc3 14 ♖xc3 bc ∓ Spielmann-Euwe, match 1932.

¹⁴ **11 ♘f3** g6 12 0-0-0 ♕f6 13 h3 ♘e5 14 ♘d4 b6 15 ♔b1 ♗b7 16 a3 f4 ∓ Pfleger-Parma, Bamberg 1962.
11 0-0 b6 12 ♘f3 ♗b7 13 ♖ad1 (13 ♖fd1 g5 14 ♘b5 g4 15 ♘e1 ♕f6 ∓ Selman-Euwe, 1931) 13 ... ♕e7 14 ♘a4 (14 a3 f4 15 ef ♖xf4 16 ♖d3 ♘d4 ∓ Stahlberg-Eliskases, Harzburg 1939) 14 ... ♖b8 = Stahlberg-Loveki, Jurata 1937.

¹⁵ **11 ...** ♕e7 12 ♘f3 a6 13 ♔b1 d6 14 ♘a4 ♗a7 15 ♘b6 ± Fine-Mitchell, Hastings 1935/36.
11 ... a6 12 ♘f3 ♕a5 13 ♔b1 ♖b8 14 ♘d4! ± Gipslis.

¹⁶ **13 a3?!** ♖c8 14 ♔b1 ♗e7 15 ♕a2 a6 16 c5 bc ∓ Plezi-Sultan Khan, Liège 1930.
13 ♔b1 ♕e7 14 ♖d2 ♖ac8 = Verlinsky-Romanovsky, USSR Ch 1925.
13 ♖d2 ♕e7 14 ♖fd1 ♖fd8 15 a3 ♖ac8 16 ♕c2 ♕e8 = Belavenets-Lilienthal, match 1935.

1 d4 ♘f6 2 c4 e6 3 ♘c3 ♗b4 *continued*

	4	5	6	7	8	9	10	11	12	
4	♕b3	e3[18]	♘f3[20]	a3[21]	♗xc4	♗b5[22]	♗xc6[24]	ed[25]	0-0	∞
	♘c6[17]	d5[19]	0-0	dc	♗d6	e5[23]	ed	bc	♗g4[26]	
5	...	♘f3	♗g5[28]	♗xf6[30]	e3[31]	♗xc4	0-0	♕c2	♖ad1	∞
	...	d5[27]	h6[29]	♕xf6	dc[32]	0-0	♕e7[33]	♗d6	♔h8![34]	
6	♘f3	bc	g3	♗g2	0-0	a4	♘d2	♔xg2	e4	=
	♗xc3+[35]	b6[36]	♗b7	d6[37]	♘bd7	a5	♗xg2	0-0	e5[38]	
7	...	d5[39]	♗d2	e3	♗d3	♘xd5[42]	cd	♕xd2		=
	c5	d6[40]	0-0	♘a6	ed[41]	♘xd5	♗xd2+	♘c7[43]		
8	...	♕c2	a3	♕xc3	e3[44]	b4	♗b2	♕c2	♗e2	=
	b6	♗b7	♗xc3+	d6	0-0	♘bd7	♘e4	f5	♘g5[45]	
9	g3	♘f3[46]	♘xd4	♕d3	♘b3[49]	♕e3	bc	♗g2	0-0	∞∞
	c5	cd[47]	♘e4[48]	♕a5	♕f5[50]	♘xc3	♗e7	0-0	♘c6!?[51]	
10	...	♗g2	♘f3	0-0	♖e1	a3[53]	♕a4	♘xb5	♘c3	∞
	0-0	d5	dc	♘c6	♖b8!?[52]	♗e7	b5!?	a6	♘xd4[54]	

[17] 4 ... ♗xc3+? 5 ♕xc3 ♘e4 6 ♕c2 d5 7 ♘f3 c5 8 dc ♕a5+ 9 ♘d2 ♘c6 10 e3 0-0 11 a3 ♘xd2 12 ♗xd2 ± Taimanov.

[18] 5 d5?! ed 6 cd ♘d4 7 ♕d1 c5 8 a3 ♗a5 9 b4 cb 10 ab ♗b6 11 e3 ♘f5 12 ♘f3 d6 ∓ Dittman-Bachtiar, Leipzig Ol 1960.

[19] **5 ... a5** 6 ♗d2 d5 7 ♘f3 0-0 8 ♗e2 ♗d7 9 cd a4 10 ♕c4 ♗xc3 11 ♗xc3 ed 12 ♕d3 ♘e6 13 0-0 ♘a7 = Vuković-Simanović, Yugoslav Ch 1948/49.

5 ... 0-0 6 ♗d3 b6 7 ♘e2 ♗a6 8 a3 ♗e7 9 ♕d1 ♗b7 10 e4 d6 11 0-0 e5 12 c5 ♘b8 13 f4 = Stahlberg-Lilienthal, Budapest 1934.

[20] **6 c5** e5 7 ♗b5 0-0 8 ♘e2 ♗xc3+ 9 bc ♗f5 10 ♘g3 ♗g6 11 0-0 h5 12 ♕a4 h4 ∓ Euwe-Romanovsky, Leningrad 1934.

6 cd ed 7 ♗d3 0-0 8 ♗d2 ♖e8 9 ♘ge2 a6 10 h3 ♗f8 11 0-0 b5 ∓ Troitzky-Ragozin, USSR 1938.

6 ♗d2 0-0 7 0-0-0 ♗e7 8 cd ed 9 f3 ♗e6 10 g4 ♘a5 11 ♕c2 c5 ∓ Tolush-Sokolsky, USSR 1936.

[21] **7 ♗d3** dc 8 ♗xc4 ♗d6 9 ♘b5 ♘a5 10 ♕a4 ♗xc4 11 ♕xc4 ♗d7 = Stahlberg-Keres, match 1938.

7 ♗d2 dc 8 ♗xc4 ♗d6 9 ♘b5 ♘e4 10 ♘xd6 cd 11 0-0 b6 = Tolush-Keres, USSR 1939.

[22] **9 ♕c2** e5 =.

9 ♘b5 ♘e4 = Gipslis.

[23] 9 ... ♕e7 10 ♗xc6! bc 11 e4 ± Lipnitsky.

[24] 10 d5 ♘e7 11 e4 a6 12 ♗e2 c6 = Gipslis.

[25] **11 ♗xb7** ♖b8 12 ♗d4 ♗xb7 ∓.

11 ♘xd4 bc 12 ♘xc6 ♕d7 13 ♘d4 ♕g4 ∓ Capablanca-Ragozin, Moscow 1935.

[26] 13 ♘e5 c5 14 ♗g5 (14 ♘xg4 ♘xg4 15 h3 cd ∓) 14 ... ♗e6 15 d5 ♗xd5 16 ♘xd5 ♗xe5 17 ♖ad1 ♕b8 ∞ Trifunović-Barcza, Yugoslavia v Hungary 1947.

[27] **5 ... a5** 6 ♗d2 d6 7 ♕c2 e5 8 d5 ♘e7 9 e4 ♘g6 10 g3 0-0 11 h4 ± Taimanov.

5 ... d6 6 d5! ♗xc3+ 7 ♕xc3 ed 8 cd ♘xd5 9 ♕xg7 ♕f6 10 ♕xf6 ♘xf6 11 b3 ♘e4 12 ♗b2 0-0 13 ♘d2 ♘xd2 14 ♔xd2 f6 15 ♖c1 ± Alatortsev-Ragozin, USSR 1932.

[28] 6 a3 dc 7 ♕xc4 ♗d6 8 ♗g5 h6 9 ♗h4 g5 10 ♗g3 ♗xg3 11 hg g4 12 ♘e5 ♕xd4 = Schwarz.

6 ... dc 7 ♕xc4 ♕d5 8 ♕xd5 ed 9 ♗xf6 gf
10 a3 ♗xc3+ 11 bc ♗e6 12 e3 ♘a5 13 ♗d3 c5
14 ♔e2 ♔e7 ∞ Lipnitsky.

30 7 ♗h4 g5 8 ♗g3 g4 ∓.

31 8 cd ♘xd4 9 ♘xd4 ♕xd4 10 ♖d1 ♕b6 11 a3
♗xc3+ 12 ♕xc3 0-0 ∓ Rabinovich-Ragozin,
USSR 1937.

32 8 ... a5 9 a3 a4 10 ♕c2 ♗xc3+ 11 ♕xc3 0-0
12 ♗d3 ♗d7 13 0-0 ± Smetan-Schweber,
Buenos Aires 1972.

8 ... 0-0 9 cd ed 10 ♕xd5 ♖e8 11 ♗e2 g5
12 0-0 g4 13 ♘d2 ♗xd4 14 ed ♗xc3 15 bc ♖xe2
16 ♘e4 ♕e7 17 ♘g3 ± Euwe-Szabo, Hastings
1949/50.

33 10 ... ♗d6 11 ♗b5 ♗d7 12 ♖fd1 a6 13 ♗e2
♖ab8 14 ♖ac1 ± Szabo-Haag, Hungarian Ch
1959.

34 12 ... e5? 13 ♘d5 ♕e8 14 ♘f6+ gf 15 ♕g6+.

12 ... a6 13 e4 b5 14 ♗e2 ♘b4 15 ♕d2 c5
16 d5 ± Szabo-Prins, Stockholm IZ 1952.

12 ... ♔h8! 13 a3 e5 14 ♘d5 ♕e8 ∞
Eliskases-Fischer, Buenos Aires 1960.

35 4 ... 0-0 5 ♗g5 h6 6 ♗h4 c5 7 e3 cd 8 ♘xd4
♘c6 9 ♖c1 ♗e7 (9 ... ♘e5!? 10 ♗e2 ♘g6
11 ♗xf6 ♕xf6 12 a3 ♗e7 ∞ Zuckerman-Tisdall,
New York 1980) 10 ♗e2 ♘xd4 11 ♕xd4 d5
12 0-0 dc 13 ♖fd1 ± Navarovsky-Flesch,
Szombathely 1966.

4 ... ♘e4 5 ♕c2 f5 6 g3 b6 7 ♗g2 ♗b7 8 ♘d2
♗xc3 9 bc ♘d6 10 ♗xb7 ♘xb7 11 e4 0-0 12 0-0
♘c6 ± Balogh-Keres, corr. 1936.

4 ... d6 5 ♗g5 h6 6 ♗h4 ♗xc3+ 7 bc ♘bd7
8 ♘d2 ♕e7 9 e4 e5 10 ♗d3 ♘f8 11 ♕a4+ ♗d7
12 ♕b3 b6 13 c5 ♘g6 14 cd ± Borisenko-
Lublinsky, USSR Ch 1950.

36 5 ... d6 6 ♗g5 (6 g3 0-0 7 ♗g2 ♕e7 8 ♗a3
♘bd7 9 ♘d2 e5 10 0-0 ♖e8 11 e3 c5 ± Lasker-
Henneberger, Zürich 1934) 6 ... h6 7 ♗h4 g5
8 ♗g3 ♘e4 9 ♘d2 ♘xg3 ± Gipslis.

37 7 ... 0-0 8 0-0 d6 9 d5 ed 10 ♘h4
♘e4 11 cd ♖e8 12 ♗b2 b5 13 a4 ♕g5
14 ab ♕xd5 15 ♕a4 ∞ Euwe-Alekhine, match
1937.

7 ... c5 8 0-0 d6 9 ♗f4 0-0 Alekhine-Sämisch,
Triberg 1921.

38 Havasi-Tartakower, Debrecen 1925.

39 5 g3 – 4 g3.

5 dc ♗xc3+ 6 bc ♕a5 7 e3 0-0 8 ♘d4 ♘e4
9 ♗b2 ♘xc5 10 ♘b3 ♕c7 = Alekhine-Keres,
1936.

40 5 ... ed?! 6 cd d6 7 e3 ♘bd7 8 a3 ♗xc3+ 9 bc
0-0 10 c4 b5 11 cb ♘b6 12 ♗b2 ♘bxd5 13 ♗c4 ±

Szabo-Donner, Wageningen 1957.

5 ... ♗xc3+ 6 bc d6 7 e3 e5 8 ♕c2 ♕e7 9 ♗e2
0-0 10 ♘d2 e4 11 h3 (intending g4) ∞.

5 ... b5!? 6 de fe 7 cb d5 8 e3 ♘e4 ∞
Antoshin-Garcia, Sochi 1964.

41 8 ... ♘c7 9 de fe 10 a3 ♗a5 11 ♖b1 a6
12 b4 ± Korchnoi-Nedeljković, Baden 1957.

42 9 cd? ♘c7 10 e4 ♖e8 ∓ Gipslis/Taimanov.

43 Taimanov.

44 8 ♗g5 ♘bd7 9 e3 ♕e7 10 ♗d3 e5 11 de ♘xe5
12 ♘xe5 ♕xe5 = Bogoljubow-Matanović, BRD
v Yugoslavia 1957.

45 13 c5 ♗e4 = Korchnoi-Simagin, USSR Ch
1960.

46 5 d5 b5 (5 ... ♘e4 6 ♗d2 ♘xd2 7 ♕xd2 d6
8 de ♗xe6 9 a3 ♗a5 10 0-0-0 ♘c6 11 e3 ♕f6 ∓
Prins-Matanović, Stockholm IZ 1952) 6 ♗g2
♗b7 7 e4 bc 8 ♘e2 ed 9 ed d6 10 0-0 ♘bd7
11 a3 ♗xc3 12 ♘xc3 0-0 ∓ Keres-Veresov,
USSR Ch 1940.

47 5 ... ♘e4 6 ♕d3 ♕a5 7 ♕xe4 ♗xc3+ 8 ♗d2
♗xd2+ 9 ♕xd2 ♘c6 10 dc (10 d5?! ♘d4 11 ♗g2
♘b3 12 ♖d1 ♕xa2 ∓) 10 ... b6 11 ♗g2 ♗b7
12 ♕f4 ♕xc5 13 a3 ± Tukmakov-Hermlin, USSR
1977.

48 6 ... 0-0 7 ♗g2 d5 8 cd ♘xd5 9 ♗d2 ♘xc3 =.
9 ... ♗xc3 10 bc e5 =.

49 8 ♘c2 ♗xc3+ 9 bc ♘c5 10 e3 (10 ♕d2 b6
11 ♗g2 ♗b7 12 ♗xb7 ♘xb7 13 ♗a3 ♘c6 14 0-0
d6 15 ♖ab1 ♕a4 ∓ Lombard-Rogoff, Biel IZ
1976) 10 ... b6 11 ♗h3 0-0 12 0-0 ♗b7 13 ♘d4
♕a4 ∓ Romanishin-G.Garcia, Caracas 1976.

50 8 ... ♘xc3 9 ♗d2! (9 ♘xa5 ♘e4+ 10 ♗d2
♗xd2+ 11 ♕xd2 ♘xd2 =) 9 ... ♘e4 10 ♕xe4
♗xd2+ 11 ♘xd2 0-0 12 ♗g2 ♘c6 ± Tukmakov-
Fernandez, Decin 1977.

51 12 ... ♘a6 13 c5! ♗xc5 (13 ... ♘xc5? 14 g4;
13 ... d5 14 cd ♗xd6 15 ♖d1 ♗e7 16 ♗e4 ±
Ribli-Langeweg, 1978) 14 ♘xc5 ♕xc5 15 ♕xc5
♘xc5 16 ♗a3 d6 (16 ... ♘a4 17 c4!!) 17 ♖fd1
♖b8 18 ♖d4 b6 19 ♖b1 ♗b7 20 ♗xc5 ♗xg2
21 ♔xg2 bc 22 ♖xb8 ♖xb8 23 ♖d7 ±
Donchenko-Shakarov, USSR 1976

12 ... ♘c6!? 13 c5 b6 14 cb ab 15 ♕xb6
♗a6 ∞ Palatnik.

52 8 ... ♖e8 9 e4 e5 10 ♘xe5 ♘xe5 11 de ♕xd1
12 ♖xd1 ♖xe5 13 ♗f4 ± Kaplan.

53 9 e4 b5 10 e5 ♘d5 11 ♘g5 ♗e7 12 ♘ge4
♘cb4 13 ♗f1 ♗d7 (De Roode-Christiansen,
Amsterdam II 1978) 14 a3 ♘xc3 15 bc ♘d3
16 ♗xd3 cd 17 ♕xd3 ♗c6 ∓.

54 Gulko-Tal, USSR Ch 1977.

Leningrad 1 d4 ♘f6 2 c4 e6 3 ♘c3 ♗b4 4 ♗g5

	4	5	6	7	8	9	10	11	12	
1	...	d5[2]	cd	e3	♗b5[3]	♗xd7+	♘e2	0-0	♘xc3	±
	c5[1]	ed	d6	♘bd7	♕a5	♘xd7	♘e5	♗xc3	f6[4]	
2	...	♗h4[5]	d5[6]	bc	d6	♕c2[9]	♗g3	e3	♖d1	±
	h6	c5	♗xc3+[7]	e5[8]	♘c6!	g5	♘h5	♕f6	b6[10]	
3	...	...	...	de[12]	cb	e3	♗d3[13]	ed	a3	∞
	...	...	b5[11]	fe	d5	0-0	d4	cd	♗a5[14]	
4	...	...	...	e3[15]	♗g3	♕c2	♖c1	cd	♗d3	∞
	...	...	d6	g5[16]	♘e4	♕f6[17]	ed	♗f5	♕g6[18]	
5	...	...	...	...	bc	♕c2[19]	♗d3	♗g3	♕d1[22]	∓
	...	...	...	♗xc3+	e5	0-0[20]	g5[21]	♘h5	♘xg3[23]	
6	...	...	...	...	...	f3	♗d3[24]	♕xd3	e4	=
	...	...	...	...	...	♗f5!	♗xd3	♘bd7	♘f8[25]	

[1] 4 ... ♗xc3+ 5 bc ♕e7 6 ♕c2 d6 7 e4 e5 8 ♗d3 h6 9 ♗e3 0-0 10 ♘e2 ♘c6 ± Tartakower-Nimzowitsch, Berlin 1928.

[2] 5 ♘f3 cd 6 ♘xd4 0-0 7 ♖c1 ♘c6 8 e3 d5 9 a3 ♗e7 10 cd ♘xd4 11 ♕xd4 ♘xd5 = Gulko-Tal, Biel IZ 1976.

[3] 8 ♗d3 ♕a5 9 ♘e2 ♘xd5 10 0-0 ♗xc3 11 bc c4! 12 ♗f5 ♘7f6 (12 ... f6 13 ♘d4! ♗e7! 14 ♗xd7+ ♗xd7 15 ♗f4 0-0 16 ♗xd6 ± Timman-Karpov, Amsterdam 1976) 13 ♗xc8 ♖xc8 14 ♗xf6 ♘xf6 15 ♕xd6 ♕c5 = Timman.

[4] 13 ♗f4 0-0 14 ♘e4 ♕d8 15 ♕d2 ± Spassky-Hasin, USSR Ch 1961.

[5] 5 ♗xf6 ♕xf6 6 ♖c1 c5 7 dc ♘a6 8 ♘f3 ♗xc5 9 a3 ♗xc3+ 10 ♖xc3 b6 11 g3 ♗b7 12 ♗g2 0-0 13 0-0 = L.Grigorian-Balashov, USSR 1967.
5 ... ♗xc3+ (Alekhine) 6 bc ♕xf6 7 g3 d6 8 ♗g2 0-0 9 ♘f3 e5 10 0-0 ♕e7 11 ♘d2 c5 12 ♘b3 ♘d7 ∓ Bronstein-Grigorian, Moscow 1976.

[6] 6 ♖c1 cd 7 ♕xd4 g5 8 ♗g3 ♘c6 ∓.

[7] 6 ... ♘xd5?! 7 ♗xd8 ♘xc3 8 ♕b3 ♘e4+ 9 ♔d1 ♘xf2+ 10 ♔c1! ± ♘xh1 11 a3 ♗e1 12 ♘f3 ♗f2 13 ♗c7 d5 ± Zak.

[8] 7 ... d6 8 de ♗xe6 9 e3 0-0 10 ♘f3 d5 11 ♗e2 ± Zak.

[9] 9 e3 g5 10 ♗g3 ♘e4 11 ♗xe5!? (11 f3 ♘xg3 12 hg ♕f6 13 e4 h5 14 ♕d2 b6 15 g4 h4 16 ♘h3 ♖g8 = Spassky-Timman, Tallinn 1973) 11 ... ♘xe5 12 ♕d5 ♕f6 13 ♕xe4 0-0 ∞.

[10] 12 ... ♕e6 13 ♗e2 ♘g7 14 e4 ± Taimanov.
12 ... b6 13 ♗e2 ♘xg3 14 hg ♗b7 15 ♗f3 0-0-0 16 ♘e2? h5! ∓ Bagirov-Keene, Tbilisi 1974. 14 fg!? ♗b7 15 ♗f3 0-0-0 16 ♘e2 ± Taimanov.

[11] 6 ... 0-0 7 ♘f3 b5!? 8 e3 ♗b7 9 d6 g5 10 ♗g3 ♘e4 11 ♕c2 ♕a5 12 ♖c1 ♕xa2 ∞ Mititelu-Larsen, Reykjavik 1957.

[12] 7 ♖c1 bc (7 ... ed?! 8 ♗xf6! ±) 8 e4 g5 9 ♗g3 ♘xe4 10 ♗xc4 ♗xc3+ 11 bc ♕f6 = Portisch-Szily, Hungarian Ch 1959.

7 e4 ed (7 ... g5 8 ♗g3 ♘xe4 9 ♕f3 ♗xc3+ 10 bc ed 11 cd 0-0 12 ♗d3 f5 13 ♗xe4 fe ∞ Portisch-Darga, Bled 1961; 9 ♗e5 0-0 10 ♕h5 d6 11 ♗d3 ♘xc3 12 ♗xh6 ♘e4+ 13 ♗f1 de 14 ♗xe4 f5 15 ♕g6+ ± Zak) 8 ed 0-0 9 cb ♖e8+ (9 ... ♗b7 10 ♗e2 ♗xd5 ∞) 10 ♗e2 g5 11 ♗g3 ♘e4 12 ♖c1 ♕f6 13 ♗f1 ♗xc3 14 bc ♘xc3 15 ♕c2 ∞ Zak-Levin, Leningrad 1953.

[13] 10 ♘f3 ♕a5 11 ♗xf6 ♖xf6 12 ♕d2 a6 13 ba ♘c6! ∓ Spassky-Tal, Tallinn 1973.
10 a3!? intending 10 ... ♗a5 11 ♘f3.

[14] 13 b4 dc 14 ba ♗b7 15 ♘e2! ♗xg2 16 ♖g1 ♗f3 17 ♗c2 (17 ♖g3!? Basman) 17 ... ♘bd7 18 ♕d6 ♘e5!! (Keene) ∓.

[15] 7 f3 ed 8 cd 0-0 9 e4 ♘bd7 10 ♗d3 ♘e5 11 ♘e2 c4 12 ♗c2 ♗c5 13 ♕d2 ♗d7 ∓ Taimanov.

[16] 7 ... ed 8 cd 0-0 (8 ... ♘bd7 9 ♗d3 ♕a5 10 ♘e2 ♘xd5 11 0-0 ♘xc3 12 bc ♗xc3 13 ♘xc3 ♕xc3 14 ♗e2/14 ♖c1!? ∞∞) 9 ♗d3 ♘bd7 10 ♘e2 ♘e5 11 0-0 ♘g6 12 ♗g3 ♘h5 13 f4 f5 ∞.

[17] 9 ... ♗xc3+ 10 bc ♘xg3 11 hg ±.

[18] 13 ♔e2?! ♗xc3 14 bc c4! 15 ♕a4+ ♘d7 ∓ Timman. 14 ♗xe4 ♗xe4 15 ♕xc3 0-0 16 h4 g4 ∓ Timman: 17 h5!? ∞.
13 ♖d1 ♘d7 14 de ♘xg3 15 hg ♗xd3+ 16 ♕xd3 ♕xd3+ 17 ♔xd3 ♘e5+ 18 ♔e2 ∞ Timman-G.Garcia, Orense 1976.

[19] 9 f4 ef 10 ef ♕e7+! 11 ♕e2 (11 ♗e2 g5! 12 fg ♘e4 ∓) 11 ... ♕xe2+ 12 ♘xe2 ♘e4 13 ♗g3 ♘xg3 (13 ... ♘xc3? 14 ♔d2, intending ♖e1+) 14 ♗xg3 ♗f5 15 ♔d2 = Cherepkov-Taimanov, USSR 1955.
9 ♗d3 e4 10 ♗c2 g5 11 ♗g3 ♕e7 12 h4 ♖g8 13 hg hg 14 ♘e2 ♘bd7 15 ♗a4! ∞ Miles.
9 ♘f3 ♗f5 10 ♘d2 g5 11 ♗g3 ♘bd7 12 ♗e2 ♕e7 13 0-0 h5 14 f4 ef 15 ef h4 16 ♖e1!? (16 ♗f2 gf 17 ♕a4+ ♔f8 18 ♖ae1 ♘e5 ∓ Planinc-Hort, Hastings 1974/75) 16 ... hg 17 ♗f3 gh+ 18 ♔h1

♘e5 19 fe de 20 ♕e2 oo Cvetković.

[20] 9 ... g5 10 ♗g3 e4 11 h4 ♖g8 12 hg hg 13 f4 gf 14 ♗xf4 ♕e7 15 ♘h3 ♘bd7 16 ♘f2 ♘f8 = Marović-Ree, Amsterdam 1968.

[21] 10 ... ♖e8!? 11 f3 ♘bd7 12 ♘h3 e4! 13 fe ♘e5 14 ♘f2 ♘g6 15 ♗g3 ♘h5 ∓ Ghitescu-Kozma, Bratislava 1957.

[22] 12 f3!? f5 13 ♘e2 oo.

[23] 13 hg ♔g7 14 g4?! ♘d7 15 ♘e2 ♘f6 ∓

Balashov-Taimanov, Vilnius 1975. 14 e4!? ∓.

[24] 10 e4 ♗c8! intending ... g5, ... ♘b8-d7-f8-g6 =. 10 ♕b3?! b6 11 h3 ♘bd7 12 g4 ♗h7 13 ♘e2 g5 14 ♗f2 h5 ∓ Timman-Dzhindzhihashvili, Geneva 1977. 10 g4!? Keene-McCambridge, Dortmund 1982.

[25] 13 ♖b1 b6 14 ♕c2 ♘g6 = Böhm-Szabo, Amsterdam 1975.

Classical 1 d4 ♘f6 2 c4 e6 3 ♘c3 ♗b4 4 ♕c2

	4	5	6	7	8	9	10	11	12	
1	...	a3	♕xc3	♗g5[3]	e3	f3	♗d3	♘e2	0-0	∓
	0-0[1]	♗xc3+	b6[2]	♗b7	d6	♘bd7	c5	♖c8	♗a6![4]	
2	...	♗g5	♘f3	e3	♗e2	0-0	bc	♘d2	a4	∞
	...	d6[5]	♘bd7	e5[6]	♖e8	♗xc3	b6	♗b7	a5[7]	
3	...	♘f3	a3[9]	♕xc3	b3	g3	♗g2	de	♗b2	∞
	♘c6	d6[8]	♗xc3+	a5	0-0	♕e7	e5	de	♖e8[10]	
4	...	a3[11]	♕xc3	♕c2	e3	cd	♗c4	b4	♕xe4	±
	d5	♗xc3+	♘e4	♘c6[12]	e5	♕xd5	♕a5+	♘xb4	♘c2+[13]	
5	...	dc	♘f3[14]	e3[16]	♗d2	♗e2	0-0	♖fd1[18]	b3	=
	c5	0-0!	♘a6[15]	♘xc5	b6	♗b7	a5!?[17]	♕e7	♖ac8[19]	

[1] 4 ... d6 5 a3 ♗xc3+ 6 ♕xc3 0-0 7 g3 a5 8 b3! =/±.

[2] 6 ... ♕e8!? 7 f3 d6 8 e4 e5 9 d5 ♘fd7! 10 g4 a5 11 b4 ab 12 ab ♖xa1 13 ♕xa1 ♘a6 14 ♗d2 ♕e7 oo Dueball-Keene, Dortmund 1973.

[3] 7 ♘f3 ♗b7 8 b4!? d6 9 ♗b2 ♘bd7 10 e3 ♘e4 11 ♕c2 f5 12 ♗d3 =.

[4] Gheorghiu-Timman, Malta Ol 1980.

[5] 5 ... h6 6 ♗h4 c5 7 e3 cd 8 ed ♘c6 9 ♘f3 ♗e7 10 ♖d1 d5 11 a3 b6 12 ♗d3 dc = Kotov-Tolush, USSR 1947.

[6] 7 ... h6 8 ♗xf6 ♘xf6 9 ♗d3 c5 10 dc dc 11 0-0 ♗d7 12 e4 ♗xc3 13 ♕xc3 ♗c6 = Korchnoi-Petrosian, Yerevan 1965.

[7] 13 ♖ae1 h6 14 ♗h4 ♕e7 oo Larsen-Matanović, Monte Carlo 1967.

[8] 5 ... 0-0 6 ♗g5 h6 7 ♗h4 d6 8 e3 ♕e7 9 ♗e2 e5 10 d5 ♘b8 11 ♘d2 ♘bd7 12 0-0 a5 13 ♖ae1! ♖e8 ± Keres-Euwe, match (6) 1940.

[9] 6 ♗d2!? 0-0 7 a3 ♗xc3 8 ♗xc3 ♕e7 9 e3 e5 10 de de 11 b4 ♗g4 12 ♗e2 e4 13 b5! ef 14 gf ♗d7 15 bc ± Bagirov. 14 ... ♗xf3? 15 ♗xf3 ♘e5 16 ♗xb7 ♖b8 17 ♗b4 c5 18 bc ♘f3+ 19 ♔f1 ± Flohr-Keres, USSR Ch 1947.

[10] 13 0-0 ♘d7 14 ♖ad1 f6 15 e3 ♘c5 oo.

[11] 5 cd ed (5 ... ♕xd5 6 ♘f3 c5 7 ♗d2 ♗xc3 8 ♗xc3 cd 9 ♖d1! ♘c6 10 ♘xd4 0-0 11 f3 e5 12 e4 ♕c5 13 ♘xc6 bc 14 ♕d2 ± Doroshkevich-Vaganian, USSR 1970) 6 ♗g5 h6 7 ♗xf6 (7 ♗h4 c5 8 0-0-0 ♗xc3! 9 ♕xc3 g5! ∓ Keres-Botvinnik,

USSR Ch 1941) 7 ... ♗xf6 8 a3 ♗xc3+ 9 ♕xc3 0-0 10 e3 c6 11 ♘f3 ♗f5 12 ♗e2 ♘d7 13 b4 a5 14 0-0 ab 15 ab ♖fc8 (Flohr-Szabo, Saltsjöbaden 1948) 16 ♖a3 ± Bagirov.

[12] 7 ... c5 8 dc ♘c6 9 cd ed 10 ♘f3 ♗f5 11 b4 0-0 12 ♗b2 b6 13 b5 bc 14 bc ♕a5+ 15 ♘d2 ♖ab8 oo Grigorian-Gulko, USSR 1975.

[13] 13 ♔e2 ♕e1+ 14 ♔f3 ♘xa1 15 ♗b2 0-0 16 ♔g3! h6 17 h4! ♕d2 18 ♘f3 ♕xb2 19 ♘g5! ⩲ Bagirov.

[14] 6 ♗g5 ♘a6 7 a3 ♗xc3 8 ♕xc3 ♘xc5 9 ♗xf6 ♕xf6 10 ♕xf6 gf 11 f3 a5 12 e4 b6 = Kotov-Averbakh, USSR Ch 1951.

[15] 6 ... ♘c6 7 ♗g5 ♗xc5 8 e3 ♗e7 9 ♖d1 ♕a5 10 ♗e2 d5 11 0-0 dc 12 ♗xc4 ♘e5 13 ♘xe5 ♕xe5 14 ♗f4 ♕c5 15 ♘e4 ♕c6 16 ♗xf6 ± Knaak-Plachetka, E Germany v Czechoslovakia 1972.

[16] 7 ♗d2 ♘xc3 8 a3 ♗xc3 9 ♕xc3 ♘ce4 (9 ... b6 10 ♘g5 ♖e8 11 b4 h6 12 h4 ng 13 bc gh 14 ♖xh4 bc oo Reshevsky-Euwe, Amsterdam 1950) 10 e3 b6 11 ♗e2 ♗b7 12 0-0 ♖c8 13 ♗b4 ♖e8 = Kottnauer-Keres, Budapest 1952.

[17] 10 ... ♖c8 11 ♘b5 ± Flohr-Tolush, USSR Ch 1947.

10 ... ♗xc3 11 ♗xc3 d5 12 ♖ad1 ♕e7 = Boleslavsky-Plater, Moscow 1947.

[18] 11 a3? ♗xc3 12 ♗xc3 a4 ∓ Larsen.

[19] 13 ♕b2 ♘ce4 14 ♘xe4 ♘xe4 15 a3 (15 ♗e1 ♗a3 ∓) 15 ... ♘xd2 16 ♘xd2 ♗c5 17 ♗f3 = Ivkov-Larsen, Bled/Portorož 1979.

Sämisch I   1 d4 ♘f6 2 c4 e6 3 ♘c3 ♗b4 4 a3 ♗xc3+ 5 bc

	5	6	7	8	9	10	11	12	13	
1	...	f3	e4	♗d3	♘e2	♗e3	♘g3	0-0	♕e2	±
	d6	e5[1]	c5[2]	♘c6	b6	♘a5	♕c7	♗a6	0-0-0[3]	
2	...	e3[4]	cd	♘e2	♘g3	f3	♗e2	0-0	e4	±
	d5	0-0	ed[5]	c5[6]	♕c7	♖e8	b6	♗a6	cd[7]	
3	...	♘h3[8]	e3[9]	♗d2	cd	♕xd2	♔xd2	♗d3	♖hc1	=
	♘e4	c5	♕a5	cd	♘xd2	♕xd2+	b6	♗a6	♘c6[10]	
4	...	♕c2	♘h3[11]	f3	c5[13]	cb	e3[14]	♗d2	c4	=
	...	f5	0-0[12]	♘f6	b6	cb	♕c7	♘e8	♗a6[15]	
5	...	f3	e4	♗g5	♗h4[17]	♗xc4	♕a4+	♕xc4	♘e2	±
	b6	♗a6[16]	d5	h6	♗xc4	dc	♕d7	♘c6[18]	♘a5[19]	
6	...	...	...	e5[20]	♘h3[21]	♕a4	♗d3	♘f4	h4[23]	∞
	...	...	♘c6	♘g8	♘a5	h6[22]	♘e7	0-0	d6[24]	
7	...	f3[25]	e4	♗e3	♗d3	♘e2	0-0	♘g3	ef	∞
	c5	d6	♘c6	b6[26]	0-0[27]	♘e8[28]	♘a5	f5	ef[29]	
8	...	...	cd	cd[30]	c4	♗d2	♘h3	♘f4	e3	⩵
	...	d5	♘xd5	f5[31]	♕f6	♘e7[32]	♘bc6	0-0	♘g6[33]	
9	...	...	...	...	e4	♕c2	♗d3[35]	c4	♗xe3	=
	...	...	...	...	fe	e3[34]	♘d7	♘f4	♕a5+[36]	
10	...	...	...	...	♘h3	c4	♘f2[38]	e3	♗e2	∞
	...	...	...	...	0-0[37]	♕h4+	♘f6[39]	♘c6	e5[40]	
11	...	e3	♗d3	♘e2	♗b1	♘g3	f3[43]	♘f5[45]	♘d6	=
	...	♘c6[41]	e5	e4[42]	b6	♗a6	♗xc4[44]	0-0	♗d3[46]	
12	...	...	♗d3[47]	f3	♘e2	e4	e5	0-0	d5	∞
	...	b6	♗b7[48]	♘c6	♖c8	♘a5[49]	♘g8	f5	♘e7[50]	

---

[1]   6 ... ♘h5 7 ♘h3 e5 8 ♘f2 0-0 9 e4 ♘c6 10 g4 ♘f6 (Diez del Corral-Korchnoi, Buenos Aires Ol 1978) 11 ♗e3! ∞.

[2]   7 ... ♘c6 8 ♗e3 b6 9 ♗d3 ♗a6?? 10 ♕a4! ±± Sämisch-Capablanca, Carlsbad 1929.

[3]   14 f4 ±.

[4]   6 ♗g5 c5 7 cd ed 8 ♘f3 ♘bd7 9 ♕c2 ♕a5 10 ♘d2 0-0 11 e3 b6 12 ♗d3 ♗a6 = Gipslis.

[5]   7 ... ♕xd5 8 c4 ♕d6 9 ♘f3 c5 10 ♗d3 ±.

[6]   8 ... ♗f5 9 ♘g3 ♗g6 10 c4 ±.

[7]   14 cd ♗xe2 15 ♕xe2 ± Petrosian-Ghitescu, Tel Aviv Ol 1964.

[8]   6 e3 f5 7 ♕h5+! g6 8 ♕h6 ♘f6 9 f3 ♘d6 10 ♕f4 0-0 11 c5 ± Klüger-Androvitsky, Budapest 1962.

[9]   7 f3? ♘xc3 8 ♕d3 ♕h4+ ∓.
7 ♕c2 ♘a5 8 ♗b2 f5 9 f3 ♘d6 10 e3 b6 ∞ Sämisch-Kmoch, Frankfurt 1931.

[10]   Botvinnik-Tal, match 1960.

[11]   7 f3 ♕h4 8 g3 ♘xg3 9 hg ♕xh1 10 ♘h3 d6 11 ♔f2 e5 12 ♗g2 ♕h2 13 ♗f4 ef 14 gf ♘c6 15 ♖h1 ♕xh1 16 ♗xh1 ♗d7 ∓.
7 e3 b6 8 ♗d3 ♗b7 9 ♘e2 ♕h4 10 0-0 0-0 11 f3 ♗g5 12 ♗d2 ♘c6 Vladimirov-Tarasov, USSR 1957.

[12]   7 ... d6 8 f3 ♘f6 9 e4 fe 10 fe e5 11 ♘f2 0-0 12 ♗e2 c5 13 de de 14 0-0 ♘c6 15 ♗g5 ♕e8 = Botvinnik-Tal, match 1960.

[13]   9 e4 fe 10 fe e5 =.
9 e3 b6 10 ♗d3 ♘e7 11 0-0 d6 12 ♘f2 c5 13 e4 ♘c6 14 ef ef = Eliskases-Pleci, Warsaw 1935.

[14]   11 e4 fe 12 fe ♗b7 13 ♘f2 (13 ♗d3 ♘xe4) 13 ... d5 14 e5 ♘e4 ∓ Taimanov.

[15]   14 ♖c1 ♘d6 15 ♕a4 ♕c6 16 ♕xc6 ♘xc6 = Botvinnik-Tal, match 1960.

[16]   6 ... d5 7 ♗g5 ♗b7 8 e3 ♘bd7 9 ♗d3 h6 10 ♗h4 c5 11 ♘e2 ♕c7 12 cd ♘xd5 13 ♗g3 ♕c6

14 ♕d2 c4 15 ♗c2 ♘7f6 16 e4 ± Lilienthal-Eliskases, Budapest 1934.

[17] 9 ♕a4+ c6 10 ♗xf6 ♕xf6 11 cd ♗xf1 12 ♔xf1 ed 13 ed 0-0 14 dc ♘xc6 ∞ Gipslis.

[18] 12 ... ♕c6 13 ♕d3 ♘bd7 14 ♘e2 ± Lilienthal-Capablanca, Hastings 1934/35.

[19] 14 ♕d3 ♕c6 15 0-0 0-0-0 16 e5 g5 17 ef gh 18 ♕e4 ± Alekhine-Eliskases, Hastings 1933/34.

[20] 8 ♗g5 h6 9 ♗h4 ♘a5 10 ♕a4 ♕c8 11 ♗d3 (11 ♘h3 ♕b7! Taimanov) 11 ... ♕b7 12 e5 ♘xd5 13 cd ♗xd3 14 ♖d1 ♕a6 ∞ Parma.

[21] 9 ♗d3 ♘a5 10 ♕a4 f6 11 ♘h3 ♕e7 12 ef (12 f4!? Gipslis) 12 ... ♘xf6 ∓ Koberl-Bondarevsky, Szczawno Zdroj 1950.

[22] 10 ... f6!? Gipslis.
10 ... ♕h4+?! 11 g3 ♕h5.
10 ... ♘e7 11 ♗g5 h6 12 ♗h4 0-0 13 ♗d3 ♕e8! ∞.

[23] 13 0-0 d6 14 ♖d1 ♕e8 ∓ Gutman-Kärner, USSR 1975.

[24] Vuković.
13 ... f5!?
13 ... d5 14 ♗b1 ♗xc4 15 ♕c2 ± Gutman-Levchenko, USSR 1976.

[25] 6 e4 ♕a5! (6 ... ♘xe4 7 ♕g4 ∞) 7 e5 ♘e4 8 ♗d2 ♘c6 9 ♘e2 b6 10 f4 cd 11 cd ♘xd2 12 ♕xd2 ♕xd2+ 13 ♔xd2 ♗a6 ∓.

[26] 8 ... ♕a5 9 ♕d2 b6! 10 ♗d3 cd 11 cd ♕xd2+ 12 ♔xd2 ♗a6 = Gutman-Savon, USSR Ch 1977.

[27] 9 ... ♘a5 10 ♘h3! ♗a6 11 ♕e2 ♕d7 12 e5 ∞ Spassky-Hübner, Bugojno 1982.

[28] 10 ... ♗a6 11 ♘g3 ♖c8 12 ♕e2 ♘a5 13 ♖c1 ♕d7 14 0-0 ♕a4 14 ♗g5 = Lehmann-Lombardy, Leipzig 1960.

[29] 14 ♘h5 ♘c7 15 ♕e2 ♗a6 ∞ Botvinnik-Furman, USSR 1960.

[30] Keres.
8 ♕d2 ♕a5 9 ♗b2 ♘b6 10 e3 ♕a4 11 ♖b1 ♘xb2 12 ♕xb2 0-0 13 ♔f2 b6 14 ♗b5 ♗d7 15 ♗d3 ♘c6 = Steiner-Donner, Venice 1950.
8 ♕d3 ♕a5 9 ♗d2!?

[31] 8 ... ♕a5 9 e4 ♘e7! 10 ♗e3 ♕xc3+ 11 ♔f2 0-0 12 ♘e2 ♕a5 13 ♕b3 f5! 14 ♘f4 ♔h8 15 ♘xe6 15 ♘xe6 ♗xe6 15 ♕xe6 ♘bc6 ∓ Kozlovskaya-Fatalibekova, USSR 1977. 13 ♕d2 ♕xd2 14 ♗xd2 ♗a6 15 ♗e3 f5 =. 13 h4!? e5 14 ♕c1 ♗e6 15 h5 ♘bc6 16 ♖b1 ♖ab8 17 g4 ∞ Pribyl-Timoshenko, CSSR 1973.

[32] 10 ... ♘c3 11 ♘xc3 ♕xc3+ 12 ♔f2 ♕xc4 13 e3 ♕h4+ 14 g3 ♕e7 = Koblents-Buslayev, USSR 1961.

[33] 14 ♘xg6 ♕xg6 15 ♔f2 e5 16 ♗e2 ♗e6 17 ♕b3 f4 18 ♕xb7 fe+ 19 ♗xe3 (Greckin-Estrin, corr. 1971) 19 ... ♘d4 ∞.

[34] 10 ... ef 11 ♘xf3 ♕a5 12 ♗d3 ♕xc3+ 13 ♕xc3 ♘xc3 14 ♗b2 ♘d5 15 ♗xg7 ♖g8 16 ♗e5 ±.
10 ... ♕a5 11 fe ♕xc3+ 12 ♕xc3 ♘xc3 13 ♗d3 ♗d7 14 ♗d2 ♘a4 15 ♖c1 ♗c6 16 ♘f3 ♘d7 = Ruderfer-Gulko, USSR 1966.
10 ... 0-0 11 fe ♕h4+ 12 g3 ♕f6 13 ♗d3 ♕xc3+ 14 ♕xc3 ♘xc3 15 ♗f4! ± Hollis.

[35] 11 c4 ♕a5+ ∓ Bukić-Sokolov, Yugoslavia 1962.
11 ♗b2 ♘c6 12 0-0-0 ♕a5 13 h4 0-0 ∞ Vladimirov-Bikov, USSR 1968.

[36] 14 ♔f2 ♘xd3+ 15 ♕xd3 0-0 16 ♕d2 (16 ♕d6 ♘f6! ∞ Gipslis) 16 ... ♕a6 (16 ... ♕xd2 intending ... ♘xc5) 17 ♘e2 ♘f6 18 ♘g3 ♕xc4 19 ♖hc1 ♕a4 = Furman-Polugayevsky, USSR Ch 1963.

[37] 9 ... ♕a5 10 e4! fe 11 ♘g5 ♘xc3 (11 ... ef 12 ♕xf3 ♖f8 13 ♕d3 ♘c6 14 ♘e4 ±; 11 ... e3!? Gipslis) 12 ♕d4 ♘b5+ 13 ♕d2 ♕xd2+ 14 ♔xd2! (14 ♗xd2? ♘d4 ∓) 14 ... ♘d4 15 ♔c3 ± Gipslis.

[38] 11 g3? ♕xc4 12 e4 ♕c3 13 ♗d2 ♕e5 ∓.

[39] 11 ... ♕xc4? 12 e4 ♕c3 + 13 ♗d2 ♕e5 14 ♘d3 ±.

[40] 14 0-0 ♗e6 15 ♖b1 ♗f7 16 ♕a4 ♖af8 ∞ Gutman-Dzanoyev, USSR 1972.

[41] 6 ... ♕a5 7 ♗d2 ♘e4 8 ♗d3 ♘xd2 9 ♕xd2 d6 10 ♘f3 ♘c6 11 0-0 0-0 12 ♕c2 h6 13 ♘d2 ♕c7 14 f4 f5 15 d5 ± Bronstein-Boleslavsky, Moscow 1950.

[42] 8 ... d6 9 0-0 e4 10 ♗b1 0-0 11 ♘g3 ♖e8 12 f3 ef 13 ♕xf3 ♕e7 14 e4 cd 15 ♗g5 ♘e5 16 ♕d1 dc 17 ♗xf6 gf 18 ♕c1 ♔h8 ∞ Szabo-Teschner, Helsinki 1952.

[43] 11 ♕a4 ♘a5 12 dc ♗xc4 13 ♘xe4 ♘xe4 14 ♗xe4 ♖c8 ∞.
11 ♘xe4 ♘xe4 12 ♗xe4 ♗xc4 13 f3 ∞ Tal.

[44] 11 ... ef 12 ♕xf3 ♗xc4 13 ♘f5 0-0 14 e4 ∞.

[45] 12 fe d6 13 ♕f3 0-0 14 e5 de 15 ♕xc6 ed ∞.

[46] 14 ♗xd3 ed 15 ♕xd3 cd 16 cd ♘e8 17 ♘f5 d5 18 a4 ♘d6 = Spassky-Tal, USSR Ch 1958.

[47] 7 ♘e2 ♗a6 (7 ... ♘c6 8 ♘g3 ♗a6 9 e4 ♘a5 10 e5 ♘g8 11 ♘e4 ±) 8 ♘g3 ♕c7 9 e4 cd 10 cd ♗xc4 11 ♕c2 (11 ♗g5 ♗xf1 12 ♔xf1 d6 13 ♖c1 ♕b7 14 e5 de 15 de ♘d5 16 ♘h5 ∞ Taimanov) 11 ... d5 12 ♗d3 ♕c6 13 e5 ♘fd7 14 0-0 f5 15 a4 ∞ Vaganian-Gulko, USSR Ch 1977.

[48] 7 ... ♘c6 8 e4 d6 9 ♘e2 ♕d7 10 0-0 ♗a6 11 ♗g5 0-0-0 12 ♘c1 ♘a5 13 ♘b3 ♕a4 14 ♘xa5 ♕xa5 15 ♕c2 ± Geller-Lisitsin, USSR Ch 1955.

[49] 10 ... cd 11 cd ♘a5 12 ♗g5 h6 13 ♗xf6 ♕xf6 14 ♖c1 ♗a6 15 ♕a4 ± Taimanov.
10 ... d6 11 0-0 ♘d7 12 f4 e5 13 fe de 14 d5 ± Trapl-Marszalek, CSSR 1961.

[50] 14 d6 ♘g6 15 f4 0-0 ∞ Beni-O'Kelly, Amsterdam 1954.

147

Sämisch II   1 d4 ♘f6 2 c4 e6 3 ♘c3 ♗b4 4 a3 ♗xc3+ 5 bc 0-0

	6	7	8	9	10	11	12	13	14	
1	f3[1]	e4	♗g5	♘e2	♗e3	d5	g4	♕d2	♘g3	±
	d6[2]	e5	♖e8[3]	h6	c5	♘h5	♘f4	g5	♕f6[4]	
2	...	e4	♘h3[5]	e5[6]	♗g5[7]	ef	♗d3	0-0	♗h4	±
	♘e8	b6	♗a6	♘c6	f6	♘xf6	e5	h6	ed[8]	
3	...	cd[9]	e3	♘e2	g4[11]	♘f4	♗d2	♕b1	♗d3	±
	d5	ed	♗f5	c5[10]	♗d7	♕a5	♗a4	♘c6	g6[12]	
4	...	...	...	g3[13]	♗d3	♘e2	♗xa6	♕d3	c4	±
	...	...	♘h5	b6	f5[14]	♗a6	♘xa6	♕c8	c6[15]	
5	e3	♘e2[17]	♘g3	♗d3	♗xc4	♕f3	♕c6	0-0	♕xc4	=
	b6[16]	♗a6	d5	♗xc4	dc	♘bd7	♖c8	♘b8	c5[18]	
6	...	♘e2	♘g3	e4[19]	♗d3	d5[20]	♕e2	0-0	de	∞
	c5	♘c6	b6	♘e8!	♗a6	♘a5	f6![21]	♘d6	de[22]	
7	...	♗d3	♘e2[23]	0-0[24]	♕c2	cd	♘f4	c4	ed	±
	...	b6	♗b7	d6	d5	♕xd5	♕c6	cd	♘bd7[25]	
8	...	...	e4	♗g5	h4	e5	de	♖h3	♖xd3	±
	...	...	♗b7[26]	h6	d6	de	♗e4	♗xd3[27]	♕c7[28]	
9	...	...	e4	♘f3	d5	0-0	♖b1	♗h6	♘g5	±
	...	d6	♘c6	e5	♘e7[29]	♘e8[30]	g6	♘g7	♔h8[31]	
10	...	...	♘e2[32]	e4	d5	f3	g4	h4	♗h6	±
	...	♘c6	d6	e5[33]	♘e7	♘e8	f6	g6	♖f7[34]	
11	...	...	...	e4[35]	♗e3	0-0[37]	dc	♗xc4	♖e1[38]	∓
	...	...	b6	♘e8[36]	♗a6	♘a5	♘xc4	♗xc4	bc[39]	
12	...	...	...	...	e5[40]	ef	♗e3[42]	cd	♕c2	±
	...	...	...	...	f5[41]	♕xf6	cd[43]	♗a6	g6[44]	

[1] **6** ♗g5 c5 7 ♕c2 d5 =.
  6 ♕c2 d6 7 e4 e5 8 ♗d3 ♘c6 9 ♘e2 b6 10 f4 ∞ Donner-Pirc, Opatija 1953.
[2] **6 ...** ♘c6 7 e4 e5 8 ♗g5 ±.
  6 ... ♘h5 7 ♘h3 f5 8 e4 d6 (8 ... fe 9 ♗g5 intending fe ±) 9 ♗e3 f4 10 ♗f2 ♕e8 11 c5 ♔h8 12 cd cd 13 g4 ± Deze-Czom, Vrsac 1969.
[3] 8 ... ♘c6 9 ♘e2 b6 10 g4 ♗a6 11 ♘g3 h6

12 ♗e3 ♘h7 13 ♗d3 ♘a5 14 ♕e2 ± Taimanov.
[4] 15 h4 ± Tal-Matanović, Bled 1961.
[5] 8 ♗d3 ♗a6 9 f4 ♘c6 10 e5 f5 11 a4 d5 12 a3 dc 13 ♗c2 (13 ♗f8 cd intending ... ♕d5 ∓) 13 ... ♖f7 14 ♘f3 h6 =.
[6] 9 ♗d3 c5 10 0-0 ♘c6 11 ♗e3 ♘a5 12 ♕e2 ♖c8 13 e5 cd 14 ♗g5 f6 15 ♕e4 g6 16 ef ♘xf6 ∓ Toth-Flesch, Hungarian Ch 1971.

[7] **10 Wa4?** ♘a5 11 ♗e3 f6! ∓ Szabo-Taimanov, Szczawno Zdroj 1950.
10 ♗d3 ♘a5 11 ♕e2 f5 12 ♗g5 ♕c8 13 ♗e7 ♖f7 14 ♗b4 ±.

[8] 15 cd ♘xd4 (Dittman-Pachman, Marianske Lazne 1960) 16 ♗e4 ± Gipslis.

[9] 7 ♗g5!? h6 8 ♗h4 c5 9 e3 ♕a5 10 ♕d2 ±.

[10] 9 ... ♘bd7 10 ♘g3 ♗g6 11 ♗d3 c5 12 0-0 ♖e8 13 ♖e1 ♗c7 14 ♗xg6 hg 15 e4 ± Botvinnik-Tal, match 1960.

[11] 10 ♘g3 ♗g6 11 ♗d3 ♘c6 12 0-0 ♕d7 13 ♖a2 ♖fe8 14 ♖e2 ♖ad8 15 ♗b2 cd 16 cd ♘h5 = Portisch-Matanović, Yugoslavia v Hungary 1959.

[12] 15 h4 ± Taimanov.

[13] 9 ♕c2 ♖e8 10 g4 ♘f4 11 h4 c5 12 ♗f2 ♗g6 13 ♗d3 ± Gheorghiu-Fischer, Havana Ol 1966.

[14] 10 ... ♗a6 11 ♗xa6 ♘xa6 12 ♕d3 ♘b8 13 e4 ±.

[15] 15 0-0 ♘c7 16 ♗d2 ± Gheorghiu-Averbakh, Mar del Plata 1965.

[16] 6 ... ♘c6 7 ♗d3 e5 8 ♘e2 e4 9 ♗b1 b6 10 ♘g3 ♗a6 11 ♘xe4 ♘xe4 12 ♗xe4 ♗xc4 13 ♗d3 ♗xd3 14 ♕xd3 d5 = Havarinen-Vukčević, Leningrad 1960.

[17] 7 ♗d3 ♗b7 8 ♘f3 ♗e4 9 0-0 f5 10 ♕c2 d6 11 ♘e1 ♕h4 12 f3 ♘g5 13 f4 ♘e4 14 ♘f3 ♕h5 15 ♘d2 ♘xd2 16 ♗xd2 ♕g6 ±.

[18] 15 ♕e2 cd = Toran-Bisguier, Leipzig Ol 1960.

[19] 9 d5 ♘a5 10 e4 d6! =.

[20] 11 0-0 ♘a5 12 ♕e2 cd 13 cd ♖c8 14 ♗d2 ♘b3 15 ♖ad1 ♘xd4 16 ♕h5 f6 17 ♗c3 g6 18 ♕h6 ♗b3 19 f4 ∞ Geller-Durasević, USSR v Yugoslavia 1956.
11 ♗e3 ♘a5 12 ♕e2 ♖c8 13 d5 ♕h4 ∓ Geller-Smyslov, Amsterdam C 1956.

[21] **12 ... ♘d6** 13 e5 ♖e8 14 ed ed 15 ♗e3 d4 16 ♕h5 ±±.
12 ... ♕h4 13 0-0 ♘d6 14 e5 ♘dxc4 15 ♘e4 ±.

[22] 15 e5 ♘dxc4 16 ef ∞ Gipslis.

[23] 8 ♘f3 ♗b7 9 0-0 d6 10 a4 ♘bd7 11 ♕c2 ♖c8 = Jimenez-Filip, Havana 1967.

[24] 9 f3 ♘c6 10 e4 ♘e8 11 0-0 ♖c8 12 e5 f5 13 ef ♕xf6 14 ♗e3 cd 15 cd ♘d6 = Balanel-Voiculescu, Bucharest 1953.

[25] 15 ♗b2 ♖fe8 ± Euwe-Reshevsky, Zürich C 1953.

[26] 8 ... ♘e8 9 ♕h5 d6 10 e5 g6 (10 ... f5!? Gipslis) 11 ♕f3 d5 12 ♗h6 ♘g7 13 ♕f6 ♘h5 14 ♕xd8 ♖xd8 15 g4 ± Szabo-Foldi, Hungarian Ch 1955.

[27] 13 ... hg 14 hg ♗xd3 15 gf ♗g6 16 ♕g4 ±±.

[28] 15 ♗xf6 gf 16 ef ♕e5+ 17 ♔f1 ♕xf6 18 ♕g4+ ♔h7 19 ♖ad1 ± Gipslis. 16 f4!? Bronstein.

[29] 10 ... ♘a5 11 ♗g5 h6 12 ♗h4 ♗g4 13 h3 ♗xf3 14 ♕xf3 g5 15 ♗g3 ♔g7 16 h4 ± Gipslis.

[30] 11 ... ♘g6 12 ♕c2 ♘h5 13 g3 ♗h3 14 ♖e1 h6 15 ♔h1 ♕c8 16 ♘g1 ± Sanguinetti-Castillo, Mar del Plata 1948.

[31] 15 f4 ef 16 ♕d2 ± Geller-Suetin, USSR Ch 1952.

[32] 8 e4 cd 9 cd ♘xd4 10 e5 ♕a5 (10 ... ♘e8!?) 11 ♔f1 ♘e8 12 ♗d2 ♕d8 13 ♗b4 d6 14 ♗h7+ ♔xh7 15 ♕xd4 a5 16 ♗xd6 ♘xd6 17 ed ♗d7 18 ♘f3 f6 ∞ Euwe.

[33] 9 ... ♘e8 10 0-0 b6 11 f4 ♗a6? 12 f5 e5 13 f6! ± Bronstein-Najdorf, Candidates' 1950. 11 ... f5! ∞.

[34] 15 ♕d2 ± Stahlberg-Bolbochan, Mar del Plata 1946.

[35] **9 ♘g3** ♗a6 10 0-0 ♘a5 11 ♕e2 d6 12 d5 ed 13 cd c4 14 ♗c2 ♘xd5 15 ♗xh7+ ♔xh7 16 ♕h5+ ♔g8 = Beni-Müller, Gastein 1948.
9 0-0 ♗a6 10 e4 e5 11 f4 ed 12 cd cd 13 ♘g3 d6 14 e5 ♘e8 15 ♕h5 ± Riumin-Panov, USSR Ch 1934.

[36] 9 ... d6 10 f3 e5 11 0-0 ♕e7 12 ♗g5 h6 13 ♗e3 ♗d7 14 ♔h1 ♖ac8 15 g4 ± Kotov-Plater, Moscow 1947.

[37] 11 ♘g3 ♘a5 12 ♕e2 ♖c8 13 ♖c1 ♘d6! 14 e5 cd 15 ♗xd4 ♘f5 16 ♕g4 ♘xd4 ∓ Polugayevsky-Furman, Sochi 1958.

[38] 14 cb ab ∓ Ciocaltea-Geller, Szczawno Zdroj 1957.

[39] 15 ♗xc5 d6 ± Lengyel.

[40] 10 0-0 ♗a6 11 ♕a4 ♕c8 12 ♗e3 ♘a5 13 dc d6 14 ♘g3 dc 15 e5 f5 16 ef ♘xf6 = Szabo-Portisch, Hungary 1959.

[41] **10 ... d6** 11 ♕c2 h6!? (11 ... f5!? Gipslis).
10 ... ♗a6 11 ♕c2?! h6 12 0-0 ♖c8 13 ♘g3 cd 14 cd d6 15 ♕e2 de 16 ♗b2 ♘xd4 ∓ Littlewood-Gheorghiu, Hastings 1965/66. 11 ♘g3!? cd 12 cd ♘xd4 13 ♗b2 ♘c6 14 ♕h5 g6 ∞.

[42] 12 0-0 ♗a6 13 ♘g3 ♘d6 14 dc ♘xc4 15 ♘e5 ♕e5 16 ♕e2 ♘ca5 17 ♕g4 ± Starek-Somogyi, Budapest 1961.

[43] 12 ... ♗a6!? 13 ♕c2 g6 14 h4! ♘d6 15 h5 ♘xc4 16 hg hg 17 ♗xc4 ♗xc4 18 ♖h6 ♘e7! 19 ♘f4 ♕g5 =.

[44] 15 0-0 ♖c8 16 c5 ♗xd3 17 ♕xd3 ± Averbakh-Taimanov, USSR Ch 1948.

	Nimzowitsch		1 d4 ♘f6 2 c4 e6 3 ♘c3 ♗b4 4 e3 b6						
	5	6	7	8	9	10	11	12	13
1	♘e2	a3	♘f4²	cd	♔xf1	♘cxd5	♕h5	♘e6	♕e5	∞
	♗a6	♗e7!?¹	d5³	♗xf1	♘xd5⁴	ed	c6	g6	♗f6⁵	
2	...	♘g3	bc	♗a3⁷	♗xc4	e4⁹	0-0	d5	de	=
	...	♗xc3+⁶	d5	♗xc4⁸	dc	♕d7	♕b5!	♘bd7	fe¹⁰	
3	...	♕c2¹¹	a3¹³	♘xc3	♕xc3	b4¹⁶	♗b2	d5	♖d1	=
	♘e4	♗b7¹²	♗xc3+¹⁴	♘xc3¹⁵	0-0	d6	♘d7	♘f6	♕e7¹⁷	
4	♗d3	♘f3	0-0	♕c2¹⁹	bc	♘d2	f3	♗xd2	e4	=
	♗b7	♘e4	f5¹⁸	♗xc3²⁰	0-0	♕h4²¹	♘xd2	♘c6	fe²²	
5	...	...	0-0	a3²³	b4	♗xc4	♗b2	b5	♖e1	=
	...	0-0	d5	♗d6²⁴	dc	♘bd7	a5	e5	e4²⁵	
6	...	...	...	♘a4²⁶	ed	♗f4	♖c1	♖e1	♘c3	=
	...	...	c5	cd²⁷	♖e8	♗f8	d6	♘bd7	a6²⁸	

[1] 6 ... ♗xc3+ 7 ♘xc3 d5 8 b3 0-0 9 ♗e2 (9 a4 ♘c6 10 ♗a3 ♖e8 11 ♗e2 Fischer) 9 ... ♘c6 10 a4 ♖e8 (10 ... ♕d7 11 0-0 ♖fd8 intending ... e5; 10 ... dc 11 ♗a3 ♖e8 12 b4 ♘e7 13 b5 ♗b7 14 0-0 ± Fischer) 11 ♗b2 dc 12 bc ♘a5 13 ♘b5 c6 14 ♘a3 ∞ Taimanov-Kuzmin, USSR Ch 1975.

[2] 7 ♘g3 d5 8 cd ♗xf1 9 ♘xf1 ed 10 ♘g3 ♕d7 11 ♕f3 ♘c6 12 0-0 g6! 13 ♗d2 0-0 14 ♘ce2 h5! intending ... h4 ∓ Botvinnik-Bronstein, match 1951.

[3] 7 ... 0-0!? 8 e4 d6 9 d5 e5 10 ♘h3 c6! ∞ Taimanov.

[4] 9 ... ed 10 g4 g5!? 11 ♘h5 ♘xh5 12 gh ♖f8! ∞.

[5] 14 ♘xd8+ ♗xe5 15 ♘xf7 ♔xf7 16 de ♘d7 17 f4 ♘c5 ∞ Timman-Hübner, Montreal 1979.

[6] 6 ... 0-0 7 e4 ♘c6 (7 ... d5 8 cd ♗xf1 9 ♔xf1 ♗xc3 10 bc ed 11 e5 ♘e4 12 f3 ♘xg3+ 13 hg f5 14 ef ♕xf6 15 ♖h5 c6 16 ♕d3 ♕g6! 17 ♕xg6 hg 18 ♖e5 ± Gligorić-Hecht, Berlin 1971) 8 ♗d3 e5 9 d5! ♗xc3+ 10 bc ♘a5 11 ♕e2 c6 12 ♘f5 ♘e8 13 f4 ♕c7 14 fe ♕xe5 15 0-0 ± Spassky-Hübner, Munich 1979.

6 ... h5!? 7 h4 ♗b7 8 ♗d2! ±.

[7] 8 cd ♗xf1 9 ♔xf1 ♖xd5 10 ♕d3 ♘bd7 11 e4 ♕a5 12 e5 ♘d5 13 c4!? ♘b4 = Gligorić-Portisch, Wijk aan Zee 1975.

8 ♕f3 0-0 9 cd ♕xd5! 10 e4 ♕b7 11 ♗e2 ♗xe2 12 ♕xe2 c5 = Lombard-Larsen, Biel IZ 1976.

[8] 8 ... dc 9 e4 ♕d7 10 ♗e2 ♘c6 11 ♕c2 0-0-0 12 0-0 h5 13 ♖fd1 h4 14 ♘f1 (Portisch-Fischer, Siegen Ol 1970) 14 ... h3!? 15 g3 ♘a5 16 ♗b4 ♗b7 17 f3 ♘c6 ∞.

[9] 10 ♕a4+ ♕d7 11 ♕xc4 ♕c6! = Lukacs-Farago, Hungarian Ch 1976.

[10] 14 e5 ♕xe5 15 ♖e1 ♕d5! = Szabo-Hort, Wijk aan Zee 1973.

[11] 6 f3 ♗xc3+ 7 bc ♘d6 = Pritchett.

[12] 6 ... f5 7 a3 ♗xc3+ 8 ♕xc3 ♗b7 9 d5 ♘xc3 10 ♕xc3 ♕f6 11 ♕xf6 gf 12 b4 a5 = Gligorić-Andersson, Manila 1974.

[13] 7 f3 ♗xc3+ 8 bc ♘d6 9 ♘g3 ♕h4 = Taimanov-Levin, USSR 1976.

[14] 7 ... ♘xc3 8 ab (8 ♕xc3 ♗xc3+) 8 ... ♘xe2 9 ♗xe2 ♕g5 10 ♖g1 ± Taimanov.

[15] 8 ... f5 – 6 ... f5.

[16] 10 f3? ♕h4+! 11 g3 ♕h5 12 e4 f5! ∓ Farago-Kuzmin, Polanica Zdroj 1977.

10 b3 d6 11 ♗b2 ♘d7 12 0-0-0 ♕e7 13 h4 f5 = I.Ivanov-Psakhis, Vladivostok 1978.

[17] 14 ♗e2 c6 15 dc ♗xc6 16 0-0 ♖ac8 = Ivkov-Korchnoi, Amsterdam 1976.

[18] 7 ... ♗xc3 8 bc f5 9 ♖e1! ±.

7 ... ♘xc3 8 bc ♗xc3 9 ♖b1 ♘c6 10 ♖b3 ♗a5 11 e4 h6 12 d5 ♘e7 13 ♗b2 0-0 14 ♘e5! = Balashov-Romanishin, Lvov 1978.

[19] 8 d5!? ♗xc3 9 bc ♘c5! 10 ♗a3 ♘ba6 11 ♗c2 0-0 12 ♘d4 ♘f6 13 f3 ♕e7! = Taimanov.

8 ♗xe4 fe 9 ♘d2 ♗xc3 10 bc 0-0! 11 ♕g4 ♖f5! 12 d5 (12 ♘xe4 h5 ∓∓) 12 ... ♖g5 ∓ Gligorić-Larsen, Havana 1967.

[20] 8 ... ♘xc3 9 bc ♗xf3 10 gf ♕g5+ 11 ♔h1 ♗d6 12 f4 ♕h6 = Winter-Capablanca, Ramsgate 1929.

[21] 10 ... d5!? 11 cd ed 12 f3! ♘d6 13 ♗a3 ±.

[22] Rabinovich-Alekhine, Moscow 1920. 14 fe e5! 15 d5 ♘e7 16 c5! ♘g6 17 cb ab =.

[23] 8 cd ed 9 ♗d2 ♗d6 10 ♖c1 a6 11 ♘e5 c5 12 ♕f3 ♘bd7! = Gligorić.

[24] 8 ... ♗xc3 9 bc dc 10 ♗xc4 c5 =.

[25] 14 ♘d2 ♕e7 15 ♗e2 ♖ad8 = Portisch-Petrosian, Lone Pine 1978.

[26] 8 ♗d2 cd 9 ed d5 10 cd ♗xc3 11 bc ♕xd5 12 ♖e1 ♘bd7 13 ♗f4 ♖ac8 14 c4 ♕h5 15 ♗d6 ♖fd8 = Browne-Andersson, Wijk aan Zee 1976.

[27] 8 ... ♕e7!? Botvinnik.

[28] 14 a3 h6 15 b4 = Gulko-Matanović, Biel 1976.

	5	6	7	8	9	10	11	12	13	
1	♘e2	a3	♘xc3	ed	♗xc4	♗e3	0-0	♕d3[3]	♖ad1	±
	d5[1]	♗xc3+[2]	cd	dc	♘c6	0-0	b6	♗b7	h6[4]	
2	♗d3	♘f3	♗d2	d5	e4	g3	♕c2	0-0-0	♗e2	±
	♘c6	d6	e5	♘e7	♘g6	h5!	h4	♗g4	♕d7[5]	

1 d4 ♘f6 2 c4 e6 3 ♘c3 ♗b4 4 e3 c5 5 ♗d3 ♘c6 6 ♘f3 ♗xc3+ 7 bc d6

	8	9	10	11	12	13	14	15	16	
3	e4	d5[6]	♘d2[7]	♕b3	0-0[9]	g3	♖e1			=
	e5	♘e7	♕a5[8]	0-0	0-0	♗h3	f5[10]			
4	...	...	♘h4	f4![12]	♘xg6	0-0[14]	♕e1	♕g3	f5	=
	...	...	h6[11]	♘g6![13]	fg	0-0	♗d7	♕e8	g5[15]	
5	0-0	d5[16]	♕c2	♘e1[17]	e4	g3	ef	♗xf5		=
	e5	♘e7	0-0	♕e8[18]	♘h5	f5	♗xf5	♖xf5[19]		
6	...	♘d2	cd	ed	♖e1+	♗a3	♘b3	♖e3[21]		±
	...	cd	ed	♘xd4	♘e6[20]	0-0	♕d7			
7	...	...	♘b3	f4	♗e2	h3	♗d2[22]	♕e1	g4	∞
	...	0-0	b6	e4	♕d7	♘e7	♘f5	g6	♘g7[23]	

[1] 5 ... cd 6 ed d5 7 c5 ♘e4 8 ♗d2 ♘xd2 9 ♕xd2 b6! 10 a3 ♗xc3 11 ♘xc3 bc 12 dc a5 13 ♗b5+ ♗d7 14 ♖c1 a4 =. 6 ... 0-0!? 7 a3 ♗e7 8 d5 ed 9 cd ♖e8 (9 ... ♗c5!?) 10 ♗e3 (10 d6!?; 10 h3!? intending g4) 10 ... ♗g4 (10 ... d6 11 h3 ♗bd7 12 ♘g3 ± Kasparov-Andersson, Moscow 1981) 11 ♗d4 ♗f6 12 h3 ♘e5 13 ♘e4! ± Ree-Ligterink, Dutch Ch 1982.

[2] 6 ... cd 7 ab dc 8 ♘xc3 0-0 9 b3 ± Gligorić-Rellstab, Hastings 1973/74. 7 ed ♗e7 8 c5 b6 9 b4 (Torre-Pinter, Hastings 1980/81 9 ... bc 10 dc 0-0!?.

[3] 12 ♕f3 ♗b7 13 ♗d3 ♕d7 14 ♕h3 ♘xd4? 15 ♖ad1! Keene.

[4] 14 f3 ♘e7 (14 ... ♖c8 intending ... ♖c7-d7, Larsen) 15 ♗f2 ♘fd5 16 ♗a2 ♘f4 ± Korchnoi-Karpov, match 1978.

[5] 14 ♕d3 0-0-0 (Taimanov-Romanishin, USSR Ch 1976) 15 b3 intending ♔b2, a3 ±.

[6] 9 h3 h6 10 0-0 0-0 ∞. 10 ♕e2!? Keene-Ligterink, Lloyds Bank 1981.

[7] 10 0-0 ♘g6 11 ♘e1 0-0 12 g3 ♗h3 13 ♘g2 h6 14 f3 ♘h7 15 ♖f2 f5 16 ef ♗xf5 ∓ Shamkovich-Moiseyev, Moscow 1968.

[8] 10 ... ♗d7 11 ♘f1 ♕c7 12 ♘g3 0-0-0 = Gligorić-Andersson, Tilburg 1977.

[9] 12 ♘f1 ♗h5! 13 ♘e3 ♘f4 14 ♗c2 f5 = Gligorić-Sosonko, Tilburg 1977.

[10] 14 ... ♕c7 15 ♕d1 g6 16 ♘f1 ♕d7!? 17 ♗h6 ♘g7 18 f4! ± Gligorić-Timman, Tilburg 1977.

14 ... f5 = Pritchett.

[11] 10 ... ♘g6 11 ♘f5!

10 ... 0-0 11 0-0! h6 12 ♕f3! ♘g6 13 ♘f5 ♗xf5 14 ♗xf5 ♘h7 15 ♖b1 ♕e7 16 g3 ± Hort-Adamski, Polanica Zdroj 1977.

[12] 11 g3 g5 12 ♘g2 ♕a5 13 ♕b3 (13 ♗d2!) 13 ... ♗h3 14 0-0 0-0 = Najdorf-Hübner, Wijk aan Zee 1971.

11 f3 ♕a5 12 ♗d2 g5 13 ♘f5 ♗xf5 14 ef ♗d7 = Donner-Timman, Amsterdam 1981.

[13] 11 ... ef 12 ♗xf4 g5 13 e5! ♘g4 14 e6! ± Spassky.

[14] 13 fe? de 14 ♗e3 b6 15 0-0 0-0 16 a4?! a5! ∓ Spassky-Fischer, match (5) 1972.

[15] 17 ♕f3 ♕h5 = Tarjan-Dzhindzhihashvili, Hastings 1977/78.

[16] 9 ♘g5!? 0-0 10 f4 cd 11 cd ed 12 ed d5! 13 c5 h6! =.

[17] 11 ♘h4 ♖e8 12 e4 h6 13 f4 ♘g6! 14 ♘xg6 fg 15 fe de ∓ Kruger-Lukov, Bulgaria 1977.

[18] 11 ... ♘g6 12 f4 ef 13 ef ♖e8 14 h3 ♘h5 =.

[19] Farago-Portisch, Budapest 1975.

[20] 12 ... ♗e6 13 ♗b2 ♘c6 14 ♘e4 ♘xe4 15 ♗xe4 ±.

[21] 15 ♖e3 ± Portisch-Timman, Wijk aan Zee 1978.

[22] 14 ♕e1 h5 15 ♗d2 ♕f5 16 ♔h2 ♕h7! 17 a4 ♘f5 18 g3 a5 ∓ Johner-Nimzowitsch, Dresden 1926.

[23] 17 ♕h4 ♘fe8 18 a4 f5 19 g5 ∞ Nimzowitsch.

Taimanov   1 d4 ♘f6 2 c4 e6 3 ♘c3 ♗b4 4 e3 ♘c6

	5	6	7	8	9	10	11	12	13	
1	♘e2[1]	a3	cd	♘f4	♕b3!?[4]	♕a2	b4	♗xc4	♕xc4	∞
	d5	♗e7[2]	ed	0-0[3]	♘a5	c6[5]	♘c4	dc	a5[6]	
2	♗d3	♘e2[8]	ed	c5!?[10]	0-0	bc	♘g3	♗a3	♕f3	±
	e5?![7]	ed[9]	d5	0-0	♗xc3	h6	b6	♖e8	♗g4[11]	
3	♘f3	♗d3	0-0[12]	h3!	♗xc4	e4	♗e3	♘xd4	♖e1[13]	=
	0-0	d5	a6	dc	♗d6	e5	ed	♗d7	♘e5[14]	
4	...	...	...	♗xc4	♗b5[16]	♗xc6	ed[18]	♗g5	♖e1	=
	...	...	dc	♗d6[15]	e5![17]	ed	bc	♖e8	♖xe1+[19]	

[1] **5 a3 ♗xc3+ – Sämisch.**
   5 ♗d2!?
[2] 6 ... ♗f8!? 7 cd (7 ♘g1!? g6 8 ♘f3 ♗g7 Taimanov) 7 ... ed 8 ♘f4 ♘e7 9 b4 a6 10 g3 c6 11 ♗g2 ♘f5 12 0-0 ♗d6! = Osnos-Taimanov, Tbilisi 1967.
[3] 8 ... ♗f5 9 ♕b3!
[4] 9 ♗e2 ♗f5 10 g4! ♗e6 11 g5 ♘d7 12 h4 ♘b6 13 ♗d3 ±. 9 ... ♘b8!? intending ... c6 Botvinnik.
[5] 10 ... ♗e6 11 ♘xe6 fe = Pritchett.
[6] Taimanov.
[7] 5 ... d5 6 a3 dc 7 ♗xc4 ♗d6 8 f4! ± Keene-Fedorowicz, New York 1981.
[8] 6 d5!? e4?! 7 ♕c2 ♘e5 ∞ Darga-Pachman, European Team Ch 1957.
[9] 6 ... d5!? 7 0-0 dc 8 ♗xc4 ed 9 ed 0-0 10 ♗g5 ♗e7 = Pritchett. 7 cd ♘xd5 8 e4 ♘b6 9 d5 ♘e7 10 a3 ♗d6 11 ♗g5 h6 12 ♗h4 c6! = Lipnitsky-Borisenko, USSR Ch 1950.
[10] 8 cd ♘xd5 9 0-0-0-0 10 a3 ♗e7 11 ♕b3 ♘f6 12 ♖d1 a6 13 h3 ♗d6 14 ♗g5 h6 = Matanović-Taimanov, Stockholm 1951.
[11] 14 ♕f4 ♘e7 15 ♖ae1 ♗e6 16 ♘c1 bc

[17] ♗xc5 ± Gligorić-Pachman, Havana Ol 1966.
[12] 7 a3 dc 8 ♗xc4 ♗d6 9 b4 e5 10 ♗b2 ♗g4 11 d5 ♘e7 12 h3 ♗d7 13 ♘g5 (Botvinnik-Tal, 3rd match game 1961) 13 ... h6! 14 ♘ge4 ♘xe4 15 ♘xe4 f5! Pritchett.   11 de ♘xe5 12 ♗e2 ♕e7 13 ♘b5 ♖fd8 14 ♕c2 a6 = Botvinnik-Tal, 5th match game 1961.
[13] Taimanov-Fischer, Buenos Aires 1960.
[14] 14 ♗b3 ♘g6 = Taimanov.
[15] 8 ... ♕e8!? 9 a3 (9 e4!? ♗xc3 10 bc ♘xe4 11 ♗d3 f5 ∞ Taimanov) 9 ... ♗d6 10 e4 e5 11 d5 ♘e7 12 h3 ± Pritchett.
[16] 9 ♘b5 ♗e7 10 ♕c2 a6 11 ♘c3 ♗d6 = Medina-Zuckerman, Malaga 1968.
   9 e4 e5 10 d5 ♘e7 11 ♗g5 ♘g6 12 ♖c1 a6 =.
   9 h3!? e5 10 ♕c2 ♕e7 11 ♗d2 ♗d7 12 ♖ae1 ♖ae8 = Bolbochan-Pachman, Helsinki 1952.
[17] 9 ... ♕e7 10 e4 e5 11 ♗xc6 bc 12 de (12 ♗g5!?) 12 ... ♗xe5 13 ♘xe5 ♕xe5 ∞ Lipnitsky.
[18] 11 ♗xb7 ♗xb7 12 ♘xd4 ♗d7 13 ♘bd5 ♗c6 14 f3 ♗e5! ∞ Furman-Lipnitsky, USSR 1951.
   11 ♕xd4 bc 12 ♗xc6 ♕e8 13 ♘d4 ♗b7 14 ♘f5 ♗e5 15 ♕c2 ♗e6 16 f3 g6 17 ♘d4 ♕d6+∓.
[19] 14 ♕xe1 ♗f5 15 ♘e5 c5! = Pritchett.

1 d4 ♘f6 2 c4 e6 3 ♘c3 ♗b4 4 e3 0-0 5 ♗d3

	5	6	7	8	9	10	11	12	13	
1	...	♘e2	0-0[2]	♘g3	bc	♕c2	d5	f4	ef	±
	d6[1]	e5	♖e8[3]	♗xc3	c5[4]	h6	♘bd7	ef	♘f8[5]	
2	...	cd	♘e2	0-0[6]	a3	ab	b5![7]	♘xc3[9]	♗e2	±
	d5	ed	c5	♘c6	cd	dc	♘e5[8]	♕c7[10]	♖d8[11]	
3	...	a3	♗xh7+	ab	b5	♘f3	♔f1	♘d2	♘xc4	∞
	...	dc[12]	♘xh7[13]	♘c6	♘b4	♘d3+	♘f6[14]	e5	ed	
4	...	...	bc	cd	♘e2	f3	0-0	♘g3	♖a2	∞
	...	♗c3+	c5[15]	ed[16]	♖e8[17]	♘c6	b6[18]	♘a5	♘b7![19]	
5	...	...	...	...	...	0-0	♘g3	♕xd3	f3	=
	...	...	...	...	b6	♗a6[20]	♗xd3	♘c6	♕d7[21]	
6	...	...	...	...	...	...	♗xa6	♕d3[22]	f3	±
	...	...	...	...	...	...	♘xa6	♘c7	♖e8[23]	

	5	6	7	8	9	10	11	12	13	
7	...	...	...	♗xc4	♘e2[25]	0-0	♗b2	♗a2	♖e1	±
	...	...	dc	c5[24]	♘c6	♕c7	♖d8	b6	♗b7[26]	
8	...	...	...	...	...	0-0[27]	♗b2	♖c1[28]	♗a2	=
	...	...	...	...	e5	♘c6	♕c7	♘a5	c4[29]	
9	...	♘e2	a3[30]	ed	♗xc4	0-0	♗a2	♘f4	d5	=
	...	c5	cd	dc	♗d6[31]	♘bd7	♘b6	♗d7	♗xf4[32]	
10	...	...	0-0	ed	♗xc4	♕d3	a4	♗b3		=
	...	...	cd	dc[33]	♘bd7[34]	a6[35]	♘b6[36]	♘bd5[37]		

---

[1] 5 ... ♗c3+ 6 bc d6 7 ♘e2 ♕e7 8 0-0 e5 9 f3 c5 10 e4 ±.

[2] 7 d5?! ♗g4 8 f3 e4! 9 fg ed 10 ♘g3 ♘a6 ∓.

[3] 7 ... c6 8 a3 ♗a5 9 b4 ♗c7 10 ♕c2 ± Taimanov-Golombek, Moscow Ol 1956.

[4] 9 ... e4 10 ♗c2 c6 ± Mecking-Schweber, Mar del Plata 1969.

[5] Reshevsky-Keres, AVRO 1938.

[6] 8 a3 cd 9 ab dc 10 ♘xc3 ♗g4 = Botvinnik.

[7] 11 bc ♘e5 12 ♗c2 ♗d7 13 ♖a5 ♖e8 = Goldberg-Taimanov, USSR Ch 1949.

[8] 11 ... cb 12 ♗xb2 ♘b4 (12 ... ♘e7 13 ♘d4 ±) 13 ♗xh7+ ♔h7 (13 ... ♘h7 14 ♕d4 ±) 14 ♗xf6 ♕xf6 15 ♕b1+ ±.

[9] 12 bc ♗g4 13 f3 ♗d7 14 ♗a3 ± Rayković-Vuković, Smederevska Palanka 1971.

[10] Better is 12 ... ♗g4 or 12 ... ♗xd3.

[11] 14 ♕d4 ± Keene-Langeweg, Holland 1980.

[12] 6 ... ♗e7 7 cd ed 8 b4 b6 9 ♘ge2 c5 10 b5 a6 11 0-0 ab 12 ♗xb5 ± Petrosian-Antoshin, USSR 1957.

[13] 7 ... ♔xh7 8 ab ♘c6 9 ♘f3 ♘xb4 10 0-0 c5 11 ♘e5 ♕e7 12 ♘xc4 ± Petrosian-Sosonko, Biel IZ 1976.

[14] 11 ... ♘xc1? 12 ♖xc1 ♗d7 13 ♘e5 ♕e8 14 ♕a4 ± Balashov-Averbakh, USSR Ch 1970.

[15] 7 ... e5 8 cd ♕xd5 9 f3 ed 10 ed c5 11 ♘e2 cd 12 ♘xd4 ± Furman-Holmov, USSR Ch 1963.

[16] 8 ... ♕xd5 9 ♕f3 cd 10 ♕xd5 ed 11 cd b6 12 f3 ♗a6 13 ♔e2 ± Shamkovich-Tolush, USSR 1957.

[17] 9 ... ♗g4 10 f3 ♗h5 11 ♘f4 ♗g6 12 ♖b1 b6 13 ♖b2 ♘c6 14 g4 ± Reshevsky-Fischer, Los Angeles (match) 1961.

[18] 11 ... a6 12 ♕e1 b5 13 ♕f2 ♗e6 14 h3 ♖a7 15 ♗d2 ♕b6 16 ♖fb1 ± Lilienthal-Ragozin, Moscow 1935.
    11 ... ♘e7 12 g4! h6 13 ♕e1 ±.

[19] Black intends ... h5 and ... ♘d6.

[20] 10 ... ♗b7 11 f3 ♘c6 12 ♘g3 ♖e8 13 ♖a2 cd 14 cd ♖c8 15 ♖e2 ♖c7 16 ♗b2 ± Keene-Purdy, Sydney 1979.

[21] 14 ♗d2?! ♖ad8 15 ♖ad1 ♘e8 16 ♗e1 ♘d6! 17 e4 ♘c4 ∓ Byrne-Stean, London 1979.

[22] 14 ♗b2 = Stean.

[22] 12 ♗b2 ♕d7 13 a4 ♖fe8 14 ♕d3 c4 15 ♕c2 ± Botvinnik-Capablanca, AVRO 1938. 13 ... cd 14 cd ♖fc8 = Botvinnik.

[23] 13 ... ♕e8 14 a4 ♕c6 15 c4 ± Lilienthal-Benko, Moscow v Budapest 1949.
    13 ... ♖e8 14 ♘g3 ♘e6 15 ♗b2 ♕d7 16 ♖ae1 ± Tomić-Szabo, Vinkovci 1970.

[24] 8 ... e5 9 ♘f3 ♘c6 10 0-0 e4 11 ♘d2 ♘a5 12 ♗e2 ± Eliskases-Opocensky, Nanheim 1935.

[25] 9 ♗b2 ♕a5 10 ♕d2 ♘e4 11 ♕c2 ♘d6 12 ♗d3 cd 13 ed e5 ∞ Botvinnik.

[26] 14 ♘g3 ♖d7 15 ♕e2 ♖ad8 16 ♖ad1 ± Petrosian-Korchnoi, match 1980.

[27] 10 de? ♕xd1+ 11 ♔xd1 ♘g4 ∓.
    10 d5 b5 11 ♗xb5 ♕xd5 =.

[28] 12 ♗a2 ♖d8 13 ♕c2 ♗g4 14 ♘g3 ♕e7 =/∓ Seirawan-Speelman, London 1982.

[29] 14 ♘g3 ♖e8 15 ♕e2 ♗d7 = .

[30] 7 cd cd 8 ed ♘xd5 9 0-0 ♘c6 10 a3 ♗e7 11 ♕c2 h6 12 ♖d1 ♘xc3 13 bc b6 = H.Steiner-Evans, USA 1952.

[31] 9 ... ♗e7 10 0-0 ♘bd7 11 ♗f4 ♘b6 12 ♗b3 ♘bd5 13 ♗e5 ± J.Bolbochan-Martin, Buenos Aires 1946.

[32] 13 ... e5? 14 ♘e6 ± Botvinnik.
    13 ... ♗xf4 14 ♗xf4 ♘fxd5 15 ♘xd5 ed 16 ♗xd5 ♕f6 17 ♗c7 ♘xd5 18 ♕xd5 ♗c6 19 ♕e5 ½-½ Hübner-Hort, Wijk aan Zee 1975.

[33] 8 ... ♘c6 9 ♗g5 ♗e7 10 cd ♘xd5 11 ♗xe7 ♘dxe7 = Bolbochan-Najdorf, Buenos Aires (match) 1949.

[34] 9 ... ♘c6 10 ♗g5 ♗e7 11 a3 b6 12 ♕d3 ♗b7 13 ♖ad1 ♘d5 = Soos-Portisch, Balatonfüred 1959.

[35] 10 ... b6 11 a3 ♗e7 12 ♗e3 ♗b7 13 ♖ac1 ♘g4?! 14 ♗f4 e5 15 ♗g3! ± Christianen-Browne, US Ch 1980. 12 ♖d1 ♗b7 13 ♕h3! ♖e8 14 ♗a2 ± Petrosian-Miles, Tilburg 1981 – 14 ... ♖c8 15 d5 ±.

[36] 11 ... b6 12 ♗g5 ♗b7 13 ♖ac1 ♗e7 14 ♖fd1 ± Petrosian-Bronstein, Tallinn 1979.

[37] Petrosian.

1 d4 ♘f6 2 c4 e6 3 ♘c3 ♗b4 4 e3 0-0 5 ♘f3¹ d5

	6	7	8	9	10	11	12	13	14	
1	♗d2 c5²	a3³ ♗xc3	♗xc3 ♘e4	♖c1 ♘xc3	♖xc3 cd	ed ♘c6	♗e2⁴ dc	♗xc4 ♕f6	0-0 ♖d8⁵	=
2	a3 ♗xc3+⁶	bc c5⁷	♗b2⁸ ♘c6	♖c1 ♖e8	♗d3 dc	♗xc4 e5	de ♕xd1+	♖xd1 ♘xe5	♘xe5 ♖xe5⁹	=
3	... ♗e7	♗d3¹⁰ b6¹¹	0-0 c5	b3¹² ♘c6	♗b2 ♗b7	cd ed	♘e2 ♘e4	dc bc	♕c2 ♕b6¹³	=
4	♗d3 ♘c6¹⁴	a3 dc¹⁵	♗xc4 ♗d6	b4¹⁶ e5	♗b2 ♗g4	de¹⁷ ♘xe5	♗e2 ♘xf3+¹⁸	♗xf3 ♗xf3	♕xf3 ♗e5!¹⁹	=
5	... ...	0-0 dc²⁰	♗xc4 ♗d6	♗b5 e5²¹	♗xc6 ed	ed bc	♗g5 h6	♗h4 ♖b8	♕c2 ♖b6²²	±
6	... b6	0-0²³ ♗b7	a3²⁴ ♗d6²⁵	b4 dc	♗xc4 ♘bd7	♗b2 a5²⁶	b5 ♕e7	♘e2 ♖ad8	♘g3 ♘e4²⁷	=
7	... ...	... ...	cd ed²⁸	♘e5²⁹ ♗d6³⁰	f4 c5	♖f3³¹ g6	♗d2 ♘c6	♖h3 cd	♗xc6 ♗xc6³²	=
8	... ...	... ...	... ...	a3 ♗d6³³	b4 ♖e8	♕b3 a6	a4³⁴ ♘c6	♗a3 a5	b5 ♘b4³⁵	=
9	... c5	a3 cd³⁶	ed³⁷ ♗xc3+	bc dc	♗xc4 ♕c7	♕d3 ♘bd7	0-0 b6³⁸	♖fe1 ♗b7	♗a2 ♖ac8³⁹	∓
10	... ...	0-0 ♘bd7	a3 ♗a5⁴⁰	cd⁴¹ ed	b4! cb	♘b5 ♘b8⁴²	ab ♗xb4	♖xa7 ♖xa7	♘xa7 ♗e6⁴³	±
11	... ...	... b6	cd⁴⁴ ed	♘e5 ♗b7⁴⁵	♗d2 ♘c6	a3 ♗xc3	♗xc3 ♖e8	♘xc6 ♗xc6	dc!⁴⁶ bc⁴⁷	±
12	... ...	... ...	... ...	... ♖e8!	♗d2⁴⁸ ♗a6	♗xa6 ♘xa6	♕a4 ♕c8	♖fc1⁴⁹ ♕b7	♕c6 ♖ab8⁵⁰	=
13	... ...	... ...	... ...	dc bc⁵¹	♘e2 ♗b7	b3 ♘bd7⁵²	♗b2 ♗a5	♘g3 g6	♖c1 ♖c8⁵³	±

---

¹ 5 ♘e2 (Reshevsky) 5 ... d5 6 a3 ♗e7 7 cd ed (7 ... ♘xd5 8 ♕c2 ±) 8 g3 c6 9 ♗g2 ♗f5 10 0-0 ♗d6? (10 ... ♖e8! = Timman) 11 f3 ♕e7 12 e4! ± Petrosian-Timman, Bugojno 1982.

² 6 ... ♘c6!? 7 ♖c1 a6 8 a3 ♗d6 9 c5 ♗e7 10 ♗d3 ♖e8 11 b4 ± Hort-Nowak, Havirov 1970.

³ 7 ♕c2 Alekhine.

⁴ 12 c5 e5! Alekhine.

⁵ Alekhine-Kmoch, San Remo 1930.

⁶ 6 ... ♗d6 7 c5 ♗e7 8 b4 ♘e4 9 ♗b2 ♘d7 10 ♗d3 ± Petrosian-Fischer, Yugoslavia C 1959.

⁷ 7 ... dc? 8 ♗xc4 c5 9 ♕d3 ♘bd7 10 e4 ±/±.

⁸ 8 ♗d3 – Main Line.

⁹ Geller-Spassky, match 1965.

154

10 7 b4 a5 8 b5 c5 9 bc bc 10 c5 ♘bd7 11 ♕c2 ♕c7 12 ♕c2 ♕c7 13 ♗e2 e5 = Furman-Holmov, USSR 1953.

11 7 ... c5 8 0-0 dc 9 ♗xc4 ♘c6 10 ♗d3 cd 11 ed b6 12 b4 ± Lipnitsky-Polyak, USSR 1949.

12 9 cd ed 10 dc bc 11 e4 de 12 ♘xe4 ♗a6 = Smyslov-Keres, USSR Ch 1949.

13 Bronstein-Furman, USSR Ch 1948.

14 6 ... ♘bd7 7 a3 dc 8 ♗xc4 ♗d6 9 b4 e5 10 ♗b2 ± Botvinnik-van Scheltinga, Wijk aan Zee 1969.

6 ... ♘c6 – see also Taimanov.

15 7 ... ♗xc3+ 8 bc ♘a5 9 ♘d2 c5 10 0-0 b6 11 cd ed 12 f3 ± Reshevsky-Fischer, match 1961.

16 9 0-0 e5 10 h3 ♗f5 11 d5 ♘e7 12 ♘d2 c6 = Geller-Furman, USSR Ch 1955.

17 11 d5 ♘e7 12 h3 ♗d7 13 ♘g5 h6! (13 ... ♗g6? 14 ♘e6! fe 15 de ♔h8 16 ed ± Botvinnik-Tal, match 1961) 14 ♘ge4 ♘xe4 = Schwarz.

18 12 ... ♕e7?! 13 ♘b5 ♖ad8 14 ♕c2 a6 15 ♘xd6 cd 16 ♕d1 ± Botvinnik-Tal, match 1961.

19 15 ♖d1 ♖c8 16 0-0 c6 =.

20 7 ... a6 8 h3 h6 9 a3 dc 10 ♗xc4 ♗d6 11 e4 e5 12 ♗e3 ± Portisch-Emma, Mar del Plata 1966.

21 9 ... ♗d7 10 e4 ± Kotov.

22 Furman-Kopilov, USSR 1954.

23 7 cd ed – 8 cd. 7 ... ♘xd5? 8 ♕c2 h6 9 a3 ♗xc3+ 10 bc ♘d7 11 c4 ± Landau-Prins, Margate 1938.

7 a3 ♗xc3+ 8 bc ♗a6 9 cd ♗xd3 10 ♕xd3 e5 = Yudovich.

24 8 ♗d2 c5 9 cd cd! 10 ed ♘xd5 11 ♕e2 ♘f6 = Toran-Szabo, Palma de Mallorca 1969.

25 8 ... ♗xc3 9 bc dc 10 ♗xc4 ♘c6 11 ♖e1 ♘a5 12 ♗d3 ♗e4 13 ♗f1 c5 14 ♘e5 ± Gligorić-Loftsson, USA 1972.

26 11 ... ♕e7 12 ♘b5 a6 13 ♘xd6 cd 14 b5! ± Gligorić-Donner, match 1968.

27 Olafsson-Bisguier, Stockholm IZ 1962. See also Nimzowitsch Variation.

28 8 ... ♘xd5 9 ♕c2 ±.

29 9 ♗d2 ♘bd7 10 ♖c1 a6 11 ♘e5 ♘xe5 (11 ... ♗d6 12 f4 ♘e4 13 ♘xe4 de 14 ♗c4 ± Gligorić-Pirc, Zagreb 1955) 12 de ♘d7 13 e6 (13 f4?! ♘c5 14 ♗c2 d4 ∓ Taimanov) 13 ... ♘f6 (13 ... fe?! 14 ♕g4 ♕e7 15 ♘xd5! ±) 14 ♘e2 ♗xd2 15 ef+ ♔xf7 16 ♕xd2 = Gligorić-Filip, Zagreb 1955.

30 9 ... ♘bd7 10 f4 c5 11 ♕f3 (11 ♗f5 g6 12 ♗h3 ♗xc3 13 bc ♘xe5 14 de ♘e4 ∓ Portisch-Rogoff, Las Palmas 1976) 11 ... ♗xc3 12 bc ♘e4 oo Yudovich.

31 11 ♕f3 ♘c6 12 ♕h3 g6 13 ♗d2 cd 14 ♘xc6

♗xc6 15 ed ♘e4 16 ♗xe4 de 17 f5 ♗c5! 18 ♗e3 ♗xd4 19 ♖ad1 ♗xe3+ 20 ♕xe3 ♕e7! ∓ Farago-Lerner, Kiev 1978.

32 15 ed ♘e4 16 f5 ♕f6 17 ♗xe4 de (17 ... ♕xd4+? 18 ♗e3 ±±) 18 ♕g4 ♗xf5 19 ♕h4? h5 ∓ Knaak-Petrosian, Tallinn 1979. 19 ♕xf5 gf 20 ♖f1 = Petrosian.

33 9 ... ♗xc3?! 10 bc ♘bd7 11 c4 c5 12 ♗b2 ♖c8 13 ♖c1 ±.

34 12 ♗b2 ♘bd7 13 ♖fe1 c6 14 e4 de 15 ♘xe4 ♘xe4 = Taimanov.

35 Taimanov-Averbakh, USSR 1953.

36 7 ... ♗xc3+ 8 bc dc 9 ♗xc4 ♕c7 10 ♗a2 b6 11 0-0 ♗b7 12 ♘e5! ± Bagirov-Makarichev, USSR 1979.

37 8 ab?! dc 9 c5 (9 bc ♕c7 10 ♕b3 e5 ∓) 9 ... b6! 10 ♕c2 bc! (10 ... ♗b7?! 11 ♕xc3 ♕c7 12 ♘d4 a6 13 cb ♕xb6 14 ♕c5 ± Korchnoi-Padevsky, Wijk aan Zee 1968) 11 bc cb 12 ♗xb2 ♘c6 ∓.

38 12 ... e5 13 ♘xe5 ♘xe5 14 de ♕xe5 = Donner-Unzicker, Brunnen 1966.

39 15 ♘d2 =.

40 8 ... cd 9 ♘xd5! ed 10 ab dc 11 ♗xc4 ♘b6 12 ♗b3 de 13 ♗xe3 ± Tal-Tolush, USSR 1958.

8 ... dc 9 ab cd 10 ♗xh7+ ♔xh7 11 ♕d4 ♘b6 12 e4 ± Antoshin-Estrin, USSR 1957.

41 10 ♘e5 cd! 11 ed ♗xc3 12 bc ♕c7 13 ♘xd7 ♗xd7 14 ♕c2 ♖fe8 15 f3 h6 Donner-Korchnoi, Wijk aan Zee 1968.

42 11 ... ♗c7 12 ♕c2 ♗b8 13 ab ± Damjanović-Barczay, Sarajevo 1969.

11 ... a6 12 ♕b3 ba 13 ♘d6 ♗c7 14 ♗xa3 ± Gligorić-Damjanović, Yugoslavia 1968.

43 Tukmakov-Tal, USSR 1970.

44 8 a3 ♗xc3 9 bc ♗a6 10 cd ed 11 ♘e5 ♗xd3 = Donner-Pomar, Leysin 1967.

45 9 ... ♗xc3!? 10 bc ♗a6 11 ♗a3 ♖e8 12 ♖c1 ♗xd3 13 ♕xd3 c4 oo Parma.

46 14 ♖c1?! c4 15 ♗b1 b5 16 ♖e1 ♘e4 17 f3 ♘xc3 18 ♖xc3 ♕b6 ∓ Gligorić-Spassky, Bugojno 1978.

47 15 b4! d4 16 ed cd 17 ♗b2 (17 ♗xd4?? ♕d5 ∓∓) 17 ... ♕d5 18 f3 ♘g4 (18 ... a5 19 ♖c1 ± Gligorić-Bukić, Yugoslavia 1979) 19 ♕d2 ♘e3 20 ♖fc1 ± Gligorić-Ljubojević, Belgrade (match) 1979.

48 10 ♘e2!? Forintos.

49 13 ♘b5 ♖e6 14 ♗xb4 ♘xb4 = Forintos.

50 Portisch-Spassky, Geneva (match) 1977.

51 9 ... ♗xc3 10 bc bc 11 c4 ±.

52 11 ... d4 12 a3 ♗a5 13 b4 ♗c7 14 bc ± Gligorić-Keres, Moscow Ol 1956.

53 Gligorić-Szabo, Moscow Ol 1956.

1 d4 ♘f6 2 c4 e6 3 ♘c3 ♗b4 4 e3 0-0 5 ♗d3 c5 6 ♘f3 d5 7 0-0 dc 8 ♗xc4

	8	9	10	11	12	13	14	15	16	
1	...	♗d3[1]	♘e4	ed	♕e2	♗e3	de	♘xe5	♘xf6+	±
	♕e7	♘c6	cd	h6	♖d8	e5	♘xe5	♕xe5	♕xf6[2]	
2	...	a3	♕d3[3]	♖d1	♗a2	♕e2	e4	d5	♘xd4	±
	♘c6	♗a5!?	a6	b5	c4!?[4]	♕e8	e5	♘d4	ed[5]	
3	...	♕e2[7]	♖d1	a3	bc	a4!	♗b3	c4	ed	±
	♗d7[6]	♗c6	♕e7	♗xc3[8]	♘bd7	♖fc8	♕e8	cd	♘b6[9]	
4	...	♕e2[10]	d5	de	ef+	bc	e4	♖e1	♗xb5	∞
	b6	♘bd7[11]	♗xc3	♘e5	♔h8	♗g4	♕e7	b5	♘h5[12]	
5	...	♕e2	a3[13]	♗d3[14]	b4	ed	♗g5	♘e4	♘c5	±
	♘bd7	a6	♗a5	b5	cd	♗b6	♗b7	♕b8	♗xc5[15]	
6	...	ed	♗g5[16]	♕e2[17]	bc	♗d3	c4	♗e4	♕xe4	=
	cd	b6	♗b7	♗xc3!	♘bd7	♕c7	♘g4	♗xe4	♘gf6[18]	
7	...	...	...	♖e1	♖c1	♕b3	♘e5	de		=
	...	...	...	♘bd7[19]	♖c8	♗e7![20]	♘xe5	♘d7		

[1] 9 a3 ♗a5!? 10 ♕e2 ♖d8 11 ♗d2 cd 12 ed ♘c6 13 ♗e3 a6 14 ♖ad1 ½-½ Rajković-Bukić, Yugoslav Ch 1981.

[2] 17 ♗e4 ± Olafsson-O'Kelly, Dundee 1967.

[3] 10 ♗a2 a6?! 11 ♖b1 ♗b6 12 ♕c2! ± Polugayevsky-Karpov, match 1974. 10 ... ♗b6!?

[4] 12 ... ♗b6 13 dc ♕xd3 14 ♖xd3 ♗xc5 15 b4 ♗b6 16 ♗b2 ± Danner-Luczak, Haide 1981.

[5] 17 ♖xd4 ♗b6 18 ♗e3 ± Knaak-Lechtynsky, Halle 1981.

[6] Bronstein (intending ... ♗c6).

[7] 9 a3 ♗xc3 (9 ... ♗a5 10 ♕e2 ♗c6 11 ♖d1 ♕e7 ∞ Knaak-Vilela, Halle 1981) 10 bc ♗c6 = Taimanov-Wade, Buenos Aires 1960.
     9 ♗d3 ♗c6 10 ♘e5 ♘bd7 11 ♘xc6 bc 12 ♕f3 cd 13 ed ♘d5 ∞ Holmov.

[8] 11 ... ♗a5 12 ♗d2 ± Korchnoi-Matanović, Palma de Mallorca 1968.

[9] 17 a5 ± Gligorić-Taimanov, Montilla 1977.

[10] 9 a3 cd 10 ab dc 11 ♕xd8 ♖xd8 12 bc ♘e4 = Gligorić-Filip, Varna Ol 1962.
     9 ♗d3 ♘bd7 10 a3 cd 11 ed ♗xc3 12 bc ♗b7 13 ♖e1 ♕c7 14 ♗d2 ∞ Reshevsky-Donner, Santa Monica 1966.

[11] 9 ... ♗b7 10 ♖d1 ♕c8 11 ♘b5 cd 12 ♘bxd4 ♘c6 = Reshevsky-Mednis, US Ch 1963/64.

[12] 17 ♗g5 (Gligorić-H.Olafsson, Lone Pine 1979) 17 ... ♘xf3+!?
     17 ♗c4! ∞/± Knaak-Vadasz, Trnava 1981.

[13] 10 a4 ♕c7 11 ♗a2 b5 12 ♗d3 ♗a5 13 ab ab 14 ♗xb5 ♗b7 15 ♖d1 ♖fb8! = Portisch-Karpov, Moscow 1981.

[14] 11 ♗a2 cd 12 ed ♗xc3! 13 bc b5 = Psakhis-Kasparov, USSR Ch 1981.

[15] 17 dc ♗xf3 18 ♕xf3 ♘e5 19 ♕h3 ± Vaganian-Platonov, USSR Ch 1971.

[16] 10 ♕e2 ♗b7 11 ♖d1 ♘bd7 12 ♗d2 ♖c8 13 ♗a6?! ♗xa6 14 ♕xa6 ♗xc3 15 bc ♖c7! ∓ Taimanov-Karpov, USSR Team Ch 1973.

[17] 11 ♖c1 ♘bd7 12 ♗e2 ♖c8 13 ♘e5 h6 14 ♘xd7 ♕xd7 15 ♗xf6 gf 16 ♖fd1 ♕c6 17 ♕g4+ ♔h7 18 ♘d5!! ± (18 ... ed 19 ♗d3+) Taimanov-Browne, Wijk aan Zee 1981.
     ... ♗e7! is safer on moves 11 and 12.

[18] Petrosian-Karpov, Milan 1975.

[19] 11 ... ♗xc3 12 bc ♘bd7 13 ♗d3 ♖c8 14 ♖c1 ♕c7 15 ♗h4 =/± Portisch-Browne, Tilburg 1978.

[20] 13 ... ♕e7?! 14 ♗d5! ±/± Browne-Ljubojević, Tilburg 1978.

Main Line 1 d4 Nf6 2 c4 e6 3 Nc3 Bb4 4 e3 0-0 5 Nf3 d5 6 Bd3 c5 7 0-0 Nc6 8 a3 Bxc3 9 bc

	9	10	11	12	13	14	15	16	17	
1	...	cd[1]	Bb2[2]	Bc2	Qe1	Nd2	Qxd2	f3	e4	=
	b6	ed	c4	Bg4[3]	Ne4[4]	Bxd2	f5[5]	Bh5	fe	
2	...	...	Ne5	Nxc6	f3	Qe2[7]	a4	Bc2	Qf2	±
	...	...	Qc7[6]	Qxc6	a5	Bb7	c4	Rfe8	Qe6[8]	
3	...	Qe2?!	Bxc4	Nxe5[9]	de	f3[10]	a4?![11]	Bb2	Bxf6	∓
	Qc7	dc	e5	Nxe5	Qxe5	Bd7	Qxc3	Ba5	gf[12]	
4	...	cd	a4	Ba3	Bc2	Qe1	Bxe4[14]	Nd2	f3	=
	...	ed	Re8	c4	Ne4	Qd8[13]	Rxe4	Re8	Qa5[15]	
5	...	...	Nh4	a4[17]	Ba3	Bc2[18]	Nf5[19]	Nxe4	Ng3	±
	...	...	Ne7[16]	Re8	c4	Ng6	Ne4	Rxe4	Re8[20]	
6	...	Bxc4	Ne5[21]	de	f4	Bd3	a4[22]	Qc2[23]	Bxh7+	∓
	dc	Qe7	Nxe5	Nd7	Nb6	Bd7	Rad8	Bxa4!	Kh8[24]	
7	...	...	Bb2[25]	Be2[26]	Qc2	de	c4[27]	gf	Rfd1	=
	...	Qc7	e5	Rd8	Bg4	Nxe5	Nxf3+	Bh3	Qc6[28]	

---

[1] **10** Ne5 Ne5 11 de dc 12 Bxc4 Qxd1 13 Rxd1 Ng4 =.
  10 Qc2 Ba6 11 cd Bxd3 12 Qxd3 ed = Taimanov.

[2] **11 dc** bc 12 c4 dc 13 Bxc4 Na5 14 Be2 Qxd1 15 Rxd1 Rb8 16 Bd3 Bb7 = R.Byrne-Skold, Helsinki Ol 1952.
  11 Qe2?! c4 12 Bc2 Bg4 13 h3 Bh5 14 Re1 Re8 15 Bd1 Ne4 16 Qc2 Na5 ∓ Lopez Esnaola-Alekhine, Spain 1941.

[3] 12 ... b5 13 Qe1 Be6 14 Nh4 Ne4 15 f3 Nd2 16 Qxd2 Qxh4 17 e4 ± Janošević-Puc, Yugoslav Ch 1953.

[4] 13 ... Bxf3?! 14 gf Qd7 15 Kg2 Rae8 16 Rg1 Nh5 17 Qf1 f5 18 Kh1 Sverdlovsk v Novosibirsk, 1954.

[5] 15 ... Bh5? 16 f3 Bg6 17 e4 Qd7 18 Rae1 f5 • 19 ed! ± Smyslov-Petrosian, Zürich C 1953.

[6] 11 ... Ne5 12 de Ng4 (12 ... Ne4!?) 13 f4 f5 14 Be2 Nh6 15 Ra2 ± Korchnoi-Gurgenidze, USSR Ch 1959.

[7] 14 a4 Ba6 15 Bxa6 Rxa6 = Lindblom-Persitz, Leipzig Ol 1960.

[8] Gligorić-Persitz, Hastings 1968/69.

[9] 12 d5 e4! 13 dc Ng4 14 g3 ef 15 Qxf3 Ne5 ∓ Ilivitsky-Levenfish, USSR 1953.

[10] 14 Bb2 Ng4 15 g3 Qh5 ∓ Byrne, Mednis.

[11] 15 Bd2 ∓ Byrne, Mednis.

[12] Fraguela-Byrne, Torremolinos 1976.

[13] 14 ... Re6 15 Nh4 Qd8 16 f3 Nd2 17 Qxd2 Qxh4 18 e4 Rh6 19 g3 ± Unzicker-Keller, Zürich 1975.

[14] 15 Nd2!? Nxc3 (15 ... f5!?) 16 Nxc4! ±.

[15] 18 Bb2 b5 = Bannik-Averbakh, USSR Ch 1958.

[16] 11 ... Re8 12 f3 b6 13 Ra2 a5 (13 ... Bb7!? Hort) 14 Re2 Bb7 15 Bb2 Rad8 16 Qe1 ± Portisch-Hort, Niksić 1978.

[17] 12 g3!? Bh3 13 Re1 Ng6 14 Ng2 Qd7 15 f3 ± Gligorić-Averbakh, Yugoslavia v USSR 1963.

[18] 14 Bb1!? intending Ra2-e2 Cabrilo.

[19] 15 Nxg6?! hg 16 Re1 Bf5! ∓.

[20] 18 Qh5 ± Portisch-Byrne, Bugojno 1978.

[21] 11 a4!? ∞ Portisch-Miles, Tilburg 1981.

[22] 15 c4!?

[23] 16 a5!? b5 17 ab Bxd3 Chandler.

[24] 18 Rxa4 Nxa4 19 Rf3 g6 20 Rh3 Kg7 ∓ Chandler-Speelman, Brighton 1979.

[25] **11** Re1 e5 12 d5 Na5 13 d6 Qd8 14 Nxe5 Nxc4 15 Nxc4 Be6 16 Nb2 Ne4 = Panno-Szabo, Buenos Aires 1955.
  11 a4 e5 12 Ba3 e4 13 Nd2 b6 14 dc Rd8 15 cb ab 16 Qc2 Ng4 17 g3 Nce5 18 Be2 Bf5 ∞ Taimanov.

[26] 12 h3 e4 13 Nd2 Ne7 14 Qc2 Bf5 = Novosibirsk v Sverdlovsk 1958.

[27] 15 Nxe5!?

[28] **18** Rxd8+ Rxd8 19 Kh1 (19 Rd1 =) 19 ... Rd6 20 Qc3 Nh5 21 Qe5 Bg4 22 e4?! f6 23 Qc3 Nf4 ∓ Lim-Tisdall, Hastings II 1976/77.
  18 Qc3 Nh5 (18 ... Ne8? 19 Kh1 Qf6 20 Rd5 ± Krogius-Lutikov, USSR 1957) intending ... Qg6+ ∞.

Main Line *continued* 1 d4 ♘f6 2 c4 e6 3 ♘c3 ♝b4
4 e3 0-0 5 ♘f3 d5 6 ♝d3 c5 7 0-0 ♘c6 8 a3 ♝xc3 9 bc

	9	10	11	12	13	14	15	16	17	
8	...	♝xc4	♝a2	h3[29]	♘h2	f3	cd	d5[33]	fe[34]	±
	dc	♛c7	e5	e4[30]	♘a5[31]	cd[32]	♝e6	♖fd8		
9	...	...	♝e2	♛c2	de[35]	♘e1[36]	e4[38]	f3	♔h1	=
	...	...	♖d8	e5	♘xe5	c4[37]	♝g4	♛c5+	♝e6[39]	
10	...	...	♝d3	♛c2	e4	♝xc4	cd	♝d3[42]	♝xc2	=
	...	...	e5	♖e8[40]	c4!	ed	♘a5[41]	♛xc2	♘xe4[43]	
11	...	...	...	...	♘xe5	de	f3	e4	♔h1	±
	...	...	...	...	♘xe5	♛xe5[44]	♝d7[45]	h6[46]	♖ad8[47]	
12	...	...	♝b5	♝e2	♝b2	♘d2	a4[50]	♛c2	♖fc1	=
	...	...	a6[48]	e5	e4[49]	♝f5	♖fd8	♖ac8	cd[51]	

[29] 12 ♛c2 ♝g4 13 de ♘xe5 14 ♘e1 ♖ad8 15 f3 ♝e6 16 c4 ± Portisch-Sosonko, Tilburg 1978.

[30] 12 ... ♝f5 13 d5 ♖ad8 14 ♛e2 ♘e7 15 c4 ♘g6 16 ♝b2 ± Simagin-Hasin, USSR Ch 1965.

[31] 13 ... ♝f5 14 ♘g4 ♘g4 15 hg ♝g6 16 a4 ♖ad8! (16 ... ♖fd8 17 f4! ef 18 ♛xf3 ±) 17 ♛e2 (17 f4 ef 18 ♛xf3 ♖fe8 19 ♝a3 cd 20 cd ♖xd4! 21 ed ♘xd4 =) 17 ... ♖fe8 18 ♝a3 b6 19 ♖ad1 ♔h8 20 ♖d2 f5 21 gf ♝xf5 = Kagan-Shakarov, corr. 1977.

[32] 14 ... b6! 15 fe ♘xe4 16 ♛d3 ♝b7 17 c4 ♛g3 ∓ Keene-Zaltsman, New York 1980.

[33] 16 ♝xe6? fe 17 ♝d2 ♘c4 ∓ Keene-Romanishin, Gausdal 1979.

[34] Pytel.

[35] 13 ♝b2 – row 7.

[36] 14 c4 ♘xf3+ 15 ♝xf3 ♘g4 16 ♝xg4 ♝xg4 =.

[37] 14 ... ♘eg4 15 g3 ♛e5 16 ♘g2 ♝f5 17 ♛b2 ♛c7 18 f3 ♘e5 19 e4 ± Botvinnik-Padevsky, Varna Ol 1962.

[38] 14 f4?! ♘d3! 15 ♘xd3 ♝f5 ∓ Filip.

[39] Taimanov.

[40] 12 ... ♝g4 13 ♘xe5 ♝xe5 14 de ♛xe5 15 f3 ♝d7 16 a4 ♖fe8 17 e4 ± Tal.

[41] 15 ... ♘xe4 16 ♝d3 ♘f6 17 ♝g5 ± Filip.

[42] 16 e5 ♛xc4 17 ♛xc4 ♘xc4 18 ef gf 19 ♝h6 ♝e6 ∓.

[43] 18 ♖e1 ♝f5 19 ♝f4 ♘d6 = Donner-Larsen, The Hague (match) 1958.

[44] 14 ... ♖xe5? 15 c4 ♖h5 16 f4 ± Ojanen-Cuartas, Havana Ol 1966.

[45] 15 ... ♝e6 16 e4 ♖ad8 17 ♖b1 b6 18 ♖b2 c4 19 ♝e2 ♛c5+ 20 ♔h1 ♝d7 (20 ... ♘d7! intending ... ♘c5 Podgayets) 21 a4 ± Podgayets-Karyakin, USSR 1978.

[46] **16 ... ♝a4?** 17 ♛xa4 ♛xc3 18 ♛b3 ♛xa1 19 ♝b2 ±±.
16 ... ♖ad8!? 17 a4 (17 f4 ♛c7 18 e5 c4 =) 17 ... ♝c6 18 ♝c4 ♖d7 19 ♛b3 ♖ed8 20 ♖a2 ♘h5 21 g3 ♘xg3! 22 hg ♖d2 = Portisch-Spassky, Geneva (match) 1977.

[47] 18 a4 ♘c6 19 ♝e3 b6 20 ♖fb1! ± Podgayets-Donchenko, USSR 1978.

[48] 11 ... ♝d7 12 a4 a6 13 ♝e2 ♖fd8 14 ♝a3 e5 15 ♛c2 cd 16 cd ed 17 ♝e7 with attack, Lerner-Zaichik, USSR 1978.

[49] 13 ... ♝g4 14 ♘xe5 ♝xe2 15 ♛xe2 ♘xe5 16 de ♛xe5 17 c4 ± Minev.

[50] 14 ♘b3!?

[51] 18 cd ♘xd4 19 ♛xc7 ♘xe2+ 20 ♔f1 ♘xc1 ∞ Portisch-Spassky, match 1980.

	4	5	6	7	8	9	10	11	12	
1	...	Bg5[1]	e3[2]	Bd3[3]	0-0	ed	Bxf6	cd	Ne5	=
	Bb7	Be7	c5!	0-0	cd	d5[4]	Bxf6	ed	Nc6	
2	...	...	Bh4[5]	e3[7]	Be2	Nxd4	0-0	Ndb5[10]	Nd6	=
	...	h6	Be7[6]	c5[8]	cd	0-0[9]	Nc6	Rc8	Bxd6[11]	
3	...	Bg5[12]	Bh4	e3[13]	bc	Bd3[14]	0-0	Nd2	Bg3	∞
	Bb4	h6	Bb7	Bxc3+	d6	Nbd7	Qe7[15]	g5	h5[16]	
4	...	...	...	...	Bg3	Qc2[17]	bc	hg	Nd2	∞
	...	...	...	g5	Ne4	Bxc3[18]	Nxg3	Nc6![19]	Qe7[20]	
5	...	...	...	...	...	...	...	Bd3	d5[22]	=
	...	...	...	...	...	...	d6	f5[21]		

[1] 5 Bf4!? Bb4 6 Qb3 ∞ Korchnoi.

[2] 6 Qc2 c5 (6 ... d5 – Queen's Gambit) 7 Rd1 Nc6 8 e3 0-0 9 dc bc 10 Be2 b6 11 0-0 Qb8 12 Rd2 h6 = Pachman-Najdorf, Netanya 1975.

[3] 7 Bxf6?! Bxf6 8 d5 0-0 9 d6 Bxc3+ 10 bc f5 11 Be2 Qf6 ∓ Korchnoi-Taimanov, USSR Ch 1963.

  7 dc bc 8 Bd3 0-0 9 0-0 d6 10 Qe2 Nbd7 11 Rfd1 Rb8 12 b3 Re8 ∞ Furman-Planinc, Portorož 1975.

[4] 9 ... Bxf3!? 10 Qxf3 Nc6 11 Ne2 d5 =.

[5] 6 Bxf6 Qxf6 7 e4!? Bb4 8 Bd3 c5 9 0-0 cd 10 Nb5 Qd8 11 Nbxd4 0-0 12 Qe2 Nc6 13 Rad1 ± Geller-Boleslavsky, Zürich C 1953. 8 ... Bxc3+!? 9 bc d6 Geller.

[6] 6 ... g5!? 7 Bg3 Nh5 8 e3 (8 Be5? Rg8 9 e3 d6 10 Bg3 Nd7 11 Nd2 Ndf6 ∓ Qi-Speelman, China 1981; 8 Qc2 Nxg3 9 hg Nc6 10 0-0-0 g4 11 Ne1 Qg5+ 12 e3 0-0-0 = Uhlmann-Taimanov, Havana 1964) 8 ... Bg7 (8 ... Nxg3?! 9 hg Bg7 10 g4! ± Bobotsov-Polugayevsky, Beverwijk 1966) 9 Be5 f6 10 Bg3 Nxg3 11 hg f5 ∞.

[7] 7 Qc2 c5! 8 e4 cd 9 Nxd4 Nc6 10 Nxc6 Bxc6 11 Rd1 Qc7 12 Be2 Qf4 = Rajna-Liebert, Szolnok 1975.

[8] 7 ... 0-0 8 Be2 c5 9 0-0 d6 10 dc bc 11 Qc2 Nbd7 12 Rfd1 Qb6 13 Rd2 Rfd8 14 Rad1 Bc6 15 Bg3! ± Karpov-Polugayevsky, Bugojno 1980.

  7 ... Ne4 8 Bg3! Bb4 (8 ... Nxg3 9 hg ± Malich-Damjanović, Sochi 1965) 9 Qc2 Bxc3+ 10 bc d6 11 Nd2! ± Matanović-Korchnoi, Belgrade 1964.

[9] 9 ... g5?! 10 Bg3 Bxg2 11 Rg1 Nc6 12 Ndb5 ∞/ ±.

[10] 11 Rc1 Nxd4 12 Qxd4 Ne4! = Spassky-Keres, match 1965.

  11 Bf3!? Nxd4! 12 Bxb7 Rb8 13 Ba6 Nf5 =.

[11] 13 Qxd6 Ne4 = Spassky-Keres, Tallinn 1973.

[12] 5 Qc2 Bb7 6 a3 Bxc3+ 7 Qxc3!? d6 8 e3 Nbd7 9 b4 0-0 10 Bb2 ± Miles-Andersson, Wijk aan Zee 1981.

  5 Qb3 c5 6 e3 Ba6 7 a3 Ba5 8 Bd2 0-0 9 0-0-0 ∞ Browne-Korchnoi, Chicago 1982.

[13] 7 Qc2 c5 8 a3 Be4! = Malich-Keres, Varna Ol 1962.

  7 Qb3 Qe7.

  7 Nd2 c5 =.

[14] 9 Nd2 Qe7 (9 ... g5 10 Bg3 h5 11 h4! ±) 10 f3 e5 11 e4 Nbd7 12 Bd3 g5 ∓ Botvinnik-Keres, USSR Ch 1940.   12 ... Nf8?! 13 c5! Tal-Hecht, Varna Ol 1962.

[15] 10 ... g5?! 11 Bg3 Ne4 12 Nd2! ± Tolush-Taimanov, USSR Ch 1956.

[16] Borik-Speelman, Dortmund 1981.

[17] 9 Nd2!? Bxc3 (9 ... Nxc3 10 bc Bxc3 11 Rc1 Bb4 12 h4 gh ∞ Stein-Langeweg, Amsterdam 1969; 11 h4!? Bxa1 12 Qxa1 intending d5 ∞) 10 bc f5 (10 ... Nxg3 11 hg d6 12 Bd3!? – Jelen-Cebalo, Yugoslav Ch 1981 – 12 ... Bxg2 13 Rh2 Bb7 14 Qc2 Nd7 15 Be4 d5! + Cebalo) 11 f3 Nxd2! 12 Kxd2 d6 ∞ Vaisman-Foisor, Bucharest 1981.

[18] 9 ... f5?! 10 Bd3 Bxc3+ 11 bc Nxg3?! 12 hg Nc6 13 d5 Na5 14 g4! ± Keene-Burger, New York 1981.

[19] 11 ... Qe7!? 12 Bd3 Nc6 13 Rb1 0-0-0 14 c5 d6 15 cb cb 16 c4 Kb8 (Karpov-Speelman, London 1982) 17 Rb5! ∞.

[20] 13 c5!? Na5 14 f3 h5 ∞ Ubilava-Haritonov, USSR 1981.

  13 Nb3? Qa3! ∓.

  13 Qb2 g4 14 Nb3 Qg5 ∓ Langeweg-Karpov, Amsterdam 1981.

[21] 11 ... Nxg3 12 hg Nd7 ∞.

[22] 12 ... ed 13 cd Bxd5 14 Nd4 Qf6 15 f3 Nc5 16 Bxf5 Nbd7 17 Nb5 0-0-0 18 Rd1! ± Ribli-Seirawan, Malta Ol 1980.

  12 ... Nd7! 13 Nxe4 fe 14 Qxe4 Qf6 = Hort-Bellin, Hastings 1975/76.

Queen's Indian and Bogoljubow-Indian

Another beneficiary of recent fashion, the Queen's Indian is now, with the Sicilian, arguably one of the two most popular openings in master practice. This is partially due to the great difficulties White experiences in achieving substantial success against the Nimzo-Indian, leading to attention being focused on schemes involving ♘f3. The other factor in the Queen's Indian's rise to prominence is the discovery and refinement of double-edged systems with 4 ... ♗a6 against White's classical system of 4 g3. Once thought to be a reliable defence because of its solidity, the Queen's Indian is now respected for its resilience and activity in counterplay.

Popularised by Nimzowitsch (who also authored 4 ... ♗a6! against the Classical Variation), the ideas behind the Queen's Indian are eminently logical. Black's scheme of development exerts pressure on the key square e4, and the combined influence of the ♘f6 and the fianchettoed queen's bishop makes the acquisition of this square, an integral part of successful White strategy, extremely difficult to achieve.

The latest attempt by White to prove advantage, 4 a3, popularised by Petrosian, Gheorghiu and, lately, Kasparov, can lead to positions directly related to the Benoni. Another complex occurs if Black responds with ... d5, accepting a slightly disadvantageous pawn structure but gaining dynamic equality through excellent piece activity.

English GM Miles employed 4 ♗f4 with good success, but Black now appears well prepared to handle this system. 4 e3 and 4 ♘c3 + 5 ♗g5 (see page 159 for the latter) have much in common with the Nimzo-Indian, into which they may easily transpose. These attempts steer the game away from more traditional paths but it is doubtful that they confer a significant advantage on the first player. It is safe to assume that this defence is not likely to decrease in popularity until White decides to bypass it and face up to the Nimzo.

Similar in style to the Queen's Indian is the solid **Bogoljubow-Indian** (3 ♘f3 ♗b4+), while a sharper alternative for Black is the **Blumenfeld Gambit** (3 ♘f3 c5 4 d5 b5).

	4 e3 and Miles System					1 d4 ♘f6 2 c4 e6 3 ♘f3 b6				
	4	5	6	7	8	9	10	11	12	
1	e3	♗d3	♘bd2	0-0	dc	a3	b3	♗b2	♕e2	±
	♗b7	♗b4+[1]	c5[2]	0-0	♗xc5	a5	♘c6	d5[3]		
2	...	...	0-0	b3[4]	♗b2	♘c3[5]	cd	♖c1	♕e2	=
	...	d5	♗d6	0-0	♘bd7	c5	ed	♕e7	♖ad8[6]	
3	...	...	0-0	b3	♗b2	ed	♘bd2	♖c1	♖e1	∞
	...	c5	♗e7	0-0	cd	d5	♘c6	♖e8	♖c8[7]	
4	...	...	...	♘c3	ed	b3	♗b2	♕e2	♗xc3	=
	...	...	...	cd[8]	d5	♘e4	♘d7	♘xc3	0-0[9]	
5	...	...	♘c3	0-0	b3[10]	♗b2	♕e2	ed	♗b1	∞
	...	♗e7	d5	0-0	c5	♘c6[11]	cd	♘b4	dc[12]	
6	...	...	...	...	...	...	♖c1	ed	♖e1	=
	...	...	...	...	...	...	cd	♖c8	♘b4[13]	
7	♗f4	e3	♘bd2	♗e5	♘xe4	♗g3[15]	♕xf3	♗d1	a3	±
	♗b7	♘e4[14]	g5	f6	♗xe4	♗xf3	♗b4+	♘c6	♗e7[16]	
8	...	...	♘c3	♗g3	♗d3	♕c2[17]	♗e4	♕xe4		=
	...	♗e7	♘h5	d6	♘d7	g6	♗xe4[18]	0-0[19]		

	4	5	6	7	8	9	10	11	12	
9	...	...	h3	♘bd2[20]	♘xe4	♘d2	♛c2	dc	♘xe4	±
	...	...	♘e4	f5	fe	0-0	c5	bc	♘c6[21]	
10	...	...	...	♘c3	cd	♗d3	0-0	♘e5	♛f3	=
	...	...	0-0	d5	ed[22]	♘bd7	a6	♖e8	♗d6[23]	
11	...	...	...	...	...	...	0-0	♘e5	♛f3[25]	±
	...	...	...	...	...	c5	♘c6	a6[24]		
12	...	...	...	♘c3[26]	♗xd4[27]	♘bd5	♘d6[28]	♗xd6	♗xe7	∞/=
	...	...	c5	cd	0-0	♘e8	♘xd6	♘a6	♛xe7[29]	
13	...	...	♘bd2	♗d3[30]	0-0	e4	♘xd4	♗g3	♛e2	=
	...	♗b4+	♗e7	c5	0-0	cd	d6	♘bd7	a6[31]	
14	...	...	♘fd2	a3[32]	♘c3	cd[34]	♘xd5	♖c1	dc	=
	...	...	0-0	♗e7[33]	d5	♘xd5[35]	♗xd5	c5	♗xc5[36]	

---

[1] 5 ... ♘e4 6 0-0 f5 7 ♘fd2 ♗e7 8 ♘c3 ♘xc3 9 bc 0-0 10 e4 ± Simagin-Goldenov, USSR Ch 1952.

[2] 6 ... 0-0 7 0-0 d5 8 a3 ♗e7 9 b3 ♘bd7 10 ♗b2 c5 11 ♛e2 ± Christiansen-Garcia, Linares 1981.

[3] Gheorghiu-Larsen, Las Palmas 1972.

[4] 7 ♘c3 0-0 8 cd ed 9 b3 a6 10 ♗b2 ♘bd7 11 ♛c2 ♖e8 12 ♖ac1 ♘e4 = Simagin-Polugayevsky, Moscow 1966.

[5] 9 ♘e5 c5 10 ♛e2 ♛c7 11 f4 ♘e4 = Filip-Botvinnik, Varna Ol 1962.
 9 ♘bd2 ♗e7 10 ♖c1 ♖ad8 11 ♛c2 c5 12 cd ed 13 dc?! bc ∞/∓ Spassky-Tal, Montreal 1979.

[6] 13 ♖fd1 ♘e4 = Petrosian-Polugayevsky, USSR Ch 1970.

[7] 13 a3 ∞ Petrosian-Tal, USSR Ch 1976.

[8] 7 ... d5 8 cd! ed 9 ♗b5+ ± Kotov-Botvinnik, USSR Ch 1944.

[9] 13 ♖ac1 ♖c8 14 ♗b2 ♗f6 = Szabo-Unzicker, Göteborg IZ 1955.

[10] 8 ♛e2 c5 9 dc bc 10 ♖d1 ♛b6 = Korchnoi-Mecking, Augusta (match) 1974.

[11] 9 ... cd 10 ♘xd4 dc 11 ♗xc4 a6 12 ♗e2 b5 13 ♗f3 ♖a7 14 ♗xb7 ♖xb7 = Petrosian-Karpov, San Antonio 1972.

[12] 13 bc ♗xf3 14 gf (Grigorian-Karpov, USSR Ch 1976) 14 ... ♘h5 ∞ Polugayevsky.

[13] 13 ♗f1 ♘e4 14 a3 ♗xc3 15 ♖xc3 ♘c6 = Keres-Smyslov, Zürich C 1953.

[14] 5 ... c5 6 d5! ed 7 ♘c3 ±/±.

[15] Geller. 9 ♘xg5? ♗b4+ 10 ♔e2 ♗g6 ∓∓.

[16] 13 ♗d3 intending ♔e2, ♖hd1, ♔f1 etc ±.

[17] 9 0-0 g6 10 h3 ♘xg3 11 fg 0-0 ∓ Spassky-Karpov, Montreal 1979.

[18] 10 ... c6 11 d5! ±.

[19] Miles-Andersson, Amsterdam 1978.

[20] 7 ♘fd2 0-0 8 ♗d3 ♘xd2 9 ♘xd2 ♗xg2 10 ♖g1 ♗b7 11 ♗h6 ♗f6 12 ♛g4 ± Geller.

[21] 13 ♘c3 ♘d4 14 ♛d2 ♖xf4 15 ef ♛a5 16 0-0-0 ± Geller.

[22] 8 ... ♘xd5!? 9 ♘xd5 ♗xd5 10 ♗d3! ♗b4+ 11 ♔e2 ♗d6 12 ♗xd6 cd!? (12 ... ♛xd6 13 ♛c2 h6 14 ♖hc1 Geller; 12 ... ♗xf3+ 13 ♔xf3 ♛xd6 14 ♛c2 f5 15 ♖ac1 f4 16 ♛xc7! ± Miles-Rivas, Amsterdam Z 1978) 13 ♛c2 h6 14 ♖hc1 ♘c6 (14 ... ♗c6 – Miles-Reshevsky, Lone Pine 1979 – 15 ♗e4 ♗b5+ 16 ♔e1 d5 17 ♗d3 ± Geller) 15 e4 ♗b4!? Geller.

[23] 13 ♘g4 ♗xf4 14 ♛xf4 ♘xg4 15 ♛xg4 ♘f6 16 ♛f5 ±/= Geller.

[24] 11 ... c4 12 ♗c2 a6 13 g4 b5 14 g5 ♘e8 15 ♛g4 g6 16 ♖ad1! ♘g7 17 h4 ± Miles-Spassky, Montilla 1978.

[25] Miles-Spassky, Buenos Aires Ol 1978.

[26] 7 ♗d3 cd 8 ed d5 Geller.
 7 dc bc 8 ♘c3 0-0 9 ♗e2 ♘c6 10 0-0 d5 11 cd ed 12 ♖c1 d4 13 ♘a4 ♘d5 14 ♛b3 ♗b4 Lputian-A.Ivanov, USSR 1979.

[27] 8 ed 0-0 9 ♗e2 d5 = Geller.

[28] 10 ♗xb8 ♖xb8 11 ♘xa7 ♘f6 12 ♘ab5 d5 ∞ Geller.

[29] 13 ♛d2 ♖fd8 ∞/= – Djurić-Ornstein, Pamporovo 1981.

[30] 7 h3 d5 8 ♖c1 ♘bd7 9 ♗d3 c5 10 0-0 0-0 = Rivas-Azmaiparashivili, Gröningen 1980.

[31] 13 ♖ad1 g6 14 h3 ♘c5 = Hübner-Andersson, Buenos Aires Ol 1978.

[32] 7 ♗d3 d5 8 0-0 c5 9 a3 ♗xd2 10 ♘xd2 cd 11 ed ♘c6 12 ♘f3 dc 13 ♗xc4 ♖c8 ∓ Miles-Andersson, Buenos Aires Ol 1978.

[33] 7 ... ♗xd2+ 8 ♘xd2 d5 9 ♖c1 ♘bd7 10 b4 dc 11 ♘xc4 ♘d5 12 ♗g3 f5! = Geller.

[34] 9 ♛f3 c5 10 dc bc 11 0-0-0 ♛b6 12 ♗d3 d4 13 ♘ce4 ♘xe4 14 ♗xe4 ♗xe4 15 ♘xe4 ♘c6 =/∓ Geller.

[35] 9 ... ed!? Geller.

[36] **12 ... bc!?** intending 13 ♗c4 ♗f6 and ... ♗xb2/... ♗xg2 Geller.
 12 ... ♗xc5 13 ♗c4 ♗b7 14 0-0 ♗d6! = Miles-Hübner, England v West Germany 1979.

1 d4 ♘f6 2 c4 e6 3 ♘f3 b6 4 g3 ♗a6

	5	6	7	8	9	10	11	12	13	
1	♕c2[1]	♗g2[3]	0-0[4]	♖d1	♕a4[5]	♘a3[6]	♕xa3	♘xd4		∓
	c5[2]	♘c6	cd	♖c8	♘a5	♗xa3[7]	♗xc4	♕xe7[8]		
2	♘bd2	e4[9]	e5	♗g2	0-0	♘b3	♘xe5	♔xg2	♕xd4	±
	c5	cd[10]	♘g8	♗b7	d6[11]	de	♗xg2	♘d7	♘gf6[12]	
3	...	...	...	...	...	♘xd4!	♔xg2	ed	♕f3	±
	...	...	...	...	...	♗xg2	a6[13]	♗xd6	♖a7[14]	
4	...	♗g2	0-0[15]	b3	♘e5	♗b2	cd	♘dc4		=
	d5	♗e7	0-0	♘bd7[16]	♗b7	c5	♘xd5	cd[17]		
5	...	♕c2[18]	♗g2	a3?![20]	♘xd2	dc	b4[21]	0-0	ab	=
	♗b4	0-0[19]	d5	♗xd2+	c5	bc	♘bd7	cb	♗xc4[22]	
6	...	♗g2	0-0	♕c2[24]	cd	♘e5	♘df3	♗f4	dc[25]	±
	♗b7	♗e7[23]	0-0	d5	ed	c5	♘bd7	♘e4		
7	♕a4	♘c3[26]	cb	♘xb5	♘c3[28]	♗d2[29]	♗g2	♖b1	a3	=
	c6	b5[27]	cb	♕b6	♗b4	0-0	♘c6	♖ab8	♗xc3[30]	
8	...	♘c3	e4[31]	♗d3	cd	e5	0-0	♕c2	♗e2	∞
	♗e7	0-0	♗b7!?[32]	d5	ed	♘e4	c5	c4!	♘a6[33]	
9	...	♗g2	0-0	♘xd4	♔xg2	♘c3	♖d1	♗f4	f3	∞
	♗b7	c5	cd[34]	♗xg2	♗e7[35]	0-0	♕c7[36]	♕b7+	a6[37]	
10	b3	♗g2[39]	0-0	♗b2	cd	dc	♘c3	♘e1		=
	d5[38]	c5[40]	♘c6	♖c8	ed	♗xc5[41]	0-0	♖e8[42]		
11	...	♗d2	♗g2[44]	♘c3[46]	0-0	cd	a4	♘e1[49]	♘d3	∓
	♗b4+	♗e7[43]	c6[45]	d5	♘bd7[47]	cd	♗b7[48]	0-0	♘e4[50]	
12	...	...	...	cd	♘c3	♘xd5	0-0[51]	♗f4	♖c1	=
	...	...	d5	♘xd5	0-0	ed	♘d7	♖e8	c5[52]	

---

[1] **5 ♗g2?** ♗xc4 6 0-0? (6 ♘fd2 ♗d5 7 e4) 6 ... ♗d5 ∓ Naegeli-Nimzowitsch, Zürich 1934.
    5 ♕b3 ♘c6 6 ♘bd2 ♘a5 7 ♕c2 c5 8 e4 cd 9 e5 ♘g8 (9 ... ♘g4!?) 10 ♗d3 ∞ Timman-Polugayevsky, Bugojno 1982.

[2] 5 ... d5 6 ♘bd2 ♗e7 7 ♗g2 0-0 8 0-0 c5 = Udovčić-Rakić, Yugoslav Ch 1957.

[3] 6 d5? ed 7 cd ♗b7 (7 ... ♘xd5?? 8 ♕e4+ ±±) 8 ♗g5 (8 e4 ♕e7 9 ♘c3 ♗xd5 ∓) 8 ... ♗xd5 9 ♘c3 ♗b7 ∓ Grigorian-Keres, USSR 1967.

[4] **7 dc** ♗c5 8 0-0 ♖c8 9 ♕a4 ♗b7 10 ♘c3 0-0 = Beutelhoff-Kupreichik, Dortmund 1975.

[5] 9 ♘xd4 ♘xd4 10 ♖xd4 ♘c5 11 ♖d1 ♗f2+ ∓∓.

[6] 10 b3!?

[7] 10 ... ♗xc4!? 11 b4 (11 ♘xd4 intending 12 b4 Geller) 11 ... ♘d5 12 ba! ♘c3 13 ♕c2 ♗a6 14 ♕b3 ♘xe2+ ∞ Sveshnikov.

[8] Krogius-Kuzminikh, Leningrad 1951. 13 b3 ♕xa3 14 ♗xa3 ♗a6 15 e4! ∞ Geller.

[9] 6 ♗g2 ♘c6 7 dc bc (7 ... ♗xc5 8 0-0 0-0 9 a3 ♗b7 10 b4 ♗e7 11 ♗b2 ± Bronstein-Taimanov, Zürich C 1953) 8 0-0 ♗e7 9 b3 0-0 10 ♗b2 ♗b7 = Bolbochan-Keres, Varna Ol 1962.

[10] **6 ... ♗b7** 7 d5 ed 8 ed ♗e7 9 ♗g2 d6 10 0-0 0-0 11 b3 ♘bd7 12 ♗b2 ± Sosonko-Helmers, Reykjavik 1980.
    6 ... d6!? 7 ♗g2 (7 d5 ed 8 ed ♕e7+ 9 ♗e2 g6 =) 7 ... ♘c6 (7 ... cd!?) 8 d5 ∞.

[11] 9 ... ♘e7 10 ♖e1 ♘f5 12 g4 ♘e7 13 ♘e4 ± Uhlmann-Thorbergsson, Reykjavik 1968.

¹² 14 ♗f4 ± Adamski-Spassov, Warsaw 1980.

¹³ 11 ... de 12 ♕f3 ♘d7 13 ♘b5 ±.

¹⁴ 14 ♘e4 ♖d7 15 ♖d1 ♘e7 16 ♘g5 ± Sosonko-Gheorghiu, Wijk aan Zee 1981.

¹⁵ 7 ♕a4+ c6 8 cd ed 9 ♘e5 ± Vaganian-Kuzmin, USSR 1971. 8 ... b5! = Matanović/Ugrinović.

¹⁶ 8 ... c5 9 ♗b2 ♘c6 10 dc bc 11 cd ed 12 ♖e1 ♗b7 13 ♖c1 ± Hübner-Sosonko, Biel IZ 1976.

¹⁷ Dzhindzhihashvili – Polugayevsky, USSR 1971.

¹⁸ **6 ♕b3 c5!** (6 ... ♘c6 7 d5 ± Kasparov-Speelman, Malta Ol 1980) 7 a3 ♗xd2+ 8 ♗xd2 ♘c6 9 d5 ♘a5 10 ♗xa5 ba 11 de fe 12 ♕c2 ♖b8 ∓ Fedorowicz-Seirawan, USA 1981.

6 ♕a4!? c5 7 a3 ♗xd2+ 8 ♗xd2 cd 9 ♘xd4 ♗b7 = Walden-Miles, London 1981.

¹⁹ **6 ... ♗b7!?** 7 ♗g2 ♗e4 8 ♕d1 (8 ♕b3) 8 ... ♗xd2+ 9 ♗xd2 d6 10 0-0 ♘bd7 11 ♗c3 ♕e7 = Pirc-Nimzowitsch, Bled 1931.

6 ... c5 7 e4 cd 8 e5 ♗b7 9 ♗g2 ♘e4 10 0-0 ♗xd2 11 ♗xd2 ♗xd2 12 ♕xd2 ♗xf3 13 ♗xf3 ♘c6 14 ♖fe1 ♕c7 15 ♗xc6 dc 16 ♕xd4 ♖d8 = Alburt-Seirawan, USA 1981. 7 ♗g2 0-0 8 a3 ♗xd2+ 9 ♗xd2 d5 10 cd ed 11 dc ♕e7 = Najdorf-Seirawan, Mar del Plata 1982.

²⁰ 8 0-0!? Geller.

²¹ 11 cd ed 12 ♕xc5 ♖e8 13 ♗f3 (13 e3 ♘bd7) 13 ... ♘bd7 14 ♕d6 ♖e6! 15 ♕f4 ♘e5 ∓.

²² 14 ♘c4 ♖c8 = Korchnoi-Parma, USSR v Yugoslavia 1971.

²³ 6 ... c5 7 e4 cd (7 ... ♘xe4 8 ♘e5!) 8 e5 ♘g8 – row 3. 8 ... ♘g4 9 0-0 ♕c7 (9 ... ♗c5 intending ... ♘e3!?) 10 ♖e1 ± Dorfman-Platonov, USSR 1980.

²⁴ 8 b3 c5 (8 ... d5!? 9 cd ed 10 ♘e5 ♘bd7 11 ♗b2 c5 ∞/± Najdorf-Franco, Mar del Plata 1982) 9 ♗b2 a6 10 e3 cd 11 ♘xd4 ♕c7 = Gheorghiu-Timman, Wijk aan Zee 1981.

²⁵ Kasparov-Gheorghiu, Moscow 1981.

²⁶ 6 ♗g2 b5 7 cb cb 8 ♕d1 ♘c6 = Smejkal-Kavalek, Czechoslovakia 1968.

²⁷ 6 ... ♗e7 7 ♗g2 0-0 8 0-0 d5 9 cd cd 10 ♗f4 ♕d7 11 ♕xd7 ♘bxd7 12 ♖c1 ± Polugayevsky-Eberlein, USA 1978.

²⁸ 9 e3 ♗b7 10 ♗e2 ♘c6 11 ♕c4! (11 ♕b3?! ♕b7 ∓) 11 ... ♕b7 12 0-0 a6 13 ♘c3 ♗xf3 14 ♗xf3 ♕xf3 15 ♕c8+ ♔e7 ∞∞ Klüger-Portisch, Hungary 1958.

²⁹ 10 ♗g2 0-0 11 0-0 (11 ♕c2 ♘c6 12 0-0 ♖fc8 13 a3 ♗xc3 14 bc ♘d5 15 ♖d1 ♘ce7 ∓ Tukmakov-Gulko, USSR Ch 1977; 15 ♘g5!?) 11 ... ♗xc3 12 bc ♗xe2 = Bagirov-Zaichik, Kirovakan 1978.

³⁰ 14 ♗xc3 ♖fc8 15 ♕c2 ♘e7 16 0-0 ♘ed5 17 ♖fc1 ♕b3! = Kuzmin-Mednis, Riga IZ 1979.

³¹ 7 ♗g2 c6 8 ♗f4 ♕c8 9 ♖c1! (9 0-0 d5! =) 9 ... ♕b7 10 d5! ± Bukić-Polugayevsky, Skopje 1968.

³² 7 ... d5 8 cd ♗xf1 9 ♔xf1 ed 10 e5 ♘e4 = Toran-Matanović, Beverwijk 1956.

³³ Antoshin-Speelman, Frunze 1979.

³⁴ 7 ... ♗e7 8 ♘c3 0-0 9 ♖d1 a6 10 ♗f4 d6 11 dc bc ± Gheorghiu-Keene, Montilla 1974.

³⁵ 9 ... ♕c8 10 ♗f4 ♗c5 11 ♘b5 ♕c6+ 12 f3 0-0 13 ♖d1 ± Kuzmin-Kärner, USSR 1972.

³⁶ 11 ... ♕c8 12 ♘db5 ♕c6+ 13 f3 ♖c8 14 ♗f4 ♘e8 15 ♖ac1 ♗f8 16 e4 h6 17 ♘e2 d6 ½-½ Timman-Ribli, Tilburg 1978.

³⁷ 14 e4 d6 15 ♘de2 ♖d8 16 ♖d2 ♘c6 = Browne-Andersson, Buenos Aires 1978.

³⁸ 5 ... ♗e7 6 ♗g2 c6 7 0-0 0-0 8 ♘bd2 d5 9 ♗b2 ♘bd7 10 ♖e1 c5 11 e4 de 12 ♘xe4 ♘xe4 13 ♖xe4 ♗b7 = Savon-Polugayevsky, USSR Ch 1967.

³⁹ 6 cd ed 7 ♗g2 ♗b4 8 ♗d2 ♗xd2+ 9 ♘bxd2 0-0 10 0-0 c5 = Tarasov-Holmov, USSR 1957.

⁴⁰ 6 ... dc 7 ♘e5 ♗b4+ 8 ♗d2 (8 ♔f1!? c6 9 ♘xc6 ♘xc6 10 ♗xc6+ ♔e7 11 a3! ♗c5 12 ♗b2 ♖c8 13 ♗f3 ♕d7! ∞ Kouatly-Saeed, Sharjan Z 1981) 8 ... ♕xd4 9 ♗xb4 ♕xa1 10 ♗c3 ♕xa2 11 bc!! ♗xc4 12 ♘xc4! ± Fedorowicz-Plaskett, Thessaloniki 1981.

⁴¹ 10 ... bc?! 11 ♘c3 ♗e7 12 ♖c1 ±.

⁴² Westerinen-Johannessen, Gausdal 1973.

⁴³ 6 ... ♗xd2+ 7 ♘bxd2 (7 ♕xd2!?) 7 ... d5 8 ♗g2 0-0 9 0-0 ♘bd7 10 ♖e1 c5 11 e4 de 12 ♘xe4 ♘xe4 = Zilber-Vitolins, USSR 1973.

⁴⁴ 7 ♘c3 c6 8 e4 d5 9 e5 (9 ♕c2 de 10 ♘xe4 ♗b7 = Gheorghiu-Ribli, Herkulana Z 1982) 9 ... ♘e4 10 ♗d3 ♗xc3 11 ♗xc3 c5 = Tarjan-Polugayevsky, Riga IZ 1979.

⁴⁵ 7 ... d5 8 cd ed (8 ... ♘xd5 – row 12) 9 ♘c3 0-0 10 0-0 ♘bd7 11 ♘e5 ± Petrosian-Korchnoi, Il Ciocco (match) 1977.

⁴⁶ 8 0-0 d5 9 ♘c3 (9 ♘e5!? 0-0 10 ♗c3 ♘fd7 11 ♘xd7 ♘xd7 12 ♘d2 ∞ Rukavina-Dizdar, Yugoslav Ch 1982) 9 ... 0-0 10 ♘bd2 ♘bd7 11 ♖e1 c5 = Korchnoi-Tal, USSR Ch 1972.

⁴⁷ 9 ... 0-0 10 cd?! (10 ♘e5 ♘fd7 =) 10 ... cd 11 ♕b1? (11 ♕c1!?) 11 ... ♘c6 12 a3 ♖c8 13 ♖c1 ♖e8 14 e3 h6 15 ♕b2 ♗d6 ∓ O'Kelly-Miles, England 1978.

⁴⁸ 11 ... 0-0 12 ♘b5 ♘e4 13 ♕c2 ♗xb5 14 ab ♘d6 15 ♕d3 ± Browne.

⁴⁹ Better is 12 ♗f4 – Browne.

⁵⁰ Benjamin-Browne, Philadelphia 1979.

⁵¹ 11 ♘e5!?

⁵² 13 ... ♗d6?! 14 ♗xd6 ♗xe2 15 ♗c7 ♕f6 16 ♗e5 ± Timman.

13 ... c5 14 dc ♗xc5 15 ♖c2 ♘f6 = Ree-Timman, Wijk aan Zee 1980.

1 d4 Nf6 2 c4 e6 3 Nf3 b6 4 g3 Bb7[1] 5 Bg2

	5	6	7	8	9	10	11	12	13	
1	...	d5	Nh4	Nc3	0-0	Bg5[5]	Bf4	cd	Rc1	±
	c5[2]	ed[3]	g6[4]	Bg7	0-0	Qc7	Qc8[6]	Ne8	d6[7]	
2		0-0[8]	d5[10]	cd	Nc3	e4	e5	Nd5	Nh4	±
	Qc8	c5[9]	ed	Bd5[11]	Bc6	Be7	Ne4[12]	h6	Ng5[13]	
3		Nbd2	0-0	Bxd2	Qxd2	Rfd1	Rac1[16]	Ne1	Nxg2	=
	Bb4+	Ne4[14]	Nxd2	Bxd2	d6[15]	0-0	Nd7	Bxg2	Qe7[17]	
4	...	...	0-0[18]	a3	b4	bc[21]	dc	Bb2	Ne5	=
	...	0-0	d5[19]	Be7	c5[20]	bc	Bxc5	Nbd7	Nxe5[22]	
5	...	Bd2	Nbxd2	0-0	Qc2[25]	e4	Rfe1	Rad1	Nb1	±
	...	Bxd2+[23]	d6[24]	0-0	Nbd7	e5	Qe7[26]	Rfd8	c6[27]	
6	...	...	Qd2	Nc3[29]	Nxe4	0-0	Rac1	cd	b4	±
	...	...	0-0[28]	Ne4	Bxe4	d5?![30]	Nd7	Bxd5	Nf6[31]	
7	...	...	Nc3[32]	0-0	Ne5[35]	Kxg2	e3	Qf3	ed	±
	...	Be7	0-0[33]	Na6[34]	Bxg2	Qb8	c5	cd[36]	Nb4[37]	
8	...	Nc3	Qc2[39]	d5	Ng5	Qd1	cd	0-0	Nf3	±
	Be7	0-0[38]	c5[40]	ed	g6[41]	d6	Na6	Nd7	Nc7[42]	
9	...	...	Bd2	0-0	Rc1[44]	d5[46]	cd	Nxd2	Nde4![47]	±
	...	Ne4	Bf6[43]	0-0	c5[45]	ed	Nxd2	d6	Be7[48]	
10	...	0-0	d5[49]	Nd4[50]	cd[52]	Bxd5	e4	Nc3	Nf5	∞
	...	0-0	ed	Bc6[51]	Bxd5	Nxd5	Nb4[53]	Bf6[54]	Re8[55]	
11	...	...	...	Nh4[56]	cd	Nf5	e4	Nc3	Bg5	±
	...	...	...	c6[57]	Nxd5	Nf6[58]	d5	de[59]	h6[60]	
12	...	...	...	...	...	Nc3	Bf5	Bf4	Rc1[61]	=/±
	...	...	...	...	cd	Na6	Nc7	Bc5	Bc6[62]	

[1] 4 ... Bb4+ 5 Bd2 Bxd2+ 6 Qxd2 Ba6 intending ... c5 or ... c6 and ... d5.

[2] 5 ... g6 6 0-0 Bg7 7 Qc2 0-0 8 Nc3 d6 9 e4 ± Milev-Simagin, Moscow 1959.

[3] 6 ... b5 7 0-0 bc 8 e4! Nxe4 9 de fe 10 Ng5 ± Guimard-Opocensky, Prague 1946.

[4] 7 ... Be7 8 0-0 0-0 9 cd d6 10 Nc3 ± Florian-Csom, Gyula 1965.

[5] 10 Bf4 d6 = Knežević.

[6] 11 ... d6? 12 Bb5 ±.

[7] 14 a3 Nd7 15 b4 ± Tal-Ljubojević, Riga IZ 1979.

[8] 6 Nc3 Bb4

[9] 6 ... Nc6 7 Nc3 d6 8 a3 ± Lilienthal-Romih, Paris 1930.

[10] 7 Nc3 cd 8 Qxd4 Bc5 = Glass-Steiner, Vienna 1935.

[11] 8 ... Nd5 9 e4 Nc7 (9 ... Nf6 10 Nc3 intending 11 e5 ±) 10 Nh4 Nc6 11 Nf5 g6 12 Nd6+ Bxd6 13 Qxd6 Ne6 14 Nc3 ± Budo-Gothilf, Moscow 1935.

[12] 11 ... Bg8 12 Re1 ± Fine-Landau, Ostend 1937.

[13] **13 ... Bxh4?** 14 gh ±±.
13 ... Ng5 14 Nxe7 ± Katetov-Pachman, Moravska Ostrava 1946.

[14] 6 ... c5 7 a3 Bxd2+ 8 Bxd2 (8 Qxd2 cd 9 0-0 0-0 10 Qxd4 Nc6 11 Qd3 d5 = Uhlmann-Parma, Skopje/Ohrid 1968) 8 ... 0-0 (8 ... cd?! 9 Bb4! Na6 10 Bd6 Ne4 11 Be5 0-0 12 0-0 d6 13 Bxd4 ± Gheorghiu-Hecht, West Germany v Romania 1979) 9 dc bc 10 b4 a5! = Matanović.

[15] 9 ... 0-0 10 Qc2 Nc6 11 Rad1 d6 12 d5 Horowitz-Denker, New York 1946.

[16] 11 b4!?

[17] 14 e4 Rad8 = Réti-Capablanca, Bad Kissingen 1928.

[18] 7 a3 Bxd2+ 8 Bxd2 c5 – note 14. 8 ... d6!? 9 0-0 Nbd7 10 Qc2 Qe7 11 Bc3 c5 12 dc dc = Tukmakov-Gipslis, USSR Ch 1970.

[19] 7 ... Bxd2 8 Qxd2 d6 9 b3 Nbd7 10 Bb2 ± Alekhine-Alexander, Nottingham 1936.

[20] 9 ... a5?! 10 b5 c5 11 Bb2 Nbd7 12 Ne5 ± Alekhine-Colle, Scarborough 1926.

[21] 10 b5 a6 11 dc bc 12 Bb2 Nbd7 13 a4 dc 14 Nxc4 ab = Peev-Partos, Bulgaria v Romania 1972.

[22] 14 Be5 Ng4 15 Bc3 Rb8 = Rubinstein-Alekhine, Semmering 1926.

23 6 ... ♕e7 7 0-0 ♗xd2 (7 ... 0-0 8 ♗f4 ♗d6 9 ♘xd6 ♕xd6 10 ♘c3 ♕e7 11 ♕c2 ± Becker-Reinhardt, Stuttgart 1939) 8 ♕xd2 0-0 9 ♘c3 d5 (9 ... ♘e4 10 ♘xe4 ♗xe4 11 ♕f4 ± Sosonko) 10 cd ♘xd5 11 ♖ac1 ± Sosonko-Hecht, Malta Ol 1980.

6 ... a5 7 0-0 0-0 8 ♗f4 ± Benko-Lengyel, Malaga 1969.

24 7 ... d5 8 ♘e5 ± Matanović/Ugrinović.

25 9 ♖e1 ♘bd7 10 e4 e5 11 ♕c2 a5 12 ♖ad1 ed 13 ♘xd4 ♘c5 14 ♘b1! ♖e8 15 ♘c3 ±.

26 11 ... c6.

11 ... c5!? Cvetković.

27 13 ... c5 14 de ♘xe5 15 ♘c3 ± Kuzmin-Larsen, Riga IZ 1979.

13 ... c6 ± Cvetković.

28 7 ... ♘e4 8 ♕e3 ± Matanović/Ugrinović.

29 8 0-0 d5 9 ♘e5 ♕c8 10 cd ♗xd5 11 ♗xd5 ed 12 ♘c3 ♕h3 = Alatortsev-Romanovsky, USSR 1931.

30 10 ... d6 Timman.

31 13 ... ♖c8? 14 ♖fd1 ♕e7 15 ♘h4! ± Timman-Hübner, Tilburg 1980.

13 ... ♘f6 14 ♖fd1 a5 15 b5 a4 16 ♘e5 ♗xg2 ± Timman.

32 7 0-0 c5 8 ♘c3 cd 9 ♘xd4 ♗xg2 10 ♔xg2 ♕c8 11 b3 ♕b7+ 12 f3 d5 = Bertok-Castro, Budapest 1960.

33 7 ... c5 8 d5 ± Matanović.

34 8 ... ♘e4 9 d5 ♘xd2 10 ♕xd2 ♘a6 11 e4 ± Holmov-Lilienthal, USSR Ch 1949.

8 ... d5 9 cd ♘xd5 10 ♕c2 ♘d7 11 ♖fd1 c5 12 dc ♘xc5 13 ♗f4 ± Tukmakov-Balashov, USSR Ch 1970.

35 9 ♗f4 ♘e4 10 ♘xe4 ♗xe4 11 ♕a4 ♕c8 12 ♖ac1 c5 13 ♖fd1 ♖e8 = Georgadze-Romanishin, USSR 1979.

36 12 ... ♘b4 13 ♘e4 ♘xe4 14 ♕xe4 ♕c7 15 ♗xb4 cb 16 ♖ac1 ± Lerner.

37 14 ♗g5! ± Lerner-Romanishin, USSR Ch 1979.

38 6 ... c5 7 d5 ed 8 cd d6 9 ♘d2 ± Tukmakov-Damjanović, Buenos Aires 1970.

39 7 ♕d3 d5 8 cd ♘xd5 9 ♘xd5 ed 10 0-0 ♘d7 11 ♖d1 ♖e8 12 ♗e3 c5 (12 ... ♗d6 13 ♖ac1 ± Korchnoi-Karpov, match 1974) 13 dc bc 14 ♘e1 ♘b6 15 ♖ac1 ♖c8 = Botvinnik.

40 7 ... d5 8 cd ♘xd5 9 0-0 ♘d7 10 ♘xd5 ed 11 ♖d1 ♘f6 12 ♘e5 c5 13 dc ♗xc5 14 ♘d3 ± Karpov-Spassky, USSR 1975.

41 9 ... ♘c6 10 ♘xd5 g6 11 ♕d2! (11 ♘h3 ♘b4 oo Dzhindzhihashvili-Shamkovich, USSR 1973) 11 ... ♖b8 ± Matanović. 11 ... ♘xd5 12 ♗xd5 ♖b8? (12 ... ♗xg5 ±) 13 ♘xh7! ±± Korchnoi-Karpov, match 1974.

42 Korchnoi-Karpov, match 1974.

43 7 ... d5 8 cd ed 9 0-0 0-0 10 ♗f4 ± Matanović.

7 ... f5 8 d5 ♗f6 9 ♕c2 ♘a6 10 0-0 ± Benko-Matanović, Winnipeg 1967.

44 9 ♕c2 ♘xd2 10 ♕xd2 d6 11 ♖ad1 ♘d7 12 ♖e1 ♗xg2 13 ♕xg2 (13 ♔xg2!?) 13 ... ♕e7 = Korchnoi-Karpov, match 1974.

45 9 ... d6 10 d5 ♘xd2 11 ♘xd2 e5 12 ♘de4 ±.

46 10 ♘e1 ♘d6 11 ♗xb7 ♘xb7 12 d5 ed 13 cd d6 14 ♘d3 ♖e8 oo Ribli-Timman, Amsterdam 1980.

47 13 ♘c4 ♗a6! =.

48 13 ... ♖e8? 14 ♕d2 a6 15 b4 ± Kasparov-Ligterink, Malta Ol 1980.

13 ... ♗e7 14 f4 ♘d7 15 g4 ±.

49 7 ♕d3 c5 8 dc bc 9 ♘c3 ♘c6 10 e4 d6 = Tartakower-O'Kelly, Amsterdam 1950.

7 ♗f4 d6 8 ♕c2 c5 9 ♖d1 ♘c6 (9 ... cd 10 ♖xd4 ♘c6 11 ♖d1 ♕c7 12 ♘c3 ♕b8 13 ♖d2 ± Hort-Augustin, Harrachov 1966) 10 dc bc 11 ♘c3 ♕b8 oo Matanović.

50 Pomar.

51 8 ... ♘c6 9 cd ♘xd4 10 ♕xd4 c5 11 ♕d3 (11 dc dc 12 ♕a4 ± Sosonko) 11 ... d6 12 a4 (12 ♘c3 a6 13 a4 b5! 14 ab ab 15 ♖xa8 ♖xa8 16 ♘xb5 ♘xd5 17 ♗xd5 ♗xd5 18 ♘c7 ♗e4! = Sveshnikov) 12 ... a6 13 ♘a3 b5 14 ♗f4 b4 15 ♘c4 ± Polugayevsky-Korchnoi, match 1980.

52 9 ♘xc6 dc 10 ♕c2 oo Sveshnikov.

53 11 ... ♘f6 12 e5 ♘e8 13 ♕f3 c6 14 ♖d1 ♕c7 15 ♗f4 ♗c5 16 ♘f5 ♔h8 17 e6 ± Pomar-Kupper, Munich Ol 1958.

54 12 ... ♘8c6 13 ♘f5 ♘e5 14 f4 ♘g6 15 ♕g4 ± Uhlmann-Padevsky, Monte Carlo 1968.

55 13 ... g6 14 ♘h6+ ± Uhlmann-Kurajica, Hastings 1966/67.

13 ... ♖e8 14 f4 (14 ♗f4 oo Sveshnikov) 14 ... d6 15 ♕g4 ♘8c6 16 e5 de 17 fe (17 ♘e4? ef 18 ♘h6+ ♔f8 19 ♘xf6 ♕xf6 20 ♖xf4 ♖e1+! 21 ♔g2 ♘e5! ∓ Polugayevsky-Korchnoi, match 1980) 17 ... ♖xe5 18 ♗f4 oo Sveshnikov.

56 Polugayevsky.

57 8 ... ♘e4 9 cd ♗xh4 10 ♗xe4 ± Sveshnikov.

58 10 ... ♗c5?! 11 e4 ♗e7 12 ♘xg7! ♔xg7 13 b4 ♗xb4 14 ♕d4+ ± Polugayevsky-Korchnoi, match 1980.

10 ... ♗f6 11 ♖e1! ♗a6 12 e4 ♘e7 13 ♘e3 ♗e5 14 ♘g4 ♗c7 15 e5 d5?! 16 ♗g5 ♗c8 17 ♘f6+! Timman-Portisch, London 1982.

10 ... ♘c7 11 ♘c3 d5 12 e4 ♗f6 13 ed cd 14 ♗f4 ± Kasparov-Marjanović, Malta Ol 1980.

59 12 ... ♘bd7?! 13 ♗g5 ± Matanović.

60 14 ♗f4! ♗a6 15 ♖e1 ♗b4 16 ♕b3 ♗xc3 17 ♕xc3 ♕d3 18 ♘xh6+ ♔h8 19 ♕xd3 ed 20 ♗d6 ± Sturua-Kengis, USSR 1981.

61 13 ♗xc7?! ♕xc7 14 ♘xd5 ♗xd5 15 ♗xd5 ♖ae8 16 e4 ♕e5 ∓ Byrne/Mednis.

62 14 ♘a4 g6 15 ♘xc5 bc 16 ♗xc7 ♕xc7 17 ♘e7+ ♔g7 18 ♘xd5 ♗xd5 19 ♗xd5 ♖ab8 =/± Belyavsky-Spassky, Baden 1980.

165

1 d4 ♘f6 2 c4 e6 3 ♘f3 b6 4 g3 ♗b7 5 ♗g2 ♗e7 6 0-0 0-0 7 ♘c3

	7	8	9	10	11	12	13	14	15	
1	... d5[1]	cd[2] ed[3]	♖e1[4] ♘a6[5]	♗g5[6] c6[7]	♕a4 ♘c7	♘e5 b5[8]	♕b3 ♘e6	♘f3 c5	♗f6[9] ♗f6[10]	=
2	... ...	♘e5 ♘a6![11]	cd[12] ed	♘d3 h6!?[13]	♘f4 ♕d7	♗e3 ♖fd8	♖c1 c5[14]			∞
3	... ♘e4	♘xe4[15] ♗xe4	♗f4 d6	♕d2 ♘d7	♖fd1[16] ♕e8[17]	b4[18] f5	♖ac1 ♖d8	♗g5 ♗xg2	♔xg2 ♗xg5[19]	=
4	... ...	... ...	♘e1 d5[20]	b3[21] ♗xg2	♔xg2 c5	dc dc	♕xd8 ♖xd8	cb ab	bc ♖c8[22]	=
5	... ...	♕c2 ♘xc3[23]	bc ♘c6[24]	♘d2[25] ♘a5	♗xb7 ♘xb7	e4 d5[26]	cd ed	e5 ♕d7	f4 f5[27]	⩱
6	... ...	... ...	♕c3 d6[28]	♕c2 f5[29]	♘e1[30] ♗xg2	♘xg2 ♕d7[31]	e4 fe	♕xe4 d5	♕g4 ♗d6[32]	±
7	... ...	... ...	... ♗e4	♖d1[33] f5[34]	♕e3[35] ♗f6	♗d2 a5	♗c3 d5	cd ed	a3 ♖e8[36]	=
8	... ...	... ...	... ...	♗f4 ♘c6[37]	♖fd1 d5	♘e5 ♘xe5	♗xe5 ♗xg2	♔xg2 c6	♖ac1[38]	=
9	... ...	... ...	... c5	♗e3[39] d6[40]	♖fd1 ♘d7	♖ac1[41] ♖c8	d5 ed	cd ♖e8	b4 ♗f6[42]	=
10	... ...	... ...	... ...	♖d1 d6	b3 ♕c7[43]	♗b2 ♗f6	♕d2[44] ♖d8	dc dc	♕f4 ♘a6[45]	=
11	... ...	... ...	... f5	d5[46] ♗f6[47]	♕c2 ♘a6[48]	♖d1 ♕e7	♘d4 ♘c5	♗e3 ♗xd4	♗xd4 d6[49]	=
12	... ...	... ...	... ...	b3 ♗f6[50]	♗b2[51] d6[52]	♖ad1 a5[53]	♘e1 ♗xg2	♘xg2 ♘c6	♕d2[54] ♕d7[55]	=

---

[1] 7 ... c5 8 d5 ed 9 cd d6 10 ♘d2 ♘a6 11 ♘c4 ± Smyslov-Dominguez, Las Palmas 1972.

7 ... ♕c8 8 ♗g5 c5 9 d5 ed 10 cd d6 11 e4 ♘bd7 12 ♖e1 ± Holmov-Stolyar, USSR Ch 1957.

[2] 8 ♗f4 dc 9 ♕a4 ♘d5 10 ♘e5 ♘xc3 11 bc ♗xg2 12 ♔xg2 ♕d5+ ∓ Sapi-Kovacs, Hungarian Ch 1963.

[3] 8 ... ♘xd5!? 9 ♘xd5 ♗xd5 (9 ... ed 10 ♘e1 ♘d7 11 ♘d3 ± Ivkov) 10 ♗f4 ♗d6 11 ♗xd6 cd 12 ♘e1 = Beni-Tartakower, Dubrovnik Ol 1950.

[4] 9 ♘e5 – row 2.

9 ♕b3 ♘c6 10 ♗g5 ♘a5 11 ♕c2 h6 12 ♗f4 ♖e8 13 ♘e5 ♗d6 14 ♘d3 ♘c6 = Panno-Larsen, Copenhagen 1953.

[5] 9 ... c5 10 ♗e3 (10 dc Parma) 10 ... ♘a6 11 ♖c1 ♘c7 12 dc bc 13 ♘a4 d4 14 ♗g5 ♘e6

(14 ... ♘e4?! 15 ♗xe7 ♕xe7 16 ♘d2 ± Parma) 15 ♗xf6 = Portisch-Karpov, Tilburg 1979.

[6] 10 ♗e3 c6 11 ♘e5 ♘d7 12 ♘d3 ♖e8 13 ♕a4?! ♗f6 14 ♖ad1 ♘c7 15 ♘b4 b5 ∓ Panno-Petrosian, Buenos Aires (*Clarin*) 1979.

[7] 10 ... c5 11 dc ♘xc5 12 ♘d4 ± Minev.

[8] 12 ... ♕e8 13 e4! ± Minev.

[9] 15 dc ♗xc5 16 ♕d1 b4 ∞ Minev.

[10] 16 dc ♖b8 17 ♖ad1 d4 18 e3 ♘xc5 = Portisch-Spassky, match 1980.

[11] 8 ... ♘bd7 9 cd ed (9 ... ♘xe5 10 d6! ±±) 10 ♕a4 ± Najdorf-Wexler, Buenos Aires 1965.

8 ... ♘e4 9 cd ed 10 ♘xe4 ♗xe4 de 11 ♕c2 f5 12 ♗e3 ± Euwe-Capablanca, AVRO 1938.

8 ... c6 9 e4! ♘bd7 (9 ... dc 10 ♘xc4 ♗a6 11 b3 b5 12 ♘e5 b4 13 ♘e2 ♗xe2 14 ♕xe2 ♕xd4 15 ♗b2 ∞∞) 10 ♘xc6! ♗xc6 11 ed ♗b7 12 d6 ±

Langeweg-Ivkov, Wijk aan Zee 1972.
[12] 9 ♗e3 c5 10 ♖c1 ♘e4 11 cd ed 12 ♘xe4 de 13 dc ♗xc5 = Browne-Tal, Las Palmas 1977.
[13] 10 ... ♘e4 11 ♗f4 ♘xc3 12 bc c6 13 e4 de 14 ♗xe4 ± Bukić-Lengyel, Stip 1977.

10 ... c5 11 dc bc 12 ♗g5 ♖b8 (12 ... h6!?) 13 ♕a4 c4 14 ♗xf6 ♗xf6 15 ♘f4 ± Kavalek-Ljubojević, Montreal 1979.
[14] Loginov-Psakhis, USSR Teams' Ch 1981.
[15] 8 ♗d2 - previous section.
[16] 11 b4 ♗f6 (11 ... ♕c8 = Matanović/Ugrinović) 12 ♖fd1 ♕e7 13 ♖ac1 ♖ad8 14 ♕e3 ± Uhlmann-Yanofsky, Siegen Ol 1970.
[17] 11 ... h6 12 ♘e1 f5 13 ♗xe4 (13 f3 ∞) 13 ... fe 14 ♕c2 ♘f6 15 f3 g5 ∓ Hug-Hort, Skopje Ol 1972.
[18] 12 ♕e3 f5 13 ♘e1 ♕g6 14 ♕b3 ♖ad8 15 ♗e3 ♘f6 = Uhlmann-Smyslov, Palma de Mallorca IZ 1970.
[19] Molnar-Podgayets, Hungarian Ch 1950.
[20] 9 ... ♗xg2 10 ♘xg2 d5 11 ♕a4 ♕d7 (11 ... c5 12 ♗e3 ♕d7 13 ♕xd7 ♘xd7 14 cd ed 15 ♘f4 ± Petrosian-Botvinnik, match 1963) 12 ♕xd7 ♘xd7 13 cd ed 14 ♗f4 c5 15 dc ♘xc5 = Polugayevsky-Smyslov, Sochi 1974.
[21] 10 f3 ♗g6 11 e4 de 12 fe e5! = Suetin.

10 cd ♗xg2 11 ♔xg2 ♕d5+ 12 ♘f3 ♕b7 13 ♗e3 ♖d8 = Benko-Smyslov, Venice 1974.
[22] 16 ♘f3 ♖xc4 = Smyslov-Karpov, USSR 1976.
[23] 8 ... f5 9 ♘e5 ± Matanović.

8 ... d5 9 cd ♘xc3 10 ♕xc3 ed 11 ♖d1 ± Szabo-Platz, Budapest 1952.
[24] 9 ... c5 10 d5 d6 11 a4 ♘d7 12 ♘d2 a6 13 ♖b1 ♕c7 13 f4 ± Panov-Chekhover, USSR Ch 1939.
[25] 10 e4 ♘a5 11 ♘d2 d6 12 ♖e1 e5 13 f4 ♗f6 14 d5 c6 15 ♗f1 ♖c8 ∓ May-Najdorf, Budapest 1936.
[26] 12 ... d6 13 ♘b3 ♗f6 14 f4 e5 15 ♗b2 ♕d7 16 a4 a5 17 ♘d2 ± Averbakh-Pogacs, Szczawno Zdroj 1950.
[27] Geller.
[28] 9 ... ♕c8 10 ♗f4 d6 11 ♖fe1 f5 12 ♖ad1 a5 13 a3 ± Smyslov-Larsen, Havana 1967.
[29] 10 ... ♘d7 11 e4 e5 12 b3 ♗f6 13 ♗b2 Maroczy-Takacs, Vienna 1922.
[30] 11 d5 e5 12 e4 fe 13 ♕xe4 ♘d7 14 ♗d2 a5 15 b3 ♗f6 16 ♕e3 ♗c5 ½-½ Gligorić-Najdorf, Moscow 1967.
[31] 12 ... c6 13 e4 ♘a6 14 ef ef 15 ♕a4 ± Alekhine-Keres, Buenos Aires Ol 1939.
[32] Averbakh-Bilek, Palma de Mallorca 1972.
[33] 10 ♘e5 ♗xg2 11 ♘xg2 ♘c6 (11 ... d6 12 ♕f3 d5 13 ♗f4 f6 14 ♘g4 ± Bolbochan-Luckis, Sao Paulo 1941) 12 ♘xc6 dc 13 ♗f4 = Udovčić-Janošević, Yugoslav Ch 1951.
[34] 10 ... ♗f6 11 ♕e3 d5 12 ♗d2 ♘d7 13 ♗c3 c6

14 ♖ac1 ♕c7 15 ♘d2 ♗xg2 16 ♔xg2 ♕b7 = Najdorf-Petrosian, Wijk aan Zee 1971.
[35] 11 ♘e1 ♗xg2 12 ♘xg2 ♗f6 13 ♕c2 ♕e8 = Ardid-Alekhine, Germany 1944.

11 ♕b3 ♘c6 12 d5 ♘a5 13 ♕a4 ed 14 cd ♗f6 = Guimard-Stahlberg, Buenos Aires 1943.
[36] Kramer-O'Kelly, Hilversum 1947.
[37] 10 ... c6 11 ♖fd1 d6 12 ♖ac1 ♕d7 13 ♗f1 ♖c8 = Heilemann-Kostro, corr. 1975.
[38] Petrosian-Korchnoi, match 1977.
[39] 10 dc bc 11 ♖d1 d6 12 b3 ♘c6 13 ♗b2 ♗f6 = Najdorf-Gheorghiu, Buenos Aires 1970.
[40] 10 ... ♗f6 11 ♖fd1 ♗xf3 12 ♗xf3 ♘c6 = Tal-Korchnoi, match 1968. 11 ♕d3 ± Matanović.
[41] 12 ♕c2 ♕c7 13 dc bc 14 ♗g5 ♘f6 15 ♘e1 ♗xg2 = Debarnot-Kuzmin, Nice Ol 1974.
[42] Larsen-Karpov, Amsterdam 1980.
[43] 11 ... ♗f6 12 ♗b2 ♕e7 13 ♕d2 ♖d8 14 ♖ac1 ♘d7 15 ♘e1 ♗xg2 16 ♘xg2 cd = Panno-Csom, Palma de Mallorca 1971. 13 ♖d2 ♘c6 14 ♕c2 ♘b4 15 ♕b1 ♖ac8 = Hort-Korchnoi, Hastings 1975/76. 13 ♕c2 ♘c6 14 e4 g6 15 d5 ♘b4 16 ♗xf6 ♕xf6 17 ♕d2 ±.
[44] 13 ♕c2 ♘d7 14 ♖d2 cd 15 ♗d4 ♖fd8 16 ♖ad1 ♖ac8 - Bagirov-Balashov, Lvov 1978. 14 e4 ♖fd8 15 ♕e2 Karpov.
[45] 16 ♕xc7 ♘xc7 = Timman-Karpov, Amsterdam 1980.
[46] 10 ♘e1 ♗g2 11 ♘g2 ♗f6 12 ♗e3 ♘c6 13 ♖ad1 a5 14 ♕d2 ♕e8 = Yudovich-Lilienthal, USSR 1949.

10 ♖d1 ♗f6 11 ♗f4 d6 12 b4 ♕e7 13 ♖ac1 ♘d7 = Hort-Belkadi, Lugano Ol 1968.
[47] 10 ... ed 11 ♘e1 d4 (11 ... ♗f6 12 ♕d2 ♔h8 13 ♖b1 ± Averbakh-Kots, USSR 1955) 12 ♕xd4 ♗xg2 13 ♘xg2 ♕d5 ♗f7 15 ♗e3 ± Krogius-Lisitsin, USSR 1955.

10 ... ♘a6!? Euwe.
[48] 11 ... ed !? 12 ♘e1 ♘c6 ∞ Matanović.
[49] 16 b4 ♘d7 17 a4 a5 = Krogius-Holmov, USSR Ch 1965.
[50] 10 ... ♕e8 11 ♗b2 d6 12 ♘e1 ♗xg2 13 ♘xg2 ♗g5 14 ♖ae1 ♘d7 15 f4 ♗f6 16 e4 ± Stupica-Matanović, Yugoslav Ch 1969.
[51] 11 ♗a3 d6 (11 ... c5!? Tukmakov) 12 ♖ad1 ♘c6 13 ♕c2 ♘e7 14 ♘e1 ♗g2 15 ♘g2 e5 16 de ♗e5 17 c5! ± Tukmakov-Stean, Las Palmas 1978.
[52] 11 ... ♘c6 12 ♕d2 ♘e7 13 ♘e1 ♗xg2 14 ♘xg2 g5 15 ♖ad1 g6 16 f3 ♕e7 17 e4 ± Pirc-Euwe, Amsterdam Ol 1954.
[53] 12 ... ♘c6 13 ♕e3 intending ♘e1-d3 ± Sveshnikov.
[54] 15 ♕f3 ♕d7 16 ♘f4 ♗xd4 17 ♗xd4 ♘xd4 18 ♖xd4 e5 = Polugayevsky-Korchnoi, match 1980.
[55] 16 d5 ♘d8 17 ♗xf6 ♖xf6 18 de ♘xe6 = Polugayevsky-Korchnoi, match 1980.

1 d4 ♘f6 2 c4 e6 3 ♘f3 b6 4 a3

	4	5	6	7	8	9	10	11	12	
1	...	e3	♘c3[2]	♗d3	0-0	b4	♗b2	d5	cd	∞
	c5	a6!?[1]	♗b7	♗e7	d6	♘bd7	0-0	ed	b5[3]	
2	...	d5	♕c2[5]	cd	e4	♗d3	0-0	♗g5![8]	♗h4	±
	...	♗a6[4]	ed[6]	♗b7[7]	♕e7	♘xd5	♘c7	f6	♘c6[9]	
3	...	e3[10]	♘bd2	b4	♗b2	♕a4	♖c1	♗e2	dc	=
	♗a6	d5	♗e7	0-0	♘bd7	♕c8	c5	dc	bc[11]	
4	...	♕c2	cd	♘c3	g3	♗g2	0-0	♖e1	♗g5[13]	±
	...	d5[12]	ed	c6	♗d6!	0-0	♘bd7	♖e8		
5	...	♘c3	d5!	cd	e4	♗g5	♕a4+	e5[15]		±
	♗b7	c5	ed	d6	g6?![14]	a6	♘bd7			
6	...	...	gf	f4	f5!	♗g2	cd	♕d3	♗g5	±
	...	♗xf3	♗e7	d5	ef	0-0[16]	♗d6	g6	♖e8[17]	
7	...	...	d5	cd	e4[19]	♗d3	0-0	ed	d6	±
	...	♗e7	ed[18]	0-0	♖e8	c6	cd	♘a6	♗f8[20]	
8	...	...	♘xe4	e3[21]	♗d3	♕xd3	e4[23]	♕xc4	dc	±
	...	♘e4	♗xe4	♗e7[22]	♗xd3	d5	dc[24]	c5	♗xc5[25]	

1 d4 ♘f6 2 c4 e6 3 ♘f3 b6 4 a3 ♗b7 5 ♘c3 g6

	6	7	8	9	10	11	12	13	14	
9	e3[26]	♗e2	0-0	cd	b4!	a4	♕b3	bc	♕a3	±
	♗g7	0-0	d5	ed?![27]	♘bd7	♘e4	c5	♘dxc5	♘xc3[28]	
10	d5	g3[30]	♗g2	de	♗f4	♕c2				⩱
	♗g7[29]	0-0	c6	de	c5[31]					

168

[1] 5 ... cd 6 ed d5 7 Nc3 Be7 8 cd Nxd5 9 Bb5+ Bd7 10 Bd3 Bc6 (10 ... Nxc3 11 bc Nc6 12 0-0 Bf6 13 Re1 ± Speelman-Andersson, Hastings 1980/81) 11 Ne5! ± Gheorghiu-Skrobek, Warsaw Z 1979.

5 ... Bb7 6 Nc3 cd 7 ed d5 8 Bg5 Be7 9 Bxf6 Bxf6 10 cd (Ree-Ligterink, Graz 1979) 10 ... ed 11 Bb5+ Bc6! 12 Qe2+ Kf8 13 Bxc6 Nxc6 14 Ne5 Bxe5 15 Qxe5 Qe8 = Geller.

5 ... g6 6 Nc3 Bg7 7 e4 cd (7 ... Bb7 8 d5 ed 9 ed ± Vaganian-van der Wiel, Baden 1980) 8 Nxd4 0-0 ∞ Miles-Timman, Amsterdam 1981.

[2] 6 Be2 Bb7 7 0-0 Be7 8 Nc3 cd 9 Nxd4 0-0 10 Qc2!? Alburt-Korchnoi, Wijk aan Zee 1980.

[3] Timman-Korchnoi, Wijk aan Zee 1980.

[4] 5 ... ed 6 cd g6 (6 ... d6 7 Nc3 Bg6 8 e4 ± Lputian-Psahis, USSR Ch 1980/81) 7 Nc3 Bg7 8 Bg5 0-0 9 e4 d6 10 Nd2 Re8 (10 ... h6 11 Bf4± Franco-Giardelli, Mar del Plata 1982) 11 Be2± Olafsson-Andersson, Las Palmas 1975.

[5] 6 b3 ed 7 cd g6 8 Bb2 Bg7 9 e4 Bxf1 10 Kxf1 d6 = Panno-Miles, Puerto Madryn 1980.

[6] 6 ... Qe7 7 Bg5! ed 8 Nc3! Bxc4 9 e4 h6 (Kasparov-van der Wiel, Graz 1981) 10 Bh4! ±.

[7] 7 ... g6 8 Nc3 d6 9 g3 Bg7 10 Bg2 0-0 11 0-0 Nbd7 (11 ... b5!? 12 Re1 Nbd7 13 h3 Re8 ∞ van der Sterren-Stehouwer, Dutch Ch 1981; 11 ... Re8 12 Re1 ± Lputian-Belyavsky, USSR Ch 1980/81) 12 Bf4 Qe7 13 a4 ± Franco-Andersson, Mar del Plata 1982. 9 Bf4!? Bg7 10 Qa4+ Qd7 11 Bxd6 Qxa4 12 Nxa4 Nxd5 13 0-0-0 Ne7 (13 ... Nf6!?) 14 e4! Bxf1 15 Rhxf1 Nc6 16 Nc3 (Kasparov-Gligorić, Bugojno 1982) 16 ... Bxc3! 17 bc f6 =.

[8] 11 Nc3 Qd8!? 12 Nd5 Ne6 13 b3 (13 Ne5 Nc6 14 f4 ∞ Cvitan-Short, World Junior Ch 1981) 13 ... Be7 14 Bb2 Nc6 ∞ Cebalo-Dizdar, Yugoslav Ch 1982.

[9] 12 ... Ne6 13 Nc3 Qf7 14 Bg3 Nc6 15 Bc4 Be7 16 Rad1 ± Burger-Short, Brighton 1981. 12 ... Nc6 13 Nc3! 0-0-0 14 Rfe1 g5!? (14 ... Qf7!?) 15 Nd5! ±/± Henley-Maninang, Indonesia 1982.

[10] 5 Qa4 c5 (5 ... Bb7!?) 6 Bf4 (6 d5 ed 7 cd b5!?) 6 ... Bb7 7 dc Bxc5 8 Nc3 0-0 8 e3 d5 = Trikaliotis-Sanguinetti, Lugano Ol 1968.

[11] 13 b5 Bb7 14 Qc2 Rd8! = Gheorghiu-Romanishin, Riga IZ 1979.

[12] 5 ... c5 6 d5 – 4 ... c5.

[13] Petrosian-Korchnoi, match 1980.

[14] 8 ... Be7!?

[15] Inkiov-Flesch, Bucharest 1981.

[16] 9 ... c6 10 cd cd 11 Qa4+ Qd7 12 Qxd7+ Nbxd7 13 Nxd5 Nxd5 14 Bxd5 ±.

[17] 13 h4 Nbd7 14 h5 Rb8 (Petrosian-Spassky, match 1966) 15 Qh3! ±.

[18] 6 ... d6 7 e4 0-0 (7 ... c6 8 de fe 9 Ng5 Bc8 10 f4 ± Petrosian-Keres, Zürich 1961) 8 Bd3 c5 9 0-0 ed 10 cd ± Keene-Ostojić, Hastings 1967/68.

[19] 8 g3 Re8 9 Bg2 Bf8 10 0-0± Gaprindashvili-Ioseliani, match (2) 1980.

[20] 13 b4 ± Marjanović-Forintos, Bar 1980.

[21] 7 Bf4 Be7 8 e3 0-0 (8 ... c5 9 d5 ±) 9 Bd3 Bxd3 10 Qxd3 d6 11 0-0 Nd7 = Chen-Liang, China 1981.

7 Nd2!? Bb7 (7 ... Bg6?!. 8 g3 intending Bg2 ± Kasparov-Andersson, Tilburg 1981) 8 e4 Qf6 (8 ... d5!? 9 cd ed 10 e5 c5 Geller) 9 d5 Bc5 10 Nf3 Qg6 11 b4! ± Tseitlin-Zilberstein, USSR 1977.

[22] 7 ... c5 8 d5 ed 9 cd Qf6 ∞ Timman-Ljubojević, Amsterdam 1978. 8 Bd3 Bxd3 (8 ... d5!? Geller) 9 Qxd3 cd 10 Qxd4! ± Gheorghiu-Andersson, London 1980.

[23] 10 cd Qxd5 11 e4 Qb7 = Smyslov-Panno, Palma de Mallorca IZ 1970.

10 0-0 0-0 11 e4 (11 b4!? c6! 12 e4 a5! Tatai-Pomar, Barcelona 1979) 11 ... de 12 Qxe4 ± Timman-Andersson, Wijk aan Zee 1981.

[24] 10 ... c6 Geller.

[25] 13 0-0 0-0 (Gheorghiu-Kudrin, USA 1979) 14 b4 Be7 15 Bf4 ± Geller.

[26] 6 Bg5 h6 7 Bh4 Bg7 8 e3 d6 9 d5 0-0 = Portisch-Spassky, match 1980.

[27] 9 ... Nxd5!? 10 Qc2 c5 = Geller.

[28] 15 Qxc3 Qf6 16 a5! ± Chernikov-Smyslov, Moscow 1966.

[29] 6 ...ed 7 cd Bg7 8 g3 0-0 9 Bg2 c5 10 0-0 d6 11 h3 a6 12 a4 Langeweg-Kavalek, Amsterdam 1981.

[30] 7 e4!?

[31] Langeweg-Speelman, Dortmund 1981.

1 d4 ♘f6 2 c4 e6 3 ♘f3 b6 4 a3 ♗b7 5 ♘c3 d5

	6	7	8	9	10	11	12	13	14	
1	♗g5[1]	cd[2]	♗xe7	♘xd5	♖c1	e3	♗d3	dc	♖xc5	=
	♗e7	♘xd5	♕xe7	♗xd5	0-0	♖c8	c5	♖xc5	♕xc5[3]	
2	cd	e3[4]	♗d3	0-0	♘xd5	♘xd4	♕h5![6]	♕h3[7]		±
	♘xd5	♘d7	c5[5]	cd	♗xd5	♗d6	g6			
3	...	...	♕a4+	♕c2	bc	♗d3				=
	...	♗e7	♕d7!	♘xc3!	c5	♕c7[8]				
4	...	...	♗b5+	♗d3	e4	bc	♗e3!	0-0	♘d2[11]	±
	...	...	c6[9]	♘d7	♘xc3	c5[10]	♕c7	0-0		
5	...	...	...	...	♕a4+[12]	♕c2	bc	♗b2	c4[13]	±
	...	...	...	c5	♕d7	♘xc3	♘c6	♖c8		
6	...	...	...	...	bc	0-0	♕e2	♗b2	♖ad1	±
	...	...	...	♘xc3	c5	♘c6[14]	0-0	♖c8	cd[15]	
7	...	...	...	...	e4[16]	bc	0-0[17]	cd	♗e3[20]	∞
	...	...	...	0-0	♘xc3	c5	cd[18]	♘c6[19]	♖c8[21]	
8	...	b4	b5	e3	♕b3	♗d3	0-0[22]	a4	♗a3	=
	ed	a5	♗d6	♘bd7	0-0	♘e4	♖e8	♘df6	♘xc3[23]	
9	...	e3	♗e2[24]	b4	0-0	♕b3	♖b1	a4	b5	∓
	...	♘bd7	♗d6	0-0[25]	a6	♕e7	♘e4	♘df6	♘xc3[26]	
10	...	♗g5	e3[28]	♗d3	♖c1	0-0	♗b1	♖e1	♗xe7	=
	...	♗e7[27]	0-0	♘bd7	c5	a6[29]	♖e8	♘e4	♕xe7[30]	
11	...	g3	♗g2[32]	0-0	♗f4[34]	♘e5	dc	♘c4	♗xc7	=
	...	♗e7[31]	0-0	♘a6[33]	c5	♘c7[35]	bc	♖b8![36]	♕xc7[37]	
12	...	♗f4	e3	♗e2[38]	♘e5	0-0	dc	♗f3	♘d3	∞
	...	♗e7	0-0	c5	♘c6	♖c8[39]	bc	♗d6	♗a6[40]	
13	...	...	♗g3[41]	e3	♗d3[43]	0-0	hg	dc	b4!	=
	...	♗d6	0-0[42]	c5	♖e8	♗xg3	♘bd7	bc	d4![44]	

---

[1] 6 e3 ♗e7 7 b4 0-0 8 c5 ♘e4! 9 ♗b2 bc 10 bc ♕c8 11 ♗d3 f5 12 ♘e2 ♗f6 13 ♖c1 ♗a6! ∓ Shamkovich-Nikitin, Moscow 1966.

[2] 7 ♗xf6!? ♗xf6 8 cd ed 9 g3!? Kuligowski-Wells, Lone Pine 1981.
7 e3 0-0 8 ♗d3 (8 ♖c1 ♘bd7 = Gligorić-Karpov, Linares 1981) 8 ... ♘bd7 = Peev-Mititelu, Bulgaria v Romania 1971.

[3] Petrosian-Polugayevsky, USSR Ch 1969.

[4] 7 ♕c2!? intending e4 Portisch.

[5] 8 ... ♘xc3 9 bc ♗d6 10 e4 e5 11 ♗g5 ±/± Browne-Sunye, Wijk aan Zee 1980.

[6] 12 e4 ♗b7 13 ♕e2 0-0 = Timman-Hort, Malta Ol 1980.

[7] Butnoris-Sokolov, USSR 1981.

[8] Psakhis-Dorfman, Yerevan Z 1982.

[9] 8 ... ♘d7? 9 ♘xd5 ed 10 ♘e5 ±.

[10] 11 ... ♕c7!? 12 0-0 0-0 13 ♕e2 e5 Ivkov-Whitehead, Lone Pine 1981.

[11] Vaganian-Makarichev, USSR 1979.

[12]   10 ♘xd5 ♕xd5 (10 ... ed!?) 11 dc! ♗xc5
(11 ... ♕xc5 12 ♗d2 ♘c6 13 ♖c1 ♕d6 14 ♕c2
♖c8 15 0-0 ± Petrosian-Smyslov, USSR Ch
1961) 12 ♗b5+ ♔e7 13 ♕e2 ±/= Gheorghiu-
Karpov, Moscow 1981.

[13]   Timman-Petrosian, Moscow 1981.

[14]   11 ... 0-0 12 ♕c2! g6 13 e4 ♘c6 (13 ... ♕c7
14 ♕e2 ♖d8 15 h4 ± Polugayevsky-Petrosian,
Moscow 1981) 14 ♗h6 ♖e8 15 ♖fd1 ± Kasparov-
Petrosian, Moscow 1981.

[15]   15 cd ♘a5?! 16 e4 f6 17 d5! ± Browne-
Dzhindzhihashvili, Chicago 1982.

[16]   10 ♕c2 h6 (Vaganian-Timman, Rio de
Janeiro IZ 1979) 11 e4! ±.

[17]   12 h4 cd 13 cd ♗a6! = Lputian-Georgadze,
USSR Ch 1980/81.
   12 ♗e3 ♕c7 13 h4!? cd 14 cd ♕c3+
15 ♔f1 ∞ Vaganian-Kuzmin, USSR 1980.
   12 ♕e2 cd 13 cd ♕c8 14 ♗b2 ♗a6 ∞
Browne-Portisch, Mar del Plata 1981.

[18]   12 ... ♘c6 13 d5 ed 14 ed ♘a5 15 c4 b5 ∞.
13 ♗e3 cd 14 cd – 12 ... cd.
   12 ... ♘d7!? 13 ♕e2 ♖c8 14 ♗b2 ♕c7
15 ♘d2 ± Gheorghiu-Browne, Novi Sad 1979.
   12 ... h6 13 ♗f4 ± Kasparov-Marjanović,
Banja Luka 1979.
   12 ... ♕c7 13 ♕e2 ♘d7 14 ♖d1 ♖fe8 15 a4!
♖ac8 16 ♗b5! ♖ed8 17 d5! ± Spiridonov-
Foisor, Bucharest 1980.

[19]   13 ... ♘d7 14 ♕e2 ♖c8 15 ♗b2 ♕c7
16 ♕e3 ± Kasparov-Aakesson, World Jr Ch
1980.

[20]   14 ♗b2 ♗f6 15 e5 ♗e7 16 ♕e2 ♘a5 17 ♘d2
♕d5 18 f4 f5 ∞ Ftacnik-Farago, Herkulana Z
1982.

[21]   14 ... ♗f6?! 15 ♗b1! ♖c8 16 ♕d3 g6
17 ♗a2 ± Furman-Panno, Madrid 1973.
   14 ... ♖c8 15 ♕e2 ♘a5 16 ♖fe1 ♔h8
(16 ... ♖c3 17 a4 ♘b3!? 18 ♖ad1 ♕a8 19 ♘d2
♖d8 = Lputian-Georgadze, USSR 1981; 16 ...
♕d6 17 d5 ed 18 e5 ♕e6 19 ♘d4 ♕xe5 20 ♘f5 ∞∞
Kasparov-Najdorf, Bugojno 1982) 17 h4 (17 a4
f5 ∞ Schmidt-Smyslov, Warsaw 1980) 17 ...
♗xh4 18 ♖ad1 ♗e7 ∞ Kasparov-Groszpeter,
Graz 1981.

[22]   12 ♘xd5 ♘dc5 13 dc ♗xc5 14 ♗xh7+ ♔xh7
15 ♕c2+ f5! 16 ♘c3 ♗e4! Geller.

[23]   15 ♕xc3 ♘e4 = Gheorghiu-Bobotsov,
Siegen Ol 1970.

[24]   8 ♗d3!?
   8 b4 intending ♗d3.

[25]   9 ... ♘e4?! 10 ♕b3! ±.

[26]   15 ♕xc3 ♘e4 ∓ Spassky-Petrosian, match

1969.

[27]   7 ... ♘bd7!? 8 g3 ♗e7 9 ♗xf6 ♘xf6 10 ♕a4+
c6 11 ♗g2 0-0 ∞ Reshevsky-Seirawan, US Ch
1981.

[28]   8 ♗xf6 ♗xf6 9 g3 0-0 10 ♗g2 ♖e8 11 0-0
♘a6 12 b4 c5 = Kasparov-Bukić, Banja Luka
1979.

[29]   11 ... ♖e8!?
   11 ... h6?! 12 ♗f4 ♘e4 13 ♗b1 ± Timman-
Hübner, Wijk aan Zee 1975.

[30]   Spraggett-Browne, USA 1979.

[31]   7 ... ♗d6 8 ♗g2 0-0 9 0-0 ♖e8 10 ♗g5 ♘bd7
11 ♘b5 h6 12 ♘xd6 cd 13 ♗xf6 ♘xf6 14 ♘e1 ±
Kasparov-A.Ivanov, USSR 1981.

[32]   8 ♕a4+ c6 (8 ... ♘bd7? 9 ♘e5!; 8 ... ♕d7
9 ♕xd7+ ♘bxd7 10 ♘b5 ±) 9 ♗g2 0-0 10 0-0 c5
11 ♖d1 ± Dorfman-Romanishin, USSR Ch 1981.

[33]   9 ... c5 10 ♗f4!? (10 ♕c2 ♕c8 11 ♖d1 ♖d8
12 ♗f4 ♘a6 13 ♖ac1 ♘c7 = Rodriguez-
Yudasin, Minsk 1982) 10 ... ♘c6 11 dc bc 12 ♘e5
(12 ♖c1 ♕d7 ∞ Lputian-Dziuban, USSR 1981)
12 ... ♘d4 13 b4 ∞ Ftacnik-Möhring, Trnava
1979.

[34]   10 b4!? c6? 11 b5! ♕c7 12 bc ♗xc6 13 ♕b3
♘e6 14 a4! ± Matera-Zaltsman, New York
1980.

[35]   11 ... ♘e4 12 ♘xe4 de 13 dc ♘xc5 ∞
Vaganian-Gulko, Lvov 1978.

[36]   13 ... ♘e6? 14 ♗e5 ♘d4 15 ♘e3! ♘e4
16 ♘exd5 ± Vaganian-Janetschek, Baden
1980.

[37]   15 ♘xd5 ♗xd5 16 ♗xd5 ♖fd8 17 e4 ♘xd5!
18 ed ♕b7 = Gheorghiu-Parma, Istanbul 1980.

[38]   9 ♗d3 c5 10 0-0 ♘bd7 (10 ... ♘a6 11 ♗e5
♘c7 12 ♕a4 ± Inkiov-Augustin, Lodz Z 1979)
11 ♘e5 cd 12 ed ♘e4 ∞ Browne-Kudrin, US Ch
1981.

[39]   11 ... cd 12 ed a6 13 ♖c1 ♖c8 14 ♘xc6
(14 ♘a4 ♘xe5 15 ♖xc8 ♗xc8 16 ♗xe5 ♘d7
17 ♗g3 ½-½ Portisch-Karpov, Montreal 1979)
14 ... ♖xc6 15 ♕b3 ± Portisch-Spassky, London
1982.

[40]   Portisch-Hübner, match (6) 1980.

[41]   8 ♗xd6 ♕xd6 9 g3 (9 ♖c1 ♕e7 10 g3 0-0
11 ♗g2 c5 12 ♕d2 ♘c6 = Browne-Ivanov, Los
Angeles 1982) 9 ... 0-0 10 ♗g2 c5 11 0-0 ♘bd7
12 ♖c1 a6 = Christiansen-Seirawan, London
1982.
   8 g3!? ♗xf4 9 gf ±.

[42]   8 ... a6 9 e3 0-0 10 ♖c1 ♖e8 11 ♗d3 ♗e7
12 b4! ± Miles-Panno, Puerto Madryn 1980.

[43]   10 ♗e2 ♕e7 = Ivkov-Gligorić, Vrbas 1980.

[44]   Portisch-Tal, Montreal 1979.

171

	3	4	5	6	7	8	9	10	11	
1	...	d5²	de⁴	cb	e3⁵	♘c3	e4!	♘g5	♕c2	±
	c5¹	b5³	fe	d5	♗d6	♗b7	de⁶	♗d5	♘bd7	
2	...	...	♗g5	♗xf6	♘c3	♘b5	e4	e5	♗d3!	±
	...	...	h6⁷	♕xf6	b4	♘a6	g5	♕f4	g4⁸	
3	...	♘bd2⁹	e3¹¹	a3	♕xd2	♗e2	b3	♗b2	0-0	=
	♗b4+	b6¹⁰	♗b7	♗xd2+	0-0	d6	♘bd7	♕e7	♘e4¹²	
4	...	♗d2	g3¹⁴	♗g2	♘bxd2	0-0	e4	d5	b4¹⁶	±
	...	♕e7¹³	♘c6¹⁵	♗xd2+	d6	0-0	e5	♘b8		
5	...	...	g3¹⁷	♗g2	0-0	♕c2	♘c3	e4	♖fe1	±
	...	a5	d6¹⁸	♘bd7	e5	0-0	♖e8	c6	♕c7¹⁹	
6	...	...	♕xd2²⁰	♘c3	e3	♗d3²²	e4	♘xe4	♗xe4	±
	...	♗xd2+	0-0	d5²¹	♘bd7	c6	de	♘xe4	♕e7²³	

¹ **3 ... d5** – 1 d4 d5 2 c4 e6 3 ♘f3 ♘f6.
  3 ... ♘e4 4 ♘fd2 ♗b4 5 ♕c2 d5 6 ♘c3 f5 7 ♘dxe4 fe 8 ♗f4 0-0 9 e3 ± Alekhine-Marshall, New York 1927.

² 4 ♘c3 cd 5 ♘xd4 – 1 c4 c5 2 ♘f3 ♘f6 3 d4 cd 4 ♘xd4 e6 5 ♘c3.

³ 4 ... ed 5 cd b5 (5 ... d6 – Benoni) 6 ♗g5 ♕b6!? (6 ... ♕a5 7 ♘c3 ♘e4 8 ♗d2 ♕xd2 9 ♘xd2 ± Browne-Ljubojević, Buenos Aires 1979) 7 ♘c3 b4 8 ♗xf6 ♕xf6 9 ♘e4 ∞ Browne.

⁴ 5 e4!? ♘xe4 6 de fe 7 ♗d3 ♘f6 8 ♘g5 (intending 9 ♗xh7!) 8 ... ♕e7 9 cb d5 ∞ Gipslis.
  5 a4 bc (5 ... ed!? 6 cd b4 ∞) 6 ♘c3 ♗b7 7 e4! ♘xe4 8 ♘xe4 ed 9 ♘c3 d4 10 ♗xc4 dc 11 ♗xf7+ ♔xf7 12 ♕b3+ ∞ Rubinstein-Spielmann, Vienna 1922.

⁵ 7 ♗g5 ♗e7 8 e3 ♘bd7 9 ♘c3 ♗b7 10 ♗e2 0-0 11 0-0 ♕c7! ∞ Kan-Goldenov, USSR 1946.

⁶ 9 ... d4? 10 e5 ±.
  9 ... ♘bd7!?

⁷ 5 ... ed 6 cd d6 7 e4! a6 8 a4 ♗e7 (8 ... b4 9 ♘bd2 ±) 9 ♗xf6 ♗xf6 10 ab ♗xb2 11 ♖a2 ♗f6 12 ♘bd2 ± Vaganian-K.Grigorian, USSR Ch 1971.
  5 ... ♕a5+ 6 ♕d2 (6 ♘c3 ♘e4 7 ♗d2! ±) 6 ... ♕xd2+ 7 ♘bxd2 bc 8 ♗xf6 gf 9 e4 ±.

⁸ 12 ♕d2 ♕xd2+ 13 ♘xd2 ± Polugayevsky-Ljubojević, Manila 1975.

⁹ 4 ♘c3 – 1 d4 ♘f6 2 c4 e6 3 ♘c3 ♗b4 4 ♘f3.

¹⁰ 4 ... d6 5 g3 (5 e3 0-0 6 ♗e2 ♕e7 7 0-0 ♗xd2 8 ♘xd2 e5 =) 5 ... ♘c6 6 ♗g2 0-0 7 0-0 ♗xd2 (7 ... e5 8 d5 ♗xd2 9 ♕xd2 ♗e7 10 ♘e1 ♘d7 11 f4 f5 12 ♘f3 ± Quinteros-Hecht, Wijk aan Zee 1974) 8 ♕xd2 ♘e4 9 ♕e3 f5 10 b3 a5 ± Polugayevsky-Razuvayev, Moscow 1967.
  4 ... d5 5 a3 (5 ♕a4+ ♘c6 6 a3 ♗e7 7 e3 ♗d7 8 ♕c2 a5 =) 5 ... ♗e7 6 e3 0-0 7 ♗d3 (7 b4 a5 8 b5 c5 9 bc bc 10 ♕c2 c5 11 dc ♘bd7 12 c6 ♘c5 = Gurgenidze-Gipslis, USSR 1974) 7 ... b6

8 0-0 c5 9 bc cd 10 ed ♗b7 11 ♗b2 ♘bd7 12 ♖e1 ♖e8 13 ♘e5 ± Korchnoi-Ivkov, Sousse IZ 1967.
  4 ... c5 5 a3 ♗xd2+ 6 ♗xd2 cd (6 ... d6 7 ♕c2 ♘c6 8 e3 ± Gipslis) 7 ♕xd4 ♘c6 8 ♗c3 0-0 9 ♕c2 d5 10 e3 ♗d7 = Timman-Ivkov, Rio de Janeiro IZ 1979.
  4 ... 0-0 5 g3 (5 a3 ♗xd2+ 6 ♗xd2 b6 =) 5 ... c5 6 dc ♗xc5 7 ♗g2 ♘c6 8 0-0 d5 9 a3 ♗d6 10 ♕c2 ♕e7 11 cd ed 12 ♘b3 ♗b6 =.

¹¹ 5 g3 ♗b7 6 ♗g2 0-0 =.

¹² 12 ♕c2 f5 13 ♖ad1 ♘df6 = Baumbach-Lein, Moscow 1970.

¹³ 4 ... ♗e7 5 g3 d5 6 ♗g2 0-0 7 0-0 c6 8 ♕c2 ♘bd7 9 ♖d1 b6 10 a4 ♗a6 11 b3 ± Polugayevsky-Korchnoi, Evian (match) 1977.

¹⁴ 5 a3 ♗xd2+ 6 ♕xd2 0-0 7 ♘c3 d6 8 e4 e5 =.
  5 e3 ♗xd2+ 6 ♕xd2 0-0 7 ♘c3 d6 8 ♗e2 e5 =.

¹⁵ 5 ... ♗xd2+ 6 ♕xd2 d5 7 ♗g2 0-0 8 0-0 dc 9 ♘a3 ♖d8 (9 ... c5 10 dc ♕xc5 11 ♖ac1 ♘c6 12 ♘xc4 ± Kasparov-Petrosian, Bugojno 1982) 10 ♕c2 c5 11 dc ♕xc5 12 ♖fd1 ♘c6 13 ♕xc4 ♕xc4 14 ♘xc4 ± Ivkov-Andersson, Bugojno 1982.

¹⁶ 11 ♘e1 a5 12 ♘d3 ♗a6 13 b3 b6 14 a3 ± Petrosian-Tal, Las Palmas 1975.
  11 b4 ±.

¹⁷ 5 ♘c3 b6 6 e3 ♗b7 7 ♗d3 0-0 8 0-0 d6 9 ♕e2 ♘bd7 10 e4 ± Lengyel-Lehmann, Solingen 1968.

¹⁸ 5 ... d5 6 ♗g2 dc 7 ♕c2 ♘c6 8 ♕xc4 =/± Browne-Smyslov, Las Palmas IZ 1982.

¹⁹ 12 b3 b5 13 cb cb 14 ♖ac1 ± Kovacs-Gipslis, Lublin 1969.

²⁰ 5 ♘bxd2 d6 6 e4 0-0 7 ♗d3 e5 =.

²¹ 6 ... d6 7 g3 (7 e3 ♕e7 8 ♗e2 e5 9 0-0 e4! 10 ♘e1 ♖e8 ∞) 7 ... ♘c6 8 ♗g2 e5 9 d5 ♘e7 10 e4 a6 11 0-0 b5 12 cb ab 13 b4 ± Razuvayev-Makarichev, USSR 1972.

²² 8 ♖c1 c6 9 ♗d3 ♕e7 10 0-0 dc 11 ♗xc4 e5 12 e4 ed 13 ♕xd4 ±.

²³ 12 0-0 ± Voronkov.

Pirc and Modern Defences

Pirc (1 e4 d6 2 d4 ♘f6)

The paternity claims to this defence have been numerous but in common parlance Pirc has won out over Robatsch, Ufimtsev and other more peripheral characters. It was not until relatively recently that the merits of Black's system became clearly understood. Disparaged for many years as passive and eccentric, the mechanics of Pirc counterplay are now well defined. Ideally, the strategy is to undermine and explode the White centre and to establish the latent power of the fianchettoed king's bishop. As is the case with defences of a hypermodern turn, White is allowed a superiority in space which it is his task to maintain.

The first player has a wide choice of weapons, but the toughest questions are posed by the Austrian Attack (3 ♘c3 g6 4 f4). White tries to enforce a central clamp, followed by direct kingside hostilities. Black requires thorough preparation and strong nerves to avoid a lasting inferiority. More subtle but no less threatening is the Classical Variation (3 ♘c3 g6 4 ♘f3 ♗g7 5 ♗e2). White restricts his ambitions to ensuring that his space advantage will endure – a humble goal which, however, he can almost certainly achieve. Still, his edge is not intimidating and the Pirc devotee can attain a solid position, though full equality is a more difficult matter.

Other tries for White (4 ♗c4, 4 ♗g5 4 ♗e3) carry their own brand of trouble but are less likely to procure a pull against accurate play. Nonetheless, there is always danger involved in provocative defence and Black must be well prepared to cope with an opponent bent on his outright destruction.

Modern (1 e4 g6 2 d4 d6 or 2 ... ♗g7)

Blood-brother of the Pirc in strategical aim, the Modern embraces subtle differences in move order. Co-author Keene has, for example, used this possibility to forge a new system against the Austrian Attack. The major difference between the Pirc and the Modern is that the lack of pressure on e4 (usually exerted by Black's recalcitrant king's knight) allows White to play 3 c4 and steer the game into channels that approximate to, or transpose into, the King's Indian Defence. Very interesting play can result from Black attempts to pressure White's d-pawn with an early ... ♘c6 or ... c5. This defence gives ample scope for innovation and improvisation, often of a highly tactical nature. It is a truly 'modern' system and has allowed players with a creative temperament (particularly Suttles and Timman) to pose problems at an early stage of the game. White must beware of reflex response in order to emerge with an edge.

		Pirc		1 e4 d6 2 d4 ♘f6 3 ♘c3 g6					
	4	5	6	7	8	9	10	11	12	
1	♗e2	g4[1]	g5	h4	d5	h5[3]	h6	bc	♕d4	∞
	♗g7	♘a6[2]	♘d7	c5	c4	♘ac5	♗xc3+	f6	♕a5[4]	
2	h4	f3	♗e3	♕d2	a4	♖xa4	♗h6	♕xh6	♘ge2	±
	♗g7	♘c6[5]	a6?!	b5	ba	♗b7	♗xh6	e5!	♕e7[6]	
3	...	♗e2[7]	♗g5[9]	♕d2	0-0-0	f4	♗f3	♘ce2	f5	∞
	...	h5[8]	c6[10]	♕c7	♘bd7	b5	b4	a5[11]	gf[12]	
4	♗e3	f3	♕c1[14]	♗d3[15]	♘ge2	g4[16]	de	♘g3	h4	∞
	c6	♕b6!?[13]	♗g7	0-0	♕c7	e5	de	b5	b4[17]	
5	...	f3	♕d2	♗d3[18]	♘ge2[19]	a4	0-0	♔h1	♘g3	=
	♗g7	c6	b5!	♘bd7	a6	♗b7	0-0	♕c7	e5[20]	
6	♗g5[21]	♕d2[23]	f4	♘f3[24]	♗d3	f5	♘e2	0-0	c3	∞
	♗g7[22]	c6	0-0	b5	♗g4[25]	b4	♘bd7	c5	bc[26]	
7	♗f4	♕d2	0-0-0	♗h6	♗xg7	f4	a3	e5	♘ge2	±
	♗g7	0-0	c6[27]	♕a5	♔xg7	♗e6	b5	♘d5	♘d7[28]	
8	♗c4	♕e2[29]	♗b3	♘f3	a4	h3	0-0	e5	♘xd5[31]	±
	♗g7	c6[30]	0-0	a5	♘a6	♕b6	♘c7	♘fd5		
9	g3	♗g2	♘ge2[33]	0-0	h3[35]	♖e1	♘xd4	♗f4[37]		=
	♗g7	0-0[32]	e5	♘bd7[34]	♖e8	ed[36]	♘c5	♘e6[38]		
10	...	...	...	...	...	♗e3	g4	♗xd4	♘g3	±
	...	...	...	...	...	♕e7[39]	ed	♘c5	c6[40]	
11	♘f3	h3?!	♗e3	a4	♗e2	0-0	♘d2	de	♕c1	=
	♗g7	0-0[41]	c6	a5	♘a6	♘b4	e5	de	♗e6[42]	

---

1 Chinese Variation.

2 5 ... h6?! 6 h3 c5 7 d5 0-0 8 h4! e6 9 g5 hg 10 hg ♘e8?! (10 ... ♘h7 intending ... ♖e8, ... ♘f8 ±) 11 ♕d3! ± Liu Wenzhe-Donner, Buenos Aires Ol 1978.

3 9 ♗xc4 ♕c7 ∞ Nunn.

4 13 ♗d2 0-0 14 f4 b5 15 ♘f3 ♕c7 ∞ Katalimov-Tseitlin, USSR 1978.

5 5 ... h5 6 ♗c4 c6 7 ♗b3 ♕c7 8 ♗e3 e5?! 9 ♕d2 b5 10 de de 11 ♘h3 ♗xh3 12 ♖xh3 ♘bd7 13 0-0-0 a5 14 a4! b4 15 ♘b1 0-0 16 ♕f2 ± Mariotti-Pribyl, Italy 1978.
    5 ... c6 intending ... b5 Nunn.

6 13 d5 ♘b8 14 ♖b4 ± Mariotti-Botterill, Ostend 1975.

7 Mariotti Variation, also arising from 4 ♗e2 ♗g7 5 h4.

8 5 ... ♘c6 6 h5 gh 7 ♗e3 ♘g4 8 ♖xh5 ♘xe3 9 fe e6 10 ♕d2 ♗d7 11 0-0-0 ♕e7 12 ♘f3 0-0-0 = Sax-Simić, Vrnjačka Banja 1974.

5 ... c5?! 6 dc ♕a5 7 ♔f1 ♕xc5 8 ♗e3 ♕a5 9 h5 gh 10 ♘h3! ±/ ± Balashov-Pfleger, Munich 1979.

9   6 ♘h3 ♘c6! 7 ♘g5 0-0 8 ♗e3 e5 9 d5 ♘d4! 10 ♗xd4 ed 11 ♕xd4 c6 ∞/∓ Wade-Smyslov, Havana 1965.

10   6 ... ♘c6 7 ♕d2 ♘h7 8 ♗e3 e5 9 ♘f3 ♗g4 10 d5 ♘e7 ∞.

11   Sax-Kestler, Nice Ol 1974.

12   13 ef ♘b6 14 ♘g3 ♘c4 15 ♕e2 d5 16 ♘xh5 ∞.

13   5 ... ♘bd7 6 ♕d2 b5 7 ♘ge2 ♘b6 8 b3 ♕c7 9 g4 e5 10 ♗g2 b4 11 ♘d1 a5 12 0-0 c5 13 d5 h5 14 g5 ♘h7 15 a3 ♗a6 = Hennings-Smyslov, Havana 1967.

14   6 ♕d2 ♘xb2 7 ♖b1 ♕a3 8 ♗c4 ♘bd7 9 ♘ge2 ♗g7 10 0-0 0-0 11 g4 ♕a5 ∞.

15   7 ♘ge2 0-0 8 ♘f4 ♕a5 9 ♗e2 e5 10 de de 11 ♘d3 ♘bd7 12 0-0 ♖e8 13 a4 ♘f8 ∓ Lipnitsky-Bronstein, USSR Ch 1951.

16   9 0-0 e5 10 ♔h1 ♖e8 11 ♕d2 ♘bd7 12 ♖ad1 b5 13 ♘g3 ♘f8 = Yurkov-Tomson, USSR 1962.

17   13 ♘a4 c5 14 ♗xc5 ♖d8 ∞ Parma.

18   7 0-0-0 ♕a5 8 ♔b1 ♘bd7 9 ♗h6 ♗xh6 10 ♕xh6 ♘b6 = Platonov-Savon, USSR 1968.

19   8 ♗d1 e5 9 c3 a6 10 ♘e2 0-0 11 0-0 d5 12 ♗f2 ♗f7 13 a3 ♖e8 ∓ Hecht-Forintos, Siegen Ol 1970.

20   13 de de 14 ♕f2 ♖fe8 = Geller-Hort, Amsterdam 1970.

21   Panov or Opatija Variation.

22   4 ... c6 5 ♕d2 b5 6 ♗d3 h6! 7 ♗e3 (7 ♗h4 g5 8 ♗g3 ♘h5 ∓) 7 ... ♘g4 8 ♗f4 e5 9 de de 10 ♗g3 h5 (10 ... ♘d7 11 ♘f3 ♕e7 12 ♗h4 ♘e6 13 a4 b4 14 ♘d1 a5 ∞ Tseitlin-Karasev, Leningrad 1977) 11 ♘f3 h4! = Liberzon-Torre, Nice Ol 1974.

23   5 f4 h6 6 ♗h4 c5 7 e5 ♘h5 8 dc ♘xf4 9 ed g5 10 ♗f2 0-0 11 g3 ♘g6 12 ♕d2 ed 13 0-0-0 ♕f6 14 cd ♗g4 15 ♗d4 ♘e5 ∞ Mednis-Parma, Norristown 1973.

24   7 0-0-0 b5 8 e5 (8 ♗d3 ♕a5 9 ♔b1 b4 10 ♘ce2 ♕a6 ∓) 8 ... b4 9 ef ef 10 ♗h4 bc 11 ♕xc3 ♘b6 12 ♘f3 ♕a6 13 ♗c4 d5 ∓ Nikitin-Liberzon, USSR 1963.

25   8 ... ♘bd7 9 0-0 ♘b6 10 e5 b4 11 ♘e2 ♘fd5 12 f5 c5 13 ♗h6 ± Soltis-Botterill, Graz 1972.

26   13 bc ♕a5 14 ♕f4 cd 15 cd ♕a4 ∞ Browne-Hort, Madrid 1973.

27   6 ... ♘c6!? 7 ♗b5 ♘a5 8 ♗e2?! (8 h4!) 8 ...

♘g4 9 ♗xg4 ♗xg4 10 f3 ♗d7 11 h4 ♘c4 ∓ Grabczewski-Smyslov, Polanica Zdroj 1968.

28   13 ♘xd5 ♕xd2+ 14 ♖xd2 ♗xd5 15 ♘c3 ± Kuzmin-Adorjan, Budapest 1968.

29   5 ♘f3 0-0 6 ♕e2 (6 0-0 ♘xe4! 7 ♘xe4 d5) 6 ... ♗g4 (6 ... c6 transposes to row 8) 7 e5 ♘h5! =.

30   5 ... ♘c6!? 6 e5 ♘d7 (6 ... ♘xd4 7 ef ♘xe2 8 fg ♖g8 9 gxe2 ♖xg7 10 ♗h6 ♖g8 11 0-0-0 ♗e6! ∞; 6 ... ♘h5? 7 ♗b5!) 7 ♘f3 ♘b6 8 ♗b3 0-0 9 h3 ♘a5 10 ♗f4 ♘xb3 11 ab f6 =.

31   Gligorić-Dimitriević, Krk 1976.

32   5 ... e5? 6 de de 7 ♕xd8+ ♔xd8 8 ♘f3 ♘bd7 9 b3 ♘e8 10 ♗b2 f6 11 0-0-0 c6 12 ♘e1 ♔e7 13 ♘d3 intending f4 ± Geller-Lerner, USSR 1979.

33   6 ♘f3 ♘bd7 (6 ... ♗g4 7 ♗e3 ♘c6 8 h3 ♗xf3 9 ♕xf3 e5 10 de de 11 0-0 ♘d4 12 ♕d1 ♕e7 13 ♘b1 h5! 14 ♘d2 h4 = Spassky-Timman, Tilburg 1978; 6 ... c5 7 0-0 – Sicilian Dragon) 7 0-0 e5 8 a4 c6 9 b3 ♖e8 10 ♗a3 ed 11 ♘xd4 ♘c5 12 ♖e1 ♘g4 13 ♕d2 ♘e6 14 ♘de2 ♕f6 ∞ Spassky-Gligorić, Montilla 1978.

34   7 ... c6 8 h3 a5 9 ♗e3! ♘db7 10 ♕d2 ♖e8 11 ♖ad1 ♕c7 12 f4! ed 13 ♗xd4± Lein-Donner, Amsterdam 1979.

7 ... ♘a6?! 8 ♖e1 c6 9 h3 ♖e8 10 ♗g5 h6 11 ♗e3 ♕c7 12 ♕d2 ♔h7 13 ♖ad1 ± Karpov-Timman, Montreal 1979.

35   8 ♖e1 c6 9 b3 ♕c7 10 ♗b2 ♖e8 11 a4 a5 12 ♕d2 ♘f8? (12 ... ed 13 ♘xd4 ♘c5 ±) 13 d5! c5 14 ♘b5 ♕d8 15 ♘ec3 ± (intending ♘d1-e3-c4) Lombard-Hoi, Buenos Aires Ol 1978.

36   9 ... c6 Nunn.

37   11 ♘b3!?

38   11 ... ♘h5?! 12 ♗e3 ♘f6 13 f3 a5 14 ♕d2 ♘fd7 15 ♖ad1 a4 16 ♘bd5 ± Bisguier-Taulbut, Lone Pine 1978.

11 ... ♘e6 =.

39   9 ... b6 10 d5! ♗b7 11 ♕d2± Gufeld-Torre, Baku 1980.

9 ... c6 10 a4 a5 11 ♕d2 ± Speelman-Nunn, British Ch 1979.

40   A.Ivanov-Zaichik, USSR 1977.

41   5 ... a6 6 ♗d3 ♘fd7 7 ♘e2 c5 8 c3 ♘c6 9 0-0 b5 10 ♗e3 0-0 11 ♕d2 ± Spassky-van der Wiel, Baden 1980.

42   13 b3 ♘d7 = Kuzmin-Pribyl, Varna 1976.

	6	7	8	9	10	11	12	13	14	
1	...	d5	♗f4[2]	a4	♖e1	♗c4	♗g5	♕d3		±
	c5[1]	♘a6	♘c7	b6	♗b7	♘h5	♘f6	a6		
2	...	e5	♗f4	♖e1[4]	h3	♗d3	♗e3	de		=
	♘bd7	♘e8	c6[3]	♘b6	♘c7	♘e6	de	♘d7[5]		
3	...	d5	♖e1	de	♗f4	h3	♕d2	♗h2	e5	±
	♘c6	♘b8	e5	♗xe6	♘c6[6]	h6	g5[7]	d5	♘e4[8]	
4	...	...	...	h3	♗g5	a4	dc	♘d4[9]		±/±
	...	...	c6	♗d7	a5	♘a6	♗xc6			
5	...	...	♖e1[10]	a3	de[12]	♘d4[13]				±
	...	♘b4?!	e6[11]	♘a6	♗xe6					
6	...	♖e1[14]	e5	♘xe5	♗c4	♕f3	♘e4[17]			±
	c6	♕c7[15]	de	♖d8?![16]	♘d5	e6				
7	...	a4	a5	de	♗e3	♗d2	♕c1	♗g5	♗d2	±/±
	...	♕c7[18]	e5	de	♘g4?!	♖d8	♕e7	f6	♕f8[19]	
8	...	h3	a4	de	♗e3	♕d3	a5!	ab	♖xa7	±/±
	...	♘bd7	e5	de	♕e7	♘b6[20]	♗e6	♖fd8	♖xd3[21]	
9	...	...	a4	♗e3	♕d2	♗h6	♗xg7			=
	...	♕c7	a5[22]	♘a6	♘b4	e5	♔xg7[23]			

[1] 6 ... b6 7 ♖e1 ♗b7 8 e5 ♘d5 9 ♘xd5 ♗xd5 10 c4 ± Marić-Quinteros, Bar 1977.

6 ... ♘a6 7 ♖e1 c5 8 e5 ♘g4 9 ed ♕xd6 10 ♘e4 ♕c7 11 ♗xa6 ba 12 ♘xc5 e5! 13 h3 ± Geller-Sax, Budapest 1973.

6 ... a5 7 h3 ♘a6 8 ♗f4 c6 9 ♕d2 b5 10 e5 de 11 ♘xe5 ♗b7 12 ♗f3 ♕b6 13 a4   b4 14 ♘e2 ± Stean-Larsen, Las Palmas 1978.

6 ... a6!? 7 ♖e1 ♘c6 8 d5 ♘e5 9 ♘xe5 de 10 ♗e3 ♕d6 11 ♕d3! ± Miles-Kavalek, Amsterdam 1977.

[2] 8 ♖e1 ♘c7 9 a4 b6 10 h3 ♗b7 11 ♗f4 a6 12 ♗c4 ♕d7 13 e5 ♘h5 14 ♗g5 f6 ∞ Belyavsky-Torre, Moscow 1981.

[3] 8 ... c5?! 9 ♖e1 cd 10 ♕xd4 de 11 ♘xe5 ♕b6 12 ♘xb6 ♘xb6 13 a4 ± Sosonko-Botterill, Ostend 1975.

[4] 9 ♕d2!? Nunn.

[5] Weinstein-Nunn, Amsterdam II 1975.

[6] 10 ... h6?! 11 ♘d4 ♗d7 12 ♕d2 ♔h7 13 e5! ± Tal-Petrosian, USSR 1974.

[7] Geller-Kuzmin, USSR 1974.

[8] 15 ♕e3 ± Geller.

[9] Liberzon-Janetschek, Vienna (Tungsram) 1980.

[10] 8 h3 e6 9 ♗g5 h6 10 ♗e3 ed 11 ed ± Gipslis-Vadasz, Budapest 1977.

[11] 8 ... e5!?

[12] Tseshkovsky-Parma, Ljubljana/Portorož 1977.

[13] Nunn.

[14] 7 e5!? de 8 ♘xe5 ♗e6 9 ♗f4 ♘bd7 10 ♕d2 ± Smyslov-Bilek, Venice 1974.

[15] 7 ... ♗g4 8 ♗g5 ♘a5 9 ♕d2 ♘bd7 10 ♖ad1 e5 11 d5 ± Andersson-Uhlmann, Nikšić 1978.

[16] 9 ... ♗e6 intending ... ♘bd7 Nunn.

9 ... ♘fd7!? 10 ♘c4 ♘b6 11 ♘e4 ♗f5 12 ♗f1 ♘8d7 13 ♗g5 ♗xe4! 14 ♖xe4 ♘f6 = Keres.

[17] Diesen-Shamkovich, New York 1976.

[18] 7 .. a5 8 ♖e1 ♘a6 9 ♗f1 ♗b4 (9 ... ♗g4!? 10 h3 ♗xf3 11 ♕xf3 ♘d7 = Poutiainen-Planinc, Nizza 1974) 10 ♘b1! ♗g4 11 ♘bd2 e5 12 c3 ± Miles-Panno, Amsterdam 1977.

[19] Tringov-Keene, Rovinj/Zagreb 1975.

[20] 11 ... ♘h5!? intending ... ♘f4 ∞.

[21] 15 ♖xa8+ ♖d8 16 ♖xd8+ ♕xd8 17 ♘xe5 ±/± Browne-Eising, Mannheim 1975.

[22] 8 ... e5 9 de de 10 ♗c4 a5 11 ♗e3 ♘a6 12 ♕e2 ♕e7 13 ♖ad1 ±/= Bonsch-Uhlmann, GDR Ch 1976.

8 ... ♘bd7 9 a5 ♖d8 10 ♗e3 ♘f8 11 ♕d2 ♗d7 12 ♖fd1 ♗e8 13 b4 e5 (Chiburdanidze-Gaprindashvili, match 1978) 14 d5 =.

[23] Qi-Torre, China v Philippines 1975.

	Classical Pirc II			1 e4 d6 2 d4 ♘f6 3 ♘c3 g6 4 ♘f3 ♗g7 5 ♗e2 0-0 6 0-0 ♗g4					
	7	8	9	10	11	12	13	14	15	
1	♗g5	♕d2	♘d5	♘xf6+	♗e3	h3	♗xf3	♗xf4		=
	♘c6	♘d7[1]	♘f6	ef	f5	♗xf3	f4	♘xd4[2]		
2	♗e3	d5	♗xf3	♗e2	f4	dc	♕d2	♗f3		±
	♘c6	♗xf3	♘e5	c6	♘ed7	bc	a5	♘b6[3]		
3	...	♕d3[4]	d5	h3[7]	♘d2	♘c4	f4	♖xf4		∞
	...	e5[5]	♘e7[6]	♗c8	♘d7	f5!?	ef	g5[8]		
4	...	♕d2	♖ad1	de[9]	h3	♗xf3	♘a4	c3	♕c2	±
	...	♖e8	e5	de	♗xf3	a6	♕e7	♖ed8		
5	...	...	de	♖ad1	♕c1	♖xd8+	♖d1	h3	♗xf3	±/=
	...	e5	de	♕c8	♖d8	♕xd8[10]	♕f8	♗xf3	h5[11]	

	1 e4 d6 2 d4 ♘f6 3 ♘c3 g6 4 ♘f3 ♗g7 5 ♗e2 0-0 6 0-0 ♗g4 7 ♗e3 ♘c6 8 ♕d2 e5 9 d5								
	9	10	11	12	13	14	15	16	17	
6	...	♖ad1	h3	♗xf3	a4	♗e2	a5	b4	ef	±
	♘b8?![12]	♘bd7	♗xf3	♔h8	♘g8	a6	♕e7	f5	gf[13]	
7	...	♖ad1[14]	♗h6[16]	♗xg7	♘e1	f4	♕xf4	♘d3		=
	♘e7	♗d7[15]	♘c8[17]	♔xg7	c5	ef	♕e7	♘b6[18]		
8	...	...	h3	♘h2	f4	♘f3	♘xe4	fe	♗g5	±
	...	...	♘e8	f5	♔h8[19]	fe	♘f5	de	♕c8[20]	

[1] 8 ... e5 9 de de 10 ♕xd8 ♖axd8 11 ♗xf6 ♗xf6 12 ♘d5 ♔g7 13 ♘xc7 ♗xf3 14 ♗xf3 ♖d2 ∞ Shashin.

[2] Byrne-Sigurjonsson, Geneva 1977.

[3] Urzica-Tseshkovsky, Moscow 1977. 15 ♕d3!? ±.

[4] 8 ♘d2!? ♗xe2 9 ♕xe2 e5 10 d5 ♘e7 11 a4 c6! 12 dc bc 13 ♖fd1 d5 ∞ Taimanov-Gufeld, USSR 1978.

[5] 8 ... ♘d7! 9 ♘d2 ♘b4 10 ♕c4 ♗xe2 11 ♘xe2 c5! 12 dc dc 13 ♖ad1 ♕c7 14 ♘f3 b6 15 c3 ♘c6 16 ♗f4 ♘de5 = Polugayevsky-Sax, Buenos Aires Ol 1978.

[6] 9 ... ♘b4 10 ♕d2 a5 11 h3 ♗d7 12 ♗g5 ♕e8 13 ♘h2 ♔h8 14 a3 ♘a6 15 ♗h6 ♗xh6 16 ♕xh6 ♘g8 17 ♕e3 ± Karpov-Korchnoi, match 1978.

[7] 10 ♘d2!? ♗xe2 11 ♕xe2 ♕c8 12 f3 ♘h5.

[8] Gligorić-Nunn, Vienna (Tungsram) 1980.

[9] 10 d5 ♗xf3 11 ♗xf3 ♘d4! ∞.

[10] 12 ... ♖xd8!? Pritchett-Keene, China 1981.

[11] 15 ... a6 16 ♘b1! ♖d8 17 ♖xd8 ♕xd8 18 c3 ♕d3 19 ♘d2 ♗f8 20 ♕b1! ± Petrosian-Sax, Tallinn 1979.

15 ... ♖d8 16 ♘b5 ♖c8 17 c3 ± Andersson-Qi, Buenos Aires Ol 1978.

15 ... h5!? intending ... ♔h7, ... ♗h6.

[12] 9 ... ♗xf3 10 ♗xf3 ♘d4!? 11 ♗xd4 ed 12 ♕xd4 ♘d7 13 ♕d2 f5 14 ef gf 15 ♗e2 f4 16 ♗g4 ♘e5 17 ♗e6+ ♔h8 18 ♘e4 ♕h4 19 ♖fe1 ± Belyavsky-Zilberman, USSR 1979.

[13] 18 f4 (Tal-Hort, Montreal 1979) 18 ... ef ∓/=.

[14] 10 a4 ♗d7 11 a5 a6 12 ♘e1 ♘h5 (12 ... ♘e8 13 f3 f5 14 g3 ♘f6 15 ♘d3 ♖f7 ∞ Rogoff-Timman, Malaga 1971) 13 ♘d3 f5 14 f3 ♘f6 15 b4 f4 16 ♗f2 g5 = Geller-Vasyukov, Kislovodsk 1968.

[15] 10 ... ♗xf3 11 ♗xf3 ♘d7 12 ♗e2 f5 13 f4 a6 14 g4 g5 15 ef ef 16 ♗d4 ♗xd4+ 17 ♕xd4 ± Planinc-Sigurjonsson, Ljubljana/Portorož 1977.

10 ... b5!? 11 b4 a5 12 a3 ab 13 ab ♖a3 intending ... ♖xc3/... ♘xe4. 11 ♗xb5 ♗xf3 12 gf ♘h5 ∞.

10 ... ♘d7 11 ♘g5 ♗xe2 12 ♘xe2 h6 13 ♘h3 ♔h7 14 ♘g3 f5 15 f4 ± Spassky-Parma, Havana Ol 1966.

[16] 11 ♘e1 ♘g4 (11 ... b5! =) 12 ♗xg4 ♗xg4 13 f3 ♗d7 14 f4 ♗g4 15 ♖b1 c6 16 h3 (16 fe de 17 ♗c5 cd? 18 ♕g5 ±± Liberzon-Chandler, Hastings 1980/81; 17 ... ♖e8 18 ♕f2 f6 ∞) 16 ... ♗d7 ∞/= Torre-Chandler, Penang 1978.

[17] 11 ... ♗xh6 12 ♕xh6 ♔h8 13 ♘e1 ± Planinc-Ree, Wijk aan Zee 1974.

11 ... ♘h5 12 ♗xg7 ♔xg7 13 g3 ♗h3 14 ♖fe1 h6 15 ♘h4 ♘f6 16 f4 ± Haag-Botterill, Birmingham 1975.

11 ... ♘e8!?

[18] Groszpeter-Mednis, Budapest 1978.

[19] 13 ... ef 14 ♗xf4 ♘f6 15 ef ♗xf5 16 ♗f3 ♘d7 17 g4! ♗xc2 18 ♖de1 ± Vogt.

[20] 18 g4 ♘fd6 19 ♘xe5!? ±.

	5	6	7	8	9	10	11	12	13	
1	...	dc	♝d3	♛e2	♝e3	0-0	♛e1	♜xf3	♛h4	±
	c5	♛a5	♛xc5	0-0	♛c7	♝g4	♝xf3	a6	♞bd7[2]	
2	...	...	...	...	...		♔h1!	fe	♛e1	±
	...	...	...	...	...	♞bd7	e5	de	♞c5[3]	
3	...	...	...	...	...	0-0	h3	♛xf3	a3	=
	...	...	...	...	♛a5	♝g4[4]	♝xf3	♞c6	♞d7[5]	
4	...	♝b5+[6]	♝xd7+	d5	0-0	♛e2	a4!	♜d1	a5	±/=
	...	♝d7	♞fxd7	♞a6	0-0	♞c7	a6	♜b8	b5[7]	
5	...	...	e5	♝xd7+	d5	h3	♞xe4	♞xf6+	0-0	=
	...	...	♞g4	♛xd7	de	e4	♞f6	♝xf6	0-0[8]	
6	...	...	...	h3	♞xb5	♞c3	♛xd4	♛e4	g4	±
	...	...	...	♝xb5	♛a5+?![9]	cd	♞c6	♞h6	0-0-0[10]	
7	...	...	...	...	♛xd4	♛d5	♞g5	♛xb7	bc	±/±
	...	...	...	cd	de[11]	e4	♞h6	♝xc3+	♝xb5[12]	
8	...	...	...	e6	ef+	♞xb5	♞c3	♞xd4	♛xd4	=
	...	...	...	♝xb5	♔d7	♛a5+	cd	♝xd4	♞c6[13]	
9	...	♝e2	dc	0-0	♔h1	♛e1	♝d3	e5	fe	=
	0-0	c5	♛a5	♛xc5+	♞bd7	a6	b5	de	♞g4[14]	
10	...	e5	de	♔xd1	♝c4	♝e3	♜f1	♝e2	ef	=
	...	de	♛xd1+	♞h5	♞c6	♝g4	♞a5	f6	♝xf6[15]	
11	...	...	h4	h5	hg	gf+	♝c4	♞g5	♞xf7	=
	...	♞fd7	c5	cd	dc	♜xf7	e6	♞f8[16]	♔xf7[17]	
12	...	♝e3	e5	♝g1	h3	♛xd4	0-0-0	g4	♞d5	±
	...	♞a6[18]	♞g4	c5	cd	♞h6	♛a5	♝d7	♛xa2[19]	
13	...	...	♝d3	h3	de	fe	♝g5	♝e7	♝xf8	±/=
	...	c6	♞bd7	e5	de	♞e8	♛b6	♞xe5	♔xf8[20]	

[1]   5 e5 de 6 de (6 fe ♞d5 =) 6 ... ♛xd1+ 7 ♔xd1 ♞g4 8 ♔e1 f6 =.
5 ♝c4 c5 6 e5 ♞fd7 7 ed 0-0 =.

[2]   14 g4 e6 15 ♜af1 ± van der Wiel-Wilder, Lone Pine 1979.

[3]   13 ... b6 14 ♛h4 ♝b7 15 ♝g5 ± Tseshkovsky-Peev, Moscow 1977.
13 ... ♞c5 14 ♛h4! intending ♝g5 ± Nunn.

[4]   10 ... ♞c6 11 h3! ±.

[5]   14 b4?! ♛d8 15 ♞e2 ♝xa1 16 ♜xa1 ∓ Ljubojević-Torre, Manila 1975.
14 ♝d2 ♛b6+ 15 ♔h1 ♞c5 16 ♜ab1 ♞xd3 17 cd f5! (17 ... e6 18 f5! ef 19 ef ♞d4 20 ♛g3 ♞xf5 21 ♜xf5 gf 22 ♞d5 f4! 23 ♞f6+! ♔h8 24 ♛h4 h6 25 ♝c3! ±) 18 ♞d5 ♛d8 19 ♝c3 (19 ef gf 20 ♜fe1 e6! = Nunn) 19 ... e6 20 ♝xg7 ♔xg7 =.

[6]   6 e5 ♞fd7 7 e6!? (7 ed 0-0 8 ♝e3 ed 9 ♛d2 ♞c6 = Matulović-Sigurjonsson, Vraca 1975) 7 ... fe 8 ♞g5 ♞f6 9 dc ♞c6 10 ♝c4 d5 11 ♝b5 d4! ∞ Vasyukov-Tseshkovsky, USSR 1974.

[7]   14 ab ♞xb6 15 ♝d2 ♛c8? 16 ♝e1! ± Hort-Torre, Polanica Zdroj 1977. 15 ... e6! = Fridstein.

[8]   14 c4 e6 = Adorjan-Pfleger, Lanzarote 1975.

[9]   9 ... de! 10 hg ♛a5+ ∞ Tseitlin. 11 ♔f2 e4!. 11 c3 e4! 12 ♛e2 ef 13 ♞d6+ ♔d7 14 ♞xb7 ∞.

[10]   14 0-0 de 15 fe (Timman-Sigurjonsson, Geneva 1977) 15 ... f5! 16 ef ef 17 ♝f4 ♜he8 ± Sigurjonsson.

[11]   9 ... ♝xb5 – 8 ... ♝xb5.

[12]   14 ♛xa8 ♝c6 15 ♛xa7 0-0 16 g4! ± Sigurjonsson-Vogt, Cienfuegos 1976.

[13]   14 ♛c4! ♛b6! 15 ♛e2 h5 16 ♝d2 ♞d4 17 ♛d3 ♞f5 18 ♞e4 ♜ac8 19 ♝c3 hf8 20 0-0-0 ♛e3+ = van Wijgerden-Timman, Amsterdam 1977.

[14] 14 e6 ♘de5! = Fridstein.
[15] Unzicker-Pfleger, Munich 1979.
[16] 12... ♘xe5 13 ♕h5 ♕a5 14 fe ♕xe5 15 ♗e2 ♖f5 16 g4 ± Sorokin.
[17] 14 ♕h5+ ♔g8 15 f5 ♕a5 ∞ A.Schneider-Forgacs, Hungary 1975.
[18] 6... c5 7 dc ♕a5 8 ♗d3 ♘g4 9 ♗d2 ♕xc5 10 ♕e2 ♘f6 11 0-0-0 ♘a6 12 e5 de 13 fe ♘g4 14 ♖de1 ± Tal-Mednis, Riga IZ 1979.

6... ♘c6 7 ♗e2 ♘g4 8 ♗g1 e5 9 fe de 10 d5 ♘b8 11 h3 ♘f6 ∞ Balashov-Tseshkovsky, USSR 1976. 7 ♕d2 (±) e5 (7... ♗g4 8 0-0-0! d5 9 h3) 8 de de 9 ♕xd8 ♖xd8 10 fe Karpov-Christiansen, Linares 1981.
[19] 14 ♘xe7+ ♔h8 15 ♕xd6 ♕a1+ 16 ♔d2 ♕a5+ 17 ♔e3 ± Tseshkovsky-Vadasz, Malgrat de Mar/Calella 1978.
[20] Nunn.

Pirc: Austrian Attack II	1 e4 d6 2 d4 ♘f6 3 ♘c3 g6 4 f4 ♗g7 5 ♘f3 0-0 6 ♗d3							
	6	7	8	9	10	11	12	13	14	

#	6	7	8	9	10	11	12	13	14	
1	...	h3	♕xf3	♗e3	e5	0-0-0	dc	cd	a3!	±
	♗g4[1]	♗xf3	♘c6	♘d7[2]	♘b4	c5	♕a5	ed	de[3]	
2	...	e5	e6[4]	♘g5	♕e2	♗c4	♗b3			∞
	♘a6	♘d7	fe	♘f6	♘b4	d5	♕d7[5]			
3	...	0-0	d5	♔h1[6]	a4	♕e1	♕h4	ab		±
	...	c5	♖b8	♘c7	b6	a6	b5	ab		
4	...	e5[7]	fe	♗e3	♗e2	ef[8]	0-0	h3	♗xf3	=
	♘c6	de	♘h5!	♗g4	f6	ef	f5	♗xf3	f4[9]	
5	...	...	de	♗d2	♕e2	♗e4	♗d3[10]			=
	...	...	♘d5	♘b6	♘b4	f5				
6	...	0-0	de[11]	f5	♗g5	♔h1	♕xd3	cd		±
	...	e5	de	♘b4	♕d6	♘xd3	♕xd3	c6[12]		
7	...	...	e5	♗e3!	de	ef	h3	♕xf3	♘e2	±
	...	♗g4	♘h5?	de	f6	♗xf6	♗xf3	♗d4	e5[13]	
8	...	...	...	de	h3	bc	♗e3	♕e2	♖ad1	±/=
	...	...	...	♘d5	♘xc3	♗f5	♕d7	♖ad8	♗xd3[14]	

[1] 6... c6?! 7 0-0 b5 8 f5 a6 9 ♕e1 e5 10 de de 11 ♗g5 h6 12 ♗xf6 ♕xf6 13 fg fg 14 a4 ♗b7 15 ♕g3 ♘d7 16 ab ab 17 ♖xa8 ♖xa8 18 ♘h4 ± Damjanović-Nikolić, Yugoslavia 1965.

[2] 9... e5?! 10 de de 11 f5 gf 12 ♕xf5 ♘d4 13 ♕f2 ± Fischer-Benko, USA 1964.

[3] 15 ab ♕a1+ 16 ♔d2 ♕xb2 17 ♘d5 ef 18 ♕xf4 ♖ad8 19 ♖b1 e5 20 ♕xe5 ± Byrne-Korchnoi, Moscow 1975.

[4] 8 ♘e4!? ♘b4 (8... c5!?) 9 ♗e2 ♘b6 10 c3 ♗f5 11 ♘fg5 d5 12 ♘g3! ♘c2+ 13 ♔f2 ♘xa1 14 ♘xf5 gf 15 ♗d3 ± Mednis-Vadasz, Budapest 1976.
8 ♗e3 ♘b4 9 ♗e2 ♘b6 = Timman-Nunn, London 1982.

[5] Nunn.

[6] 9 ♕e1 ♘b4 10 ♕h4 b5 11 a3 ♘xd3 12 cd ♗g4! 13 f5 ♕c8! ∓ Nunn-van der Sterren, Ramsgate 1981.

[7] 7 ♗e3 e5 8 fe de 9 d5 ♘e7 10 h3 c6 11 dc ♘xc6 = Martin-Adorjan, Las Palmas 1977.

[8] 11 e6!? f5! 12 d5 ♘b4 13 ♗c4 ♗xf3 14 gf ♕d6 ∞ Fridstein.

[9] 15 ♗f2 ♘g3 16 ♖e1 ♘f5 = Nunn.

[10] 12 ef? ef 13 a3 f5! 14 ab fe 15 ♘e5 ♗xe5 16 fe ♕h4+ 17 g3 ♕h3 ∓ Pinter-Adorjan, Hungary 1975.

[11] 8 fe de 9 d5 ♘e7 10 ♘xe5 fxd5 11 ♘xf7! ± Yudovich-Luik, USSR 1968. 10... c6!

[12] Sax-Torre, Rio de Janeiro IZ 1979.

[13] 15 ♘xd4 ± Mednis-Vadasz, Budapest 1978.

[14] 15 cd b5! 16 d4 ♕d5 17 c4 bc 18 ♖c1 ±/= Parma-Eising, Mannheim 1975.

179

Modern I   1 e4 g6 2 d4 ♗g7

	3	4	5	6	7	8	9	10	11	
1	♘f3 / b6¹	c4 / ♗b7	♘c3 / d6	♗e2 / ♘d7	0-0 / e6	♗e3 / ♘e7	♕c2 / h6	♖ad1 / 0-0	d5 / e5²	±
2	c3 / b6³	♗e3⁴ / ♗b7	♘d2 / ♘f6⁵	♗d3 / 0-0	f4 / d6	♘h3 / e5	0-0 / ed	cd / ♖e8	f5!⁶	±
3	♘c3 / c5⁷	d5⁸ / d6	♗e3 / ♘f6	f3 / ♘a6	♕d2 / ♘c7	♘h3!? / ♗xh3	gh / 0-0	♖g1 / ♕d7	0-0-0 / b5⁹	∞
4	♘f3 / c5	c4 / d6	♘c3 / ♕a5	♗e2 / ♗g4	0-0 / ♗xf3	♗xf3 / cd	b4!? / ♕d8	♘b5 / ♘c6	♗b2 / e5¹⁰	$\overline{\infty}$
5	... / ...	♘c3 / ♕a5	d5¹¹ / ♗xc3+	bc / ♘f6	♗e2 / ♘xe4	0-0 / d6	♗d3 / ♘f6	♖e1 / ♗g4	h3 / ♗xf3¹²	=
6	♘c3 / d6	♗e3 / c6	♕d2 / b5	♗d3¹³ / a5	a3 / ♗a6	♘f3 / ♘d7	0-0!¹⁴ / 0-0	♗h6 / ♘gf6	♗xg7 / ♔xg7¹⁵	±
7	... / ...	... / ...	... / ...	0-0-0! / ♘d7	♔b1 / ♘b6	♗d3 / ♖b8	♘f3 / ♘c4?!	♗xc4 / bc	e5!¹⁶	±
8	... / ...	... / a6	♕d2¹⁷ / ♘d7¹⁸	♘f3 / b5	a4 / b4	♘e2 / ♘gf6	♘g3 / h5!	♘g5 / h4	♘e2 / ♘g4¹⁹	∞
9	c3 / d6	♘f3 / ♘f6	♘bd2²⁰ / 0-0	♗e2 / b6!?²¹	0-0 / e6²²	♖e1 / ♗b7	♗d3 / c5	dc / bc	e5 / de²³	⩱
10	♘f3 / d6	♗c4 / ♘f6	♕e2 / c6²⁴	♗b3 / e5!?	de / de	0-0²⁵ / ♕c7	♖d1 / 0-0	♘bd2 / ♘bd7	♘c4 / ♘c5!²⁶	=
11	... / ...	... / ...	... / ...	... / 0-0	0-0 / ♘a6!?	♖d1 / ♘c7	e5 / ♘fd5	c4 / ♘b6	h3 / d5²⁷	=
12	... / ...	... / ...	... / ...	... / ...	... / ♗g4	h3²⁸ / ♗xf3	♕xf3 / ♘bd7²⁹	c3 / e5	♗g5 / ♕a5³⁰	∞
13	... / ...	... / ...	... / ...	... / ...	... / a5	c3!³¹ / ♗g4	h3 / ♗xf3	♕xf3 / e6	♗g5 / ♘bd7³²	±/=
14	... / ...	... / ...	... / ...	... / ...	♗g5! / h6³³	♗h4 / e5	de / de	♘bd2 / ♕c7	♘c4 / ♘h5³⁴	=
15	... / ...	♘c3 / ♗g4	♗e3³⁵ / ♘c6³⁶	♗e2³⁷ / e5³⁸	d5³⁹ / ♘ce7	♘d2!⁴⁰ / ♗d7	0-0 / f5	f4 / fe	♘dxe4 / ♘f5⁴¹	±/±
16	... / ...	... / c6⁴²	♗e2⁴³ / ♘d7⁴⁴	0-0⁴⁵ / ♘h6	♖e1 / ♕c7	a4 / 0-0	h3 / ♔h8	♗c4 / e5	de / de⁴⁶	±

[1] Mongredien's Line – not quite as bad as it looks. See also 1 ... b6 for further details.

[2] 12 ♕c1 ♔h7 13 g3 ± Petrosian-Spassky, match (12) 1966.

[3] See row 9 and Modern II rows 4-10 for more "modern" treatments of 3 c3.

[4] 4 ♘f3 ♗b7 5 ♗d3 d6 6 0-0 ♘d7 7 a4!? (7 ♘bd2; 7 ♗e3) 7 ... e5 8 a5 ♘e7 ∞ Ardiansyah-Larsen, Siegen Ol 1970.

[5] 5 ... d6 intending ... ♘d7, ... e5.

[6] S.Garcia-Larsen, Siegen Ol 1970.

[7] Rows 3-5 (Modern plus quick ... c5) have been christened the "Pterodactyl Variation" by Canadian masters. There are obvious transpositional possibilities to many other openings, e.g. Sicilian, Benoni etc.

[8] 4 ♘f3 ♘f6 (4 ... cd – Accelerated Fianchetto) 5 d5 (5 e5 ♘g4 6 h3 cd 7 ♕xd4 ♘h6 8 ♗xh6 ♗xh6 9 e6 ∞) 5 ... 0-0! 6 ♗d2 (6 e5 ♘g4 7 ♗f4 d6 =) 6 ... d6 7 ♗e2 ♘a6 8 0-0 ♘c7 9 a4 b6 10 ♘c4 ♗a6! = Browne-Gheorghiu, London 1980.
4 dc ♕a5 5 ♗d2 ♕xc5 6 ♘d5 is an interesting pawn offer.

[9] 12 ♘e2 b4 13 ♘g3 ♕a4 14 ♗c4 ♘d7 ∞ Ravi Kumar-Keene, Manchester 1981.

[10] Murey-Keene, Manchester 1981.

[11] 5 ♗e3 ♘f6 6 ♕d2 ♘c6 (6 ... cd!?) 7 dc ♘g4 8 ♗c4 ♘xe3 9 ♕xe3 ±.
5 dc ♗xc3+ 6 bc ♕xc3+ 7 ♗d2 (7 ♕d2!? ♕xa1 8 c3 ∞) 7 ... ♕xc5 ∞.

[12] 12 ♕xf3 ♘bd7 13 ♗f4 0-0 14 ♖xe7 ♕xc3 15 ♖d1 c4 = Gobet-Keene, London 1981.

[13] 6 h4!? h5 7 ♘h3 intending ♘g5.

[14] 9 d5? cd (Dueball-Hübner, Zehlendorf 1970) 10 ♘xd5 ♘gf6 11 ♘d4 ♖c8 12 0-0 0-0-0 ∞ Hübner.

[15] Hübner.

[16] Hartston-Keene, Cambridge 1968.

[17] 5 f3 ♘d7 6 ♕d2 b5 7 a4 b4 8 ♘d1 ♖b8 ∞ Balinas-Ivkov, Lugano Ol 1968.

[18] 5 ... b5 6 a4 b4 7 ♘d1 (7 ♘d5 a5 8 ♗c4 intending h4 is more aggressive) 7 ... a5 8 f3 ♘f6 9 ♗d3 ♘bd7 10 ♘e2 c5 11 c3 0-0 12 0-0 bc 13 bc ♗a6 = Hartston-Keene, England 1971.

[19] Hort-Keene, Dortmund 1982.

[20] Geller's System.
5 ♗d3 0-0 6 0-0 ♘c6 7 ♘bd2 e5 8 de de 9 ♘c4 ♘h5 ∞.

[21] 6 ... c5 7 dc dc 8 0-0 ♘c6 9 ♕c2 b6 10 ♘c4 ♗b7 11 a4 ± Petrosian-Mecking, Palma de

Mallorca 1969.
6 ... ♘c6 7 0-0 e5 8 de ♘xe5 9 ♘xe5 de 10 ♕c2 ♗h6 =.

[22] 7 ... ♗b7 8 ♕c2 e6 (8 ... c5 9 a4 ♕c8 10 a5 ±) 9 a4 c5 10 a5! ± Velimirović-Nunn, Moscow 1977.

[23] 12 ♘xe5 ♘c6 13 ♘dc4 ♘xe5 14 ♘xe5 ♕c7 ∓ Filip-Bronstein, Moscow 1967.

[24] 5 ... 0-0 6 0-0 ♗g4 7 e5!? (7 ♘bd2; 7 c3) 7 ... de (7 ... ♘e8!? intending 8 e6 d5 Marić) 8 de ♘fd7 9 e6 ♘e5 10 ef+ ♔h8 11 ♕xe5!? ∞ Jansa-Gaprindashvili, Göteborg 1968.
5 ... ♘c6!? Keene.

[25] 8 a4 0-0 9 ♘bd2 ♕c7 10 ♘c4 ♘bd7 11 c3 a5 12 0-0 ♘c5 13 ♗c2 ♘h5 = Ivkov-Donner, Beverwijk 1963.

[26] Milić.

[27] Ciric-Hort, Krems 1967. 12 c5!?

[28] 8 ♘bd2 d5?! (8 ... ♘a6!?; 8 ... e5!?) 9 c3 ♘bd7 10 e5 ± Savon-Shamkovich, Leningrad 1971.

[29] 9 ... d5 10 e5 ♘fd7 (Kärner-Gurgenidze, Pärnu 1967) 11 ♗g5! ±.

[30] 12 ♗e3 d5 ∞ Hübner-Mecking, Wijk aan Zee 1971.

[31] 8 a4? ♗g4 9 ♘bd2 d5! ∓ Matanović-Botvinnik, Belgrade 1969.

[32] Ardiansyah-Keene, Siegen Ol 1970.

[33] 7 ... e5 8 de de 9 ♘bd2 ♕c7 10 ♘c4 (Matulović-Hübner, Athens 1969) 10 ... ♘h5! (Ničevski) ∞.

[34] Matulović-Botvinnik, USSR v Rest of the World 1970.

[35] 5 ♗e2 ♘c6 6 d5 ♗xf3 7 ♗xf3 (Kolarov-Orev, Bulgarian Ch 1958) 7 ... ♘e5 =.

[36] 5 ... c6 6 h3 ♗xf3 7 ♕xf3 ±.

[37] 6 ♗b5 a6 7 ♗xc6+ bc 8 h3 ♗xf3 9 ♕xf3 ♖b8 = Gligorić-Robatsch, Moscow Ol 1956.

[38] 6 ... e6!?

[39] 7 de ±.

[40] 8 ♘g1 Taimanov.

[41] 12 ♗c1 (Yanofsky-Henin, Winnipeg 1958) 12 ... ♕e7 13 ♗b5! c6 14 ♗d3 ±.

[42] Suttles Variation.

[43] 5 ♗g5 ♘f6 – Pirc.

[44] 4 ... ♘f6 – Pirc.

[45] 6 a4 a5! 7 0-0 ♕c7 8 ♗e3 ♘gf6 9 ♘d2 d5 (Benko-Kurajica, Malaga 1970) 10 ed ♘xd5 11 ♘xd5 cd 12 ♘b1 intending ♘c3 ± Kurajica.

[46] 12 ♗e3 f5 13 ♗g5 f4 14 ♗e7 ♖e8 15 ♕d6 ± Jimenez-Suttles, Palma de Mallorca IZ 1970.

	3	4	5	6	7	8	9	10	11	
17	♘c3	f4[47]	dc!	bc	♕xd8+	♗c4[49]	f5	fg	♘f3	±/±
	d6	c5	♗xc3+[48]	dc	♔xd8	e6	♘c6	hg	♔e7[50]	
18	...	...	♘f3[51]	♗e2	e5	♘e4	c3	dc	♘f2	⩱
	...	c6	♗g4	♕b6	♘h6[52]	0-0	c5	♕c6	de[53]	
19	...	...	...	♗e3	♕d2[54]	gf	0-0-0[55]	♔b1[56]	f5	±/±
	...	...	...	♕b6	♗xf3	♘d7	♕a5	b5	♘gf6[57]	
20	...	...	♗e3[58]	♗e2[59]	♘f3	e5[61]	♗g1	♘g5[62]	♗f3	∞
	...	♘c6	♘f6	0-0	a6![60]	♘g4	b5	♘h6	♗d7![63]	

[47] Pseudo-Austrian Attack.

[48] 5 ... dc 6 ♕xd8+ ♔xd8 7 ♗e3±/± O'Kelly-Castillo, Paris 1963.

[49] 8 ♗e3 – note 48.

[50] 12 0-0 ±/± Brinck Claussen-Larsen, Danish Ch 1963.

[51] 5 ♗e3 ♕b6 6 ♖b1 f5 7 e5 de 8 fe ♗xe5 9 ♗c4 ∞.

   5 ♗c4 b5 6 ♗b3 b4 7 ♘a4 ♘f6 8 e5 ♘d5 9 ♘f3 (Bronstein-Yukhtman, Tbilisi 1959) 9 ... 0-0! = Fridstein.

[52] 7 ... ♘d7!? 8 ♗g5 ♗xe2 9 ♕xe2 ♘f8!? ∞ Papapostolu-Ghizdavu, Athens 1971.

[53] Terentiev-Shaposhnikov, USSR 1961.

[54] 7 ♖b1 ♘f6 8 ♕d2 d5 = Marić.

   7 ♕d3 ♘f6! 8 0-0-0 d5 9 e5 ♘e4! = Suetin-Gufeld, Tbilisi 1969/70.

[55] 9 ♗c4 e6 10 ♗b3 d5 11 ♘e2 ♕a6! = Murey-Alexeyeva, Moscow 1965.

   9 ♗h3 ♘gf6 (9 ... ♕a6!?) 10 e5 ♘d5 11 ♘xd5 cd =. 10 0-0! ♕c7 11 ♘e2 e6 (11 ... 0-0!? intending ... c5) 12 c4 0-0 13 ♘g3 c5 14 dc ♗xc5 15 f5 ± Knox-Keene, England 1971.

[56] 10 f5!? b5 11 e5!? b4 12 f6!? ♗gxf6 13 ef bc (13 ... ♘xf6 14 ♘e4! ±/±) 14 fg cd+ 15 ♗xd2 ♕xd2+ 16 ♖xd2 ♖g8 ⩱/∓ Keene.

[57] 12 ♗d3 b4 13 ♘e2 0-0 (13 ... c5!?) 14 h4! and White's attack is the more dangerous.

[58] 5 d5 ♘d4!

   5 ♘f3 ♗g4! 6 ♗e3 ♗xf3 7 gf d5 8 e5 (8 ♘xd5 e6; 8 ed ♘b4 9 ♗b5+ ♔f8 10 ♗c4 ♘f6 intending ... ♘bxd5) 8 ... e6 9 ♕d2 ♘ge7 ∓ Talianov-Ufimtsev, USSR 1965.

[59] 6 h3!? 0-0 7 g4!? e5 8 de de 9 f5 gf (9 ... h6!?) 10 gf (Fischer-Udovčić, Zagreb 1970; 10 ef ♘d4 11 ♗g2 ♕e7 12 ♕d2 ♖d8 13 ♕f2 h6 14 0-0-0 c5 ∞ Arnason-Keene, London 1981) 10 ... ♕xd1+ 11 ♖xd1 ♘d4 =.

   6 ♘f3 0-0 7 ♕d2 ± – Austrian Attack I, note 18.

[60] Bednarski-Keene, Hanover 1976.

[61] 8 d5 ♘a7! 9 a4 c5 (9 ... e6!? Davies) 10 ♘d2 (Georgadze-Keene, Baguio 1980) 10 ... ♖b8! intending ... b5.

[62] 10 h3 ♘h6 11 ♗f2 ♗b7 ∞ Balashov-Keene, Skara 1980.

[63] 11 ♕e2 b4 12 ♘ce4 f6 13 e6 ♗e8 14 ♘h3 f5 15 ♘eg5 ♘xd4! ∓ I.Wells-Keene, Morecambe 1980.

   11 ♗f2 b4 12 ♘e2 f6 13 e6 (13 ♗xc6 fg 14 ♗xa8 ♕xa8 ∞∞) 13 ... fg 14 ed ♕xd7 15 ♕d3 d5 ∞ Lein-Keene, New York 1981.

	3	4	5	6	7	8	9	10	11	
1	f4	e5	♘e2	♘g3	♗e2	dc	c3	♘d2	♘b3	=
	d5	♗f5[1]	e6	♘e7	c5	♕a5+	♕xc5	♘bc6	♕b6[2]	
2	...	♘f3	dc	♘bd2	♘b3	♘fd2	♕f3	♗d3	♘c4	∞
	d6	c5[3]	♕a5+	♕xc5	♕b4+	♘f6	0-0	♕b6	♕c7[4]	
3	...	d5	♘f3	♘c3[5]	♗e2	a4	de[7]	0-0		=
	c5	d6	♘f6	0-0	a6[6]	e6	♗xe6	d5		
4	c3	ed[8]	♘f3[9]	dc	♔xd1	♗e3?![10]	♘bd2	♗c4	fe	∞
	d5	♕xd5	c5!	♕xd1+	♘f6	0-0	♘g4	♘xe3+	♗g4[11]	
5	...	♘d2	♘xe4	♗c4	♗g5	♘1f3	♗e4	♗xf6+[13]	0-0	=
	...	de[12]	♘d7	♘df6	♘d5	h6	♘gf6	ef!	0-0[14]	
6	...	f4	♘f3	♗c4	0-0	fe	b3	♗a3	♘xe5![16]	±
	d6[15]	♘d7	e5	♕e7	♘gf6	de	0-0	c5	♘xe5[17]	
7	...	...	dc	cd[19]	e5	♕xd8+	fe	♘f3	♗g5+	=
	...	c5[18]	♘f6	ed	de	♔xd8	♖e8	♘g4[20]	f6[21]	
8	...	...	de	g3	ed	♕e2	♘xe2[22]	♘a3	♗g2[23]	±
	...	e5	♕h4+	♕e7	♕xe4+	♕xe2+	cd	♗d7	♗c6[24]	
9	...	...	e5	fe	♘f3	♗c4	0-0	♕xd4[26]	♗g5	∞
	...	♘f6	de[25]	♘d5	0-0	c5!	cd	e6	♘c6[27]	
10	...	...	♗d3	♘f3	cd	♘c3	0-0	♗e3		=
	...	...	e5![28]	ed[29]	0-0	♘c6	♗g4	♖e8[30]		

[1]   4 ... h5!? 5 c4 c6 6 ♘c3 ♘h6 7 cd cd 8 ♕b3 ♘c6! ∞ Wolfsson-Sakharov, Alger 1969.

[2]   Chistiakov-Kremenetsky, match 1968.

[3]   4 ... c6!? 5 ♗d3 ♗g4 6 c3 ♘d7 7 0-0 d5 8 e5 e6 ∞ Chetnikov-Ageichenko, USSR 1970.
   4 ... ♘f6 5 e5 – Alekhine's Defence, 4 Pawns' Attack.

[4]   Suetin-Polugayevsky, USSR Ch 1963.

[5]   6 ♗b5+ ♘bd7! ∓ Sherwin-Benko, USA 1966.

[6]   7 ... e6!

[7]   9 0-0?! ed! ∓ Sarapu-Ivkov, Sousse IZ 1967.

[8]   4 e5?! c5! = McAlpine-Keene, Lugano Ol 1968.

[9]   5 ♗e2!? (Benko) 5 ... c5 6 ♗f3 ♕e6+ 7 ♘e2 ± Benko-Ciocaltea, Malaga 1971.

[10]   8 h3! ±.

[11]   Nilsson-Gaprindashvili, Göteborg 1968.

[12]   4 ... c5 5 dc ♘f6 6 ed ♕xd5 7 ♘b3! ±.

[13]   10 ♘c5! Gufeld.

[14]   12 ♖e1 c6 = Tal-Gufeld, USSR 1970.

[15]   Often arising from 1 e4 d6 2 d4 g6 3 c3 ♗g7.

[16]   11 ♘bd2? b6 12 ♕e1 ♗b7 = Hübner-Suttles, Palma de Mallorca IZ 1970.

[17]   12 ♗xc5 ♕c7 13 ♗xf8 ± Hübner.

[18]   "Pterodactyl" Variation.

[19]   6 ♘f3 0-0 7 e5 ♘e4 8 cd ed ∞ Ghizdavu-Day, Jerusalem 1967.   7 ♗d3 ♘bd7 – note 28.

[20]   10 ... ♘c6 11 ♗b5 ♗d7 12 ♗xc6 bc 13 0-0 ± Stein-Suttles, Sousse IZ 1967.

[21]   12 ♗h4 ♘xe5 13 ♘xe5 ♖xe5+ 16 ♔f2 ♖f5+! =.

[22]   9 ♗xe2 cd 10 ♘a3 ±.

[23]   11 ♗e3 ♗c6 =. Kurajica-Suttles, Belgrade 1969.

[24]   12 0-0 ±.

[25]   5 ... ♘d5 6 ♘f3 0-0 (6 ... ♗f5; 6 ... e6) 7 ♗c4 (7 ♗d3 c5!? 8 ♗e4 ♘ac7 9 dc de!? Lehmann-Ivkov, Palma de Mallorca 1968) 7 ... c6 8 0-0 a5 9 a4 ♘a6 10 ♘a3 ♘ac7 11 ♕e2 ♔h8! ∞ Bogdanović-Kotov, Sochi 1967.

[26]   10 cd ♘c6 =.

[27]   Konstantinopolsky-Kotov, Moscow 1967.

[28]   5 ... c5 6 dc 0-0 7 ♘f3 (7 cd ed intending ... ♖e8) 7 ... ♘bd7 8 cd ed intending ... ♘c5 ∞.

[29]   6 ... ef 7 ♗xf4 0-0 8 0-0 c5 = R.Byrne-Donner, San Juan 1969.

[30]   Tseshkovsky-Tseitlin, Novosibirsk 1971.

Modern II *continued* 1 e4 g6 2 d4 ♗g7 3 c4 d6 4 ♘c3

	4	5	6	7	8	9	10	11	12	
11	...	♘f3[31]	♗e3	♗e2	♗xf3	0-0	g3	h3	♗g2	±
	c6	♗g4	♘d7	♗xf3	♘gf6	a6	h5	e5	0-0[32]	
12	...	ef	♘f3[34]	♗e2	0-0	d5	♘g5	♗d3	♘e2	±
	f5	♗xf5[33]	♘h6	0-0	♘a6	c5	♘c7	♗d7	♘f7[35]	
13	...	♘f3	d5	♗e2	0-0	a3	♖b1	♔h1	♘e1	±
	e5	♗g4	a5[36]	♘a6	♘e7	0-0	c5	♗d7	f5[37]	
14	♗e3	♗xd4	f3![38]	♗e3	♘ge2	♘f4	♕b3	♖d1		=/∞
	...	ed!	♘f6	♘c6	0-0	♘e5	c6	♘fd7	♕h4+![39]	
15	...	de	♕xd8+	♗g5+[40]	0-0-0+	♗e3	♗xh6	h4	h5	=
	...	de	♔xd8	f6	♘d7	♗h6!	♗xh6	c6	♔e7[41]	
16	...	d5	♗e3	♗xh6	♕d2	h3	♗d3	♘ge2	a3	=
	...	♘d7!?[42]	♗h6	♘xh6	♘g4	♘gf6	a6	♕e7	c6[43]	
17	...	♘f3[44]	♗e2[45]	0-0	♖e1[47]	♗f1	de	b3	♘b5	=
	♘d7	e5	♘e7[46]	0-0	h6	♔h7	de	c5	♘c6[48]	
18	...	♘ge2[49]	d5	♘g3[50]	♗d3	h4	a3	♗g5	♕d2	±
	♘c6	e5	♘ce7	c5	h5	a6	♘f6	0-0	♘h7[51]	
19	...	♗e3	d5![53]	g4	gf!	♕h5+	ef	♕f3	♘b5	∞
	...	e5[52]	♘ce7![54]	f5	gf	♘g6[55]	♕h4	♘6e7	♔d8	
20	...	...	...	...	h3	g5	♕d2	♘f3	0-0-0	∞
	...	...	...	♘f6![56]	h5	♘h7	0-0	♗d7	♕b8![57]	
21	...	...	...	...	g5!	h4	gh	♗xh6	♕d2	∞
	...	...	...	...	♘d7[58]	h5	♗xh6	♗xh6	♖xh6	

[31] 5 f4 ♕b6! 6 ♘f3 ♗g4 7 d5 ♘f6 = Uhlmann-Olafsson, Reykjavik 1968.

[32] Schmid-Bronstein, Monaco 1969.

[33] 5 ... gf?! 6 ♕h5+ ♔f8 intending ... ♘f6 ±.

[34] 6 ♗d3 ♗xd4 7 ♗xf5 ♗xc3+ 8 bc gf 9 ♕h5+ ♔d7 = Portisch-Bilek, Sousse IZ 1967.

[35] Polugayevsky-Bilek, Lipeck 1968.

[36] 6 ... ♘e7 7 ♗e2 0-0 8 ♘d2 ♗c8! = Cobo-Ivkov, Havana Ol 1966.

[37] Korchnoi-Hübner, Wijk aan Zee 1971.

[38] 7 ♗e2 0-0 8 ♘f3 ♘c6 =.

[39] Donner-Ivkov, Wijk aan Zee 1971.

[40] 7 f4!? ♗e6 (7 ... ♘c6 8 fe ♗e6 9 ♗g5+ ♔c8 10 ♘f3 h6 ∓ Uhlmann-Larsen, Aarhus 1971; 7 ... ♘d7 8 ♘f3 c6 9 ♗e2 f6 10 0-0 ♔e8 11 g3 ± Hübner-Benko, Hungary 1978) 8 ♘f3 (8 fe ♘c6) 8 ... ♘d7 9 ♗e2 h6 10 0-0 ♘e7 11 ♘d2 ± Tarjan-Mestel, Hastings 1977/78. 9 ... c6!?

[41] 13 hg hg 14 ♘f3 ♘f8 15 ♘h4 ♗e6 = Janošević-Benko, Majdanpek 1976.

[42] 5 ... ♘f6 – King's Indian Defence.

[43] Ivkov-Panno, Caracas 1970.

[44] 5 f4 e5 6 d5 – King's Indian Defence. 5 ♘ge2!? e5 6 ♗e3 – cf. KI Sämisch.

[45] 6 g3 ♘e7 7 ♗g2 0-0 8 0-0 ♘c6 = Velimirović.

[46] 6 ... c6 7 0-0 ♘h6 ∞.

[47] 8 ♗e3 f5! 9 ef gf 10 de de 11 ♗g5 h6 12 ♗h4 ± Kozma-Plachetka, Luhacovice 1969.

[48] 13 ♘d6 ± Filip-Suttles, Palma IZ 1970.

[49] 5 d5 ♘d4 (5 ... ♘b8!? Hartoch) 6 ♗e3 c5 7 ♘ge2 ♕b6 8 ♘a4 (8 ♕d2 ♘f6! ∞; 8 ♘xd4 cd 9 ♘a4 ♕a5+ 10 ♗d2 ±; 9 ... de!? 10 ♘xb6 ef+ 11 ♔xf2 ab ∓ !?) 8 ... ♕a5+ 9 ♗d2 ♕a6 10 ♘xd4 ±.

[50] 7 h4 h5 8 g3 intending ♗h3 ± *Archives*.

[51] 13 ♗h6! ±/= Forintos-Uhlmann, Monaco 1968.

[52] 5 ... ♘h6?! 6 h3 f5 7 ♕d2 ♘f7 8 d5 ±/± Lehmann-Shamkovich, Palma 1966.

5 ... ♘f6!? (Keene) 6 f3 – King's Indian Sämisch. 6 ♗e2 e5 7 d5 ♘d4 8 ♗xd4 ed 9 ♕xd4 0-0 ∞ Ligterink-Keene, Rotterdam 1981. 6 d5 ♘e5 7 f4 ♘ed7 ∞ Tal-Christiansen, Wijk aan Zee 1982. 7 ... ♘eg4!? 8 ♗d2 ♘h5! ∞.

[53] 6 ♘ge2 ♘h6 7 f3 f5 8 ♕d2 ♘f7 9 0-0-0 0-0 10 ♔b1 a6 11 d5 ±.

[54] 6 ... ♘d4 7 ♘ge2 ♘xe2 8 ♗xe2 ±.

[55] 9 ... ♔f8 10 ♗h3 ±/±.

[56] 7 ... f6 8 h4 ♘h6 9 g5 ♘f7 10 gf ♗xf6 11 ♕f3 ♗g7 12 0-0-0 ♖f8 ±/± Polugayevsky-Zaitsev, Moscow 1969.

7 ... a6 8 f3 f5 9 c5 ♘f6 10 h3 0-0 11 ♕d2 ±.

7 ... c5!?

[57] 13 ♔b1 ♖d8 14 c5 ♘c8! ∞.

[58] 8 ... ♘h5!? intending ... ♘f4.

1 e4: Miscellaneous, Centre Counter and Nimzowitsch Defences

1 ... g5 and 1 ... a6. These highly unusual first moves have been championed by the irrepressible English IM Michael Basman. They are of great psychological value but are positionally suspect, though it must be noted that Basman's compatriot Miles adopted 1 ... a6 to defeat Karpov. The moves remain, despite this success, rather distrusted by the public in general and should be recommended only to the adventurous.

1 ... b6. This move enjoyed a brief revival at the hands of American IM Regan and Yugoslav GM Sahović. Unfortunately, the attention it received unearthed more accurate lines for White and it is currently considered insufficient.

1 ... d5. The Centre Counter, or Scandinavian, has been much maligned over the years and it is a defence that deserves a better reputation. Having re-earned its name thanks to the efforts of the enterprising Dane Bent Larsen, it has made strides towards respectability, particularly after it was used by Larsen to defeat Karpov. White, with proper preparation, should be able to keep the edge.

1 ... ♘c6. The Nimzowitsch Defence, envisaged by its namesake as a system akin to the French, has never been fully accepted as a dependable opening. Nevertheless it is sound and offers the maverick spirit a great deal of foreign territory to explore.

1 e4: Miscellaneous Defences and Centre Counter — 1 e4

	1	2	3	4	5	6	7	8	9	
1	...	d4[2]	♘f3[3]	♗d3[4]	♕e2	a4	dc[7]	e5[9]	0-0	±
	a6[1]	b5	♗b7	♘f6[5]	e6	c5!?[6]	♗xc5[8]	♘g4	b4[10]	
2	...	...	...	...	...	c3	0-0	e5[11]	♗c2	±
	...	...	...	...	...	c5	♘c6	c4	♘d5[12]	
3	...	d4	♗d3[14]	ef	♕h5+	fg	gh+	♘f3!	♕g6[15]	±
	b6[13]	♗b7	f5?!	♗xg2	g6	♗g7	♔f8	♘f6		
4	...	...	...	♘f3	c3	♕e2	cd	♘bd2	e5	±
	...	...	e6	c5[16]	♘f6[17]	cd	♗b4+	d5	♘fd7[18]	

---

[1] St George's Defence.
   1 ... f6 2 d4 e6 3 c4 ♘e7 4 ♘c3 d5 5 ♘f3 ±.

[2] 2 c4 (Miles) 2 ... c5! 3 ♘f3 ± – O'Kelly Sicilian. 2 ... b5!? Basman.

[3] 3 a4 ♗b7 4 ab ab 5 ♖xa8 ♖xa8 6 ♘d2 e6 7 ♗xb5 f5 (Chandler-Basman, London 1979) 8 ♕h5+ g6 9 ♕e2 ± Miles. 4 ... ♗xe4! 5 ba ♗b7 ∓ Miles.

[4] 4 e5!? (Chandler) 4 ... e6 (4 ... d6!?) 5 c4 bc 6 ♗xc4 ♗b4+ 7 ♘c3 ♘e7 Miles.

[5] 4 ... e6 5 ♘bd2 c5 6 dc ♗xc5 7 ♘b3 ♗d6 8 a4 ± Spielmann-Hartingsvelt, 1934.

[6] 6 ... b4!? Miles.

[7] 7 e5!? c4 ∞.
   7 c3 c4!? 8 ♗c2 d5 intending ... b4 Miles.
   7 ab ab 8 ♖xa8 ♗xa8 9 e5 c4 10 ef cd 11 fg ♗xg7 12 ♕xd3 ♕a5+!? ∞ Miles.

[8] 7 ... b4!? Miles.

[9] 8 ♘bd2 b4 9 e5 ♘d5 10 ♘e4 ♗e7 ∓ Karpov-Miles, Skara 1980.

[10] 10 h3 h5!? 11 ♘bd2! intending ♘e4, ♗e4.

[11] 8 d5 ♘e7 9 de de 10 e5 ♘fd5 11 ♘g5 ♘g6 12 f4 c4! = De Rosende-Hodgson, Hastings II 1980/81.

[12] 10 b3 ±.

[13] Owen's Defence.

[14] 3 ♘c3 e6 4 ♘f3 ♗b4 ±.

[15] 9 ... ♗xh1 10 ♗h6 ♖xh7 11 ♘g5 ±±.
   9 ... ♗xf3 10 ♖g1 ♖xh7 11 ♕g3! ♗e4 12 ♗xe4 ♘xe4 13 ♕f3+ ♔g8 14 ♕xe4 ±.

[16] 4 ... g6 5 c3 ♗g7 6 ♗e3 d6 7 ♘bd2 ♘e7 8 0-0 0-0 9 ♕e2 ± Owen-Mongredien, London 1862.

[17] 5 ... d6? 6 0-0 ♘d7 7 ♖e1 ♘e7 8 ♗g5 ♕c7 9 ♘a3 ♘g6 10 h4 ± Mattison-Tartakower, Carlsbad 1929.

[18] Hübner-Larsen, Bugojno 1978.

	1	2	3	4	5	6	7	8	9	
5	... d6	d4 f5[19]	♘c3 fe	♘xe4[20] ♗f5	♘g3 ♗g6	♗d3 ♗xd3	♕xd3 ♕d7	♘f3 ♘c6	d5 ♘e5[21]	±
6	... g5[22]	d4 h6	♗d3[23] d6	♘e2 c5	c3 ♘c6	0-0 ♘f6	♘d2 ♕c7[24]	b4! b6[25]		±
7	... d5[26]	ed ♘f6	♗b5+ ♗d7	♗c4 ♗g4[27]	f3 ♗f5	♘c3 ♘bd7	♕e2 ♘b6	♗b3 ♕d7!	d6 ♕xd6[28]	∞
8	... ...	... ...	d4 ♘xd5	♘f3[29] ♗g4[30]	♗e2 ♘c6	c4 ♘b6	0-0 e6	♘c3![31] ♗b4[32]	d5 ♘e7[33]	±
9	... ...	... ♕xd5	♘c3 ♕d8[34]	d4 ♘f6	♗c4 ♗f5	♕f3! ♕c8	♗g5! ♗xc2	♖c1 ♗g6	♘ge2 ♘bd7[35]	∞/±
10	... ...	... ...	... ♕a5	d4 ♘f6[36]	♘f3 c6[37]	♗c4[38] ♗f5	♕e2 e6	♗d2 ♗b4[39]	a3 ♗g4![40]	∞
11	... ...	... ...	... ...	... ...	♗c4 ♘c6[41]	d5 ♘e5	♗b3 c6[42]	♕e2 ♘ed7	♗d2 cd[43]	±

[19] Balogh's Defence.
  2 ... ♘f6 – Pirc.
  2 ... g6 – Modern.
[20] 4 f3!?
[21] 9 ... ♘b4 10 ♕b3! a5 11 a3 ±±.
  9 ... ♘e5 10 ♘xe5 de 11 ♕e4 ♘f6 12 ♕xe5±.
[22] Basmaniac or Borg Defence.
[23] 3 h4!? gh 4 ♖xh4 (4 ♘c3 c6 5 ♗d3 d5 6 e5 ♕b6 ∞ Tucker-Basman, England 1980) 4 ... d5 5 ed e6!? 6 ♖h5 ♘f6 7 de ♗xe6 8 ♘c3? ♘xh5 9 ♕xh5 ♗b4 10 ♘e2 ♘c6 11 ♗e3 ♕d7 12 a3 ♗g4 ∓ Speelman-Basman, British Ch 1980.
  8 ♖e5!? 8 ♖h1!? intending ♘f3.
  3 f4 ♗g7 4 c3 gf 5 ♗xf4 c5 6 dc b6!? ∞.
[24] 7 ... ♗d7!? Basman.
[25] Nunn-Basman, British Ch 1980.
[26] Centre Counter or Scandinavian Defence.
[27] 4 ... b5!? 5 ♗b3! ♗g4 6 ♘f3 ♗xd5 7 ♘c3 ♘xc3 8 ♘e5!
[28] 10 ♘b5 ♕d7 11 ♕e5 0-0-0 12 ♘xa7+ ♔b8 13 ♘b5 ♘fd5 14 a4 e6! = Peters.
[29] 5 c4 ♘b6 6 c5 ♘6d7! intending ... e6, ... ♗e7, ... 0-0 =.
[30] 4 ... g6 5 ♗e2 ♗g7 6 0-0 0-0 7 ♖e1 ♘c6 8 c3 ♗f5 9 ♘a3 ♖e8 10 ♗b5 ± Marović.
[31] 8 b3 ♗xf3 9 ♗xf3 ♘xd4 10 ♗xb7 ♖b8 11 ♗e3! c5! (11 ... ♖xb7 12 ♕xd4 ♕xd4 13 ♗xd4 c5 14 ♗e7 15 ♘c3 0-0 16 ♖ad1 ♖c8 17 ♖d3 ± Dely-Karaklajić, Belgrade 1965)

[ ] 12 ♗e4 f5! 13 ♗d3 ♗e7 = Peters.
[32] 8 ... ♗xf3 9 ♗xf3 ♘xc4 10 d5! ed 11 ♖e1+ ♗e7 12 ♘xd5 ♘d6 13 ♗f4 ± J.Whitehead-Peters, USA 1978.
[33] Taulbut-Peters, Hastings 1978/79. 10 ♕b3 a5 11 ♖d1 ± Peters.
[34] 3 ... ♕d6 4 d4 ♘f6 5 ♘f3 a6 6 ♗e3± Karpov-Lutikov, USSR 1979. 4 ... c6!?
[35] 10 0-0 ∞/± Fischer-Addison, Palma 1970.
[36] 4 ... e5 5 ♘f3 ♗g4 6 h3 ed 7 ♕xd4 ♗xf3 8 ♕e3+ ♗e7 9 ♕xf3 ± Keene.
[37] 5 ... ♗g4 6 h3 ♗h5 (6 ... ♗xf3 7 ♕xf3 c6 8 ♗c4 ±/± Botvinnik-Konstantinopolsky, USSR 1952) 7 g4 ♗g6 8 ♘e5 e6 9 ♗g2 c6 10 h4 ♘bd7 11 ♘c4 ♕a6 12 ♗f1 ± Karpov-Larsen, Mar del Plata 1982.
[38] 6 ♘e5 ♗f5 7 g4 ♗e6! 8 ♘c4 ♕c7 9 ♘e3 ♘bd7 10 g5 ♘d5 = Matanović-Janicijevski, Vrsac 1979.
[39] 8 ... ♘bd7?! 9 d5! ± Spassky-Larsen, Montreal 1979.
[40] 10 0-0-0 ♗xc3 11 ♗xc3 ♕h5 ∞ Psakhis-Kurajica, Sarajevo 1981.
[41] 5 ... ♗g4? 6 f3 ♗f5 7 ♘ge2 ♘bd7 8 g4 ♗g6 9 h4 h6 10 ♘f4 ± Kavalek-Larsen, Beverwijk 1967.
[42] 7 ... ♗g4 8 f3 ♗f5 9 ♕e2 ♘ed7 10 g4 ♗g6 11 ♗d2 ± Aronin-Klaman, USSR 1956.
[43] 10 ♘xd5 ♕d8 ± Aronin.

Nimzowitsch Defence   1 e4 ♘c6

#	2	3	4	5	6	7	8	9	10	
1	♘f3[1]	d4	♘c3	d5[5]	♗g5	♕d2	de	♗e2	0-0-0[6]	±
	d6[2]	♘f6[3]	♗g4[4]	♘b8	♘bd7	e5	fe	♗e7		
2	♗c4	♘c3[7]	d3	♗b5	♘xe4[9]	♗e3[10]	de	♖xd1		=
	♘f6	e6[8]	d5	de	♗e7	♘xe4	♕xd1+	♗d7		
3	d4	e5	f4!	♘e2	♘g3	fe	♘xf5	♗b5	♗e2	±
	d5[11]	f6	♗f5	e6	fe[12]	♕d7[13]	ef	a6	g6[14]	
4	...	...	c3[15]	♘e2	♘f4	♘h5	♕xh5	♕h3	♗b5	±
	...	♗f5	e6[16]	♗g6[17]	♗e7[18]	♘xh5	g6	♕d7	a6[19]	
5	...	♘c3	e5	♘f3	♘e2	g3[22]				±
	...	e6[20]	♘ge7[21]	b6	♗a6					
6	...	...	d5	♗c4[23]	♗g5	♗f4	♕e2![25]			±
	...	de	♘b8	♘f6	h6	a6[24]				
7	...	...	...	♕d4[26]	♕a4+	♕b3	♗e3	0-0-0	♘ge2	±
	...	...	♘e5	♘g6	♗d7	♕c8[27]	♘f6	a6	e6[28]	
8	...	...	...	...	♕xe4	♗c4[29]	♕e2	♘f3	h3	∞
	...	...	...	...	a6	♘f6	♕d6	♗g4	♗xf3[30]	

[1] 2 f4 d5 3 e5 d4 4 ♘f3 ♗f5 5 ♗b5 e6 ∞ Coates-Smith, British Ch 1978.
  2 ♗b5!?

[2] **2 ... e6** 3 d4 d5 4 ♘bd2 ± – French.
  2 ... e5 – 1 ... e5.

[3] **3 ... g6** – Pirc!?
  3 ... ♗g4 4 ♗b5! ±.

[4] 4 ... a6!? Harding.

[5] 5 ♗b5! Larsen.

[6] McKay-Kostro, Nice Ol 1974.

[7] 3 d3 e6 4 ♘c3 d5 5 ed ed 6 ♗b3 ♗e7 Myers.

[8] 3 ... ♘xe4!? Myers.

[9] 6 ♗xc6+!? bc 7 ♘xe4 ♘xe4 8 de ♕xd1+ 9 ♔xd1 ♗a6 ∞/∓ Harding.

[10] 7 ♘e2 ♗d7! ∓ Keres.

[11] 2 ... e5 3 ♘f3 – Scotch. 3 d5 ♘ce7 4 c4 ♘g6 5 f3 ♗c5 6 h4 d6 7 h5 ± Reshevsky-Mikenas, Stockholm 1937.

[12] 6 ... ♘h6!? Myers.

[13] 7 ... ♗g6 8 h4! ± Larsen.

[14] 11 0-0 ♘h6 12 ♗xh6 ♖xh6 13 ♕d2 ± Kolste-Nimzowitsch, Baden Baden 1925.

[15] 4 g4 ♗e4! 5 f3 ♗g6 6 ♗e3 e6 7 c3 ♗e7 8 ♘h3 ♗h4+ 9 ♗f2 h5 ∓ Beisser-Braune, corr. 1963-64.
  4 ♘e2 e6 5 ♘g3 ♗g6 6 h4 f6 7 h5 ♗f7 8 f4 ♕d7 9 c3 0-0-0 10 ♗e3 ♔b8 11 ♘d2 ♘h6 (Shashin-Vinogradov, USSR 1967) 12 ♗b5!? Larsen. 6 ... h5 7 ♘e2 ♗f5 8 ♗f4 g6 9 c3 ♕d7 10 ♘d2 ± Romanishin-Mariotti, Leningrad 1977.

[16] 4 ... ♕d7!? 5 ♗b5 a6 (5 ... e6) 6 ♗a4 f6 7 f4 ♘h6 8 ♘f3 e6 9 h3 b5 ∞.

[17] 5 ... ♘ge7 6 ♘g3 ♗g6 7 ♗d3 ♕d7 8 ♕f3 ♗xd3 9 ♕xd3 ♘g6 10 h4 f5 11 ef!? (11 h5 ♘ge7 = Harding) 11 ... gf 12 f4!? intending f5 ∞.

[18] 6 ... ♗f5 7 h4 ♗e7 8 h5 ♗h6 9 ♘d2 ♗g5 10 ♘h3 ± Harding.

[19] 11 ♗a4 0-0-0 12 0-0 h5 13 b4 ♘h6 14 ♘d2 ♘f5 15 ♕d3 ♖dg8 16 ♘b3! ±.

[20] 3 ... e5 4 de d4 5 ♘d5 f5 6 ef6 ♘xf6 7 ♗g5 ♗e6 8 ♗xf6 gf 9 ♗c4 ♗f7 10 ♘f3 ±.

[21] 4 ... ♗b4 5 ♕g4! ±/±.

[22] Intending ♗h3.

[23] 5 f3 e6! 6 ♗c4 ♘f6 7 ♗g5 ♗b4 8 ♕d4 ♘c6 9 ♗b5 0-0 =.

[24] 7 ... g6 8 ♕d2 c6 9 0-0-0 b5 10 dc! ♕xd2+ 11 ♖xd2 bc 12 ♗xb8 ♖xb8 13 c7 ±.

[25] Larsen.

[26] 5 ♘xe4 c6 6 c4 (6 dc ♕xd1+ ∓) 6 ... cd 7 ♕xd5 =.
  5 f3 e6 6 ♗f4 (6 f4!?) ♘g6 7 ♗g3 ♗d6 (7 ... ef!?) 8 ♗b5+ ♗d7 9 de fe ∞ Harding.
  5 ♗f4 ♘g6 6 ♗g3 f5 (6 ... a6 7 h4 h5 8 ♘xe4 e5 9 de ♗xe6 10 ♘f3 ±; 7 ♗c4 f5 8 h4 b5 9 ♗b3 f4 ∞) 7 h4 (7 ♘h3!?) 7 ... e5 8 h5 ♘f4 9 ♗xf4 ef 10 ♕d2 ♗d6 ∞ Anderson-Crouch, Hallsberg 1974.

[27] 7 ... ♘f6 8 ♕xb7 ♘b8 9 ♕xb8+ ♖xb8 10 ♗c4 ±/± Harding.

[28] Harding.

[29] 7 ♕a4+ ♗d7 8 ♕b3 ♖b8!?

[30] 11 ♕xf3 ♘e5 12 ♕e2 ♘xc4 13 ♕xc4 b5 14 ♕e2 b4 15 ♘e4 ♕xd5 16 ♘xf6+ gf (Robatsch-Lutikov, Beverwijk 1967) 17 ♗f4 ∞.

Alekhine's Defence

Alekhine's Defence, in the best hypermodern tradition, attempts to lure White's centre forward in order to fix and, later, to sabotage it. In practice, the defence leads to positions of an obscure order, but there are several ways for White to maintain an edge and the choice is a matter of temperament. Of modern GMs only Alburt, Kneževic and Bagirov seem comfortable with the difficult and unique problems native to the defence.

	2	3	4	5	6	7	8	9	10	
1	♘c3[1]	ed	♗c4	♗b3	♘f3	0-0	d4	♘e4	♕d3	=
	d5	♘xd5	♘b6	♘c6	e6[2]	♗e7	0-0	♘a5	♘xb3[3]	
2	...	...	...	♘f3	0-0	d4	♘e4	♕e2	♖d1	=
	...	...	e6	♗e7	0-0	b6	♗b7	♘d7	c5[4]	
3	...	e5	ef	fg	♕xd2[5]	♗xd2	0-0-0	♗b5		=
		d4	dc	cd+	♕xd2+	♗xg7	♘c6	♗d7[6]		
4	...	...	♘ce2	d3[8]	b4	♘f3	bc	♗b2		∞
	...	♘e4	d4[7]	♘c5	♘e6	c5!	♘c6	b6[9]		
5	...	...	f4[10]	♘f3	g3[11]	♗g2	0-0	d3		=
	...	♘fd7	e6	c5	♘c6	♗e7	0-0	f6![12]		
6	e5	♘c3[14]	♘xd5	d4	♘f3	♗e2[15]	♗f4	0-0		=
	♘d5[13]	e6	ed	d6	♘c6	♗e7	0-0	f6![16]		
7	...	...	d4	♘f3	♘xe5	bc	♗f4	♘c4		=
	...	...	d6	de	♘xc3	♘d7	c5[17]	♘b6[18]		
8	...	...	bc	f4	♘f3	d4	♗e2	0-0	fe	∓
	...	♘xc3	c5[19]	d6	g6	♗g7	0-0	de	♘c6[20]	
9	...	...	dc	♘f3[21]	♕xd8+	♘xe5	♗c4	♗e3[22]	♘d3	=
	...	...	d6	de	♔xd8	♔e8	e6	♗d6	♗d7[23]	

	5	6	7	8	9	10	11	12	13	
					1 e4 ♘f6 2 e5 ♘d5 3 c4 ♘b6 4 c5 ♘d5					
10	♘c3	dc	cd[24]	♗c4[25]	♗f4	♗xe5	♕xd8	♘f3[26]		±
	♘xc3	d6	ed	♗e7	de	0-0	♗xd8			
11	...	♘xd5[27]	d4	cd	♘f3	♗e2	0-0	♗f4		=
	e6	ed	d6[28]	cd	♘c6	♗e7	0-0	♗g4[29]		
12	...	♗c4[30]	♕b3[31]	♘xd5	♗xd5	♗xb7	♕xb7	♕c8+	♕c7+	∞
	c6	d6	de	cd	e6	♗xb7	♕d5![32]	♔e7	♔f6[33]	
13	♗c4	♘c3	dc	♗f4	♕g4	♗xg5[37]	♗h3[38]	f4	fe	∞
	e6	♘xc3[34]	♘c6[35]	♗xc5[36]	g5	♖g8	♗e7	♘xe5	♗xg5[39]	
14	...	d4	cb	♘f3	♗xa6	0-0	♘c3	a3		=
	...	b6[40]	ab	♗a6	♘xa6	♗e7	♘ab4	0-0[41]		

[1] 2 ♗c4 ♘xe4 3 ♗xf7+ ♔xf7 4 ♕h5+ ♔g8 5 ♕d5+ e6 6 ♕xe4 d5 7 ♕e2 c5 ∓ Bagirov.
  2 d3 e5 3 f4 ♘c6 4 ♘f3 d5! 5 ed ♘xd5 6 fe ♗g4 7 ♗e2 ♗xf3 8 ♗xf3 ♕h4+ (Maroczy-Alekhine, New York 1924) 9 g3 ♕d4 10 ♕e2 0-0-0 11 c3 ♕xe5 12 0-0 ♕xe2 13 ♗xe2 ♗e7 =/∓ Bagirov.

[2] 6 ... ♗f5 7 d4 e6 = Lein-Alburt, New York 1980.

[3] 11 ab ♘d5 = Rogoff-Doda, Polanica Zdroj 1975.

[4] Bisguier-Keres, Tallinn 1971. 11 dc ♘xc5 = Bagirov.

[5] 6 ♗xd2 ♗xg7 7 ♕h5 (7 ♕f3!?) ♕d4 8 c3 ♕e4+ 9 ♗e3 ♘c6 = Honfi-Larsen, Copenhagen 1965.

[6] Chekhov-Barlow, Tjentiste 1975.

[7] 4 ... ♘c5 5 d4 ♘e6 6 f4 g6 7 ♘f3 c5 8 c3 ♘c6 9 ♗e3 c4 oo Lyublinsky-Mikenas, USSR Ch 1950.

[8] 5 c3! ± Sahović-Gliksman, Yugoslavia 1963.

[9] Filzer-Bronstein, Moscow 1959.

[10] 4 d4 c5 5 ♗b5 ♘c6 6 ♘f3 a6 7 ♗xc6 bc 8 e6! fe 9 0-0 ± Bogoljubow-Alekhine, Carlsbad 1923. 4 ... e6/5 ... e6/6 ... e6 – French.
  4 ♘xd5 ♘xe5 5 ♘e3 c5 6 f4 (6 b3 ♘ec6 7 ♗b2 e5! ∓ Groszpeter-Suba, Kecskemet 1979) 6 ... ♘ec6 7 ♘f3 ♕c7 8 g3 e6 = Tartakower-Landau, Rotterdam 1930.
  4 e6 fe 5 d4 ♘f6 6 ♘f3 g6 7 ♘e5 ♗g7 8 h4 c5 ∓ Suttles-Mecking, Sousse IZ 1967.

[11] 6 ♗e2 ♗e7 7 0-0-0-0 8 ♕e1 ♘c6 9 ♕g3 f5 = Berndtson-Grünfeld, Kecskemet 1928.

[12] 9 ... ♘b6? 10 ♘e2 d4 11 g4 ± Nimzowitsch-Alekhine, Semmering 1926.
  9 ... f6! = Bagirov.

[13] 2 ... ♘g8!? 3 d4 d6 4 ♘f3 g6 5 ♘c3 ♗g7 6 ♗c4 c6 7 h3 ± Boleslavsky-Petrosian, USSR 1966. 4 ... ♗g4 5 h3 ♗f5 6 ♗d3 ♕d7 7 ed ed 8 ♗xf5 ♕xf5 9 0-0 ± Smejkal-Vesely, CSSR 1968.

[14] 3 ♗c4 ♘b6 4 ♗b3 c5 5 ♕e2 ♘c6 6 ♘f3 d5 7 ed e6! 8 ♘c3 ♗xd6 9 ♘e4 ♗e7 10 d3 ♘d5 11 0-0 0-0 =/∓ Yates-Rubinstein, Dresden 1926.

[15] 7 ♗f4 de 8 de ♗c5 9 ♕d2 ♘e7 10 0-0-0 c6 11 ♗e3 ♕b6 = Byrne-Jansson, Skopje Ol 1972.

[16] Sämisch-Alekhine, Budapest 1921.

[17] 8 ... ♗e7?! 9 ♗d3 ♘xe5 10 ♗xe5 ± Andersson-Kraidman, Siegen Ol 1970.

[18] Bagirov.

[19] 4 ... d6 5 f4 de 6 fe ♕d5 7 ♘f3 ♘c6 8 d4 ♗g4 9 ♗e2 e6 10 0-0 ♗e7 11 ♘g5 ± Bilek-Larsen, Sousse IZ 1967.

[20] 11 ♗f4 ♗g4 ∓ Hennings-Gipslis, Havana 1971.

[21] 5 ♗c4 ♘c6 6 ♘f3 de 7 ♗xd8+ ♘xd8 8 ♘xe5 f6 9 ♘d3 e5 10 0-0 ♗e6 11 ♗b3 ♗d6 ∓ Nezhmetdinov-Spassky, Tbilisi 1959.

[22] 9 f4 ♘d7 10 ♘xd7 ♗xd7 11 ♗e3 ♗d6 12 0-0 ♔e7 13 ♖ae1 ♖he8 14 ♗d3 f5 15 c4 = Sarapu-Hort, Sousse IZ 1967.

[23] 11 0-0-0 ♗c6 = Radulov-Jansa, Orebro 1966.

[24] 7 ♗c4 d5 8 ♕xd5 ♕xd5 9 ♗xd5 e6 10 ♗e4 ♗xc5 = Alekhine-Fine, Pasadena 1932.
  7 ♗g5? de 8 ♕b3 ♕d7 9 ♖d1 ♕f5 10 ♗c4 ♘d7! 11 ♘f3 e6 12 ♖xd7 (12 0-0 ♗xc5 13 ♖fe1 e4 14 ♕c2 ♗xf2+! ∓ Shakarov-Sideifzade, USSR 1970) 12 ... ♕e4+! 13 ♔d2 (13 ♔d1 ♗xd7 14 ♖e1 ♖e8 15. ♘xe5 ♕a4 ∓) 13 ... ♗xd7 14 ♖e1 ♗c6 15 ♘xe5 ♗xc5 ∓.

[25] 8 ♘f3 ♗e7 9 ♗c4 de 10 ♕xd8+ ♗xd8 11 ♘xe5 0-0 = Bagirov.

[26] Krogius-A.Zaitsev, Rostov 1971.

[27] 6 d4 d6 7 cd cd 8 ♘f3 ♘c6 – Sicilian, Alapin-Sveshnikov Variation.

[28] 7 ... b6 8 ♗e3 bc 9 dc c6 10 ♗d3 ♘a6 11 ♕c1 ♕a5+ 12 ♗d2 oo/± Hennings-Smejkal, Kapfenberg 1970.

[29] Ničevski-Vasyukov, Skopje 1969.

[30] 6 ♘xd5 cd 7 d4 d6 8 cd ed 9 ♘f3 – row 11.

[31] 7 ♘xd5?! cd 8 ♗xd5 e6! 9 ♗f3 de 10 b4 e4! ∓ Kopilov.

[32] 11 ... ♘d7 12 b4! ♖b8 13 ♕e4 f5 14 ♕c4 ±.

[33] 14 d4 ♘c6 oo Sveshnikov-Palatnik, Chelyabinsk 1974.

[34] 6 ... ♗xc5 7 d4 ♗b4 8 ♗xd5 ed 9 ♕g4 ♔f8 10 ♘f3 d6 11 ♕g3 ♘c6 12 0-0 oo Bagirov.
  6 ... d6 7 ♘xd5 ed 8 ♗xd5 c6 9 ♗xf7+ ♔xf7 10 cd ♕e8 11 ♕f3+ ♔g8 12 ♕e3 ♗e6 13 ♘e2 ♘d7 14 0-0 ♗xe5! 15 ♕xe5 ♗c4 16 ♕xe8 ♖xe8 =/oo Vasyukov-Spassky, Tbilisi 1959.

[35] 7 ... ♗xc5 8 ♕g4 ±.

[36] 8 ... b6 9 cb ab 10 ♘f3 ♗e7 11 0-0 0-0 12 ♕e2 ± Markland-Ghizdavu, Reggio Emilia 1973.

[37] 10 ♕xg5 ♕xg5 11 ♗xg5 ♘xe5! 12 ♗f6 ♘xc4 13 ♗xh8 ♘xb2 +/∓ Ciocaltea-Orev, Sofia 1962.

[38] 11 f4 ♘xe5 12 ♕h4 ♖xg5 13 fg ♘xc4 13 ♕xc4 ♕xg5 14 ♘e2 d6! ∓ Gulko-Spizyn, Moscow 1963.
  11 ♗xd8 ♖xg4 13 ♗e2 ♖xg2 14 ♗xc7 b6 oo Lees-Ribli, England 1971.

[39] 14 ♕h5 ♗g7 15 0-0 ♕e7 16 ♖f3 b6 17 ♖g3 h6 oo Angelov-Popov, Sofia 1972.

[40] 6 ... d6 7 cd cd – Sicilian, Alapin-Sveshnikov Variation.

[41] Machulsky-Gurgenidze, Kirovabad 1973.

	Alekhine II: 4 c4		1 e4 ♘f6 2 e5 ♘d5 3 d4 d6 4 c4¹ ♘b6						
	5	6	7	8	9	10	11	12	13	
1	ed	♘f3	♗e2	0-0	♗e3²	♘c3³	b3	c5	b4	∞
	cd	g6	♗g7	0-0	♘c6	♗g4	d5	♘c8	a6⁴	
2	...	♘c3	♗e3⁵	♗d3	♘ge2	0-0	f3	b3	♕xd3	=
	...	g6	♗g7	0-0	♘c6	♗g4	♗f5	♗xd3	e6!⁶	
3	...	♘c3	♗d3	♘ge2	0-0	♗e3	b3	♘g3	♕xd3⁷	=
	ed	g6	♗g7	0-0	♘c6	♘e7	♗f5	♗xd3		
4	...	...	h3⁸	♘f3	♗e2	0-0	♗f4			=
	...	♗e7	0-0	♗f6⁹	♖e8	♘c6	♗f5¹⁰			
5	f4	♘c3	fe	♗e3¹¹	♘f3	dc	e6	♕c2	♗e2¹³	∞
	g6	de	♗g7	0-0	c5¹²	♘d7	fe	♕a5		
6	...	♘c3	♗e3	ed	♘f3	♗e2	♖c1¹⁵	b3	0-0¹⁶	±
	♗f5¹⁴	e6	♘a6	cd	♗e7	0-0	♘d7	♘c7		
7	...	...	...	♘f3	♗d3	♕xd3	b3	bc	0-0¹⁸	±
	...	...	♗e7	0-0	♗xd3¹⁷	d5	dc	♘c6		
8	...	fe	d5	♘c3¹⁹	cd	g3	♗b5+!²⁰	♕e2	e6!	±
	de	c5	e6	ed	♕h4+	♕d4	♗d7	♘bxd5	fe²¹	
9	...	...	...	...	...	♘f3	♕d4²²	gf	♗xc4	∞
	...	...	...	...	c4	♗g4	♗xf3	♗b4	0-0²³	
10	...	...	♘c3	♘f3	♗e2	0-0	♗e3	♘xe5	♘f3	=
	...	♗f5	e6	♗e7	0-0	f6²⁴	fe	♘8d7	h6²⁵	
11	...	...	...	...	♗e3	♗e2²⁶	0-0	♘xd4	♗xd4	∞
	...	...	...	...	♗b4	c5	♘c6	cd²⁷	♗c2²⁸	
12	...	...	...	...	♗d3	0-0	c5	bc²⁹		±
	...	...	...	...	♗g4	♘c6	♗xc3			
13	...	...	♘f3	e6	c5	♗b5	♘bd2³¹	♕a4	♘e5	∓
	...	♘c6	♗g4	fe	♘d5³⁰	♕d7	g6	♗g7	♗xe5³²	
14	...	...	♗e3	♘c3	♘f3	d5!³⁴	cd	♘d4	♘xd5	±
	...	...	♗f5	e6	♕d7³³	ed	♘b4	♘6xd5	♕xd5³⁵	
15	...	...	...	...	...	♗e2	0-0	ef³⁶	♕d2	±
	...	...	...	...	♗e7	0-0	f6	♗xf6	♕e7³⁷	

[1] 4 ♗g5 de 5 de ♘c6 6 ♗b5 ♗f5 7 ♘f3 ♘b4! =
L.Steiner-Alekhine, Budapest 1921.

4 ed ♕xd6! 5 ♘f3 ♗g4 6 ♗e2 ♘c6 7 0-0
0-0-0 8 c3 ♘f4 9 ♗xf4 ♕xf4 10 b4 (Yates-
Kmoch, Budapest 1926) 10 ... e6 = Bagirov.

4 f4 ♗f5 5 ♘f3 e6 6 ♗d3 ♗xd3 7 ♕xd3 c5
8 dc ♕a5+ 9 ♗d2 ♕xc5 = Bohosian-Orev,
Pernik 1975.

4 ♗c4 ♘b6 5 ♗b3 ♗f5 6 ♕f3 ♕c8 7 ♘h3
♘c6! 8 c3 e6! 9 ♘g5 ♗e7 = Arnason-Alburt,
Lone Pine 1980.

[2] 9 h3 ♘c6 10 ♘c3 ♗f5 11 ♗e3 d5 12 c5 ♘c4
13 ♗xc4 dc 14 ♕a4 e5! 15 ♖fd1 ♗xd4 16 ♘xd4
ed 17 ♗xd4 ♗xd4 18 ♕xc4 ♗xf2+ = Baikov-
Dzhailov, USSR 1980.

[3] 10 ♘bd2 d5 11 c5 ♘d7 12 ♕b3 e5 13 de
♘dxe5 14 ♘xe5 ♘xe5 15 ♖fd1 ♘g4 16 ♗xg4
♗xg4 ∞ Ničevski-Jansa, Athens 1969.

[4] 14 ♖b1 e6 15 a4 ♘8e7 16 b5 ab 17 ab ♗xf3
18 ♗xf3 ♗a5 19 ♗e2 ♘f5 20 ♕d2 h6 21 ♖fd1
♖e8 22 b6 ∞ ½-½ Klovan-Bagirov, Alma Ata
1969.

[5] 7 h4 h5 8 ♗e3 ♗g7 9 ♗d3 ♘c6 10 ♘ge2 0-0
11 ♕b3 e5 12 d5 ♘d4 = Kadrev-Orev, Sofia
1963.

[6] Minić-Gipslis, Erevan 1971.

[7] Bagirov.

[8] 7 ♘f3 0-0 8 ♗e2 ♗g4 9 b3 ♘c6 10 ♗e3 ♗f6
11 0-0 d5! =.

[9] 8 ... ♘c6 9 ♗e2 ♗f5 10 0-0 h6 11 b3 ♗f6
12 ♗e3 ± Marić-Buljovčić, Yugoslavia 1969.

[10] Matanović-Larsen, Palma de Mallorca 1969.

[11] 8 ♘f3 ♗g4 9 c5 ♘d5 10 ♗c4 e6 11 0-0 ♘xc3
12 bc 0-0 ± Parma-Schiffer, Berlin 1971.

[12] 9 ... c6 10 ♗e2 f6 11 ef ef 12 0-0 ♖e8 13 ♕d2
♗e6 14 b3 ♗f7 15 ♖ad1 ♘8d7 = Parniani-
Sjoby, Varna Ol 1962.

[13] Bagirov.

[14] Trifunović Variation.

[15] 11 0-0 ♖c8 12 b3 ♘d5! ∓ Wade-Trifunović,
Lemington 1951.

[16] Gasić-Mikhalchishin, Sarajevo 1970.

[17] 9 ... d5 10 ♗xf5 ef 11 c5 ♘c4 12 ♗f2 ♘xb2
13 ♕b1 ♘c4 14 ♕xb7 ± Stein-Mikenas, Erevan
1962.

[18] Bagirov.

[19] 8 d6 ♕h4+ 9 g3 ♕e4+ 10 ♕e2 ♕xh1 11 ♘f3
♘c6! 12 ♘bd2 ♘d7! 13 ♔f2 ♘dxe5! 14 ♘xe5
♕xh2+ 15 ♗g2 ♘d4 16 ♕d1 ♗xd6 17 ♘f1
♕xg2+ 18 ♔xg2 ♗xe5 ∓ Nekrasov/Tokar v
Argunov/Yudin, Orenburg 1931.

[20] 11 ♕xd4 cd 12 ♘b5 ♘xd5 13 ♗c4 ♘b6
14 ♗b3 ♘a6 15 ♘f3 ♗d7 16 ♗fxd4 ♗c5
17 ♘d6+ ♗xd6 18 ed ♘c5 ±/± Bagirov.

[21] 14 ♕xe6+ ♗e7 15 ♘f3 ± Ljubojević-Moses,
Dresden 1969.

[22] 11 ♗e2 ♗b4 12 0-0 0-0 13 ♘g5 ♗xe2

14 ♕xe2 h6 15 e6! ±/ ± Silakov-Bagirov, Baku
1969.

[23] 14 ♖g1 g6 15 ♗g5 ♕c7 16 ♗b3 ♗c5 17 ♕f4
♗xg1 18 d6 ♕c5 19 ♘e4 ♕d4 20 ♖d1 ♕xb2
21 e6 ♘8d7 22 e7 ♕xh2 23 ef♕+ ♖xf8 ∞
Grünfeld-Ljubojević, Riga IZ 1979.

[24] 10 ... ♘c6 11 ♗e3 f6!? – row 15.

[25] Suetin-Mikenas, Vilnius 1961.

[26] 10 ♕b3 ♕e7 11 a3 (11 d5!? Bagirov) 11 ... cd
12 ♘xd4 ♗c5! ∓ Suetin-Stein, Kislovodsk 1972.

[27] 11 ... 0-0 12 dc (Krasnov-Kimelfeld, Moscow
1972) 12 ... ♗xc3! Bagirov.

[28] 14 ♕d2 ♖c8 ∞ Pritchard-Williams, England
1972.

[29] Velimirović-Martz, Vrnjačka Banja 1973.

[30] 9 ... ♘d7 10 ♗c4 (10 ♗e2 e5 11 0-0 ed
12 ♘g5 ♗xe2 13 ♕xe2 ♘de5 14 ♘e6 ♕d7
15 ♕h5+ g6 16 ♕xh7 ♕xe6 17 ♕xh8 ♘d7
18 ♗h6 0-0-0 19 ♗xf8 ♕e3+ 20 ♔h1 ♘xf8 ∞
Bagirov) 10 ... ♗xf3 11 gf e5 12 ♕b3 ± Levenfish.

[31] 11 0-0!?

[32] 14 de ♘e3! 15 ♕e4 0-0 (15 ... ♕d4 16 ♗xc6+
bc 17 ♕xd4 ♗c2+ = Ilyin Zhenevsky-Levenfish,
Leningrad 1936) 16 ♕xe3 ♘b4! ∓∓.

[33] Tartakower Variation.

9 ... ♘b4 10 ♖c1 c5 11 ♗e2 (11 d5 ed 12 cd
♘4xd5 13 ♗g5 ♗e7 14 ♗b5+ ♔f8! ∓ Euwe)
11 ... ♗e7 12 0-0 0-0 13 a3 cd 14 ♘xd4 ♘c6
15 ♘xf5 ef 16 ♖xf5 g6 17 ♖f1 ♗g5 18 ♗c5 ♖e8
19 ♕xd8 ♖axd8 20 ♖cd1 ♖xe5 21 ♘e4 ♖xd1
(Keres-Sajtar, Prague 1943) 22 ♖xd1 ♗e7
23 ♗xe7 ♖xe7 24 c5 ± Bagirov.

[34] 10 ♗e2 0-0-0 11 0-0 ♗g4 12 c5 ♘d5 13 ♘xd5
♖xd5 14 ♗g5 ♗xe2 15 ♕xe2 ♖xd4 16 ♗xd4
♕xd4+ 17 ♔h1 ♗d2 ∞ Honfi-Ghizdavu,
Bucharest 1973. 11 ... f6 12 d5 ♘xe5 13 ♘xe5
fe 14 a4 a5 15 ♘b5 ♗b4 16 d6 c5 17 ♗d2!?
♕xd6!? 18 ♘xd6+ ♖xd6 19 ♗xb4 ♖xd1
20 ♖fxd1 cb 21 g4 ♗c2 ∞∞ Shakhmatny Listok
1929. 17 ♕c1 intending ♗d2!? Bagirov.

[35] 13 ... ♘xd5? 14 ♘xf5 ♗b4+ 15 ♔e2! 0-0-0
16 ♘d6+ cd 17 ♕xd5 ±.

13 ... ♕xd5 14 ♘xf5 ♕xe5 15 ♖c1 ♕xf5
16 ♖xc7 ♕e6 17 ♗b5+ ± Tagman-Benko,
Budapest 1948.

[36] 12 d5 ♘xe5 13 ♘xe5 fe 14 g4 ♗g6 15 de c6
16 ♕b3 ♗g5 17 ♗c5 ♕d2 = Sziliki-Popov,
Varna 1958. 12 ... ed! 13 cd ♘xe5 ∓ Bagirov.

[37] 13 ... ♖f7?!

13 ... ♕e7 14 ♖ad1 ♖ad8 15 ♕c1 ♖d7?!
16 ♔h1 ♖fd8 17 d5! (17 c5? ♘d5 18 ♘xd5
♖xd5 19 ♗c4 ♖5d7 20 ♘g5 ♘xd4! 21 ♖xf5
♕xf5 22 ♘xd7 ♖xd7 23 ♗xe6+ ♕xe6! ∓
Shakarov) 17 ... ed 18 cd ♗xc3 19 dc ♖xd1
20 ♗xd1 ♗xb2 21 ♕xb2 ♕xe3 22 cb ± Euwe.
15 ... h6 16 ♔h1 ♔h8 17 h3 ♗h7 = Medina-
Smyslov, Hastings 1970.

Alekhine II: 4 c4 *continued*   1 e4 Nf6 2 e5 Nd5 3 d4 d6
4 c4 Nb6 5 f4 de 6 fe Nc6 7 Be3 Bf5 8 Nc3 e6 9 Nf3 Be7 10 d5

	10	11	12	13	14	15	16	17	18	
16	...	cd[38]	Nd4	e6[39]	de	Qg4	g3	0-0-0	gh	±
	ed	Nb4	Bd7	fe	Bc6	Bh4+	Bxh1[40]	Qf6	0-0[41]	
17	...	Nd4	a3[42]	Nxe6	ab	Na4[44]	Nxb6	Rxa8	d6	∞
	Nb4	Bg6	c5![43]	fe	cb	0-0	ab	Qxa8	Bd8[45]	
18	...	Rc1	a3	ab	Bxd4	Nxd4	Nxf5	Be2	c5	±
	...	ed[46]	c5!?[47]	d4	cd	Qb8	Qxe5+	Qxf5	Nd7[48]	

[38] 11 Bxb6!? ab 12 cd Nb4 13 Nd4 Bg6 (Majerić-Rogulj, Zagreb 1981) 14 Bb5+ Kf8 15 0-0 Bc5 oo Alburt.

[39] 13 Qf3!? (Littlewood-Cafferty, British Ch 1979) 13 ... 0-0! Alburt.

[40] 16 ... Bf6 17 0-0-0! Gligorić.

[41] **19 Bg5** Qxf1! 20 Rxf1 (20 e7 Nxa2+! 21 Nxa2 Qc4+ 22 Nc3 Rf1 ∓ Kupreichik-Alburt, Odessa 1974) 20 ... Rxf1+ 21 Kd2 Nc4+ 22 Ke2 Raf8 23 Nd1 Nc2! ∓.
19 Bb5! Qe5!? (19 ... Bf3 20 Nxf3 Qxf3 21 Qxf3 Rxf3 22 Bxb6 intending e7 ± Bagirov; 19 ... Bc6 20 Bg5! Qe5 21 e7 Rfe8 22 Nf5! ± Marjanović-Rogulj, Yugoslavia 1975) 20 Bh6 (20 Bg5 c5 21 e7 cd 22 efQ+= Rxf8 += Veröci-Alexandria, Wijk aan Zee 1977) 20 ... c5 21 Rg1 cd 22 Qxg7+ Qxg7 23 Bxg7 Rf2 24 Bxd4+ Rg2 25 Rxh1 ± Kveinis-Panchenko, USSR 1979.

[42] 12 Rc1 ed 13 cd 0-0 =+.

[43] 12 ... Na6 13 de fe 14 Qg4 ±/± Bagirov.

[44] 15 Nb5 0-0 16 Rxa7 Rxa7 17 Nxa7 ed 18 cd Nxd5 19 Bc4 Bf7 20 Bf2 Qc7 21 Qd4 Nf4 Bagirov.

[45] 19 Be2 b3 20 Rf1! Qa5+ 21 Qd2 Qxe5 22 Rxf8+ Kxf8 23 Bf4 Qa5 24 d7 Be4 25 Bd6+ Kf7 26 Bb4 Qe5 27 Qe3 Qf5 28 Qxb3 Bxg2 oo.

[46] 11 ... 0-0 12 a3 Na6 13 Bd3 Bc5 14 Bxc5 Nxc5 15 Bxf5 ef 16 b4 Ne4 17 Qd4 ± Parma-Mikhalchishin, Sarajevo 1971.

[47] A.Petrosian. 12 ... Nc4!? 13 Bxc4 dc 14 14 ab Qxd1+ 15 Rxd1 Bxb4 16 0-0 Bd3 (Kostro-Hlousek, Luhacovice 1971) 17 Rf2! ± Bagirov.

[48] **19 Bg4** Qe5+ 20 Qe2 Qxe2+ 21 Kxe2 Ne5 oo/± Bagirov.
19 Nd5 Bd8 20 Rc3 0-0 21 Ne3 ± Velimirović-Marović, Yugoslavia 1977.

Alekhine III: 4 ♘f3   1 e4 ♘f6 2 e5 ♘d5 3 d4 d6 4 ♘f3

	4	5	6	7	8	9	10	11	12	
1	...	c4	e6	♗g5[1]	♗d3	♗xh7	♘xh7	♘a3	♘xc4	∓
	♘c6	♘b6	fe	e5	♘xd4	♖xh7	♗f5	♘xc4!	♘c2+[2]	
2	...	♗d3	0-0	c4	♕xd3	ed	♖fe1+	a4	b3	±/±
	♗f5	♕d7	♘c6[3]	♗xd3	♘b6	ed	♘e7	♕c6	h6[4]	
3	...	♘xe5	♘xf7!	♕h5+	c4!	d5+	♕h3[7]	♕a3	♗e3	∞
	de[5]	♘d7[6]	♔xf7	♔e6	♘5f6	♔d6	♘c5	e5	b6[8]	
4	...	...	c4[9]	♗e2	♘c3	♗f4[10]	0-0	♕d2	♖ad1	±
	...	g6	♘f6	♗g7	0-0	c6	♘a6	♗f5	♕c8[11]	
5	...	a4[12]	♗b5+	♗e2	h3	0-0	♗f4	♗g3[13]		±
	♘b6	a5	c6	g6	♗g7	0-0	♘d5			
6	...	♘g5	de	♗c4	e6	♘xe6	♘d2	0-0		∞
	g6	de[14]	♗g7	c6	♗xe6	fe	♘d7	♕b6[15]		
7	...	...	♗c4	♕e2	0-0	de	♘f3	♘bd2	h3	=
	...	c6	♗g7	0-0	de[16]	h6	♗g4	♕c7	♗xf3[17]	
8	...	♗c4	♗b3	♘g5[20]	0-0	c3	f4	♘f3	fe	±
	...	♘b6[18]	♗g7[19]	d5	♘c6	0-0[21]	f6	fe	♗f5[22]	

[1] 7 h4!? e5 8 d5 ♘d4 9 ♘xd4 ed 10 ♕xd4 ♕d7 10 ♗e2 e5 11 de ♕xe6   12 ♖h3! ∞/± Nei-Honfi, Budapest 1969.

[2] 13 ♔f1 ♘xa1 ∓ Volfl-Podgorny, corr. 1979.

[3] 6 ... ♘b4 7 ♗xf5 ♘xf5 8 c3 ♘c2 9 ♘h4 ♕e4 10 ♘d2 ♕d3 11 ♖b1 de 12 ♘df3 ± Kavalek-Ljubojević, Hilversum 1973.

[4] 13 ♘c3 0-0-0 14 a5 ±/± Becker-Grünfeld, Vienna 1927.

[5] Larsen Variation.

[6] 5 ... e6 6 ♕f3 ♕f6 7 ♕g3 h6 8 ♘c3 ♘b4 9 ♗b5+ c6 10 ♗a4 ♗d7 (Tal-Larsen, Bled 1965) 11 ♘e4 ± Tal.

[7] 10 ♕f7 ♘b8! 11 c5+ (11 ♗f4+ e5 12 c5+ ♔xc5 13 b4+ ♔d6 14 ♗e3 b6 15 ♗c5+ bc 16 bc+ ♔xc5 17 d6 ♕e8 18 ♕xc7+ ♔c6 19 ♕d8 ♕e4+ 20 ♗e2 ♘c6 ∓ Bagirov) 11 ... ♔xc5 12 ♗e3+ ♔d6 13 ♘a3 a6 14 ♗d7 15 d6 ±±.

10 c5+!? ♘xc5 11 ♗f4+ ♗d7 12 ♗b5+ c6 13 dc+ bc 14 ♕xc5 ♕b6! 15 ♕xb6 ab 16 ♗c4 ±/±.

[8] 13 ♘c3 ♗e7 14 b4 ♘cd7 ∞ Bagirov.

[9] 6 ♗c4 ♗e6 7 ♘c3 (7 0-0 ♗g7 8 ♖e1 0-0 9 ♘d2 ♗d7 10 ♘ef3! ♘7f6 11 ♗f1 c6 12 c4 ♘c7 13 b3 ± Unzicker-Williams, Buenos Aires Ol 1978; 8 ♕e2 0-0 9 ♗b3 a5!?) 7 ... ♗g7 8 ♘e4 ♗xe5 9 de ♘c6 10 ♘c5 ♘e3! = Bagirov.

[10] 9 ♗e3 ♘bd7 =/± Ljubojević-Williams, Nice Ol 1974.

[11] 13 ♗h6 ± Dolmatov-Kengis, USSR 1980.

[12] 5 ♗d3!? ♘c6 6 ed ♕xd6 7 0-0 ♗g4 8 c3 ±.
5 ... g6! 6 ♗f4 ♘c6 7 0-0-0-0 = Penrose-Cafferty, England 1964.

[13] Ciocaltea-Hecht, Dortmund 1973.

[14] 5 ... f6 6 c4 ♘b6 7 e6 fg 8 d5 ♗g7 9 a4 a5 10 h4 gh 11 ♖xh4 ± O'Kelly-Golombek, Amsterdam 1951.

[15] Penrose-Cafferty, England 1968.   12 ♕e2!

[16] 8 ... e6!? 9 ♘c3 ♗xc3 10 bc d5 11 ♗d3 c5 12 ♕g4 ±/± Vasyukov-Larsen, Moscow 1959.

[17] 13 ♘xf3 e6 = Bagirov.

[18] 5 ... c6 6 h3 (6 ed ♕xd6 7 0-0 ♗g7 8 ♘bd2 ±) 6 ... ♗g7 7 ♕e2 0-0 8 0-0 de 9 de ♕c7 10 ♖e1 a5 11 a4 ♘a6 12 ♘bd2 ± Matulović-Kovačević, Yugoslavia 1976.

[19] 6 ... a5 7 a4 ♗g7 8 ♘g5 d5 (8 ... e6 9 f4 ± Kasparov-Palatnik, USSR 1978) 9 0-0 0-0 10 ♖e1 ♘c6 11 c3 f6 12 ef ef 13 ♘e6 ±.   7 e6!? ♗xe6 (7 ... f6? 8 ♘g5! ±) 8 ♗xe6 fe 9 ♘g5 ♘c6 10 ♘xe6 ♕d7 11 ♘g7+ ♔d8 12 ♘xf8 ♖xf8 13 ♘c3 ♘c6 14 ♗h6 ♖f5 15 0-0-0 ± Kapengut-Palatnik, USSR 1977.

[20] 7 ♕e2 ♘c6 (7 ... 0-0!? 8 e6 d5 9 ef+ ♖xf7) 8 0-0 0-0 (8 ... de 9 ♘d4 10 ♘xd4 ♕xd4 11 e6 ♗xe6 12 ♗xe6 fe 13 ♘d2 ± Geller-Alburt, USSR Ch 1975) 9 h3 de 10 de ♘d4 11 ♘xd4 ♕xd4 12 ♖e1 ± Boleslavsky.

[21] 9 ... h6 10 ♘f3 ♗g4 11 h3 ±.
9 ... f6 10 ef ef 11 ♖e1+ ♘e7 12 ♘e6 ±.
9 ... ♗f5 10 g4! ♗xb1 11 ♕f3! 0-0 12 ♖xb1 ♕d7 13 ♗c2 ♘d8 14 ♕h3 h6 15 f4! ± Olafsson-Larsen, Reykjavik 1978.

[22] 13 ♘h4 ± Panchenko-Uusi, USSR 1980.
13 ♘bd2 ♕d7 14 ♖f2 ♘a5 15 ♗c2 ♗xc2 16 ♕xc2 (Karpov-Torre, Leningrad 1973) 16 ... ♗h6 ±.

Alekhine III: 4 ♘f3 *continued*   1 e4 ♘f6 2 e5 ♘d5 3 d4 d6 4 ♘f3 ♗g4

	5	6	7	8	9	10	11	12	13	
1	h3[1]	♕xf3	de	♗c4[3]	♕e4	♗e3	0-0	♕xh4	♗b5	∓
	♗xf3	de	e6[2]	♘c6[4]	♘de7	♘f5	♕h4!	♘xh4	♘f5[5]	
2	c4[6]	♗e2	c5	cb[8]	♗xf3	♕xf3	0-0	♕xb7	♗e3	∓
	♘b6	de	e4[7]	ef	♗xf3	♘c6![9]	♘xd4	ab	♖b8[10]	
3	♗e2	♘g5[11]	♕xe2	de	0-0	♖d1[13]	♘f3	♘bd2	♘c4[15]	±
	c6	♗xe2[12]	de	e6	♘d7	♕c7	♘e7[14]	♘g6		
4	...	c4	ed[16]	d5[17]	♗xf3	♗e2	0-0	♘d2	♕c2	=
	♘c6	♘b6	ed	♗xf3	♘e5	♗e7[18]	0-0	♖e8	♗f8[19]	
5	...	0-0	h3	♗xf3	de	♖xd1	b3[20]	♗b2[21]		±
	...	♘b6	♗xf3	de	♕xd1	e6	♗e7			
6	...	0-0	c4	ed	d5!	cd	gf	♗b5+	♕d4	±
	e6	♘c6	♘b6[22]	cd	ed	♗xf3	♘e5[23]	♘ed7	♕f6[24]	

1 e4 ♘f6 2 e5 ♘d5 3 d4 d6 4 ♘f3 ♗g4 5 ♗e2 e6 6 0-0 ♗e7 7 c4 ♘b6

	8	9	10	11	12	13	14	15	16	
7	ed	b3	♘c3	♗e3[26]	c5	b4	♖b1	a4[28]		∓
	cd	♘c6	0-0[25]	d5!	♘c8	a6[27]	♗f6	♘8e7[29]		
8	...	...	♘bd2	♗b2	c5	a3	b4	♖e1[31]	♘f1	∓
	...	...	0-0	d5[30]	♘d7	a6	♕c7	b6!	♗f6[32]	
9	...	♘c3	♗e3	d5!	♗xf3	de	♗g4	♗xe6+	♗xb6[34]	±
	...	0-0	♘c6	♗xf3[33]	♘e5	fe	♘exc4	♔h8	♗xb6[35]	
10	...	...	...	c5	♗xf3	♗f4[36]	b3	♖c1	♘a4	=
	...	...	d5	♗xf3	♘c4	♘c6	♘4a5	b6	♗f6[37]	
11	h3	ed	♘bd2	b3	♗b2	c5	a3	b4	♖e1	=
	♗h5	cd	♘c6	0-0	d5[38]	♘d7	f6	a6	♗f7[39]	
12	...	♘c3	♗e3[40]	c5[42]	♗xf3	♗f4[43]	b3	♖c1	dc	∞
	...	0-0	d5[41]	♗xf3	♘c4	b6[44]	♘a5	bc	♘ac6[45]	
13	...	...	...	...	gf	b4[46]	f4	fe	♗d3	±/±
	...	...	...	...	♘c8	f6	fe	♕e8	♗d8[47]	
14	♘c3	♗e3	c5	gf	f4	♗d3!				∞
	0-0	d5[48]	♗xf3	♘c8	♘c6	g6[49]				

---

[1] Panov Variation.

[2] 7 ... ♘c6?! 8 ♗b5.

[3] 8 a3 ♘d7 9 ♕g3 h5 10 ♘d2 h4 11 ♕b3 ♖h5 12 ♘f3 ♘xe5 ∓ Panov-Mikenas, Moscow 1943.
  8 ♕e4 ♘d7 9 ♗c4 ♘c5 10 ♕e2 ♘b6 11 ♗b3 a5 12 a3 ♘xb3 13 cb ♗e7 ∓ Kupreichik-Bagirov, Vitebsk 1970.

[4] 8 ... ♘d7 9 ♕e2 ♘b6 10 ♗b3 ♘c5 Bagirov.

[5] 14 ♗xc6+ bc 15 ♘d2 ♘xe3 16 fe ♖d8 ∓ Zhuravlev-Alburt, Odessa 1974.

[6] Alekhine's Variation for White.

[7] 7 ... ♘6d7 7 ♘xe5 ♗xe2 8 ♕xe2 ♘xe5 9 de ♘c6 10 ♗f4 (11 e6!? Bagirov) 11 ... ♕d5 12 0-0 e6 13 ♘c3 ♘d4 14 ♗g4 ♕c6 15 ♖ac1 ♗e7 16 b4 ± Lukhin-Rotman, Irkutsk 1956.

[8] 8 ♘g5 ♗xe2 9 ♕xe2 ♘d5 10 0-0 ♘c6

11 ♖d1 (Alekhine) 11 ... e6 intending ... ♗e7 = Bagirov.

[9] 10 ... ab 10 ♕xb7 ♘d7 11 ♗f4 e5 12 ♗xe5 ♘xe5 14 de ♗b4+ 15 ♘c3 ♗xc3+ 16 bc ± Alekhine-Euwe, Amsterdam 1935.

[10] 14 ♕e4 ♘b5! ∓ Bagirov.

[11] 6 0-0 ♗xf3 7 ♗xf3 de 8 de e6 9 ♕e2 ♘d7 (9 ... ♕c7 10 ♖e1 ♘d7 11 g3! a5 12 a4 ♗b4 13 c3 ♗e7 14 ♘d2 0-0 15 ♘b3 ♖fd8 16 h4 ± Tukmakov-Bagirov, Rostov on Don 1971) 10 ♖e1 ♕c7 11 ♘d2 ♗c5 12 c4 ♘e7 13 ♘c3 a5 = Matanović-Knežević, Yugslavia 1972.

[12] 6 ... ♗f5 7 ♗g4!? (7 e6 fe 8 g4 ♗g6 9 ♘d3 ♗xd3 10 ♕xd3 g6 11 0-0 ♕d7 12 ♖e1 ♘a6 13 ♕f3 ♘ac7 14 ♕f7+ ♔d8 15 ♖xe6+ ♗xe6 16 ♕xe6 ♕xe6 17 ♖xe6 ∓ Doronov-Pavlov, corr. 1978/79) 7 ... ♗xg4 8 ♕xg4 ♕xg4 9 de e6 10 0-0 ♘d7 11 c4 ♗b4 (11 ... ♘e7) 12 ♕e2 a5 13 ♘c3 ♕c7 14 a3 ♘a6 15 ♗f4 = Bagirov.

[13] 10 c4 ♗e7 11 ♘c3 ♘f5 12 ♘f3 ♕c7 13 ♖e1 ♗b4 14 ♗d2 0-0 = Bagirov.

[14] 11 ... b5 12 c4 ±.

[15] Tseshkovsky-Hort, Manila IZ 1976.

[16] 7 e6 fe 8 ♘c3 g6 9 ♗g5 ♗xe2 10 ♘xe2 ♕d7 11 d5 ed 12 cd ♘b4 13 0-0 ♘4xd5 ∓ Simagin-Fridstein, Moscow 1947.

[17] 8 0-0 ♗e7 9 ♘c3 0-0 10 b3 ♗f6 11 ♗e3 d5 12 c5 ♘c8 13 h3 ♗e6 14 b4 a6! 15 ♖b1 ♘e7 16 g4 h6 ∞ Estrin-Gik, Dubna 1968.

[18] 10 ... ♕h4 11 0-0 h5 12 ♘d2 g6 13 f4 ♘g4 14 ♘f3 ♕f6 15 ♖e1 0-0-0 16 a4 ± Karpov-Alburt, Malta Ol 1980.

[19] 14 ♘e4 h6 15 b3 = Koz-Steinberg, Kiev 1958.

[20] Novopashin-Mikenas, Erevan 1962.
11 ♗xc6+ bc ±.

[21] Bagirov.

[22] 7 ... ♘de7 8 ed ♕xd6 9 ♘c3 ♗xf3 10 ♗xf3 0-0-0 11 ♘b5 ♕d7 12 ♕b3 a6 13 ♘a7+ ♔b8 14 ♘xc6+ ♘xc6 15 ♗e3 ♖e8 16 ♖fd1 ♘d8 17 d5 ± Matulović-Knežević, Bajonok 1975.

[23] 11 ... ♘e7 12 ♖e1 ±.

[24] 14 ♖e1+ ♗e7 15 ♕xf6 gf 16 ♘c3 (Vogt-Uddenfeld, Skopje Ol 1972) 16 ... ♔d8 17 f4 ±.

[25] 10 ... ♗f6 11 ♗e3 d5 12 c5 ♘d7 13 b4 ♗xb4 14 ♖b1 ♘c6 15 ♖xb7 ♗xf3 16 ♗xf3 0-0 17 ♕a4 ±.

[26] 11 ♗b2 d5 12 c5 ♗xf3 13 ♗xf3 ♘d7 14 ♕d2 ♗f6 15 ♘a4 ♖e8 Nyholm-Grünfeld, 1927.

[27] 13 ... ♘xb4? 14 ♕b3! ±.

[28] Mikhalchishin-Hort, Banja Luka 1974.

[29] 16 b5 ♘a5 17 ♗f4 ♘f5 18 ♘e5 ♗xe2 19 ♘xe2 ab 20 ab ♗xe5 21 ♗xe5 ♘c4 22 ♗f4 ♖a5 ∓ Bagirov.

[30] 11 ... ♕b8!? 12 ♘e1 ♗xe2 13 ♕xe2 d5 14 c5 ♘d7 15 ♘d3 ♗f6 16 ♘f3 b6 17 b4 bc 18 bc ♕b5 ∓ Pacl-Bagirov, Wroclaw 1976.

[31] 15 ♖c1 ♗f6 intending ... ♖fd8, ... e5.

[32] Makarichev-Palatnik, Daugavpils 1979.

[33] 11 ... ed 12 ♘xd5! ♘xd5 13 ♕xd5 ♗f6 14 ♕d2! ♕a5 15 ♖fd1 ♖fe8 16 ♕c2! ± Matanović-Ghizdavu, Bath 1973.

[34] 16 ♗d4 ♘xb2! 17 ♕c2 ♗f6! 18 ♗xb6 ♕xb6 19 ♘e4 ♕d4 ∓ Bikhovsky-Bagirov, Vilnus 1966.

[35] 17 ♕b3 ♗f6 18 ♖ad1 ± Timman-Bagirov, Tbilisi 1971.

[36] 13 b3 ♘xe3 14 fe ♘c6 15 a3 b6 16 cb ab 17 ♘b5 ♗g5 = Radojević-Bagirov, Polanica Zdroj 1969.

[37] 17 ♗e3 b5 18 ♘c3 (Sax-Hecht, Wijk aan Zee 1973) 18 ... b4 19 ♘e2 ♘e7 intending ... ♘ac6 = Bagirov.

[38] 12 ... ♕b8 13 ♗c3 a5 14 a3 ♖fc8 15 ♖c1 ♗g6 16 ♖e1 ♗f6 17 ♗f1 d5 = Bertok-Kovačević, Belgrade 1976.

[39] 17 ♘f1 b6! = Medina-Hecht, Malaga 1972.

[40] 10 ♗f4!? de ∞ Bagirov.

[41] 10 ... ♘c6 11 ed cd 12 d5 ed 13 ♘xd5 ♗xf3 (13 ... ♘xd5 14 ♕xd5 ♗g6 15 ♖ad1 ±) 14 ♗xb6 ab 15 ♗xf3 ± Gulko-Kakageldiev, USSR 1974.

[42] 11 cd ♘xd5 12 ♕b3 ♘b6 (12 ... ♘xe3 13 fe b6 14 d5 ± Georgadze-Alburt, Tbilisi 1977) 13 d5!? (13 ♖fd1 c6 14 a4 a5 15 ♗g5 ♗xf3 16 ♗xe7 ♕xe7 17 ♗xf3 ♕b4 = Holmov-Palatnik, USSR 1979) 13 ... ♘xd5 14 ♖fd1 ±. 11 ... ed 12 ♘e1 (12 ♗d3 ♘c6 13 g4 ♗g6 14 ♗f5 ♕e8 15 ♘e2 f6 = Gulko-Bagirov, USSR Ch 1977; 12 g4!? ♗g6 13 ♘d2 ♘c6 14 f4 f5 15 ♖f2 intending ♘f1-g3) 12 ... ♗xe2 13 ♕xe2 ± Plachetka-Bagirov, Kirovakan 1978.

[43] 13 b3 ♘xe3 14 fe (Spassky-Fischer, match 1972) 14 ... ♘c6 15 ♖b1 a5 16 a3 b6 17 b4 ab 18 ab bc 19 bc ♖a3 = Petrosian.

[44] 13 ... ♘c6 14 b3 ♘4a5 15 ♖c1 b6 16 ♘a4 f6 17 ♖e1 (17 ef ♗xf6 18 ♗e3 ♘e7! 19 ♕d2 ♘ac6 20 ♗g4 ♘f5 = Belyavsky-Alburt, Kiev 1978) 17 ... ♕d7 18 ♗g4 ♖ae8 19 b4! b5 20 ba ba 21 ♕xa4 fe 22 de ♖b8 23 ♗d2 ± Tukmakov-Neckar, Leningrad 1974.

[45] 17 ♖e1 ♗g5 18 ♘xd5!? (18 ♕d2 = Lukhin-Bagirov, Moscow 1979) 18 ... ed 19 ♗xg5 ♕xg5 20 ♗xd5 ♔h8! (Kavalek-Schmidt, Nice Ol 1974) 21 ♕e2! a5 22 ♕e4 ♗a6 23 f4 ∞.

[46] 13 f4 ♘c6 14 b4 ♗h4 15 b5 ♘a5 = Dorfman-Bagirov, USSR 1978.

[47] Matanović-Vukić, Novi Sad 1975.

[48] 9 ... a5!? Alburt.

[49] 13 ... ♗xc5! 14 dc d4 15 ♕h5!? (15 ♗xh7+! – Smyslov – ♔xh7 16 ♕h5+ ♔g8 17 ♘e4 de 18 ♖ad1 e2 19 ♖xd8 ef+ 20 ♔xf1 ♖xd8 21 ♘g5 ±±) 15 ... g6 16 ♕h6 dc 17 ♖ad1 ± Shamkovich-Alburt, New York 1980.

13 ... g6 ∞ Smyslov.

French Defence

The French is a defence in the truest sense of the word, appealing to players who are content to endure cramped or passive positions in the hope of emerging with a superior pawn structure or an eventual counterattack. It was honed into a formidable weapon by ex-World Champion Botvinnik and the defence's most dedicated and successful practitioners are now undoubtedly Uhlmann and Korchnoi. As the times and the players setting opening trends change, so do the popularity and assessments of White's main choices against this opening.

The **Winawer Variation** (3 ♘c3 ♗b4), the most dynamic and double-edged option, saddles White with a gashed pawn formation in return for the bishop pair and an advantage in space. In the heyday of such players as Tal, Spassky and Fischer the Winawer was the usual topic of discussion in the French.

Today the most frequently seen line is the **Tarrasch Variation** (3 ♘d2). Once thought to be harmless, the fine points of this method of attack have been demonstrated time and again by the World Champion, who excels in the simple positions that result. In contrast to the Winawer, the Tarrasch is less direct but cedes no positional defects. It allows Black a greater degree of freedom at the cost of strategical weaknesses (usually in the form of an isolated queen's pawn) and leaves him with long-term difficulties in achieving full equality.

The **Advance Variation** (3 e5), advocated by Nimzowitsch, has waned in popularity. It is not without its dangers for the second player, and it must be studied carefully by anyone who wishes to employ the defence in tournament play.

The **Classical Variation** (3 ♘c3 ♘f6) is also very rarely seen nowadays but it offers a viable alternative to the complexities of the Winawer.

The **MacCutcheon Variation** (4 ♗g5 ♗b4) currently suffers from neglect, since it may involve Black in the disadvantages of the Winawer without its compensatory chances for counterattack. However, this line still holds unclear possibilities for those who wish to study it.

	French I: Miscellaneous and Exchange Variation							1 e4 e6		
	2	3	4	5	6	7	8	9	10	
1	b3[1]	♗b2	♘c3	♕e2[2]	0-0-0	d3[3]	♕e1	♗xd3	♘ce2	=
	d5	de!	♘f6	♗e7	♘c6	♘d4	ed	♗d7	c5[4]	
2	♘c3	g3	♗g2	d3	de	♘xd1	f3	♔f2[5]		=
	d5	de	♗d7	♗c6	♕xd1+	♘f6	♗b4+			
3	♘f3	♘c3[6]	♘e2	c3	bc	♘g3	d4	♗d3	cd[8]	=
	d5	d4[7]	c5	dc	♘f6	♗e7	♘c6	cd		
4	♕e2[9]	b3[10]	♗b2[11]	♗xf6[12]	e5	♕g4	f4	c3	♘f3	=
	♗e7	d5	♗f6	♘xf6	♘fd7	0-0[13]	♘c6	d4!	f5[14]	
5	d3	♘d2	g3	de	♗g2	♘gf3	0-0	c3		=
	d5[15]	♘f6	de[16]	♗c5	e5	♘c6	0-0	a5[17]		
6	...	...	♘gf3	g3	♗g2	0-0	e5	♖e1	♘f1	=
	...	...	b6	♗b7	♗e7	c5	♘fd7	♘c6	♕c7[18]	

	4	5	6	7	8	9	10	11	12	
7	♘f3	♗d3	0-0	♘c3	♖e1					=
	♘f6[20]	♗d6	0-0	h6	c6[21]					
8	♗d3	♘f3	0-0	c3	♖e1	♘bd2	h3	♘f1	♗g5[23]	=
	♗d6[22]	♗g4	♘c6	♘ge7	♕d7	0-0	♗f5	♖ae8		
9	...	♘c3!?	h3	♕h5	♘ge2	♗f4!?				∞
	...	c6	♘e7	♕b6	♗e6[24]					
10	...	c3	♕f3[25]	♗f4[27]	h3	♕xf4	♘e2	♕g5		=
	♘c6!	♗d6	♘ce7[26]	♘f6	♗xf4	0-0	♘g6			
11	♘c3	♗d3	♘ge2	♗f4	♕d2	0-0-0	♘g3	♕xd3		=
	♘f6[28]	♘c6	♗e7	0-0	♘b4	♘e8	♘xd3+	c6[29]		

[1]   2 c4 d5 3 cd ed 4 ed ♘f6 5 ♕a4+ ♘bd7 6 ♘c3 ♗e7 = Czerniak-Michel, Cordoba 1942. 3 ed cd 4 d4 ♘f6 5 ♘f3 ♗e7 6 ♘c3 0-0 7 ♗e3 c6 8 ♗d3 dc 9 ♗xc4 ♘bd7 10 0-0 ♘b6 11 ♗b3 ♘bd5 = Velimirović-Uhlmann, Skopje 1976.

2 g3 d5 3 ♗g2 de 4 ♗xe4 ♘f6 5 ♗g2 e5 =.

2 e5 c5 3 f4 ♘c6 4 ♘f3 ♘h6 5 g3 ♗e7 6 ♗g2 0-0 7 d3 f6 8 ef ♗xf6 9 0-0 ♘f7 10 c3 (Steinitz-Schwarz, Vienna 1882) 10 ... d5 =.

2 f4 d5 3 e5 c5 4 ♘f3 ♘c6 5 c3 f5!? Atwood-Philidor, 1794. 2 ... c5 – 1 e4 c5 2 f4 e6.

[2] 5 f3!? ef 6 ♘xf3 ∞. 5 ... ♗c5! Harding.

[3] 7 ♘xe4 ♘d4 intending ... a5, ... a4 $\mp$ Keres.

[4] Kärner-Ritov, Tallinn 1972.

[5] 9 c3? ♗c5 $\mp$ Castro-Szabo, Costa Brava 1976.

9 ♔f2 =.

[6] 3 e5 c5 4 b4!? cb 5 d4 ♗d7 6 a3 ♕a5! 7 ♗d3 ♗b5 8 ab!? ♕xa1 9 ♗xb5+ ♘c6 10 ♗d2 with insufficient compensation, Day-Hübner, World Junior Ch 1967.

[7] 3 ... de 4 ♘xe4 – Rubinstein System.

3 ... ♘f6 4 e5 ♘e4!? 5 ♗e2 ♗c5 6 d4 ♗e7 7 ♘g3 c5 8 ♗d3 ♘g5!? ∞ Vogt-Romanishin, Leningrad 1977.

[8] Ljubojević-S.Garcia, Palma de Mallorca 1977.

[9] Chigorin.

[10] 3 g3 d5 4 d3 ♘f6 5 ♗g2 0-0 =.

3 ♘c3 d5 4 d3 ♘f6 5 g3 b6 6 ♗g2 ♗b7 = Chigorin-Maroczy, Nuremburg 1896.

3 ♕g4!? ♗f6 4 f4 d5 5 e5 h5 6 ♕d1 ♗e7 = Alapin.

[11] 4 ed ed 5 ♗b2 ♘f6 6 ♗xf6 gf 7 ♘f3 ♘c6 8 d4 ♗g4 9 c3 ♕d7 = Vasyukov.

[12] 5 e5 ♗e7 6 ♕g4 ♗f8 7 ♘f3 c5 8 ♗b5+ ♗d7 9 ♗xd7+ ♕xd7 10 ♘c3 ♘c6 11 0-0 ♘ge7 Chigorin-Tarrasch, match (14) 1893.

[13] 7 ... g6 8 f4 c5 Botvinnik.

[14] 10 ... dc?! 11 ♘xc3 ♘c5 12 d4 f5 13 ef ♕xf6 14 ♖d1 ♕d7 15 ♗d3! ♕h6 16 0-0! ± Chigorin-Tarrasch, match (22) 1893.

10 ... f6!? 11 ♕xe6+ ♔h8; 11 ef ♕xf6; 11 cd ♘b6 Vasyukov.

10 ... f5 = Vasyukov.

[15] 2 ... c5 3 ♘f3 ♘c6 – 1 e4 c5 2 d3 ♘c6.

2 ... b6 3 g3 ♗b7 4 ♗g2 c5 5 ♘f3 ♘f6 6 0-0 ♗e7 7 e5 ♘d5 ∞ Kavalek-Korchnoi, Wijk aan Zee 1978.

[16] 4 ... c5 5 ♘gf3 ♘c6 – 1 e4 c5 2 d3 ♘c6 3 ♘f3 e6.

4 ... ♘c6!?

[17] Vasyukov-Tal, USSR Ch 1961 and Kagan-Vaganian, Rio de Janeiro IZ 1979.

[18] 11 ♕e2 h6 12 h4 0-0-0 = Bobekov-Vankov, Bulgaria 1977.

[19] 3 ♗d3 de 4 ♗xe4 ♘f6 =.

3 ♗e3 de 4 f3 ef 5 ♘xf3 ♘f6 $\mp$.

[20] 4 ... ♗d6 5 c4! (Paulsen) ♘f6 6 ♘c3 ±.

[21] Abrahams.

[22] 4 ... c5!? 5 ♘f3 ♘c6 6 ♕e2+ ♗e7 7 dc ♘f6 8 h3 0-0 9 0-0 ♗xc5 10 c3 ♖e8 11 ♕c2 ♕d6 = (intending ... ♗b6-c7) 12 ♘bd2?? ♕g3!! 13 ♗f5 ♖e2 14 ♘d4 ♘xd4 0-1 Tatai-Korchnoi, Beersheva 1978.

[23] 12 ♗g5 = Korchnoi.

[24] Grob-Szabo, Hastings 1947/48.

[25] 6 ♕c2 ♕f6! intending ... ♘ge7, ... ♗f5 Botterill.

6 ♘f3 ♘ge7 Nimzowitsch.

6 ♘e2 ♕f6!? Alekhine, or 6 ... ♘f6 Nimzowitsch.

[26] 6 ... ♘f6 7 h3 ♗e6 = Spielmann-Réti, 1921.

[27] 7 ♗g5 h6 8 ♗h4 ♗e6 intending ... 0-0-0 Korchnoi.

7 ♘e2 ♘g6 intending 8 ♘f4 ♕e7+, or.8 0-0 ♕h4 9 h3 ♘8e7 Harding.

[28] Svenonius Variation.

[29] Yukhtman-Korchnoi, USSR 1957.

	3	4	5	6	7	8	9	10	11	
1	...	c4	♗xc4	♘f3	♗g5	♘c3	♗xe7	d5	♗xd5	∞
	b6[1]	dc	♗b7	♘e7	♕d7	h6	♗xe7	ed	♗xd5[2]	
2	...	♘f3	c3	♗d3	♗xa6	♕d3[3]	♘bd2	0-0	b3![4]	=
	...	♘e7	♕d7	♗a6	♘xa6	♘b8	♘bc6	♘g6		
3	...	...	c4	♘c3	♗e2	0-0	♗xc4	♗e3	d5	∞
	...	...	♕d7	♗b7	♘bc6	dc	0-0-0![5]	♘f5	♘xe3[6]	
4	...	...	...	...	cd	♗d3	0-0	bc	♘xd4[7]	±
	...	...	...	...	♘xd5	c5	♘xc3	cd		
5	...	♕g4[8]	♘f3	♗d3	♗f4[9]	0-0	♖e1	♕xf4		∓
	c5	cd	♘c6	♕c7	♘ge7	♘g6	♘xf4	f6![10]		
6	...	dc[11]	♘f3[12]	♗d3	♕e2[13]	♘xe5	♕xe5	♕e2	♘d2	=
	...	♘c6	♗xc5	f6	fe	♘xe5	♕f6	♘e7	0-0[14]	
7	...	♘f3	♗d3	0-0	♗f4	♗g3	♖e1	♘bd2	h4	∓
	...	♘c6	cd	♘ge7	♘g6	♕b6	♕xb2	♗b4	♗c3[15]	
8	...	c3	♘f3	♗d3	0-0	cd	♗e2[16]			±
	...	♘e7	♘ec6	♘d7	cd	♘b4				
9	...	...	♘f3	♗e2	0-0	♕xe2	♕d1	♖e1	♘bd2	∞
	...	♕b6	♗d7[17]	♗b5	♗xe2	♕a6	c4[18]	♘c6	0-0-0[19]	
10	...	...	...	...	c4	♗xc4	♘bd2	a3	♕e2	±
	...	...	...	...	♗xc4	♕b4+!	dc	♕b5	cd[20]	
11	...	...	...	a3	c4!	♗xc4	d5	de!		±
	...	...	...	♗b5	♗xc4	dc	♘e7[21]			
12	...	...	...	♘a3	♗e2	cd	♔f1	♘c2	♘xb4	±
	...	...	...	♘c6	cd	♗b4+	f6[22]	fe	♘xb4[23]	

---

1 e4 e6 2 d4 d5 3 e5 c5 4 c3 ♘c6 5 ♘f3 ♕b6

	6	7	8	9	10	11	12	13	14	
13	♗d3	cd	♘c3	♘xd4	0-0[24]	♖e1	♘xd5	♕g4	♗d2	∓
	cd	♗d7	♘xd4	♕xd4	♕xe5	♕b8	♗d6	♔f8	h5[25]	
14	...	...	...	...	...	♕e2	♔h1	f4	♖d1	∞
	...	...	...	...	a6	♘e7	♘c6	♘b4	♘xd3[26]	
15	...	...	...	...	...	♔h1	f4	♗e3		∓
	...	...	...	...	...	♕xe5	♕d6	♗e7[27]		
16	...	...	...	...	...	♖e1	♗e3	♕f3	♗c5	∓
	...	...	...	...	...	♘e7	♕xe5	♗c6	♕f6	

	6	7	8	9	10	11	12	13	14	
17	♗e2	cd	♘c3	♔f1	♘a4	g4	♘xh4	♔g2	gf	∓
	cd[28]	♘h6	♘f5	♗e7	♕d8	♘h4	♗xh4	f5!	ef[29]	
18	...	...	...	♘a4	♗d2	♗c3	a3	♘xc3	ab	∞
	...	...	...	♗b4+	♕a5	b5	♗xc3+	b4	♕xb4	
19	a3	♘bd2	ef	g3	♗g2	0-0	♖b1	b3		=
	c4[30]	f6	♘xf6	♗d6	0-0	♗d7	♕c7	b5[31]		
20	...	g3	ef	♗g2[32]	0-0	♕e2	♘e5	de	♗e3	±
	...	f6	♘xf6	♗d6	0-0	♔h8[33]	♗xe5[34]	♘d7	♘c5[35]	

---

[1] 3 ... ♗d7!? 4 ♘f3 a6 Basman.

[2] 12 ♕xd5 c6 =.

[3] 8 a4!?

[4] 11 ♖e1 f5! ∓ Hedman-Romanishin, Cienfuegos 1977.
   11 b3! =.

[5] 9 ... ♘a5? 10 ♗b5 ± Sax-Short, London 1980.

[6] 12 fe ♘a5 13 ♗b5 ♕e7 14 d6 cd 15 b4 ∞ Sax.

[7] Kupreichik-Vaganian, USSR 1980.

[8] 4 ♗b5+? ♘c6 5 ♗xc6+ bc 6 c3 ♕b6 ∓ Le Lionnais.

[9] 7 0-0 ♘xe5 8 ♘xe5 ♕xe5 9 ♗f4 ♕f6 10 ♗g5 ♕e5 =.

[10] Holford-Heidenfeld, South African Ch 1947.

[11] Steinitz.

[12] 5 ♗f4 ♗xc5 6 ♗d3 ♕b6! =.

[13] 7 ♗f4? fe 8 ♘xe5 ♕f6 ∓.
   7 ef ♘xf6 ∓ Heidenfeld.

[14] Zubarev-Grigoriev match (11) 1923.

[15] 12 ♖b1 ♕xa2 13 ♘g5 ♗xd2 14 ♕xd2 ♕a5 ∓ Wise-Lightfoot, British Ch 1976.

[16] Schwarz.

[17] Wade Variation.

[18] 9 ... ♘d7 10 ♗e3 ♖c8 11 ♘bd2 ♘e7 12 dc ♘xc5 13 ♗xc5 ♖xc5 14 ♘d4 ± Sabitov-Zhivodov, corr. 1975/77.

[19] Hecht-Karpov, Bath 1973.

[20] 12 ♘xd4 ♕d5 13 ♘4f3 ♘d7 14 ♘xc4 ♖c8 15 ♘e3 ± Pinter-Ornstein, Budapest 1977. 13 ... ♘c6!? (Minić) ±.

[21] Formanek-Sahović, Lone Pine 1977.

[22] 9 ... ♘h6!?

[23] 12 de ♗b5 13 a3 (Schmid-Wade, match 1950) 13 ... ♗xe2+ 14 ♕xe2 ♘c6 15 ♗e3 d4 (Wade) ±.

[24] Milner Barry Gambit.

[25] 15 ♕h3 ♗c6 16 ♘b4 ♘f6! ∓ Messere-Endzelins, corr. 1975/77.

[26] 15 ♖xd3 ♕b6 (15 ... ♕c4 16 f5!?) 16 ♗e3 ♗c5 17 ♗xc5 ♕xc5 18 f5 d4 ∞ Messere-Dijkstra, corr. 1975/77.

[27] Wade-Menvielle, Palma de Mallorca 1966.

[28] 6 ... ♘h6 7 ♗xh6 ♕xb2? 8 ♗e3 ♕xa1 9 ♕c2 cd 10 ♘xd4 ± Wills-Spodny, Skara 1980. 7 ... gh ∞.

[29] 15 ♖g1 0-0 ∓.

[30] 6 ... a5 7 ♗e2 ±.

[31] Bastian-Sprotte, West Germany 1980.

[32] 9 ♗h3 ♘a5 10 ♘bd2 ♗d6 11 ♕e2 0-0 12 ♗xe6+ ♔h8 13 ♗xc8 ♖axc8 14 0-0 ♖ce8 ∞ Botterill.

[33] 11 ... ♘a5!? 12 ♘bd2 ♗d7 13 ♘e5 ♗e8 ∓.

[34] 12 ... ♘a5 13 ♘d2 ♗xe5 14 ♕xe5 ± Botterill.

[35] 15 ♘d2 ♕a5 16 f4 ♗d7 (Alexander-Uhlmann, Munich Ol 1958) 17 ♘f3 ±.

	3	4	5	6	7	8	9	10	11	
1	...	♘xe4	♘f3	♗d3[2]	♘xf6+	0-0[3]	c3	cd	♕e2	±
	de	♘d7[1]	♗e7	♘gf6	♗xf6	c5	cd	0-0	♘b6[4]	
2	...	...	...	♘xf6+[5]	♗g5	♗d3	♘e5[7]	♗b5+	♗e2[8]	±
	...	...	♘gf6	♘xf6	♗e7	b6![6]	♗b7	c6!		
3	...	e5[9]	♘xe4	♗e3[10]	dc	♕g4	♗b5+!	0-0-0	♗xd3	±
	♘f6	♘e4	de	c5	♘d7	♘xc5	♗d7[11]	♘d3+	ed[12]	
4	...	...	♕g4[13]	♘f3	♘xd4	♕g3	♗b5	♗xc6+	♗e3	∓
	...	♘fd7	c5	cd	♘xe5	♘bc6	a6	♘xc6	♗e7[14]	
5	...	...	f4	♘f3[15]	♗e3	♘xd4	♕d2	♗xd4	♕xd4[17]	±
	...	...	c5	♘c6	cd[16]	♗c5	♘xd4	♗xd4		
6	...	♗g5	♘xe4	♗xf6	♕d3	0-0-0	♘c3	f4	g4	±
	...	de[18]	♗e7	gf[19]	b6	♗b7	c6	f5	fg[20]	
7	...	...	e5	h4[22]	♗xe7[24]	f4![25]	♘f3	♘b5	♖b1[26]	∞
	...	♗e7	♘fd7[21]	c5[23]	♔xe7	♕b6	♕xb2	a6	♕xa2[27]	
8	...	...	...	...	...	♘b5	♘c7	♘xa8	♕xd4[28]	±
	...	...	...	...	♕xe7	0-0	cd	f6	♘c6	
9	...	...	...	...	hg	♘h3[29]	♘f4	♕d2		=
	...	...	...	♗xg5!	♕xg5	♕e7	♘c6!	b6!		
10	...	...	...	♗xe7	♕d2[30]	f4[31]	♘f3	dc	0-0-0	±
	...	...	...	♕xe7	0-0	c5	♘c6	♘xc5	a6[32]	

	8	9	10	11	12	13	14	15	16	
11	♘f3	♗d3[34]	ef	♘g5	♗xh7+	♕d2[35]	♔xd2	♔e1	h4	∞
	c5	f5	♕xf6	♕xf4!	♔h8	♕xd2+	♖xf2+	♖xg2	cd![36]	
12	...	...	♗xh7+	♘g5+	fg	♕d3+	♕xc3	h4[37]		∞/∓
	...	cd!	♔xh7	♕xg5!	dc	♔g8	♘c6			
13	...	dc!	♗d3	ef	g3	0-0	♕d2	♖ae1	cd[40]	±
	...	f6	♘c6	♕xf6[38]	♘xc5	♗d7[39]	♗e8	♘xd3		

[1] 4 ... b6 5 ♕f3 c6 6 ♗g5! ± Tal.
4 ... e5 5 ♘f3 ♗g4 6 ♗c4 f6 7 0-0 ±.
4 ... ♘c6 5 ♘f3 ♗e7 6 c3 ♘f6 7 ♗d3 0-0 8 ♕c2 ±.
4 ... ♗d7 5 ♘f3 ♗c6 6 ♗d3 ♘d7 7 ♘e5 ± Suetin. 7 0-0 ±.
4 ... ♕d5 5 ♗d3 ♘f6 6 ♘g3 ±.
4 ... ♘f6 5 ♘xf6+ ♕xf6 6 ♘f3 h6 7 ♗d3 ♗d6 8 0-0 ♘c6 9 c3 ±.

[2] 6 ♗c4 ♘gf6 7 ♘xf6+ ♘xf6 8 ♕e2 ♕e7 9 ♗f4 c5 10 d5 ed.

[3] 8 ♕e2 ♕e7 9 0-0 c5 10 c3 cd 11 cd ♘b6 12 ♗d2 ♗d7 13 ♘e5 ± Lightfoot-Clarke, British Ch 1974.

[4] Intending ♘d5 ±. 11 ... ♕a5?! 12 ♗f4 ♕h5 13 ♖ac1 ±.

[5] 6 ♗d3 ♗e7 – 5 ... ♗e7.

[6] 8 ... c5 9 ♕e2! ±.
8 ... 0-0 9 ♕e2 ±.

[7] 9 ♕e2!?
9 0-0!?

[8] Kmoch.

[9] Steinitz.
4 ed ♘xd5 5 ♘f3 c5 6 ♘xd5 ♕xd5 7 ♗e3 ♘d7! 8 c4 ♕d6 Shamkovich.

[10] 6 ♗c4 c5 7 d5! ♘d7 8 de fe 9 f4! ef 10 ♘xf3 ♘b6 11 ♕xd8+ ♔xd8 (Kostro-Pytel, Poland 1973) 12 ♗d3! intending 0-0 ±.

[11] 9 ... ♘d7 10 ♘e2 ♕a5+ 11 ♘c3 a6 12 ♗xd7+ ♗xd7 13 ♗d4 ♗c6 ∞ A.Ivanov-Malanyuk, USSR 1981.

[12] 12 ♖xe3 ± Matulović-Maksimović, Nice 1977.

[13] 5 ♘f3 c5 6 dc ♘c6 7 ♗f4 ♗xc5 8 ♗d3 f6 9 ef ♘xf6 10 0-0 0-0 = Spassky-Petrosian, match (9) 1966.

[14] Estrin-Lilienthal, Baku 1951.

[15] 6 dc ♘c6 7 ♘f3 ♗xc5 8 ♗d3 a6 9 ♕e2 ♕c7 10 ♗d2 b5 11 a3 ♖b8 12 ♘d1 ♘b6 13 b4 ♗e7 14 0-0 (Boleslavsky-Pachman, Stockholm 1948) 14 ... ♘c4! = Pachman.

[16] 7 ... a6 8 dc ♗xc5 9 ♗xc5 ♘xc5 10 ♕d2 intending 0-0-0 ± Keres.
7 ... ♗e7 8 dc ♘xc5 9 ♘d4 ♗d7 10 a3 ±.
7 ... ♕b6 8 ♗a4 ♕a5+ 9 c3 cd 10 b4 ♘xb4 11 cb ♗xb4+ 12 ♗d2 ± (12 ... b6!? Haag).

[17] Tal-Stahlberg, Stockholm 1961.

[18] Burn Variation.

[19] 6 ... ♗xf6 7 ♘f3 ♘d7 8 ♕d2 b6 9 ♗b5 ♗b7 10 ♘xf6+ gf 11 ♕c3 ♕e7 12 ♕xc7 ♕b4+ 13 c3 ♕xb5 14 ♕xb7 ♕xb2 15 0-0 ♖d8 16 c4 ♕a3 17 ♖fe1 0-0 ± L.Steiner-Stahlberg, Saltsjöbaden 1948.

[20] Bronstein-Chistyakov, Moscow Ch 1978.

[21] 5 ... ♘g8 6 ♗e3 b6 7 h4! h5 8 ♗e2 g6 9 ♘f3 ♗a6 10 ♕d2 ♗xe2 11 ♘xe2 ♘c6! (11 ... c5? 12 c4 ±) 12 0-0 ♕d7 13 b3 ♗a3! 14 c4 ±.
5 ... ♘e4 (Tartakower) 6 ♗xe7 ♕xe7 7 ♘xe4 de 8 ♕e2! b6 9 0-0-0 ♗b7 10 g3 c5 11 ♗g2 ± Milner Barry-van den Bosch, England v Holland 1947.

[22] Albin-Chatard Attack.

[23] 6 ... h6 7 ♕h5 a6 8 0-0-0 c5 9 dc ♘xc5 10 ♘f3 ± Nikitin-Gusev, USSR 1960.
6 ... a6 7 ♕g4 ♗xg5 8 hg c5 9 g6 f5 =.
6 ... f6 7 ef ♘xf6 8 ♘f3 c5 9 dc ♘c6 10 ♗b5 ± Keres.

[24] 7 ♘b5 f6 8 ♗d3 a6 9 ♕h5+ ♔f8 10 ♖h3 ab 11 ♗h6! gh 12 ♕xh6+ ♔f7 13 ♕h5+ ½-½.

[25] 8 ♕g4 ♔f8 9 ♘f3 cd 10 ♕xd4 ♕b6 11 ♕xb6 ab! =.

[26] 11 ♘c7 ♕b4+ 12 ♔f2 ♖a7 13 c4! ± Keres.

[27] 12 ♘d6 ♕a5+ 13 ♔f2 ♘c6 14 ♖h3 cd 15 ♗d3 ♕c7 16 ♕c1! ∞ Matulović-Zaradić, Zagreb 1955.

[28] 11 ♘c7!? fe 12 ♘b5 ♘f6 ∞ Stahlberg. 12 ... a6? 13 ♘a7 ♕b4+ 14 ♕d2 ±.

[29] 8 ♘f3!? ♕e7 9 ♗d3 a6 10 ♕d2 c5 11 dc ♘c6 12 0-0-0 ♕xc5 13 ♕g5 ∞ Mrs Fagan-Richmond, London 1896.

[30] 7 ♕h5 0-0! ∓.
7 ♕g4 0-0 8 ♘f3 c5 9 ♗d3 f5 10 ef ♖xf6! ∓ Bernstein-Lasker, Zürich 1934.
7 ♘b5 ♘b6 =.

[31] 8 ♘ce2 c5 9 c3 f6 =.
8 ♘d1 f6 9 f4 c5 10 c3 ♘c6 ∓.

[32] Gligorić-Stahlberg, 1949. 11 ... ♗d7!? Keres.

[33] 7 ... a6 8 ♕g4 g6 (8 ... f5 9 ef ♘xf6 10 ♕g5 0-0 11 0-0-0 ±) 9 ♘f3 c5 10 dc ♘c6 11 ♗d3 ♘xc5 12 0-0 ♘b4 13 ♘e1 ± Matanović-Fuderer, Zagreb 1955.

[34] 9 ♘b5? cd 10 ♘c7 ♘xe5 11 ♘xa8 ♘xf3+ 12 ♕xf3 ♕b4+ ∓ Bronstein.

[35] 13 ♕h5 ♘f6! ∓ (13 ... ♕f2+? 14 ♔d1 ♘f6 15 ♕h3 e5 16 ♗f5+ intending 17 ♗xc8! ±±) 14 ♘f7+ ♖xf7 15 ♕xf7 ♔xh7 Heidenfeld.

[36] 17 ♘e2! e5 18 ♔f1 ∞/±.

[37] Heidenfeld.

[38] 11 ... ♖xf6 12 ♕d2 ♘xc5 13 0-0 ± Bronstein-Yanofsky, Stockholm 1948.

[39] 13 ... b6 14 ♕d2 ♗b7 15 ♖ae1 ♖ad8 intending ... ♘e4 ∞.

[40] Shabanov-Osnos, USSR 1951.

201

French III *continued*   1 e4 e6 2 d4 d5 3 ♘c3 ♘f6 4 ♗g5 ♗b4[41]

	5	6	7	8	9	10	11	12	13	
14	ed	♗xf6	bc	♕d2	c4	♘e2	f3			=
	♕xd5[42]	♗xc3+	gf	♘d7	♕e4+	b6	♕c6			
15	e5	♗e3[43]	♕g4	a3!	♘ge2	dc	0-0-0	♘xc3		∞
	h6	♘e4	♔f8	♗a5	c5	♘c6	♘xc3	♘xe5[44]		
16	...	♗d2	bc[45]	♕g4	♗d3	♔xd2	h4	♖h3	♖g3	±
	...	♗xc3	♘e4	♔f8	♘xd2	c5	♕a5	cd	♕xc3+[46]	

1 e4 e6 2 d4 d5 3 ♘c3 ♘f6 4 ♗g5 ♗b4 5 e5 h6 6 ♗d2 ♗xc3 7 bc ♘e4

	8	9	10	11	12	13	14	15	16	
17	♕g4	♗e3	♗d3	dc	♘f3	♔f1	♗xe4	♕xe4	♕d4	∞
	g6	♘xc3	c5	♕a5	♘e4+	♗d7	de	♗c6	♘a6[47]	
18	...	♗c1	♗d3	dc	♗d2	h3	♕xa4	♗b5+	♗xa4	=
	...	♘xc3	c5	♕a5	♕a4	h5	♘xa4	♗d7	♗xa4[48]	
19	...	h4	♗d3	♔xd2	♖h3[49]	♗xg6	♖g3[50]	♗h7	♕f4	∓
	...	c5	♘xd2	♘c6	♕a5	♘xd4!	♖f8	♗d7	0-0-0[51]	
20	...	♗d3	♔xd2	♖b1	♘f3	cd	♔e2[53]	♕f4	♖hc1	∞
	...	♘xd2	c5	♘c6	cd	♕a5+[52]	b6	♗a6	♖c8[54]	

---

[41] MacCutcheon Variation.

[42] 5 ... ♗xc3+!? 6 bc ed 7 ♕f3 ♕e7+! Harding.

[43] Janowski.

6 ♗c1 ♘e4 7 ♕g4 ♔f8 8 ♘ge2 c5 9 a3 ♗a5 10 dc ♘xc3 11 ♘xc3 d4 12 b4 dc 13 ba ♘c6! Harding.

6 ♗h4 g5 7 ♗g3 ♘e4 8 ♘ge2 f5 9 ef ♕xf6 10 ♕d3 ♘c6 11 0-0-0 ♘xg3 12 ♘xg3 ♗d7 13 ♗e2 0-0-0 (Purdy-Miller, Australia 1955) 14 ♘h5 ♕f7 15 f4 (Schwarz) ∞.

6 ♗xf6 gf 7 ♘f3 f5 8 ♗d3 c5 ⩱ Steinitz-MacCutcheon, Manhattan 1885.

6 ef hg 7 fg ♖g8 8 h4 gh 9 ♕g4 ♕f6 10 ♖xh4 ♕xg7 11 ♕xg7 ♖xg7 12 ♖h8+ ♔d7 13 ♘f3 ♘c6 ∞ Keres.

[44] 13 ♕g3 ♗c7 14 ♗f4 ∞.

13 ♕f4!?

[45] 7 ♗xc3 ♘e4 8 ♗b4 c5! 9 ♗xc5 ♘xc5

10 dc ♕a5+ 11 c3 ♕xc5 12 ♕d4 ♕c7! ⩱ Bogoljubow-Réti, Kiel 1921.

[46] 14 ♗e2 ♖g8 15 ♖e1 b6 16 ♔f1 ♕c7 17 ♘f3 ♗a6 ± Fuchs-Sliwa, Zinnowitz 1967.

[47] Fjelstad-Savermann, corr. 1974/76.

[48] 17 ♖b1 = Harding.

[49] 12 ♘f3 ♕a5! (intending ... cd) 13 dc ♗d7. 13 ♖he1 ♗d7 intending ... 0-0-0 ⩱.

[50] 14 ♔d1 ♖g8 15 ♗xf7+ ♔xf7 16 ♕h5+ ♔e7 ⩱.

14 ♘f3 ♖g8 15 ♗xf7+ ♔xf7 16 ♕h5+ ♔e7 17 ♘xd4 cd 18 ♖f3 ♖f8 ⩱.

[51] 17 ♕xh6 ♗b5! ⩱.

[52] 13 ... ♕e7!? Euwe.

[53] 14 ♗e3 b6!? 15 ♕f4 ♗a6 16 ♖he1 ± Barcza.

[54] 17 ♔f1 ♕a3 18 ♔g1 ♗xd3 19 cd ♕xd3 20 ♖b3 ♕f5 21 ♕d2 (Matulović-Tsvetkov, Varna 1965) 21 ... g5! ∞.

	4	5	6	7	8	9	10	11	12	
1	ed[1]	♗d3[3]	♘ge2	0-0	♗f4[4]	♗xf5	♕d3			=
	ed[2]	♘c6	♘ge7!	0-0	♗f5	♘xf5	♕d7![5]			
2	♕g4	♕xg7	♕h6	♕e3	a3[6]	bc	cd			∞
	♘f6	♖g8	♖g6	c5!	♗xc3+	cd	♘xe4			
3	a3	bc	♕g4	♕xg7	♕h6	♘e2	♗g5[8]	♕h4[9]	♘g3	∓
	♗xc3+	de	♘f6	♖g8	♘bd7![7]	b6	♕e7	♗b7	h6![10]	
4	♗d3	♗xe4	♗f3	♘e2	a3	bc	♗g5	♗xc6+	cd	=
	de[11]	♘f6	c5	♘c6	♗xc3+	e5!	ed	bc	cd[12]	
5	♗d2[13]	♕g4	0-0-0[15]	♕e2!	♘xe4	♖xd2	h4![16]			∞
	de[14]	♕xd4	h5!	♗d7	♗xd2+	♕b4				
6	...	...	♕xg7	♕h6	0-0-0	♕h4	♕h3	♗e2!		=
	...	♘f6	♖g8	♕xd4[17]	♗f8![18]	♖g4	♕xf2	♖g6[19]		
7	♘ge2[20]	a3	♘xe4	♘2g3[21]	c3	♘xf6+	d5	c4![22]	♗e2	=
	de	♗e7	♘f6	♘c6	e5	♗xf6	♘e7	0-0	♘g6[23]	
8	...	...	...	♗f4	♕d3	.0-0-0[24]	♘2c3	♘xd5	♘c3[25]	=
	...	...	♘c6	♘f6	0-0	b6	♘d5	ed		

[1]   Exchange Winawer.
[2]   4 ... ♕xd5?! – 3 ed ♕xd5.
[3]   **5 ♕f3?!** (Larsen) ♕e7+! 6 ♕e3 ♘c6 ∓ Ajala-Farago, Harrachov 1967.
  5 ♘f3 ♘e7 6 ♗d3 ♘bc6 7 h3 ♗f5 ∓ Mannheimer-Nimzowitsch, Frankfurt 1930.
[4]   8 ♘g3 f5! ∓ Eley-Uhlmann, Hastings 1972/73.
[5]   Ivashin-Boleslavsky, USSR 1942.
[6]   8 ♗d2 ♘g4 9 ♕d3 ♘c6 10 h3 c4 ∓. 10 ♘ge2 cd 11 ♘xd4 ♘xf2! ∓.
[7]   8 ... b6 9 ♗g5 ♖g6 10 ♕h4 ♗b7 11 ♘e2 h6 12 ♗xh6 ♕d5 (Watson-Whiteley, Bristol 1968; 11 ... ♖g4 ±) 13 ♗d2! ±/±.
[8]   10 ♘g3 ∞ Mednis.
[9]   11 ♘f4 ♘g4! ∓/∓.
[10]   Fischer-Kovačević, Zagreb 1970.
[11]   4 ... c5 5 ed ed (5 ... ♕xd5 6 ♗d2 ♗xc3 7 ♗xc3 cd 8 ♗xd4 ♕xg2 9 ♕f3 ♕xf3 10 ♘xf3 f6 11 ♖g1 ♔f7 12 ♘d2! ♕e7 13 ♗c5! ± Mazurenko-Kac, corr. 1979) 6 dc ♘c6 7 ♘f3 ♗xc5 =.
[12]   Hort-Pietzsch, Kecskemet 1964.
[13]   Müller-Zhuravlev Gambit.
[14]   4 ... ♘f6 5 e5 ♗xc3 6 ♗xc3 ♘e4 7 ♗d2 c5 =.
[15]   **6 ♘ge2** ♕f6! 7 a3 =/∞.
  6 ♘f3 ♘h6 7 ♕f4 e5! =.

[16]   **10 a3?!** ♕e7 11 ♘f3 (Cherepkov-Hasin, Mosow 1962) 11 ... ♘f6! ∓.
  10 h4! intending ♖h3.
[17]   7 ... ♖g6?! 8 ♕h4!
[18]   8 ... ♖g6 9 ♕h4 ♗g4 10 ♕h3 ♕xf2 11 ♗e3! ♕f5 (11 ... ♕h4 12 ♕xh4 ♖xh4 13 ♗g5 ±±) 12 ♗b5+! c6 13 ♖f1 ♕e5 14 ♖xf6 ♗xc3 15 ♕xg4 ♗xb2+ 16 ♔b1 ♕xf6 17 ♕g8+ ♔d7 18 ♗g5 ±±.
[19]   **11 ... ♖h4** 12 ♕xh4! ♕xh4 13 g3 ♕h6! 14 ♗xh6 ♗xh6+ 15 ♔b1 ♗d7 ±.
  11 ... ♖g6 12 g4 ♕d4! 13 ♗e3! ♕e5! 14 ♗d4 ♕f4+! etc.
[20]   Alekhine Variation.
[21]   **7 ♘xf6+** ♗xf6 8 ♗e3 0-0 9 ♕d2 e5 = Kurajica-Petrosian, Zagreb 1970.
  7 ♕d3 0-0 8 ♗f4 ♘d5 9 ♗d2 b6 10 c4 ♗a6 11 b4 ♘f6 12 ♘2g3 ♘bd7 ∓ Biriescu-Uhlmann, Bucharest 1978.
[22]   11 ♗c4 0-0 12 0-0 ♘f5 = Hort-Uhlmann, Skopje Ol 1972.
[23]   13 ♘h5 ♗g5! = Pachman-Bronstein, Saltsjöbaden 1948.
[24]   9 g3!? ♘xe4 10 ♕xe4 ♗d7 11 0-0-0 ♗d6 12 ♗g2 = Ghinda-Uhlmann, Bucharest 1978.
[25]   Stoica-Uhlmann, Bucharest 1978.

	4	5	6	7	8	9	10	11	12	
9	e5	a3²⁶	bc	♕g4!	h4!	♕f3	♕h3	g4	♗g5	±
	♘e7	♗xc3+	b6²⁷	♘g6	h5	♘xh4²⁸	♘f5	♘e7	♗a6²⁹	
10	...	♕g4³⁰	♕g3	a3³¹	♘f3³²	♗d3	♘e2	h4	♗d2	=
	♕d7	f5	b6	♗f8	♗b7	♘c6	0-0-0	♘h6	♗e7³³	

1 e4 e6 2 d4 d5 3 ♘c3 ♗b4 4 e5 ♕d7 5 a3 ♗xc3+

	6	7	8	9	10	11	12	13	14	
11	bc	♘h3	♗xa6	♕g4	♕h5+	♕e2	c4	c3	cd	∓
	b6	♗a6³⁴	♘xa6	f5	g6!	♘b8	♘c6	♘ge7	♘xd5³⁵	
12	...	a4	♗xa6	♕g4	♕h5+	♕e2	h4³⁶	♘h3	♘f4	=
	...	♗a6	♘xa6	f5	g6!	♘b8	h6	♘c6	♘ge7³⁷	
13	...	♕g4!	♕g3	♗xa6	♘e2!	a4	h4	♕d3	♗g5	±
	...	f5	♗a6	♘xa6	♔f7³⁸	♘e7	c5	♕b7	cd³⁹	

1 e4 e6 2 d4 d5 3 ♘c3 ♗b4 4 e5

	4	5	6	7	8	9	10	11	12	
14	...	♗d2	♗xa6	a3	♕e2	♘d1!?⁴⁰	c3	♘f3	cd	=
	b6	♗a6	♘xa6	♗f8	♕c8!?	c5	♘e7	cd	♕c4⁴¹	
15	...	♘h3!?	♘f4	♗e2	0-0	♘a4	c3	b4	♗d3	=
	...	♕d7	♘c6	♗b7	0-0-0	♗f8	f6	♘h6!	♘f7⁴²	
16	...	a3	f4⁴³	♘f3	♗d3	0-0	♗xa6	♕d3	♘e2⁴⁴	±
	...	♗f8	♘e7	♘f5	h5	♗a6	♘xa6	♘b8		
17	...	♕g4	♗g5⁴⁵	0-0-0⁴⁶	♗e3	♘ge2	♕h3	♗g5	f4	=
	...	♗f8	♕d7	h6!	♗a6	h5	g6	♗e7	♘h6⁴⁷	
18	...	♗d2⁴⁸	♘b5	♕xd2	♘xd4⁵⁰	♘f3	♕xd4	♗d3	♕e3	=
	c5	♘c6⁴⁹	♗xd2+	♘xd4!	cd	♘e7	0-0	♘c6	f5⁵¹	
19	...	dc⁵²	♘f3⁵³	♗d3	a3	b4	ab	0-0	♖b1	=
	...	♘e7	♘bc6	d4!	♗a5	♘xb4!	♗xb4	♗xc3	♕c7⁵⁴	
20	...	♕g4	dc	♗d2	♘f3	♕h4	♕xd8	♘a4!		=
	...	♘e7	♘bc6	0-0	f5!	♘g6!	♖xd8	♗d7⁵⁵		
21	...	a3	♕g4!?⁵⁷	dc	bc	♕xg7?!⁵⁸	♕xh7			∞/∓
	...	♗a5⁵⁶	♘e7	♗xc3+	♘d7	♖g8	♕c7⁵⁹			
22	...	...	b4	♕g4	♕xg7⁶⁰	♕xh7	ba	♘f3	♖b1!⁶¹	=
	...	...	cd	♘e7	♖g8	dc	♘bc6	♕xa5	♕c7⁶²	
23	...	...	...	...	...	...	...	♘f3	♗b5	∞/=
	...	...	...	...	...	...	♘d7	♕c7	a6⁶³	
24	...	...	...	...	...	...	...	f4	♘f3	∞
	...	...	...	...	...	...	...	♕xa5	♘f8⁶⁴	

²⁶ **5 ♕g4** ♘f5 (5 ... c5! – 4 ... c5 5 a3 ♗xc3+
6 bc ♘e7 7 ♕g4) 6 ♘f3! ♘c6 (6 ... c5 7 dc!)
7 ♗d3 h5 8 ♕f4 ♘ce7 9 ♘h4 (9 a3 ♗xc3+ –
4 ... c5 5 a3 ♗xc3+ 6 bc ♘e7 7 ♕g4 ♘f5 8 ♗d3
h5) 9 ... ♘g6 10 ♕xg6 fg (Pushkar-Sakharov,
Ukraine Ch 1964) 11 ♗xf5!? ∞.

5 ♗d2 b6 6 ♘f3 ♕d7 – 4 ... ♕d7.
²⁷ 5 ... c5! – 4 ... c5.
²⁸ 9 ... ♗a6 10 ♗xa6 ♘xa6 11 ♗g5 ♕d7
12 a4 ± Ivkov-Byrne, Havana Ol 1966.
²⁹ 13 ♗xa6 ♘xa6 14 ♕d3 ♘b8 15 ♖xh5! ♖xh5
16 gh ♔d7 17 c4! ± Matulović-Antoshin,
Yugoslavia v USSR 1964.
³⁰ **5 ♗d2** b6 6 ♘f3 ♗a6 7 ♗xa6 ♘xa6 8 0-0
♘b8 9 ♘e2 ± Geller-Karpov, USSR Ch 1976.
6 ... c6 7 ♗e2 ♗a6 8 0-0 ♘e7 9 ♗xa6 ♘xa6
10 ♘e2 ♗xd2 11 ♕xd2 c5 = Hartston-Timman,
Teesside 1975.

5 ♘e2 f6!? Szabo-Seirawan, Lone Pine 1977.
³¹ **7 ♗d2** ♗a6 8 ♗xa6 ♘xa6 9 ♕d3 ♘b8 10 a3
♗f8!

7 h4 ♗b7 8 ♗d3 ♘c6 9 ♘e2 0-0-0 =
Olafsson-Petrosian, Bled 1961.
³² **8 ♘h3** ♘c6 9 ♗e3 ♗b7 10 ♘f4 ±.

8 ♗d3 ♗a6 9 ♘ge2 ± Keres.
³³ 13 ♘g5 ♖df8 = Nyman-Lundquist, corr.
1963.
³⁴ 7 ... ♘e7 8 a4 ♗a6 9 ♗xa6 ♘xa6 10 0-0
♘b8 =/∓ Karpov-Seirawan, Mar del Plata 1982.
³⁵ 15 ♗b2 b5!! ∞/∓.
³⁶ 12 ♘f3 ♘c6 13 c4 ♘a5 14 cd ♕xd5 15 0-0 h6
16 ♗d2 ♘c4 17 ♖ab1 c6 = Smailbegović-Ivkov,
Sarajevo 1962.
³⁷ 15 g4 0-0-0 16 gf ♘xf5! 17 ♕xg6 ♖hg8 18 h5
♘a5 = Razuvayev-Lebredo, Cienfuegos 1975.
³⁸ 10 ... ♘b8 11 ♘f4 intending ♘xe6, ♕xg7.
³⁹ 15 ♗xe7 ♔xe7 16 cd ♔f7 17 c3 ±
Sveshnikov-Gulko, USSR Ch 1976.
⁴⁰ 9 b4 c5!
⁴¹ 13 ♘e3 ♕xe2+ 14 ♔xe2 ♘g6 15 g3 =.
⁴² 13 f4 f5 = Ivanović-Planinc, Yugoslav Ch
1978.
⁴³ 6 ♘f3 ♘e7 7 ♗d3 ♘bc6 8 0-0 ♗b7 9 ♗d2
♕d7 10 b4 ♘g6 11 ♖e1 0-0-0 = Nedeljković-
Petrosian, Vienna 1957.
⁴⁴ **12 ♘d1?!** c5 ∓ Kupper-Petrosian, Venice
1967.

12 ♘e2! ±.
⁴⁵ **6 ♘f3** ♕d7 7 a4 (7 ♗b5 c6 8 ♗d3 ♗a6

9 h4 ± Honfi-Lebredo, Cienfuegos 1976)
7 ... ♘c6 (7 ... ♗a6 8 ♘b5 ♘e7 9 ♗e2 ♘f5 10 0-0
c6 = Postnikova-Skegina, Moscow 1966) 8 ♗d2
(8 ♗e2 ♘b4!?) 8 ... ♘ge7 9 ♗e2 ♘f5 = Tal-
Petrosian, USSR Ch 1977.

6 a4 ♗a6 7 ♘b5 ♕d7 8 ♗e2 ♗b7 9 b3
a6 10 ♘a3 c5 11 c3 ♘c6 12 ♘f3 (Ljubojević-
Andersson, Hilversum 1973) 12 ... cd 13 cd
♘b4 =.

6 ♘h3 ♕d7 7 ♘f4 g6 =/∞.

6 h4 ♗a6 7 ♖h3 ♗xf1 8 ♔xf1 ♕d7 =.
⁴⁶ **7 f4** ♗a6 8 ♗xa6 ♘xa6 =.

7 ♘f3 ♗a6 8 ♗xa6 ♘xa6 9 0-0 h6! 10 ♗f4
♘e7 11 ♖fd1 0-0-0 12 ♘e1 (Moe-Cuartas,
Siegen Ol 1970) 12 ... ♔b7! =.
⁴⁷ 13 ♗xh6 ♖xh6 14 g4 ♗f8! 15 g5 = Shatskes-
Shashin, Moscow Ch 1965.
⁴⁸ Bogoljubow Variation.
⁴⁹ 5 ... ♘e7 6 a3 ♗xc3 7 ♗xc3 ♘bc6 8 ♘f3 cd
9 ♗xd4 a5 = Uhlmann. 6 ♘b5 ♗xd2+
7 ♕xd2 0-0 8 ♘f3 (8 ♘d6?! cd! 9 ♘f3 ♘bc6
10 ♘xd4 f6! ∓; 8 dc!? ♕d7 9 f4 ♘xc5 10 ♗d3
♕b6 11 0-0 ♘c6! =) 8 ... a6 9 ♘c3 cd 10 ♘xd4
♘bc6 11 f4 ♘xd4 12 ♕xd4 ♘c6 = Omari-Golz,
Leipzig Ol 1960.
⁵⁰ 8 ♘d6+ ♔f8 9 0-0-0 ♘c6 10 f4 f6 ∓ Moles.
⁵¹ **13 0-0** ♗d7 = Aronin-Petrosian, USSR Ch
preliminaries 1949.

13 0-0-0 ♗d7 14 ♔b1 ♗e8 = Michel-
Trifunović, Mar del Plata 1952.
⁵² Soltis.
⁵³ 6 ♕g4 – 5 ♕g4.
⁵⁴ Pachman.
⁵⁵ Mednis.
⁵⁶ Swiss Variation.
⁵⁷ 6 ♗d2 ♘c6 7 ♘b5 ♗xd2+ 8 ♕xd2 ♘xd4
9 ♘xd4 cd 10 ♘f3 ♘e7 (Fuchs-Golz, 1962)
11 ♕xd4 0-0 12 ♗d3 ♘c6 13 ♕e3 f5 14 0-0 ♗d7
15 c4 ± Uhlmann.
⁵⁸ 9 ♘f3! ♘g6 ∞.
⁵⁹ 11 ♘f3 ♘xe5 12 ♗e2 ♘xf3+ 13 ♗xf3 ♕xc5
∓. 12 ♕h5 ♘xf3+ 13 ♔xf3 ♗d7 14 ♗f4 e5 ∞.
⁶⁰ 8 ♘b5 ♗c7 9 ♕xg7 ♖g8 10 ♕xh7 ±
Timman-Hug, Nice Ol 1974.
⁶¹ 12 ♘g5!? (Fischer) ♖f8 13 f4 ♗d7 ∞/±.
⁶² 13 ♗f4 ♗d7 14 ♗g3 0-0 15 ♗d3 ♖df8 =.
⁶³ 13 ♗xd7+ ♗xd7 14 0-0 d4! ∞/=.
⁶⁴ 13 ♕d3 ♗d7 14 ♗g5 ♘f5! 15 g4 ♘h6 16 h3
0-0-0 ∞ Ježek-Olexa, Czechoslovakia 1954.

205

	6	7	8	9	10	11	12	13	14	
1	...	♕g4	♕xg7	♕xh7	f4	♖b1[2]	♘f3	♗g5	♗xa6	±
	♘c6	♘ge7	♖g8	cd[1]	♕a5	b6	♗a6	♖f8	♕xa6[3]	
2	...	♗d2	♕g4	♕d1	h4	h5	♖h4	♗xa6	♖f4![4]	±
	♕a5	♕a4	♔f8	b6	♘e7	h6	♗a6	♘xa6		
3	...	♕g4	♘f3[6]	♗e2	0-0	♕h3	a4	♗a3	a5	∓
	♕c7	f6![5]	c4!	♘c6	♕f7	♘ge7	♗d7	0-0-0	h5[7]	
4	...	♘f3	a4	♗e2	ef	c4!	0-0	dc!	♗xc4[10]	±
	...	♘d7[8]	♘e7	f6[9]	gf	0-0	dc	♘xc5		
5	...	...	♕d2	a4	ef	♗e2	♕h6[11]	♘h4	♗h5	=
	...	♘e7	♘bc6	f6	gf	c4	♘g6	♖g8	♕g7[12]	
6	...	...	♗e2	a4[13]	♗xa6	0-0	a5!	♗a3	♕e2	=
	...	...	b6	♗a6	♘xa6	♘b8	ba!	♘d7	0-0[14]	
7	...	...	a4	♗a3	cd	♕d2	♔xd2[16]			=
	...	...	♘bc6[15]	cd!	♕a5+	♕xd2				
8	...	♘f3	♗d3[17]	0-0[18]	♗e2	♖e1	♗f1	♕d2		∓
	♘e7	♗d7	♗a4!	c4	♘bc6	h6	♕a5	0-0-0[19]		
9	...	...	a4	♗d3	0-0	♗e2	♗d2	♖b1	♖a1	=
	...	♘bc6	♗d7	♕a5	c4	♕xc3	♕b2[20]	♕a3	♕b2	
10	...	...	♗d2	♘g5	♘h3	♘f4	♘h5	♗e2[22]	0-0	±
	♕a5	c4?![21]	h6	♗d7	♗a4	♖g8		♘d7	0-0-0[23]	
11	...	a4	♘f3	♕d2	♗d3[25]	ef	dc	c4!	♗xc4	=
	...	♘bc6	♕a5	♗d7[24]	f6	gf	e5	dc	0-0-0[26]	
12	...	...	...	♗d2	♗e2	0-0[29]	♖e1	ef	♗f1	=
	...	...	...	♗d7[27]	c4[28]	0-0-0[30]	f5	gf	♘xf5[31]	
13	...	♕g4	♘f3	♗d3	ef[32]	♗g5	♕h4	0-0	♗xe7!	±
	...	0-0!?	♘bc6	f5	♖xf6	♖f7!	h6	c4		
14	...	...	♗d3	♕f4!	cd	♕xh4	♗g5!	♘e2	c3[33]	±
	...	♘f5	h5	cd	♕h4	♘xh4	♘f5	♘c6		
15	...	...	♕xg7	♕xh7	♘e2!	♘g3	♘h5	f4[34]		±
	...	cd	♖g8	♕a5	dc	♘d7	d4			

	9	10	11	12	13	14	15	16	17	
16	♕xh7	♕d3	♘e2	♗f4	♕xe4	cd	♗g3			=
	cd	♕xe5+	♘bc6	♕e4	de	♘d5!	♘a5			
17	...	♔d1	♘f3	♘g5	f4	fg	h4!	h5	♗b5+	∞/=
	...	♘bc6[35]	dc	♘xe5[36]	♖xg5!?[37]	♘5g6	e5	♘f8	♘c6[38]	
18	...	♘e2	♗f4	♖b1	h4	♕d3	♗g5	♕xc3	♘d4	=
	...	♘bc6	♗d7	dc	0-0-0	♘g6	♘gxe5	♖df8	♘xd4[39]	
19	...	...	f4	h3[40]	g4	♕d3	♖b1	fe	♖g1	∞
	...	...	♗d7	dc	0-0-0	d4	♘xe5!	♗c6	♘g6[41]	

1   9 ... ♕c7 10 ♕d3 cd 11 cd ♘xe5 ∞.
2   11 ♘e2 dc 12 ♕d3 ♘b4.
3   15 ♕h5 ± Kunz-Boch, corr. 1959.
4   Fischer-Hook, Siegen Ol 1970.
5   7 ... f5?! 8 ♕g3 cd 9 cd ♘e7 10 ♗d2 0-0
11 ♗d3 b6 12 ♘e2 ♗a6 13 ♘f4 ♕d7 14 h4 ♗xd3
15 ♕xd3 ♖c8 16 ♖h3 ♖c4! = Konstantinopolsky-
Smith, corr. 1960.
6   8 ♗b5+!? ♔f8!? ∞.
7   Matulović-Byrne, Sousse IZ 1967.
8   7 ... ♗d7 8 a4 ♘e7 (8 ... ♘c6 9 ♗d3 cd
10 cd ♘xd4 11 0-0 ♘xf3+ 12 ♕xf3 ±
Shamkovich-Hasin, USSR 1962) 9 ♗e2 ♘bc6
10 0-0 f6 11 ef gf 12 c4 0-0-0 13 ♗a3 ± Gufeld-
Bagirov, USSR 1960 and Liberzon-Panchenko,
USSR 1972.
9   9 ... cd 10 cd ♘b6!? Moles.
10   Rakić-Lengyel, Belgrade v Budapest 1957.
11   12 0-0/12 ♘h4 =.
12   15 ♕e3 ♘ce7 = Smyslov-Bondarevsky,
Pärnu 1948.
13   9 0-0 ♗a6 10 ♗xa6 ♘xa6 11 a4 = Liberzon-
Bronstein, USSR 1966.   11 ♕e2!?
14   15 ♖fe1 ♖fc8 =.
15   8 ... b6 9 ♗b5+ ♗d7 10 ♗d3 ♘bc6 11 0-0 h6
12 ♖e1 0-0 13 ♗d2 (13 ♗xh6?? gh! 14 ♕d2 ♔g7
15 ♕f4 ♘g8! 16 ♖e3 ♘3e7 17 ♘h4 ♘g6 18 ♖g3
♗e8 19 ♖e1 c4! = Sutton-Moles, Skopje Ol
1972) 13 ... c4 14 ♗f1 f6 = Moles.   12 ♗a3
♘a5 13 dc bc 14 ♘d2 0-0 15 ♘b3 ♘xb3 16 cb
f6! ∞.
16   Schwarz.
17   8 a4 – 7 a4.
18   9 dc!? Farago.
19   Gutierrez-Farago, Kikinda 1978.
20   With a draw.
21   8 ... ♘bc6 9 g3! ± Sigurjonsson-Watson,
New York 1977.
    8 ... ♗d7 9 a4 – 7 a4.
22   13 g4 ♘d7! 14 f4 0-0-0 15 ♗h3 f5! =
Tarnowski-Ivkov, Varna Ol 1962.
23   15 ♗g4 ±.
24   9 ... 0-0 10 ♗d3 b6 11 ♗a3 ♗a6 12 ♗xa6
♕xa6 = Kostro-Kanko, Budapest 1959.
    9 ... f6 10 ef gf 11 ♗a3 =.
25   10 ♗e2 f6 11 ef gf 12 dc 0-0-0 13 0-0 e5
14 ♗a3 ♖hg8 15 ♖fb1 ♘g6 16 g3 = Hartston-

Hutchings, Swansea 1972.
26   15 0-0 ♖xc5 16 ♗b3 e4!? (16 ... ♘f5 =) 17
♗a3 ♕h5 ∞ Weiner-Emmerich, corr. 1970/73.
27   9 ... c4 10 g3 ♗d7 11 ♗h3 0-0-0 12 0-0 h6
13 ♘h4 ± Ratsch-Liebert, Berlin 1962.
28   10 ... f6 11 c4 (11 ef!? Hartoch) 11 ... ♕c7
12 cd ♘xd5 13 c4 ♘de7 14 ef gf 15 dc 0-0-0
16 ♗c3 e5! = Timman-Korchnoi, match (3)
1976.
    10 ... 0-0 11 0-0 ♕c7 12 ♖e1 h6 13 ♕c1! f6
14 ef ♖xf6 15 ♕a3 ± Timman.
29   11 ♘g5 h6 (11 ... 0-0 12 0-0 f6 13 ef ♖xf6
14 ♗g4 ± Timman-Uhlmann, Skopje 1976;
11 ... f6?? 12 ♗h5+! ♘g6 13 ♘xh7 ±±) 12 ♘h3
0-0-0 13 ♘f4 g6 14 0-0 ♔b8 15 ♕e1 ♘c8 16
♗c1 ♘b6 17 ♗a3 ± Liberzon-van den Broeck,
Reykjavik 1975.
30   11 ... f6 12 ♖e1 fe (12 ... 0-0 13 ♕b1! ±
Ciocaltea-Grizov, Israel 1975) 13 ♘xe5 0-0 14
♗f1 ♖ae8 15 f3 ♘c8 16 ♕e2 ♘b6 17 ♖eb1 ∞
Ciocaltea.
31   Suetin-Uhlmann, W Germany v Byelorussia
1967.
32   10 ♕g3 ♕a5 11 ♗d2 cd 12 cd ♕a4! =
Klovan-Vaganian, Aktiubinsk 1970.
33   Yanofsky-Uhlmann, Stockholm IZ 1962.
34   Timman-Korchnoi, match (5) 1976.
35   10 ... ♘d7 11 ♘f3 ♘xe5 (11 ... dc!?) 12 ♗f4
♕xc3 13 ♘xe5 ♕xa1+ 14 ♗c1 ♖f8 15 ♗d3!
♗d7 16 ♔e2! 0-0-0 17 ♘xf7 ♖xf7 18 ♕xf7 ♖e8
19 ♖e1 e5 20 ♔f1 e4 21 ♗e2 ♕c3 22 ♗g5 ♕xa3
(Matulovic-Jahr, Reggio Emilia 1974) 23 ♖d1! ±.
36   12 ... ♖f8? 13 f4 ♗d7 14 ♗d3! ±.
    12 ... ♕xe5 (Korchnoi) 13 ♕xf7+ ♔d7
14 h4 ± or 14 f4 ±.
37   13 ... f6 14 ♗b5+ ♗d7 (14 ... ♔d8 Euwe)
15 ♘xe6 ♕b6 ∞.   14 fe fg 15 ♕h5+ ♔d8! =.
38   18 ♕g7 ♗g4+ 19 ♔e1 0-0-0 20 ♕xc6 ♕xc6
21 h6 d4 22 ♔f2 ♗f5 23 h7 ∞/=.
39   18 ♕xd4 = Bakali-Uhlmann, Lugano Ol
1968.
40   12 g3 0-0-0 13 ♕d3 dc 14 ♘xc3 a6 15 ♖b1
♘a5 16 ♗g2 = Hartmann-Golz, Leipzig Ol
1960.
    12 ♖b1 dc 13 ♕d3 – 12 ♕d3 dc 13 ♖b1.
41   Byrne-Uhlmann, Monte Carlo 1968.
    18 ♕g3! ♗e4! Larsen.

207

	9	10	11	12	13	14	15	16	17	
20	...	...	...	Qd3	Ng3[42]	Be2	Nxf5	0-0	Bf3	=
	...	...	...	dc	0-0-0	Nf5	ef	d4	Be6[43]	
21	...	...	...	...	Qxc3	Rb1!	Qc4	Bd2	Rxb7	=
	...	...	...	...	Nf5	d4[44]	Qa5+	Qxa3	Ne3![45]	
22	...	...	...	...	Nxc3	Rb1	h4	Rh3	h5	∞
	...	...	...	...	a6[46]	Na5![47]	Nf5	0-0-0	Nc4[48]	
23	...	...	...	...	h4	h5[49]	h6	h7	Rb1	∞
	...	...	...	...	Nf5	0-0-0	Rg6	Rh8	d4[50]	
24	...	...	...	...	Rb1	h3!	g4	Qh7!	Kf2	±
	...	...	...	...	Nf5	d4	Nh4	Nf3+	0-0-0[51]	
25	...	...	...	...	...	Nxd4	Qxd4	Qf2	Rb4[52]	±
	...	...	...	...	d4	Nxd4	Nf5	Qc6!	Qd5[53]	
26	...	...	...	...	...	Nxc3	Nb5	Rxb5		∞/=
	...	...	...	...	0-0-0	Na5	Bxb5			
27	...	...	...	...	...	Qxc3	Rg1!	g4	ef	±
	...	...	...	...	...	Nf5	f6	Nh6	Rxg4[54]	

[42]   13 Be3?! d4!? (13 ... Nf5!?) 14 Bf2 0-0-0 15 Nxd4 Nxd4 16 Qxd4 b6 (16 ... Bc6 17 Qxa7 Rd2 18 Bb6 Qb8 ∞ Keene) 17 Bh4 Bb5 18 Qe4 Bxf1 (Spassky-Korchnoi, 2nd match game 1977) 19 Qa8+ Kd7 20 0-0-0+ Nd5 21 Rxd5+ ed 22 Qxd5+ Kc8 23 Qa8+ = Keene.

[43]   Burnevsky-Zagorovsky, Russian Z 1969.

[44]   14 ... 0-0-0 - row 27.

[45]   Portisch.
18 Bxe3 de 19 Qc3 Qxc3+ 20 Nxc3 Nd4 21 Ne4 Bc6 22 Nd6+ Kd8 23 Nxf7+ =.

[46]   13 ... Nf5!? 14 Rb1 N3d4 ∞ Moles.

[47]   14 ... Rc8 15 h4! (Schmidt) Nf5 16 Rh3 ±.

[48]   17 ... Rg4?! 18 Qf3! Moles.
17 ... Nc4 18 Rb4 b5!? intending ... Qc5, ... Bc6, ... a5 ∞ Moles.   18 ... Bc6 19 Ne2 ±

Hort-Uhlmann, Hastings 1970/71.

[49]   14 Qxc3 Rac8!? 15 Ra2 N3d4 16 Qxc7 Rxc7 17 Nxd4 Nxd4 18 Kf2 Ba4 = Zagorovsky-Ruttner, corr. 1968/71.

[50]   17 ... f6 18 ef Be8 ∞/±.
17 ... d4 18 Rb5 (intending Qh3, g4) ∞.

[51]   18 Kxf3 Nxe5+ ±.

[52]   17 Rg1 Qe4+ 18 Qe2 Qd4 19 Qf2 Qe4+ 20 Qe2 =.

[53]   18 Rg1 Bc6 19 Bd3 Rd8 20 Rc4! Rh8 21 h3 Nh4 22 Rc5 Qa2 23 Rxc3 Qa1 24 Kd2 Nf5 (Matanović-Rolland, Le Havre 1966) 25 Qxa7!? / 25 g4!?

[54]   18 Be3 Rxg1 19 Bxg1 Nf5 20 Rd1! Rf8 21 Qd3 (Mecking-Uhlmann, Manila IZ 1976) 21 ... Nd6 intending ... Ne4 ± Minić.

	3	4	5	6	7	8	9	10	11	
1	...	♘gf3	e5	♗d3	c3	0-0	dc	♗c2	♘b3	±
	♗e7[1]	♘f6[2]	♘fd7	c5	♘c6	♕b6	♘xc5	a5	♕c7[3]	
2	...	♘gf3[5]	e5	♗b5	0-0	♗d3	c3	♗c2		∞/±
	♘c6[4]	♘f6	♘d7[6]	a5	♘a7	c5	c4	b5		
3	...	...	...	♗e2	ef	♘f1	♘e3	0-0	h3	=
	...	...	...	f6	♕xf6	♗d6	0-0	♔h8!?	♕g6[7]	
4	...	...	...	♗d3	♘g5	de	♕h5+	♗xg6+	f4	∞
	...	...	...	f6	♘dxe5![8]	fg	g6!	♔d7	gf[9]	
5	...	...	...	♘b3	a4[11]	h4[13]				±
	...	...	...	a5[10]	b6[12]					
6		e5	f4	c3	♘df3	g3	♗h3![18]	♘e2[19]		±
	♘f6	♘fd7[14]	c5[15]	♘c6[16]	♕b6[17]	♗e7	0-0			

[1] 3 ... b6 4 ♘gf3 ♗a6!? 5 ♗xa6 ♘xa6 6 c3! ±.
3 ... ♘e7 4 ♘gf3 ♗g6 5 h4! h5 6 g3 c5 7 ♗g2 ♘c6 8 c3 ± Matanović-Garcia, Banja Luka 1979.
3 ... g6 4 ♘gf3 ♘e7 5 h4! h6 6 h5 ± Geller-Makarov, Ukraine Ch 1959.
3 ... ♘d7 4 ♘gf3 ♘gf6 5 e5 ♘g8 6 ♗d3 c5 7 c4! ± Bolěslavsky-Goldenov, USSR 1955.
3 ... f5 4 ef ef 5 ♗d3 ♗d6 6 ♘df3 ♘f6 7 ♘e2 ±.
[2] 4 ... de – Rubinstein Variation.
[3] 12 ♖e1 ♘xb3 13 ab ± Keene/Taulbut.
[4] Guimard Variation.
[5] 4 c3 e5 5 de ♘xe5 6 ♘gf3 ♘xf3+ 7 ♕xf3 ± Pachman.
[6] 5 ... ♘e4 6 c3 ♘xd2 7 ♗xd2 b6 8 ♗d3 h6 9 b4 ♗b7 10 a4 a5 11 ♖b1 ± Keene/Taulbut.
[7] 12 ♗d3 ♕h5 13 ♗e2 ♕g6 ½-½ Radulov-Ivkov, Malta Ol 1980.
[8] 7 ... fg?! 8 ♕h5+ g6 9 ♗xg6+! hg 10 ♕xg6+ ♔e7 11 ♘e4!! ± Chiburdanidze-Zatulovskaya, Tbilisi Z 1976.
[9] 12 ♗d3 ♘b4 ∞ Faibisovich-Monin, USSR 1979.
[10] 6 ... ♗e7 7 h4 h6 8 ♗f4 ♘cb8 9 ♖h3 ± Shamkovich-Mednis, Cleveland 1975.
6 ... f6 7 ♗b5 fe 8 de ♗e7 9 ♗f4 ± Pachman-De Ruyter, Hilversum 1947.
[11] 7 ♗f4!? Keene/Taulbut.
[12] 7 ... ♗e7 8 ♗b5 ♘cb8 9 h4! h6 10 c3 b6 11 h5 ± Delaune-Seirawan, USA 1979.
[13] Pytel.

8 c3 ♗e7 9 ♗d3 ♗a6 10 ♗xa6 ♖xa6 11 0-0 ♖a8 = Hübner-Larsen, Montreal 1979.
8 ♗f4 ♗e7 9 c3 ± Kupreichik-Böhm, Polanica Zdroj 1981.
[14] 4 ... ♘g8 5 ♗d3 c5 6 c3 ♘c6 7 ♘e2 ♗d7 8 0-0 ♕c7 9 ♘f3 c4 10 ♗c2 h6 11 ♖e1 0-0-0 12 b3 ± Stein-Bagirov, USSR Ch 1963.
4 ... ♘e4 5 ♘xe4?! de 6 ♗e3 c5 7 dc ♘d7 8 ♕g4 ♘xc5 9 ♗xc5 ♗xc5 10 ♕xg7 ♕a5+ 11 c3 ♖f8 12 ♘e2 ♗d7 13 ♕f6 ♗a4 14 ♘g3 (Tringov-Bednarski, Varna 1972) 14 ... ♗a3! 15 ♖b1 ♖d8! ∓ Pytel. 9 ♗b5+ ♘d7 10 ♘e2 ♕a5+ 11 ♘c3 a6 12 ♗xd7+ ♗xd7 13 ♗d4 ♗c6 ∞ A.Ivanov-Malanyuk, USSR 1981. 5-♗d3 ♘xd2 6 ♗xd2 c5 7 dc ♘d7 8 ♘f3 ♘xc5 9 0-0 ± Tan-Hug, Petropolis IZ 1973.
[15] 5 ... b6 6 ♘df3 ♗a6 7 ♘e2 ♘c6 8 g4! ± Gipslis-Taimanov, USSR 1972.
[16] 6 ... b6 7 ♘df3 ♗a6 8 ♗xa6 ♘xa6 9 f5! ± Matanović-Panno, Yugoslav Ch 1962.
6 ... f5 7 ♘df3 ♗e7 8 h4 h5 9 ♘g5 ♘f8 10 ♗e3 ± Westerinen-Keene, Alicante 1975.
[17] 7 ... f5 8 ♗d3 ♗e7 9 ♘e2 0-0 10 h3 a5 11 g4 ± Inkiov-Ambrož, Herculana Z 1982.
7 ... ♗e7 8 ♗d3 ♕a5 9 ♗d2 ♕b6 10 ♘e2 = Keres.
7 ... ♕a5 8 dc!? ♕xc5 9 ♗d3 ♗e7 10 ♘e2 ♕b6 11 ♘ed4 ♘xd4 12 ♘xd4 ± Minić-Yudovich, Zagreb 1970.
[18] 9 ♘e2 cd! 10 cd f6 ∞ Liberzon-Uhlmann, Liepzig 1965.
[19] Sznapik-Farago, Herculana Z 1982.

1 e4 e6 2 d4 d5 3 ♞d2 ♞f6 4 e5 ♞fd7 5 f4 c5 6 c3 ♞c6 7 ♞df3 cd 8 cd

	8	9	10	11	12	13	14	15	16	
1	...	g3!	♔f2	♔g2	♝d3	♞e2	h3	g4[1]		±
	♛b6	♝b4+	f5	♛d8	♞b6	♝d7	♝e7	g6		
2	...	...	♝h3	fe	♔f1	♔g2![2]	de	♝f4		∞
	...	f6	fe	♝b4+	0-0!?	♞dxe5	♞xe5	♞c4[3]		
3	...	...	♝d3!	fe	♔f1	♔g2![4]				±
	...	...	fe	♝b4+	0-0					
4	...	g4!	gh	♞e2	♞g3	h4!	h5	♞xh5		±
	♞b6[5]	h5	♜xh5	g6	♜h8	♝e7	gh			
5	...	♝d3	♞e2	0-0	a3	b3	♔h1	♜g1	♝b2	±
	h5	♞b6	♝d7	a5!	♝e7	g6	♔f8	♔g7[6]		

1 e4 e6 2 d4 d5 3 ♞d2 ♞f6 4 e5 ♞fd7 5 ♝d3 c5 6 c3 ♞c6 7 ♞e2[7]

	7	8	9	10	11	12	13	14	15	
6	...	0-0	cd	♞f3	♝g5[8]	h4	♝xe7			±
	a5!?	cd	a4	♞b6	♝e7	♞b4!				
7	...	...	...	♞f3	♝d2	♜e1	♝b1			=
	...	...	♞b6	♝d7	♝e7	♞b4	♞c4[9]			
8	...	cd	0-0	♞f3	♞f4	h3[11]				=
	cd	♞b6	♝d7[10]	♝e7	♜c8	g6!				
9	...	...	...	f4	♞f3	♔h1	♝b1	♜g1	♛xe2	±
	...	...	...	g6!	h5	♞b4	♝b5	♝xe2	♛c7[12]	
10	...	...	...	a3	b3[13]	b4	f4	g4	f5	∞
	...	...	...	a5	a4	♝e7	g6![14]	h5	ef[15]	
11	...	...	♞f4	♛h5+	ef+![16]	♞g6+	♛xh8	0-0	♞b3	∞
	...	f6	♞xd4	♔e7	♞xf6	hg	♔f7	e5	♞f5[17]	
12	...	...	ef	♞f3	♝d2	♛xd2	0-0	de	♞xe5	±
	...	...	♛xf6	♝b4+	♝xd2+	0-0	e5	♞dxe5	♞xe5[18]	
13	...	...	...	♞f3	0-0	♞c3	♝g5	♝h4		∞
	...	...	♞xf6	♝d6[19]	♛c7	a6	0-0	♝d7[20]		
14	...	...	...	...	...	♝g5	♝h4	de	♞xe5	=
	...	...	...	...	...	0-0	e5	♞xe5	♝xe5[21]	
15	...	...	♞f3	♞c3!?	de	♝e3	♞b5	♔f1	♜b1	∞
	...	♛b6	f6	fe	g6	♛xb2[22]	♝b4+	0-0	♛xa2[23]	

1 e4 e6 2 d4 d5 3 Nd2 Nf6 4 e5 Nfd7 5 Bd3 c5
6 c3 Nc6 7 Ne2 cd 8 cd Qb6 9 Nf3 f6 10 ef Nxf6

	11	12	13	14	15	16	17	18	19	
16	0-0	Nf4[24]	Re1	Be3![25]	g3	Rc1	Ng5!	Nf3	Ng6[28]	±
	Bd6	0-0	Bd7	Qc7[26]	Rae8	Qb8	h6	Ne4[27]		
17	...	Nc3	Be3	a3	h3[31]	Re1	Rc1	Rc2	Rce2	±
	...	0-0[29]	Bd7[30]	Qd8	Rc8	Kh8	Qe8	a6	Rc7[32]	

---

[1] Liberzon-Uhlmann, Leipzig 1965.
[2] 13 Bxe6+ Kh8 intending ... Ndxe5!
[3] Intending Rxf4.
[4] Intending 13 ... Nxd4?! 14 Nxd4 Nxe5 ± Medina-Keene, Torremolinos 1976.
[5] 8 ... a5!?
[6] Balinas-Lim Kok Ann, Manila 1968.
[7] 7 Ngf3 Qb6 8 0-0 cd 9 cd Nxd4 10 Nxd4 Qxd4 11 Nf3 Qb6 12 Qa4 Qb4 13 Qc2 Qc5 14 Qe2 Be7 15 Be3 ∞.
[8] 11 Nc3 Bb4! 12 Be2 Bd7 13 h4 Be7 14 h5 (Balashov-Bukal, Karlovac 1979) 14 ... h6! ±.
[9] Bajović-Enklaar, Hastings II 1980/81.
[10] 9 ... a5 – row 7.
[11] 12 Nh5 g6 13 Nf6+ Bxf6 14 ef Qxf6 15 Bg5 Qg7 ∓.
[12] 16 a3 ± Matanović-Wade, Stockholm 1952.
[13] 11 Nf3 Be7 12 Ng3 h5! =.
[14] 13 ... f5 14 ef Bxf6 ± Ivkov-Hecht, Vrsac 1973.
[15] 16 gf Bxf5 17 Bxf5 gf 18 Rxf5 Qd7 ∞ Keene/Taulbut.
[16] 11 Ng6+ hg 12 ef+ Kxf6 13 Qxh8 Kf7 14 0-0 Nc5 ∓ Barle-Portisch, Portorož 1973.
[17] 16 Bg5 Qb6 17 Rac1 (Belyavsky-Cuartas, Bogota 1979) 17 ... a5! ∞ Keene/Taulbut.
[18] 16 Nd4 ± Trifunović-Matanović, Belgrade 1954.
[19] 10 ... Qb6 – 8 ... Qb6.
[20] 14 ... g6!? 15 Bg3 Bxg3 16 hg Qg7! 17 Qd2 (17 Na4!?) 17 ... Ng4 18 Rac1 (18 Rad1) 18 ... Rxf3! 19 gf Nxd4 ∓ Weinstein-Bradford, Lone Pine 1979.
   14 ... Bd7 15 Qe1 Kh8 16 Rc1 Bf4 17 Bg3 Nh5 18 Bxf4?! (18 Rc2) 18 ... Qxf4 19 Bb1

(Matulović-Marjanović, Yugoslav Ch 1979) 19 ... g5! ∞.
[21] 16 Bg3 Bxg3 17 Nxg3 Qb6 18 Qd2 Bd7 19 Rad1 Rad8 = Radulov-Vaganian, Leningrad 1977.
[22] 12 ... Qa5 13 Bd2 Ndxe5 (13 ... Bg7! ∞) 14 Bxe5 Nxe5 15 Bb5+ Bd7 16 Qe2! Bg7! 17 f4! ± Shamkovich-Watson, USA 1976.
   12 ... Bc5!?
[23] 16 Nc7 Rb8 17 Nxe6 Rxf3 18 Rxf3 Ndxe5 (18 ... Ncxe5 19 Qe2 Qxe2 20 Bxe2 ±) 19 Qf6 Bxe6 20 Qxe6+ Kg7 21 Bd4 ±.
[24] 12 b3 0-0 13 Bb2 Bd7 14 Ng3 Kh8 15 Rb1 a5 = Florian-Uhlmann, Balatonfüred 1959.
   12 Ng3 0-0 13 Re1 Kh8! =.
   12 Bd2 0-0 13 Bc3 Bd7 14 Qd2 =.
   12 Rb1 0-0 13 Bf4 Nxd4! =.
[25] 13 Nxe6 Rfe8 14 Bf5 Bb4! 15 Bd2 Bxd2 16 Qxd2 Ne7 17 Bxg7! Kxg7 18 Qg5+ Kg6 19 Bxd7 Nxd7 20 h4 ∞.
[26] 13 ... Ne4!? 14 g3 (14 Bxe4 Bxf4 15 Bc2 Qc7 =) 14 ... Qxb2 15 Rb1 Qxa2 16 Ne2!? ∞.
[27] 17 ... Ng4 18 Ng6!
[28] Georgiev-Farago, Dubna 1979.
[29] 12 ... Bd7 13 Be3 0-0-0 14 Nb5 ±.
[30] 12 ... Qxb2 13 Nb5 ±.
   12 ... Ng4 13 Bxh7+ ±.
   12 ... Qd8 13 Bg5 Bd7 14 Re1 Qb8 15 Bh4 a6 16 Rc1 b5 17 Bb1 Bf4 18 Bg3 ± Karpov-Hort, Budapest 1973.
[31] 14 b4!? e5? (14 ... Rc8) 15 Nxd5! Nxd5 16 Bc4 Be6 17 Ng5 ed (Grünfeld-Watson, Gausdal 1980) 18 Nxe6! (Grünfeld) Bxh2+ 19 Kh1 Qd6 20 Nxf8 ±.
[32] 19 Bb1 ± Geller-Uhlmann, Skopje 1968.

	4	5	6	7	8	9	10	11	12	
1	dc	Nb3[1]	ed	Bb5+	Bxd7+	c4	c5			=
	Bxc5	Bb6	Nf6[2]	Bd7	Qxd7	ed	Bc7[3]			
2	Ngf3	Bb5	e5	dc	0-0	Re1	Bxc6	Nb3	ef	±
	Nc6[4]	Bd6[5]	Bb8	Ne7	0-0	Ng6	bc	f6	Qxf6[6]	
3	...	...	Nxd4	Nxc6	Bd3	Qe2	Nf3	0-0	Re1	±
	...	cd	Bd7	bc	Qc7	Ne7	Ng6	Bd6	Rb8[7]	
4	ed	Ngf3	Bc4	0-0	Nb3	Nbxd4	Nxd4	Bb3	c3	±
	Qxd5	cd	Qd6[8]	Nf6	Nc6	Nxd4	a6[9]	Be7	0-0[10]	
5	...	Bb5+	Qe2+	Bxd7+	dc	Nb3	Nxe2	Nbd4[11]		±
	ed	Bd7	Qe7	Qxd7	Nxd7	Nxc5	Qxe2+	Na4		
6	...	...	...	dc	Nb3	Be3	Nf3	Nxc5!	Qd2	±
	...	...	Be7	Nf6	0-0	Re8	Bxc5	Qa5+	Qxb5[12]	
7	...	...	...	...	...	...	...	Bd3	Nfd4	±
	...	...	...	...	...	...	a6	Ba4	Nbd7[13]	
8	...	...	Qe2+	Ngf3	0-0	Re1[14]	Bxc6	Ng5[15]		±
	...	Nc6	Be6	Nf6	Be7	0-0	bc			
9	...	...	...	dc	Nb3	Nf3	Be3	0-0-0[17]	Bc4	∞
	...	...	Be7	Nf6	0-0	Ne4![16]	Re8	Nxc5	Nxb3+[18]	
10	...	...	...	...	...	Be3	0-0-0	a3	Nf3	=
	...	...	...	...	...	Re8	a5	Bd7	Na7[19]	
11	...	Ngf3	Bb5+	Bxd7+	0-0	dc	Nd4	Nf5	Nb3	±
	...	Nf6	Bd7	Nbxd7	Be7	Nxc5	0-0	Re8	Ne6[20]	
12	...	...	c4[21]	cd	Bc4	Bb3				=
	...	a6	Nf6	cd	b5	Qe7+				
13	...	...	Bb5	0-0	dc[24]	Nb3	Re1	Be3	c3	±
	...	Nc6	Bd6[22]	Nge7[23]	Bxc5	Bb6	0-0	Bf5	Be4[25]	

	10	11	12	13	14	15	16	17	18	
14	Bd2[26]	Nc3	Nbd4	Be2	Ne1[27]	Nxe2	Nf3[28]			=
	0-0	Bg4	Bh5	Ng6	Bxe2	Re8				
15	Bxc6+	Qd4	Bf4	Qd2	Bxd6[30]	a4	Qd4	a5	Qd3	∓
	bc[29]	0-0	Nf5	Qb6	Nxd6	Ne4	Be6	Qb5	Qb4[31]	
16	Bg5	Bh4?!	Bd3	a4[32]	Bxf5	Ng3	hg			∓
	0-0	Qb6	a5!	Nf5	Bxf5	Bxg3	Be4[33]			
17	...	Re1	Bd3	c3	h3	Be2	Nfd4	Bd3	Nxd4	=
	...	a6[34]	Bg4	Qc7	Bh5	Rfe8	Bg6	Nxd4	Nc6![35]	
18	Nbd4	Be3[36]	Qd2	h3	Nh4	Nxg6	Bxc6	c4		±/∞
	0-0	Bg4	Qc7	Bh5	Bg6	hg	bc	Qd7!		
19	...	Bg5	Be3	Re1	Bf1	h3	c3	a4	a5!?[37]	=
	...	f6	Ne5	a6	Kh8	Bd7	Rc8	Re8		
20	...	c3	Qa4	Be3	Be2	Qxd4	Qd2	Rad1	Bb6	±
	...	Bg4	Qd7[38]	a6	Nxd4	Nc6	Rfe8	Rad8	Bc7[39]	

212

[1] 5 Bd3 Nf6 6 Qe2 Nc6 7 Ngf3 0-0 8 0-0 Bb6 9 e5 Nd7 10 c4 Bc7 =/∓ Ghinda-Farago, Herculana Z 1982.

[2] 6 ... ed 7 Nf3 Nc6 8 Bb5 Ne7 9 0-0 0-0 10 Nfd4 a6 = Haag-Korchnoi, Gyula 1965.

[3] Steinitz-Lasker,Nuremburg 1896.

[4] 4 ... de 5 Nxe4 cd 6 Qxd4 Qxd4 7 Nxd4 ± Grünfeld-Tartakower, Debrecen 1925.

4 ... Nf6 5 ed Nxd5 6 Nb3 cd 7 Nbxd4 Be7 8 g3 0-0 9 Bg2 Nf6 10 0-0 Nc6 11 c3 Qb6 12 Qb3 ± Keres-Stahlberg, Budapest 1952.

4 ... a6 5 ed – 4 ed.

[5] 5 ... a6 6 ed ab 7 dc bc 8 dc Bxc5 9 0-0 ±.

5 ... de 6 Nxe4 Bd7 7 Bg5 Qa5+ 8 Nc3 cd 9 Nxd4 Be7 10 Qd2 Nf6 11 0-0-0 ±.

[6] 13 c4! ± Estrin-Kuligowski, Leipzig 1976.

[7] 13 c4 ±.

[8] 6 ... Qh5?! 7 0-0 Nc6 8 Nb3 Nf6 9 Nbxd4 Nxd4 10 Nxd4 Qxd1 11 Rxd1 ± Lipnitsky-Chistiakov, Kiev 1950.

6 ... Qc5 7 0-0 Nc6 8 Qe2 Nf6 9 Nb3 Qb6 10 Rd1 Bc5 11 a4 ± Keres-Stahlberg, Buenos Aires 1939.

6 ... Qd8 7 0-0 Nc6 8 Nb3 Nf6 9 Qe2 a6 10 Rd1 b5 11 Nbxd4 Nxd4 12 Rxd4 Qb6 13 Bd3 Bb7 14 a4 Bc5 15 Rh4 b4 16 a5! ± Sax-Andersson, Hilversum 1973.

[9] 10 ... Be7 11 c3 Bd7 12 Re1 ± Balashov-Spassky, Munich 1979.

[10] 13 Qf3 ± Jansa-Petrosian, Moscow 1977.

[11] Parma-Vaganian, Yugoslavia v USSR 1971.

[12] 13 0-0-0 Bg4!? (13 ... b6 14 Nxd7 Nbxd7 15 Kb1 Ne4 16 Qd3 Qxd3 17 Rxd3 Ndf6 18 h3 ± Karpov-Korchnoi, 22nd match game 1978) 14 h3 Bh5 15 g4 Bg6 16 Nh4 Na6 17 Nxg6 hg 18 Bxa6 Qxa6 19 Kb1 ± Tseshkovsky-Vaganian, Lvov 1978.

[13] 13 0-0-0! Nxc5 14 Nf5 Bf8 15 Nxc5 Bxc5 16 Qf3 Bxe3+ 17 Nxe3 ± Tal-Portisch, Montreal 1979.

[14] 9 Ng5!?

9 Ne5!?

[15] Iglitsky-Verlinsky, USSR 1937.

[16] 9 ... Re8!? 10 Ne3 a6 (10 ... Ne4! – 9 ... Ne4!) 11 Bd3! Ne4 12 0-0-0 Nxc5 13 Bc4 Nxb3+ 14 Bxb3 Be6 ±/∞.

[17] 11 0-0 Nxc5 12 Qd1 Ne4 = Gerstenfeld-Boleslavsky, USSR Ch 1940.

[18] 13 Bxb3 Be6 ±/∞ Florian-Katetov, Prague 1943.

[19] 13 Nfd4 Ne4 =.

[20] 13 Be3 Qc7 14 c3 ± Geller-Stahlberg, Zürich C 1953.

[21] 6 Be2 c4 7 0-0 Bd6 8 b3 (8 Re1 Ne7 9 Nf1 Nbc6 10 Bg5 0-0 11 c3 f6 12 Bd2 b5 = Gipslis-Korchnoi, Tallinn 1967; 12 Bh4!?) 8 ... cb (8 ... b5!?) 9 ab Ne7 10 Re1 Nbc6 11 Nf1 0-0 12 Ne3 ± Geller-Korchnoi, Moscow 1975.

6 dc Bxc5 7 Nb3 Ba7 8 Bd3 Qe7+ 9 Be2 Nf6 10 0-0 0-0 11 Nfd4 (11 Bg5!? Keres) 11 ... Nc6 12 Re1 Ne4 13 Be3 Ne5 = Cirić-Korchnoi, Yugoslavia v USSR 1967.

[22] 6 ... Qe7+ 7 Be2 cd 8 0-0 Qd8 9 Nb3 Bd6 10 Nbxd4 ±.

6 ... c4 7 Qe2+ Qe7 8 b3 ± Fuchs-Uhlmann, Berlin 1962.

[23] 7 ... cd 8 Nb3 Ne7 9 Nbxd4 transposes.

[24] 8 c4 0-0! 9 dc Bxc5 =.

[25] 13 Nbd4 Qd6 14 Bf1 Qf6 15 Qa4 h6 16 Rad1 ± Ghizdavu-Botez, Romania 1972.

[26] 10 Bd3 0-0 11 Nbd4 Re8! ∓.

10 Be3 0-0 11 Nd2 Bg4 12 Be2 Bxf3 13 Bxf3 Ne5 = Gligorić-Petrosian, Stockholm IZ 1952.

[27] 14 g3!? Ljubojević.

[28] Ljubojević-Petrosian, Milan 1975.

[29] 10 ... Nxc6 11 Re1+ ± Averbakh-Botvinnik, USSR Ch 1951.

[30] 14 Rfe1!?

[31] Velimirović-Kraidman, Kragujevac 1974.

[32] 13 c3 a4 14 Nbd4 Ng6 15 Nb5 Bf4 ∓ Zhidkov-Gulko, Daugavpils 1974.

13 c4 a4 14 cd Nb4 15 Nbd4 Nxd3 16 Qxd3 Ra5 = Wittman-Vaganian, Student Ol 1974.

[33] Balashov-Gulko, Moscow Ch 1974.

[34] 11 ... f6 12 Bh4 Qb6 13 Be2 Be6 14 Bg3 Ne5 15 Nxe5 intending Bf3/Bd3.

11 ... Bg4 12 h3 Bh5 13 Bxc6 bc 14 Nbd4 Rc8 15 c4 h6 16 Bxe7 Bxe7 17 g4! ± Peters-Ervin, Lone Pine 1978.

11 ... Qc7 12 c3 a6 13 Be2 Be6 14 Bxe7 Bxe7 15 Nfd4 ± Balashov-Portisch, Bugojno 1978. 12 ... h6 13 Bxe7 Bxe7 14 Nbd4 a6 15 Bd3 ± Hübner-Korchnoi, South Africa 1981.

[35] Holmov-Uhlmann, Halle 1978.

[36] 11 h3 Nxd4 12 Qxd4 Bf5 = Tukmakov-Uhlmann, Hastings 1972/73.

11 b3 Nxd4 12 Nxd4 Be5.

11 Bd3 Ng6 12 Bg5 Be7 13 Bxe7 Qxe7 14 Re1 Qf6 = Jansa-Matanović, Varna Ol 1962.

[37] 18 Nxe5? fe 19 Qf3 h6 ∓ Geller-Uhlmann, Amsterdam 1970.

18 a5!? =.

[38] 12 ... Bh5 13 Re1 Qc7 14 h3 Bg6 15 Bg5 a6 16 Bf1 h6 17 Bxe7 Nxe7 18 Rad1 ± Karpov-Korchnoi, match (4) 1974.

[39] Karpov-Korchnoi, match (16) 1974.

213

Caro-Kann

Christened in honour of the analytical efforts of H.Caro of Berlin and M.Kann of Vienna who adopted the opening towards the end of the 19th century, the Caro-Kann is another opening that owes a great deal of its present status to the work of Botvinnik. Although it has a reputation for being unnecessarily dull, as the theory of this defence has developed so it has expanded to include variations ranging from the quiet to the chaotic. Every year this once maligned defence adds new converts to its ranks and its adherents include GMs of a wide variety of tastes – Andersson, Larsen, Speelman and Seirawan, to name just a few.

The Classical System (**2 d4 d5 3 ♘c3 de 4 ♘xe4 ♗f5**) continues to attract players who prefer to postpone the fight until they have secured a solid position and who enjoy chipping away at the ambitiously advanced boundaries of White's position. White must tread a narrow line between aggression and over-extension. Black must always be wary of the retribution that such a provocative stance can entail.

Recent attention has been focused on the sharp system championed by Bent Larsen (**2 d4 d5 3 ♘c3 de 4 ♘xe4 ♘f6 5 ♘xf6+ gf**). Black's unorthodox pawn structure allows him many chances for tactical counterplay along the half-open g-file. His results with this system have, to date, been impressive indeed.

For the more peacefully inclined, **5 ... ef** offers chances of a solid equality and is a favourite of GM Ulf Andersson. Korchnoi has used this variation with success as well, finding the kingside pawn mass useful both for defence and attack. **2 d4 d5 3 ♘c3 de 4 ♘xe4 ♘d7** is also in tune with the basically solid mood of the Caro-Kann. Unambitious, it nevertheless poses problems as far as White's intentions to demonstrate an opening advantage are concerned.

Alternative attempts to handle the Caro-Kann are the Two Knights, **2 ♘c3 d5 3 ♘f3**, the Exchange Variation, **2 d4 d5 3 ed cd** (both of which were tried by Fischer), the Advance, **2 d4 d5 3 e5** and the Panov-Botvinnik Attack, **2 d4 d5 3 ed cd 4 c4**. The last two are White's sharpest options. Black must be theoretically prepared and, in the case of the Panov-Botvinnik, conversant with the various transpositional possibilities in order to equalise.

214

	2	3	4	5	6	7	8	9	10	
1	d3[1]	g3[2]	♗g2	♘d2	♘gf3	0-0	ed	♖e1	♘f1	=
	e5	♘f6	d5	♗d6	♘bd7	0-0	cd	♖e8	h6[3]	
2	...	♘d2	♘gf3	g3	♗g2	0-0	♖e1	b4	ba	=
	d5	g6[4]	♗g7	e5	♘e7	0-0	♘d7	a5	de![5]	
3	c4[6]	ed	cd	♘c3	d4	♘f3[9]	♗d3	0-0	♕e2	=
	d5[7]	cd	♕xd5	♕d6[8]	♘f6	e6	♗e7	♘c6	0-0[10]	
4	...	...	...	♕a4+	♘c3	♘f3[12]	♕b3![13]	♗c4	♕a3	±
	...	...	♘f6	♘bd7[11]	g6	♗g7	0-0	♘c5	b6[14]	
5	...	...	...	♘c3	d4	♗b5+[15]	♕a4	bc	♘f3	=/±
	...	...	...	♘xd5	g6	♘c6	♘xc3	♗g7	0-0[16]	
6	...	...	...	♗b5+	♘c3	♕a4[19]	♗e2	♕d4		=
	...	...	...	♘bd7[17]	a6[18]	♖b8![20]	b5	♘b6[21]		

[1] Breyer Variation.

[2] 3 ♘f3 d6 5 g3 ♘f6 5 ♗g2 ♗e7 6 0-0 0-0 7 ♘c3 ♕c7 8 a4 a5 9 d4 ♘a6 10 h3 = Shamkovich-Barcza, Salgotarjan 1967.

[3] Stein-Barcza, Tallinn 1977.

[4] 3 ... e5 4 ♘gf3 ♗d6 5 ♗e2 ♘e7 6 0-0 0-0 7 d4 ed 8 ♘xd4 ♕c7 = Pirttimäki-Campora, Graz 1981.

3 ... de 4 de e5 5 ♘gf3 ♗c5 6 ♘xe5! ♗xf2+ 7 ♔xf2 ♕d4+ 8 ♔e1 ♕xe5 9 ♘c4! ±.

3 ... ♕c7!? 4 ♘gf3 ♗g4 = Lobron-Keene, Dortmund 1980.

[5] 10 ... ♕xa5?! 11 ♗b2 ♕c7 12 a4! ♖e8 13 d4! ± Ciocaltea-Kozma, Satu Mare 1977.

10 ...de! 11 ♘xe4 ♕xa5 12 ♗b2 ♕c7 13 ♘ed2 c5 14 ♘c4 ♘c6 = Bischoff-Greenfield, Graz 1981.

[6] "English" Variation.

[7] 2 ... e5!? 3 d4 d6! 4 ♘f3 ♘d7 5 ♘c3 ♘gf6.

[8] 5 ... ♕a5!? 6 d4 ♘f6 7 ♘f3 g6 8 ♗c4 ♗g7 9 ♕b3 0-0 10 ♘e5 e6 = Salonen-Panzeri, Graz 1981.

[9] 7 ♘ge2!? (Sax-Speelman, Skara 1980) 7 ... g6!?.

[10] Iskov-Seirawan, London 1981.

[11] 5 ... ♗d7 6 ♕b3 ♘a6 7 d4 ♕b6 8 ♗c4 ♖c8 ∞

Szabo-Sliwa, Szczawno Zdroj 1957.

[12] 7 g3 ♗g7 8 ♗g2 0-0 9 ♘ge2 ♘b6 10 ♕b3 a5 11 ♘f4 a4 12 ♕b5 ♗d7 13 ♕b4 ♖e8 14 0-0 ♗f8 15 ♕d4 ♗f5 16 ♕e5 ♗g7 ∞ Suetin-Gurgenidze, Kislovodsk 1972.

7 d4!? ♗g7 8 ♕b3 0-0 9 ♗g5 ♘b6 10 ♗xf6 ♗xf6 11 ♘f3 (Larsen-Karpov, Montreal 1979) 11 ... e6 12 d6 ∞ Larsen.

[13] 8 ♘e5 0-0 9 ♘xd7 ♘xd7 10 ♕b3 e6 11 ♗e2 ed 12 d4 ♘e4 13 ♘xe4 de ½-½ Kuzmin-Razuvayev, USSR Ch 1981.

[14] 11 0-0 ♗b7 12 d4 ± Kuzmin-Dolmatov, USSR Ch 1980.

[15] 7 ♗c4 ♘b6 8 ♗b3 ±.

For others see Panov-Botvinnik, 5 ... g6.

[16] Karpov-Miles, Amsterdam 1981.

[17] 5 ... ♗d7 6 ♗c4 ♕c7 7 d3! ♘xd5 8 ♗xd5 ♕e5+ 9 ♗e4! ± Soltis.

[18] 6 ... g6 7 d4 ♗g7 8 d6 ed 9 ♕e2+ ♕e7 10 ♗f4 ♕xe2+ 11 ♘gxe2 ♔e7! =.

[19] 7 ♗a4?! b5! =.

7 ♗xd7+ ♕xd7 8 ♕b3 ♗g4 9 ♘ge2 b5 = Varnusz-Flesch, Hungary 1963.

[20] 7 ... g6 8 ♘f3 ♗g7 9 0-0 0-0 10 ♗xd7 ♗xd7 11 ♕b3 ± Evdokimov-Gorenstein, corr. 1962.

[21] Intending ... ♗b7, ... ♘bxd5 = Soltis.

Caro-Kann: Two Knights 1 e4 c6 2 ♘c3 d5 3 ♘f3

	3	4	5	6	7	8	9	10	11	
1	...	♘xe4	♘g3	b3	♗b2	♗b5	0-0	♕e2	♗xc6	=
	de[1]	♘f6	c5	♘c6	e6	♗d7	♗e7	0-0	♗xc6[2]	
2	...	...	♘xf6+	g3[4]	♗g2	h3	b3	♗b2		=
	...	...	gf[3]	♗g4[5]	♕d7	♗e6	♘a6	0-0-0[6]		
3	...	h3	ed	♗b5+[7]	g4	♘e5	d4	♕e2	h4[8]	∞
	♗g4	♗h5	cd	♘c6	♗g6	♖c8	e6	♗b4		
4	...	...	♕xf3	g3	♗g2	♕e2	♘xe4	♗xe4	♗g2	∞
	...	♗xf3	e6	♘f6	de	♘bd7	♘xe4	♗e7	0-0[9]	
5	...	...	...	d4	♘xe4	♗d3	♗e3	0-0-0	♔b1	∞
	...	...	...	de	♕xd4	♘d7	♕d5	♘gf6[10]		
6	...	...	...	d3	♗e2	♕g3	0-0	♗f4	♖ab1	±
	...	...	♘f6	e6	♘bd7	g6	♗g7	♕b6[11]	0-0[12]	
7	...	...	...	...	♕g3!?	♗e2	e5	♕xe5	a3	±
	...	...	...	...	♘bd7	♗b4!?	♘xe5	d4	♗a5[13]	
8	...	...	...	d4[14]	♕e3!	♘xe4	♕xe4	♕d3	♗e2	±
	...	...	...	de	♘bd7[15]	♘xe4	♘f6	e6[16]	♗e7[17]	

Caro-Kann: Fantasy 1 e4 c6 2 d4 d5 3 f3

	3	4	5	6	7	8	9	10	11	
9	...	♘c3	♗e3	a3	bc	♕d2[19]				∞
	e6	♗b4[18]	de	♗xc3+	♕a5					
10	...	c3	♘a3	♗e3	fe	♕f3	0-0-0	♘h3		=
	g6	♗g7	♘d7	de	♘gf6	0-0	♕a5	b5[20]		
11	...	fe	♘f3	c3	♗d3	♕e2	♘bd2	0-0		=
	de	e5	♗e6	♘f6	♘bd7	♗d6	♕e7	0-0-0[21]		

Caro-Kann: Advance 1 e4 c6 2 d4 d5 3 e5 ♗f5

	4	5	6	7	8	9	10	11	12	
12	c3[22]	♘f3[23]	♗e2	♘a3	0-0	♘c2	♘xh4	♕xe2		=
	e6	♘d7	♗e7	♗g4	♘f5	♘h4	♗xe2	♕xh4[24]		
13	h4	c4!?[26]	♖xb1	a3	♘f3	♗g5	cd	♗d3[27]		±
	h5[25]	♗xb1?!	e6	♘d7	g6	♗e7	cd			
14	♗d3	♕xd3	♘c3	♘ge2	♘f4[28]	♘xd3	♗e3	f4	♗f2	=
	♗xd3	e6	♕b6	♕a6	♕xd3	♘d7	♘e7	♘f5	h5[29]	
15	♘c3	g4	♘ge2	h4[32]	♖h3	♘g3	♗g5	a3![35]		±
	e6[30]	♗g6	♗b4[31]	♗e4	h5	c5[33]	♕b6[34]			
16	...	...	...	♘f4[36]	de[38]	h4	♘d3	♗g5	♗d2	∞
	...	...	f6	fe[37]	♗f7	♘d7	h5	♕a5	♕c7[39]	
17	...	...	...	h4	♘xd4[41]	♗b5+	♗g5	f4	♕xg4	∓
	...	...	c5	cd[40]	h5	♘d7	♗e7[42]	hg	♗xg5![43]	
18	...	...	...	♗e3	dc	♘d4	f4!?	♗b5+	♗g1	=
	...	...	...	♘c6	♘xe5	♘f6!?[44]	♘exg4!?	♔e7	♕c7[45]	
19	...	...	...	...	...	♘b5	♘c7+	♘xa8	♘g3	∞
	...	...	...	...	♕h4!?	♗e4	♔d7	♗xh1	♕xh2[46]	

1 3 ... ♘f6 4 e5 ±.

2 12 ♘e5 ♕c7 = Lutikov-Botvinnik, USSR 1966.

3 5 ... ef 6 ♗c4 ♗e7 7 0-0-0-0 8 d4 ♗d6 9 ♗b3 ♘d7 10 ♖e1 ♕c7 11 c4 c5 = Boleslavsky.

4 6 d4 – 2 d4 d5 3 ♘d2 de 4 ♘xe4 ♘f6 5 ♘xf6+ gf.
   6 ♗c4 ♖g8!? 7 g3 ♗g4 8 h3 ♗h5 9 g4 ♗g6 10 d3 e6 = Wejbora-Karp, Graz 1981.

5 6 ... ♗f5!? 7 ♗g2 ♕d7 8 0-0 ♘a6 9 ♖e1 0-0-0 10 d3 ♗h3! =/∓ Westerinen-Chandler, Brighton 1981.
   6 ... e5 7 ♗g2 ♗e6 8 0-0 ♘d7 9 d4 ♕c7 10 ♕e2 0-0-0 ±/= Westerinen-Chandler, Bochum 1981.

6 Rauzer-Konstantinopolsky, USSR Ch 1937.

7 6 d4!? ♘c6 7 g4 ♗g6 8 ♘e5 e6 9 h4 f6 10 h5 oo Ghinda-Chandler, Bochum 1981.

8 11 ... ♗xc3+ 12 bc ♕a5 13 ♗b2! ♘e7 14 h5 ♗e4 15 f3 f6 16 fe fe 17 0-0 oo Boleslavsky.
   11 ... ♘e7!? 12 h5 ♗e4 13 f3 0-0 14 ♗xc6 ♘xc6 15 ♘xc6 ♖xc6 16 0-0 ♗xc3 17 bc ♖xc3 18 ♗d2 ♖xc2 19 fe de oo Durao-Silva, Portugal 1978.

9 12 0-0 ♘f6 13 ♖b1 a6 14 d3 ♖e8 15 h4 ♘b6 16 ♕h5 ♘d5 oo Kudrin-Ekstöm, Graz 1981.

10 Milić-Golombek, Opatija 1953.
    10 ... ♕xa2!? oo.

11 10 ... 0-0 11 ♗d6 ♖e8 12 e5 ±.

12 12 ♗f3 e5! 13 ♗d2 de 14 de a5 = Karpov-Portisch, Montreal 1979.
    12 e5! ♘e8 13 ♖fe1 ±.

13 12 ♗f3 0-0 13 0-0 dc 14 bc ♘d5 15 ♗d2 ♖e8 16 a4 ± Velikov-Spiridonov, Pernik 1981.

14 6 g3 ♘xe4 7 ♘xe4 de 8 ♕xe4 ♕d5 =.

15 7 ... ♕a5 8 ♗d2 ♕f5 9 0-0-0 e6 10 f3 ef 11 g4 ♕a5 12 ♗c4 oo Messing-Nemet, Yugoslavia 1967.

16 10 ... ♕d5!? 11 c4 ♕d6 12 ♗e2 ♗e3 13 d5 (Fischer-Keres, Bled 1961) 13 ... cd 14 cd ♕xd5 15 ♕xd5 ♘xd5 16 ♗b5+ ♗e7 17 0-0 oo ECO.

17 12 0-0 0-0 ± Boleslavsky.

18 4 ... ♘f6 5 e5 ♘fd7 6 f4 c5 – French, 3 ♘c3 ♘f6 4 e5.

19 Tartakower-Flohr, Kemeri 1937.

20 Vinogradov-Kopylov, USSR 1946.

21 Kasparian-Holmov, USSR 1949.

22 4 ♘e2 e6 5 ♘g3 ♗g6 6 h4 h6 7 h5 ♗h7 8 ♗d3 ♗xd3 9 cd ♕b6 = Grünfeld-Campora, Graz 1981.
    4 g4? ♗e4! 5 f3 ♗g6 6 h4 h5! ∓.
    4 c4 e6! 5 ♘c3 dc 6 ♗xc4 ♘d7 =.

23 5 ♗e3 ♘d7 6 ♘f3 ♘e7 7 ♘bd2 ♕c7 =.

24 Ambrož-Meduna, Herculana Z 1982.

25 4 ... h6 5 g4 ♗d7 6 h5 e6 7 f4 c5 8 c3 ♘c6 9 ♘f3 ♕b6 10 ♔f2! 0-0-0! 11 ♘g3 (Okhotnik-Berezhnoy, USSR 1981) 11 ... ♔b8! oo.

26 5 ♘e2?! e6 6 ♘g3 ♗g6 7 ♗e2 c5! ∓ Espig-Vadasz, Trnava 1979.

27 Spassky-Seirawan, London 1982.

28 8 ♕h3 ♘e7! ∓.

29 13 ♔e2 b6 14 b4 a5 15 a3 = Boleslavsky.

30 4 ... ♕d7!? 5 ♘ge2 (5 ♗e3! ±) 5 ... e6 6 ♘g3 ♘e7 7 ♗e3 ♕c7 8 ♗d3 ♗xd3 9 cd ♘d7 10 0-0 a6! ∓ Taulbut-Miles, Ramsgate 1981.
    4 ... h5 5 ♗e2 e6 6 ♗xh5 c5 7 ♗e2 cd 8 ♘b5 ± Nunn-Seirawan, Mexico IZ 1982.

31 6 ... ♗e7!? 7 ♘f4 c5 8 dc d4 9 ♘xg6 hg 10 ♘e4 ♗xc5 11 ♘xc5 ♕d5 12 ♘xb7 ♕xh1 13 ♘d6+ ♔f8 14 ♕xd4 oo Nunn-Chandler, Wiesbaden 1981.
    6 ... h6 7 h4! c5?! 8 h5 ♗h7 9 ♗e3 ♘c6 10 f4 ± Boleslavsky.

32 7 ♘f4!? oo van der Wiel-Hort, Bochum 1981.

33 9 ... ♘d7 10 ♘xh5! g6 11 ♗g5 ♕a5 12 ♘f4 c5 oo Plaskett-Roos, Graz 1981.

34 10 ... f6 11 ♗d2±/± Vasyukov-Razuvayev, USSR Ch 1980/81.

35 11 ♘xe4 cd! ∓ Day-Vranesic, Canadian Ch 1981. 11 a3! Day.

36 7 h4!? fe 8 h5 ♗f7 9 de ♘d7 10 f4 ♗c5 oo/± van der Wiel-Messa, Graz 1981.

37 7 ... ♗f7!? 8 ef gf 9 ♕e2 ♕e7 10 ♘d3 ♘d7 11 g5 fg 12 ♖c1 h6 13 f4! oo Braga-Garcia Palermo, Mar del Plata 1982.

38 8 ♘xe6!? ♕e7 9 ♘xf8 ed+ 10 ♗e2 dc 11 ♘xg6 hg 12 ♕d3 ♘f6 13 ♕xc3 ♘bd7 oo/= Nunn-Andersson, London 1982.

39 Kinlay-Freeman, London 1980.

40 7 ... h6 8 ♘f4 ♗h7 9 ♗e3 (9 g5!?) 9 ... ♘e7 10 dc ♘ec6 11 ♗b5 ♘d7 12 ♕e2 ♕c7 13 0-0 oo Korchnoi-Bivshev, USSR 1951.

41 8 ♕xd4 ♘c6 9 ♕a4 h5 10 ♘f4 ♗h7 11 ♘xh5 a6 intending ... b5 oo Boleslavsky.

42 10 ... ♕c7 oo.

43 13 fg ♗h5 14 ♕h3 ♘e7 15 ♔d2 ♖c8 ∓ Hort-Seirawan, Bad Kissingen 1980.

44 9 ... ♖c8 10 f4 ♘c4 11 ♗xc4 dc 12 f5 ± van der Sterren-Blow, Marbella Z 1982.
    9 ... a6?! 10 f4 ♘c4 11 ♗xc4 dc 12 f5 ef 13 gf ♕e7 14 ♔d2! ±/± van der Wiel-Timman, Wijk aan Zee 1982.
    9 ... ♘d7!? 10 ♗b5 a6 11 ♗a4 ♗xc5 12 ♘xe6 fe 13 ♗xd7+ ♕xd7 14 ♗xc5 =/∓ Ady-Speelman, Westergate 1982.
    9 ... ♘c6 10 ♗b5 ♖c8 11 ♕e2 ♘f6 12 0-0-0 ♗xc5 13 h4! h5 14 g5 ♘d7 15 ♘xe6! fe 16 ♗xc5 ♘xc5 17 ♖xd5 ± Kuijf-van den Berg, Amsterdam 1982.

45 13 c6 b6 14 ♕e2 ♕xf4 15 c7 ♘e4 16 ♘c6+ ♔d6 17 h3 ♕g3+ 18 ♔f1 ♕f4+ =/oo Braga-Timman, Mar del Plata 1982.

46 13 b4 ♗h6 14 ♕e2 ♗e7 15 b5 ♘xe5 ½-½ van der Wiel-Sosonko, Amsterdam 1982.

Caro-Kann: Exchange   1 e4 c6 2 d4 d5 3 ed cd 4 ♗d3

	4	5	6	7	8	9	10	11	12	
1	...	c3	♗f4	♘f3	0-0	♖e1	♘bd2	b4	a4	∞
	g6	♗g7	♘h6	0-0	♘c6	♔h8!	f6	a6	e5[1]	
2	...	c3	♘f3	♗f4	♕c1	0-0	♖e1	♘d2	♘f1	±
	♘c6	g6	♗g7	♘h6	♘f5	0-0	♖e8	f6	e5[2]	
3	...	...	♗f4	♕b3	♘d2	♘gf3	♘e5	♗xe5	♕c2	±
	...	♘f6	♗g4	♕c8[3]	e6	♗e7[4]	♘xe5	0-0	♗f5[5]	
4	...	...	...	♘d2[6]	h3	♘gf3	♕e2	0-0	♗h2	±
	...	...	g6	♗g7	0-0	♗f5	♖c8	♘h5	♗h6[7]	

[1] Hort-Bellon, Montilla 1978.

[2] 13 de fe 14 ♗g5 ± Pantavos-Pasman, Graz 1981.

[3] 7 ... ♘a5 8 ♕a4+ ♗d7 9 ♕c2 e6 10 ♘f3 ♕b6 11 a4! ± Fischer-Petrosian, USSR v Rest of the World 1970.

[4] 9 ... ♗h5!? 10 ♘e5 ♗e7 11 0-0-0-0 (Sznapik-Seirawan, Malta Ol 1980) 12 ♕c2 ♗g6 13 ♘xg6 hg 14 ♘f3 ± Sznapik.

[5] 13 ♗xf5 ef 14 ♕b3 ♕c6 (Nezhmetdinov-Shamkovich, USSR 1970) 15 a4 ± ECO.

[6] 7 ♘f3 ♗g7 8 ♘bd2 ♘h5 9 ♗e3 0-0 10 0-0 f5 11 ♘b3 f4!? 12 ♗d2 ♗g4 13 ♗e2 ♕d6 14 ♖e1 ♖ae8 = Upton-Campora, Graz 1981.

[7] 13 ♗xf5 gf 14 ♘e5 ± Benjamin-Santo Roman, Graz 1981.

Caro-Kann: Panov-Botvinnik   1 e4 c6 2 d4 d5 3 ed cd 4 c4 ♘f6

	5	6	7	8	9	10	11	12	13	
1	♘c3	♘f3	cd	♕b3	gf	♕xb7	♗b5+	♕c6+	♕xb5	=
	♘c6	♗g4	♘xd5	♗xf3	e6[1]	♘xd4	♘xb5	♔e7	♕d7[2]	
2	...	♗g5	♗xf6[4]	cd	♕d2	bc	♘e2[5]	♗f4	♗e2	∞
	...	♕a5[3]	ef	♗b4	♗xc3	♕xd5	0-0	♕d6[6]	♗f5[7]	
3	...	♗g5	♘f3	cd	♘xg5	♗c4	♘f3	♖xd4	♘ce2	∞∞
	g6	♗g7	♘e4	♘xg5	0-0	e5	ed	♕h4	♗g4[8]	
4	...	cd	♕b3	♗b5+[9]	♘f3	♘e5	♘xd7	♗e3	0-0	=
	...	♘xd5	♘b6	♗d7	♗g7	0-0	♘8xd7	♘f6	♘fd5[10]	
5	...	♕b3	cd	g3[11]	♗g2	♘ge2	♘f4[13]	0-0	♘fe2	∞
	...	♗g7	0-0	♘bd7[12]	♘b6	♗f5	h6	g5	♕d7[14]	
6	...	...	...	♗e2	♗f3	♗f4[15]	♖d1			∞
	...	...	...	♘bd7	♘b6	♗f5![16]	♕d7[17]			
7	...	...	...	...	...	♗g5	♗xf6	♘xf3	0-0	=
	...	...	...	...	...	♗g4	♗xf3	ef[18]	♕d7![19]	

1 e4 c6 2 d4 d5 3 ed cd 4 c4 ♘f6 5 ♘c3 e6

	6	7	8	9	10	11	12	13	14	
8	♘f3	c5[21]	♗d3	b4	♘a4	h4	♘g5	♔f1	♘xe6	∞
	♗e7[20]	0-0	b6	a5	♘fd7	f5	♕e8	ab	♘xc5[22]	
9	...	♗g5	c5	b4	a3	♗xe7	♘xe4[24]	♘e5		=
	...	0-0[23]	b6	a5	♘e4	♕xe7	de	♘d7[25]		
10	...	cd	♗b5+	♗xd7+[27]	0-0	♕b3	♗g5	♖fe1[28]		±
	...	ed[26]	♗d7	♘bxd7	0-0	♘b6	♖e8			

[1] 9 ... ♘b6 10 d5 ♘d4 11 ♕d1 e5 12 de fe 13 ♗e3 ♗c5 14 b4 ♕f6 15 bc ♘xf3+ 16 ♔e2 0-0 17 cb ♕xc3 18 ♗g2 ♕c4+ 19 ♕d3 ± Zhuravlev-Gutman, USSR 1972. 10 ♗e3 e6 11 ♖g1 ♗b4 12 ♗b5! ± Elvest-Kasparov, USSR 1979.

[2] 14 ♕a5 ♗xc3! 15 ♕xc3 f6 16 ♗e3 ♔f7 17 0-0 ♗e7 18 ♖ac1 ♕d5! ∞/= Tseitlin-Kasparov, USSR 1978.

[3] 6 ... ♗g4 7 ♗e2 ♗xe2 8 ♘gxe2 ±/ ±.

6 ... e6 7 ♘f3 ♗e7 8 c5 0-0 9 ♖c1 ♘e4 10 ♗xe7 ♘xe7 ∞/=; 7 cd ed 8 ♘f3 ♗e7 9 ♗b5 ±.

6 ... ♕b6 7 cd ♘xd4 8 ♗e3 e5 9 de ♗c5 10 ef+ ♔e7 11 ♗c4 ♖d8 12 ♘f3 ±/ ± Romanov-Flerov, corr. 1963.

[4] 7 ♕d2 e5 8 ♗xf6 gf 9 ♘f3 ±. 7 ... ♗f5!? intending 8 ♗xf6 gf 9 ♘xd5 ♕xd2+ 10 ♔xd2 ♗h6+ ∞.

7 ♘f3 ♗g4 8 ♕b3!? 0-0-0 9 ♗xf6 ef!? ∞.

[5] 11 ♘f3 ♗g4 12 ♗e2 0-0 = Gufeld.

[6] 12 ... ♕a5? 13 ♗e2 ♖d8 14 ♖d1 ♗f5 15 0-0 ♖ac8 16 ♕b2! ± Sveshnikov-Bagirov, USSR Ch 1978.

[7] 14 0-0 ♖ac8 ∞ Gufeld.

[8] 14 ♖c1 ♘d7 ∞.

[9] 8 d5!? ± Mednis.

[10] 13 ... e6? 14 d5 ± Mesing-Atanasov, Varna 1973.

13 ... ♘fd5 14 ♘xd5 ♘xd5 = Botvinnik.

[11] 8 ♗g5 ♕a5 9 ♗xf6 ef 10 0-0-0 ♘d7 11 ♔b1 ♘b6 = Tal-Bronstein, USSR Ch 1961.

[12] 8 ... e6 9 de ♘c6 10 ef+ ♔h8 11 ♘ge2 ♕e7 12 ♗e3 ♘g4 13 ♔d2 ♗e6 14 d5 ♗xf7 ∞ Gheorghiu-Johannessen, Havana Ol 1966.

[13] 11 0-0 ♗d3 intending ... ♗c4 = Botvinnik.

[14] 14 f4 g4 15 a4 ∞ Botvinnik.

[15] 10 ♘ge2!? ♗g4 11 ♘xg4 ♘xg4 12 a4 ♘f6 13 ♘f4 ♕d7 14 a5 ♘c8 15 0-0 ♘d6 16 ♖e1 (Hort-Gipslis, Prague 1974) 16 ... ♖ac8 ∞.

[16] 10 ... ♗g4 11 ♗xg4 ♘xg4 12 ♘f3 ♘f6 13 d6 ± Botvinnik.

[17] Panov/Estrin.

[18] 12 ... ♗xf6 13 a4 ♕c7 14 0-0 ♖fd8 15 a5 ♕c4 16 ♖a3 ± Botvinnik.

[19] 14 ♖ac1 ♗h6! 15 ♖c2 ♗f4 ∞/=.
14 ♖fc1 ♖ad8 =.

[20] 6 ... ♗b4!? 7 cd ♘xd5 8 ♗d2 ♘c6 = Bordonada-F.Olafsson, Manila 1979.

[21] 7 ♗d3!? dc 8 ♗xc4 0-0 9 0-0 ♘c6 10 a3 a6! 11 ♖e1 b5 12 ♗a2 ♗b7 13 ♗g5 b4 14 ♘a4! ba 15 ba ♗xa3 16 d5! ed 17 ♗xf6 ♕xf6! (17 ... gf 18 ♗b1 intending 19 ♕d3 ±±) 18 ♘b6 ♖ad8 19 ♘xd5 ♕d6 20 ♗g5! ∞ Boudy-Szilagyi, Varna 1979.

[22] 15 ♘axc5 bc 16 ♘xf8 c4 17 ♘xh7 cd 18 ♘g5 ♗a6 19 ♔g1 ♘c6 20 ♕f3 ∞ Karlsson-Mahlin, corr. 1970.

[23] 7 ... ♘c6 8 ♖c1 0-0 9 c5 ♘e4 10 ♗xe7 ♕xe7 11 ♗e2 ±.

[24] 12 ♘a4? ab 13 ab bc 14 bc ♕a7 ∓ Kan-Makagonov, USSR Ch 1939.

[25] 13 ... ♖d8 14 ♗b5±/ ± Hort-Cirić, Amsterdam 1970.

13 ... ♘d7 = Botvinnik.

[26] 7 ... ♘xd5 – Semi-Tarrasch.

[27] 9 ♕b3 ± Botvinnik.

[28] Botvinnik.

	4	5	6	7	8	9	10	11	12	
1	e5[1]	f4	♘f3	h3[2]	♕xf3	g3	♕f2	♗d3	♘e2	=
	♗g7	h5!	♗g4	♗xf3	e6	♕b6!	♘e7	♘d7	0-0-0[3]	
2	...	♘f3[4]	♗e2	♗f4	♕d2	h3	♘xe5	♘xf7	♗e3	=
	...	♘h6[5]	f6	♘f7	0-0	fe	♘d7	♖xf7	e5[6]	
3	♘f3	h3	♘xe4	♘xf6+	♗c4	0-0				±
	♗g7	de	♘f6[7]	ef[8]	0-0[9]	♕c7[10]				
4	...	...	♗d3[11]	♘xe4	♗xe4	0-0	c3[13]	♗c2		±
	...	♘f6	de	♘xe4	♘d7[12]	0-0	c5	♕c7[14]		
5	...	...	♗f4![15]	♘xe4	♕d2[16]	c3	g4	♘xd6	♗xd6	∞
	...	♘h6	de	0-0	♘f5	♘d7	♘d6	ed	♖e8+[17]	
6	...	♗d3	♘xe4	0-0	♘xf6+	h3	♖e1	c3		=
	...	de[18]	♘d7[19]	♘gf6	♘xf6	0-0	♕d6	c5![20]		
7	ed	♘f3[21]	♗f4[22]	♘b5	h3	♕xf3	♗d3	c3	h4	±
	cd	♗g7	♗g4	♘a6	♗xf3[23]	♘f6	0-0	♘e8[24]		

	4	5	6	7	8	9	10	11	12	
8	c3[25]	e5	g3[27]	h4	♗e2	♘gf3	♘g5	♕a4+	♗b5	=
	♘f6[26]	♘h5	♘g7	h5	♗f5	e6	c5	♘c6	♕c8[28]	
9	♘gf3	h3	♗d3	0-0	♖e1	c4	♘f1[31]	♗xe4	dc	±
	♗g7[29]	♘h6	0-0	f6[30]	♘f7	e6	de	c5	♕xd1[32]	
10	...	...	e5	♗d3[33]	♗xd2	♕e2	♗b5+	dc	dc	±
	...	♘f6	♘e4	♘xd2	♘xd2	b6[34]	c5	♔f8[35]	bc[36]	
11	...	♗d3	♕e2	e5	♘b3	a4	h3	0-0		±
	...	♘d7![37]	♘df6	♘h5	a5	♗f8!?	♘g7	♗f5[38]		
12	...	c3	♗d3	♘xe4	♘xf6+	0-0	♖e1	♕e2	♗f4	±
	...	♘d7	de	♘gf6	♘xf6	0-0	b6	e6	♗b7[39]	

[1] 4 ♗e3 ♗g7 5 e5 ♘h6 6 f4 f6 7 ♘f3 ♗g4
8 ♗e2 0-0 9 ♘d2 fe 10 fe ♕d7 = Weitz/
Konstantinopolsky.

[2] 7 ♗e2 e6 8 ♗e3 ♘h6 9 ♕d2 (9 0-0 ♘f5
10 ♗f2 ♗h6 11 ♕d2 ♘d7 =) 9 ... ♘f5 10 ♗f2
♘d7 11 g3 ♗f8 12 h3 ♗xf3 13 ♗xf3 ±
Marjanović-Ciocaltea, Istanbul 1980.

[3] Fischer-Petrosian, USSR v Rest of the World
1970. 12 ♗d2 ♘f5 13 ♗xf5 gf 14 0-0-0
(Fischer) =.

[4] 5 ♗d3 ♘h6!? intending ... f6, ... ♘f7.

[5] 5 ... ♗f5 6 ♗d3 ♗xd3 7 ♕xd3 ♘h6
8 e6! ±/± Stepanian-Kishev, USSR 1977.

[6] Bellin-Gipslis, Sukhumi 1977.

[7] 6 ... ♘d7 7 ♗c4! ♘gf6 8 ♘xf6+ ♗xf6 9 0-0
0-0 10 ♖e1! ♗f5 (10 ... c5!?) 11 ♘e5 ♗e4
12 ♗g5 ♗d5 13 ♗d3 ♗e6 14 c3 ♘d7 15 ♘f3 ±
Tal-Kolarov, European Team Ch 1970.
  6 ... ♗f5 7 ♗g3 ♘f6!? 8 ♗xf5 gf 9 ♗d3 e6
10 ♕e2 c5 11 dc ♕a5+ (Sahović-Botvinnik,
Belgrade 1969) 12 c3 ♕xc5 13 ♗e3 ±. 7 ♘c5!
♘d7 8 ♘xd7 ♕xd7 9 ♘e5 ♕d5 10 c4 ± Urzica-
Honfi, Bucharest 1975.

[8] 7 ... ♗xf6?! 8 ♗c4 ♕d6 9 ♕e2 a5 10 0-0 b5
11 ♗d3 ♗f5 12 a4 b4 13 ♗c4 ±/± Vasyukov-
Basman, Zolotiye Peski 1971.

[9] 8 ... ♕e7+ 9 ♕e2 ♕xe2+ 10 ♔xe2 ± Chekhov-
Bronstein, USSR Ch 1974.

[10] Intending ... ♘b8-d7-b6 or c6-c5 Weitz/
Konstantinopolsky.

[11] 6 e5 ♘e4 7 ♘xe4 de 8 ♗g5 c5 9 dc ♕a5+
10 ♗d2 ♕xc5 11 ♗c3 ♘d7 (11 ... e3 12 f4 ±)
12 ♘xe4 (12 ♗d4!? ♕a5+ 13 b4 ♕xb4+ 14 c3
intending e6 ± Boleslavsky) 12 ... ♕c6 13 ♕e2
♗xe5 14 ♗xe5 ♘xe5 15 f4 ♘d7 16 0-0-0 0-0
17 ♘c3 e6 18 ♘e4 ± Mnatsakanian-Zilberman,
USSR 1979.

[12] 8 ... ♗f5 9 ♗xf5 ♕a5+ 10 c3 ♕xf5 11 0-0 ±
Kochiev-Zilberman, Chelyabinsk 1975.

[13] 10 ♖e1 c5 11 c3 cd 12 cd ♘f6 13 ♗c2
(Mariotti-Tseshkovsky, Manila 1976) 13 ... b6
14 ♗f4 ♗b7 15 ♗e5 = Weitz/Konstantinopolsky.

[14] 11 ... cd?! 12 ♘xd4 e5 13 ♘b5 a6 14 ♘d6 ±
Bronstein-Tseshkovsky, USSR Ch 1974.
  11 ... ♕c7 12 ♖e1 ♘f6 13 dc ♕xc5 14 ♗e3
♕c7 15 ♗d4 ± Shakarov-Kanzler, USSR 1979.

[15] 6 ♗d3 f6 7 0-0 0-0 8 ♖e1 ♗f7 9 ♕e2 e5
10 ♗e3 f5! ∓ Kotz-Lutikov, Dnepropetrovsk
1970.
  6 e5 f6 7 ♗f4 0-0 8 ♕d2 ♗f7 9 0-0-0 ±.

[16] 8 ♗d3 ♘f5 9 c3 ±.

[17] 13 ♗e2 ♘b6 14 ♗e5 f6 15 ♗f4 ♘c4 16 ♕c2

♗e6 (intending ... ♗d5) ∞.

[18] 5 ... ♗g4 6 ed cd 7 h3 ♗xf3 8 ♕xf3 e6 9 ♘e2
♘c6 10 c3 ♘ge7 11 0-0 0-0 12 ♗g5 f6 13 ♗d2
e5 14 de fe 15 ♕g4 ±/± Klovan-Rytov,
Leningrad 1974.

[19] 6 ... ♘f6 7 ♘xf6+ ef 8 ♕e2+ ♕e7 9 ♕xe7+
♔xe7 ±.

[20] Kneževič-Tseshkovsky, Erevan 1980.

[21] 5 ♗f4 ♗g7 6 ♗b5 ♗a6 7 ♕e2 ♘f6 8 ♘d6+
♔f8 9 ♗xc8 ♖xc8 10 c3 ♘c7 11 f3 ♘ce8 12 g4 h5
13 g5 ♘d7 14 ♗h3 e6 ∞ Nurmanedov-
Botvinnik, USSR 1966.

[22] 6 ♗b5+ ♗d7 7 ♕e2 ♘f6 8 ♗g5 0-0 9 ♗xf6 ef
10 ♗xd7 ♕xd7 11 0-0 (Leonidov-Kogan,
Moscow 1969) 11 ... ♘c6! 12 ♕b5 ♖fd8 =.
  6 ♘e5 ♘f6 7 ♕f3 0-0 8 ♗d3 ♘c6 9 ♘xc6 bc
10 0-0 ♘d7 11 ♕f4 ♕b6 12 ♖e1 ♖e8 13 ♘e2
e5! ∓ Lazarević-Gaprindashvili, Yugoslavia v
USSR 1970.

[23] 8 ... ♗d7!?

[24] Soltis-Brasket, New York 1977.

[25] 4 h3 de 5 ♘xe4 ♘d7 6 ♘f3 ♘gf6 =.

[26] 4 ... ♗g7 5 ♗d3 ♘h6 6 h3 0-0 7 ♘gf3 c5
8 dc ♘d7 9 ed ♘xc5 10 ♗c4 ± Peresishkin-
Rashkovsky, Moscow 1974.

[27] 6 ♘df3 ♗g7 7 h3 ♕b6 8 ♕e2 ♘a6 9 a4 ♕d8
10 ♘g3 h5 11 ♗xa6 ba ∞ A.Ivanov-Gurgenidze,
Daugavpils 1977.

[28] 13 ♘b3 ♗c2! = Georgadze-Gurgenidze,
Tbilisi 1974.

[29] 4 ... de 5 ♘xe4 ♗f5 6 ♘g3 ♗g4 7 ♗c4 e6
8 c3 ♘d7 9 h3 ♗xf3 10 ♕xf3 ♘gf6 11 0-0 ♗g7
12 ♖e1 0-0 ± Adorjan-Benko, Wijk aan Zee
1972.

[30] 7 ... a5 8 a4 ♘a6 9 ♖e1 c5 10 e5 cd 11 ♘xd4
♘c5 12 ♘2f3 ♘f5 13 ♗d2 ♘xd4 14 ♘xd4 f6 =
Tukmakov-Spassky, Moscow 1971.

[31] 10 b3 ♘d7 11 ♗b2 dc 12 ♗xc4 ♖e8 =
Kovačević-Tringov, Vinkovci 1976.

[32] 13 ♖xd1 f5 14 ♗c2 ♘a6 15 ♖b1 ♘xc5 16 b4
♘d7 17 c5 ± Vasyukov-Gurgenidze, USSR 1973.

[33] 7 ♘xe4 – row 4, note 11.

[34] 8 ... ♕b6 9 b4! ± Kozlov-Machulsky, Lvov
1975.

[35] 10 ... ♗d7 11 e6!? ∞.

[36] Intending ... ♗b7, e6, ♕c7, ♘d7, h6, ♔g8,
♔h7 etc.

[37] 5 ... de 6 ♘xe4 ♗g4 7 c3 ♘f6 8 h3 ♗xf3
9 ♘xf6+ ♗xf6 10 ♕xf3 ± Panchenko-Zaichik,
Lenigrad 1976.

[38] Razuvayev-Gurgenidze, Moscow 1974.

[39] 13 ♖ad1 ± Ligterink-Gipslis, Jurmala 1978.

	6	7	8	9	10	11	12	13	14	
1	c3[3]	♗d3	♘e2[4]	0-0	♘g3	♗e3	♕c2	♖fe1		=
	♗d6	0-0	♖e8	♕c7	♘d7	♘f8	♗e6	♖ed8[5]		
2	♗c4	♕e2+	♕xe7+	♘e2	♗d3	♗f4	♗xd6+	b3	c4	±
	♗d6	♕e7[6]	♔xe7	♗e6[7]	♘d7[8]	♘b6[9]	♔xd6	♔c7	♖ad8[10]	
3	...	♕h5[11]	♘e2	♗b3	0-0	♕f3	♗d2!?[12]			∞
	♘d7	♕e7+	♘b6	♗e6	g6	0-0-0				
4	...	♕e2	♘xe2	♗xe6	♗f4	0-0-0	c4	♖he1	b3	=
	♕e7+	♕xe2+	♗e6	fe	♔f7	♘d7	♗e7	♘b6	♖he8[13]	
5	...	...	♗b3	♗f4	0-0-0	♔b1[15]				∞
	...	♗e6	♘a6[14]	0-0-0	♘b4					

	6	7	8	9	10	11	12	13	14	
6	♗e2[17]	♗f3	♘e2	♗xg4	0-0	f3	♗e3![18]	♕d3	♖ad1	=
	♖g8!	e5	♗g4	♖xg4	♕d5	♖g6	♘d7	♘b6	0-0-0[19]	
7	♗c4	♘e2[20]	♘g3	h4[21]	♗f4	♕d2	♗xd6	0-0-0	♖he1	=
	♗f5	e6	♗g6	h5!	♗d6	♕c7	♕xd6	♘d7	0-0-0[22]	
8	♗f4	♗c4	♘f3[23]	0-0	♗xd6	♘h4	f4	c3	♕e2	=
	♗f5	e6	♖g8	♗d6	♕xd6	♗g6	f5!	♘d7	0-0-0[24]	
9	♘e2	♘g3	h4	♗e2	c3	b4	♘xh5	♗xh5	♗g4	∞∞
	♗f5[25]	♗g6	h5![26]	♘d7	♕a5	♕c7	♗xh5	a5	ab[27]	
10	c3	♘e2[29]	♘g3[31]	h4	h5	♗e3	♕d2	♗xh6	♕xh6	=
	♗f5[28]	e6[30]	♗g6	h6	♗h7	♘d7	♕a5	♗xh6	0-0-0[32]	
11	...	...	♘g3[33]	♗e2	♕xe2	♘e4	f3	♗e3	0-0	=
	...	h5	♗g4	♗xe2	♕d5	♘d7	0-0-0	♗h6	♗xe3+[34]	
12	♘f3	♗e2[35]	0-0	c4	d5	♘d4[37]	♗e3	♘b3!	♕e1	±
	♗f5	e6[36]	♕c7	♘d7	0-0-0	♗g6	e5	♔b8	♖g8[38]	
13	...	♗d3	♗e2	0-0	c4	d5	♗e3	♘h4	♗f4	∞
	...	♗g4!?[39]	♕c7	♘d7	0-0-0	♖g8	c5	♘e5	♗d7[40]	
14	...	♗e2	0-0[41]	c4	d5	♗e3	h3	♕c2	♖ad1	=
	♗g4	e6	♕c7	♘d7	c5	♗d6	h5	0-0-0	♗f5[42]	
15	...	...	h3[43]	0-0	d5	c4[44]	♗e3	♗xb6	♗xf3	±
	...	♕c7	♗h5	♘d7	♖d8	♘b6	♗xf3	ab	cd[45]	
16	...	...	...	...	c4	d5!	♘d4[46]	♗e3		=
	...	...	...	e6	♘d7	0-0-0!	♗g6!	c5[47]		
17	...	...	...	...	...	...	dc	♕a4		∞
	...	...	...	...	...	...	bc	♗c5![48]		

1 5 Ng3 c5 (5 ... h5!?; 5 ... g6!?) 6 Nf3 e6
7 Bd3 Nc6 =.

2 Tartakower Variation.

3 6 g3 Qd5 7 Nf3 Bd6 8 Bg2 0-0 9 0-0 Qh5
10 c4 Bg4 = Boleslavsky.

4 8 Qc2 Re8+ 9 Ne2 g6 10 h4 c5! (10 ... Nd7?
11 h5 Nf8 12 Bh6! Be6 13 0-0-0 Qc7 14 c4! ±
Sznapik-Kostro, Poland 1980) 11 h5 f5 12 hg
hg ∞ Planinc-Puc, Chachak 1969.

5 Byrne-Lein, Brazil 1979.

6 7 ... Be7 8 Nf3 Bg4 9 c3 ± Bogoljubow-
Alekhine, 1942.

7 9 ... Re8 10 0-0 Bf5 11 c3 ± Pachman-
Dobias, Brno 1944.

8 10 ... c5 11 Be3 c4 12 Be4 ± Klovan-
A.Zaitsev, USSR 1969.

9 11 ... b5 12 a4 a6 13 Be4 ± Bikhovsky-
Goldberg, USSR 1963.

10 15 Kd2 Rhe8 16 Rae1 Nc8 17 Kc3 ±
Matulović-Smyslov, Siegen Ol 1970.

11 7 Ne2 b5!? 8 Nb3 Nb6 9 0-0 Be7 10 Ng3 a5
11 c3 a4 12 Nc2 0-0 13 Qf3 Nd5 14 Re1 Re8
15 Bd2 g6 ∞ Sel-Alhadhradi, Graz 1981.
7 ... Bd6 8 Bf4 Nb6 9 Nb3 0-0 10 0-0 Bg4
11 f3 Bxf4 12 Nxf4 Bf5 13 c3 Qc7 14 Nd3
Rad8 15 Re1 g6 16 Nc5 Nd5 = Liberzon-
Korchnoi, Lone Pine 1979.

12 Intending Ba5.

13 Martinović-Knežević, Yugoslav Ch 1981.

14 8 ... Bxb3 9 ab Qxe2+ 10 Nxe2 Bd6
11 Bf4! ±.

15 Analysis.

16 Bronstein-Larsen Variation.

17 6 Qd3!? Na6 7 a3 Nc7 8 Ne2 h5 9 h4 Bg4 =
Barczay-Bronstein, Tallinn 1981.
6 g3!? Bf5 7 Bg2 Qd7 intending ... Na6,
... 0-0-0 and a kingside attack with ... Bh3
plus ... h5.

18 12 b3 Nd7 13 c4 Qe6 14 Re1 Rg8 =
Timman-Bellon, Amsterdam Z 1978.

19 15 Qf5+ Qd7 = Paolozzi-Burger, New
York 1979.

20 7 Bf4 Qb6!? 8 Bb3 a5 9 a4 Bg7 10 Nf3 0-0
11 0-0 Na6 12 Re1 e6 13 Nh4 Bg6 14 Be3
Qc7 = Lau-Keene, Clare Benedict 1979.

21 9 f4 f5! = ECO.

22 ECO.

23 8 Qd2 Bd6 9 Bg3 Qc7 10 Nf3 Nd7 11 0-0-0
0-0-0 = Krutikhin-Voronkov, USSR 1952.

24 ECO.

25 6 ... h5 7 Qd3! Qa5+ 8 Bd2 Qf5 9 Qg3!
Qxd3 10 Bxd3 h4 11 Ne4 Bg7 12 c3 Bg4?
13 f4! Qh5 14 0-0 Nd7 15 f5! Nf8 16 Rae1 1-0
Maeder-Engel, corr. 1978/81.

26 8 ... h6 9 h5 Bh7 10 c3 e6 11 Be3 Nd7
12 Qd2 Qa5 13 Be2 0-0-0 14 Bxh6 Bxh6
15 Qxh6 (Mecking-Larsen, San Antonio 1972)
15 ...e5! ∞ Larsen.

27 15 cb f5!? ∞ Bosković-Rohde, New York
1979.

28 6 ... b6!? Voronkov.

29 7 Bc4 e6 8 Ne2 h5 9 Ng3 Bg6 10 Qe2 Nd7
11 f4 f5 = Ciocaltea-Pachman, Moscow 1956.
7 Nf3 – 6 Nf3.

30 7 ... Nd7!? 8 Ng3 Bg6 9 h4 h6 10 h5 Bh7
11 Bd3 Bxd3 12 Qxd3 Qc7 13 Qf3! e6
14 Bf4 ± Adorjan-Hübner, match 1980.

31 8 h4!? h5 9 Nf4 Bg4 10 Be2 Be2 11 Qxe2
Nd7?! 12 d5! cd 13 Nxd5 ± Bielczyk-
Kaikamdzhozov, Zamardi 1978.

32 15 Qd2 e5 16 Be2 f5 17 de Qxe5 18 Rh4
Nc5 19 Qe3 Qxe3 ∞ Roos-Cirić, Manchester
1981.

33 8 Nf4 h4 9 Bc4 e6 10 0-0 Nd7 11 Re1 Qc7
12 Qf3 0-0-0 =/∓ Guerra-Kaspret, Graz 1981.
8 h4 Nd7 9 Ng3 Bg4 10 Be2 Bxe2 11 Qxe2
Qa5 12 0-0 0-0-0 = Averbakh-Sokolsky, USSR
Ch 1950.

34 15 Qxe3 Nb6 16 b3 h4 = T.Horvath-
Plachetka, Keszthely 1981.

35 7 c3 Nd7 8 g3 Qa5 (intending 9 Bg2 Qa6)
9 Qe2!? ∞.

36 7 ... Nd7 8 0-0 Qc7 9 c4 0-0-0 (9 ... e6 10 d5
Rg8 11 de Bxe6 12 Kh1 0-0-0 13 Qa4 Nb8
14 Be3 c5 15 Rad1 Bd6 16 Rd2 f5 17 Qd1 Ne5
18 Nxe5 Bxe5 19 Rxd8+ Rxd8 20 Qc2 Bd4 ∞
Gy.Horvath-Chandler, Keszthely 1981) 10 Qa4
Kb8 11 b4 Rg8 12 Nh4 Bg4 13 f3 Bh3 14 Be3
Nb6 15 Qb3 e5 = Kosten-Chandler, London
1981.

37 11 Be3 c5 12 b4 Rg8 13 bc Bxc5 14 Nd4
Bh3 15 g3 Bxf1 16 Bxf1 Ne5 ∓ Spassky-
Larsen, Buenos Aires 1979.

38 15 dc Be4 16 f3 ± Cirić-Dlugy, Manchester
1981.

39 7 ... Bxd3 8 Qxd3 Qc7 9 0-0 Nd7 10 d5! ±
(10 c4 e6 11 d5 0-0-0 12 de fe 13 Qe2 ±) Peters.
7 ... e6 8 0-0 (8 Bxf5!?) 8 ... Bg6 9 c4 Qd7
10 Bf4 Qa5 11 Qb3 0-0-0 12 Qxg6 hg 13 c5 g5
14 Bg3 g4 15 Ne1 e5 16 Qc4 ed 17 b4 ±/±
Slaheddine-Kaspret, Graz 1981.
7 ... Bg6 8 0-0 (Radulov-Larsen, Hastings
1971/72) 8 ... e6 9 c4 Na6!? Peters.

40 15 Bg3 f5 ∞.

41 8 h3 Bh5 9 0-0 Bd6!?

42 15 Bd3 Bxd3 16 Qxd3 Ne5 17 Nxe5
Bxe5 = Michimata-Campora, Graz 1981.

43 8 Be3 Nd7 9 c4 e6 10 0-0 Rg8 11 Re1
Bd6 12 g3 0-0-0 13 c5 Be7 14 b4 Ne5 ∓∓
Oswald-Roos, Manchester 1981.

44 11 Qd4 (Pachman) 11 ... cd 12 Qxa7 Qb6
∞/±.

45 Smyslov-Pachman, Amsterdam 1964.

46 12 Qd4!? cd 13 Qxa7 Qb6! ∞/=.

47 Peters.

48 Peters.

223

Caro-Kann with 4 ... ♘d7   1 e4 c6 2 d4 d5 3 ♘c3 de 4 ♘xe4 ♘d7

	5	6	7	8	9	10	11	12	13	
1	♘f3	♘xf6+	♘e5	♗e2[2]	0-0	c4!	♗e3	♘f3	h3	=
	♘gf6	♘xf6	♗e6[1]	g6	♗g7	0-0	♘d7	♗g4	♗xf3[3]	
2	...	...	...	♘d3[4]	c3	♗f4	♕d2	♗e2	de	=
	...	...	♘d7	g6![5]	♗g7	♕a5	0-0	e5	♘xe5[6]	
3	...	♘g3	♗d3	c3[7]	♘xd4	♗b5+	♕e2	0-0		=
	...	e6	c5	cd[8]	♘c5	♗d7	♗e7	0-0		
4	♗c4	♘xf6+	♘f3	0-0[9]	♗g5[10]	♕e2	♖ad1	h3	♕xf3	±
	♘gf6	♘xf6	♗f5	e6	♗e7	♗g4	0-0	♗xf3	♘d5[11]	
5	...	...	...	♕e2[12]	♗g5	0-0-0	h3	♕xf3	♗xe7	±
	...	...	...	e6	♗e7	♗g4[13]	♗xf3	♘d5	♕xe7[14]	
6	...	♘g5	♕e2[16]	♗d3[17]	♘5f3	dc[18]	♗d2[19]	0-0-0	♘h3	±
	...	e6[15]	♘b6	h6	c5	♘bd7	♗xc5	♕c7[20]	g5[21]	
7	...	...	...	...	...	...	c6	♗d2	♘d4	±
	...	...	...	...	...	...	bc	♗e7	♕b6[22]	
8	...	...	...	...	...	...	♘e5	♘gf3	0-0	=
	...	...	...	...	...	♗xc5	♘bd7	♕c7[23]	0-0[24]	

[1] 7... ♗f5 8 c3 ♗g6 (8 ... e6 9 g4! ♗g6 10 h4 h5 11 g5 ♘d5 12 ♘xg6 fg 13 ♕c2 ± Karpov-Hort, Bugojno 1978) 9 h4 ♘d7 10 ♘c4 h5 11 ♗g5 f6 12 ♗f4 b5 13 ♗d3 ♗xd3 14 ♕xd3 ♔f7 15 ♘e3 ♘b6 16 0-0 e6 17 ♖fe1 ± Karpov-Spassky, Bad Kissingen 1980.

[2] 8 c3 g6 9 ♗c4 ♗xc4 10 ♘xc4 ♗g7 11 0-0 0-0 12 ♖e1 ♖c8 13 ♕e2 ♖e8 14 ♗f4 ♕d5 15 ♗e5 c5 16 dc ♕xc5 = Barczay-Razuvayev, Keszthely 1981.

[3] 14 ♗xf3 ± Hort.

[4] 8 ♘f3 ♘f6! =.
8 ♗f4!? ♘xe5 9 ♗xe5 ♕d5.

[5] 8 ... e6 9 ♗f4 ♗e7 10 ♗e2 0-0 11 0-0 b6 12 ♗f3 ♗b7 13 ♖e1 ± Kavalek-Bleiman, Netanya 1971.

[6] 14 ♘xe5 ♗xe5 15 ♗g5 ♗e6 16 0-0 ♗g7 = Karpov-Sosonko, Amsterdam 1980.

[7] 8 0-0 ♗e7 9 b3 cd 10 ♘xd4 0-0 11 ♗b2 ♘c5 = Plachetka-Chandler, Keszthely 1981.

[8] 8 ... ♕c7 9 0-0 ♗d6 10 ♖e1 0-0 11 ♕e2 b6

12 ♘e5! ♗b7 13 ♗g5 h6 14 ♗f4 ±/± Gurgenidze-Bagirov, Tbilisi 1980.

[9] 8 c3 e6 9 ♕e2 ♗g4 10 h3 ♗xf3 11 ♕xf3 ♕c7 12 0-0 ♗e7 = Mnatsakanian-Filip, Erevan 1965.

[10] 9 h3 ♗e7 10 ♕e2 0-0 = Reshevsky-Smyslov, Palma de Mallorca IZ 1970.

[11] Larsen-Filip, Palma de Mallorca IZ 1970. 14 ♗e3! Larsen.

[12] 8 ♘e5 e6 9 0-0 ♗d6 10 ♕e2 0-0 11 ♗g5 ♕c7 = Spassky-Ilivitsky, Sochi 1965.

[13] 10 ... h6 11 ♗h4 ♘e4 12 g4! ♗h7 13 ♗g3 ♘xg3 14 fg ♕c7 15 ♘e5 ♗d6 16 h4 ± Tal-Füster, Portorož IZ 1958.

[14] 14 ♔b1 ♖d8 15 ♘e4 b5 16 ♗d3 a5 17 c3 ♕d6 18 g3 b4 19 c4 ± Fischer-Petrosian, Bled 1961.

[15] 6 ... ♘d5 7 ♘1f3 h6 8 ♘e4 ♘7b6 9 ♗b3 ♗f5 10 ♘g3 ♗h7 11 0-0 e6 12 ♘e5 ±.

[16] 7 ♘e2 h6 8 ♘f3 ♗d6 9 0-0 ♕c7 10 ♖e1 0-0 11 ♘c3 b5! 12 ♗d3 ♗b7 13 ♘e4 ♘xe4 14 ♖xe4 c5 ∞ Boleslavsky.

[17] 8 ♗b3 h6 9 ♘5f3 a5! =/∞ Tal-Petrosian, USSR Ch 1973.

[18] 10 ♗e3 ♘bd5 11 ♘e5 ♘xe3 12 fe ♗d6 =.

[19] 11 ♘e5 ♘xe5 12 ♕xe5 ♕a5+ = Hazai-Barczay, Keszthely 1981.

11 b4 b6 12 ♘d4 ♘d5! (12... bc?? 13 ♘c6 ♕c7 14 ♕xe6+ fe 15 ♗g6 mate) 13 ♗b2 (13 ♘xe6!? fe 14 ♗g6+ $\overline{\overline{\infty}}$) 13... ♗xb4! 14 ♗e4 (14 c6 ♘xd3+ 15 ♕xd3 ♘c5 16 ♕f3 ♗a6! Speelman) 14... ♗a6 15 ♕f3 ♘xc5 16 ♗xa8? (16 ♘c6! ♘e4! 17 ♕xd8 ♘xc2+ 18 ♔d1 ♖xd8+ 19 ♔xc2 ♖c8+ = Balashov) 16... ♘xc2+! 17 ♘xc2 ♘d3+ 18 ♔d2 ♘xb2+ 19 ♔c1 ♘d3+ 20 ♔b1 ♗c5 ∓ van der Wiel-Balashov, Malta Ol 1980.

[20] 12... 0-0 13 ♘h3 ♕c7 14 g4 ±/ ± Fedorov-Volchek, USSR 1981.

[21] 14 ♘e1 ±.

[22] 14 ♘gf3 c5 15 ♘b5 0-0 16 0-0 ♗b7 17 a4 ±.

[23] 12... ♘xe5 13 ♘xe5 0-0 14 ♗d2 ♕d5 **15 0-0** ♗d4. **15 f4?** b5! intending ... ♗b7 $\overline{+}$. **15 0-0-0** ♕xa2 16 c3 ∞, e.g. 16 ... b5 17 ♗xh6 ♗b7 18 ♘d7 ♘xd7 19 ♕g4 ♕a1+ 20 ♗b1 g6 21 ♖xd7 ♗a3 22 ba ♕xc3+ 23 ♔d1 ♖fd8 24 ♖d2.

[24] **14 ♖e1** ♖e8 15 ♗f4 ♗d6 = Horvath-Navarovsky, Hungarian Ch 1980.

14 ♗f4 ♗d6 15 ♘xd7 ♗xd7 16 ♗xd6 ♕xd6 17 ♘e5 ♖fd8 = Velikov-Spiridonov, Herculana Z 1982.

Caro-Kann: Classical (Introduction)				1 e4 c6 2 d4 d5 3 ♘c3 de 4 ♘xe4 ♗f5				
	5	6	7	8	9	10	11	12	13
1	♘c5[1]	♗d3	♘xd3	♘f3	0-0	♖e1	c4	♗f4	♘fe5	=
	♕c7[2]	♗xd3	♘d7	e6	♘gf6	♗e7	0-0	♗d6	♖fd8[3]	
2	♘g3	♘1e2	♘f4	♘xg6	♘e4	g3	♗g2	♗xe4	0-0	=
	♗g6	e6[4]	♗d6	hg	♗e7	♘f6	♘xe4	♘d7	♕a5[5]	
3	...	♗c4	♘1e2	0-0[6]	f4	♗d3	♕xd3	b3	♗b2	=
	...	e6	♘f6	♗d6	♕d7	♗xd3	g6	♘a6	♗e7[7]	
4	...	♘f3	♗d3	0-0	c4	♗xg6	♕a4	b4	♖e1[9]	∞
	...	♘d7	e6	♕c7[8]	0-0-0	hg	♔b8	♘h6	♘f5[10]	
5	...	h4	♘h3	♘f4	♗c4	0-0	♘gh5	♖e1	c3	=
	...	h6	♘f6[11]	♗h7	e6	♗d6	0-0	♖e8	♘bd7[12]	
6	...	...	♘f3	♗d3	♕xd3	♗d2	0-0-0	♔b1	c4	=
	...	...	♘d7	♗xd3	♕c7	e6	♘gf6	0-0-0	c5[13]	

[1] 5 ♗d3 ♘d7 6 ♘f3 ♘gf6 =.

[2] 5... e5!? 6 ♘xb7 ♕e7 7 ♘a5 ed+ 8 ♗e2 ♕b4+ 9 ♗d2 ♕xb2 10 ♗d3 ♗xd3 11 cd ♗b4 ∞ Klovan-Machulsky, USSR 1978.

[3] Sigurjonsson-Burger, Brighton 1981.

[4] 6... ♘d7 7 h4 h6 8 ♘f4 ♗h7 9 ♗c4 e5! 10 ♕e2 ♕e7 11 de ♕xe5 12 ♗e3 ♗c5 = Tal-Botvinnik, match 1960.

[5] Byrne-Kavalek, US Ch (Z) 1981.

[6] 8 ♘f4 ♗d6 9 ♗b3 ♕c7 10 ♕f3 ♘bd7 11 h4 e5 12 ♘xg6 hg 13 ♗e3 0-0-0 ∞.

[7] Van der Wiel-Seirawan, Baden 1980.

[8] 8 ... ♘gf6 9 ♖e1 ♗e7 10 c4 0-0 11 ♗xg6 hg 12 ♗f4 ± Najdorf-Kotov, Zürich C 1953.

[9] 13 ♕b3 ♘f5 14 a4 e5 15 de ♘xe5 16 ♘xe5 ♕xe5 17 ♗b2 ♕c7 ∞ Dückstein-Petrosian, Varna Ol 1962.

[10] 14 ♕b3 ∞ Neuronov-Mandzhdaladze, USSR 1980.

[11] 7 ... e5 8 de ♕a5+ 9 ♗d2 ♕xe5+ 10 ♗e2 ♕xb2 11 0-0 ♕xc2 12 ♕e1 ♗e7 13 ♖c1 ♕a4 14 ♘f4 ± Espig-Bohnisch, East German Ch 1979.

[12] Bellon-Seirawan, Las Palmas 1981.

[13] Parma-Ivkov, Yugoslavia 1964.

225

Caro-Kann: Classical 1 e4 c6 2 d4 d5 3 ♘c3 de 4 ♘xe4 ♗f5
5 ♘g3 ♗g6 6 h4 h6 7 h5 ♗h7 8 ♘f3 ♘d7 9 ♗d3 ♗xd3 10 ♕xd3 ♕c7

	11	12	13	14	15	16	17	18	19	
1	♖h4	♗f4	♗xd6	♘e4	♕a3	ba	♘c5[3]	dc	♖b1	=
	e6[1]	♗d6[2]	♕xd6	♕e7	♕xa3	♔e7	♘xc5	a5	♖a7![4]	
2	0-0	c4[5]	d5[7]	♕d4	♗f4	♕xc4[9]	♗xd6	♕xf7[10]		=
	e6	0-0-0[6]	♘c5[8]	ed	dc!	♗d6	♕xd6			
3	♗d2	♕e2	0-0-0	♖h4[12]	♗f4[14]	d5	c4			∞
	e6	♘gf6	c5!?[11]	♖c8[13]	♕a5	♕xa2	♗e7![15]			
4	...	...	...	♘e5	♗a5[17]	♗xb6[18]	c4	♘e4	♕xe4	=
	...	...	0-0-0	♘b6[16]	♖d5	ab	♖d8[19]	♘xe4	♗d6[20]	
5	...		...	...	...	...	f4	♔b1	c3[22]	∞
	...	...	...	...	...	...	♗d6[21]	♖d8	c5![23]	
6	...	...	c4	♘e5[25]	de	f4	0-0-0	♔b1		∞
	...	0-0-0[24]	♘xe5[26]	♘d7	♘c5	♘d3+	♘xb2![27]			
7	...	c4	c5[28]	♕a3[30]	♕xa7	♗a5	♔f1	♕xc5	♗xc7	=
	...	♘gf6	0-0-0!?[29]	e5!	ed	♖e8+	♗xc5	♘xc5	♔xc7[31]	
8	...	0-0-0	c4	♗c3	♔b1	♘xd4	♘b3[32]	♕f3	♖xd1	∞
	...	♘gf6	0-0-0	c5	cd	a6	♘c5[33]	♖xd1+	♗e7[34]	
9	...		♘e4[35]	g3	♕xe4	♔b1	♕e2!	♖he1	♘e5	±
	...		0-0-0	♘xe4[36]	♗e7[37]	♖he8	♗d6	♘f6[38]	c5[39]	
10	...	...	...	...	...	♕e2	c4	♗c3[41]	♘xd4[42]	=
	...	...	...	...	♘f6	♗d6[40]	c5	cd	a6[43]	
11	...		...	♔b1	♘xf6+	dc	♕e2	♘e5		∞
	...	...	♗e7	c5	♘xf6	♗xc5	0-0	♖fd8[44]		

1 e4 c6 2 d4 d5 3 ♘c3 de 4 ♘xe4 ♗f5 5 ♘g3 ♗g6
6 h4 h6 7 h5 ♗h7 8 ♘f3 ♘d7 9 ♗d3 ♗xd3 10 ♕xd3 e6

	11	12	13	14	15	16	17	18	19	
12	♗f4	c3[45]	a4	0-0	♖fe1	♘e5[47]	de	♗d2	♘e4	∓
	♕a5+	♘gf6	c5	♗e7![46]	0-0	♘xe5	♘d5	♖fd8	♘f6	
13	...	0-0-0	♔b1[48]	♘e4	♕xe4	♕e2	♘e5			∞
	♘gf6	♗e7	a5	♘xe4	♘f6	a4	♕d5[49]			
14	♗d2	0-0-0	♘e4[52]	♕xe4	♕e2	c4				=
	♘gf6[50]	♗e7[51]	♘xe4	♘f6	♕d5	♕f5[53]				

[1] 11 ... ♘gf6 12 ♗f4 ♕a5+ 13 ♗d2 ♕b5 14 ♕xb5 cb = Sax-Hort, Tilburg 1979.

[2] 12 ... ♕a5+ 13 ♗d2 ♕b6 14 0-0-0 ♗e7 15 ♖hh1 ♘gf6 = Gilezetdinov-Shakarov, corr. 1976.

[3] 17 ♖b1 ♖b8 18 ♘c5 ♗xc5 19 dc a5 20 ♘e5 ♘f6 21 ♖d4 ♖hc8 22 ♖b3 ♖c7 23 g4 ♖d8 =

Bellon-Pomar, Olot 1975.

[4] 20 ♘e5! ♘f6 21 ♖d4 ♖c8! 22 a4 ♖c7 23 ♖bd1 ♖a6! = Harper-Seirawan, USA 1980.

[5] 12 ♕e2 ♘gf6 13 ♘e5 ♗d6 14 ♖e1 0-0 = Vitolins-Kivlan, USSR 1980.

[6] 12 ... ♘gf6!? intending ... 0-0.

[7] 13 b4!? ♗xb4 14 ♖b1 ♗d6 15 ♘e4 ∞

Vitolins-Okhotnik, USSR 1980.

[8] 13 ... ♘b6 14 ♗e3 ed 15 c5 ♘c4 16 ♗d4 ± Mikhalchishin.

[9] 16 ♗xc7 ♖xd4 17 ♘xd4 ♔xc7 18 ♖ac1 b5 ∓ Mikhalchishin.

[10] 18 b4? ♘e6 19 b5 ♘e7 ∓ Vitolins-Mikhalchishin, USSR Ch 1979.
18 ♕xf7 =.

[11] 13 ... ♗d6?! 14 ♘f5 ♗f4 15 ♗xf4 (15 ♘xg7+ ♔f8 16 ♘xe6+ fe 17 ♕xe6 ♖e8 18 ♕f5 ♗xd2+ 19 ♖xd2 ♖g8 ∞) 15 ... ♕xf4+ 16 ♘e3 ± Ivanović-Vukić, Yugoslav Ch 1978.

[12] 14 ♔b1 ♗e7 =.
14 c4 cd 15 ♖xd4 ♖c8 16 ♔b1 ♗c5 17 ♗c3 0-0 = Marjanović-Seirawan, Niš 1979.
14 ♘f5!? 0-0-0 15 ♘e3 ∞ Faibisovich-Okhotnik, USSR 1979.

[13] 14 ... ♗e7 15 dc ♘xc5 = Butnoris-Bagirov, USSR 1975.

[14] 15 dc ♘xc5 16 ♖c4 b5 17 ♖d4 ½-½ Spassky-Portisch, Tilburg 1978.
15 ♘f5 cd 16 ♘3xd4 ♕c4! 17 ♕xc4 ∓ Gaprindashvili-Chiburdanidze, match 1978.

[15] Shakarov-Asriyan, corr. 1973.

[16] 14 ... ♘xe5 15 de ♘d7 16 f4 ♗e7 17 ♘e4 ♘c5 18 ♘c3 f6 19 ef ♗xf6 20 ♕c4 ♕b6 21 b4 ♘a6 22 ♘e4 ± Spassky-Petrosian, match 1966.

[17] 15 ♖h4 ♗d6 16 ♗a5 ♗xe5 17 de ♖xd1+ 18 ♔xd1 ♘fd7 19 ♖e4 ♕d8! 20 ♔c1 ♘c5 21 ♖g4 ♕d5 ∓ Privorotsky-Makogonov, USSR 1969. 16 ♘f1 =.

[18] 16 b4?! ♖xa5 17 ba ♗a3+ 18 ♔b1 ♘a4 ∞.

[19] 17 ... ♖a5 18 ♔b1 ♗d6 19 f4 ♖d8 20 ♖d2 b5 21 c5 ♗xe5 22 fe ♖a4! ∞ Marczell-Shakarov, corr. 1977.

[20] 20 ♘f3 ♗e7 intending ... ♗f6 =.
20 f4 f5 21 ♕e2 ♗xe5 22 ♕xe5 ♕xe5 23 de g5! (23 ... ♖hg8? 24 ♖xd8+! ± Martin-Pomar, Las Palmas 1977) 24 hg ♖dg8 =.

[21] 17 ... ♖d8!?

[22] 19 c4 ♖a5 – note 19.

[23] 19 ... ♔b8?! 20 ♘f1 ± Romanishin-Bagirov, Lvov 1978.
19 ... c5! ∞.

[24] 13 ... ♗d6 14 ♘f5 ♗f4 15 ♗xf4 ♕xf4 16 ♘e3 c5! 17 ♘d5 ♘xd5 18 cd 0-0 19 de ♖fe8 20 0-0 ♖xe6 21 ♕b5 ♕c7! = Tal-Portisch, Bugojno 1978.

[25] 14 c5 ♖g8 15 b4 g6 ∞ Karpov-Hort, Portorož/Ljubljana 1975.

[26] 14 ... ♘b8!? 15 ♗c3 c5 16 0-0-0 ♘c6 =.

[27] Klovan-Andreyev, corr. 1976.

[28] 13 ♕e2 ♗d6 14 ♘f5 0-0 15 ♘xd6 ♕xd6 16 0-0-0 b5 17 g4 bc 18 g5 hg 19 h6 g6 20 h7+ ♘xh7 21 ♘xg5 ♘xg5 22 ♗xg5 c3! 23 ♕e5!! cb+ 24 ♔b1 ♕xe5 29 de f6 30 ♖xd7 fg = Kasparov.
13 0-0-0 b5 14 c5 (14 ♘c5 ♘xc5 15 dc ♕xc5! 16 ♖he1 bc 17 ♕c2 ♕b5 ∓ Hanov-

Shakarov, USSR 1979) 14 ... 0-0-0 ∞.

[29] 13 ... b6 14 b4 a5 15 cb ♕xb6 16 ba ♕a6! 17 ♕xa6 ♖xa6 18 ♘e5 ♗d6 ∞ Rom-Porath, Israel 1976.

[30] 14 ♕e2 – note 25.
14 b4 e5 ∞.

[31] Kayumov-Shakarov, USSR 1976.

[32] 17 ♕e2 ♗d6 18 ♘f1 ♘c5 19 ♘b3 ♘xb3 = Reshevsky-Sherwin, US Ch 1966/67.

[33] 17 ... ♗e7 18 ♗a5 b6 19 ♗c3 ♘c5 20 ♕f3 ♕b7 21 ♕xb7+ ♔xb7 22 ♘xc5 bc 23 f3 ± Spassky-Portisch, match (9) 1980.

[34] 20 ♗a5 ♕e5 21 ♖e1 ♕d6! ∞ Minev.

[35] 13 ♔b1 0-0-0 14 c4 c5 15 ♕e2 ♗d6 16 ♘e4 ♘xe4 17 ♕xe4 ♘f6 (17 ... ♗e7 = Matulović-Hort, Sousse IZ 1967) 18 ♕e2 ♕c6!?

[36] 14 ... c5? 15 ♗f4 c4 16 ♗xc7! cd 17 ♗xd8 ♘xe4 18 ♖h4! ±.
14 ... ♘xc5 ♗xc5 16 c4!?± (16 ♔b1 ♗d6 17 c4 c5 18 ♗c3 a6 = Trifunović; 16 ♕e2!? ♗xd4 17 ♗f4).

[37] 15 ... c5 16 dc ♘xc5 17 ♕c4! ±.

[38] 18 ... ♖e7 19 c4 c5 20 ♗c3 ♘f6 21 ♘e5 cd (Kasparov-Vukić, Skara 1980) 22 ♗xd4! ±.

[39] Geller-Kasparov, USSR Ch 1978.
20 ♗c1!? ±.

[40] 16 ... c5 17 dc ♘xc5 18 ♖h4! ± Tal-Hübner, Montreal 1979.

[41] 18 ♔b1 cd 19 ♘xd4 ♗xg3! 20 ♘b5 ♕e5 ∞.

[42] 19 ♗xd4 ♕a5!? 20 ♔b1 ♗c7 21 c5 ♕a4 22 b3 ♕c6 23 ♘e5 ♗xe5 24 ♗xe5 (Polovodin-Haritonov, USSR 1980) 24 ... ♖xd1+ 25 ♖xd1 ♖d8 = Polovodin.

[43] 20 ♖d2 ♕c5 21 ♔c2 ♗c7 22 g4 ♗a5 23 ♘b3 ♕c6 = Cabrilo-Vadasz, 1981.

[44] Hübner-Korchnoi, match (1) 1980.

[45] 12 ♗d2 ♕c7 – 10 ... ♕c7.

[46] 14 ... ♖c8 15 ♖fe1 (15 ♕b5 ♕b6 16 ♖fe1 ± Gaprindashvili) 15 ... c4 (15 ... ♗e7!?) 16 ♕c2 ♗e7 (16 ... ♗xh5 17 ♘xh5 ♕xh5 18 ♕e4 b6 19 ♕b7 ± Gaprindashvili) 17 ♘e5 0-0 18 ♘f5 ∞ Gaprindashvili-Nikolac, Wijk aan Zee 1979.

[47] 16 ♘f5 ♖fe8 17 ♗xh6+ gh 18 ♘e5 ♗xe5 19 de ♘h7 20 ♗xh6 ♗f8 ∓ Vitolins-Kivlan, USSR 1978.

[48] 13 ♖he1 a5 14 c4 (14 ♘e5 a4? 15 ♘g6!! ±± Belyavsky-Larsen, Tilburg 1981; 14 ... 0-0! Tal) 14 ... b5! 15 c5 ♘d5 16 ♗e5 0-0 17 ♘e4 ♘7f6 18 ♗xf6 ♘xf6 19 ♗xf6 ♗xf6 ∓ Tal-Larsen, Tilburg 1980.

[49] Torre-Karpov, Moscow 1981.

[50] 11 ... ♕c7 – 10 ... ♕c7.

[51] 12 ... c5? 13 ♖he1 ♗e7 14 d5! ± Kavalek-Hübner, Montreal 1979.

[52] 13 ♖he1 a5 14 ♕e2 0-0 15 ♔b1 ♕b6 = Hübner-Larsen, Tilburg 1980.

[53] Karpov-Larsen, Linares 1981.

Sicilian Defence

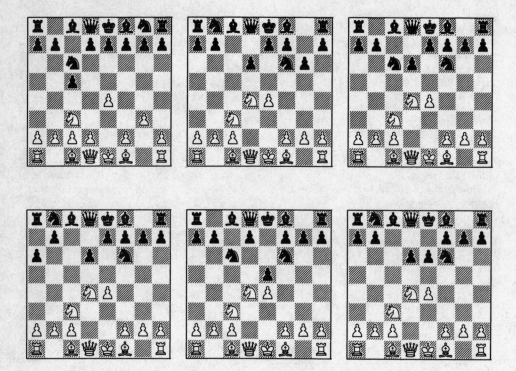

The most popular reply to 1 e4, the Sicilian steers clear of symmetrical defence in favour of a more dynamic pawn structure. By trading his c-pawn for White's d-pawn Black guarantees pressure down the half open c-file and chances to fashion his central pawn majority into a strong centre. In return for these long-term possibilities White gets a lead in development which, combined with an edge in space and the half-open d-file, can lead to quick and violent attacks.

The balance is delicate in this opening and through continuous tournament practice many recurring tactical themes for attack and defence have been mapped. A classic example is Black's c-file pressure culminating in an exchange sacrifice on c3 to undermine White's pawn centre. This idea cuts across all variations of the Sicilian but is predominant in the Scheveningen and Dragon.

White's initiative can reach hurricane proportions if Black neglects his king safety or piece development while engaged in more esoteric pursuits. Black's most reliable stratagem in the face of White storming his bastions is to fall back on a truism that will serve the Sicilian player well, and that is the wisdom of meeting a flank attack with a reaction in the centre. Here Black's central preponderance makes this an extremely effective tack, and a well-timed blow in this sector of the board can completely turn the game around.

Another critical theme for the defence is the acquisition of the e5 square. Whether or not Black can seize this post for defence is often the difference between success and failure for the attack.

A common strategical formation is the stationing of White pawns on c4 and e4, the well-known 'Maroczy Bind'. White's strategy is ambitious, attempting to restrict Black's expansion on the queenside and in the centre. This ambition entails an added responsibility in that White must exercise eternal vigilance on a number of fronts to maintain his grip on the position. However, if White is up to the task Black suffers from his lack of space and may be slowly strangled.

In the **Closed Sicilian** (2 ♘c3 ♘c6 3 g3), White's refusal to trade a centre pawn for Black's c-pawn leads to a slow, strategical battle where the first player has a choice of a gradual kingside storm or erecting a formidable centre with c3 and d4. Generally, Black relies on a full-scale onslaught on the queenside to provide adequate counterplay. Although not without danger for Black, the closed systems have never caught on as a really serious threat to the Sicilian.

Open Systems

The **Dragon** (2 ♘f3 d6 3 d4 cd 4 ♘xd4 ♘f6 5 ♘c3 g6) is in many ways the most logically motivated of Sicilians, emphasizing quick development and with all of Black's pieces seeking aggressive posts. The acid test has always been the Yugoslav attack, a direct and unabashed attempt to give mate. Like so many popular variations, the Yugoslav Dragon has acquired a vast body of theory, and the play in this line is so complex that it is foolhardy to enter into it without doing one's 'homework'. World-renowned specialists in this line are Miles, Mestel and Gufeld.

Against the two knights' formation (2 ♘f3 d6 3 d4 cd 4 ♘xd4 ♘f6 5 ♘c3 ♘c6) White's main choices are the **Sozin/Velimirović Attack** (6 ♗c4) and the **Richter-Rauzer** (6 ♗g5). Both variations rest their hopes on producing dividends through the use of violence. The play is razor-sharp, characterised in most cases by castling on opposite sides and full-scale attacks. Theory is not as extensive here as in variations like the Najdorf or Dragon and defence depends on a sophisticated combination of defence and counterattack.

The **Najdorf** (2 ♘f3 d6 3 d4 cd 4 ♘xd4 ♘f6 5 ♘c3 a6) is fraught with dangers for both sides and requires considerable expertise. It tends to attract sharp and ambitious players who intend to specialise in the intricacies of this defence. Fischer, Polugayevsky and Browne are good examples of players devoted to the Najdorf, and it has served each of them well.

The **Pilnik/Pelikan/Lasker/Sveshnikov** (2 ♘f3 ♘c6 3 d4 cd 4 ♘d4 ♘f6 5 ♘c3 e5) is the latest rage, the result of tremendous successes scored by the Soviet GM Sveshnikov who has devoted lifelong energies to forging a complex and aggressive system that has served him faithfully throughout his career. Black accepts an odd pawn structure and a gaping hole on d5 in return for the bishop pair and a wealth of possibilities for active counterplay. It leads to lively play and is a volatile and difficult variation for both sides to handle.

The **Taimanov** (2 ♘f3 e6 3 d4 cd 4 ♘xd4 ♘c6), like its close relative the Kan, may transpose into the Scheveningen at several junctures. In its own territory, however, it offers scope for sophisticated manoeuvring and it justifiably bears the name of Soviet GM Mark Taimanov, who has constantly discovered imaginative new strategical possibilities, infusing the line with his own brand of defensive versatility.

In the **Kan** (2 ♘f3 e6 3 d4 cd 4 ♘xd4 a6) Black essays slow development to construct a pawn shell that he hopes will deter aggressive demonstrations from White's more active pieces. Miles, Karpov and Gheorghiu are the masters of the options that this extremely flexible variation has to offer.

The **Scheveningen** (2 ♘f3 e6 3 d4 cd 4 ♘xd4 ♘f6 5 ♘c3 d6) is the classic Sicilian. Black is subjected to persistent pressure on the kingside in return for counterplay on the queenside and the c-file. The defender must exercise great care in order not to succumb to direct attack, but he has rich opportunities for counterattack as the reward for success.

	2	3	4	5	6	7	8	9	10	
1	b3[1]	♗b2	♗b5+	♗xd7+	♗xf6	♕h5	♘e2	♕xg4	♘bc3	∞
	d6[2]	♘f6[3]	♗d7	♕xd7	gf	♖g8[4]	♕g4	♖xg4	♘c6[5]	
2	b4	a3	ed[6]	♘f3	ab	♗a3	♘xa3	♘b5	♗c4	∓
	cb	d5!	♕xd5	e5	♗xb4	♗xa3	♘c6	♕d8	♘f6[7]	
3	f4	♘f3	a4	♗e2[9]	d3	0-0	♘c3	h3	♗e3	=
	d6[8]	a6	♘c6	♘f6	e6	♗e7	0-0	♖b8	b5[10]	
4	...	ed	♘c3	♘f3	♗b5+	♕e2	♘e5	♕c4	♕xc5	∞∞
	d5	♕xd5	♕d8	♘f6[11]	♗d7	g6	♗g7	0-0!	♗f5![12]	
5	g3	ed	♘f3	♗g2	♔f1	h3	♘c3	♕e2	d3	∞
	d5[13]	♕xd5	♗g4	♕e6+	♕d6!?[14]	♗d7	e5	f6	♘e7[15]	
6	♘e2	♘bc3[16]	ed	♘xd5	d4	♕xd4	♘xd4	♗e3	0-0-0	±
	♘f6	d5?![17]	♘xd5	♕xd5	cd	♕xd4	a6	♗d7	♘c6[18]	
7	d3	♘f3[19]	g3	♘bd2	♗g2	0-0	♖e1	e5	♘f1	±/∞
	♘c6	e6	d5[20]	♘f6[21]	♗e7	0-0	b5	♘d7[22]	a5[23]	

[1] 2 ♗c4 e6 3 ♕e2 ♘c6 4 c3 ♗e7 5 d3 d5 6 ♗b3 ♘f6 =.

[2] 2 ... e6 3 ♗b2 ♘c6 4 ♘f3 d6 5 d4 cd 6 ♘xd4 ♘f6 7 ♗d3 (7 ♘xc6 bc 8 e5!? Polugayevsky) 7 ... ♗d7 ±/= Nei-Knaak, Tallinn 1979.

[3] 3 ... ♘c6 4 ♗b5 ♗d7 5 f4 ♘f6 6 ♘c3 a6 7 ♗e2 b5 8 ♗f3 ♖c8 9 ♘d5 ± Passerotti-Csom, Rome 1979.

[4] 7 ... ♘c6 8 ♘e2!? Polugayevsky.

[5] 11 0-0 ♗h6! ∞/= Shichovany-Lapenis, Beltsy 1979.

[6] 5 e5 ♘c6 6 d4 ♕b6 7 ♗e3 ♗f5 ∓ Orienter-Grünfeld, Vienna 1946.

[7] ECO.

[8] 2 ... ♘c6 3 ♘f3 e6 4 ♗b5 g6 5 ♗xc6 bc 6 c4 ♗g7 7 ♕e2 ♕b6 8 e5 ♘h6 9 ♘c3 ♘f5 10 ♘e4 ± Williams-Staunton, London 1851. 5 ... dc 6 d3 ♗g7 7 0-0 ♘e7 8 ♘c3 0-0 9 ♕e1 b6 10 a4 ♗a6 (Larsen-Perez, Amsterdam IZ 1964) 11 b3! ±.
2 ... ♘f6 3 ♘c3 d5 4 e5 d4 5 ef dc 6 fg cd+ 7 ♕xd2 ♕xd2+ 8 ♗xd2 ♗xg7 9 0-0-0 ♗f5 10 ♘e2 ± Miles-Plachetka, Dubna 1976.
2 ... e6 3 ♘f3 d5 4 ed ed 5 ♗e2 (5 ♗b5+) 5 ... ♗d6 6 c3 ♘c6 = Horwitz-Staunton, London 1846.

[9] 5 ♗c4?! e6 6 ♘c3 ♘f6! 7 ♕e2 ♗e7 8 d3 d5!

[10] 11 ab ab 12 ♕d2 b4 13 ♘d1 = ECO.

[11] 5 ... ♘c6?! 6 ♗b5 ♗d7 7 0-0 ♘f6 8 ♘e5±/± Westerinen-Tseshkovsky, Sochi 1981.

[12] Westerinen-Polugayevsky, Sochi 1981.

[13] 2 ... e6 3 ♗g2 d5 4 ed ed 5 d4! cd 6 ♘e2 ±.
2 ... g6 3 ♗g2 ♗g7 4 d3 d6 5 f4 ♘c6 6 c3 e6 7 ♘f3 ♘ge7 8 0-0 d5 ∞ Chandler-Cebalo, Vršac 1981.

[14] 6 ... ♗h3 7 d4 cd 8 ♗xd4 ♕d7 9 ♘c3 ♘c6 10 ♘xc6 ♕xc6 = Pachman-Taimanov, Buenos Aires 1960.

[15] Chandler-Levin, England 1981.

[16] 3 e5 ♘g4 4 d4 cd 5 ♕xd4 d6 6 ed ♘c6 7 de ♕xe7 8 ♕f4 g6 = Lutikov-Bronstein, USSR 1971.

[17] 2 ... d6/♘c6/e6 3 d4!

[18] 11 ♘b3 ± Keres-Kotov, Moscow 1947.

[19] 3 f4 g6 4 c3 ♗g7 5 ♗e3 d6 6 ♗e2 ♘f6 7 ♘d2 0-0 8 g4 b5 9 a3 ♗b7 10 ♗f3! a5 11 h4 (The "Big Clamp") ±/∞ Day-Benko, New York 1980. With White's early choices, such as d3 and f4, clearly interchangeable, there are frequent transpositional possibilities in the lines examined in this section, and between them and the Closed Sicilian.

[20] 4 ... g6 5 ♗g2 (5 d4!?) 5 ... ♗g7 6 0-0 ♘ge7 7 ♖e1 0-0 8 e5 b6 9 ♘c3 d6! 10 ed ♕xd6 11 ♗f4 ♕d8 12 ♕d2 ♗b7 13 ♗h6 ♘f5 =/∓ Lee-Keene, Bristol 1968. 7 c3 0-0 8 d4 ± Fischer-Durao, Havana Ol 1966.

[21] 5 ... ♗d6 6 ♗g2 ♘ge7 7 0-0 0-0 8 ♘h4 b6 9 f4 de 10 de ♗a6 11 ♖e1 c4 12 c3 ± Fischer-Ivkov, Santa Monica 1966. 9 ... f6! =.

[22] 9 ... ♘e8 10 ♘f1 a5 11 h4 a4 12 ♗f4 a3 13 b3 b4!? intending ... ♘a7-b5.

[23] 11 h4 b4 12 ♗f4 ♗a6 13 ♘e3 a4 (intending ... a3) 14 a3 ♗b5! ∞ Damjanović-Uhlmann, Monaco 1968. 13 ♘g5!? ♕e8 14 ♕g4 a4?? 15 ♘xe6! 1-0 Bronstein-Uhlmann, Moscow 1971 (14 ... ♗xg5! ±).

It is advisable to compare notes 20-23 with King's Indian Attack lines in the Réti and French sections.

	Smith-Morra Gambit			1 e4 c5 2 d4 cd 3 c3					
	3	4	5	6	7	8	9	10	11
1	...	♗xd3	c4	♘f3	0-0	h3!	♘c3	♗e3	♖c1	±
	d3[1]	♘c6!?[2]	g6	♗g7	d6	♘f6	♘d7	♘c5!?[3]	♘xd3[4]
2	...	♘xc3	♘f3	♗c4	e5!?	♘xe5	♕d5	bc	♕d6	∞
	dc	♘c6	g6	♗g7	♘xe5[5]	♗xe5	♗xc3+	e6
3	...	...	...	...	0-0	♕e2	h3[6]	♖fd1	♗g5	∞
	...	...	...	...	d6	♘f6	0-0	♘d7
4	...	...	...	♗c4	0-0	♕e2	♖d1	♗f4[9]	♖ac1	∞
	...	...	e6	d6[7]	♘f6	a6[8]	♕c7	♗e7	♕b8[10]
5	...	...	♘f3[11]	♗c4	0-0	♗g5?![13]	♗f4	♗g3	a3	∓
	...	e6	♗c5[12]	♘e7	0-0	f6	♘g6	♘c6	♘ge5[14]

---

[1] **3 ...** ♘f6 4 e5 ♘d5 – 2 c3 ♘f6 3 e5 ♘d5 4 d4 cd.

  3 ... d5!? 4 ed ♘f6!? (4 ... ♕xd5 – 2 c3) 5 ♗b5+ ♗d7 6 ♗c4 dc 7 ♘xc3 ♗a6 8 ♘f3 ♕a5 ± Chandler-van der Wiel, Wijk aan Zee 1982.

[2] **4 ...** d6 5 c4 ♘f6 6 ♘c3 e6 7 ♘f3 ♘c6 8 0-0 ♗e7 9 ♗g5! ±.

[3] **10 ...** 0-0 11 ♗e2 ±.

  10 ... ♘de5 11 ♖c1 ±.

[4] 12 ♕xd3 0-0 13 ♕d2 ± Chandler-Sunye, Wijk aan Zee 1982.

[5] 7 ... ♕a5 8 0-0 ♘xe5 9 ♘xe5 ♗xe5 10 ♘d5 e6 11 ♖e1 f6 12 ♗b3 ♔f7 13 ♖xe5! ± Sokolov-Petek, Yugoslavia 1955.

[6] 9 e5 de! 10 ♖d1 ♕a5! ∓.

[7] **6 ...** a6 7 0-0 ♘ge7 8 ♗g5! d6 9 ♕d2 h6 10 ♗h4 g5 11 ♗g3 ♘g6 12 ♖fd1 e5 13 ♘d5 ♗g4

[8] ♗e2 ± Tarassov-Shestakov, corr. 1971.

  6 ... ♗b4 7 0-0 ♘ge7 (7 ... ♗xc3!?) 8 ♘b5 d5 9 ed ed 10 ♗xd5 ± Zaitsev-Furman, USSR 1973.

[8] 8 ... ♗e7 9 ♖fd1 e5 10 h3 (10 ♗e3!?) 10 ... 0-0 11 ♗e3 ♗e6 12 ♗xe6 fe 13 ♖c1 ♖c8 14 b4! a6 15 b5 ab 16 ♕xb5 ♕d7! 17 ♘a4 ♘d4! = Pokovčik-Gligorić, Yugoslavia 1970.

[9] 10 ♗g5 (Fischer-Korchnoi, Buenos Aires 1960) 10 ... ♗e7 11 ♖ac1 0-0 12 ♗b3 h6 13 ♗f4 e5! =.

[10] 12 ♗b3 0-0 13 ♗g3 ♘e5! 14 h3 b5 ∞/= Rodionov-Gik, Moscow 1970.

[11] 5 ♗c4!? a6 (5 ... ♗c5!?) 6 ♘f3 b5 7 ♗b3 ♗b7 8 ♕e2 ± Matulović-Scocco, Italy 1955.

[12] 5 ... ♕c7!? 6 ♕e2 a6 7 ♘f3 ♗b4 ∞.

[13] 8 ♘a4!?/8 ♗f4!?/8 e5!? ∞ Flesch.

[14] 12 ♗a2 a6 ∓ Chandler-Timman, Wijk aan Zee 1982.

	2	3	4	5	6	7	8	9	10	
1	... b6[1]	d4 ♗b7	♗d3[2] ♘f6[3]	♘d2[4] cd	cd ♘c6	♘e2[5] g6	0-0 ♗g7	a3 0-0	f4 ♖c8[6]	∞
2	... e6	d4[7] d5	ed ed	♘f3 ♗d6	dc[8] ♗xc5	♗e2 ♘c6	0-0 ♘ge7	♘bd2 0-0	♘b3 ♗b6[9]	=
3	... d5	ed ♕xd5	d4 cd	cd ♘c6	♘f3 ♗g4[10]	♘c3! ♗xf3	gf! ♕xd4	♕xd4 ♘xd4	♘b5 e5[11]	±
4	... ...	... ...	... ♘f6	♘f3 ♗g4[12]	♗e2 e6	h3[13] ♗h5	0-0 ♗e7	♗e3 cd	cd ♘c6	=
5	... ...	... ...	... ...	... ...	... ...	0-0 ♘c6	♘a3 cd	♘b5 ♖c8	♘bxd4 ♘xd4[14]	=
6	... ...	... ...	... ♘c6	♘f3 ♗g4	♗e2 cd	cd e6	♘c3 ♕a5[15]	0-0 ♘f6	♕b3 ♕b4[16]	±
7	... ...	... ...	... e6	♘f3 ♘c6	♗e2[17] ♘f6	♘a3 ♕d8	♘c2 b6!?	♗b5 ♗d7	♕e2 cd[18]	=
8	... ♘f6	e5[19] ♘d5	d4[20] cd	♗c4!? ♕c7[21]	♕e2 ♘b6	♗d3 ♘c6	♘f3 g6[22]	0-0 dc	♘xc3 ♗g7[23]	∞
9	... ...	... ...	... ...	♕xd4 e6	♗c4 ♘c6	♕e4 ♘de7![24]	♘f3 ♘g6	♗b5 ♕c7	♗xc6 ♕xc6[25]	∓
10	... ...	... ...	... ...	... ...	♘f3 ♘c6	♕e4 d6	♘bd2 de[26]	♘xe5 ♘xe5	♕xe5 ♘f6[27]	=
11	... ...	... ...	... ...	... ...	... ...	... f5	♕e2[28] ♕c7	g3 d6	ed ♗xd6[29]	∞
12	... ...	... ...	... ...	cd d6	♘f3 ♘c6	♗c4[30] e6	0-0 ♗e7[31]	♕e2[32] 0-0	♘c3[33] ♘xc3[34]	∞
13	... ...	... ...	... ...	... ...	... ...	... ♘b6[35]	♗b5 de	♘xe5 ♗d7	♘c3[36] ♘xe5[37]	=
14	... ...	... ...	... ...	... ...	♗c4 ♘b6	♗b3 de	♕h5 e6	de ♘c6	♘c3! g6[38]	∞

¹ 2 ... g6 3 d4 cd 4 cd d5 5 e5 (5 ed – Caro-Kann, Panov) 5 ... ♘c6 6 ♘c3 ♗g7 7 ♗e2 (7 ♘f3 ♗g4 = Bhend-Bilek, Kecskemet 1964) 7 ... ♘h6 8 h3 0-0!? (8 ... f6 9 ef ef 10 ♘f3! ± Groszpeter, Regan, Budapest 1978) ∞ Chandler.

2 ... ♕a5!? 3 ♘f3 ♘c6 4 d4 cd 5 b4 ♕c7 ∞ Sveshnikov-Tseshkovsky, USSR Ch 1981.

2 ... d6!? 3 d4 ♘f6 4 dc ♘c6 5 f3! d5 6 ed ± Novotnikov-Razuvayev, USSR 1981.

² 4 d5 ♘f6 5 ♗d3 c4! =.

³ 4 ... e6 5 ♘f3 ♘f6 6 ♕e2 cd 7 cd ♗b4+ (7 ... ♘c6 8 a3! ±) 8 ♘bd2 ± Hübner-Larsen, Bugojno 1978.

⁴ 5 ♕e2 cd 6 cd ♘c6 7 ♘f3 ♘b4! 8 ♘c3 ♘xd3+ 9 ♕xd3 e6 = Chandler-Speelman, British Ch 1976.

⁵ 7 ♘gf3 ♘b4 8 ♗b1 ♗a6 9 ♘e5!? Miles.

⁶ 11 h3 ∞ Zhuravlev-Murey, USSR 1974.

⁷ 3 ♘f3 d5 4 d3!? de 5 de ♕xd1+ 6 ♔xd1 ± Lombardy.

⁸ 6 ♗b5+ ♗d7 7 ♗xd7+ ♕xd7 8 0-0 ♘e7 =.

6 ♗e3 c4 7 b3 cb 8 ab ♘e7 9 c4 ♘bc6 10 c5 ♗c7 11 ♘c3 0-0 12 ♗d3 ♗f5 = Short-Kasparov, Dortmund 1980.

⁹ Padevsky-Karpov, Nice Ol 1974.

¹⁰ 6 ... e5 7 ♘c3 ♗b4 8 ♗d2 ♗xc3 9 ♗xc3 e4 10 ♘e5 (10 ♘d2 ♘f6 11 ♗c4 ♕g5 12 d5 ♘e5 13 ♗b5+ ♗d7 ∞) 10 ... ♘xe5 11 de ♘e7 12 ♕a4+ ♗d7 13 ♕b4! a5 14 ♕b6 ♕c6 (14 ... ♗c6? 15 ♖d1 ♕xa2 16 ♕c5 ±) 15 ♗xa5 ♕d5 16 ♗c3 ♖xa2 17 ♖d1 ±.

¹¹ 10 ... ♘c2+ 11 ♔d1 ♘xa1 12 ♘c7+ ♔d7 13 ♘xa8 g6!? (Crouch-Balinas, London 1979) 14 ♗b5+! ± Chandler.

10 ... e5! 11 ♘c7+ ♔d7 12 ♘xa8 ♗b4+ 13 ♔d1!? ± Rozenberg.

¹² 5 ... e6!? 6 ♗d3 ♗e7 7 0-0 0-0 8 ♕e2 cd 9 cd ♘c6 = Braga-Karpov, Mar del Plata 1982.

¹³ 7 ♘a3 ♘c6 8 ♘b5 ♕d8 9 dc ♗xc5 ±/=.

¹⁴ 11 ♘xd4 ♘xe2 12 ♕xe2 ♗e7 = Buljovčić-Olafsson, Novi Sad 1976.

¹⁵ 8 ... ♗b4 9 0-0 ♕a5 10 a3! ♘f6 11 d5! ± Alekhine-Podgorny, Prague 1942.

¹⁶ 11 ♗g5 ♗e7 12 ♕xb4 ♗xb4 13 ♗b5+ ± Kernan-Muniz, Teesside 1973.

¹⁷ 6 ♘a3 ♕d8 7 ♘c2 ♘f6 8 ♗d3 ±.

6 ♗d3 ♘f6 7 0-0 cd 8 cd ♗e7 9 ♘c3 ♕d8 – Semi-Tarrasch.

¹⁸ 11 ♘cxd4 ♘xd4 12 ♘xd4 ♗c5 = Sveshnikov-Dorfman, USSR 1979.

¹⁹ 3 ♗d3!? ♘c6 4 ♘f3 c4! 5 ♗c2 d5 6 e5 ♘d7 7 ♕e2 e6 ∞ ECO.

²⁰ 4 ♘f3 ♘c6 5 ♘a3 g6 6 g3 ♗g7 7 ♗g2 ♘c7! 8 ♕e2 0-0 9 0-0 d6 =/+ Bisguier-Fischer, Stockholm IZ 1962.

²¹ 5 ... ♘b6 6 ♗b3 d6 7 cd de 8 ♕h5 e6 9 de ♘c6 10 ♘f3 ♕d3! + Marić-Radulov, Novi Sad 1974.

²² 8 ... d5?! 9 ed ♕xd6 10 ♘xd4 ♘xd4 11 cd ± Braga-Larsen, Mar del Plata 1982.

²³ Miles-Sax, Bath 1973.

²⁴ 7 ... d6 8 ed ♘f6 9 ♕e2 ♗xd6 10 ♗g5 b6!? =.

²⁵ 11 ♕xc6 bc 12 0-0 f6 13 ♖e1 ♗b7 + Semenyuk-Yuferov, USSR 1977.

²⁶ 8 ... ♗d7 9 ed ♗xd6 10 ♘c4 ♗c7 11 ♘ce5 ♘f6 12 ♕e2 ± Vorotnikov-Lichenko, USSR 1975.

²⁷ 10 ... ♕d6 11 ♗b5+ ♗d7 12 ♗xd7+ ♕xd7 13 0-0 ♕d6 14 ♕xd6 ♗xd6 15 ♘e4 ± Jacobs-Tarjan, US Jr Ch 1970.

10 ... ♘f6 11 ♗b5+ ♗d7 12 a4 a6 13 ♗xd7+ ♕xd7 14 0-0 ♗d6 15 ♕e2 ♕c7 16 h3 = Sveshnikov-Geller, USSR Ch 1979.

²⁸ 8 ef ♘xf6 9 ♕h4 e5! 10 ♗g5 d5 11 ♗b5 ♗d6 12 c4 0-0! 13 0-0 e4 14 cd ef 15 dc fg + Hort-Miles, England 1979.

²⁹ 11 ♗g2 0-0 12 ♘bd2 ♘f6 13 ♘c4 e5 14 ♘xd6 ♕xd6 15 ♗e3 f4!? ∞.

³⁰ 7 ♘c3 de (7 ... ♘xc3 8 bc de 9 d5 ±) 8 de ♘db4! 9 a3 ♕xd1+ 10 ♔xd1 ♘a6 11 b4 ♘c7 ∞ Radovici-Ghinda, Romania 1975.

³¹ 8 ... ♘c7!? 9 ♕e2 b6 10 a3!? Chandler.

³² 9 a3! ± Kurajica-Robatsch, Tuzla 1981.

³³ 10 a3 ♕b6 11 ♖d1 ∞ Sveshnikov-Timoshenko, USSR 1975.

10 ♕e4 ♔h8!? 11 ♗xd5 ed 12 ♕xd5 de = Chekhov-Dorfman, USSR Ch 1975.

³⁴ 11 bc de 12 de b6 13 ♕e4 ♗b7 14 ♗d3 g6 15 ♗h6 ♖e8 ∞/=.

³⁵ 7 ... de!? 8 ♗xd5 ♕xd5 9 ♘c3 ♕d6 10 d5 ♘d4 11 ♘xd4 cd 12 ♕xd4 e5 13 ♕d3 ♗d7 14 0-0 (14 f4 f5! Regan) 14 ... f5! 15 ♖e1 ♗f7! ∞ Regan-Grünfeld, Philadelphia 1979.

³⁶ 10 ♗xc6 ♗xc6 11 ♘xc6 bc 12 0-0 g6 13 ♖e1 ♗g7 14 ♗g5 0-0 15 ♗xe7 ♕xd4 16 ♘c3 ♕xd1 17 ♖axd1 ♖fe8 = Regan-Adorjan, Budapest 1978.

10 ♘xd7 ♕xd7 11 ♘c3 e6 12 0-0 a6 13 ♗xc6 ♕xc6 14 ♖e1 (Sveshnikov-Popov, Lvov 1973) 14 ... ♗b4 + Speelman/Regan.

³⁷ 10 ... e6?! 11 ♗xc6 ♗xc6 12 ♘xc6 bc 13 ♕g4 ± Sveshnikov-Browne, Novi Sad 1979.

10 ... ♘xe5! 11 de ♗xb5 12 ♘xb5 ♕xd1+ 13 ♔xd1 ♘d5 = Sveshnikov-Kasparov, USSR Ch 1979.

³⁸ 10 ... ♘b4 11 ♗g5! ♘d3+ 12 ♔e2! ♕d4 13 ♘f3! ±/± Papp-Cserna, Hungary 1981.

10 ... g6!? 11 ♕g5 ♕xg5 12 ♗xg5 ♗g7 ∞ Florian.

	2	3	4	5	6	7	8	9	10	
1	...	f4	♘f3	♗c4[3]	0-0	f5	d3	♕e1	ef	∞
	d6[1]	♘c6[2]	g6	♗g7	e6[4]	ef	♘ge7	h6	♗xf5![5]	
2	...	f4	♘f3	♗c4[6]	f5	fe	d3	0-0	♗e3	=
	♘c6	g6	♗g7	e6!	♘ge7	de[7]	0-0	♘d4!	♘ec6[8]	
3	...	...	♘f3	♗b5	♕e2	♘xe4	♗xc6+	b3	♗b2	±
	...	e6	d5[9]	♘ge7[10]	de	a6	♘xc6	♗e7	0-0[11]	

[1]   2 ... e6 3 g3 d5 4 ed ed 5 ♗g2 ♘f6 6 ♘ge2 d4 7 ♘e4 ♘xe4 8 ♗xe4 ♘d7! 9 d3 ♘f6 10 ♗g2 ♗d6 = Spassky-Korchnoi, match 1968.

[2]   3 ... g6 4 d4 cd 5 ♕xd4 ♘f6 6 e5 ♘c6 7 ♗b5 de (7 ... ♘h5!? Romanishin-Portisch, Tilburg 1979) 8 ♕xd8+ ♔xd8 9 fe ♘xe5 10 ♗f4 ♘ed7 11 0-0-0 a6 12 ♗c4 e6 13 a4 ∞ Gulko-Kuligowski, Buenos Aires Ol 1978.

[3]   5 ♗b5 ♗d7 6 0-0 ♗g7 7 d3 ♘f6 8 ♗xc6 ♗xc6 9 ♕e1 0-0 10 ♗d2 e6 11 e5! ±.

[4]   6 ... ♘f6 7 d3 0-0 8 f5 gf 9 ♕e1 fe 10 de ♗g4 11 ♕h4 ♗xf3 12 ♖xf3 ∞ Hodgson-Nunn, London 1978.

[5]   11 g4 ♗xg4 12 ♗xf7+ ♖xf7 13 ♘e5+ ♔g8 14 ♘xg4 ♕d7 15 ♕g3 ∞ Sznapik-Kuligowski, Warsaw 1978.

[6]   5 ♗b5 ♘d4! 6 ♘xd4 cd 7 ♘e2 e6 8 c3 dc 9 dc a6 10 ♗d3 d5 11 ♗e3 ♘e7 = Rossolimo-Hort, Wijk aan Zee 1968.

[7]   7 ... fe 8 d3 d5 (8 ... 0-0 9 ♗g5?! h6 10 ♗h4 g5 ∓ Hebden-Speelman, British Ch 1982) 9 ♗b3 0-0 10 0-0 h6 11 ♕e1 ♘d4 12 ♘xd4 ♖xf1+ 13 ♕xf1 cd ∞ Nunn-Inkiov, Varna 1977. 9 ... b5!? Wibe-Keene, Gausdal 1979.

[8]   11 ♕d2 ♘a5 =.

[9]   4 ... d6 5 ♗b5!? ♗d7 6 ♗xc6 ♗xc6 7 d3 ♘f6 8 0-0 ♗e7 9 e5!? ∞ Klovsky-Azmaiparashvili, Moscow 1979.

[10]   5 ... ♘f6 6 e5 ♘d7 7 ♗xc6 bc 8 0-0 c4!? 9 b3 ♗a6 10 bc ♗xc4 ∞ Bangiev-Tukmakov, USSR 1979.

[11]   11 0-0 ± Rossolimo-Zuckerman, USA 1966.

	6	7	8	9	10	11	12	13	14	
1	♘h3[1]	0-0	f3	♗xh3	♗e3	♕d2	♖ac1	♘d1	♕e2	=
	♘f6[2]	♗g4[3]	♗xh3	0-0	♘e8[4]	♘c7	b6	d5	e6[5]	
2	♗e3	h3[7]	♕d2	♘ce2	c3	f4				±
	♘f6[6]	0-0	♘d4[8]	e5	♘e6					
3	...	♕d2[9]	♘d1[11]	c3	♘e2	0-0[12]	f4	♘f2	♘h3	±
	e6	♘d4[10]	e5	♘c6	♗g4	♘ge7	0-0	♗e6	♕c8[13]	
4	...	♕d2	f4	♘f3	0-0	♗xf4	♖xf3	♗h6	♗xg7	=
	e5	♘ge7[14]	♘d4	0-0	ef[15]	♘xf3+	♗e6	♘c6	♔xg7[16]	
5	f4	♘f3	0-0	h3[19]	a3!	♗e3	ab	♘e2	b3![21]	±
	♘f6[17]	0-0	♖b8[18]	b5	a5	b4	ab	♗b7[20]	♖a8[22]	
6	...	♘f3	0-0	♗d2[25]	♖b1	a3	a4	♘xa4	♗xd4	∓
	e6	♘ge7[23]	0-0[24]	♖b8	b5	a5[26]	ba!	♘d4	♗xd4+[27]	
7	...	...	...	♗e3	♖b1[28]	♘e2	♗xf3	♗g2	♘c1	∞
	...	...	...	♘d4	♘ec6[29]	♗xf3+	♘d4[30]	♕a5	♕a4![31]	
8	...	♘h3[32]	0-0	♘xf4[34]	♘fd5	♘xd5	♘f4	c3	a3	=
	e5	♘ge7	ef[33]	0-0	♘xd5	♗e6	♗d7	b5	a5[35]	

[1]   6 ♘ge2 e5 (6 ... ♘f6 7 0-0 ♖b8 8 h3 e5 = Shishov-Polugayevsky, USSR 1972) 7 0-0 ♘ge7 8 ♗e3 0-0 9 f4 ♘d4 10 ♕d2 ♗e6 11 ♖ae1 ♕d7 12 ♘c1 ♖ad8 13 ♘d1 b6 14 c3 ♘dc6 = Holmov-Tal, USSR Ch 1964.

[2]   6 ... h5!? 7 f4! Smyslov-Romanishin, USSR 1976.

[3]   7 ... 0-0!? 8 f4 ♗g4 9 ♕d2 ♘d4 10 ♔h1 ♕d7 (Medina-Benko, Malaga 1970) 11 ♘f2 = Geller.

[4]   10 ... ♘d4?! 11 ♗xd4 cd 12 ♘e2 intending c3 ± Geller.

[5]   Spassky-Petrosian, match 1966.

[6]   6 ... e6?! (Kinderman-Speelman, Dortmund 1981) 7 ♘ge2 ♘ge7 8 ♕d2 h6 9 0-0 ± Speelman.
    6 ... ♖b8 7 ♕d2 b5 8 ♘f3 b4 9 ♘d1 ♘d4 10 ♘h4 e5 11 f4 ef 12 ♗xf4 ♘e7 13 0-0 (13 c3!?) 13 ... h6! 14 ♗e3 ± Smyslov-Portisch, match 1971.

[7]   7 ♕c1 ♘d4 8 ♘d1 e5 9 c3 ♘e6 10 ♗h6 0-0 11 ♗xg7 ♘xg7 12 ♘e2 (Pachman-Olafsson, Portorož 1958) 12 ... d5! =.

[8*]   8 ... ♘e8!? Pachman.

[9]   7 ♘h3 ♘ge7 8 0-0 0-0 9 ♕d2 e5 (9 ... ♖b8 10 ♗h6 b5 11 ♖ae1 ♘d4 12 ♗xg7 ♔xg7 13 f4 ± Suttles-Padevsky, Lugano Ol 1968) 10 ♗h6 f6! 11 ♗xg7 ♔xg7 12 f4 ♗e6 = Geller.

[10]   7 ... ♕a5 8 ♘ge2 ♘d4 9 0-0 ♘xe2+ 10 ♕xe2 ♗xc3 11 bc ♕xc3 12 ♖ab1 ♘e7 13 ♗h6 ♘c6 14 e5 ∞.
    7 ... ♘ge7 8 ♗h6 ♗xh6 9 ♕xh6 ♘d4 10 0-0-0 ♘ec6 11 ♘ge2 ♗d7 12 ♕g7 ± Ljubojević-Quinteros, Mar del Plata 1981.
    7 ... ♖b8 8 ♘h3 ♘d4 9 0-0 ♘e7 10 ♘d1! b6 11 c3 ♘dc6 12 ♗h6 0-0 13 ♗xg7 ♔xg7 14 ♘e3 ± Pacis-Shamkovich, Malta 1980.

[11]   8 ♘ge2 ♘e7 9 0-0 0-0 10 f4 f5 11 ♖ae1 ♖b8 12 ♘d1 b5 = Kopilov-Petrosian, USSR Ch 1949.

[12]   11 f3 ♗e6 =.

[13]   15 ♘g5 ♗d7 16 ♖ac1 f6 17 ♘f3 f5 18 fe ♘xe5 19 ♘xe5 de 20 d4 ± Hort-Kurajica, Zagreb 1958.

[14]   7 ... ♗e6!? 8 f4 ♘ge7 9 ♘f3 ♘d4 10 0-0 0-0 11 ♖ae1 (11 ♖f2!? Hort) 11 ... ♘xf3+ 12 ♗xf3 ♕d7 = Hort-Tal, Wijk aan Zee 1968.

[15]   10 ... ♗g4 11 ♘h4 ef 12 ♗xf4 ♕d7 = Pachman-Bogdanović, Sarajevo 1963.

[16]   15 ♖af1 ♕e7 = Smyslov-Tal, Leningrad 1962.

[17]   6 ... ♖b8 7 ♘f3 b5 8 0-0 b4 9 ♘d5 e6 10 ♘e3 ♘ge7 11 a3 a5 12 ab ab 13 f5 (13 g4!?) 13 ... ef 14 ef ♗xf5 15 ♘xf5 ♘xf5 16 ♘g5 ± Kopilov-Belov, USSR 1963.
    6 ... b6!? 7 ♘f3 ♗b7 8 0-0 ♕d7 9 f5 ± Bernstein-Fischer, Netanya 1968.
    6 ... f5 7 ♘f3 ♘f6 8 0-0 0-0 9 ♔h1 ♗d7 10 ♗e3 ♖b8 11 ♕e2 b5 12 ♗g1 b4 13 ♘d1 ♘e8 14 c3 (Smyslov-Larsen, Munich Ol 1958)

[14] ... ♕c8!? intending ... ♕a6 Boleslavsky.
    6 ... ♘h6!? 7 ♘f3 0-0 8 0-0 ♖b8 9 ♗e3 b5 10 ♕c1? (10 ♖b1) 10 ... ♘g4! 11 ♗d2 ♘d4! ∓ Edmonds-Keene, England 1982.

[18]   8 ... ♘e8 9 h3 ♘c7 (9 ... f5!?) 10 ♗e3 b6 11 ♕d2 ♗b7 12 f5 d5 13 ♗h6! ± Smyslov-Ilivitsky, USSR 1952.

[19]   9 ♘h4 ♘d4 10 f5 b5 11 ♗g5 b4 12 ♘b1 ♘d7 13 ♘d2 ♘e5 14 ♔h1 a5 15 ♖b1 = Spassky-Geller, match 1968.   12 ♘e2 ♘xe2+ 13 ♕xe2 ♘d7 14 ♖ab1 ♘e5 15 ♕d2 a5 16 ♗h6 ♗d7 17 ♘f3 ♘xf3+ 18 ♖xf3 f6 = Petrosian/Suetin.

[20]   13 ... ♘e8 14 ♖b1 ♘c7 15 f5 ♘b5 16 ♕d2 ♘bd4 17 ♘h4 ♘xe2+ 18 ♕xe2 ♘e5 19 ♘f3 ♘xf3+ 20 ♕xf3 ± Reshevsky-Korchnoi, match 1968.

[21]   14 ♕d2 ♖a8 15 ♖ab1 ♕a5 = Spassky-Geller, match 1968.

[22]   15 ♖c1 ♖a2 16 g4 e6 (16 ... ♕a8 17 ♕e1 ♕a6 18 ♕f2 ♖a7 19 f5 ♘b5 20 fg hg 21 ♘g5 ♘a3 22 ♕h4 ± Spassky-Geller, match 1968; 16 ... ♘d7!?) 17 ♕g3 ♖e8 18 f5 ±.

[23]   7 ... ♖b8 8 0-0 ♘ge7 9 e5! de 10 fe ♘xe5 11 ♗f4 ♘xf3+ 12 ♖xf3 ± Bronstein-Keres, Zürich C 1953.

[24]   8 ... ♗d7 9 ♗e3 ♘d4 10 ♖b1 ♖c8 11 ♗f2 ♘ec6 12 ♘e2 ♕a5 (12 ... 0-0) 13 ♘exd4 ♘xd4 14 c3! ± Spassky-Hort, West Germany 1981.

[25]   9 a3 ♗d7 10 ♖b1 ♖c8 11 ♗d2 ♘d4 12 ♘e2 = Spassky-Geller, match 1968.

[26]   11 ... f5?! 12 ♗e3 ♘c7 13 ♗f2 ♔h8 14 ♖e1 b4 15 ab cb 16 ♘e2 fe 17 de e5 18 ♕d2 ♗e6 19 ♘c1! ± Spassky-Larsen, match 1968.

[27]   15 ♔h1 ♗d7 16 c3 ♗g7 17 ♕c2 ♕c7 ∓ Tarve-K.Grigorian, USSR 1972.

[28]   10 ♕d2 d5 (10 ... ♖b8 11 g4 f5 12 gf gf 13 ♔h1 ♘g6 14 ♖g1 b5 = Wade-Matulović, Skopje 1968) 11 ed ed (Wade-Matanović, Vinkovci 1968) 12 ♗f2 ∓ Matanović/Parma.

[29]   10 ... ♖b8 11 ♘e2 ♘xf3+ 12 ♗xf3 b6 13 g4 f5 14 ♘g3 ♗b7 15 c3 ♕d7 = Ničevski-Bukić, Yugoslav Ch 1981.
    10 ... ♗d7 11 ♘e2 ♘xf3+ 12 ♗xf3 ♕c7 13 ♕d2 ♖ad8 14 c4 b6 15 g4 f5 = Christiansen-Andersson, Mar del Plata 1981.

[30]   12 ... b6 (Karpov-Quinteros, Buenos Aires 1980) 13 d4 cd 14 ♘xd4 ♘xd4 15 ♗xd4 ♕c7 16 ♗xg7 ♔xg7 17 e5 d5 ±.

[31]   Balashov-Rashkovsky, USSR Ch 1980/81.

[32]   7 ♘f3 ♘ge7 8 0-0 0-0 9 ♖b1 ♖b8 10 a3 b5 11 h3 ± Zaichik-Forintos, Kirkovan 1978.

[33]   8 ... 0-0? 9 f5!
    8 ... ♘d4 9 f5!? gf 10 ♘g5!? h6 11 ef hg 12 f6 ♗f8 13 fe ♗xe7 14 ♘d5 ∞ Seret-Birnboim, Malta Ol 1980.

[34]   9 ♗xf4!? 0-0 10 ♕d2 Portisch.

[35]   15 ♗e3 ♘e5 16 h3 = Bilek-Evans, Lugano Ol 1968.

1 e4 c5 2 ♘f3

	2	3	4	5	6	7	8	9	10	
1	...	d4	♘xd4	♘c3[1]	♗d3	f4	♘f3	0-0	♕e1	±
	b6	cd	♗b7	a6	g6	♗g7	d6	♘f6	0-0[2]	
2	...	d4[3]	♘xd4	♘c3	♗g5!?[4]	♕d2	0-0-0	f4		∞
	♕c7	cd	♘f6	a6	e6	♗e7	0-0	♘c6		
3	...	♗c4	0-0	c3	d4	e5	♘xe5	de	♔xd1	±
	g6	♘c6[5]	♗g7	d6	♘f6	de	♘xe5[6]	♕xd1+	♘d7[7]	
4	...	d4	♘xd4	♘c3	♘f3	♗c4[8]	♗b3[9]	0-0	bc	=
	a6	cd	♘f6	e5	♗b4	♕c7	0-0	♗xc3	d6[10]	
5	...	c3	ed	d4	♗e2	0-0	♗e3	cd	♘c3	±
	...	d5[11]	♕xd5	♘f6[12]	e6	♗e7[13]	cd	♘c6	♕d6[14]	
6	...	c4	d4	♘xd4	♘c3	♘f5	cd	ef	♗d3	±
	...	♘c6[15]	cd	♘f6	e5[16]	d5	♗xf5	♘d4	♘xd5[17]	
7	...	♘c3	d4	ed	♘xd5	♗e3	♘xd4	♕xd4	♗xd4	±
	♘f6[18]	♘c6[19]	d5?!	♘xd5	♕xd5	cd	♘xd4[20]	♕xd4	♗d7[21]	
8	...	e5	d4[22]	♕xd4	♗c4[23]	♕e4	0-0	♘xe5	♘xc6	∞
	...	♘d5	cd	e6	♘c6	d6	de	♘f6	♕c7[24]	
9	...	...	♘c3	dc	♗f4	♕d2[25]	0-0-0	h4	♗d3	±
	...	...	♘xc3	♘c6	e6	♕c7	h6	b6	♗b7[26]	
10	...	...	...	♘xd5[27]	d4	dc	♕xd5	♗c4	♔e2	∞
	...	...	e6	ed	♘c6	♗xc5	♕b6	♗xf2+	0-0[28]	
11	...	...	...	...	...	...	...	ed	♗c4[29]	±
	...	...	...	...	...	...	d6!?	♕b6	♗xf2+[30]	

236

¹ 5 ♗d3 d6 6 0-0 ♘f6 7 ♘c3 e6 8 ♕e2 ♗e7
9 ♗b5+ ♘fd7 10 ♕g4 0-0 11 ♗e3 ♘f6 = Bakulin-
Volovich, USSR 1964.
² 11 ♕h4 ♘bd7 12 ♗d2 ±.
³ 3 ♘c3 a6 4 d3 e6 5 g3 ♘c6 6 ♗g2 ♘f6 7 0-0
♗e7 8 ♘h4 d6 9 f4 ± Durao-Ghubash, Malta Ol
1980.
⁴ 6 g3!?
   6 ♗d3!?
   6 ♗e2!?
⁵ 3 ... ♗g7 4 c3 ♕c7 (4 ... e6 5 d4 cd 6 ♗g5!?;
6 ♗f4!?; 5 h4!?) 5 0-0 d6 6 d4 ♘f6 7 e5 de 8 de
♘g4 9 ♗f4 0-0 10 ♖e1 ♘c6 11 ♕e2 ♘a5
12 ♗d3 ±/± Stein-Bilek, Bucharest 1961.
⁶ 8 ... 0-0 9 ♘xc6 bc 10 dc ♕c7 11 ♘d2 ±
Dünhaupt-Behnke, corr. 1969.
⁷ 11 e6! ±.
⁸ 7 ♗d2 d6 8 ♗d3 ♘bd7 9 a3 ♗xc3 10 ♗xc3
♘c5 ∓ P.Schmidt-O'Kelly, Beverwijk 1949.
⁹ 8 ♕d3 b5 9 ♗b3 ♗b7 10 ♗d2 ♗xc3
11 ♗xc3 d6 12 ♘g5 0-0 13 0-0-0 ∞ Alexander-
Prins, Berne 1962.   12 0-0-0!? Sokolov.
¹⁰ Gligorić/Sokolov.
¹¹ 3 ... ♘f6 4 e5 ♘d5 5 d4 cd 6 cd d6 7 ♗c4 ±
(... a6 is not useful here – compare this line with
Sicilian: 2 c3).
¹² 5 ... ♗g4!? 6 ♗e2 e6 7 0-0 ♘f6 8 ♗e3 (8 c4
♕d6 9 ♕b3 ± Suetin) 8 ... cd (8 ... ♘bd7!?
9 c4 ♕d6 ∞ O'Kelly) 9 cd ♘c6 10 ♘c3
♕a5! (10 ... ♕d7 11 ♘e5 ± Unzicker-Beni,
Dubrovnik Ol 1950) 11 h3 ♗h5 12 a3 ♗e7 13 b4 ∞
Lhagva-Camara, Malta Ol 1980.
¹³ 7 ... cd 8 ♘xd4 ♗e7 9 ♘d2 0-0 10 ♘c4 ±
Gipslis-Taimanov, USSR Ch 1967.
¹⁴ 11 ♘d2 ♘b4 12 ♘de4 ♘xe4 13 ♖xe4 ♕d8
14 ♗f3 ± Cirić-Taimanov, Rostov 1961.
¹⁵ 3 ... d6 4 d4 cd 5 ♘xd4 ♘f6 transposes to
the Maroczy Bind.
¹⁶ 6 ... e6 7 ♘xc6 bc 8 e5 ♘g8 9 ♗f4 ♗b4
10 ♗d3 ♘e7 11 0-0 d5 12 ed ♗xd6 13 ♗xd6
♕xd6 14 ♖e1 ± Navarro-Bueno, Cienfuegos
1980.
¹⁷ 11 0-0 ♗b4 12 ♗e4! ♘xc3 13 bc ♗xc3
14 ♖b1 ± Kupper-Tordion, Swiss Ch 1956.
¹⁸ Rubinstein/Nimzowitsch.

¹⁹ 3 ... d5 4 ed ♘xd5 5 ♗b5+ ♗d7 6 ♘e5 ♗xb5
7 ♕f3 f6 8 ♗xb5 ♘a6 9 ♕h5+ g6 10 ♘xg6 hg
11 ♕xh8 ♕d7 12 ♘c3 ♕e6+ 13 ♔f1 ♘ab4
14 ♕h3 ± Sozin-Kirilov, USSR Ch 1931.
²⁰ 8 ... ♕a5+ 9 c3! ♘xd4 10 b4! ♕e5 11 ♕xd4·
♕xd4 12 ♗xd4 f6 13 f4 ± Spassky-Pribyl,
Tallinn 1973.
     8 ... e5 9 ♘b5 ±.
²¹ 11 ♗c4 e6 12 0-0 ± Cirić-Rejfir, European
Team Ch 1961.
²² 4 c4 ♘c7 5 d4 cd 6 ♕xd4 ♘c6 =.
²³ 6 a3 ♘c6 7 ♕e4 b6!? ∞.
²⁴ 11 ♕f3 ♗d7 ∞ Timoshenko-Garcia Palermo,
Havana 1981.
²⁵ 7 ♗c4 ♕c7 8 0-0 b6 9 ♖e1 h6 10 ♘d2 d5
11 ed ±.
²⁶ 11 ♕e2 0-0-0 12 ♘d2 d5 13 ed ± Tsarenkov-
Ketslokh, USSR 1972.
²⁷ 5 ♘e4 f5 6 ♘c3!? d6 7 ♘xd5 ed 8 d4 ♘c6 ∞
Tompa-Cuibus, Hungary 1973.   5 ... ♘c6 6 c4
♘b6 7 b3 (7 b4!? ♘xb4 8 ♗b2 – Gurgenidze-
Mnatsakanian, Tbilisi-Sukhumi 1977 – 8 ...
d5 9 ed f5 ∞) 7 ... d5 8 ed ♗xd6 9 d4 f5
10 ♘xd6+ ± Gipslis-Mnatsakanian, USSR 1977.
²⁸ 11 ♖f1 ♗c5 12 ♘g5 ♘d4+ 13 ♔d1 ♘e6
14 c3 (14 ♕e4 ♘xg5 15 ♗xg5 d5! ∓ Torre-
Ljubojević, Manila IZ 1976; 14 ♘e4!? d6
15 ed ♖d8! ∞) 14 ... d6 15 b4 ♘xg5 (15 ... ♗g1!?)
16 bc ♕a5! ∞ Minić-Bjelajac, Yugoslav Ch
1977.   12 c3?! d6! 13 b4 ♗xb4! ∞ Planinc-
Pribyl, Majdanpek 1976.
     11 ♖d1 d6 12 ed ♗e6 13 ♕e4 – note 30.
²⁹ 10 ♕e4+ ♗e6 11 d7+ ♔xd7 12 ♗e3 ♗xe3
13 ♖d1+ ♔c7 14 fe ♖ad8!? (14 ... ♕xb2
15 ♕f4+ ♔c8 16 ♔f2 ♖d8 ∞ Tolush) 15 ♕f4+
♔c8 16 ♘d4 ♘xd4 17 ♖xd4 ♖xd4 ∓.
³⁰ 11 ♗e2 0-0 12 ♖d1 ♗e6 13 ♕b5 ♘d4+
14 ♘xd4 ♗xd4 15 ♗f3 ♗xc4 16 ♕xc4 ♗e5
(Pokros-Rozhkov, corr. 1964) 17 ♕d5 ±. 16 ...
♗g1!? 17 ♔g3 ♖ac8 18 ♕d3 ♖fd8 (Smith-
Regan, USA 1978; 18 ... ♖c6!?) 19 ♖xg1 ±.
     13 ♕e4 ♖ae8 14 ♔f1 ♗d7! (Parma-Pribyl,
Czechoslovakia 1974) 15 ♕d5 ♘b4! (Waldowski)
16 ♕h5 (16 ♕d2 ♗e3 17 ♕c3 ♗xc1 18 ♖axc1
♖c8! ∓ Peters) 16 ... ♘xc2 17 ♖b1 ♗e3 ∓.

	3	4	5	6	7	8	9	10	11	
1	b4	d4[1]	♗d3	0-0	♘bd2	e5	♘e1	♕g4	♘df3	∓
	cb	♘f6	e6	♗e7	d5	♘fd7	♘c6	0-0	f5[2]	
2	c3	♗d3[3]	♗c2	d3	♘bd2	h3	0-0	♖e1[4]	♘f1	=
	♘f6	♘c6	♗g4	g6	♗g7	♗d7	0-0	♖c8	b5[5]	
3	♘c3	e5	♘xe5	♗b5+	♘xd7	0-0	d4	♕xd4	♗f4	=
	♘f6[6]	de	e6	♗d7	♘bxd7	♗e7	cd	0-0	♘b6[7]	
4	♗b5+	d4	0-0[9]	♕e2	♗g5	♗xf6	♘xd4	♗xd7+	♘c3	±
	♘d7	♘f6[8]	♘xe4	♘f6	cd	gf	a6	♗xd7	♕a5[10]	
5	...	0-0	e5[12]	♘xe5	d4[13]	♗f4	♘d2	♗xc6	♘dc4	±
	♘c6	♘f6[11]	de	♕c7	e6	♗d6	0-0	bc	♗a6[14]	
6	...	♗xd7+[15]	0-0[16]	♕e2[17]	c3	d4	e5	ed	♖d1	=
	♗d7	♘xd7	♘gf6	e6	♗e7	0-0	♘e8	♘xd6	cd[18]	
7	...	...	0-0[19]	c3	d4[21]	d5	♖e1	♗g5	c4	∞
	...	♕xd7	♘c6[20]	♘f6	♘xe4[22]	♘b8	♘f6	♘a6	e5!?[23]	
8	...	...	c4	0-0	d4	♘xd4	♗e3	f3	♘c3	∞/=
	...	...	♘c6[24]	g6	cd	♗g7	♘f6[25]	0-0	♖fd8![26]	
9	d4	♕xd4	♗e3[29]	♘c3	0-0-0[32]	♕d2	♕e1	♗g5	♔b1	∞
	cd[27]	a6[28]	♘d7[30]	♘gf6[31]	e5	b5	♗b7	♕c7	♗e7[33]	
10	...	...	♗b5	♕d3	♗xc6[35]	♘d4[36]	c4	♘a3		±
	...	♘c6	♕d7[34]	a6	♕xc6	♕c7	b5			
11	...	...	...	♗xc6	♘c3[37]	♗g5	0-0-0	♖he1	♔b1	∞/=
	...	...	♗d7	♗xc6	♘f6	e6	♗e7	0-0	♕c7[38]	
12	...	♘xd4	f3	♗b5+	♘f5	ed	♗xd7+	♘e3	c4	=
	...	♘f6	e5[39]	♘bd7[40]	d5	a6	♕xd7	b5	♗c5[41]	

---

[1]   4 a3? ♘f6 ∓.

[2]   Corden-Gligorić, Hastings 1969/70.

[3]   4 e5 ♘d5 – 2 c3.
    4 ♕c2 e5! Estrin.
    4 ♗b5+ ♗d7 5 ♗xd7+ – 3 ♗b5+.
    4 ♗e2!?

[4]   10 ♘h2 b5 11 f4 b4 12 ♘c4 d5 ∓ Bisguier-Fischer, US Ch 1967.

[5]   Grefe-Miles, Lone Pine 1980.

[6]   3 ... a6 4 g3 b5 5 ♗g2 ♗b7 6 d3 g6 7 0-0 ♗g7 8 ♘h4 ∞ Mecking-Ljubojević, Vršac 1971.

[7]   Holmov-Geller, USSR 1973.

[8]   4 ... cd 5 ♕xd4 ♘f6 6 ♗g5 e6 7 ♘c3 ♗e7 8 0-0 a6 9 ♗xd7+ ♗xd7 10 ♖ad1 ♗c6 11 ♖fe1 ± Boleslavsky.

[9]   5 ♘c3 cd 6 ♕xd4 g6 7 e5 ±.

[10]   12 ♕f3 ± (12 ... 0-0-0? 13 b4! ±±).

[11]   4 ... ♗g4 5 h3 ♗h5 6 c3 (6 g4!? ♗g6 7 d4 ∞) 6 ... ♘f6 (6 ... ♕b6 7 ♘a3 e5 8 d4 cd 9 cd 0-0-0 10 g4! ♗g6 11 d5 ♘d4 12 ♗e3 ♘xf3+ 13 ♕xf3 ±)

7 d4 ± Boleslavsky-Petrosian, USSR 1953.

[12] 5 ♖e1 e5 6 c3 ♗d7 7 d4 ♕c7 8 ♗g5 ♗e7 9 ♗xf6 ♗xf6 10 dc dc 11 ♗xc6 (O'Kelly-Najdorf, Amsterdam 1950) 11 ... bc = Polugayevsky.

[13] 7 ♕f3!? Ravinsky.

[14] 12 dc ♗xc5 =.
12 ♘xd6! ♕xd6 (12 ... ♗xf1 13 dc =) 13 ♖e1 ±/∞.

[15] 4 a4 ♘c6 5 0-0 ♘f6 6 ♖e1 e6 7 c3 a6 8 ♗f1 ♗e7 9 d4 cd 10 cd d5 11 e5 ♘e4 = Siaperas-Robatsch, Skopje Ol 1972.

[16] 5 c4 ♘gf6 6 ♘c3 a6 7 0-0 g6 8 d4 cd 9 ♘xd4 ♖c8 = Short-Stean, London 1980. 6 ... ♘e5!? Miles.

[17] 6 ♖e1 e6 7 d4 cd 8 ♕xd4 ♗e7 9 c4 0-0 10 ♘c3 a6 = Peters-Fedorowicz, Lone Pine 1980.

[18] 12 ♘xd4 = Lechtynsky-Csom, Malta Ol 1980.

[19] 5 c3 ♘f6 6 d3 e6 7 0-0 ♗e7 8 ♕e2 0-0 9 d4 ♘c6 10 ♖d1 cd 11 cd d5 12 e5 ♘e4 = Bronstein-Kottnauer, Prague v Moscow 1946.

[20] 5 ... ♘f6 6 e5 de 7 ♘xe5 ♕c8 8 ♕f3 e6 9 ♘c3 ♗e7 10 d3 ±/= Hug-Savon, Petropolis 1973.

[21] 7 ♖e1 e6 8 d4 cd 9 cd d5 10 e5 ♘e4 11 ♘bd2 ♘xd2 = Segal-Ciocaltea, Dortmund 1980.

[22] 7 ... cd 8 cd d5 (8 ... e6 9 d5 ♘e5 10 de ♘xf3+ 11 ♕xf3 fe 12 ♖d1 ± Nogueiras-Garcia Palérmo, Bayamo 1980) 9 e5 ♘g8 10 a3 e6 11 b4 ± Fedorov-Zaichik, USSR 1974.

[23] 11 ... ♘c7 12 ♘c3 e6 = Ivkov-Mecking, Vršac 1971.
11 ... e5!? 12 de fe 13 ♘c3 ♗e7 14 ♕c2 ♘c7 15 ♖ad1 a6 ∞/∓ Cording-Holm, Hamburg 1980.

[24] 5 ... e5 6 ♘c3 g6 7 d3 ♗g7 8 a3 ♘c6 9 ♖b1 ♘ge7 10 b4 b6 11 0-0 0-0 12 ♘d5 ♘xd5 13 cd ♘d4 14 ♘xd4 cd 15 ♗d2 ♖ac8 16 ♕b3 ± Spassky-R.Byrne, match 1974.

[25] 9 ... ♘h6 10 f3 f5 11 ♘c3 fe 12 ♕d2 ♘f7 13 ♘xe4 0-0 14 ♖ad1 ± Nei-Spassky, Tallinn 1973.

[26] 11 ... ♖ac8?! 12 b3 ± Blau-Fischer, Zürich 1959.
11 ... ♖fd8! 12 ♕d2 e6 13 ♖fd1 d5 ∞/= Biriescu-Schneider, Zamardi 1980.

[27] 3 ... ♘f6 4 dc (4 ♘c3 cd – 3 ... cd) 4 ... ♘xe4 5 cd e6 (5 ... ♕xd6?! 6 ♗d3 ±; 5 ... ♘xd6 6 ♗f4 e6 7 ♘c3 ♘c6 8 ♕d2 ±/±) 6 ♕d3! ♘xd6 7 ♘c3 ±/± Cortlever-Kottnauer, Beverwijk 1947.

[28] 4 ... ♘f6?! 5 e5 ♘c6 6 ♗b5 ♕a5+ 7 ♘c3 ♕xb5 8 ♘xb5 ♘xd4 9 ♘fxd4 de 10 ♘c7+ ♔d8 11 ♘xa8 ed 12 ♗f4 ± Szabo-Toran, Hastings 1957/58.
4 ... ♗d7 5 c4 ♘c6 6 ♕d2 g6 7 b3 ♗g7 8 ♗b2 ♘f6 9 ♘c3 0-0 10 ♗e2 ♕a5 11 ♖b1 a6 13 a3! ±/± Vasyukov-Zhelyandinov, USSR Ch 1967.

[29] 5 ♗g5 ♘c6 6 ♕d2 h6 7 ♗h4 g5 8 ♗g3 ♗g7 ∞.
5 c4 ♘c6 6 ♕d2 g6 7 ♘c3 (7 h3; 7 b3) 7 ... ♗h6 8 ♕d1 ♗g7 9 h3 ♘f6 10 ♗e2 0-0 = Tringov-Bilek, Skopje Ol 1972.

[30] 5 ... ♘c6 6 ♕b6 (6 ♕d2 ♘f6 7 ♘c3 ♘g4 ∞ Panchenko) 6 ... ♕xb6 7 ♗xb6 ♘f6 8 ♘c3 ♘d7 9 ♗e3 e6 10 a4 ♗e7 11 0-0-0 ♘ce5 ∞.

[31] 6 ... e6 7 0-0-0 ♘gf6 8 h3 ♗e7 9 g4 0-0 10 g5 ♘e8 11 h4 b5 ∞ Hropov-Nepomnashi, Leningrad Ch 1982.

[32] 7 ♗c4 e6 8 0-0-0 ♕c7 9 ♗b3 (Mark Tseitlin-Lukin, Leningrad Ch 1982) 9 ... b5 / ♕g4!? ∞.

[33] 12 ♗d3 h6 13 ♗xf6 ♗xf6 14 a3 ♕b6 ∞ Mark Tseitlin-Nepomnashi, Leningrad Ch 1982.

[34] 5 ... ♗g4 6 ♘bd2 (6 ♘c3 ♗xf3 7 gf ♘f6 8 ♗g5 a6/e6 ∞/=; 6 a4 ♕d7 7 ♘d4 ♖c8 =) 6 ... e6 7 0-0 ♘ge7 = Polovodin-Vitolins, USSR 1981.
5 ... a6?! 6 ♗xc6+ bc 7 0-0 e5 8 ♕d3 ♗e7 9 c4 ± Karpov-Szabo, Budapest 1973.

[35] 7 ♗a4!? Ciocaltea-Tringov, Istanbul 1980.

[36] 8 c4 b5! Schneider-Ribli, Buenos Aires Ol 1978.

[37] 7 c4 f5!? (7 ... ♘f6 8 ♘c3 g6 9 0-0 ♗g7 10 ♕d3 0-0 11 ♘d4 ♖c8 12 b3 =/± Padevsky-Ghitescu, Reykjavik 1969) 8 ef (8 ♘c3 e5 9 ♕d3 fe 10 ♘xe4 ♘f6 11 ♘xf6+ gf; 11 ♘g3 ♕d7 12 0-0 0-0-0 13 ♕e2 h5 ∞ Polovets) 8 ... ♕a5+ 9 ♘c3 ♕xf5 10 ♘d5 (Zakharov-Tseitlin, Odessa 1971) 10 ... e5!? 11 ♗e3 ♗xd5 ∞/= Polovets.

[38] 12 ♕d2 ♖fc8! 13 ♘d4 ♕b6 ∞/∓ Vasyukov-Ubilava, USSR 1981.

[39] 5 ... g6 6 c4 ±.
5 ... e6 6 c4 ♘c6 7 ♘c3 ♗e7 8 ♗e3 0-0 9 ♘c2 d5 =/∞.

[40] 6 ... ♗d7 7 ♗xd7+ ♘bxd7 8 ♗f5 d5 9 ed ♕a5+ 10 ♘c3 ♘b6 11 ♕e2 0-0-0 ∞ Böök-Solmanis, Kemeri-Riga 1947.

[41] 12 ♘c3 0-0! 13 cb ab = Bely-Navarovszky, Hungary 1954.

Dragon I   1 e4 c5 2 Nf3 d6 3 d4 cd 4 Nxd4 Nf6 5 Nc3 g6

	6	7	8	9	10	11	12	13	14	
1	g3[1]	Nde2[2]	Bg2	0-0	Re1	f3				=/±
	Nc6	Bg7[3]	Bd7[4]	Qc8	Bg4	Bh3[5]				
2	f4[6]	Be2	Be3[7]	Bf3	Qe2	Nb3	Bxg4	g3	Qxg4	=
	Nbd7	Bg7	0-0	Nb6	e5	Ng4	Qh4+	Qxg4	Bxg4	
3	...	Bb5[8]	0-0	Nd5	ed	Bxd7+	Qxd4			=
	Nc6	Qc7![9]	Bd7	Nxd5	Nxd4	Kxd7	Qc5[10]			
4	...	Nxc6	e5	ed[12]	Be3	Qf3	0-0-0	Bd4	h4	=
	...	bc	Nd7[11]	ed	Be7[13]	d5	Bf6	0-0	Rb8[14]	
5	...	e5	fe	e6	Bb5+	ef+	0-0+	Nxc6	Qxd8	=
	Bg7	de?![15]	Nfd7[16]	Ne5	Nbc6	Kxf7	Bf6	bc	Rxd8[17]	
6	Be2	0-0	Nb3	Kh1[18]	a4	f4	f5	cb	Be3	∓
	Bg7	Nc6	0-0	a5[19]	Be6	Qb6	Bxb3	Qb4	Nd7	
7	...	Be3	Nb3[20]	f4	a4	Bf3[22]	0-0	Bd4	Rf2	=
	...	Nc6	0-0	a5[21]	Be6	Nb4	Nd7	Bc4	e5[23]	
8	...	...	Qd2	0-0-0[24]	ed	Nxc6	Nxd5	Qxd5	Qxa8	=
	...	...	0-0	d5[25]	Nxd5	bc	cd	Qc7	Bf5[26]	
9	...	...	...	0-0	Bxg4	f4[28]	Bxd4	Be3	Rxf4	
	...	...	...	Ng4[27]	Bxg4	Nxd4	e5	ef	Be6	

1 e4 c5 2 Nf3 d6 3 d4 cd 4 Nxd4 Nf6 5 Nc3 g6 6 Be2 Bg7 7 Be3 Nc6 8 0-0 0-0[29]

	9	10	11	12	13	14	15	16	17	
10	f4[30]	e5!?[31]	fe	Nf5	Nxe7+	Bd4	Bxe5	Qd4	Bxg7+	∞/∓
	Qb6	de	Nxe5	Qxb2	Kh8	Qb4!	Qxe7	Nh5	Nxg7[32]	
11	Nb3	a4	f4[33]	f5	cb	Bc4	Qe2	Bb5[34]		±
	a5	Be6	Rc8	Bxb3	Nb4	Nd7	Ne5			
12	...	f4	f5	Nxa5[36]	Qxe2	g4	g5[37]	gf	Qxe3	=
	Be6	Na5[35]	Bc4	Qxe2	Qxa5	Rac8	Rxc3!	Rxe3	Bxf6[38]	
13	...	...	h3[39]	Nd4	Bxd4	f5	e5	f6	ef	=
	...	...	Qc8	Rd8[40]	Nxd4	Bc4	d5!	Ne4	ef	Bf8[41]	

---

[1] 6 Bg5 Bg7 7 Qd2 Nc6 8 0-0-0 0-0 (8 ... Nxe4!? 9 Nxe4 Bxd4 ∞ Ragozin) 9 Nxc6 bc 10 e5 (Rauzer-Kan, USSR 1936) 10 ... Nd5 =.
  6 Nd5 Bg7! =.
  6 h3 Bg7 7 Be3 Nc6 8 g4!? 0-0 9 g5 Ne8 10 h4 Nc7 11 f4 e5! 12 Nde2 (Lasker-Napier, Cambridge Springs 1904) 12 ... Bg4 ∓.
[2] 7 Bg2 Nxd4! 8 Qxd4 Bg7 =.
[3] 7 ... h5!? 8 h3 Bd7 9 Bg2 Qc8 ∞.
[4] 8 ... 0-0 9 0-0 Bd7 10 h3 (Geller-Pachman, Malta Ol 1980) 10 ... Rc8 11 Nd5 Ne5 ∞.
  8 ... Rb8 9 a4 a6 10 0-0 b5 11 ab ab 12 Nd5 0-0 13 Bg5 ± Nunn-Miles, Baden bei Wien 1980.
[5] T.Clarke-W.Watson, British Ch 1982.
[6] Levenfish.
[7] 8 0-0 0-0 9 Nf3! Nb6 10 e5 ∞.
[8] 7 Be2 / 7 Be3 – Classical.
[9] 7 ... Bd7 8 Nxc6 Bxc6 (8 ... bc 9 e5 Nd5 10 Nxd5 cd 11 Qf3 e6 12 0-0 Bg7 13 c3! 0-0 14 Qg3 Qc7 15 ed Qxd6 16 Be3 ± Olafsson-Panchenko, Las Palmas 1978) 9 e5 de 10 fe Ne4 11 Nxe4 Bxe4 12 0-0 Bg7 (Penrose-Barden, Hastings 1957/58) 13 Bf4 0-0 = Geller.
[10] Levy.

[11] **8 ... de** 9 ♕xd8+ ♔xd8 10 fe ♘g4 11 ♗f4 ♗g7 12 0-0-0+ ♗d7! 13 e6 fe 14 ♘e4 e5 15 ♗e2! ± Heidenfeld. 11 ... ♗e6 12 ♘e4 ♗g7 13 ♘c5 ♗xe5 14 0-0-0+ ± Levy.

8 ... ♗g4 9 ♗e2 ♗xe2 10 ♕xe2 de 11 fe ♘d5 12 e6! f5 13 ♘xd5 ♕xd5 14 ♗g5! intending ♖d1-d7 ± Euwe.

8 ... ♘g4 9 ♗e2 h5 10 h3 ♘h6 11 ♗e3 ± Lyublinsky-Aronin, Moscow Ch 1947.

[12] 9 ♕f3 ♗g7! 10 ♕xc6 (10 ♗b5 0-0!) 10 ... ♖b8 11 ♗e3 0-0 ∓.

[13] **10 ... ♕e7** 11 ♕d4 ♗g7 12 ♕xg7 ♕xe3+ 13 ♗e2 ♖f8 14 ♖f1 ♗a6 15 ♖f3 ♕g1+ 16 ♗f1 ♗xf1 17 0-0-0 0-0-0 18 ♖dxf1 ♕xg2 19 ♕d4! ♘b6 20 h3 (Nicolav-Georgieva, Gori 1970) 20 ... g5!? (Levy) 21 ♕e4 d5 2 ♕f5+ ± Keene.

10 ... ♘f6! 11 ♕d2 ♗g7 12 0-0-0 d5 13 ♘c5 e6 14 ♕d4 ♕a5 ∞ Nunn-Miles, London 1982.

[14] 15 ♕f2 ♖b4 16 ♗xf6 ♘xf6 17 a3 (Tal-Lisitsin, USSR Ch 1956) 17 ... ♖b7 = Geller.

[15] **7 ... ♘g4** 8 ♗b5+ ♔f8 9 h3 ♘h6 10 ♗e3 ♘c6 11 ed ♘xd4 12 ♗xd4 ♕xd6 13 ♗g7+ ♔xg7 14 ♕xd6 ± Levenfish-Rabinovich, USSR Ch 1939.

7 ... ♘h5 8 ♗b5+ ♗d7 9 e6 fe! 10 ♘xe6 ♗xc3+ 11 bc ♕c8! 12 ♕d3 (12 ♗xd7+ ♘xd7!) 12 ... ♗xb5 13 ♕xb5+ ♘c6 14 ♘g5 h6 15 ♘f3 ♕f5 16 ♕xb7 ♕e4+ 17 ♔f2 ♖b8! = Trifunović.

[16] **8 ... ♘g4** 9 ♗b5+ ♘c6 (9 ... ♔f8?? 10 ♘e6+ 1-0 – many games!) 10 ♘xc6 ♕xd1+ 11 ♖xd1 a6 12 ♗a4 ♗d7 13 h3 ♘h6 14 ♘xe7! ±.

[17] 15 ♗a4 ♗a6 16 ♖e1 c5! Gufeld.

[18] 9 ♗g5 a6 10 f4 b5 11 ♗f3 b4 12 ♘a4 ♗d7 13 ♖f2!? ∞ Mencinger-Petursson, Ljubljana 1981.

[19] 9 ... a6!? 10 f4 b5 11 ♗f3 ♗d7 12 ♗e3 ♖c8 13 ♖f2 ♕c7 14 ♖d2 b4 15 ♘a4 ♖b8 16 ♕g1 ♗g4 = Lobron-Keene, Dortmund 1982.

[20] 8 h4 h5 9 f3 0-0 10 ♕d2 d5 11 ♘xc6 bc 12 e5 ♘e8 13 f4 f6 14 0-0-0 (14 g4!? – Botvinnik – hg 15 0-0-0 fe 16 fe ♕a5! ∞) 14 ... fe 15 fe ♗xe5 16 g4 ♗xg4 17 ♗xg4 hg 18 h5 g5! = Smyslov-Botvinnik, match 1958.

[21] 9 ... ♗e6 10 g4!? ♘a5 (10 ... d5!? ∞; 10 ... ♘d7) 11 g5 ♘d7 12 ♗d4 f6 13 h4 fg 14 ♗xg7 ♔xg7 15 f5 ♕b6! = Boleslavsky.

[22] 11 ♘d4 ♕b6! 12 ♘xe6 ♕xe3 13 ♘xf8 ♘g4! ∓ Gufeld.

[23] 15 ♘db5 ef 16 ♗xf4 ♗xb5 17 ab ♗e5 = Gufeld.

[24] 9 ♘b3 ♗g4 10 ♗f4 a5 11 a4 ♗e6 = Grechkin-Saigin, ½-f USSR Ch 1949.

[25] 9 ... ♘xd4 10 ♗xd4 ♗e6 11 ♔b1 ♖c8 12 h4 ♗c4 (Smyslov-Konstantinopolsky, USSR 1945) 13 h5 ±.

[26] 15 ♕xf8+ ♔xf8 16 ♖d2 = Wade-Wotkowsky-Heidelberg 1949.

[27] 9 ... d5 10 ♘xc6 bc 11 e5 ♗e8 12 f4 f6 13 ef ef 14 ♗f3 ♗e6 15 ♘a4 ♘d6 16 ♘c5 ♗f7 = Bonch Osmolovsky-Kopilov, USSR 1953.

10 ♖fd1 ♖xd4 11 ♕xd4 ♘xe4 12 ♕xd5 ♘d6 ∓ Vasyukov-Gufeld, USSR Ch 1959.

[28] **11 ♘d5** ♗d7 12 c4 ♘e5 13 b3 e6 14 ♘c3 ♕a5 15 h3 a6 16 a4 f5 17 f4 ♘f7 = Boleslavsky.

11 ♘xc6 bc 12 ♗h6 ♕a5 13 ♗xg7 ♔xg7 14 ♖fe1 ♗e6 15 ♖ad1 ♖ac8 16 b3 ♖fd8 = Sergeant-Landau, Hastings 1938/39.

[29] 8 ... h5 9 h3 ♗d7 10 ♕d2 ♘c8 11 f4 ♗f8 12 ♖ad1 h4 13 ♘xc6 bc 14 e5 ± Tarrasch-Bird, Hastings 1895.

[30] **9 h3** d5! 10 ed ♘xd5 11 ♘xd5 ♕xd5 12 ♗f3 ♕a5! ∓ Ravinsky-Lisitsin, USSR Ch 1944.

9 ♔h1 d5 10 ed ♘b4 11 d6 ♕xd6 12 ♘db5 ♕b8 13 a4 ♗f5 ∞ Sampouw-Mascarinas, Wellington 1978.

9 f3 d5 =.

[31] 10 ♕d3 ♘g4 (10 ... ♕xb2 11 ♖ab1 ♕a3 12 ♘xc6 bc 13 ♘d5!; 11 a3 ♕xe4! ∞) 11 ♘d5 ♗xd4 12 ♗xg4 (12 ♘xb6? ♗xe3+) 12 ... ♗xe3+ 13 ♕xe3 ♕xe3+! 14 ♘xe3 = P.Cramling-Keene, London 1982.

[32] 18 ♗d3 ♗e6 ∓/∞ Levy.

[33] 11 ♘d4 ♘xd4 12 ♗xd4 ♕c8 ∞.

[34] Gufeld.

[35] 10 ... b5!? 11 ♗f3 (11 f5 ♗xb3 12 ab b4 ±) 11 ... ♕d7 12 h3 ♗c4 13 e5 ♘e8 14 ♖f2 ♖c8 15 ♗g4 e6 16 ♖d2 h5 (Liberzon-Miles, Baden bei Wien 1980) 17 ♗f3 d5 18 ♘e4! ± Liberzon.

[36] **12 g4** ♖c8 13 ♗xa7 (13 e5 de 14 ♕xd8 ♖fxd8 15 ♘xa5 ♗xe2 16 ♘xe2 ♖xc2 17 ♖fd1 – Aitken-Footner, British Ch 1962 – 17 ... ♖xd1+ 18 ♖xd1 ♗xg4 ∓ Golombek) 13 ... ♗xe2 14 ♕xe2 ♘c4 =.

12 ♗d3 ♗xd3 13 cd d5 14 ♘xa5 ♕xa5 15 e5 d4! 16 ♗xd4 ♘d7 ∞/∓ Rantanen-Helmers, Kringsja 1978.

[37] 15 ♗d4 ♕b4 16 ♖ad1 ♕c4 ∞/= Boleslavsky.

[38] 18 c3 ♖c8 19 a3 ♗c4 20 ♖ae1 b5 21 ♖f3 ♕c7 22 fg fg 23 ♖h3 h5! = Filipowicz-Hollis, Marianske Lazne 1962.

[39] **11 ♔h1** ♖d8 (11 ... a5 12 ♘d4 a4!?) 12 ♗g1 d5 13 e5 ♘e4 14 ♘b5 g5! ∞ Timman-Tarjan, Banja Luka 1974.

11 ♕e1 ♘b4! 12 ♘d4 ♗c4 13 a3 ♗xe2 14 ♕xe2 ♘c6 15 ♖ad1 ♖e8/♘g4 ∞ Gufeld.

[40] 11 ... a5 12 a4! ♘b4 13 ♘d4 ♗c4 14 ♘db5 ±/± Gufeld.

[41] 18 ♗xc4 ♕xc4 = Geller-Lipnitsky, Kiev 1950.

	6	7	8	9	10	11	12	13	14	
1	♗e3	f3[2]	♕d2[3]	e5	f4	0-0-0!	fe	♘f3	♘xd5	±
	♗g7[1]	0-0	d5?![4]	♘e8[5]	f6	fe	♘c6	♗g4	♖xf3[6]	
2	...	...	♗c4[7]	♗b3	♕d2	♗h6	♕xh6	0-0-0	cb	±
	...	a6	b5	♗b7	♘bd7	♗xh6	♘c5	♘xb3+	♕b6[8]	
3	...	...	♗c4	♕e2	♗d3	♘b3	0-0	♖fd1	♗xc4	=
	...	♘c6	0-0	♘a5[9]	e5	♗e6	♖c8!	♘c4	♗xc4[10]	
4	...	...	♕d2	g4[12]	♗xd4	0-0-0[13]	♔b1[14]	a3	h4	=
	...	...	0-0[11]	♘xd4	♗e6	♕a5	♖fc8	♗c4	♗xf1[15]	
5	...	...	...	0-0-0	♗xd4	♔b1[17]	g4[18]	g5[19]	♘b5	=
	...	...	...	♘xd4[16]	♗e6	♕c7	♖fc8	♘h5	♕d8[20]	
6	...	...	...	...	...	...	h4	h5!	a3[21]	±
	...	...	...	...	...	...	♖fc8	♕a5	♘d7[22]	

	9	10	11	12	13	14	15	16	17	
7	0-0-0	ed[23]	♘xc6	♗d4[24]	♗c5	♘xd5[25]	♕xd5	♖xd5	♖d6!	=
	d5	♘xd5	bc	e5	♖e8	cd	♕xd5	♗e6	♗xa2![26]	
8	...	...	...	...	...	♘e4[27]	h4	g4	♕c3	∞
	...	...	...	...	♗e6	♖e8	h6	♘f4[28]	♗d5[29]	
9	...	...	...	...	...	...	g4[30]	gf	♖g1[31]	=
	...	...	...	...	...	♖b8!?	f5	gf	fe[32]	
10	♗c4	♗xd4	♗b3	0-0-0	♔b1	♖he1	cb	♗xf6	♗xc3	±
	♘xd4[33]	♗e6	♕a5	b5	♖fc8[34]	♗xb3	b4	bc	♗xc3[35]	
11	...	♗b3	0-0-0	♗g5!?[37]	♕e2	♔xb2				∞
	♗d7	♖c8[36]	♘e5	♘c4[38]	♘xb2!	♖xc3!				
12	...	h4	♗b3	♗h6	♕xh6	bc	♕d2[40]	0-0	♖ae1	=
	...	♖c8[39]	♘e5	♗xh6	♖xc3!	♕a5	♖c8	♖xc3	♕c5[41]	
13	...	0-0-0	♗b3	g4[42]	♔b1	h4	♕d3	♕d2[44]	♕d3	=
	...	♕a5	♖fc8	♘e5	b5[43]	♘c4	♘e5	♘c4		
14	...	...	...	♔b1	♗g5	♗xc4	♘b3[47]	♖he1	bc[48]	±
	...	...	...	♘e5[45]	♘c4[46]	♖xc4	♕e5	♖xc3		

[1] 6 ... ♘g4?? 7 ♗b5+ ±±.

[2] 7 ♗c4 ♘g4! 8 ♗b5+ ♔f8 = Sköld-Botvinnik, Stockholm 1962.

[3] 8 ♘b3 ♗e6 9 ♕d2 ♘bd7! 10 0-0-0 ♘b6 11 g4 ♖c8 12 ♗h6 ♗h8! Panov-Simagin, Moscow 1943.
   8 ♗c4 a6!? 9 ♗b3 ♘bd7 10 ♕d2 ♘c5 ∞ Dorfman-Gufeld, USSR 1981.

[4] 8 ... ♗e6 9 ♘xe6 fe (Fischer-Mednis, New York 1965) 10 e5!? ♘e8 11 ed ed 12 0-0-0 ±.

[5] 9 ... ♘fd7!? 10 f4 ♘b6 11 ♗e2 ♘c6 12 0-0!? (Popović-Sax, Vršac 1981) 12 ... ♘c4 =.

12 0-0-0 ♗d7 13 ♘b3 ∞.

[6] 15 gf ♗xf3 16 ♗g2! ♗xd1 17 ♖xd1 ♗xe5 ∞/± Rosinow-Meyer, corr. 1958.

[7] 8 ♕d2 b5 9 a4! ba (9 ... b4 10 ♘a2 a5 11 ♗b5+ ♗d7 12 c3 ±) 10 ♘xa4 ± Boleslavsky-Ufimtsev, USSR Ch 1947.

[8] 15 ♔b1 0-0-0 16 b4! ♔b8 17 ♘b3 ± Krutikhin-Botvinnik, USSR 1963.

[9] 9 ... ♘e5 10 ♗b3 a6 11 0-0-0?! b5 =.

[10] 15 ♕f2 b6 16 ♖d2 ♕c7 17 a4 ♘c6 18 a5 ♖b8 = Miles.

[11] 8 ... ♗d7 9 ♗c4 ♖c8 10 ♗b3 ♘e5 11 0-0-0

♘c4 12 ♗xc4 ♖xc4 13 ♘b3 ♕c7 (13 ... 0-0 14 e5!) 14 ♗d4 ♗e6 15 e5 de 16 ♗xe5 ♕c8 ∞ Gufeld.

[12] 9 h4 d5! ∞.

[13] 11 ♘d5 ♗xd5 12 ed ♖c8 13 h4 ♕c7 14 ♖h2 ± Karpov-Mestel, London 1982.

[14] 12 a3 ♖ab8 13 h4 ♖fc8 14 ♘d5 ♕xd2+ 15 ♖xd2 ♗xd5 16 ed ± Karpov-Miles, London 1982. 13 ... b5 ∞.

[15] 15 ♖hxf1 ♖c4! = Gufeld.

[16] 9 ... ♗e6? 10 ♘xe6 fe 11 g3 ± Byrne-van der Wiel, Baden 1980.

[17] 11 ♘d5 ♗xd5 12 ed ♕c7 13 ♔b1 (13 h4? ♖fc8 14 h5?? ♗h6! 0-1 Hall-W.Watson, British Ch 1979; 13 g4 ♖ac8 14 c3 ♕a5 15 g5 ♘h5 16 ♗xg7 ♘xg7! = Timman-Sosonko, Wijk aan Zee 1978) 13 ... ♖fc8 14 ♖c1! a6 15 c4 ± Ginsburg-Kudrin, USA 1980.

[18] 12 ♗b5!?

[19] 13 h4 ♕a5 14 a3 ♖ab8 15 h5 b5 16 h6 ♗h8 17 ♖xf6 ♗xf6 18 ♘d5 b4!! 19 ab ♕a4 ∓∓ Ostermeyer-Sosonko, Mannheim 1975.

[20] 15 ♗xg7 ♘xg7 16 ♘d4 ♖c5 = Hort-Sosonko, Tilburg 1979.

[21] 14 hg hg 15 a3 ♖ab8 16 ♘e2 ♕a4 ∞ Ivanović-Velimirović, Yugoslav Ch 1981.

[22] 15 f4 ♗xd4 16 ♕xd4 ♘f6 17 f5! ± Dolmatov-Vasyukov, USSR Ch 1981.

[23] 10 h4!? de 11 h5 ♘xh5? 12 g4 ♘g3? 13 ♕h2! Rasidović-Wagman, Biel 1981. 11 ... ♘xd4 12 ♗xd4 ♘xh5 ∓ (12 ... e5 ∞).

[24] 12 ♘xd5 cd 13 ♕xd5 ♕c7! 14 ♕c5 (14 ♕xa8?! ♗f5 15 ♕xf8+ ♔xf8 16 ♖d2 h5 ∓) 14 ... ♕b7 (14 ... ♕b8!?) 15 b3 (15 ♕a3 ♗f5 16 ♗a6 ♕c7 17 ♕c5 ♕b6 18 ♕xb6 ab 19 ♗c4 ♖fc8 20 ♗b3 ♖xa2! =) 15 ... ♗f5 16 ♗d3 ♖ac8 17 ♕xa7 ♗xd3 18 ♕xb7 ♖xc2+ =.

[25] 14 ♘e4 f5 15 ♘d6 ♗f8 16 ♘xe8 ♗xc5 17 c4 f4!. 16 ♗c4 ♗e6 17 ♗b7 ♕h4! 18 ♗xd5 cd 19 ♗xf8 ♔xf8 20 ♘c5 ♗f7 ∓ Fedorowicz-Sosonko, Lone Pine 1981. 16 c4 ♗xd6 = Velimirović-Miles, Vrbas 1980.

[26] 18 b3 ♖ec8 19 ♖d5 a5! = A.Ivanov-Peshina, USSR 1980.

[27] 14 ♗xf8!? ♕xf8 15 ♔b1 ♖b8 ∞∞.
14 ♗c4 ♘xc3 (14 ... ♕h4!?) 15 ♕xc3 ♕g5+ 16 ♗e3 ♕xg2 =.

[28] 16 ... ♕c7 17 g5! h5 18 ♗c4 ♖ed8 19 ♕e1! ♖ab8 20 ♖h2 ± Maeder-Nesis, corr. 1980.

[29] 18 h5 (Psakhis-Vasyukov, USSR Ch 1981) 18 ... f5 ∞.

[30] 15 ♗xf8 ♕xf8 16 ♕a5 f5 17 ♘c5 e4 18 c3 ♗xc3! 19 bc ♕h6+ 20 ♖d2 ♖b1+! ∓.
15 h4 f5 16 ♘g5 e4 17 c3 ♕a5 ∞.

[31] 17 ♘g5 e4! 18 c3 ♖xb2 19 ♔xb2 ♕a5 ∞ Velimirović-Gufeld, Vinkovci 1982.

[32] 18 ♕h6 ♕f6 19 ♖xg7+ ♕xg7 20 ♕xe6+ (20 ♗xf8 ♔xf8!) 20 ... ♔h8 21 ♗xf8 ♕g5+ = Dolmatov-Schneider, Euro-Club 1982.

[33] 9 ... a6 10 ♗b3 ♘xd4 11 ♗xd4 b5 12 a4 ±.
9 ... ♘a5 10 ♗b3 a6 11 h4 ♘xb3 12 ab ♗d7 13 h5 ♖c8 14 ♗h6 ± Spassky-Geller, match 1965.
9 ... ♘d7 10 h4 ♘a5 11 ♗b3 ♘e5 12 ♕e2 h5 13 0-0-0 ♗d7 14 g4 (Mikhalchishin-Barczay, Cienfuegos 1981) 14 ... hg ∞.

[34] 13 ... b4 14 ♘d5!? ♗xd5 15 ed ♕b5 16 ♕d3 ♕b7 17 ♖he1 a5 18 ♗a4 ±.

[35] 17 ... ♖xc3? 18 ♖e2! ♖c5 19 b4 ±.
17 ... ♗xc3 18 bc ♖xc3 19 ♖e3 ± Tal-Portisch, European Team Ch 1961.

[36] 10 ... ♕b8 11 0-0!
10 ... ♘xd4 11 ♗xd4 b5 12 h4 (12 0-0-0 a5 ∓; 12 0-0 a5 =; 12 a4 b4 13 ♘d5 ♘xd5 14 ed =) 12 ... a5 13 a4! ba 14 ♘xa4 e5! ∞.

[37] 12 ♗h6 ♘xh6 13 ♕xh6 ♖xc3! ∞.
12 g4 ♘c4 13 ♗xc4 ♖xc4 14 ♔b1 b5! ∞.
12 ♕e2 a6 intending ... b5, ... b4, ... a5 ∞.

[38] 12 ... b5!?

[39] 10 ... ♕a5 11 ♗b3 ♖fc8 12 g4 ♘e5 13 h5?! ♖c4! 14 ♗xc4 ♘xc4 15 ♕c1 d5! ∞ Martinov-Lusgin, corr. 1979.

[40] 15 ♘e2 ♕c5 (15 ... ♗b5!?; 15 ... ♖c8!? Gufeld) 16 h5 ♘xh5 17 0-0-0 ♘f6 18 ♘f4! e6 19 ♔b1 ♖c8 20 ♕g5! ♔g7 21 ♘h5+ ♘xh5 22 ♖xh5 ♖h8 23 f4 ± Veingold-Yuferov, Klaipeda 1976.

[41] 18 ♖e3 ♖xe3 19 ♕xe3 b5 = (19 ... a5 =) Vasyukov-Parma, Yugoslavia 1973.

[42] 12 h4 ♘e5 13 h5 ♘xh5 and now:
14 g4 ♘f6 15 ♗h6 ♖xc3 16 bc ♗xh6 17 ♖xh6 ♖c8 18 ♔b2 (Tal-Wade, Palma 1966) 18 ... ♕b6 =.
14 ♔b1 ♖xc3 15 ♕xc3 ♕xc3 16 bc ♖c8 17 ♔b2 a5 = Spassky-Stein, RSFSR v Ukraine 1967.
14 ♘d5 ♕xd2+ 15 ♖xd2 ♗f8 16 g4 ♘f6 17 ♗h6! ♗xh6 18 ♖xh6 ♘xd5 19 ♗xd5 ♖ab8 20 ♖xh7 e6 21 ♗b3 ♔e7 =.
14 ♗h6!? ♗xh6! (14 ... ♘d3+!? 15 ♔b1 ♘xb2 ∞) 15 ♕xh6 ♖xc3 16 bc ♖c8! =.

[43] 13 ... ♘c4 14 ♗xc4 ♖xc4 15 ♗b3 ♕d8 16 e5! ±.

[44] 16 ♕e2?! ♖xc3! ∓.

[45] 12 ... ♖ab8 13 g4 (13 h4!? ±) 13 ... b5 14 h4 b4 15 ♘d5 ♘xd5 16 ed ♘xd4 17 ♗xd4 ♗xd4 18 ♕xd4 ♕c5 19 ♕d2 ± Schmidt-Bobotsov, Varna 1967.

[46] 13 ... ♕d8!? Ribli.
13 ... ♖c5!? Miles.

[47] 15 ♗xf6!? ♗xf6 16 ♘d5 ± Boleslavsky.

[48] Insufficient compensation – Euwe.

	9	10	11	12	13	14	15	16	17	
15	...	...	...	h4	g4	♗xc4	h5[49]	hg	♘b3![52]	±
	...	...	♖ac8	♘e5	♘c4	♖xc4	♖fc8[50]	hg[51]	♕a6[53]	
16	...	...	♗b3[54]	♘db5[56]	♗xa4	♕e2				∞
	...	♕b8	a5[55]	a4!?	♘a5	♖c8[57]				
17	...	...	♗b3	♗h6	♗xc4	h4	♗xg7	♔b1	♘ce2[59]	∞
	...	♕c7	♘e5[58]	♘c4	♕xc4	b5	♔xg7	b4		

49 15 ♔b1 ♖fc8 16 ♘b3 ♕a6 17 h5 ♗e6! 18 hg fg 19 ♗h6 ♗h8 = Pokojowczyk-Rigo, Balatontapolca 1981.

50 16 ... ♖xc3!?

51 16 ... fg 17 ♘b3 ♕a6 18 e5 ♘e8 19 ♕h2 h5 20 ♗d4 ± Timoshenko-Veselovsky, USSR 1980.

52 **17 ♗h6?** ♘xe4!
17 ♘de2? ♗e6! 18 ♔b1 ♘xg4! 19 ♗d4 ♘e5 20 ♕e3 b5 21 b3 b4 ∓.
17 ♔b1 ♖xc3 18 bc (18 ♘b3 ♘xe4!!) 18 ... ♗xg4 19 fg ♘xe4 ∓.

53 18 e5! de 19 ♗h6! (19 g5 ♗f5 20 gf ♗xf6 ∞)
19 ... ♗h8 and now:
20 ♗f8 ♖xf8! ⹂⹂ Pirisi-Rigo, Budapest 1980.
20 g5 ♗g7 21 ♗xf6 ♗xf6 22 ♕xd7 e4 23 ♔b1! ef (Pirisi-Sapi, Budapest 1980) 24 g5!! ♗xg5 25 ♘e4 ♖xc2 26 ♘xg5 ♕f6 27 ♕d8+! ±±.

20 ... ♘xg4!? 21 ♕xd7! ♘f2 22 ♖xh8+!? ♔xh8 23 ♖d2! ♖4c7 24 ♕b5 ±.

54 **11 g4** b5! 12 ♗b3 (12 ♘cxb5? ♘e5 13 ♗e2 ♘xf3 ∓) 12 ... a5 13 ♘d5 ♕b7 = Gufeld.
11 h4 b5 12 ♗b3 (12 ♘cxb5 ♖c8/d5!?; 12 ♘dxb5 ♖c8 13 ♗e2 ♘b4 ∞, or 13 ♗b3 ♘a5 14 ♘d4 ♘xb3+ intending 15 ... a5 – Gufeld) 12 ... ♘a5 ∞ Miles.
11 ♘d5 ♘xd5 12 ♗xd5 ♕c7 13 h4 ♖fc8 = Fischer.

55 11 ... ♖c8!?

56 12 a4 ♖c8 13 ♘db5 ± Sosonko-Browne, Wijk aan Zee 1975.

57 Gufeld.

58 11 ... ♖fc8 12 h4 ♘e5 13 ♗h6 ♗h8 14 h5 ♘c4 15 hg fg 16 ♗g5 b5 17 ♗xc4 ♕xc4 18 ♗xf6 ♗xf6 19 ♘d5! ♗xd4 20 ♘xe7+ ± Lilienthal.

59 Agnello-Miles, Malta 1973. 17 ... e5 ∞ Miles.

**Dragon III   1 e4 c5 2 ♘f3 d6 3 d4 cd 4 ♘xd4 ♘f6 5 ♘c3 g6
6 ♗e3 ♗g7 7 f3 0-0 8 ♕d2 ♘c6 9 ♗c4 ♗d7 10 0-0-0 ♖c8 11 ♗b3 ♘e5**

	12	13	14	15	16	17	18	19	20	
1	h4	a4[1]	♗xc4	b3	♘db5	♘xb5	♔b1	g4	♕g2	±
	a5	♘c4	♖xc4	♖c8	♗xb5	h5	♘d7	♘f6	hg[2]	
2	...	♗xc4[3]	g4[4]	h5	hg	♔b1	♘b3	♗d4!	♕h2	±
	♘c4	♖xc4	♕c7[5]	♖c8	fg	♕a5[6]	♘e5	♕e6	♕f7[7]	
3	...	...	...	h5	♘d5	ed	♔b1	hg[10]	♕h2	±
	...	...	b5	b4	♘xd5[8]	♕a5	♕xd5[9]	fg[11]	♕e5[12]	
4	...	...	...	e5![13]	fg	♘de2	♗g5[15]			∞
	...	...	h5	♘xg4[14]	♗xg4	♗xe5				
5	...	...	h5	g4	♗h6[16]	♕e3![18]	bc[20]	♗xg7	♘e2[21]	∓
	...	...	♘xh5	♘f6	♘xe4[17]	♖xc3[19]	♘f6	♔xg7	♕a5[22]	
6	...	...	...	...	♘de2[23]	♗h6[25]	e5[26]	fg[27]	♗f4	∓
	...	...	...	...	♖e8[24]	♗h8	♘xg4	♗xe5[28]	♕a5[29]	
7	...	...	...	...	e5	fg	♖dg1[30]	♖xg4	♖xh5	=
	...	...	...	...	♘xg4!	♗xg4	de	h5!	♖xd4![31]	
8	...	...	...	...	♘d5[32]	ed	b3	♕h2[35]	gh	∞
	...	...	...	...	♘xd5[33]	♕b6[34]	♖c5	h5	♖fc8	
9	...	...	...	...	♖dg1	♘ce2[37]	♘f5[38]	ef[39]		∞
	...	...	...	...	♖e8[36]	e5	♗xf5	♖a4!?[40]		

¹ **13 h5** a4 14 ♘xa4 ♗xa4 15 ♗xa4 ♘c4 (Gufeld) =.

13 g4 b5 14 h5 a4 15 ♗d5 b4 16 ♘ce2 ♘xd5 17 ed ♘c4 ∓ Mestrović-Osvath, corr. Ol 1974.

² **21 fg?** ♕d7 22 ♖dg1 ♕e6! Gufeld.

21 h5 gf 22 ♕xf3 ♕d7 23 h6! ± Gernud-Edelsberg, corr. 1974.

³ **13 ♕d3** ♘xe3 14 ♕xe3 ♕b6! ∞/= A.Zaitsev-Honfi, RSFSR v Hungary 1963.

⁴ **14 ♔b1** ♕c7! 15 g4 ♖c8 16 g5 ♘h5. 15 h5 ♖c8 ∞ Boleslavsky.

⁵ 14 ... ♕a5 – see earlier ... ♕a5 systems.

⁶ 17 ... ♖xc3 18 ♕xc3 ♕xc3 19 bc ♖xc3 ∓.

⁷ **21 e5!** de 22 ♗xe5 ♗e6 23 ♘d4 ♖xc3 24 bc! ± Nesis-Oechslein, corr. 1977/79.

⁸ 16 ... e6!? 17 ♘xf6+ ♕xf6 18 hg hg 19 ♕h2 ♖fc8 ∞ Kokkonen-Nesis, corr. 1978.

⁹ 18 ... ♖fc8 19 hg fg 20 ♕h2 ±/± Byrne-Ciocaltea, Hastings 1971/72.

¹⁰ 19 ♕h2!? Byrne.

¹¹ 19 ... hg 20 ♕h2 ♖fc8 21 ♕h7+ ♔f8 22 ♗h6! ±±.

¹² 21 ♕xh7+ ♔f7 22 ♖h6 ± Peters-Belyavsky, Caracas 1976.

¹³ **15 gh** ♘xh5 16 ♘de2 (16 ♖dg1 e6 17 ♘de2 d5 ∓/∓ Bellin-Sosonko, Amsterdam 1973) 16 ... ♕a5 17 ♗h6 ♗e6 18 ♗xg7 ± Kostro-Rodriguez, Haifa Ol 1976. 17 ... ♗xc3! 18 ♘xc3 ♖fc8 intending ... ♖xc3! Lepeshkin.

¹⁴ 15 ... de 16 ♘b3! intending g5, ♘c5 ±/± Adorjan-Sosonko, Wijk aan Zee 1974.

¹⁵ Gufeld.

¹⁶ **16 ♘b3!?** Gufeld.

16 ♕h2 ♖xc3 17 bc ♕a5 18 ♘b3 ♕a3+ 19 ♔b1 ♗e6 20 ♗d4 ♖c8 ∓ Rantanen-Rodriguez, Haifa Ol 1976.

¹⁷ 16 ... ♖xc3 17 ♗xg7 ♔xg7 18 ♕h6+ ♔g8 19 g5! ±/± Gufeld.

¹⁸ **17 fe** ♘xd4 18 ♕h2 ♖xd1+ 19 ♘xd1 e6! 20 ♗xg7 ♕g5+! ∓∓ Gufeld.

17 ♘xe4 ♖xd4 18 ♕h2 ♗e5! ∞/∓.

17 ♕h2 ♗e5!?

17 ♕f4 ♘xc3! 18 bc ♗e5! Gufeld.

¹⁹ 17 ... ♘f6 18 ♗xg7 ♔xg7 19 ♘d5!

17 ... ♘xc3 18 ♗xg7 ♔xg7 19 ♕h6+ ♔f6 20 g5+ ±±.

²⁰ 18 ♕xe4? ♗xh6+ 19 ♖xh6 e5! 20 ♖dh1 ♖c4! 21 ♖xh7 ♖xd4 22 ♕e3 ♖f4! ∓ Trofimov-Nesis, corr. 1971/72.

²¹ **20 ♖h2** ♕c7! (20 ... ♖g8 21 ♘e2 ♗h8 22 ♕xa7 ♗c6 23 ♘d4 ±) 21 ♕xe7 ♕xc3 22 ♕xd6 ♖c8 = Gufeld.

20 ♕h6+ ♗h8 21 ♘e2 ♖g8 22 ♕e3 a6 23 ♘g3 ± Ivanović-Tatai, Budva Z 1982.

²² **20 ... ♖g8** 21 ♘g3 ♗h8 22 g5!? (22 ♕d4 ♕b6 =) 22 ... ♘e8! 23 ♖he1! ±/±.

20 ... ♕a5! 21 ♘g3 ♖c8 22 ♕h6+ ♔g8! 23 ♖d3 ♖xc3! 24 g5 ♕a3+ 25 ♔b1 ♕b4+

²³ Chukman.

²⁴ 16 ... ♕a5 17 ♗h6! ♗xh6 18 ♕xh6 ♖fc8 19 ♖d3 ♗e6! (19 ... ♘4c5 20 g5! ♖xg5 21 ♖d5! ± Karpov-Korchnoi, match 1974; 19 ... ♖8c5! Karpov) 20 g5 ♘h5 21 ♘g3 ♗e5 22 ♘xh5! gh 23 ♕xh5 ♔f8!? (23 ... ♕g7 24 f4 d5 25 ♖hd1 b5 – Jambon-Nesis, corr. 1975 – 26 ♖1d2! ♕g6 27 ♕h6! ± Geller) 24 ♕h2 ♕xg5+ 25 f4 ♕f6 26 f5 ♖xc3 27 bc ♗xa2 28 ♕xh7 ♔e8 29 ♕h8+ ♔d7 30 ♕xf6 ef ±/= Nagornov-Nesis, corr. 1975/77.

²⁵ 17 e5 ♘xg4! 18 fg ♗xg4 19 ed (19 e6!? ♗xe6 20 ♗d4 ♖xd4! 21 ♘xd4 ♗g4 ∞∞ W.Watson; 19 ♕d3? ♕c8 20 ed ed 21 ♖de1 ♗f5 22 ♕d2 b5! ∓/∓ Berner-Schneider, Hungary 1976) 19 ... ♕xd6! ∓/∓ Gufeld.

²⁶ **18 ♕e1** b5! 19 b3 ♖c8 20 ♔b1 ♕a5 ∓/∓ Hartston-Sosonko, Hastings 1975/76.

18 ♗g5!? Gobet-Swoboda, Berne 1981.

18 ♕g5!? Hund.

²⁷ 19 ed ♘xh6 20 ♕xh6 ♗g7! ∓ Ostojić-Tarjan, Torremolinos 1974.

²⁸ 19 ... ♗xg4 20 ed! ♕xd6! 21 ♕xd6 ed 22 ♖xd6 ♗g7 23 ♗xg7 ♔xg7 24 ♘d4! h5 25 ♔d2 ♖cc8 26 ♖e1! ♖ed8 27 ♖d5 ±/± Matulović-Tarjan, Majdanpek 1976.

²⁹ 21 ♗xe5 ♕xe5 22 ♘d5 ♖xg4 (22 ... ♗xg4 23 ♖de1!) 23 ♘ec3 ♕g5 24 ♖de1! h5! ∓/∓ Lekrog-Nesis, corr. 1977/79.

³⁰ 18 ♗h6 ♗xe5! 19 ♗xf8 ♗xd1! ∓/∓.

³¹ 21 ♗xd4 ed 22 ♘e4 gh 23 ♖xg7+ ♔xg7 24 ♕g5+ =.

³² Geller.

³³ 16 ... e6 17 ♘xf6+ ♕xf6 18 ♕h2 ♖fc8 19 ♕xh7+ ♔f8 (Geller-Ivkov, Amsterdam 1974) 20 ♔b1! Gufeld.

³⁴ 19 ... ♕c7?! 18 ♕h2! h5 19 gh ♖c8 20 hg fg (Ristić-Meresescu, Balkaniad 1975) 21 ♔b1! ±.

³⁵ 19 ♗h6 ♕a5 20 ♕e3 ♕c3! 21 ♕xc3 ♖xc3 ∓ Vogt-Rodriguez, Halle 1974.

³⁶ 16 ... ♗e6 17 ♘f5 ♗xf5 18 gf ♕a5 19 ♗h6!? ♖fc8 20 ♗xg7 ♖xc3! ∞/=. 17 ♘ce2! ±/± Gufeld.

³⁷ 17 ♘f5 ♗xf5 18 gf ♕a5 19 ♗h6 ♖xc3! (19 ... ♖ec8 – note 36) =.

17 g5 ♘h5 18 ♕xh5 (18 ♘d5 e6!) 18 ... gh 19 ♘d5 ♕h8! 20 b3 ♖c8 21 ♕h2 e6 22 ♘f4 ♗e5 23 ♕xh5 ♖g8 24 ♕xf7 ♕f8! ∓ Gufeld.

³⁸ 18 ♘b3 ♗e6 19 ♘g3 d5! 20 g5 ♘h5 21 ♘xh5 gh 22 ♕h2 de 23 ♕xh5 ♖xc2+! ∓ Kiselev-Nesis, corr. 1971/72.

³⁹ Gufeld.

19 gf d5! ∓/∓.

⁴⁰ 19 ... e4 20 f4.

19 ... ♖a4!? intending ... ♕a5 ∞∞.

Dragon IV   1 e4 c5 2 ♘f3 d6 3 d4 cd 4 ♘xd4 ♘f6 5 ♘c3 g6 6 ♗e3 ♗g7 7 f3 ♘c6 8 ♕d2 0-0 9 ♗c4 ♗d7 10 0-0-0 ♖c8 11 ♗b3 ♘e5 12 h4 h5!?

	13	14	15	16	17	18	19	20	21	
1	♔b1[1]	♗xc4[2]	♘de2	♗h6	♗xg7	♘d5	ed	♖he1	♘d4	∞
	♘c4	♖xc4	b5	b4[3]	♔xg7	♘xd5	♕a5	♗f5[4]	♕xd5	
2	♗g5	g4	♗xf6[6]	h5	♘d5[7]					∞
	♖c5[5]	hg	♗xf6	g5						
3	...	...	f4	♕e2	f5!					∞
	...	...	♘c4	b5[8]						
4	...	♘de2?	♗xf6	f4	♗xc4	e5	ed			∓
	...	b5	♗xf6	♘c4	♖xc4	♗g7	♗g4[9]			
5	...	f4	♕d3	e5?!	♘e4	♘xd6	fe	♗xd5!	♖xd3	±
	...	♘c4	b5	♘g4[10]	♖d5?!	♘gxe5	♘xe5	♘xd3+	♕b6[11]	
6	...	...	...	...	...	ed	♖he1?![12]	♘xd6	f5	∓
	...	...	...	...	♖c8!	f6	ed	♗h7!	♘xd6[13]	
7	...	...	...	...	♗xf6	ef	♘e4	c3[14]		∓
	...	...	...	♕b6!	ef	♗xf6	♗g7	♖d5![15]		
8	...	...	...	♗xf6!?	e5	♘e4	e6	♘xe6	♔b1	∞∞
	...	...	...	♗xf6	♗g7	♖c8	♗xe6	♗xb2+	fe[16]	
9	...	♖he1	f4	♗xc4	♗xf6	e5	e6	ef+	♘e6	±
	...	b5	♘c4	bc?!	♗xf6	♗g7	♗c8	♖xf7	♗xe6[17]	
10	...	...	...	...	e5!?[18]	ef	♕e2	fe	ef♕+	∞∞
	...	...	...	♖xc4	b4[19]	bc	♖xd4	♕a5	♔xf8[20]	
11	♗h6	♕xh6	bc	♔b2[22]	♕d2	♔a1	a3	♔b2	♖h3	=
	♗xh6	♖xc3!	♕a5[21]	♖c8	♕b6	a5[23]	♕c5	♗e8[24]	♕b6[25]	

---

[1] 13 g4 hg 14 h5 ♘xh5 15 ♗h6 e6 16 ♖dg1 ♕f6 17 ♗xg7 ♕xg7 18 fg ♘f6 ∓ Sampouw-Sosonko, Indonesia 1982.

[2] 14 ♕d3?! ♘xe3 15 ♕xe3 ♖c5 16 ♖he1 b5!? 17 ♘dxb5 ♕b6 18 ♘d4 ♖b8 ∞ Pritchett-Miles, British Ch 1982.

[3] 16 ... ♕a5! 17 ♗g5 b4 18 ♘d5 ♘xd5 19 ♕xd5 ♖c5 20 ♕d3 ♗e6 ∓ Suetin-Szabo, Leningrad 1967.

[4] 20 ... ♖e8!? ∞.

[5] **13 ... ♘h7?!** 14 ♗h6 ♗xh6 15 ♕xh6 ♖xc3 16 bc ♕a5 17 ♘e2 ± Tal-Mista, Dubna 1973.

13 ... ♘c4!? 14 ♗xc4 ♖xc4 15 e5 (15 ♘b3!? Polugayevsky) 15 ... de 16 ♘b3 ♖c7 17 ♘b5 ♗f5! 18 ♘xc7 ♖xc7 ∞. 14 ♕e2 ♕a5! intending ... a6 and ... e5.

[6] 15 h5?! ♘xh5 16 ♘d5 ♖e8 17 ♖xh5 gh 18 ♕h2 gf 19 ♕xh5 ♗g4 20 ♕h4 ♖xd5 21 ♗xd5 ♕b6 ∓ W.Watson-Mestel, England 1978.

[7] Georgadze-Miles, Dortmund 1979.

17 ... gf!? ∞.

17 ... ♖xd5!?

[8] Westerinen-Mestel, Esbjerg 1979. 17 e5 de 18 ♘dxb5 ♗xb2 19 ♔xb2 ♕a5! ∞.

[9] J.Whitehead-Miles, Lone Pine 1980.

[10] 16 ... de? 17 ♗xf6 ♗xf6 18 ♘dxb5 ± Klovan-Gufeld, USSR 1978.

[11] 22 ♗xe7! ± Ljubojević-Miles, Riga IZ 1979.

[12] 19 ♘g3!? ∓.

[13] 22 fg+ ♔h8 23 ♗f4 ♘e5 24 ♗xe5 fe 25 ♘f3 e4 26 ♕xd6 ef ∓∓ Ljubojević-Miles, Malta Ol 1980.

[14] 20 ♘xc5 dc ∓.

[15] A.Rodriguez-Gufeld, Barcelona 1979.

[16] 22 ♘g5 ♖f6 23 ♖he1 ♔h8! ∞ Pokojowczyk-Mestel, Malta Ol 1980.

[17] 22 ♖xe6 ♕a5 23 ♕e3! ± Karpov-Sosonko, Tilburg 1979.

[18] 17 ♗xf6? ♗xf6 18 e5 ♗g7 19 ♘cxb5 ♕b8! ∓ Nunn-Miles, London 1980.

[19] 17 ... ♘h7!? 18 ed ♗xd4 19 de ♕a5 20 ef♕+ ♘xf8 ∞ Matanović.

[20] Gufeld.

[21] 15 ... ♕c7!? intending ... a5 ∞.

[22] 16 g4!? ♕xc3 17 ♔b1 a5 18 gh a4 19 hg ab 20 cb fg 21 h5 ♘xh5! 22 ♖xh5! =.

16 ♔b1!?

[23] 18 ... ♕a5 19 ♔b2 ♕b6 =.

[24] 20 ... d5! Spassky.

[25] Spassky-Mestel, London 1982.

Boleslavsky and Miscellaneous 6th Moves
1 e4 c5 2 ♘f3 d6 3 d4 cd 4 ♘xd4 ♘f6 5 ♘c3 ♘c6

	6	7	8	9	10	11	12	13	14	
1	f4	♘b3[2]	♕e2	♗e3	g4	g5[3]	a4	h4	h5	=
	♕b6[1]	e6	♗e7	♕c7	a6	♘d7	b6	♘c5	♘b4[4]	
2	♗e3	♗b5	fe[6]	0-0	♗xc6	e5[7]	♕h5	ed	♘e4	=
	♘g4[5]	♘xe3	♗d7	e6	bc	♗e7	0-0	♗xd6	♗e7[8]	
3	g3	f3	♗e3	g4	h4	♖g1	g5	♕d2	0-0-0	∞
	♗g4[9]	♗d7	e6[10]	h6	a6	b5	♘h5	♖ab8	hg[11]	
4	♗e2	♘b3[13]	0-0	f4[14]	a4[16]	♔h1	f5	♗g5	♗xf6	±/=
	e5[12]	♗e7	0-0	a5[15]	♘b4[17]	♗e6	♗d7	♗c6	♗xf6[18]	
5	...	...	...	♔h1	f4	♗xf4	e5	♗d3	bc	±
	...	...	...	♗e6	ef	d5	♘e4	♘xc3[19]	♖c8[20]	

[1] 6 ... g6 – Dragon.
   6 ... e6 – Scheveningen.
[2] 7 ♗e3 ♕xb2 8 ♘db5 ♗g4 9 ♕b1 ∞ Martin-Tatai, Las Palmas 1977.
[3] 11 0-0-0 b5 12 g5 ♘d7 13 h4 ♗b7 14 ♗h3 ∞ Kirov-Pähtz, Bialistok 1979.
[4] Kochiev-Belyavsky, USSR 1978.
[5] 6 ... e5!?
[6] 8 ♘xc6 ♘xd1 9 ♘xd8+ ♔xd8 10 ♖xd1 =.
[7] 11 ♕f3 ♕f6 12 ♕xf6 gf 13 ♖xf6 ♗g7 ∞.
[8] Gipslis-Tukmakov, USSR 1979.
[9] See note 1.
[10] 8 ... g6 9 ♕d2 ♗g7 10 0-0-0 ♖c8 11 g4 ♘e5 12 h4 ∞ Mestel-Christiansen, Hastings 1978/79.
[11] 15 hg ♘xd4 16 ♕xd4 b4 17 ♘b1 e5 ∞ Mestel-Timman, Lone Pine 1978.
[12] Boleslavsky.

[13] 7 ♘xc6 bc 8 0-0 ♗e7 9 ♕d3 ♗d7 10 ♕g3 0-0 = Bogoljubow-Gligorić, England 1951.
   7 ♘f3 h6 8 0-0 ♗e7 9 b3 0-0 10 ♗b2 a6 11 ♘d2 ♘d4 12 ♗d3 b5 ∞ Smyslov-Timman, Tilburg 1977.
[14] 9 ♗e3 ♗e6 10 ♗f3 ♘a5 11 ♘xa5 ♕xa5 12 ♕d2 ♖fc8 13 ♖fd1 ♕b4 = Boleslavsky-Euwe, Zürich C 1953.
[15] 9 ... ef 10 ♗xf4 ♘e5 ∞.
[16] 10 ♗e3 a4!
[17] 10 ... ef 11 ♗xf4 ♗e6!? Polugayevsky.
[18] 15 ♘d5 ±/= Barczay-Spassov, Warsaw 1979.
[19] 13 ... f5 14 ef ♘xf6 15 ♕e1 ♕d7 16 ♘a4 ♗f7 17 ♘ac5 ± Bronstein-Levenfish, USSR 1949.
[20] 15 ♘d4 ♕d7 16 ♖b1 ♘xd4 17 cd ± Karpov-Timman, Bad Lauterberg 1977.

Richter-Rauzer I   1 e4 c5 2 ♘f3 d6 3 d4 cd 4 ♘xd4 ♘f6 5 ♘c3 ♘c6 6 ♗g5

	6	7	8	9	10	11	12	13	14	
1	...	♗xf6[1]	♘b3	♕h5	♖d1	♗e2	0-0	♔h1[2]		∞
	a6	gf	e6	♕b6	♗d7	♗e7	0-0-0			
2	...	♕d2	0-0-0	♗f4	♘xc6[5]	♕e1[6]	♗c4	♗b3	♔b1	∞
	e6	a6[3]	h6	♗d7[4]	♗xc6	♕a5	♗e7	0-0-0	♕c7[7]	
3	...	...	...	♗e3	♗xd4	f3	♔b1	h4	♘a4	∞
	...	...	...	♘xd4	b5	♗e7	0-0	b4	e5[8]	

[1] 7 ♕d2 ♘xd4 8 ♕xd4 ♕a5 9 ♗xf6 gf 10 0-0-0 ♗e6 11 ♔b1 ♖c8 12 f4 ♖xc3 13 ♕xc3 ♕xa2+ 14 ♔c1 ♗h6 15 g3 ♕a1+ 16 ♔d2 ♕a4 17 ♗d3 ± Holmov-Barczay, USSR 1979. 7 ... e6 – rows 2-9.
[2] Rogulj-Ghitescu, Bucharest 1979.
   13 ... ♖dg8! ∞.
[3] 7 ... ♗e7 8 0-0-0 a6 9 f4 ♕c7 10 ♗e2 ± Tal-Larsen, Montreal 1979.

[4] 9 ... e5?? 10 ♘xc6 and 11 ♗xe5 ++.
[5] 10 ♗g3!? ♘xd4 11 ♕xd4 ♗c6 12 ♕e3 ♕c7 13 ♗e2 ♗e7 14 e5 de 15 ♗xe5 ♕a5 16 f4 0-0 17 ♗f3 ± Tringov-D.Pavlović, Niš 1981.
[6] 11 f3 d5!? 12 ♕e1 ♗b4 ∞ Sidef Zade-Makarichev, USSR Ch 1979.
[7] 15 f3 ♖he8 ∞ Dvoiris-Hasin, Katan 1980.
[8] 15 ♗e3 ♖b8 ∞ Shamkovich-Christiansen, US Ch 1980.

Richter-Rauzer I *continued* **1 e4 c5 2 Nf3 d6 3 d4 cd 4 Nxd4 Nf6 5 Nc3 Nc6 6 Bg5**

	6	7	8	9	10	11	12	13	14	
4	...	Qd2	0-0-0	Be3	Bxd4	f4	Bxf6	Bd3	Kb1	=
	e6	a6	h6	Nxd4	b5	Bb7[9]	gf	Qb6	Be7[10]	
5	...	...	...	f4	Bxf6	Nxc6[12]	Qe1	Bd3	Kb1[14]	±
	...	...	Bd7	b5	gf[11]	Bxc6	Be7[13]	Qb6		
6	...	...	...	...	...	g3	Nce2	Kb1	Bg2[16]	±
	...	...	...	...	...	Qb6	0-0-0[15]	Kb8		
7	...	...	...	...	Nf3	Bxf6[17]	Kb1	f5	g3	±
	...	...	...	Be7	b5	gf	Qb6	0-0-0	Kb8[18]	
8	...	...	...	...	Bh4[19]	Qe1	Nf5	Nxd6+	Rxd6	±
	...	...	...	h6	Nxe4	Nf6	Qa5	Bxd6	Qc7[20]	
9	...	...	...	...	...	fg	Nf3[21]	g6[22]	gf+	∞
	...	...	...	...	g5!?	Ng4	Be7	Bxh4	Kxf7[23]	

1 e4 c5 2 Nf3 d6 3 d4 cd 4 Nxd4 Nf6 5 Nc3 Nc6 6 Bg5 Bd7

	7	8	9	10	11	12	13	14	15	
10	Bxf6!?	Nf5	Bb5	Bxc6	Qd3	0-0	b4!	Rfd1	Rab1[25]	∞
	gf	Qa5	a6	bc	Rb8?![24]	Rg8	Qc7	Rxb4		
11	Qd2[26]	0-0-0	Qxd4	f4	e5	fe	Bd2	Bxc3	b4![28]	±
	Rc8	Nxd4	Qa5	e6[27]	de	Rxc3	Qxa2	g6		
12	...	...	...	...	...	...	Bb5[29]	Nxd5	Nc3!?[30]	∓
	...	...	...	...	...	Bc6!	Nd5	Bxb5	Bc5![31]	
13	...	...	...	...	...	...	Nb5!?	ef	h4!	∞
	...	...	...	...	...	...	Bxb5[32]	Bc6	Rg8![33]	

[9] **11 ... b4** 12 Bxf6 Qxf6 13 Ne2 Rb8 14 Nd4 Rb6 15 Bc4 ± Tal-Radulov, Malta Ol 1980.
11 ... Be7!?

[10] 15 f5 e5 = Jansa-Spassov, Sochi 1980.

[11] 10 ... Qxf6? 11 e5! ±.

[12] 11 Kb1 Qb6 12 Nce2 0-0-0 13 g3 h5 14 Bg2 Kb8 15 Rhf1 Ne7 16 Nb3 Bc6 17 Ned4 ± Timman-Torre, Rio de Janeiro IZ 1979.

[13] 12 ... b4? 13 Nd5! ±.

[14] **14 ... Qc5** 15 Rf1 h5 16 Rd2!? ± Jansa-Cabrilo, Kladovo 1980.
14 ... h5 15 f5 b4 16 Ne2 e5 17 Qg3 Bf8 18 Qf3 Qc5 19 Nc1 ± Sveshnikov-Ghitescu, Sochi 1979.
14 ... a5 15 Qe2 b4 16 Nb5 Rb8 17 c4 bc 18 Nxc3 ± Suetin-Panchenko, USSR 1979.

[15] 12 ... Rc8!? ∞/±.

[16] Sax-Ribli, Warsaw 1979. 14 ... Be7! ∞/±.

[17] 11 e5!? b4 12 ef bc 13 Rxc3 gf 14 Bh4 d5 15 Kb1 Na5 16 f5 Rc8 17 Qd2 (Planinc-Spassov, Polanica Zdroj 1979) 17 ... Qc7! 18 Bd3 Nc4 ∞ Gufeld.

[18] 15 fe fe 16 Bh3 Rc8 17 Qe1 Qc5 18 Ne2 d5 19 ed Nb4 20 Nfd4! ± Matulović-Mednis, Smederevo 1981.

[19] 10 Bxf6 Qxf6 11 Nf3 Qd8! 12 Kb1 Be7 13 h4 Qb6 14 Rh3 0-0-0 15 Qe1 Kb8 = Marjanović-Kupreichik, Belgrade 1979.

[20] 15 Qd2 Ne7 16 Bxf6 gf 17 Ne4 (Kais-Kudrasov, USSR 1979) 17 ... Ng8! intending ... 0-0-0, ... Bc6 ±.

[21] 12 Be2 Nge5 13 Nf3 Be7 14 Bg3 hg 15 Rhf1 b5 16 Nxe5 Nxe5 ∞ Lerner-Kupreichik, Odessa 1974.

[22] 13 g3 Nxh2! 14 Rxh2 hg 15 e5 d5 = Matulović-Banas, Stip 1979.

[23] 15 Qf4+ Bf6 16 Qxg4 Be7 ∞ Klovan-Bielczyk, Polanica Zdroj 1980.

[24] 11 ... Rg8!? 12 0-0 Rg5!? ∞ Adorjan.

[25] Plaskett-Lombardy, USA 1979.

[26] **7 Nb3** h6 8 Bh4 Rc8 9 Be2 g5! ∞ Damjanović-Stein, Tallinn 1969.
7 Be2 e6 8 Ndb5 Qb8 9 a4 Be7 10 Qd2 a6 = Spassky-Hort, Moscow 1971.

[27] 10 ... h6?! and now:
11 Bh4 g5 12 e5! gh 13 ef e6 14 Be2 Bc6 15 Rhe1 Rg8 16 Bf3 ± Karpov-Byrne, Hastings 1971/72.
11 Bxf6 gf 12 f5! h5 13 Kb1 (13 g3! ± Dolmatov) 13 ... Qc5 14 Qd3 ± Dolmatov-

Dorfman, USSR Ch 1981.

[28] 15 ... ♘d5 16 ♗c4 ♗h6+ 17 ♖d2! ± Belyavsky-Ubilava, USSR 1978.

[29] 13 ♗xf6 gf 14 ♘e4 ♖d8! 15 ♘xf6+ ♔e7 16 ♕xd8+ ♖xd8 17 ♖xd8 ♔xd8 ∞ Dolmatov-Ruderfer, USSR 1981. 16 ♕h4 ♖xd1+ 17 ♔xd1 ♔d8! ∞.

[30] 15 ♕xa7 ♗b4! (15 ... ♕xa7?? 16 ♘c7+!) 16 ♕xb7 0-0 17 ♘xb4 ♕xb4 18 ♖d2 ♕a5 19 a3 ♗c6 20 ♕b4 ♕xe5 ∞ Peshina-Azmaiparashvili, USSR 1981.

[31] 15 ... ♗c6?! 16 ♖hf1! ♗b4 17 ♘e4 ♗d5 18 ♘d6+ ♗xd6 19 ed f6 20 ♗xf6! gf 21 ♖xf6 ± Belyavsky-Yudasin, USSR Ch 1981.

15 ... ♗c5! 16 ♕g4 ♗b4! 17 ♘xb5 ♕xb5 (Dolmatov-Yudasin, USSR Ch 1981) 18 ♖d4 ♕c6! 19 ♕e4 ♕xe4 20 ♖xe4 ♗e7 ∓ Yudasin.

[32] 13 ... ♘d5? 14 ♕xa7!

[33] 16 ♗c4 gf 17 ♖he1!? (17 ♗xf6 ♖xg2 18 ♖he1 ♗h6+ 19 ♔b1 ♖d2 = Yudasin) 17 ... fg 18 ♗xe6 fe (Kupreichik-Yudasin, USSR Ch 1981) 19 ♕f6! ♕xe1! 20 ♖xe1 ♖c7! ∞ Yudasin.

Richter-Rauzer II   1 e4 c5 2 ♘f3 d6 3 d4 cd 4 ♘xd4 ♘f6
5 ♘c3 ♘c6 6 ♗g5 e6 7 ♕d2 ♗e7 8 0-0-0 0-0

	9	10	11	12	13	14	15	16	17	
1	f3	h4	♕xd4	♔b1	♕d2	♘e2	♘c1	g4	♗xf6	∞
	a6!	♘xd4	♕a5	b5	b4	e5	♗e6	♖fd8	♗xf6[1]	
2	♘b3	♗e3[3]	f3	g4	♔b1	f4	♕f2	♘e2	♗g2	∞
	♕b6[2]	♕c7	a6	b5	♘d7	♘b6	♘a4	♗b7	♖ac8[4]	
3	f4	♕xd4	♗h4	♗c4	fe	♕d3	♗b3?!	♗xe6	♕h3	∓
	♘xd4[5]	h6!?[6]	♕a5	e5	de	♕c5	♗e6	fe	♕c6![7]	
4	...	♗h4	♘f5	ef	♔b1	♗xf6[9]	♘d5	♖xd2	♘xf6+	±
	h6	e5	♗xf5	♕a5	♖ad8[8]	♗xf6	♕xd2	ef	gf[10]	
5	...	...	♘db5	♗xe7	♖xd8	♗c7	♖d3	♗xd6	♘c7!	=
	...	♗d7	♘xe4[11]	♘xd2	♘xf1	♘e3	♘xg2	♖fc8	♖ab8[12]	
6	...	...	♘f3	♔b1![13]	g4![14]	♗d3!	a3	♘d5!	♘xe7+	±
	...	...	♕a5	♖fc8	b5	♘b4	♘xd3	♕xd2	♔f8[15]	
7	...	...	...	...	♕e1	♗d3	g4	a3	♖xd3[17]	±
	...	...	...	♖fd8	♗e8	♘b4?![16]	♖ac8	♘xd3		

[1] 18 g5 ♗e7 ∞ Tringov-Kupreichik, Plovdiv 1980.

[2] 9 ... h6 10 ♗xf6 ♗xf6 11 ♕xd6 ♗xc3 12 bc ♕h4 13 f4! ♖d8 14 g3 ♕f6 15 ♕c5 ♖xd1+ 16 ♔xd1 e5 17 f5 b6 ± Kuzmin-Tseshkovsky, USSR Ch 1981.

[3] 10 f3 a6 11 h4!? ♖d8 12 g4 d5 13 ed ♘xd5 14 ♗xe7 ♘dxe7 15 ♗d3 e5 16 h5! ± Gipslis-Bielczyk, Riga 1981. 14 ... ♘cxe7! ∞.

[4] Karpov-Sosonko, Waddinxveen 1979.

[5] 9 ... e5!? 10 ♘f5! ♗xf5 11 ef ♖c8 12 ♔b1 ♖e8 13 ♗b5 e4 14 ♖he1 ♕b6 15 ♗xc6! ♕xc6 16 ♗xf6 ♗xf6 17 ♘d5 ♕c4 18 c3 ± Pritchett-Diez del Corral, Malta Ol 1980. 13 ... ♕a5!?

[6] 10 ... ♕a5 11 ♗c4 ♗d7 12 e5 de 13 fe ♗c6 14 ♗d2 ♘d7 15 ♘d5 ♕d8 16 ♘xe7+ ♕xe7 17 ♖he1 ♗b6! ∞ A.Rodriguez-Armas, Bayamo 1980.

[7] Ochoa-Gonzalez, Cuba 1981. 15 ♗xf6!? ∞.

[8] 13 ... ♖fe8!? 14 g4 ef 15 ♗xf4 d5 16 g5 hg 17 ♗xg5 d4 18 ♗xf6 ♗xf6 19 ♘e4 ± Karpov-Timman, London 1982.

[9] 14 ♗d3!? d5! 15 fe ♘xe5 16 ♖he1 d4 17 ♘e4 ♕b6 18 ♗xf6 ♗xf6 19 ♕f4 ♖fe8 ∞/± Hübner-Sosonko, Tilburg 1980.

[10] van der Wiel-Ligterink, Dutch Ch 1981.

[11] 11 ... d5!? 12 ed ♘xd5 13 ♘xd5 ed 14 ♗xe7 ♘xe7 15 ♘d4 ♖c8 (Belyavsky-Kupreichik, USSR Ch 1981) 16 ♗d3! ∞.

[12] 18 h4 ♘a5! 19 ♖g1 (van der Wiel-Fedorowicz, Graz 1981) 19 ... ♘c4! =.

[13] 12 ♗c4?! b5 13 ♗xb5 ♖fc8 14 ♗c4 ♘b4 15 ♕e2 ♖xc4! 16 ♕xc4 ♖c8 17 ♕b3 ♘xe4! ∓ Tseshkovsky-Kupreichik, USSR Ch 1979.

12 ♕e1 ♖fd8 13 e5 de 14 fe ♘h7! 15 ♗xe7 ♘xe7 16 ♘d5 (16 ♗d3? ♗c6 ∓ Karpov-Timman, Buenos Aires 1980) 16 ... ♘c6 17 ♕xa5 ♘xa5 =.

[14] 13 ♖g1 b5! ∞ Yudasin.

13 ♗d3 d5! 14 ed ♘b4 15 a3 ♘bxd5 16 ♘xd5 ♕xd5 17 ♘e5 ♗a4 ∞ Byrne-Kupreichik, Reykjavik 1980.

[15] 18 ♖xd2 ♔xe7 19 ♖xd3 ±/±± Dolmatov-Belyavsky, USSR Ch 1981.

[16] 14 ... ♖ac8!? Minić/Sindik.

[17] Mnatsakanian-Tukmakov, Erevan 1980. 17 ... b5 18 e5 de 19 fe ♖xd3 20 cd ♘d5 ±.

	6	7	8	9	10	11	12	13	14	
1	...	0-0[1]	♘xc6	f4	♔h1	♕f3	h3	♘a4	♗b3	∞/±
	♗d7	g6[2]	bc[3]	♕b6+	♘g4	♗g7	h5	♕d4	0-0-0[4]	
2	...	♘xc6	0-0	b3[6]	♗b2	♕e2	♘a4	f4	♖f3	∞
	♕b6	bc	e6[5]	♗e7	0-0	♘d7![7]	♕c7	♗b7!	♖ae8[8]	
3	...	♘de2	0-0	♗b3	♘g3[10]	♗g5	♕d2	♖ad1	♖fe1	∞
	...	e6	♗e7	0-0[9]	♘a5	♕c7	a6	♖d8	b5![11]	
4	...	♘b3	♗e3	f4	0-0	♗d3[12]	♕f3	♖ae1	♕h3	=
	...	e6	♕c7	♗e7	a6	b5[13]	♗b7	♘b4	e5![14]	
5	...	♘db5	♗e3	♘d4	0-0	♗b3	f4	f5!	♗xd4	=/±
	...	a6	♕a5[15]	e6[16]	♗e7	0-0	♗d7	♘xd4	♖ac8[17]	

[1]   7 ♗b3 g6 8 f3 ♘a5 9 ♗g5 ♗g7 10 ♕d2 h6 11 ♗e3 ♖c8 12 0-0-0 ♘c4 = Fischer.

[2]   7 ... e6 8 ♔h1 ♗e7 9 f4 0-0 10 f5! ±/± Euwe.

[3]   8 ... ♘xc6 9 ♘d5 ♗g7 10 ♗g5 ♗xd5 11 ed 0-0 12 ♕e2 ± Euwe.

[4]   Mititelu.

[5]   8 ... g6 9 b3 ♗g7 10 ♗b2 0-0 11 ♕d3 a5 12 ♖ae1 ♗a6 13 e5 de 14 ♘a4 ♗xc4 =.

[6]   9 ♗g5 ♗c5! 10 ♗xf6 ♕xc4 ∓.

[7]   11 ... e5?! 12 ♔h1 ♕c7 13 ♖ae1 ♘d7 14 ♘a4 ♗b7 15 ♗d3 ♖fe8 16 c4 ± Karpov-Stein, Moscow 1971.

[8]   15 ♖af1 g6 16 ♗d3 intending c4 ∞.

[9]   9 ... a6 10 ♕d3 0-0 11 ♕g3! ♔h8 12 ♗g5 ♕c7 13 ♖ad1 ± Ljubojević-Radulov, 1975.

[10]   10 ♔h1 ♘a5 11 ♗g5 ♗c5 12 f4 b5 13 ♘g3

♗b7! 14 ♘h5 b4! 15 ♘a4 ♕c7 16 ♘xf6+ ♗xf6 17 ♗xf6 gf 18 ♕g4+ ♔h8 19 ♕h4 ♖g8 ∓.

[11]   15 ♘f5!? ef 16 ♗xf6 ♘xb3! 17 ab ♗xf6 18 ♘d5 ♕d7! ∞ Ljubojević-Ribli, 1972.

[12]   11 a4 b6 12 ♗d3 ♗b7 13 ♕f3 ♘b4 =.

[13]   11 ... 0-0?! 12 g4! b5 13 g5 ♘e8 14 ♕h5! g6 15 ♕h6 ± Fischer-Saidy, USA 1967.

[14]   15 a3 ♘xd3 16 cd 0-0 17 ♖c1 ♕d8 =.

[15]   8 ... ♕d8 9 ♘d4 ♘g4!? (9 ... e6 10 ♕e2 – Velimirović Attack) 10 ♘xc6 bc 11 ♗g5! ♕b6 12 ♕d2 h6 13 ♗h4 g5 14 ♗g3! ∞.

[16]   9 ... ♘xe4 10 ♕f3 f5 11 ♘xc6 bc 12 0-0-0! d5 13 ♘xd5! cd 14 ♗xd5 ♖b8 15 ♗c6+ ♔f7 16 ♗xe4 ± Bednarski-Minev, 1975.

[17]   15 fe ♘xe6 16 ♘d5 ♗xd5 17 ed ♖ce8 18 c3 ♗d8! =/± Bilek-Hort, Göteborg 1971.

	7	8	9	10	11	12	13	14	15	
1	a3	♗a2	0-0	f4	f5[2]	♘de2	♘g3	♗e3[4]	♗xb6	∓
	♗e7	0-0	b5	♗b7	e5	♘bd7![3]	♖c8	♘b6	♕xb6+[5]	
2	♗b3	f4	♕f3	f5	♗e3	♗xd4	♗e3	a3	0-0[8]	±
	♗e7[6]	0-0	♕c7[7]	♘c6	♘xd4	e5	b5	♗b7		
3	...	0-0[9]	♖e1	♗g5	♗h4?![12]	♗g3	♘f3	♗d5	♘xe5	∓
	b5	♗b7[10]	♘bd7[11]	h6	g5![13]	♘e5	♕c7	ed	de[14]	
4	...	...	♕f3[15]	♗e3[17]	♕g3	♖fe1	a3	♘xc6	♗h6	=
	...	♗e7	♕b6[16]	♗b7	♗d7	♘c6	0-0	♗xc6	♘e8[18]	
5	...	...	f4	e5[19]	fe	♗e3	ef	♕e1![22]	♕xe3	∞
	...	...	♗b7!?	de	♗c5	♘c6[20]	♗xd4[21]	♘xe3+	♕d4[23]	
6	...	...	...	e5	fe	♕h5	♘xc6	♗e3[25]	♖f3	∞
	...	...	0-0	de	♘fd7	♘c6[24]	♕b6+	♘xc6	♗b7[26]	
7	...	...	...	...	...	♗e3!?	♕h5	♗xc4	♖ad1![28]	∞
	...	...	...	...	...	♘xe5[27]	♘c4	bc	♕c7[29]	

[1] 6 ... b5!? 7 ♗b3 e6 transposes but avoids row 1.

[2] 11 ♖e1 ♘bd7 12 e5 de 13 fe ♘e8 14 ♘xe6 fe 15 ♗xe6+ ♔h8 16 ♕xd7 (16 ♗xd7? ♗c5+ 17 ♗e3 ♕g5! ∓∓) 16 ... ♗c5+ 17 ♗e3 ♕b6! = Honfi-Schneider, Hungary 1976.

[3] 12 ... ♘xe4 13 ♘xe4 ♗xe4 14 ♘g3 intending ♘h5 ∞.

[4] 14 ♗g5 ♗xc3! 15 bc ♘xe4 16 ♘xe4 ♗xe4 17 ♗xe7 ♕xe7 18 c4 ♖c8! 19 ♕e2 ♘f6 20 ♖ac1 h5! 21 cb ab 22 ♕xb5 ♕a7+ 23 ♔h1 h4 ∓ Ermenkov-Portisch, Skara 1980.

[5] 16 ♔h1 ♕e3! 17 ♘d5 ♗xd5 18 ♗xd5 ♖d8 ∓ Robatsch-Fischer, Havana 1965.

[6] 7 ... ♘bd7? 8 f4 ♗c5 9 f5! ±.

[7] 9 ... ♘c6 10 ♗e3 ♕c7 11 g4! ♖e8 12 g5 ♘xd4 13 ♗xd4 ♘d7 14 0-0-0 b5 15 g6! ± Ermenkov-Peev, Bulgarian Ch 1976.

[8] Honfi-Blubaum, West Germany 1979. 15 ... ♖ac8!? ± Nunn.

[9] 8 f4 ♗b7 9 f5 e5 10 ♘de2 ♘bd7 11 ♗g5 ♗e7 12 ♗g3 ♖c8 13 ♘h5 (13 0-0?! h5! ∓ R.Byrne-Fischer, Sousse IZ 1967) 13 ... ♘xh5! 14 ♕xh5 0-0 ∓.

[10] 8 ... b4?! 9 ♘a4 ♗b7!? (9 ... ♘xe4 10 ♖e1 ♘f6 11 ♗g5 ♗e7 12 ♘f5! ef 13 ♗xf6 gf 14 ♕d5 ±) 10 ♖e1 ♘bd7! 11 a3! ♘xe4 12 ♘xe6! fe 13 ♗xe6 ♘df6 14 f3 d5 15 fe de 16 ab ±/± de Firmian-Hort, Baden Baden 1981. 13 ... ♗e7!? 14 ♕d4 ♘ef6 15 ab ∞ de Firmian.

[11] 9 ... ♗e7? 10 ♗xe6!
9 ... b4? 10 ♘d5 ♘bd7 11 ♗g5 ±.
9 ... ♘c6 10 a4 b4 11 ♘xc6 ♗xc6 12 ♘d5 ± Vasyukov-Averkin, USSR Ch 1969.

[12] 11 ♗xf6!? intending 11 ... ♕xf6 12 a4 b4 13 ♘a2 a5 14 c3 ±, or 11 ... ♘xf6 12 a4 (12 ♕f3!?).

[13] 11 ... ♘c5 12 ♗d5! ± Fischer-Rubinetti, Palma IZ 1970.

[14] 16 ♗xe5 ♕xe5 17 ed ♗d6 18 ♕d4 ♘d7 19 ♖xe5+ ♗xe5 20 ♕b4 0-0-0 21 a4 ba! ∓/∓ Plaskett-Tukmakov, Malta 1980.

[15] 9 a4 b4 10 ♘a2 0-0 11 ♘xb4 ♗b7 12 c3 a5 13 ♘d3 ♗xe4 14 ♖e1 ♘a6 = Kavalek-Andersson, Tilburg 1980. 10 ... ♕b6!? 11 ♗e3 ♕b7 12 f3 ♗d7 =/∞ Stean.

[16] 9 ... ♕c7!? 10 ♕g3 ♘c6 11 ♗e3 0-0 12 ♘xc6 ♕xc6 13 ♗h6 ♘e8 14 ♘d5 ♗d8 15 ♖fe1 ♕b7 16 ♘c3 ½-½ Balashov-Tukmakov, USSR Ch 1971 (=/∓ Nunn).

[17] 10 ♗g5!? 0-0 11 ♖ad1 ♘bd7 12 ♕g3 ♘c5 13 ♗h6 ♘e8 14 ♗d5 ed 15 ♘xd5 ♕d8 16 ♘c6

♗h4 17 ♘de7+ ♕xe7 18 ♘xe7+ ♗xe7 ∓ Brooks-Browne, USA 1982.

[18] 16 ♖ad1 ♔h8 17 ♗f4 ♖g8!? 18 ♗g5 ♗xg5 19 ♕xg5 a5 = Wedberg-Grünfeld, Lucerne 1979.

[19] 10 ♗e3!?

[20] 12 ... ♗xd4!? 13 ♗xd4 (13 ♕xd4 ♕xd4 14 ♗xd4 ♘c6 15 ef ♗xd4 16 fg ♖g8 =/∓) 13 ... ♘c6 14 ♖f4 ♕c7! 15 ♕e2 0-0-0 ∓ Nunn-Kosten, London 1980.

[21] 13 ... ♘xd4 14 fg ♖g8 15 ♖xf7! ♘xb3 16 ♕h5 ♗xe3+ 17 ♔h1 ♗xg2+ 18 ♔xg2 ♕g5+ 19 ♕xg5 ♗xg5 20 ♖af1 ± Marjanović-Dieks, Gröningen 1972/73.

[22] 14 fg ♗xe3+ 15 ♔h1 ♖g8 16 ♗xe6! ♖xg7! 17 ♗xf7+ ♖xf7 18 ♕h5 ♕d7! 19 ♘e4 ♔f8 20 ♘d6 ♖f2! ∓ Nunn.

[23] 16 ♖ae1 ♖d8 17 ♘e4 gf 18 ♗xf6+ ♔e7 19 ♘d5+!? ♖xd5 20 ♗xd5 ♕xd5 21 ♖d1 (Romanishin-Shashin, USSR 1974) 21 ... ♕e5 ∞ Nunn.

[24] 12 ... ♗c5!? 13 ♗e3 ♗xd4 14 ♗xd4 ♘c6 15 ♖ad1 ♘xd4 16 ♖xd4 ♕b6 17 ♖f4 ♕c5! 18 ♘d5 ♖a7!? (18 ... ♗b7 19 ♖h4 h6 20 ♘f6+ ♗xf6 21 ef ♕g5! = McKay-Scrimgour, Scottish Ch 1974) 19 ♔h1 ed 20 ♖d3 ♘xe5! ∓ Socaciu-Dominte, Romania 1980.
12 ... ♘c5 13 ♗e3 ♘xb3 14 cb ♗b7 15 ♖ad1 ♕e8 =/∓ Nunn.

[25] 14 ♔h1 ♕xc6 15 ♖f3 ♗b7 16 ♗f4 ♘c5 17 ♖g3 b4 (Adorjan-Hecht, Amsterdam 1977) 18 ♖g1! =. 17 ... f5!? 18 ef ♖xf6 19 ♗e5 ♖f7 ∓ Liberzon. 16 ♗e3 – row 6 (note 26).

[26] 16 ♔h1 ♘c5 (16 ... b4!? 17 ♗a4 ♕c7 18 ♖h3 h6 19 ♗xd7 bc 20 ♖xh6 cb ∓∓ Nunn) 17 ♖e1 a5 18 ♖g3 a4 19 ♗xc5 ♘xc5 20 ♖xg7+ =.
16 ♖af1!? ♘c5 17 ♖1f2 ♗xe3 18 ♖xe3 ♕c7! ∞ Nunn.

[27] 12 ... ♘c5 13 ♕g4!
12 ... ♗g5? 13 ♕xg5 ♕xg5 14 ♘xe6! ±.
12 ... ♕c7? 13 ♖xf7! ♖xf7 14 ♘xe6 ♕xe5 15 ♗d4 ♕f5 16 ♘xg7 ♕f4 17 ♘e6 ♕f5 18 ♘g7 ♕f4 19 ♘e2! ♕e4 20 ♕f1 ♕f6 21 ♗xf6 ♘xf6 (Nogueiras-Tarjan, Bogota 1979) 27 ♖d1! ± Nunn.

[28] 15 ♖f3? g6 ∓ Tarjan-Byrne, US Ch 1981.

[29] 16 ♖f3 g6 17 ♕h6 f5 18 ♘xf5!? ♖xf5 19 ♖xf5 gf 20 ♗d4 e5 21 ♘d5 ♕d6 22 ♘xe7+ ♕xe7 23 ♗xe5 ∞ de Firmian-Ribli, Baden Baden 1981. 18 ♗f4!? de Firmian.

251

Velimirović I 1 e4 c5 2 ♘f3 d6 3 d4 cd 4 ♘xd4 ♘f6 5 ♘c3 ♘c6 6 ♗c4 e6 7 ♗e3 ♗e7 8 ♕e2

	8	9	10	11	12	13	14	15	16	
1	...	0-0-0	♘xe6!?[1]	ed	de	♗d5	♕c4	/		±
	0-0	d5	fe	♘a5	♕c7[2]	♘c6!				
2	...	...	♗b3	♖hg1[4]	g4	g5	♕h5	♘a4	♘b6	=
	...	a6	♕e8!?[3]	♘d7	♘c5	b5	b4	♘xe4	♖b8[5]	
3	...	...	♗xd4	e5	♗xe5	♘b5[6]	♗c3	♖d4	♗xb5	±
	...	♘xd4	♕a5	de	b6	♗a6	♕a4	♗xb5	♕xa2[7]	
4	...	...	f4!	f5!	♗xd4	♗f2[8]				±
	...	♗d7	♕b8	♘xd4	e5					
5	...	...	♗b3[9]	♘xd4	♔b1[10]	f4	♖hf1	f5!	fe	±
	...	♕a5	♘xd4	♗d7	♗c6[11]	♖ad8	b5	b4	bc[12]	
6	...	...	♗b3	♖hg1[13]	g4	g5	ab	f4[14]	♘f5!?	∞
	...	♕c7	a6	b5	♘a5	♘xb3+	♘d7	b4	♘c5!	
7	...	...	...	...	...	♘xc6	♘d5!?	g5!	♗xd5	∞
	...	...	...	...	b4	♕xc6	ed	♘xe4	♕a4![15]	
8	...	...	...	g4	♖xd4	g5	♕h5[17]	♖hg1	♕h6	∞
	...	...	...	♘xd4[16]	♘d7	b5	♖fd8!	g6	♗f8[18]	
9	...	...	...	♔b1	♕h5	g4	cb!	♖hg1	♖xd4	=
	...	...	...	♘d7	♘c5	♘xb3	♗d7	♘xd4	f6![19]	

---

[1] 10 ♘f3!? ♘xe4 11 ♘xe4 ♕a5 12 ♗d2 ♕a4 13 ♗d3 de 14 ♕xe4 ♕xe4 15 ♗xe4 f6 (15 ... ♗d7 16 ♗g5! ±) 16 ♗e3 e5 17 ♗d5+ ♔h8 intending ... ♗d7, ... ♖fd8 =.

[2] 12 ... ♕e8 13 ♗b5 ♘c6 14 ♖he1 a6 15 ♗c4 b5 16 ♗b3 ♘a5 17 ♗d5 ♖b8 ∞.

[3] Belyavsky.

[4] 11 f4 ♘d7 12 g4 ♘c5 13 ♔b1 b5 14 f5 ♗f6 15 fe fe 16 ♘f5! ± Velimirović-Spassov, Yugoslavia 1974. 14 ... ♘xb3! 15 ab ♗d7 ∞.

[5] 17 ♘xc8 ♕xc8 18 ♖g4 d5 19 ♖h4 h6 20 ♖xe4 de 21 gh g6 22 ♘xc6 ♕xc6 23 ♕e5 f6 24 ♕xe6+ ♕xe6 25 ♗xe6+ (Harding) 25 ... ♔h8 26 ♖d7 ♗d8 27 ♗c5 ♗b6! 28 ♗xf8 ♖xf8 = Euwe.

[6] 13 ♗b5 a6! 14 ♗c6 ♖a7 15 ♗b8 ♗b7! 16 ♗xa7 ♗xc6 ∓.

[7] 17 ♖hd1 ± Bogdanović-Shamkovich, Yugoslavia v USSR 1963.

[8] Analysis.

[9] 10 f4 ∓ ♘xd4 11 ♖xd4 ♗d7! 12 ♖f1 ♗c6 13 f5 d5! ∓.

[10] **12 g4 e5!**
12 f4!?

[11] **12 ... b5** 13 ♗xf6 ♗xf6 14 ♖xd6 ±.
12 ... ♖ad8 13 ♕e3! b6 14 ♗xf6! gf 15 ♘d5!! ♖fe8 16 ♕h6! ±± Fischer.

[12] 17 ef+ ♔h8 18 ♖f5! ♕b4 19 ♕f1! ♘xe4 (Fischer-Geller, Skopje 1967) 20 ♕f4! ± Fischer.

[13] 11 f4 ♘xd4 12 ♖xd4 b5 13 ♖hf1 ♖ab8 14 a3 ♗d7 15 f5 a5 =/∓.

[14] **15 h4** b4 16 ♘a4 ♗b7 17 g6 hg 18 h5 e5! ∓.
15 ♕h5 g6 16 ♕h6 ♖e8 17 ♖g3 ♗f8 ∞.
15 ♘f5!? ef 16 ♘d5 ♕d8 17 ef ♖e8 18 g6!?

[15] **17 ♗xa8** ♘c3 18 bc ♗e6! ∞.
17 ♗xe4? ♗e6! =/∓.

[16] 11 ... ♘d7 and now:
12 ♘f5!? ef 13 ♘d5 ♕d8 14 gf ♘a5 15 ♖hg1 ♘xb3+ 16 ab ±. 12 ... ♘c5! ±/=.
12 g5 ♘c5 13 ♖hg1 ♗d7 14 ♖g3! ♖fc8 15 ♕h5 g6 16 ♕h6 ♗f8 17 ♕h4 ♗e7 ∞.

[17] 14 e5 de 15 ♖h4 ♖d8 16 ♕h5 ♘f8 17 ♘e4! ♗b7 18 ♘f6+! ♗xf6! 19 gf ♗xh1 20 fg ♔xg7 21 ♗h6+ ♔g8 22 ♕g5+ ♘g6 23 ♕f6 ♖d1+!! 24 ♔xd1 ♕d8+ ∓∓.

[18] 17 ♕h4 ♗e7 =. 17 ... ♘c5!?

[19] 17 ♖c1 (Velimirović) 17 ... ♕d8 =.

	8	9	10	11	12	13	14	15	16	
1	...	Bb3	g4	g5	f4!?[3]	Na4	f5	Ne6[4]	fe	∞
	Qc7[2]	Na5	b5	Nd7	b4	Bb7	e5	fe	Nc5![5]	
2	...	0-0-0	Bd3[7]	a3[8]	f4	Rhf1	g4	ed	Nxd5	∓
	...	Na5[6]	b5!	Bb7	Be7	0-0	d5!	Nxd5	Bxd5[9]	
3	...	...	...	g4	Nb1	Nd2	e5	f4	f5	∓
	...	...	...	b4	Bb7	d5	Qxe5	Qd6	e5[10]	
4	...	...	Bb3[11]	g4!	g5	ab	h4[13]	Na2!	h5!	∞
	...	Be7	Na5[12]	b5	Nxb3+	Nd7	b4	Bb7	Qa5[14]	
5	...	...	...	...	...	...	Nf5!?	Nd5	ef	∞
	...	...	...	...	...	...	ef	Qd8	Bb7[15]	

[1]   8 Bb3 Be7 9 f4 0-0 10 0-0 Nxd4 11 Bxd4 b5 12 e5 de 13 fe Nd7 14 Ne4 Bb7 15 Nd6 Bxd6 16 ed Qg5 17 Rf2 a5! = Sax-Timman, London 1980.

[2]   8 ... Na5 9 Bd3 b5 10 b4! ± de Firmian-Zaltsman, Lone Pine 1979.
8 ... Bd7 9 0-0-0 b5 10 Bb3 Qb8 11 g4 Nxd4 12 Bxd4 e5 13 g5! ed 14 gf dc 15 e5! cb+ 16 Kb1 ±.

[3]   12 Bxe6 fe 13 Nxe6 Qc4! 14 Qxc4 Nxc4 15 Nc7+ Kd8 17 Nxa8 Nxe3 18 fe Bb7 ∓.
12 Nxe6 fe 13 Bxe6 Ne5 14 Nd5 Qc4! 15 Nxf6+ gf 16 Bxc4 Bg4! 17 Bxb5+ Kf7 18 Bxa6 Bxe2 19 Kxe2 Nac4 oo. 16 Qh5+? Ke7 17 Rxc4 Bg4 18 gf+ Kd7! ∓.

[4]   15 Nf3!? Nxb3 16 cb Bxe4 17 0-0 Qb7 18 Nd2 Bc6 19 Rf2 Qb5! ∓ Rot-Kasparov, World Jr Ch 1980.

[5]   17 Nxc5 dc 18 Bd5 0-0-0 19 0-0-0 oo.

[6]   9 ... b5 10 Nxc6 ±/±.

[7]   10 Bb3 b5 11 g4 (11 f3 Be7 12 g4 0-0 13 g5 Nh5! 14 f4 g6 15 f5 b4! 16 Nb1 Nxb3+ 17 ab e5! 18 f6 ed 19 fe Qxe7 20 Bxd4 a5 21 Rhg1 Re8 ∓ Tal-Gipslis, Riga 1981) 11 ... Nxb3+ 12 ab Bb7!? (12 ... g6 13 g5 Nh5!?).

[8]   11 f4 b4 12 Nb1 e5 (12 ... Nb7!?) 13 Nf5 g6 14 fe de 15 Bg5 Nd7 oo Ljubojević-Musil, Yugoslavia 1975.

[9]   17 Kb1 Nc4 ∓ Tisdall-Dorfman, Mexico 1977.

[10]   17 Bf4 Nd7 ∓ Shlekis-Alvanov, USSR 1977.

[11]   10 Rhg1 and now:
10 ... b5 11 Nxc6 Qxc6 12 Nxb5 Nxe4 13 Na7 Qb7 14 Nxc8 Qxc8 ±.
10 ... 0-0 11 g4 Nxe4 12 Nxe4 d5 13 Bd3 de 14 Bxe4 e5 15 Nf5 Be6 16 Qf3! ±.
10 ... Na5 11 Bd3 b5 12 a3 e5!? 13 Nf5 Bxf5 14 ed d5 =.   11 Bb3 Be7 – rows 4-5.

[12]   10 ... Bd7 11 g4 Nxd4 12 Rxd4 Bc6 13 g5 Nd7 14 f4 Nc5 15 Rhd1 Nxb3+ 16 ab 0-0-0 17 Qf2 b5 18 f5 ±.
10 ... b5 11 Nxc6 Qxc6 12 Bd4 Bb7 (12 ... 0-0 13 Nd5! ±) 13 Rhe1 0-0 14 f4 ± Hübner-Hort, Bamberg 1972.

[13]   14 b4?! 0-0 15 f4 a5 16 Ncxb5 Qb7 17 f5 ab! 18 f6 gf 19 Rhg1 Kh8 20 gf Nxf6 21 Bh6 Rg8 ∓ Kristiansen-Tukmakov, Graz 1972.

[14]   17 Kb1 Bxe4 18 f3 Bf5 (18 ... Bd5!?) 19 Nxb4! Qxb4 20 Nxf5 ef 21 Bd4! ±.

[15]   17 f6! gf 18 Rhe1 Bxd5 (18 ... 0-0 19 gf Nxf6 20 Nxe7+ Qxe7 21 Rg1+ Kh8 22 Bd4! ±) 19 Rxd5 Rg8 (19 ... 0-0 20 gf Bxf6 21 Rg1+ Kh8 22 Rh5! ±) and now:
20 Bf4 Kf8 21 Bxd6!? Bxd6 22 Rxd6 Rxg5! oo/∓. 21 Qh5! (Matanović-Musil, Yugoslavia 1973) 21 ... Qa5 =.
20 Bd2 Kf8 21 Qh5! Rg7! ∓.
20 h4 Rc8! 21 Bf4 Kf8 22 gf Nxf6 23 Rf5 Rc5! ∓.
20 gf Nxf6 21 Rf5 Ng4!? (21 ... Rg6 22 Bb6! Qd7 23 Qf3 Rb8 24 Rxf6 Rxb6 25 Qa8+ ± Kupreichik-Belyavsky, USSR 1974) 22 Bg5 Ne5 oo.   21 ... Nd7 oo.

Najdorf I   1 e4 c5 2 ♘f3 d6 3 d4 cd 4 ♘xd4 ♘f6 5 ♘c3 a6

	6	7	8	9	10	11	12	13	14	
1	h3[1]	g4	ed	♘de2	♗g2	♗d2	♘e4	0-0	b3	∓
	e6[2]	d5	♘xd5	♗b4	0-0	♘b6!	♗e7	♘c6	f5[3]	
2	g3	♘de2	a4	ab	♖xa8	♗g2	♗g5	♘xb5	♗xe4	=
	e5	b5[4]	♗b7!	ab	♗xa8	♗e7	♘bd7	♗xe4	♘xe4[5]	
3	♗e3	♘b3[6]	♕d2	f3	g4[8]	g5[9]	♘e2[10]	♘g3	♗xf4	∞
	e5	♗e6	♘bd7	♗e7[7]	b5	b4	♘h5	♘f4	ef[11]	
4	a4	♘f3	♗g5	♘d2	♗h4	♗g3	♗c4	♗xe6	♕e2	∞
	e5	♕c7!	♘bd7	h6	g5	♘c5	♗e6	fe	♗e7[12]	
5	f4	♘f3	a4	♗d3	0-0	♘h4[15]	f5	ed	♗e2	∞
	e5[13]	♕c7	♘bd7[14]	♗e7	0-0	g6	d5	e4	♗d6[16]	
6	...	...	a4[17]	♗c4	0-0	♔h1	♗d5	♘d4[19]		∞
	...	♘bd7	♗e7	0-0	♕b6+	ef	♘g4!?[18]	♘de5!		
7	...	♘f3	♗d3	0-0	♕e1	f5!?[21]	♕h4[22]			∞
	♕c7	♘bd7	g6	♗g7[20]	0-0	b5				

---

[1]   6 ♗c4 – Sozin-Najdorf.

[2]   6 ... e5?! 7 ♘de2 ♗e6 8 g4 ♗e7 9 ♗g2 0-0 10 ♘g3 ±.

6 ... g6 7 g4 ♗g7 8 g5 ♘h5 9 ♗e2 e5! =.

6 ... ♘c6 7 g4 ♘xd4 8 ♕xd4 e5 9 ♕d3 ♗e7 10 ♗g5 ♘d7 11 ♗e3 ± Fischer-Bolbochan, Stockholm IZ 1962.

6 ... ♕b6!?

[3]   Kurajica-Najdorf, Hastings 1971/72.

[4]   7 ... ♘bd7 8 a4 ♗e7 9 ♗g2 0-0 (9 ... b6 10 h3! ∞) 10 0-0 ♖b8 11 h3 b5 12 ab ab (Mestel-Balashov, Moscow 1977) 13 b4!? Balashov.

[5]   15 ♗xe7 ♕a5+= Ligterink-Stean, Haifa Ol 1976.

[6]   7 ♘f3 ♕c7 8 ♗g5 ♘bd7 9 a4 h6! 10 ♗h4 g5 11 ♗g3 ♘c5 12 ♘d2 ♗e6 ∓ Shamkovich-Sunye, Lone Pine 1977.

[7]   9 ... b5 10 a4 b4 11 ♘d5 ♘xd5 12 ed ♘b6 13 ♗xb6 ♕xb6 14 a5 ♕b7 15 ♗c4 ♗e7 16 ♖a4 ♖b8 17 ♘c1 ♗d8! = Gufeld-Gaprindashvili, USSR 1981.   17 ♕d3 ♕a7!? ∞ Tseshkovsky.

[8]   10 0-0-0 b5 11 g4 ♘b6 12 g5 ♘fd7 ∓ Stean.

[9]   11 a4!? b4 12 ♘d5 ∞ Nunn-Morris, Manchester 1980.

[10]   12 ♘a4 ♘h5 13 ♕xb4 d5 14 ♕a5 ♗xg5 = Stean.

[11]   15 ♘h5 ∞ Nunn.

[12]   15 0-0 ♘cd7 16 ♖fd1 ♖c8 ∞ Chandler-Maninang, Indonesia 1982.

[13]   6 ... g6? 7 e5 de 8 fe ♘d5 9 e6!

6 ... e6 7 ♗e2 ♗e7 8 ♗e3 – Scheveningen.

[14]   8 ... ♗e6!? 9 f5 ♗c4 10 ♘d2! d5! 11 ♘xc4 dc 12 ♕e2 ♗b4 13 ♗d2 0-0 14 ♕xc4 ♕xc4 15 ♗xc4 ♗xc3 = Georgadze.

[15]   11 ♔h1 ef 12 ♗xf4 ♗e5 (Georgadze-Nemet, USSR v Yugoslavia 1979) 13 ♘d4 ♗e6 14 a5 ±/=.

[16]   15 g3 b6 ∞ Sax-Andersson, London 1980.

[17]   8 ♗c4 b5! 9 ♗d5 ♖b8 (Hort-Andersson, Wijk aan Zee 1979) 10 a3 ♗e7 11 0-0-0 0-0 12 ♔h1 a5 = Nunn.

[18]   12 ... ♘e5 =.

[19]   van der Wiel-Ribli, Amsterdam 1980.

[20]   9 ... e5 10 ♕e1 b5 11 ♔h1 ♗b7 (Tukmakov-Tal, Leningrad IZ 1973) 12 a4 b4 13 ♘d1 ±.

[21]   11 ♔h1 e5?! (11 ... e6!? =) 12 ♕h4 (12 f5!? b5 13 a3 ♗b7 14 ♗g5 ♗c6 15 ♘d2 ♕b7 16 ♕h4 ± Shamkovich-Grefe, USA 1978; 14 ... h6!? Nunn) 12 ... b5 13 fe de 14 ♗h6 ♗b7 15 ♘g5 ♕d6! 16 g4 ♖fc8 17 ♗xg7 ♔xg7 18 ♕h6+ ♔g8 19 ♘xf7 ♗xf7 (Manetta-Cabarkapa, West Germany 1975) 20 ♕xh7+ ∞ Nunn.

[22]   Velikov-Valenti, Pernik 1979. 12 ... ♘c5 ∞ Nunn.

254

	7	8	9	10	11	12	13	14	15	
1	♘f3[2]	0-0	a4	b3	♗b2	♖e1	♗f1	♕d2[5]		±
	h6[3]	♗e6[4]	♘c6	♖c8	♗e7	0-0	♕c7			
2	♘b3	f4	g4!	a3	g5	fg	♗g4	♗xe6	♕f3	±
	♗e6	♕c7[6]	b5[7]	h6	hg	♘fd7	♖h4	fe	♘c6[8]	
3	...	♗g5[9]	♗xf6	♕d3[10]	♘d5	0-0	♘xe7	♖fd1		∓
	♗e7	♗e6	♗xf6	♘c6	♗g5	♘e7!	♕xe7	♖d8[11]		
4	...	0-0	♔h1[12]	a4	f4	♗f3	♕e2	♖d1	g4	=
	...	0-0	♘c6	b6	♗b7	♘b4	♕c7	♖fe8!	d5[13]	
5	...	...	♗e3	a4[14]	a5	♕d2	♖fc1	♗f3	♖a4!	±
	...	...	♗e6	♘bd7	♖c8	♕c7	♕c6	♗c4	♖fd8[15]	
6	...	...	a4	f4	♔h1[17]	a5[18]	♗xf4	♘d5	ed	±
	...	...	♗e6	♕c7[16]	♘bd7	ef	♘e5	♗xd5	♘c4[19]	

[1]   6 ... ♘bd7 7 f4 (7 0-0 g6?! 8 f4 ♗g7 9 ♗e3 0-0 ±; 7 ... e6) 7 ... e5 (7 ... b5!? Nunn) 8 ♘f5 ♘c5 9 ♘g3 ♕b6 10 ♖b1! ♗d7 11 fe de 12 ♗e3 ± Olafsson-Sax, Novi Sad 1976.

[2]   7 ♘f5? ♘xe4 8 ♘xg7+ ♗xg7 9 ♘xe4 d5 ∓.

[3]   7 ... ♗e6 8 ♗g5 ♕c7 9 ♘xe6 fe ±.

7 ... ♕c7 8 ♗g5 ♘bd7 9 a4 b6 10 0-0 ♗e7 11 ♘d2 ♗b7 12 ♗c4 0-0 13 ♕e2 ± Westerinen-Browne, Mannheim 1975.

[4]   8 ... ♗e7 9 a4 ♕c7 10 ♘d2 ±/=.

[5]   Smyslov-Tukmakov, USSR Ch 1977.

[6]   8 ... ♘c6 9 f5 ♗xb3 10 ab ±.

[7]   9 ... ef 10 g5 ♘fd7 11 ♗xf4 ♘c6 12 ♕d2 ± Olafsson-Kavalek, Las Palmas 1974.

9 ... h6 10 g5 hg 11 fg ♘fd7 12 ♗g4 intending g6 ± Gurevich-Balashov, USSR 1973.

[8]   16 ♕g3 ± Hardicsay-Hradeczky, Hungary 1976.

[9]   8 f4 0-0 9 g4 ef 10 g5 ♘fd7 = Nunn.

[10]   10 ♘d5 ♘d7 =/∓ Unzicker-Fischer, Santa Monica 1966.

10 0-0 0-0 11 ♕d3 ♘c6 ∞.

[11]   Arnason-Kaplan, World Jr Ch 1980.

[12]   9 ♗g5 ♗e6! 10 f4 ef 11 ♗xf6 ♘c6 12 ♔h1 d5

13 e5 ♘d7 14 ♘xd5 ♘dxe5 15 c4 ♗g5 = Byrne-Browne, US Ch 1980.

[13]   16 g5 ♘d7 = Shalnyev-Yuferov, USSR 1978.

[14]   10 ♕d2 ♘c6!? (10 ... d5?! 11 ed ♘xd5 12 ♘xd5 ♗xd5 13 ♖fd1 ♗c6 14 ♗a5! ±) 11 ♖fd1 (11 a4 d5) 11 ... a5!? ∞ Suetin.

[15]   16 ♖b4 ♕c7 17 ♘d5 ♘xd5 18 ed f5 19 ♗e2 ± Karpov-Portisch, London 1982.

[16]   10 ... ef 11 ♗xf4 ♘c6 12 ♔h1 ♖c8 (12 ... d5!?) 13 ♘d4 ♘e5 ∞ Belyavsky-Tal, USSR Ch 1975.
13 ♗d3!?

[17]   11 f5 ♗c4 12 a5 ♘bd7 13 ♗e3 (Tal-Fischer, Curaçao C 1962) 13 ... ♖fc8 14 ♗xc4 ∞.

[18]   12 f5 ♗c4 13 a5 b5 14 ab ♘xb6 15 ♗g5 (15 ♗e3 ♖fc8 16 ♗xb6 ♕xb6 17 ♗xc4 ♖xc4 18 ♕e2 ♖ac8 19 ♖a2 ♗d8! 20 ♖fa1 ♕b7! = Karpov-Stoica, Graz 1972) 15 ... ♗xe2 16 ♕xe2 ♕c4 17 ♕d1 ± Kaplan.

12 ♗e3 ef 13 ♖xf4 ♘e5 14 a5 ♖ac8 15 ♘d4 ♘fd7 ∞ Tal-Grigorian, USSR Ch 1974.

[19]   15 ... ♖fe8 16 c4 ♗f8 17 ♖c1 ♘fd7 18 ♕d2 g6 19 ♘d4 b6?! 20 ♘c6 ± Mestel-Nemet, Skara 1980.

15 ... ♘c4 ± Mestel.

Najdorf III   1 e4 c5 2 Nf3 d6 3 d4 cd 4 Nxd4 Nf6 5 Nc3 a6 6 Bg5

	6	7	8	9	10	11	12	13	14	
1	...	Bxf6[1]	Be2[2]	Nb3	0-0	Bh5	Kh1	Rab1		=
	Nc6	gf	Qb6[3]	e6	Bd7	Ne5	Nc4	Rc8[4]		
2	...	Bc4!	Qd2	0-0[6]	Rad1	Bh4	Be2	Bxf6	f4	±
	Nbd7	Qa5[5]	e6	Be7[7]	h6[8]	Ne5[9]	b5	gf	b4[10]	
3	...	Qf3	0-0-0	Qg3	Bxb5	Ndxb5	Nxd6+	Qxd6	Rxd6	±
	e6	Nbd7	Qc7	b5?![11]	ab	Qb8	Bxd6	Qxd6	h6[12]	
4	...	...	Bh4[13]	0-0-0	Be2	Rhe1[16]	Bg3	Qe3	a3	∓
	...	h6!	Nbd7	Qc7[14]	Be7[15]	g5	Ne5	b5	Rb8[17]	
5	...	Qd3	0-0-0	f4	e5	fe	Qg3	Ncxb5[19]	Bxb5	∓
	...	Nbd7[18]	b5	Bb7	de	Nxe5	Ned7	ab	Rxa2![20]	
6	...	f4	Qf3	0-0-0	Rxd4	Bc4[23]	Rhd1	Qe2	Bh4	±
	...	Bd7[21]	Nc6	Nxd4[22]	Bc6	Be7	Qa5	h6	e5[24]	
7	...	...	Bxf6[25]	Be2	Qd3!?[26]	Qxd4	Qd2	Rf1	0-0-0	±
	...	Qc7	gf	Nc6	Nxd4[27]	Qc5!	Bd7	Rc8	b5[28]	
8	...	...	...	Qf3	0-0-0[30]	e5	Ncb5![32]	Bxb5+	Nxe6![35] Qh3	±±
	...	...	...	b5[29]	b4[31]	Bb7	ab[33]	Nfd7[34]	fe Kf7[36]	

1 e4 c5 2 Nf3 d6 3 d4 cd 4 Nxd4 Nf6 5 Nc3 a6 6 Bg5 e6 7 f4 Nbd7

	8	9	10	11	12	13	14	15	16	
9	Qe2[37]	0-0-0[38]	f5	Nd5	ed	Qh5!	Nc6	Qxg5	Qh5+	∞
	Qc7	b5[39]	e5	Nxd5	Nc5	Be7	Bxg5+	f6	Qf7[40]	
10	Qf3	0-0-0	e5	Qh3	Nxe6	Qxe6+	Bxf6[41]	Be2	Nd5[43]	=
	Qc7	b5	Bb7	de	fe	Be7	gf[42]	h5!	Bxd5[44]	
11	...	...	Bd3	Rhe1	Nd5!?	Nc6!!	ed+	dc	Bxf6	±±
	...	...	Bb7	Qb6[45]	ed?![46]	Bxc6[47]	Be7	Nc5	gf[48]	
12	...	...	Bxb5	e5	Ndxb5	Qe2[50]	fe	Ne4[51]		∞/∓
	...	...	ab	Bb7!?[49]	Qc8!	de	Nd5	Ra6![52]		
13	...	...	...	Ndxb5	e5	ef[53]	Bh6	Nxd6+	Kb1	±
	...	...	...	Qb8	Ra5	gf	Bxh6	Be7	Nb6[54]	

[1] 7 Qd2 (White's best) – Richter-Rauzer.

[2] 8 Qd2 h5! ∓ Nunn.

[3] 8 ... Rg8!? 9 g3 Bh3 ∓ Nunn.

[4] Nunn-Quinteros, England 1977.

[5] 7 ... b5? 8 Bd5! Nxd5 9 Nxd5 Bb7 10 0-0 intending 11 a4 ± Nunn.

[6] 9 0-0-0 b5 10 Bb3 Bb7 11 Rhe1 0-0-0 12 a3 Be7 13 Kb1 Qb6 14 f3 Kb8 15 Be3 Nc5 16 Ba2 (Gulko-Petrosian, Moscow 1976) 16 ... Nc7 ± Nunn.

[7] 9 ... b5?! 10 Bd5! ed 11 ed Nc5 12 Rfe1+ Kd7 13 a3 ∞∞.

9 ...h6 10 Bh4 g5 11 Bg3 Nh5 12 Nxe6! fe 13 Nxe6 Nxg3 14 fg Ne5 15 Rxf8+ Rxf8 16 Qxd6 Rf6 (Tal-Petrosian, Bled 1959) 17 Qc7! ± Nunn.

[8] 10 ... Nc5?! 11 Rfe1 Bd7 12 a3 Qc7 13 b4 Na4 14 Nxa4 Bxa4 15 Bxe6! fe 16 Nxe6 Qxc2

[17] Qd4 ± Tal-Polugayevsky, Riga 1959.

[9] 11 ... Nxe4 12 Nxe4 Qxd2 13 Nxd6+ Bxd6 14 Rxd2 ± Nunn.

11 ... g5 12 Bg3 Ne5 13 Be2! Bd7 14 f4! ±.

[10] 15 Nb1 Qc5 16 Kh1 Nc4 17 Bxc4 Qxc4 18 b3 Qc5 19 c3! ± Nunn.

[11] 9 ... Be7 10 f4 h6 – Najdorf IV, row 9.

[12] Bronstein-Najdorf, Buenos Aires 1954.

[13] 8 Bxf6 Qxf6 9 Qxf6 gf 10 0-0-0 b5 11 a3 Bb7 = Sidorov-Polugayevsky, corr. 1953.

8 Be3 Nbd7 9 Qg3 e5 10 Nb3 b5 11 f3 Qc7 12 Qf2 b4 13 Nd1 d5 ∓ J.Littlewood-Nunn, British Ch 1979.

[14] 9 ... Ne5 10 Qe3 g5 11 Bg3 Qc7 12 Be2 Be7 13 Rhf1 b5 14 a3 Rb8 15 f4 gf 16 Rxf4 h5 17 h3 b4 18 ab Rxb4 19 Bh4? Nfg4! ∓ Kupreichik-Grigorian, USSR 1976. 10 Qe2! =.

[15] 10 ... b5? 11 e5! Bb7 12 Nxe6! Qc8 (12 ... fe

13 Qh5+!) 13 Nxg7+ Kxg7 14 Qg3 ±±.

[16] 11 Qe3 g5 12 Bg3 Ne5 13 h4 Rg8 14 hg hg ∓ Liberzon-Portisch, Skara 1980.

[17] Tal-Platonov, USSR 1959.

[18] 7 ... b5!? 8 0-0-0 b4 9 e5?! bc 10 ef gf 11 Qf3 fg 12 Qxa8 Qb6! ∓ Neuronov-Zaichik, USSR 1979.

[19] 13 Bxf6 gf 14 Be2 b4 15 Bh5 Bh6+ 16 Kb1 bc! 17 Nxe6 Qb6 18 Bxf7+ Kxf7 19 Rxd7+ Ke8! ∓ Nunn.

[20] 15 Kb1 Qa8 16 Nb3 Bd5 17 Bxf6 Ra1+! (17 ... gf? 18 Bxd7+ Kxd7 19 c4!) 18 Nxa1 Qa2+ 19 Kc1 Qxa1+ 20 Kd2 Qa5+ ∓ Katalimov-Gofstein, USSR 1977.

[21] 7 ... Nc6 8 Be2 h6 9 Bh4 Qb6 10 Nb3 Qe3 11 Bxf6 gf 12 g3 Be7 13 Qd3 ± Ljubojević-Andersson, Stockholm 1980.

[22] 9 ... Be7 10 e5! de 11 Nxc6 ±.
9 ... Qc7 10 Nxc6 bc 11 Bc4 Be7 12 Rd3 e5 13 Bxf6 Bxf6 14 Rhd1 ± Keres-Panno, Amsterdam 1956.

[23] 11 f5!? Qa5 12 Bxf6 gf 13 Be2 ± Nunn.

[24] 15 Bxf6 Bxf6 16 Rxd6 ef 17 Nd5 Bxd5 18 R1xd5 ± Panno-Lombardy, Varna 1958.

[25] 8 Bd3 Be7 9 Nf3 (9 Qe2 h6! ∓ intending 10 Bh4 Nxe4!; 9 Qf3 – Najdorf IV) 9 ... Nbd7 10 Qe2 h6 11 Bh4 e5! oo. 9 ... Qb6!?

[26] 10 Nb3 Qb6 11 Qd2 h5 12 a4 Na5 13 Nxa5 Qxa5 = Tal-Balashov, USSR Ch 1977.

[27] 10 ... Qb6 11 Nb3 h5 12 0-0-0 Bd7? 13 Nd2! Nb4 14 Qh3 Rc8 15 Kb1 a5 16 Nc4 Qc5 17 a3 Na6 18 Rd2! ± A.Rodriguez-Csom, Berlin 1979.

[28] Tal-Tukmakov, USSR Ch 1978. 15 Bf3 ± Tal.

[29] 8 ... Nc6!? 9 0-0-0 Bd7 10 Bc4 Be7 11 Bb3 Na5 12 Rhe1 0-0 13 Kb1 Qh8 14 e5 ± Sax-Masić, Baja 1971.

[30] 9 Bxf6 gf 10 0-0-0 b4 11 Nd5 ed 12 ed Qc5! 13 Bd3 Ra7 14 Bf5 Kd8 oo Dorfman-Yuferov, USSR 1978.

[31] 9 ... Nbd7 – rows 10-13.
9 ... Bb7 10 Bd3 Nbd7 – rows 10-13.

[32] 11 Qh3 de 12 Ncb5 ab 13 fe (13 Bxb5+ Bc6! 14 fe Bxb5 15 ef Bd7! 16 Bf5 gf! 17 Bxf6 Rg8 ∓ Psakhis-Tukmakov, USSR Ch 1st L 1979) 13 ... Nfd7 14 Nxe6 Qb6 15 Nd4 oo Nunn.

[33] 11 ... Qb6!? 12 Qh3! de 13 fe ab 14 ef Rxa2 15 Bxb5+ Nc6 16 Nxe6 Ra1+ 17 Kd2 Qf2+ 18 Be2 ± Nunn.

[34] 12 ... Nbd7 13 Qh3 b3 14 Qxb3 Bd5 15 c4 Ne4 16 Qc2 Rxa2 17 Kb1 Qa7 18 Nb3 Ba8 19 c5! ± Kosten-Kuligowski, Lewisham 1981.

[35] 13 Qh3? b3! 14 Qxb3 Bd5 ∓∓. 14 ab de 15 Nxe6 Ra1+ 16 Kd2 Rxd1+ 17 Rxd1 Qd6+ ∓∓ Nunn.

[36] 15 f5 Be4 16 fe+ Kg8 17 Qb3 Bxc2 18 Qxc2 Qxc2+ 19 Kxc2 Nxe5 20 e7 Bxe7 21 Bxe7 Nbc6 22 Bxd6 ±± Georgiev-Kasparov, Malta Ol 1980.

[37] 8 Bc4 Qb6 9 Bb3 Be7 10 f5 Nc5! 11 fe fe 12 Be3 Qc7 13 0-0 b5 14 a3 Nxb3 15 cb 0-0 16 b4 Qd7 17 Qe2 Bb7 = Bronstein-Savon, Moscow 1970.

[38] 9 g4 b5 10 a3 Be7 11 Bg2 Bb7 12 0-0-0 Nb6 13 Bh4 h6 14 Bg3 0-0-0 15 Bf3 g5 16 fg hg 17 e5! oo Kuzmin-Stean, Hastings 1973/74.

[39] 9 ... Be7 10 g4 (10 Nf3!? Nb6 11 Qe1! ± Spassky) 10 ... b5 11 Bg2 b4! 12 e5 bc 13 ef gf 14 Bxa8 fg 15 Qf3 gf 16 Bc6 cb+ 17 Kb1 0-0 18 Bxd7 (Kuzmin-Dorfman, USSR 1978) 18 ... Bxd7! ∓.

[40] 17 Qf3 Bb7 18 Kb1 0-0 19 g4 oo Tukmakov-Browne, Madrid 1973.

[41] 14 Bxb5!? ab 15 Nxb5 Nc6 16 Nd6+ Kd8 17 fe! Kc7 18 Kb1! Bf8 oo Nunn.
14 Nxb5?! ab 15 Nxb5 Be4! 16 c4 0-0-0 17 Qxe7 h6 18 Bxf6 gf ∓ Zhelyandinov-Gutman, USSR 1970.

[42] 14 ... Nxf6? 15 Nxb5+ Kf8 16 fe Bc8 17 Nd5 ±±.

[43] 16 Bf3!? Tal.

[44] 17 Rxd5 Nb6 18 Rxh5+ Rxh5 19 Qg8+ Bf8 20 Qe6+ =. 18 Bd3?! Kf8! 19 Bg6 Kg7 20 Qf7+ Kh6 21 Bf5 Rag8 ∓ Stean/Nunn.

[45] 11 ... 0-0-0 12 a3 (12 Qh3 b4 13 Nd5!? ed 14 e5 de 15 fe Bc5! 16 ef Bxd4 ∓ S.Garcia-Dorfman, Polanica Zdroj 1978) 12 ... Be7 13 Qf1!? (Petrushin-Vitolins, USSR 1978) 13 ... Kb8! oo/±.

[46] 12 ... Qxd4!? 13 Bxf6 gf 14 Bxb5 Qa7!? 15 Nxf6+ Ke7 16 Bxd7 Kxf6 17 e5+ Kxe7 oo.

[47] 13 ... d4 14 e5!

[48] 17 Bf5 Qc7 18 b4 Ne6 19 Qh5 Ng7 20 Bd7+ Kf8 21 Qh6 d5 22 Rxe7 Qxe7 23 Re1+ Kf8 24 Qxf6 Kg8 29 Re7 ±± Chiburdanidze-Dvoris, USSR 1980.

[49] 11 ... Ra5 12 ef (12 Ndxb5 Qb8 – row 13) 12 ... gf 13 Rhe1 b4! 14 Nc6 Rg8! 15 Ne4 Rxa2 16 Kb1 Bb7 17 Nxf6+ Nxf6 18 Bxf6 Rg6! ∓∓ Semkov-Georgiev, Varna 1977.

[50] 13 ef!? Bxf3 14 fg Rg8! 15 gfQ+ Kxf8 16 gf Rg6 ∓ Nunn.

[51] 15 Nxd5 Bxd5 16 Rxd5 ed 17 e6 Nf6 18 e7 Ne4 ∓∓. 18 Bxf6 gf 19 e7 Bh6+ ∓∓ Nunn.

[52] 15 ... Qc6?? 16 Rxd5! ±± intending 16 ... ed 17 Nc7+! Qxc7 18 Nd6+.
15 ... Ra6! oo/∓ Nunn.

[53] 13 Nd4 Bb7 14 Qh3 Nd5 15 Nxe6! Nxc3 oo Nunn. 14 ... Nxe5!? oo Nunn.

[54] 16 Rd8!? oo Bagirov.
16 ... Qb6 17 Nce4 Na4 18 Nxc8+ Rxc8 19 Qa3+ Nc5 20 Nxa5 Nxe4 21 Qa3+ Nc5 22 g3 f5 23 Rhe1 ± Psakhis-Anikayev, USSR 1979.

Najdorf IV 1 e4 c5 2 Nf3 d6 3 d4 cd 4 Nxd4
Nf6 5 Nc3 a6 6 Bg5 e6 7 f4 Be7 8 Qf3 h6

	9	10	11	12	13	14	15	16	17	
1	Bh4	fg	Nxe6[3]	Qh5+	Bb5!	0-0+[5]	g6	Rf7	Qxh6	=
	g5[1]	Nfd7[2]	fe	Kf8	Rh7[4]	Kg8	Rg7	Bxh4	Qf6![6]	
2	...	...	Qh5	Bg3	Be2[8]	Bxe5	Nf3	Nd1	c3	∞
	...	...	Ne5[7]	Bxg5	Qb6[9]	de	Qxb2[10]	Qb4+[11]	Qe7[12]	

1 e4 c5 2 Nf3 d6 3 d4 cd 4 Nxd4 Nf6 5 Nc3
a6 6 Bg5 e6 7 f4 Be7 8 Qf3 Qc7 9 0-0-0 Nbd7

	10	11	12	13	14	15	16	17	18	
3	Bd3	Rhe1	Nd5	ed	Rxe6+[16]	Nxe6![18]	Qh5+	Qxg5	Kb1	∞
	b5	Bb7[13]	Nxd5[14]	Bxg5[15]	fe[17]	Qb6![19]	g6	Qe3+	Kf7[20]	
4	...	...	Qg3	Nd5	e5[22]	fe	e6[24]	ef+	Rxe7+	=
	...	...	b4[21]	ed	de	Nh5[23]	Nxg3	Kxf7[25]	Kg8[26]	
5	...	Bh4	fg[27]	Qe2	Nf3	Qxf3[29]	Bg3	Bxe5	Be2	±
	h6	g5	Ne5	Nfg4	Nxf3[28]	hg	Ne5	de	Bd7[30]	
6	...	Qh3[31]	f5![33]	Nde2!	Kb1	Be3	g4	Qf3		±
	...	Nb6[32]	e5	Bd7	Bc6	Nbd7	0-0-0	b5[34]		
7	g4	Bxf6[36]	g5	f5	f6[39]	gf	Qh5[40]	a3[42]		∞
	b5[35]	Nxf6[37]	Nd7	Nc5[38]	gf	Bf8	Bd7[41]	Qa5![43]		
8	...	...	...	a3	Bh3[45]	Rhg1	ab	f5	f6	=
	...	...	...	Rb8[44]	Nc5	b4	Rxb4	Qb7![46]	gf[47]	
9	Qg3	Bh4	fg	Qe3	Kb1[50]	Bf2	Qd2	Nf3	Be3[52]	=
	h6![48]	g5	Nh5[49]	Qc5	hg	Ne5	Qc7	Rg8[51]	g4[53]	
10	Be2	Bxf6[55]	e5	ef[56]	Bxf3	Bxa8	Bxd5[58]	Rxd4	Re1+	=
	b5![54]	Nxf6	Bb7	Bxf3	Bxf6[57]	d5	Bxd4!	ed	Kf8[59]	

---

1 Göteborg Variation.

2 10 ... Nh7 11 Bg3 hg 12 0-0-0 Nf8 13 Be2! Qg6 14 Rhf1 ±.

3 11 Bg3 Ne5! 12 Qf2 hg 13 Be2 Qb6 14 0-0-0 Nbc6 15 Na4 Qa7 = Stein-Calvo, Las Palmas 1973.

4 **13 ...** Ne5 14 Bg3! Rh7 15 Bxe5 de 16 Rd1 Bd7! 17 g6 Rg7 18 0-0+ Kg8 19 Bc4 Qc8 20 Bb3 ±/∞ Nunn.

13 ... Kg7 14 0-0 Ne5 15 Bg3 Ng6 16 gh+ Rxh6 17 Rf7+ Kxf7 18 Qxh6 ±± Spassky-Pilnik and Keres-Najdorf, Göteborg IZ 1955.

5 14 Qg6!? Rf7 15 Qxh6+ Kg8 16 Rf1 Rxf1+ 17 Rxf1 Ne5 18 Bc4! Nxc4 = Timman-Stean, London 1973.

6 18 Rxf6 Bxf6 19 Be2 Ne5 20 Nh5 Bd7 21 Rf1 Be7 22 Rf7! = Gaspariants-Eidlin, Moscow 1971.

7 11 ... Bxg5? 12 Bxg5 Qxg5 13 Nxe6! ±.

8 **13** Nf3!? Nbd7 14 Nxg5 Qxg5 15 Nd1! Qe7 16 Qd4 b5 17 0-0-0 ±/± Radulov-Inkiov, Bulgarian Ch 1976.

13 h4 Bf6 14 Be2 Nbc6! = Nunn.

9 **13 ...** Nbc6 14 Nxc6 bc 15 0-0 Ra7 16 Bxe5 de 17 Rf3 ±.

13 ... Bd7 14 h4 Nf6 15 0-0-0 ± Nunn.

10 15 ... Rf8 16 Nxg5 Qxb2 17 0-0! hg 18 Rxf7! Rxf7 19 Rf1 Qb6+ 20 Kh1 Qc7 21 Qh8+ ±± Nunn.

11 16 ... Qxa1 17 Nxg5 Rf8 18 Nxf7 Nd7! ∞ Parma-Minić, Yugoslavia 1968.

12 18 0-0 Rh7 19 Nf2 Nd7 20 Ng4 Nf6! 21 Nxf6+ (Sakharov-Nasibulin, USSR 1979) 21 ... Bxf6! ∞.

13 11 ... b4?! 12 Nd5! ed 13 Nf5 h6 14 Bh4 g5 15 e5 de 16 fe Nxe5 17 Rxe5 Bxf5 18 Qxf5 =.

14 12 ... ed!? 13 Nf5 Bf8! 14 Qg3 de 15 Bxe4 Bxe4 16 Rxe4 Rc8 17 Re2 Qc4 18 Nxe7 ±± Garcia-Boudy, Cienfuegos 1973. 16 ... Qc5! (Nunn) intending 17 Bh6 Nxe4 18 Qxg7+ Ke8 19 Qxh8+ Kf8 ∓ is untested.

15 13 ... Bxd5? 14 Qxd5 ed 15 Rxe7+ Kf8 16 Bf5 Rd8 17 Be6! ±±.

16 14 Nxe6? fe 15 Qh5+ Kf8 16 fg Ne5 17 Bxh7 Qc4! ∓∓ Miscević-Masić, Vršac 1973.

17 14 ... Be7 15 Re2 Nf6 16 Rde1 0-0

17 ♖xe7 ±.

18 15 ♕h5+ g6! 16 ♗xg6+ hg 17 ♕xh8+ ♘f8
18 ♘xe6 ♗xf4+! 19 ♔xf4 0-0-0! ∓ Nunn.

19 15 ... ♕a5? 16 ♕h5+ g6 17 ♕xg5 ♖g8
18 ♖d2! ♘f8 19 ♘xf8 ♕d8 20 ♘xh7 ±±
Velimirović-Ljubojević, Yugoslav Ch 1972.

20 19 ♕h6 ♖ag8! 20 ♘g5+ ♔e8 21 ♕h4! ♔d8
22 ♖e1 ♕b6 ∞ Nunn.

21 12 ... 0-0-0 13 ♗xb5 ab 14 ♘dxb5 ♕c5
(14 ... ♕b6 15 e5 d5 16 f5! ♕h5 17 ♕h4 ♗xg5+
18 ♕xg5 ± Velimirović-Al Kazzaz, Nice Ol
1974) 15 e5 de 16 fe ♘d5 17 ♗xe7 ♕xe7
18 ♘d6+ ♔b8 19 ♘xd5 ed 20 e6 ±± Nunn.

22 14 ed ♘d8 15 ♕e3 ♘b6 16 ♘f5 ♘bxd5
17 ♕e2!? ♕c5 18 ♗c4 ∞ Geller.

23 15 ... 0-0-0 16 ♘f5! ♗xe5 17 ♘xe7+ ♕xe7
18 ♖xe5 ♕c7 19 ♗f4 ±± Petryk-Gadalinski,
Poland 1977.

24 16 ♕h4!? ♗xg5+ 17 ♕xg5 g6 18 e6 ♘c5
19 ef+ ♔xf7 20 ♖f1+ ♔g8 ∞ Nunn.

25 17 ... ♔d8 18 ♖xe7 ♕f4 19 ♖e3+ ♕xg5
20 ♘e6+ ♔c8 21 ♘xg5 ♘e4 22 ♘xe4 ± Nunn.

26 19 hg ♕xg3 20 ♘e6 ♕e5 21 ♖f1 ♘f8!
22 ♗f5 ♗c8 23 ♖e8 ♔f7 = Nunn.

27 12 e5!? gh 13 ef ♘xf6 14 f5 e5 15 ♘de2 ♗d7
16 ♗e4 ♖g8!? ∞/∓ Nunn.

28 14 ... hg 15 ♗g3 ♗d7 16 h3 ♘xf3 17 hg
♖xh1 18 ♖xh1 ♘h4 19 ♖f1! ± Minić-Hort,
Virovitica 1979.

29 15 gf hg 16 ♗g3 ♘e5 17 h4 gh 18 f4 ♘xd3+
19 ♖xd3 ♗d7 20 ♕e1 ♗b5 21 ♖d1 (Ljubojević-
Browne, Wijk aan Zee 1976) 21 ... ♗f6! =.

30 19 ♖d3 ♗c6 20 ♖f1 ♖h7 21 ♕f2! ±
Matulović-Browne, Skopje Ol 1970.

31 11 h4!? ♘c5 (11 ... hg 12 hg ♖f8 13 gf ♗xf6
14 ♘de2 ♘c5 15 ♔b1 ∞/± Silman-Tarjan,
Lone Pine 1979) 12 f5 hg?! (12 ... ♗d7!?) 13 hg
♖xh1 14 ♗hd7 15 ♗h8+ ♘f8 16 f6 f6 =
Angantysson-Petursson, Icelandic Ch 1976.

32 11 ... ♖g8 12 e5 hg 13 ef gf6 14 f5 ± Nunn.

33 12 ♖hf1 ♗d7 13 ♗h4 ♖c8 14 ♕g3 e5! 15 fe
de 16 ♘f5 ♗xf5 17 ♗xf6 ♗xf6 18 ♖xf5 ♕e7 =
Timman-Browne, Amsterdam 1976.

34 17 ... ♘c5? 18 ♗xc5 dc 19 ♗c4 ± Browne-
Grefe, Lone Pine 1976.

17 ... b5 ± Nunn.

35 10 ... h6?! 11 ♗xf6 ♗xf6 12 h4 ♕b6 13 ♘ce2
♘c5 14 g5 ♗e7 15 ♖g1 hg 16 hg ±. 13 ... g5!?

36 11 a3 ♖b8 12 ♗h4 ♘c5 13 ♗xf6 gf (13 ...
♗xf6 14 ♗xb5+!) 14 f5 b4 ∞ Stean-Momeni,
Teesside 1973.

37 11 ... gf!? 12 f5! ♘e5 13 ♕h3 0-0 14 ♘ce2
♔h8 15 ♘f4 ♖g8 16 fe (16 ♖g1 ♕b7! Fischer)
16 ... fe 17 ♘fxe6 ♖xe6 18 ♖xe6 ♕d7 19 ♘d4
♕xg4 = Spassky-Donner, Leiden 1970.

38 13 ... ♗xg5+ 14 ♔b1 ♘e5 15 ♕h5 ♕e7
16 ♘xe6 ♗xe6 17 fe g6 18 ef+ ♔xf7 19 ♕e2
♔g7 = Ervin-Gligorić, USA 1972.

39 14 h4!? b4 15 ♘ce2 e5 16 f6 ed 17 fe d3!
18 cd! ♘xd3+ = Geszosz-Bielczyk, Poland
1970/71.

40 16 ♗h3 b4 17 ♘d5 (17 ♘ce2 ♗b7 =) 17 ...
ed 18 ed ♗xh3 19 ♖he1+ ♔d8 20 ♘c6+ ♔c8
21 ♕xh3+ ♕d7 22 ♕h4 a5 =.

41 16 ... b4!? 17 ♘d5 ed 18 ed ♗d7 19 ♖e1+
♔d8 20 ♔b1! ♖c8 21 ♕xf7 ∞.

42 17 ♗h3 b4 18 ♘ce2 (18 ♘d5 ed 19 ed 0-0-0
20 ♘c6 ♖e8 ∓) 18 ... 0-0-0 19 ♕xf7 ♗h6+
20 ♔b1 ♖df8 21 ♕e7 ♖e8 =.

43 17 ... 0-0-0 ∞.

17 ... ♖g8 ∞.

17 ... ♕a5!? 18 ♘b3!? ♗xb3+ 19 cb ♖c8 =
Matulović-de Firmian, Niš 1981. 18 ♗e2! (18 ♖g1
b4 19 ab ♘b3+ ∓∓) 18 ... b4 19 ab ♕xb4
20 ♖hf1 intending ♕xf7+! ∞ de Firmian.

44 13 ... ♗b7 14 ♗h3 ♕c4 15 ♖he1 g6 16 ♔b1
♘b6 17 ♕g3 ± Sapunov-Pavlov, Bulgaria 1976.

45 14 h4 b4 15 ab ♖xb4 16 ♗h3 ♕b6! 17 ♘f5!?
♗f8! 18 ♘e3 ♕a5 ∓ Necesany-Zagorovsky,
corr. 1974.

46 17 ... ♕b6 18 fe fe 19 ♘xe6 ♗xe6 20 ♗xe6
♘xe6 21 ♘d5 ± Nunn.

47 19 gf ♗f8 20 b3 a5 21 ♕h5 a4 22 ♘a2 ab
23 ♘xb4 ♕xb4 24 cb ♘xb3+ 25 ♔xb3 ♕c3+ =.
22 ... ♖xd4!? Nunn.

48 10 ... ♘c5? 11 ♗d3 h6 12 ♗h4 0-0 13 ♘f3!
intending e5 ± Nunn.

49 12 ... ♖g8?! 13 ♗e2 ♘e5 14 ♘f3 ♘fd7
15 g6! ♖xg6 16 ♕h3 ± Nunn.

50 14 ♕d2 ♗xg5! =.

14 ♗e2 ♘f4! 15 ♕xf4 hg 16 ♕f2 ♖xh4 =.

51 17 ... ♘xf3 18 gf ♗d7 19 h4! gh 20 ♗e2 0-0-0
21 ♗xh4 ± Westerinen-Petursson, Reykjavik
1976.

52 18 h4 g4 19 ♘xe5 de 20 ♕h6 ♘f6 21 ♗e3
g6 22 ♕h8+ ♖g8 23 ♕h6 ½-½ Balashov-
Browne, Manila IZ 1976.

53 19 ♘xe5 de 20 ♗d3 b5 21 ♖hf1 ♗d7 22 ♕f2
♖g7 = Chiburdanidze-Gavrikov, USSR 1980.

54 10 ... h6 11 ♗h4 ♖g8 12 ♗g3 b5 13 e5 ♗b7
14 ♕f1 de 15 fe ♘d5 16 ♘xd5 ♗xd5 17 ♗f3 ±
Tal-Ljubojević, Bugojno 1980.

55 11 e5 ♗b7 12 ♕g3 de 13 fe ♕xe5 14 ♗f4
♕c5 15 ♗e3 ♕e5 16 ♗f4 ♕c5 17 ♗e3 ♕c8!
18 ♖hf1 0-0 19 ♗d3 ♘c5 ∓ Kuzmin-
Gheorghiu, Riga IZ 1979.

56 13 ♕g3 de 14 fe ♘d7 15 ♗f3 ♗xf3 16 gf g6!
17 f4 ♕b7 18 h4 0-0-0 ∓ Larsen-Portisch,
Manila 1974.

57 14 ... ♖c8!? 15 fe b4 ∞ Nunn.

58 16 ♗c6+ ♔e7 17 ♘ce2 ♖c8!

16 ♘ce2 0-0 17 ♗c6 ♗xd4 18 ♘xd4 ♕xf4+
19 ♔b1 ♕c7 =/∓ Nunn.

59 19 ♖e5 g6 20 ♘xd5 ♕d6 21 c3 ♔g7 22 g4
♖c8 23 g5 ♕d7! 24 f5 gf 25 ♖f4 ♕a7! =
Richardson-Zagorovsky, corr. 1972/76.

259

Najdorf V: Poisoned Pawn 1 e4 c5 2 ♘f3 d6
3 d4 cd 4 ♘xd4 ♘f6 5 ♘c3 a6 6 ♗g5 e7 7 f4 ♕b6

	8	9	10	11	12	13	14	15	16	
1	♘b3	♕f3[2]	0-0-0	♗e2[4]	♗xf6	e5	♕g3	fe	♗f3[6]	=
	♗e7[1]	♘bd7	♕c7[3]	b5[5]	♘xf6	♗b7	de	♘d7	0-0[7]	
2	♕d2[8]	♘b3	♗xf6	♗e2[9]	0-0	♖f3!?[10]	♔h1	♖d1		∞
	♕xb2	♕a3	gf	♘c6	♗d7	♗g7	0-0	♖ac8[11]		
3	...	...	♗d3	♗xf6[13]	0-0	♘b1[14]	c4	♘c3	♖ab1[15]	∞/±
	...	♘c6[12]	♕a3	gf	♗d7	♕a4!	♕b4	♘a5		
4	...	...	♗xf6	♘a4[16]	♘b6	♘c4	♔f2[17]	♗d3	♘b6	=
	...	...	gf	♕a3	♖b8	♕a4	e5[18]	♗e6[19]	♕b4[20]	

1 e4 c5 2 ♘f3 d6 3 d4 cd 4 ♘xd4 ♘f6 5 ♘c3
a6 6 ♗g5 e7 7 f4 ♕b6 8 ♕d2 ♕xb2 9 ♖b1 ♕a3

	10	11	12	13	14	15	16	17	18	
5	♗xf6[21]	♗e2	♘xc6	0-0	♔h1	f5[23]	ef	♗xa6	♖xf5	=/±
	gf	♘c6[22]	bc	♕a5	♗e7	ef	♗xf5	♕xa6	d5[24]	
6	e5?!	fe	♗c4[25]	0-0[26]	♖be1	♘xc6	♕f4	♔h1		∓
	de	♘fd7	♕a5!	♘xe5![27]	♘bc6	♘xc6	♗c5+	0-0[28]		
7	f5	fe	♘xc6	e5	♘xd5	♗e2	0-0	c4	♔h1	∞/±
	♘c6[29]	fe	bc	♘d5	cd	de	♖a7![30]	♕c5+	d4[31]	
8	...	...	...	...	♗xf6	♘e4	♗e2	♖b3	c4	∞/=
	...	...	...	de[32]	gf	♗e7[33]	h5	♕a4	f5[34]	
9	...	...	...	...	...	...	...	♘xf6+!		∞/±
	...	...	...	...	...	...	...		♗xf6[35]	
10	...	...	...	...	...		♖d1[36]	♗e2[37]	0-0	∞/=
	...	...	...	...	♕xa2!?	♗e7		0-0	f5[38]	

[1] **8 ...** ♕e3+ 9 ♕e2 ♕xe2+ 10 ♗xe2 ♘bd7 11 0-0-0 b5 ∞.

8 ... ♘bd7 9 ♕e2 ♕c7 10 g4! ♗e7 11 0-0-0 h6 12 ♗h4 g5 13 fg ♘h7 14 ♗g3 hg 15 e5! ± Kupreichik-Tal, USSR Ch 1979.

[2] **9** ♕e2?! h6 intending 10 ♗h4 ♘xe4!

9 e5 ♕e3+ 10 ♕e2 ♕xe2+ 11 ♗xe2 de 12 fe ♘fd7 ∓.

[3] **10** ... h6 11 ♗h4 ♕c7 12 ♗g3 b5 13 e5 ♗b7 14 ♕e2 ♘d5 15 ♘xd5 ♗xd5 16 ♖xd5 ed 17 e6 ∞ Nunn.

[4] **11** ♗d3 h6 12 ♗h4 g5 =.

[5] **11** ... h6 12 ♗h4 g5 13 fg ♘e5 14 ♕f2 ♘fg4 15 ♗xg4 ♘xg4 16 ♕f4 ♘e5 17 gh!? ♘g6 18 ♗xe7 ♘xf4 19 ♗xd6 ♕b6 20 ♗xf4 ∞ Timman-Hulak, Amsterdam 1977.

[6] **16** ♕xg7 ♘xe5 ∓.

16 ♖xd7 ♔xd7! 17 ♖d1+ ♔c8 18 ♕xg7 ♖f8 ∓.

[7] Nunn.

[8] **8** f5?! ♕xb2 9 ♘a4 ♕a3 10 c3 ♗d7 11 fe fe

[12] ♗xf6 gf 13 ♕h5+ ♔e7 14 ♗c4 ♕xa4 ∓ Murei-Pinter, Malta Ol 1980.

[9] **11** ♗d3 ♘d7 12 0-0 ♘c5 13 ♔h1 ♗d7 14 f5 0-0-0 = Hulak-Tringov, Bar 1977.

[10] **13** ♘b1 ♕b4 14 ♕e3 ♘e7 15 a3 ♕a4 16 f5 ♖c8 17 ♗d3 ∞ Matulović-Lederman, Le Havre 1977. 17 ... d5!? Shamkovich. 17 ... ♕c6 18 ♘1d2 ♖g8!? Minić.

[11] Maryasin-Rashkovsky, USSR 1979.

[12] **9** ... ♘bd7!? 10 ♗xf6 gf 11 ♗e2 ♘c5 12 0-0 ♗d7 13 ♖ab1 ♕a3 ∞ Nunn. 11 ... b5!?

[13] **11** 0-0 ♗d7 12 ♖ae1 0-0-0 13 ♗h4 ♗e7 14 ♗f2 ♘g4 15 ♗b6 ♕b4 16 ♗xd8 ♗xd8 ± Sakharov-Dementiev, USSR 1972.

[14] **13** ♕e3 ♕b4 14 ♘e2!? Shamkovich.

[15] **16** ... ♘xb3 17 ♖xb3 ♕c5+ 18 ♔h1 ♗c6 19 ♘d5 ed 20 ed ♗d7 21 ♖xb7 ♔d8 22 ♕b2! ±.

[16] **11** ♗e2 d5 12 ♘a4 ♕a3 13 ♘b6 d4 14 0-0 ♖b8 15 ♘c4 ♕b4 16 ♕d1 b5 ∓/∓ Nunn-Portisch, Toluca IZ 1982. 11 ... f5!?

[17] **14** ♗e2 d5 15 ed ed 16 ♘b6 ♕b4 17 ♖xd5

♕xd2+ 18 ♔xd2 ♗g7 19 ♔e3 0-0 20 c4 a5 21 a4
♖e8+ = Rodriguez-Marjanović, Vrnjačka Banja
1977.

18 14 ... ♗e7!? 15 a3 b5 16 ♘xd6+ ♔f8 ∞/∓.

14 ... f5? 15 a3! ♗g7 16 e5 b5 17 ♘xd6+ ♔f8
18 g4 b4 19 ♗g2 ± Timman-H.Olafsson,
Reykjavik 1976.

19 15 ... ef!? 16 ♕xf4 ♘e5 17 ♘b6 ♖c6 18 ♘d5
♘g4+ 19 ♔e2 ♖h6 20 ♕f1 ♗g7 ∞ Fernandez-
Nunn, Budapest 1978.

20 17 ♖xb4 ♘xb4 18 f5 ♗d7 19 a3 ♘xd3 20 cd
♗c6 = Ligterink-Barczay, Wijk aan Zee 1977.

21 10 ♗e2!? ♘bd7 11 0-0 ♗e7 12 f5 e5 13 ♘b3
♕b4 14 ♗e3!? ♘xe4 15 ♘xe4 ♕xe4 16 ♘a5 d5
17 ♗f3 ♕xe3+ 18 ♕xe3 ♗c5 19 ♕xc5 ♘xc5
20 ♗xd5 ± Sax-Browne, Wijk aan Zee 1981.
10 ... ♘c6!?. 10 ... ♗e7!?

22 11 ... h5 12 0-0 ♘d7 13 ♔h1 ♘c5 14 ♖f3
♕a5 15 ♘b3 ♕c7 ∞ Velimirović-Tringov,
Osijek 1978. 14 e5!? Nunn.

11 ... ♗g7 12 f5 0-0 13 0-0 ♘c6 14 ♘xc6 bc
15 ♔h1 ♕a5 16 ♖f3 ∞/± Zinser-Buljovčić,
Reggio Emilia 1967.

23 15 ♖f3 ♖a7! 16 f5 ♗b7 17 ♖bf1 h5 =
Parma-Bertok, Vrnjačka Banja 1962.

24 19 ♖e1 ♕b7 (Matanović-Bertok, Yugoslav
Ch 1962) 20 ♕h6! ± Nunn.

25 12 ♗e2 ♗b4 13 ♖b3 ♕a5 14 0-0-0-0 15 ♗f6
♘xf6 16 ef ♖d8 17 fg (Mahia-Quinteros,
Buenos Aires 1980) 17 ... ♗c5! ∓∓.

12 ♘e4 h6 13 ♗b5?! (Platonov-Minić,
USSR v Yugoslavia 1968) 13 ... hg 14 ♖b3 ♕xa2
15 ♕c3 ♘c6! 16 ♗xc6 bc 17 ♕xc6 ♕a1+ 18 ♔e2
♕xd4 19 ♕xa8 ♕c4+ ∓∓ Nunn.

26 13 ♘xe6? fe 14 ♗xe6 ♕xe5+ 15 ♕e3 ♕xe3+
16 ♗xe3 ♘c6 17 ♘d5 ♗d6 18 0-0 ♘f6! ∓
Mazzoni-Fischer, Monaco 1967.

13 ♗xe6 fe! 14 ♘xe6 (14 0-0 ♘xe5 15 ♔h1
♘bc6 16 ♘xc6 bc 17 ♕f4 ♕f5 18 ♕d7
♗d6 ∓∓) 14 ... ♘xe5! 15 ♘d5 (15 ♗d8 ♘f3+!
16 gf ♕e5+ 17 ♔d1 ♗xe6 18 ♖e1 ♕f5 ∓
Shalomon-Murei, corr. 1970) 15 ... ♕xd2+
16 ♔xd2 ♔d7 17 ♘ec7 ♖a7 18 ♖he1 ♘c4+
(intending ... b5) ∓.

27 13 ... ♗c5 14 ♘d5! ♗xd4+ 15 ♕xd4 ♘c6
16 ♕f4 dxe5 17 ♖be1 ♗c5+ 18 ♔h1 ♕xc4
19 ♘c7+ ♔f8 20 ♘xa8 h6! ±/∞ Norton-
Freeman, New Zealand Jr Ch 1978.

28 Boleslavsky.

29 10 ... b5 11 fe fe 12 ♖b3 ♕a5 (12 ... ♕c5?
13 ♘cxb5 ♘xe4 14 ♕a5! ± Velimirović-
Marjanović, Yugoslav Ch 1979) 13 ♗xf6 gf
14 ♗e2 b4 15 0-0 ♗g7 16 ♘d1 0-0 (Hartston-
Lee, England 1967) 17 ♘c4 ± Hartston.

30 16 ... ♗c5+ 17 ♔h1 ♖f8 18 c4 ♖xf1+
19 ♖xf1 ♗b7 20 ♕c2 e4 21 ♗g4 ♗c8 22 cd ♕d3

23 ♕c1 e5 24 ♖d1 ♕b5 ∓ Lilienthal, ± Nunn.

31 19 ♗h5+ g6 20 ♗d1 ♗e7 21 ♗a4+ ♔d8
22 ♖f7 h6 23 ♗xh6 e4 24 h3!? (Timman-Sunye,
Wijk aan Zee 1980) 24 ... ♖b7!? Nunn.
22 ... e4!? 23 ♖xe7 ♖xe7 24 ♗f6 e5 25 ♗xh8 e3
26 ♕e2 ♖f7 (Sergyan-Nagy, corr. 1981)
27 ♔g1 ∞ Botlik. 27 h3!?

32 13 ... ♘d7?! 14 ed ♗xd6 15 ♗d3 ♖b8
16 ♖d1 ♕e5+ 17 ♘e4 ♗c5 18 ♗f4 ♗b4 19 c3
♗xc3 (∞ Kasparov) 20 ♕xc3 ♕xf4 21 ♘d6+
♔d8 22 ♗e4 (± Nunn) Vitolins-Peresipkin,
Kiev 1974.

33 15 ... ♕e7 16 ♗e2 h5 17 ♕d1! ±.

15 ... f5? 16 ♗e2 fe 17 ♗h5+ ♔e7 18 0-0 ♕d6
19 ♖f7+ ♔d8 20 ♖xf8+ ±±.

34 19 ♘g3 h4 20 ♘h5 ♖a7 (20 ... ♗d8!?)
21 ♖b8 ♔f7 22 0-0 ♖b7 23 ♖xc8 ♖xc8 24 ♕h6
♖g8 25 ♗f4!? ∞/=.

19 0-0 fe 20 ♕c3 ♕xa2 21 ♗d1 ♗c5+ 22 ♔h1
♖f8 23 ♗xh5+ ♔d8 24 ♖d1+ ♗d4 25 ♖xd4+ ed
26 ♕xd4+ ♗d7 27 ♕b6+ ♗e7 28 ♕c5+ ♔f6
29 ♕d4+ e5 30 ♕xd7 ♕xb3 31 ♕d6+ ♔g7
32 ♕g6+ =.

19 ♘d6+? ♗xd6 20 ♕xd6 ♕a5+ 21 ♔f2
♖a7 22 ♖b8 ♔f7 23 ♖d1 ♖d7! ∓ Matulović-
Stean-Vršac 1979.

35 19 c4 and now:

19 ... c5 20 0-0 ♕d7 21 ♕xd7+ ♗xd7
22 ♖xf6 h4! 23 ♖e3 ♔e7 =/± Rogulj-Stean,
Yugoslavia 1980.

19 ... ♗h4+ 20 g3 ♗e7 21 0-0 ♖a7 22 ♖b8
♖c7 23 ♕d3 ♗c5+ 24 ♔h1 ♗e7 25 ♕e4!? ♔d6
26 ♖d1+ ♕xd1 27 ♗xd1 h4 28 ♕d3+ ♗d4
29 c5+! ±/±± Belyavsky-Hübner, Tilburg
1981.

19 ... ♖a7 20 0-0 ♖f7 21 ♕c3 (21 ♕d6 ♗e7
22 ♕xe5 ♖xf1+ 23 ♗xf1 ♖h7 24 ♖b8 ♔d7
25 ♕d4+ ♗d6 26 ♕a7+ ♔d8! 27 ♖xc8+ ♗xc8
28 ♕xh7 ♗c5+ 29 ♔h1 ♕xa2 ∓ Chiburdanidze-
Alexandria, match 1981) 21 ... c5 22 ♖xf6 ♖xf6
23 ♕xe5 ♖fh6 24 ♕xc5 ♗f7 25 ♕e5 ♕d7
26 ♖f3+ ♗e8 27 ♖g3 ♕d2 28 ♕c5 ♗d7
29 ♖g7 =.

36 16 ♘xf6+ ♗f7 17 ♖b3 (17 ♖d1 a5! ∓) 17 ...
♕a1+ 18 ♔e2 ♕d4 19 ♕g5 (Matulović-Nunn,
Helsinki 1981) 19 ... e4! 20 ♕g4 ♗g7 ∓ Nunn.

37 17 ♗d3 0-0 18 0-0 f5 19 ♕h6 ♖f7 20 ♖f3
♔h8! 21 ♖h3 ♗d7 22 ♔h1 ♖g8 23 ♘c3 ♕a5
24 ♗xf5 ef 25 ♖xd7 ♕c5 ∓ Velimirović-
Polaizer, Maribor 1980.

38 19 ♕h6 ♕xc2 20 ♖d3 ♕xe2 21 ♖g3+ ♔f7
22 ♖xf5+ ef 23 ♖g7+ ♔e8 24 ♕xc6+ ♔d8
25 ♕b6+ = Velimirović-Ftacnik, Vršac 1981.

For more detail on these complex lines the
reader should consult John Nunn's *Sicilian
Defence: Najdorf Variation* (Batsford 1982).

	8	9	10	11	12	13	14	15	16	
1	a3?!¹ / ♗b7²	♗e2 / ♘bd7	♗f3 / ♕b6	♕d2 / ♖c8	♗h4 / ♘c5	♗f2 / b4	ab / ♕xb4	0-0 / ♗e7	♖ad1 / 0-0³	∓
2	e5 / de	fe / ♕c7	♗xb5+ / ab	ef / ♕e5+	♕e2 / ♕xg5	♘dxb5 / ♖a5!	fg / ♗xg7⁴	♘e4 / ♕e5	♘bd6+ / ♔e7⁵	±
3	... / ...	... / ...	ef / ♕e5+	♗e2 / ♕xg5	0-0 / ♕e5	♘f3⁶ / ♗c5+	♔h1 / ♕xf6	♘e4 / ♕e7	♘fg5⁷ / ♕	∞
4	... / ...	... / ...	... / ...	... / ...	♕d3 / ♕xf6	♖f1 / ♕e5	♖d1⁸ / ♖a7⁹	♘f3 / ♕c7	♘g5 / f5¹⁰	±
5	... / ...	... / ...	♕e2 / ♘fd7	0-0-0 / ♗b7	♘xe6 / fe	♕h5+¹¹ / g6	♕g4 / ♕xe5¹²	♗d3 / ♘c5	♕h4 / ♘bd7¹³	=
6	... / ...	... / ...	... / ...	... / ...	♕g4 / ♕b6	♗e2 / ♘xe5	♕h3 / ♘bd7	♗h5 / g6	♗f3 / ♘xf3¹⁴	∞
7	... / ...	... / ...	... / ...	... / ...	... / ...	... / h6	♕h3 / ♘xe5	♖he1 / ♘bd7	♗h4 / g5¹⁵	∞
8	... / ...	... / ...	... / ...	... / ...	... / ♕xe5	♗e2!?¹⁶ / ♗c5¹⁷	♘f3 / ♗e3+¹⁸	♔b1 / h5	♘xe5 / hg¹⁹	±
9	... / ...	... / ...	... / ...	... / ♘c6	♘xc6 / ♕xc6	♕d3 / h6	♗h4 / ♗b7	♗e2 / ♕c7	♖he1²⁰ / ♘c5!²¹	∞

¹ 8 ♗e2 b4 9 ♘a4 ♗e7 10 ♗f3 ♖a7 11 0-0 ♗d7 12 b3 ♗xa4 13 ba 0-0 14 ♘b3 ♘bd7 ∓ Suetin-Polugayevsky, USSR Ch 1960.
  8 ♗d3 ♘bd7 9 f5 e5 10 ♘c6 ♕b6 11 ♘b4 ♗b7 12 ♗e2 ♗e7 13 0-0-0 ♖c8 14 ♗xf6 ♘xf6 15 g4 ♗a5 16 a3 ♖xc3 17 bc d5! ∓ Spassky-Polugayevsky, USSR Ch 1960.

² 8 ... ♘bd7 9 ♕f3 ♗b7 10 0-0-0 ♖c8 11 f5 e5 12 ♘de2 ♕c7 13 ♖d2 ♗e7 14 h4 0-0 ∓ Ervin-Browne, New York 1974.

³ Koska-Cetkovsky, Brno 1978.

⁴ 14 ... ♕xg7!? ∞ Polugayevsky.

⁵ 17 0-0 f5 18 ♖ad1 ♖d5 19 ♕c4 ± Tal-Polugayevky, match 1980. 17 ... f6!?

⁶ 13 ♗h5!? g6 14 ♗f3 ♖a7 15 ♘e4 ∞ Kavalek-Polugayevsky, Bugojno 1980.
  13 ♔h1 ♖a7 14 fg ♗xg7 15 ♗f3 = Polugayevsky.
  13 ♗f3 ♖a7 14 ♘c6 ♘xc6 15 ♗xc6+ ♗d7 16 ♗xd7+ ♖xd7 17 ♕f3 ♗d6 18 ♕h3 (18 g3 ♕xf6 19 ♕a8+ ♔d8 20 ♕xa6 b4 21 ♘e4 0-0 ∓ Mariotti-Ribli, Manila 1976) 18 ... b4! 19 fg ♖g8 20 ♘a4 ♕xg7 ∓ Nunn.

⁷ 16 ... 0-0 17 ♘xf7! ♖xf7 18 ♖xf7 ♗xf7 19 ♗h5+ ♔g8 20 ♘xc5 (Belyavsky-Polugayevsky, USSR 1979) 20 ... ♖a7! ±.
  16 ... f5! 17 ♗h5+ g6 18 ♘xh7 ♗f7! ∞.

⁸ 14 0-0-0?! ♖a7 15 ♘f3 ♗f4+ ∓ Gheorghiu-Ljubojević, Amsterdam 1975.

⁹ 14 ... ♕c7? 15 ♗h5! g6 16 ♗f3 ♖a7 17 ♘c6 ♘xc6 18 ♗xc6+ ♗d7 (Belyavsky-Polugayevsky, Moscow 1981) 19 ♗xd7+! ♕xd7 20 ♕e3 ±±.

¹⁰ 17 ♕d4! h5 18 ♖xf5!? ef 19 ♘d5 ♕d7 (Tal-Polugayevsky, match 1980) 20 ♖d3! ±. 19 ... ♕a5+!?

¹¹ 13 ♕g4 ♘xe5 14 ♗d3 ♗e7 15 ♗xe7 ♔xe7 16 ♖he1 h5 17 ♕h4+ ♕f6 18 ♕b4+ ♔d8 19 ♗e4 ∞/∓ Nunn.

¹² 14 ... ♗e7 15 ♗xe7 ♘xe5 16 ♗d8!? ♘xg4 17 ♗xc7 0-0 18 ♖e1 ± Nunn.
  14 ... ♘c5!? ∞ Nunn.

¹³ 17 ♖he1 ♕g7 18 ♗e4 ♘xe4 19 ♘xe4 ♗e7 20 ♗xe7 ♕xe7 21 ♘d6+ ♔d8 22 ♘f7+ = Nunn.

¹⁴ 16 ... ♗xf3 17 ♘xf3 ±.
  16 ... ♘xf3!? 17 ♘xf3 ♗g7 ∞ Nunn.

¹⁵ 17 ♘xe6! gh (17 ... fe 18 ♗f2! ♕xf2 19 ♕xe6+ ♔d8 20 ♗xb5 ♕xe1 21 ♖xe1 ab 22 ♖xe5 ♘xe5 23 ♕xe5 ±± Kasparov) 18 ♗h5 ♗d6 19 ♕f5 ∞ Nunn/van der Vliet. 19 ... b4!?. 19 ... ♖c8!?

¹⁶ 13 ♗xb5!? ab 14 ♘cxb5 f5 15 ♕h4 ♘a6!? (15 ... ♖xa2 16 ♔b1 ♗a5 17 ♗f4 ♕f6 18 ♗g5 ♕e5 = Nunn) 16 ♖he1 ♗e4 17 g4 (Georgiev-Soylu, Istanbul 1980) 17 ... ♖c8! ∞ Georgiev.

¹⁷ 13 ... ♘f6 14 ♗xf6 ♕xf6 15 ♘cxb5 ±±.
  14 ... gf 15 ♖he1 ±.

¹⁸ 14 ... ♕c7 15 ♗f4 ±.
  14 ... ♕f5 15 ♕h4 ±.

¹⁹ 17 ♘xf7 ♔xf7 18 ♗xe3 ♘f6 ±.

²⁰ 16 ♖hf1!? ±/∞.

²¹ 17 ♕h3 b4 18 ♘b5! ab! 19 ♗xb5+ ♗c6 20 ♕f3 ♘b3+! ∞/= Grünfeld-Polugayevsky, Riga IZ 1979. 21 ab! ♖a1+ 22 ♔d2 ♕d7+ 23 ♔e3 ♗c5+ 24 ♔f4 g5+ 25 ♔g3 ♖xd1 26 ♗xc6 ♖xe1 27 ♗xd7+ ♔f8! ∞/= Polugayevsky.

Sicilian: 2 ... Nc6   **1 e4 c5 2 Nf3 Nc6 3 Bb5**

	3	4	5	6	7	8	9	10	11	
1	... a6[1]	Bxc6 dc[2]	h3[3] e5	d3[4] Bd6	a4 a5	Nbd2 Ne7	Nc4 f6	Nh4 0-0	g4 Bc7[5]	±
2	... Qb6	Nc3[6] e6	0-0 Nge7[7]	Re1 Nd4	Bc4[8] Nec6	d3 d6[9]	Nxd4 cd	Ne2 Na5[10]	c3 Nxc4[11]	±
3	... d6	0-0[12] Bd7	c3[13] Nf6	Re1 a6	Bf1 g6	d4 cd	cd d5	e5 Ne4	Nc3 Nxc3	∞
4	... Nf6	Nc3[14] Bd4[15]	e5 Nxb5	Nxb5 Nd5	0-0[16] a6	c4!? Nb4[17]	Nc3 d6			∞
5	... e6	0-0[18] Nge7	c3[19] a6[20]	Ba4 b5[21]	Bc2 Bb7	d3 Ng6	Ng5!? f6	Nh3 Bd6	f4 0-0[22]	±

[1] 3 ... Qc7 4 0-0 Nf6 (4 ... a6 5 Bxc6 Qxc6 6 d4 cd 7 Nxd4 Qc7 8 Nc3 e6!? 9 e5 ±; 4 ... e6 5 c3 Nf6 6 Re1 a6 7 Bxc6 Qxc6 ∞) 5 Nc3 e6 6 Re1 d6 7 d4 cd 8 Nd5 ed 9 ed+ Be7 10 Nxd4 Nxd5 11 Nxc6 bc 12 Qxd5 Bb7 = Westerinen.

[2] 4 ... bc 5 d3 d6 6 0-0 (6 b3 !? e5 7 Bb2 Be7 ∞) 6 ... Bg4 ∞. 6 c3!?

[3] 5 d3 Nf6 6 0-0 Bg4 7 Nbd2 e6 8 Nc4 Qc7 9 Bg5 b5 10 Ne3 Nh5 11 Bh4 Bd6 12 Bg3 ± Rossolimo-Lundin, Bad Gastein 1948. 5 ... Qc7!? intending ... e5.

[4] 6 0-0 f6 7 d3 Be6 8 a4 Qd7 9 a5 0-0-0 10 b3 g5 11 Be3 Ne7! 12 Bxc5 Ng6 ∞ Boleslavsky.

[5] 12 Be3 b6 13 Qe2 Be6 14 b3 Qd7 15 Rg1 Kh8 16 0-0-0 Qe8 (Vasyukov-Zhelyandinov, Havana II 1967) 17 Nf5 ±.

[6] 4 Na3 Nf6 5 Be2 a6 =.
    4 a4 e6 5 0-0 Nf6 6 e5 Nd5 7 Nc3 Be7 8 Bc4! ±.
    4 Qe2 e6 5 0-0 Nge7 6 c3 a6 7 Ba4 Bg6 8 Rd1 Be7 9 d4 ± Gufeld-Radev, Tbilisi 1971.
    4 Ba4 g6 5 0-0 Bg7 6 c3 e6 7 Re1 Nge7 (Sax-Miles, London 1975) 8 Na3! ±.

[7] 5 ... a6 6 Bxc6 Qxc6 7 d4 cd 8 Qxd4 b5 9 Re1 Bb7 (Kapengut-Kupreichik, USSR Ch 1978) 10 a4 ±.
    5 ... Nf6 6 Re1 d6 7 e5 de 8 Nxe5 ±.

[8] 7 a4! a6 (7 ... Nec6 8 Nd5!) 8 Bc4 ± Inkiov-Helmers, Lodz 1978.

[9] 8 ... Be7 9 Nd5 Nxf3+ 10 Qxf3 Nd4 11 Qg3 ed 12 ed Kf8 13 Rxe7! ±± Semenyuk-Yailian, USSR 1981.

[10] 10 ... Be7!?
    10 ... g6!?

[11] 12 dc dc 13 Nxc3 Be7 14 b3 0-0 15 Be3 ± Kudriashov-Korchnoi, USSR 1965.

[12] 4 Bxc6+ bc 5 0-0 e5 6 c3 g5!? ∞.

[13] 5 c4 Nf6 6 Nc3 Be5 7 d3 g6 8 Nxe5 de 9 Be3 = Gurgenidze-Timoshenko, USSR 1977.

[14] 4 Bxc6 dc 5 d3 g6 6 h3 Bg7 7 Nc3 0-0 8 Be3 b6 9 Qd2 Ne8 10 h4 Bg4 11 h5 ∞.
    4 e5 Nd5 5 Nc3 Nc7 6 Bxc6 dc 7 h3 g6 8 0-0 Bg7 9 Ne4 b6 = Adorjan-Sveshnikov, Sochi 1976.
    4 Qe2 g6 5 Nc3! Bg7 6 e5 Ng4 7 Bxc6 dc 8 h3 Nh6 9 g4! ± Ermenkov-Tukmakov, Vrnjačka Banja 1979.

[15] 4 ... g6 5 h3 Nd4 (5 ... Bg7 6 e5! ± Kuzmin-Timoshenko, USSR 1977) 6 e5 Nxb5 7 Nxb5 Nd5 8 Qe2 Nc7 (8 ... Nf4!?) 9 d4 Nxb5 10 Qxb5 cd 11 Bg5! h6 12 Bf4! ± Egin-Tukmakov, USSR 1979.

[16] 7 Ng5 h6 8 Ne4 a6 9 Nbc3 e6 10 0-0 Nxc3 11 dc Qc7 ∞ Zaitsev-Sveshnikov, Sochi 1980.

[17] 8 ... Nc7 9 Nxc7+ Qxc7 10 d4 ±.
    8 ... Nb6?! 9 Nc3 d5 (9 ... Nxc4 10 d4 cd 11 Bxd4 b5 12 a4 Bb7 13 ab ab 14 Rxa8 Bxa8 15 Nxb5 ±) 10 d4! ± Sax-Sveshnikov, Hastings 1977/78.

[18] 4 Bxc6 bc 5 0-0 Ne7 6 b3 (6 c4 Ng6 7 d4 cd 8 Qxd4 c5 9 Qd3 Be7 10 Nc3 0-0 11 b3 ± Vasyukov-Gaprindashvili, USSR 1981) 6 ... Ng6 7 Bb2 f6 8 d4 cd 9 Nxd4 Bc5? (9 ... Be7) 10 c4 0-0 11 Nc3 Qc7 12 Kh1 Be7 13 Rc1 Bb7 14 Rc2 ± Timman-Visier, Las Palmas 1977.

[19] 5 b3 Nd4 (5 ... Ng6 6 Bb2 f6 7 Nc3 Be7 8 Re1 0-0 9 Bf1! ±) 6 Nxd4 cd 7 c3 Qb6 8 Qe2 a6 9 Bc4 Nc6 10 Bb2 Bc5 11 b4 0-0 12 a4 ±/± Plaskett-Braga, Graz 1981.
    5 Re1 a6 6 Bxc6 Qxc6 7 d4 cd 8 Nxd4 d6 9 Nc3 ± Christiansen-Bellon, Torremolinos 1978.

[20] 5 ... d5 6 ed Qxd5 (6 ... Nxd5 7 d4 cd 8 cd Be7 9 Nc3 0-0 10 Re1 Bd7 11 Nxd5 ed 12 Qb3 ± Vasyukov-Timoshenko, USSR 1975) 7 d4 cd 8 c4! ± Timman-Sveshnikov, Wijk aan Zee 1981.

[21] 6 ... c4!?
    6 ... d6 7 d4 cd 8 cd d5 9 Nc3 ± Kozlov-Peshina, USSR 1979.
    6 ... d5 7 ed Qxd5 8 d4 Bd7 9 Re1 Rd8 10 c4! Qxc4 11 Nbd2 Qd5 12 Bb3 Qh5 13 Ne4! Nf5 14 dc ± Spassky-Timman, Amsterdam 1977.

[22] 12 Be3 Nce7 13 Nd2 Rc8 14 a4 ±.

	3	4	5	6	7	8	9	10	11	
6	...	♘c3	0-0	♗xc6	d4	♘xd4	♘xc6[24]	♕g4	f4	∞
	e6	♘ge7[23]	a6	♘xc6	cd	d6	bc	♕f6	♗e7[25]	
7	...	0-0	c3[26]	♖e1	d4	cd	e5	♘c3	bc	±
	g6	♗g7	♘f6[27]	0-0	cd	d5	♘e4	♘xc3[28]	♗a5[29]	
8	...	...	♖e1	♗xc6[31]	d3	♘bd2	♘c4	b4	a3	=
	...	...	e5[30]	dc	♕e7	♘h6[32]	f6	cb!	0-0	

[23] 4 ... ♘d4 5 a4!? (5 ♘xd4 cd 6 ♘e2 ♕g5 ∓ Dorfman) 5 ... ♘e7 6 ♘xd4 cd 7 ♘e2 a6 8 ♗c4 d5 9 ed ♘xd5 ± Dorfman-Taimanov, USSR 1976.

[24] 9 ♗e3 ♗e7 10 ♕e2 0-0 11 f4 ♗d7 = Kozlov-Sveshnikov, USSR 1978.

[25] Tseitlin-Vukhman, Leningrad Ch 1976.

[26] 5 ♘e2 ♘f6!? (5 ... e5) 6 e5 ♘d5 7 ♕c4 ±.

[27] 5 ... e5 6 d4!? cd 7 cd ed 8 ♗f4 a6 9 ♗a4 b5 10 ♗b3 d6 11 a4 b4 12 ♘bd2 ±.

[28] 10 ... ♗f5 11 ♘h4 ♗d7 12 ♗d3 ± Levchenko-Klovan, Latvian Ch 1980.

[29] 12 ♕a4 a6 13 ♗f1 ± Sax-Janošević,

Madonna di Campiglio 1974.

[30] 5 ... e6!? 6 ♗xc6 dc 7 e5 ♘e7 8 d3 ♘f5 9 ♗g5 ♕c7 10 h3 ±.

  5 ... ♘f6 6 e5 (6 ♘c3 0-0 7 h3 ♘d4! =;   7 e5 ♘e8 8 ♗xc6 dc 9 d3 ±) 6 ... ♘d5 7 b3 (7 ♘c3; 7 d3) 7 ... 0-0 8 ♗b2 ♘c7 9 ♗xc6 dc 10 d3 f5!? ∞ Kengis-Peshina, Vilnius 1979.

[31] **6 b4!?** ♘xb4! 7 ♗b2 ♕b6 8 ♘a3 a6 ∞.

  6 c3 ♘ge7 7 d4 cd 8 cd ed 9 ♗f4 a6 10 ♗f1 d6 11 ♘bd2 0-0 12 h3 ± Castro-Geller, Biel IZ 1976.

[32] 8 ... ♘f6 9 ♘c4 ♗d7 10 ♗d2 0-0 11 a3 b6 12 b4 ♗a6 13 ♗c3 ± Torre-Timman, Moscow 1981.

		Accelerated Fianchetto I			**1 e4 c5 2 ♘f3 ♘c6 3 d4 cd 4 ♘xd4 g6**					
	5	6	7	8	9	10	11	12	13	
1	♘xc6[1]	♕d4[2]	e5	c4[4]	♕e4	♘c3	f4	♗d2		=
	bc	♘f6!	♘d5[3]	♕b6	♘c7	♗g7	0-0	d5[5]		
2	♘c3	♘xc6[6]	e5	♗c4	♕f3	♗f4	0-0	♖ad1	♖fe1	±
	♘f6?!	bc[7]	♘g8[8]	♗g7[9]	f5	♖b8[10]	e6	♕c7	♘e7[11]	
3	...	♗e3	♘xc6	e5	f4[12]	♕d2[14]	0-0-0	♗c4	h4	∓
	♗g7	♘f6	bc	♘g8	♘h6![13]	0-0	♕a5!	♖b8	d6[15]	
4	...	...	...	...	♘xd5	♕xd5	♗xa7[16]	♗d4	♗d3	=
	...	...	...	♘d5!?	cd	♖b8	♖xb2	♖xc2	e6[17]	
5	...	...	♗e2[18]	0-0[19]	ed	♘xd5	♗f3	♘xc6	♗xc6	=
	...	...	0-0	d5	♘xd5	♕xd5	♕a5	bc	♖b8[20]	
6	...	...	♗c4	♗b3[22]	f3	♕d2	0-0-0	g4	♔b1	∞
	...	...	0-0[21]	♕a5[23]	b6[24]	♗a6	♖ac8	♘e5	♖c4!?[25]	
7	...	...	...	0-0[26]	♗b3	h3[27]	f4	♗xd4	♕d3	=
	...	...	♕a5	0-0	d6	♗d7	♘xd4[28]	♗c6	♖ad8[29]	
8	...	...	...	...	♘b3	♗e2[30]	f4	♗f3	♘b5	=
	...	...	...	...	♕c7	d6	b6![31]	♗b7	♕c8[32]	

[1] 5 &c4 ♕a5+! (5 ... &g7 6 c3 ♕b6 7 ♘b5 intending &e3, ♕d5; 6 ... ♘f6 =) 6 ♘c3 &g7 =/∓ Ivanović-Rajković, Yugoslav Ch 1981.
[2] 6 &e3 &g7 (6 ... ♘f6 =) 7 &d4 ♘f6 8 e5 ♘d5 (8 ... ♘g8 9 &c4 f6 10 ♕f3 ± Koch-Mannsfeld, East Germnay 1956) 9 c4 ♘f4 =/∓.
[3] 7 ... ♘g8 =.
7 ... ♘h5 =.
[4] 8 &c4 ♕b6!
8 e6 f6 9 ed+ &xd7 10 &c4 e5 11 ♕e4 ∞. [5] Chestyakov-Veresov, USSR 1953. 12 ... ♕xb2!?. 12 ... d6 =.
[6] 6 &c4 &g7 7 &e3 = (see below).
[7] 6 ... dc 7 ♕xd8+ &xd8 8 &c4 ± Gligorić-Kristinsson, Reykjavik 1967.
[8] 7 ... ♘d5 8 ♘xd5 ed 9 ♕xd5 ♖b8 10 e6! ± Euwe.
[9] 8 ... ♕a5 9 ♕e2 &g7 10 f4 ♘h6 11 &d2 0-0 12 0-0-0 ♕c7 13 g4 d5 14 ed ed 15 f5 ± Siyanovsky-Sherbakov, USSR 1960.
[10] 10 ... ♕a5 11 0-0 &xe5? 12 b4 ♕c7 13 ♘b5 ♕b8 14 &xe5 ♕xe5 15 ♖fe1 ♕b8 16 ♕c3 ± Karakas-Polihroniade, Beverwijk 1966.
10 ... e6 11 g4!? Euwe/Vreeken.
[11] 14 b3 0-0 15 ♕e3 ± Andersson-Bilek, Teesside 1972.
[12] 9 &d4 ♕a5 10 e6 ♘f6 11 ef+ &xf7 12 &c4+ d5 13 &b3 ♖e8 14 f4 c5 ∓ Plater-Vasyukov, Poland v USSR 1955. 10 &c4!?
[13] 9 ... h5!?
[14] 10 &e2 0-0 11 0-0 ♘f5 12 &f2 h5! =/∓ Murmamedov-Gurgenidze, USSR 1960.
[15] 14 h5 ♘f5 15 hg hg 16 g4 ♘xe3 17 ♕xe3 &xg4 18 ♖dg1 &f5+ Ravinsky-Zilberstein, Leningrad 1963.
[16] 11 &c4 0-0 12 f4 d6 (12 ... ♕c7!?; 12 ... e6!?) 13 &b3 a5 14 0-0 &b7 15 ♕c4 ♖c8 16 ♕d3 (Gheorghiu-Forintos, Ljubljana 1969) 16 ... de 17 ♕xd8 ♖fxd8 18 fe &d5 19 &f4 &xb3 20 cb ♖c2 =.
[17] 14 ♕a8 ♖c6 15 0-0 (15 &b5 ♖a6!? 16 &xa6 ♕a5+ 17 &f1 0-0! 18 ♕e4 &a6+ 19 &g1 d6! ∓ Volshok) 15 ... &a6 16 ♕xd8+ &xd8 = Belyavsky.
[18] 7 f4 d6 8 &e2 ♕b6 9 ♕d3 ♕xb2 10 0-0 0-0 11 ♖ab1 ♕a3 12 ♘xc6 bc 13 ♘d5 ♕xd3 =.
7 ♘b3 0-0 8 &e2 a5 9 a4 (9 0-0 a4 =) 9 ... ♘b4 10 0-0 d5 11 e5 ♘e4 12 f4 f6! Euwe/Vreeken.
7 f3 0-0 8 ♘b3 a5 9 &b5 d5! =/∓ Ruble-Aronson, USSR 1957.

[19] 8 ♕d2 d5! =.
[20] Euwe/Vreeken.
[21] 7 ... ♘a5 8 &xf7+ &xf7 9 e5 d5 10 ef &xf6 11 ♕f3 e6 12 0-0-0 &g7 13 h4 ♘c6 14 h5 ± Shaposhnikov-Altschuler, corr. 1963.
7 ... d6 8 f3 ♕b6!? 9 ♘f5 ♕xb2 10 ♘xg7+ &f8 11 ♘d5 ♘xd5 12 &xd5 &xg7 13 ♖b1 ♕c3+ 14 &f2 ♕a5 15 ♖c1 ∞.
[22] 8 0-0 ♘xe4! 9 ♘xe4 d5 =.
8 ♘xc6 dc =.
8 f3 ♕b6! ∓.
[23] 8 ... ♘a5 9 e5! ±.
8 ... e6 9 ♘xc6 dc (9 ... bc 10 &c5!) 10 e5 ♕xd1+ 11 ♖xd1 ♘g4 12 &c5 ♖e8 13 f4 ±.
8 ... d5 9 ed ♘a5 10 ♕d2! b6 11 0-0-0 &b7 12 &h6 ♘xb3+ 13 ♘xb3 a5 14 a4 ♕d6 15 &xg7 &xg7 16 ♕d4 &g8 17 ♖he1 ±.
8 ... ♕c7 9 f3 a6 10 ♕d2 b5 11 0-0-0 &b7 12 h4 ♖fc8 13 h5 ±/± Shishov-Voronkov, USSR 1969.
8 ... b6 9 f3 &a6 10 ♕d2 ♕b8 11 0-0-0 ♖d8 ∞ Yudovich-Simagin, Moscow 1962.
8 ... ♘g4? 9 ♕xg4 ♘xd4 10 ♕d1 ♘xb3 11 ab ±.
8 ... a5 9 f3! (9 a4? ♘g4! 10 ♕xg4 ♘xd4 11 ♕d1 ♘xb3 12 cb ∓) 9 ... d5!? ∞.
[24] 9 ... e6 10 ♕d2 d5 11 ed ±.
[25] 14 g5 ♘h5 15 ♘d5 e6 ∞ Veresov.
[26] 8 f3!? ♕b4 9 ♘xc6 bc 10 &b3 d5 11 ed ♘xd5 12 &xd5 cd 13 ♕xd5 ♕xb2 14 ♕c6+! (14 ♕xa8 0-0) 14 ... &f8 ∞ Hattleback-Watt, Ybbs 1968.
[27] 10 f3 &d7 11 ♕e1 ♖ac8 12 ♖c1 ♖fd8 = Spassky-Gurgenidze, USSR 1960.
[28] 11 ... ♖ac8 12 ♘f3! ± Kurajica-Kuijpers, Wijk aan Zee 1970.
11 ... ♕h5!? 12 ♕d2 b5 13 ♘xc6 &xc6 14 &d4 b4 = Levitina-Alexandria, match 1975.
[29] 14 ♖ad1 ♘d7 15 &xg7 &xg7 = Martin-Bellon, Olot 1974.
[30] 10 &g5!? a5 11 a3 a4 12 ♘d2 ♕a5 13 ♘d5 d6 14 c3 ± Kupreichik-Veremeshik, USSR 1976.
[31] 11 ... a5 12 a4 ♘b4 13 ♖f2! ± Fischer-Olafsson, Bled 1961.
11 ... ♖d8!? 12 &f3 (12 g4 d5! ∞) 12 ... e5!? 13 fe ♘xe5 14 ♘b5 ♕e7 15 &xa7 ♘xf3+ 16 ♕xf3 &g4 17 ♕g3 ♕d7 =.
[32] 14 c4 ♘b4 15 ♘d2 ♘d7 16 ♖b1 a6 17 ♘c3 &xc3! 18 bc ♘d3 19 ♕e2 ♘3c5 = Klovan-Veremeshik, USSR 1979.

265

	5	6	7	8	9	10	11	12	13	
1	...	♘c3	♕xd4	♗e2[2]	0-0[3]	♕e3[4]	♗d2	♖fd1	a4	±
	♘f6	♘xd4	d6	♗g7	0-0	♗d7	a6	♕b8	a5[5]	
2	...	...	...	♗e3	f3	♕d2	♖c1	♘d5	♘xe7+	±
	...	...	...	♗g7	0-0	♗e6[6]	♕a5	♕xa7[7]	♔h8[8]	
3	...	♘c2	♗e2	♘c3	♗d2[10]	0-0	b3	f3	♔h1	±
	♗g7	d6	♘f6[9]	♘d7	0-0	♘c5	♗d7	a5	b6[11]	
4	...	...	...	ef	0-0	♘d2[12]	♘f3	♘e3	♘xf5	∓
	...	...	f5!?	♗xf5	♘h6	0-0	♕d7	♔h8	♘xf5[13]	
5	...	♗e3	♗e2[14]	♕d2	♗xg4	♘c3	0-0	♖ac1[16]	b3	±
	...	♘h6	d6[15]	♘g4	♗xg4	0-0	♕a5	♖fc8	a6[17]	
6	...	...	♘c3	♕xg4	♕d1	♘b5	♕d2[21]	♗d3	cd	±
	...	♘f6	♘g4	♘xd4[18]	e5[19]	0-0[20]	♕h4[22]	d5!	♘xb5[23]	
7	...	...	...	♗e2	♕d2[24]	f3	0-0-0	♔b1	b3[26]	±
	...	...	0-0	b6	♗b7	e6[25]	♖c8	♘a5		
8	...	...	...	...	0-0	♕d2	♗xd4	f3	♗e3![29]	±
	...	...	...	d6	♗d7[27]	♘xd4[28]	♗c6	♘d7		

[1] See also English: Hedghog Systems.

[2] 8 c5 ♗g7 9 ♗b5+ ♗d7 10 cd 0-0 11 0-0 ♗xb5 12 ♘xb5 a6 13 ♘c3 ♘e8 14 ♕b4 ♘xd6 = Bogdanović-Ankerst, Yugoslavia 1965.

8 f3 ♗g7 9 ♗g5!? 0-0 10 ♕d2 ♗e6 11 ♖c1 ♕a5 12 b3 ♖fc8 13 ♗e2 a6 14 ♘a4! ♕xd2+ 15 ♔xd2 ± Karpov-Kavalek, Nice Ol 1974.

[3] 9 ♗d2 0-0 10 ♕e3 e6 11 0-0 d5 12 cd ed 13 ed ♖e8 14 ♕g3 ± Keres-Barczay, Budapest 1970.

9 ♗g5 h6 (9 ... 0-0 10 ♕e3!? a6 11 0-0 ♗d7 12 ♖fd1 ± Murei-Gelfer, Israeli Ch 1980; 9 ... ♗e6 10 ♖c1 ♕a5 11 ♕d2 ♖c8 12 f3! ± Geller-Stean, Teesside 1975) 10 ♗e3 0-0 11 ♕d2 ♔h7 12 0-0 ♗e6 13 ♗d4 (13 ♖ac1 ♕a5 14 f4 ♖ac8 15 b3 a6 16 f5 ♗d7 = Gulko-Petrosian, Biel IZ 1976) 13 ... ♖c8 14 b3 a6 15 ♕e3! ±/= Timman-Ribli, Amsterdam 1973.

[4] 10 ♗g5 ♗e6 11 ♕d2 ♕a5 12 ♖c1 ♖fc8 13 b3 a6 14 f4 ♖c5!? 15 ♗f3 ♖ac8 16 ♕e3 b5 17 e5 ± Psakhis-Pigusov, USSR 1979.

[5] 14 ♖ac1 ± Ivkov-Browne, Wijk aan Zee 1972.

[6] 10 ... ♕a5 11 a3 ♗e6 12 b4 ♕d8 13 ♖c1 ♖c8

14 ♘b5 a6 15 ♘d4 ±/± Savon-Tal, USSR 1972.

[7] 12 ... ♕xd2+ 13 ♔xd2 ♗d5 14 cd ♖fc8 15 ♖xc8 ♖xc8 16 g3! ♖c7 17 ♘h3 ♘d7 18 ♖c1 ♖xc1 19 ♔xc1 ± Kurajica-Huguet, Malaga 1976.

[8] 14 ♗e2 ♘g8 15 ♘d5 ± Schmidt-Andersson, Warsaw 1973.

[9] 7 ... ♘h6 8 g4 ♕a5+ 9 ♗d2 ♕e5 10 ♘c3 f5 11 f4 ± Euwe/Vreeken.

[10] 9 ♕d2 0-0 10 0-0 ♘c5 11 b3 f5 = Karpov-Kaplan, San Antonio 1972.

[11] Timman-Miles, Wijk aan Zee 1978. 13 ... ♘b4!?

[12] 10 ♘c3 0-0 =.

[13] Alexander-Botvinnik, Amsterdam Ol 1954.

[14] 7 ♘c3 0-0?! (7 ... d6 8 ♗e2 f5! = Kovačević-Barcza, Zagreb 1982) 8 ♗e2 d6 (8 ... f5 9 ef ♗xd4 10 ♗xh6! ♖xf5 11 0-0 ±/±) 9 0-0 f5 10 ef ♘xd4 11 ♗xd4 ♗xd4 12 ♕xd4 ♘xf5 13 ♕d2 ± Vilela-Estevez, Cienfuegos 1980.

[15] 7 ... f5 8 ef ♘xf5 9 ♘xf5! ± Unzicker-Filip, Baden Baden 1957.

[16] 12 f4 ♘xd4 13 ♗xd4 ± Petrosian-Heinicke, Vienna 1957.

[17] **14 f4!** ±.

14 ♘xc6!? ♖xc6 15 ♗h6 ♖ac8 16 ♗xg7 ♔xg7 19 ♕b2 f6 20 ♘d5 ±/± Kasparov-Ivanov, USSR 1978.

[18] 8 ... ♗xd4 9 ♗xd4 ♘xd4 10 0-0-0 e5 11 ♕g3 d6 12 f4 f6 13 f5! ♔f7 14 ♘b5! ♗xb5 15 cb ♕c7+ 16 ♔b1 ♗d7 (Mestel-Karlsson, Las Palmas IZ 1982) 17 ♖c1! ±.

[19] 9 ... ♘c6 10 ♕d2 ♕a5 11 ♖c1 0-0 12 ♗e2 d6 13 0-0 ♗e6 14 f4! ♖ac8 15 a3 f5 16 ef gf 17 ♖f3! ♔h8 18 ♗f2 ♗g8 19 ♖d1 ± Janošević-Udovčić, Yugoslavia 1962.

9 ... ♗e6 10 ♖c1 b6 (10 ... d6 11 b4! 0-0 12 ♗e2 a5 13 a3 ab 14 ab ♗d7 15 0-0 ♗c6 16 ♕d2 ± Portisch-Pfleger, Manila 1974) 11 ♗d3 ♗b7 12 ♖b1 0-0 13 0-0 d6 14 f4 ♘c5 15 f5! ±/± Olafsson-Hübner, Wijk aan Zee 1971.

[20] 10 ... ♘xb5 11 cb ♕e7 12 ♕d2 0-0 13 ♖d1 ♖d8 14 b6! a6 15 ♗c4 ± Neikirch-Szilagyi, Sofia 1957.

[21] 11 ♘xd4? ed 12 ♗xd4 ♕a5+ 13 ♔e2 ♖e8 14 f3 d5! 15 ♗xg7 ♖xe4+ 16 ♔f2 ♕c5+ 17 ♔g3 ♕e3 ∓∓ Euwe/Vreeken.

[22] 11 ... ♕e7 12 0-0-0! ±.

[23] 14 ♗xb5 ♕xe4 15 0-0 ♖d8 16 ♖fd1 (16 d6 ±) 16 ... ♕f5 (16 ... ♗e6? 17 f3!! ±± Penrose-Lees, British Ch 1965: 17 ... ♕xd5 18 ♕e2; 17 ... ♕h4 18 ♗g5) 17 ♖ac1 ♗d7 18 ♗e2 e4 19 ♖c7 ± Gufeld-Espig, Sukhumi 1972.

[24] 9 0-0 ♗b7 10 f3 ♘h5 intending ... ♘f4 = Gonzales-Fernandez, Buenos Aires Ol 1978.

[25] 10 ... ♘e8!? intending ... ♗xd4, ... e5.

[26] Nyman-Abramov, corr. 1967.

[27] 9 ... ♘xd4 10 ♗xd4 ♗e6 11 f4 ±.

[28] 10 ... a5 11 ♘db5 a4 12 f4 ♕a5 13 c5! ± Timman-Larsen, Las Palmas IZ 1982.

[29] Gheorghiu-Smejkal, Moscow 1981.

	Löwenthal	1 e4 c5 2 ♘f3 ♘c6 3 d4 cd 4 ♘xd4 e5								
	5	6	7	8	9	10	11	12	13	
1	♘xc6[1]	♗c4	♗g5	0-0	♗xf6	♘c3	♔h1	♕d2	♖ad1	∞
	bc	♘f6	♗c5	h6	♕xf6	a5	d6	g5	♔e7[2]	
2	♘b5	♘d6+	♕xd6	♕c7[4]	♘c3	♗d3	0-0	♘a4!	♕xc6+	±
	a6[3]	♗xd6	♕f6	♘ge7	♘b4	d5	d4	♕c6	♘exc6[5]	
3	...	...	...	♕d1[6]	♘c3	♘xd5[7]	♗e3[8]	♘c7+[9]	♖c1[10]	±
	...	...	...	♕g6	d5	♕xe4+	♘d4	♔e7	♗g4[11]	
4	...	...	...	...	h4	♗g5	ed	♗xe7		±
	...	...	...	...	♘ge7	h5	d5	♘b4	♔xe7[12]	

[1] **5** ♘b3 ♗b4+ 6 c3 ♗e7 =.

5 ♘f5 d5! 6 ♘xd5 ♕xd5 7 ed ♗xf5 8 dc bc =.

5 ♘f3 ♘f6 6 ♘c3 ♗b4 – 4 ... ♘f6 5 ♘c3 e5 6 ♘f3 ♗b4.

[2] 14 ♘a4 ♗d4 15 ♕d3 ∞ Macdonnell-Labourdonnais, match 1839.

[3] **5** ... ♘f6 6 ♘5c3 (6 ♗g5 ♗c5 7 ♘d6+?! ♗xd6 8 ♕xd6 ♘xe4, or 7 ♗xf6 ♕xf6 8 ♕d2 0-0 9 ♘c7 ♖b8 10 ♘d5 ♕g6 11 ♘1c3 b5! 12 ♗xb5 ♘d4 ∞ Nunn; 6 ♘1c3! ±) 6 ... h6 7 ♗e3 ♗b4 8 a3 ♕a5 9 ab! ♕xa1 10 ♕d6 ♘xe4 11 ♘xe4! ♕xb1+ 12 ♔d2 ♕xb2 13 b5 ♘b4 14 ♗c5! ∞ Nunn-Anthony, England 1981.

[4] **8** ♕xf6 ♘xf6 9 ♘c3 ♘b4 10 ♗d3 ♘xd3+ 11 cd h6! 12 ♗e3 d6 =.

8 ♗a3 ♘ge7 9 ♘c3 ♖b8 10 ♗e3 b5 11 ♘d5 ♘xd5 12 ed b4 ±.

[5] 14 ♘b6 ♖b8 15 f4 ±/= Boleslavsky.

[6] **8** ♕d2 ♕g6 9 ♘c3 d5 10 ♕g5! ±. 8 ... ♘ge7 9 ♘c3 d6 10 ♗c4 ±.

[7] **10** ed ♘b4 11 ♗d3 ♘xd3+ 12 ♕xd3 ♕xg2 13 ♕e4 ∞ Vogt.

10 ♕xd5 ♗e6 (10 ... ♘f6!?) 11 ♕c5 ♘f6 12 ♕e3 ♘b4 ∓.

[8] **11** ♘e3 ♘f6 12 ♗d3 ♗b4+ 13 c3 ♕e7 14 0-0 0-0 15 ♘f5 ♗xf5 16 ♗xf5 e4 ∓ Damjanović-Wittmann, Graz 1979.

11 ♗e2!?

[9] **12** c4!? ♘xc2+ 13 ♔d2 ♘xe3 14 fe ♘f6! 15 ♘xf6+ gf 16 ♕f3 ♗f5 ∞ Chiburdanidze.

[10] **13** ♕d3 ♘xc2+ 14 ♔d2 ♕xd3+! 15 ♗xd3 ♘xe3 16 ♘xa8 ♘d5! 17 ♖ac1 ♘gf6 18 ♘c7 ♘b4! (18 ... ♘f4 19 ♖he1 ♘xd3?! 20 ♔xd3 ± van der Wiel-Carlier, Dutch Ch 1980) 19 a3 ♘xd3 20 ♔xd3 ♗d7 intending ... ♗c6 ∓.

13 ♘xa8 ♘xc2+ 14 ♔d2 ♘xe3! 15 fe ♘f6! 16 ♖c1 ♘b4+ 17 ♔e2 ♗g4+ 18 ♔f2 ♖xa8 ∞ Zaitsev-Watzka, Graz 1979.

[11] 14 ♕d3 ♕xd3 15 ♗xd3 ♖d8 16 h3 ♗c8 17 f4! intending 0-0 ± Liberzon-Franzoni, Biel 1980.

[12] 14 d6+! ♔d8 15 ♗d3! ♘xd3+ 16 ♕xd3 ♕xd3 17 cd ±.

	Lasker-Pelikan		1 e4 c5 2 ♘f3 ♘c6 3 d4 cd 4 ♘xd4 ♘f6 5 ♘c3 e5						
	6	**7**	**8**	**9**	**10**	**11**	**12**	**13**	**14**	
1	♘f5	ed	dc	♗d3	♗e2	♗g5	♗h4[1]	♗g3		∓
	d5	♗xf5	bc	e4	♗d6	h6	g5	♗f4[2]		
2	♘f3[3]	♗c4	0-0	♘d5	♘xb4	c3	♕d3	♗b3	♗c2	=
	♗b4	0-0	d6[4]	h6	♘xb4	♘c6	♕c7	♘a5	d5![5]	
3	♘b3	♗c4[6]	0-0	♕d3	♕xc4	♘d5	♕xd5			=
	♗b4	d6![7]	♗e6	♗xc4	♖c8	♘xd5	0-0			
4	♘db5	♘d6+![9]	♕xd6	♘b5[10]	♘xd6+	♘f5+	b3	♗a3+	ed[12]	±
	h6[8]	♗xd6	♕e7	♕xd6[11]	♗e7	♔f8	d5	♔g8		
5	...	a4	♘a3	♘c4[15]	♗d3	♗e3	0-0	♖e1	♗e2	=
	d6[13]	a6	♗e6[14]	♖c8	♘b4	♗e7	0-0	♕c7	♕c5[16]	
6	...	♘d5	ed	c3	a4	♗d3				∞
	...	♘xd5	♘e7	♘f5[17]	♗e7	0-0[18]				
7	...	...	...	c4	♘c3	♗d3	♕xd3	0-0	♗e3	=
	...	...	♘b8	a6[19]	♗f5[20]	♗xd3	♗e7	0-0	♘d7[21]	
8	...	♗g5	♗xf6	♘d5[22]	c3[23]	♘a3	ed			∞
	...	♗e6	gf	♖c8	a6	♗xd5[24]	♘e7[25]			
9	...	...	♘d5	♘bc3[27]	♗xf6	ed	♗d3	0-0	♘b1	±
	...	...	♖c8[26]	♘xd5	♕xf6	♘d4	♕d8	♗e7	a6[28]	
10	...	...	♗xf6	♘a3	♘xd5!	ba	♗c4	♕d2	♔xd2	±
	...	a6	gf	d5[29]	♗xa3	♗e6[30]	♕a5+	♕xd2+[31]	0-0-0[32]	
11	...	...	...	...	♕h5[34]	♘axb5[35]	♗xb5	♗c4[36]	♘d5	∞/±
	...	...	...	f5[33]	b5!?	ab	♗b7	♕f6[37]	♕g6[38]	
12	...	...	...	...	...	0-0-0[39]	♘xd5[41]	ba	♗c4	±
	...	...	...	...	d5	♘d4[40]	♗xa3	♗e6	♖c8[42]	
13	...	...	♘a3	♘c4	♘e3[44]	♗xf6	♘cd5	c3	♗e2	∞/±
	...	...	♗e6[43]	♖c8	♗e7[45]	♗xf6	♗g5	0-0	g6[46]	
14	...	...	...	...	♗xf6	♘e3	♘ed5[49]	♗d3	♕h5	∞
	...	...	...	...	gf[47]	♗h6[48]	♘d4	♖g8	♖g6[50]	
15	...	...	...	...	...	♗d3!?	♘e3[52]	0-0	fe	±
	...	...	...	...	...	♘e7[51]	♗h6	♗xe3	♕b6[53]	

[1]   Lutikov-Sveshnikov, USSR 1976.
[2]   Sveshnikov.
[3]   6 ♘xc6 bc 7 ♗c4 ♗b4 8 ♗g5 ♗xc3+ 9 bc ♕a5! ∓ Gligorić/Sokolov.

   6 ♘de2 ♗c5 (6 ... d5 7 ed ♘b4 8 ♗g5 ♗c5 9 a3 ♗g4! 10 ♗xd8 ♗xf2+ =; 9 ♘g3 ±) 7 ♘g3 d6 8 ♗e2 ♗e6 9 0-0 a6 ∞.

[4]   8 ... ♗xc3 9 bc ♘xe4 10 ♗a3 d6 11 ♕e1 f5 12 ♖b1 ♕a5 13 ♘h4! (Domnitz-Kchouk, Varna Ol 1962) 13 ... ♕xa3 14 ♘xf5 ♘f6 ∞∞.

[5]   Ortega-Zinn, Berlin 1968.

[6]   7 ♗d3 d5! 8 ed ♘xd5 9 ♗d2 ♗xc3! =.

   7 ♗g5 h6 8 ♗xf6 ♗xc3+ 9 bc ♕xf6 10 ♗d3 ♘e7 = Marjanović-Urzica, Groningen 1972/73.

[7]   7 ... ♘xe4!? 8 0-0 (8 ♗xf7+?! ♔xf7 9 ♕d5+ ♔f8 10 ♕xe4 d5 =; 8 ♕d5!?) 8 ... ♘xc3 9 bc ♗e7 10 f4 (Spassky-Kagan, Student Ol 1955) 10 ... d6! ±.

   7 ... 0-0 8 0-0 ♗xc3 9 bc ♘xe4 10 ♗a3 d6 11 ♕d3! ± Kopayev-Korchnoi, USSR 1952.

[8]   Haberditz Variation.

   6 ... a6 7 ♘d6+ ♗xd6 8 ♕xd6 ♕e7 9 ♕d1 ±.

6 ... ♗c5 7 ♗e3! ♗xe3 8 ♘d6+ ♔f8 9 fe ♕b6 10 ♘c4 ♗c5 11 ♕d6+ ♔xd6 12 ♘xd6 ± Bivshev-Abramov, USSR 1951.

6 ... ♗b4 7 a3 ♗xc3+ 8 ♘xc3 d6 9 ♗g5 ±/±.

[9] 7 ♗c4 a6 8 ♘d6+ ♗xd6 9 ♕xd6 ♕e7 10 ♕xe7+ ♔xe7 = Karpov-Hug, Graz 1972.

[10] 9 ♕xe7+ ♔xe7 10 b3 ± Tringov-Gheorghiu, Bulgaria v Romania 1972.

[11] 9 ... 0-0 10 ♕xe7 ♘xe7 11 ♘d6 ± Marić. 9 ... ♘xe4? 10 ♘c7+ ±±.

[12] Spassky-Gheorghiu, Bath 1973.

[13] Pelikan Variation.

[14] 8 ... ♗g4!? 9 f3 ♗e6 10 ♗c4 ♗c8 ∞ Reinhardt-Pelikan, Argentinian Ch 1955.

[15] 9 ♗g5 ♖c8 10 ♘c4 ♘d4 11 ♗xf6 ♕xf6 12 ♘e3 = Savon-Tseshkovsky, Sochi 1975.

9 ♗c4 ♖c8 10 ♗g5 ♘b4 11 b3 ♗e7 12 ♗xf6 ♗xf6 13 0-0 0-0 = Price-Speelman, Israel 1977.

[16] Gufeld-Filipenko, USSR 1978.

[17] 9 ... ♘g6 10 ♕a4! ♗d7 11 ♕c4! ±/± Kisin.

[18] 11 ... ♘h4 12 0-0 ♘g6 13 f4! ± Gulko-Gurgenidze, USSR 1979.

11 ... 0-0 Gulko.

[19] 9 ... ♗e7 10 ♗d3 0-0 11 0-0 ♘d7 12 ♕c2 g6 13 ♗h6 ♖e8 14 f4 ± Chandler-Cramling, World Jr Ch 1977.

[20] 10 ... ♗e7 11 ♗e2 0-0 12 0-0 f5 13 f4 = Tal-Tseshkovsky, Riga IZ 1979.

[21] 15 b4 ♖c8 16 ♖fd1 f5 = Veselovsky-Chekhov, USSR 1978.

[22] 9 ♕d2 a6 10 ♘a3 b5 11 ♘d5 f5 12 ef ♗xf5 13 ♗d3 ♗e6 14 ♗e4 f5 15 ♗f3 h5! ∓ Hojnik-Zamecnik, Czechoslovakia v Poland corr. 1976.

[23] 10 ♘bc3 f5 11 ef ♗xf5 12 ♗d3 ♗e6 = Skacel-Zamecnik, corr. 1976.

[24] 11 ... b5 12 ♘c2 ♗g7 13 ♘ce3 ♖b8 14 ♗d3 ± R.Rodriguez-Kestler, Haifa Ol 1976.

[25] Intending ... f5, ... ♗g7, ... 0-0, ... ♕d7.

[26] 8 ... ♗xd5 9 ed ♘e7 10 c4 a6 11 ♘c3 ♘f5 12 ♗d3 ♘d4 13 0-0 ±/±.

[27] 9 ♗xf6 – row 8.

9 c4 a6 10 ♘bc3 ♘d4 11 ♗e3 ♗xd5 12 cd g6 13 ♗xd4 ed 14 ♕xd4 ♗g7 ∞∞.

[28] 15 a4 g6 16 c3 ♘f5 17 ♗xf5 gf ∓ Kupka-Polak, Poland 1976.

[29] Pelikan.

[30] 11 ... ♖g8 12 ♕d2 ♗e6 13 g3 (13 ♖b1!?) 13 ... f5 14 ♗g2 fe 15 ♗xe4 ♘d4 ∓ Rossetto-Pelikan, Mar del Plata 1956. 12 g3! f5 13 ef ♗xf5 14 ♗g2 ♕a5+ 15 c3! ± Suetin.

[31] 13 ... 0-0-0 14 ♖d1 ♕xa3 15 0-0 ♖hg8 16 ♕e3 ♕xe3 17 fe ♔b8 18 ♗b3 ♖g6 19 ♘b6 ± Fischer-Rossetto, Buenos Aires 1960.

[32] 15 ♖ad1 f5 16 f3 ♖hg8 17 g3 ♔b8 18 ♔e3 ± Stein-Benko, Curaçao 1970.

[33] Janowski.

[34] 10 ef ♗xf5 11 ♘d5 b5 – Chelyabinsk Variation.

10 ♗d3 ♗g7 11 0-0 fe 12 ♗xe4 0-0 ∓ Mukhin-Timoshenko, USSR 1979.

10 ♗c4!? ♕g5 (10 ... ♗g7 11 ♕h5 0-0 12 ef ♘d4 13 ♗d3 ± Fischer-Soltis, New York 1971) 11 g3 (Kirilov-Ilkov, Sofia 1973) 11 ... ♘d4!? ∞.

10 ♘c4 fe 11 ♘xe4 ♘d4 12 c3 d5 13 ♘xe5 de 14 ♕xd4 ♕xd4 15 cd f6 16 ♘c4 ♗e6 ∞∞ Bazen-Pelikan, Argentinian Ch 1961.

[35] 11 ♘d5 fe ∓.

11 ef b4 12 ♗c4 ♖a7! ∓ Harding/Markland.

[36] 13 ♕xf5 ♗g7 14 0-0-0 0-0 15 ♗xc6 ♗xc6 ∓ Levchenkov-Sveshnikov, Latvia v RSFSR 1969.

[37] 13 ... ♕d7 14 ♘d5 ♖d8 15 ♘c3 =.

[38] 15 ♘c7+ ♔d8 16 ♕xg6 fg 17 ♘xa8 ♗xa8 18 ♗d5 ♔c7 ∞/± Tarrasch-Janowski, Vienna 1898.

[39] 11 ♘c4 d4! ∓.

11 ♘xd5? ♗xa3 12 ba ♕a5+ 13 c3 ♗e6 ∓.

[40] 11 ... ♗xa3 12 ♘xd5 ♗e6 13 ♗c4 ♘d4 14 ♖he1 ♖c8 15 ♖xd4! ± Pripis-Malinin, USSR 1975.

[41] 12 ef ♗xf5! 13 ♖xd4? ed 14 ♕xf5 dc 15 ♕e5+ ♕e7 ∓∓ Harding/Markland.

[42] 14 ... ♕a5 15 ♖xd4 ed 16 ♕g5 ♕xa3+ 17 ♔d1 ± Hamilton.

14 ... ♖c8 15 ♖xd4! ed 16 ef! ♗xd5 17 ♖e1+ ± Hamilton-Davis, Australia 1975.

[43] Bird Variation.

[44] 10 ♘d5 ♗xd5 11 ♗xf6 gf 12 ♕xd5 b5!? 13 ♘e3 ♗h6! 14 ♕d2 ♘d4 15 c3 ♗xe3 ∞ Sznapik-Matulović, Smederevo 1981.

[45] 10 ... ♕b6!? 11 ♖b1 (11 ♗xf6!? ♕xb2 12 ♘cd5 ♗xd5 13 ♘xd5 ♘b4 14 ♗d3 ♘xd5 15 ed ♕c3+ 16 ♔f1 ∞∞) 11 ... ♘xe4! 12 ♘xe4 h6 13 c3! (13 ♕h5 d5 14 ♘d2 g6! 15 ♕h4 ♗g7 16 ♗f6 g5! ∓ Day) 13 ... hg 14 ♗c4 ♘d8 15 ♗b3 ∞∞ Benjamin-Ginsburg, New York 1981.

[46] Ciocaltea-Simić, Athens 1981.

[47] 10 ... ♕xf6?! 11 ♘b6! (11 ♘xd6+?! ♗xd6 12 ♕xd6 ♘d4 ∞∞) 11 ... ♖b8 12 ♘cd5 ± Karpov-Nunn, London 1982.

[48] 11 ... ♘e7 12 ♗d3 ♕b6 13 0-0 ♕xb2 14 ♘cd5 ♗xd5 15 ed ♕d4 16 ♕f3 ♕f4 17 ♕h3 (Lombardy-Markland, Nice Ol 1974) 17 ... ♕h6!? ∞. 16 ♖b1 ♖c7 ∞ Jansa-Matulović, Smederevo 1981.

[49] 12 ♘cd5 ♗xe3 13 ♘xe3 ♕b6 14 ♗d3 ♕b4+! 15 ♕d2 ♕xb2 16 0-0 ♕d4 17 ♖ab1 ∞∞/∞ Hakki-Tisdall, Hamar 1981.

12 ♗d3!? ♗xe3 13 fe ♕b6 14 ♕c1 ♖g8!? 15 0-0 ♖g6 ∞ Arnason-Tisdall, New York 1981.

[50] 15 h3 ♘d7! 16 ♔f1! ♖c6 17 a4 ♕g8 ∞ Grünfeld-Tisdall, New York 1981.

[51] 11 ... ♘d4? 12 ♘e3 intending ♘cd5, c3 ± Rodriguez.

[52] 12 ♕e2!? intending 0-0-0 A.Rodriguez.

[53] 15 ♕f3 h5! 16 ♘d5 ♗xd5 17 ed ♖h6 18 ♖ab1 ± Tseshkovsky-Chandler, Minsk 1982.

	9	10	11	12	13	14	15	16	17
16	♘d5[55]	♗xf6[57]	c3[58]	♘c2	a4	♖xa4	♗c4	0-0	ef	=
	♗e7[56]	♗xf6	0-0[59]	♗g5[60]	ba	a5	♔h8![61]	f5	♗xf5[62]	
17	♗xf6	♘d5	♗xb5	♘xb5	♘dc7+	♖xa8	♖f1	♕e2	♘ac7	∓
	gf	f5	ab	♕g5!?[63]	♔d8	♕xg2	♕xe4+	♕a4!	♘d4![64]	
18	...	...	♘xb5	♗xb5	ef	a4	♗xd7+	c3	♘e3	=
	...	...	ab	♗d7	♗g7	♘d4	♕xd7	♕b7	♗h6[65]	
19	...	...	♗d3	♕h5[66]	0-0	c4	♗xc4	♖ac1	b3	=
	...	...	♗e6	♗g7	f4	bc[67]	0-0	♖b8	♕d7[68]	
20	...	...	...	...	...	♔h1	♘b1	♘d2	g4[69]	±
	...	...	...	...	...	♖b8	h6	0-0		
21	...	...	ef	♗d3[70]	♕e2	♕e3	f3	g3	♕xf3	∞
	...	...	♗xf5	e4!	♘d4	♗g7	♕h4+	♘xf3+	ef[71]	
22	...	...	...	c3	♘c2	a4[72]	ab	♖xa8	♗xb5	=
	...	...	...	♗e6	♗h6	0-0	ab	♕xa8	♘d4![73]	
23	...	...	...	...	♘c2	♘ce3	g4[75]	♗g2	♕d3[77]	=
	...	...	...	...	♗g7	0-0[74]	♗e6	♘e7[76]	♖c8	♘xd5[78]	

[54]   Chelyabinsk Variation.

[55]   9 ♘ab1 ♗e7 10 ♗xf6 ♗xf6 11 a4 b4 12 ♘d5 ♗g5 13 ♗c4 0-0 14 0-0 ♗e6 (14 ... ♗b7 15 ♘d2 ♖c8 ∞ Mnatsakanian-Georgadze, Tbilisi-Sukhumi 1977) 15 ♘d2 ♘e7 16 ♘f3 ♗xd5 17 ♗xd5 ♘xd5 18 ♕xd5 ♗e7 = Rodriguez-Jokšić, Prshtina 1977.

[56]   9 ... ♗e6 10 ♗xf6 gf 11 c4 b4 12 ♕a4 ♗d7 13 ♘b5 ab 14 ♕xa8 ♕xa8 15 ♘c7+ ♔d8 16 ♘xa8 ∞/± Harding/Markland.
      9 ... ♕a5+ 10 ♗d2 ♕d8 11 ♘xf6+ ♕xf6 12 c4 (12 ♗d3 d5! 13 ed ♘b4 14 ♗e4 ♕h4 – Smyslov-Kuzmin, USSR Ch 1977 – 15 ♕e2 f5 16 d6! Tal) 12 ... ♕g6 13 f3 ♗e7 14 cb ♗h4+ 15 g3 ♗xg3+ 16 hg ♕xg3+ 17 ♔e2 ♘d4+ 18 ♔e3 f5 19 ef ♗xf5 20 ♗c3! ±/±. 11 c4!? ♘xe4 12 cb ♗e6 13 ♗c4 ± Belyavsky-van der Wiel, Moscow IZ 1982.

[57]   10 ♘xe7 ♘xe7 (10 ... ♕xe7 11 ♗d3 0-0 12 0-0 h6 13 ♗h4 ♗b7 14 c3 ♕e6 ½-½ Grünfeld-Adorjan, Riga IZ 1979) 11 ♗xf6 gf 12 c4 ♗b7 13 ♗d3 bc 14 ♗xc4 d5 15 ed ♕xd5 16 ♘d6+ ♔f8 = Ljubojević-Tseshkovsky, Riga IZ 1979.

[58]   11 c4 b4 12 ♘c2 a5 13 ♗e2 0-0 14 0-0 ♗g5 15 ♗g4 ♗e6 = Bennett-Speelman, London 1976.
      11 g3 0-0 12 ♗g2 ♗g5 13 0-0 ∞.

[59]   11 ... ♗g5 12 ♘c2 ♖b8 13 a4! ba 14 ♘cb4 ♘xb4 15 ♘xb4 0-0 16 ♘c6 ♕b6 17 ♘xb8 ♕xb2 18 ♗e2 ♕xc3+ 19 ♔f1 ♗e6 20 h4 ±± Nunn-Borik, Dortmund 1979.

[60]   12 ... ♖b8 13 ♗e2 ♗g5 14 0-0 ♗e6 15 ♕d3 f5 16 ♗f3 g6 = Sigurjonsson-Ligterink, Wijk aan Zee 1971.

[61]   15 ... ♖b8 16 ♖a2 ♔h8 17 ♘ce3! ♘e7 18 0-0 ± Tseshkovsky-Vukić, Banja Luka 1981.

[62]   Geller-Sveshnikov, USSR Ch 1977.

[63]   12 ... ♖a4 13 ♘bc7+ ♔d7 14 0-0 (14 c4 ♖xc4 15 ♕h5 ♘d4! 16 ♕xf7+ ♔c6 17 ♘b4+ ♔b7! 18 ♘b5+ ♕d7! ∓ Brüggeman-Gauglitz, West Germany 1982) 14 ... ♕g5! 15 c4 ♖g8 16 g3 ♖a7! ∞/∓ Dittmar-Antoskiewicz, corr. 1981. 13 c4!? ♕a5+ 14 b4 ♖xb4 15 0-0 ♖xc4 ∞ S.Szilayi-Müllner, corr. 1980.
      12 ... ♕a5+!? 13 c3 ♕a4 ∞.

[64]   18 ♘xd4 ed 19 ♕b5 ♕xc2 20 ♘d5 ♖h6 ∓ Honfi-Horvath, Subotica 1978.

[65]   18 cd ♗xe3 19 fe ♕xg2 20 ♖f1 ♕xb2 ½-½ Nunn-Adorjan, Skara 1980.

[66]   12 c4 ♕a5+ 13 ♔f1 fe 14 ♘xe4 ♗g7 15 ♘e3 ♖c8 16 ♕xd6 ♘d4 17 ♗b7 ♖d8 = Unzicker-Adorjan, Munich 1979.

[67]   14 ... b4 15 ♘c2 ± Pinkas-Weider, Polish Ch 1979.

[68]   18 ♖fd1 ♘d4 19 ♘c2 ♘xc2 20 ♖xc2 = Tukmakov-Sveshnikov, USSR Ch 1978.

[69]   Wedberg-Bouaziz, Gausdal 1980.

[70]   12 ♕f3 ♘d4 13 ♘c7+ ♕xc7 14 ♕xa8+ ♔e7 15 c3 b4 16 cb ♕b6! 17 ♖xa6 ♕xb4+ 18 ♔f1 ♕d2 19 h4! ♗h6 20 ♕b7+ ♔f6 21 ♖e1 = Kurkin-Azletsky, USSR 1978.

[71]   18 gh ♗xd3 19 cd ♗xb2 20 ♔f2 ♗xa1 21 ♖xa1 ♖c8 ∞/∓ Browne-Adorjan, Amsterdam 1978.

[72]   14 g4 0-0 15 ♗g2 ♕h4 16 ♘de3 ♖ac8 17 ♗e4 d5! ∓ Pinter-F.Portisch, Budapest 1976.
      14 g3!?

[73] Sigurjonsson-Sax, Ljubljana-Portorož 1977.
[74] 13 ... ♗e6 14 ♘ce3 (14 a4 0-0! 15 ab ab 16 ♖xa8 ♕xa8 17 ♗xb5 ♘d4! ∓ Rajna-Tisdall, Hastings 1976/77) 14 ... ♘e7 15 ♘xe7 ♕xe7 16 ♗e2 0-0 17 ♘f3 ♖ab8 18 ♕d2 e4 19 ♗xe4 d5! = Kaplan-Rocha, Sao Paulo 1977.
[75] 15 g3 f5 16 ♗h3 = Sigurjonsson-Rohde, New York 1977.
[76] 15 ... ♗h6 16 ♗g2 ♖a7 17 ♕f3 ♗xe3 18 ♘f6+ ♔g7 19 ♘h5+ ♔h8 20 ♕xe3 d5 (Stanciu-Sveshnikov, Bucharest 1976) 21 ♕h6 ♖g8 22 ♘f6 ♖g7 23 0-0-0 ±.

15 ... ♖a7 16 ♗g2 ♘e7 17 ♕d3! ♘xd5 18 ♗xd5 ±.
15 ... ♗xd5 16 ♘xd5 ♘e7 17 ♗g2 ♘xd5 18 ♗xd5 ♖a7 ∞ Suetin.
15 ... ♕h4 16 ♗g2 e4! 17 ♗xe4 ♘e5 18 h3 f5 19 ♗xf5 ♗xf5 20 gf ♕e4 21 ♘e7+ ♔h8 ∞ Trabattoni-Sveshnikov, Marina Romea 1977.
[77] 17 h4 ♘xd5 18 ♗xd5 ♕f6 ∞ Gheorghiu-Piasetski, Orense 1977.
[78] 18 ♗xd5 ♗xd5 19 ♘xd5 ♖c4! 20 ♘e3 ♖f4 21 h3 b4 22 c4 = Ciocaltea-Tatai, Amsterdam 1976.

Sicilian 2 ... e6: Introduction   1 e4 c5 2 ♘f3 e6

	3	4	5	6	7	8	9	10	11	
1	b3[1]	e5	♗b2[2]	c4	h4	g3	♗g2	0-0!?[3]	♘xe5	∞
	♘f6	♘d5	♘c6	♘f4	h5	♘g6	♕c7	♘gxe5	♘xe5[4]	
2	...	♗b5+[5]	0-0	♖e1	♗f1[6]	c4	♘c3	d4	♘xd4	=
	d6	♘d7	♘f6	♗e7	b6	♗b7	0-0	cd	a6[7]	
3	d4	♘xd4	♗d3	♘xc6	0-0[11]	♘d2	♕e2	g3	c4	=
	cd	♘f6[8]	♘c6[9]	bc[10]	d5	♗d6	♕c7	0-0	♖e8[12]	

1 e4 c5 2 ♘f3 e6 3 d4 cd 4 ♘xd4 ♘f6 5 ♘c3 ♗b4 6 e5[13] ♘d5[14]

	7	8	9	10	11	12	13	14	15	
4	♗d2	bc	♗d3	ed	♕h5	♕xd5				=
	♘xc3	♗a5	d6[15]	♕xd6	♕d5	ed[16]				
5	♕g4	♗d3[18]	0-0!	bc	♖b1	♘b5	♗a3+	♖fd1	♘d6[19]	∞/±
	♔f8[17]	d6	♘xc3	♗xc3	de	♗a5	♔g8	♕f6		
6	...	a3	bc	♕g3	♗e2	♗e3	♖d1			∞
	g5!?	♗xc3+	♕c7	♘f4![20]	♕xe5	♘c6				

[1] 3 ♘c3 ♘c6 4 ♗b5 - 2 ... ♘c6 3 ♗b5 ♘f6 4 ♘c3.
3 g3 b6 4 ♗g2 ♗b7 5 ♘c3 d6 6 0-0 ♘f6 7 d4 cd 8 ♘xd4 ♗e7 9 f4 ♕d7 ∞.
[2] 5 ♗c4 b6 6 ♘c3 ♘xc3 7 dc ♘c6 8 ♗f4 ♗e7 9 ♕d2 0-0 10 0-0-0 f6 11 ef gf 12 ♗d6± Kaspret-Hoeksema, European Jr Ch 1980.
[3] 10 ♕e2!?
[4] 12 d4 cd 13 ♕xd4 ♘g4 14 ♘c3 ∞ Cuartas-Hess, Dortmund 1980.
[5] 4 ♗b2 ♘f6 5 ♗b5+ ♘bd7 6 ♕e2 ♗e7 7 0-0 0-0 8 c3 a6 = Böhnisch-Hesse, E Germany 1980.
[6] 7 c3 a6 8 ♗f1 b5 9 d4 ♗b7 10 ♗d3 ♕c7 11 ♗b2 c4 12 ♗c2 e5 13 ♘bd2 0-0 14 ♕e2 ± Makarichev-Lerner, USSR Ch 1979. 11 ... e5 =.
[7] 12 ♗b2 ♖e8 13 ♕d2 ♗c7 14 ♖ad1 ♖ad8 = Paulsen-Gheorghiu, London 1980.
[8] 4 ... ♗c5 5 ♗b3 ♗b6 6 ♘c3 ♘e7 7 ♗f4 0-0? 8 ♗d6 f5?! 9 e5 ± Timman-Basman, Hastings 1973/74 and Morphy-Paulsen, New York 1857. 7 ... d5!? ∞.
[9] 5 ... a6 - 4 ... a6.
[10] 6 ... dc 7 0-0 e5 8 ♔h1 ♗e6 9 f4 ef 10 ♗xf4 ♗e7 11 ♘d2 ♘d7 =.
[11] 7 c4 e5! 8 0-0 ♗e7 9 ♘c3 0-0 10 ♗e3 d6 11 f3 ♗e6 12 ♕c2 ♕c7 = Karaklaić-Lengyel, Reggio Emilia 1979/80.
[12] Radulov-Nunn, Malta Ol 1980.
[13] 6 ♗d3 e5 7 ♘f5 0-0 8 ♘e3 d6! 9 0-0 ♗e6 10 ♗d2 ♗c5 = Taimanov.
[14] 6 ... ♘e4 7 ♕g4 ♘xc3 (7 ... ♕a5 8 ♕xg7 ♗xc3+ 9 bc ♕xc3+ 10 ♔e2 ±) 8 ♕xg7 ♖f8 9 a3 ♘b5+ 10 ab ♘xd4 11 ♗g5 ♕b6 12 ♗h6 ♕xb4+ 13 c3 ± Szabo-Mikenas, Kemeri 1939.
[15] 9 ... ♘c6 10 ♘xc6 dc 11 0-0 ♕c7 12 ♖e1 ♗d7 13 ♕g4 g6 14 ♕g5 ± Levchenkov-Zhuravlev, Latvian Ch 1980.
[16] Adorjan-Bednarski, Polanica Zdroj 1971.
[17] 7 ... 0-0!?
[18] 8 a3 ♗a5 9 ♗d2 ♘xc3 10 bc ♕c7 11 ♕g3 ♘c6 12 f4 ♘xd4 13 cd ± Boleslavsky.
[19] Veröci-Glaz, Malta Ol 1980.
[20] 10 ... ♘xc3+ 11 ♕xc3 ♘xc3 12 ♗xg5 ±.
10 ... ♘f4 Taimanov.

2 ... e6: 4 Knights   1 e4 c5 2 Nf3 e6 3 d4 cd 4 Nxd4 Nf6 5 Nc3 Nc6

	6	7	8	9	10	11	12	13	14	
1	Be2[1]	0-0	bc	Bd3	Ba3	cd	Qc1	Rb1	Bb4	∞
	Bb4[2]	Bxc3[3]	Nxe4	d5	Nxd4	Qa5	Bd7	Bc6	Qc7[4]	
2	g3	ed[6]	Bg2	Nxc6	Kxd1	Be3	Na4			=
	d5[5]	Nxd5	Ndb4[7]	Qxd1+	bc[8]	Be7	e5[9]			
3	Ndb5	Bf4	Qf3[11]	Nc7+	0-0-0[12]	bc	Qxe4	Bxc7	Bb5	±
	Bb4[10]	Nxe4	d5	Kf8	Bxc3	g5[13]	Qxc7	de	Kg7[14]	
4	...	a3	Nxc3	ed[15]	Bd3	0-0	Ne2	Bf4	c4	±
	...	Bxc3+	d5	ed	0-0	d4!	Qd6	Qd5	dc[16]	
5	Nxc6	e5	Ne4	f4	Bd3[19]	Qe2	ef	Nxf6+	c3	∓
	bc	Nd5	Qc7![17]	Qb6[18]	Be7[20]	f5[21]	Nxf6	Bxf6	Rb8	
6	...	...	...	...	c4	Ke2	Nf2!	Bf3	Be3	=
	...	...	...	...	Bb4+	f5	Ba6[22]	Ne7	Bc5[23]	

[1] 6 Bg5!? Qa5 (6... Be7!?; 6... h6!?) 7 Bxf6 gf 8 Nb5 ± Radulov-Skrobek, Pamporovo 1981.
6 Be3 Bb4!? (6 ... d6 – Scheveningen) 7 Nxc6 bc 8 e5 Nd5 9 Bd2 Qc7 10 f4 Qb6 11 Qf3 0-0 ∞ Spassky-Hübner, Tilburg 1981.

[2] 6 ... d6 – Scheveningen.

[3] 7 ... 0-0 8 Nxc6 bc 9 e5 Nd5 =.

[4] 15 Qa3 a5 16 Bxe4 de 17 c4 f6 18 Bd6 Qd7 ∞ Geller-Hasin, USSR 1961.

[5] 6 ... d6 – Scheveningen.

[6] 7 Bg2 Qb6 8 Be3 Bc5 (8... Qxb2? 9 Ndb5 ±) 9 Na4 Qa5+ 10 c3 Bxd4 11 Bxd4 = Romanishin-Tseshkovsky, Tallinn 1979.

[7] 8 ... Nxc3 9 bc Qxd4 10 Qxd4 Be7 11 Qxd8+ Bxd8 ± Dolmatov-Sveshnikov, USSR 1979.

[8] 10 ... Nxc6 =.

[9] Jansa-Sveshnikov, Sochi 1980.

[10] 6 ... d6 7 Bf4 e5 8 Bg5 – Lasker-Pelikan.

[11] 8 Nc7+ transposes to the row.

[12] 10 Nxa8 e5! 11 Bg3 Nd4! ∓.

[13] 11 ... Rb8 12 Bc4! ∞/± Pickett.

[14] 15 h4! g4 16 Rhe1 ± Urzica-Ilijin, Romanian Ch 1974.

[15] 9 Bd3 Ne5! 10 Be2 Nxe4 11 Nxe4 de 12 Qxd8+ Kxd8 13 Bf4 Nc6 14 0-0-0+ Ke8 = Nezhmetdinov-Ilivitsky, USSR 1952.

[16] 15 Nxc3 Qd4 16 Ne2 Qd5 17 Qc2 Be6 18 Rad1 Qb3 =.

[17] 8 ... f5 9 Nd6+ (9 ef Nxf6 10 Nd6+ Bxd6 11 Qxd6 Qb6 12 Bd3 c5 13 Bf4±; 11 ... Ba6 12 Bxa6 Qa5+ 13 Bd2 ±) 9 ... Bxd6 10 ed Qb6 11 c4 ± Byrne-Day, Buenos Aires Ol 1978.

[18] 9 ... f5!? 10 ef Nxf6 11 Nxf6+ gf 12 Qh5+ Kd8 13 Bd2 ± Kurajica-Rossolimo, Montilla 1972.

[19] 10 Qf3 Be7 11 Bd3 Ba6 12 Bxa6 Qxa6 13 Bd2 f5 ∓ Polugayevsky.

[20] 10 ... Ba6 11 a3 Be7 12 Qe2 Bxd3 13 Qxd3 f5 14 Nf2 Bc5 15 0-0 a5 ∓ Tseshkovsky-Sveshnikov, USSR 1978.

[21] 11 ... 0-0?! 12 c4 f5 13 cd! fe 14 Qxe4 Qb4+ ± Spassky-Adorjan, Baden 1980.

[22] 12 ... Bc5 13 Nd3 Be3 14 Qb3! Nxf1 15 Qxb6 Bxb6! =/∞ A.Ivanov-Peshina, USSR 1981.

[23] 15 Bxc5 Qxc5 16 Qd6 Qb6 17 b3 c5 Gorelov-Sveshnikov, USSR 1981.

Taimanov   1 e4 c5 2 Nf3 e6 3 d4 cd 4 Nxd4 Nc6

	5	6	7	8	9	10	11	12	13	
1	Nb5[1]	c4[2]	N5c3	Be2	0-0	Bf4	Nd2	Re1	Rc1	=
	d6	Nf6	Be7	0-0	b6	Bb7	Rc8[3]	Qd7	Rfd8[4]	
2	...	...	N1c3	Na3	Be2	0-0	Be3	f4[6]	Bf3	=
	...	...	a6	Be7	0-0	b6	Ne5!?[5]	Ned7	Bb7[7]	
3	Nc3	g3[8]	Bg2	0-0	Nxc6[9]	Be3	Na4	Bh3!	Bxd7	±
	a6	Qc7	Nf6	h6?!	dc	e5	Nd7	b5	Bxd7[10]	

	5	6	7	8	9	10	11	12	13	
4	...	...	...	...	♖e1	♕xd4	♕d1	h3!?	♗e3	=
	...	...	...	♗e7	♘xd4	♗c5	d6	♘d7!	0-0[11]	
5	...	♗e3	♗d3	0-0	h3[13]	f4!?	♘f5!	♘xg7+	♗xc5	∞
	...	♕c7[12]	♘f6	♘e5	♗c5	♘c6	♗e7!	♔f8	♕xc5+[14]	
6	...	...	...	♕e2	g3	♘b3	f4	bc	c4	∞
	...	...	...	♗d6[15]	♗e5	0-0	♗xc3+	d6	b6[16]	
7	...	...	♗e2	0-0	♘a4	c4	♕c2!	c5!		±
	...	...	♘f6	♗b4[17]	♘e7[18]	♘xe4	f5	♘d5[19]		
8	...	♗e2	♗f4[20]	♘xc6[21]	♗d6	♕xd6	0-0-0	♖xd6	♖hd1	±
	...	♘ge7	♘g6	bc	♗xd6	♕e7	♕xd6	♔d8	♔c7[22]	
9	...	...	♘b3	♘xa5[24]	0-0	a3	♗e3	f4	♕e1[25]	=
	...	...	♘a5[23]	♕xa5	♘c6	d6	♗e7	0-0		

---

[1] 5 c4 ♘f6 6 ♘c3 ♗b4 7 ♘xc6 (7 f3 d5) 7 ... bc 8 ♗d3 e5 =.

[2] 6 ♗f4 e5 7 ♗e3 ♘f6 8 ♗g5 ♗e6 (8 ... ♕a5+ 9 ♕d2! ±) 9 ♘d2 ♗e7 10 ♗xf6 ♗xf6 11 ♘c4 0-0 12 ♕xd6 ♕c8 = Peresipkin-Timoshenko, USSR 1973.

[3] 11 ... ♘e5 12 ♖e1 ♘g6 13 ♗g3 ♕d7 14 a3 ♖fd8 =.

[4] Gipslis-Averbakh, USSR 1978.

[5] 11 ... ♗b7!? 12 ♕b3! ♘d7 13 ♖fd1 ♗c5 14 ♕c2 ♗f6 15 ♖ac1 ♘e5 16 ♘ab1 ± Karpov-Olafsson, Amsterdam 1976.
11 ... ♗d7!?
11 ... ♕c7!?

[6] 12 f3!? ♗b7 13 ♕e1 ♖e8 14 ♕f2 ♘ed7! = Tal-Polugayevsky, match 1980.
12 ♕b3!? ♘ed7 13 ♖fd1 ♗b7 14 f3 ♖c8 15 ♔h1 ♖e8 16 ♖d2 ± Gufeld-N.Popov, USSR 1980.

[7] 14 ♕e2 ♕c7 (14 ... ♖e8!?) 15 ♖ac1 ♖ac8 16 g4 ♘c5 17 ♔g2 (Tseshkovsky-Kasparov, Minsk 1979) 17 ... d5! ∞.

[8] 6 ♗e2 ♘xd4 7 ♕xd4 ♘e7 8 ♗f4 ♘c6 9 ♕d2 b5 (9 ... ♕a5 10 0-0 ♘e5 11 a3 ♗e7 12 ♗e3 ♕c7 13 ♕d4 0-0 14 ♕b6 ± Krogius-Chukayev, USSR 1963) 10 0-0 ♗e7 11 ♖ad1 ± Boleslavsky-Táimanov, USSR 1967.

[9] 9 ♘b3! d6 10 a4 ♗e7 11 a5 0-0 12 ♗e3 ♘e5 13 ♗b6 ♕b8 14 ♕e2 (14 ♘d2!?) 14 ... ♘fd7 15 ♘a4 ♘xb6 16 ♘xb6 ♖a7 (Popović-Rajković, Kladovo 1980) 17 ♘d2! ±.

[10] 14 ♘b6 ± Popović-Cebalo, Yugoslav Ch 1980.

[11] 14 ♕d2 ♘e5 15 ♗xc5 ♕xc5 = Shamkovich-Timman, Rio de Janeiro IZ 1979.

[12] 6 ... ♘f6 7 ♗d3 d5 8 ed ed 9 0-0 ♗d6! 10 ♘xc6?! (10 ♗e2/h3) 10 ... bc 11 ♗d4 0-0

[12] ♕f3!? ♗e6 13 ♖fe1 c5 14 ♗xf6 ♕xf6 15 ♕xf6 gf 16 ♖ad1 ♖fd8 = Spassky-Fischer, match 1972.

[13] 9 ♘f3!? d6 10 a4 b6 11 ♘d2 ♗b7 12 ♗e2 (Ljubojević-Najdorf, Buenos Aires, 1979) 12 ... ♗e7 13 f4 ♘ed7 =.

[14] 14 ♔h1 ♔xg7 15 e5 =/∞ Monin-Loginov, USSR 1978.

[15] 8 ... b5 9 0-0 ♗b7 10 h3 ♗e7 (10 ... ♘e5!?) 11 f4 d6 12 ♘f3 0-0 13 a3 ± Romanishin-Balashov, USSR Ch 1979.

[16] Rajna-Jansa, Sarajevo 1979.

[17] 8 ... d6 – Scheveningen.

[18] 9 ... 0-0 10 ♘xc6 bc 11 ♘b6 ♖b8 12 ♘xc8 ♖fxc8 13 ♗xa6 ♖d8 14 ♗d3 ♗d6 15 ♔h1 ♗e5 16 c3 ♖xb2 17 ♕c1 ♘g4 18 f4 ♘xe3 19 ♕xb2 ♗xf4 20 ♕f2 ± Tal-Liberzon, Skara 1980.

[19] Kolker-Semeniuk, corr. 1979. 13 ♗h5+! g6 14 ♗f3 ±.

[20] 7 ♗e3 b5 8 0-0 ♘xd4 9 ♕xd4 ♘c6 10 ♕d2 ♗e7 11 ♖ad1 0-0 12 f4 d6 13 ♗d3 (Velimirović-Bukić, Vrbas 1980) 13 ... ♗b8 =.
7 f4 b5 8 0-0 ♗b7 9 ♔h1 (9 ♘b3!?) 9 ... ♘xd4 10 ♕xd4 ♘c6 11 ♕f2 ♗e7 12 ♗e3 0-0 13 ♖ad1 ♖c8 14 ♗f3 (14 a4!? b4 15 ♘b1 ♗b8) 14 ... ♘b8!? = Gufeld-Vasyukov, USSR 1975.

[21] 8 g3 ♗e7 9 0-0 (9 ♘b3!?) 9 ... d6 10 ♕d2 0-0 11 ♖ad1 ♕b6 12 ♘b3 ♖d8 13 ♔h1 ♕c7 14 a4 ♗f8 15 f4 ♗d7 16 ♗h5! ± Balashov-Olafsson, Buenos Aires 1980.

[22] 14 g3 (Adorjan-G.Garcia, Banja Luka 1979) 14 ... ♘e7!? 15 ♖6d2 d5 ±.

[23] 7 ... ♘g6 8 ♗e3 b5 9 0-0 ♕c7 10 ♕d2 (Sisniega-Romanishin, Mexico 1980) 10 ... ♗e7 11 ♖ad1 0-0 12 f4 d6 13 ♗d3!? =.

[24] 8 0-0!? ∞.

[25] Ivanović-Bukić, Vrbas 1980.

	5	6	7	8	9	10	11	12	13	
1	g3	♘f3	ed	♗g2	0-0	♘c3	♘d4			=
	d5	♘f6	ed	♘c6	♗e7	0-0[1]				
2	♗e2	♘c3	♕d3[2]	e5	0-0	bc	c4	♕e3	♗a3	∞
	♘f6	♗b4	d5	♘e4	♗xc3	♘d7	0-0	♖e8	♕a5[3]	
3	♘d2	e5	♗c4[5]	ed	0-0	♘2f3	♕e2	♗g5	h3	=
	♘f6[4]	♘d5	d6	♘f6	♗xd6	♕c7	♕c7	♘g4	♘e5[6]	
4	c4	♘c3	♘c2	bc	♕d3[8]	f3	♗a3	♕e3	f4	∞∞
	♘f6	♗b4[7]	♗xc3+	♕a5	♕e5	d5	de	♘c6	♕a5[9]	
5	...	...	e5	♕g4	a3	bc	♕g3	ed	♕xd6	=
	...	...	♘e4[10]	♘xc3	♗f8	♕a5	d6	♗xd6!	♕xc3+[11]	
6	...	...	♗d2	e5	♗xc3	♕c2[12]	ed	♕xc3	0-0-0	=
	...	...	0-0	♗xc3	♘e4	d5	♘xc3	♕xd6	♕f4+[13]	
7	...	...	♗d3	♘c2![14]	bc	ed	♗a3	♕e2	0-0	=
	...	...	♘c6	♗xc3+	d5	ed	♗e6	♕c7	0-0-0![15]	
8	♘c3	♗d3	0-0	♕h5	♘xc6	♗f4	♗g3	a4	♘d5	±
	b5	♗b7	♘e7[16]	♘bc6[17]	♗xc6	♘g6	♕b6	b4	♗xd5[18]	
9	...	g3	♗g2	0-0	f4	g4	♘xc6[20]	g5	f5[21]	∞/∓
	♕c7	♘f6[19]	♗e7	0-0	d6	♘c6	bc	♘e8	ef[22]	
10	...	♗e2	f4	e5	0-0	bc	♘b3	♗b2	f5	∞∞
	...	♘f6	♗b4	♘e4	♘xc3	♕xc3	♕c7	♘c6	♗e7[23]	
11	...	...	0-0	♕d3	♘xc6	f4	e5	♕h3	bc	±
	...	...	♗b4[24]	♘c6	dc[25]	0-0	♖d8	♗xc3	♘d7[26]	
12	...	...	♗f3	0-0	♘xc6[27]	a4	ab[28]	e5	♘xb5	=
	...	b5	♗b7	♘c6	dc	♗d6	cb	♗xe5	ab[29]	
13	...	f4	a3	♗d3	♘b3	0-0	♗e3	♕f3		=
	...	b5	♗b7	♘c6	d6	♘f6	♗e7	0-0[30]		
14	...	♗d3	0-0	♖e1	♗g5	♗xf6	♘d5	ed+	♕f3	±
	...	b5	♗b7	d6[31]	♘f6[32]	gf	ed	♔d8	♗e7[33]	
15	...	...	♘xc6[34]	0-0	♕e2	♗g5[36]	f4	e5	♗xe7	±
	...	♘c6	bc	♘f6	d5[35]	♗b7	♗e7	♘d7	♔xe7[37]	

[1] Czerniak-Gheorghiu, Bucharest 1966.

[2] 7 0-0 ♗xc3 8 bc ♘xe4 9 ♗f3 ♘c5 10 ♗a3 (Soloviev-Moiseyev, USSR 1956) 10 ... ♕c7 11 ♘b3 d6 12 ♕d4 e5 ∓ Taimanov.

[3] 14 cd ed ∞ Evans-Portisch, Stockholm IZ 1952.

[4] 5 ... d6 6 ♗d3 ♘f6 7 0-0 ♗e7 8 c4 0-0 9 b3 ♘bd7 10 ♗b2 ♕c7 11 ♖c1 b6 12 ♕e2 ♗b7 13 ♗b1 ♖fe8 14 ♖fd1 ± Kapengut-Grigorian, USSR Ch 1971.

[5] 7 ♗d3 ♕c7 8 0-0 ♕xe5 9 ♘f5 ♕c7 10 ♖e1 ♘e7 11 ♕f3 ♘xf5 12 ♗xf5 ♘c6 ∞ Sydor-Gipslis, Lublin 1969.

[6] 14 ♘xe5 ♗xe5 = Geller-Gipslis, Sousse IZ 1967.

[7] 6 ... ♕c7 7 a3 b6 (7 ... ♘c6!? 8 ♗e3 ♗e7 9 ♖c1 ♘e5 10 ♗e2 ♘g6 11 0-0 b6 ±/= Torre-Karpov, Bad Lauterberg 1977) 8 ♗d3 ♗b7 9 0-0 ♘c6 10 ♘xc6 ♗xc6 11 ♕e2 ♗e7 12 f4 ± Krnić-Taimanov, Vrnjačka Banja 1974) 12 ... ♗c5+ 13 ♔h1 ♗d4 14 ♗d5! ±.

6 ... d6 7 ♗e2 ♗e7 8 ♗e3 0-0 9 0-0 ♘bd7 10 ♖c1 ♖e8 11 f4 ♗f8 12 ♘b3! ± Barua-Gheorghiu, London 1981.

[8] 9 f3 d5 10 cd ed 11 e5 ♕xc3+ 12 ♗f2 ♘fd7 13 ♗a3 ♘c6 ∓ Hasin-Furman, USSR 1957.

[9] 14 ♗e2 e5 15 0-0 ef 16 ♖xf4 ∞ Kertesz-Forintos, Hungary 1966.

[10] 7 ... ♕a5 8 ef ♗xc3+ 9 bc ♕xc3+ 10 ♕d2 ♕xa1 11 ♗e2 ♘c6! 12 fg ♖g8 13 ♘xc6 bc! 14 0-0 ♕xg7 15 g3 d5 16 ♗a3 ♕g5 17 ♕b4 ♕d8 18 cd cd 19 ♖c1 ± (Nielsen-Arlauskas, corr. 1959) 19 ... ♗d7 20 ♖c7 ♖c8 21 ♖b7 ♖c6 22 ♗h5 ± Boleslavsky. 20 ... ♖b8!? 21 ♕d6 ♖c8! 22 ♖b7 ♖c6 23 ♕b4 ±/∞.

[11] 14 ♗d2! ♕xa1+ 15 ♔e2 ♕b2 16 ♔e3 ♘c6 17 ♘xc6 ♕b6+ 18 ♕d4 ♕xc6 19 ♕xg7 ♕c5+ = Berczy-Neistadt, corr. 1959.

[12] 10 ♗b4 d6 11 ♕e2 ♕b6 12 ♘c2 ♘c6 13 a3 d5! 14 f3 ♘c5 15 ♕e3 d4 16 ♘xd4 ♘xb4 17 ab ♕xb4+ = Korchnoi-Furman, USSR 1957.

[13] 14 ♕e3 ♕xe3+ 15 fe ♘d7 = Boleslavsky-Kotov, USSR Ch 1957.

[14] 8 ♗c2 ♕c7 9 0-0 0-0! (9 ... ♘xd4 10 ♕xd4 ♘g4 11 e5 ♘xe5 12 ♘e4! ±/± Chiburdanidze-Fischdick, Belgrade 1979) 10 ♗g5 (10 ♔h1 ♘xd4 11 ♕xd4 ♘g4! 12 f4 ♗c5 13 ♕d3 ♘f2+ 14 ♖xf2 ♗xf2 15 e5 g6 16 ♘e4 ♗h4 17 ♗d2 b5! ∓/∓ Mestel-Miles, British Ch 1979) 10 ... ♗e7!? (10 ... ♘xd4 11 ♗xf6! ± Dimitrov-Popov, Bulgarian Ch 1961).

8 ♘xc6 dc 9 e5 ♕a5 10 ef ♗xc3 11 bc ♕xc3+ 12 ♗d2 (12 ♕d2 ♕xa1 13 fg ♕xg7 14 0-0 e5 15 f4 ♗g4 ∞ Tal) 12 ... ♕xd3 13 fg ♖g8 14 ♗h6 ♕c3+ 15 ♔f1 ♕f6! 16 ♕c1 e5 ∞ Paulsen-Farago, Svendborg 1981.

[15] 14 c5 ♖he8 15 ♘d4 ♘e4 16 ♗xe4 de 17 ♕xe4 ♘xd4 18 cd ♗c4 19 ♕g4+ ♕d7 = Khachaturov-Kan, USSR 1955.

[16] 7 ... b4 8 ♘a4 ♘f6 9 ♖e1 d5 10 e5 ♘e4 11 c4 ♘c5 12 ♘xc5 ♗xc5 13 ♗e3 ♘d7 14 ♕g4 ± Bikhovsky-Suetin, USSR 1966.

7 ... d6 8 ♖e1 ♘d7 9 a4 ba 10 ♖xa4 ♘gf6 11 ♗d2 ♗e7 12 ♘b3 0-0 13 ♘a5 ± Keres-Najdorf, Los Angeles 1963.

[17] 8 ... ♗g6 9 ♘f3 ♘c6 10 ♗e3 ♕c7 11 ♘g5 ±.

[18] 13 ... ed?! 14 ed ♗b7 15 ♖fe1+ ♔d8 16 ♗xg6 fg 17 ♕e5 ± Taimanov.

13 ... ♗xd5 14 ed ♗e7 (Suetin-Gipslis, USSR 1966) 15 a5 ♕c5 16 ♕e2 ±.

[19] 6 ... b5 7 ♗g2 ♗b7 8 0-0 ♘f6 9 ♖e1 d6 10 a4 b4 11 ♘d5 ed 12 ed+ ♔d8 13 ♗g5 ♗c8 14 ♗xf6+ gf 15 ♕h5 ± Quinones-Higashi, Siegen Ol 1970.

6 ... ♗b4 7 ♗e2 ♗e7 8 ♗g2 ♘f6 9 0-0 ♘c6 10 h3 d6 ∞ Kudrin-Kavalek, US Ch Z 1981.

[20] 11 ♘b3 b5 12 g5 ♘d7 13 a3 ♗b7 14 ♕h5 ♖fe8 ∞ Padevsky-Neikirch, Varna 1972.

[21] 13 ♗e3 ♖b8 14 b3 d5 15 f5 ♗d6 16 ♕h5 ef 17 ed ♗e5 = Garcia-Gheorghiu, Bucharest 1971.

[22] 14 ef d5 ∞/∓ Browne-Quinteros, Mar del Plata 1971.

[23] 14 f6 gf 15 ef ♗f8 16 ♗h5 d6 ∞∞ Jansa-Castro, Lugano Ol 1968.

[24] 7 ... d6 – Scheveningen.

[25] 9 ... bc!? 10 ♗g5 d5 11 f4 ♗b7 12 f5 0-0 13 ♗xf6 gf 14 ♕h3 ♔h8! 15 ♕h6 ♕e5 ∓ Lanz-Suetin, Brno 1975.

[26] 14 ♗e3 ± Olafsson-Pilnik, match 1957.

[27] 9 ♖e1 ♗d6!? (9 ... ♘e5 10 ♗f4 d6 11 a4 ba 12 ♗h5! g6 13 ♗e2 ♘f6 14 ♖xa4 ± Panchenko-Agzamov, Vilnius 1978) 10 g3 ♘xd4 11 ♕xd4 ♗e5 12 ♕d3 ♘e7! =/∞ Panchenko-Miles, Las Palmas 1978.

[28] 11 g3! ♘e5 (11 ... ♘f6!?) 12 ♗g2 ♘f6 13 f4 ♖ad8 14 ♕f3 ± Liberzon-Torre, Bad Lauterberg 1977.

[29] 14 ♖xa8+ ♗xa8 15 ♗xa8 ♗xh2+ 16 ♔h1 ♗d6 = Estrin-Polugayevsky, USSR 1964.

[30] Franco-Miles, Buenos Aires 1980.

[31] 8 ... ♘c6 9 ♘xc6 ♕xc6 10 a4 b4 11 ♘d5 ♘f6 12 ♗d2 ♘xd5 13 ed ♕c5 14 ♗e4 f5 15 ♗f3 ± Tal-Gipslis, USSR Ch 1958.

[32] 9 ... ♗e7 10 ♗xe7 ♘xe7 11 ♗xb5 ab 12 ♘dxb5 ♕b6 13 ♘d6+ ♔f8 14 ♘xb7 ±± Taimanov.

[33] 14 ♘f5 ♖e8 15 ♗xe7 ♖xe7 16 ♕xf6 ±.

[34] 7 ♘b3/7 ♗e2 –Scheveningen.

[35] 9 ... e5?! 10 f4 ♗d6 11 ♔h1 h6 12 ♗d2 0-0 13 ♖ae1 ♖e8 14 f5 ♗b4 15 g4 d5 16 g5 ± Bistrich-Lazarevich, USSR 1979.

[36] 10 f4 ♗e7 11 ♗d2 0-0 12 ♖ae1 ♖e8 13 ♔h1 ♗f8 = Spassky-Liptay, Marianske Lazne 1962.

[37] 14 ♘a4 c5 15 c4 ± Spassky-Petrosian, Palma de Mallorca 1969.

	5	6	7	8	9	10	11	12	13	
Kan II		1 e4 c5 2 Nf3 e6 3 d4 cd 4 Nxd4 a6 5 Bd3								
1	...	c4[1]	Nxc6	Nc3	f4	Qxd3[2]				±
	Ne7	Nbc6	Nxc6	Ne5	Nxd3+	d6				
2	...	Nxc6[3]	0-0	c4	Nc3	cd	ed	Qa4+	Re1[5]	±
	Nc6	bc	d5[4]	Nf6	Be7	cd	ed	Qd7		
3	...	...	Nd2	Qh5	Nc4	Bg5	Qe2	Bh4	0-0	∞
	...	dc	e5	Bd6	Qc7!?	Nf6	h6	Qe7	g5[6]	
4	...	...	0-0[7]	Nd2	a4	Qf3	Nc4	Ne3		±
	...	...	e5	Qc7	Nf6	Bc5[8]	0-0	Re8[9]		
5	...	0-0	Nxc6	c4[10]	Nc3	Re1	Bg5	Qd2		±
	Qc7	Nc6?!	Qxc6	g6	Bg7	Ne7	d6			
6	...	Nc3	Be3	Qd2	Nb3	Bh6!	h4	Bxg7	Nxe4	±
	g6	Bg7	Ne7	d5[11]	Nbc6	0-0	de	Kxg7	f5!?[12]	
7	...	...	...	Nb3[13]	ed	Bc5	Be3	0-0	Re1	±
	...	...	Nc6	d5	ed	b6	Nge7	0-0	Ra7[14]	
8	...	0-0	c3[15]	Na3!?	Bg5	Qe2	Nc4	a4		=
	...	Bg7	d6	Nf6	0-0	Nbd7	Qc7	h6[16]		
9	...	c4	Nb3[17]	Nc3	Bf4	Be2	Be3	0-0		±
	...	Bg7	d6	Nf6	0-0	e5	Be6	Nc6[18]		
10	...	c3	Be3	Nd2	0-0	N2f3	Nxc6	Bxa7	e5	±
	Bc5	Nc6[19]	Ba7	Nf6	0-0	d6[20]	bc	Rxa7		
11	...	Nb3	Qe2!	Be3	Qxe3	Nc3[22]	0-0-0	Rd2	Rhd1	±
	...	Ba7	Nc6	Bxe3	Nf6[21]	d6	b5[23]	0-0	Qc7[24]	
12	...	...	0-0	Qe2	Be3	c4[26]	Nc3	Qxe3	Rfd1	±
	...	Bb6	Nc6[25]	d6	Nf6	0-0	Bxe3	b6	Rb8[27]	

	7	8	9	10	11	12	13	14	15	
		1 e4 c5 2 Nf3 e6 3 d4 cd 4 Nxd4 a6 5 Bd3 Nf6 6 0-0 Qc7[28]								
13	c4	b3[30]	Bb2	Nc3	Nxc6	Rc1!	Re1	f4	e5	±
	d6[29]	Be7	Bd7	Nc6	Bxc6[31]	Qb8	Bd7[32]	0-0	Ne8[33]	
14	...	Nxc6	f4	Kh1[35]	Qc2	Nc3[36]	e5	Bxf4	c5!?	±
	Nc6	dc[34]	e5	Bg4	0-0-0	ef	Qxe5	Qa5[37]		
15	Qe2	f4	Kh1	Nc3	a4[39]					=
	d6[38]	Nbd7	Be7	b5						
16	...	c4	Nc3[40]	Be3	Rac1	Nxc6	f4[41]	Rfd1	a3![43]	±
	...	g6	Bg7	0-0	Nc6	bc	c5	Bb7[42]		
17	...	...	...	...	...	Bb1	f4	b4	Bd3	=
	...	...	...	...	Nbd7	b6	Bb7	Rac8	e5![44]	
18	...	...	...	...	...	f3	Qf2	Rfd1	Bf1	±
	...	...	...	...	...	b6	Bb7	Rac8	Ne5![45]	
19	...	...	...	...	...	...				=
	...	...	...	...	...	Ne5![46]				

276

[1] 6 0-0 ♘bc6 7 ♘xc6 ♘xc6 8 ♕g4 ♘e5 9 ♕g3 ♘d3 10 cd b5 11 a4 b4 12 ♗g5 f6 13 ♗e3 ± Bednarski-Banas, Netanya 1973.

[2] Romm-Pachman, Netanya 1973.

[3] 6 ♗e3 ♘f6 7 0-0 ♘e5 8 h3 d5 9 ♘d2 de 10 ♘xe4 ♘d5 oo Taimanov.

[4] 7 ... e5 8 f4 ♗c5+ 9 ♔h1 ♘e7 10 ♕h5 ♘g6 11 f5 ♘f4 12 ♗xf4 ef 13 f6 ± Ravinsky-Vorotnikov, USSR 1963.

[5] Fischer-Petrosian, match 1971.

[6] Ligterink-Miles, Lone Pine 1980.

[7] 7 f4 e5 8 f5 b5 9 a4 ♗b7 10 ♗e3 ♘f6 11 ♘d2 ♕c7 12 ♕e2 ♘d7 13 ♕f2 ♗e7 14 0-0 ± Matulović-Popov, Zagreb 1973.

[8] 10 ... h5?! 11 ♘c4 ♗e6 12 a5 ♗c5 13 ♗e3 ♗xe3 14 ♕xe3 ± Parma-Damjanović, Yugoslav Ch 1960.

[9] Keres-Tal, Yugoslavia C 1959.

[10] Karpov.

[11] 8 ... 0-0 9 h4 ± Karpov.

[12] 14 ♘c3 h6 ± Commons-Peev, Primorsko 1976.

[13] 8 ♘ce2!?

[14] 14 ♕e2 ♕c7 15 h3 ± Gipslis-Poutiainen, Tallinn 1977.

[15] 7 ♗e3 ♘e7 8 ♘c3 0-0 9 ♕d2 ±.
  7 ♘f3!? ♘e7 8 ♘c3 ♕c7 9 ♗e3 ♘bc6 10 ♕d2 ± Suetin-Miles, Dubna 1976.

[16] Ginsburg-Rajković, Lone Pine 1980.

[17] 7 ♗e3!? ♘e7 8 ♘c3 d5 9 ed ed 10 0-0 0-0 11 ♖c1 ♖e8 ± Jansa-Miles, Hastings 1976/77.

[18] 13 ♖c1 intending f3 ± Ljubojević-Rajković, Yugoslavia 1980.

[19] 6 ... ♘e7 7 0-0 0-0 8 ♕h5 d6 9 ♘d2 ♘d7 10 ♘2b3 ♘f6 11 ♕e2 ♗a7 12 ♗g5 ♘g6 13 ♖ad1 h6 14 ♗c1 ♕c7 (Geller-Taimanov, Moscow 1969) 15 ♗c2 e5 16 ♘f5 ♗xf5 17 ef ♘f4 18 ♕f3 ± Karpov.
  6 ... d5 7 ♘d2! ♗xd4 8 cd de 9 ♘xe4 ♘c6 10 ♗e3 ± Karpov.

[20] 10 ... ♘g4?! 11 ♗g5 f6 12 ♗h4 ♕e8 intending ... ♘ge5 ±.

[21] 9 ... ♘ge7 10 c4 d6 11 ♘c3 ±/± Karpov.

[22] 10 c4 0-0 = Botterill-Hübner, Graz 1972.

[23] 11 ... 0-0 12 f4 ♕c7 13 g4! (13 ♖hg1?! b5 14 g4 b4 15 g5 ♘e8 oo Arnason-Suetin, Erevan 1980) 13 ... b5 (13 ... ♗xg4?! 14 ♕g3!) 14 g5 ♘d7 15 f5! b4 16 ♘ce2 a5 17 ♕h3 ef 18 ef ♘de5 19 ♘f4! ±/oo Kengis-Nevednichy, Moscow 1979.

[24] 14 f4 b4 15 ♘e2 e5 16 fe de 17 ♖f1 ♘d7 18 ♘g3 ♘b6 19 ♘f5 ± Byrne-Larsen, Biel 1976.

[25] 7 ... ♘e7 8 ♕e2 ♘bc6 9 ♗e3 0-0 (9 ... d5!? Suetin) 10 ♗xb6 ♕xb6 11 ♘c3 d6 12 ♖ad1 ♘e5

13 ♔h1 ± Panchenko-Suetin, Erevan 1980.

[26] 10 ♗xb6 ♕xb6 11 ♘1d2 0-0 12 ♔h1 e5 13 f4 ♗g4 14 ♕e1 ef 15 ♖xf4 ♘e5 = Ostojić-Portisch, Beverwijk 1969.

[27] 14 ♗e2 ♕e7 15 ♖d2 ♖d8 16 ♖ad1 ± Parma-Benko, Reggio Emilia 1971.

[28] 6 ... d6 7 c4 ♗e7 8 ♘c3 0-0 9 ♕e2 (9 ♗e3 ♘bd7 10 ♖c1 ♖e8 11 a3?! ♗f8 12 ♗b1 b6! 13 ♕e2 ♗b7 14 ♖fd1 ♖c8 15 ♗g5 ♕c7 16 ♗a2 ♕b8 17 f3 d5! oo/∓ Ljubojević-Gheorghiu, London 1980) 9 ... ♗d7 10 f4 ♘c6 11 ♘f3 e5 12 f5 ♘d4 13 ♕f2!? ♘xf3+ 13 gf! ± Fedorowicz-Miles, Lone Pine 1980.

[29] 7 ... ♗d6 8 ♔h1 ♘c6 9 ♘xc6 dc 10 ♗e3 e5 11 c5 ♗e7 12 f3 ± Belyavsky-Smyslov, Moscow 1973.
  7 ... ♗e7 8 b3!? d6 9 ♗b2 ♗d7 – 7 ... d6.

[30] 8 ♘c3 ♗e7 9 ♗e3 ♘bd7 10 ♖c1 b6 11 f4 g6 12 b3 ♗b7 13 ♗b1 0-0 14 ♕f3 ♖fe8 15 ♔h1 ♗f8 = Kuijpers-Popov, Wijk aan Zee 1979.

[31] 11 ... bc ± Karpov.

[32] 13 ... 0-0 14 ♘d5! ed 15 ed ± Karpov.

[33] 16 ♘e4 ± Sveshnikov-Gorchakov, Kiev 1973.

[34] 8 ... bc 9 ♘c3 d6 10 ♕e2 ♗e7 11 ♗g5 h6 12 ♗d2 e5 13 b4 0-0 14 ♖fc1 a5 15 b5! ± Kuzmin-Grigorian, Baku 1972.

[35] 10 f5 h5!? 11 h3? ♗c5+ 12 ♔h1 ♘g4! 13 ♕e2 ♕b6 oo.

[36] 12 fe ♕xe5 13 ♗f4 ♕d4.
  12 f5 ♕d7 13 ♗e2 ♗xe2 14 ♕xe2 ♕d3 15 ♕xd3 ♖xd3 16 ♘c3 ♗b4 ∓ Karpov.

[37] Karpov.

[38] 7 ... ♗d6 8 ♔h1 ♘c6 9 ♘xc6 dc 10 f4 e5 11 ♘d2! ± Bagirov-Korchnoi, USSR 1960.

[39] 11 e5? de 12 fe ♕xe5! 13 ♕f3 ♗d6! 14 g3 ♖b8 15 ♘c6 ♗b7 ∓ Tseitlin-Dementiev, Riga 1970.
  11 a4!? = Karpov.

[40] 9 b4!? ♘c6 10 ♘xc6 ♕xc6 11 ♗b2 ♗g7 12 ♘d2 0-0 13 ♖ac1 ± Zaitsev.

[41] 13 c5 d5 14 ed ♘xd5 = Karpov.

[42] 14 ... ♖b8!?
  14 ... ♗d7!?

[43] Karpov-Hübner, Leningrad IZ 1973.

[44] 16 ♘d5 ♕d8 17 fe ♘xd5! (=) 18 cd ♘xe5 19 ♗xa6 ♖xc1 20 ♗xc1 ♖xa6 21 ♕xa6 ♕h4 22 ♕e2 ♘g4 23 ♘f3 ♗d4+ 24 ♔h1 ♘f2+ 25 ♔g1 ♘h3+ Karpov.

[45] 16 ♖c2 ♖fe8 17 ♖cd2 ♗f8 18 ♘db5! ab 19 ♘xb5 ♕b8 20 ♘xd6 ± Musil-Karpov, Portorož-Ljubljana 1975.

[46] Karpov.

277

Scheveningen: 6 f4			1 e4 c5 2 ♘f3 e6 3 d4 cd 4 ♘xd4 ♘f6 5 ♘c3 d6 6 f4[1]						
	6	7	8	9	10	11	12	13	14
1	... ♗e7[2]	♗e3 0-0	♕f3 e5	♘f5 ♗xf5	ef ♕a5[3]	0-0-0[4] e4	♕h3 ♖c8	♗d4 ♘c6	♗c4 ♕b4[5]	±
2	... a6	♗e3[6] ♕c7	g4[7] d5!	e5 ♘fd7	a3[8] g5!?	f5 ♕xe5!?[9]	♕d2 ♗c5	0-0-0 ♘c6	h4 ♗xd4[10]	∞
3	... ...	... b5	♕f3 ♗b7	♗d3[11] ♘bd7[12]	g4[13] b4	♘e2 e5!?	♘b3 d5	♘g3 ♕c7!?	g5 ♘xe4[14]	∞
4	... ♘c6	♗e3 ♗e7	♗e2 0-0	♕d2!? e5![15]	♘f3[16] ef	♗xf4 ♗g4!	0-0-0 ♖e8	h3 ♗h5	♖he1 ♕a5[17]	=
5	... ...	... ...	♕f3 ♕c7	0-0-0 0-0[18]	g4[19] ♘xd4!	♗xd4 e5	fe de	♕g3! ♘g4![20]	♘d5[21]	∞
6	... ...	... ...	... ...	♗d3 a6	0-0[22] 0-0	♔h1[23] ♗d7	♖ae1[24] b5	a3[25] ♖ab8!	♘xc6 ♗xc6[26]	=
7	... ...	... ...	... ♗d7	0-0-0[27] 0-0	♖hg1 ♘xd4	♗xd4 ♗c6	g4 d5!?[28]	e5 ♘e4!	♔b1 ♗c5!?[29]	=/±
8	... ...	... ...	... e5	♘xc6[30] bc	fe de[31]	♗c4 0-0	h3! ♗e6!?[32]	♗xe6 fe	♕e2 ♕b8[33]	=
9	... ...	... ...	... ...	... ...	f5! ♕a5[34]	♗c4[35] ♖b8[36]	0-0-0[37] 0-0[38]	♗b3 ♖xb3!?[39]	cb d5[40]	∞
10	... ...	... ...	... ...	... ...	... ...	... ♗a6!?	♗b3 0-0	0-0-0 ♘d7	g4 ♘c5[41]	∞

[1] 6 ♗b5+ (Vitolins) ♘bd7 7 ♗g5 ♕b6 8 ♗xf6 gf 9 ♕d3 a6 10 ♗xd7+ ♗xd7 11 0-0 ♕a5 ∞ Bagirov. 6 ... ♗d7!?

[2] 6 ... ♕b6 7 ♘b3 ♘c6 8 ♗e2 ♗e7 9 ♗f3 0-0 10 ♕e2 ± Timoshenko-Mikhalchishin, USSR 1973.

[3] 10 ... e4?! 11 ♘xe4 ♘xe4 12 ♕xe4 d5 (12 ... ♗h4+ 13 g3 ♖e8 14 ♕xb7 ♖xe3+ 15 ♔f2 ±) 13 ♕d3 ♘c6 14 a3! ♗f6 15 0-0-0 ♖e8 16 ♔b1 ± Yudasin-Lukin, USSR 1981.

[4] 11 ♕xb7!? ♘bd7 12 ♕a6 ♕c7 13 0-0-0 ♖fc8 ∞∞.

[5] 15 ♗xf6 ♗xf6 16 ♗b3 ♘d4 17 ♘d5! ♖xc2+! 18 ♔b1 ♘xb3 19 ♘xf6+ gf 20 ♖xc2 ♖c8+ 21 ♔b1 ♘d2+ 22 ♔a1 ♖c2 23 ♖a3! ± Kupreichik-Sigurjonsson, Reykjavik 1980.

[6] 7 ♗d3 ♘c6 8 ♘f3 ♗e7 9 0-0 ♕c7 10 ♔h1 b5 12 f5 ♗d7 13 ♗f4 ♘c5 =.

[7] 8 ♕f3 b5! 9 ♗d3 ♗b7 10 g4 ♘fd7 11 0-0-0 b4 12 ♘ce2 ♘c5 13 ♔b1 ♘bd7 14 ♖hf1 g6 =

278

Kupreichik-Zilberstein, USSR 1976.

[8] 10 Wf3 Bb4! 11 Ne2 Nc6 12 0-0-0 Nb6 =.

[9] 11 ... Nxe5 12 We2 Nbc6 13 0-0-0 Be7 14 Bg2 Bd7 15 Bxd5! ± Keres-Bilek, 1960.

[10] 15 Bxd4 Nxd4 16 Wxd4 Wxd4 17 Rxd4 gh! ∞/∓.

[11] 9 a3 Nbd7 10 Bd3 Be7 11 0-0-0-0 12 Rae1 Rc8 13 Wh3 Nc5! 14 Bf2 g6 =.

[12] 9 ... Be7 10 g4 g6!? 11 g5 Nh5 12 0-0-0 Nd7 13 f5 Ne5 14 Wh3 b4 = Platonov-Dzhindzhihashvili, USSR 1974.

[13] 10 0-0 b4 11 Nce2 Nc5 12 Ng3 (Christiansen-Reshevsky, USA 1977) 12 ... Be7! =.

[14] 15 Nxe4 Rc8!? 16 Ng3 d4 17 Be4 Bxe4 18 Wxe4 de 19 0-0-0 ∞.

[15] 9 ... a6 10 0-0-0 Wc7 11 g4 b5 (11 ... Nxd4?! 12 Bxd4 e5 13 Be3 b5 14 a3 Bxg4 15 Bxg4 Nxg4 16 Nd5 Wb7 17 Rhg1 ±) 12 g5 Nfd7 13 f5 b4 14 f6 gf 15 Rhg1! f5 Itkis-Popov, 1977. 16 g6! ∞.

[16] 10 Nf5 Nxe4! 11 Nxe7+ Wxe7 12 Nxe4 ef =.

10 Nb3!?

[17] 15 Bb5 Rac8 16 Kb1 Bf8 = Ghinda-Jansa, Bucharest 1982.

[18] 9 ... a6 10 g4! 0-0 11 g5 Nd7 12 Rhg1 b5 13 Wh5 b4! 14 Nce2 g6! 15 Wh6 Re8! 16 Rg3 Bf8 ∞.

9 ... Nxd4 10 Bxd4 e5 11 fe! Bg4 12 Wg3 Bxd1 13 Wxg7 Rf8 14 ef ±.

[19] 10 Ndb5!? Wb8 11 g4 a6 12 Nd4 Nxd4 13 Bxd4 e5! 14 g5 Bg4! 15 Wg3! ed 16 gf dc 17 fe cb+ 18 Kb1 Bxd1 19 efW+ Wxf8 20 Rg1 g6! ∞/∓.

[20] 13 ... Bd6 14 Be3! Bb4 15 g5 Nh5 16 Nd5! Nxg3 17 Nxc7 Nxf1 18 Rhxf1 Bh3 19 Nxa8 ± Grünfeld-Dur, Graz 1981.

[21] 14 ... Wd8 intending ... Bh4, ... Wg5+.

14 ... Wd6!? ∞.

[22] 10 Nb3 b5 11 0-0 Bb7 12 Rae1 Nb4! 13 a3 Nxd3 14 cd d5 =/∓.

[23] 11 Rae1!? Nxd4 12 Bxd4 e5 13 fe de 14 Wg3 Be6! (15 Wxe5? Bd6 16 Wg5 Bxh2+; 15 Bxe5 Wc5+ 16 Kh1 Ng4!) 15 Kh1 Nd7 16 Be3 Rfe8 =.

[24] 12 Wg3!? b5 13 e5 de 14 Nxc6 Bxc6 15 fe Nd7 16 Bf4 Nc5 17 Bh6 g6 18 Bxf8 Bxf8 ∞.

[25] 13 g4 Nxd4 14 Bxd4 e5 15 fe de 16 Nd5 Wd6!

[26] 15 Wh3! Rbd8! 16 Bd4 e5! 17 fe de =

Novopashin-Korchnoi, USSR 1962.

[27] 9 g4?! Nxd4 10 Bxd4 e5! 11 fe de 12 Bxe5 Wa5! ∓/∓.

[28] 12 ... Wa5 13 g5 Nd7 14 Wh5 Rfd8 15 f5 ef 16 Bc4! ±.

[29] Kasparov/Nikitin.

[30] 9 Nf5 Bxf5 10 ef Nd4 11 Bxd4 ed 12 Nb5 Wa5+ 13 c3 dc =.

9 Nde2 g4 10 Wf2 Wa5 11 Ng3 0-0 12 h3 ef 13 Bxf4 Be6 =.

9 fe Nxe5!? (9 ... de 10 Nf5 Bxf5 11 ef Nd4 12 Bxd4 ed 13 0-0-0 ±) 10 Bb5+ Kf8!? 11 We2 Nfg4 12 Bf4 a6 13 Ba4 Ng6 14 Bg3 h5 = Ruderfer-Lepeshkin, USSR 1966. 10 ... Nfd7!?

[31] 10 ... Ng4!? 11 ed Wxd6 12 Bf4 Ne5 13 Wg3 Bf6 ∞ Zaitsev.

[32] 12 ... Ne8!? 13 0-0 Nd6 14 Bd3 Be6 15 b3 Wa5 16 Ne2 c5 =.

[33] 15 Rab1 Ne8 16 Bf2 Nd6 17 0-0 Wb4 18 a3 Wc4! 19 Rfe1 Bd8! =.

[34] 10 ... d5?! 11 ed Nxd5 12 Bb5! Nxe3 13 Bxc6+ Kf8 14 Wxe3 Rb8 15 Rd1 Wc7 16 Nd5 Wxc6 17 Nxe7 ±.

10 ... 0-0 11 0-0-0 d5 (11 ... Nd7 12 h4! Nb6 13 g4! ±) 12 ed cd 13 Bc4! e4 14 We2 ± Ree-Reshevsky, Nice Ol 1974.

[35] 11 g4 d5 12 Bd2 Bb4 =.

11 0-0-0 d5!? 12 ed Bb4 13 Bd2 0-0 14 dc Rb8 ∞. 11 ... Ba6!? intending ... 0-0-0.

[36] 11 ... Bb7 12 0-0-0 0-0 13 g4! d5 14 g5 d4! 15 gf Bxf6 16 Bd2 dc 17 Bxc3 ±.

11 ... d5?! 12 ed Bb4 13 Bd2 e4 14 Nxe4 Bxd2+ 15 Nxd2 0-0 16 0-0-0 cd 17 Bb3 ±.

[37] 12 Bb3 d5! 13 Bd2 Bb4! 14 0-0-0 d4 15 Nb1 0-0 16 a3 Bxd2+ 17 Nxd2 Nd7 = Sigurjonsson-Olafsson, Reykjavik 1976.

[38] 12 ...d5!? 13 ed Rxb2! (13 ... Ba3? 14 ba Wxc3 15 Bxa7! Wb2+ 16 Kd2 ±) 14 d6! (14 Kxb2 Wa3+ 15 Kb1 Wxc3 16 Bb3 cd ∞) 14 ... e4! 15 Nxe4 Rxc2+ 16 Kxc2 Bxf5 17 Rd4 Bxd6 18 Rf1 Bg6 19 Rxd6! Bxe4+ 20 Wxe4 ±±.

[39] 13 ... Nd7!? 14 g4 Nc5 15 Bxc5 dc! 16 h4 Rb4! 17 a3 Rd4! =.

[40] 15 ed cd 16 Rxd5! Nxd5 17 Nxd5 Bd6 18 Nf6+ Gaprindashvili-Hartoch, Amsterdam II 1976.

[41] 15 Bxc5 dc 16 h4 c4! 17 Ba4 Rac8 ∓.

15 g5! Nxb3+ 16 cb d5 ∞.

For the uncredited analysis above Kasparov was aided by his second Nikitin.

	Scheveningen: Keres Attack			1 e4 c5 2 ♘f3 e6 3 d4 cd 4 ♘xd4 ♘f6 5 ♘c3 d6 6 g4 a6					
	7	8	9	10	11	12	13	14	15	
1	♗e3	g5	gf	fg	b4!	♖g1	♕h5!	b5	ba	±
	b5?!¹	b4?!²	bc	♗xg7	♗b7	♗f6	♕e7	♗xe4	d5³	
2	...	♕e2!?	a3	f3	h4	ed	♘xd5	0-0-0	♔b1⁴	∞
	h6	b5	♗b7	♘bd7	d5!?	♘xd5	♗xd5	♖c8		
3	...	♖g1!?	♕f3	h4	g5	♕g3	♗xg5	hg	♘b3	∞
	...	♗e7	♕c7	♘fd7	♘e5	hg	♗xg5	♘bc6	♗d7⁵	
4	...	♕f3	♕h3	♘f5⁷	g5!?⁸	ef	0-0-0	gf	♗xc4	∓
	...	♘bd7	e5⁶	g6	gf	d5	d4	dc	♕xf6⁹	
5	...	...	♖g1	♕h3	f4	fe	♘f5	♘xg7+	♗xh6	∞
	...	♘c6	♘e5!¹⁰	♘g6!	e5	de	♗b4	♔f8	♔g8!	
6	...	♘f5	g5!!	ef	♕f3	0-0-0				∞
	e5!	g6	gf	d5	d4	♕c7				
7	g5¹¹	♖g1¹²	a3	♖g3¹³	♗g2	b3	♗b2	♘de2	h4	∞
	♘fd7	b5	♘b6	♗b7	♘8d7	g6	e5!	h6	hg¹⁴	

				1 e4 c5 2 ♘f3 e6 3 d4 cd 4 ♘xd4 ♘f6 5 ♘c3 d6 6 g4 h6					
	7	8	9	10	11	12	13	14	15	
8	♗g2¹⁵	h3	♗e3	f4	♗f2	b3	♕d3	0-0		±
	♘c6	♗e7¹⁶	♘e5	♘c4	♗d7	♕a5	♘a3	♖c8¹⁷		
9	h4	♖g1	ed¹⁹	♘xd5	♗g2	♗d2	♗e3	♘xc6!	♗xc6+	±
	♘c6¹⁸	d5	♘xd5	♕xd5	♕a5+	♕e5+	♗d7	♗xc6	bc²⁰	
10	...	...	♗b5	ed	♘xd5	♗e3!	♕e2	♗xd4+	♗xd7+	±
	...	...	♗d7	♘xd5	ed	♕xh4²¹	♘xd4	♕e7	♔xd7²²	
11	g5	♗xg5	♕d2²⁴	♘b3	0-0-0	h4	♗e2	f4	h5	±
	hg	♘c6²³	♕b6	a6	♗d7	♕c7	♗e7	0-0-0	♔b8²⁵	

				1 e4 c5 2 ♘f3 e6 3 d4 cd 4 ♘xd4 ♘f6 5 ♘c3 d6 6 g4 ♘c6					
	7	8	9	10	11	12	13	14	15	
12	g5²⁶	♘db5	♗f4	♕h5	♗g3²⁷	♘d4	0-0-0	♔b1	♖g1	∓
	♘d7	♘b6	♘e5	♘g6	a6	♗e7	♗xg5+	0-0	♗f6²⁸	
13	...	♗e3	♖g1²⁹	♕h5	♕e2	♘b3	0-0-0³¹	♘c5	♘xe6³²	∞
	...	♗e7	♘b6!³⁰	g6	e5	♗e6	♘c4	♘xe3		
14	...	...	♕d2	ed	0-0-0	♗b5	♘b3			∞
	...	♘b6!?	d5!?	ed	♗e7	♗d7	♗e6³³			
15	...	...	h4³⁴	♕e2	♘xc6	♗d4	0-0-0	a3	♖h3³⁵	±
	...	a6	♕c7	b5	♕xc6	♗b7	0-0-0	♘b6		
16	...	...	♕d2	0-0-0	♕xd4	h4	♔b1	♘a4	b3³⁶	±
	...	...	♕c7	♘xd4	b5	♖b8	b4	♗b7		

[1] **7 ... d5** 8 e5 Nd7 9 f4 Be7 10 Qf3 Nc6 11 0-0-0 g5! = Tseshkovsky-Palatnik, USSR 1980.
7 ... h5!?

[2] 8 ... Nfd7 transposes below.

[3] Rigo-Barczay, Hungarian Ch 1980.

[4] Sax-Ghinda, Warsaw Z 1979.

[5] 16 0-0-0 0-0-0 17 f4 Ng6 oo Velimirović-Hübner, Rio de Janeiro IZ 1979.

[6] 9 ... Nc5 10 f3 e5 11 Nb3 Be6 12 0-0-0 Nxb3+ 13 ab Qa5 14 Kb1 Rc8 oo. 12 Nxc5 dc 13 Qg3 Bd6! 14 0-0-0 Qe7 =.

[7] 10 Nb3 Nb6 11 f3 Be6 =.

[8] 11 Ng3? Nb6 12 Be2 h5 $\mp$ Ermenkov-Polugayevsky, Buenos Aires Ol 1978.

[9] 16 f4 Nc5 $\mp$ Sax-Gheorghiu, Wijk aan Zee 1981.

[10] 9 ... g5 10 0-0-0 Ne5 11 Qe2 Nfd7 12 f4 gf 13 Bxf4 $\pm$ Sax-Ghinda, Herkulana Z 1982.

[11] 7 Bg2 Nc6 8 Nxc6?! bc 9 e5 Nd5! 10 ed Qxd6 11 Ne4 Qc7 12 c4 Nf4! 13 Bxf4 Qxf4 14 Nf6+ Ke7! $\mp$ Planinc-Ribli, Wijk aan Zee 1973.

[12] 8 Bg2 b5 (8 ... Nc6 – 6 ... Nc6) 9 f4 (9 Be3 $\pm$) 9 ... Bb7 10 f5!? (10 0-0 / 10 a3 $\pm$) 10 ... b4 11 fe bc 12 ef+ Kxf7 13 0-0+ Ke8! 14 Ne6! Qb6+ 15 Kh1 oo/$\pm$.
8 Bc4 Nb6! 9 Be2 e5 10 Nb3 Be6 11 Be3 Be7 =.
8 f4 Nc6! 9 Be3 Be7 – 6 ... Nc6.

[13] 10 Qg4!? Ginsburg.

[14] 16 hg Be7 17 Qd2 Nc5 oo Brüggemann-Espig, East German Ch 1979.

[15] 7 Rg1 Nc6 8 Be3 d5 9 Bb5 Nd7 10 ed ed 11 Qe2 Nb4! 12 Nxc6 Bxc6! =.

[16] 8 ... Bd7 9 Be3 Be7 10 Qe2 (10 Nde2 0-0 11 0-0 Na5 =; 10 ... g5 =) 10 ... a6 11 f4 Qc7 12 Qf2! $\pm$.

[17] Hort-Andersson, Malta Ol 1980.

[18] 7 ... Be7 8 Qf3! (8 Rg1 d5 9 Bb5+ Kf8!) 8 ... h5! 9 gh Nxh5 10 Bg5 Nc6 11 0-0-0!? (11 Nxc6!) 11 ... Bxg5 12 hg Qxg5+ 13 Kb1 Nxd4 14 Rxd4 Bd7! 15 Rxd6 Bc6 oo/=.

Ljubojević-Timman, Montreal 1979.

[19] 9 Nxc6 bc 10 g5 hg 11 hg Nd7 oo Ivanović-Sznapik, 1981.

[20] 16 Qd4! $\pm$ Belyavsky-Ghinda, Bucharest 1980.

[21] 12 ... Be7 13 Qd2 (13 Qe2!?) 13 ... Bxh4 14 0-0-0 Bf6 15 Nf5 Bxf5 16 gf a6 17 Bxc6+ bc 18 Bc5 $\pm$ Karpov-Spassky, Tilburg 1980.

[22] **16 Qxe7+** Bxe7 17 Bxg7 Rhe8! 18 0-0-0 Bg5+ 19 Kb1 Nc6 oo/=.
16 Be3 Rd8 17 0-0-0 Nc8 $\pm$.

[23] 8 ... a6 9 Bg2 Bd7 10 Qe2 Be7 10 0-0-0 Qc7 $\pm$/=.

[24] 9 h4! Qb6 10 Nb3!? a6 11 Qe2 Qc7 12 0-0-0 b5 13 Bh3 b4!? 14 Nd5 ed 15 ed+ Ne7 oo.

[25] 16 Bf3 Bc8 17 Qe3 $\pm$ Spassky-Ribli, Manila IZ 1976. 17 Bh4!? Kinlay.

[26] 7 Bg2? Nxd4 intending ... e5 $\mp$.

[27] 11 Be3 a6 12 Nd4 d5! 13 0-0-0 Bb4 14 Nde2 0-0 13 h4 Nc4 14 ed Qa5 oo.

[28] 16 f4 (Chiburdanidze-Kozlovskaya, USSR 1979) 16 ... e5! 17 fe Qxe5 $\mp$.

[29] 9 h4 0-0 10 Qd2 (10 f4 d5!? Magerramov) 10 ... a6 11 0-0-0 Nxd4 12 Bxd4 b5 13 a3! Bb7 14 f4 Qa5 oo.

[30] 9 ... a6 10 Qd2 0-0 11 0-0-0 Nxd4 12 Bxd4 b5 13 a3 Rb8 14 Qg3 Re8 =. 13 f4 b4 14 Na4 Qa5 15 b3 Bb7 16 Bg2 e5! =.

[31] 13 Bxb6 ab! 14 Nd5 Bxd5 15 ed Nd4! 16 Nxd4 ed 17 Qb5+ Kf8!

[32] **15 ... Nxd1** 16 Nxd8 Nxc3 17 bc Rxd8 oo.
15 ... fe =.

[33] **13 ... Nc4?!** 14 Qxd5 Nxe3 15 fe a6 16 Bxc4 Be6 17 Qe4 $\pm$ Krementsky-Andrianov, USSR 1980.
13 ... Be6! oo/=.

[34] 8 a4 Nde5 9 Nb3 d5!? 10 ed ed 11 Qxd5 Bg4! 12 Bg2 Qxd5 13 Bxd5 Nb4 14 Be4 f5 oo Bronstein-Tal, USSR 1976.

[35] Korsunsky-Eingorn, USSR 1979.

[36] Hort-Andersson, Amsterdam 1973.

For the uncredited analysis above Kasparov was aided by his second Nikitin.

	8	9	10	11	12	13	14	15	16	
1	...	♗e3	♕e1[1]	♗f3[2]	e5	fe	♕g3	♘xf3[4]	♗xc5	∓
	a6	♕c7	b5	♗b7	de	♘fd7[3]	♗xf3	♗c5	♘xc5[5]	
2	...	♔h1!	♕e1	♗f3	e5	f5[8]	fe	ef+	♘xf3	±
	...	♕c7	b5[6]	♗b7	♘e8[7]	de[9]	♗xf3[10]	♖xf7	♘d7[11]	
3	...	♗e3	♕e1[12]	♗xd4	♕g3	f5	♗e3	♘xe4	♗h6!	∞
	♘c6	♗d7	♘xd4	♗c6	g6	e5	♘xe4	♗xe4	♕b6+[13]	
4	...	...	♕e1	♗xd4	♗e3[14]	♖xf4	♕g3	♗d4	♖af1	∞/∓
	...	♕c7	♘xd4	e5	ef	♗e6	♘d7	♘e5	a6[15]	
5	...	...	♔h1	♕xd4[16]	a4[17]	♕d2	♗xf4	♖fd1	a5	=/±
	...	...	♘xd4	a6	e5	ef	♗e6	♖fd8	♖ac8	
6	...	...	♘b3[18]	♗xf4[20]	♔h1	e5	♘xd5	c4	♕c1[22]	=
	...	e5	ef[19]	♗e6	d5!	♘d7[21]	♘dxe5	♗g5!	♗xf4[23]	

	10	11	12	13	14	15	16	17	18	
7	♕e1	♗xd4	♖d1[25]	♗f3	e5	fe	♗xb7	♘e4	♕g3![28]	±/=
	♘xd4[24]	b5	♗b7[26]	♕c7	de	♘d7	♕xb7	♕c7![27]	♔h8[29]	
8	...	♕g3	♗xd4	♖ae1[31]	a3	♗d3	♕h3[32]	fe	♗xe5	∓
	♗d7	♘xd4[30]	♗c6	b5	♕d7	a5	e5!	de	♕xh3[33]	
9	...	♖d1	♗xd4	♗f3!	e5	ed	♗xc6	♕g3	♔h1	=
	...	♘xd4	♗c6	♕c7	♘d7!?	♗xd6	♕xc6	g6	♗c5[34]	
10	♔h1	♕e1	♕g3	a3[35]	e5!	fe	♖xf6!	♗f4	♗xe5	±
	♕c7	♗d7	b5	♖ab8[36]	de[37]	♘xe5	♗xf6	♕b6	♗xe5[38]	
11	...	...	♗xd4	a3	♕g3	♖ae1	♗d3	ab[39]	♘e2	=
	...	♘xd4	b5	♗b7	♗c6	♕b7	b4	♕xb4	♕b7[40]	

[1] **10** ♔h1 ♘bd7 11 a4 b6 12 ♗f3 ♗b7 13 ♕e2 ♘c5 14 e5 ♘fe4 15 ♘xe4 ♘xe4 16 ed (Timoshenko-Bonsch, Varna 1977) 16 ... ♘xd6! =.
10 g4?! ♘c6 11 g5 ♘d7 12 f5 ♘de5 13 f6 ♗d8 14 fg ♔xg7 15 ♕d2 b5 ∓ Sax-Stean, Moscow 1977.

[2] 11 e5? de 12 fe ♕xe5 13 ♗f3 ♗c5! 14 ♕f2 (14 ♗xa8? ♘g4!) 14 ... ♖a7 15 ♖fe1 ♖c7 ∓ Zapata-Sigurjonsson, Bogota 1978.

[3] 13 ... ♘e8 14 ♗xb7?! ♕xb7 15 ♘f3 ♘d7 16 ♖d1 ♖c8 =/∓ Unzicker-Karpov, Bad Kissingen 1980. 14 ♕g3! ♘d7 15 ♖ad1 ∞/±.

[4] 15 ♕xf3 ♘b6 16 ♔h1 ♘8d7! =/∓. 16 ♕g4!? Nunn.

[5] 17 ♖ae1 ♘c6 18 ♘g5 ♖ad8 19 ♖f6 ♘xe5! ∓.

[6] 10 ... ♘bd7!? 11 ♗f3 ♖e8 12 a4 ♘f8 13 ♘b3 ♖b8 14 g4 ♘b6 15 g5 ♘fd7 16 ♗g2 ♘c4 ∞ Timoshenko-Vilela, Decin 1978.

[7] 12 ... de 13 fe ♘fd7 14 ♕g3 ♔h8 15 ♗f4 ♘c6 16 ♘xc6! ♗xc6 17 ♘e4 ± Ugrinović.

[8] 13 ♕g3!? ♘d7 14 a3 ♖c8 15 ♗e3 ♘b6 16 ♖ae1 ♘c4 17 ♗xb7 ♕xb7 18 ♗c1 ∞/± Sznapik-Jansa, Warsaw 1979.

[9] 13 ... ♗xf3 14 ♘xf3 b4 15 f6 gf 16 ed ♗xd6 17 ♘e4 ♔h8 18 ♗d2! ♘c6 (Karpov-Ermenkov, Skara 1980) 19 c3!: a5 20 ♖c1 ± Ermenkov.

[10] 14 ... ed? 15 ♘d5! ♗xd5 16 ♗xd5 ♘c6 17 ef+ ♔h8 18 ♗xc6 ♕xc6 19 ♕xe7 ± Jansa-Lombard, Czechoslovakia v Switzerland 1978.

[11] 17 ♗g5! ♖xf3 18 ♖xf3 ♗xg5 19 ♕e4 ♘b6 20 ♘d5 ± Sznapik-Georgiev, Herkulana Z 1982.

[12] **10** ♘db5 ♕b8 11 a4 ♖d8 12 ♗f3 ♘b4 13 ♕e2 e5! 14 ♖ad1 a6 15 ♘a3 b5! ∞ Nunn.
10 ♘b3 - rows 14-16.

[13] 17 ♔h1 ♖fc8 18 ♗d3 ♗xd3 19 cd ♗f8 (Bodach-Möhring, E Germany 1978) 20 ♕h3!? ♖c2 21 f6 ♕c6 22 ♖f3 ♔h8 23 ♖g1 ♕c8! 24 ♕h4 ♖xh6 25 ♕xh6 ♕f8 intending ... ♖ac8 ∞/=.

[14] 12 fe de 13 ♕g3 ♗c5 14 ♗xc5 ♕xc5+ 15 ♔h1 ♔h8 16 ♖xf6 gf 17 ♕h4 ♖g8 =. 16 ♗d3 ♗e6 17 ♕h4 ♘g8! 18 ♗e2 ♖ad8 ∓ Unzicker-Andersson, Munich 1979.

[15] 17 a4 ♖ac8 18 ♔h1 ♕d8 19 ♗d3 ♗g5 ∞/∓ Ermenkov-Andersson, Skara 1980.

[16] 11 ♗xd4 e5! =.

[17] **12** ♖ad1 e5! 13 ♕d3 b5 14 fe de 15 ♗g5 ♗b7 = Belyavsky-Kochiev, Minsk 1976.
12 e5!? Nunn.

[18] 10 fe de 11 ♘f5± Geller-Kasparov, Moscow IZ 1982.

[19] 10 ... a5 11 a4! ♘b4 12 ♔h1! ♗d7 13 ♗f3 ♕c7 14 ♖f2 ♖fe8 15 ♖d2 ±.

[20] 11 ♖xf4 ♘e8! 12 ♕d2 ♗f6! 13 ♖f2 ♗e5 = Geller-Andersson, London 1982.

[21] 13 ... ♘e4!? 14 ♗d3 f5! 15 ef ♗xf6! 16 ♘xe4 de 17 ♘c5 ed 18 ♘xe6 dc = Tseshkovsky-Tukmakov, USSR 1981.

[22] 16 ♘c5 ♗xf4 17 ♖xf4 b6! 18 ♘e4 b5! 19 b3 bc 20 ♗xc4 ♔h8! =/∓ Geller-Kasparov, USSR 1981.

[23] 17 ♘xf4 ♕e7 18 ♖c3 ♖ad8 = Kuzmin-Kasparov, USSR 1981.

[24] 10 ... ♕c7 - rows 9-11 and 14-18.

[25] 12 a3 - next row.

[26] 12 ... ♕c7 13 e5 de 14 fe ♘d7 15 ♘e4 ♗b7 16 ♘f6+ ♔h8 17 ♗d3! h6 18 b4!! ♖fd8 19 ♘h5 ♗f8 20 c3! ♗xb4 21 ♕g3 ±/±± A.Ivanov-Magerramov, USSR 1980.

[27] 17 ... ♖ad8 18 ♖d3 ♕c6 19 ♖g3 ♕xc2 20 ♕e3 ♕c4 21 b3 ♕d5 22 ♘f6+ ♗xf6 23 ef g6 24 ♖g4! ± Tal-Andersson, match 1976.

[28] 18 ♘f6+ ♔h8 19 ♘xd7 ♕xd7 20 ♖d3 ♖ac8 21 c3 b4 22 ♖h3 bc = Olafsson-Panno, Buenos Aires 1980.

[29] 19 ♘d6!? ♕g8! 20 ♖xf7 ♖xf7 21 ♘xf7 ♕xc2 22 ♕g4 ♕g6 ±/= Kasparov/Nikitin.

[30] 11 ... ♕c7 12 e5 de 13 fe ♘xe5 14 ♗f4 ♗d6 15 ♖ad1 ♕b8 16 ♖d3 ♘e8 17 ♘e4 ∞ Ljubojević-Andersson, Wijk aan Zee 1976. 12 ♘f3 b5 13 e5 ♘e8 14 ♖ad1 ♖d8 15 ♘e4 f5 ∞ Tal-Andersson, match 1976.

[31] 13 ♗d3 b5 14 a3 ♕d7 15 ♖f3 a5 16 ♕h3 e5! 17 fe de 18 ♗xe5 ♘c5+ 19 ♔h1 ♕xh3 20 ♖xh3 ♘g4 21 ♗g3 b4 22 ♘d5 ba 23 ba f5 ∞ Vukčević-H.Olafsson, Reykjavik 1976.

[32] **16** ♖f3 g6! 17 f5 e5 18 ♗e3? b4 19 ♗c4 ♘h5! ∓ Nunn-Hartston, match 1981. 18 ♗f2 b4 ∓.
16 e5!? Nunn.

[33] 19 gh b4 20 ab ab 21 ♘d1 ♗c5+ 22 ♘f2 ♖ae8! ∓ Vukčević-Sigurjonsson, Reykjavik 1976.

[34] Kasparov/Nikitin.

[35] 13 e5!? de 14 fe ♘xe5 15 ♗h6 ♘e8 16 ♗f4 ♗d6! ∞.

[36] 13 ... ♘xd4! - next row.

[37] 14 ... ♘e8 15 ♗d3 b4 16 ♘e4 ba 17 ba g6 18 ♘f3 ♘a5 19 ♗d4 ♗b5 20 ed ♖xd6 21 ♘f6+ ♗xf6 22 ♗xf6 ♗xd3 23 cd ♖b5 24 ♖ae1 ± Hartston-Karpov, Nice Ol 1974.

[38] 19 ♕xe5 b4 20 ab f6 21 ♕c5 ± Kasparov-Korsunsky, USSR 1978.

[39] 17 ♘d1 ba 18 ba ♘h5 19 ♕g4 ♘f6 20 ♗xf6 ♗xf6 21 e5 de 22 fe ♗e7 23 ♕h3 h6 24 ♖f4 ♖ad8 25 ♖g4 ♗c5! = Mednis-Jansa, Budapest 1978.

[40] 19 e5 ♘h5 20 ♕h3 g6 21 ♘g3 de 22 ♗xe5 ♘g7 23 ♗c3 (Sax-Jansa, Budapest 1976) 23 ... ♗b4! =.

	10	11	12	13	14	15	16	17	18	
12	♔h1	♕e1	a3	♗f3[41]	♗xd4	♗e3[42]	♖d1	♘d5	ed	=
	♗d7!	b5	♕b8!	♘xd4	e5	♗c6	♖e8	♗xd5	ef[43]	
13	...	...	...	♗d3	♘xc6	ab	♘d5[45]	ed	♖fxe1	∞
	...	...	...	b4[44]	♗xc6	♕xb4	♘xd5	♕xe1	♗xd5[46]	
14	a4	♔h1	♘b3	♗f3[47]	♕e2	g4	g5	♗g2	f5	∞
	♗d7	♕c7	b6	♖fd8	♗e8	♘d7	♗f8	♘b4	♘c5![48]	
15	...	...	...	♕e1!?	♘d4	♕g3	e5	♗d2[49]		±
	...	...	...	♘b4	♖fc8	♔h8	♘fd5			
16	...	...	♘b3![50]	♘d2![51]	♕e1	♕f2	♖fc1[52]	♗b6	♗f3	∞
	...	♖c8	♘a5	♕c7	♘c6	♘b4	♗c6	♕b8	d5[53]	
17	...	♔h1	♗f3![54]	♕e1	♘b3	♗xf4	♕g3	♖ad1	♘d5	±
	♕c7	♖e8	♖b8	e5[55]	ef	♗e6	♔h8	♖bd8	♗xd5[56]	
18	...	...	♕e1[57]	♗xd4	♗g1[58]	a5!	♗b6	♖xf4	♕f2[60]	=
	...	♖d8!	♘xd4	e5	ef	♖e8	♕b8	d5[59]		

[41] **13 ♖d1!?** ♘xd4 14 ♗xd4 ♗c6 15 ♕g3 ♕b7 16 ♗f3 ♖ad8 17 ♖fe1 g6! ∞ Kasparov/Nikitin.
13 ♕g3 b4 14 ab ♕xb4 15 ♘xc6 ♗xc6 16 e5 ♘e4 17 ♘xe4 ♗xe4 = Kavalek-Larsen, Solingen 1970. 16 ... de!? 17 fe ♘e4 18 ♘xe4 ♗xe4 19 ♖xa6 ♖xa6 20 ♗xa6 Tompa-Sax, Hungary 1977. 20 ... ♕xb2! ∓.

[42] 15 ♘d5 ♗xd5 16 ed ed! 17 ♕xe7 ♗f5 18 ♖ac1 ♖e8 ∓ Szabo-Larsen, Costa Brava 1976.

[43] 19 ♗xf4 ♕c7 20 c3 ♗f8 = De Boer-Tompa, Biel 1978.

[44] 13 ... ♘xd4? 14 ♗xd4 e5 15 ♘d5 ♘xd5 16 ed ed 17 ♕xe7. 14 ... ♗c6 15 e5 de 16 fe ♘d7 17 b4! ♔h8 18 ♕e2 ±/± Dobosz-Jansa, Trencianske Teplice 1979.

[45] 16 e5 de 17 fe ♕g4!

[46] 19 ♖xa6 ∞ Kasparov/Nikitin.

[47] 13 g4?! d5 14 ed ♘b4 15 de ♗xe6 16 ♘d4 ♗c4 17 ♗xc4 ♕xc4 18 ♕f3 ♗c5 = Hartston-Pritchett, British Ch 1980.

[48] 19 fe fe 20 ♗h3 ♗d7 21 g6 (Chiburdanidze-A.Rodriguez, Barcelona 1979) 21 ... ♘c6! ∞.

[49] Klovan-Petkevich, USSR 1979.

[50] 12 ♕e1 ♘b4! 13 ♕g3 ♖xc3! 14 bc ♘xe4 15 ♕e1 ♘d5 16 ♗f3 ♘dxc3 17 ♘e2 ♗f6 18 ♗d4 ♗xd4 19 ♘xd4 f5 =/∓ Jansa-Polugayevsky, Skara 1980.

[51] 13 e5?! ♘e8 14 ♘xa5 ♕xa5 15 ♗f3 ♗c6 16 ♗d4 de 17 fe ♖d8 =/∓ Geller-Polugayevsky, USSR Ch 1978.

[52] 16 ♘b3!? Nunn.

[53] Vujačić-Cvetković, Yugoslavia 1980.

[54] 12 ♕e1 ♘xd4 13 ♗xd4 e5 14 fe de 15 ♕g3 ♗d8! 16 ♗e3 ♔h8 17 ♗g5 ♗e6 18 ♖ad1! ♘g8! 19 ♗e3 = Tal-Andersson, match 1976.

[55] 13 ... ♘xd4 14 ♗xd4 e5 15 ♗a7 ♖a8 16 ♗e3 ♗e6 17 ♕g3 ef 18 ♗xf4 ♘d7 19 ♗g4 ± Dolmatov-Timoshenko, USSR 1979.

[56] 19 ed ♘e5 20 ♘d4 ♘fd7 21 ♘f5 ♗f8 ± Kasparov/Nikitin.

[57] 12 ♗f3 ♘e5! 13 ♗e2 b6 14 ♘b3 ♘ed7 15 ♗f3 ♗b7 16 ♕e2 ♖ac8.
12 ♘b3 b6 13 ♕e1 ♖b8 14 ♕f2! ♘b4 15 ♗f3 e5! 16 a5 ba 17 ♖xa5 ♘c6 18 ♖c4 (Reshevsky-Ree, Amsterdam 1978) 18 ... ♘b4! 19 b3 ♘d7 = Reshevsky.

[58] 14 ♗e3 ef 15 ♗xf4 ♗e6 16 ♕g3 ♘d7! 17 ♗d3 ♘e5 18 ♘d5 ♗xd5 19 ed g6 20 c3 ♗f6! ∓ Karpov-Ribli, Leningrad 1977.
14 fe de 15 ♗e3 ♗e6 16 ♕g3 ♕a5! = Raman-Kasparov, USSR 1978.

[59] 17 ... ♗e6 18 ♕d2 ♘d7 19 ♗e3 ♗g5! = Kasparov/Nikitin.

[60] Geller-Tal, USSR 1977. 18 ... ♗e6! 19 ♗d3 de! 20 ♘xe4 ♘d5! = Kasparov/Nikitin.

1 e4 e5 Miscellaneous

Centre Game (1 e4 e5 2 d4 ed 3 ♕xd4)   The early development of White's queen is a serious breach of the basic rules of development and not surprisingly he forfeits the initiative rather quickly. It is almost never seen in modern practice.

Bishop's Opening (2 ♗c4)   As more and more KP players become frustrated by the diminishing returns of allowing the Petroff, the Bishop's Opening is bound to gain in popularity. Modern treatment steers the game into channels closely akin to the Giuoco Pianissimo or the Two Knights. Black has several paths to equality but present tastes prefer the latent possibilities of this system to the static formations arising from the Petroff.

	2	3	4	5	6	7	8	9	10	
1	♘e2[1]	♘bc3[2]	♘a4	d4	d5	♕d3	g3	c4		=
	♘c6	♗c5	♗e7	♘f6	♘b8	d6	♘bd7	c5[3]		
2	d4	c3[4]	♗c4	♗xb2	♗xd5	♗xf7+	♕xd8	♕d2	♘xd2	=
	ed	dc[5]	cb	d5!	♘f6[6]	♔xf7	♗b4+	♗xd2+	♖e8[7]	
3	...	♕xd4[8]	♕e3	♘c3	♗d2	0-0-0	♗c4	f3[9]	♗b3	=
	...	♘c6	♘f6	♗b4	0-0	♖e8	d6	♘e5	♗e6[10]	
4	♗c4	d3[11]	♘f3	♗b3[13]	♘c3	♘e2				±
	♘f6	c6[12]	d5	♗d6[14]	d4	c5[15]				
5	...	...	...	...	♗d2	♘bxd2	0-0	♖e1	h3	±
	...	...	...	♗b4+	♗xd2+	♕c7	0-0	♗g4[16]	♗xf3[17]	
6	...	d4	♘f3	♕xd4	♗g5	♘c3	0-0-0	♖he1	♗d3	∞
	...	ed	♘xe4	♘f6!	♗e7	c6!	d5	♗e6[18]	♘bd7[19]	

[1]   2 c3 d5 =.
[2]   3 d4 ed 4 ♘xd4 – Scotch.
[3]   Alapin-Chigorin, Berlin 1897.
[4]   Danish Gambit.
[5]   3 ... d5!? Horowitz.
[6]   6... ♗b4+ 7 ♘c3 ♗xc3+ 8 ♗xc3 ♘f6 9 ♕f3 ♘xd5 10 ed 0-0 ∞ Kaikamdzhozov/Minev.
[7]   Nyholm-Tartakower, Baden 1914.
[8]   Centre Game.
[9]   9 ♘f3 ♗e6 10 ♖xe6 ♖xe6 11 ♘g5 ♖e8 12 f4 h6 13 h4 ♕c8 ∓ Tartakower-Reshevsky, Kemeri 1937.
[10]   Spielmann-Eliskases, Semmering 1937. 11 ♘d5 = Larsen.
[11]   3 ♘c3 – Vienna.

[12]   3 ... ♘c6 4 ♘c3 ♗c5 5 f4 – King's Gambit.
[13]   5 ed cd 6 ♗b3 ♗b4+ 7 c3 ♗d6 8 ♗g5 ♗e6 9 d4 e4 = Adams-Steiner, St Louis 1941.
[14]   5 ... de? 6 ♘g5! ♗c5 7 ♘xf7 ♕b6 8 0-0 ♘g4 (Taulbut-Westerinen, Brighton 1981) 9 d4! ±±.
[15]   Intending ... ♘c6 ± Nunn. 7 ... ♘a6? 8 c3 dc 9 bc 0-0 10 0-0 ♘c5 11 ♗c2 ♗g4 (Nunn-Korchnoi, Johannesburg 1981) 12 ♘e1 ± Nunn.
[16]   9 ... ♘bd7 10 d4 ±.
[17]   11 ♕xf3 de 12 ♘xe4 ♘xe4 13 ♖xe4 ♘d7 14 d4! ± Vogt-Romanishin, Riga 1981.
[18]   9 ... 0-0 10 ♕h4 ♘bd7 11 ♗d3 g6 12 ♖e2! =.
[19]   11 ♕h4 ♘c5 12 ♘d4 ♘g8! 13 ♗xe7 ♕xe7 14 ♕g3 g6 15 ♘ce2 ∞ Keres.

King's Gambit

A weapon of incomparable danger in the hands of the great attacking players of the 19th century, the King's Gambit was responsible for many gems of sacrificial daring in the romantic days of chess history. But it would be only a matter of time before the elements that provided White with virulent attacks (quick development, excessive materialism) were used against him to rob the gambit of its venom. Today the defender has learned how to reach equality with the timely return of the gambit pawn in order to successfully mobilise his forces, but crucial also are his attempts to hold the pawn without going to lengths to acquire more material. Nonetheless, there is still scope here for investigation, and free spirits like Bronstein, Fischer and Spassky have been known to essay the old gambit when in an appropriately violent mood.

King's Gambit (Introduction) 1 e4 e5 2 f4

	2	3	4	5	6	7	8	9	10	
1	...	Nf3	Nc3	Bc4	d3	h3	Qxf3	Qg3	fe	=
	Bc5[1]	d6	Nf6[2]	Nc6	Bg4	Bxf3	Nd4	0-0!	de[3]	
2	...	...	...	...	...	Na4	Nxc5	c3	gf	±
	...	...	...	...	...	Nd4[4]	dc	Nxf3+	Bh5[5]	
3	...	...	...	...	...	fe[6]	Bg5	Bxf6	Nd5	=
	...	...	...	...	a6	de	Qd6	Qxf6	Qd6[7]	
4	...	...	c3	fe	d4	Bc4	e5	cd	Bd2	∞
	...	...	f5[8]	de	ed	Nf6[9]	Ne4	Bb4+	Nxd2[10]	
5	...	...	...	fe	a4	b4	Bc4			=
	...	...	Bb6!	de	Nc6	a6	Be6[11]			
6	...	ed[13]	Nc3	fe	Ne4	Bd3	Qe2[15]			±
	d5[12]	c6	cd[14]	d4	Qd5	Nc6				
7	...	...	d3	de![17]	Nf3[18]	Qe2	Nc3	Be3	Bxc5	±
	...	e4	Nf6[16]	Nxe4	Bc5	Bf5	Qe7	Nxc3	Nxe2[19]	
8	...	Qf3[20]	c3	d4	e5	Bxf4	ef[22]	Bd3[23]		=
	ef	Nc6[21]	Nf6	d5	Ne4	f6	Nxf6			
9	...	Nc3[24]	Ke2	Nxd5	Nf3	d4	e5	Bxf4	c4[25]	∓
	...	Qh4+	d5	Bg4+	Bd6	Nc6	0-0-0	Nge7	Bb4[26]	
10	...	d4[27]	ed	Ke2[28]	Nf3	c4	Nc3	dc	Kd2[29]	∞
	...	d5	Qh4+	Bd6	Bg4	c5	Nf6	Bxc5		
11	...	Be2[30]	ed	Nf3[33]	0-0	Nc3	Nxd5	d4[34]		=
	...	d5[31]	Nf6[32]	Be7	0-0	Nxd5	Qxd5			
12	...	Bc4[35]	Bxd5	Nc3	Nf3	dc	Bc4	Kxd1	Bxf4	=
	...	d5[36]	Nf6	Bb4	Bxc3	c6	Qxd1+	0-0	Nxe4[37]	
13	...	...	Kf1	d4	Qf3	g3	Qxh5[39]	Be2	e5	=
	...	Qh4+	c6[38]	g5	Nf6	Qh5	Nxh5	Nf6	Nd5[40]	
14	...	...	Nc3	Qf3[43]	ed	d3	Qf2	Kf1[44]		=
	...	Nf6[41]	c6[42]	d5	Bd6	Bg4	0-0	Re8+		

[1] **2 ...** d6 3 ♘c3 ♘f6 4 ♘f3 ♘c6 5 ♗b5
♗d7 6 d3 ef 7 ♗xf4 ♗e7 8 0-0 0-0 9 d4
♗e8 10 ♕d2 ♘d7 11 ♖ae1 ♘f6 ±.

2 ... c5!? (?!) intending 3 ... ♘c6, 4 ... d6.

2 ... ♕h4+ (Keene) 3 g3 ♕e4 4 ♘c3 ef
5 ♕f3 fg 6 ♗g3 ♗d7 7 ♕xg3 ∞ *ECO.*

[2] 4 ... ♘c6 5 ♗b5 ♘ge7 6 ♘a4 ♗b6
7 ♘xb6 ab 8 d3 0-0 9 0-0 ef 10 ♗xf4 d5
11 ed ♘xd5 = Levenfish. 11 e5 ♘g6 12
♗g3 ♗g4 13 d4 ±.

[3] 11 ♗g5 ♕d6 12 0-0-0 ♘h5 13 ♕h4
♘f4 14 ♗xf4 ef =.

[4] 7 ... ♗b6 8 ♘xb6 ab 9 c3 d5 10 ed
♘xd5 11 h3 ± Spielmann-Przepiorka, Nuremberg 1906.

[5] 11 ♕e2 ♕d6 12 fe ♕xe5 13 f4 ♕e7
14 ♕g2 0-0-0 15 0-0 ± Korchnoi.

[6] 7 f5 h6! 8 ♕e2 ♗d7 9 ♗e3 ♘d4 10
♗xd4 ed 11 ♘d1 0-0 12 0-0 d5 $\mp$ Tolush-
Furman, USSR 1946.

[7] Spielmann-Yates, Moscow 1925.

[8] 4 ... ♘f6 5 fe de 6 ♘xe5 ♕e7 7 d4 ♗d6
8 ♗c4 ♘xe4 9 ♘xd6+ cd! (9 ... ♘xd6+ 10
♕e2 ±) ∞.

[9] 7 ... ♘c6 8 b4 ♗b6 9 ♕b3 ♘h6 10 ♗g5
♕d6 11 ♘bd2 dc 12 ♕xc3 ♗d4 13 ♘xd4
♕xd4 14 ♕xd4 ♘xd4 15 0-0-0 ♘f7 16
♗e3 ± Korchnoi.

[10] 11 ♘bxd2 ♘d7 12 ♕b3 ♕e7 13 0-0-0
♘b6 14 a3 ♗xd2+ 15 ♖xd2 c6 16 d5 ♕c5
17 ♖c2 ♘xc4 18 ♖xc4 ♕xd5 19 ♖d1 ∞ *ECO.*

[11] Spielmann-Eliskases, 1937.

[12] Falkbeer.

[13] 3 ♘f3 de 4 ♘xe5 ♗d6 5 d4 ed 6 ♗xd3
♘f6 7 0-0 0-0 8 ♘c3 ♘bd7 9 ♘c4 ♗c5
10 ♘xd6 ♕xd6 11 f5 ♘xd3 = Radchenko.

[14] 4 ... ef 5 ♘f3 ♘f6 6 d4 ♗d6 7 ♕e2+
♕e7 8 ♕xe7+ ♗xe7 9 ♘e5 ♘xd5 10 ♘xd5+
cd 11 ♗xf4 f6 12 ♘d3 ± Tatenbaum-Estrin,
Moscow 1959.

[15] Opocensky-P.Johner, Baden 1914.

[16] 4 ... ♕xd5 5 ♕e2 f5 6 ♘c3 ♗b4 7 ♗d2
♗xc3 8 ♗xc3 ♘f6 9 de ♕xe4 10 ♕xe4 fe
11 ♗c4 ± Keres.

[17] 5 ♕e2 ♗f5 (5 ... ♗g4 6 ♕e3 ♕xd5
7 ♕xe4+ ♗e7 8 f5 ♘f6 9 ♕xb7 ♘bd7 ∞)
6 de ♘xe4 7 ♘c3 ♕e7 8 ♗d2 ♗xc3 =.

[18] 6 ♗e3 ♗d6 7 ♘f3 0-0 8 ♗c4 ♘d7
9 0-0 ♖e8 10 ♖e1 ♘ef6 11 ♔h1 ♘g4 12
♗g1 ♘b6 13 ♗b3 ♗xf4 $\mp$ Bronstein-Unzicker,
Moscow Ol 1956.

[19] 11 ♗xe7 ♘xf4 12 ♗a3! ♘d5 13 0-0-0 c6
14 ♘g5 ± Kuznetsov-Pozarsky, USSR 1963.

[20] Breyer Gambit.

[21] 3 ... ♕h4+ 4 g3 fg 5 hg ♕f6 6 ♘c3
(6 ♗c4!? ♘c6!) 6 ... ♕xf3 7 ♘xf3 ♗e7
8 ♘d5 ♗d8 9 b3 ♘e7! (9 ... ♘f6 10 ♗b2
♘xd5 11 ed 0-0 12 d6 ± Breyer) 10 ♗b2

0-0 11 ♘f4 ∞.

[22] 8 ♗b5?! ♗e7 9 ef ♗xf6 10 ♘e2 0-0
11 0-0 g5! $\mp$ Spielmann-Tarrasch, Berlin 1920.

[23] Estrin.

[24] Keres Gambit.

[25] Spassky-Furman, ½f USSR Ch 1959.

[26] 11 ♗g3 ♕h5 12 ♘xe7 ♗xe7 Korchnoi.

[27] Rosentreter Gambit.

[28] 5 ♔d2 ♗d6 6 ♕e1+! ♕xe1+ 7 ♔xe1 =
Keres.

[29] Mason-Kurschner, Nuremberg 1882.

[30] Tartakower or Lesser Bishop's Gambit.

[31] 3 ... ♘e7 4 ♘c3! d5 5 ed ♘xd5 6 ♘xd5
♕xd5 7 ♘f3 transposes.

3 ... h6? 4 d4! ± N.Littlewood-Zwaig,
Tel Aviv Ol 1964.

[32] 4 ... ♘e7 5 c4! c6 6 d4 ♘g6 7 ♘c3
♗b4 8 ♗f3 ∞.

[33] 5 d4 ♘xd5 6 ♘f3 ♗b4+ 7 c3 ♗e7
8 0-0 0-0 $\mp$ Tartakower-Alekhine, New York
1924.

[34] Transposing to 3 ♘f3 d5.

[35] Bishop's Gambit.

[36] Bledow Variation 3 ... f5!? 4 ♕e2! ♕h4+
5 ♔d1 fe 6 ♕xe4+ ♗e7 7 ♘f3! ♕h5 8 ♖e1
♘c6 9 ♗xg8! ♖xg8 10 ♘c3 d6 11 ♘d5!
♗f5 12 ♘c4 ♗c2+ 13 ♔e2! ♘e5 14 ♕xc7
♕f7 15 ♕xb7 ♖d8 16 ♔f1 ♗d3+ 17 ♔g1
♔f8 18 ♘d4 ± Glazkov.

[37] 11 ♖e1 = Bilguer.

[38] 4 ... ♘f6 5 ♘f3 ♕h5 6 ♕e1! d6 7 e5 de
8 ♘xe5 ♗e6 9 ♘xf7 ♕xf7 10 ♗e6 ± Bilguer.

4 ... g5 (Lopez, 1561) 5 ♘c3 ♘e7 6 d4
♗g7 7 g3 fg 8 ♔g2!

4 ... d6 (Cozio, 1766) 5 ♘c3 ♗e6 6 ♕e2
c6 7 ♘f3 ♕e7 8 d4 ♗xc4 9 ♕xc4 g5 (Fischer-
Evans, US Ch 1963/64) 10 h4! gh 11 ♘e1
♗h6 12 ♘d3 ± Korchnoi.

[39] 8 e5?! d5 9 ♕xh5 ♘xh5 10 ♗e2 ♘g7! 11
gf ♘e6! 12 fg ♘d4 13 ♗d3 ♗f5 $\mp$ Holmov.

[40] 11 c4 ♘e3+ 12 ♗xe3 fe = Korchnoi.

[41] Lopez Defence (1561).

[42] 4 ... ♗b4 5 e5 d5 6 ♗b5+ c6 7 ef
cb 8 ♕e2+! (8 fg ♖g8 9 ♕e2+ ♗e6 10
♕xb5+ ♕d7 11 ♕xb7 ♖c8 12 ♘f3 ♖xg7 13
0-0 ♗h3 $\mp$ Castro-Karpov, Stockholm 1969)
8 ... ♗e6 9 ♕xb5+ ♘c6 10 ♘f3 ♗xc3
(10 ... ♕xf6 11 ♕xb7 ♖c8 12 ♘d5 ± Carlsen-
Kolisch, 1862) 11 bc! ♕c7 12 fg ♖g8 13 c4!
intending ♗b2 ± Glazkov.

[43] 5 d4 ♗b4 6 e5 ♘e4! 7 ♕f3 d5 8 ed
0-0 9 ♘ge2 ♕h4+! 10 g3 fg 11 hg ♕g4 12
♕xg4 ♗xg4 13 ♗d3 ♖e8 $\mp$ Keres.

[44] 10 ... b5 11 ♗b3 b4 12 ♘ce2 ♘xd5
13 ♗xd5 cd 14 ♕g3 ♗xe2+ 15 ♘xe2 ♕f6
16 ♕g5! Keres.

10 ... ♗xf4 11 ♕xf4 cd 12 ♘xd5 ♘xd5
13 ♗xd5 ♕xd5 14 ♕xg4 ♘c6 = Euwe.

287

	3	4	5	6	7	8	9	10	11	
1	... ♘f6[1]	e5 ♘h5[2]	♗e2 d6![3]	0-0 de	♘xe5 ♕d4+	♔h1 ♘f6	♘d3 ♗d6	c3[4]		±
2	... ...	... ...	d4 d6	♕e2[5] d5	c4 ♗e6	cd ♗xd5	♘c3 ♘c6	♗d2! ♗b4	♘xd5 ♕xd5[6]	±
3	... h6[7]	d4 g5	g3[8] fg	♘c3!? d6[9]	h4 g4	♘g1 g2[10]	♗xg2 ♗e7	h5 ♗h4+	♔e2 ♗g5[11]	∞
4	... d6[12]	♘c3!? g5?![13]	h4 g4	♘g5 h6[14]	♘xf7 ♔xf7	d4 f3	♗c4+ ♔e8	gf ♘f6	♗f4 ♕e7[15]	∞
5	... ...	d4 g5	h4![16] g4	♘g1! ♗h6	♘c3 c6	♘ge2 ♕f6	g3 f3	♘f4[17]		∞
6	... ♗e7[18]	♗c4 ♗h4+[19]	♔f1 d5	♗xd5 ♘f6	♘c3[20] ♘xd5[21]	♘xd5 f5	♘xh4 ♕xh4	♘xc7+ ♔d8	♘xa8 fe[22]	=
7	... ...	♘c3 ♘f6	e5?![23] ♘g4	d4 ♘e3	♗xe3 fe	♗c4 d6	0-0 0-0	♕d3 ♘c6	ed ♗xd6[24]	=
8	... ...	♗e2! ♗h4+[25]	♔f1 ♗e7	d4 g5	h4 g4	♘e5 h5	♗c4 ♖h7[26]	♗xf4!		±
9	... g5	♘c3[27] g4[28]	♘e5[29] ♕h4+	g3 fg	♕xg4 ♕xg4![30]	♘xg4 d5	♗h3! de	♘f6+ ♔d8	♗xc8 ♔xc8[31]	∞
10	... ...	d4 g4[32]	♘e5[33] ♕h4+	g3 fg	♕xg4 ♕xg4[34]	♘xg4 d5	♘e3 de	hg ♘c6	♗g2![35]		∞
11	... ...	♗c4 g4	0-0[36] gf	♕xf3 ♕f6	e5?![37] ♕xe5	♗xf7+[38] ♔xf7	d4 ♕xd4+	♗e3 ♕f6	♗xf4 ♘e7[39]	∓
12	... ...	... d6	d4[40] h6	0-0 ♗g7	g3[41] ♘c6	c3 g4	♘h4 f3	♕b3 ♕d7![42]	♘d2 ♘a5[43]	∓
13	... ...	... ♗g7	h4[44] h6[45]	d4 d6	c3[46] ♘c6	♕b3 ♕e7	0-0 ♘f6	hg hg	♘xg5 ♘xd4![47]	∓
14	... ...	h4 g4	♘g5[48] h6[49]	♘xf7 ♔xf7	♗c4+ d5	♗xd5+ ♔e8	d4 ♘f6[50]	♘c3 f3	gf ♗b4[51]	∓

[1]   3 ... ♘e7 4 d4 d5 5 ♘c3 de 6 ♘xe4 ♘g6 7 h4! ♗e7 8 h5 ♘h4 9 ♗xf4 ♗g4 10 h6! ± Kuznetsov–Bonch-Osmolovsky, Moscow 1964.

　　3 ... f5 4 e5! d5 5 d4 g5 6 h4 g4 7 ♘g1 f3 (7 ... ♗e7 8 ♗xf4 ♗xh4+ 9 g3 ±) 8 ♗g5! fg 9 ♗xg2 ♗e7 10 ♘c3 ♗e6 11 ♘ge2 ♕d7 12 ♘f4 c6 13 ♗f1 ±.

[2]   4 ... ♘e4 5 d3 ♘g5 6 ♗xf4 ♘e6 7 ♗g3 d5 (7 ... d6!? intending 8 ... de, 9 ... ♘bd7) 8 ♘c3 d4 (8 ... c5!?, 8 ... ♗b4!?) 9 ♘e4 ♘c6 10 ♗e2 ♗e7 11 0-0 0-0 12 ♕d2 ± Tolush–Averbakh, Kislovodsk 1960.

[3]   5 ... g5 6 0-0 ♖g8 7 d4 d5 8 ♕d3 ♖g6 9 ♘h4 ♖h6 10 ♗xh5 ♖xh5 11 ♘f5 ♕d7 12 g4 fg 13 ♘xg3 ± Glazkov.

[4]   Intending ♘xf4 ±/±.

[5]   6 ♘c3 de 7 ♕e2 ♗g4 8 ♕xe5+ ♗e7 9 ♘d5 ♘c6 10 ♗b5 0-0 11 ♗xc6 d6!

　　6 ♗c4 ♘c6! 7 ♘c3 de 8 ♕e2 ♗g4! 9 d5 (9 ♗b5 Keres) 9 ... ♗xf3 10 ♕xf3 ♕h4+ 11 g3 ♘d4 12 ♕e4 ♘xg3 13 hg ♕xg3+ 14 ♔d1 0-0-0 ∓.

[6]   12 0-0-0 ♕xa2 13 d5! ±.

[7]   Anti-Kieseritzky System.

[8]   Others transpose elsewhere.

[9]   6 ... gh 7 ♖xh2 ♗g7 8 ♗c4 d6 9 ♘xg5 ±.

　　6 ... ♗g7 7 hg d5 8 ♘xd5 ♗g4 9 ♗c4 ± Spassky–Gibbs, Leningrad 1960.

　　6 ... g4 7 hg! gf 8 ♕xf3 ♕f6 9 ♗f4 ∞/± Kardino.

[10]   8 ... ♗e7 9 ♗g2 ♗xh4 10 ♗f4 ♕f6 11 ♕d2 intending 12 0-0-0 ∞ Korchnoi.

[11]   12 ♗xg5 ♕xg5 13 ♕d2 (13 ♕d3!?)

288

13 ... ♕xd2+ 14 ♔xd2 ♘e7 15 ♘ge2 ∞ Korchnoi.

12 Fischer's Defence or Fischer's Bust.

13 4 ... h6 (Korchnoi) 5 h4 ♗g4 6 d4 ♗xf3 7 ♕xf3 ♗e7 8 ♗xf4 ♗xh4+ 9 g3 ♗g5 10 0-0-0 ∞ Analysis.

14 6 ... f6 7 ♘h3 gh 8 ♕h5+ ♔d7 9 ♕f5+ ♔e7 10 ♘d5+ ♔f7 11 ♕h5+ ♔g7 12 gh ♘e7 13 ♖g1+ ♔g6 14 ♘xf4 ♕e8 15 ♕d5 ±± Bhend.

15 12 ♕d3 ♗e6 ∞ Bhend.

16 5 ♗c4 transposes to the Hanstein Gambit, or 5 ... g4!? 6 ♗xf4 gf 7 ♕xf3 ∞ Dal-Danberg, Sweden 1968.

17 Bhend.

18 Cunningham Gambit.

19 4 ... ♘f6 5 e5 ♘g4 6 ♘c3 ♗h4+ 7 ♔f1 0-0 8 d4! ♘e3 9 ♗xe3 fe 10 ♕d3 ♗f2 11 h4! ± Glazkov; 6 ... d6! 7 d4 de 8 de ♕xd1+ 9 ♔xd1 ♗e6 10 ♗xe6 fe 11 h3 ♘h6 12 ♗xf4 ♘f5 = ECO.

20 7 ♗b3!? (Korchnoi) intending 7 ... ♗g4 8 d3! (8 ♗xf7+ ♔xf7 9 ♘e5+ ♔e8 10 ♕xg4 ♘f6 ∓); 7 ... 0-0! intending ... ♘xe4 ∞.

21 7 ... 0-0 8 d3!

22 12 ♕e1 ♕h5! 13 ♕xe4 ♖e8 14 ♕f3 ♕e5 15 ♔f2 ♕c5+ 16 ♔f1 (Anderson-Horseman, British Ch 1954) 16 ... ♕e5! = (17 ♕f2!? f3! ∓).

23 5 ♗e2! will transpose to row 24.

24 12 ♘e4 ♗e7 = Korchnoi.

25 4 ... ♘f6 5 ♘c3 d5 transposes to row 24.
4 ... d5 5 ed ♘f6 6 0-0 0-0 7 c4! c6 8 dc ♘xc6 9 d4 ♗g4 10 d5 ±.

26 Solntsev-Vasilchuk, USSR 1957.

27 Quaade Gambit.

28 4 ... ♗g7! – Philidor and Hanstein Gambits.
4 ... d6 – Fischer Defence.

29 5 ♗c4 (the MacDonnell Gambit) 5 ... gf 6 ♕xf3 d6! 7 0-0 ♗e6 8 ♘d5 c6 9 ♕c3 cd 10 ♕xh8 dc 11 ♕xg8 ♕b6+ 12 ♔h1 ♘c6 13 b3 ♕d4 ∓ Malkin (1911).

30 7 ... g2+? 8 ♕xh4 gh♕ 9 ♕h5 ♗d6 10 ♕xf7+ ♔d8 11 d4! ♘e7 12 ♗g5 ±± Keres.

31 12 ♘cxe4 gh 13 ♖xh2 ∞ Schmidt (1884).

32 4 ... ♗g7! transposes to the Philidor or Hanstein Gambits.
4 ... h6 5 ♘c3 ♗g7 6 g3 d6 7 gf g4 8 ♘g1 ♕h4+ 9 ♔e2 ♘c6 10 ♗e3 g3 11 ♘f3 ♗g4 12 ♔d2 ♗xf3 13 ♕xf3 ♘d4 14 ♕xg3 ± Bhend.

33 5 ♗xf4!? gf 6 ♕xf3 ∞ Keene-Milner Barry Blackheath 1980.

34 7 ... g2+? 8 ♕xh4 gh♕ 9 ♘c3! d6 10 ♘xf7 ♗e7 (10 ... ♔xf7 11 ♕h5+ ♔g7 12 ♕f2!! ±±) 11 ♕h5 ♘f6 12 ♘d6+ ♔d8 13 ♘f7+ with a draw by perpetual check.

35 11 ♗b5 ♗g7 12 d5 a6 13 ♗a4 b5 ∓ Schmidt (1884); 11 ... ♗d7! ∓ ECO.

36 Muzio-Polerio Gambit. Also available are:
5 ♘c3 fg 5 ♕xf3 (the MacDonnell Gambit – note 27).
5 ♗xf7+ (the Lolli Gambit) 5 ... ♔xf7 6 ♘e5+ ♔e8 7 ♕xg4 ♘f6 8 ♕xf4 d6 9 ♘f3 ♖g8 10 0-0 ♖g4 11 ♕e3 ♖xe4 ∓ Schmidt (1886).
5 d4 (the Ghulam-Kassim Gambit) 5 ... gf 6 ♕xf3 (6 ♗xf4 d5!) 6 ... d5 7 ♗xd5 ♘f6 8 0-0 c6 9 ♗xf7+ ♔xf7 10 ♕xf4 ♗g7 11 e5 ♖f8 12 ef ♔g8! ∓∓.
5 ♘e5 (the Salvio Gambit) 5 ... ♕h4+ 6 ♔e2 (6 ♔f1!?) 6 ... f3+!? 7 gf gf+ 8 ♔d3 (8 ♘xf3 ♕xe4+) intending 8 ... f2 9 ♗xf7+ ♔d8 10 ♗h5! ∞; 6 ... ♘c6!? 7 ♘xf7 ♗c5 8 ♕f1!; 7 ♘xf7 ♗c5 8 ♕e1 g3 9 ♘xh8 ♗f2 10 ♕d1 ♘f6 11 d4 d5 ∓∓.

37 7 c3! ♘c6 8 d4 ♘xd4 9 ♗xf7+ ♕xf7 10 cd ♗h6 11 ♘c3 d6 12 ♘d5 ♗e6 13 ♘xf4 ♗xf4 14 ♗xf4 0-0-0 15 d5 ♗d7 16 ♕c3 ♕f6 = ECO.

38 8 d3? ♗h6 9 ♘c3 ♘e7 10 ♗d2 ♘bc6 11 ♖ae1 ♕f5 12 ♘d5 ♔d8 13 ♕e2 b5! 14 ♘xe7 ♕c5+ 15 ♖f2 ♕xe7! ∓ Korchnoi.

39 12 ♘c3 ♗h6! intending ♗g6 14 g4 ♗e7 15 ♔h1 ♕h4 (Schüssler-Akvist, Sweden 1976) 16 ♕e3 ♘c6 ∞; 16 ... ♔g8! 17 ♗e5 b6 intending ... ♗b7 ∓.

40 The Hanstein Gambit.

41 7 ♘c3 ♗e6! 8 ♗xe6 fe 9 e5 ♘c6! ∓.
7 c3 ♘c6! – 7 g3.

42 10 ... ♕e7?! 11 ♗f4! ♘f6 12 ♘d2 ♘h5 13 ♗e3 ♗f6 14 ♘dxf3 gf 15 ♖xf3 ± Korchnoi.

43 12 ♕c2 ♘xc4 13 ♘xc4 ♘e7 14 ♘e3 ♕f6 ∓ Kaplan-Karpov, Stockholm 1969.

44 5 0-0 h6 6 d4 d6 7 c3 (7 ♘c3 ♘c6! ∓) 7 ... ♘c6 8 g3 g4 9 ♘h4 f3 10 ♘d2 ♘f6! 11 ♘f5 ♗xf5 12 ef 0-0 13 ♗d3 (Heuer-Vilard, USSR 1964) 13 ... d5! =.

45 Philidor Gambit.

46 7 ♘c3 ♘c6 8 ♘e2 ♕e7 9 ♕d3 ♗d7 10 ♗d2 0-0-0 11 ♘c3 (11 0-0-0 – Keres – ♘f6!) 11 ... ♖e8 12 d5 ♘e5 13 ♘xe5 de 14 0-0-0 ♘f6 ∓ Anderssen-Neumann, 1866.

47 Zak/Korchnoi.

48 Allgaier Gambit.

49 5 ... ♘f6 (Schlechter Variation) 6 e5 ♕e7 7 ♕e2 ♘h5 8 ♕xg4 (simplest) 8 ... ♕xe5+ (8 ... ♘g3 9 ♕xf4 ♘xh1 10 ♘c3 c6 11 ♗c4 ±) 9 ♗e2 ♘g3 10 d4 ♕xe2+ 11 ♕xe2 ♘xe2 12 ♔xe2 ±.

50 9 ... f3 10 gf ♘f6 (10 ... ♗e7 11 0-0 ±) 11 ♘c3 – 9 ... ♘f6.

51 12 ♗b3 ♘c6 13 ♗e3 gf 14 ♕d3 ♕e7 15 e5 ♘g4 16 0-0-0 ♗xc3 ∓ Zak/Korchnoi.

	3	4	5	6	7	8	9	10	11	
15	...	...	♘e5⁵²	♗c4	d4	♘xf7!	♗xf7+	♗xf4⁵⁴		±
	...	...	h5⁵³	♖h7	d6	♖xf7	♔xf7			
16	...	...	...	♘xg4	♘f2	d4	♗e2	♘c3⁵⁷	♘xg4	±
	...	...	d6⁵⁵	h5⁵⁶	♘f6	♗h6	♘c6	♗g4	♗xg4⁵⁸	
17	...	...	...	♗c4	ed	d4⁶⁰	0-0	♕e1	♖xe1	=
	...	...	♘f6⁵⁹	d5	♗d6	♘h5!⁶¹	♕xh4	♕xe1	0-0⁶²	
18	...	...	...	d4	♘d3	♘c3	♗xf4	♘xe4	♔f2	±
	...	...	...	d6	♗g7	0-0	♘xe4	♖e8	♖xe4⁶³	
19	...	...	...	...	...	♗xf4	c3!	♘d2	♘xe4	∞̄
	...	...	...	...	♘xe4	♗g7	0-0	♖e8	♖xe4+⁶⁴	
20	...	...	...	...	...	...	♕e2	c3	♘d2	=
	...	...	...	...	...	♕e7	♗g7	h5	♘xd2⁶⁵	
21	...	...	...	d4	♘xg4	♕xg4	c3	♗xf4	♕f3	=
	...	...	♗g7!⁶⁶	d6	♗xg4	♗xd4	♗e5	♘f6	♘bd7⁶⁷	
22	...	ed	♘c3	d4	♗d3	0-0	♘e4	c4	♗xe3	±
	d5⁶⁸	♗d6	♘e7	0-0	♘d7	h6	♘xd5	♘e3	fe⁶⁹	
23	...	♘c3	♘xd5	d4	c4	♗e2	0-0	♖e1		=
	...	♘f6	♘xd5⁷⁰	♕xd5	♗e7	♕e4+	♘c6	♗f5	0-0-0⁷¹	
24	...	...	...	...	...	♗e2!	0-0			=
	...	...	...	...	...	0-0⁷²				
25	...	...	♗b5+	dc	d4	0-0	♘bd2	♘c4	♗xc6	±
	...	...	c6	♘xc6⁷³	♗d6	0-0	♗g4	♘c7	bc⁷⁴	

⁵² Kieseritzky Gambit.

⁵³ The Long Whip.

⁵⁴ Stanley-Fraser, 1837.

⁵⁵ Green Variation.

⁵⁶ 6 ... ♗e7 7 d4 ♗xh4+ 8 ♘f2 ♕g5 9 ♘c3 ♘f6 10 ♕f3 ± Steinitz-Green, London 1864.

⁵⁷ Intending ♕d3, ♗d2, 0-0-0.

⁵⁸ 12 ♕d3 ±.

⁵⁹ Berlin Defence.

⁶⁰ 8 0-0!? (the Rice Gambit) 8 ... ♗xe5 9 ♖e1 ♕e7! 10 c3 ♘h5! 11 d4 ♘d7 12 de (12 ♕xg4 ♘df6!) 12 ... ♘xe5 13 b3 0-0! 14 ♗a3 ♘f3+ 15 gf ♕xh4 16 ♖e5 ♗f5 (16 ... ♕g3+ draws) 17 ♘d2 ♕g3+ 18 ♔f1 ♕h2 19 ♗xf8 g3 20 ♗c5 g2+ 21 ♔e1 g1♕+ (21 ... ♕h4+ draws after 22 ♔e2 ♘g3+) 22 ♗xg1 ♕xg1+ 23 ♗f1 ♘g3 ∞ Capablanca.

⁶¹ Staunton.

⁶² 12 ♗d3 ♖e8 13 ♗d2 f6 14 ♘c4 = Zak/Korchnoi.

⁶³ 12 c3 ♕f6 13 g3 ♗h6 14 ♗d3 ♗xf4

15 ♗xf4 ♖xf4+ 16 gf ♕xf4+ 17 ♔e2! (Rubinstein) 17 ... g3 18 ♕d2! ±.

⁶⁴ 12 ♔f2 ♕f6 13 g3 ♗h6 14 ♕d2 intending ♗g2 ∞̄ Zak/Korchnoi.

⁶⁵ 12 ♔xd2 ♕xe2+ 13 ♗xe2 ♘c6 =.

⁶⁶ Paulsen.

⁶⁷ 12 g3 ♕e7 13 ♘d2 =.

⁶⁸ Scandinavian Variation.

⁶⁹ 12 c5 ± Spassky-Bronstein, Leningrad 1960.

⁷⁰ 5 ... ♗d6 6 ♗c4 0-0 7 0-0 ♘bd7 8 d4! ±.

⁷¹ 12 ♗f1 ♕c2 13 ♗xc2 ♗xc2 = Spielmann-Milner Barry, Margate 1938.

⁷² If here 8 ... g5 9 c4! and White has excellent attacking chances, according to Zak/Korchnoi, although Korchnoi gives 8 ... g5 ∓ in *ECO*.

⁷³ 6 ... bc 7 ♗c4 ♘d5 8 0-0 ♗d6 9 ♘c3 ♗e6 10 ♘e4 ♗c7 11 ♗b3 0-0 12 d4 ± Tal-Haubt, 1960.

⁷⁴ 12 ♕d3 ♕d5 13 ♘fe5 ± *ECO*.

Vienna

Another opening whose heyday has passed, the Vienna's original scheme was to effect a sort of delayed King's Gambit. Unfortunately, this hesitation does nothing to improve White's attacking chances and Black secures at least equality by striking out in the centre. When seen in modern tournament play, White usually opts for Smyslov's preference 3 g3. This quiet positional continuation is more in keeping with the orderly sentiments of contemporary play, but this also seems too indirect to provide White with a real advantage.

	2	3	4	5	6	7	8	9	10	
	Vienna	1 e4 e5 2 ♘c3								
1	...	♘a4	♔xf2	♔e3	♔d3	♔c3	d4![1]	♔b3	♕e2	=
	♗c5	♗xf2+	♕h4+	♕f4+	d5	♕xe4	ed+	♘c6	♘a5+[2]	
2	...	♘f3	d4	♘xd4	♗g5	♗h4	♘xc6	♗d3		±
	...	d6	ed	♘f6	h6	♘c6	bc			
3	...	f4	♘f3	h4[3]	♘g5	♘xf7	d4	♗xf4	♗e2	∓
	♘c6	ef	g5	g4	h6	♔xf7	d5	♗b4	♗xc3+[4]	
4	...	g3	♗g2	♘ge2	0-0	d3	♗e3	fe		=
	...	♗c5	♘ge7	0-0	a6	d6	♗xe3	f5[5]		
5	...	♗c4	♕g4!	♕f3	♘ge2	d3	♕g3	f4	♘d5	±
	...	♗c5[6]	g6	♘f6	d6	♗g4	h6	♕e7[7]	♘xd5[8]	
6	...	g3	ed	♗g2	bc	♘e2	0-0	d3	f4	±
	♘f6	d5	♘xd5	♘xc3	♗d6	0-0	c6	♘d7	ef[9]	
7	...	...	♗g2	♘ge2	0-0	d3	♗g5	♘xg3![10]	♘h5	∓
	...	♗c5	d6	♘c6	h5	h4	hg	♘d4!	♘e6[11]	
8	...	...	...	♘f3	d3	♘a4	h3	c3	♔xf2[12]	±
	...	...	...	♘c6	♗g4	♘d7	♗h5	♗xf2+		
9	...	...	...	♘ge2	ed	dc				∞
	...	...	0-0	d5	c6!?	♘xc6[13]				
10	...	...	...	d3	♘ge2	0-0	ed	♔h1		=
	...	...	...	♖e8	c6	d5	♘xd5	♗g4[14]		
11	...	a3!?[15]	ed	♕h5!	♘f3	dc	♗c4	♕h4	♗g5[17]	±
	...	d5?![16]	♘xd5	♕d6	♘xc3	♘d7	g6	♗e7		
12	...	...	♘f3	d4	♗e2	0-0	h3	♗e3		±
	...	g6!	d6	♘bd7[18]	♗g7	0-0	c6	♕c7		

---

1   8 ♔b3 ♘a6 9 a3 ♕a4+ 10 ♔xa4 ♘c5+ Hamppe-Meitner, Vienna 1870; 8 ... ♘c6!?
2   11 ♔b4 ♘c6+ 12 ♔b3 =; 12 ♔a3!? ∞.
3   5 d4 g4 6 ♗c4 gf 7 0-0 d5 8 ed ♗g4 9 ♕d2 ♘ce7 10 ♗xf4 ♘h6! ∓ Keres.
4   Keres.
5   Konstantinopolsky.
6   3 ... ♘f6 - 1 e4 e5 2 ♘c3 ♘f6 3 ♗c4 ♘c6.
7   Larsen-Portisch, Santa Monica 1966.
8   11 ♕xg4 ♘e3 12 ♗xe3 ♗xe3 ±.
9   11 ♗xf4 ♘e5 12 ♖b1 ♖b8 13 c4 ± Spassky-Karpov, Tilburg 1979.
10   9 hg ♗g4 10 ♕d2 ♕d7 11 ♘a4 ♗h3! ∓ Nunn.
11   11 ♘xg7+! ♔xg7 12 ♘d5 ♘xd5! 13 ♗xd8 ♘f4 14 ♗g5 ♘ge6 15 ♗xf4 ♗xf4 16 ♔h1 ∓ Augustin-Nunn, Moscow 1977.
    11 ♗xf6 gf 12 ♘d5 ∞ ECO.
12   Averbakh-Spassky, USSR Ch 1963.
13   Gunsberg-Pollock, Hastings 1895.
14   Portisch-Toran, Malaga 1961.
15   Mengarini's Opening.
16   3 ... ♘c6 4 ♘c3 - Four Knight's.
17   Myers.
18   Evans.

	Vienna 1 e4 e5 2 ♘c3 ♘f6 3 ♗c4								
	3	4	5	6	7	8	9	10	11
1	... ♗b4	♘f3 d6	0-0 0-0	d3 ♗xc3[1]	bc ♗e6	♗xe6 fe	♕e2 ♘bd7	♘g5 ♕e7	=
2	... ♗c5	d3 d6	f4 ♗e6	♗xe6[2] fe	fe de	♕e2 ♘c6	♗e3 ♗xe3	♕xe3 0-0[3]	=
3	... ♘xe4	♕h5 ♘d6	♗b3 ♘c6!?[4]	♘b5 g6	♕f3 f5!	♕d5 ♕e7	♘xc7+ ♔d8	♘xa8 b6	♘xb6[5] ab[6]	∞
4	... ...	... ...	♕xe5+ ♕e7	♕xe7+ ♗xe7	♗b3 ♘f5	♘f3 c6	0-0 d5	♖e1 0-0[7]	=

	Vienna 1 e4 e5 2 ♘c3 ♘f6 3 f4								
	3	4	5	6	7	8	9	10	11
5	... d5[8]	fe[9] ♘xe4	♕f3 f5	d3 ♘xc3	bc d4	♕g3 ♘c6	♗e2 ♗e6	♗f3 ♕d7	♘e2 0-0-0![10]	∞/∓
6	... ...	... ...	d3 ♗b4	de ♕h4+	♔e2 ♗xc3	bc ♗g4+	♘f3 de	♕d4 ♗h5[11]	=
7	... ...	... ...	♘f3 ♗e7	♕e2 ♘xc3	dc 0-0	♗f4 c5	0-0-0 ♕a5!	♔b1 ♘c6[12]	♕b5 ♗e6[13]	=

[1] 6 ... ♗e6?! 7 ♗xe6 fe 8 ♘e2 ♘bd7 9 c3 ♗a5 10 a4 c6 11 ♘g3 ♕e7 12 ♕e2 h6 13 d4 ± Larsen-Smyslov, Las Palmas 1972.

[2] 6 ♗b3 ♘c6 7 f5 ♗xb3 8 ab h6 intending ... d5 ∓ Mieses-Scheve, Monte Carlo 1901.

[3] Spielmann-Tarrasch, Bad Kissingen 1928.

[4] 5 ... ♗e7 6 ♘f3 0-0 7 h4! ♘c6 8 ♘g5 h6 9 ♕g6 ♗xg5 10 hg ♕xg5 11 ♕xg5 hg 12 d3 ⊙⊙ Gufeld-Tarve, Tallinn 1969.

[5] 11 d3 ♗b7 12 h4 f4 13 ♕f3 ♘d4 14 ♕g4 ♗h6 15 ♘h3 ♘6f5 16 ♘g5 d5! (Miller-Statham, corr. 1979; 16 ... ♗xg5 17 hg f3 18 g3 ♕b4+ 19 ♔d1 ♘xc2 20 ♕xb4 ♘xb4 ∞/± Trajković) 17 c3 (17 0-0 ♗xg5! ∓) 17 ... ♘xb3! 18 ab ♗xa8; 13 ... ♗h6! 14 ♗d5 ♗xa8 15 ♕g4 ♖f8 ∓ Konstantinopolsky.

[6] 12 ♕f3 ♗b7 13 d3 ♘d4 14 ♕h3 e4 15 ♗e3 ed 16 0-0-0 ♘xc2 17 ♗xb6+ ♔e8 18 ♕xd3 ♗h6+ 19 ♔b1 ♗e4 20 ♗xc2 ♗xd3 21 ♗xd3 ♗g7 ∞ Yudelevich-Poselnikov, corr. 1974.

[7] Sämisch-Rubinstein, Hanover 1926.

[8] 3 ... d6 4 fe de 5 ♘f3 ±.

[9] 4 ed ef 5 d4 ♗d6 6 ♕e2+ ♔f8! ∓ Inkiov-Pinter, Herkulana Z 1982.

[10] 12 0-0 ♗c5 13 c4 ♗xc4 14 ♘f4 ♘xe5!? 15 dc d3+ 16 ♔h1 dc ∞/∓ Vorotnikov-Kapengut, USSR 1975.

[11] Chigorin-Caro, Vienna 1898.

[12] Janošević-Baretić, Yugoslavia 1977.

[13] 12 ♕xa5 ♘xa5 13 ♘g5 ♗xg5 14 ♗xg5 ♘c6 = Rajković.

Philidor   Latvian   Petroff

The Philidor and Latvian have never achieved a great following simply because they present the second player with difficulties in equalising. Philidor's Defence suffers from being too passive, though it does have a few wild side variants. Larsen's variation has the most promise, an interesting attempt to inject life into an essentially inferior defence. Critical here is White's attempt to score the point by force, castling long and initiating a full scale assault against the opposing king. At present there has been insufficient testing to reach a definite conclusion regarding the viability of Larsen's plan with an early ... g6.

The Latvian Gambit (sometimes also known as the Greco Counter Gambit in honour of the Italian master who analysed it in the seventeenth century) has never been considered quite respectable. 2 ... f5, introducing a kind of King's Gambit in reverse, is a highly provocative move which at one time analysts claimed to have refuted outright. But resources have been found for Black which, although not good enough for complete equality, at least offer him a playable game. The gambit has useful surprise value since there is no simple way for White to gain an advantage and few players as White will have bothered to commit to memory an antidote to such a rare counterthrust. 3 d4 (row 1), 3 ef (row 2), 3 ♘xe5 (rows 3-6) and 3 ♗c4 (rows 7 and 8) all offer White some advantage. 3 ♗c4 is generally considered White's most promising move but perhaps the less usual 4 ♘g5!? (note 1) deserves more tests.

The third member of this section, Petroff's Defence, is another animal entirely. Originally envisaged by its inventors Petroff and Jaenisch (the defence bears Petroff's name, perhaps because he defeated co-author Jaenisch in a match) as a lively counterattacking alternative to 2 ... ♘c6, it has since been viewed as a colourless drawing variation. Recent attention has been focused on the merits of this defence after Larsen's use of it to defeat World Champion Karpov. The Petroff is not without its possibilities as a winning attempt for Black and its reputation as a rock-solid choice for equality has not diminished. It is an extremely difficult nut to crack and, currently enjoying a resurgence in popularity, it has even found its way into Karpov's repertoire. In essence, it remains an opening geared for static equilibrium, and in this respect it is a particularly efficient defence.

	3	4	5	6	7	8	9	10	11	
1	♗c4	0-0	♖e1	d4	♘xd4	a4?!	♘b3	♕e2	♗xe6!?[2]	∓
	♗e7	♘f6	0-0	ed	a6	c5	♗e6	♘c6		
2	d4	♗c4	♘xe5	♕h5+	♘xg6	♕e5+	♗b5+	♘xe7	♕xe7+	±
	f5	fe	d5	g6	♘f6	♗e7	c6	♕xe7	♔xe7[3]	
3	...	♗c4	0-0	de	♘g5[4]	♕h5	♕xg5	♗xg5	♗d2[6]	±
	♘d7	c6	♗e7	de	♗xg5[5]	g6	♕xg5	h6		
4	...	♘xd4[7]	c4	♘c3	♗e3	h4!	♕d2	0-0-0[9]		±
	ed	g6[8]	♗g7	♘c6	♘ge7	h6	♘e5			
5	...	de	♕d5![10]	♗g5[11]	ed	♘c3	0-0-0	h3	♗e2	±
	♘f6	♘xe4	♘c5	♕d7[12]	♗xd6	0-0	♕g4	♕h5	♗e6[13]	
6	...	♘c3	♗c4	0-0	♕e2	a4	h3[15]	♖d1	de[16]	±
	...	♘bd7[14]	♗e7	0-0	c6	♕c7	b6	♗b7	♘xe5	
7	...	...	♘xd4	♗f4	♕d2	0-0-0	ed	♘f5	♕e3[18]	±
	...	ed	♗e7	0-0	a6[17]	d5	♘xd5	♘xf4		
8	...	...	...	♗g5[19]	♕d2	♗f4	♗g3	♗e2	hg	∞
	...	...	g6	♗g7	h6	g5	♘h5	♘xg3	♘c6[20]	

[1]   2 ...d5?! 3 ♘xe5 de 4 ♗c4 ♕g5 5 ♗xf7+ ♔e7 6 d4 ♕xg2 7 ♖f1 ♗h3 8 ♗c4 ♘f6 9 ♗f4 ± Lob-Eliskases, corr. 1932.
      2 ... ♕e7?! 3 ♘c3 c6 4 d4 d6 5 ♗g5 ♘f6 6 ♕e2 ± Georgadze-Kupreichik, USSR 1971.

[2]   11 ♘c3?! ♗b4! ∓ Mestel-Georgadze, Hastings 1979/80.

[3]   12 ♗e2 ♖g8 13 g3 ± Keres.

[4]   7 ♘c3 h6 8 ♕e2 ♕c7 9 ♗e3 b5 10 ♗b3 ♘gf6 11 a3 ♘c5 ∓ Thomas-Alekhine, Hastings 1933/34.

[5]   7 ... ♘h6 8 ♗e6 fe 9 ♗xh6 ♘b6 10 ♕h5+ ♔f8 11 ♗b3 gh 12 ♖ad1 ∞/± Matulović-Tomović, Sombor 1957.

[6]   Steiner-Brinckmann, Budapest 1929.

[7]   4 ♕xd4 ♘c6 5 ♗b5 ±.

[8]   Larsen.

[9]   Westerinen-Wahlbom, Gausdal 1978.

[10]   5 ♗c4 c6! =.

[11]   6 ♘g5 ♕e7 ∞ Keres.

[12]   6 ... ♗e7 7 ed ♕xd6 8 ♘c3 ± Steiner-Holzhausen, Berlin 1928.

[13]   12 ♕d2 h6 13 ♗f4 ± Keres.

[14]   4 ... ♗g4 5 ♗e2 ♘bd7 6 0-0 c6 7 ♗e3 ♗e7 8 ♘h4 ♗xe2 9 ♕xe2 g6 10 ♖ad1 0-0 11 g3 ♘e8 12 de ± Haag-Titkos, Hungary 1979.

[15]   9 ♗a2!? b6 10 ♗e3 ♗b7 11 ♘h4 ± Zaitsev-Durao, Sochi 1977.

[16]   Klompus-Schonmann, corr. 1961-63.

[17]   7 ... d5 8 ed ♘xd5 9 ♘xd5 ♕xd5 10 ♘b5 ♕e4+ 11 ♗e2 ♘a6 12 0-0 ±/ ± Kirilov-Darznieks, Riga 1972.

[18]   Keres.

[19]   6 ♗e3 ♗g7 7 ♕d2 0-0 8 0-0-0 ♖e8 9 f3 ♘c6 ± Unzicker-Keene, Moscow 1977.

[20]   12 ♗b5 ♗d7 13 ♘de2 ♕f6 ∞ Hennings-Radulov, Siegen Ol 1970.

Latvian Gambit   1 e4 e5 2 ♘f3 f5

	3	4	5	6	7	8	9	10	11	
1	d4!?	♘xe5[1]	♗e2[2]	♘g4	♘c3	♗g5	♗xe7	♗xg4		±
	fe	♘f6	d6	♗e7[3]	♘bd7	♘xg4	♕xe7	♘f6[4]		
2	ef	♘e5[6]	♗e2[7]	♗h5+	♘f7	♘c3[8]	♘d5+	♕xh5	f6	±
	e4[5]	♘f6	d6	♔e7	♕e8	♘xh5	♔d7[9]	♖g8	♘a6[10]	
3	♘xe5	♘xc6![11]	♘c3	d3	♗g5	f3	♗e2	♗d2[13]	ef	±
	♘c6	dc	♕e7![12]	♘f6	♗d7	0-0-0	h6	g5	♗xf5	
4	...	♘c4	♘c3	d3[15]	♘e3	♕xc2				±
	♕f6	fe	♕e6[14]	ed+[16]	dc					
5	...	...	...	♘e3[17]	♘xe4	♘g3[18]	h4	d4	c3	∞
	...	...	♕f7!	c6	d5	h5!	g6	♗g7	♘e7[19]	
6	...	d4	♘c4	♘e3	d5	♗e2				±
	...	d6	fe	♘c6[20]	♘e5					
7	♗c4	d4	♘e5	♗e2	0-0	f3!	♗xf3	♕e2[22]		∞
	♘f6[21]	fe	d5	♗e6	♗d6	ef	0-0			
8	...	♘e5	♕h5	♘xg5	♕xg6+[24]	♗xd5	♘c3	b3	♕f7	±
	fe	d5[23]	g6	hg	♔d7![25]	♘f6	♕e7	♖h6![26]	♕xf7[27]	

[1] 4 ♘g5!? ed 5 ♕xd4 d5 (5 ... ♘f6 6 ♗c4 ±) 6 ♗e2 (6 ♕e5+ ♗e7 7 ♗e2 h5 8 ♗f4 c6 9 ♘c3 ♕d7! ∞ Redolfi-Atars, corr. 1973) 6 ... h5 7 ♗f4 c6 8 ♘c3 ♕e7 9 0-0-0 ±.

[2] 5 ♘c3 d6 6 ♗c4 ♗f5 7 ♗e2 ♗e7 8 0-0 0-0 9 ♗e3 ♘bd7 10 f3 ♗g6! = Luna-Atars, corr. 1973.
　5 ♗c4 d5 6 ♗b3 ♗e6 (6 ... ♘c6? 7 c4 ±) 7 ♗g5 ♗e7 8 0-0 0-0 9 f3 ef 10 ♘xf3 Keres. 8 ... ♘bd7!?
　5 ♗g5 d6 6 ♘c4 ♗e7 7 ♗e2 0-0 8 0-0 c6 9 ♘c3 d5 10 ♘e3 ♘bd7 ±.

[3] 6 ... ♘xg4? 7 ♗xg4 ♘d7 8 ♘c3 ♘f6 9 ♗xc8 ♕xc8 10 0-0 ± Romanishin-van Riemsdyk, Riga IZ 1979.

[4] Kapitaniak.

[5] 3 ... ♘c6 4 ♗b5 ♗c5 5 0-0 (5 ♗xc6? dc 6 ♘xe5 ♗xf5 7 ♕h5+ g6 8 ♘xg6 hg! 9 ♕xh8 ♕e7+ 10 ♔d1 ♗xf2 11 ♕xg8+ ♗d7 12 ♕c4 ♖e8 0-1 Schlechter-Chigorin, 1878) 5 ... e4 6 d4 ±.
　3 ... d6 4 d4 e4 5 ♘g5 ♗xf5 6 f3 ♕e7 7 fe ♗xe4 8 ♘xe4 ♕xe4+ 9 ♗e2 ± Schmigalle-Bandick, corr. 1976.
　3 ... ♗c5!? 4 d4! ±.

[6] 4 ♘d4?! ♕f6 5 ♕h5+ g6 6 fg hg 7 ♕d5? ♘e7 8 ♕xe4 ♖h4 9 g4 d5! ∓ Evans-Grivainis, Munich 1958.
　4 ♕e2 ♕e7 5 ♘d4 ♕e5 6 ♘b5 ±.

[7] 5 g4 ♕e7! 6 ♘c4 d5 7 ♘e3 d4 8 ♘g2 h5! 9 g5 ♘g4 ∓ Vashegui-Grob, corr. 1970.

[8] 8 ♘xh8 ♕xh5 (8 ... ♘xh5 9 d3 ed 10 0-0 ±) 9 ♕xh5 ♘xh5 10 g4 ± Garcia-Kapitaniak, corr. 1978.

[9] 9 ... ♔xf7 10 ♕h5+ g6 11 fg+ ♔g7

12 ♘xc7 ±.

[10] 12 0-0 c6 13 ♘e5+ de 14 f7 ♕e6 15 fg♕ ♕xg8 16 ♘e3 ±.

[11] 4 ♕h5+? g6 5 ♘xg6 ♘f6 6 ♕h3 hg! 7 ♕xh8 ♕e7 8 ♕h4 d5! 9 d3 ♘d4 ∓ Pannullo-Ravaro, corr. 1976.

[12] 5 ... ♗c5 6 ♗c4 ♗xf2+ 7 ♔f1! ±.

[13] 10 ♗e3?! ♘b8 11 0-0 g5! 12 ♕e1 f4 ∓ Janikowski-Kapitaniak, Poland 1979.

[14] 5 ... ♕g6 6 d3 ♗b4 7 ♗d2 ♗xc3 8 ♗xc3 ±.
　5 ... d6 6 d3 ed 7 ♗xd3 ±.

[15] 6 ♘e3!? c6 7 d3 d5 8 de de 9 ♗c4 ± Strautins-Gabrans, Latvia 1971.

[16] 6 ... ♗b4 7 ♘e3 ♗e7 8 ♗d2 0-0 9 de! ♕g6 10 ♗c4+ ♔h8 11 0-0 ♗xc3 12 ♗xc3 ♕xe4 13 ♗d3 ± Kapitaniak.

[17] 6 d4 ♘f6 7 ♗e2 d5 8 ♘e5! ±.

[18] 8 ♘g5!? ♕f6 9 ♘f3 d4 10 ♘c4 ∞.

[19] 12 ♕f3 ♗f6 ∞ Arnlins-Anderson, 1973.

[20] 6 ... c6 7 ♗c4 d5 8 ♗b3 ♗e6 9 c4 ±.

[21] 3 ... b5?! 4 ♗b3! fe 5 d4! ± (5 ... ef 6 ♕f3 ±±).

[22] Purins-Morgado, corr. 1976.

[23] 4 ... ♗g5 5 d4 ♕xg2 6 ♕h5+ g6 7 ♗f7+ ♔d8 8 ♗xg6 ♕xh1+ 9 ♔e2 c6 10 ♘c3 ♘f6 11 ♕g5! ± Pupols-Dreiburg, USA 1956.
　4 ... ♘f6!? 5 ♗f7 ♕e7 6 ♘xh8 d5 7 ♗e2 ♘c6 8 d3! ± Petersson-Ortiz, corr. 1974.

[24] 7 ♕xh8 ♗f7 ∞.

[25] 7 ... ♔e7? 8 d4 ♘f6 9 ♗g5 ♕d6 10 ♘c3 ± Keast-Skrastins, corr. 1976.

[26] 10 ... ♘a6? 11 ♗a3 ±.

[27] 12 ♗xf7 ♘c6 13 ♗b2 ♔e7 14 ♗c4 ♗f5 15 0-0-0 ± Kapitaniak.

Petroff's Defence   1 e4 e5 2 ♘f3 ♘f6

#	3	4	5	6	7	8	9	10	11	
1	♗c4	♘c3[1]	dc	0-0	♘h4	f4	f5	♗e3[4]	♕f3	∓
	♘xe4	♘xc3[2]	f6	d6[3]	g6	♕e7	♕g7	♘c6	♗e7[5]	
2	d3	♗e2	♘bd2	0-0	c3	♕c2	♖e1	♘f1		=/∓
	♘c6	d5[6]	♗e7	0-0	♗e6	h6[7]	♘d7	f5[8]		
3	♘c3	♘xe5	♗e2	♘d3	dc	0-0	♘f4	♗e3	♗d3	=
	♗b4[9]	0-0	♖e8	♗xc3	♘xe4	d5!?[10]	c6	♘d6	♗f5[11]	
4	...	♗c4	0-0	d3	bc	ed	♖e1	♗d2	♖b1	=
	...	0-0	♘c6[12]	♗xc3	d5	♘xd5	♗g4	♕d6	♘b6[13]	
5	♘xe5	d4	♘f3	♗e2	0-0	♗d3	♖e1			±
	♕e7[14]	d6[15]	♘xe4	♕d8	♗e7	♘f6				
6	...	♕e2	♕xe4	d4	de[17]	♗b5!?[18]	♘c3	♗f4	♗xc6[20]	∞
	♘xe4[16]	♕e7	d6	de	♘c6	♗d7	0-0-0	g5[19]	♗xc6[21]	
7	...	...	...	f4	fe[23]	d4[24]	de	♗f4	♗g3	±
	...	...	...	de[22]	f6	fe	♘c6	g5	♗g7[25]	
8	...	♘xf7[26]	d4	♘c3[28]	♗c4+					∞
	d6	♔xf7	♗e7[27]	♖e8						
9	...	♘c4	♕e2[29]	d3	♗g5	♘c3	0-0-0	♗xf6	♘d5	=
	...	♘e4	♕e7	♘f6	♗e6[30]	♘c6	h6	♕xf6	♕g5+[31]	
10	...	♘f3	♕e2	d3	♗g5	♘c3	♗xe2	♗h4	♘e4	=
	...	♘xe4	♕e7	♘f6	♘bd7[32]	♕xe2+	h6	c6[33]	♗e7[34]	
11	...	...	c4	♘c3[35]	♘xe4[37]	♗e2	0-0			=
	...	...	♗e7	♗f5[36]	♗xe4	♘c6	0-0[38]			
12	...	...	d4	♗d3	0-0	c4[40]	cd[42]	♘c3	♖e1	=
	...	...	d5[39]	♗d6	0-0	♗g4[41]	f5	♘d7!	♘df6![43]	
13	...	...	...	...	...	...	♘c3[44]	♗xc4	h3	±
	...	...	...	...	...	♘f6	dc	♗g4	♗h5[45]	
14	...	...	...	...	0-0	♖e1	c4[48]	cd[49]	♘c3	±
	...	...	...	♗e7	♘c6[46]	♗g4[47]	♘f6	♘xd5	0-0[49]	
15	...	...	...	...	...	♗b5[50]	♘bd2	♘f1		=
	...	...	...	...	...	♗f5	♘f6![51]	0-0	♘e7[52]	
16	...	...	...	...	...	...	c4!	♗f1	a3	±
	...	...	...	...	...	...	♘b4	0-0	♘c6[53]	
17	d4	♗d3	♘xe5	0-0	♘c3	bc	♖e1	g3[57]		±
	♘xe4	d5	♗d6[54]	0-0	♘xc3	♕h4[55]	♘c6[56]			
18	...	...	...	...	c4	de	cd[58]	♕c2	♗xe4	±
	...	...	...	...	♗xe5	♘c6	♕xd5	♘b4	♘xc2[59]	

---

1 Boden's Gambit (1851).
  4 ♕e2 d5! =.
  4 d3 ♘f6 5 ♘xe5 d5 6 ♗b3 ♗d6 =.
  4 ♘xe5? ♗e7 ∓.

2 4 ... d5 5 ♗xd5 ♘f6 =.

3 6 ... ♕e7 7 ♖e1 ∞.
  6 ... g6 7 ♖e1 d6 8 b4 ∞.
  6 ... ♘c6 7 ♘h4 g6 8 f4 f5 9 ♘f3 e4 10 ♘g5 ♗c5+ 11 ♔h1 ♕f6 ∓ Marco-Schlechter, Berlin 1897.

4 10 b4!?

5 12 b4 ♘d8 13 ♗b3 c6 14 ♕g3 g5

15 Rae1 Nf7 16 Nf3 Bd7 17 Qf2 b6 18 h4 h6 19 Qe2 0-0 ∓ Meyer-Schlamm, corr. 1899.

[6] 4 ... Bc5? 5 0-0 d6 6 c3 Bb6 7 Qc2 Bg4 8 b4 ± Hanham-Gossip, New York 1889.

[7] 8 ... Nd7 9 b4 a6 10 a3 f6 11 Bb2 Kh8 12 Rfd1 Qe8 = Kozomara-Milich, Yugoslav Ch 1957.

[8] Bogatyrchuk-Kan, Moscow 1925.

[9] 3 ... Nc6 – Four Knights.

[10] 8 ... d6 9 Nf4 Nd7 10 Be3 =.

[11] Ed. Lasker-Marshall, Lake Hopatcong 1926.

[12] 5 ... c6 6 d3 d5 7 Bb3 a5 8 a3 =.
5 ... d6 6 d3 c6 =.

[13] 12 Bb5 Rae8 13 Bxc6 bc 14 c4 (Bernstein-Alekhine, match 1934) 14 ... Bxf3 =.

[14] Lopez Variation (1561).

[15] 4 ... Nxe4 5 Be2 Qd8 6 0-0 Be7 7 d3 Nf6 8 d4 0-0 =.

[16] Damiano Variation.

[17] 7 Nxe5 Qxe5+ 8 de Nc6 9 Bb5 Bd7 =. 8 ... Bf5 ∞∞.

[18] 8 Nc3 Qxe5 9 Qxe5+ Nxe5 10 Bf4 Bd6 11 Bg3! ±/= Vasyukov-Chekhov, USSR Ch 1975.

[19] 10 ... a6 11 Bc4 ± Sax-Hulak, Budapest 1975.

[20] 11 Nd5 Qc5.

[21] 12 Qf5+ Qd7! 13 Qxd7+ (13 Qxg5 Be7!) 13 ... Rxd7 14 Bxg5 Rg8 ∞ (=/∓).

[22] 6 ... Nc6!? 7 Bb5 Bd7 ∞∞.

[23] 7 Qxe5 Qxe5+ 8 fe Nc6 9 Bb5 Bd7 =.

[24] 8 Nc3 Qxe5 9 Qxe5+ fe 10 d4 Bb4 11 Bc4 ±/=.

[25] 12 Nc3 Bxe5 13 Bxe5 Qxe5 14 0-0-0 0-0 15 Qxe5 Nxe5 16 Re1 Ng6± Cafferty/Hooper.

[26] Cochrane's Gambit.

[27] 5 ... g6 6 Nc3 Bg7 7 Bc4+ Be6 8 Bxe6+ Kxe6 9 f4 ∞ Vitolins-Anikayev, USSR 1979.
5 ... d5 6 Be8! Kochiev.

[28] 6 e5? de 7 Bc4+ Be6 ∓.

[29] 5 Nc3 Nxc3 6 bc g6 7 d4 Bg7 8 h4 0-0 9 Bg5 Qe8+ 10 Ne3 c5 11 h5 Nc6 ∞.

[30] 7 ... Qxe2+ 8 Bxe2 Be7 9 Nc3 Bd7 10 0-0-0 h6 = Vitolins-Kochiev, USSR Ch 1979.

[31] 12 Nce3 ½-½ Ljubojević-Hort, Bugojno 1980.

[32] 7 ... Qxe2+ 8 Bxe2 Be7 9 Nc3 Bd7 10 0-0-0 Nc6 11 d4 h6 12 Bh4 0-0-0 13 Bc4 Rhf8 14 Rhe1 ±/= Fine-Alexander, Hastings 1935/36.

[33] 10 ... Be7 11 0-0-0 Nb6 12 h3 Nbd5 = Zaitsev-Holmov, Riga 1968.

[34] 12 0-0-0 d5 = Gufeld-Savon, Moscow 1970.

[35] 6 d4 0-0 7 Bd3 Bb4+ = Keres.

[36] 6 ... Nxc3 7 dc Nc6 8 Bd3 Ne5 9 Nxe5 de

10 Qc2 Bg5 11 0-0 Be6 12 Rd1 Rxc1 13 Raxc1 Qg5 = Maroczy-Marshall, San Sebastian 1911.

[37] 7 Nd5 0-0 8 d3 Nf6 = Keres.
7 Nd4!?

[38] Keres.

[39] 5 ... Be7 6 Bd3 Nf6 7 h3 0-0 8 0-0 Nc6 9 c3 Re8 10 Re1 Bd3 11 Bf4 h6 12 Nbd2 Bf8 13 Qc2 ± Polgar-Toth, Kecskemet 1972.

[40] 8 Nc3 Nxc3 9 bc Bg4 10 Rb1 Nd7 11 h3 Bh5 12 c4 (12 Rxb7 Nb6 13 Bb5 ∞∞) 12 ... dc = Leonhardt-Marshall, Carlsbad 1911.

[41] 8 ... c6 9 Qc2 Na6 10 Bxe4 de 11 Qxe4 Re8 12 Qd3! Bb4 13 Qb3 ± Keres.

[42] 9 Re1 f5 10 Nc3?! Bxh2+ 11 Kxh2 Nf2 intending ... Nxd3, ... Bxf3, ... Qh4+ ∓.

[43] Keres.

[44] 9 Bg5 ± ECO.

[45] 12 Re1 ±.

[46] 7 ... Bf5 8 Re1 0-0 9 c4 c6 10 Qb3 dc 11 Bxc4 ± Keres.

[47] 8 ... Nd6 9 Bf4 0-0 10 c3 Be6 11 Nbd2 ± R.Byrne-Reshevsky, New York Z 1972.

[48] 9 c3 f5 10 Qb3 Nb3 0-0 11 Nbd2 (11 Qxb7 Rf6) 11 ... Kh8 12 h3 Bxf3 13 Nxf3 Nb8 ∞∞.

[49] 10 Nc3 0-0 11 cd Nxd5 12 h3 (12 Be4 Be6 13 Qd6 h6 14 Bxh7+ Kh8 15 Bf4 ∞ Belyavsky-Yusupov, USSR Ch 1981) 12 ... Be6 13 a3 Nxc3 14 bc Bf6 15 Qc2 g6 ± Vasyukov-Vladimirov, USSR Ch 1st L 1981.

[50] 9 Nc3!? Nxc3 10 bc Bxd3 ∞∞.
9 a3!?
9 Nbd2 Nxd2 10 Qxd2 Bxd3 11 Qxd3 0-0 12 c3 Qd7 13 Bf4 a6!? 14 Re3 Rae8 15 Rae1 Bd8! 16 h3 ± Kasparov-Karpov, USSR Special Teams Ch 1981.

[51] 9 ... 0-0 10 Bxc6 dc 11 Ne5 Bh4 12 Be3 (Timman-Portisch, Moscow 1981) 12 ... f6! ∞∞.

[52] 12 c3 Bg6 13 Bd3 Nd6 14 Bxf5 Nxf5 = Karpov-Korchnoi, match (4) 1981.

[53] 12 Nc3 ± Karpov-Portisch, Turin 1982.

[54] 5 ... Be7 6 Qe2 Nd6 7 Qh5 ± Keres.
5 ... Nd7 6 Qe2 (6 Bxf7 Nxf7 7 Qh5+ Be7 8 Qe2 Kf7 9 Qh5+ ½-½ Nunn-Balashov, Malta Ol 1980; 6 Nxd7 Bxd7 7 0-0 Qh4 8 Qe1 0-0-0 =/∞ Timoshenko-Nogueiras, Havana 1981) 6 ... Nxe5 7 Bxe4 de 8 Qxe4 Qe6 9 Qxe5 Qd7 10 Nc3 0-0-0 11 Be3 Bb4 12 0-0 f6 = Unzicker-Rogoff, Amsterdam II 1980.

[55] 8 ... Nd7 9 Re1 ± Keres.

[56] 9 ... Nd7 10 g3 Qh3 11 Bf1 ± Smyslov-Lilienthal, Leningrad 1941.

[57] Boleslavsky. 10 Rb1 Nxe5 11 de Bc5 12 Be3 Bxe3 13 Rxe3 c5 ±/= Kapengut-Karasser, Leningrad 1971.

[58] 9 f4 Nb4 10 cd Qxd5 11 Bxe4 Qxe4 12 Nc3 Qg6 13 Be3 ± Damjanović-Trifunović, Vrnjacka Banja 1963.

[59] 12 Bxd5 Bf5 13 g4! ±/=.

1 e4 e5 2 ♘f3 ♘f6 3 d4 ed 4 e5 ♘e4

	5	6	7	8	9	10	11	12	13	
19	♕e2[60]	♘xd4	♘xc6[62]	♘c3	♗e3	♖d1	♖d2	f4		∓
	♘c5[61]	♘c6	dc[63]	♗f5	h5[64]	♕e7	♘d7	0-0-0[65]		
20	♕xd4	ed	♗d3	♕f4	0-0	♘c3[66]	♗e3	♗c5![67]	♖ad1	∓
	d5	♘xd6	♘c6	g6	♗g7	0-0	♗e6	♖e8![68]	♕f6![69]	
21	...	...	...	...	♘c3	♗e3[70]	0-0-0	♘g5[72]	♗xf4	=
	...	...	...	...	♗g7	♗e6	♕f6[71]	♕xf4	0-0[73]	
22	...	...	♘c3	♕f4	♗d2[75]	♗e2	0-0-0	h4	♖he1	=/±
	...	...	♘c6[74]	g6	♕e7+!	♗e6	♗g7	h6	♕f6[76]	
23	...	...	...	...	♗d3[77]	♘d4	♘xc6	♗e3	0-0[78]	=/±
	...	...	...	♗e6	g6	♗g7	bc	0-0	♖b8	
24	...	...	...	...	♗b5	♗e3[81]	♘xb5	♕xb4	c3	=/±
	...	...	...	♗f5[79]	♕e7+[80]	♘xb5	♕b4+	♗xb4+	♗d6![82]	

[60] Steinitz Variation. 5 ♗b5 ♘c6 6 0-0 ♗e7 – Spanish.

[61] 5 ... ♗b4+ 6 ♘bd2 ♘xd2 7 ♗xd2 ♗xd2+ 8 ♕xd2 d6 9 ♕xd4 ♘c6 10 ♗b5 ♗d7 11 ♗xc6 ♗xc6 12 0-0-0 ± Boleslavsky.

[62] 7 ♗e3 ♘xd4! 8 ♗xd4 ♕h4 ∞/= Tal-Holmov, Alma-Ata 1969.

[63] 7 ... bc 8 ♘c3 ♗a6 9 ♕g4 (9 ♕e3 ♗xf1 10 ♖xf1 ♕h4 ∞/=) 9 ... ♗xf1 10 ♖xf1 d6 11 ♗e3 ♕d7 12 ♕g3 de =/± Boleslavsky.

[64] 9 ... ♕e7 10 g4 ♗d7 11 0-0-0 ∞.

[65] Klyavin-Vistanetskis, Tbilisi 1962.

[66] 10 ♖e1 ♗e6 11 ♘c3 (11 ♗g5 0-0! 12 ♘xe6 fe 13 ♕g4 ♗d4! 14 ♕xe6+ ♔h8 15 ♖e2 ♕h4 16 g3 ♕h5 ∓∓ Bonch-Osmolovsky) 11 ... 0-0 12 ♗e3 ♖e8 13 ♖ad1 (Simagin-Vesovich, corr. 1963-66) 13 ... ♕f6 =.

[67] 12 ♘g5 ♖e8 13 ♖ad1 ♕f6 14 ♕xf6 ♗xf6 15 ♘xe6 fe 16 ♘b5 (Larsen-Trifunović, Dortmund 1961) 16 ... ♖ac8 ± Toth.

[68] 12 ... ♕f6 13 ♕xf6 ♗xf6 14 ♘b5 ± Unzicker-Jimenez, Leipzig Ol 1960.

[69] 14 ♗xd6 cd 15 ♕xd6 ♖ed8 (15 ... ♗f8 16 ♕g3 ♗b4 ∞∞) 16 ♕g3 ♕e7 17 ♘g5 ♗xc3! 18 bc ♗xa2 ∓ Hermlin-Maslov, USSR 1970.

[70] 10 ♗d2 ♕e7+ 11 ♔f1 ♗e6 12 ♖e1 0-0 13 h4 ♕f6 ∓ Yudovich-Gusakov, Perm 1960.

[71] 11 ... 0-0? 12 ♗c5 ♖e8 13 ♗b5 a6 14 ♗xc6 bc 15 ♘d4 ± Zuckerman-Balshan, Dresden 1969.

[72] 12 ♕xf6 ♗xf6 13 ♘b5 ♗xb5 14 ♗xb5 0-0 15 ♗xc6 bc 16 ♗d4 ♗e7 = Toth. 13 ♘g5 ♗xc3! 14 ♘xe6 ♗xb2+ 15 ♔xb2 fe 16 h4 ∞/∓ Toth.

[73] Intending ... ♗xc3 or ... ♘b4. 14 ♘xe6 fe 15 ♗g3 ♗e5! =/± Toth.

[74] 7 ... ♗f5 8 ♕e5+ ♕e7 9 ♘d5 ♕xe5+ 10 ♘xe5 f6 11 ♘f3 (11 ♘xc7+ ♔d8 12 ♘xa8 fe ∓ Toth) 11 ... ♔d7 12 ♗f4 ♘c6 13 0-0-0 ♖d8 14 ♘e3 ♗e6 15 ♗b5 ± Bronstein-Borisenko, Moscow 1961.

[75] 9 ♗b5 ♗g7 10 ♗xc6+ bc 11 0-0 0-0 12 ♗e3 ♖b8! 13 ♖ab1 a5 14 ♗c5 ♖e8 15 ♘d4 ♗e5 16 ♕f3 ♕h4 17 g3 ♕h3 18 ♖fe1 ♗b7 19 ♘ce2 (Gurgenidze-Borisenko, USSR 1971) 19 ... ♘e4! 20 ♕xe4 ♗d6 ∓ Zaitsev. 19 ♘b3!?

[76] ... 14 ♗d3 ♕xf4 15 ♗xf4 0-0-0 = Keres-Trifunović, Bled 1961.

[77] 9 ♗d2 g6 (9 ... ♗e7 10 0-0-0 0-0 11 ♗d3 = Toth) 10 0-0-0 ♗g7 11 ♗d3 0-0 12 h4 ♕f6 13 ♕h2 ♘e5 14 ♗g5 ♘xf3 15 gf (15 ♗xf6 =) 15 ... ♕xf3 16 h5 ♗xh5 17 ♕xh5 gh 18 ♖dg1 f5 19 ♖xh5 ♗f7 20 ♘e2! (Krogius-Holmov, Tiflis 1959) 20 ... ♗c4 Toth.
    9 ♗e3 ♘f5! 10 ♗b5 ♗b4+ 11 ♗d2 ♗xd2+ 12 ♘xd2 0-0!? (12 ... ♘d6 =) 13 0-0-0 ♖c8 14 ♘f3 ♕e7 15 ♗d3 a6 16 ♘c3 ♕b4 ∞ Fuderer-Bronstein, Kiev 1959. 13 ♘xc7 ♘fd4! ∞ Toth.

[78] Pietzsch-Vistanetskis, Riga 1961.

[79] Pillsbury Variation.

[80] 9 ... ♗e7 10 ♘d4 ♗d7 11 ♗xc6 ♗xc6 12 ♘xc6 bc 13 0-0 ± Chigorin-Pillsbury, St Petersburg 1895.

[81] 10 ♔f1 (Tal) 10 ... ♗e4 11 ♗a4 0-0-0 12 ♗e3 (Suetin-Borisenko, Riga 1968) 12 ... ♗xf3 13 ♕xf3 ♘e5; 13 gf ♘e5 14 ♖e1 ♕e6! Toth.

[82] 14 0-0-0 0-0-0! 15 ♗xa7 ♖xa7 16 ♘xa7+ ♔b8 17 ♘b5 ♗f4+ 18 ♘d2 c5 ∞ Holmov.
    14 ♘xd6+ cd 15 0-0-0! ♗e6 16 ♖xd6 (16 b3 ♗e7 17 ♖d2 ♖hd8 18 h3 b6 19 ♖hd1 d5 = Zhuravlev-Borisenko, Riga 1968) 16 ... ♗xa2 17 ♗c5! ± Matulović-Holmov, Sochi 1968. 15 ... ♔e7!? Spassky.

Ponziani and Modern Bishop's Opening

The Ponziani is a very old opening which is presently enjoying a small revival of interest. Well-analysed by Ponziani in 1769, it never really caught on as a major weapon in the white arsenal. The plan is to build a pawn centre as quickly as possible, but Black can equalise with straightforward developing moves such as 3 ... ♘f6 or Romanishin's 3 ... ♗e7!?, while the standard reply 3 ... d5, properly handled, is also fully adequate.

The position after 1 e4 e5 2 ♗c4 ♘f6 3 d3 ♘c6 4 ♘f3, or 1 e4 e5 2 ♘f3 ♘c6 3 ♗c4 ♘f6 4 d3, commanded little attention from theorists and practical players until quite recently, when it began to appear in the repertoire of Nunn and several young Soviet players. Frequently play transposes into the Giuoco Piano if Black responds with 4 ... ♗c5, but many original variations have been developed. The game often takes on characteristics of the Ruy Lopez, especially when White plays c3 and brings the bishop back to c2 via b3.

			Ponziani		1 e4 e5 2 ♘f3 ♘c6 3 c3					
	3	4	5	6	7	8	9	10	11	
1	...	d4[1]	♘xe5	♘g4	♗f4	♘e3	♘a3	♕b3	♘ac2	±
	f5	fe	♕f6[2]	♕g6	d6	♘f6	♗e7	a6	♘d8[3]	
2	...	♗b5	♘xe5	♕a4	♖f1	♗xc6+	♕xc6+	♕xa8+	♘c6+	∓
	d5	de	♕g5![4]	♕xg2	♗h3!	bc	♔d8!	♔e7	♔f6![5]	
3	...	♕a4	♗b5	ed	d4	c4	d5[7]	gf	dc	∞
	...	f6[6]	♘ge7	♕xd5	e4!?	♕d7!	ef	♕h3	b6[8]	
4	...	...	ed	♕d1	♕xf3	d4[9]	♕d1	c4	♘c3	∞̄
	...	♗d7	♘d4	♘xf3+	f5	e4	♗d6	b6	♘f6[10]	
5	...	...	♗b5	d4[11]	ed	0-0	c4[12]	♖e1	♘e5	∓
	...	♕d6!	♗d7	♘f6	♕xd5	e4	♕h5	♗e7	♘xe5[13]	
6	...	d4	cd	ed	♗b5+	♗xd7+[15]	0-0	♘e5	♕g4	=
	♗e7!?[14]	ed!	d5	♘b4	♗d7	♕xd7	♘xd5	♕d6	♗f6[16]	
7	...	d4	d5	♘xe5	♕d4	♕xe4	♗e2	♕d3	♗e3	=
	♘f6	♘xe4[17]	♘b8[18]	♗d6!	0-0	♗xe5	♖e8	d6	♘a6[19]	
8	...	...	h3[20]	♗e3	d5	♗d3	c4	♗xc5	♘c3	=
	...	d6	♗e7	0-0	♘b8	♘bd7	♘c5	dc	♗d6[21]	

299

[1] 4 ef Qf6! =.

[2] 5 ... Nf6 6 Bb5 Be7 7 0-0 a6 8 Ba4 ±.

[3] 12 Bg3 Nf7 13 Bc4 ± Zagorovsky.

[4] 5 ... Bd7 6 Nxd7 Qxd7 7 d4 ed 8 Qxd3 Qxd3 9 Bxd3 ± Keres.
5 ... Qd5 6 Qa4 Nge7 7 f4 ef 8 Nxf3 ±.

[5] 12 Qxd8+ Kg6 13 Ne5+ Kh5 14 Bd1 Qxf1+ 15 Kc2 Bd6 ∓ Zagorovsky.

[6] 4 ... de?! 5 Nxe5 Qd5 6 Nxc6 bc 7 Bc4 Qd7 8 d3 ed 9 0-0 Bd6 11 Nd2 Ne7 12 Ne4 0-0 12 Rd1 ± Ljubojević-Karpov, Portorož 1975.

[7] 9 Ng1 a6! 10 Ne2 Rb8 = Zagorovsky.
9 Nfd2!?

[8] 12 Qd1 Ng6 ∞/∓ Zagorovsky.

[9] 8 Bc4 Bd6 9 d3 ∞.

[10] Zagorovsky.

[11] 6 ed Qxd5 7 0-0 Be7! intending ... Nf6 Zagorovsky.

[12] 9 Ng5 h6! 10 Bc4 Nxd4! ∞/ ∓ Zagorovsky.

[13] 12 de Qxe5 13 Bxd7+ Nxd7 ∓.

[14] Romanishin.

[15] 8 Bc4 Bf5!? 9 Qa4+ Kf8 ∞.

[16] Sax-Romanishin, Tilburg 1979.

[17] 4 ... ed 5 e5 – Scotch Gambit.
4 ... d5!?

[18] 5 ... Bc5 6 dc Bxf2+ 7 Ke2 bc 8 Qa4 f5 9 Nbd2 0-0 10 Nxe4 fe 11 Qxe4 d5 12 Qxe5! Re8 13 Qxe8+ Qxe8+ 14 Kxf2 ± Makarichev-Perenyi, Zalaegerszeg 1973.
5 ... Ne7 6 Nxe5 Ng6 7 Qd4 Qf6 8 Qxe4 Qxe5 9 Qxe5+ Nxe5 10 Nd2 ± Velimirović-Smejkal, Rio de Janeiro IZ 1979.

[19] Zhukhovitsky.

[20] 5 Bb5 Bd7 6 Nbd2 Be7 – Ruy Lopez.

[21] 12 g4 = Velimirović-Tal, Yugoslavia v USSR 1979.

Modern Bishop's Opening   1 e4 e5 2 Bc4 Nf6 3 d3 Nc6 4 Nf3

	4	5	6	7	8	9	10	11	12	
1	...	Nc3[1]	a3	h3	Be3	Qd2	g4	Rg1		∞
	h6!?	d6	g6!?[2]	Bg7	0-0	Kh7	Nd7	Nb6[3]		
2	...	Nc3[4]	h3	0-0[5]	Bb3	ab	Be3	Nd2	ed	=
	Be7	d6	0-0	Na5	Nxb3	c5	Be6	d5	Nxd5[6]	
3	...	Nbd2	c3	Bb3	Nf1	Bd5	Be3	Bc4	Ng3	=
	...	0-0	d6	Nd7[7]	Nc5	Bf6	Ne7	Ne6	d5![8]	
4	...	0-0	Re1[19]	c3	Bb5	Bxd7	d4	cd	e5	
	...	0-0	d6	Na5!?	Bd7	Qxd7	ed	d5	Ne4	
5	...	Bb3	0-0	c3	Nbd2	Qxb3	Re1	Nf1	Qc2	=
	...	0-0[10]	d6[11]	Be6[12]	Nxb3	Rb8	Nd7	Nc5	d5[13]	
6	...	c3[15]	0-0	Re1	Bb3	Nbd2	Nf1	Qxb3	Ng3	±
	Bc5[14]	a6	d6	Ba7	0-0	Be6	Bxb3	Qc8	Re8[16]	

[1] 5 Bb3 d6 6 c3 g6 7 Nbd2 Bg7 8 Nf1 d5 9 Qe2 Be6 10 Ng3 Ne7 11 h4 0-0-0 = Gipslis-Eingorn, Tallinn 1980.
5 0-0 d6 6 c3 g6 7 d4 Qe7 8 Nbd2 Bg7 9 Re1 0-0 10 h3 Bd7 11 Nf1 Rae8 = Nunn-Spassky, London 1982.

[2] 6 ... Be7 7 Be3 0-0 8 h3 Be6 9 Nd5 Bxd5 10 ed Nb8 11 Nh4 c6 12 dc bc 13 Nf3 d5 ∞ Herzog-Hazai, Keszthely 1981.

[3] Spassky-Belyavsky, USSR 1981.

[4] 5 c3?! d5 6 ed Nxd5 7 Qb3 0-0 8 Bxd5 Na5! 9 Bxf7+ Rxf7 10 Qc2 Bf5 ∓.

[5] 7 a3 Nd4! 8 Nxd4 ed 9 Ne2 c5 10 c3 d5! =.

[6] 13 Nxd5 Bxd5 = Zita-Smyslov, Prague v Moscow 1946.

[7] 7 ... Be6!? Zagorovsky.

[8] Bronstein-Nei, Tallinn 1973.

[9] 6 c3 d5! = Zagorovsky.

[10] 5 ... d5!? 6 Nbd2 0-0 7 0-0 de 8 de Bc5 = Gaprindashvili-Chiburdanidze, match 1978.

[11] 6 ... d5!? 7 ed Nxd5 8 Re1 Bg4 9 h3 Bh5 10 g4 Bg6 11 Nxe5 Nxe5 12 Rxe5 c6!? (12 ... Nb6 = Dolmatov-Chekhov, USSR 1981) 13 Bxd5! cd?! (13 ... Bd6!? Psakhis) 14 Qf3! ± Kudrin-Psakhis, Graz 1981.

[12] 7 ... Bg4 8 h3 Bh5 9 Nbd2 Bd7 10 Bc2 Bg6 11 d4 ed 12 Nxd4 Nxd4 13 cd ½-½ Djurić-Bronstein, Tallinn 1981.
7 ... a5 8 Re1 Nd7 9 Be3 Bf6 = Makarichev-Faibisovich, USSR 1978.

[13] 13 Ne3 de 14 de Qd3 15 Qxd3 Nxd3 = Dolmatov-Klovan, USSR 1981.

[14] See 1 e4 e5 Miscellaneous and Giuoco Piano for more on the Bishop's Opening.

[15] 5 0-0 d6 6 c3 Qe7?! 7 Nbd2 a6 8 Bb3 0-0 9 Re1 Be6 10 Nf1 Ba7 11 Bc2 Kh8 12 Ng3 ± Nunn-Olafsson, England v Iceland 1982.

[16] Karpov-Korchnoi, match (10) 1981.

3 Knights   4 Knights   Scotch

This assortment of double KP openings has fallen into disuse. The Three and Four Knights are not without their pitfalls, but with a working knowledge of theory Black can work his way through to a very comfortable equality. Old-fashioned romanticism like the Belgrade Gambit of the Four Knights can be found in these quiet systems but Black has a variety of methods to defuse these volatile lines.

The Scotch has received attention from those KP players who have become dissatisfied with the well trodden paths of the Ruy Lopez, but White has yet to prove an advantage here.

Three Knights and Four Knights (incl. Scotch Four Knights)							1 e4 e5 2 ♘f3 ♘c6 3 ♘c3		
3	4	5	6	7	8	9	10	11	
1 …	♘d5	♘xb4	♘xe5	d4	a3	ab	♕xd4	♕xe4	±
♗b4	♘f6[1]	♘xb4	♕e7	d6	de	ed	♕xe4+	♘xe4[2]	
2 …	d4	♘xd4	♗e3	♘xc6!	e5	♗d4!	♕e2	ef	±
g6	ed	♗g7	♘f6	bc	♘g8	♕e7	f6	♘xf6[3]	
3 …	…	♘d5	♗g5	♘xd4[5]	♘c3	♗f4[8]	♕d2	0-0-0	=
…	…	♗g7	♘ce7[4]	c6[6]	h6[7]	d5	♘f6	♘xe4[9]	

[1] Schlechter's Variation.
[2] 12 ♗f4 c6 13 ♗d3 ♘f6 14 c4 ± Keres.
[3] Keres.
[4] 6 … f6 7 ♗f4 d6 8 ♘xd4 ♘ge7 9 ♗c4 ♘e5 10 ♗b3 c6 11 ♘e3 ♕a5 12 c3 ± Gershman-Tukmakov, USSR 1966.
[5] 7 e5 h6 8 ♗xe7 ♘xe7 9 ♕xd4 ♘xd5 10 ♕xd5 d6 =.

[6] 7 … h6 8 ♗e3 ♘xd5 9 ed (Czerniak-Romanishin, Göteborg 1971) 9 … d6! =.
[7] 8 … ♕a5 9 ♕d2 h6 10 ♗e3 ±.
[8] 9 ♗e3 ♘f6 10 ♗c4 0-0 11 e5 ♘e8 12 ♕d2 d5 ∓ Tarve-Keres, Pärnu 1971.
[9] 12 ♘xe4 de 13 ♗c4 ♘f5 14 ♘b3 ♕xd2 15 ♘xd2 = Lehmann-Keres, West Germany v USSR 1960.

	3	4	5	6	7	8	9	10	11	
4	...	♗e2	d3	ed	♗d2	bc	0-0			=
	♘f6	♗b4	d5	♘xd5	♘xc3	♗d6	0-0[10]			
5	...	♗b5	0-0	d3	♘e2	c3	♘g3	♗a4	d4	=
	...	♗b4[11]	0-0	d6	♘e7	♗a5	c6	♘g6	d5![12]	
6	...	...	...	...	♗g5	bc	♖e1	d4	♗c1	=
	...	...	...	...	♗xc3	♕e7	♘d8!	♘e6	c5[13]	
7	...	d4	d5	♘xe5	♗b5+	♘d3[15]	bc	♕f3		∞
	...	♗b4[14]	♘e7	d6!	♔f8	♗xc3+	♘xe4	♘f6		
8	...	...	♘xe5!	♕g4	♕xg7	a3	ab	♔d2	♔xc3	∞
	...	...	♘xe4![16]	♘xc3	♖f8	♘xd4[17]	♘xc2+	♘xa1	a5![18]	
9	...	...	♘d5[19]	♕e2[20]	♘g5[21]	cd	♕h5+	♕h4	de	∓
	...	ed	♘xe4	f5	d3!	♘d4	g6	c6!	cd[22]	
10	...	...	♘xd4	♘xe4	f3	♗b5	0-0	♗xc6	fe!	±
	...	...	♘xe4	♕e7	d5	♗d7	de	bc	0-0-0[23]	
11	...	...	...	♗e3	♗e2	♕d2	♗xg4	h3	0-0-0[24]	±
	...	...	♗c5	♗b6	d6	♘g4	♗xg4	♗d7		
12	...	...	...	♘xc6	♗d3	♗g5	♗h4	0-0	f4[25]	±
	...	...	♗b4!	bc	d6	h6	♕e7	0-0		
13	...	...	...	...	...	0-0	♗g5	♗h4	♗g3[27]	±
	...	...	...	...	0-0	♖e8	h6	g5[26]		
14	...	...	...	...	...	ed![28]	♕e2	♕xe7+	0-0	±
	...	...	...	...	d5	♕e7+	cd	♔xe7	♖d8[29]	
15	...	...	...	...	...	...	0-0	♗g5	♘b5	=
	...	...	...	...	...	cd	0-0	♗e6	c5[30]	

[10] Balla-Grünfeld, Pistyan 1922.

[11] 4 ... ♗c5?! 5 0-0 0-0 6 ♘xe5 ♘xe5 7 d4 ♗d6 8 f4 ♘c6 9 e5 ♗b4 10 d5 a6 11 ♗e2 ♗c5+ 12 ♔h1 ♘xd5 13 ♕xd5 ± Shaposhnikov-Borisenko, corr. 1956.

[12] Sveshnikov-Yusupov, USSR Ch 1979.
11 ... ♖e8 12 ♗b3 h6 13 h3 ♗e6 14 ♖e1 ±.

[13] 12 d5 ♘c7 13 ♗d3 b5! 14 c4 ♗d7 15 ♗g5 h6 16 ♗h4 ♖fb8 17 ♘d2 ♘ce8 = Barendregt-van den Berg, Amsterdam 1950.

[14] This option is not available with the move order 3 d4 ed 4 ♘xd4 ♘f6 5 ♘c3.

[15] 8 ♘f3 ♘xe4 9 ♕d4 (9 0-0 ♗xc3!) 9 ... ♘xc3 10 bc ♗c5 =.

[16] 5 ... ♕e7 (5 ... 0-0!?) 6 ♕d3 ♘xe5 7 de ♕xe5 8 ♗d2 0-0 9 0-0-0 ±.

[17] 8 ... ♗a5 9 ♘xc6 dc 10 ♕e5+ ♕e7 11 ♕xe7+ ♔xe7 12 ♗d2 ±.

[18] Angantysson-Polgar, Dresden 1969.

[19] Belgrade Gambit.

[20] 6 ♗c4 ♗e7 7 ♘xd4 0-0 8 ♗b5! (Kenworthy-van der Sterren, Ramsgate 1981) 8 ... ♘e5 9 ♘bxc7 ♘xc4 10 ♘xa8 b5! ∞ Nunn.

[21] 7 ♗f4!? d6 8 0-0-0! ∞∞.

[22] 12 ed ♗g7! (intending ... h6) 13 ♕g3 0-0! 14 d6 b5! + Panov/Estrin.

[23] 11 ... g6 12 ♗e3 ♗g7 13 ♘b3! ± Euwe.
11 ... 0-0-0 12 ♕d3! ±.

[24] 11 0-0-0 ± Botterill/Harding.

[25] 11 f4 ± Wade-Gereben, Monte Carlo 1967.

[26] 10 ... d6!? 11 f4 ♗b7! 12 ♕f3! intending ♖ae1 ±.

[27] Pomar-Ljubojević, Las Palmas 1979.

[28] 8 e5?! ♘g4! (8 ... ♘e4 9 ♗xe4 ♗xc3+ =) 9 ♗f4 f6! ∓ Davie-Gligorić, Dundee 1967.

[29] 11 0-0 ♖d8 12 ♘g5! ± Hort-Spassky, Varna Ol 1962.

[30] 12 a3 ♗a5 13 b4 cb 14 ab ♗xb4 (Krogius-Shianovsky, Leningrad 1960) 15 ♖a6!? h6! = (15 ... ♕c8? 16 ♗xf6! ♕xa6 17 ♗xh7+!).

	4	5	6	7	8	9	10	11	12	
1	c3	ed[2]	cd	♘c3	♗e2	♗xf3	♗e3[3]	bc	♔f1	=
	d5	♕xd5	♗b4+	♗g4	♗xf3!	♕c4!	♗xc3+	♕xc3+	♕c4+[4]	
2	...	♗xd3[5]	♗f4![6]	h3	♘bd2	♕c2				±
		d3	d6	♗e7	♘f6	♗d7				
3	...	♗c4	♗xb2	0-0[8]	♗xe6	♕b3	♘g5	f4	f5[10]	∓
	dc	cb!	d6![7]	♗e6	fe	♕d7![9]	♘d8	♘f6	e5[11]	
4	...	♘xc3	♗c4[13]	0-0[14]	bc	♕b3[16]	♗xf7+	gf	♗xg8	±
	...	♗b4![12]	d6	♗xc3	♗g4[15]	♗xf3	♔f8	♘e5	♖xg8[17]	
5	...	...	...	...	...	e5	♘xe5	♕b3	♗a3	∓
	...	...	...	...	♕e7	♘xe5	de	♘f6	c5[18]	
6	♗c4	c3!?	0-0	b4	a4	a5	♕b3	b5!	♘xe5	±
	♗c5[19]	d3?![20]	d6[21]	♗b6	a6	♗a7	♕f6	♘e5	de[22]	
7	♘xd4	♕xd4	♗c4	♕d5[23]	♘c3[24]					±
	♘xd4	♕e7!	♘c6	♕f6						

[1] **3 ... d5?!** 4 ♘xe5! ♘xe5 5 de de 6 ♕xd8+ ♔xd8 7 ♘c3 ♗b4 8 ♗d2 intending 0-0-0 ±.
3 ... ♘xd4 4 ♘xd4 – 3 ... ed 4 ♘xd4 ♘xd4.

[2] 5 ♗d3!? de 6 ♗xe4 ♘f6 7 ♗xc6+ bc 8 ♗d2 = Smit.

[3] 10 ♗xc6+ bc 11 ♕e2+ ♕xe2+ 12 ♔xe2 0-0-0 13 ♗e3 ♘e7 = Emma-Vogt, Skopje Ol 1972.
10 ♕b3 ♕xb3 11 ab ♘ge7 12 0-0 a6 13 ♖a4 ♗d6 14 ♗g5 f6 15 ♗h5+ ♘g6 16 ♖e1+ ♘ce7 17 ♗d2 0-0-0 = Ljubojević-Ree, Amsterdam 1972.

[4] 13 ♔g1 ♘ge7 14 ♖c1 ♖xa2 15 ♖a1 ♕c4 16 ♖c1 = (½-½) Marshall-Capablanca, Lake Hopatcong 1926.

[5] 5 ♕xd3 d6 6 ♗e2 ♘f6 7 0-0 g6 8 ♗g5 h6 (Smit) =.

[6] **6 0-0** ♘f6 7 ♘bd2 ♗e7 8 ♘d4 0-0 9 f4 ±. 6 ... ♘e5! =.
6 ♘d4 ♘f6 7 f4 ♗g4!? 8 ♕b3 ♘a5!?. 7 ... ♗e7 8 0-0 0-0 9 ♕c2 g6 10 ♘d2 ♘xd4 11 cd d5 12 e5 ♘g4 13 ♘f3 ♘h6 14 h3 (Botterill/Harding) 14 ... c5!?
6 h3 g6! 7 ♗g5 ♘f6 8 ♘bd2 ♗g7 9 ♘d4 0-0 10 ♘xc6 bc 11 f4 ♖b8 12 0-0 ♕e8! 13 ♕e1 ♘d7 14 ♖b1 ♘c5 = Raaste-Westerinen, Helsinki 1979.

[7] 6 ... ♗b4+!?

[8] 7 ♕b3 ♕d7! (intending ... ♘a5) 8 ♗c3 ♘f6! ∓ Smit.
7 ♘c3 ♗e7 8 ♕b3 ♘h6 9 ♘d5 f6 10 0-0 ♘a5 ∓ Csom-Barczay, Hungary 1967.

[9] 9 ... ♕c8 10 ♘g5 ♘d8 11 f4 ±.

[10] 12 e5 de 13 fe ♘d5 14 ♘d2 (Krantz-Sellberg, corr. 1974) 14 ... ♗e7! ∓.

[11] 13 ♘c3 h6 14 ♘e6 c6 15 ♖ad1 ♘xe6

16 fe ♕c7 17 ♔h1 ♗e7 ∓ E.Szabo-Kocsis, corr. 1979.

[12] **5 ... ♗c5** 6 ♗c4 d6 7 ♗g5 ♘ge7 (7 ... ♕d7!?) 8 ♘d5 f6 9 ♗xf6 gf 10 ♘xf6+ ♔f8 11 ♕c1! (Keres) ±.
5 ... d6 6 ♗c4 ♘f6 7 ♕b3 ♕d7 8 ♘g5 ±.

[13] 6 ♗g5 ♘ge7 (6 ... ♗e7) 7 ♕c2 d6 8 0-0-0 ♗xc3 9 ♕xc3 0-0 10 h4 ♗e6 11 h5 h6 ∓ Gufeld-Stein, USSR 1959.

[14] 7 ♕b3 ♗xc3+ 8 bc ♕d7 ∓ Minev-Korchnoi, Moscow 1960.

[15] 8 ... ♘f6 and 8 ... ♗e6 are playable.

[16] 9 ♗xf7+? ♔xf7 10 ♘g5+ ♔xg5! ∓∓.
9 ♗a3 ♘f6 10 ♗b5 0-0 11 ♗xc6 bc 12 e5 ♘d5 ∓ Penrose-Smyslov, Munich 1958.

[17] 13 f4 (13 ♕xb7 g5!) 13 ... ♘f3+ 14 ♔g2 ♘h4+ 15 ♔h1 ♕d7 16 f5 ♖e8 (Ciocaltea-Karaklajić, Smederevska Palanka 1971) 17 ♕xb7 ♖a4 18 f3 ♕c2 19 ♕b2 ♕d3 20 ♕f2 g5 21 ♗xg5 ♖xe4 22 ♗xh4 ♖e2 23 ♕xa7 ± Milukas-Sutkus, corr. 1976.

[18] 13 ♗b5+ ♔f8! ∓ Joksić-Medancić, Catanzaro 1979.

[19] **4 ... ♘f6!** transposes to the Scotch (Gambit) Variation of the Two Knights' Defence.
4 ... ♗b4+? 5 c3! dc 6 0-0! ±.

[20] 5 ... ♘f6! – Italian II, row 6 ff. This is Black's last chance to equalise.

[21] 6 ... ♘f6!? 7 ♕xd3 ±.

[22] 13 ba ba 14 ♕a4+! ♗d7 15 ♕d1 ♘e7 16 ♕xd3 ♗c8 17 ♘a3 ± Sveshnikov-A.Petrosian, USSR 1974.

[23] 7 ♕e3! Harding/Botterill.

[24] Edinburgh v London, 1826-28. 8 0-0! Lewis.

303

	4	5	6	7	8	9	10	11	12	
8	♘xd4	c3	♗c4[26]	♗b3	f4	♘f5	ef	♕d5		±
	♗b4+[25]	♗e7	♘e5	d6	♘g6	♗xf5	♘h4	♘h6[27]		
9	...	♘c3[28]	♗e3	♕d2	0-0-0	♘xc6	♗d4	♕xd4		=
	g6!?	♗g7	d6![29]	♘f6	♘g4	bc	♗xd4	♕f6[30]		
10	...	♘b5![32]	♕f3	♘xc7+	♘xa8	♗d3!	♗xe4!	♔f1	♕d3	±
	♕h4	♗c5	♘f6[33]	♔d8	♖e8!	♘xe4	♖xe4+	♘d4	♘b3![34]	
11	...	...	♕e2	♘xd4	c3	g3	♗g2[36]			±/±
	...	...	♘d4[35]	♗xd4	♗b6	♕e7				
12	...	...	♗e2[37]	0-0	♘1c3	♘d4[39]				∞/±
	...	...	♕xe4+	♔d8[38]	a6	♕e8				
13	...	...	c3	♘d2	♘a3	♕e2	g3	f3	♘dc4	±
	...	♗b4+	♗a5[40]	a6	♗b6	d6	♕g4	♕e6	♗a7[41]	
14	...	...	♗d2	♗e2	0-0	♘1c3	g3	♘d5![42]	♘xf6	±
	...	...	♕xe4+	♔d8	♘f6	♕h4	♕h3	♗xd2	gf[43]	
15	...	...	...	...	...	♘xd2	g3	♘c4	♗f3![45]	±
	...	...	...	...	♗xd2	♕f4[44]	♕h6	♘ge7		

25 4 ... ♕f6 5 ♘b5 ♗c5 6 ♕e2 ♗b6 7 ♘c3 ♘ge7 8 ♗e3 ♗a5 ± Kupreichik-Nei, USSR 1975.

26 6 ♗f4 d6 7 ♘d2 ♘f6 8 ♗e2 ± Harding/Botterill.

27 Messing-Planinc, Yugoslav Ch 1968.

28 5 c4! ± Evans.

29 6 ... ♘f6 7 ♘xc6! bc 8 e5 ♘g8 9 ♗f4! (9 f4!? f6 10 ♕d2 fe 11 fe ♗xe5 12 0-0-0 ∞ Sabanov-Vorotnikov, USSR 1977) 9 ... ♕e7 10 ♕e2! ± Harding/Botterill.

30 Bellon-Karpov, Las Palmas 1976.

31 Steinitz Variation.

32 5 ♘c3 ♗b4 6 ♘db5 ♕xe4+ 7 ♗e2 ♗xc3+ 8 ♘xc3 ♕d4 (8 ... ♕e7!? intending 9 ♘b5 ♕d8) 9 ♗d3 ♘b4 10 0-0! ♘xd3 11 ♘b5 ♕c4 12 ♕xd3 ♕xd3 13 cd ♔d8 14 ♗f4 d6 15 ♖ac1 ♗d7 16 ♘xc7 ♖c8 = Steinitz, improved at move 10 by Harding/Botterill.

5 ♕d3 ♘f6 6 ♘xc6 dc 7 ♘c3 ♗b4 8 ♗d2! ± Maczuski-Kolisch, Paris 1863.

5 ♘f3 ♕xe4+ 6 ♗e2 ♕e7! (Evans) 7 ♘c3 ♘f6 8 ♗g5 ♕d8! 9 ♘d5 ♗e7 ∓ (insufficient

compensation – Evans).

33 6 ... ♗b6!?

34 6 ... ♘d4 7 ♘xd4 ♗xd4 8 c3 ♗b6 9 ♗e3 ±.

34 13 ♗e3 ♗xe3 14 fe ♘xa1 ± (15 ♘d2 ♖a4 16 ♔e2 ♖xa2 17 ♕d6 ±±).

35 6 ... ♗b6 7 ♗e3 ♗a5+ 8 ♗d2 ♗xd2+ 9 ♘xd2 ♕d8 10 0-0-0 ± Rosenthal-Winawer, 1867.

36 Harding/Botterill.

37 6 ♗e3 ♕e5! 7 ♘d2 d5 8 ♘f3 ♕e7 9 ♕xd5 ♗e6 (O'Hanlon-Mikenas, Buenos Aires Ol 1939) 10 ♕d2 ♖d8 11 ♗d3 ♘b4 ∓.

38 6 ... ♗b4+ – row 14.

39 Staunton.

40 6 ... ♕xe4+ 7 ♗e2 ♗a5 8 0-0 ±.

41 13 ♗e3 ± Radulov-G.Garcia, Torremolinos 1975.

42 11 ♘xc7?! ♘xc7 12 ♘d5+ ♘xd5 13 ♗g4 ♕xg4 14 ♕xg4 ♗xd2 15 ♖fd1 (Potter and Steinitz) 15 ... ♗h6! 16 ♖xd5 d6 ∓.

43 13 ♕xd2 d6 14 ♖ad1 ± Harding/Botterill.

44 9 ... ♕g6 10 ♘c4 intending 11 ♗f3 ±.

45 Botterill-Staples, Manchester 1974.

Scotch II   1 e4 e5 2 ♘f3 ♘c6 3 d4 ed 4 ♘xd4

	4	5	6	7	8	9	10	11	12	
1	... ♘f6	♘xc6 bc	♗d3[1] d5!	♕e2[2] de!	♗xe4[3] ♘xe4	♕xe4+ ♕e7[4]				∓
2	... ...	... ...	♘d2 ♗c5[5]	♗d3! d5	0-0 0-0	c4![6] ♕e7	♕c2 h6	b3 ♗d4	♖b1[7]	±
3	... ...	... ...	... d5!	♗d3[8] ♗d6!	0-0 0-0	h3 ♖e8!	ed cd[9]			±

1 e4 e5 2 ♘f3 ♘c6 3 d4 ed 4 ♘xd4 ♘f6 5 ♘xc6 bc 6 e5[10]

	6	7	8	9	10	11	12	13	14	
4	... ♘d5	♗d3 d6	ed cd	0-0 ♗e7	♗e4 ♕c7	♗xd5 cd	♘c3[11]			±
5	... ♘e4	♕f3! ♕h4[12]	g3 ♘g5	♕e2[13] ♕e4	♗xg5! ♕xh1	♘c3 h6	♗f4 ♕xh2	♘e4 ♗e7	0-0-0 0-0[14]	±
6	... ♕e7!	♕e2 ♘g8	b3! g6[15]	♗a3 ♕e6	♗xf8 ♔xf8	♘c3 f6	f4 d5	0-0-0![16]		±
7	... ...	... ♘d5	♘d2 ♗b7[17]	♘b3[18] 0-0-0	c4 ♘b6	♗d2 ♖e8	f4 f6	a4 ♗a6	♕e4 ♕f7[19]	∓
8	... ...	... ...	c4 ♘b6	♘d2[20] ♕e6	b3 ♗e7	♗b2[21] 0-0	♕e4 d5	ed cd[22]		=
9	... ...	... ...	... ♕b4+	♘d2 ♘f4	♕e4 ♘e6	♗e2[23] a5	0-0 a4	♘f3[24] ♗e7	♖b1 0-0[25]	=

1   5 ♘c3 – Scotch Four Knights.

2   7 ♘d2 – row 2.
7 ed?! cd =.
7 e5?! ♘g4 8 ♗f4 ♗c5 ∓.

3   8 ♘d2 ♗b4! 9 ♗xe4 0-0 10 c3 ♗d6 11 ♗xc6 ♖b8 12 0-0 ♗xh2+ 13 ♔xh2 ♕d6+ ∓∓ Grüber-Euwe, Vienna 1921.

4   Mieses-Teichmann, Berlin 1924.

5   6 ... d6 7 ♗d3 g6 8 0-0 ♗g7 9 ♘c3 0-0 = Bilek-Szabo, Budapest 1954.

6   9 ♕f3 ♘g4 10 ed ♕d6 11 ♕g3 ♕xg3 12 hg cd 13 ♘b3 ♗b6 14 ♗f4 (Tartakower-Jacobsen, Copenhagen 1923) 14 ... ♗e6 15 ♗a6! intending a4-a5 Keres.

7   Analysis by Harding/Botterill.

8   7 ed cd 8 ♗b5+ ♗d7 Sefc-Dittman, Dresden 1956 (=).

9   Botterill-Dilworth, Manchester 1975.

10   Mieses Variation.

11   Arseniev-Veselov, USSR 1960.

12   7 ... ♘c5 8 ♗c4 ♘e6 9 0-0 ♕h4 10 ♘d2 ± Wade-Balanel, Bucharest 1954.
7 ... ♗g5 8 ♕g3 ♘e6 9 ♗d3 d5 (9 ... f6 10 ♕h4 Tarrasch) 10 0-0 g6 11 ♘d2 f5 12 ♘b3 ♗g7 13 f4 0-0 14 ♕f2 ♖e8 15 ♗e3 a5 16 ♘d4 ± Bednarsky-Prameshuber, Kecskemet 1964.

13   9 ♕e3 ♕d4 10 ♗g2 ♘e6 ± Troianescu-Radelescu, Bucharest 1955.

14   15 ♕f3 ± Gusakov-Efimov, USSR 1959.

15   8 ... f6 Tarrasch.

16   Harding/Botterill.
13 ed ♕xd6 = Savon-Razuvayev, USSR Ch 1972.

17   8 ... ♘f4?! (Kaikamdzhozov) 9 ♕e3! ♘d5 10 ♕e4! intending c4 ±. 9 ... ♘g6 10 ♘f3 d6 (10 ... d5 11 b4! ±) 11 ed cd 12 ♗e2 ±. 9 ... ♘e6 10 f4! ±.

18   9 c4 ♘b6 – 8 c4 ♘b6 9 ♘d2 ♗b7.

19   15 c5 ♗xf1 16 cb ab! 17 a5 b5! ∓.

20   9 ♘c3 ♕e6 10 b3 ♗b4 11 ♗b2 0-0 (11 ... a5!?) 12 0-0-0 ♖e8 = Harding/Botterill.
9 ♗f4!? Botterill.

21   11 g3 d5 12 cd cd 13 ♗g2 0-0 14 0-0 a5! = Hort-Kostro, Varna 1969.

22   Bednarsky-Gligorić, Havana 1967.

23   11 f4 ♗b7 12 a3 ♕b6 13 ♘f3 c5 14 ♕d3 oo Walbrodt-Marco, Hastings 1895.

24   13 f4!? ♗b7 14 f5 ♘c5 15 ♕h4!
13 ♗g4!? Botterill/Harding.

25   15 ♘d4 ♘xd4 = Botterill-Rumens, Birmingham 1975.

1 e4 e5 2 ♘f3 ♘c6 3 d4 ed 4 ♘xd4 ♘f6 5 ♘xc6 bc 6 e5 *continued*

	6	7	8	9	10	11	12	13	14	
10	...	...	...	♕e4	♘c3	♕xf5	♗xc4	0-0		∓
	...	...	♗a6	♘b6[26]	f5!?	♗xc4	♘xc4	g6[27]		
11	...	...	...	♘d2[28]	b3[29]	♗b2	0-0-0	♕e4	f4	±/∞
	...	...	...	g6	♗g7	0-0[30]	♖ab8[31]	♘b6	♖fe8[32]	
12	...	...	...	...	b3	♗b2	0-0-0[34]	f4	♕f2![37]	±
	...	...	...	♘b6	0-0-0	g6[33]	♗g7[35]	♖he8[36]	♗b7!?[38]	

1 e4 e5 2 ♘f3 ♘c6 3 d4 ed 4 ♘xd4 ♗c5

	5	6	7	8	9	10	11	12	13	
13	♗e3[39]	c3[40]	g3	♗g2	♘b5	♘xc7+	fe[42]	♘d5		=
	♕f6	♘ge7!	d5!	de[41]	♗xe3	♔f8	♖b8	♕g5[43]		
14	...	...	f4	cd	♘c3	d5	♗c5	♗b5+	dc	±
	...	...	♗xd4[44]	d5	de[45]	♘f5	♘ce7	c6	bc[46]	
15	♘b3	g3	♗g2	0-0	h3	a4[47]				±
	♗e7	♘f6	0-0	♖e8	a5					
16	...	c3[49]	g3[50]	♗g2	0-0	f4	h3	♘1d2	♘d4	±
	♗b4+[48]	♗e7	♘f6	0-0[51]	♖e8	d6	♗f8	g6	♗g7[52]	

1 e4 e5 2 ♘f3 ♘c6 3 d4 ed 4 ♘xd4 ♗c5 5 ♘b3 ♗b6

	6	7	8	9	10	11	12	13	14	
17	♘c3[53]	♗e2[54]	0-0	♕d3	♕g3	hg	♗d3			∓
	d6	♕h4	♘f6	0-0	♕xg3	♘b4[55]				
18	...	♗g5[57]	♕d2	♗e3	0-0-0	f3	♕xe3	♘d4	♕xd4	±
	♘f6[56]	d6[58]	h6	0-0	♕e7	♗xe3	a5	♘xd4	♖e8[59]	
19	a4	♕e2	a5	♘xd4	c3	g3	♗g2	0-0	a6!	±
	♕f6[60]	♘ge7[61]	♘d4	♗xd4	♗e5[62]	c6	0-0	d5[63]	ba[64]	
20	...	♘c3	♕e2	♘d5!?[67]	ed+	h4!	g4!	♗g2	c3	±
	a5	♕f6[65]	♘ge7[66]	♘xd5	♘e7	h6[68]	d6	♗d7	0-0-0[69]	
21	...	♘c3	♕e2	♘d5	ed+	a5	h4	♖a4!	g4[71]	±/∞
	a6	♕f6	♘ge7	♘xd5	♘e7	♗a7	h6[70]	0-0	d6![72]	
22	...	...	♗g5[73]	♕h4	♕d2[74]	0-0-0	f4[75]			±
	...	♘ge7	f6	0-0	d6	♗d7				
23	...	...	♗g5	♕e2	♗h4	♘xd4	♕d2	♗d3	f4!?[79]	±/=
	...	♘f6[76]	d6	h6	♘xd4	♗xd4	♗e5[77]	♗e6[78]	♗xc3[80]	
24	...	...	♕e2[81]	♘d5	g3	♗e3	♕xe3	0-0-0[82]		±
	...	d6	♗e6	♗a7	♕d7	♗xe3	0-0-0			

---

26 9 ... ♘f6 10 ♕e2 ♘d5 =.
27 Sveshnikov-Zaitsev, USSR 1975.
28 9 b3 ♘b6 10 ♗b2 0-0-0 11 ♘d2 transposes to row 12.
29 10 ♘c3 ♗g7 11 ♗g5 (Barczay-Pogacs, Hungarian Ch 1964) 11 ... ♕b4+ 12 ♕d2

♛xd2+ 13 ♚xd2 ♞b6 14 b3 ± Botterill/
Harding.

30 11 ... 0-0-0 – row 12.

31 12 ... ♖fe8! Harding/Botterill.

32 15 ♛c2 d5 16 h4! ±/∞ Zverev-Lisenkov,
USSR corr.

33 11 ... d6 12 ed ♛xe2+ 13 ♗xe2 cd
14 0-0-0 ±.

34 12 ♞e4 ♗g7 13 f4 ♖he8 14 ♛d2 d6
(14 ... d5!?; 14 ... f5!?) 15 ♛a5 de! 16 ♛xa6+
♚b8 17 f5 gf 18 ♞d2 ♖xd2! 19 ♚xd2 ♖d8+ ∓
Gaidakov-Tui, Latvia 1975.

35 12 ... ♗h6!? intending ... ♖he8 Evans.

36 13 ... d5 (Evans) 14 ♛e3! ±.

37 Naroditsky-Makarov, Moscow 1962.

38 Keres.

39 5 ♞xc6 ♛f6! 6 ♛e2 (6 f4!? = Larsen-
Brinck-Claussen, Copenhagen 1979) 6 ... bc
7 ♞c3 ♞e7 =.

5 ♞f5?! d5! (5 ... ♛f6!? = Ljubojević-
Karpov, Montreal 1979) 6 ♞xg7+ (6 ♞c3!?)
6 ... ♚f8 ∓.

40 6 ♞b5 ♗xe3! 7 fe (The Blumenfeld Attack)
7 ... ♛h4+ 8 g3 ♛d8 9 ♛g4 ♚f8 10 ♛f4 d6 ∓
Mieses-Schelfhout, Amsterdam 1946.

41 8 ... ♗xd4 9 cd de = Parma.

42 11 0-0 ♖b8 12 fe ♛d6!

43 Klovan-Romanishin, Odessa 1974.

44 7 ... d6 8 ♗b5! ±/±.

45 9 ... 0-0! Botterill/Harding (=!?).

46 14 ♞d5 ± Brat.

47 Bastrikov-Bannik, USSR 1952.

48 Romanishin Variation.

49 6 ♗d2?! ♗xd2+ 7 ♛xd2 ♞f6 8 ♞c3 0-0
9 0-0-0 ♖e8! 10 f3 d6 11 g4 ♗e6 12 g5 ♞d7
13 h4 a5! 14 ♗b5 ♞b4 ∓ Biriescu-Ciocaltea,
Satu Mare 1979.

50 7 f4 d6 8 ♗d3 d5 9 e5 h5! = Urzica-
Romanishin, Gröningen 1972.

7 ♞d4 ♗f6 8 g3 ♞ge7 9 ♗g2 0-0 10 0-0
d6 = Radulov-Keres, Budapest 1970.

7 ♗f4 d6 8 ♞d2 ♞f6 9 ♗e2 0-0 10 0-0
♖e8 11 ♖e1 ♗f8 12 ♗f1 g6 13 ♛c2 ± Pfleger-
O'Kelly, Montilla 1973.

51 8 ... h5?! 9 h3 d6 10 c4 ± Kuprechik-
Romanishin, Odessa 1974.

52 14 ♚h2 ± Grotkov-Tarasov, Agler 1969.

53 Generally transposing below, but this row
gives exceptions.

54 7 a4! – below.

55 Paoli-Keres, Dortmund 1973.

56 6 ... ♞ge7 (Radulov) 7 ♗g5 0-0 8 ♛d2 d6
9 0-0 f6 =.

57 7 ♗d3 is promising: 7 ... d5 8 ♗g5! h6
9 ♗xf6 ♛xf6 10 ♛e2 (or 10 0-0) Botterill/
Harding.

58 Botterill and Harding suggest 7 ... h6!?

59 15 g4 ± Radulov-Matanović, Helsinki 1972.

60 6 ... ♛h4 7 ♛e2 d6 8 a5 ♗g4 9 ♛d2 ♗c5
10 ♗b5 ♞e7 11 ♞xc5 dc 12 0-0 0-0 13 c3 ±
Damjanović-Kolarov, 1964.

61 7 ... ♞d4 8 ♗xd4 ♗xd4 9 c3 ♗c5 10 e5
♛c6 11 ♞d2 ♗e7 12 ♞f3 ±/± Arulaid-
Barcza, Tallinn 1969.

62 10 ... ♗c5 11 e5 ♛c6 12 ♞d2 a6
(Damjanović-Barcza, Tallinn 1969) 13 ♞b3
♗a7 14 ♗e3 ± Harding/Botterill.

63 Barczay-Greshkin, corr. 1966-67.

64 15 ed ♞xd5 16 ♞d2 ♗c7 17 ♞e4 ±.

65 7 ... d6!?
   7 ... ♞ge7!?

66 8 ... ♞b4 9 ♞d5!? (9 ♞b5!? intending c3
– Parma) 9 ... ♞xd5 10 ed+ ♞e7 11 c4 ±
Stern-Kolarov, corr. 1971-72.

67 9 ♗e3 ♞b4 10 0-0-0 0-0 11 f4 d5 ∞
Musil-Ilijevski, Yugoslav Ch 1968. 9 ... ♗xe3
10 ♛xe3 0-0 11 0-0-0 ♞b4 ∞.

68 11 ... d6 12 ♗g5 ♛e5 13 ♛xe5 de 14 c4!?/
14 ♗b5+/ 14 0-0-0!? ±/± in each case.

69 15 ♗e3 ♗xe3 16 fe ♛e7 17 0-0-0 ±
Stupina-Viner, USSR 1978.

70 12 ... 0-0 13 ♗g5 ♛xb2 14 ♗xe7 ♖e8
15 ♚d1! d6 16 ♗f6 ♖xe2 17 ♗xb2 ♖xf2
18 ♗d4 ±± Barczay-Sapi, Budapest 1964.

12 ... d6 13 ♖a4! ♛f5! 14 ♖e4 ♗xf2+
15 ♚d1 ♛xd5+ 16 ♞d2 ♗f5! 17 c4!! ±
Stoica-Orlowski, Poland 1970.

71 14 d6!? Keres.

72 14 ... ♞xd5 15 g5 ♛c6 (15 ... ♛d8 16 gh!)
16 ♖c4! ♞c3 17 ♖xc3! ♛xh1 18 gh ±
Botterill/Harding.

14 ... ♛d6 15 g5 h5 16 ♗g2 ♞xd5 17 0-0
♛c6 18 ♞e4 ± Botterill/Harding.

14 ... d6! 15 g5 ♛f5!! 16 ♗g2!! ♞xd5
(16 ... ♞d7!? 17 ♖f4 ♛e5 18 ♛xe5 de 19 ♖c4)
17 ♞d4 ♛e5 18 ♛xe5 de 19 ♗xd5 ± Botterill/
Harding.

73 8 a5 ♗a7 9 ♗g5 0-0 10 ♛d2 d6 11 0-0-0
♗e6 12 ♞d5 ±/± Hort-Portisch, Monaco
1969.

74 10 ♗e2 d6 11 0-0 ♞g6 12 ♗g3 ± Barczay-
Addison, Havana Ol 1966.

75 Radulov-Portisch, Budapest 1970.

76 Geller Variation.

77 12 ... ♗a7? 13 ♞d5! ±±.

78 Tseitlin-Geller, USSR Ch 1971.

79 Botterill/Harding.

80 15 ♛xc3 ♖xe4 16 ♗xd8 ♞xc3 17 ♗xc7
♞d5 18 ♗xd6 ♖d8 19 ♗e5 f6 20 f5! ♗c8
21 ♗g3 (21 ♗c3!?) 21 ... ♞b4 (21 ... ♞e3!?)
22 0-0-0 =. Analysis by Botterill/Harding.

81 8 ♗e2 ♛h4 (8 ... ♞ge7?! Ivanović-Tal,
Tallinn 1979) 9 0-0 ♞ge7 10 a5 ♗a7 11 ♖a4
♞e5 12 ♞d4 ♗d7 13 ♖a3 0-0 = Zhitenev-
Lhagkva, Moscow 1972.

82 Analysis by Botterill/Harding.

307

Giuoco Piano (Italian)   2 Knights

The Giuoco Piano eyes the sensitive f7 square and simply continues development. It is schizophrenic in character, ranging in mood from the exceedingly quiet (Giuoco Pianissimo) 4 d3 to the untamed pyrotechnics of the Evans Gambit. One of the oldest of openings, it has been analysed in detail and there appear to be few surprises left in several lines, particularly those beginning 4 c3, 5 d4. A perusal of the Giuoco's large and long standing body of theory will unearth several paths to equality for Black.

For the more daring, Black can liven the play with 3 ... ♘f6, initiating a much sharper struggle in the shape of the Two Knights' Defence. White may head back to the calm of the Giuoco with 4 d3 or plunge into a maelstrom of complications with 4 ♘g5, when he must be ready to cope with the main lines stemming from 4 ... d5 as well as the obscurities of 4 ... ♗c5!?, the Wilkes/Barre Variation. At present, these discussions are usually conducted in correspondence rather than over-the-board circles due to the intensely confusing positions that result. Theory (and there is a great deal of it available) has yet to reach a definite conclusion concerning these hair-raising lines.

	Giuoco Piano I		1 e4 e5 2 ♘f3 ♘c6 3 ♗c4						
	3	4	5	6	7	8	9	10	11
1	...	d4	de[3]	♗d5!?[4]	♘g5	c3	♗b3	g3	h3	±
	♗e7[1]	d6[2]	de	♗d6	♘h6	♘e7	♘g6	♕e7	♗d7[5]	
2	...	c3[7]	d4[9]	♗e3	♕b3	♘bd2	de[10]			±
	d6[6]	♗g4[8]	♕e7	♘f6	♘d8	g6				
3	...	♘c3[12]	d3[13]	♗g5[14]	♘d5[15]	dc	♘xf6+	♗h4[17]		=
	♗c5[11]	♘f6	d6	♘a5	♘xc4	c6![16]	gf	♖g8[18]		
4	...	d3	c3[19]	b4[20]	a4	♘bd2	0-0	♗b3	♘c4	=
	...	♘f6	d6	♗b6	a6[21]	0-0	♘e7[22]	♘g6	♗a7[23]	
5	...	b4[24]	a4[26]	♘c3	♘d5!	ed	dc	♕xf3	♔d1	±
	...	♗b6[25]	a6[27]	♘f6[28]	♘xd5	e4	ef[29]	♕e7+	dc[30]	

	1 e4 e5 2 ♘f3 ♘c6 3 ♗c4 ♗c5 4 b4 ♗xb4								
	5	6	7	8	9	10	11	12	13
6	c3[31]	d4	0-0[32]	cd	d5!?	♗b2	♗d3	♘c3	♘e2	∓
	♗c5	ed	d6[33]	♗b6	♘a5![34]	♘e7	0-0	♘g6[35]	c5[36]	
7	...	...	...	...	h3	♖e1	♗a3	♘c3	♖c1[37]	∞
	...	...	...	...	♘f6	h6	0-0	♖e8		

[1] Hungarian Defence.
  3 ... f5 4 d4 fe 5 ♘xe5 d5 6 ♗b5 ♘ge7
  7 0-0 a6 8 ♗xc6+ bc 9 f3 ♗f5 10 ♘c3 ±

Bilguer Handbuch.
  3 ... g6 4 d4 ed 5 c3! dc 6 ♘xc3 ♗g7
  7 ♕b3 ♕e7 8 ♘d5! ♕xe4+ 9 ♗e2 ♔d8

(9 ... ♘a5 10 ♕d1!) 10 0-0 ♕xe2 11 ♗g5+ f6 12 ♖fe1 ♕xe1+ 13 ♖xe1 fg 14 ♘xg5 ♘h6 15 ♕h3! ♖f8 16 ♕h4 ±± Unzicker.

3 ... ♘d4 4 0-0 d6 5 ♘xd4 ed 6 c3 ± Keres.

2 4 ... ed 5 ♘xd4 d6 6 0-0 ♘f6 7 ♘c3 0-0 8 h3 ♖e8 9 ♖e1 ♗f8 10 ♗g5 h6 (Estrin-Chaplinsky, Moscow 1970) 11 ♘xc6 bc 12 ♗h4 ♗e6 13 ♗d3 ± Harding/Botterill.

3 5 d5 ♘b8 6 ♗d3 ♘f6 7 c4 0-0 8 h3 ♘bd7 9 ♘c3 ♘e8 10 0-0 ±.

5 ♘c3 ♘f6 6 h3 0-0 7 0-0 ± Tal-Filip, Miskolc 1963.

4 6 ♕xd8+ ♖xd8 7 ♘c3 a6 8 ♗e3 ♗e6 9 ♗xe6 fe 10 0-0-0 h6 11 ♖d2 ± Vasyukov-Tseshkovsky, USSR 1975.

5 12 ♕e2 0-0-0 13 ♘f3 ± Bronstein-Reshevsky, Petropolis IZ 1973.

6 Paris Defence.

7 4 d4 ♗g4 5 c3 ♕e7 tranposes to the text. 5 h3! ±. 5 ... ♕d7 6 d5 ±.

8 4 ... ♕e7 5 d4 g6 Alekhine.

4 ... ♗e6 Tartakower.

9 5 ♕b3 ♕d7 6 ♘g5?! (6 ♗xf7+ ♕xf7 7 ♕xb7 ♕d7 8 ♕xa8 ♗xf3 9 gf ♕xf3 10 ♖g1 ♕xe4+ 11 ♔d1 ♕f3+ = Sozin) 6 ... ♘h6 7 ♘xf7 ♘xf7 8 ♗xf7+ ♕xf7 9 ♕xb7 ♔d7 10 ♕xa8 ♘c4 11 f3 ♗xf3! 12 gf ♘d4! 13 d3? (13 cd ♕xc1 ∓) 13 ... ♕xd3 14 cd ♗e7 15 ♕xh8 ♗h4 mate, Rodzinski-Alekhine, Paris 1913.

10 Levenfish-Tolush, Leningrad 1939.

11 Giuoco Piano.

12 4 ♗xf7+ ♔xf7 5 ♘xe5+ (the Jerome Gambit) 5 ... ♘xe5 6 ♕h5+ ♔f8 7 ♕xe5 d6 ∓.

4 d4 ♗xd4! 5 ♘xd4 ♘xd4 6 f4 d5! ∓ Fatirni-Spielmann, Baden 1914.

4 0-0 ♘f6 5 d4 ♗xd4 6 ♘xd4 ♘xd4 7 ♗g5 ♕e7 8 ♘c3 c6 9 f4 d6 10 ♕d2 ♘e6 ∓ Markland-Reshevsky, London 1973.

13 Giuoco Pianissimo.

14 Canal Variation.

6 0-0 ♗g4!

6 h3 ♘a5! 7 ♗g5 ♘xc4 8 dc ♗e6 9 ♘d5 c6 10 ♘xf6+ gf ∓.

6 ♗e3 ♗b6! 7 ♕d2 ♗e6 =.

15 7 ♗xf6 ♕xf6 8 ♘d5 ♕d8 ∓.

7 ♗b3 c6! 8 ♘a4 ♗b4+ 9 c3 ♘xb3 intending ... ♗a5 ∓ Harding/Botterill.

16 8 ... ♗xf2+!? 9 ♔xf2 (9 ♔e2 – Keres – 9 ... ♗b6 10 ♖f1 h6 11 ♗h4 ♗e6! Harding/Botterill) 9 ... ♘xe4+ 10 ♔g1 ♘xg5 11 ♘xg5 c6 12 ♕h5 g6 13 ♕h6 (13 ♕f3 f5! ∓) 13 ... cd 14 ♕g7 ♕xg5 15 ♕xh8+ ♔e7 16 h4! = Unzicker.

17 10 ♗e3 ♕b6 11 ♕d2 ♗e6 12 0-0-0 0-0-0 ∓ Korchnoi-Bronstein, USSR Ch 1952.

18 Eliskases-Bronstein, Mar del Plata 1960.

10 ... ♕d7 11 ♗xf6 ♖g8 12 ♗h4! ♖xg2?!

13 ♗g3 ♕g4 14 ♘d2! ± Harding/Botterill.

19 5 0-0 d6 6 ♗g5 h6 7 ♗h4 g5! 8 ♗g3 h5! 9 h4! ♗g4 10 c3 (10 hg h4!) 10 ... ♕d7! ∓ Dubois-Steinitz, London 1862.

20 Blackburne/Bird Variation.

6 ♗e3 ♗b6 (6 ... ♗xe3!?) 7 ♗bd2 ♗e6!? (7 ... ♘e7, Mason-Gunsberg, New York 1889) 8 ♕e2 (8 ♗b3) (Blackburne-Chigorin, London 1883) 8 ... 0-0! =.

21 7 ... a5 8 b5 ♗b8 (8 ... ♘e7!? 9 ♗e3 ♗xe3 10 fe c6 11 0-0 0-0 – Bird-Zukertort, London 1883 – 12 ♖a2!?, 12 ♕e1!?) 9 0-0 0-0 10 ♗g5 h6 11 ♗h4 g5 12 ♘xg5!? (Keres) 12 ... hg 13 ♗xg5 ♘bd7 (13 ... ♗e6 14 ♕f3 ♘bd7 15 ♕g3!) 14 ♔h1 intending f4 ∞/± Harding/Botterill.

22 9 ... ♕e7!? intending ... ♗e6 Pirc.

23 12 ♖a2 h6 13 ♖e1 ♖e8 14 h3 ♗e6 = Ljubojević-Furman, Ljubljana/Portorož 1975.

24 Evans Gambit.

25 4 ... ♗e7 5 c3 ♘f6 6 ♕b3 0-0 7 d3 ± Harding/Botterill.

4 ... d5!? 5 ed! ♕xb4 6 ♗a3! ± Keres.

26 5 ♗b2 d6 6 a4 a6 7 b5 ab 8 ab ♖xa1 9 ♗xa1 ♘d4! ∓ Tartakower-Schlechter, Baden 1914.

5 b5?! ♘a5 6 ♘xe5 (6 ♗e2 d5!) 6 ... ♘h6! 7 d4 d6 8 ♗xh6 gh 9 ♗xf7+ (9 ♘xf7 ♕f6 ∓ Max Lange) 9 ... ♔e7 10 ♘c3 de 11 ♕f3 ♗g4! 12 ♕xg4 ♘xf7 (Max Lange) 13 ♘d5 (Keres) 13 ... ♖f8 14 de ♕g5 15 ♕d7+ ♔g6! 16 ♘e7+ ♔g7! 17 ♘f5+ ♔h8 (intending ... ♖d8, ... ♕d2+) ∓ Unzicker.

27 5 ... a5 6 b5 ♘d4 7 ♘xd4 ♗xd4 8 c3 intending d4 ± Keres.

5 ... ♘xb4? 6 a5 ♗c5 7 c3 ±.

28 6 ... ♘xb4 7 ♘xe5 ♕g5 8 ♕f3 ±.

6 ... d6 7 ♘d5 ♗a7! 8 d3 h6 9 ♗e3! ± Panov/Estrin.

29 9 ... 0-0 10 ♗b2 ± Sokolsky-Goldenov, Kiev 1945.

30 12 ♖e1 ♗e6 ± Panov.

31 5 0-0?! ♘f6 6 d4 ed 7 c3 dc 8 e5 d5 ∓ Pinkus-Marshall, New York 1926.

32 7 cd ♗b4+ 8 ♗d2 or 8 ♗f1 ±.

33 7 ... d3 8 ♘g5! ♘h6 9 ♘xf7! ♘xf7 10 ♗xf7+ ♔xf7 11 ♕h5+ g6 12 ♕xc5 ± Duhrssen-Kramer, Ebensee 1930.

34 9 ... ♘ce7 10 e5! de 11 ♘xe5 ♘f6 12 d6! ♕xd6 13 ♘xf7 ±.

35 12 ... c6 13 ♘e2 f5 (13 ... cd 14 ed ♗f5) 14 ♖c1 fe 15 ♗xe4 ♗f5 16 ♗xf5 ♖xf5 17 dc bc 18 ♘ed4 ± Anderssen-Steinitz, match (1) London 1866.

36 14 ♕d2 ♗c7! 15 ♖ac1 ♖b8 16 ♘g3 f6 17 ♘f5 b5 18 ♔h1 c4! ∓ W.Paulsen-Anderssen, Barmen 1869.

37 Mariotti-Gligorić, Venice 1971.

1 e4 e5 2 ♘f3 ♘c6 3 ♗c4 ♗c5 4 b4 ♗xb4 *continued*

	5	6	7	8	9	10	11	12	13	
8	c3	d4	0-0	cd	♘c3!	♗g5	♗xf7+	♘d5	♗xe7	=
	♗c5	ed	d6	♗b6	♕a5	♘e7[38]	♕xf7	♖e8!	♖xe7[39]	
9	...	d4	0-0	♘g5[41]	f4	e5	de			∞
	♗d6!?[40]	♕e7	♘f6	0-0	ef	♘xe5!	♗xe5![42]			
10	...	d4	♘xe5	♘xc4	ed	♘e3	0-0	c4		=
	♗e7	♘a5	♘xc4	d5	♕xd5	♕d7[43]	♘f6	b5![44]		
11	...	♕b3	d4	♕b5![45]	♗xh6	♕xc4	de	♕b5+		==
	...	♘h6	♘a5	♘xc4	gh[46]	d6[47]	♗e6	♕d7![48]		
12	...	♕b3	0-0	d4	de	♘xe5	a4	♔h1		∞
	♗a5	♕f6[49]	♗b6	d6	♘xe5	de	a6	♘e7[50]		
13	...	d4[51]	0-0	de	♕b3![53]	♗g5	♗d5	♗xe7	♗xc6	∞
	...	d6	♗b6![52]	de	♕f6	♕g6	♘ge7	♔xe7	♕xc6[54]	
14	...	...	♕b3!	0-0	♗b5?![56]	♗xc6	de	♕c2		∓
	...	...	♕d7[55]	♗b6!	a6	♕xc6	♗e6	0-0-0[57]		
15	...	...	...	de!	♘bd2	♕c2	♘xc4	♘fxe5	♗a3!	±
	...	...	...	♗b6	♘a5[58]	♘xc4	de	♕e6	♘e7![59]	
16	...	...	...	...	0-0	♖d1![60]	a4!	a5	♗a3	=
	...	...	...	de	♗b6	♕e7	a6![61]	♗c5	♗xa3[62]	

[38] 10 ... ♕d7!? 11 ♗d3 ∞ (==).

[39] 14 ♘g5+ ♔g8 15 ♕h5 h6 16 ♘g6! hg 17 ♘f6+ ♔f8 18 ♘h7+ ♔g8 19 ♘f6+ = Chigorin.

[40] Stone-Ware Defence.

[41] 8 ♘bd2 (Halilbeily-Shishov, USSR 1958) 8 ... 0-0 9 0-0 ♖e8 ∞ (=!?) Analysis.

[42] Analysis by Botterill/Harding. If 12 ♕b3 or 12 ♔h1 then 12 ... d5! ∞.

[43] **10 ... ♕d8** 11 0-0 ♘f6 12 c4 0-0 13 ♘c3 ± Tartakower-Trifunović, Paris 1950.

10 ... ♕a5 11 0-0 ♘f6 12 c4 (12 ♖e1 ♗e6 13 c4 c6 14 ♗b2 0-0-0 ∞/= Porreca-Euwe, Bern 1957) 12 ... 0-0! = Cafferty.

[44] Nunn.

12 ... 0-0 13 ♘c3 c6 14 d5 cd 15 ♘cxd5 ♘xd5 16 ♘xd5 ♖d8 17 ♖b1 ♖c6 18 ♕d4 ♗e6 19 ♖b3 ± Nunn-Larsen, London 1980.

[45] 8 ♕a4?! ♘xc4 9 ♕xc4 ♘g4! ∓. 9 ♗xh6? ♗b6! ∓.

[46] 9 ... ♘d6?! 10 ♕xe5 ±.

[47] 10 ... ed 11 cd ==.

[48] **12 ... ♔f8?!** 13 ♕xb7 ♗g7 14 0-0 ♕d7 15 ed ♗xd6 16 e5 ♖hb8 17 ♕e4 ♗e7 18 ♘bd2 ± Harding-Hodgson, corr. 1974-75.

12 ... ♕d7! 13 ♕xb7 0-0 14 ♕a6 (14 ♘bd2 de 15 ♘xe5 ♕d6 16 ♘f3 ♗f6 intending ... ♕d3 ∞/∓) ∞.

[49] 6 ... ♕f6 7 0-0 ♗b6 8 d4 ed 9 e5 ♕g6 10 cd (10 ♗a3!?) 10 ... ♘xd4 11 ♘xd4 ♗xd4 12 ♘c3 ♘h6 (Bird-Chigorin, Hastings 1895) 13 ♗a3! ± Harding/Botterill.

[50] Nunn-Hübner, Johannesburg 1981.

[51] 6 0-0 d6! 7 d4 – 6 d4.

[52] Lasker's Defence.

[53] **9 ♗xf7+?** ♔xf7 10 ♘xe5+ ♔e8! 11 ♕h5+ g6 12 ♘xg6 ♘f6 13 ♕h6 ♖g8 14 ♘h4 ♘e5! ∓∓ Panov/Estrin.

9 ♕xd8+ ♘xd8 10 ♘xe5 ♘f6! Lasker.

[54] 14 ♘xe5 ♕e6 (Chigorin) 15 ♘c4 ∞ Keres.

[55] 7 ... ♕e7 8 d5 ♘d4 9 ♕a4+! ♕d7 10 ♕xa5 b6 11 ♘xd4 ba 12 ♗b5 ed 13 ♗xd7+ ♔xd7 14 cd ± Harding/Botterill.

[56] 9 de!?

[57] Keres.

[58] 9 ... de 10 ♗a3 ♘a5 11 ♕b4 c5 12 ♕b2 ♘xc4 13 ♘xc4 c6 (13 ... ♕e6!? Euwe) 14 ♖d1 ♕f6 15 ♘d6+ ∞ Sokolsky-Schumacher, corr. 1954.

[59] Intending ... 0-0. 14 ♕a4+ ♗d7 15 ♘xd7 ♕xd7 16 ♘xb6 cb 17 ♕xd7+ ♔xd7 18 0-0-0+ ♔e8 ± Harding/Botterill.

[60] 10 ♗a3 ♘a5 11 ♘xe5 ♘xb3 12 ab ♕e6! 13 ♗xe6 ♗xe6 == Sokolsky.

[61] 11 ... a5 12 ♗d5 ♗g4 ∞/± Shaposhnikov-Veltmander, USSR 1958.

[62] 14 ♘xa3 ♘f6 15 ♗d5 0-0 16 ♘c4 ♗d7 ∞/=.

	4	5	6	7	8	9	10	11	12	
1	...	d4	cd	♘c3	♗e3	♗b3	♕d3	0-0	♖ae1³	±
	d6	ed	♗b6¹	♘f6²	♗g4	0-0	♖e8	♗h5		
2	...	d4	0-0	a4	de	♘xe5	♕f3	a5	♖e1	±
	♕f6	♗b6⁴	h6	a6	♘xe5	♕xe5	♘f6⁵	♗a7	d6⁶	
3	...	d4!	0-0!	e5	b4	a4	♗a3	cb	♕b3	±
	♕e7⁷	ed?!	d3⁸	h6	♗b6	a5	ab	♘xb4	♗c5⁹	
4	...	...	d5!?	d6¹¹	♕xd6	♘a3	♗d5	♘c4	♘h4	∓
	...	♗b6	♘d8¹⁰	♕xd6	cd	♘e6	♘f6	♗c7	g6¹²	
5	...	...	♗g5!¹³	d5!	d6!	♘a3¹⁶	♘c2	♔e2	♘h4	±
	...	...	♘f6¹⁴	♘d8	cd¹⁵	a6¹⁷	♗xf2+¹⁸	♗c5	♘e6¹⁹	
6	...	d4²⁰	e5	♗b5	cd²¹	♘c3	0-0	♗e3	ef²²	=
	♘f6	ed	d5!	♘e4	♗b6	0-0	♗g4	f5	♘xc3²³	
7	...	...	0-0	cd	dc	♕xd8+²⁴	♖d1+	♗e3	♘a3	=
	...	...	♘xe4!	d5!	dc	♔xd8!²⁵	♗d7	♔e7	♗e6	

	7	8	9	10	11	12	13	14	15	
8	♘c3²⁶	ed	0-0	♗g5	♗xd5²⁸	♘xd5	♗e7	♖e1+	♕e2	∞
	d5	♘xd5	♗e6²⁷	♗e7	♗xd5²⁹	♕xd5	♔xe7³⁰	♘f8	g6!³¹	

¹ 6 ... ♗b4+ 7 ♘c3 ♘f6 8 ♗g5 ±.

² 7 ... ♗g4 8 ♗b5! ±.

³ Leonhardt-Teichmann, London 1904.

⁴ 5 ... ed? 6 e5! ♕g6 7 cd ♕xg2 8 ♖g1 ♗b4+ 9 ♘c3 ♕h3 10 ♗xf7+! ± Bilguer Handbuch.

⁵ 10 ... ♕f6 11 ♕xf6 ♘xf6 12 e5 ± Keres.

⁶ 13 ♗f4 ± intending e5 – Euwe.

⁷ Lewis Defence.

⁸ 6 ... ♘e5 7 ♘xe5 ♕xe5 8 f4! dc+ 9 ♔h1 cb 10 fe ba♕ 11 ♕d5! ±± Harding/Botterill.
6 ... dc 7 ♘xc3 d6 8 ♘d5 ±.

⁹ 13 ♘c3 ± Rossolimo-Evans, Hastings 1949/50.

¹⁰ 6 ... ♘b8?! 7 d6! ±.

¹¹ 7 0-0!? Keres.

¹² 13 ♖h6 ♘xd5 14 ed ♘c5 ∓.

¹³ Mestel's Variation.

¹⁴ 6 ... f6 7 ♗e3 ed 8 cd ♕xe4 9 ♘c3 ♕e7 10 ♘d5 ∞/ ±.

¹⁵ 8 ... ♕xd6 9 ♕xd6 cd 10 ♗xf6 gf 11 ♘h4 ± Mestel.

¹⁶ 16 ♘h4? ♗xf2+!.

¹⁷ Or else 10 ♘b5.

¹⁸ 10 ... h6 11 ♗xf6 ♕xf6 12 ♘b4 ± Harding/Botterill.

¹⁹ 13 ♘f5 ± Mestel-Doyle, Dublin 1975.

²⁰ 5 d3 – 4 d3 ♘f6 5 c3 (Italian I, row 4).

²¹ 8 ♘xd4 ♗d7 9 ♗xc6 bc 10 0-0 f6! ∓ Bouteville-Larsen, Le Havre 1966.

²² Cordel-Schallop, Berlin 1880.

²³ 13 bc ♗xf6 = Unzicker.

²⁴ 9 ♕e2 ♕d3! 10 ♖e1 f5 11 ♘bd2 0-0 12 ♘xe4 fe 13 ♕xe4 ♗f5 14 ♕f4 ♖ae8 = Popov.

²⁵ 9 ... ♘xd8 10 ♖e1 f5 11 ♘c3 0-0 12 ♘xe4 fe 13 ♖xe4 ± Popov-Schneider, corr. Ol 1972-74.

²⁶ Greco's Attack.

²⁷ 9 ... ♘xc3 10 bc ♗xc3 (10 ... ♗e7 11 ♗f4! Neishtadt) 11 ♕b3! ♗xa1 12 ♗xf7+ ♔f8 13 ♗a3+ ± Bilguer Handbuch.
9 ... ♗b6 10 ♖e1+ ♗e7 11 ♗b3 0-0 12 d5 ♘a5 13 ♗c2 ♘ac4 14 ♕d3 ± Steinitz-Blackburne, Nuremberg 1896.
9 ... ♗xc3 10 bc 0-0 11 ♕c2 h6 12 ♖e1 ♗e6 13 ♗xh6 ♕d7!? (13 ... gh 14 ♖xe6! – Steinitz – fe 15 ♕g6+ ± Samuels-Klein, 1929) 14 ♗d2 ♗f5 15 ♗d3 ± Steinitz-Schiffers, match (2) 1896.

²⁸ 11 ♗xe7 ♘cxe7 12 ♘e4 0-0 ∞.

²⁹ 11 ... ♗xg5 12 ♗xe6 fe 13 ♕b3! ± Neishtadt.

³⁰ 13 ... ♘xe7 14 ♖e1 f6 15 ♕e2 (15 ♕a4+ ♔f7! 16 ♖ac1 ♗d6! 17 ♕b3+ ♗d5 18 ♘d2 ± I.Zaitsev).

³¹ Intending ... ♔g7, ... ♖he8 – Wade.

	7	8	9	10	11	12	13	14	15	
9	...	...	...	...	...	♗xe7	♖e1	♕e2	♘xd5	±
	...	...	...	...	...	♘xe7	f6	c6[32]	cd[33]	
10	...	0-0	bc	cb	♖e1+	♗g5	♕e2!	♗f4	♕xc4+	±
	♘xe4!	♘xc3	d5[34]	dc	♘e7	f6	♗g4[35]	♔f7	♘d5[36]	
11	...	...	d5![37]	dc	♘e5!	♕g4	b4!	♗b2	♕xc4	∞
	...	♗xc3!	♗a5[38]	bc	♘d6[39]	♕f6[40]	♗xb4[41]	♘xc4	♗e7[42]	
12	...	...	...	♖e1![43]	♖xe4	♗g5[45]	♘xg5	♘xh7!	♕h5+	∞
	...	...	♗f6!	♘e7![44]	d6!	♗xg5	0-0[46]	♔xh7[47]	♔g8[48]	
13	...	...	...	...	...	...	...	♗b5+[49]	♕e2[50]	∓
	...	...	...	...	...	...	h6!	♗d7	♗xb5![51]	
14	♔f1	ed	♘c3	bc	♗xf7+[52]	♕b3+	♕xc3			∓
	d5!	♘xd5	♘xc3	♗xc3	♔xf7	♗e6	♕d5[53]			
15	♗d2	♗xb4	♗xf7+!	♕b3+	♘e5+	♕xb4	♕a3!	♘f3	0-0	±
	♘xe4	♘xb4	♔xf7	d5	♔e6[54]	c5	cd	♕b6	♔f7[55]	
16	...	♘bxd2	ed	♕b3	0-0	♖fe1	a4!	a5	♘xb3	=
	♗xd2+!	d5!	♘xd5	♘ce7?!	0-0	c6[56]	♕b6!	♕xb3	♖d8![57]	
17	...	...	...	...	...	♘e5!	♘e4	♖ad1	♗xb3	±
	...	...	...	...	...	c6	♕b6	♕xb3	♖d8[58]	
18	...	...	...	...	♕a4+	♕b3[59]	♕a4+			=
	...	...	...	♘a5!	♘c6	♘a5	♘c6[60]			

[32] 14 ... ♗xf3 15 ♕xf3 c6 16 ♕e4 ♕d7 17 d5 ♔f7 18 dc ♘xc6 19 ♖ad1 ± I.Zaitsev.

[33] 16 ♖ac1 ♕d7 (16 ... ♕d6 17 ♕c2 0-0 18 ♕c7) 17 ♘e5!? or 17 ♕e3 ♔f7 18 ♕f4 ± I.Zaitsev.

[34] 9 ... ♗xc3 10 ♗a3! d6 11 ♖c1 ± Aitken 1937.

[35] 13 ... fg 14 ♕xc4 ±.

[36] 16 ♘d2! ♗e6 17 ♗g3 ♖e8 18 ♘e4 ± Sakharov.

[37] The Möller Attack.

[38] 9 ... ♘e5 10 bc ♘xc4 11 ♕d4 f5 12 ♕xc4 d6 13 ♘d4 0-0 14 f3 ♘c5 15 ♖e1 ♔h8 16 ♗a3 ± Romanov-Kotkov, corr. 1964.

[39] 11 ... 0-0 12 ♘xf7 ♖xf7 13 ♗xf7+ ♔xf7 14 ♕h5+ ±±.

[40] 12 ... 0-0 13 ♗g5! ♕e8 14 ♗f6! ±±.

[41] 13 ... ♕xe5 14 ♗f4 ♕f6 15 ♖ae1+ ♔f8 16 ♗g5 ♕g6 17 ♗e7+ ♔g8 18 ♗xd6 ♗b7 19 ♕xd7 h5 20 ♗c5 ± Bilguer Handbuch.

[42] Analysis by Harding/Botterill.

[43] 10 dc? bc 11 ♖e1 d5 ∓.

[44] 10 ... 0-0 11 ♖xe4 ♘e7 12 d6! (12 g4!? d6 13 g5 ♗e5) 12 ... cd 13 ♕xd6 ♘f5 14 ♕d5 ♘e7 15 ♕d6 = (draw).

[45] 12 g4 0-0 – note 44.

[46] The Therkatz Variation.

[47] 14 ... ♗f5 15 ♖h4 ♖e8 16 ♕h5 ♗g6 17 ♖d4 ♗e5 18 f4 ♘xf4! ∞.

[48] 16 ♖h4 f5 ∞.

[49] 14 ♕h5 0-0 15 ♖ae1 (Rennie-Chalupetsky, Raab 1907) 15 ... ♘f5! 16 ♘xf7 ♕f6! ∓ Zak.

[50] 15 ♗xd7+ transposes.

[51] 16 ♕xb5+ ♘d7 17 ♕e2 ♔f8! 18 ♘xf7 ♔xf7 19 ♖e1 ♘g8! 20 ♖e6 ♔f8! ∓ Barczay-Portisch, Hungarian Ch 1968/69.

[52] 11 ♕b3 (Lord) 11 ... ♗xa1 12 ♗xf7+ ♔f8 13 ♗a3+ ♘e7 14 ♘g5 ♕xd4 15 ♗g8 ♕f4 ∓∓ Harding/Botterill.

[53] Unzicker.

[54] 11 ... ♔e8 12 ♕xb4 ♕g5 13 0-0 ♖h3 14 g3 ♗xf1 15 ♕xb7 ♖c1 16 ♕xa8+ ♔e7 17 ♘c3! ±.

[55] 16 ♖d1 d3 17 ♘e5+ ♔f6 18 ♘xd3 ♗g4 19 ♖e1 ♖ac8 20 ♘c3! ± Harding/Botterill.

[56] 12 ... ♘b6 13 ♗d3 ♗f5!?

[57] Rossolimo-Unzicker, Heidelberg 1949.

[58] 16 ♖fe1 ± Miles-Korchnoi, South Africa 1979.

[59] 12 ♘e5 0-0 13 ♘xc6 ♕e8+! ∓.

[60] Miles-Korchnoi, South Africa 1979.

Two Knights I 1 e4 e5 2 Nf3 Nc6 3 Bc4 Nf6

	4	5	6	7	8	9	10	11	12	
1	d4[1]	Ng5[2]	ed	Kf1	Qxd4	Qxc4	Nf3[4]			=
	ed	d5![3]	Qe7+!	Ne5	Nxc4	h6	Bd7[5]			
2	...	0-0	Re1[7]	Nc3!?[9]	Bxd5	Bxe4	Rxe4+			=
	...	Nxe4[6]	d5![8]	dc3	Bf5[10]	Bxe4	Be7[11]			
3	...	...	...	...	Rxe4+	Nxd4	Rf4	Nxc6	Nxd1	=
	...	...	...	dc4	Be7[12]	f5	0-0	Qxd1+	bc[13]	
4	...	...	...	...	...	Bh6!?	Nxc6	Rd4		∓
	...	...	...	...	...	0-0![14]	bc	Qe8[15]		
5	...	...	...	Bxd5	Nc3	Nxe4[17]	Bd2[18]	Bg5	Bf6!?[19]	=
	...	...	...	Qxd5	Qa5[16]	Be6	Qd5!	Bd6!	0-0![20]	
6	...	...	e5	ef	Re1+	Ng5	Nc3	Nce4	g4	=
	...	Bc5[21]	d5![22]	dc	Be6[23]	Qd5	Qf5[24]	0-0-0!	Qe5[25]	

[1] 4 Nc3 Nxe4 5 0-0 Nxc3 6 dc f6 7 Re1 (7 Nh4 g6 8 f4 f5! =) 7 ... d6 8 Nh4 (8 b4!?) 8 ... g6 9 f4 Qe7 10 f5 Qg7 11 Re3 Ne7 ∓ Keres-Nielsen, corr. 1935/36. 4 ... Bc5 – 3 ... Bc5.
4 0-0 Bc5 – 3 ... Bc5.
4 d3 – Modern Bishop's Opening.

[2] 5 Nxd4 Nxe4! 6 Qh5! Nf6 7 Nf3 (7 Nb5 Bb4+! 8 c3 Ba5) 7 ... Bb4+ 8 c3 Qe7 9 0-0 Bc5 = Estrin.

[3] 5 ... Ne5 6 Nxd4! Nxc4 7 Qxc4 d5 8 ed Qxd5 9 Qe2+! Be6 10 0-0 0-0-0 11 Nc3! Qc4 12 Nxe6 Qxe6 13 Qxe6+ fe 14 Be3 h6 15 Nb5 a6 16 Nd4 ± Pfleger-Rinder, West Germany 1965.

[4] 10 Nc3 hg 11 Bxg5 Bc5 12 Qe2!? Keres.

[5] Intending ... 0-0-0 Archives 1953.

[6] 5 ... d6 6 Nxd4 Be7 7 Nc3 0-0 8 h3 Re8 (8 ... Nxd4 9 Qxd4 Be6 10 Bxe6 fe 11 e5 Nd7 12 ed cd ± Tarrasch-Taubenhaus, Ostend 1905) 9 Re1 Bf8 10 Bg5 h6 11 Bh4 Ne5 12 Bf1 ± Estrin-Chaplinsky, Moscow 1970.
5 ... Bc4 – Scotch Gambit.
5 ... Be7 6 Re1 ± Harding/Botterill.

[7] 6 Nc3 Nxc3! (6 ... dc? 7 Bxf7+ Kxf7 8 Qd5+ Ke8 9 Re1 ±) 7 bc d5 8 Bb5 Be7 ∓ Novopashin-Nezhmetdinov, Kislovodsk 1966.

[8] 6 ... Be7 7 Rxe4! d5 8 Rxe7+ Nxe7 9 Bf1 c5 10 b4 ± Estrin.

[9] Canal Variation.

[10] 8 ... Be6 9 Bxe4 (9 Rxe4? Ne7! ∓∓) 9 ... Bb4 10 b3 Qxd1 11 Rxd1 h6 (11 ... Bd7 intending ... 0-0-0 Keres) 12 Bf4 ∞ Podtserob-Hmelnitsky, corr. 1953.

[11] Gligorić.

[12] 8 ... Be6 9 Nxd4 Nxd4 10 Rxd4 (Canal-Johner, Trieste 1923) 10 ... Qf6! Estrin, intending 11 Ne4? Qxd4! 12 Rxd4 Rd8.

[13] 13 Rxc4 Bd6 (13 ... c5 14 Be3 Be6 15 Ra4 a6 16 Ra5 c4 17 Bc5 Bd6 = Filipowicz) 14 Nc3 = Botvinnik.

[14] 10 ... Kf7!? 11 Qh5+ g6 12 Nxc6 ∞ Garcia-Taulbut, Madrid 1982.

[15] 13 Bf4 Qf7! ∓ Nicholson-Blackstock, London League 1977. But if he approaches from row 5 (note 16) Black has no pawn at c4, and therefore ±!

[16] 8 ... Qd8 9 Rxe4+ Be6 (9 ... Be7 – rows 3 and 4) 10 Nxd4 Nxd4 11 Rxd4 Qc8 12 Bg5 ± Tringov-Rosetto, Amsterdam 1964.

[17] 9 Rxe4+ Be6 10 Nxd4 0-0-0 11 Be3 Nxd4 12 Rxd4 Bc5 ∓ Estrin.

[18] 10 Neg5 0-0-0 11 Nxe6 fe 12 Rxe6 Qf5 13 Qe2 h6 14 Bd2 Qxc2 = Bogoljubow.

[19] 12 c3 0-0 = Littlewood-Medina, Hastings 1969/70.

[20] 13 Nxd4 Nxd4 14 Qxd4 Qxd4 15 Bxd4 = Marić-Djurasević, Yugoslav Ch 1956.

[21] Max Lange. Now 6 c3 transposes to Giuoco Piano II, row 7.

[22] 6 ... Ng4 (Steinitz Variation) 7 Bf4 d6! 8 ed Bxd6 (8 ... cd!?) 9 Re1+ Kf8 10 Bxd6+ Qxd6 11 c3! Qc5 12 Nxd4! Nxd4 13 Qxd4 Qxd4 14 cd Bd7 15 Nc3 ± Harding/Botterill.

[23] 8 ... Kf8 9 Bg5 gf 10 Bh6+ Kg8 11 Nc3! Bf8 12 Nxd4 Bxh6! 13 Nxc6 Qd1 14 Ne7+ Kg7 15 Raxd1 Be6 16 Ned5 Bxd5 17 Nxd5 Rhe8 = Harding/Botterill.

[24] 10 ... dc? 11 Qxd5 ±±.

[25] 13 Nxe6 fe 14 Bg5 (14 fg Rhg8 15 Bh6! d3! 16 c3 d2! 17 Re2 Rd3 = Marshall-Leonhardt, San Sebastian 1911) 14 ... g6! 15 f7! Be7! = Kliesch-Teblis, East Germany v Romania corr. 1972.

Two Knights II   1 e4 e5 2 Nf3 Nc6 3 Bc4 Nf6 4 Ng5

	4	5	6	7	8	9	10	11	12	
1	...	Nxf7	Kxf2	Bg1[2]	g3	Nxh8[3]	Qe1[4]	Qe3	Bb5	±
	Bc5[1]	Bxf2+!	Nxe4+	Qh4	Nxg3	d5!	Qd4+	Nxh1	Qg4+[5]	
2	...	Bxf7+	Bd5!	c3	d4	Bxc6	0-0	cd	e5[8]	±
	...	Ke7	d6[6]	Rf8	ed	bc	h6[7]	Bb6		
3	...	ed	Bxb5	Nc3!	Qf3	Nxf3	0-0	Bxc6	Nxe5	=
	d5	b5[9]	Qxd5	Qxg2	Qxf3	Bd7	Bd6	Bxc6	Bxe5[10]	
4	...	...	Bb5+[11]	Qe2	Nc3[12]	0-0	dc			∞
		Na5	Bd7	Be7!	0-0	c6![13]	Nxc6[14]			
5	...	...	...	dc	Qf3	Bd3[16]	Ne4	Ng3		∞
	...	...	c6	bc	Rb8[15]	h6!	Nd5	g6		
6	...	...	...	...	Be2	Nf3	Ne5	d4[17]	Nxd3	∞
	...	...	...	...	h6	e4	Bd6	ed	Qc7[18]	
7	...	...	...	...	...	Nh3	0-0	d3	Nc3	∞
	...	...	...	...	...	Bc5[19]	0-0	Nb7	Bb6[20]	

1 e4 e5 2 Nf3 Nc6 3 Bc4 Nf6 4 Ng5 d5 5 ed Nd4

	6	7	8	9	10	11	12	13	14	
8	c3[21]	Bf1	Nxf7	cd	Bxb5[22]	Qe2	Bxe2	Bc4+		∞
	b5!	Nxd5	Kxf7	ed!	Qe7+	Qxe2+	Bb4	Be6[23]		
9	...	...	cd	Bxb5+[24]	Qf3	0-0	Nc3	dc	Bxg5+	∞
	...	...	Qxg5	Kd8	Bb7	Rb8	Nxc3	Bxf3	f6[25]	
10	...	...	...	...		Bc6	Bxa8[27]	Qd3[28]	Be4[29]	∓
					ed	Nf6[26]	Bg4	Qe5+	Nxe4[30]	
11	...	...	Ne4	Bxb5+	Bxd7+	0-0	d4	cd	Nbc3[31]	±
	...	...	Ne6	Bd7	Qxd7	Be7	ed	0-0		

1 e4 e5 2 Nf3 Nc6 3 Bc4 Nf6 4 Ng5 d5 5 ed Nd4 6 c3 b5 7 Bf1 Nxd5 8 Ne4 Qh4![32] 9 g3 Bg4 10 f3 e4![33] 11 cd Bd6 12 Bxb5+ Kd8

	13	14	15	16	17	18	19	20	21	
12	0-0	Qb3	a3	ab[35]	Ra5!	ba	Qb8+[37]	Rxf3	Rf1	∓
	ef	Nb4![34]	Rb8!	Rxb5[36]	Rxa5	Re8	Bc8	Re1+	Bxg3[38]	
13	...	...	Rxf3!	Be2![39]	Qxf3[40]	Qh1	Qf1	Nf5		∓
	...	...	c6!!	Bxf3	Qxd4+	Bc5	Nc2	Qf2[41]		
14	...	Rxf3	a4[42]	Bf1[43]	Nc3	d3	Be2[44]	Bxf3	Bxe3	=
	...	Rb8	a6	Re8	c6	f5!	Bxf3	Ne3	Rxe3[45]	
15	Qb3	Qd1	Bc6	Bxd5[46]	Qxg3	hg	Rg1	Nc3	Qc2	=
	Bxg3+	Be6	ef	fg[47]	Qxg3	Bxd5	Re8!	Bf3+	Rb8[48]	

[1] The Wilkes-Barre Variation or Traxler Counterattack.

4 ... Nxe4 5 Bxf7+! Ke7 6 d4! d5 (6 ... h6 7 Nxe4 Kxf7 8 d5) 7 Nc3! (Lepeshkin) 7 ... Nxc3 8 bc Nd6 9 a4 Kd8 10 Bg8! ± Estrin.

[2] 7 Ke3? Qh4! 8 g3 (8 Qf3 Nf6 0-1 Jentzsch-Nosotta, corr. 1956) 8 ... Nxg3 9 hg Qd4+ ∓ Ostrava-Kutna, Gora 1959.

[3] 9 hg? Qxg3+ 10 Kf1 Rf8 11 Qh5 d5! 12 Bxd5 Nb4! 13 Bc4 b5! ∓ Klem-Hentsgen, corr. 1969.

[4] 10 Qf3 (Estrin) 10 ... Qd4+ 11 Qe3 - 10 Qe1. 10 ... Nf5! 11 Bxd5 Ncd4 12 Qe4 Qg5+ ∓ Lepeshkin.

[5] 13 Kxh1 d4 (Krc-Sapundzhiev, corr. 1965/66) 14 Qe2! (Lepeshkin) ±.

6 6 ... ♖f8 7 ♘f3 ♕e8!? 8 c3 ♕h5 9 0-0
(9 d4 ed 10 ♗xc6 bc ∞) 9 ... d6 10 d4 ♗g4
(Stein-E.Kristiansen, Gausdal 1980) 11 dc
♘xd5 12 ed ♖xf3 13 cd+ cd 14 dc bc?! ±±
Pytel. 14 ... ♖af8!? 15 ♕d2! ∞/± Whiteley.
7 ... ♘d4 8 ♘xd4 ♗xd4 9 0-0 c6 10 c3
♗b6 11 ♗b3 ♘xe4 12 d4 ed 13 ♖e1 d5
14 ♗g5+! ±/± Harding/Botterill.

7 10 ... dc? 11 ♕e2! ± Estrin.

8 Estrin. In spite of the better evaluation of
row 1, this line provides a simpler and safer
method for gaining the advantage.

9 Ulvestad Variation.
5 ... ♘xd5 6 ♘xf7 (Fegatello or Fried Liver
Attack) 6 ... ♔xf7 7 ♕f3+ ♔e6 8 ♘c3 ♘cb4!
9 a3! ♘xc2+ 10 ♔d1 ♘d4 11 ♗xd5+ ♔d6 12
♕f7 ♕e7 13 ♘e4+ ♔d7 14 ♘c5+ ♔d6 15
♘xb7+ ♗xb7 16 ♕xe7+ ♗xe7 17 ♗xb7 ♖ab8
18 ♗e4 ♘b3 19 ♖b1 ± "Sovremenny Debut".
6 d4 ♗b4+ 7 c3 ♗e7 8 ♘xf7 ♔xf7 9 ♕f3+
♔e6 10 ♕e4! ± Barden/Keffler.
5 ... ♗g4 6 ♘xf7! ♕e7 (6 ... ♗xd1? 7
♘xd8 ♘d4 8 ♘xd1 ♘g4 9 ♘f1 ♘xh2 10 ♘e6!
♘xe6 11 ♖e1 ±± Gerasimov) 7 d6 cd 8 f3
♖g8 9 ♘xd6+ ♔xd6 10 fg ♖h8 11 d3 ♕c5
(Gerasimov) 12 g5 ± Estrin.

10 13 ♖e1 0-0 14 ♖xe5 ± Turmurbator-
Hemmansy, Singapore 1969.

11 Polerio Variation.
6 d3 h6 7 ♘f3 e4 8 ♕e2 ♘xc4 9 dc =
Korchnoi-Suetin, ½-f USSR Ch 1952.

12 8 d4 ed 9 b4 0-0 10 ba ♗b4+ 11 ♔d1 ♖e8
∞∞ Kurkin-Mantevfel, corr. 1966/67.

13 9 ... ♗xb5 10 ♕xb5 c6 11 dc bc 12 ♕e2
♘e8 13 ♘f3 ♗d6 14 d3 ± Byelov-Kopilov,
Saratov 1966.

14 Estrin.

15 Colman's Defence.

16 9 ♗xc6+ ♘xc6 10 ♕xc6+ ♘d7 ∓.

17 Estrin-Ragozin, Moscow 1955.
11 f4 ef! 12 ♘xf3 0-0! ∞∞/∓ Estrin-Strand,
corr. 1966.

18 13 f4 0-0 14 0-0 ♖e8 15 ♘c3 ♗f5 16 b3
♖ad8 17 ♗d2 ♘b7 18 h3 = Anderssen-
von Neumann, Berlin 1886.
13 b3 0-0 14 ♗b2 ♘d5 (14 ... ♗f5!?) 15
♘c3 ♘f4 (Honfi-Tal, Sarajevo 1966) 16 0-0
(Tal) ∞.

19 9 ... ♗e7 10 0-0 0-0 11 d3 ♖b8 12 ♔h1 c5
13 ♘g1 ♘c6 (Klaman-Faibisovich, USSR
1979) 14 f4!? ∞.

20 13 ♔h1 ♘c5 14 f4 e4 ∞∞ Hamann-Geller,
Kislovodsk 1966.

21 6 ♘c3 h6 7 ♘f3 ♗g4 8 ♗e2 ♗xf3
9 ♗xf3 ♗b4 10 0-0 0-0 11 ♖e1 ♖e8 =.

22 10 ♕f3+ ♘f6! 11 ♕xa8 ♗c5 12 ♗xb5
♖e8+! 13 ♔f1! ± Berliner.

23 Suetin-Ravinsky, USSR 1949.

24 9 ♕b3 ed 10 ♗xb5+ ♔d8 11 ♗c6 ♗e6! 12
♗xa8 ♕xg2 13 ♖f1 ♕e4+ 14 ♔d1 d3 ∓∓
Vasiliev-Kocheguro, USSR 1959.
9 ♘c3! ed 10 ♗xb5+ ♗d7 11 ♗xd7+
♔xd7 12 0-0! = van der Wiel-Timman,
Amsterdam 1980.

25 15 gf ♖xb5! 16 ♗c1 ed 17 ♖d1 ♗d6
18 ♖xd4 ♖e8 ∞∞ Estrin.

26 11 ... ♘b4! 12 ♗xa8 ♘c2+ 13 ♔d1!? (13
♔f1 ♗a6+ 14 ♔g1 ♘xa1 ∓) 13 ... ♗g4 14
♔xc2 ♗xf3 15 ♗xf3 ♕c5+ 16 ♔d1 d3 17 ♘c3
♕xf2 ∓ Rothman-Schiller, New York 1981.

27 12 0-0! ∞.

28 13 ♕g3 ♗d6 14 f4 ♖e8+ 15 ♔f1 ♘h5!
16 ♕f2 (16 fg ♘xg3 ∓∓) 16 ... ♘xf4 ∓
Berliner.

29 14 ♔f1 ♗c5 (intending ... ♖e8) 15 g3
♗h3+ 16 ♗g2 ♗f5! 17 ♕e2 ♕xe2+ 18 ♔xe2
♖e8+ 19 ♔d1 ♘g4 ∓ Berliner.

30 15 0-0 ♗d6 16 f4 (16 g3 ±) 16 ... ♕d5 17
♘c3 ♘c5 18 ♕g3 (18 ♘xd5 ♘xd3 ∓∓) 18 ...
dc 19 ♕xg4 ♕d4+ 20 ♔h1 ♘d3 21 dc (21 ♕f3
c2! ∓∓) 21 ... ♘f2+ 22 ♖xf2 ♕xf2 intending
... ♖e8 ∓∓ Berliner.

31 Spassky-Shamkovich, USSR 1960.

32 The Berliner Variation.

33 10 ... ♘f5 11 ♗xb5+ ♔d8 12 0-0! ♗c5+
13 d4 ed 14 ♘e4! ± Kopilov.

34 14 ... ♘f4 15 ♖xf3 ♖b8 16 ♖xf4 ♖xb5 17
♕xb5 ♗xf4 18 ♕d5+ ♗d7 19 ♘f1 ±± Estrin-
Nielsen, corr. 1973.

35 16 ♗c4 ♗xg3 17 hg ♕xg3 18 ♖f2 (18
♖xf3 ∓) 18 ... ♖e8 19 ab ♖e1+ 20 ♗f1 ♖xf1+
21 ♔xf1 fg+ ∓∓ Berliner.

36 Intending ... ♖h5.

37 19 ♖xf3 ♗xf3 20 ♕xf3 ♕xd4+ ∓∓.

38 22 hg ♕xd4+ ∓∓.

39 16 ♗xc6? ♘xc6 17 ♕b7 ♗xf3! ∓∓.
16 a3 ♗xf3 17 ♕xf3 ♖e8 18 ♘c3 ♖e1+ 19
♔f2 ♘c2! 20 ♘e2 ♗xg3+ 21 ♕xg3 ♕xg3+ 22
hg cb ∓ Berliner.

40 17 ♗xf3 ♖e8 ∓∓.

41 Analysis by Berliner, as are notes 42-48.

42 15 ♗f1 ♖e8 16 ♘c3 c6 17 d3 ♘xc3
18 bc ♖b5! 19 ♗e2 ♖h5 =.

43 16 ♗xa6 ♖e8 17 ♘c3 ♘b4 18 ♗f1 ♗xf3
19 ♕xf3 ♘c2 20 ♖b1 ♖e1 21 d3 ♕xd4+ 22
♔h1 ♕xc3! 23 bc ♖xb1 24 ♗d2 ♖ed1 25 ♗f4
♘e3! 26 ♗xd6 ♘xf1 =.

44 19 ♗d2 ♖xb2 20 ♕c1 ♖xd2! 21 ♕xd2
♗xf3 ∓.
19 ♘ce2 ♗e6 20 ♖f2 g5 21 ♕d2 ♘e3 ∓.

45 22 ♘ce2! ♖xb2! 23 ♖b1 ♖bxe2 24 ♘xe2
♖xe2 25 ♗xe2 ♕xh2+ ½-½.

46 16 ♗xa8 fg 17 ♖g1 ♕g4+ ∓∓.

47 16 ... ♕h5?! 17 ♕xf3! ♗g4 18 ♗xa8 ±.

48 22 d3 ♖b6 23 ♗f4 (23 ♗d2 ♖g6 24 ♗e1
♖h6! ∓) 23 ... h5 =/∞.

Ruy Lopez (Spanish)

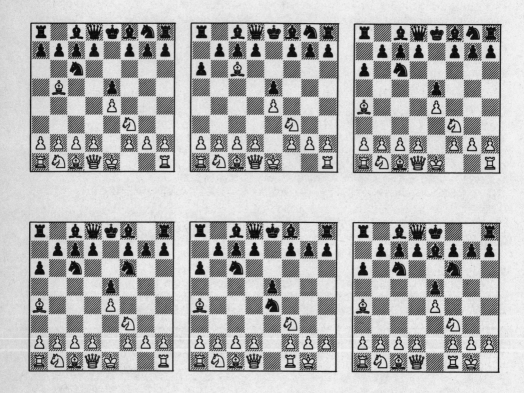

Analysed by the Spanish priest Ruy Lopez in 1561, this opening, with its idea of direct pressure on the Black KP, has been continuously popular with the players and theoreticians. Clearly the Lopez has weathered the test of time and despite long scrutiny by generations of chess thinkers it retains its strategical complexity. Mastery of either side of the opening requires the positional virtuosity of a truly mature player and it is no accident that the Lopez has figured in the repertoire of nearly every major figure in chess history, and current champion Karpov's ease in handling both sides is testimony to its continuing vitality.

It is more common that one specialises in the White side of the Lopez, because of the lasting pull it affords to players versed in its mysteries. Defending the Lopez can take a wide variety of forms, from the stolid classicism of the Closed Defence to the violent aggression of the Schliemann or the Marshall. Although 3 ... a6 is the automatic choice in modern practice, the older defences which omit this swipe at the Lopez bishop are not without merit.

3 ... ♘d4. Bird's Defence conceals a multiplicity of tricks to swing on the unwary Lopez player, but theory claims a small edge for White if he can steer clear of the pitfalls. An

obscure and probably underestimated defence.

3 ... **♗c5 Classical Defence**. The oldest of Black's options against the Lopez, it offers the second player reasonable chances and leads to an early skirmish of complications.

3 ... **f5!?** Theoretically doubtful but often successful in practice, the **Schliemann Defence** enjoys sporadic revivals before returning to hibernation. Perhaps this is because the element of surprise is a helpful addition to its arcane complications. A sharp variation offering great risk to both players.

3 ... **d6 Steinitz Defence**. Fully playable but more than a little passive and cramped. Only recommended for those willing to suffer a few indignities for the prospect of eventually exploiting the indiscretions of an overzealous attacker.

3 ... **♘ge7**. The **Cozio Defence** has never enjoyed a real following, although Larsen has used it with success. Relatively unexplored.

3 ... **♘f6 Berlin Defence**. Another neglected but solid defence – Black's chances for equality are fairly promising but White enjoys a small though lingering advantage.

3 ... **g6 Smyslov Defence**. A solid and resilient variation which received attention when ex-world champion Vasily Smyslov scored some surprisingly good results with it. Perhaps insufficient for complete equality, it is both complex and uninvestigated.

3 ... **a6 4 ♗xc6**. The **Exchange Variation** was a feared weapon in the hands of Bobby Fischer but his success was probably due in greater part to his own powerful technique rather than the advantages of the opening. It has now fallen into disuse and is once again regarded as safe and uninspired.

3 ... **a6 4 ♗a4 ♘f6 5 0-0 ♘xe4 Open Variation**. Foregoing the slow, subtle manoeuvring of the closed defences, the Open Ruy gives Black rapid development and free piece play in return for a static pawn formation. A large body of theory has coalesced as a result of the World Championship matches between Karpov and Korchnoi, where both combatants unveiled new ideas for their respective sides of the opening. At present Karpov seems to have won the theoretical debate and White maintains an edge.

Marshall Counterattack. Frank Marshall's ingenious attempt to overrun the Lopez by force has attracted theoreticians for years and now one must be very well prepared to cope with the reams of analysis available to Black. It appears White can emerge with advantage but this is a nerve-wracking business and an examination of one of the Anti-Marshall systems may appeal to the practical player.

Closed Ruy Lopez. The classical battleground of the Ruy Lopez, both players must be ready to handle the subtle strategical demands of the position and Black can choose from a wide assortment of different systems. His position is resilient and has survived over a hundred years of protracted struggle.

			Ruy Lopez: Introduction		1 e4 e5 2 ♘f3 ♘c6 3 ♗b5				
	3	4	5	6	7	8	9	10	11	
1	...	0-0	c3	♗xc6	b4	b5	♘xe5²			±
	♗b4¹	♘ge7	♗a5	♘xc6	♗b6	♘a5				
2	...	d4	♘xd4	♛xd4	e5	♘c3	♘d5	0-0⁶		±
	g5³	♘xd4⁴	ed	♛f6	♛g6⁵	♗e7	♗d8			
3	...	0-0	d4	a3⁸	♗c4	h3	♘c3⁹			±
	f6⁷	♘ge7	♘g6	♗e7	d6	♗d7				

¹ Alapin's Variation.
² Geller-Taimanov, Zürich C 1953.
³ Brentano's Variation.
⁴ 4 ... g4 5 ♘xe5 ♘xe5 6 de ♛h4 7 ♘c3 c6
8 ♗c4 ±.
⁵ 7 ... ♛e7!?
⁶ Adam-Herzog, corr. 1937.
⁷ Nuremberg Variation.
⁸ 6 ♘c3 a6 7 ♗c4 ♘a5 8 ♗e2 c6 9 ♗e3
b5 10 d5 c5 11 d6 ± Schlechter-Steinitz,
Nuremberg 1896.
⁹ Tarrasch-Steinitz, Nuremberg 1896.

	3	4	5	6	7	8	9	10	11	
4	...	♘c3	d3	♘xd4	♕e2	♗a4	0-0	b4	a3	±
	♕f6	♘ge7	♘d4	ed	c6[10]	d5	g6	♕d6	♗g4[11]	
5	...	0-0[13]	c3	d4	cd	ed	♖e1+	♗g5		±
	♘ge7[12]	g6[14]	♗g7	ed	d5	♘xd5	♗e6	♕d6		
6	...	d4	♗g5	♗h4[18]	♘xd4	♗c4	♗e2	ed	♕d2	∞
	g6[15]	ed[16]	f6[17]	♗g7	♘ge7	♘a5!	d5!	♘xd5	c5[19]	
7	...	c3	d4	0-0	de	♗e3	♘bd2	♗c5	♕e2	±
	...	d6	♗d7	♗g7	de	♘f6	0-0	♖e8		
8	...	...	...	...	♕b3!	♕a4	♗e2	♕c2	♗e3	±
	...	...	...	...	♘a5	c6[20]	b5	♘e7	0-0[21]	
9	...	♘xd4	0-0	d3[23]	♗c4	f4	e5	♗xf7+!	fe	±
	♘d4[22]	ed	♗c5	c6	d6	♘f6	de	♔xf7	♕d5[24]	
10	...	...	...	♗c4	♖e1	d3	♘d2	♘f3[25]		±
	...	...	c6	♘f6	d6	♗e7	0-0			
11	...	d4	♘c3	♘xd4	♗xc6	♕d3	♗g5	0-0-0		±
	d6[26]	♗d7[27]	ed[28]	♘f6[29]	bc	♗e7	0-0			
12	...	0-0	♘xd4	c3	d4	♗a4	♘a3	♗c2	♗g5	±
	♗c5[30]	♘d4[31]	♗xd4	♗b6	c6	d6	♘f6	♗e6	h6[32]	
13	...	c3	0-0	d4	cd	ed	♖e1+	a4	♗xc6+	±
	...	♘ge7	♗b6	ed	d5	♘xd5	♗e6	a6	bc[33]	
14	...	...	d4	e5	0-0	♘xd4	f3	♗e3	f4	±
	...	♘f6	ed	♘e4[34]	d5	0-0	♘g5	♘e6	f6[35]	
15	...	...	d4	♗xc6	♘fd2	de	fe	♕h5+	♕f3	±
	...	f5	fe	dc[36]	♗d6[37]	e3	♗c5	g6	♕h4[38]+	
16	...	0-0	♘xe5!	♕e2	d4	dc	b4![43]			±
	♘f6[39]	♗c5[40]	♘xe4[41]	♘xe5	♕e7[42]	♘xc5				
17	...	...	...	...	♕xe4	d4	♕g4	♕h5+	♕d1	±
	...	...	...	...	♕e7	♘c6[44]	f5	g6	♘xd4[45]	
18	...	...	d4	♘c3	♘xd4	♗xc6[47]	b3	♗b2	♖e1	±
	...	d6	♗d7[46]	ed	♗e7	bc	0-0	♖e8	♗f8[48]	
19	...	...	...	...	♗xc6[49]	♕d3	♘xd4	♗g5	♖ae1	±
	...	...	...	♗e7	♗xc6	ed	♗d7[50]	0-0	h6[51]	
20	...	...	♖e1	♘xe5	♕h5!?[52]	♕d3	♘xg6!	♗xg6	♕xg6+	∞
	...	♘xe4	♘d6	♗e7	0-0	g6	fg	hg	♔h8[53]	
21	...	...	d4	♗xc6	de	♕e2	♗e3[55]	♘c3	♖fe1	±
	...	...	♘d6[54]	dc	♘e4!	♘c5	♗g4	♕e7	♕e6![56]	
22	...	...	...	♕e2	♗xc6	de	♘c3	♖e1	♘d4[58]	±
	...	...	♗e7	♘d6	bc[57]	♘b7	0-0	♘c5	♘e6[59]	

[10] 7 ... a6!? 8 Bc4 b5 9 Bb3 c5!? (±).

[11] 12 Bb2 ± Bogoljubow-Ed. Lasker, New York 1924.

[12] Cozio Defence.

[13] 4 Nc3 Ng6 5 d4 ed 6 Nxd4 Bc5 7 Be3 Bxd4 8 Bxd4 0-0 9 Be3 d6 10 0-0 Kh8 11 Qd2 f5 12 f4 ± Barczay-Sydory, Lublin 1969.

[14] 4 ... Ng6 5 c3 d6 6 d4 Bd7 7 Ng5!? ± Zukertort-Anderssen, 1867.

4 ... a6 5 Bc4 Ng6 6 d4 Be7 7 Nxe5 ± Westerinen-Larsen, Siegen Ol 1970.

[15] Smyslov System.

[16] 4 ... Nxd4 5 Nxd4 ed 6 Qxd4 Qf6 7 e5 Qb6 8 Qd3 c6 9 Bc4 Qa5+ 10 Nc3 Qxe5+ 11 Be3 d5 12 0-0-0 ± I.Zaitsev-Sutyeyev, 1968.

[17] 5 ... Be7 6 Bxe7 Ngxe7 7 Nxd4 d5 8 Nc3 de 9 Nxe4 0-0 10 Be2 Nxc6 11 Nxc6 bc 12 0-0 = Boleslavsky-Trifunović, Yugoslavia 1956.

[18] 6 Bf4 Bb4+ 7 Nbd2 Nge7 (7 ... a6?! 8 Bc4 d6 9 0-0 Qe7 10 Bd5 Bg4 11 c3 ± Marco-Pillsbury, Vienna 1898) 8 0-0 a6 9 Bc4 Na5 ∞. 8 ... 0-0!? 9 Bc4+ Kh8 10 Nb3 d5!?

[19] Dely-Smyslov, Szdonok 1975.

[20] 8 ... Nc6!?

[21] 12 de de 13 a4 ± Kupreichik-Smyslov, USSR Ch 1976.

[22] Bird's Defence.

[23] 6 b4!? Gipslis.

[24] 12 ef gf 13 Nd2 ± Kasparov-Roizman, USSR 1978.

[25] Liberzon-Henley, Lone Pine 1980.

[26] Steinitz Defence.

[27] 4 ... ed 5 Qxd4 Bd7 6 Bxc6 Bxc6 7 Nc3 Nf6 8 Bg5 Be7 9 0-0-0 0-0 10 Rhe1 Re8 11 Kb1 ± Parma-S.Nikolić, Yugoslav Ch 1969.

[28] 5 ... Nf6 6 Bxc6! Bxc6 7 Qd3 Nd7 8 Be3 ed 9 Nxd4 f6 10 Nh4 ± Nimzowitsch-Steiner, Niendorf 1927.

[29] 6 ... g6 7 Be3 Bg7 8 Qd2 Nf6 9 Bxc6 bc 10 Bh6 Bxh6 11 Qxh6 Ng4 12 Qd2 Qh4 13 g3 ± Holmov-Kimelfeld, USSR 1970.

[30] Classical Defence.

[31] 4 ... Qf6!? 5 d3 h6 (5 ... Nd4 6 Nxd4 Bxd4 7 Nd2 c6 8 Ba4 d6 9 c3 Bb6 10 Nc4! g5 11 Nxb6 ab 12 Be3 b5 13 Bb3 Ne7 14 d4 ± Gipslis-Gulko, Tallinn 1976).

[32] 12 Bxf6 ± Portisch-Spassky, Budapest v Leningrad 1961.

[33] 12 Bg5 Qd6 13 Nbd2 ± Keres.

[34] 6 ... Nd5 7 0-0 0-0 8 cd Bb6 9 Bc4 Nce7 10 Bg5 Qe8 11 Qb3 c6 12 Nbd2 ± Smyslov-Barcza, Helsinki Ol 1952.

[35] 12 Kh1 Bxd4 13 cd fe 14 de d4 15 Bc1 ± Nezhmetdinov-Valentinov, USSR 1963.

[36] 6 ... ef 7 Bxf3 ed 8 0-0! ± Torre-Tatai, Haifa Ol 1976.

[37] 7 ... Qg5 8 dc Qxg2 9 Qh5+ Kd8 10 Rf1 Bh3 11 Qxe5 Nf6 12 Qg3 ± Keres.

[38] 12 g3 Qh3 13 Ne4 ± Liberzon-Giterman, USSR 1968.

[39] Berlin or Rio de Janeiro Defence.

[40] 4 ... Be7!? 5 d4 ed (5 ... a6 6 de! Nxe5 7 Ba4 Nxf3+ 8 Qxf3 0-0 9 e5! Geller-Olafsson, Wijk aan Zee 1969) 6 Qe2 0-0 7 e5 Ne8 8 Rd1 d5 9 c3! Bf5 10 cd Nb4 11 Na3 c6 12 Ba4 ± Keres.

[41] 5 ... Nxe5 6 d4 c6 7 de Nxe4 8 Bd3 d5 9 ed Nf6 10 Bg5 Qxd6 11 Nc3 Be6 12 Bxf6 gf 13 Ne4 Qe5 14 Nxc5 Qxc5 15 Qf3 ± Shamkovich-Aronin, USSR 1962.

[42] 7 ... Be7 8 de Nxc5 9 Rd1 0-0 10 Bc4 c6 11 a4! Kh8 12 Ba3 Qe8 13 Rh3 f6 14 b4 Ne6 15 Nc3 fe 16 Bd3 ± O'Kelly-Dückstein, Zürich 1960.

[43] Gipslis-Gonsoir, Hradec Kralove 1977/78.

[44] 8 ... Ng6 9 Bxd7+ Bxd7 10 Qxb7 0-0.

[45] 12 b4 Bb6 13 c4 Qe2 (13 ... 0-0 14 c5 Nxb5 15 cb c6 16 a4 ± Timoshenko-Donchenko, USSR Ch 1976) 14 Ba4 Qxd1 15 Bxd1 ±.

[46] 5 ... ed 6 Nxd4 Bd7 7 Bxc6 bc 8 Qf3 c5 9 Nf5 Bxf5 10 Qxf5 Qd7 11 Qf3 Bg4 12 Qd3! ± Keres.

[47] 8 Bf4 0-0 9 Bxc6 bc 10 e5 Ne8 11 Qf3 d5 12 Rad1 g6 13 Bh6 Ng7 14 Rfe1 Rb8 15 b3 ± Geller-Shamkovich, Riga 1968.

[48] 12 Qd3 g6 13 Rad1 Bg7 14 Bc1 Ng4 15 h3 Ne5 16 Qg3 c5 17 Nde2 Nc6 ± (17 ... f5?! 18 Bg5! ± Klovan-Klousky, USSR 1967.

[49] 7 Bg5 0-0 (7 ... ed 8 Nxd4 0-0 9 Bxc6 bc 10 Qd3 h6 11 Bh4 Nh7 12 Bxe7 Qxe7 13 f4 ± Keres) 8 de Nxe5 9 Bxd7 Nfxd7 10 Bxe7 Nxf3+ 11 Qxf3 Qxe7 12 Nd5 Qd8 13 Rad1 Re8 14 Rfe1 Nb6 15 Qc3! ± Schlechter-Lasker, match 1910.

[50] 9 ... 0-0 10 Nf5! Bd7 11 Nxe7+ Qxe7 12 Bg5 ± Keres.

[51] 12 Bh4 Nh7 13 Bxe7 Qxe7 14 Nd5 Qd8 15 c4! ± Lasker-Capablanca, match 1921.

[52] 7 Bf1 0-0 8 Nc3 Nxe5 9 Rxe5 Bf6 10 Re3 g6 11 b3 b6! 12 Ba3 c5 13 Qg4 Bd4 14 Re2 Bb7 = Shamkovich-Martz, Lone Pine 1979.

[53] 12 b3! ∞ Shamkovich-Blohm, USA 1977.

[54] 5 ... a6 6 Ba4 – 3 ... a6.

[55] 9 Bg5 Be7 10 Rd1 Bd7 11 e6!? ∞ Gulko.

[56] ± (±/=) Gulko-Reshevsky, Vilnius 1978.

[57] 7 ... dc 8 de Nf5 9 Rd1 Bd7 10 Nc3 0-0 11 Ne4 Qc8 12 h3 ± Geller-Bronstein, Moscow 1967.

[58] 11 Be3 Ne6 12 Rad1 d5 13 ed cd 14 Nd4 Bd7 15 Nf5 d5 16 Nxe7+ Qxe7 17 Qd2! ± Karpov-Korchnoi, match (2) 1981.

[59] 12 Be3 Nxd4 13 Bxd4 c5 14 Be3 d5 15 ed Bxd6 16 Ne4 Bb7 17 Nxd6 cd 18 Rad1 Qf6 19 c4 Rfe8 20 Qg4 (Tarrasch-Lasker, match 1908) 20 ... Re6! ± Keres.

Ruy Lopez: Schliemann 1 e4 e5 2 ♘f3 ♘c6 3 ♗b5 f5

	4	5	6	7	8	9	10	11	12	
1	ef	♕e2	♗xc6	♘d4	♘f3	♘c3	d3	♘d2	♘de4	∞
	e4	♕e7	dc	♕e5	♕xf5[1]	♘f6	♗b4	0-0	♕g6[2]	
2	d4	♘xe5	de	♘c3	♘xe4	ed	♕d4	♗g5	♘g3[4]	∞
	fe	♘xe5	c6	cb	d5	♘f6	♗e7[3]	♗f5	♗xc2[5]	
3	d3	de	0-0	♗xc6	♘xe5	♕e2	♘d3	♘c3	♖e1	∞
	fe	♘f6	♗c5[6]	bc	0-0	♕e7	♗a6	♗d4	♖ae8[7]	
4	♘c3	ef	♘xe5	0-0	♘f3	♘xd4	♗e2	d3	♗f4	±
	♘f6	♘d4[8]	♗c5	0-0	c6[9]	♗xd4	d5	♗xf5	♕d7[10]	
5	...	♘xe4	♘xf6+	0-0!	♘xd4	b3[12]	♘d3	c4	bc!	±
	fe	♘f6	♕xf6	♘d4?![11]	ed	c6	d5	dc4	♗e7![13]	
6	...	...	♕e2	♘xf6+	d4	de	♗xc6[14]	e6	0-0	∞
	...	...	d5	gf	♗g7	0-0	bc	♖e8	♖xe6[15]	
7	...	...	♘xe5	♘xc6	♕e2	f4	g3	♘e5+	♗c4	±
	...	d5	de	♕g5[16]	♘f6	♕h4+[17]	♕h3	c6	♗c5[18]	
8	...	...	...	...	c4	♘xa7+	♗xd7+	♕h5+!	♕a5	±/±
	...	...	...	♕d5	♕d6	♗d7[19]	♕xd7	♔d8[20]	♔e8[21]	
9	...	0-0	♘xb5	♘xe5	♕h5+	♕h4	♕f4!	♕xe4[23]		±
	♘d4	♘xb5[22]	fe	♘e7!	g6	♗g7	♖f8			
10	...	ef	♘xb5	d4	♘g5	f3	♕e2[25]	fe		∞
	...	♘xb5[24]	d6	e4	♗xf5	♕d7	0-0-0	♖e8		
11	...	♗a4	0-0	♘xe5	ef	♘e2	♘xd4	♗f3		∞
	...	♘f6	♗c5	0-0	d5	♕d6!	♗xd4	♗g4[26]		
12	...	...	...	...	...	♘f3	♘xd4	♘e2	c3	∞
	...	...	...	...	...	♗xf5	♗xd4	♗g4!	♕e7![27]	
13	...	...	ef	0-0	♘xd4[28]	♘e2	d3[29]			±
	...	...	♗c5	0-0	ed	d5				
14	...	♗c4	0-0	♖e1	♕xf3	g3	d4	de	♕h5+[31]	±
	...	c6	d6[30]	♘xf3+	f4	♕f6	g5	de		

[1] 8 ... ♕e7 = (drawing by repetition).

[2] 13 0-0 ♗h3 14 f3 Nikolić-Marić, Yugoslavia 1965.

[3] 10 ... ♘xe4 11 ♕xe4+ ♔f7 12 ♗f4 ♕e8 ±.

[4] 12 0-0-0 ∞.

[5] 13 ♕d2 ∞ Kaiszauri-Marić, Sandefjord 1975.

[6] 6 ... d6 7 ♘c3 ♗e7 8 ♕d3 ♗g4 9 h3 ♗xf3 10 ♕xf3 0-0 11 ♕d1 ♔h8 12 ♗e3 ± Pilnik-Rubinetti, Mar del Plata 1971.

[7] 13 e5 ∞ Schneider-Grünfeld, Beersheva 1980.

[8] 5 ... ♗c5 6 0-0 0-0 7 ♘xe5 ♘xe5 8 d4 ♗xd4 9 ♕xd4 d6 10 ♗f4 ♗xf5 11 ♗xe5 de 12 ♕xe5 ♗xc2 13 ♗c4+! ♔h8 14 ♘b5 ± Stein-Nadezlin, USSR 1963.

[9] 8 ... ♘xf3+ 9 ♕xf3 d5 10 ♗d3 c6 11 b3 ±/±

Timman-Lombardy, Amsterdam 1974.

[10] 13 ♕d2 ± Minić.

[11] 7 ... ♗e7!? (7 ... ♗d6!?) 8 ♗xc6 dc 9 ♕e1 e4!? 10 ♕xe4 ∞ Shamkovich/Schiller.

[12] 9 ♖e1+ ♗e7 10 ♕e2 c6 11 ♗d3 d5 12 b3 0-0 = Adorjan-Parma, Moscow 1977.

[13] 13 ♕c2 g6 14 c5 0-0 15 ♗b2 ± Tal.

[14] 10 ef ♖e8 11 ♗e3 ♕xf6 ∞∞.

[15] 13 ♕d3 c5 14 ♖d1 c6 ∞ Tseshkovsky-Parma, Bled/Portorož 1979.

[16] 7 ... bc 8 ♗xc6+ ♗d7 9 ♕h5+ ♔e7 10 ♕e5+ ♗e6 11 f4 ef 12 0-0 ♖b8 13 d4 ♘f6 14 d5 ± Gipslis-Tringov, Varna Ol 1962.

[17] 9 ... ♗xf4 10 ♘e5+ c6 11 d4 ♕h4+ 12 g3 ♕h3 13 ♗c4 ♗e6 14 ♗g5! ± Yudovich-Boey, corr. 1975.

[18] 13 d3 ♘g4 14 ♘f7 ♗f2+ 15 ♔d1 e3 16

♕f3 ♘h6 17 ♕e4+ ♔f8 18 ♗xe3 ♗g4+ 19 ♔d2 ♖e8 20 ♘e5 1-0 Timman-Böhm, Wijk aan Zee 1980. 16 ... ♘f6! 17 f5! ♖f8 (Nunn-Rumens, London 1977) 18 ♗xe3! ±.

[19] 9 ... c6 10 ♘xc8 ♖xc8 11 ♗a4 ± Bivshev-Krutinich, USSR 1953.

[20] 11 ... g6?! 12 ♕e5+ ♔f7 13 ♗b5! c6 14 ♕d4! ♕e7 15 ♘c3 ♘f6 16 0-0 ♖d8 17 ♕e3 ±.

[21] 13 0-0 ♘f6 14 d3 ed 15 ♗e3 ±/±.

[22] 6 ♗c4 – 5 ♗c4.

[23] Chiburdanidze-Gaprindashvili, USSR 1980.

[24] 5 ... ♘f6 6 0-0 ♘xb5 7 ♘xb5 d6 8 d4 e4 9 ♘g5 ♗f5 10 f3 ± Parma-Dantar, Yugoslavia 1980.

[25] 10 fe ♕xb5 11 ef 0-0-0 ∞ Keres.

[26] Marjanović-Parma, Yugoslavia 1979.

[27] 13 ♗b5 ♖ae8 (13 ... c6 O.Rodriguez) 14 cd ♗e2 15 ♗xe2 ♕xe2 ∞/= Stoica-Ciocaltea, Bucharest 1980.

[28] 8 d3 d5 9 ♘xe5 ± Tringov-Grünfeld, Skara 1980.

[29] Keres.

[30] 6 ... ♘f6 7 ♘xe5!? fe 8 ♘f7 ♕e7 9 ♘xh8 d5 10 ♗e2 ♗f5 ± Geller-O.Rodriguez, Las Palmas 1976.

[31] Keres.

	Ruy Lopez: Exchange			1 e4 e5 2 ♘f3 ♘c6 3 ♗b5 a6 4 ♗xc6					
	4	5	6	7	8	9	10	11	12	
1	...	d4	♕xd4	e5	0-0	♘bd2	♘b3	♕c3		±
	bc	ed	♕f6[1]	♕g6	♗b7	0-0-0	c5	f6[2]		
2	...	♘c3	d4	♗e3	♕d3	0-0-0	h4	♘d2!	g3	±
	...	d6	f6	♘e7[3]	♗e6	♘g6	h5	a5	ed[4]	
3	...	♘c3	d4[5]	♕xd4[6]	♘xd4	♗e3	♘de2	a3	f3	=
	dc	f6	ed	♕xd4	♗d7	♗b4	♘e7	♗d6	0-0-0[7]	
4	...	0-0	d4	♕xd4	b3![9]	♗a3	♘xd6	c4	♘c3	±
	...	♗d6[8]	ed	f6	♗e6	♘h6[10]	cd[11]	0-0	♘f7[12]	
5	...	...	d4	♘xd4	♗e3	♘d2	ef	♘2f3	♘h4	±
	...	♘e7	ed	♕d6	♕g6	f5	♗xf5	0-0-0	♕f6[13]	
6	...	...	h3	♕xf3	d3	♘d2	♘c4	♗d2	b4	±
	...	♗g4	♗xf3	♕d7[14]	f6	0-0-0	h5[15]	♔b8	g5[16]	

[1] 6 ... d6 7 0-0 ♘e7 8 b4! ♘g6 9 ♗g5 f6 10 ♗e3 ♗e7 11 ♘bd2 ± Grigoriev-Panov, USSR 1933.

[2] Krogius-Lutikov, USSR 1965.

[3] 7 ... ♖b8 8 ♕d3 ♖xb2 9 de fe 10 ♘xe5 ± Gipslis.

[4] 13 ♗xd4 ♘e5 14 ♕f1 ♕b8 15 f4 ± Padevsky-Daskalov, Bulgarian Ch 1972.

[5] 6 d3 ♗d6 7 ♗e3 c5 8 ♗e2 ♘e7 9 ♘g3 ♗e6 10 c3 ♕d7 = Romanovsky-Botvinnik, Moscow 1935.

[6] 7 ♘xd4 c5 8 ♘de2 ♕xd1+ 9 ♘xd1 ♗e6 = Ragozin-Levenfish, USSR 1929.

[7] Flores-Geller, Lugano Ol 1968.

[8] 5 ... ♗e7 6 d3! ♗f6 7 ♗e3 ♘e7 8 h3! (8 d4 ♗g4 9 c3 ♗xf3 10 ♕xf3 ed 11 cd ♗xd4 12 ♖d1 c5 13 ♘a3 ♘c6 ∓ Gipslis – insufficient compensation) 8 ... ♘g6 9 ♘c3 0-0 10 ♕d2 (10 d4!?) ± Georgadze-Novopashin, USSR 1975.

5 ... ♕e7 6 d4 ed 7 ♕xd4! ♗g4 8 ♗f4 (8 ♘e5!? Gipslis) 8 ... ♗xf3 9 gf ♘f6 10 ♘c3 ♘h5 11 ♗g3 ± Dvoretsky-Smyslov, Odessa 1974.

5 ... ♕f6 6 d4 ed 7 ♗g5! ♕g6 8 ♕xd4 ♗d6 9 ♘bd2 ♗e6 10 ♖e1 ♘e7 (Gipslis-Romanishin, USSR 1972) 11 ♘c4! ♖ad8 12 ♘xd6+ cd 13 e5! ± Gipslis.

[9] 8 e5 fe 9 ♘xe5 ♕f6! 10 ♘d2 (10 ♘f3 ♘e7 11 ♗g5 ♕xd4 12 ♘xd4 c5 13 ♘b3 ♗f5 14 ♘a3 b5! + Suradiradja-Pytel, Kikinda 1976) 10 ... ♘e7 11 ♘df3 h6 12 h3 = Matanović-Gligorić, Yugoslav Ch 1975.

[10] 9 ... ♘e7 10 ♗xd6 ♕xd6 11 ♘c3 0-0 12 ♘a4 ♗g4 13 ♕c4+ ♔h8 14 e5 ∞ Iskov-Westerinen, Denmark 1979.

[11] 10 ... ♕xd6 11 ♕xd6 cd 12 c4 ± Gipslis.

[12] 13 ♕e3 ♖e8 14 ♘d4 ♗d7 15 ♕d3 ± Kagan-Zwaig, Hastings 1976/77.

[13] 13 ♘hxf5 ± Georgadze-Zaitsev, 1972.

[14] 7 ... ♕f6 8 ♕g3 0-0-0 9 d3 ♘e7 10 ♘c3 ♕e6 11 f4 ef 12 ♗xf4 ♖d7 13 ♕f2 ♗b8 14 ♘a4 ± Perez-Milić, Zeevenaar 1961.

[15] 10 ... ♘e7 11 ♗d2 ♕e6 12 a4 g5 13 ♕g3 ± Hug-Teschner, Berlin 1971.

[16] 13 a4 g4 14 ♕g3 ± Bronstein-Nei, Tallinn 1971.

	4	5	6	7	8	9	10	11	12	
7	...	0-0	h3	d3![17]	♘bd2[18]	♖e1	d4	hg	♘h2	±
	dc	♗g4	h5	♕f6	♘e7	♘g6	♗d6[19]	hg	♖xh2[20]	
8	...	...	d4	♘xd4	♗e3	♘b3	♕xd6	♖e1		=
	...	♕d6	ed	♗d7	c5![21]	♗b5![22]	♗xd6	b6		

1 e4 e5 2 ♘f3 ♘c6 3 ♗b5 a6 4 ♗xc6 dc 5 0-0 f6

	6	7	8	9	10	11	12	13	14	
9	d4	♘xd4	♕h5+[23]	♕f3	♔xh2	♖d1	♗f4	♕b3	ab	±
	ed	♗d6	g6	♗xh2+[24]	♕xd4	♕c4	♕f7	♕xb3	♗e6[25]	
10	...	...	♗e3	♕h5[27]	♘f5	f4	♕xf5	♘d2	♖ae1[30]	±
	...	♘e7[26]	♘g6	♗d6[28]	0-0	♗xf5[29]	♕e7	♖ad8		
11	...	c3	♘bd2[31]	h3	♘b3	♘a5	♘h2	de	♕e2	∞
	♗g4	♗d6	♘h6[32]	♗e6	♘f7	♕c8	c5	fe	b5[33]	
12	...	de	♖xd1	♖d3	gf[35]	♘d2	f4	♘f3	e5[37]	±
	...	♕xd1	fe	♗xf3[34]	♗d6[36]	b5	ef	♘e7		

[17] 7 c3 ♕f6 (7 ... ♕d3!? 8 hg hg 9 ♘xe5 ♗d6 10 ♘xd3 ♗h2+ =) 8 d4 ♗xf3 9 ♕xf3 ♕xf3 10 gf ed 11 cd 0-0-0 12 ♗e3 f5! = Marović.

[18] 8 ♗e3 ♗d6 9 ♘bd2 ♘e7 10 ♖e1 ♗d7 11 d4! ♘g6 12 ♘c4 ♕e6 13 ♕d3 0-0-0 14 ♖ad1 ±/ ± Fedorowicz-Böhm, USA 1977.   8 ... ♗xf3 9 ♕xf3 ♕xf3 10 gf ♗d6 11 ♔h1 f5 12 ef ♘e7 13 ♖g1 0-0 14 ♘d2 ♖xf5 ∓ Larsen-Mjagmasuren, Siegen Ol 1970.

[19] 10 ... ♗xf3 11 ♘xf3 0-0-0 12 ♗e3 ♖d7 13 ♕d2 ♘g6 14 b4! ± Tatai-Jean, Monte Carlo 1967.

[20] 13 ♕xg4 ♖h4 14 ♕f5 ♘e7 15 ♕xf6 gf (Schmid-Tseshkovsky, USSR 1971) 16 c3!? ± Gipslis.

[21] 8 ... ♕g6?! 9 ♘d2 0-0-0 10 ♕e2 h5 11 f3 h4 12 ♘c4 ♕h5 13 ♖fd1 ± Gipslis.
8 ... 0-0-0!?
8 ... c5! Euwe.

[22] 9 ... b6 ±.

[23] 8 ♗e3 ♘e7 9 ♘d2 0-0 10 ♘c4 ♘g6 11 c3 ♖e8 12 f3 ♗f8 Damjanović-Portisch, Palma de Mallorca 1967.
8 ♘c3 ♘e7 9 ♕h5+ ♘g6 10 ♘f5 0-0 11 ♖d1 ♘e5 12 f4 ♘f7 13 ♘xd6 cd 14 ♗e3 ♕e7 15 ♗b6! ± Hort-Gligorić, Skopje 1968.

[24] 9 ... h5 10 ♕d3 ♕e7 11 f4 ♗c5 12 ♗e3! ± Pytel-Gromczewski, Polish Ch 1971.

[25] 15 ♗xc7 ± Hecht-Gligorić, Teesside 1972.

[26] 7 ... c5 8 ♘b3 ♕xd1 9 ♖xd1 ♗d7 (9 ... ♗d6 10 ♘a5 ♘h6 11 ♗xh6 gh 12 ♘c4 ± Bagirov-Keres, USSR 1967) 10 ♗f4 0-0-0 11 ♘c3 ♗e6

12 ♖xd8+ ♔xd8 13 a4 ♗xb3 14 cb ♘e7 15 ♖d1+ ♔c8 ± Vitolins-Kakagaldiev, 1972.

[27] 9 ♘d2 ♗d6 10 ♘c4 0-0 11 ♕d3 ♘e5 12 ♘xe5 ♗xe5 13 f4 ± Fischer-Unzicker, Siegen Ol 1970.

[28] 9 ... ♕e7 10 ♘d2 ♕f7 11 f4!
9 ... ♕d7 10 ♘f5 ♕f7 11 ♘d2 ♘e5 12 ♕xf7+ ♔xf7 13 ♘g3! ♘g6 14 f4 a5 15 ♘f3 ± Gipslis-Letelier, Havana 1971.

[29] 11 ... ♕e8 12 ♘d2 ♗xf5 13 ♕xf5 ♖d8 (Hartston-Unzicker, Vienna 1972) 14 ♖ae1! ±.

[30] Gipslis-Savon, USSR Ch 1969.

[31] 8 ♗e3 ♕e7 9 ♘bd2 0-0-0 10 ♕c2 ed 11 cd ♖e8 12 e5 ♗b4 13 h3 ♗e6 14 ♘e4 ♕f7 15 a3 ♗b3 16 ♕b1 ♗f8 17 ♘ed2 ♗d5 18 b4 ♕g6 (Smyslov-Geller, USSR Ch 1973) 19 ♕xg6 = Geller. 13 ♗f4!

[32] 8 ... ♕e7 9 ♘c4 ♘h6 10 ♕b3 b5 11 de ♗xf3 12 ed bc 13 ♕xc4 ♕xe4 14 ♕xe4 ♗xe4 15 ♖e1 ± Gipslis.

[33] 15 f4 ∞ Kopilov-Kuuskmaa, corr. 1970.

[34] 9 ... ♗d6!? 10 ♘bd2 ♘f6 11 ♘c4 0-0 12 ♘cxe5 ♗h5 13 ♗f4? ♗xf3 0-1 Hübner-Tal, Wijk aan Zee 1982. 12 ♘fxe5!

[35] 10 ♖xf3 ♘f6 11 ♘c3 ♗b4 12 ♗g5 ♗xc3 13 bc ♖f8! 14 ♗xf6 ♖xf6 15 ♖xf6 gf 16 ♖d1 (Fischer-Smyslov, Monte Carlo 1967) 16 ... a5! 17 ♖d3 a4 18 ♕h3 ♖a5! = Gipslis.

[36] 10 ... ♘f6 11 ♘d2 b5 12 a4 ♗d6 13 ♘b3 c5 (13 ... 0-0 14 ♖c3! ± Adorjan-Tringov, Varna 1972) 14 ♘a5 c4 15 ♖d1 ± Gipslis.

[37] Sorokin-Jovčić, corr. 1977.

	4	5	6	7	8	9	10	11	12	
1	...	d4	♘xd4	♕xd4	e5	♘c3				±
	g5[1]	♘xd4	ed	♕f6	♕g6					
2	...	c3	0-0[3]	d4	cd	ed	♗b3[4]	d5	♗d2[5]	±
	♗b4[2]	♗a5	♘ge7	ed	d5	♕xd5	♕h5	♘a7		
3	...	♘xe5	♗b3	♘g4	h3	d3	♘e3[8]			±
	♘d4[6]	b5	♕g5[7]	d5	h5	♕g6				
4	...	d4	e5	0-0	♗b3	ed	♖e1	♘bd2	a4	±
	f5[9]	ed[10]	♗c5	♘ge7	d5[11]	♕xd6	h6	b5	♖b8[12]	
5	...	♗b3	0-0	d4	♘xd4	♗d2	♕e1	♘xb3	♘a5	±
	b5	♘a5	d6	ed[13]	♗b7	c5[14]	♘xb3	♗e7	♖a7[15]	
6	...	d4	♗b3	♘xd4	c3	♘xc3	0-0[17]	♖e1	♗g5[18]	∞
	d6	b5	♘xd4	ed	dc[16]	♘f6	♗e7	0-0		
7	...	c4	♘c3[19]	d4	♗e3	de	♘xe5	♗xd7+		=
	...	♗d7	g6[20]	♗g7[21]	♘f6	♘xe5	de	♕xd7[22]		
8	...	♘c3	h3	♕xf3	d3	0-0	♗xc6+	b4		=
	...	♗g4	♘f6[23]	♗xf3	♗e7	♘d7	♘c5	bc	♘e6[24]	

[1] Brentano Variation.
4 ... ♕f6 5 ♘c3 ♘ge7 6 d3 ♘d4 7 ♘xd4 ed 8 ♘e2 ±.
4 ... ♗e7 5 0-0 d6 6 c4 ♘f6 7 d4 0-0 8 ♘c3 ed 9 ♘xd4 ♘a5 10 ♕d3! ♘g4 11 ♘d5! ± Kupreichik-Romanishin, USSR Ch 1979.

[2] Alapin Variation.

[3] 6 ♘a3 b5 7 ♗b3 ♗b6 8 0-0 0-0 9 d4 d6 = Evans-H.Steiner, match 1952.

[4] 10 ♘c3 ♗xc3! 11 bc ♗g4 12 ♕d3 ♗xf3 13 ♕xf3 ♕xf3 14 gf 0-0-0! ∞/= Owens-Mengarini, Asbury Park 1961.

[5] Mengarini.

[6] Bird.

[7] 6 ... d5!? Rabar.

[8] Rabar.

[9] Schliemann Deferred.

[10] 5 ... fe 6 ♘xe5 ♕h4 7 0-0 ♘f6 8 ♘c3 ♘d8 9 f3 b5 10 ♗b3 d6 11 ♘d5 ♖a7 12 g3 ♕h3 13 ♘f4 ♕h6 14 ♘e6 ± Romanovsky-Matsukevich, USSR 1968.

[11] 8 ... ♘a5 9 c3 ♘xb3 10 ♕xb3 d5 11 ed ♕xd6 12 cd ♗b6 13 ♖e1 h6 14 ♘c3 ♔f8 15 ♗f4 ± Fuderer-O'Kelly, Bled 1951.

[12] 13 ab ab 14 ♘f1 ♘d8 15 c3 ♗d7 16 cd ♗xd4 17 ♖e2 f4 18 ♖d2 ♗g4 19 ♘d4 ± Moiseyev-Andreyev, corr. 1968.

[13] 7 ... ♘xb3 8 ab f6 9 c4! bc 10 bc ♘e7 11 ♘c3 ♘g6 12 ♗e3 ♗e7 13 b4 ± Pfeiffer-Barcza, Sofia 1957.

[14] 9 ... ♘xb3 10 ♘xb3 ♗e7 11 ♘a5 ♗c8 12 ♖e1 c5 13 b4 ♕c7 14 a4 ♘c6 15 ab ab 16 ♘c3 ♖xa5 17 ♘d5 ± Kapengut-Alburt, USSR 1967.

[15] 13 a4 b4 14 ♘xb7 ♖xb7 15 ♕e2 ♖b6 16 ♖d1 ± Platonov-Savon, USSR Ch 1969.

[16] 8 ... ♗b7 9 cd ♘f6 10 f3 ♗e7 11 0-0 0-0 12 ♘c3 c5 13 ♗e3 ± Zaitsev-Estrin, USSR 1968.

[17] 10 e5? de 11 ♗xf7+ ♔e7 12 ♗d5 ♘xd5 13 ♘xd5+ ♔e6 ∓ Zlotnik-Mikliayev, USSR 1968.

[18] Rabar.

[19] 6 d4 ♘xd4 7 ♘xd4 ed 8 ♗xd7+ ♕xd7 9 ♕xd4 ♘f6 10 0-0 ♗e7 11 ♘c3.

[20] 6 ... ♘f6 7 d4 ♗e7 8 0-0 ed 9 ♘xd4 ♘xd4 10 ♗xd7+ ♘xd7 11 ♕xd4 ♗f6 12 ♕d2 0-0 13 ♘d5 ♖e8 14 f3 ♗e5 15 ♕c2 c6 16 ♘e3 (Janošević-Filip, Harrachov 1966) 16 ... ♗d4 = Rabar.

[21] 7 ... ed 8 ♘xd4 ♗g7 9 ♗e3 ♘ge7 10 0-0 0-0 11 ♖c1 ♘xd4 12 ♗xd4 ♗a4 13 ♘xa4 ♗xd4 14 ♕xd4 ♘c6 ± Keres.

[22] Levenfish.

[23] 6 ... g6 7 d3 ♗g7 8 ♘d5 h6 9 b4 ♔f8 10 ♗b2 ♘ge7 11 h3 ♗xf3 12 ♕xf3 ♘d4 = Konstantinopolsky-Petrosian, USSR 1956.

[24] 13 ♗e3 c5 = Medina-Portisch, Hastings 1969/70.

	4	5	6	7	8	9	10	11	12	
9	...	0-0	h3	d4²⁶	♗b3	hg	♘g5	♗d5	c3²⁸	±
	d6	♗g4	h5²⁵	b5	♘xd4	hg	♘h6	♘e7²⁷		
10	...	...	...	...	...	...	...	f4	♖xf3	±
	...	...	...	...	...	...	...	gf	♘xf3+²⁹		
11	...	...	d4	♗b3	♘xd4	c3	♕h5³¹	♘xc3	♕f3	∞
	...	♗d7	b5	♘xd4	ed	dc³⁰	♕e7	♘f6	♗e6³²	
12	...	♗xc6+	d4	♗e3	b3	♕d2	♘c3	0-0-0³⁴		±
	...	bc	f6	♖b8³³	g6	♗g7	♘e7			
13	...	...	...	...	c4	♘c3	♕a4³⁵	♕a5	♘d2	=
	...	...	...	♘e7	♘g6	♗e7	♗d7	♗g4	0-0³⁶	
14	...	...	...	...	♘c3	♕d3	h4	0-0-0	♖dg1	∞
	...	...	...	...	♘g6	♗e7	h5	a5³⁷	♗d7³⁸	
15	...	...	...	...	...	♕e2	h4	de	♘xe5	±
	...	...	...	...	...	♗e7	h5	♘xe5	fe³⁹	
16	...	c3	ef	d4	♘g5⁴⁰	f3	f4	0-0	♘f3	∞
	...	f5	♗xf5	e4	d5	e3⁴¹	♘f6	♗d6	b5⁴²	
17	...	...	...	0-0	♖e1⁴³	♗c2⁴⁴	♕xc2	d4	de	±
	...	...	...	♗d3	♗e7	♗xc2	♘f6	0-0	♘xe5⁴⁵	
18	...	...	d4	0-0	♗e3⁴⁶	♘bd2	a3	♖e1	cd	∞
	...	♗d7	♘ge7	♘g6	♗e7	0-0	♔h8	ed	f5⁴⁷	
19	...	...	...	♗b3	♗e3	♗xg5	♘xg5	♘xf7	♗d5+	∞
	...	...	...	h6	g5	hg	♘d5⁴⁸	♔xf7	♔e8⁴⁹	
20	...	...	...	...	♘h4	♗c2	♘f5	ef	0-0	∞
	...	...	...	...	♘a5⁵⁰	g5	♘xf5	♘c6	♗g7⁵¹	
21	...	...	...	...	♘bd2	♘c4	0-0⁵²	♘e3	♗xe3	=
	...	...	...	...	♘g6	♗e7	♗g5⁵³	♗xe3	0-0⁵⁴	
22	...	...	...	de	♗g5⁵⁵	♗e3	♘bd2	♘f1		=
	...	...	g6	de	f6	♘h6	♘g4	b5⁵⁶		
23	...	...	...	0-0	de⁵⁷	♗g5	♘a3⁵⁹	♗e3	♕c1	∞
	...	...	...	♗g7	de	♘ge7⁵⁸	h6	0-0	♔h7⁶⁰	
24	...	...	...	...	...	♗e3	♘bd2	♗c5⁶²	♗c2	±
	...	...	...	...	...	♘f6⁶¹	0-0	♖e8	b6⁶³	

25   6 ... ♗h5 7 c3 ♘f6 8 ♖e1 ♗e7 9 ♗xc6+ bc 10 d4 ♘d7 11 g4 ♗g6 12 ♕a4 ± Matulović-Ciocaltea, Bucharest 1966.

26   7 c4 ♕f6 8 ♕b3 0-0-0 9 ♗xc6 bc 10 hg hg 11 ♘h2 ♕g6 12 ♕g3 ♘f6 Faibisovich-Vorotnikov, USSR 1972.

27   11 ... c6 12 c3 cd 13 cd ♗e7 14 de ♗xg5 ± Ciocaltea.

28   Stoica-Ciocaltea, Bucharest 1980.

29   13 ♕xf3 ♕f6 14 ♘c3 c6 (Shashin-Vorotnikov, USSR 1973) 15 a4 ± Rabar.

30   9 ... d3 10 a4!? (Rabar) ±.

31   10 ♘xc3 ♘f6 11 f4 ♗e6 12 ♕f3 Vlianov-Stolyar, USSR 1965.

32   13 ♘d5 ♗xd5 14 ed ♕d7 15 a4 ∞ Mieses-Schlechter, Hastings 1895.

33   7 ... g6 8 ♕d2 ♗g7 9 ♘c3 ♘e7 10 h3 0-0 11 ♗h6 ± Matulović-Mestrović, Yugoslav Ch 1964.   11 ... ♗e6!? Matanović.

34   Levenfish.

35   10 h4 h5 11 ♕a4 ♗d7 12 c5 ♕b8 13 0-0-0 a5 14 de fe 15 ♘d2 ♖a6 16 ♕c4 ♗c8 17 g3 ♕b4 18 ♕e2 ♖a8 ∞ Walther-Keres, Zürich 1959.

36   Ortega-Ciocaltea, Havana 1962.

37   11 ... ♗e6 12 de ♘xe5 13 ♘xe5 fe 14 f4 ef 15 ♗xf4 0-0 ∞ Ornstein-Westerinen, Stockholm 1971/72.

38   13 de fe 14 g3 ♕b8 15 ♗g5 ♗f6 ∞. 15 ... ♕b6!? 16 ♗xe7 ♘xe7 17 ♘g5 ♖f8 18 ♖f1 ± Matanović-Blau, Munich Ol 1958. 15 ... ♗f6 ∞ Matanović.

39   13 ♕c4 ± Ciocaltea-Sliwa, Moscow 1956.

40   8 0-0 ef 9 ♖e1+ ♗e7 10 ♕xf3 ♗d7 11 ♗b3 ♘f6 12 ♗g5 ♗g4 13 ♕f4 ♕d7 14 f3 ♗f5 15 g4 ♗g6 16 ♗xf6 gf 17 ♗e6 ∞ Radchenko.

41   9 ... h6 10 fe hg 11 ef ♗d6 12 ♘d2 ♕f6 13 ♗c2 0-0-0 14 ♘f3 ♖e8+ ∞ Castaldi-Porreca, corr 1956.

42   12 ... 0-0 13 ♘e5 ♗xe5 14 de ♗g4 15 ♕d3 e2 16 ♖e1 ♘h5 17 ♘a3 (Kinnmark-Ciocaltea, Halle 1967) 17 ... ♘e7 18 h3 ♗e6 ∞ Rabar.
     12 ... b5 13 ♘e5 ♗xe5 14 fe ♗g4 15 ♕e1 e2 16 ♖f2 ba = Bannik-Gufeld, USSR 1961.

43   8 ♕b3 b5 9 ♕d5 ♘d4 10 cd ♘e7 11 ♕e6 ♗xf1 12 ♗b3 ♗c4 13 ♗xc4 bc 14 de de 15 ♘c3 ♕d6 16 ♕xc4 ∞ Gerasin-Kuzhnetsov, USSR 1963.

44   9 ♖e3 e4 10 ♘e1 ♗g5 11 ♖h3 (11 ♖g3 ♘h6 12 ♕h5+ ♘f7 13 ♘xd3 ed 14 ♖xd3 0-0 ∞ Korn) 11 ... ♘f6 12 ♘xd3 ed 13 ♖xd3 0-0 14 ♖h3 ♕e7 15 ♘a3 ♖ae8 16 ♘c2 ♘e4 = Smyslov-Lutikov, USSR 1961.

45   13 ♘xe5 de 14 ♘d2 ± Bannik-Estrin, USSR 1963.

46   8 d5 ♘b8 9 c4 ♗e7 10 ♘c3 h6 11 ♗e3 ♗g5 12 ♖e1 ♗xe3 13 ♖xe3 0-0 = Trifunović-Keres, Yugoslavia v USSR 1956.

47   13 ef ♗xf5 14 ♖c1 d5 15 ♗xc6 bc 16 ♖xc6 ♗d6 ∞ Boleslavsky-Tarasov, USSR 1957.

48   10 ... d5 11 ed ♘a5 12 d6! ±.

49   Keres.

50   8 ... ed 9 cd ♘xd4 10 ♕xd4 ♘c6 11 ♕d5 ♕xh4 12 ♕xf7+ ♔d8 13 ♘c3 ♘e5 14 ♕d5 ♕g4 15 0-0 ♗c6 16 ♕d1 ♕xd1 17 ♖xd1 g5 = Vasyukov-Gurgenidze, USSR 1959.

51   13 d5 ♘e7 14 ♕f3 f6 15 c4 h5 16 ♗xg5 ♕c8! 17 ♘c3 fg 18 f6 0-0 19 ♕xh5 ♖xf6 20 ♗h7+ ♔f8 21 ♘e4 ♖h6 22 ♕f3+ ♗f5 ∞ Konstantinopolsky-Aratovsky, USSR 1957.

52   10 ♘e3 ♗g5 11 ♘d5 ♗xc1 12 ♕xc1 ♗g4 13 ♕e3 ♗xf3 14 gf ♘ce7 15 de ♘xd5 16 ed de 17 f4 ♘xf4 18 ♕xe5 ♕e7 ∓ Litsberger-Keres, Stockholm 1966.

53   10 ... 0-0 11 ♘e3 ♖e8 12 ♖e1 ± Bronstein-Keres, USSR Ch 1948.

54   Fischer-Pachman, Mar del Plata 1959.

55   8 ♗e3 ♘f6 9 ♘bd2 ♘g4 10 ♗g5 ♗e7 = Eliskases-Thomas, Podebrady 1936.

56   Bronstein-Sakharov, USSR Ch 1960.

57   8 d5 ♘ce7 9 ♗xd7+ ♕xd7 10 c4 h6 11 ♘c3 f5 ± Fischer-Filip, Curaçao C 1962.

58   9 ... ♘f6 10 ♘bd2 ♕e7 11 b4 0-0 12 ♗b3 (Gligorić-Sliwa, Moscow Ol 1956) 12 ... ♗e6! 13 ♘c4 h6 = Euwe.

59   10 ♕d3 h6 11 ♗e3 b6 12 ♖d1 ♕c8 = Aronin-Bronstein, USSR Ch 1959.

60   13 ♘c2 f5 14 ef gf 15 ♖d1 ♕e8 (Zheliandinov-Nezhmetdinov, USSR 1959) 16 ♘b4!? Byrne.

61   9 ... ♘ge7 10 ♗c5 b6 11 ♗a3 b5 12 ♗c2 0-0 13 ♘bd2 ♘a5 14 ♕e2 ± Hasin-Siyanovsky, USSR 1957.

62   11 ♖e1 ♖e8 12 ♗g5 h6 13 ♗h4 b5 = Suetin-Sakharov, USSR Ch 1960.

63   13 ♗a3 ± Parma-Darga, Bled 1961.

	5	6	7	8	9	10	11	12	13	
1	d4[1]	0-0	e5	b4!?[2]	a3	♗b3	c3[4]	♘xc3		∓
	ed	♗e7	♘e4	0-0[3]	b5	d5	♘xc3	dc[5]		
2	...	...	...	♘xd4	♘f5	♗xc6[7]	♘xe7+	♖e1		=
	...	...	...	0-0[6]	d5	bc	♕xe7	♖e8[8]		
3	...	...	♖e1	e5	♖xe5[9]	♖e1	♘xd4	♕f3	♘c6	=
	...	...	b5	♘xe5	d6[10]	ba	♗d7	0-0	♗xc6[11]	
4	...	...	...	e5	c3	♘xc3	ed	♗g5[13]	♗xc6	=
	...	...	0-0	♘e8	dc	d6	♗xd6[12]	♘f6	bc[14]	
5	...	...	...	...	♗f4	♗xc6	♕xd4	♘xd4	♘f3	=
	...	...	...	...	f6[15]	dc	♕xd4	f5	g6[16]	
6	0-0	♘xe5	d4	♖e1	♖xe4	c4	♘c3	♖e2	f3	±
	♗c5	♘xe5[17]	♘xe4	♗e7	♘g6	0-0	f5[18]	f4	d6[19]	
7	...	♗b3	♖e1	c3	d4	♘bd2	cd	♘xd4	♘f3	=
	b5[20]	♗b7	♗c5[21]	d6	♗b6	ed	♘xd4	♗xd4	♗b6[22]	
8	...	...	...	...	...	♘h4	♗g5	d5	♗xf6	=
	...	...	...	...	...	♕d7![23]	0-0-0	♘e7	gf[24]	

	10	11	12	13	14	15	16	17	18	
9	a3	♗c2	♗g5	♗h4	♕d3	cd	♗g3[26]	d5	dc	=
	♕e7[25]	0-0	h6	♖fe8	ed	g5	g4	gf!	♗xc6[27]	
10	♗e3	♘bd2	de	ef	♕xd2	♗d5	a4	♘xe5	ab	=
	0-0	♖e8	♗xe3	♗xd2	♕xf6	♖ab8	♘e5	♕xe5	ab[28]	
11	a4	ab[30]	♖xa8	♗g5	♘a3	cd	♗c2	♘b1		=
	0-0[29]	ab	♕xa8[31]	♘d7[32]	ed	♘a5	b4	♖e8[33]		
12	...	ab[34]	♖xa8	d5[35]	♘a3	♗e3[36]	♖xe3	♘xb5	dc	=
	h6	ab	♕xa8	♘e7	0-0	♗xe3	♖d8	c6	♗xc6[37]	
13	♗g5	♗h4[38]	a4	♗g3	ab	♘a3	♕d3	c4	♘h4	±
	h6	♕e7	g5	0-0-0[39]	ab	♘a7	♕e8[40]	g4	♗xd4[41]	
14	...	...	a4	ab	♘a3	♗g3	h4	♘xg5	♗xf7	±
	...	♕d7	0-0-0	ab	g5	h5[42]	♖dg8	ed	♖xg5[43]	
15	...	...	a4[44]	ab	♖xa8	cd	♘c3[46]	♗g3	♗c2[47]	=
	...	0-0	ed[45]	ab	♗xa8	♖e8	g5	♘a5	b4[48]	

1. 5 d3 b5 6 Bb3 Be7 7 c3 d5 8 Qe2 de 9 de 0-0 =.
5 Qe2 Be7 6 c3 d6 7 d4 Bd7 8 0-0 – 5 0-0 Be7.
5 Nc3 b5 6 Bb3 Bb7 7 Bd5 b4 8 Bxc6 dc 9 Ne2 Nxe4 10 Nxe5 Bd6 ∓ Schlechter-Vidmar, Carlsbad 1911.
2. Torre.
3. 8 ... Nc3 9 Nxc3 dc 10 a3 0-0 11 Qd3 b5 12 Bb3 a5 = Santos-Henao, Colombia 1976.
4. 11 Nxd4 Nxe5 12 Bf4 Ng6 13 Nc6 Qe8 14 Nxe7+ Qxe7 15 Bxd5 Rd8 16 Bxa8 Rxd1 17 Rxd1 Rxf2 18 Bxf2 Nxf4 ∓ Nunn.
5. Egenberger-Klovan, corr. 1977.
6. 8 ... Nc5 9 Nf5 0-0 10 Qg4 g6 11 Bxc6 dc 12 Nxe7+ Qxe7 13 Qg3 Re8 = Vujakovic-Karpov, Sochi 1968.
7. 10 ed Bxf5! 11 de Nxe7 12 Bb3 Qxd1 13 Rxd1 Rad8 14 Re1 Nc5 15 Nc3 = Ljubojevic-Karpov, Milan 1975.
8. Johnke-Karpov, Stockholm 1969.
9. 9 Nxe5 ba 10 Qxd4 0-0 11 Qxa4 Rb8 12 a3 Rb6 = Zotos-Ivarsson, Haifa 1970.
10. 9 ... ba 10 Nxd4 0-0 11 Nc3 Re8 12 Bg5 Bb7 13 Nf5 Bf8 14 Rxe8 Qxe8 15 Bxf6 Qe6 16 Bxg7 Qxf5 = Adorjan. 17 Bxf8 ± Nunn.
11. 14 Qxc6 Nd7! 15 Nc3 Bf6! 16 Bd2 a3 17 b3 Bd4 = Sax-Smejkal, Amsterdam 1979.
12. 11 ... Nxd6 12 Bf4 b5 13 Bb3 Nc4 14 Nd5! ± Romanishin-Tukmakov, USSR Ch 1978.
13. 12 Bc2 Bg4 13 Qd3 g6 14 Bg5 Nb4! 15 Qc4 Qd7 ∓ Povah-Flear, London 1980.
14. 14 Qa4 h6 = Short-Bellin, British Ch 1979.
15. 9 ... b5!? 10 Bb3 d5 11 c3 Bg4 12 h3 Bh5 13 g4 Bg6 14 cd Bb4 15 Bg3 ± Donaldson-Opl, Graz 1978.
16. Lanka-Schneider, Jurmala 1978.
17. 6 ... Nxe4 7 Nxc6 dc 8 Qe2 Qe7 9 Re1 Nf6 10 d4 Qxe2 11 Rxe2+ Be7 12 Bb3 Nd5 13 c4 ± Hort and Pribyl.
18. 11 ... c6 12 d5! f5 13 Re1 ± Szabolcsi-Lengyel, Hungary 1972.
19. 14 Bc2 ± Kashdan-Milner Barry, 1932.
20. Archangelsk Variation.
21. 7 ... Be7 8 c3 d5 9 ed Nxd5 10 Nxe5 Nxe5 11 Rxe5 Nf4 12 d4 Nxg2 13 Qe2 h6 14 Qh5 g6 15 Qh3 Qd6! 16 Nd2 Nh4 17 Ne4 Qxe5! 18 de Bxe4 19 Bd1 g5 20 Be3 g4 ∞ Matsukevich. 8 d3 0-0 – 5 ... Be7.
22. 14 Bg5 0-0 15 Qd2 Qd7 16 Bxf6 gf = Petrushin-Matsukevich, USSR 1970.
23. 10 ... Ne7 11 Qf3 h6 12 Nd2 Qd7 13 Nf1 Qg4 14 Qxg4 Nxg4 15 f3 ± Kapengut-Kupreichik, USSR 1973.
24. 14 Qf3 Rhg8 15 g3 Qh3 16 Kh1 Rg4 = Kapengut-Malanyuk, USSR 1978.
25. 10 ... 0-0 11 Bc2 Nd7 12 Qd3 Re8 13 Nbd2 Nf8 14 b4 Ng6 15 Nf1 ± Suetin-Malich, USSR 1965.
26. 16 Nxg5 hg 17 Bxg5 Nxd4! Matsukevich.
27. 19 gf Nd7 = Matsukevich.
28. 19 Bxb7 Rxb7 = Zaitsev-Matsukevich, USSR 1972.
29. 10 ... ba 11 Bxa4 0-0 12 Bg5 h6 13 Bh4 Qe7 14 Na3 g5 15 Bg3 Nxe4 16 Rxe4! ±/± I.Zaitsev.
30. 11 Bg5 h6 12 Bh4 – 10 Bg5.
31. 12 ... Bxa8 13 d5 Ne7 14 Bg5 Ng6 15 Bh4 Nxh4 16 Bxh4 h6 = Bednarski-Levy, 1969.
32. 13 ... Na5!? 14 Bxf6 Qxb3 15 Ng5! gf 16 Qxh7! ±.
33. Milić-Stein, 1963.
34. 11 Qd3 0-0 12 d5 Ne7 13 Na3 Ng4 14 Re2 f5 15 ef Bxf5 16 Nc2 Rf7 17 Nb4 Nf6 = Tseshkovsky-Kozlov, USSR 1973.
35. 13 Na3 ed 14 cd 0-0 15 Nxb5 Na5 16 d5 Nxb3 17 Qxb3 Nxe4! Matsukevich.
36. 15 Nxb5 Ng4 16 Be3 Nxe3 17 fe f5 18 ef Nxf5 19 Qd3 Nxe3! 20 Rxe3 Qa1+ ∓ Matsukevich.
37. 19 Nc7 Qa5! 20 Nd5 Qexd5 21 ed Bxd5 22 Bxd5 Rxd5 23 Rd3 Nf4 =/∓ Burnevsky-Matsukevich, USSR 1971.
38. 11 Bxf6 Qxf6 12 Bd5 Rb8 13 Nbd2 0-0 14 Nb3 Ne7 15 Bxb7 Rxb7 = Kuksov-Kozlov, USSR 1978.
39. 13 ... h5 14 ab! ab 15 Rxa8+ Bxa8 16 h4 g4 17 Ng5 0-0 18 Qd3! ± Prokofiev-Zauernayev, USSR 1975.
40. 16 ... c6 17 c4 b4 18 c5! dc 19 Nc4 ±/±.
41. 19 Bxb5 Nxb5 20 cb ± Kuakeler-Meleghegyi, corr. 1979.
42. 15 ... ed 16 Nxb5 Rde8 16 Nbxd4 Nxd4 17 Nxd4 Nxe4 18 Ba4! ± Karpov-Tseshkovsky, USSR 1976. 16 ... gh!? 17 Bxh4 Rh6.∞
43. 19 hg h4 20 Bh2 ± Chiburdanidze-Kaiszauri, USSR 1978.
44. 12 Qd3 Na5 13 Bc2 c5 14 d5 (14 de de 15 Qxd8 Raxd8 16 Nxe5 g5 17 Bg3 Nxe4! Matsukevich) 14 ... c4 15 Qe2 g6 16 Nbd2 Rc8 17 Rac1 Kg7 18 b4 ∞ Mecking-Planinc 1971.
45. 12 ... Na5 13 Bc2 Qe7 14 Nbd2 c5 15 d5 c4 16 Qe2 Rfb8 17 Nf1 Bc8 18 Ne3 g6 19 h3 Kg7 = Vasyukov-Kuzmin, USSR 1972.
46. 16 d5?! Ne5 17 Nxe5 de 18 Qe2 g5 19 Bg3 c6 20 dc Bxc6 21 Nd2 Qd4 ∓ Tukmakov-Kupreichik, USSR 1975.
47. 18 d5 Nxb3 19 Qxb3 Ba5.
48. 19 Na4 Bxe4 20 Nxb6 cb 21 Bxe4 Rxe4 22 Rxe4 Nxe4 23 Qe1 f5! = Honfi-Gromchevsky, USSR 1975.

	6	7	8	9	10	11	12	13	14	
1	d4[1]	Re1	Nxd4![3]	Nxc6	Kh1	Rxe4+	Qd8+	Nxd8+	Kxh2	±
	ed[2]	d5	Bd6	Bxh2+	Qh4	de	Qxd8	Kxd8	Be6[4]	
2	...	Re1[5]	Rxe4	Nxe5	Bxb5+	Rxe5	Nc3[6]	Re1		∞
	Be7	b5	d5	Nxe5	ab	0-0	c6			
3	...	...	d5[7]	Nxe5	c3[8]	Nd3	Be3	Rxe3	Bb3	±
	...	f5	Na5	0-0	Bc5	Ba7	Bxe3	b5	Nxb3[9]	
4	...	d5	Re1	Rxe4	Nc3	Re1	Nxa4	b3	Bb2	∓
	b5	Ne7!	ba!	d6	f5	Ng6[10]	Be7	0-0	Bb7[11]	
5	...	...	Re1[12]	Nc3	Nxe4	Rxe4	Bxe6	Nxd4!	Qg4	±
	...	Bb3 ed	d5	Be6	de	Be7	fe	0-0	Nxd4[13]	
6	...	...	c4[14]	cd	Nxe5	de				=
	...	d5	Be6[15]	Bxd5	Nxe5	c6[16]				
7	...	...	a4	Nxd4	ab[17]	c3	cd	Nc3	ba	=
	...	...	Nxd4!	ed	Bc5	0-0	Bb6	Bb7	Rxa6![18]	
8	...	...	Nxe5	de	Be3[20]	Nd2[21]	Qxd2	Qc3		=
	...	...	Nxe5	c6![19]	Be7	Nxd2[22]	0-0	Bb7[23]		
9	...	...	...	de	Be3	Nd4![25]	Qe1	ab	b4[26]	±
	...	...	...	Be6	Na5[24]	Qd7	Nxb3	Be7		
10	...	...	...	Nbd2[27]	c3	Bxe6	cd	Ne4[28]	Be3	±
	...	...	...	Nc5	d4	Nxe6	Ncxd4	Be7[29]	Nf5[30]	
11	...	...	...	...	...	Ng5	Nxe6	bc		∞
	...	...	...	...	...	dc[31]	fe	Qd3![32]		
12	...	...	...	...	Nxe4	Ng5	Rxd1	ab	Bxe3	±
	...	...	...	Bc5!?	de	Qxd1	Bxb3	e3	Bxe3[33]	

	10	11	12	13	14	15	16	17	18	
13	c4	Ba4	Nc3	e6	Bxc6	Ne5	Qh5+	Nxg6	Qxh8+	∞/∓
	bc	Bd7	Nc5	fe	Bxc6	Qd6	g6	hg	Kd7[35]	
14	Rd1	Bxd5[36]	Nc3	Rxd8+	Qe3	b3	Ne4	Ne1	Bb2	=
	Nc5	Bxd5	Bc4!	Rxd8	b4	Be6[37]	Rd1+	Nd4	Nxc2[38]	
15	...	Be3	ab[39]	Nc3	Bg5	Nb1				∞
	...	Nxb3	Qc8	Nb4	c5[40]	d4[41]				
16	...	...	c4	Bxc4	Bxd5![42]	Nc3![43]	Qxf3	b4	ba	=
	...	0-0	bc	Na5	Bxd5	Bxf3	Qe8	Nd7[44]	Nxe5[45]	
17	...	c4	Bxc4	Be3	Qxe3	Bb3	Qe2	Nc3	bc	±
	0-0	bc	Bc5[46]	Bxe3	Qb8	Qb6	Rad8	Nxc3	Ne7[47]	
18	...	...	...	...	...	...	Ne1[48]	Qxb6	f3	=
	...	...	...	...	...	Na5	Qb6	cb	Nxb3[49]	
19	...	...	...	...	...	...	...			∞
	...	...	...	...	...	...	f5![50]			
20	...	...	...	Nc3!	bc	ef[52]	Ng5[53]	Bxg5	Be3	∞
	...	...	Qd7[51]	Nxc3	f6	Bxf6	Bxg5	h6!	Qd6[54]	

[1] 6 Ʀe1 Ꙩc5 7 Ꙩxe5 Ꙩxe5 8 Ʀxe5+ Ꙅe7
9 Ꙩc3 0-0 =.

[2] Riga Variation.

[3] 8 Ꙅg5 Ꙅe7 9 Ꙅxe7 ꙅxe7! ∞ Krause.

[4] 15 Ꙅe3 f5 16 Ꙩc3 ꙅe7 17 g4! g6 18
ꙅg3! ± Capablanca Ed Lasker, New York 1915.

[5] 7 ꙳e2 f5 8 de 0-0 9 Ꙅe3 ꙅh8 10 Ꙩbd2
Ꙩc5 11 Ꙅxc5 Ꙅxc5 12 c3 ꙳e7 13 b4 Ꙅa7
14 Ʀfe1 Ꙩd8 15 Ꙩf1 b5 16 Ꙅb3 Ꙅb7 17
Ꙩe3 Ꙩe6 18 Ꙩd5 ± Romanishin-Smejkal,
Leningrad 1977.

[6] Kondratiev-Suetin, USSR 1965.

[7] 8 de 0-0 9 Ꙅb3+ ꙅh8 10 Ꙩc3! Ꙩxc3 11 bc
꙳e8 12 Ꙅg5 f4 13 ꙳d3 Ꙅxg5 14 ꙳xg5 ꙳h5
(Rohde-Bisguier, New York 1976) 15 Ꙩf3 d6
16 ed Ꙅf5 17 ꙳d5 Ʀad8 18 Ꙩe5! (Nunn) ±.

[8] 10 d6 Ꙅxd6 11 ꙳d5+ ꙅh8 12 Ꙩf7+ Ʀxf7
13 ꙳xf7 Ꙅxh2+ 14 ꙅf1 b5 15 Ꙅb3 Ꙅxb3
16 ab Ꙅb7 17 Ꙩc3 ꙳h4 ∓ Planinc-Parma,
Banja Luka 1976. 17 g3!? ∞ Parma.

[9] 15 ab ± Ledermann-Pytel, Le Havre 1977.

[10] 11 ... a3 12 b3! =.

[11] 15 Ꙩc3 ꙅh8 ∓ (intending ... Ꙩf4, ... g5).

[12] 8 Ꙩxd4!? Keres (±/ ±).

[13] 15 Ʀxd4 ꙳c8 16 Ʀe4 Ʀf6 ± Fischer-
Trifunović, Bled 1961.

[14] 8 Ʀe1? Ꙅe6 9 Ꙩxe5 Ꙩxe5 10 de Ꙅe7 ∓.

   8 Ꙩc3 Ꙩxc3 9 bc e4 10 Ꙅg5 Ꙅf5 11 f3
e3 =/∓ Shatskes-Zhuravlev, Riga 1962.

[15] 8 ... dc 9 Ꙅc2 Ꙩf6 10 de ꙳xd1 11 Ʀxd1
Ꙩd7 12 Ꙅe4 Ꙅb7 ∞.

[16] Vitolins-Sideifzade, USSR 1979.

[17] 10 Ꙩc3 Ꙩxc3 11 bc c5! 12 ab Ꙅe7
(Spielmann-Tarrasch, San Sebastian 1912) 13
꙳f3 Ꙅe6 = (∓!? Keres).

[18] 15 Ʀxa6 Ꙅxa6 16 Ʀe1 Ꙅb7 Lasker-
Schlechter, match (8) 1910.

[19] 9 ... Ꙅb7 10 c3 Ꙅc5 11 Ꙩd2 ꙳h4 12 Ꙩxe4
de 13 e6 fe 14 Ꙅxe6 Ʀd8 15 ꙳e2 ±/=.

[20] 10 c3 Ꙅf5 11 Ꙅc2 Ꙅg6 =.

[21] 11 c3 0-0 12 f3 Ꙩc5 13 Ꙅc2 Ꙩe6 (13 ... f5
14 ef Ʀxf6 Barle-Tukmakov, 1976) 14 ꙳d3!
g6 15 Ꙅh6 Ꙩg7 16 Ꙅxg7 ꙅxg7 17 f4 Ꙅf5
18 ꙳e2 Ꙅxc2 19 ꙳xc2 f5 = Tukmakov.

[22] 11 ... Ꙩc5!? (Korchnoi) is more active.

[23] Fischer-Addison, US Ch 1966/67.

[24] 9 ... Ꙅe7! 10 c3 – main lines.

[25] 10 Ꙩbd2 Ꙩxd2 11 ꙳xd2 c5 12 c3
Ꙅe7 = Rosselli-Canal, Trieste 1923.

[26] Kupreichik-Slucki, USSR 1979.

[27] 9 a4 Ꙩa5! 10 ab ab 11 Ꙩd4 Ꙅc5 12 c3 0-0
13 f3 (13 Ꙅc2 ꙳h4 14 b4!?) 13 ... f6! 14 fe fe
15 Ʀxf8+ ꙳xf8 16 ed Ꙅf7 = Korchnoi.

[28] 13 a4 Ꙅc5! (13 ... Ꙅe7 14 Ꙩxd4 ± Karpov-
Korchnoi, match 1981) 14 Ꙩb3 Ꙩxb3 15 ꙳xb3
0-0 16 ab ab 17 ꙳xb5 Ʀb8 ∞ Kasparov.

[29] ?! (Keene). 13 ... ꙳d5!

[30] 14 ... Ꙩxf3+? 15 ꙳xf3 0-0 16 Ʀfd1 ±

Karpov-Korchnoi, match (14) 1981.

   14 ... Ꙩf5 15 ꙳c2 ± Karpov-Korchnoi,
match (16) 1981.

[31] 11 ... ꙳xg5 12 ꙳f3 0-0-0 13 Ꙅxe6+ fe
14 ꙳xc6 ꙳e5! 15 b4 ꙳d5! 16 ꙳xd5 ed 17 bc
dc 18 Ꙩb3 d4 ∞ Timman-Smyslov, West
Germany 1979.

[32] Karpov-Korchnoi, match (10) 1978.

   14 c4!? (Keene) 14 ... Ꙩd4 15 ꙳g4 0-0-0
16 cb ab ∞ Shamkovich.

[33] 15 fe Ꙩxe5 16 Ʀd5! ± Shamkovich.

[34] 9 ... Ꙅc5?!

   9 ... Ꙩc5 10 Ʀd1 Ꙩxb3 (10 ... Ꙅe7 –
9 ... Ꙅe7) 11 ab ꙳c8 12 c4!

[35] 19 ꙳g7 d4 Abrashin-Radchenko, 1954.

[36] 11 c4 d4! 12 cb Ꙩxb3 13 ab ab 14 Ʀxa8
꙳xa8 15 ꙳xd4! (15 Ꙅg5!? Mecking) 15 ...
Ꙩxd4 16 Ꙅxd4 0-0 17 ꙳xb5 c5! 18 Ʀd1 ꙳e4
19 Ꙩc3 ꙳xe5 20 ꙳b7 = Korchnoi.

[37] 15 ... bc? 16 Ꙅa3! ±± Suetin-Gurgenidze,
Voroshilovgrad 1955.

[38] 19 ꙳e2 Ʀxa1 20 Ꙅxa1 Ꙩxa1 (20 ... Ꙩxe1
21 ꙳xe1 Ꙩxe4 22 ꙳xe4 0-0 Radchenko)
21 Ꙩxc5 Ꙅxc5 22 Ꙩd3 Ꙅb6 23 Ꙩxb4 0-0
(23 ... a5 = Keres) 24 Ꙩc6 f6 25 h4 fe 27 ꙳xe5
Ʀf6! = Suetin-Boleslavsky, USSR Ch 1958.

[39] 12 cb Ꙩa5! Stahlberg, intending ... Ꙩb7
and ... c5.

[40] 14 ... h6 15 Ꙅxe7 ꙅxe7 16 Ꙩb1 c5 17 c3
Ꙩc6 18 ꙳e3 Ꙩb8 19 b4 ± Matanović-Rabar,
Yugoslav Ch 1951.

[41] Korchnoi.

[42] 14 Ꙅxc5 Ꙅxc5 15 Ꙅxa6 f6 ∞/∓.

[43] 15 b4 Ꙅxf3! 16 gf ꙳e8 17 Ꙅxc5 Ꙅxc5
18 bc =.

[44] 17 ... Ꙩa4 18 Ꙩd5! ± Jansa.

[45] 19 ꙳f5 Ꙩg6 20 Ʀac1 Ꙅa3 = Hübner-
Korchnoi, match (5) 1973.

[46] 12 ... dc 13 Ʀxd8 Ʀfxd8 14 Ꙩc3 Ꙩxc3
15 bc ± Augustin-Petras, corr. 1968.

[47] 19 Ʀab1 ꙳a5 20 c4 ± Vogt-Strobel, Varna
1975.

[48] 16 Ꙩbd2 ꙳a7 17 Ꙩd4 Ꙩxd2 18 ꙳xd2
꙳b6 19 ꙳e2!? c5 20 ꙳d3 g6 21 Ꙩxe6 fe
22 ꙳g3 ∞ Korchnoi.

   16 Ꙩd4!? Pritchett.

[49] 19 ab Ꙩc5 20 b4 Ꙩd7 21 Ꙩd3 (Karpov-
Korchnoi, 12th match game 1978) 21 ...
Ʀfc8 =.

[50] Kuuskmaa.

[51] Ekstrom Variation.

[52] 15 Ꙅxa6 Ꙩxe5 16 Ꙩd4 Ꙅg4 17 f3 Ꙅh5 ∞/=
Fedorov-Semenyuk, Kharkov 1970.

[53] 16 ꙳xe6+ ꙳xe6 17 Ꙅxd5 ꙳xd5 18 Ʀxd5
Ꙩb4 19 Ʀc5 Ꙩc2 = Larsen.

   16 Ꙅg5 ꙅh8! Fischer.

[54] 19 Ꙅb3 Ꙩe5 20 Ʀd4 c5 21 Ʀf4 Ꙩd7 22 Ʀd1
꙳c6 23 ꙳d2 Ꙩf6 24 Ʀh4 Ʀa7 ∞ Korchnoi.

	9	10	11	12	13	14	15	16	17	
1	...	a4[1]	ab	♘xe5	♘d2[3]					∞
	g6!?	♗g7[2]	♘xe5	♗xe5						
2	...	♘d4[5]	f4	f5	♗c2[8]	♖e1+	♗xe4	♖xe4+	f6	∞
	♘c5[4]	♘xe5[6]	♘ed3[7]	♗c8	♘xc1	♘e4	de	♗e7	gf	
3	...	♗c2	♖e1[9]	h3	e6	cd	♕xf3	♕h5+	♗xg6+	±
	...	♗g4	d4[10]	♗h5	fe	♗xf3	♘xd4	g6	hg[11]	
4	...	...	...	♘bd2	♘b3	h3	♗f5	♗e3	♗c5	∞
	...	...	♗e7	♕d7	♘e6	♗h5	♘cd8	a5[12]	a4[13]	
5	...	♕e2	♗f4[14]	♘bd2	♕xd2	♗c2	h3	♕d3	♕xf3	∞
	♗c5	0-0	♕d7[15]	♘xd2	d4	♗g4	♗xf3	g6	♖ad8[16]	
6	...	♕d3[17]	♘bd2[19]	ef	♘g5[20]	♕g3	♗c2![22]	♘b3	♗f4	∞
	...	0-0[18]	f5	♘xf6	♘e5[21]	♕d6	♖ae8	♗b6	♗d7[23]	
7	...	♘bd2	♕e2	♘xe4[24]	♘g5	♘xe4	♕xd3	♘xc5	♗e3	=
	...	0-0	♗f5!	de	♘xe5	♕d3	♘xd3	♘xc5	♘xb3[25]	

	11	12	13	14	15	16	17	18	19	
8	...	♘b3	♘fd4	cd[27]	♗e3	♘d2[28]	♖b1	♘xe4	♖xb2	=
	♗f5[26]	♗g6	♗xd4	a5	a4!	a3	ab	♗xe4	♕d7[29]	
9	...	...	♘xc5	♖e1	h3[31]	♗f4	♗d2	♗f4		=
	...	♗g4	♘xc5	♗h5[30]	♖e8	♘e6!	♘c5	♘e6[32]		
10	...	...	h3	g4	♗xe4!	♘xc5	♗f4	♖axd1	♖d7	±
	...	...	♗h5	♗g6	de	ef	♕xd1!	♘d8!	♘e6[33]	
11	...	♕xd2	ef[34]	♕e2![35]	♗e3	♖ad1				±
	♘xd2	f6	♖xf6	h6	♕d6	♘e5[36]				
12	...	♖xf2	♘f1[38]	♔xf2	♔g1	♗g5	♘d4	♕d2		=
	♘xf2[37]	f6	♗xf2+	fe	e4	♕d7	♗g4	♘e5[39]		

[1]   10 ♘bd2 ♘c5 11 ♕e1 ♗g7 12 ♘c2 0-0 13 ♘b3 ♗xb3 14 ♗xb3 ♖e8 15 ♗f4 ♘a5 = Kashdan-Ulvestad, USA 1946.

[2]   10 ... ♖b8 11 ab ab 12 ♕e2 ± Fuderer.

[3]   Karasev-Shamkovich, USSR 1968.

[4]   Berlin Defence.

[5]   10 ♖e1 ♘xb3 11 ab ♗e7 12 b4 0-0 13 ♘d4 ♘xd4 14 ♕xd4 a5 ∓ Goldenov-Makogonov, USSR Ch 1947.

      10 ♗g5 ♕d7 11 ♗c2 h6 12 ♗f4 ♗g4 13 ♘bd2 (Matanović-Lehmann, Zevenaar 1961) 13 ... ♘e6! intending ... ♗c5.

[6]   10 ... ♘xd4 11 cd ♘xb3 12 ♕xb3 c5 13 dc ♗xc5 14 ♕g3 ♕c7 15 ♗f4 ♗d4 16 ♖c1 ♕b6 ± Korchnoi.   17 ♘c3 ±.

[7]   11 ... ♘c4 12 f5 ♗d7 13 ♕h5!? ♘e4 14 ♘d2 ♘f6 15 ♗g5 ♗e7 16 ♕xg7 ♖g8 17 ♕h6 c5 18 ♘4f3 ±/ ± Mukhin-Ruderfer, Riga 1972.

[8]   13 ♘c6!? ♕f6 14 ♗xd5 ♗b7 15 ♕f3 ♗d6 ∞.

[9]   11 ♕e2 ♕d7 (11 ... ♗e7 – row 4) 12 ♖d1 ♖d8 13 b4 ♘e6 14 a4 ♗e7 15 ab ab 16 ♗d3 ♗xf3 17 gf ♗g5 18 ♗xb5 ♗xc1 19 ♖xc1 0-0 ∞ Liberzon-Gurevich, USSR 1964.

[10] 11 ... ♕d7 12 ♘bd2 ♖d8 13 h3 ♗f5 14 ♘f1 ♗e7 15 ♘g3 ♗g6 16 ♘d4 ± O'Connell.

[11] 18 ♕xh8 ± Unzicker-Lehmann, 1953.

[12] 16 ... ♘b7 17 ♕e2 c5 18 ♖ad1 ♖d8 19 ♘bd2! ± Sigurjonsson-Stean, Munich 1979.

[13] 18 ♗xe7 ♕xe7 19 ♘bd2 c6 ∞ Karpov-Korchnoi, match (28) 1978.

[14] 11 ♘bd2 – 10 ♘bd2.

      11 ♗e3 f6 12 ♘d4 ♗xd4 13 cd fe 14 de ♕e7 = Gligorić-Unzicker, Oberhausen 1961.

[15] 11 ... h6? 12 ♘bd2 ♘xd2 13 ♕xd2 ♘e7 14 ♘d4 ± Jansson-Vymetal, Sweden 1970.

[16] 18 ♖fe1 ∞.

[17] Motzko Variation.

[18] 10 ... f6 transposes.

[19] 11 ♗e3 f6 12 ef ♕xf6 13 ♘bd2 ♘e5 14 ♘xe5 ♕xe5 15 ♗d4 ♗xd4 16 cd ♕d6 17 ♖ac1 (Tal-Langeweg, Wijk aan Zee 1968) 17 ... c5! =.

[20] 13 a4 ♖b8 14 ab ab 15 ♗c2 ♗f7 16 ♘b3 ♗d6 17 ♘bd4 ♘xd4 18 ♕xd4 c5 19 ♕h4 ♘e4 20 ♗g5! = Puc-Milić, Yugoslav Ch 1946.

[21] 13 ... ♕e7? 14 ♘xe6 ♕xe6 15 ♘e4 ±± Shamkovich-Garcia, New York 1980.

[22] 15 ♖e1 ♘fg4 16 ♘de4 de 17 ♖xe6+ ♔h8 18 ♘xe4 ♕xe6 19 ♘xc5 ♘f3+ ∓∓ Breyer-Spielmann, Pistyan 1912.

[23] 17 ... ♗g4?! 18 ♘d4 ± Thiele-Karker, corr. Ol 1968-70.

      17 ... ♗d7 18 ♘d4! (18 ♖ae1 ♘h5 19 ♗xe5 ♘xg3 20 ♗xd6 ♖xe1 21 ♗xh7+ ♔h8 22 ♗xg3! ♖e2) 18 ... ♘h5 19 ♗xe5 ♖xe5 20 ♗xh7+ ♔h8 21 ♕h4 ♕h6! ∞ (Sapundzhiev) 22 ♘df3 ♖e7 intending ... ♘f4 ∞.

[24] 12 a4 ♖b8 13 ab ab 14 ♖a6 ♗b6 15 ♘xe4 de 16 ♘g5 ♘xe5 17 ♘xe4 ♕h4 18 ♘g5 ♖be8 ∓ Wolf-Maroczy, Oostende 1905.

[25] 18 ab a5 ½-½ Boleslavsky-Botvinnik, USSR Ch 1941.

[26] The Baguio Variation.

[27] 14 ♘xd4 ♘e7 15 f3 ♘c5 16 f4 ♗xc2 17 ♕xc2 ♘e4 18 b4 ♖c8 19 ♗a3 ♘g6 ∓ Georgsson-Pioch, corr. 1975.

[28] 16 ♘c1 a3 17 b3 f6! 18 ef ♕xf6 19 ♘e2 ♘b4 = Karpov-Korchnoi, match (6) 1981.

[29] 20 ♗xe4 de 21 ♖xb5 ♗xd4 22 ♖c5 ♖fd8 = Ivanov-Yusupov, USSR 1979.

[30] 14 ... d4 15 h3 ♗h5 16 cd ±/= Karpov-Korchnoi, match (2) 1978.   16 b4!? and 17 ♗b1 may lead to a slight edge (Shamkovich).

[31] 15 ♗g5 ♗xf3 16 ♕xf3 ♕xg5 17 ♕xd5 (Bronstein-Flohr, Moscow 1944) 17 ... ♖ae8! =.

[32] ½-½ Karpov-Korchnoi, match (4) 1978.

[33] 20 ♘xe6 fe 21 ♗e3 ♖ac8 (Karpov-Korchnoi, match (14) 1978) 22 ♗c5! ± Timoshchenko-Sideifzade, USSR 1979.

[34] 13 ♕d3 g6 14 ef ♗f5 15 ♕d1 ♗xc2 16 ♕xc2 ♕xf6 17 ♗h6 ± Korchnoi.

[35] 14 b4 ♗b6 15 a4 ♖b8 16 ♕e2 ♕d7 17 ♗g5 ♗f7 18 ♖ad1 ♗g4 19 ♗b3 ♗xf3 20 gf ♘e7 21 a5! ± Klovan-Shereshevsky, USSR 1974.

[36] de Vega-Mosete, corr. 1950.

[37] The Dilworth Attack.

[38] 13 ♘b3 ♗xf2+ 14 ♔xf2 fe 15 ♔g1 ♗g4 ∓.

      13 ♕e1 fe 14 ♘b3 ♗xf2+ 15 ♕xf2 ♗f5 16 ♗xf5 ♖xf5 ∓ Tsvetkov-Trifunović, Hilversum 1947.

      13 ♕e2 fe 14 ♘b3 ♗xf2+ 15 ♕xf2 e4 (15 ... ♗g4!?) 16 ♕e1 ♗g4 17 ♘fd4 ♘e5 ∓ Kluger-Szabo, Hungary Ch 1946.

[39] Esnaola-Albareda, corr. 1947.

331

1 e4 e5 2 ♘f3 ♘c6 3 ♗b5 a6 4 ♗a4 ♘f6 5 0-0 ♘xe4
6 d4 b5 7 ♗b3 d5 8 de ♗e6 9 c3 ♗c5 10 ♘bd2 0-0 11 ♗c2

	11	12	13	14	15	16	17	18	19	
13	...	♖xf2	ef	♕f1!?[40]	♘b3	♕xf2	♘bd4	h3[41]	♘xf3	∞
	♘xf2	f6	♕xf6	♖ae8!	♗xf2+	♘e5	♗g4	♘xf3+	♗xf3[42]	
14	...	...	...	♔xf2	♘b3	♘bd4[43]	♗b3[45]	♘xf3	♔g1	∓
	...	...	♗xf2+	♕xf6	♘e5	♗g4[44]	♗xf3[46]	♕h4+	c6	
15	...	...	...	...	♘f1	♗e3[47]	♗d4[48]	♔g1		∓
	...	...	...	...	♘e5	♖ae8	♕h4+[49]	♘xf3+		
16	...	...	...	...	♔g1	♘f1	♗e3	gf	♕xf3	∓
	...	...	...	...	♖ae8[50]	♘e5	♘xf3+	♕xf3	♖xf3[51]	
17	...	...	...	...	...	♕f1	h3	♘b3		∞
	...	...	...	...	...	♔h8	♗f7	♗h5[52]		
18	...	♘b3[53]	♘fd4[54]	♘xd4	cd	f3	hg[56]	♕d3	♕xf5	∞
	f5	♗b6	♘xd4	♗xd4	f4	♘g3![55]	fg	♗f5	♖xf5[57]	
19	...	...	...	...	♕xd4!	♕d1	f3	a4	cb	∞
	...	...	...	...	c5	f4	♘g5	b4[58]	c4![59]	

---

1 e4 e5 2 ♘f3 ♘c6 3 ♗b5 a6 4 ♗a4 ♘f6 5 0-0
♘xe4 6 d4 b5 7 ♗b3 d5 8 de ♗e6 9 c3 ♗e7

	10	11	12	13	14	15	16	17	18	
20	♗e3	♘bd2	♘xe4	♕d5!	♗xd5	♗xc6	♔xg2	a4	ab	±
	0-0	♗g4	de	♕xd5[60]	ef	fg	♖ad8	f6	ab[61]	
21	...	...	♕xd2	♕d3[62]	♗c2	♗h6	♕e2	♘d4	♘xc2	=
	...	♘xd2	♕d7	♘a5	g6	♗f5	♖fe8	♗xc2	♗d6[63]	
22	♘bd2	♗c2[64]	♘b3[65]	♘bd4	♘xd4	♘xe6	f3	a4[67]	♗xg5	=
	0-0	f5	♕d7	♘xd4[66]	c5	♕xe6	♘g5	g6[68]	♗xg5[69]	
23	...	♕e2!	♘d4	♘xc6	♖axc1	♘xe7+	f4	ef	♕e3	±
	...	♘c5[70]	♘xb3	♘xc1	♕d7	♕xe7	f5[71]	♕xf6	♗f5[72]	
24	...	...	...	♗c2	ef	♘2b3	♘xd4	f3	♕f2	=
	...	...	♕d7	f6	♗xf6	♘xd4	♗g4	♖ae8	♗h5[73]	

40 14 ♘b3 – 13 ... ♗xf2+.
    14 ♘f1 – 13 ... ♗xf2+.
41 18 ♕g3 c5! ∓.
    18 b4 ♕b6 ∓.
    18 ♗g5 ♕b6 19 ♕h4 ♖xf3 ∓.
42 20 gf ♕xf3 21 ♕xf3 ♖xf3 22 ♔g2 ♖ef8 23 ♗b3 c6 ∞ (±).
43 16 ♘c5 ♗g4 17 ♕xd5+ ♔h8 18 ♕e4 g6 19 ♔g3 ♘xf3 20 ♕xg4 ♖g1! ∓∓ Nightingale-Ritson Morry, corr. 1944.
44 16 ... ♖ae8 17 ♘xe6 ♕xe6 18 ♔g1 ♘xf3+ 19 gf ♕e1+ 20 ♕xe1 ♖xe1+ 21 ♔f2 ♖fe8 22 ♗d3 ♖h1 23 a4 b4! (23 ... ♖ee1 24 ab! ♖xc1 25 ♖xc1 ♖xc1 26 ba ∞) 24 ♗xa6 ♖ee1 25 cb ♖xc1 26 ♖xc1 ♖xc1 ∞ (±).
45 17 b4 ♖ae8 18 ♗d2 ♕h4+ 19 ♔g1 ♕h5 20 a4 ba 21 ♖xa4 ♗xf3 22 ♘xf3 ♖xf3 23 ♗f4 ♖f8 24 ♕xd5+ ♔h8 0-1 Thomas-Schiller, New York 1980.
46 17 ... ♖ad8 18 ♔g1 ♕b6 19 ♔h1 c5 20 ♗g5! ± Perez-Mocete, corr. 1947.
    17 ... ♘c4!?
47 16 ♔g1 ♖ae8 17 ♗e3 ♘xf3+ 18 ♕xf3 ♕xf3 19 gf ♖xf3 ∞.
48 17 ♗c5 ♖f7 18 ♘d2 ♗f5 19 ♔g1 ♘xf3 20 ♘xf3 ♗e4 Korchnoi.
49 17 ... ♗g4 18 ♘d2 ♕f4!? 19 ♔g1 ♘xf3+ 20 ♘xf3 (20 gf ♗h3!) 20 ... c6 ∞ Balashov-Tukmakov, USSR 1977.
50 15 ... ♘e5? 16 ♘xe5! ±.
51 20 ♗d4 ♗h3 21 ♘g3 g6 22 ♖d1 c6 23 ♗d3 ♗g4 24 ♖d2 ♖e1+ 25 ♔g2 ♖f7 26 ♗e2 ♗xe2 27 ♘xe2 ♖e7 28 ♘g3 a5 ∓ Plaskett-Condie, Hastings II 1980/81.
52 Kozlov-Estrin, USSR 1973.
53 12 ef ♘xf6 (12 ... ♘xf2 – Dilworth) 13 ♘b3 ♗b6 14 ♘g5 ♕d7 15 ♘xe6 ♕xe6 16 ♘d4 ♕xd4 17 cd ♘e4 18 ♗e3 c6 = Malishev-Druganov, corr. 1954.
54 13 a4 ♕d7 14 ab ab 15 ♖xa8 ♖xa8 16 ♗e3 ♗xe3 17 fe b4! ∓. 14 ♘fd4 ♘xd4 15 ♘xd4 c5! = Suetin-Nei, USSR Ch 1966/67.
55 Fleißig-Mackenzie, Vienna 1882.
56 17 ♖f2 ♕h4 18 ♕d3 ♗f5 19 ♗xf4 ♖xf4! = Napolitano-Sapundzhiev, corr. 1972.
57 20 ♗xf5 ♕h4 21 ♘h3 ♕xd4+ 22 ♔h1 ♕xe5 23 ♗d2 ♕xb2 24 ♗f4 d4! ∞/∞̄ – Baturinsky-Estrin, corr. 1946.
58 18 ... ba 19 ♖xa4 c4 20 b3! ± Haag-Estrin, corr. 1979.
59 19 ... cb 20 ♕d4 ♗f5 21 ♗b3 ♘e6 22 ♕xd5 ♕b6+ 23 ♔h1 ♖ad8 24 a5! ♕a7 25 ♕c6 ±± Korchnoi.
    19 ... c4! 20 ♕d4 ♗f5 ∞ (∓!?).
60 13 ... ef 14 ♘xc6 fg 15 ♕xg2 ♕d7 16 ♗h6 gh 17 f3 h5 (17 ... ♗c5+ 18 ♔h1 ♖ae8 19 ♖ae1 ±) 18 ♖ad1 ♕f5 19 fg ♕e5 20 ♖de1! ± Kasparov-Yusupov, USSR Ch 1979.
61 19 ♗xb5 fe 20 ♗c4+ ± Alekhine-Teichmann, match (4) 1921.
62 13 ♗g5 ♖ad8 14 ♖fe1 ♖fe8 = Suetin.
63 Keres-Dyckhoff, corr. Ol 1935/36.
64 11 ♖e1 ♘c5 12 ♗c2 d4 ∓ Johner-Euwe, Zürich 1934.
65 12 ef ♘xf6 13 ♘b3 (13 ♘g5 ♗g4 14 f3 ♗c8 ∓ Kotov-Averbakh, USSR 1952) 13 ... ♗g4 14 ♕d3 ♘e4 15 ♘bd4 ♘xd4 16 ♘xd4 ♗d6 17 h3! = Ragozin-Ravinsky, Moscow 1947.
66 13 ... ♘a5!? 14 ♘xe6 ♕xe6 15 ♘d4 ♕e5 16 f3 ♗d6 17 g3 f4! = Boleslavsky-Zagorovsky, USSR 1954.
67 17 ♗xg5 ♗xg5 18 f4 ♗e7 19 ♕f3!? c4 ∞ Korsunsky-Chekhov, USSR 1978.
68 17 ... c4 18 ab ♕b6+!? 19 ♔h1 ♕xb5 = Korchnoi.
69 19 f4 ♗e7 20 ♕f3 b4 21 ♖fe1 ♖fd8 22 cb c4 = Balashov-Korchnoi, BRD 1980.
70 11 ... ♘xd2?! 12 ♕xd2 ♘a5 (12 ... f6!?) 13 ♗c2 ♘c4 14 ♕d3 g6 15 ♗h6 ♖e8 16 ♕d4 ± Scholl-Zuidema, Dutch Ch 1967.
71 16 ... g6!? 17 b4! d4! O'Connell.
72 19 ♕d4 ± Janošević-Lukić, Yugoslav Ch 1955.
73 19 ♘e2 ♕d6 = Seibold-Ohls, corr. 1929/31.

Ruy Lopez   1 e4 e5 2 ♘f3 ♘c6 3 ♗b5 a6 4 ♗a4 ♘f6 5 0-0 ♗e7

	6	7	8	9	10	11	12	13	14	
1	♗xc6[1]	♘c3	h3	g4[2]	♘xe5[3]	♘xg6	dc	♕xd8+		=
	dc	♗g4	♗h5	♗g6	♘xe4	♘xc3	hg	♖xd8[4]		
2	...	♕e1	d4	♘xd4	♕e3	♘c3	♖d1	b4	♘f5	=
	...	♘d7	ed	♘c5![5]	0-0	♖e8	♗d6	♘d7	♘e5[6]	
3	...	d3	♘bd2	♘c4	♘h4[8]	♕f3[9]	♕g3	♗e3	♘f5	±
	...	♘d7	0-0	f6[7]	♘c5	♖e8	♔h8	♘e6	♗f8[10]	
4	♕e2	♗b3	a4	ab	♘c3	h3	d3			=
	b5	0-0	♖b8	ab	d6	♗d7	♕e8[11]			
5	...	...	c3	d3[13]	♖e1	♘bd2	♘f1	♗g5		=
	...	...	d5[12]	♖e8	♗b7	♕d7	♖ad8	♘a5[14]		
6	♖e1	♗xc6+	d4	♘xd4	♘c3	♗f4	h3	♘b3		±
	d6	bc	ed[15]	♗d7	0-0	♖e8	c5	a5[16]		
7	...	c3	d4	♘bd2	♘f1[17]	♘g3	a3[18]	♗c2	b4[19]	±
	...	0-0	♗d7	♖e8	h6	♗f8	♘a5	c5		
8	...	♗b3	a4	♗a2	c3[21]	d3	♘a3	♗g5	ab	±
	b5	d6	♘a5[20]	c5	c4	♗d7[22]	0-0[23]	♕c7	ab[24]	

1 e4 e5 2 ♘f3 ♘c6 3 ♗b5 a6 4 ♗a4 ♘f6 5 0-0 ♗e7 6 ♖e1 b5 7 ♗b3 0-0

	8	9	10	11	12	13	14	15	16	
9	a4[25]	d4[26]	de	♘bd2	h3	♕xf3	♕g3	♘f3	cb[27]	±
	b4	d6	de	♗g4	♗xf3	♘d4	♘d7	♘xb3		
10	...	d3	♘c3	♗a2	♘e2	♗d2[28]	♘g3	♘f1		=
	♗b7	d6	♘a5	b4	c5	♖e8[29]	g6	♗f8		
11	...	...	♗d2	c3	♘xc3	d4	♕xb3	♕c2		=
	...	...	b4	bc	♘a5	♘xb3	♖b8	d5[30]		
12	c3	ed	dc	d4!	♕f3	♗f4	♗xd5	♘d2[32]		±
	d5	e4	ef	fg[31]	♗e6	♗d5	♕xd5			
13	...	...	♘xe5	♖xe5	d4	♖e1	h3	♕f3	♗e3	±
	...	♘xd5	♘xe5	♘f6	♗d6	♘g4	♕h4	h5[33]	♘xe3[34]	
14	...	...	...	...	g3	♖e1	d4	♖e4[35]	♕f3	∓
	...	...	...	c6	♗d6	♕d7!	♕h3	g5!	♗f5[36]	

1 e4 e5 2 ♘f3 ♘c6 3 ♗b5 a6 4 ♗a4 ♘f6 5 0-0 ♗e7 6 ♖e1 b5 7 ♗b3 0-0 8 c3 d5
9 ed ♘xd5 10 ♘xe5 ♘xe5 11 ♖xe5 c6 12 d4 ♗d6 13 ♖e1 ♕h4 14 g3 ♕h3

	15	16	17	18	19	20	21	22	23	
15	♗e3[37]	♕d3	♘d2	c4	♗xf4	♕f1	♔h1			∓
	♗g4	♖ae8[38]	♖e6	♗f4![39]	♘xf4[40]	♘e2+	♕h6[41]			
16	...	...	...	...	cd	♕e4	♔f1	dc+		∞
	...	...	...	...	♖h6	♕xh2+	f5	♔h8[42]		
17	...	...	...	♗xd5	a4	c4[43]	cd	♗xd2		∞
	...	...	...	cd	ba	♗b4!	♗xd2	♖b6[44]		
18	...	...	...	a4	♕f1	f4	♖xa4	♖xa6	♖xc6[46]	±
	...	...	...	f5!	♕h5	ba	g5	gf!?[45]	fe[47]	
19		...	...	...	...	...	...	♗xd5	♕g2	∞
		...	...	...	...	...	♖b8	cd	♕e8[48]	

[1] 6 d4 – 5 d4.

[2] 9 ♕e2 ♕c8 10 d3 h6 11 ♘d1 ♘h7 12 g4 ♗xg4 13 hg ♕xg4+ 14 ♔h2 ♕h5+ ½-½ Tal-Keres, Bled 1961.

[3] 10 ♕e2 ♘d7 11 d4 ed 12 ♘xd4 h5! 13 ♘f5 hg 14 hg ♗d6 ∓ Sax-Ivkov, Rio de Janeiro IZ 1979.

[4] Matulović-Spassky, Yugoslavia v USSR 1965.

[5] 9 ... 0-0 10 ♘c3 ♘b6 11 ♗e3 ♘c4 12 ♖d1 ♕e8 13 ♗c1 ♗b4 14 a3 ♗a5 15 ♖d3 ± Pribyl-Hamann, Prague 1972.

[6] Hasin-Geller, Kislovodsk 1968.

[7] 9 ... ♗f6 10 ♗d2 ♖e8 11 ♘c3 c5 12 a4 b6 13 h3 g6 14 ♘h2 ♗g7 15 ♕d2 ♘b8 16 f4 f6 17 fe fe 18 ♕f2! ± Kostro-Adorjan, Polanica Zdroj 1970.

[8] 10 d4 ed 11 ♘xd4 ♘e5 12 ♘xe5 fe = Vuković-Gligorić, Yugoslavia 1949.

[9] 11 ♘f5 ♗xf5 12 ef ♕d7 13 ♕g4 b5 14 ♘e3 ♖fe8 15 b3 ♕d4 16 ♗d2 ♕xg4 17 ♘xg4 ♘b7 = Gheorghiu-Portisch, Moscow 1967.

[10] 15 a4 c5 16 f4 ef 17 ♗xf4 ♘xf4 18 ♕xf4 ± Hort-Lengyel, Wijk aan Zee 1971.

[11] Treybal-Alekhine, Pistyan 1922.

[12] 8 ... d6 9 a4 ♗g4 10 h3 ♗xf3 11 ♕xf3 ♘a5 12 ♗c2 c5 13 ♖e1 ± Cirić-Tomović, Yugoslavia 1963.

[13] 9 ed ♗g4 10 dc e4 11 d4 ef 12 gf ♗h5 13 ♗f4 ♖e8 ∞ Foltys-Keres, Salzburg 1943.

[14] Keres-Geller, Budapest 1952.

[15] 8 ... ♘d7 9 ♘bd2 f6 10 ♘c4 ♘b6 11 ♘a5 ♗d7 12 c4 0-0 13 ♗e3 ♕e8 14 c5 ♘c8 15 ♖c1 ♖b8 16 ♕c2 ± Hasin-Littlewood, Hastings 1963/64.

[16] Holmov.

13 ... ♗e6 14 e5! de 15 ♗xe5 ♗d6 16 ♕f3! ± Kapengut-Holmov, USSR Ch 1972.

[17] 10 a3 ♗f8 11 b4 d5 12 ♗b3 ♗g4 13 ed ♘xd5 14 ♗b2 ♘xf3 15 ♗xd5 ♘xd5 16 c4 ♗xf3 17 cd ♗xd1 18 dc ♗a4 19 cb ♖ab8 20 de ♖xb7 ∞ Smyslov-Gligorić, Yugoslavia 1959.

[18] 12 h3 ♘a5 13 ♗c2 c5 14 d5 b5 15 b3 ♘b7 16 ♗e3 g6 17 ♕d2 h5 ± Tal-Gligorić, Hastings 1963/64.

[19] Suetin-Tseshkovsky, USSR 1971.

[20] 8 ... b4 9 c3 bc 10 bc ♘a5 (10 ... 0-0!?) 11 ♗a2 c6 12 d4 ♕c7 13 ♘g5 0-0 14 f4 ± Matanović-Gligorić, Yugoslav Ch 1958.

[21] 10 ab ab 11 d3 ♗g4 12 ♗g5 ♘c6 13 ♘bd2 0-0 14 ♗xf6 ♗xf6 15 h3 ♗d7 ∓ Balashov-Belyavsky, USSR Ch 1979.

[22] 11 ... ♗b7!?

[23] 12 ... h6!?

[24] 15 ♕e2 ± Balashov-Torre, Lone Pine 1980.

[25] 8 d3 d6 9 c3 =.

[26] 9 d3 d6 10 ♘bd2 ♖b8 11 ♘c4 ♗e6 12 č3 ♘d7 13 ♗e3 bc 14 bc = Keres.

[27] Westerinen-Ivkov, Wijk aan Zee 1970.

[28] 13 ♘g3 ♖b8 14 ♘d2 ♘e8 15 c3 bc 16 bc ♗c8 17 ♘f3 ♗f6 18 ♗e3 g6 = Gipslis-Ivkov, Zagreb 1965.

[29] 13 ... ♖b8 14 ♘g3 ♗c8 15 ♘f1 ♗e6 16 ♗xe6 fe 17 ♘e3 h6 18 ♘c4! ♘xc4 19 dc ♕e8 20 g3 ♕c6 21 ♘h4!? ♗xe4 22 ♘g6 ♗f7 23 ♕f3! ± Kurajica-Littlewood, Borovo 1980.

[30] Matulović-Reshevsky, Maribor 1967.

[31] 11 ... ♗d6 12 ♕f3 ♖e8 13 ♗d2 ♗g4 14 ♕d3 ♖xe1 15 ♗xe1 ♕e8 16 ♘d2 ♕c6 17 f3 ± Haller-Dal, corr. 1970.

[32] Tal.

[33] 15 ... ♘xf2 16 ♗d2! ♗b7 17 ♖xb7 ♘d3 18 ♖e2 ♖ae8 19 ♕f3 ♖xe2 20 ♕xe2 ♕g3 (Chemoine-Prameshuber, Munich Ol 1958) 21 ♕f3! ♕xh2+ 22 ♔f1 ♕h1+ 23 ♔e2 ♘xb2 24 ♗e3 ± Euwe.

[34] 17 ♖xe3 ♕xf4 18 ♕xf4 ♗xf4 19 ♖e1 ♗f5 20 ♘a3 ± Tal.

[35] 15 ♗e3 – 12 d4.

[36] 17 ♗xd5 cd 18 ♖e3 ♗e4 19 ♖xe4 de 20 ♕f6 ♕g4! ∓ Blackstock-Radovici, England 1972.

[37] 15 ♕d3 ♗f5 16 ♕f1 ♕h5 17 ♗e3 ♗h3 18 ♗d1 ♕f5 19 ♕e2 ♖ae8 20 ♘d2 c5 21 a3 cd 22 cd ♗f4 23 ♕f3 ♗xe3 24 fe ♕xf3 25 ♗xf3 ♘xe3 ½-½ Boleslavsky-Bronstein, match 1950.

[38] 16 ... f5 17 f4 g5 18 ♕f1 ♕h5 19 ♘d2 ♖ae8 20 ♕g2! gf 21 ♗d5+! ♔h8 22 ♗xf4 ♗xf4 23 ♗xc6! ♗e3+ 24 ♔h1 ♗h3 25 ♕e2! ♗g4 26 ♗xe8 ♖xe8 27 ♕xe3 ± Boleslavsky.

[39] 18 ... bc 19 ♘xc4 ♗f4 20 ♕f1 ♕h6 21 ♗c1! ♗h3 22 ♖xe6 fe 23 ♕d1 ♗xc1 24 ♖xc1 ♕f6 25 f3 ♕xf3 26 ♕xf3 ♖xf3 27 ♘e5 ♖f8 28 ♘xc6 ± Byrne-Geller, Las Palmas 1976.

[40] 19 ... ♗e2? 20 cd ± Dvoiris-Liflyandchik, USSR 1975.

[41] Yudovich.

[42] Sideifzade-Poleshchuk, corr. 1978.

[43] 20 ♕f1 ♖b8 ∓ Tal.

[44] Tal.

[45] 22 ... ♘h8 23 ♖xc6! ♘xe3 24 ♕f2 ♘d1 25 ♗xd1 ♖xe1+ 26 ♕xe1 ♖e8 27 ♕f1 ♗xd1 28 ♖xd6 ±± Tal.

[46] 23 ♗xf4 ♗xf4 24 ♖xc6 ♗e3+ 25 ♖xe3 ♖xe3 26 ♗xd5+ ♔h8 27 ♕f4 = Tal-Geller, USSR Ch 1975.

[47] 23 ... fg 24 hg ♗xg3 25 ♕g2 ±.

23 ... fe 24 ♗xd5 ed 25 ♖xe6! ± Gutman.

[48] 24 ♕xd5 ♔h8 25 ♔f2 g5 26 ♖xa6 ♖xb2 27 ♖a2 ∞ Tal, Gutman.

Ruy Lopez: 9 d4   1 e4 e5 2 ♘f3 ♘c6 3 ♗b5 a6 4 ♗a4
♘f6 5 0-0 ♗e7 6 ♖e1 b5 7 ♗b3 d6 8 c3 0-0 9 d4

	9	10	11	12	13	14	15	16	17	
1	...	cd	♘c3!	gf	♗c2	♘e2	d5	♘g3	♗h6	±
	ed[1]	♗g4	♗xf3[2]	♘a5	b4	c5	♘e8	g6	♘g7[3]	
2	...	♗e3[4]	cd	♗c2	♗c1	b3	♘bd2	h3	♗b2	=
	♗g4	ed	♘a5	♘c4[5]	c5	♘b6	♖c8	♗h5	♘fd7[6]	
3	...	...	ed	♗xd4	cd	♘c3	a3	bc	♗a2	∞
	...	d5	ed!	♘xd4	♗b4	a5	♗xc3	a4	♕d6[7]	
4	...	d5	♗c2	dc	♘bd2	h3	♘f1	♘g5	♘g3	=
	...	♘a5	c6[8]	♕c7!	♕xc6	♗e6	♖fe8	♗d7	g6[9]	
5	...	...	...	h3	♕xf3	ed	♘d2	♘f1	♘g3	=
	...	...	...	♗xf3!?[10]	cd	♘c4!	♘b6	♘bxd5[11]	♘c7[12]	
6	...	...	...	...		dc	♘bd2	♘f1[13]	♘g3	=
	...	...	...	...	♖c8	♕c7!	♕xc6	♘c4	♖fe8[14]	

---

[1]   **9 ...** ♘a5?! 10 ♗c2 ♗g4 11 h3 ♗h5 12 g4 ♗g6 13 de de 14 ♕xd8 ♖fxd8 15 ♘xe5 ±.
    9 ... ♗b7 10 ♘bd2 ♘d7 11 ♘f1 ♗f6 12 ♘e3 ± ECO.

[2]   11 ... ♘a5 12 ♗c2 c5 13 dc dc 14 e5! ± Lasker-Bogoljubow, Moravska Ostrava 1923.

[3]   Karpinsky-Pillsbury, USA 1901.

[4]   10 h3 ♗xf3 11 gf ♘a5 12 ♗c2 ♘h5 13 f4 ♘xf4 14 ♗xf4 ef 15 ♘d2 c5 16 ♘f3 ♘c6 17 ♕d2 cd 18 cd $\overline{\overline{\infty}}$ Dubinin-Antoshin, USSR 1962.

[5]   12 ... c5 13 ♘bd2 cd 14 ♗xd4 ♘c6 15 ♗e3 d5 = Sosonko-Ree, Wijk aan Zee 1974.

[6]   Klovan-Geller, USSR Ch 1975.

[7]   18 h3 (Gulko-Geller, Lvov 1978) 18 ... ♗h5!? ∞ Ravinsky.

[8]   11 ... ♕c8 12 h3 ♗d7 13 ♘bd2 c6 14 dc ♕xc6 15 ♘f1 ♖fe8! 16 ♘g3 ♘c4 17 ♘f5 ♗xf5 18 ef ♗f8 ∞ Ligterink-Smejkal, Amsterdam 1979.

[9]   Mednis-Byrne, US Ch 1974.

[10]   **12 ...** ♗d7 13 ♘xe5! ±.
    12 ... ♗h5 13 dc ♕c7 14 ♘bd2! ±.

[11]   16 ... ♘e8? 17 a4! ba 18 ♘g3! ± – Tseshkovsky-Belyavsky, USSR Ch 1978.

[12]   18 ♘f5 ♘e6 19 a4 b4! = Kurajica-Smejkal, Yugoslavia 1978.

[13]   15 ♖e3 g6 16 b4 ♘c4 = Soltis-Reshevsky, US Ch 1977.

[14]   Timman-Spassky, Montreal 1979.

| | Ruy Lopez: Smyslov   1 e4 e5 2 ♘f3 ♘c6 3 ♗b5 a6 4 ♗a4 | | | | | | | |
| | ♘f6 5 0-0 ♗e7 6 ♖e1 b5 7 ♗b3 0-0 8 c3 d6 9 h3 h6 | | | | | | | |

	10	11	12	13	14	15	16	17	18	
1	d4	♗e3[1]	♘bd2	♕b1	a3	♗a2	b4	♕xb3	♕c2	=
	♖e8	♗f8	♗d7	♖b8	a5	a4	ab	♗e6	♗xa2[2]	
2	...	♘bd2	a3	♗c2	♘f1	d5	c4	♘e3		=
	...	♗f8	♗d7[3]	g6	♗g7	♘e7	c6	♖f8![4]		
3	...	...	♗c2	♗d3!	b3	♗b2	d5	c4[5]		±
	...	...	♗d7	♕b8	g6	♗g7	♘d8			
4	...	...	♘f1	♘g3	♗c2	b3	cd	♗b2	♕d2![6]	±
	...	...	♗d7	♘a5	c5	cd	♘c6	♖c8		
5	...	...	...	...	...	...	d5	♗e3	♕d2	±
	...	...	...	...	...	♘c6	♘e7	g6	♔h7[7]	
6	...	...	...	...	...	a4	b3	ab	d5	=
	...	...	...	...	♘c4	c5	♘a5	ab	♕c7[8]	
7	...	...	...	...	...	b3!	♘h2[9]	f4	cd	±
	...	...	...	...	...	♘b6	c5	cd	♖c8[10]	
8	...	...	...	♘g3	♗c2	b3![11]	♗d2	d5	a4	=
	...	...	♗b7	♘a5	♘c4	♘b6	c5	g6	ba[12]	
9	...	...	...	...	...	...	a4!	♘xe5	♘xe4	±
	...	...	...	...	...	...	d5	de	♘xe4[13]	

---

1 11 a4 ♗d7 12 ab ab 13 ♖xa8 ♕xa8 14 ♘a3 ♕b8 15 ♗a2 ♗f8 = Gligorić-Porath, Tel Aviv Ol 1964.
2 19 ♖xa2 = Savon-Geller, Petropolis 1973.
3 12 ... ♗b7 – 9 ... ♗b7 10 d4 ♖e8 11 ♘bd2 ♗f8 12 a3 h6.
4 Krogius.
5 Savon-Geller, Lvov 1978.
6 Gufeld-Savon, Vilnius 1975.
7 19 ♘h2 ♗g7 20 f4 ef ± Sigurjonsson-Smejkal, Raach 1969.
8 19 ♗e3 g6 20 ♘d2 ♗g7 = Jansa-Geller, Lugano Ol 1968.
9 16 ♗b2 c5 17 de de 18 c4 ♕c7 19 ♘d2 ♖ad8 20 ♕e2 ♘h7 ∞ Tal-Geller, Moscow 1967.
10 19 ♘f3 ed 20 ♗b2 ♗c6 21 ♘xd4 ± Liberzon-Darga, Amsterdam 1969.
11 15 a4 d5 16 ♘xe5 ♘xe4 17 ab ab 18 ♖xa8 ♗xa8 ∞.
12 19 ba a5 20 ♗d3 c4 = Damjanović-Gligorić, Venice 1971.
13 19 ♗xe4 ♗xe4 20 ♖xe4 f6 21 ♘c6 ♕d5 22 ♖xe8 ♖xe8 23 ab ab ± Gligorić.

Ruy Lopez: Flohr-Zaitsev   1 e4 e5 2 ♘f3 ♘c6 3 ♗b5 a6
4 ♗a4 ♘f6 5 0-0 ♗e7 6 ♖e1 b5 7 ♗b3 d6 8 c3 0-0 9 h3 ♗b7

	10	11	12	13	14	15	16	17	18	
1	d4	a4	d5	♗a2	♗g5	♗xf6	♗xd5	♕xd5		=
	♖e8[1]	♗f8[2]	♘a5[3]	c6	cd	♕xf6	♗xd5	♕e6[4]		
2	...	♗g5	♗xe7	♘bd2	a4	♗c2	ab	d5	♕e2	=
	...	♘d7	♕xe7	♘f6	♘a5	c5	ab	c4	♕c7[5]	
3	...	♘g5	f4	♗xf4	♗c2	ed[6]	♕h5	♗g3	♕f3	∓
	...	♖f8	ef	♘a5	♘d5	♗xg5	h6	g6	♘c4[7]	
4	...	...	♘f3	♘bd2[9]	♘g5[10]	d5	♗c2	b4	♘xc4	=
	...	...	♖e8[8]	♗f8	♖e7	♘a5![11]	c6	♘c4	bc[12]	
5	...	♘bd2	♗c2	d5[14]	b3	c4	a4[16]	♗a3	cd	=
	...	♗f8	g6[13]	♘b8	c6[15]	♘bd7	♕c7	cd	♖ec8[17]	
6	...	...	a3!	♗c2	b4	♘b3	♗b2	d5	♘a5	∞
	...	...	♕d7[18]	g6	♗g7	♘h5	♖e7	♘d8	♗c8[19]	
7	...	...	♗c2	b4	bc	♘xe5	cd			∞
	...	...	♕c8	♘d8	c5	dc	cd	♕c3[20]		
8	...	...		♗c2	b4	♗b2	bc	cd	♗c3	=/∞
	...	...	h6	♘b8	♘bd7	c5	ed!?[21]	dc	♗d6[22]	
9	...	...	...	...	...	...	c4	cb	♘xd4	±/=
						g6	ed	ab	♘c6[23]	

[1] **10 ... ♕d7!?**
10 ... ♘d7 11 ♘bd2 ♘f6 12 ♘f1 ♖e8 13 ♘g3 g6 14 ♗h6 ♘a5 15 ♗c2 c5 16 d5 ♘c4 17 ♕c1 ± Ljubojević-Karpov, Turin 1982.

[2] 11 ... h6 12 ♘a3 ♗f8 13 d5 ♘a7 14 ♘c2 c6 15 ♘b4 c5 16 ♘c2 ♗c8 = Hübner-Portisch, Tilburg 1980.

[3] 12 ... ♘b8 13 ab ab 14 ♖xa8 ♗xa8 15 ♘a3! c6 16 ♗g5 ♘bd7 17 dc ♗xc6 18 ♘c2 ± Grünfeld-Smejkal, Skara 1980.

[4] Tseshkovsky-Karpov, USSR 1980.

[5] 19 ♖a3 ♖a6 20 ♖ea1 ♖ea8 ½-½ Byrne-Gligorić, Baden bei Wien 1980.

[6] **15** ♘xh7 ♘xf4.
15 ♕h5 h6 Gligorić.

[7] Ljubojević-Gligorić, match (5) 1979.

[8] 12 ... h6 – 9 ... h6 (Smyslov Variation).

[9] 9 ♘g5 ♖f8 =.

[10] **14** ♗c2 – 11 ♘bd2.
14 a3 – 11 ♘bd2.

[11] 15 ... ♘b8 16 ♘f1 h6 17 ♘f3 c6 18 ♘e3 ♖e8 19 ♘h4 ± Vasyukov-Torre, Reykjavik 1980.

[12] 19 dc ♗xc6 20 a4 ♗b7! = (∓!?) Timman-Karpov, Bugojno 1980.

[13] 12 ... h6 – 9 ... h6 Smyslov's Variation).

[14] 13 b3 d5! 14 de ♘xe5 15 ♘xe5 ♖xe5 16 ♘f3 ♖xe4! 17 ♗xe4 ♘xe4 18 ♕c2 ♗g7 19 ♗b2 ♕f6! = Rodriguez-Belyavsky, Bogota 1979.

[15] 14 ... ♗g7 15 ♘f1 c6 16 c4 cd 17 cd ♘bd7 18 ♗e3 ♖c8 19 a4 ♘c5 20 ♘3d2 ba 21 b4 ± Karpov-Balashov, USSR 1976.

[16] 16 ♘f1 bc 17 bc ♘c5 18 ♖b1 ♕c7 19 ♗a3 ♘fd7 20 ♘3d2 ♖ec8 = Timoshchenko-Klovan, USSR 1979.

[17] 19 ♗d3 ♘c5 20 ♗f1 ♕b6 21 ♕b1 (22 ♕e2 b4 22 ♘c4 ♕a7 23 ♗xb4 ♘cxe4 24 a5 ♘xd5 Geller-Ivkov, Las Palmas 1979) 21 ... ♗h6 22 ♗b4 ♘fd7 23 ♖c1 (Ljubojević-Gligorić, match (7) 1979) 23 ... ♗f8 intending ... f5 (Gligorić) =.

[18] 12 ... g6 13 ♗a2 ♗g7 14 b4 ♘b8 15 de de 16 ♗b2 ♘bd7 17 c4 ± Matanović-Ivkov, match (3) 1978.   14 ... a5! 15 d5 ♘e7 16 ♘b3 ab 17 cb ♘xe4! 18 ♖xe4 ♗xd5 19 ♖e1 e4 ∞/= Chiburdanidze-A.Ivanov, USSR 1980.

[19] 19 a4 ♖b8 20 ab ab 21 c4 ∞ Dorfman-Malevinsky, USSR 1980.

[20] Karpov-Romanishin, USSR 1980.

[21] 16 ... dc 17 de?! (17 ♘xe5 ♘xe5 18 de ♘d7 19 f4 ♕h4 20 ♕f3 Gligorić) 17 ... ♘h5! = Tal-Romanishin, Riga 1978.

[22] Dvoiris-Podgayets, USSR 1980.

[23] **19** ♘4b3 ♖c8 20 a4 ba 21 ♖xa4 ♗a8 22 ♕a1 ♘h5! = Hübner-Kavalek, Tilburg 1979.

19 a4 ba 20 ♗xa4 ♖c8 21 ♖c1 c5 22 bc dc 23 ♘4f3 ♗c6 24 ♗xc6 ♖xc6 25 ♘c4 ♘b6 26 ♕xd8 ♖xd8 ½-½ (±/=) Timman-Karpov, Tilburg 1979.

Ruy Lopez: Breyer   1 e4 e5 2 ♘f3 ♘c6 3 ♗b5 a6 4 ♗a4
♘f6 5 0-0 ♗e7 6 ♖e1 b5 7 ♗b3 d6 8 c3 0-0 9 h3 ♘b8

	10	11	12	13	14	15	16	17	18	
1	d3[1]	♘bd2	♘f1	♘g3[2]	a4	♘f5[3]	g4	♗c2	cb	±
	c5	♘c6	h6	♖e8	♗d7	♗f8	♘a5	b4	cb[4]	
2	...	♘bd2	♘f1	♗c2	♘g3	♗h6!	♕d2	♖ad1	d4	±
	♘bd7	a5	a4	♖e8[5]	g6[6]	♗f8	♗b7	♕e7	♗xh6[8]	
3	...	...	♘f1	♗c2	♘g3[10]	♗h6!	♗xf8	♕d2	d4[12]	±/±
	...	♗b7	♘c5[9]	♖e8	g6	♗f8	♔xf8[11]	♔g7		

1 e4 e5 2 ♘f3 ♘c6 3 ♗b5 a6 4 ♗a4 ♘f6 5 0-0 ♗e7 6 ♖e1 b5 7 ♗b3 d6
8 c3 0-0 9 h3 ♘b8 10 d3 ♘bd7 11 ♘bd2 ♗b7 12 ♘f1 ♘c5 13 ♗c2 ♖e8 14 ♘g3 ♗f8

	15	16	17	18	19	20	21	22	23	
4	♘h2	♕f3	♘f5	g4	g5	de	h4	♘g4	h5	∞
	d5[13]	♘e6[14]	♔h8!	c5	de	♘d7	♕c7	c4	♘ec5[15]	
5	...	...	...	ed[16]	♕g3	♕xe5	♘e7	♘xd5	cd	∞
	...	...	...	♗xd5	♘h5!	♕d7	♘f6	♘d4	♘xd5[17]	
6	b4	♗b3[19]	a4	♕c2	ed	♕a2	dc	♕c2	♕xc3	∓
	♘cd7[18]	h6[20]	c5	d5!	♘xd5	c4	♘xc3	ba	ab[21]	
7	...	d4	a4[23]	♗d3	de	♘xe5				=
	...	g6![22]	♗g7	ba	♘xe5[24]	♖xe5[25]				

[1]   10 a4 (Matulović) 10 ... ♗b7 11 d3 ♘bd7 12 ab ab 13 ♖xa8 ♗xa8 14 ♘a3 ♘c6 15 ♘c2 = Matulović-Matanović, Yugoslav Ch 1972.

[2]   13 d4 ♗d7 14 dc dc 15 ♘e3 c4 16 ♗c2 ♗e6 17 ♕e2 ♕c7 18 g4 ♗c5 = Tal-Tukmakov, Moscow 1971.

[3]   15 ♗e3 ♗f8 16 ♘d2 ♘a5 17 ♗c2 d5! ∓ Stein-Karpov, USSR Ch 1970.

[4]   19 d4 ± Ciocaltea-Ree, Skopje Ol 1972.

[5]   13 ... c5 14 ♘3h2 ♘b6 15 f4 ef 16 ♗xf4 ♘e8 17 ♘f3 a3 18 b3 d5 19 d4 ± Kudriashov-Zakharov, USSR 1974.

[6]   14 ... ♗f8 15 ♘f5 ♘c5 16 ♘h2 ♘e6 17 d4 ± Zukharov-Krogius, RSFSR Ch 1955.

[7]   17 ... ♘b6 (Parma-O'Kelly, Havana 1965) 18 ♗xf8! ±.

[8]   19 ♕xh6 ♘f8 20 d5 ±.

[9]   12 ... c5 13 ♘g3 g6 14 ♗h6 ♖e8 15 ♕d2 ♗f8 (Holmov-Chukayev, Lithuanian Ch 1955) 16 d4!

[10]   14 ♘e3 ♗f8 15 b4 ♘cd7 16 ♗b3 c5 17 ♘g5 c4 18 dc h6 = Spassky.
14 ♘3h2 d5 15 ♕f3 ♘e6 16 ♘g4 ♘xg4 17 ♕xg4 ♗f8 18 ♕g3 f6 = Parma-Wade, Skopje 1968.

[11]   16 ... ♖xf8 17 d4!

[12]   Unzicker-Padevsky, Tel Aviv Ol 1964.

[13]   15 ... g6 (15 ... ♘e6!?) 16 f4 ef 17 ♗xf4 ♘e6 18 ♗d2 ♗g7 19 d4 c5 20 d5 ♘f8 21 ♗f4 ♕e7 22 ♖f1 h5 = Gheorghiu-Portisch, Monte Carlo 1969.

[14]   16 ... g6 17 ♗g5 ♗e7 18 h4! h5 19 ed ♗xd5 20 ♘e4 ♘fxe4 21 ♗xe7 ♕xe7 22 de ♗c6 23 ♕e3 a5 = Sanakoyev-Zagorovsky, corr. 1968/71.

[15]   24 g6 ∞ Ciocaltea-O'Kelly, Havana 1965.

[16]   18 ♘g4 ♘xg4 19 ♕xg4 c5 20 h4 ♕c7 (Shamkovich-O'Kelly, Palma de Mallorca 1966) 21 h5 ♖ad8 22 ♖e3 =.

[17]   24 ♘f3 ½-½ (!) Tringov-Filip, Siegen Ol 1970.

[18]   15 ... ♘e6 16 a4 (16 d4 ♘d7!?) 16 ... g6 17 ♗e3 ♗g7 18 ♕c1 c5 19 bc ♘xc5 20 ab ab 21 ♕b2 ♗c6 = Bronstein-Krogius, USSR Ch 1964/65.

[19]   16 ♘f5 (Westerinen) 16 ... a5 17 ♗d2 ab 18 cb d5 19 ♗b3 h6 20 ♘3h4 ♔h7 =/∓ Westerinen-Smejkal, Tallinn 1971.

[20]   16 ... a5 17 a3! ±.

[21]   Gaprindashvili-Spassky, Göteborg 1971.

[22]   16 ... a5 17 a3 ab 18 cb ed 19 ♘xd4 d5 20 ♗g5 ±/± Ivkov-Lengyel, Amsterdam IZ 1964.
16 ... h6 17 ♗d2 ♘b6 18 ♗d3 ± Karpov-Gligorić, San Antonio 1972.

[23]   17 ♗b3 ♗g7 =.
17 de de! 18 ♕e2 c5 19 a3 ♕c7 20 ♗b2 ♘b6 = Lee-Parma, Siegen Ol 1970.
17 ♗g5 h6! 18 ♗d2 ♗g7 19 ♕c1 ♔h7 20 a4 ♘b6 21 a5 ♘c4 = Kuzmin-Furman, USSR Ch 1965.

[24]   19 ... de?! 20 ♖xa4 ± Keres-Matanović, Winnipeg 1967.

[25]   Blackstock.

	10	11	12	13	14	15	16	17	18	
8	...	c4²⁶	♘c3	a3	♘xd4	♗a2	♗xc4	ed	♗a2	=
	♘bd7	♗b7²⁷	c6²⁸	ed²⁹	♘c5!³⁰	bc	d5	cd	♘fe4³¹	
9	...	...	de	♘xe5	♘c3³²	♗d5	ed	♗e3	♖c1	=
	...	c5	♘xe5	de	♕b6³³	♗xd5	♗d6	f5	f4³⁴	
10	...	...	♕c2³⁵	♘c3	♘e2	♘exd4	♗e2³⁶	♘g3	♕e2	∓
	...	c6	♗b7	b4	ed	g6	♘c5	a5	♘fd7³⁷	
11	...	...	cb	♘c3	♗g5	de	♘xe5	♗xf6	♕h5³⁹	=
	...	...	ab	♗a6!³⁸	h6	♘xe5	de	♗xf6		
12	...	...	c5	cd	♗g5	♗xf6⁴²	♕xd4⁴³	♕c3		=
	...	...	♕c7⁴⁰	♗xd6	ed!⁴¹	gf	♗c5	a5⁴⁴		
13	...	♗g5	♘bd2	♗h4⁴⁶	a4⁴⁷	♕e2	♗c2	b4	♗g3⁴⁹	=
	...	♗b7	h6!⁴⁵	c5	♕c7⁴⁸	c4	♖fe8	♘f8		
14	...	♘h4	♘f5	♕f3⁵¹	♕xf5	♖xe4	♕xe4	♗d2	♘xd2⁵²	±
	...	♘xe4	♘df6⁵⁰	♗xf5	ed	♘xe4	♗g5	♗xd2		
15	...	...	♗h6	f4⁵³	♘f3	♗c2	♘bd2	♗xf8⁵⁴		=
	...	g6	♖e8	c5!	c4	♗b7	♗f8			

	12	13	14	15	16	17	18	19	20	
16	...	♘f1⁵⁶	♘g3⁵⁷	d5	b3⁵⁸	♕e2	♗d3	♗b5		=
	c5⁵⁵	♖e8	♗f8	g6	♘b6	a5	b4	♖e7⁵⁹		
17	...	b4	a4⁶⁰	a5	♗b2	♖b1⁶³	♗a1	♗d3⁶⁴	c4	±
	♖e8	♗f8	♘b6⁶¹	♘bd7	♖b8⁶²	♗a8	g6	♗g7	bc⁶⁵	
18	...	♘f1	♘g3⁶⁶	a4⁶⁷	d5	♗g5⁶⁹	♗e3	♕d2		=
	...	♗f8	g6	c5⁶⁸	c4	h6	♘c5	h5		
19	...	...	...	...	...	♕e2	♗xa4	♖xa4	♖a3	=
	...	...	...	...	♘b6	♘xa4	ba	♘d7!⁷⁰	♘b6⁷¹	

²⁶ Arseniev Variation.

²⁷ 11 ... b4 12 c5 (12 a3!? Ravinsky) 12 ... ♗b7 (12 ... ed 13 cd cd 14 ♘xd4 ♗b7 15 ♗f5! ♘c5 – Arseniev-Zhilin, RSFSR Ch 1957 – 16 ♗g5! Shamkovich) 13 ♕c2 ed 14 c6! d3 15 ♕c4 ♘b6 16 cb ♘xc4 17 ba♕ ♕xa8 18 ♗xc4 ♘xe4 19 ♗xd3 d5 20 a3! (20 ♘bd2 f5 ∓) 20 ... ♘c5 (Shamkovich-Ragozin, Leningrad 1957) 21 ♖xe7! ♘b3 22 ♖xc7 ± Suetin.

²⁸ 12 ... bc 13 ♗xc4 ♘b6 14 ♗b3 ed 15 ♘xd4 ♘fd7 16 ♗e3! ♘c5 17 ♘f5 ± Lenchiner-Lazarev, Ukrainian Ch 1960.

²⁹ **13 ...** ♕c7 14 ♗g5 ♖ae8 15 ♖c1 ♕b8 16 ♗a2! ± Geller-Spassky USSR Ch 1958.

13 ... ♖b8 14 ♗a2 a5 15 cb cb 16 b4 ab 17 ab ed 18 ♘xd4 d5 (Matanović-Smyslov, Yugoslavia v USSR 1956) 19 e5! ♗xb4 20 ef ♗xc3 21 fg ± Boleslavsky.

13 ... h6 14 ♗e3 ♖e8 15 ♖c1 ± Hort-Pribyl, Czech Ch 1972.

³⁰ 14 ... bc?! 15 ♗xc4 d5 (Keres) 16 ♘xc6 ♗xc6 17 ed intending d6 ± Blackstock.

³¹ 19 ♘f5 ♘xc3 20 ♘xe7+ ♕xe7 21 bc ♘e6 22 ♗xd5 ♖fd8 23 c4 ♗xd5 24 cd ♕c5 25 ♗e3 ♕xd5 ½-½ Byrne-Spassky, Baden 1980.

³² 14 ♗g5 ♗e6! 15 ♕e2 ♖b8 ∓ Georgadze-Razuvayev, USSR 1971.

³³ **14 ...** ♗d7 15 a4 bc 16 ♗xc4 ♗e6 = Suetin-Forintos, Titovo Uzice 1966.

14 ... ♕xd1 15 ♖xd1 ♖b8 16 a4 ♗e6 17 ab ab = Geller-Holmov, Kislovodsk 1972.

³⁴ 19 ♗d2 f3 =.

[35] **12 ♘bd2 ♗b7 13 ♗c2 ♘e8 14 ♕e2** ±
Byrne-Matanović, Biel 1976.   13 ... c5! 14 d5
♘b6 15 b3 ♗c8 = Matanović.

12 a4 bc 13 ♗xc4 ♘xe4! 14 ♖xe4 d5 =
Lombardy-Matanović, Leipzig Ol 1960.

12 a3 bc 13 ♗xc4 ♘xe4 14 ♖xe4 d5 =
Hübner-Lengyel, Wijk aan Zee 1971.   13 ... d5!?
14 de ♘xe4 15 ♗xd5 cd 16 ♕xd5 ♖b8
17 ♕xe4 ♘c5! ∞ Dückstein-Krogius, Le Havre
1966.

12 ♘c3 b4 13 ♘a4 c5 14 dc dc 15 a3 a5 =
Walther-Unzicker, Zürich 1959.
[36] 16 ♘h2!? Timman.
[37] Tal-Timman, Sochi 1973.
[38] 13 ... b4!? (13 ... ♗b7?! 14 ♗g5 ±) 14 ♘e2
♘xe4 15 ♕c2 ♘ef6 ∞ Tukmakov-Averbakh,
USSR Ch ½f 1972.
[39] ½-½ Hort-Jansa, Sarajevo 1972.
[40] 12 ... dc 13 de ♘e8 14 e6! ± Averbakh-
Furman, USSR Ch 1961.
[41] **14 ... h6** 15 ♗h4 ♘h7 16 ♗g3! ± Blackstock.
14 ... ♗b7 15 ♘c3 ed 16 ♘xd4 ± Blackstock.
[42] 15 ♕xd4 ♘e5 16 ♘bd2 ♘fd7 17 ♕e3 c5 ∓
Dubinin-Yudovich, corr.
[43] 16 ♘xd4 ♘e5! = Nemet-Matanović, Zagreb
1964.
[44] I. Zaitsev.
[45] 12 ... ♖e8 13 ♗c2 ♗f8 14 ♘h2 ± Shamkovich-
Kuijpers, Amsterdam 1968.
[46] 13 ♗xf6 ♗xf6 14 d5 (E. Nowak-Kozma,
Czech Ch 1964) 14 ... ♘b6 intending ... c6
Blackstock.
[47] 14 ♗g3 ♕c7 15 ♘h4 ♖fe8 16 a4 ♗f8 =
Matulović-Matanović, Vinkovci 1968.
[48] 14 ... ♖e8 15 de de 16 ♗xf6 ♘xf6 17 ab ab
18 ♖xa8 ♗xa8 19 ♘xe5 c4 ∞ Smejkal-Parma,
Siegen Ol 1970.
[49] ½-½ Kostro-Matanović, Vrnjacka Banja
1967.
[50] 12 ... ♘ef6?! 13 ♕f3 e4!. 13 ♗g5 ♘b6
14 ♘xe7+ ♕xe7 15 ♘d2 ♗b7 ∓ Shianovsky-
Gufeld, Kiev 1964.
[51] 13 ♘xe7+ ♕xe7 14 ♖e2! intending ♕e1,
f3 - Bronstein.
[52] Zakharov-Krogius, USSR 1966.
[53] 13 de ♘xe5! = Darga-O'Kelly, Bordeaux
1964.
[54] ½-½ Byrne-Portisch, Amsterdam 1969.
[55] Gligoric's Variation.
[56] 13 b3 g6 14 a4 ♘h5 15 ♘f1 ♗f6! 16 dc
♘xc5 17 ab ab 18 ♗h6 ♗g7 = Suetin-Gligorić,
Yugoslavia v USSR 1974.
[57] 14 d5 g6 15 b3 ♘b6 = Torre-Gligorić Nice
Ol 1974.
[58] 16 ♗g5 h6 17 ♗e3 ♗g7 18 b3 (18 ♕d2 h5!
19 a4 c4 = Kavalek-Gligorić, Wijk aan Zee
1975) 18 ... ♘b6 19 ♕e2 a5 20 a4 b4 21 cb cb
22 ♕b5! ± Gufeld-Psakhis, USSR Cup

1982.
[59] Jansa-Gligorić, Nice Ol 1974.
[60] 14 ♗b2 a5 15 ♗d3 c6 16 a3 ♘b6 17 ♖c1
ed 18 ♘xd4 ♘fd7 19 ♘2b3 (Tal-Karpov,
Leningrad 1972) 19 ... ♘c4 20 ♗xc4 bc 21
♘xa5 ♖xa5 ∞ Gipslis.
[61] **14 ... c5** 15 bc ed 16 cd4 dc 17 e5 ♘d5
18 ♘e4 (Balashov-Podgayets, USSR 1966)
18 ... c4 ∞.

14 ... g6 15 ♗b2 ♗g7 16 c4 ed 17 cb ab
18 ab d3 19 ♗xd3 ♘xe4 20 ♗xe4 ♗xb2
21 ♖xa8 ♕xa8 22 ♗xb7 ♖xe1+ 23 ♕xe1 ♕xb7 =
Sznapik-Romanishin, Caracas 1976.

14 ... a5 15 d5!? ±.

14 ... d5 15 ♘xe5! de 16 f4 ± Vasyukov-
Holmov, Dubna 1973.
[62] **16 ... g6** 17 ♖b1! Tringov.

16 ... ♕b8 17 ♖b1 c5 18 bc dc 19 de ♘xe5
20 c4! ± Kostro-Sznapik, Poland 1972.
[63] **17 ♕b1!?** ♘h5 18 c4 bc 19 ♘xc4 ed
20 ♗xd4 c5 ∓ Ljubojević-Karpov, Manila
1976.

17 ♖e3!? Petrosian.
[64] 19 c4 bc 20 de ♘xe5 21 ♘xe5 de 22 ♘c3
♗c6! 23 ♕e2 ♗b5 24 ♘xc4 c5 25 bc ♖c8!
26 ♗b3 ♖xc5 27 ♗b4 ♖c6 28 ♗xf8 ♖xf8
29 ♕a2 ♗xc4 30 ♗xc4 ♕c7 = Browne-
Karpov, Amsterdam 1976.
[65] 21 ♗xc4 ed!? 22 ♗xd4 ♘xe4 23 ♘xe4
♖xe4 24 ♗xa6 ♗xd4 25 ♖xd4 c5 26 ♘c2
cb 27 ♕xd6 b3?! (27 ... ♕xa5!?) 28 ♘e3
♖e6 29 ♕d4! ♖xa6 30 ♖ed1 ± Vukčević-
Kraidman, Hastings 1966/67 (note that this
line can be avoided by adopting Gligorić's
12 ... c5 and later transposing into row 18 or 19).
[66] 14 ♗g5 (Romanishin's Line) 14 ... h6 15
♗h4 ♕c8 (15 ... g6!? 16 a4 ♗g7 17 d5 ♕b8
intending ... c6 = Smejkal; 16 d5 c6 = Smejkal)
16 de de 17 ♘3h2 c5 18 ♕f3 ♕c6 19 ♖ad1 ±
Romanishin-Spassky, Tilburg 1979.   18 ... a5!?
Romanishin.
[67] 15 ♗g5 h6 16 ♗d2 ♘b6 17 b3 c5!? 18 d5
♗g7 19 ♕e2 ♗c8 ∞.

15 ♗d2 ♗g7 16 ♕c1 (16 de ♘xe5 17 ♘xe5
♖xe5 18 ♗f4 ♖e8 19 ♕d2 ♘d7 ½-½ Yanofsky-
Spassky, Lugano Ol 1968) 16 ... c5 17 ♗h6
♕e7 18 ♗xg7 ♔xg7 = Unzicker-Karpov,
Hastings 1971/72.
[68] 15 ... ♗g7 16 d5! ±.
[69] 17 ♗e3 ♘c5 18 ♕e2 (Jansa-Smejkal,
Czech Ch 1972) 18 ... ♘fd7! = Minić.
[70] 19 ... ♗c8!? 20 ♗g5! ± (Romanishin)
20 ... h6 21 ♗e3 ♖b8 22 ♖ea1 ± Geller-
Romanishin, USSR 1978.
[71] 21 c4 a5 =.

21 ♘h2!? ♗g7 22 ♘g4 ♗c8 23 c4 ♗xg4
24 hg a5! = Torre-Gligorić, Bad Lauterberg
1977.   23 ♘h6+ ♔f8 24 c4 ♕h4 ∞.

	10	11	12	13	14	15	16	17	18	
1	♗c2	d4	b3	♘bd2	b4	cd	ba	e5	de	±
	♗b7	♘c4[1]	♘b6	♘bd7[2]	ed	a5	c5	de	♘d5[3]	
2	...	d4	de	♘bd2	♕e2	g3	♘f1	a4	b3	∞
	c5	♗b7[4]	de	♕d6	♘h5	g6	♘c4	♕e6	♘d6[5]	
3	...	...	♘bd2	cd	d5	♗b1	♕e2![7]	♘f1	♗d2[8]	±
	...	...	cd	♘c6[6]	♘b4	a5	♕c7	♖fc8		
4	...	...	cd	♘c3[9]	♕e2	♗d3	♗g5	♗d2	d5[10]	±
	...	cd	♗b7	♕c7	♖ac8	♖fe8	h6	♗f8		
5	...	...	♘bd2	cd	♘b3[12]	♗d3	d5	♗f1	♘bd4![13]	±
	...	♘d7	cd	♘c6[11]	a5	♗a6	♘b4	a4		
6	...	...	...	...	...	♗e3	♘c1[14]	♘xd4	♗xd4	±
	...	...	...	...	...	a4	ed	♘xd4	♘e5[15]	
7	...	...	♘bd2	de	♘h2	♕f3	♘hf1	g4	♗g3	∞
	...	♕c7	♗d7[16]	de	♗e6	♘c4	♖fe8	♘d7	♘f8[17]	
8	...	...	...	♘f1	b3[19]	♗g5	♗xe7	♘e3	♖c1	±
	...	...	...	♖fe8[18]	g6	♘h5	♖xe7	♘f6	♘b7[20]	
9	...	...	...	b4[21]	cb	♗b2	♗b3	♖c1	♖e3[22]	±
	...	...	♖e8	cb	♘c6	♘xb4	♘d7	♕b7		
10	...	...	...	de[23]	♘h2	♕f3	♘df1	♘g3	b3	±
	...	...	♗b7	de	♖ad8[24]	♗c8	♘c4	g6	♘a5[25]	
11	...	...	...	d5[26]	a4[27]	b4	♘f1	ab	♘3h2[28]	±
	...	...	♘c6	♘d8	♖b8	c4	♘e8	ab		
12	...	...	...	dc	♘f1[29]	♘e3	♕e2	♘f5	ef	±
	...	...	...	dc	♗e6	♖ad8	c4[30]	♗xf5	♖fe8[31]	
13	...	...	...	cd	d5	♖b1	♘f1	♗e3	♖c1	=
	...	...	cd	♗b7	♗c8[32]	b4	♘b7	♗d7	♖fe8[33]	
14	...	...	...	...	♘f1	♗b1	♘g3	b3	♗b2	=
	...	...	...	...	♖ac8	♖fe8[34]	♘d7	♘d7	♗f6[35]	
15	...	...	...	...	...	♗d3	de	♘g3	ef	∞̄
	...	...	...	...	...	d5[36]	♘xe4	f5	♗xf6[37]	
16	...	...	...	...	...	♖e2	de	♘g3	ef	±
	...	...	...	...	...	d5[38]	♘xe4	f5[39]	♗xf6[40]	
17	...	...	...	...	a3[41]	d5[43]	♘f1	♗d3		=
	...	...	...	♘c6	♗d7[42]	♘a5	♘h5[44]	g6[45]		
18	...	...	...	...	♘b3	♗e3[46]	♘bd2	♗b1		=
	...	...	...	...	a5	a4	♘b4![47]	♗d7[48]		

[1] 11 ... ed 12 cd d5 13 e5 Ne4 14 Nc3 f6 15 ef Bxf6 16 Nxe4 de 17 Bxe4 Bxe4 18 Rxe4 c5 19 d5 ± Fischer.

[2] 13 ... ed 14 cd c5!? Fischer.

[3] 19 Ne4 Bb4 20 Bb1 Rxa5 21 Qe2 (Fischer-Stein, Sousse IZ 1967) 21 ... Re8 intending ... Nf8 ± Matanović.

[4] 11 ... Nc6 12 Nbd2 Qb6 13 dc dc 14 Nf1 Be6 15 Ne3 Rad8 16 Qe2 c4 17 Ng5 g6 18 a4 ± Tal-Bronstein, USSR Ch 1959.

[5] 19 g4 Bg7 20 Ng3 f5 21 ef Qd5 22 Ne4 gf oo Boleslavsky-Mnatsakanian, USSR 1963.

[6] 13 ... Rc8 14 Nf1 d5 15 de Nxe4 16 N1d2 Nc4 17 Nxc4 Rxc4 18 Bb3 Rc8 19 Nd4 Kh8 20 Qg4 Bc5 21 Be3 ± Aronin-Simagin, USSR 1960.

[7] 16 Nf1 Bc8 17 Ng3 Na6 18 Bd3 Bd7 19 Be3 Qb8 20 Rc1 Rc8 21 Rxc8 Qxc8 = Hoelscher-Henrotay, corr. 1961/62.

[8] Matanović.

[9] 13 d5 Bc8 14 Nbd2 g6 15 b4 Bb7 16 a4 Bd7 17 ab ± Fischer-Weinstein, US Ch 1963.

[10] Stein-Yudovich, USSR v Yugoslavia 1963.

[11] 13 ... Nf6 14 Nf1 ed 15 Nxd4 Ne5 16 Ne3 g6 17 Nd5 Bg7 18 a4 ± Kotkov-Zhukovitsky, USSR 1964.

[12] 14 d5 Nb4 15 Bb1 a5 16 Nf1 Nc5 17 Ng3 g6 18 Bh6 Re8 19 Qd2 Bf8 = Cirić-Lengyel, Amsterdam 1968.

[13] Shamkovich-Benjamin, USA 1976.

[14] 16 Nbd2 ed 17 Nxd4 Nxd4 18 Bxd4 Ne5 19 Nf1 Be6 20 Ne3 Nc6 21 Nc3 b4 22 Nd2 ± Gligorić-Reshevsky, Tel Aviv Ol 1964.

[15] 19 Ne2 Nc6 20 Bc3 Be6 21 b3 b4 22 Nd4 Nxd4 23 Bxd4 ab 24 Bxb3 ± Matanović-Lengyel, Belgrade 1969.

[16] 12 ... Rd8 13 Nf1 d5 14 de de 15 N1d2 ef 16 ef Bxf6 17 Qf3 Be6 18 Ne4 Be7 19 Qh5 ± Smyslov-Filip, Amsterdam C 1956.

[17] 19 Ndf1 Ng6 20 Nh5 Rad8 21 b3 Nb6 oo Simagin-Szabo, Moscow 1963.

[18] 13 ... Nc4 14 Ne3 Nxe3 15 Bxe3 Be6 16 Nd2 Re8 17 f4 Rad8 18 fe de 19 d5 Bd7 20 c4 Rb8 21 a4 ± Tal-Petrosian, USSR Ch 1958.

[19] 14 Ne3 g6 15 Bd2 Bf8 16 Rc1 Nc6 17 d5 Ne7 18 c4 ± Olafsson-Sliwa, Marianske Lazne 1961.

[20] 19 b4 c4 20 a4 ± Stein-Matanović, Tel Aviv Ol 1964.

[21] 13 Nf1 Bf8 14 Bg5 Nd7 15 b3 Nb6 16 Rc1 Be6 17 Bd2 f6 18 c4 Nb7 19 de de 20 Bd3 ± Geller-Ivkov, USSR v Yugoslavia 1967.

[22] Keres.

[23] 13 Nf1 Rfe8 14 d5 Bc8 15 Ne3 Bf8 16 Bh1 g6 17 g4 Bg7 18 Rg1 Kh8 19 Ng5 Nb7 = Boleslavsky-Smyslov, Warsaw 1947.

[24] 14 ... Rfd8 15 Qf3 c4 16 Ndf1 b4 17 Ng3 ±

Sanguinetti-Cardoso, Portorož IZ 1958.

[25] 19 Bh6 ± Stein-Bannik, USSR Ch 1961.

[26] 13 a3 Bd7 14 b4 cd 15 cd Rfc8 16 Bb3 a5 = Gufeld-Karpov, USSR 1971.

[27] 14 c4 Bd7 15 Bd3 g6 16 Nf1 Nh5 17 Bh6 Ng7 = Spassky-Scholl, Amsterdam 1970.

[28] Karpov-Spassky, USSR Ch 1973.

[29] 14 a4 Be6 15 Ng5 Rad8 16 Nxe6 fe 17 Qe2 c4 = Unzicker-Holaszek, Vienna 1967.

[30] 16 ... g6 17 Ng5 Bc8 18 a4 Qb7 19 ab ab 20 h4 ± Smyslov-Botvinnik, match 1957.

[31] 19 Ng5 Nb8 20 Be3 Nbd7 21 a4 ± Ivkov-Mecking, Sousse IZ 1967.

[32] 14 ... Rac8 15 Bb1 Nd7 16 Nf1 Nc4 17 Re2 Ncb6 18 Nc2 Rc8 19 Ne3 g6 20 Nd2 Na4 21 b3 Nac5 22 b4 Na4 ± Tal-Petrosian, USSR Ch 1959.

[33] 19 Qd2 Qa5 20 Bb1 Bd8 = Gligorić-Reshevsky, match 1952.

[34] 15 ... d5!? 16 ed ed 17 Bg5 h6 18 Bxh6 gh 19 Qd2 Rfd8 20 Qxh6 Rxd5 21 Re4 Rh5 22 Rg4+ Nxg4 23 Qxh5 Nf6 24 Qg5+ Kf8 25 Qh6+ Ke8 26 Bf5 ± Thelen.

[35] Panov.

[36] 15 ... Nc6 16 Ne3 Rfe8 17 d5 Nb4 18 Bb1 a5 19 Qe2 Nd7 20 Bd2 Qb6 21 a3 Na6 22 b4 ± Fischer.

[37] 19 Bxe4 de 20 Nxe4 Rcd8 21 Qe2 h6 oo Matanović.

[38] 15 ... Rfe8 16 Ng3 g6 17 b3 Nc6 18 Bb2 Bf8 19 Qd2 Bg7 20 Rd1 Qb6 21 Bb1 ± Matanović-Keres, Vienna 1957.

[39] 17 ... Rfd8 18 Nf5 ± Matanović. 17 ... Nxg3 18 fg ± Matanović.

[40] 19 Nxe4 de 20 Nxe4 Rxe4 21 Rxe4 Qc2 22 Qd5+! Kh8 23 Ne1 ± Aronin.

[41] 14 d5 Nb4 15 Bb1 a5 16 Nf1 Bd7 17 N3h2 Rfc8 18 Ne3 g6 19 Nd2 Na6 20 Qf3 Qd8 21 b3 = Stein-Reshevsky, Mar del Plata 1966.

[42] 14 ... Bd8 15 b4 Qa7 16 Nb3 Bb6 17 Be3 Re8 18 de de = I.Zaitsev-Holmov, USSR 1967.

[43] 15 Nb3 Rfc8 16 Be3 a5 17 Rc1 a4 = Keres-Borisenko, USSR 1967.

[44] 16 ... Rfc8 17 Bd3 Bd8 18 Ng3 Qa7 19 Rf1 Bb6 20 Nh4 g6 21 Kh1! ± Tseshkovsky-Dorfman, USSR Ch 1978.

[45] 18 Bh6 Rfc8 19 Ne3 Qd8 = Botvinnik-Smyslov, USSR Ch 1940. 19 ... Nf4!? 20 Bf1 Qb6 ∓ Matanović.

[46] 15 Bd2 Bd7 16 d5 Nd8 17 Rc1 Nb7 18 Qe2 Qb8 = Geller-Kuzmin, USSR Ch 1977.

[47] 16 ... Be6 17 a3 Na5 18 Bd3 Qb8 19 Qe2 ± Szilagyi-Forintos, Hungarian Ch 1966.

[48] 18 a3 Nc6 19 Bd3 (19 Ba2 Rac8 20 Rc1 Qb8 21 Qe2 h6 22 de de 23 Nh4 Rfd8 24 Qf3 b4! ∓ Tal-Spassky, Bugojno 1978) 19 ... Na5 20 Rc1 Qb8 21 Qe2 Re8 22 Rc2 Bd8 23 de de = Tal-Kuzmin, Leningrad 1977.

Index